THE
WRITER'S
HANDBOOK
2000

Barry Turner has worked on both sides of publishing, as an editor and marketing director and as an author. He started his career as a journalist with *The Observer* before moving on to television and radio. He has written over twenty books including *A Place in the Country*, which inspired a television series, and a best-selling biography of the actor, Richard Burton.

His recent work includes a radio play, travel articles, serialising books for *The Times*, editing the magazine *Country* and writing a one-man show based on the life of the legendary theatre critic, James Agate. This is his thirteenth year as editor of *The Writer's Handbook* and his second as editor of *The Statesman's Yearbook*.

THE WRITER'S COMPANION

The essential guide to being published

Barry Turner

The Writer's Companion is a route map through the media jungle, an indispensable guide for established writers and newcomers alike who seek to make the best commercial use of their talents.

Drawing on the cumulative experiences of its sister volume, *The Writer's Handbook,* which is now in its thirteenth year, *The Writer's Companion* is packed with a wealth of practical advice taking in:

- book publishing
- freelance journalism
- film and television
- radio drama
- theatre and poetry

Everyday concerns, financial and legal, from how to avoid contractual pitfalls to minimising the risk of libel are given full coverage and there is up-to-date advice on raising funds for creative projects on stage and screen.

THE
WRITER'S
HANDBOOK
2000

EDITOR

BARRY TURNER

First published 1988
This edition published 1999 by
Macmillan
an imprint of Macmillan Publishers Ltd,
25 Eccleston Place, London SW1W 9NF
and Basingstoke
Associated companies throughout the world
www.macmillan.co.uk

10 9 8 7 6 5 4 3 2 1

A CIP catalogue record for this book is available from the British Library

ISBN 0–333–725751

Credits

Publisher *Morven Knowles*
Editor *Barry Turner*
Editorial Assistant *Jill Fenner*
Poetry Editor *Peter Finch*
Contributors *P. D. James*
　　　　　Minette Walters
　　　　　Graham King
　　　　　Elizabeth Buchan
　　　　　Philip Pullman
Tax and Finance Advisor *Pat Kernon*
Production *Dominic Saraceno*

Typeset by Heronwood Press, Medstead, Hants
Printed and bound in Great Britain by Mackays of Chatham plc, Kent

Contents

Dialling Codes

National dialling codes change on 22 April 2000 for the following cities:

Cardiff	01222 XXX XXX	becomes	029 20XX XXXX
Coventry	01203 XXX XXX	becomes	024 76XX XXXX
London	0171 XXX XXXX	becomes	020 7XXX XXXX
London	0181 XXX XXXX	becomes	020 8XXX XXXX
Portsmouth	01705 XXX XXX	becomes	023 92XX XXXX
Southampton	01703 XXX XXX	becomes	023 80XX XXXX

Northern Ireland will have area code 028 followed by new eight-digit numbers:

e.g. Belfast   01232 XXX XXX becomes 028 90XX XXXX

For more information, including all new Northern Ireland numbers, call Freefone 0800 731 0202; Website: http://www.numberchange.bt

If you would like an entry in *The Writer's Handbook 2001*, please write or send a fax to:

***The Writer's Handbook*,**
34 Ufton Road,
London N1 5BX.
Fax 0171 241 0118

From Pitch to Publication

The only book that *really* tells you how to sell your publication

CAROLE BLAKE

How to master the publishing system, get published successfully and stay published – from one of Britain's leading literary agents

Carole Blake has been responsible for launching the international careers of many bestselling novelists. In her new book she offers a complete guide to identifying the market for your work, pitching it successfully to agents and publishers, and then navigating all the publishing stages from signing the contract to receiving your royalties

From Pitch to Publication includes:

- What agents want: five essentials for a good submission package
- Three key elements of a successful synopsis
- What your publishers will – and won't – do for your book
- What should – and shouldn't – be in your publishing contract
- Troubleshooting: problems with your agent or publisher

A MACMILLAN PAPERBACK £12.99

Available from all good bookshops, or order direct by calling Book Services by Post on 01624 675137

Introduction

P. D. James

As the relatively new President of the **Society of Authors**, it is a particular pleasure to contribute to this special 2000 edition of *The Writer's Handbook*. A recent report in *The Bookseller* suggested that in the 1990s more changes took place in the book trade than in the rest of the century. It is hardly surprising that many writers, caught up in this maelstrom, seem bewitched, bothered and bewildered. Never has reliable, accurate and up-to-date information and advice been more important.

Most changes – we must face it – are outside our control. Authors will always be critical of publishers, often with good reason. But I think that we should also recognise that, partly through the efforts of writers' organisations, some aspects of publishing have improved. When my first book was published there was an aura of relaxed amiability, verging on lethargy, about publishing. For too long subtle class distinctions were rife. Editors reigned supreme and hardly deigned to communicate with their sales departments. The pendulum may have swung too far in favour of accountants and sales departments, I'm inclined to think that it has, but there does seem to be much better coordination between departments, resulting in more effective marketing – at least of lead titles. Publishing, once the leisurely occupation for gentlemen, has become as frenetic as any other commercial enterprise. Whether this increased activity has led to greater efficiency is, perhaps, open to question.

The transformation of bookselling, too, has been breathtaking. The chain booksellers have expanded aggressively and imaginatively. The speed and efficiency of book distribution have improved (though not enough), aided by competition from rapidly expanding and highly efficient wholesalers. Sales via the Internet are increasing exponentially.

It is hard to reconcile all this change, dynamism and apparent growth with the perception of writers, many of whom see their royalties declining and find that they are being dropped by publishers for no very obvious reason. No doubt to some extent the malaise stems from the widening gulf between those few authors who are fortunate to have their books promoted vigorously and the many mid-list authors who see their books published passively, with little detectable commitment, publicity or drive. The large booksellers have pressurised publishers into giving ever-bigger discounts. Publishers have then tried to recover profitability by paying lower royalties. Like farmers in their struggle with the big retailers, it is the small businesses that get pushed around.

Authorship is by nature an insecure profession. We need – and have every reason to expect – to be nurtured by our editors; to be made to feel that we are part of the publishing team and not just supplier of the 'product' in its raw form.

In a changing world, the principles of publishing, as far as authors are concerned, remain the same. They can be summed up in one word: communication.

I have been fortunate to be with the same publishing house, Faber, for thirty-seven years, and have worked with only two editors. My present editor, Rosemary Goud, although retired, still returns to edit each new novel. I know how fortunate I am. One hears many horror stories, usually involving the conglomerates and their latest acquisitions or disposals; of authors suffering two or three changes of editor in the process of writing a book. The author is then left feeling that the book has lost its prime advocate within the publishing house, enthusiasm has vanished and it is almost impossible to find out what is going on. This is a recipe for frustration and bad feeling. Writing is a lonely and precarious business. If we can't get support and encouragement from our editor, where can we look for it?

Even if you are lucky enough to deal continuously with only one editor, the chances are you will find your editor becoming less accessible. It is a paradox that in a business that is all about communication, letters so often languish unanswered, and voice-mail messages vanish, apparently into cyberspace. Part of the problem is that editors are put under increasing pressure in the constant mêlée of restructuring, cost-cuttings and rationalisations to which the conglomerates are so prone. We need to see a revival in the status, fortunes and job security of editors.

Royalty departments have also been squeezed. Computers enable publishers to have immediate access to sales and royalty data. Yet nothing has been done to improve the frequency or speed with which authors are paid. Nor has the information given to us become any more intelligible. We take the information on trust, try to close our minds to niggling worries about inaccuracies and get on with our next book. The Society of Authors conducts regular random royalty audits on behalf of its members. You will not be surprised to hear that 14 out of 15 audits have resulted in authors receiving a cheque.

In turbulent conditions, it is double important to wear a seat belt. One safety feature available to writers is the Society of Authors, with its expert staff on hand to give guidance not only on contracts but on every sort of business issue and problem that may arise. The Society is more than an association of writers and a strong advocate for the written word. We who are members know that we receive a personal service from staff we regard as our friends. (Details are given on page 512.) I commend the Society to you, just as I recommend this excellent Handbook, edited with such panache by its founder Barry Turner.

P. D. James has been awarded major prizes for her crime writing in Great Britain, America, Italy and Scandinavia. In 1999 she was homoured by the Mystery Writers of America with the Grand Master Award for her lifetime's work. She was created a life peer in 1991. Recent publications include Devices and Desires, The Children of Men, Original Sin *and* A Certain Justice. *Faber & Faber will publish her memoirs,* A Time To Be In Earnest, *in November 1999.*

UK Publishers

AA Publishing
The Automobile Association, Fanum House, Basingstoke, Hampshire RG21 4EA
☎0990 448866   Fax 01256 491555
Managing Director *John Howard*
Editorial Director *Michael Buttler*

Publishes maps, atlases and guidebooks, motoring, travel and leisure. About 100 titles a year.

Abacus
See **Little, Brown & Co (UK)**

ABC-Clio Ltd
Old Clarendon Ironworks, 35a Great Clarendon Street, Oxford OX2 6AT
☎01865 311350   Fax 01865 311358
Email: oxford@abc-clio.ltd.uk
Website:www.abc-clio.com
Managing Director *Tony Sloggett*
Editorial Director *Dr Robert G. Neville*

Formerly Clio Press Ltd. *Publishes* academic and general reference works, social sciences and humanities. Markets, outside North America, the CD-ROM publications and reference books of the American parent company. Art Bibliographies *S. Pape.* SERIES *World Bibliographical; Clio Montessori.*
Royalties paid twice-yearly.

Abington Publishing
See **Woodhead Publishing Ltd**

Absolute Classics
See **Oberon Books**

Absolute Press
Scarborough House, 29 James Street West, Bath BA1 2BT
☎01225 316013   Fax 01225 445836
Email: sales@absolutepress.demon.co.uk
Managing/Editorial Director *Jon Croft*

FOUNDED 1979. *Publishes* food and wine-related subjects as well as travel guides and the *Streetwise Maps* series of city maps. About 10 titles a year. Lead title for 1999: *Icons – 50 Twentieth Century Gay Icons. Outlines,* launched in summer 1997, is a new series of monographs on gay and lesbian creative artists. No unsolicited mss. Synopses and ideas for books welcome.
Royalties paid twice-yearly.

Abson Books London
5 Sidney Square, London E1 2EY
☎0171 790 4737   Fax 0171 790 7346
Email: absonbooks@aol.com
Chairman *M. J. Ellison*

FOUNDED 1971 in Bristol. *Publishes* language glossaries and curiosities. No unsolicited mss; synopses and ideas for books welcome.
Royalties paid twice-yearly.

Academic Press
See **Harcourt Brace and Company Ltd**

Academy Group Ltd
42 Leinster Gardens, London W2 3AN
☎0171 262 5097   Fax 0171 262 5093
Chairman *John Jarvis*
Managing Editor *Maggie Toy*
Approx. Annual Turnover £2 million

FOUNDED 1969. Became part of John Wiley & Sons, Inc. group in 1997. *Publishes* architecture and design. Welcomes unsolicited mss, synopses and ideas.
Royalties paid annually.

Acair Ltd
Unit 7, 7 James Street, Stornoway, Isle of Lewis, Scotland HS1 2QN
☎01851 703020   Fax 01851 703294

Specialising in matters pertaining to the Gaidhealtachd, Acair publishes books in Gaelic and English on Scottish history, culture and the Gaelic language. 75% of their children's books are targeted at primary school usage and are published exclusively in Gaelic.
Royalties paid twice-yearly.

Actinic Press
See **Cressrelles Publishing Co. Ltd**

Addison Wesley Longman Ltd
See **Pearson Education**

Adelphi
See **David Campbell Publishers Ltd**

Adlard Coles Nautical
See **A & C Black (Publishers) Ltd**

Adlib
See **Scholastic Ltd**

African Books Collective

The Jam Factory, 27 Park End Street, Oxford OX1 1HU
☎01865 726686   Fax 01865 793298
Email: abc@dial.pipex.com
Website:www.africanbookscollective.com

FOUNDED 1990. Collectively owned by its 17 founder member publishers. Exclusive distribution in N. America, UK, Europe and Commonwealth countries outside Africa for 42 African member publishers. Concentration is on scholarly/academic, literature and children's books. Mainly concerned with the promotion and dissemination of African-published material outside Africa. Supplies African-published books to African libraries and organisations.

Age Concern Books

1268 London Road, London SW16 4ER
☎0181 765 7200   Fax 0181 765 7211
Approx. Annual Turnover £500,000

Publishing arm of Age Concern England. *Publishes* related non-fiction only. No fiction. About 18 titles a year. Unsolicited mss, synopses and ideas welcome.

Airlife Publishing Ltd

101 Longden Road, Shrewsbury, Shropshire SY3 9EB
☎01743 235651   Fax 01743 232944
Email: airlife@airlifebooks.com

Executive Chairman *J. W. B. Gibbs*
Editorial Head *Peter Coles*
Approx. Annual Turnover £3 million

IMPRINTS
Airlife Specialist aviation titles for pilots, historians and enthusiasts. Also naval and military history. About 60 titles a year. TITLES *Combat Carriers; Air War Korea; Airlife's Airliner Series; Special Operations Aviation.*

Swan Hill Press Country pursuits, horse riding, mountaineering, fishing, natural history and decorative art. About 35 titles a year. TITLES *Salmon, Trout and Charr of the World; Encyclopedia of Falconry; The Healthy Horse.*

Waterline Books Practical sailing books for yachtsmen, nautical history and narrative. About 10 titles a year. TITLES *Cost Conscious Cruiser; Traditional British Fishing Boats; Yachtsman's Guide to the Collision Rules.* Unsolicited mss, synopses and ideas for books welcome.

Royalties paid annually; twice-yearly by arrangement.

Ian Allan Publishing Ltd

Riverdene Business Park, Molesey Road, Hersham, Surrey KT12 4RG
☎01932 266600   Fax 01932 266601
Chairman *David Allan*
Managing Director *Tony Saunders*

Specialist transport publisher – atlases, maps, railway, aviation, road transport, military, maritime, reference. About 80 titles a year. Send sample chapter and synopsis (with s.a.e.). Manages distribution and sales for third party publishers.

IMPRINTS **Dial House** sporting titles; **OPC** railway titles.

J. A. Allen & Co. Ltd

1 Lower Grosvenor Place, Buckingham Palace Road, London SW1W 0EL
☎01255 679388   Fax 01255 670848

Executive Director *Caroline Burt*
Editor *Jane Lake*
Approx. Annual Turnover £750,000

FOUNDED 1926 as part of J. A. Allen & Co. (The Horseman's Bookshop) Ltd, it became independent in 1960 and was acquired by **Robert Hale Ltd** in 1999. *Publishes* equine and equestrian non-fiction. About 20 titles a year. Mostly commissioned, but willing to consider unsolicited mss of technical/instructional material related to all aspects of horses and horsemanship.

Royalties paid twice-yearly.

Allen Lane

See **Penguin UK**

Allison & Busby

114 New Cavendish Street, London W1M 7FD
☎0171 636 2942   Fax 0171 323 2023

Publishing Director *Roderick Dymott*
Editor *David Shelley*

FOUNDED 1967. *Publishes* literary fiction and non-fiction, writers' guides, crime and translations. IMPRINTS **Alternatives** Biography, history, topical issues, mind, body and spirit, the paranormal, health and hobbies; **London House** Popular history, biography. About 60 titles a year. Send synopsis with two sample chapters, not full mss. No replies without s.a.e.

Alternatives

See **Allison & Busby**

Amber Lane Press Ltd

Cheorl House, Church Street, Charlbury, Oxfordshire OX7 3PR
☎01608 810024   Fax 01608 810024
Chairman *Brian Clark*

Managing Director/Editorial Head
Judith Scott

FOUNDED 1979 to publish modern play texts. *Publishes* plays and books on the theatre. About 4 titles a year. TITLES *Strange Fruit* Caryl Phillips; *The Best of Friends* Hugh Whitemore (play texts); *Japanese Theater from the Origin to the Present* Shoji Noma; *Prokofiev* David Gutman. 'Expressly *not* interested in poetry.' No unsolicited mss. Synopses and ideas welcome.
Royalties paid twice-yearly.

AMCD (Publishers) Ltd

PO Box 182, Altrincham, Cheshire WA15 9UA
☎0161 434 5105   Fax 0161 434 5105
Email: 100625.3570@compuserve.com

Managing Director *John Stewart Adams*

FOUNDED 1988. *Publishes* financial directories, books on China, local history, business books. Took over the Jensen Business Books imprint in 1993 and is well placed in electronic reference after developing its own software. In conjunction with JHC (Technology) Ltd, AMCD offers publishers access to the electronic book market with their reference, dictionary and directory Pop-Up© software packages which can handle most languages. About 5 titles a year. TITLES *Financing China's Electricity; Around Haunted Croydon; Buying and Selling a Shop; Handguide to the Placenames of Alderley Edge.* Ideas for business books and books on European History, China or the Far East welcome in synopsis form (no mss). No poetry, fiction or historical romance. Final mss must be on disk.
Royalties paid twice yearly.

Amsco

See **Omnibus Press**

Anchor

See **Transworld Publishers Ltd**

Andersen Press Ltd

20 Vauxhall Bridge Road, London SW1V 2SA
☎0171 840 8701/840 8700 (editorial)
Fax 0171 233 6263

Managing Director/Publisher *Klaus Flugge*
Editorial Director *Janice Thomson*
Editor, Fiction *Audrey Adams*

FOUNDED 1976 by Klaus Flugge and named after Hans Christian Andersen. *Publishes* children's high-quality picture books and hardback fiction. Seventy per cent of their books are sold as co-productions abroad. TITLES *Elmer* David McKee; *Greyfriars Bobby* Ruth Brown; *I Want My Potty* Tony Ross; *Badger's Parting Gifts* Susan Varley;

Teddy, Where Are You? Ralph Steadman; *Jack's Fantastic Voyage* Michael Foreman; *Suddenly!* Colin McNaughton; *Junk* Melvin Burgess. Unsolicited mss welcome for picture books; synopsis in the first instance for books for young readers up to age 12. No poetry or short stories.
Royalties paid twice-yearly.

Anness Publishing Ltd

Hermes House, 88–89 Blackfriars Road, London SE1 8HA
☎0171 401 2077   Fax 0171 633 9499

Chairman/Managing Director *Paul Anness*
Publisher/Partner *Joanna Lorenz*

FOUNDED 1989. *Publishes* highly illustrated co-edition titles: general non-fiction – cookery, crafts, interior design, gardening, photography, decorating, lifestyle and children's. About 400 titles a year. IMPRINTS **Lorenz Books**; **Old Forge Gift Collection**; **Hermes House**; **Sebastian Kelly**.

Antique Collectors' Club

5 Church Street, Woodbridge, Suffolk IP12 1DS
☎01394 385501   Fax 01394 384434

Managing Director *Diana Steel*
Director *Brian Cotton*

FOUNDED 1966. Has a five-figure membership spread over the United Kingdom and the world. The Club's magazine *Antique Collecting* is sold on a subscription basis (currently £19.50 *p.a.*) and is published 10 times a year. It is sent free to members who may also buy the Club's books at special pre-publication prices. *Publishes* specialist books on antiques and collecting. The price guide series was introduced in 1968 with the first edition of *The Price Guide to Antique Furniture*. Subject areas include furniture, silver/jewellery, metalwork, glass, textiles, art reference, ceramics, horology. Also books on architecture and gardening. RECENT TITLES *Starting to Collect Series: Antique Silver* Ian Pickford; *British Prints, Automobilia: 20th Century International Reference and Price Guide* Gordon Gardiner and Alistair Morris; *Dictionary and Price Guide* Ian Mackenzie. Unsolicited synopses and ideas for books welcome. No mss.
Royalties paid quarterly as a rule, but can vary.

Anvil Press Poetry Ltd

Neptune House, 70 Royal Hill, London SE10 8RF
☎0181 469 3033   Fax 0181 469 3363
Email: anvil@cix.co.uk

Editorial Director *Peter Jay*

FOUNDED 1968 to promote English-language and foreign poetry, both classic and contemporary, in translation. English list includes Peter Levi, Dick Davis and Carol Ann Duffy. Translated books include Bei Dao, Celan, Dante, Lalic. Preliminary enquiry required for translations. Unsolicited book-length collections of poems are welcome from writers whose work has appeared in poetry magazines. Please enclose adequate return postage.

Authors' Rating With a little help from the Arts Council, Anvil has become one of the foremost publishers of living poets. An American distributor will help overseas sales. But what is really needed is an injection of fresh capital.

Apollos
See **Inter-Varsity Press**

Apple
See **Quarto Publishing** under **UK Packagers**

Appletree Press Ltd
19–21 Alfred Street, Belfast BT2 8DL
☎01232 243074   Fax 01232 246756
Managing Director *John Murphy*
Creative Manager *Rob Blackwell*
FOUNDED 1974. *Publishes* cookery and other small-format gift books, plus general non-fiction of Irish and Scottish interest. TITLES *Little Cookbook* series (about 40 titles); *Ireland: The Complete Guide*. No unsolicited mss; send initial letter or synopsis.
   Royalties paid twice-yearly in the first year, annually thereafter. For the *Little Cookbook* series, a standard fee is paid.

Arc Publications
Nanholme Mill, Shaw Wood Road, Todmorden, Lancashire OL14 6DA
☎01706 812338   Fax 01706 818948
Publishers *Rosemary Jones, Angela Jarman*
General Editor *Tony Ward*
Associate Editors *John Kinsella* (International), *David Morley* (UK), *Jean Boase-Beier* (Translations), *Robert Gray* (Australia)
FOUNDED in 1969 to specialise in the publication of contemporary poetry from new and established writers both in the UK and abroad. AUTHORS include John Goodby, Miklos Ragnoti (Hungary), C. K. Stead, Andrew Johnson (New Zealand), Tariq Latif, Donald Atkinson, Tomas Saluman (Slovenia), James Sutherland Smith, Gail Dendy (S. Africa). 8 titles a year. Authors submitting material should

ensure that it is compatible with the current list and should enclose s.a.e. if they wish mss to be returned.

Argentum
See **Aurum Press Ltd**

Aris & Phillips Ltd
Teddington House, Warminster, Wiltshire BA12 8PQ
☎01985 213409   Fax 01985 212910
Email: Aris.Phillips@btinternet.com
Website:www.arisandphillips.com
Managing/Editorial Director *Adrian Phillips*
Editor, Hispanic Classics *Lucinda Phillips*
FOUNDED 1972 to publish books on Egyptology. A family firm which has remained independent. *Publishes* academic, classical, oriental and hispanic. About 10 titles a year. TITLES *Mammals of Ancient Egypt* Osborn; *The Reign of Ramesses IV* A. J. Peden; *The Third Intermediate Period in Egypt (1100–650BC)* K. A. Kitchen. With such a highly specialised list, unsolicited mss and synopses are not particularly welcome, but synopses will be considered.
   Royalties paid twice-yearly.

Arkana
See **Penguin UK**

Arms & Armour Press
See **Cassell**

Arnefold
See **George Mann Books**

Arnold
See **Hodder Headline plc**

Arrow
See **Random House UK Ltd**

Artech House
Portland House, Stag Place, London SW1E 5XA
☎0171 973 8077   Fax 0171 630 0166
Email: jlancashire@artech-house.com
Website:www.artech-house.com
Managing Director (USA)
   William M. Bazzy
Senior Commissioning Editor
   Dr Julie Lancashire
FOUNDED 1969. European office of Artech House Inc., Boston. *Publishes* electronic engineering, especially telecommunications, computer

communications, computing, optoelectronics, signal processing, digital audio and video, intelligent transportation systems and technology management (books, software and videos). 50–60 titles a year. Unsolicited mss and synopses considered.

Royalties paid twice-yearly.

Ashgate Publishing Ltd

Gower House, Croft Road, Aldershot, Hampshire GU11 3HR
☎01252 331551   Fax 01252 344405
Chairman *Nigel Farrow*

FOUNDED 1967. *Publishes* in business, arts and humanities under the **Gower** imprint for professional books and social sciences under the **Ashgate** imprint for academic books.

DIVISIONS *Julia Scott* Business and management; *Sarah Markham* Social sciences; *John Irwin* Law and legal studies; *Alec McAulay* History; *John Smedley* Variorum collected studies; *Rachel Lynch* Music and literary studies; *Pamela Edwardes* Art history; *John Hindley* Aviation studies; *Jo Gooderham* Social work.

Ashmolean Museum Publications

Ashmolean Museum, Beaumont Street, Oxford OX1 2PH
☎01865 278009   Fax 01865 278018
Website:www.ashmol.ox.ac.uk
Publisher/Editorial Head *Ian Charlton*

The Ashmolean Museum, which is wholly owned by Oxford University, was FOUNDED in 1683. The first publication appeared in 1890 but publishing did not really start in earnest until the 1960s. *Publishes* European and Oriental fine and applied arts, European archaeology and ancient history, Egyptology and numismatics, for both adult and children's markets. About 8 titles a year. No fiction, American/African art, ethnography, modern art or post-medieval history. Most publications are based on and illustrated from the Museum's collections.

IMPRINTS **Ashmolean Museum Publications** and **Griffith Institute** (Egyptology imprint). Recent TITLES *Ancient Greek Pottery; Twentieth Century Painting; The Forest Fire; Techniques of Drawing; Glass; Turner Watercolours.* No unsolicited mss.

Royalties paid annually.

Aspire Publishing

8 Betony Rise, Exeter, Devon EX2 5RR
☎01392 252516   Fax 01392 252517
Email: aspire@xcentrex.force9.net
Also at: 9 Wimpole Street, London W1M 8LB

Managing Editor *Patricia Hawkes*

FOUNDED 1997. *Publishes* popular fiction, autobiography, biography and political. 11 titles in 1998. IMPRINTS **Aspire** fiction; **Greenzone** non-fiction. TITLES *In the Shadow of Saddam* Mikhael Ramadan; *Trial by Conspiracy* Jonathan Boyd Hunt; *Invaders of Privacy* Julie Burville. No unsolicited material; send s.a.e. for guidelines. Around 50% of titles are commissioned.

Associated University Presses (AUP)

See **Golden Cockerel Press Ltd**

The Athlone Press

1 Park Drive, London NW11 7SG
☎0181 458 0888   Fax 0181 201 8115
Email: athlonepress@btinternet.com
Managing Director *Doris Southam*
Editorial Head *Tristam Palmer*

FOUNDED 1949 as the publishing house of the University of London. Now wholly independent, but preserves links with the University via an academic advisory board. *Publishes* archaeology, architecture, art, economics, film studies, history, history-of-ideas, history-of-science, law, eating disorders, psychiatry, literary criticism, psychic, medical, Asia, philosophy, politics, religion, science, sociology, women's/feminist issues. Anticipated developments in the near future: more emphasis on cultural studies, history of ideas, women's/feminist studies and environmental issues, including medicine. About 35 titles a year. Unsolicited mss, synopses and ideas for academic books welcome.

Royalties paid annually. *Overseas associates* The Athlone Press, c/o Transaction Publishers, 390 Campus Drive, Somerset, NJ 08873, USA.

Atlantic Europe Publishing Co. Ltd

Greys Court Farm, Greys Court, Nr Henley on Thames, Oxon RG9 4PG
☎01491 628188   Fax 01491 628189
Email: info@AtlanticEurope.com
Website:www.AtlanticEurope.com
Directors *Dr B. J. Knapp, D. L. R. McCrae*
Websites:www.AtlanticEurope.com/
   www.curriculumVisions.com

Closely associated, since 1990, with Earthscape Editions packaging operation. *Publishes* full-colour, highly illustrated children's non-fiction in hardback for international co-editions. Not interested in any other material. Main focus is on National Curriculum titles, especially in the fields of mathematics, science, technology, social history and geography. About 25 titles a year.

Unsolicited synopses and ideas for books welcome; s.a.e. essential for return of submissions.
Royalties or fees paid depending on circumstance.

Attic Books

The Folly, Rhosgoch, Painscastle, Builth Wells, Powys LD2 3JY
☎01497 851205

Managing Director/Editorial Head
Jack Bowyer

FOUNDED 1984 by its architect owners. *Publishes* books on building crafts, architecture and engineering. Mostly technical books for the industry, dealing mainly with restoration and conservation.
Royalties paid annually.

AUP (Associated University Presses)

See **Golden Cockerel Press Ltd**

Aurum Press Ltd

25 Bedford Avenue, London WC1B 3AT
☎0171 637 3225   Fax 0171 580 2469

Managing Director *Bill McCreadie*
Editorial Director *Piers Burnett*
Approx. Annual Turnover £1.89 million

FOUNDED 1977. Formerly owned by Andrew Lloyd Webber's Really Useful Group, now owned jointly by Piers Burnett, Bill McCreadie and Sheila Murphy, all of whom worked together in the '70s for André Deutsch. Committed to producing high-quality, illustrated/non-illustrated adult non-fiction in the areas of general human interest, art and craft, lifestyle, sport and travel. About 40 titles a year.
IMPRINTS **Argentum** Practical photography books; **Jacqui Small** high-quality lifestyle books. TITLES *Sesame Street Unpaved* David Borgenicht; *Seasonal Landscapes* Keith Fenwick; *Ageless Beauty* Dayle Haddon; *The Duchess of Windsor* Greg King.
Royalties paid twice-yearly.

Autumn Publishing Ltd

North Barn, Appledram Barns, Birdham Road, Near Chichester, West Sussex PO20 7EQ
☎01243 531660   Fax 01243 774433

Managing Director *Campbell Goldsmid*
Editorial Director *Ingrid Goldsmid*

FOUNDED 1976. Publisher of highly illustrated children's books. About 50 titles a year. Unsolicited synopses and ideas for books welcome if they come within relevant subject areas.
Payment varies according to contract; generally a flat fee.

Azure

See **Society for Promoting Christian Knowledge**

B & W Publishing Ltd

29 Inverleith Row, Edinburgh EH3 5QH
☎0131 552 5555   Fax 0131 552 5566

Directors *Campbell Brown, Steven Wiggins*

FOUNDED 1990. *Publishes* general fiction and non-fiction, including memoirs, sport cookery, guidebooks. Ideas for books welcome. Send synopsis and sample chapter with s.a.e. or return postage.
Royalties paid twice-yearly.

Baillière Tindall

See **Harcourt Brace and Company Ltd**

Bantam/Bantam Press

See **Transworld Publishers Ltd**

Barefoot Books Ltd

Editorial & Rights: PO Box 95, Kingswood, Bristol BS15 5BH
☎0117 9328885   Fax 0117 9328881

Sales, Marketing & Management: 18 Highbury Terrace, London N5 1UP
☎0171 704 6492   Fax 0171 359 5798
Email: info@barefoot-books.com
Website:www.barefoot-books.com

Managing Director *Nancy Traversy*
Publisher *Tessa Strickland (at Bristol office)*
Approx. Annual Turnover £1 million

FOUNDED in 1993. *Publishes* high-quality children's picture books, particularly new and traditional stories from a wide range of cultures. 40 titles in 1999. TITLES *The Gigantic Turnip* Alexei Tolstoy; *Mary's Story* Sarah Boss; *The Barefoot Book of Stories From the Silk Road* Cherry Gilchrist. No unsolicited mss.
Royalties paid twice-yearly.

Authors' Rating Barefoot gives a whole new meaning to home publishing. Founding partners Nancy Traversy and Tessa Strickland live 100 miles apart but keep in constant and profitable contact by telephone, fax and email. An exciting new publisher of quality books for children.

Barny Books

The Cottage, Hough on the Hill, Near Grantham, Lincolnshire NG32 2BB
☎01400 250246

Managing Director/Editorial Head
Molly Burkett

Business Manager *Tom Cann*
Approx. Annual Turnover £10,000

FOUNDED with the aim of encouraging new writers and illustrators. *Publishes* mainly children's books but moving into adult fiction and non-fiction. TITLES *The Rutland Osprey* Molly Burkett; *Once Upon a Wartime* (series); *Let All the Bells Ring (50 Years of Bell Ringing)* James Dowland; *Diamond's Quest* Lillian Gillard; *Kangaroo Slow* Shealee Inglehart. Too small a concern to have the staff/resources to deal with unsolicited mss. Writers with strong ideas should approach Molly Burkett by letter in the first instance. Also runs a readership and advisory service for new writers (£10 fee for short stories or illustrations; £20 fee for full-length stories).
Royalties division of profits 50/50.

Authors' Rating A gutsy small publisher with a sense of fun which appeals to youngsters.

Barrie & Jenkins
See **Random House UK Ltd**

B. T. Batsford Ltd
583 Fulham Road, London SW6 5BY
☎0171 471 1100   Fax 0171 471 1101
Email: info@batsford.com
Website:www.batsford.com
Chairman *Gerard Mizrahi*
Chief Executive *Jules Perel*
Approx. Annual Turnover £5 million

FOUNDED in 1843 as a bookseller, and began publishing in 1874. An independent publisher until 1996 when it was bought by Labyrinth Publishing UK Ltd. A world leader in books on chess, arts and craft. *Publishes* non-fiction: archaeology, cinema, crafts and hobbies, fashion and costume, graphic design and gardening. Acquired Faber chess list in 1994 and Rushmere Wynne business books list in 1997. About 120 titles a year.
DIVISIONS **Arts & Crafts**; **Archaeology & Ancient History**; **Business**; **Chess**; **Film and Media**; **Graphic Design**; **Horticulture**.
Royalties paid twice in first year, annually thereafter.

Authors' Rating Efficiency is welcome but it should be implemented with sensitivity. In toughening up its act Batsford upset some of its authors by trying to impose a £100 threshold below which royalties would be carried forward. A close reading of contracts is recommended by the Society of Authors.

BBC Worldwide Ltd
80 Wood Lane, London W12 0TT
☎0181 576 2000   Fax 0181 576 2858
Website:www.bbcworldwide.com
Editorial Manager *Richard Larkham*
Approx. Annual Turnover £30 million

Publishes TV tie-in titles, including books which, though linked with BBC television or radio, may not simply be the 'book of the series'. Also publishes TV tie-in titles for children. Books with no television or radio link are of no interest. About 80 titles a year. TITLES *Delia Smith's How to Cook; Shooting Stars; Rhodes Around Britain.* Unsolicited mss (which come in at the rate of about 15 weekly) are rarely accepted. However, strong ideas well expressed will always be considered, and promising letters stand a chance of further scrutiny.
Royalties paid twice-yearly.

Authors' Rating The secret is to come up with an idea as commercial as the Teletubbies. Books, videos, audio cassettes, magazines, greetings cards follow in profitable succession. In other words, think big. Delia Smith did it, why not you.

Bedford Square Press
See **NCVO Publications**

Belair
See **Folens Ltd**

Bellew Publishing Co. Ltd
Nightingale Centre, 8 Balham Hill, London SW12 9EA
☎0181 673 5611   Fax 0181 675 2142
Chairman *Ian McCorquodale*
Managing Director *Ib Bellew*
Approx. Annual Turnover £600,000

FOUNDED 1983. Publisher and packager. *Publishes* craft, art and design, fiction, illustrated non-fiction, general interest, religion and politics. About 15 titles a year. TITLES *We Believe* Alfred Gilbey; *Chronicle* Alan Wall; *The Awakening of Willie Ryland* Tom Hart; *On Depiction: Critical Essays on Art* Avigdor Arikha. No unsolicited mss. Synopses with specimen chapters welcome.
Royalties paid annually.

Berg Publishers
150 Cowley Road, Oxford OX4 1JJ
☎01865 245104   Fax 01865 791165
Email: enquiry@berg.demon.co.uk
Website:www.berg.demon.co.uk
Editorial Director *Kathryn Earle*

Production Director *Sara Everett*

Also **Oswald Wolff Books** imprint. *Publishes* scholarly books in the fields of history, social sciences and humanities. About 45 titles a year. No unsolicited mss. Synopses and ideas for books welcome.

Royalties paid annually.

Berkswell Publishing Co. Ltd

PO Box 420, Warminster, Wiltshire BA12 9XB

☎01985 840189   Fax 01985 840189

Managing Director *John Stidolph*
Approx. Annual Turnover £250,000

FOUNDED 1974. *Publishes* illustrated books, royalty, heritage, country sports, biography and books about Wessex. No fiction. About 4 titles a year. Unsolicited mss, synopses and ideas for books welcome.

Royalties paid according to contract.

Berlitz Publishing Co. Ltd

4th Floor, 9–13 Grosvenor Street, London W1X 9FB

☎0171 518 8300   Fax 0171 518 8310

Website:www.berlitz.com

Chairman *H. Yokoi*
Managing Director *R. Kirkpatrick*

FOUNDED 1970. Part of Berlitz International, which also comprises language instruction and translation divisions. *Publishes* travel and language-learning products only: travel guides, phrasebooks and language courses. SERIES *Pocket Guides; Berlitz Complete Guide to Cruising and Cruise Ships; Phrase Books; Pocket Dictionaries; Business Phrase Books; Self-teach: Rush Hour Commuter Cassettes; Think & Talk; Berlitz Kids.* No unsolicited mss.

BFI Publishing

British Film Institute, 21 Stephen Street, London W1P 2LN

☎0171 255 1444   Fax 0171 436 7950

Website:www.bfi.org.uk

Head of Publishing *Andrew Lockett*
Head of Sales *John Atkinson*
Approx. Annual Turnover £500,000

FOUNDED 1982. Part of the **British Film Institute**. *Publishes* academic and general film/television-related books. About 30 titles a year. TITLES *Film Classics* (series); *Modern Classics* (series); *The Cinema Book, revised edition* eds. Pam Cook and Meike Berninck; *A Handbook of Experimental Film and Video* A. L. Rees; *BFI Film & Television Handbook* (annual) Eddie Dyja.

Unsolicited synopses and ideas preferred to complete mss.

Royalties paid annually.

BFP Books

Focus House, 497 Green Lanes, London N13 4BP

☎0181 882 3315   Fax 0181 886 5174

Chief Executive *John Tracy*
Commissioning Editor *Stewart Gibson*

FOUNDED 1982. The publishing arm of the Bureau of Freelance Photographers. *Publishes* illustrated books on photography, mainly aspects of freelancing and marketing pictures. No unsolicited mss but ideas welcome.

Clive Bingley Books

See **Library Association Publishing Ltd**

Birlinn Ltd

Unit 8 Canongate Venture, 5 New Street, Edinburgh EH8 5BH

☎0131 556 6660   Fax 0131 558 1500

Managing Editor *Hugh Andrew*

FOUNDED 1992. Acquired **John Donald Publishers** in 1999. *Publishes* Gaelic, Scottish interest and history. 80 titles in 1999. No unsolicited mss; synopses and ideas welcome.

Royalties paid.

A. & C. Black (Publishers) Ltd

35 Bedford Row, London WC1R 4JH

☎0171 242 0946   Fax 0171 831 8478

Email: enquiries@acblack.co.uk

Chairman *Charles Black*
Deputy Chairman *David Gadsby*
Managing Directors *Charles Black, Jill Coleman*
Approx. Annual Turnover £7.75 million
(Group turnover)

Publishes children's and educational books, including music, for 3–15-year-olds, arts and crafts, ceramics, fishing, ornithology, nautical, reference, sport, theatre and travel. About 125 titles a year. Acquisitions brought the Herbert Press' art, design and general books, Adlard Coles' sailing list and Christopher Helm's natural history and ornithology lists into A. & C. Black's stable.

IMPRINTS **Adlard Coles Nautical; Christopher Helm; The Herbert Press.** TITLES *New Mermaid* drama series; *Who's Who; Writers' & Artists' Yearbook; Know the Game* sports series; *Blue Guides* travel series. Initial enquiry appreciated before submission of mss.

Royalties Payment varies according to contract.

Black Ace Books

PO Box 6557, Forfar DD8 2YS
☎01307 465096   Fax 01307 465494
Managing Directors *Hunter Steele, Boo Wood*
FOUNDED 1991. *Publishes* new fiction,
Scottish and general; some non-fiction including biography, history, philosophy and psychology. 36 titles in print.

IMPRINTS **Black Ace Books, Black Ace
Paperbacks** TITLES *Succeeding at Sex and
Scotland, Or the Case of Louis Morel* Hunter
Steele; *Spitfire Girls* Carol Gould; *Count Dracula
(The Authorized Version)* Hagen Slawkberg.
Completed books only. No unsolicited mss.
No submissions from outside UK. 'Send only:
one-page covering letter, one-page synopsis,
one full page of text and large s.a.e. If possible,
include one-page recommendation from suit-
able referee such as published author, book
reviewer or university teacher of literature. No
poetry, children's, cookery, DIY, religion.'
Royalties paid twice-yearly.

Black Dagger Crime

See **Chivers Press Ltd**

Black Lace

See **Virgin Publishing Ltd**

Black Spring Press Ltd

2nd Floor, 126 Cornwall Road, London
SE1 8TQ
☎0171 401 2044   Fax 0171 401 2055
Directors *Simon Pettifar, Maja Prausnitz*
FOUNDED 1986. *Publishes* fiction, literary criti-
cism, biography. About 5 titles a year. TITLES
King Ink 2 Nick Cave; *The Mortdecai Trilogy* Kyril
Bonfiglioli; *The Tenant* Roland Topur; *Beautiful
Losers* Leonard Cohen; *The Terrible News* collec-
tion of Russian short stories by Zamyatin, Babel,
Kharms, *et al.* No unsolicited mss.
Royalties paid twice-yearly.

Black Swan

See **Transworld Publishers Ltd**

Blackstaff Press Ltd

Blackstaff House, Wildflower Way, Apollo
Road, Belfast BT12 6TA
☎01232 668074   Fax 01232 668207
Email: books@blkstaff.dnet.co.uk
Director/Editorial Head *Anne Tannahill*
FOUNDED 1971. *Publishes* mainly, but not
exclusively, Irish interest books, fiction, poetry,
history, politics, illustrated editions, natural history and humour. About 25 titles a year. Unsolicited mss considered, but preliminary submission of synopsis plus short sample of writing
preferred. Return postage *must* be enclosed.
Royalties paid twice-yearly.

Authors' Rating This Belfast publisher is
noted for a strong backlist, 'wonderfully well-
presented catalogues and promotional material'.

Blackwell Publishers Ltd

108 Cowley Road, Oxford OX4 1JF
☎01865 791100   Fax 01865 791347
Website:www.blackwellpublishers.co.uk
Chairman *Nigel Blackwell*
Managing Director *René Olivieri*
Approx. Annual Turnover £23.7 million
FOUNDED 1922. Rapid growth since the 1970s
included the establishment of a wholly owned
distribution company, Marston Book Services,
a joint venture with **Polity Press** (see entry).
The focus is on international research journals
and undergraduate textbooks in social sciences,
business and humanities; computer-aided instruction on p.c. applications. About 300 titles
a year and over 150 journals.

DIVISIONS **Books** *Philip Carpenter, Stephan
Chambers* **Journals** *Sue Corbett, Claire Andrews.*
Unsolicited synopses with specimen chapter
and table of contents welcome.
Royalties paid annually. *Overseas associates*
Blackwell Publishers Inc., Maldon, Massachu-
setts; InfoSource Inc., Orlando, Florida.

Authors' Rating Continuing expansion is
thanks largely to successful exploitation of the
US academic market where Blackwell scores
more than half its total sales.

Blackwell Science Ltd

Osney Mead, Oxford OX2 0EL
☎01865 206206   Fax 01865 721205
Website:www.blackwell-science.com
Chairman *Nigel Blackwell*
Managing Director *Robert Campbell*
Editorial Director *Peter Saugman*
Approx. Annual Turnover (Group)
     £105 million
FOUNDED 1939. Rapid growth since the 1970s
along with expansion into Europe in the late
1980s. Also owner of Danish academic publisher
Munksgaard. *Publishes* medical, professional
(including Fishing News Books) and science.
About 400 titles a year, plus 235 journals, now
available on-line. TITLES *Diseases of the Liver and
Biliary System* Sherlock; *Essential Immunology*
Roitt; *Textbook of Dermatology* Champion. Un-
solicited mss and synopses welcome.

Royalties paid annually. *Overseas subsidiaries* in USA, Australia, Japan, Hong Kong, Paris, Berlin and Vienna; editorial offices in London and Edinburgh.

Authors' Rating Blackwell Science's main business is in scientific journals, mostly produced in partnership with learned societies, and medical publishing. Much of the growth is in mainland Europe where Blackwell Science has offshoots in Berlin, Paris and Vienna.

Blake Publishing

3 Bramber Court, 2 Bramber Road, London
W14 9PB
☎0171 381 0666   Fax 0171 381 6868
Chairman *David Blake*
Managing Director *John Blake*
Approx. Annual Turnover £1 million

FOUNDED 1991 and rapidly expanding. Bought the assets of **Smith Gryphon Ltd** in 1997 when that publishing house went into receivership. *Publishes* mass-market non-fiction. No fiction, children's, specialist or non-commercial. About 30 titles a year. No unsolicited mss; synopses and ideas welcome. Please enclose s.a.e.
Royalties paid twice-yearly.

Authors' Rating Unashamedly mass-market with its celebrity titles, tailor-made for press serialisation.

Blandford Press

See **Cassell**

Bloodaxe Books Ltd

PO Box 1SN, Newcastle upon Tyne
NE99 1SN
☎01434 240500   Fax 01434 240505
Email: editor@bloodaxebooks.demon.co.uk
Website:www.bloodaxebooks.demon.co.uk
Chairman *Simon Thirsk*
Managing/Editorial Director *Neil Astley*

Publishes poetry, literature and criticism, and related titles by British, Irish, European, Commonwealth and American writers. 95 per cent of their list is poetry. About 50 titles a year. TITLES include two major anthologies, *The New Poetry* Hulse, Kennedy and Morley (ed.); *Sixty Women Poets* Linda France (ed.); *The Gaze of the Gorgon* Tony Harrison – winner of the **Whitbread Award** for poetry in 1992; *No Truth With the Furies* R. S. Thomas (**Nobel Prize** nominee); *Selected Poems* Jenny Joseph; recent collections by Selima Hill, Helen Dunmore and Peter Reading. Unsolicited poetry mss welcome; send

a sample of no more than 10 poems, 'but if you don't read contemporary poetry, don't bother'. Authors of other material should write in the first instance.
Royalties paid annually.

Authors' Rating Assisted by regional Arts Council funding, Bloodaxe is one of the liveliest and most innovative of poetry publishers with a list that takes in some of the best of the younger poets.

Bloomsbury Publishing Plc

38 Soho Square, London W1V 5DF
☎0171 494 2111   Fax 0171 434 0151
Website:www.bloomsbury.com
Chairman/Chief Executive *Nigel Newton*
Publishing Directors *Liz Calder,*
    David Reynolds, Kathy Rooney, Alan Wherry
    Matthew Hamilton, Sarah Odedina
Approx. Annual Turnover £13.7 million

FOUNDED 1986 by Nigel Newton, David Reynolds, Alan Wherry and Liz Calder. Over the following years Bloomsbury titles were to appear regularly on *The Sunday Times* bestseller list and many of its authors have gone on to win prestigious literary prizes. In 1991 Nadine Gordimer won the **Nobel Prize for Literature**; Michael Ondaatje's *The English Patient* won the 1992 **Booker Prize**; Tobias Wolff's *In Pharaoh's Army* won the Esquire/Volvo/ Waterstone's Non-Fiction Award in 1994; in 1997 Anne Michaels' *Fugitive Pieces* won both the **Orange Prize for Fiction** and the **Guardian Fiction Prize**, Joanna Traynor's *Sister Josephine* won the **SAGA Prize**, J. K. Rowling's *Harry Potter and the Philosopher's Stone* won the **Smarties Book Prize** and Jane Urquhart's *The Underpainter* won the Governor General's Prize in Canada.
Publishes literary fiction and non-fiction, including general reference. AUTHORS Margaret Atwood, T. C. Boyle, Daniel Goleman, David Guterson, John Irving, Jay McInerney, Will Self, Hunter S. Thompson, Rupert Thomson, Joanna Trollope. Unsolicited mss and synopses welcome; no poetry.
Royalties paid twice-yearly.

Authors' Rating Having started as a literary publisher, Bloomsbury now seems to be putting its energy behind reference and electronic media. Cooperation with Microsoft having got off to a good start with a new World English dictionary, further joint projects are anticipated.

Blue Bananas

See **Egmont Children's Books**

Boatswain Press
See **Kenneth Mason Publications Ltd**

Bobcat
See **Omnibus Press**

Bodley Head
See **Random House UK Ltd**

The Book Guild Ltd
Temple House, 25 High Street, Lewes, East
Sussex BN7 2LU
☎01273 472534   Fax 01273 476472
Email: info@bookguild.co.uk
Website:www.bookguild.co.uk
Chairman *George M. Nissen CBE*
Managing Director *Carol Biss*
FOUNDED 1982. *Publishes* fiction, human in-
terest, children's fiction, academic, natural
history, naval and military, biography, art.
Approx. 80 titles a year. Expanding mainstream
list, plus developing the human interest genre.

DIVISIONS/TITLES
Cookery *Famous Family Food* 50 celebrity
receipes in aid of Kidney Research Aid.
Children's *Underneath the Underground Books
1&2* Anthea Turner and Wendy Turner.
Human Interest *A Matter of Timing: Dealing
with Alzheimer's* Audrey Brown. **Biography**
Tony Hancock's Last Stand Edward Joffe; **Natural
History** *Mindful of Butterflies* Valerie Baines.
Travel *A View of China* Dora Gauss. **Fiction**
Days of Rage Desmond Meiring. **History**
Manhattan Tales 1920–1945 Isabel Butterfield.
IMPRINT **Temple House Books** Non-
fiction: *The Fitzroy* Sally Fiber; *Colditz, Last
Stop* Jack Pringle. Unsolicited mss, ideas and
synopses welcome.
Royalties paid twice-yearly.

Authors' Rating Regularly advertises for
authors who may be asked to cover their own
production costs. But in promoting its services,
The Book Guild is more up-front with its
clients than the typical vanity publisher who
promises the earth and delivers next to nothing.

Boulevard Books &
The Babel Guides
8 Aldbourne Road, London W12 0LN
☎0181 743 5278   Fax 0181 743 5278
Email: raybabel@dircon.co.uk
Website:www.raybabel.dircon.co.uk
Managing Director *Ray Keenoy*
Specialises in contemporary world fiction by
young writers in English translation. Existing or
forthcoming series of fiction from Brazil, Italy,
Latin America, Low Countries, Greece, and
elsewhere. The Babel Guides series of popular
guides to fiction in translation started in 1995.

DIVISONS
Latin American *Ray Keenoy* TITLE *Hotel
Atlantico* J. G. Noll. **Italian** *Fiorenza Conte*
TITLE *The Toy Catalogue* Sandra Petrignani.
Brazil *Dr David Treece* TITLE *From the Heart of
Brazil* (anthology). **Low Countries** *Prof. Theo
Hermans.* **Greece** *Marina Coriolano-Likourezos.*
Babel Guides to Fiction in Translation *Ray
Keenoy* Series Editor TITLES *Babel Guide to
Italian Fiction in Translation*; *Babel Guide to the
Fiction of Portugal, Brazil & Africa in Translation*;
*Babel Guide to French Fiction in English
Translation*; *Babel Guide to Jewish Fiction.*
Suggestions and proposals for translations of
contemporary fiction welcome. Also seeking
contributors to forthcoming Babel Guides (all
literatures).
Royalties paid annually.

Bounty
See **Octopus Publishing Group**

Bowker–Saur
Windsor Court, East Grinstead House, East
Grinstead, West Sussex RH19 1XA
☎01342 326972   Fax 01342 336192
Website:www.bowker-saur.com
Group Publishing Director *Gerard Dummett*
Managing Director *Charles Halpin*
Publishers *Geraldine Turpie*
Owned by Reed Elsevier, Bowker-Saur is part
of Reed Business Information in the UK.
Publishes library reference, library science,
bibliography, biography, African studies, busi-
ness and professional directories. Unsolicited
mss will not be read. Approach with ideas only.
Royalties paid annually.

Boxtree
See **Macmillan Publishers Ltd**

Marion Boyars Publishers Ltd
24 Lacy Road, London SW15 1NL
☎0181 788 9522   Fax 0181 789 8122
Editor *Karen McCrossan*
Editor, Non-fiction *Ken Hollings*
FOUNDED 1975, formerly Calder and Boyars.
Publishes biography and autobiography, economics, fiction, literature and criticism, music,
philosophy, poetry, politics and world affairs,
psychology, sociology and anthropology, theatre
and drama, film and cinema, women's studies.

About 30 titles a year. AUTHORS include Georges Bataille, Ingmar Bergman, Heinrich Böll, Hortense Calisher, Jean Cocteau, Clive Collins, Warwick Collins, Carlo Gébler, Julian Green, Ivan Illich, Pauline Kael, Ken Kesey, Kenzaburo Oe, Michael Ondaatje, Hubert Selby, Igor Stravinsky, Frederic Tuten, Eudora Welty, Judith Williamson, Tom Wiseman. Unsolicited mss not welcome for fiction or poetry; submissions from agents preferred. Unsolicited synopses and ideas welcome for non-fiction.

Royalties paid annually. *Overseas associates* Marion Boyars Publishers Inc., 237 East 39th Street, New York, NY 10016, USA.

Authors' Rating Marion Boyars caters exclusively for the intellectual top end of the book market.

Boydell & Brewer Ltd
PO Box 9, Woodbridge, Suffolk IP12 3DF
☎01394 411320

Publishes non-fiction only, principally medieval studies. All books commissioned. No unsolicited material.

BPS Books
St Andrews House, 48 Princess Road East,
Leicester LE1 7DR
☎0116 2549568   Fax 0116 2470787
Website:www.bps.org.uk
Publications Manager *Joyce Collins*
Editor *Susan Pacitti, Jon Reed*

Book publishing division of The British Psychological Society. *Publishes* a wide range of academic and applied psychology, including specialist monographs, textbooks for teachers, managers, doctors, nurses, social workers, and schools material; plus general psychology and some electronic publishing. 10–15 titles a year. Proposals considered.

Bradt Publications
41 Nortoft Road, Chalfont St Peter,
Buckinghamshire SL9 0LA
☎01494 873478   Fax 01484 873478
Email: bradtpublications@compuserve.com
Managing Director *Hilary Bradt*
Editorial Head *Tricia Hayne*
Approx. Annual Turnover £300,000

FOUNDED in 1974 by Hilary Bradt. *Specialises* in travel guides to off-beat places. 13 titles in 1998. TITLES *Guide to Ethiopia; Madagascar; Zanzibar; Cuba*, etc.; *Wildlife Guide to Madagascar; Antarctica; Rail Guide to USA; Greece; India; Backpacking Guides; By Road Guides; Climbing and Hiking in Ecuador.* No unsolicited mss; synopses and ideas for travel guidebooks welcome.

Royalties paid twice-yearly.

Brampton Publications
See **SB Publications**

Brassey's (UK) Ltd
583 Fulham Road, London SW6 5BY
☎0171 471 1100   Fax 0171 471 1101
Email: info@batsford.com
Website:www.batsford.com
Chief Executive *Jules Perel*

Began life as *Brassey's Naval Annual* in 1886 to become the most important publisher of serious defence-related material in the world. Part of **B. T. Batsford** following its acquisition by Batsford Communications in April '98. *Publishes* books and journals on defence, international relations, military history, maritime and aeronautical subjects and defence terminology. Further sports titles are being published under the **Brassey's Sports** imprint in both the UK and US.

IMPRINTS **Brassey's (UK)**; **Brassey's Inc**; **Brassey's Sports**; **Conway Maritime Press** Naval history and ship modelling; **Putnam Aeronautical Books** Technical and reference.

Royalties paid annually.

Nicholas Brealey Publishing Ltd
36 John Street, London WC1N 2AT
☎0171 430 0224   Fax 0171 404 8311
Website:www.nbrealey-books.com
Managing Director *Nicholas Brealey*

FOUNDED 1992, an independent and international non-fiction publisher focusing on high-profile, practical books for business that inspire, enable, inform and entertain. *Publishes* on the 'big picture', management, training and human resources. 20 titles a year. TITLES *Coaching for Performance; The 80/20 Principle; Reengineering the Corporation; NLP at Work; The Living Company; The Fifth Discipline Fieldbook; China Wakes; The Death of Inflation; Rethinking the Future; Intellectual Capital.* No fiction, poetry or leisure titles. No unsolicited mss; synopses and ideas welcome.

Royalties paid twice-yearly.

Authors' Rating Looks to be succeeding in breaking away from the usual computer-speak business manuals to publish information and literate texts. Lead titles have a distinct trans-Atlantic feel.

The Breedon Books Publishing Co. Ltd

44 Friar Gate, Derby DE1 1DA
☎01332 384235   Fax 01332 292755
Email: breedonbooks@netmatters.co.uk
Chairman/Managing Director
A. C. Rippon
Approx. Annual Turnover £1 million
FOUNDED 1983. *Publishes* autobiography, biography, local history, old photographs, heritage and sport. 40 titles in 1998. Unsolicited mss, synopses and ideas welcome if accompanied by s.a.e. No poetry or fiction.
Royalties paid annually.

Breese Books Ltd

164 Kensington Park Road, London
W11 2ER
☎0171 727 9426   Fax 0171 229 3395
Email: MBreese999@aol.com
Chairman/Managing Director
Martin Ranicar-Breese
FOUNDED 1975 to produce specialist conjuring books and then went on to establish a more general list. Breese Books has now closed its general publishing division and is concentrating on two specific areas: conjuring/sleight of hand/illusions and Sherlock Holmes pastiches. There is little point in submitting material on any subjects other than the above.

Authors' Rating Having cut back on his publishing programme Martin Breese is offering a Critical Eye Service to advise authors on how to make their work saleable. There are no guarantees of publication and there is a charge but for some, straight practical advice may be useful.

Brimax

See **Octopus Publishing Group**

Bristol Classical Press

See **Gerald Duckworth & Co. Ltd**

British Academic Press

See **I. B. Tauris & Co. Ltd**

The British Academy

10 Carlton House Terrace, London
SW1Y 5AH
☎0171 969 5200   Fax 0171 969 5300
Email: secretary@britac.ac.uk
Website:www.britac.ac.uk
Publications Officer *J. M. H. Rivington*
Publications Assistant *J. English*
FOUNDED 1901. The primary body for promoting scholarship in the humanities, the Academy publishes many series stemming from its own long-standing research projects, or series of lectures and conference proceedings. Main subjects include history, philosophy and archaeology. About 10–15 titles a year. SERIES *Auctores Britannici Medii Aevi; Early English Church Music; Fontes Historiae Africanae; Records of Social and Economic History.* Proposals for these series are welcome and are forwarded to the relevant project committees. The British Academy is a registered charity and does not publish for profit.
Royalties paid only when titles have covered their costs.

The British Library

96 Euston Road, London NW1 2DB
☎0171 412 7704   Fax 0171 412 7768
Managing Director *Jane Carr*
Publishing Manager *David Way*
Approx. Annual Turnover £950,000
FOUNDED 1979 as the publishing arm of The British Library's London Collections to publish works based on the historic collections and related subjects. *Publishes* bibliographical reference, manuscript studies, illustrated books based on the Library's collections, and book arts. TITLES *Historical Source Book for Scribes; New Found Lands: Maps in the History of Exploration; The British Library Writers' Lives Series; Medieval Medicine in Illuminated Manuscripts.* About 35 titles a year. Unsolicited mss, synopses and ideas welcome if related to the history of the book, book arts or bibliography. No fiction or general non-fiction.
Royalties paid annually.

British Museum Press

46 Bloomsbury Street, London WC1B 3QQ
☎0171 323 1234   Fax 0171 436 7315
Website:www.britishmuseumcompany.co.uk
Managing Director *Patrick Wright*
Head of Publishing *Emma Way*
The book publishing division of The British Museum Company Ltd. FOUNDED 1973 as British Museum Publications Ltd; relaunched 1991 as British Museum Press. *Publishes* ancient history, archaeology, ethnography, art history, exhibition catalogues, guides, children's books, and all official publications of the British Museum. Around 50 titles a year. TITLES *Egypt; Indigo; Sutton Hoo; Burial Ground of Kings; Cartier 1900–1939; Ancient Mosaics; Hieroglyphs and How to Read Them.* Synopses and ideas for books welcome.
Royalties paid twice-yearly.

The Brockhampton Press
See **Hodder Headline plc**

Andrew Brodie Publications
PO Box 23, Wellington, Somerset TA21 8YX
☎01823 665345   Fax 01823 665345
Email: andrew@abp-ltd.demon.co.uk
Website:www.abp-ltd.demon.co.uk
Chairman *Andrew Brodie*
Approx. Annual Turnover £150,000

FOUNDED 1992. *Publishes* children's books. 7 titles in 1998. TITLES *Times Tables Today; Spelling Today; Maths Today; Pink Pig Turns Brown.* Unsolicited mss, synopses and ideas for books welcome; send a letter in the first instance.
Royalties paid annually.

John Brown Publishing Ltd
The New Boathouse, 136–142 Bramley Road, London W10 6SR
☎0171 565 3000   Fax 0171 565 3055
Chairman/Managing Director *John Brown*

FOUNDED 1986. *Publishes* adult comic annuals; *Viz* magazine; strange phenomena. 10 titles in 1998. DIVISION **Fortean Times Books** *Mike Dash* TITLES *Book of Weird Sex; Book of Strange Deaths; Book of Inept Crime; Book of Exploding Pigs; Weird Year 1999; Fortean Studies Vol 4.* Does not welcome unsolicited mss.
Royalties paid twice-yearly.

Brown, Son & Ferguson, Ltd
4–10 Darnley Street, Glasgow G41 2SD
☎0141 429 1234   Fax 0141 420 1694
Email: info@skipper.co.uk
Website:www.skipper.co.uk
Chairman/Joint Managing Director
  T. Nigel Brown

FOUNDED 1850. *Specialises* in nautical textbooks, both technical and non-technical. Also Boy Scout/Girl Guide books, and Scottish one-act/three-act plays. Unsolicited mss, synopses and ideas for books welcome.
Royalties paid annually.

Bryntirion Press (formerly Evangelical Press of Wales)
Bryntirion House, Bridgend, Mid-Glamorgan CF31 4DX
☎01656 655886   Fax 01656 656095
Email: press@draco.co.uk
Chairman *Reverend S. Jones*
Managing Editor *David Kingdon*
Approx. Annual Turnover £100,000

Owned by the Evangelical Movement of Wales.

Publishes Christian books in English and Welsh. 12 titles in 1998. TITLES *God Spoke to Them; Talking it Over; Vital Questions; Welsh Calvinistic Methodism; Daniel Cast Out; Christmas Sermons.* No unsolicited mss; synopses and ideas welcome.
Royalties paid annually.

Bucknell University Press
See **Golden Cockerel Press Ltd**

Burns & Oates
See **Search Press**

Business Education Publishers Ltd
Leighton House, 10 Grange Crescent, Sunderland, Tyne & Wear SR2 7BN
☎0191 567 4963   Fax 0191 514 3277
Managing Director *P. M. Callaghan*
Approx. Annual Turnover £400,000

FOUNDED 1981. *Publishes* business education, economics and law for BTEC and GNVQ reading. Currently expanding into further and higher education, computing, community health services, travel and tourism, occasional papers for institutions and local government administration. Unsolicited mss and synopses welcome.
Royalties paid annually.

Butterworth Tolley
Tolley House, 2 Addiscombe Road, Croydon, Surrey CR9 5AF
☎0181 686 9141   Fax 0181 686 3155
Chief Executive *Neville Cusworth*
Managing Director *Kelvin Ladbrook*

Owned by Reed Elsevier Legal Division.
  DIVISIONS **Tolley Publishing; Charles Knight Publishing; Payroll Alliance; Butterworths Tax Publications**. Unsolicited mss, synopses and ideas welcome.

Butterworth-Heinemann International
See **Reed Educational & Professional Publishing**

C&B Publishing Plc
See **Collins & Brown**

Cadogan Books plc
See **David Campbell Publishers Ltd**

Calder Publications Ltd
126 Cornwall Road, London SE1 8TQ
☎0171 633 0599
Chairman/Managing Director/Editorial Head *John Calder*

Formerly John Calder (Publishers) Ltd. A publishing company which has grown around the tastes and contacts of John Calder, the iconoclast of the literary establishment. The list has a reputation for controversial and opinion-forming publications; Samuel Beckett is perhaps the most prestigious name. The list includes all of Beckett's prose and poetry. *Publishes* autobiography, biography, drama, literary fiction, literary criticism, music, opera, poetry, politics, sociology. AUTHORS Roy Calne, Marguerite Duras, Erich Fried, Trevor Hoyle, P. J. Kavanagh, Robert Pinget, Alain Robbe-Grillet, Nathalie Sarraute, Julian Semyonov, Claude Simon, Howard Barker (plays), ENO opera guides. *No new material accepted.*
Royalties paid annually.

Authors' Rating The last of the independent publishers, known for his patronage of eccentric talents, John Calder claims to be one of the few to carry the flag for the English language '... which is in great danger of disappearing under the American vernacular'.

California University Press
See **University Presses of California, Columbia & Princeton Ltd**

Cambridge University Press
The Edinburgh Building, Shaftesbury Road, Cambridge CB2 2RU
☎01223 312393   Fax 01223 315052
Website:www.cup.cam.ac.uk
Chief Executive *A. K. Wilson*
Managing Director, Publishing *R. J. Mynott*

The oldest printer and publisher in the world with established branches in the USA and Australia. Winner of The Queen's Award for Export Achievement in 1998. Over the last ten years, Cambridge has opened 15 new offices around the world and established new branches in Madrid and Cape Town. Its books are sold in more than 200 countries. Publications include the Cambridge Histories and Companions, encyclopedias and dictionaries; the **Canto** series; popular science and scientific and medical reference; major ELT courses; coursebooks for the National Curriculum; Cambridge Reading; and Cambridge Low Price Editions for the developing world. *Publishes* academic/educational and reference books for English-language markets worldwide, at all levels from primary school to postgraduate. Also ELT, Bibles and over 140 academic journals. Over 23,000 authors in 106 different countries and about 1800 new titles a year.

PUBLISHING GROUPS
Bibles *C. J. Wright* **ELT** *C. J. F. Hayes* **Education** *A. C. Gilfillan* **Humanities and Social Sciences** *A. M. C. Brown* **Medical and Professional Publishing** *R. W. A. Barling* **Journals** *C. Guettler* **Science Publishing** *A. E. Crowden.* Synopses and ideas for educational, ELT and academic books are welcomed (and preferable to the submission of unsolicited mss). No fiction or poetry.
Royalties paid twice-yearly.

Authors' Rating Not so many monographs from the obscure corners of academia but CUP has adapted to changing times and shrinking library budgets by expanding into reference, English Language Teaching and foreign language publishing.

Camden Press Ltd
46 Colebrooke Row, London N1 8AF
☎0171 226 2061   Fax 0171 226 2418
Chairman *Bob Borzello*

FOUNDED 1985. An imprint of stationery publishers, Camden Graphics. *Publishes* social issues; all books are launched in connection with major national conferences. 3 titles in 1998. DIVISION **Publishing for Change** *Bob Borzello* TITLE *Living with the Legacy of Abuse.* IMPRINT **Mindfield** *Susan Greenberg* TITLES *Hate Thy Neighbour: The Race Issue; Therapy on the Couch.* No unsolicited material. Approach by telephone in the first instance.
Royalties paid annually.

Camden Softcover Large Print
See **Chivers Press Ltd**

David Campbell Publishers Ltd
Gloucester Mansions, 140a Shaftesbury Avenue, London WC2H 8HD
☎0171 539 7600   Fax 0171 379 4060
Managing Director *David Campbell*
Approx. Annual Turnover £3.5 million

FOUNDED 1990 with the acquisition of Everyman's Library (established 1906) bought from J. M. Dent. Merged with Cadogan Books plc in 1995. *Publishes* classics of world literature, pocket poetry anthologies, music companion guides and travel guides. AUTHORS include Bulgakov, Bellow, Borges, Forster, Grass, Mann, Nabokov, Orwell, Rushdie, Updike and Waugh. No unsolicited mss. IMPRINT **Adelphi** Illustrated books.
Royalties paid annually.

Campbell Books
See **Macmillan Publishers Ltd**

Candle Books
See **Angus Hudson** under **UK Packagers**

Canongate Books Ltd
14 High Street, Edinburgh EH1 1TE
☎0131 557 5111   Fax 0131 557 5211
Website:www.canongate.co.uk
Publisher *Jamie Byng*
Approx. Annual Turnover £1.75 million
FOUNDED 1973. Independent publisher, following a management buyout in October 1994. *Publishes* a wide range of fiction and non-fiction. There is a strong Scottish slant to part of the house.
IMPRINTS **Canongate Classics** Adult paperback series dedicated solely to important works of Scottish literature; **Kelpie** Children's paperback fiction series; **Payback Press** Afro-American, Black orientated fiction and non-fiction; music, history, politics, biography and poetry; **Rebel Inc.** promotion of new writing – fiction, poetry and non-fiction – as well as underground and neglected classics. About 70 titles a year. Synopses preferred to complete mss.
Royalties paid twice-yearly.

Authors' Rating It started as a purely Scottish publisher but now extends to a wide range of new writing and contemporary issues. Bright idea of the year was to republish the Bible in its constituent parts, each with a lively and thought-provoking introduction.

Canterbury Press Norwich
See **Hymns Ancient & Modern Ltd**

Canto
See **Cambridge University Press**

Capall Bann Publishing
Freshfields, Chieveley, Berkshire RG20 8TF
☎01635 247050/248711
Fax 01635 247050/248711
Chairman *Julia Day*
Editorial Head *Jon Day*
FOUNDED 1993 with three titles and now have over 150 in print. Family-owned and -run company which *publishes* British traditions, folklore, computing, boating, animals, environmental, Celtic lore, mind, body and spirit. 40 titles in 1998. TITLES *Practical Spirituality; Celtic Lore; Handbook of Fairies; Talking to the Earth; Bruce Roberts' Boatbuilding.* Synopses and ideas

for books welcome. No fiction or poetry.
Royalties paid quarterly.

Jonathan Cape Ltd
See **Random House UK Ltd**

Carcanet Press Ltd
Conavon Court, 12–16 Blackfriars Street, Manchester M3 5BQ
☎0161 834 8730   Fax 0161 832 0084
Email: pnr@carcanet.u-net.com
Website:www.carcanet.co.uk
Chairman *Kate Gavron*
Managing Director/Editorial Director
    Michael Schmidt
Since 1969 Carcanet has grown from an undergraduate hobby into a substantial venture. Robert Gavron bought the company in 1983 and it has established strong Anglo-European and Anglo-Commonwealth links. *Publishes* poetry, academic, literary biography, fiction in translation and translations. About 50 titles a year, including the *P. N. Review* (six issues yearly). AUTHORS John Ashbery, Edwin Morgan, Elizabeth Jennings, Iain Crichton Smith, Natalia Ginzburg, Eavan Boland, Stuart Hood, Leonardo Sciascia, Christine Brooke-Rose, Pier Paolo Pasolini, C. H. Sisson, Donald Davie.
Royalties paid annually.

Authors' Rating Ever in the forefront of imaginative publishing, Carcanet has taken a step closer to the source of its literary creativity by setting up a postgraduate Writing School at Manchester Metropolitan University. (See entry under **Writers' Courses, Circles and Workshops**.)

Cardiff Academic Press
St Fagans Road, Fairwater, Cardiff CF5 3AE
☎01222 560333   Fax 01222 554909
Managing Director *R. G. Drake*
Academic publishers.

Carfax Publishing
See **Taylor & Francis Group plc**

Carlton Books Ltd
20 St Anne's Court, Wardour Street, London W1V 3AW
☎0171 734 7338
Fax 0171 434 1196/0171 734 7371
Managing Director *Jonathan Goodman*
Approx. Annual Turnover £11 million
FOUNDED 1992. Owned by Carlton Communications, Carlton books are aimed at the mass

market for subjects such as lifestyle, computer games, sport, health, puzzles, popular science and rock'n'roll. *Publishes* illustrated leisure and entertainment. Prime UK customers include the Book Club and W. H. Smith. A second arm of the company, established late 1992, was set up to create a promotional books business. No unsolicited mss; synopses and ideas welcome.

Royalties paid twice-yearly.

Authors' Rating Linked to the largest programme producer in the ITV network, Carlton Books has built a reputation on co-editions for the international market and television tie-ins. Noted for speed of taking a book from first idea to publication.

Frank Cass & Co Ltd

Newbury House, 890–900 Eastern Avenue, Newbury Park, Ilford, Essex IG2 7HH
☎0181 599 8866   Fax 0181 599 0984
Email: info@frankcass.com

Chairman *Frank Cass*
Managing Director *Stewart Cass*
Managing Editor *Andrew Humphrys* (Books Editor)

Publishes books and journals in the fields of politics, international relations, military and security studies, history, Middle East and African studies, economics, development studies. TITLES *Central Asia Meets the Middle East* ed. David Henashin; *In Pursuit of Military Excellence* Shimon Naveh; *Knowing Your Friends* Martin S. Alexander; *The Liberian Civil War* Mark Huband; *Regional Dynamics* Wiliam Field.

DIVISIONS **Woburn Press** Educational list TITLES *Her Majesty's Inspectorate of Schools Since 1944* John E. Dunford; *Going Comprehensive in England and Wales* Alan C. Kercknoff. **Vallentine Mitchell/Jewish Chronicle Publications** Books of Jewish interest TITLES *The Library of Holocaust Testimonies* series; *The Jewish Yearbook 1998* ed. Stephen Massil; *The Jewish Travel Guide*; *Soldier of Jerusalem* Uzi Narkiss. Unsolicited mss considered but synopsis with covering letter preferred.

Royalties paid annually.

Cassell

Wellington House, 125 Strand, London WC2R 0BB
☎0171 420 5555   Fax 0171 240 7261
Website:www.cassell.co.uk

Chairman/Managing Director *Philip Sturrock*
Approx. Annual Turnover £25 million

FOUNDED 1848 by John Cassell. Bought by Collier Macmillan in 1974, then by CBS Publishing Europe in 1982. Returned to independence in 1986 as Cassell plc and a string of acquisitions followed: Tycooly's book publishing division; Link House Books (now Blandford Publishing Ltd); Mansell; then Mowbray and Ward Lock, publisher of Mrs Beeton, (in print continuously since 1861); Victor Gollancz Ltd in 1992 and Pinter Publishers Ltd in February 1995. Acquired by the **Orion Publishing Group** in December 1998. *Publishes* business, education and academic, general non-fiction, primary and secondary school books, poetry, religion. About 700 titles a year.

IMPRINTS

Cassell General Books *Alison Goff* TITLES *Poems on the Underground; Cordon Bleu Complete Cookery Techniques; Cacti: The Illustrated Dictionary.*

Cassell Academic Books *Janet Joyce, Naomi Roth* TITLES *Cassell Guide to Literature in French; Supervisory Management; Reflective Teaching in Primary Schools.*

Mansell *Janet Joyce* TITLES *Index of English Literary Manuscripts; Facts About the Prime Ministers.*

Arms & Armour Press *Nick Chapman* TITLES *First World War Sourcebook; Napoleonic Weapons & Warfare; Great Battles of the Royal Navy.*

Blandford Press *Alison Goff* TITLES *piders of the World; Celebration of Maritime Art; SCeltic Art Sourcebook; Make Your Own Electric Guitar.*

Ward Lock *Alison Goff* TITLES *Mrs Beeton's Book of Cookery and Household Management; Home & Garden Style; Ward Lock Gardening Encyclopedia.*

Victor Gollancz (Orion House, 5 Upper St Martin's Lane, London WC2H 9EA) *Mike Petty* TITLES *Lost Gardens of Heligan; About a Boy* Nick Hornby; *Beat Route* Jools Holland.

Geoffrey Chapman *Ruth McCurry* TITLES *New Jerome Biblical Commentary; The Catechism of the Catholic Church.*

Mowbray *Ruth McCurry* TITLES *Why God* Bishop of Bath & Wells;.

Leicester University Press *Janet Joyce* TITLES *Museums and Popular Culture; Language of Displayed Art; Medieval Fortifications.*

Pinter *Janet Joyce* TITLES *States and Markets; European Union, Work for All?*

Castle Publications

See **Nottingham University Press**

Kyle Cathie Ltd

20 Vauxhall Bridge Road, London SW1V 2SA
☎0171 840 8793   Fax 0171 821 9258
Email: kcathie@aol.com

Publisher/Managing Director *Kyle Cathie*

Sales/Marketing Director *Julia Scott*

FOUNDED 1990 to publish and promote 'books we have personal enthusiasm for'. *Publishes* non-fiction: cookery, food and drink, health and beauty, style/design, reference and occasional books of classic poetry. TITLES *Rejuvenating a Garden* Stephen Anderton; *Patricia Wells at Home in Provence*; *Feel Fabulous Forever* Josephine Fairley and Sarah Stacey. About 25 titles a year. No unsolicited mss. 'Synopses and ideas are considered in the fields in which we publish.'
Royalties paid twice-yearly.

Catholic Truth Society
40–46 Harleyford Road, London SE11 5AY
☎0171 640 0042   Fax 0171 640 0046
Chairman *Rt. Rev. Peter Smith*
General Secretary *Fergal Martin*
Approx. Annual Turnover £500,000

FOUNDED originally in 1869 and re-founded in 1884. *Publishes* religious books – Roman Catholic and ecumencial; a variety of doctrinal, moral, biographical, devotional and liturgical publications, including a large body of Vatican documents and sources. Unsolicited mss, synopses and ideas welcome if appropriate to their list.
Royalties paid annually.

Caucasus World
See **Curzon Press Ltd**

Causeway Press Ltd
PO Box 13, 129 New Court Way, Ormskirk, Lancashire L39 5HP
☎01695 576048   Fax 01695 570714
Chairman/Managing Director *M. Haralambos*
Approx. Annual Turnover £2 million

FOUNDED in 1982. *Publishes* educational textbooks only. 12 titles in 1998. TITLES *Causeway Maths Series*; *Discovering History Series*; *Economics/Business Studies*; *Sociology in Focus*; *Causeway GNVQ*; *Design and Technology*. Unsolicited mss, synopses and ideas welcome.
Royalties paid annually.

CBA Publishing
Bowes Morrell House, 111 Walmgate, York YO1 9WA
☎01904 671417   Fax 01904 671384
Publications Officer *Kathryn Sleight*
Approx. Annual Turnover £80,000

Publishing arm of the **Council for British Archaeology**. *Publishes* academic archaeology reports, practical handbooks, yearbook, *Young Archaeologist* (the Young Archaeologists' Club magazine), *British Archaeology* (monthly magazine), monographs, archaeology and education. TITLES *St Bartholomew's Hospital; Romano-British Glass Vessels: A Handbook; Churches and Chapel: Recording Places of Worship*.
Royalties not paid.

CBD Research Ltd
Chancery House, 15 Wickham Road, Beckenham, Kent BR3 5JS
☎0181 650 7745   Fax 0181 650 0768
Email: cbdresearch@compuserver.com
Website:www.the.glen.co.uk/cbd/
Chairman *G. P. Henderson*
Managing Director *S. P. A. Henderson*
Approx. Annual Turnover £500,000

FOUNDED 1961. *Publishes* directories and other reference guides to sources of information. About 6 titles a year. No fiction.
IMPRINT **Chancery House Press** Non-fiction of an esoteric/specialist nature for 'serious researchers and the dedicated hobbyist'. Unsolicited mss, synopses and ideas welcome.
Royalties paid quarterly.

Centaur Press
See **Open Gate Press**

Century
See **Random House UK Ltd**

Chadwyck-Healey Ltd
The Quorum, Barnwell Road, Cambridge CB5 8SW
☎01223 215512   Fax 01223 215513
Website:www.chadwyck.co.uk
Chairman *Sir Charles Chadwyck-Healey*
Managing Director *Steven Hall*
Approx. Annual Turnover £8.2 million

FOUNDED 1973. *Publishes* literary full-text and humanities reference databases on microform, CD-ROM and the World Wide Web. No monographs. About 50 titles a year. TITLES *Know UK; Literature Online; The English Poetry Full-Text Database; Periodical Contents Index*. No unsolicited mss. Synopses and ideas welcome for reference works only.
Royalties paid annually.

Authors' Rating Having lead the breakthrough to CD-ROM, Chadwyck-Healey is now busily adapting to the Internet. This requires an expensive restructuring of the company's support services. But that's technology for you.

Chambers Harrap Publishers Ltd

7 Hopetoun Crescent, Edinburgh EH7 4AY
☎0131 556 5929   Fax 0131 556 5313
Managing Director *Maurice Shepherd*

Publishes dictionaries, reference, and local interest. The imprint was founded in the early 1800s to publish self-education books, but soon diversified into dictionaries and other reference works. The acquisition of Harrap Publishing Group's core business strengthened its position in the dictionary market, adding bilingual titles, covering almost all the major European languages, to its English-language dictionaries. Send synopsis with accompanying letter rather than completed mss.

Chameleon

See **André Deutsch Ltd**

Chancery House Press

See **CBD Research Ltd**

Channel 4 Books

See **Macmillan Publishers Ltd**

Geoffrey Chapman

See **Cassell**

Paul Chapman Publishing Ltd

See **Sage Publications Ltd**

Chapman Publishing

4 Broughton Place, Edinburgh EH1 3RX
☎0131 557 2207   Fax 0131 556 9565
Email: chapman-pub@ndirect.co.uk
Website: www.airstrip-one.ndirect.co.uk/
  chapman
Managing Editor *Joy Hendry*

A venture devoted to publishing works by the best of the Scottish writers, both up-and-coming and established, published in *Chapman* magazine, Scotland's leading literary quarterly. Has expanded publishing activities considerably over the last two years and is now publishing a wider range of works though the broad policy stands. *Publishes* poetry, drama, short stories, books of contemporary importance in 20th-century Scotland. About 4 titles a year. TITLES *Carlucco & the Queen of Hearts; The Blasphemer* George Rosie; *Gold of Kildonan; Songs of the Grey Coast; Whins* George Gunn; *The Collected Shorter Poems* Tom Scott; *Alien Crop* Janet Paisley; *Good Girls Don't Cry* Margaret Fulton Cook. No unsolicited mss; synopses and ideas for books welcome.
Royalties paid annually.

Chapmans Publishers

See **The Orion Publishing Group Ltd**

Charnwood

See **F. A. Thorpe (Publishing) Ltd**

Chatham Publishing

See **Gerald Duckworth & Co Ltd**

Chatto & Windus Ltd

See **Random House UK Ltd**

Cherrytree Press Children's Books

See **Chivers Press Ltd**

Child's Play (International) Ltd

Ashworth Road, Bridgemead, Swindon,
Wiltshire SN5 7YD
☎01793 616286   Fax 01793 512795
Email: allday@childs-play.com
Chairman *Michael Twinn*

FOUNDED in 1972, Child's Play is an independent publisher specialising in learning through play, whole child development, life-skills and values. *Publishes* books, games and A-V materials. TITLES *Big Hungry Bear; There Was An Old Lady; Puzzle Island; Children of the Sun; Ten Beads Tall; Pocket Pals; Great Pals; Big Books and Storysacks.* Unsolicited mss welcome. Send s.a.e. for return or response. Expect to wait two months for a reply.
   Royalties Outright or royalty payments are subject to negotiation.

Chimera Book Publishers

Sheraton House, Castle Park, Cambridge
CB3 0AX
☎01223 370012   Fax 01223 370040
Senior Editor *D. W. Stern*
Editor *R. Sabir*

Publishes fiction and non-fiction, general interest, biography, autobiography, humour, science fiction, erotica and crime. Unsolicited mss, synopses and ideas considered if accompanied by return postage.
   Royalties paid twice-yearly.

Chivers Press Ltd

Windsor Bridge Road, Bath BA2 3AX
☎01225 335336   Fax 01225 310771
Email: sales@chivers.co.uk
Website:www.chivers.co.uk
Managing Director *Julian R. Batson*
Approx. Annual Turnover £9 million

Part of the Gieves Group. *Publishes* reprints for

libraries mainly, in large-print editions, including biography and autobiography, children's, crime, fiction and spoken word cassettes. No unsolicited material.

IMPRINTS **Chivers Large Print; Gunsmoke Westerns; Galaxy Children's Large Print; Camden Softcover Large Print; Paragon Softcover Large Print; Cherrytree Press Children's Books; Windsor Large Print; Black Dagger Crime.** Chivers Audio Books (see entry under **Audio Books**.

Royalties paid twice-yearly.

Christian Focus Publications

Geanies House, Fearn, Tain, Ross-shire IV20 1TW
☎01862 871011   Fax 01862 871699
Email: efp@geanies.org.uk
Website:www.christianfocus.com

Chairman *R. W. M. Mackenzie*
Managing Director *William Mackenzie*
Editorial Head *Malcolm Maclean*
Children's Editor *Catherine Mackenzie*
Approx. Annual Turnover £900,000

FOUNDED 1979 to produce children's books for the co-edition market. Now a major producer of Christian books. *Publishes* adult and children's books, including some fiction for children but not adults. No poetry. About 70 titles a year. Unsolicited mss, synopses and ideas welcome from Christian writers. Publishes for all English-speaking markets, as well as the UK. Books produced for Australia, USA, Canada, South Africa.

IMPRINTS **Christian Focus** General books; **Mentor** Specialist books; **Christian Heritage** Classic reprints.
Royalties paid twice-yearly.

Churchill Livingstone

See **Harcourt Brace and Company Limited**

Cicerone Press

2 Police Square, Milnthorpe, Cumbria LA7 7PY
☎015395 62069   Fax 015395 63417
Email: info@cicerone.demon.co.uk

Managing Director *Dorothy Unsworth*
Editorial Director *Walt Unsworth*

FOUNDED 1969. Guidebook publisher for outdoor enthusiasts. About 30 titles a year. No fiction or poetry. TITLES *A Trekker's Handbook*; various *Country Walking* guides; *LD Footpath Guides*. No unsolicited mss; synopses and ideas considered.
Royalties paid twice-yearly.

Citron Press

Suite 155, Business Design Centre, 52 Upper Street, London N1 0QH
☎0171 288 6024   Fax 0171 288 6196
Email: <name>@citronpress.co.uk
Website:www.citronpress.co.uk

Managing Director *Nikki Connors*
Operations Director *Steve Connors*
Editorial Consultant *Fay Weldon*

The Citron Press New Authors' Co-operative was ESTABLISHED in 1998 to enable a limited number of previously unpublished authors of fiction to see their books in print. Publications are marketed by the **Citron Press Book Club**, the Internet and book shops. A membership fee of £399.95 is paid by authors who join the Co-operative although membership is not automatic. 'All submitted mss go through a two-stage assessment to evaluate quality of writing. If an author is not successful, the membership fee is refunded in full and is accompanied by a frank editorial report.' Voted one of the 'World's Best Ideas' in 1998 by the Institute of Social Innovation.
Royalties paid annually.

Authors' Rating Essentially a cooperative which charges authors for publishing their manuscripts. It is still early days – Citron only recently brought out its first batch of titles – but there are high expectations for a self-publishing exercise that tries to avoid the pitfalls of the vanity presses.

Clarendon Press

See **Oxford University Press**

Claridge Press

33 Canonbury Park South, London N1 2JW
☎0171 226 7791   Fax 0171 354 0383

Chairman/Managing Director/Editorial Head *Roger Scruton*
Managing Editor *Merrie Cave*

FOUNDED 1987. Developed from the quarterly *Salisbury Review* (see entry under **Magazines**). *Publishes* current affairs – political, philosophical and sociological – from a right-wing viewpoint. SERIES *Thinkers of our Time.* TITLES *Falsification of the Good; Understanding Youth; Some Turn to Mecca to Pray: Islamic Values in the Modern World; KGB Lawsuits; Edmund Burke and Our Present Discontents.* Unsolicited mss welcome within given subject areas.
Royalties paid according to contract.

Clarion
See **Elliot Right Way Books**

T. & T. Clark
59 George Street, Edinburgh EH2 2LQ
☎0131 225 4703   Fax 0131 220 4260
Email: ggreen@tandtclark.co.uk
Website:www.tandtclark.co.uk
Managing Director/Editorial Head
Geoffrey Green
FOUNDED 1821. *Publishes* religion, theology, law and philosophy, for academic and professional markets. About 35 titles a year, including journals. TITLES *Church Dogmatics* Karl Barth; *A Textbook of Christian Ethics* ed. Robin Gill; *Scottish Law Directory; The Law of Contracts and Related Obligations in Scotland* David M. Walker. Unsolicited mss, synopses and ideas for books welcome.
Royalties paid annually.

James Clarke & Co.
PO Box 60, Cambridge CB1 2NT
☎01223 350865   Fax 01223 366951
Email: publishing@jamesclarke.co.uk
Website:www.jamesclarke.co.uk
Managing Director *Adrian Brink*
Parent company of **The Lutterworth Press** (see entry). *Publishes* scholarly and academic works, mainly theological, directory and reference titles. TITLES *The Encyclopedia of the Early Church; Padua and the Tudors; The History of Morris Dancing; The Libraries' Directory*. Approach in writing with ideas in the first instance.

Richard Cohen Books
An Imprint of Metro Publishing Ltd,
19 Gerrard Street, London W1V 7LA
☎0171 734 1411   Fax 0171 734 1811
Consulting Publisher *Richard Cohen*
Publishes biography, current affairs, travel, history, politics, the arts, and sport. First titles published in 1995. The company went out of business in October 1998 and was reconstituted under Metro as an independent publishing division. No erotica, DIY, children's, reference or fiction. TITLES *Memoirs* Al Alvarez; *Lord Goodman* Brian Brivati; *Siegfried Sassoon* John Stuart Roberts. No unsolicited mss.
Royalties paid twice-yearly.

Authors' Rating The living proof of the precarious nature of small-scale, quality publishing Richard Cohen has been rescued yet again, this time by Metro Books. He is now a wholly-owned subsidiary of Metro. Long may his editorial talents thrive.

Peter Collin Publishing Ltd
1 Cambridge Road, Teddington, Middlesex TW11 8DT
☎0181 943 3386   Fax 0181 943 1673
Email: info@pcp.co.uk
Website:www.pcp.co.uk
Chairman *P. H. Collin*
FOUNDED 1985. *Publishes* dictionaries only, including specialised dictionaries in English for students and specialised bilingual dictionaries for translators (French, German, Swedish, Spanish, Greek, Chinese, Hungarian). About 5 titles a year. Synopses and ideas welcome. No unsolicited mss; copy must be supplied on disk.
Royalties paid twice-yearly.

Collins
See **HarperCollins Publishers Ltd**

Collins & Brown (C&B Publishing plc)
London House, Great Eastern Wharf, Parkgate Road, London SW11 4NQ
☎0171 924 2575   Fax 0171 924 7725
Chairman *Cameron Brown*
Managing Director *Kate McPhee*
Approx. Annual Turnover £21 million
FOUNDED 1989. Independent publisher. Acquired **Pavilion Books Ltd** in 1997 (see entry) and David Bennett Books in 1998. *Publishes* illustrated non-fiction: practical photography, crafts, gardening, decorating, lifestyle and cookery. No fiction, poetry or local interest. About 40 titles a year. DIVISION **C&B Children's Books**. No unsolicited mss; outlines with s.a.e. only.
Royalties paid twice-yearly.

Colonsay Books
See **House of Lochar**

Columbia University Press
See **University Presses of California, Columbia & Princeton Ltd**

Compendium Publishing Ltd
1st Floor, 43 Frith Street, London W1V 5TE
☎0171 287 4570   Fax 0171 494 0583
Email: compendium@compuserve.com
Managing Director *Alan Greene*
Editorial Director *Simon Forty*
FOUNDED 1996. *Publishes* general non-fiction:

history, reference, hobbies, children's, transport and militaria. 25 titles in 1998.

IMPRINT **Windrow & Greene** Military books. No unsolicited mss; synopses and ideas preferred.

Royalties paid twice-yearly.

Condé Nast Books
See **Random House UK Ltd**

Condor
See **Souvenir Press Ltd**

Conran Octopus
See **Octopus Publishing Group**

Constable & Co. Ltd
3 The Lanchesters, 162 Fulham Palace Road, London W6 9ER
☎0181 741 3663   Fax 0181 748 7562
Website:www.constable-publishers.co.uk
Chairman/Managing Director
Benjamin Glazebrook
Editorial Director *Carol O'Brien*
Approx. Annual Turnover £2.98 million
FOUNDED in 1890 by Archibald Constable, a grandson of Walter Scott's publisher. Controlling interest was bought by Benjamin Glazebrook in 1967 and the remaining 48% was purchased by Hutchinson, now owned by **Random House**, in 1968. A small but select publisher whose list includes Muriel Spark and Francis King. *Publishes* archaeology, architecture and design, biography and autobiography, Celtic interest, crime fiction, guidebooks, general history and military history, psychology, sociology and anthropology, travel and topography, food and wine. About 80 titles a year. Unsolicited sample chapters, synopses and ideas for books welcome. No fiction except crime. Enclose return postage.

Royalties paid twice-yearly.

Authors' Rating Keeping its distance from the conglomerates, even with Random holding a minority stake, Constable is highly regarded by authors who recognise a straight deal when they see it.

Consultants Bureau
See **Plenum Publishing Co. Ltd**

Consumers' Association
See **Which? Books/Consumers' Association**

Conway Maritime Press
See **Brassey's (UK) Ltd**

Thomas Cook Publishing
PO Box 227, Peterborough PE3 6PU
☎01733 503571   Fax 01733 503596
Head of Publishing *Kevin Fitzgerald*
Approx. Annual Turnover £1.7 million
Part of the Thomas Cook Group Ltd, publishing commenced in 1873 with the first issue of Cook's Continental Timetable. *Publishes* guidebooks, maps and timetables. About 20 titles a year. No unsolicited mss; synopses and ideas welcome as long as they are travel-related.

Royalties paid annually.

Leo Cooper
See **Pen & Sword Books Ltd**

Corgi
See **Transworld Publishers Ltd**

Cornwall Books
See **Golden Cockerel Press Ltd**

Coronet
See **Hodder Headline plc**

Countryside Books
2 Highfield Avenue, Newbury, Berkshire RG14 5DS
☎01635 43816   Fax 01635 551004
Publisher *Nicholas Battle*
FOUNDED 1976. *Publishes* local interest paperbacks on regional subjects, generally by English county. Local history, genealogy, walking and photographic, some transport. Over 250 titles available. Unsolicited mss and synopses welcome but, regretfully, no fiction, poetry, natural history or personal memories.

Royalties paid twice-yearly.

Cressrelles Publishing Co. Ltd
10 Station Road Industrial Estate, Colwall, Malvern, Worcestershire WR13 6RN
☎01684 540154   Fax 01684 540154
Managing Director *Leslie Smith*
Publishes a range of general books, drama and chiropody titles. IMPRINTS **Actinic Press** Specialises in chiropody; **J. Garnet Miller Ltd** Plays and theatre texts; **Kenyon-Deane** Plays and drama textbooks.

Cromwell Publishers
Eagle Court, Concord Business Park, Manchester M22 0RR
☎0161 932 6402   Fax 0161 932 6001
Contact *James Lansbury*
FOUNDED 1995. *Publishes* fiction and non-fiction

in paperback format: memoirs, biography, auto-biography, religion/inspirational, popular sciences, young children, health, Millennium. 'May consider some poetry.' No cookery, academic, manuals or erotica. 60 titles to date. No unsolicited mss; send synopsis and one sample chapter with return postage to New Submissions. IMPRINTS **Cromwell Children**; **Cromwell Publishing**.
Royalties paid annually.

Authors' Rating Liable to ask authors to contribute towards costs of publication.

Croom Helm
See **Routledge**

Crossway
See **Inter-Varsity Press**

The Crowood Press Ltd
The Stable Block, Crowood Lane, Ramsbury, Marlborough, Wiltshire SN8 2HR
☎01672 520320   Fax 01672 520280
Chairman *John Dennis*
Managing Director *Ken Hathaway*
Publishes sport and leisure titles, including animal and land husbandry, climbing and walking, maritime, country sports, equestrian, fishing and shooting; also chess and bridge, crafts, dogs, gardening, natural history, aviation, military history and motoring. About 70 titles a year. Preliminary letter preferred in all cases.
Royalties paid annually.

James Currey Publishers
73 Botley Road, Oxford OX2 0BS
☎01865 244111   Fax 01865 246454
Chairman/Managing Director *James Currey*
FOUNDED 1985. A small specialist publisher. *Publishes* academic books on Africa, the Caribbean and Third World: history, anthropology, economics, sociology, politics and literary criticism. Approach in writing with synopsis if material is 'relevant to our needs'.
Royalties paid annually.

Curzon Press Ltd
15 The Quadrant, Richmond, Surrey TW9 1BP
☎0181 948 4660   Fax 0181 332 6735
Managing Director *Malcolm G. Campbell*
Specialised scholarly publishing house. *Publishes* academic/scholarly books on history and archaeology, languages and linguistics, philosophy, religion and theology, sociology and anthropology, cultural studies and reference, all in the context of Africa and Asia. IMPRINTS **Caucasus World**; **Japan Library**.

Cygnus Arts
See **Golden Cockerel Press Ltd**

Dalesman Publishing Co. Ltd
Stable Courtyard, Broughton Hall, Skipton, West Yorkshire BD23 3AE
☎01756 701381   Fax 01756 701326
Email: editorial@dalesman.co.uk
Website:www.dalesman.co.uk
Editor *Terry Fletcher*
Publishers of *Dalesman, Cumbria* and *Peak and Pennine* magazines and regional books covering Yorkshire, the Lake District and the Peak District. Subjects include crafts and hobbies, geography and geology, guidebooks, history and antiquarian, humour, travel and topography. Unsolicited mss considered on all subjects. About 20 titles a year.
Royalties paid annually.

Terence Dalton Ltd
Water Street, Lavenham, Sudbury, Suffolk CO10 9RN
☎01787 247572   Fax 01787 248267
Director/Editorial Head *Elisabeth Whitehair*
FOUNDED 1967. Part of the Lavenham Group Plc, a family company. *Publishes* non-fiction and currently contract-publishes water and environment books for Chartered UK Institution. No unsolicited mss; send synopsis with two or three sample chapters. Ideas welcome.
Royalties paid annually.

The C. W. Daniel Co. Ltd
1 Church Path, Saffron Walden, Essex CB10 1JP
☎01799 521909   Fax 01799 513462
Email: daniel_publishing@dial.pipex.com
Website:www.cwdaniel.com
Managing Director *Ian Miller*
Approx. Annual Turnover £1 million
FOUNDED in 1902 by a man who knew Tolstoy, the company was taken over by its present directors in 1973. Output has increased following the acquisition in 1980 of health and healing titles from the Health Science Press, and the purchase of Neville Spearman Publishers' metaphysical list in 1985. *Publishes* New Age: alternative healing and metaphysical. About 15 titles a year. No fiction, diet or cookery. Unsolicited synopses and ideas welcome; no unsolicited mss.
Royalties paid annually.

Darf Publishers Ltd

277 West End Lane, London NW6 1QS
☎0171 431 7009   Fax 0171 431 7655
Chairman/Managing Director
   M. B. Fergiani
Editorial Head A. Bentaleb
Approx. Annual Turnover £500,000

FOUNDED 1982 to publish books and reprints on the Middle East, history, theology and travel. *Publishes* geography, history, language, literature, oriental, politics, theology and travel. About 10 titles a year. TITLES *Moslems in Spain; The Barbary Corsairs; Elementary Arabic; Travels of Ibn Battuta; Travels in Syria and the Holy Land* Burckhardt.
   Royalties paid annually. *Overseas associates* Dar Al-Fergiani, Cairo, Tripoli and Tunis.

Darton, Longman & Todd Ltd

1 Spencer Court, 140–142 Wandsworth High Street, London SW18 4JJ
☎0181 875 0155   Fax 0181 875 0133
Editorial Director Morag Reeve
Approx. Annual Turnover £1 million

FOUNDED by Michael Longman, who broke away from Longman Green in 1959 when they cut their religious list. In July 1990 DLT became a common ownership company, owned and run by staff members. The company is a leading ecumenical, predominantly Christian, publisher, with a strong emphasis on spirituality and the ministry and mission of the Church. About 50 titles a year. TITLES include *Jerusalem Bible; New Jerusalem Bible; God of Surprises; Audacity to Believe.* Sample material for books on theological or spiritual subjects considered.
   Royalties paid twice-yearly.

David & Charles Children's Books

Winchester House, 259–269 Old Marylebone Road, London NW1 5XJ
☎0171 616 7200   Fax 0171 616 7201
Editorial Director Mandy Suhr

FOUNDED 1994. Formerly Levinson Children's Books; acquired by **David & Charles Publishers** in 1997. *Publishes* novelty and picture books for the under-sevens. Unsolicited mss, synopsses and ideas welcome.
   Royalties paid twice-yearly.

David & Charles Publishers

Brunel House, Forde Road, Newton Abbot, Devon TQ12 4PU
☎01626 323200   Fax 01626 323317
Email: postmaster@dcpublishers.co.uk
Managing Director Neil Page

Approx. Annual Turnover £16.8 million

FOUNDED 1960 as a specialist company. Bought back from **Reader's Digest** in 1997 by a management team. Acquired **Godsfield Press** in June 1998. *Publishes* illustrated non-fiction for international markets, specialising in crafts, art techniques, interiors, gardening, equestrian and countryside, mind, body and spirit and children's. No fiction, poetry or memoirs. About 60 titles a year. TITLES *Jazz Up Your Junk; Garden Transformations; Crafts Made Easy Series; Badminton Horse Trials; The Organic Café Cookbook; Egg Day; Illustrated Encyclopedia of Well Being.* Unsolicited mss will be considered if return postage is included; synopsses and ideas welcome.
   Royalties paid twice-yearly.

Authors' Rating After a management buyout from Reader's Digest in 1997, David & Charles got itself together in remarkably quick time. Better marketing has brought increased rewards all round. The children's list has expanded with the purchase of Levinson's children's titles and and Godsfield Press. Further acquisitions are anticipated.

Christopher Davies Publishers Ltd

PO Box 403, Swansea, West Glamorgan SA1 4YF
☎01792 648825   Fax 01792 648825
Managing Director/Editorial Head
   Christopher T. Davies
Approx. Annual Turnover £100,000

FOUNDED 1949 to promote and expand Welsh-language publications. By the 1970s the company was publishing over 50 titles a year but a subsequent drop in Welsh sales led to the establishment of a small English list which has continued. *Publishes* biography, cookery, history, sport and literature of Welsh interest. About 4 titles a year. TITLES *English/Welsh Dictionaries; Ivor Allchurch M.B.E., Biography; Historic Gower; Who's Who in Welsh History.* No unsolicited mss. Synopses and ideas for books welcome.
   Royalties paid twice-yearly.

Authors' Rating A favourite for Celtic readers and writers.

Giles de la Mare Publishers Ltd

3 Queen Square, London WC1N 3AU
☎0171 465 7607/0045
Fax 0171 465 7535/0034
Email: gilesdelamare@dial.pipex.com
Chairman/Managing Director
   Giles de la Mare

Approx. Annual Turnover £45,000

FOUNDED 1995 and commenced publishing in April 1996. *Publishes* mainly non-fiction, especially art and architecture, biography, history, music. TITLES *Married to the Amadeus* Muriel Nissel; *Venice: An Anthology Guide* Milton Grundy; *History at War* Nobel Frankland; *Duchess of Cork Street* Lillian Browse; *The Weather of Britain* Robin Stirling; *Vermeer* Lawrence Gowing. Unsolicited mss, synopses and ideas welcome after initial telephone call.
Royalties paid twice-yearly.

Debrett's Peerage Ltd

Garfield House, 2nd Floor, 86–88 Edgware Road, London W2 2YW
☎0171 915 9633   Fax 0171 915 9628
Email: people@debretts.co.uk
Website:www.debretts.co.uk
Chairman *Christopher Haines*
Managing Director *Simone Kesseler*

FOUNDED 1769. The company's main activity (in conjunction with **Macmillan**) is the quinquennial *Debrett's Peerage and Baronetage* (published in 1995) and annual *Debrett's People of Today* (also available on CD-ROM). Debrett's general books are published under licence through **Headline**.
Royalties paid twice-yearly.

Dedalus Ltd

Langford Lodge, St Judith's Lane, Sawtry, Cambridgeshire PE17 5XE
☎01487 832382   Fax 01487 832382
Chairman *Juri Gabriel*
Managing Director *Eric Lane*
Approx. Annual Turnover £175,000

FOUNDED 1983. *Publishes* contemporary European fiction and classics and original literary fiction in the fields of magic realism, surrealism, the grotesque and bizarre. 12 titles in 1998. TITLES *The Decadent Traveller; The Arabian Nightmare* Robert Irwin; *Bad to the Bone* James Waddington; *Memoirs of a Gnostic Dwarf* David Madsen; *Music in a Foreign Language* Andrew Crumey (winner of the **Saltire Best First Book Award** in 1994). Welcomes submissions for original fiction and books suitable for its list but 'most people sending work in have no idea what kind of books Dedalus publishes and merely waste their efforts'. Particularly interested in intellectually clever and unusual fiction. A letter about the author should always accompany any submission. No replies without s.a.e.
DIVISIONS/IMPRINTS **Original Fiction in Paperback; Contemporary European**

Fiction 1992–2000; Dedalus European Classics; Empire of the Senses; Bizarre Literary Concept Books.
Royalties paid annually.

Authors' Rating A small, quality publisher which actually recognises that good books can come from foreign language writers. A recent project involves the translation of works by neglected nineteenth century French writers.

University of Delaware
See **Golden Cockerel Press Ltd**

JM Dent
See **The Orion Publishing Group Ltd**

André Deutsch Ltd
76 Dean Street, London W1V 5HA
☎0171 316 4450   Fax 0171 316 4499
Website:www.vci.co.uk
Managing Director *T. J. Forrester*
Editorial Director *Louise Dixon*
Approx. Annual Turnover £5.3 million

FOUNDED in 1950 by André Deutsch, who eventually ended his long association with the company in 1991. In 1995 the company was acquired by video and audio publisher and distributor VCI plc, who were, in 1998, acquired by the Kingfisher Group. In the past three years six distinct and successful imprints have been developed, two for children: **Madcap**, offering innovative, fun and accessible titles and **André Deutsch Classics**, a range of hardback classic books at paperback prices. For adults there is **Chameleon**, the commercial imprint that covers comedy, humour, sport, TV tie-ins, music and film, the **André Deutsch** label which covers biography, history, cookery, politics and current affairs and photography, the **Manchester United** imprint under which the company looks after all the publishing interests of the football club, and the recently acquired **Granada Books** imprint, under which the television company's books will be published.

Authors' Rating Who would have thought of Deutsch, one-time darling of the literary greats, as the publisher of Glen Hoddle, Cliff Richard and the Spice Girls. But that is what comes from association with the highly successful video and audio publisher Video Collection International, in turn owned by Kingfisher. Many Deutsch titles are linked to VCI products but there is also a thriving children's list.

Dial House
See **Ian Allan Publishing Ltd**

Disney
See **Ladybird Books Ltd**

Dolphin Book Co. Ltd
Tredwr, Llangrannog, Llandysul SA44 6BA
☎01239 654404   Fax 01239 654002
Managing Director *Martin L. Gili*
Approx. Annual Turnover £5000

FOUNDED 1957. A small publishing house specialising in Catalan, Spanish and South American books for the academic market. TITLES *Elegies de Bierville/Bierville Elegies* Carles Riba, Catalan text with English translation by J. L. Gili; *Proceedings of the First Conference on Contemporary Catalan Studies in Scotland* ed. Chris Dixon; *The Late Poetry of Pablo Neruda* Christopher Perriam; *Hispanic Linguistic Studies in Honour of F. W. Hodcroft; Salvatge cor/Savage Heart* Carles Riba; Catalan text with English translations by J. L. Gili. Unsolicited material not welcome.
  Royalties paid annually.

John Donald Publishers Ltd
Unit 8 Canongate Venture, 5 New Street, Edinburgh EH8 5BH
☎0131 556 6660   Fax 0131 558 1500
Publishing & Production *Donald Morrison*
Bought by **Birlinn Ltd** in 1999. *Publishes* academic and scholarly, agriculture, archaeology, architecture, economics, textbooks, guidebooks, local, military and social history, religious, sociology and anthropology. About 30 titles a year.
  Royalties paid annually.

Donhead Publishing Ltd
Lower Coombe, Donhead St Mary, Shaftesbury, Dorset SP7 9LY
☎01747 828422   Fax 01747 828522
Website:www.donhead.u-net.com
Contact *Jill Pearce*
FOUNDED 1990 to specialise in publishing how-to books for building practitioners; particularly interested in architectural conservation material. *Publishes* building, architecture and heritage only. 6 titles a year. TITLES *Encyclopaedia of Architectural Terms; A Good Housekeeping Guide to Churches and their Contents; Cleaning Historic Buildings; Brickwork; Practical Stone Masonry; Conservation of Timber Buildings; Surveying Historic Buildings; English Heritage Directory of Building Limes; Heritage, Conservation of Historic Brick Structures; Journal of Architectural Conservation* (3 issues yearly). Unsolicited mss, synopses and ideas welcome.

Dorling Kindersley Ltd
9 Henrietta Street, London WC2E 8PS
☎0171 836 5411   Fax 0171 836 7570
Website:www.dk.com
Chairman *Peter Kindersley*
Deputy Chairman *Christopher Davis*
Approx. Annual Turnover
  UK £29.1 million; US £36.5 million

FOUNDED 1974. Packager and publisher of illustrated non-fiction: cookery, crafts, gardening, health, travel guides, atlases, natural history and children's information and fiction. Launched a US imprint in 1991 and an Australian imprint in 1997. About 175–200 titles a year.
DIVISIONS **Adult; Children's; Interactive Learning; Vision** (video). TITLES *Eyewitness Guides; Eyewitness Travel Guides; RHS A–Z Encyclopedia of Garden Plants; BMA Complete Family Health Encyclopedia; Children's Illustrated Encyclopedia; The Way Things Work.* Unsolicited synopses/ideas for books welcome.

Authors' Rating After two years of getting it together, a restructured DK impressed the market with some wonderfully imaginative multimedia products. Small surprise then that DK should have been appointed education and reference publisher of the Millennium Experience. Writers who sign up with DK must be ready to work as part of an editorial and design team. Loners had best look elsewhere.

Doubleday
See **Transworld Publishers Ltd**

Ashley Drake Publishing Ltd
PO Box 733, Cardiff CF4 6WE
☎01222 522229   Fax 01222 522229
Email: info@adpub.softnet.co.uk
Website:www.soft.net.uk/adpub
Chairman *Ashley Drake*
Approx. Annual Turnover £70,000

FOUNDED 1995. *Publishes* academic, trade and Welsh-language books. 20 titles in 1999. No unsolicited mss; synopses and ideas for the Welsh Academic Press and Ashley Drake Publishing imprints welcome. No scientific or computing books.
IMPRINTS **Ashley Drake Publishing** Sport, music, cookery and general trade. TITLES *When Pele Broke Our Hearts – Wales and the 1958 World Cup; Welsh Names for Children – The Complete Guide.* **Welsh Academic Press** English language academic, scholarly humanities and social sciences. TITLES *The American West; The Electoral Handbook of Wales 1900–1999; Celtic Radicals*

and *Celtic Poetry Library* series. **Gwasg Addysgol Cymru** Welsh-language educational titles. TITLES *Dyddiadur Anne Frank (Diary of Anne Frank)*. **Y Ddraig Fach** Welsh-language titles for children. Welsh editions of Ladybird/Disney mini-hardbacks: *Crwca Notre Dame (Hunchback of Notre Dame); Pocahontas.*
Royalties paid annually.

Drake Educational Associates
St Fagans Road, Fairwater, Cardiff CF5 3AE
☎01222 560333   Fax 01222 554909
Managing Director *R. G. Drake*
Educational publishers.

Dryden Press
See **Harcourt Brace and Company Limited**

Gerald Duckworth & Co. Ltd
61 Frith Street, London W1V 5TA
☎0171 434 4242   Fax 0171 434 4420
Managing Director *Robin Baird-Smith*
Editorial Director *Deborah Blake*
Approx. Annual Turnover £1.7 million
FOUNDED 1898. A joint ownership company. Some of the company's early credits include authors like Hilaire Belloc, August Strindberg, Henry James and John Galsworthy. Expanding general trade list (including fiction) with specialist academic and educational imprints. 120 titles in 1998. IMPRINTS **Duckworth Literary Entertainments; Bristol Classical Press** Classical texts and modern languages; **Chatham Publishing** Maritime history. No unsolicited mss; synopses and sample chapters only. Enclose s.a.e. or return postage for response/return.
Royalties paid twice-yearly at first, annually thereafter.

Authors' Rating Celebrating its centenary, Duckworth launched into film-making, linking books (Duck Editions) with the big screen (Drake Films). Drake will commission screenplays which may be taken on to production or sold as part of a production package. Duckworth's general list has grown of late to represent more than half the output. Academic and educational titles account for the rest. Standards are high.

Duncan Petersen Publishing Limited
31 Ceylon Road, London W14 0PY
☎0171 371 2356   Fax 0171 371 2507
Directors *Andrew Duncan, Mel Petersen*
FOUNDED 1986. Publisher and packager of childcare, business, antiques, birds, nature, atlases, walking and travel books. SERIES *Charming Small Hotel Guide; Walker's Britain; Versatile Travel Guide.* Unsolicited synopses and ideas for books welcome.
Fees paid.

Martin Dunitz Ltd
The Livery House, 7–9 Pratt Street, London NW1 0AE
☎0171 482 2202   Fax 0171 267 0159
Website:www.dunitz.co.uk
Chairman/Managing Director *Martin Dunitz*
Production Director *Rosemary Allen*
Journals Manager *Ian Mellor*
FOUNDED 1978. *Publishes* specialist medical and dentistry atlases, texts, pocketbooks, slide atlases and CD-ROMs aimed at an international market. Particular areas of focus are psychiatry, neurology, cardiology, orthopaedics, dermatology, oncology and bone metabolism. The company won the Queen's Award for Export Achievement in 1991. 90–100 titles a year. Unsolicited synopses and ideas welcome but no mss. Also publishes *International Journal of Cardiovascular Interventions, International Journal of Psychiatry in Clinical Practice, Journal of Cutaneous Laser Therapy.*
Royalties paid twice-yearly.

Eagle
See **Inter Publishing Ltd**

Earthlight
See **Simon & Schuster**

Earthscan Publications
See **Kogan Page Ltd**

Ebury Press
See **Random House UK Ltd**

Edinburgh University Press
22 George Square, Edinburgh EH8 9LF
☎0131 650 4218   Fax 0131 662 0053
Website:www.eup.ed.ac.uk
Chairman *David Martin*
Editorial Director *Jackie Jones*
Director *Timothy Wright*
Publishes academic and scholarly books (and journals): gender studies, geography, history – ancient, classical, medieval and modern, Islamic studies, linguistics, literary criticism, media and cultural studies; philosophy, politics, Scottish studies, theology and religious studies. About 100 titles a year.

IMPRINT **Polygon** *Publishes* fiction and poetry, general trade books, Scottish literary, cultural and oral history.

No unsolicited mss for EUP titles; mss welcome for Polygon but must be accompanied by s.a.e. for reply/return; letter/synopsis preferred in the first instance.

Royalties paid annually.

Éditions Aubrey Walter
BCM 6159, London WC1N 3XX
Email: aubrey@gmppubs.co.uk
Director *Aubrey Walters*

Publishes visual work by gay artists and photographers, usually in the form of a monograph showcasing one artist's work. TITLES *Life and Work of Henry Scott Tuke* Emmanuel Cooper; *The Bear Cult* Chris Nelson; *Paintings* Sadao Hasegawa; *The Erotic Art of Duncan Grant.* Work may be submitted on disk, transparency, photocopy or photograph.

Payment One-off fee negotiable.

Egmont Children's Books
239 Kensington High Street, London W8 6SA
☎0171 761 3500   Fax 0171 761 3510
Email: <firstname>.<lastname>@ecb.
egmont.com
Managing Director *Jane Winterbotham*

Part of the Egmont Group (Copenhagen), Egmont Children's Books comprises the original imprints of Heinemann Young Books and Methuen Children's Books (both over 100 years old), and Hamlyn Children's Books. *Publishes* children's picture books, fiction and non-fiction; licensed characters for children. Over 250 titles in 1998.

DIVISIONS **Mammoth** Publishing Director/Deputy MD *Gill Evans* TITLES *Tintin; The Ghost of Thomas Kempe; The Little Prince.* **Heinemann**; **Methuen** Licensing Director *Susannah McFarlane* TITLES *Thomas the Tank Engine; Winnie-the-Pooh.* IMPRINTS **Blue Bananas**; **Yellow Bananas**. No unsolicited mss. Synopses and ideas welcome; approach in writing with s.a.e.

Royalties paid twice-yearly.

Authors' Rating What was once Reed Children's Books was sold to Egmont last year. The move caused the loss of the best-selling titles of Janet and Allan Ahlberg (who have gone to Penguin) but the list remains strong with such classics as Pooh, Barbar and Thomas the Tank Engine ever popular with early readers. The challenge now is to find new talent. Early signs are encouraging.

Egmont World Limited
Deanway Technology Centre, Wilmslow Road, Handforth, Cheshire SK9 3FB
☎01625 650011   Fax 01625 650040
Managing Director *Ian Findlay*
Publishing Manager *Nina Filipek*
Creative Director *David Riley*

Sister company of **Egmont Children's Books**. Part of the Egmont Group, Denmark. *Specialises* in children's books for home and international markets: activity, sticker, baby, early learning, novelty/character books and annuals. SERIES *Mr Men; I Can Learn; Learning Rewards.* 'Unsolicited material rarely used.' Does not accept responsibility for the return of unsolicited submissions.

Element Books
The Old School House, The Courtyard, Bell Street, Shaftesbury, Dorset SP7 8BP
☎01747 851448   Fax 01747 855721
Chairman/Publisher *Michael Mann*
Publisher *Julia McCutchen*
Approx. Annual Turnover £17 million

FOUNDED 1978. An independent general publisher whose aim is 'to make available knowledge and information to aid humanity in a time of major transition'. *Publishes* general non-fiction in hardback and paperback, including full-colour, illustrated gift books and children's books. 'We are interested in publishing in the areas of health and complementary therapies; self-help and personal development; psychology; world religions and spiritual traditions; divination and related areas.' TITLES *Dead Mars, Dying Earth*; *Bodyguards* Desmond Morris; *Mind Medicine* Uri Geller. Unsolicited mss, synopses and ideas welcome. No fiction or poetry. 'We are always interested to hear from authors who have an original contribution to make based on quality and integrity.'

Royalties paid twice-yearly.

Authors' Rating There is no denying Element's drive for expansion but the Society of Authors continues to worry about this publisher's administration. Two audits have revealed royalties going astray. More attention to management competence is promised.

Elliot Right Way Books
Kingswood Buildings, Lower Kingswood, Tadworth, Surrey KT20 6TD
☎01737 832202   Fax 01737 830311
Email: info@right-way.co.uk
Managing Directors *Clive Elliot,*
  Malcolm G. Elliot

FOUNDED 1946 by Andrew G. Elliot. *Publishes*

how-to titles and instruction books on a multifarious list of subjects including cookery, DIY, family financial and legal matters, family health, fishing, looking after pets, motoring, popular education, puzzles, jokes and quizzes. All the early books were entitled *The Right Way to . . .* but this format became too restrictive. No fiction, poetry or biography.

IMPRINTS **Right Way** Instructional paperbacks in B format; **Clarion** Promotional/bargain series of 'how-to' books. Unsolicited mss, synopses and ideas for books welcome.
Royalties paid annually.

Ellipsis London Ltd
2 Rufus Street, London N1 6PE
☎0171 739 3157   Fax 0171 739 3175
Email: <name>@ellipsis.co.uk
Website:www.ellipsis.com
Contact *Tom Neville*

FOUNDED 1992. Formerly a subsidiary of Zurich-based Artemis Verlags AG but now an independent publishing house. *Publishes* architecture and music; contemporary art on CD-ROM. About 30 titles a year. No unsolicited mss, synopses or ideas.
Royalties paid annually.

Aidan Ellis Publishing
Whinfield, Herbert Road, Salcombe, South Devon TQ8 8HN
☎01548 842755   Fax 01548 844356
Email: aidan@aepub.demon.co.uk
Website:www.demon.co.uk/aepub
Partners/Editorial Heads *Aidan Ellis, Lucinda Ellis*
Approx. Annual Turnover £150,000

FOUNDED in 1971. *Specialises* in general trade books and non-fiction. TITLES *Tall Ships and the Cutty Sark Races* Paul Bishop; *Trees for Your Garden* Roy Lancaster; *Garden Alpines* and *Come You Here, Boy!* Alan Bloom; *Guide du Fromage* (English edition) Pierre Androuet; *The Royal Gardens in Windsor Great Park* Charles Lyte; *Presumed Dead* Eunice Chapman. Ideas and synopses welcome (return postage please).
Royalties paid twice-yearly.

Elm Publications/Training
Seaton House, Kings Ripton, Huntingdon, Cambridgeshire PE17 2NJ
☎01487 773254   Fax 01487 773359
Managing Director *Sheila Ritchie*

FOUNDED 1977. *Publishes* textbooks, teaching aids, educational resources, educational software and languages, in the fields of business

and management for adult learners. Books and teaching/training resources are generally commissioned to meet specific business, management and other syllabuses. 'We are actively seeking good training materials for business/management, especially tested and proven.' About 30 titles a year. Ideas are welcome; first approach in writing with outline or by a brief telephone call.
Royalties paid annually.

Elsevier Science Ltd
The Boulevard, Langford Lane, Kidlington, Oxford OX5 1GB
☎01865 843000   Fax 01865 843010
Website:www.elsevier.nl
Managing Director *Gavin Howe*

Parent company **Elsevier**, Amsterdam. Now incorporates Pergamon Press. *Publishes* academic and professional reference books, scientific, technical and medical books, journals, CD-ROMs and magazines.

DIVISIONS **Elsevier Trends Division** *David Bousfield*; **Elsevier and Pergamon** *Barbara Barrett, Peter Desmond, Chris Lloyd, Paul Evans*. Unsolicited mss, synopses and ideas for books welcome.
Royalties paid annually.

Emissary Publishing
PO Box 33, Bicester, Oxfordshire OX6 7PP
☎01869 323447   Fax 01869 324096
Editorial Director *Val Miller*

FOUNDED 1992. *Publishes* mainly humorous paperback books; no poetry or children's. Runs a biennial Humorous Novel Competition in memory of the late Peter Pook and publishes the winning novel (s.a.e. for details). No unsolicited mss or synopses.
Royalties paid twice-yearly.

Empiricus Books
See **Janus Publishing Company Ltd**

Enitharmon Press
36 St George's Avenue, London N7 0HD
☎0171 607 7194   Fax 0171 607 8694
Director *Stephen Stuart-Smith*

FOUNDED 1967. An independent company with an enterprising editorial policy, Enitharmon has established itself as one of Britain's leading poetry presses. Patron of 'the new and the neglected', Enitharmon prides itself on the success of its collaborations between writers and artists. *Publishes* poetry, literary criticism, fiction, art and photography. About 20 titles a year. TITLES include

Thames Anna Adams; *And Another Thing* Edwin Brock; *Kali* Jim Dine; *Visiting Ezra Pound* Kathleen Raine; *The Children's Crusade* Paula Rego. No unsolicited mss.

Royalties paid according to contract. *Distribution* in Europe by Signature Book Representation, Manchester; in the USA by Dufour Editions Inc., Chester Springs, PA 19425.

Epworth Press
c/o Methodist Publishing House, 20 Ivatt Way, Peterborough, Cambridgeshire PE3 7PG
☎01733 332202   Fax 01733 331201
Chairman *Dr John A. Newton, CBE*
Editor *Gerald M. Burt*

Publishes Christian books only: philosophy, theology, biblical studies, pastoralia and social concern. No fiction, poetry or children's. A series based on the text of the *Revised Common Lectionary*, entitled *Companion to the RCL*, was launched in 1998 and the two new series *Exploring Methodism* and *Thinking Things Through* continue. About 10 titles a year. TITLES *Modern Methodism in England, 1932–1998* John Munsey Turner; *Is There Life After Death?* C. S. Rodd; *St Luke's Gospel* Judith Lieu. Unsolicited mss considered but write to enquire in the first instance. Authors wishing to have their mss returned must send sufficient postage.
Royalties paid annually.

Essentials
See **How To Books Ltd**

Euromonitor
60–61 Britton Street, London EC1M 5NA
☎0171 251 8024   Fax 0171 608 3149
Website:www.euromonitor.com
Chairman *R. N. Senior*
Managing Director *T. J. Fenwick*
Approx. Annual Turnover £7 million

FOUNDED 1972. International business information publisher specialising in library and professional reference books, market reports, electronic databases, journals and CD-ROMs. *Publishes* business reference, market analysis and information directories only. About 200 titles a year.

DIVISIONS **Market Direction & Reports** *S. Holmes*; **Reference Books & Directories** *S. Hunter.* TITLES *Credit & Charge Cards: The International Market*; *Europe in the Year 2000*; *European Marketing Handbook*; *European Directory of Trade and Business Associations*; *World Retail Directory and Sourcebook*.
Royalties Payment is generally by flat fee.

Europa Publications Ltd
18 Bedford Square, London WC1B 3JN
☎0171 580 8236   Fax 0171 636 1664
Website:www.europapublications.co.uk
Chairman *C. H. Martin*
Managing Director *P. A. McGinley*
Approx. Annual Turnover £5 million

Owned by MPG Ltd. FOUNDED 1926 with the publication of the first edition of *The Europa Year Book*. *Publishes* annual reference books on political, economic and commercial matters. About 3 titles a year. No fiction, biography or poetry. Enquiries in writing only.
Royalties paid annually.

Evangelical Press of Wales
See **Bryntirion Press**

Evans Brothers Ltd
2A Portman Mansions, Chiltern Street, London W1M 1LE
☎0171 935 7160   Fax 0171 487 5034
Email: sales@evansbrothers.co.uk
Managing Director *Stephen Pawley*
International Publishing Director *Brian Jones*
UK Publisher *Su Swallow*
Approx. Annual Turnover £3.5 million

FOUNDED 1908 by Robert and Edward Evans. Originally published educational journals, books for primary schools and teacher education. After rapid expansion into popular fiction and drama, both were sacrificed to a major programme of educational books for schools in East and West Africa. A new UK programme was launched in 1986 followed by the acquisition of Hamish Hamilton's non-fiction list for children in 1990. *Publishes* UK children's and educational books, and educational books for Africa, the Caribbean and Latin America. About 70 titles a year. Unsolicited mss, synopses and ideas for books welcome.

Royalties paid annually. *Overseas associates* in Kenya, Cameroon, Sierra Leone; Evans Bros (Nigeria Publishers) Ltd.

Everyman
See **The Orion Publishing Group Ltd**

Everyman's Library
See **David Campbell Publishers Ltd**

University of Exeter Press
Reed Hall, Streatham Drive, Exeter, Devon EX4 4QR
☎01392 263066   Fax 01392 263064
Email: uep@exeter.ac.uk

Website:www.ex.ac.uk/uep/
Publisher *Simon Baker*
FOUNDED 1956. *Publishes* academic books: archaeology, classical studies, history, maritime studies, English literature (especially medieval), linguistics, European studies, modern languages and literature, film history, Arabic studies and books on Exeter and the South West. About 40 titles a year. Proposals welcomed in the above subject areas.
Royalties paid annually.

Exley Publications Ltd
16 Chalk Hill, Watford, Hertfordshire
WD1 4BN
☎01923 248328   Fax 01923 818733
Managing/Editorial Director *Helen Exley*
FOUNDED 1976. Independent family company. *Publishes* gift books, quotation anthologies, social stationery and humour. All in series only – no individual titles. About 65 titles a year.
DIVISIONS **Gift Series** TITLES *To a Very Special Friend, Daughter, Mother, ...; Golf, Book Lovers, Dog, Friendship Quotations.* **Cartoon Series** TITLES *The Fanatics Guide to Golf, Cats, Dads,* etc. **Words on Series** TITLES *Courage, Joy, Hope, Serenity, Wisdom, etc.* No unsolicited mss. 'Writers needed who can create personal thank you and loving messages. Emotion that's never sugary or sentimental.'

Faber & Faber Ltd
3 Queen Square, London WC1N 3AU
☎0171 465 0045   Fax 0171 465 0034
Chairman *Matthew Evans*
Managing Director *Toby Faber*
Approx. Annual Turnover £10 million
Geoffrey Faber founded the company in the 1920s, with T. S. Eliot as an early recruit to the board. The original list was based on contemporary poetry and plays (the distinguished backlist includes Eliot, Auden and MacNeice). *Publishes* poetry and drama, children's, fiction, film, music, politics, biography, wine.
DIVISIONS
Children's *Suzy Jenvey* AUTHORS Terry Deary, Gaye Hicyilmaz, Russell Stannard; **Wine** *Toby Faber* TITLES *Burgundy; Bordeaux;* **Fiction** *Jon Riley* AUTHORS P. D. James, Peter Carey, Kazuo Ishiguro, Hanif Kureishi, Milan Kundera, John McGahern, Mario Vargas Llosa, Garrison Keillor, Caryl Phillips, Paul Auster; **Plays** *Peggy Butcher,* **Film** *Walter Donohue* AUTHORS Samuel Beckett,

Alan Bennett, David Hare, Brian Friel, Harold Pinter, Tom Stoppard, John Boorman, Joel and Ethan Coen, John Hodge, Woody Allen, Martin Scorsese, Quentin Tarantino; **Music** *Belinda Matthews* AUTHORS Humphrey Burton, Alexander Goehr, Donald Mitchell, Mark Steyn, Elizabeth Wilson; **Poetry** *Paul Keegan* AUTHORS Seamus Heaney, Ted Hughes, Douglas Dunn, Tom Paulin, Simon Armitage; **Non-fiction** *Julian Loose* AUTHORS John Carey, Adam Phillips, Darian Leader, Jenny Uglow.
Royalties paid twice-yearly.

Authors' Rating Strong identity; a Faber book is recognisable at twenty paces. The emphasis now seems to be on niche publishing in drama and film with biographies of actors and directors leading the list.

Fairleigh Dickinson University Press
See **Golden Cockerel Press**

Falmer Press
11 New Fetter Lane, London EC4P 4EE
☎0171 583 9855   Fax 0171 842 2303
Senior Commissioning Editor *Anna Clarkson*
Part of **Taylor & Francis Group**. *Publishes* educational books/materials for all levels. Largely commissioned. Unsolicited mss considered.
Royalties paid annually.

Farming Press Books & Videos
Wharfedale Road, Ipswich, Suffolk IP1 4LG
☎01473 241122   Fax 01473 242222
Manager *Alison Stevens*
Owned by United News & Media Plc. *Publishes* specialist books and videos on farming/agriculture. About 15 books and videos a year. No unsolicited mss; synopses and ideas on technical and machinery titles considered.
Royalties paid twice-yearly.

Fernhurst Books
Duke's Path, High Street, Arundel, West Sussex BN18 9AJ
☎01903 882277   Fax 01903 882715
Email: sales@fernhurstbooks.co.uk
Website:www.fernhurstbooks.co.uk
Chairman/Managing Director *Tim Davison*
FOUNDED 1979. For people who love watersports. *Publishes* practical, highly-illustrated handbooks on sailing and watersports. No unsolicited mss; synopses and ideas welcome.
Royalties paid twice-yearly.

Financial Times Management

128 Long Acre, London WC2E 9AN
☎0171 447 2000   Fax 0171 240 5771
Website:www.ftmanagement.com
Managing Director Rod Bristow

Part of Financial Times Professional Ltd. Publisher and supplier of business education and management development materials. Portfolio of products and services includes books, journals, directories, looseleafs, distance learning programmes, corporate training, CD-ROMS aimed at business education and management development in both private and public sectors. About 250 titles a year. IMPRINTS **Financial Times Pitman Publishing; Institute of Management; Nat-West Business Handbooks; Allied Dunbar; Investors Chronicle; Frameworks; Fairplace Institute of Banking & Finance; The Open College; Training Direct; HDL Training & Development**. Unsolicited mss, synopses and ideas for books and other materials welcome.
Royalties paid annually.

Findhorn Press Ltd

The Park, Findhorn, Moray IV36 3TY
☎01309 690582   Fax 01309 690036
Email: books@findhorn.org
Website:www.findhorn.org/findhornpress/
Directors Karin Bogliolo, Thierry Bogliolo
Approx. Annual Turnover £320,000

FOUNDED 1971. *Publishes* mind, body, spirit, new age and healing. 8 titles in 1998. Unsolicited synopses and ideas welcome if they come within their subject areas. No children's books, fiction or poetry.
Royalties paid twice-yearly.

Firefly Publishing

See **Helter Skelter Publishing**

First & Best in Education Ltd

Unit K, Earlstrees Court, Earlstrees Road, Corby, Northamptonshire NN17 4AX
☎01536 399004   Fax 01536 399012
Email: firstbest9@aol.com
Publisher Tony Attwood
Senior Editor Katy Charge

Publishers of over 1000 educational books of all types for all ages of children and for parents and teachers. No fiction. All books are published as being suitable for photocopying and/or as electronic books. Currently launching 10 new titles a month and 'keenly looking for new authors all the time'. TITLES *Raising Grades Through Study Skills; Children, Their Discipline and Behaviour; From Failure to Excellence*. IMPRINTS **Multi-Sensory Learning** (see entry) and **School Improvement Reports**. In the first instance send s.a.e. for details of requirements and current projects to Julia Perkins, Editorial Dept. at the address above.
Royalties paid twice-yearly.

Fitzgerald Publishing

PO Box 804, London SE13 5JF
☎0181 690 0597
Managing Editor Tim Fitzgerald
General Editor Andrew Smith

FOUNDED 1974. *Specialises* in scientific studies of insects and spiders. 1–2 titles a year. TITLES *Stick Insects of Europe & The Mediterranean; Baboon Spiders of Africa; Tarantula Classification and Identification Guide*. Unsolicited mss, synopses and ideas for books welcome. Also considers video scripts for video documentaries. New video documentary: *Desert Tarantulas*.

Fitzjames Press

See **Motor Racing Publications**

Fitzroy Dearborn Publishers

310 Regent Street, London W1R 5AJ
☎0171 636 6627   Fax 0171 636 6982
Email: postroom@fitzroydearborn.
demon.co.uk
Managing Director Daniel Kirkpatrick
Publishers Lesley Henderson, Roda Morrison
Commissioning Editors Mark Hawkins-Dady, Carol Jones

Publishes reference books: the arts, history, literature, business, science and the social sciences. About 50 titles a year. TITLES *Reader's Guide to American History* ed. Peter J. Parish; *Encyclopedia of Latin American Literature* ed. Verity Smith; *Encyclopedia of the Essay* ed. Tracy Chevalier; *Encyclopedia of Interior Design* ed. Joanna Banham. IMPRINT **Glenlake Business Books**. Unsolicited mss, synopses and ideas welcome for reference books.
Royalties paid twice-yearly. *US associate* Fitzroy Dearborn Publishers, 919 North Michigan Ave., Suite 760, Chicago, IL 60611.

Fitzwarren Publishing

PO Box 6887, London N19 3SG
☎0171 686 4129   Fax 0171 686 4129
Contact Emma Prinsley

Publishes two or three books a year, mainly layman's handbooks on legal matters. All books published so far have followed a rigid 128-page format. Written approaches and synopses from prospective authors welcome. Authors, although not necessarily legally qualified, are expected to know their subject as well as a lawyer would.

Royalties paid twice a year.

Five Star
See **Serpent's Tail**

Flame
See **Hodder Headline plc**

Flamingo
See **HarperCollins Publishers Ltd**

Flicks Books
29 Bradford Road, Trowbridge, Wiltshire BA14 9AN
☎01225 767728   Fax 01225 760418
Publishing Director *Matthew Stevens*
FOUNDED 1986. Devoted solely to publishing books on the cinema and related media. 14 titles in 1998. TITLES *Queen of the 'B's: Ida Lupino Behind the Camera* ed. Annette Kuhn; *By Angels Driven: The Films of Derek Jarman* ed. Chris Lippard. Unsolicited mss, synopses and ideas within the subject area are welcome.
Royalties paid annually or twice yearly.

Flint River Press Ltd
See **Philip Wilson Publishers Ltd**

Floris Books
15 Harrison Gardens, Edinburgh EH11 1SH
☎0131 337 2372   Fax 0131 346 7516
Email: floris@floris.demon.co.uk
Managing Director *Christian Maclean*
Editors *Christopher Moore, Gale Taylor*
Approx. Annual Turnover £350,000
FOUNDED 1977. *Publishes* books related to the Steiner movement, including arts & crafts, children's, the Christian Community, history, religious, science, social questions and Celtic studies. No unsolicited mss. Synopses and ideas for books welcome.
Royalties paid annually.

Fodor's
See **Random House UK Ltd**

Folens Limited
Albert House, Apex Business Centre, Boscombe Road, Dunstable, Bedfordshire LU5 4RL
☎01582 472788   Fax 01582 472575
Email: folens@folens.com
Website:www.folens.com

Chairman *Dirk Folens*
Managing Director *Malcolm Watson*
FOUNDED 1987. Leading educational publisher. About 150 titles a year. IMPRINTS **Folens**; **Framework**; **Belair**. Unsolicited mss, synopses and ideas for educational books welcome.
Royalties paid annually.

Fortean Times Books
See **John Brown Publishing Ltd**

G. T. Foulis & Co Ltd
See **Haynes Publishing**

W. Foulsham & Co.
The Publishing House, Bennetts Close, Slough, Berkshire SL1 5AP
☎01753 526769   Fax 01753 535003
Chairman *R. S. Belasco*
Managing Director *B. A. R. Belasco*
Approx. Annual Turnover £2.2 million
FOUNDED 1819 and now one of the few remaining independent family companies to survive takeover. *Publishes* non-fiction on most subjects including astrology, gardening, cookery, DIY, business, hobbies, sport, health and marriage. No fiction.
IMPRINT **Quantum** Mind, Body and Spirit titles. Unsolicited mss, synopses and ideas welcome. Around 60 titles a year.
Royalties paid twice-yearly.

Fount
See **HarperCollins Publishers Ltd**

Fountain Press Ltd
2 Gladstone Road, Kingston-upon-Thames, Surrey KT1 3HD
☎0181 541 4050   Fax 0181 547 3022
Managing Director *H. M. Ricketts*
Approx. Annual Turnover £750,000
FOUNDED 1923 when it was part of the Rowntree Trust Social Service. Owned by the British Electric Traction Group until 1982 when it was bought out by the present managing director. *Publishes* mainly photography and natural history. About 25 titles a year. TITLES *Photography Yearbook*; *Wildlife Photographer of the Year*; *Antique and Collectable Cameras*; *Camera Manual* (series). Unsolicited mss and synopses are welcome.
Royalties paid twice-yearly.

Authors' Rating Highly regarded for production values, Fountain has the reputation for involving authors in every stage of the publishing process.

Fourth Estate Ltd
6 Salem Road, London W2 4BU
☎0171 727 8993   Fax 0171 792 3176
Chairman/Managing Director
   Victoria Barnsley
Publishing Director *Christopher Potter*
Approx. Annual Turnover £17 million
FOUNDED 1984. Independent publisher with
strong reputation for literary fiction and up-to-
the-minute non-fiction. *Publishes* fiction, popular
science, current affairs, biography, humour, self-
help, travel, reference. About 100 titles a year.
   DIVISIONS **Literary Fiction/Non-fiction**;
General Fiction/Non-Fiction TITLES *Fermat's
Last Theorem* Simon Singh; *Nigel Slater's Real
Food* Nigel Slater; *The Giant, O'Brien* Hilary
Mantel; *Me and the Fat Man* Julie Myerson; *The
Intruder* Peter Blauner; *The Perfect Storm* Sebastian
Junger; *The Diving Bell and the Butterfly* Jean-
Dominique Bauby. No unsolicited mss; synopses
welcome. IMPRINT **Guardian Books** in associ-
ation with *The Guardian*.
   Royalties paid twice-yearly.

Authors' Rating The combination of a strong
memorable name with a talent to pick unlikely
bestsellers makes Fourth Estate one of the most
successful of the new generation of publishers.

Framework
See **Folens Limited**

Free Association Books Ltd
57 Warren Street, London W1P 5PA
☎0171 388 3182   Fax 0171 388 3187
Email: fab@fitzrovia.demon.co.uk
Managing Director/Publisher *T. E. Brown*
Publishes psychoanalysis and psychotherapy, psy-
chology, cultural studies, sexuality and gender,
women's studies, applied social sciences. TITLES
*Opium and the People; Rethinking the Trauma of
War; Making and Breaking Families; Psychoanalysis
with Children*. Always send a letter in the first
instance accompanied by a book outline.
   Royalties paid twice-yearly. *Overseas associates*
ISBS, USA; Astam, Australia.

W. H. Freeman
Macmillan Press, Houndsmill, Basingstoke,
Hampshire RG21 6XS
☎01256 329242   Fax 01256 330688
President *Robert Beiwen* (New York)
Sales Director *Elizabeth Warner*
Part of W. H. Freeman & Co., USA. *Publishes*
academic, agriculture, animal care and breeding,
archaeology, artificial intelligence, biochemistry,
biology and zoology, chemistry, computer science, economics, educational and textbooks,
engineering, geography and geology, mathematics and statistics, medical, natural history,
neuroscience, palaeontology, physics, politics
and world affairs, psychology, sociology and
anthropology, and veterinary. Freeman's editorial office is in New York (Basingstoke is a sales
and marketing office only) but unsolicited mss
can go through Basingstoke. Those which are
obviously unsuitable will be sifted out; the rest
will be forwarded to New York.
   Royalties paid annually.

Samuel French Ltd
52 Fitzroy Street, London W1P 6JR
☎0171 387 9373   Fax 0171 387 2161
Email: theatre@samuelfrench-london.co.uk
Website:www.samuelfrench-london.co.uk
Chairman *Charles R. Van Nostrand*
Managing Director *John Bedding*
FOUNDED 1830 with the object of acquiring acting rights and publishing plays. *Publishes* plays
only. About 50 titles a year. Unsolicited mss considered only after initial submission of synopsis
and specimen scene. Such material should be
addressed to the Performing Rights Department.
   Royalties paid twice-yearly for books; performing royalties paid monthly, subject to a
minimum amount.

Authors' Rating Thrives on the amateur dramatic societies who are forever in need of play
texts. Editorial advisers give serious attention to
new material but a high proportion of the list is
staged before it goes into print. Non-estab-
lished writers are advised to try one-act plays,
much in demand by the amateur dramatic societies but rarely turned out by well-known
playwrights.

David Fulton (Publishers) Ltd
Ormond House, 26/27 Boswell Street,
London WC1N 3JD
☎0171 405 5606   Fax 0171 831 4840
Email: mail@fultonbooks.co.uk
Website:www.fultonbooks.co.uk
Chairman/Managing Director *David Fulton*
Editorial Director *John Owens*
Commissioning Editor, Special
   Education *Alison Foyle*
Approx. Annual Turnover £1.25 million
FOUNDED 1987. *Publishes* non-fiction: books
for teachers and teacher training at B.Ed and
PGCE levels for early years, primary, secondary
and virtually all aspects of special education;

geography for undergraduates. In 1995, David Fulton set up a Fulton Fellowship in Special Education (see entry under **Bursaries, Fellowships and Grants**). About 65 titles a year. No unsolicited mss; synopses and ideas for books welcome.

Royalties paid twice-yearly.

Authors' Rating David Fulton has shown how niche publishing can succeed even in a difficult market. Known chiefly for books on learning difficulties, he gets most of his ideas and authors by going to education conferences.

Funfax Limited

Marsh House, Tide Mill Way, Woodbridge, Suffolk IP12 1AN
☎01394 380622   Fax 01394 380618
Publisher *Roger Priddy*
Managing Editor *Lisa Telford*
Approx. Annual Turnover £7 million

FOUNDED 1990. A wholly-owned subsidiary of **Dorling Kindersley** Holdings plcsince 1995. Formerly Henderson Publishing Ltd. *Publishes* children's books for the international mass markets; non-fiction information, novelty, puzzle and some fiction books. All ideas are generated in-house to specific formats across the range of imprints. Freelance writers are commissioned to write to an agreed brief with strict guidelines. Texts are then edited in-house to suit a particular style. Unsolicited synopses and ideas for books welcome. No mss. New authors welcome (send c.v. and introductory letter to Lucy Bater).

IMPRINTS include **Funfax**; **Fun Files**; **Quiz Quest**; **Funpax**; **Fun Box**; **Microfax**; **Mad Jack**; **Magic Jewellery**.

Gaia Books Ltd

66 Charlotte Street, London W1P 1LR
☎0171 323 4010   Fax 0171 323 0435
Also at: 20 High Street, Stroud, Gloucestershire GL5 1AS
☎01453 752985   Fax 01453 752987
Managing Director *Joss Pearson*

FOUNDED 1983. *Publishes* ecology, health, natural living and mind, body & spirit, mainly in practical self-help illustrated reference form for Britain and the international market. About 12 titles a year. TITLES *The Way of Healing; A Heritage of Flowers; The Detox Plan; The Book of Chakra Healing; Yoga Cookbook; The Healing Energies of Water.* Most projects are conceived in-house but outlines and mss with s.a.e. considered. 'From submission of an idea to project go ahead may take up to a year. Authors become involved with the Gaia team in the editorial, design and promotion work needed to create and market a book.'

Gairm Publications

29 Waterloo Street, Glasgow G2 6BZ
☎0141 221 1971   Fax 0141 221 1971
Chairman *Prof. Derick S. Thomson*

FOUNDED 1952 to publish the quarterly Gaelic periodical *Gairm* and soon moved into publishing other Gaelic material. Acquired an old Glasgow Gaelic publishing firm, Alexander MacLaren & Son, in 1970. *Publishes* a wide range of Gaelic and Gaelic-related books: dictionaries, grammars, handbooks, children's, fiction, poetry, biography, music and song. TITLES *The Companion to Gaelic Scotland; Derick Thomson's collection of poems, Meall Garbh/The Rugged Mountain.* Catalogue available.

Galaxy Children's Large Print

See **Chivers Press Ltd**

J. Garnet Miller Ltd

See **Cressrelles Publishing Co. Ltd**

Garnet Publishing Ltd

8 Southern Court, South Street, Reading, Berkshire RG1 4QS
☎0118 9597847   Fax 0118 9597356
Email: enquiries@garnet-ithaca.demon.co.uk
Managing Director *Ken Banerji*

FOUNDED 1992 and purchased Ithaca Press in the same year. *Publishes* art, architecture, photography, archive photography, cookery, travel classics, travel, comparative religion, Islamic culture and history, foreign fiction in translation. Core subjects are Middle Eastern but list is rapidly expanding to be more general. About 30 titles in 1998.

IMPRINTS **Ithaca Press** *Adel Kamal* Specialises in post-graduate academic works on the Middle East, political science and international relations. About 20 titles in 1998. TITLES *The Making of the Modern Gulf States; The Palestinian Exodus; French Imperialism in Syria; Philby of Arabia.* **Garnet Publishing** *Emma Hawker* TITLES *Arab Women Writers* series (winner of the 1995 WiP New Venture Award); *The Story of Islamic Architecture; Traditional Greek Cooking; Jerusalem: Caught in Time; World Fiction* series. Unsolicited mss not welcome – write with outline and ideas first plus current c.v.

Royalties paid twice-yearly. *Sister companies*: All Prints, Beirut; Garnet France, Paris.

The Gay Men's Press (Prowler Press Ltd)

3 Broadbent Close, 20–22 Highgate High Street, London N6 5GG
☎0181 348 9963   Fax 0181 348 0023
Email: bjorn@dircon.co.uk

Editors *Neal Cavalier-Smith, David Fernbach*

Publishes books on gay-related issues: non-fiction and a wide range of fiction from literary to popular. TITLES *Foolish Fire* Guy Willard; *Ulster Alien* Stephen Birkett; *Growing Pains* Mike Seabrook; *All the Queen's Men* Nick Elwood; *All Boys Together* Robin Yeo. Work should be submitted on disk. Send synopsis with sample chapters rather than complete mss.
Royalties negotiable.

Gazelle Books

See **Angus Hudson** under **UK Packagers**

Geddes & Grosset

David Dale House, New Lanark ML11 9DJ
☎01555 665000   Fax 01555 665694
Publisher *R. Michael Miller*
Approx. Annual Turnover £2.2 million

FOUNDED 1989. Publisher and packager of children's and reference books. Unsolicited mss, synopses and ideas welcome. No adult fiction.

Authors' Rating Geddes & Grosset came to success with Tarantula, a children's imprint launched four years ago which sells almost exclusively through supermarket chains.

Stanley Gibbons Publications

5 Parkside, Christchurch Road, Ringwood, Hampshire BH24 3SH
☎01425 472363   Fax 01425 470247
Chief Executive *A. Grodecki*
Operation Director *A. J. Pandit*
Editorial Head *D. Aggersberg*
Approx. Annual Turnover £3 million

Long-established force in the philatelic world with over a hundred years in the business. *Publishes* philatelic reference catalogues and handbooks. Approx. 15 titles a year. Reference works relating to other areas of collecting may be considered. TITLES *How to Arrange and Write Up a Stamp Collection; Stanley Gibbons British Commonwealth Stamp Catalogue; Stamps of the World.* Foreign catalogues include Japan and Korea, Portugal and Spain, Germany, Middle East, Balkans, China. Monthly publication *Gibbons Stamp Monthly* (see entry under **Magazines**). Unsolicited mss, synopses and ideas welcome.
Royalties by negotiation.

Robert Gibson & Sons Glasgow Limited

17 Fitzroy Place, Glasgow G3 7SF
☎0141 248 5674   Fax 0141 221 8219
Email: Robert.GibsonSons@btinternet.com
Chairman/Managing Director
   R. G. C. Gibson

FOUNDED 1850 and went public in 1886. *Publishes* educational books only, and has been agent for the Scottish Certificate of Education Examination Board since 1902 which, in 1997, became the Scottish Qualification Authority. About 40 titles a year. Unsolicited mss preferred to synopses/ideas.
Royalties paid annually.

Ginn & Co

See **Reed Educational & Professional Publishing**

Mary Glasgow Publications

See **Stanley Thornes (Publishers) Ltd**

Glenlake Business Books

See **Fitzroy Dearborn Publishers**

Godsfield Press Ltd

See **David & Charles Publishers**

Golden Cockerel Press Ltd

16 Barter Street, London WC1A 2AH
☎0171 405 7979   Fax 0171 404 3598
Email: lindesay@btinternet.com

Directors *Tamar Lindesay, Andrew Lindesay*

FOUNDED 1980 to distribute titles for US-based Associated University Presses Inc., New Jersey. *Publishes* academic titles mostly: art, film, history, literary criticism, music, philosophy, sociology and special interest. About 120 titles a year. IMPRINTS **AUP: Bucknell University Press; University of Delaware; Fairleigh Dickinson University Press; Lehigh University Press; Susquehanna University Press.** Also: **Cygnus Arts** Non-academic books on the arts; **Cornwall Books** Trade hardbacks. Unsolicited mss, synopses and ideas for appropriate books welcome.

Authors' Rating Very much attuned to American interests with trans-Atlantic spelling and punctuation predominating. Some writers may find the process wearisome but those who persevere win through to a wider market.

Victor Gollancz

See **Cassell**

Gomer Press

Wind Street, Llandysul, Ceredigion
SA44 4QL
☎01559 362371　　　　Fax 01559 363758
Email: gwasg@gomer.co.uk
Website:www.gomer.co.uk
Chairman/Managing Director *J. H. Lewis*

FOUNDED 1892. *Publishes* adult fiction and non-fiction, children's fiction and educational material in English and Welsh. About 100 titles a year (65 Welsh; 35 English). IMPRINTS **Gomer Press** *Bethan Matthews* **Pont Books** *Mairwen Prys Jones*. No unsolicited mss, synopses or ideas.
Royalties paid twice-yearly.

Gower

See **Ashgate Publishing Ltd**

GPC Books

See **University of Wales Press**

Graham & Trotman

See **Kluwer Law International**

Graham & Whiteside Ltd

Tuition House, 5–6 Francis Grove, London
SW19 4DT
☎0181 947 1011　　　　Fax 0181 947 1163
Email: sales@major-co-data.com
Website:www.major-co-data.com
Managing Director *Alastair M. W. Graham*

FOUNDED 1995. *Publishes* annual directories for the business and professional market with titles dating back to 1975 originally published by Graham & Trotman. TITLES 22 annual directories, including: *Major Companies of Europe; Major Companies of the Arab World; Major Companies of the Far East and Australasia*. Proposals for new projects welcome.
Royalties paid annually.

Graham-Cameron Publishing

The Studio, 23 Holt Road, Sheringham,
Norfolk NR26 8NB
☎01263 821333　　　　Fax 01263 821334
Editorial Director *Mike Graham-Cameron*
Art Director *Helen Graham-Cameron*

FOUNDED 1984 as a packaging operation. *Publishes* illustrated factual books for children, institutions and business; also biography, education and social history. TITLES *Up From the Country; In All Directions; The Holywell Story; Let's Look at Dairying*. No unsolicited mss.
Royalties paid annually. *Subsidiary company*: Graham-Cameron Illustration (agency).

Granada Books

See **André Deutsch Ltd**

Granta Books

2–3 Hanover Yard, Noel Road, London
N1 8BE
☎0171 704 9776　　　　Fax 0171 354 3469
Publisher *Frances Coady*

FOUNDED 1979. *Publishes* literary fiction and general non-fiction. About 35 titles a year. No unsolicited mss; synopses and sample chapters welcome.
Royalties paid twice-yearly.

Authors' Rating Granta has relaunched with 'a mix of new and established writers' while putting out the welcome sign for 'good writing and challenging ideas'.

W. Green (Scotland)

See **Sweet & Maxwell Ltd**

Green Books

Foxhole, Dartington, Totnes, Devon
TQ9 6EB
☎01803 863260　　　　Fax 01803 863843
Email: greenbooks@gn.apc.org
Website:www.greenbooks.co.uk
Chairman *Satish Kumar*
Managing Editor *John Elford*
Approx. Annual Turnover £200,000

FOUNDED in 1987 with the support of a number of Green organisations. Closely associated with *Resurgence* magazine. *Publishes* high-quality books on a wide range of Green issues, particularly ideas, philosophy and the practical application of Green values. No fiction or books for children. TITLES *Forest Gardening* Robert A. de J. Hart; *Eco-Renovation* Edward Harland; *The Growth Illusion* Richard Douthwaite; *The Green Lanes of England* Valerie Belsey; *The Organic Directory* ed. Clive Litchfield. No unsolicited mss. Synopses and ideas welcome.
Royalties paid twice-yearly.

Greenhill Books/ Lionel Leventhal Ltd

Park House, 1 Russell Gardens, London
NW11 9NN
☎0181 458 6314　　　　Fax 0181 905 5245
Email: LionelLeventhal@compuserve.com
Website:www.greenhillbooks.com
Managing Director *Lionel Leventhal*

FOUNDED 1984 by Lionel Leventhal (ex-**Arms & Armour Press**). *Publishes* aviation, military and naval books, and its Napoleonic Library series. Synopses and ideas for books welcome. No unsolicited mss.

Royalties paid twice-yearly.

Greenzone
See **Aspire Publishing**

Gresham Books Ltd
PO Box 61, Henley on Thames, Oxfordshire RG9 3LQ
☎01734 403789   Fax 01734 403789
Managing Director *Mary V. Green*
Approx. Annual Turnover £225,000

Bought by Mary Green from Martins Publishing Group in 1980. A small specialist publishing house. *Publishes* hymn and service books for schools and churches, also craftbound choir and orchestral folders and Records of Achievement. TITLES include music and melody editions of *Hymns for Church and School*; *The School Hymnal*; *Praise and Thanksgiving*. No unsolicited material but ideas welcome.

Griffith Institute
See **Ashmolean Museum Publications Ltd**

Grisewood & Dempsey
See **Kingfisher Publications plc**

Grub Street
The Basement, 10 Chivalry Road, London SW11 1HT
☎0171 924 3966   Fax 0171 738 1009
Managing Director *John Davies*

FOUNDED 1982. *Publishes* cookery, health, military and aviation history books. About 20 titles a year. TITLES *Moroccon Cuisine; JG26 War Diary, Volume Two; Aircraft vs Aircraft*. Unsolicited mss and synopses welcome in the above categories.

Royalties paid twice-yearly.

Guardian Books
See **Fourth Estate Ltd**

Guild of Master Craftsman Publications Ltd
166 High Street, Lewes, East Sussex BN7 1XU
☎01273 477374   Fax 01273 487692
Chairman *A.E. Phillips*
Approx. Annual Turnover £2 million

FOUNDED 1979. Part of G.M.C. Services Ltd. *Publishes* woodworking, craft and gardening books, magazines and videos. 40 titles in 1998. Unsolicited mss, synopses and ideas for books welcome. No fiction.

Royalties paid twice-yearly.

Guinness Publishing Ltd
338 Euston Road, London NW1 3BD
☎0171 891 4567   Fax 0171 891 4501
Email: Guinness_Publishing@guinness.com
Chairman *Nick Fell*
Managing Director *Christopher Irwin*
Publishing Director *Ian Castello-Cortes*
Television Director *Michael Feldman*
Approx. Annual Turnover £7 million

FOUNDED 1954 to publish *The Guinness Book of Records*, now the highest-selling copyright book in the world, published in 35 languages. The list has now expanded to about 12 major titles a year in international four-colour popular reference, music and film titles. Ideas and synopses welcome as is contact from projective researchers, editors and designers.

Gunsmoke Westerns
See **Chivers Press Ltd**

Gwasg Addysgol Cymru
See **Ashley Drake Publishing Ltd**

Gwasg Carreg Gwalch
12 Iard Yr Orsaf, Llanrwst, Conwy LL26 0EH
☎01492 642031   Fax 01492 641502
Managing Editor *Myrddin ap Dafydd*

FOUNDED in 1990. *Publishes* Welsh language; English books of Welsh interest – history, folklore, guides and walks. 70 titles in 1998. Unsolicited mss, synopses and ideas welcome.

Royalties paid.

Gwasg Prifysgol Cymru
See **University of Wales Press**

Peter Halban Publishers
42 South Molton Street, London W1Y 1HB
☎0171 491 1582   Fax 0171 629 5381
Directors *Peter Halban, Martine Halban*

FOUNDED 1986. Independent publisher. *Publishes* biography, autobiography and memoirs, history, philosophy, theology, politics, literature and criticism, Judaica and world affairs. 4–5 titles a year. No unsolicited material. Approach by letter in first instance.

Royalties paid twice-yearly for first two years, thereafter annually in December.

Robert Hale Ltd
Clerkenwell House, 45–47 Clerkenwell Green, London EC1R 0HT
☎0171 251 2661   Fax 0171 490 4958
Chairman/Managing Director *John Hale*

FOUNDED 1936. Family-owned company. *Publishes* adult fiction (but not interested in category crime, romance or science fiction) and non-fiction. No specialist material (education, law, medical or scientific). Acquired **NAG Press Ltd** in 1993 with its list of horological, gemmological, jewellery and metalwork titles. Over 200 titles a year. TITLES *The Art of Violin Making* Chris Johnson and Roy Courtnall; *A Guide to Surviving Life as a Mistress* Heather King and Jordan Hayes; *Good Owner's Clock Guide and Clock Logbook* John Moorhouse; *Combat Nurse* Eric Taylor; *Practical Paganism* Anthony Kemp and J. M. Sertori; *Roscoe, Emily and All the Little Bastards* Jill Fenson; *The Last of Sir Lancelot* Richard Gordon. Unsolicited mss, synopses and ideas for books welcome.

Royalties paid twice-yearly.

Authors' Rating Fair point. John Hale writes to suggest that previous Authors' Ratings have not made enough of this publisher's good standing with authors. Hale was generally smiled upon in a recent Society of Authors survey.

Halsgrove

Halsgrove House, Lower Moor Way,
Tiverton, Devon EX16 6SS
☎01884 243242   Fax 01884 243325
Email: sales@halsgrove.com
Joint Managing Directors *Simon Butler,*
  Steven Pugsley
Approx. Annual Turnover £1.5 million
FOUNDED in 1990 from defunct Maxwell-owned publishing group. Grown into the region's largest publishing and distribution group, specialising in books, video and audio tapes. *Publishes* local history, cookery, biography. 100 titles in 1998. No fiction or poetry. Unsolicited mss, synopses and ideas for books of regional interest welcome.

Royalties paid annually.

The Hambledon Press

102 Gloucester Avenue, London NW1 8HX
☎0171 586 0817   Fax 0171 586 9970
Email: office@hambledon.co.uk
**Chairman/Managing Director/Editorial
  Head** *Martin Sheppard*
FOUNDED 1980. *Publishes* British and European history from post-classical to modern. Currently expanding its list to include history titles with a wider appeal including more biographies. 25–30 titles a year. TITLES *The White Death: A History of Tuberculosis* Thomas Dormandy; *Victorian Girls: Lord Lyttelton's Daughters* Sheila Fletcher; *A Muse of Fire: Literature, Art and War* A. D. Harvey. No unsolicited mss; send preliminary letter. Synopses and ideas welcome.

Royalties paid annually. *Overseas associates* The Hambledon Press (USA), Ohio.

Hamilton & Co (Publishers)

10 Stratton Street, Mayfair, London W1X 5FD
☎0171 546 8646   Fax 0171 546 8570
Email: editorial@hamilton-and-co.demon.
co.uk
Managing Editor *James Dalton*
Editor *Max Hoffman*
FOUNDED 1997. *Publishes* fiction and non-fiction: memoirs, autobiography, biography, war, poetry, children's and historical. Around 60 titles a year. TITLES *Cut to the Chase* Steve Emecz; *Oxford Bitch* Barry St-John Nevill; *Tree Frog* Jason Charles. No unsolicited mss; synopses and sample chapters with return postage only.

Royalties paid annually.

Authors' Rating Liable to ask authors to contribute towards costs of publication.

Hamish Hamilton/
Hamish Hamilton Children's

See **Penguin UK**

Hamlyn Children's Books

See **Egmont Children's Books**

Hamlyn/Octopus

See **Octopus Publishing Group**

Harcourt Brace and Company Limited

24–28 Oval Road, London NW1 7DX
☎0171 424 4200 Fax 0171 482 2293/485 4752
Managing Director *Peter H. Lengemann*

Owned by US parent company. *Publishes* scientific, technical and medical books, college textbooks, educational & occupational test. No unsolicited mss. IMPRINTS **Academic Press**; **Baillière Tindall**; **Churchill Livingstone**; **Dryden Press**; **Holt Rinehart and Winston**; **Mosby International**; **T. & A. D. Poyser**; **W. B. Saunders & Co. Ltd.**; **Saunders Scientific Publications**.

Harlequin Mills & Boon Ltd

Eton House, 18–24 Paradise Road,
Richmond, Surrey TW9 1SR
☎0181 288 2800   Fax 0181 288 2899
Website:www.romance.net
Managing Director *F. Gejrot*
Editorial Director *Karin Stoecker*

Approx. Annual Turnover £21.3 million

FOUNDED 1908. Owned by the Canadian-based Torstar Group. *Publishes* romantic fiction and historical romance. Over 600 titles a year.

IMPRINTS

Mills & Boon Presents/Mills & Boon Enchanted (50–55,000 words) Contemporary romances with international settings, focusing on hero and heroine. **Mills & Boon Medical Romance** *Elizabeth Johnson* (50–55,000 words) Modern medical practice provides a unique background to love stories. **Mills & Boon Historical Romance** *Elizabeth Johnson* (75–80,000 words) Historical romances. **MIRA** *Linda Fildew* (minimum 100,000 words) Individual women's fiction.

Mills & Boon Temptation titles are acquired through the Canadian office. **Silhouette Desire**, **Special Edition**, **Sensation** and **Intrigue** imprints are handled by US-based **Silhouette Books** (see **US Publishers**). Please send query letter in the first instance. Tip sheets and guidelines for the Mills & Boon series available from the website or Harlequin Mills & Boon Editorial Dept. (please send s.a.e.).

Royalties paid twice-yearly.

Authors' Rating Still leading the way for lighweight romance but the plots are getting sexier.

Harley Books

Martins, Great Horkesley, Colchester, Essex CO6 4AH
☎01206 271216   Fax 01206 271182
Email: harley@keme.co.uk

Managing Director *Basil Harley*

FOUNDED 1983. Natural history publishers specialising in entomological and botanical books. Mostly definitive, high-quality illustrated reference works. TITLES *Aquatic Plants in Britain and Ireland; Songs of Grasshoppers and Crickets of Western Europe; The Moths and Butterflies of Great Britain and Ireland; Dragonflies of Europe; The Flora of Hampshire.*

Royalties paid twice-yearly in the first year, annually thereafter.

HarperCollins Publishers Ltd

77–85 Fulham Palace Road, London W6 8JB
☎0181 741 7070   Fax 0181 307 4440
Also at: Freepost PO Box, Glasgow G4 0NB
☎0141 772 3200   Fax 0141 306 3119
Website:www.harpercollins.co.uk

Chief Executive *Jane Friedman*

Executive Chairman/Publisher *Eddie Bell*
Group Managing Director *Les Higgins*
Approx. Annual Turnover £200 million

Publisher of high-profile authors like Jeffrey Archer, J. G. Ballard, Fay Weldon and Len Deighton. Owned by News Corporation. Since 1991 there has been a period of consolidated focus on key management issues within the HarperCollins empire. This has led to various imprints being phased out in favour of others, among them Grafton and Fontana, which have been merged under the HarperCollins paperback imprint. **Booker Prize** and **Pulitzer Prize** winners in 1997.

DIVISIONS

Trade Divisional Managing Director *Adrian Bourne*, Publishing Directors *Nick Sayers* (fiction), *Michael Fishwick* (non-fiction), *Susan Watt*. IMPRINTS **Collins Crime**; **Collins Willow** (sport) Publishing Director *Michael Doggart*; **Flamingo** (literary fiction, hardback and paperback) Publishing Director *Philip Gwyn Jones*; **HarperCollins Audiobooks** (see entry under **Audio Books**); **Harper Collins Entertainment** Publishing Director *Val Hudson*; **HarperCollins Paperbacks**; **Tolkien**; **Voyager** (science fiction/fantasy) Publishing Director *Jane Johnson*. Over 650 titles a year, hardback and paperback. No longer accepts unsolicited submissions.

Thorsons Divisional Managing Director *Eileen Campbell*. Health, nutrition, business, parenting, popular psychology, positive thinking, self-help, divination, therapy, recovery, feminism, women's issues, mythology, religion, yoga, tarot, personal development, sexual politics, biography, history, popular culture. About 250 titles a year.

Children's Divisional Managing Director *Kate Harris*. IMPRINTS **Picture Lions**; **HarperCollins Audio** (see entry under **Audio Books**); **Jets**. Quality picture books and book and tape sets for under 7s; all categories of fiction for the 6–14 age group; dictionaries for pre-school and primary. About 250 titles a year. No longer accepts unsolicited mss.

Reference Divisional Managing Director *Stephen Bray*. IMPRINTS **HarperCollins**; **Collins New Naturalist Library**; **Collins Gems**; **HC Illustrated**; **Janes** (military) Encyclopedias, guides and handbooks, phrase books and manuals on popular reference, art instruction, illustrated, cookery and wine, crafts, DIY, gardening, military, natural history, pet care, Scottish, pastimes. About 120 titles a year.

Educational Divisional Managing Director

Kate Harris. Textbook publishing for schools and FE colleges (5–18-year-olds): all subjects for primary education, including the **Letterland** imprint and the **Collins Study and Revision Guides**. Strong presence in all major secondary and curriculum areas. Sociology, business studies and economics in FE. (Former Holmes McDougall, Unwin Hyman, Mary Glasgow Primary Publications, and part of Harcourt, Brace & Co. educational imprints have been incorporated under Collins Educational.) About 90 titles a year.

Dictionaries *Kate Harris*. IMPRINTS **Collins**; **Collins Cobuild**; **Collins Gem** Includes the *Collins English Dictionary* range with dictionaries and thesauruses, *Collins Bilingual Dictionary* range (French, German, Spanish, Italian, etc.), and the *Cobuild* series of English dictionary, grammars and EFL books. About 50 titles a year.

Religious Divisional Managing Director *Eileen Campbell*. A broad-based religious publisher across all denominations. IMPRINTS **HarperCollins**; **Fount**; **Marshall Pickering** Extensive range covering both popular and academic spirituality, music and reference. Marshall Pickering, bibles, missals, prayer books, and hymn books. About 150 titles a year.

HarperCollins Cartographic Divisional Managing Director *Stephen Bray*. The cartographic division and Times Books now joined as one division. IMPRINTS **Collins**; **Collins Longman**; **Nicholson/Ordnance Survey**; **Times Atlases**; **Times Books**. Maps, atlases and guides (Collins; Collins Longman; Times Atlases); leisure maps, educational titles (Collins Longman); London titles (Nicholson); waterway guides (Nicholson/ Ordnance Survey); reference and non-fiction (Times Books). About 30 titles a year.

Broadcasting Consultancy *Eileen Campbell* Newly formed to exploit TV and film rights across the country.

Authors' Rating HarperCollins may be only a 'blip on the News Corp screen' but it is, nonetheless, Britain's largest consumer book publisher. The overlap with other media is at last bringing dividends, witness the success of the Titanic book. A new imprint, Entertainment, has been set up to exploit the television and entertainment output of News Corp. Personality authors, of whom HarperCollins has had more than its share, are finding life tougher with contracts being cancelled if deadlines are broken. Not before time, too.

Harrap

See **Chambers, Harrap Publishers**

Harvard University Press

Fitzroy House, 11 Chenies Street, London WC1E 7ET
☎0171 306 0603   Fax 0171 306 0604
Email: info@HUP-MITpress.co.uk
Website:www.hup.harvard.edu

Director *William Sisler*
General Manager *Ann Sexsmith*

European office of **Harvard University Press**, USA. *Publishes* academic and scholarly works in history, politics, philosophy, economics, literary criticism, psychology, sociology, anthropology, women's studies, biological sciences, classics, history of science, art, music, film, reference. All mss go to the American office: 79 Garden Street, Cambridge, MA 02138. (See entry under **US Publishers**.)

The Harvill Press Ltd

2 Aztec Row, Berners Road, Islington, London N1 0PW
☎0171 704 8766   Fax 0171 704 8805

Chairman *Christopher MacLehose*
Editorial Director *Guido Waldman*

FOUNDED in 1946. The Harvill list was bought by Collins in 1959, which maintained the imprint until it was returned to its original independent status in early 1995. *Publishes* literature in translation (especially Russian, Italian and French), English literature, quality thrillers, illustrated books and Africana, plus an occasional literature anthology. 60–70 titles in 1998. AUTHORS Mikhail Bulgakov, Raymond Carver, Richard Ford, Alan Garner, Peter Høeg, Robert Hughes, Giuseppe T. di Lampedusa, Peter Matthiessen, Cees Nooteboom, Boris Pasternak, Georges Perec, Aleksandr Solzhenitsyn, Marguerite Yourcenar. Mss usually submitted by foreign publishers and agents. Synopses and ideas welcome. No educational or technical books.

Royalties paid twice-yearly.

Authors' Rating Strong on translated fiction, the two-way traffic means that Harvill's English language writers tend to do well in Europe. Relations with authors are said to be close and friendly.

Haynes Publishing

Sparkford, Near Yeovil, Somerset BA22 7JJ
☎01963 440635   Fax 01963 440825
Email: info@haynes-manuals.co.uk
Website:www.haynes.com

Chairman *John H. Haynes, OBE*
Approx. Annual Turnover £28.7 million

FOUNDED in 1960 by John H. Haynes. A family-run business. The mainstay of its programme has been the *Owners' Workshop Manual*, first published in the mid 1960s and still running off the presses today. Indeed the company maintains a strong bias towards motoring and transport titles. *Publishes* DIY workshop manuals for cars and motorbikes, railway, aviation, military, maritime, model-making and general leisure. IMPRINTS **Haynes** *Matthew Minter* Workshop manuals; **Patrick Stephens Ltd** *Darryl Reach* Motoring, aviation, military, maritime, model-making; **Oxford Illustrated Press** photography, sports and games, gardening, travel and guidebooks; **Haynes** Home, DIY and leisure titles; **G. T. Foulis & Co.** Cars and motoring-related books. Unsolicited mss welcome if they come within the subject areas covered.

Royalties paid annually.

Overseas subsidiaries Haynes Manuals Inc., California, USA, Editions Haynes S.A., France, Haynes Publishing Nordiska AB, Sweden.

Hazar Publishing Ltd
147 Chiswick High Road, London W4 2DT
☎0181 742 8578   Fax 0181 994 1407
Managing Director *Gregory Hill*
Editorial Head *Marie Clayton*
Approx. Annual Turnover £700,000
FOUNDED 1993, Hazar is an independent publisher of high-quality illustrated books. *Publishes* children's picture books and pop-up books and adult non-fiction on design and architecture. About 15 titles a year.

Royalties paid twice-yearly.

Hazleton Publishing
3 Richmond Hill, Richmond, Surrey TW10 6RE
☎0181 948 5151   Fax 0181 948 4111
Publisher/Managing Director *R. F. Poulter*
Publisher of the leading Grand Prix annual *Autocourse*, now in its 49th edition. *Publishes* high-quality motor sport titles including annuals. TITLES *Motocourse; Rallycourse*. About 13 titles a year. No unsolicited mss; synopses and ideas welcome. Interested in all motor sport titles.

Royalties payment varies.

Headline
See **Hodder Headline plc**

Health Education Authority
Publishing Department, Trevelyan House, 30 Great Peter Street, London SW1P 2HW
☎0171 413 1846   Fax 0171 413 8912
Website:www.hea.org.uk

General Manager (Publishing) *Simon Boyd*
Approx. Annual Turnover £600,000
Publishes public information leaflets, training manuals, professional guides and open learning material for the Health Education Authority. Over 500 titles in print. TITLES cover nutrition, physical activity, cancer, sexual health, oral health, immunisation, alcohol, smoking, primary health care, accidents, mental health and drugs. No unsolicited mss; synopses and ideas welcome.

William Heinemann
See **Random House UK Ltd**

Heinemann Educational
See **Reed Educational & Professional Publishing**

Heinemann Young Books
See **Egmont Children's Books**

Helicon Publishing Ltd
42 Hythe Bridge Street, Oxford OX1 2EP
☎01865 204204   Fax 01865 204205
Email: admin@helicon.co.uk
Website:www.helicon.co.uk
Managing Director *David Attwooll*
Business Development Director
  Michael Upshall
Editorial Director *Hilary McGlynn*
Approx. Annual Turnover £3.5 million
FOUNDED 1992 from the management buy-out of former Random Century's reference division. Led by David Attwooll, the buy-out included the Hutchinson encyclopedia titles and databases, along with other reference titles. The Helicon list, which is distributed by Penguin, is increasing its range of reference titles, particularly in history, science and current affairs and is maintaining its lead in electronic publishing, especially in the area of on-line licensing, where it has relationships with several key UK and US blue-chip service providers. TITLES *The Hutchinson Almanac; The Hutchinson Encyclopedia*. Electronic: *The Penguin Hutchinson Reference Suite; The Hutchinson Educational Encyclopedia*.

Christopher Helm Publishers Ltd
See **A. & C. Black (Publishers) Ltd**

Helter Skelter Publishing
4 Denmark Street, London WC2H 8LL
☎0171 836 1151   Fax 0171 240 9880
Email: helter@skelter.demon.co.uk
Website:www.skelter.demon.co.uk

Contact *Sean Body*
FOUNDED 1995. *Publishes* books on music and film. About 8–10 titles a year. IMPRINTS **Helter Skelter Publishing; Firefly Publishing.** Unsolicited mss, synopses and ideas welcome.

Henderson Publishing Ltd
See **Funfax Limited**

Ian Henry Publications Ltd
20 Park Drive, Romford, Essex RM1 4LH
☎01708 749119   Fax 01708 749119
Managing Director *Ian Wilkes*
FOUNDED 1976. *Publishes* local history, transport history and Sherlockian pastiches. 8–10 titles a year. TITLES *Allergy Cookbook; Essex Under Arms; Sherlock Holmes and the Lusitania; Portrait of Foulness.* No unsolicited mss. Synopses and ideas for books welcome.
Royalties paid twice-yearly.

The Herbert Press
See **A. & C. Black (Publishers) Ltd**

Hermes House
See **Anness Publishing Ltd**

Nick Hern Books
The Glasshouse, 49a Goldhawk Road, London W12 8QP
☎0181 749 4953   Fax 0181 746 2006
Email: info@nickhernbooks.demon.co.uk
Chairman/Managing Director *Nick Hern*
Approx. Annual Turnover £300,000
FOUNDED 1988. Fully independent since 1992. *Publishes* books on theatre and film: from how-to and biography to plays and screenplays. About 30 titles a year. No unsolicited playscripts. Synopses, ideas and proposals for other theatre material welcome. Not interested in material unrelated to the theatre or cinema.

Hippo
See **Scholastic Ltd**

Historic Military Press
See **SB Publications**

HMSO
See **The Stationery Office Publishing**

Hobsons Publishing
159–173 St John Street, London EC1V 4DR
☎0171 336 6633   Fax 0171 490 2422
Chairman *Martin Morgan*
Managing Director *Christopher Letcher*

Approx. Annual Turnover £17.7 million
FOUNDED 1973. A division of Harmsworth Publishing Ltd, part of the Daily Mail & General Trust. *Publishes* course and career guides, under exclusive licence and royalty agreements for CRAC (Careers Research and Advisory Bureau); computer software; directories and specialist titles for employers, government departments and professional associations. TITLES *Graduate Employment and Training; Degree Course Guides; The Which Degree Series; Which University* (CD-ROM); *The POST-GRAD Series: The Directory of Graduate Studies; The Directory of Further Education.*

Hodder & Stoughton
See **Hodder Headline plc**

Hodder Headline plc
338 Euston Road, London NW1 3BH
☎0171 873 6000   Fax 0171 873 6024
Group Chief Executive *Tim Hely Hutchinson*
Deputy Chief Executive *Mark Opzoomer*
Approx. Annual Turnover £93.2 million
Formed in June 1993 through the merger of **Headline Book Publishing** and **Hodder & Stoughton**. Headline was formed in 1986 and had grown dramatically, whereas Hodder & Stoughton was 125 years old with a diverse range of publishing. 2,200 titles in 1997.

DIVISIONS
Headline Book Publishing Managing Director *Amanda Ridout.* **Non-fiction** Publishing Director *Heather Holden-Brown;* **Fiction** Publishing Director *Jane Morpeth;* **Headline** *Anne Williams;* **Headline Feature** *Bill Massey;* **Review** *Geraldine Cooke.* Publishes commercial and literary fiction (hardback and paperback) and popular non-fiction including biography, cinema, countryside, food and wine, popular science, TV tie-ins and sports yearbooks. IMPRINTS **Headline; Headline Feature; Review.** AUTHORS Catherine Alliott, Ronan Bennett, Raymond Blanc, Martina Cole, Josephine Cox, Lucy Ellmann, John Francome, Ken Hom, Jennifer Johnston, Cathy Kelly, Dean Koontz, James Patterson and Anthony Worrall Thompson.

Hodder & Stoughton General Managing Director *Martin Neild,* Deputy Managing Director *Sue Fletcher.* **Non-fiction** *Roland Philipps;* **Sceptre** *Carole Welch;* **Fiction** *Carolyn Mays;* **Audio** (See entry under **Audio Books**). *Publishes* commercial and literary fiction; biography, autobiography, history, self-help, humour, travel and other general interest non-fiction;

audio. IMPRINTS **Hodder & Stoughton**; **Lir**; **Coronet**; **Flame**; **New English Library**; **Sceptre**. AUTHORS Dickie Bird, Melvyn Bragg, John le Carré, Justin Cartwright, Charles Frazier, Elizabeth George, Thomas Keneally, Stephen King, Ed McBain, Malcolm Gluck, Lawrence Norfolk, Rosamunde Pilcher and Mary Stewart.

Hodder & Stoughton Educational Managing Director *Philip Walters*. **Humanities, Tests, Science & Scotland** *Lis Tribe*; **Languages, Business, Psychology, English and Mathematics** *Tim Gregson-Williams*; **Teach Yourself**; **Trade Education** *Jo Osborne*. Textbooks for the primary, secondary, tertiary and further education sectors and for self-improvement. IMPRINT **Hodder & Stoughton Educational**.

Hodder Children's Books Managing Director *Mary Tapissier*. IMPRINTS **Hodder Children's Books**; **Signature**. AUTHORS Enid Blyton, John Cunliffe, Lucy Daniels, Mick Inkpen, Hilary McKay, Joan Lingard, Jenny Oldfield, Christopher Pike.

Hodder & Stoughton Religious Managing Director *Charles Nettleton*. **Bibles & Liturgical** *Emma Sealey*; **Christian Paperbacks** *Judith Longman*. Bibles, commentaries, liturgical works (both printed and software), and a wide range of Christian paperbacks. IMPRINTS **New International Version of the Bible**; **Hodder Christian Books**.

Arnold Managing Director *Richard Stileman*. **Humanities** *Chris Wheeler*; **STM** *Nick Dunton*; **Science and Engineering** *Nicki Dennis*; **Health Sciences** *Georgina Bentliff*; **Journals** *Mary Attree*. Academic and professional books and journals.

The Brockhampton Press Managing Director *John Maxwell*. Promotional books.

Royalties paid twice-yearly.

Authors' Rating Big name authors dominate the list and together make the single biggest factor in Hodder Headline's growth. But this highly entrepreneurial publisher still has an eye for new talent. Further expansion is predicted including a move into the US market.

Holt Rinehart & Winston
See **Harcourt Brace and Company Limited**

Honeyglen Publishing Ltd
56 Durrels House, Warwick Gardens, London W14 8QB
☎0171 602 2876   Fax 0171 602 2876
Directors *N. S. Poderegin, J. Poderegin*
FOUNDED 1983. A small publishing house whose output is 'extremely limited'. *Publishes* history, philosophy of history, biography and selective fiction. No children's or science fiction. TITLES *The Soul of India; A Child of the Century* Amaury de Riencourt; *With Duncan Grant in South Turkey* Paul Roche; *Vladimir, The Russian Viking* Vladimir Volkoff; *The Dawning* Milka Bajic-Poderegin; *Quicksand* Louise Hide. Unsolicited mss welcome.

House of Lochar
Isle of Colonsay, Argyll PA61 7YR
☎01951 200232   Fax 01951 200232
Email: Lochar@colonsay.org.uk
Chairman *Kevin Byrne*
Managing Director *Georgina Hobhouse*
Approx. Annual Turnover £95,000

FOUNDED 1995 on a tiny island, taking advantage of new technology and mains electricity and taking over some 20 titles from Thomas and Lochar. About 10 titles a year. *Publishes* mostly Scottish – history, topography, transport and fiction. IMPRINTS **House of Lochar** TITLES *The Crofter and the Laird; The Clyde in Pictures; History of British Airships*. AUTHORS (fiction) Neill Gunn, Naomi Mitchison, Sandy Young. **Colonsay Books** TITLES *Summer in the Hebrides*. **West Highland Series** Mini walking guides. No poetry or books unrelated to Scotland or Celtic theme. Unsolicited mss, synopses and ideas welcome if relevant to subjects covered.

Royalties paid annually.

How To Books Ltd
3 Newtec Place, Magdalen Road, Oxford OX4 1RE
☎01865 793806   Fax 01865 248780
Email: info@howtobooks.co.uk
Website:www.howtobooks.co.uk
Publisher and Managing Director
Giles Lewis

A fast-growing independent reference publisher which publishers three popular SERIES: **How To** Practical, accessible and encouraging books to help people improve their lives and develop their skills; *Pathways* Inspiring, informative books for thoughtful readers wanting to develop themselves and realise their potential; **Essentials** Handy, crisp and approachable books teaching specifice skills to busy people. Over 50 titles a year. Subjects covered include business and management, computer basics, general reference, jobs and careers, living and working abroad, personal finance, self-development, small business, student handbooks and successful writing. New book proposals are 'very welcome. Authors are given assistance and guidance in the development of their books.'

Royalties paid annually.

The University of Hull Press/ The Lampada Press

Cottingham Road, Hull, East Yorkshire
HU6 7RX
☎01482 466532   Fax 01482 466858
Email: g.m.innes@admin.hull.ac.uk
Publisher *Glen Innes*

Publishes books of academic interest principally in the fields of history (maritime, medieval and colonial), literary and media studies, British art, music and regional studies. Also publishes the series *EastNote, Hull Studies in Jazz.* TITLES *DeepSong: Jan Garbarek* Michael Tucker; *Nonstop Flight: Artie Shaw* John White; *The Cutting Edge: Sonny Rollins* Richard Palmer; *The Naming of Parts* James S. Beggs. **The Lampada Press** publishes work of a more general interest. TITLES *Thank God I'm Not A Boy, the letters of Dora Willat 1915–18* ed. Alan Wilkinson; *Musicians in Time* Jenny Boyd. Welcomes unsolicited mss, synopses and ideas for books.

Royalties paid annually. *Overseas representatives*: Paul & Co., USA; St Clair Press, Australia.

Human Horizons

See **Souvenir Press Ltd**

Human Science Press

See **Plenum Publishing Co. Ltd**

Hunt & Thorpe

46a West Street, New Alresford, Hampshire
SO24 9AU
☎01962 736880   Fax 01962 736881
Email: JohnHuntPublishing@compuserve.com
Approx. Annual Turnover £1.5 million

Part of John Hunt Publishing. *Publishes* children's and religious titles only – about 25 a year. Unsolicited material welcome.

C. Hurst & Co.

38 King Street, London WC2E 8JZ
☎0171 240 2666   Fax 0171 240 2667
Email: hurst@atlas.co.uk
Website:www.hurstpub.co.uk
Chairman/Managing Director
  Christopher Hurst
Editorial Heads *Christopher Hurst, Michael Dwyer*

FOUNDED 1967. An independent company, cultivating a concern for literacy, detail and the visual aspects of the product. *Publishes* contemporary history, politics and social science. About 20 titles a year. TITLES *The Origins of Japanese Trade Supremacy; The Rwanda Crisis – History of a Genocide; Listening People, Yugoslavia's Bloody Collapse; Speaking Earth: Contemporary Paganism; Following Ho Chi Minh – Memoirs of a North Vietnamese Colonel.* No unsolicited mss. Synopses and ideas welcome.

Royalties paid twice in first year, annually thereafter.

Hutchinson

See **Random House UK Ltd**

Hymns Ancient & Modern Ltd

St Mary's Works, St Mary's Plain, Norwich,
Norfolk NR3 3BH
☎01603 612914   Fax 01603 624483
Chairman *Very Rev. Dr Henry Chadwick KBE*
Chief Executive *G. A. Knights*
Publisher, Canterbury Press Norwich
  Christine Smith
Publisher, RMEP *Mary Mears*
Approx. Annual Turnover £4 million

Publishes hymn books for churches, schools and other institutions. All types of liturgical and general religious books and material for religious and social education. Owns **SCM-Canterbury Press Ltd** of which **SCM Press Ltd** is a division (see entry).

  IMPRINTS **Canterbury Press Norwich** Liturgical and general religious books TITLES *Exciting Holiness; Gospel of the Lord; Women of the Passion; Rhythm of Life* series; *Re-pitching the Tent.* **Religious and Moral Education Press (RMEP)** Religious, social and moral books for primary and secondary schools, assembly material and books for teachers and administrators. **G. J. Palmer & Sons Ltd** TITLES *Church Times* (see entry under **Magazines**); *The Sign* and *Home Words* – two monthly nationwide parish magazine inserts. Ideas welcome; no unsolicited mss.

Royalties paid annually.

Icon Books Ltd

Grange Road, Duxford, Cambridge CB2 4QF
☎01763 208008   Fax 01763 208080
Managing Director *Peter Pugh*
Editorial Head *Richard Appignanesi*
Publishing Director *Jeremy Cox*

FOUNDED 1992. SERIES **Introducing** Cartoon introductions to the key figures and issues in the history of science, psychology, philosophy, religion and the arts TITLES *Introducing Psychology;*

Introducing Western Philosophy; **Critical Guides** Student guides to critical writings TITLES *James Joyce's Ulysses*; *Virginia Woolf's To the Lighthouse and The Waves*. **Critical Dictionaries** 'The most recent thinking and the issues under debate in key areas of current thought.' TITLES *The New Cosmology; Global Economics*. Launched **Spectator Guides to the Major Sports** in 1998 TITLES *Football; Cricket; Golf; Boxing*. 20 titles in 1998. No unsolicited mss; synopses and ideas for information non-fiction welcome.

Royalties paid twice yearly. *Overseas associates* Totem Books, USA.

Idol
See **Virgin Publishing Ltd**

Independent Voices
See **Souvenir Press Ltd**

The Industrial Society
Robert Hyde House, 48 Bryanston Square, London W1H 7LN
☎0171 479 2000   Fax 0171 723 7375
Email: infoserve@indusoc.demon.co.uk
Head of Publishing *Carl Upsall*
Approx. Annual Turnover (publishing division) £1.6 million

Industrial Society Publications, which is part of The Industrial Society (a registered charity committed to making work fulfilling), has been publishing books for approximately 20 years. *Specialises* in business, management, self-development, training, staff development, human resources – both books and special reports. 10 titles in 1998. TITLES *Communication Skills – A Practical Handbook; Fifty Ways to Personal Development; Body Talk – Skills of Positive Image; Navigating Complexity; Career Guides: Travel and Tourism, Sport, Retailing*. Unsolicited mss, synopses and ideas welcome. No fiction or illustrated non-fiction.

Royalties paid twice-yearly.

Institute of Personnel and Development
IPD House, Camp Road, London SW19 4UX
☎0181 263 3387   Fax 0181 263 3850
Email: publish@ipd.co.uk
Website:www.ipd.co.uk

Part of IPD Enterprises Limited. *Publishes* management and training. A list of 200 titles. Unsolicited mss, synopses and ideas welcome.

Royalties paid annually.

Inter Publishing Ltd
6–7 Leapale Road, Guildford, Surrey GU1 4JX
☎01483 306309   Fax 01483 579196
Email: eagle_indeprint@compuserve.com
Managing Director *David Wavre*
Approx. Annual Turnover £500,000

FOUNDED 1990. *Publishes* religious plus some gift and art books. About 24 titles a year
IMPRINT **Eagle**. Unsolicited mss, synopses and ideas for books welcome.

Royalties paid quarterly.

Inter-Varsity Press
38 De Montfort Street, Leicester LE1 7GP
☎0116 2551754   Fax 0116 2542044
Chairman *Ralph Evershed*
Chief Executive *Frank Entwistle*

FOUNDED mid-'30s as the publishing arm of Universities and Colleges Christian Fellowship, it has expanded to wider Christian markets worldwide. *Publishes* Christian belief and lifestyle, reference and bible commentaries. About 50 titles a year. No secular material or anything which fails to empathise with orthodox Protestant Christianity.

IMPRINTS **IVP**; **Apollos**; **Crossway** TITLES *The Bible Speaks Today; Science, Life and Christian Belief* Berry and Jeeves. No unsolicited mss; synopses and ideas welcome.

Royalties paid twice-yearly.

International Thomson Publishing
See **Thomson Learning**

Intrigue
See **Harlequin Mills & Boon Ltd**

Isis Publishing Limited
7 Centremead, Osney Mead, Oxford OX2 0ES
☎01865 250333   Fax 01865 790358
Managing Director *John Durrant*

Publishes large-print books – fiction and non-fiction; audio books (see entry under **Audio Books**). TITLES *The Colour of Magic* Terry Pratchett; *Return to Sunset House* Lady Fortescue; *Christine* Stephen King. No unsolicited mss as Isis undertakes no original publishing.

Royalties paid twice-yearly.

Ithaca Press
See **Garnet Publishing Ltd**

IVP
See **Inter-Varsity Press**

Jacqui Small
See **Aurum Press Ltd**

Arthur James Ltd
46a West Street, New Alresford, Hampshire SO24 9AU
☎01962 736880   Fax 01962 736881
Email: JohnHuntPublishing@compuserve.com
Managing Director *Mr J. Hunt*
Approx. Annual Turnover £250,000
FOUNDED in 1944 by a Fleet Street journalist, A. J. Russell. *Publishes* day books, devotional classics, psychological, healing, religious, social work and *New Testament* translations. AUTHORS Karen Armstrong, William Barclay, Jacques Duquesne, Laurence Freeman, Monica Furlong, Rosemary Harthill, Sara Maitland, Mary McAleese, Chuck Spezzano, Angela Tilby, Robert Van de Weyer, Marina Warner, John Woolley.
Royalties paid annually. *Overseas associates* Morehouse Publishing, USA; Buchanan, Australia; Omega, New Zealand.

Jane's Information Group
163 Brighton Road, Coulsdon, Surrey CR5 2HY
☎0181 700 3700   Fax 0181 763 1006
Website:www.janes.com
Managing Director *Alfred Rolington*
FOUNDED 1898 by Fred T. Jane with the publication of *All The World's Fighting Ships*. Now part of The Thomson Corporation. In recent years management, has been focusing on growth opportunities in its core business and in enhancing the performance of initiatives like Jane's information available on-line and on CD-ROM. *Publishes* magazines and yearbooks on defence, aerospace and transport topics, with details of equipment and systems; plus directories and strategic studies. Also *Jane's Defence Weekly* (see entry under **Magazines**).
DIVISIONS **Magazines** *Alan Condron* TITLES *Jane's Defence Weekly; Jane's International Defense Review; Jane's Airport Review; Jane's Defence Upgrades; Jane's Navy International.* **Publishing** *Alan Condron* TITLES *Defence, Aerospace Yearbooks; Jane's Intelligence Review; Foreign Report; Jane's Sentinel* (regional security assessment). **Transport** *Harry Puckering* TITLES *Transportation Yearbooks;* CD-ROM and electronic development and publication. Unsolicited mss, synopses and ideas for reference/yearbooks welcome.
Royalties paid twice-yearly. *Overseas associates* Jane's Information Group Inc., USA.

Janus Publishing Company Ltd
Edinburgh House, 19 Nassau Street, London W1N 7RE
☎0171 580 7664   Fax 0171 636 5756
Email: publisher@januspublishing.co.uk
Managing Director *Sandy Leung*
Publishes fiction, human interest, memoirs, philosophy, mind, body and spirit, religion and theology, social questions, popular science, history, spiritualism and the paranormal, poetry and young adults. About 400 titles in print.
IMPRINTS **Janus Books** Subsidy publishing; **Empiricus Books** Non-subsidy publishing. TITLES *The Writing Game* Rosmary Friedman; *The Essential Guide to Learning Martial Arts* Carol Anne Strange; *To Be A Saudi* Hani A. Z. Yamani; *Philby – The Hidden Years* Morris Riley. Unsolicited mss welcome.
Royalties paid twice-yearly. Agents in the USA, Australia, South Africa and Asia.
Authors' Rating Authors may be asked to cover their own productions costs but Janus seems to be moving into legitimate publishing with its Empiricus imprint.

Japan Library
See **Curzon Press Ltd**

Jarrold Publishing
Whitefriars, Norwich, Norfolk NR3 1TR
☎01603 763300   Fax 01603 662748
Chairman *Peter Jarrold*
Managing Director *Antony Jarrold*
Part of Jarrold & Sons Ltd, the printing and publishing company FOUNDED in 1770. *Publishes* cookery, UK tourism and travel, sports and leisure, history, gift books and calendars. Material tends to be of a high pictorial content. About 30 titles a year. Unsolicited mss, synopses and ideas welcome but before submitting anything, approach in writing to Donald Greig, Managing Editor.
Royalties paid twice-yearly.

Jensen Business Books
See **AMCD (Publishers) Ltd**

Jets
See **HarperCollins Publishers Ltd**

Jewish Chronicle Publications
See **Frank Cass & Co Ltd**

John Jones Publishing Ltd
Unit 12, Clwydfro Business Centre, Lon Parcwr, Ruthin LL15 1NJ
☎01824 705272   Fax 01824 705272

Email: johnjonespublishing.ltd@virgin.net
Website:www.johnjonespublishing.ltd.uk
Managing Director *John Idris Jones*
FOUNDED 1989. *Publishes* paperback non-fiction about Wales, its culture, topography and history (including autobiography), the history of the Celts and the Tudor period. Titles are specially commissioned or re-publications of important older books which have gone out of print. TITLES *Wild Wales; I Bought a Mountain; Hovel in the Hills; The Life of Shakespeare.* Approach in writing with s.a.e.

Michael Joseph
See **Penguin UK**

Kahn & Averill
9 Harrington Road, London SW7 3ES
☎0181 743 3278   Fax 0181 743 3278
Managing Director *Mr M. Kahn*
FOUNDED 1967 to publish children's titles but now specialises in music titles. A small independent publishing house. *Publishes* music and general non-fiction. No unsolicited mss; synopses and ideas for books considered.
Royalties paid twice-yearly.

Karnak House
300 Westbourne Park Road, London
W11 1EH
☎0171 243 3620   Fax 0171 243 3620
Managing Director *Amon Saba Saakana*
FOUNDED 1979. *Specialises* in African and Caribbean studies. *Publishes* anthropology, education, Egyptology, history, language and linguistics, literary criticism, music, parapsychology, prehistory. No poetry, humour or sport. About 12 titles a year. No unsolicited mss; send introduction or synopsis with one sample chapter. Synopses and ideas welcome.
Royalties paid twice-yearly. *Overseas subsidiaries* The Antef Institute, and Karnak House, Illinois, USA.

Sebastian Kelly
See **Anness Publishing Ltd**

Kelpie
See **Canongate Books Ltd**

Kenilworth Press Ltd
Addington, Buckingham, Buckinghamshire
MK18 2JR
☎01296 715101   Fax 01296 715148
Email: editorial@kenilworthpress.co.uk
Chairman/Managing Director *David Blunt*

Approx. Annual Turnover £500,000
FOUNDED 1989 with the acquisition of Threshhold Books. The UK's principal instructional equestrian publisher, producing the official books of the British Horse Society, the famous *Threshold Picture Guides*, and a range of authoritative titles sold around the world. About 10 titles a year.
IMPRINT **Kenilworth Press** TITLES *British Horse Society Manuals; Dressage with Kyra; A Modern Horse Herbal; For the Good of the Rider; Threshold Picture Guides 1–41.* Unsolicited mss, synopses and ideas welcome but only for titles concerned with the care or riding of horses or ponies.
Royalties paid twice-yearly.

Kenyon-Deane
See **Cressrelles Publishing Co. Ltd**

Laurence King
71 Great Russell Street, London WC1B 3BN
☎0171 831 6351   Fax 0171 831 8356
Email: enquiries@laurence-king.co.uk
Website:www.laurence-king.co.uk
Chairman *Robin Hyman*
Managing Director *Laurence King*
FOUNDED 1991. Publishing imprint of UK packager **Calmann & King Ltd** (see entry under **UK Packagers**). *Publishes* full-colour illustrated books on art history, the decorative arts, carpets and textiles, graphic design, architecture and interior design. Unsolicited material welcome.
Royalties paid twice-yearly.

Kingfisher Publications plc
New Penderel House, 283–288 High
Holborn, London WC1V 7HZ
☎0171 903 9999   Fax 0171 242 4979
Email: sales@kingfisherpubs.co.uk
Chairman *Bertil Hessel*
Formerly Larousse plc until 1997 when the company name changed to Kingfisher Publications plc. FOUNDED 1994 when owners, Groupe de la Cité (also publishers of the Larousse dictionaries in France), merged their UK operations of Grisewood & Dempsey and **Chambers Harrap Publishers Ltd** (see entry).
DIVISION **Kingfisher** *Ann-Janine Murtagh*, Publishing Director, Fiction, *Gill Denton* Non-fiction. Founded in 1973 by Grisewood & Dempsey Ltd. *Publishes* children's fiction and non-fiction in hardback and paperback: story books, rhymes and picture books, fiction and poetry anthologies, young non-fiction, activity

books, general series and reference. Send synopsis with accompanying letter rather than completed mss.

Royalties paid bi-annually where applicable.

Jessica Kingsley Publishers Ltd

116 Pentonville Road, London N1 9JB
☎0171 833 2307   Fax 0171 837 2917
Email: post@jkp.com
Website:www.jkp.com

Managing Director *Jessica Kingsley*
Senior Editor *Helen Parry*
Editor *Amy Lancaster-Owen*

FOUNDED 1987. Independent publisher of books for professionals and academics on social and behavioural sciences, including special needs arts therapies, child psychology, psychotherapy (including forensic psychotherapy), psychoanalysis and social work. About 85 titles a year. TITLE *Asperger Syndrome – A Guide for Parents and Professionals* Tony Attwood. 'We are actively publishing and commissioning in autism and Asperger Syndrome. We welcome suggestions for books and proposals from prospective authors. Proposals should consist of an outline of the book, a contents list, assessment of the market, and author's c.v. and should be addressed to Jessica Kingsley. Complete manuscript should not be sent.' No fiction or poetry.

Royalties paid twice-yearly.

Kingsway Publications

Lottbridge Drove, Eastbourne, East Sussex BN23 6NT
☎01323 437700   Fax 01323 411970

Chairman *Peter Fenwick*
Managing Director *John Paculabo*
Editorial Contact *Mrs C. Owen*
Approx. Annual Turnover £1.5 million

Part of Kingsway Communications Ltd, a charitable trust with Christian objectives. *Publishes* Christian books: Bibles, Christian testimonies, renewal issues. No poetry, fiction or unsolicited submissions accepted. About 40 titles a year.
IMPRINT **Kingsway** TITLES *The Life Application Bible*; *Will God Heal Me?* Ron Dunn; *The Heart of Revival* Nicky Gumbel.

Royalties paid twice-yearly.

Kluwer Law International

Sterling House, 66 Wilton Road, London SW1V 1DE
☎0171 821 1123   Fax 0171 630 5229

Director of Operations *Marcel Nieuwenhuis*

FOUNDED 1995. Parent company: Wolters Kluwer Group. Kluwer Law International con-

sists of three components: the law list of Graham & Trotman, Kluwer Law and Taxation and Martinus Nyhoff. *Publishes* international law. 200 titles a year. Unsolicited synopses and ideas for books on law at an international level welcome.

Royalties paid annually. North American sales and marketing: Kluwer Law International, 675 Massachusetts Avenue, Cambridge, MA 02139, USA.

Charles Knight Publishing

See **Butterworth Tolley**

Kogan Page Ltd

120 Pentonville Road, London N1 9JN
☎0171 278 0433   Fax 0171 837 3768/6348
Email: kpinfo@kogan-page.co.uk
Websites:www.kogan-page.co.uk
          www.earthscan.co.uk

Managing Director *Philip Kogan*
Approx. Annual Turnover £8 million

FOUNDED 1967 by Philip Kogan to publish *The Industrial Training Yearbook*. In 1992 acquired Earthscan Publications. *Publishes* business and management reference books and monographs, education and careers, marketing, personal finance, personnel, small business, training and industrial relations, transport, plus journals. Further expansion is planned, particularly in the finance and high-tech, EC publications areas, yearbooks and directories, and international business reference. About 280 titles a year.

DIVISIONS **Kogan Page** *Pauline Goodwin, Philip Mudd, Peter Chadwick*. **Earthscan Publications** *Jonathan Sinclair Wilson* Has close associations with the International Institute for Environment and Development and with the Worldwide Fund for Nature. *Publishes* Third World issues and their global implications, and general environmental titles, both popular and academic. About 50 titles a year. Unsolicited mss, synopses and ideas for books welcome.

Royalties paid twice-yearly.

Authors' Rating Long established as the businessman's friend (think how many Kogan Page books are carried on to planes and trains) this sturdily independent publisher is now looking to more expensive, multi-volume tomes. Trade organisations looking for a publishing ally put Kogan Page high on their list.

Ladybird Books

Ground Floor, 39 Stoney Street, Nottingham NG1 1LX
☎0115 9486900   Fax 0115 9486901

Managing Director *Michael Herridge*

Publishing Director *S. Barton*
International Director *D. King*
Approx. Annual Turnover £20 million

FOUNDED in the 1860s. Introduced just before the First World War, the Ladybird name and format was fully established as a result of the development of a children's list during the Second World War. In the early 1960s the commercial print side of the operation was abandoned in favour of publishing Ladybird titles only and in 1971 the company was bought by the Pearson Longman Group. Part of the Penguin Group since January 1995. *Publishes* children's home learning consumer books for the mass market internationally, with an emphasis on books for babies, toddlers, pre-school and under-8s. About 200 titles a year.

IMPRINTS **Ladybird; Picture Ladybird; Ladybird Discovery; Disney.** TITLES *Stories for Bedtime; First Favourite Tales; Read With Ladybird; Topsy and Tim; Toddler Talkabouts; Twinkle, Twinkle; Bouncy Lamb; Learn, Practise, Test; Boredom Busters; Winnie the Pooh;* plus the Ladybird audio cassette/book series (see entry under **Audio Books**). No unsolicited mss; synopses and ideas welcome; no poetry.

Authors' Rating Until last year few outsiders realised that Ladybird was part of the Penguin Group. This was because it was run as an independent unit with its own administration and even its own printer. All this changed when Penguin enforced economies of scale by rationalising editorial and closing the Loughborough print works. What effect this will have on quality and market shares remains to be seen.

The Lampada Press
See **The University of Hull Press**

Landmark Publishing Ltd
Waterloo House, 12 Compton, Ashbourne, Derbyshire DE6 1DA
☎01335 347349   Fax 01335 347303
Email: landmark@clara.net

Chairman *Mr R. Cork*
Editorial Director *Mr H. Muirhead*
Approx. Annual Turnover £250,000

FOUNDED in 1996 following the demise of Moorland Publishing. *Publishes* itinerary-based travel guides and industrial history. 17 titles in 1998. No unsolicited mss; telephone in first instance.
Royalties twice-yearly.

Larousse plc
See **Kingfisher Publications plc**

Lawrence & Wishart Ltd
99A Wallis Road, London E9 5LN
☎0181 533 2506   Fax 0181 533 7369
Email: lw@l-w-bks.demon.co.uk
Website:www.l-w-bks.co.uk

Managing Director *Sally Davison*
Editors *Sally Davison, Bertie Vitry*

FOUNDED 1936. An independent publisher with a substantial backlist. *Publishes* current affairs, cultural politics, economics, history, politics and education. 15–20 titles a year. TITLES *Between War and Peace: The Political Future of Northern Ireland; Forever England: Reflections on Masculinity and Empire; After Maastricht: A Guide to European Monetary Union.* Synopses preferred to complete mss. Ideas welcome.
Royalties paid annually, unless by arrangement.

Authors' Rating A left-wing publisher with much of interest to radical thinkers.

The Learning Institute
Honeycombe House, Bagley, Wedmore, Somerset BS28 4TD
☎01934 713563   Fax 01934 713492
Email: courses@inst.org

Managing Director *Kit Sadgrove*

FOUNDED 1994 to publish home-study courses in vocational subjects such as garden design, writing and computing. *Publishes* subjects that show the reader how to work from home, gain a new skill or enter a new career. Interests include self-improvement, interior design, hobbies, parenting, health, careers, music and investment. TITLES *Become a Freelance Photographer; Master the Art of Painting.* Authors guidelines sent on receipt of s.a.e. No unsolicited mss; send synopses and ideas only.
Royalties paid quarterly.

Lehigh University Press
See **Golden Cockerel Press Ltd**

Leicester University Press
See **Cassell**

Lennard Associates Ltd
Windmill Cottage, Mackerye End, Harpenden, Hertfordshire AL5 5DR
☎01582 715866   Fax 01582 715121
Email: orders@lenqap.demon.co.uk

Chairman/Managing Director
    Adrian Stephenson

FOUNDED 1979. Publisher of sporting yearbooks, personality books, and television associated titles. YEARBOOKS *The Cricketers' Who's Who; Formula*

One; Official PFA Footballers' Factfile; British Boxing Yearbook; European Tour Yearbook. No unsolicited mss. IMPRINTS **Lennard Publishing**; **Queen Anne Press**. Acquired the latter and most of its assets in 1992.

Payment Both fees and royalties by arrangement.

Letterland
See **HarperCollins Publishers Ltd**

Charles Letts
See **New Holland Publishers (UK) Ltd**

Levinson Children's Books
See **David & Charles Children's Books**

Dewi Lewis Publishing
8 Broomfield Road, Heaton Moor, Stockport SK4 4ND
☎0161 442 9450   Fax 0161 442 9450
Email: dewilewispublishing@compuserve.com
Website:www.dewilewispublishing.com

Contact *Dewi Lewis, Caroline Warhurst*
Approx. Annual Turnover £240,000

FOUNDED 1994. *Publishes* fiction, photography and visual arts. 16 titles in 1998. TITLES *Industry of Souls* Martin Booth (shortlisted for the 1998 **Booker Prize**); *Common Sense* Martin Parr; *New York 1954–5* William Klein. Mss in the above categories are welcome, provided return postage is enclosed; no synopses or ideas, please.

Royalties paid twice-yearly.

John Libbey & Co. Ltd
13 Smiths Yard, Summerley Street, London SW18 4HR
☎0181 947 2777   Fax 0181 947 2664
Email: libbey@earlsfield.win-uk.net

Chairman/Managing Director *John Libbey*

FOUNDED 1979. *Publishes* medical books and cinema/animation books and journals. *Specialises* in epilepsy, neurology, nuclear medicine, nutrition, obesity and oncology. Synopses and ideas welcome. *Overseas subsidiaries* John Libbey Eurotext Ltd, France; John Libbey & Co. Pty. Ltd, Australia.

Librapharm Ltd
3b Thames Court, High Street, Goring–on–Thames, Reading, Berkshire RG8 9AQ
☎01491 875252   Fax 01635 875200

Chairman *Dr R. B. Smith*
Managing Director *Dr P. L. Clarke*
Approx. Annual Turnover £500,000

FOUNDED 1995 as a partial buyout from Kluwer Academic Publishers (UK) academic list. *Publishes* medical and scientific books and periodicals. 25 titles a year. IMPRINT **Petroc Press**. TITLES *Fry's Common Diseases; Neighbour: The Inner Consultation; Current Medical Research and Opinion* (journal). Unsolicited mss, synopses and ideas for medical books welcome.

Royalties paid twice-yearly.

Library Association Publishing
7 Ridgmount Street, London WC1E 7AE
☎0171 636 7543   Fax 0171 636 3627
Email: lapublishing@la-hq.org.uk
Website:www.la-hq.org.uk/lapublishing

Chairman *Michael Curtis*
Managing Director *Janet Liebster*

Publishing arm of **The Library Association**. *Publishes* library and information science, monographs, reference, IT books and bibliography. About 35 titles a year.

IMPRINTS **Library Association Publishing**; **Clive Bingley Books** Over 200 titles in print, including *Walford's Guide to Reference Material* and *AACR2*. Unsolicited mss, synopses and ideas welcome provided material falls firmly within the company's specialist subject areas.

Royalties paid annually.

Frances Lincoln Ltd
4 Torriano Mews, Torriano Avenue, London, NW5 2RZ
☎0171 284 4009   Fax 0171 267 5249
Email: francesl@frances-lincoln.com

Managing Director *Frances Lincoln*

FOUNDED 1977. *Publishes* highly illustrated non-fiction: gardening, interiors, health, crafts, cookery; children's picture and information books, art and religion; and stationery. About 45 titles a year.

DIVISIONS **Adult Non-fiction** Kate Cave TITLES *Chatsworth* Duchess of Devonshire; *World Food Café* Chris and Carolyn Caldecott; *Gardener Cook* Chris Lloyd; **Children's General Fiction and Non-fiction** Janetta Otter-Barry TITLES *The Wanderings of Odysseus* Rosemary Sutcliffe, illus. Alan Lee; *Amazing Grace, Grace & Family* Mary Hoffman, illus. Caroline Binch; **Mind, Body and Spirit** Cathy Fischgrund TITLES *Zero Balancing* John Hanwee; *God's Stories* Lila Berg. Synopses and ideas for books considered.

Royalties paid twice-yearly.

Authors' Rating Courtesy of *The Bookseller* we now know that Frances Lincoln did not, as legend has it, start with an investment of £10.

The real figure was £100. To gardening and interior design has been added a trail-blazing children's list. Expansion is promised.

Linden Press
See **Open Gate Press**

Linford Romance/
Linford Mystery/Linford Western
See **F. A. Thorpe (Publishing) Ltd**

Lion Publishing
Peter's Way, Sandy Lane West, Oxford
OX4 5HG
☎01865 747550   Fax 01865 747568
Email: custserv@lion-publishing.co.uk
Website:www.lion-publishing.co.uk
Managing Director *Paul Clifford*
Approx. Annual Turnover £6.77 million

FOUNDED 1971. A Christian book publisher, strong on illustrated books for a popular international readership, with rights sold in over 100 languages worldwide. *Publishes* a diverse list with Christian viewpoint the common denominator. All ages, from board books for children to multi-contributor adult reference, educational, paperbacks and colour co-editions and gift books.
DIVISIONS **Adult** *Lois Rock*; **Children's** *Su Box*; **Giftlines** *Sarah Medina*. Unsolicited mss welcome provided they have a positive Christian viewpoint intended for a wide general and international readership. Synopses, proposals and ideas also welcome.
Royalties paid twice-yearly.

Authors' Rating Lion is now out of fiction and electronic publishing, a decision which is already proving beneficial to what is essentially a core publisher.

Lir
See **Hodder Headline plc**

Little, Brown & Co. (UK)
Brettenham House, Lancaster Place, London
WC2E 7EN
☎0171 911 8000   Fax 0171 911 8100
Chief Executive/Publisher *Philippa Harrison*
Approx. Annual Turnover £36.8 million

FOUNDED 1988. Part of Time-Warner Inc. Began by importing its US parent company's titles and in 1990 launched its own illustrated non-fiction list. Two years later the company took over former Macdonald & Co. *Publishes* hardback and paperback fiction, literary fiction, crime, science fiction and fantasy; and general non-fiction, including illustrated: architecture and design, fine art, photography, biography and autobiography, cinema, gardening, history, humour, travel, crafts and hobbies, reference, cookery, wines and spirits, DIY, guidebooks, natural history and nautical.
IMPRINTS **Abacus** *Richard Beswick* Literary fiction and non-fiction paperbacks; **Orbit** *Tim Holman* Science fiction and fantasy; **Little Brown/Warner** *Alan Samson, Barbara Boote, Hilary Hale* Mass-market fiction and non-fiction; **X Libris** *Sarah Shrubb* Women's erotica; **Illustrated** *Julia Charles* Hardbacks; **Virago** (see entry). Approach in writing in the first instance. No unsolicited mss.
Royalties paid twice-yearly.

Authors' Rating The continuing proof that sound profits and quality publishing can go together, Little, Brown features regularly in the bestseller list with niche titles. The erotic fiction list is adding another imprint.

Liverpool University Press
Senate House, Abercromby Square, Liverpool
L69 3BX
☎0151 794 2233   Fax 0151 794 2235
Managing Director/Editorial Head
  Robin Bloxsidge

LUP's primary activity is the publication of academic and scholarly books and journals but it also has a limited number of trade titles. Although its principal focus is on the arts and social sciences, in which it is active in a wide variety of disciplines, the LUP list includes some STM books. 30–40 titles a year. TITLES *Public Sculpture of Birmingham; The Ince Blundell Collection of Classica Sculpture; Frank Kupka: In White and Black; Jupiter's Children; A Retake Please! From 'Night Mail' to 'Western Approaches'; The Irish Border; If the Irish Ran the World; Montserrat, 1630–1730; Byron's 'Corbeau Blanc': The Life and Letters of Lady Melbourne 1751–1818.*
Royalties paid annually.

Livewire Books for Teenagers
See **The Women's Press**

London House
See **Allison & Busby**

Lonely Planet Publications
10A Spring Place, London NW5 3BH
☎0171 428 4800   Fax 0171 428 4828
Email: go@lonelyplanet.co.uk
Website:www.lonelyplanet.com
Owner *Lonely Planet (Australia)*
General Manager *Charlotte Hindle*

Editorial Head *Katharine Leck*
Approx. Annual Turnover £20 million

FOUNDED in 1973 by Tony and Maureen Wheeler to document a journey from London across Asia to Australia. Since then, Lonely Planet has grown into a global operation with headquarters in Melbourne and offices in Paris, California and London. *Publishes* travel writing and guides, phrasebooks, diving and snorkelling guides, gift travel books, restaurant guides, walking guides. 40 titles in 1998. TITLES *Shopping for Buddhas* Jeff Greenwald; *Lost Japan* Alex Kerr; *Full Circle: A South American Journey* Louis Sepúlveda; *Islands in the Clouds: Travels in the Highlands of New Guinea* Isabella Tree. No unsolicited mss; synopses and ideas welcome.
Royalties negotiable.

Lorenz Books
See **Anness Publishing Ltd**

Peter Lowe (Eurobook Ltd)
PO Box 52, Wallingford, Oxfordshire
OX10 0XU
☎01865 858333   Fax 01865 858263
Email: eurobook@compuserve.com

Managing Director *Peter Lowe*

FOUNDED 1968. *Publishes* children's natural history, popular science and illustrated adult non-fiction. No unsolicited mss; synopses and ideas (with s.a.e.) welcome. No adult fiction.

Lund Humphries Publishers Ltd
Park House, 1 Russell Gardens, London
NW11 9NN
☎0181 458 6314   Fax 0181 905 5245
Email: lhpubs@aol.com

Chairman *Lionel Leventhal*
Editorial Director *Lucy Myers*

Publisher of fine art books. First title appeared in 1895. *Publishes* art, architecture, photography, design and graphics. Also publishes exhibition catalogues in association with museums and galleries and the annual *Calendar of Art Exhibitions*. About 20 titles a year. Unsolicited mss welcome but initial introductory letter preferred. Synopses and ideas for books considered.
Royalties paid twice-yearly.

The Lutterworth Press
PO Box 60, Cambridge CB1 2NT
☎01223 350865   Fax 01223 366951
Email: publishing@lutterworth.com
Website:www.lutterworth.com

Managing Director *Adrian Brink*

The Lutterworth Press dates back to the 18th

century when it was founded by the Religious Tract Society. In the 19th century it was best known for its children's books and magazines, both religious and secular, including *The Boys' Own Paper*. Since 1984 it has been an imprint of **James Clarke & Co** (see entry). *Publishes* religious books for children and adults, children's fiction and non-fiction, adult non-fiction. TITLES *Lutterworth Dictionary of the Bible; Carol Corsa & Mickey Morgan; Never the Same Again: A History of VSO; Time to Say Goodbye.* Approach in writing with ideas in the first instance.
Royalties paid annually.

Authors' Rating Strong on evangelical books with a thriving children's list.

Lynx
See **Society for Promoting Christian Knowledge**

Macdonald & Co.
See **Little, Brown & Co. (UK)**

Macdonald Young Books
See **Wayland Publishers Ltd**

McGraw-Hill Publishing Company
McGraw-Hill House, Shoppenhangers Road, Maidenhead, Berkshire SL6 2QL
☎01628 502500   Fax 01628 770224
Email: alfred_waller@mcgraw-hill.com
Website:www.mcgraw-hill.co.uk

Group Vice President, Europe *Italo Raimondi*
Publishing Director, Europe *Alfred Waller*

FOUNDED 1899. Owned by US parent company. Began publishing in Maidenhead in 1965, having had an office in the UK since 1899. *Publishes* business and economics, accountancy, finance, computer science and business computing for the academic, student and professional markets. Around 50 titles a year. Unsolicited mss, synopses and ideas welcome.
Royalties paid twice-yearly.

Macmillan Publishers Ltd
25 Eccleston Place, London SW1W 9NF
☎0171 881 8000   Fax 0171 881 8001
Website:www.macmillan.co.uk

Chairman *Nicholas Byam Shaw*
Chief Executive *Richard Charkin*
Approx. Annual Turnover £90 million
    (Book Publishing Group)

FOUNDED 1843. Macmillan is one of the largest publishing houses in Britain, publishing approximately 1400 titles a year. In 1995, Verlagsgruppe Georg von Holtzbrink, a major German publisher, acquired a majority stake in the Macmillan Group. In 1996, Macmillan bought Boxtree, the successful media tie-in publisher and, in 1997, purchased the Heinemann English language teaching list from Reed Elsevier. Unsolicited proposals, synopses and mss are welcome in all divisions of the company (with the exception of Macmillan Children's Books). Authors who wish to send material to Macmillan General Books should note that there is a central submissions procedure in operation. Send a synopsis and the first 3–4 chapters with a covering letter and return postage to the Submissions Editor, 25 Eccleston Place, London SW1W 9NF.

Divisions

Macmillan Press Ltd Brunel Road, Houndmills, Basingstoke, Hampshire RG21 6XS ☎01256 329242 Fax 01256 3479476 Managing Director *Dominic Knight*. **Academic** *T. M. Farmiloe*; **College** *S. Kennedy*; **Business and Economics** *S. Rutt*. *Publishes* textbooks and monographs in academic, professional and vocational subjects; medical and scientific journals. Publications in both hard copy and electronic format.

Macmillan Heinemann English Language Teaching Macmillan Oxford, 4 Between Towns Road, Oxford OX4 3PP ☎01865 405700 Fax 01865 405701 Email: elt@mhelt.com Website:www.mhelt.com Managing Directors *Mike Esplen, Chris Harrison*; Publishing Directors *Sue Bale, Alison Hubert*. *Publishes* a wide range of ELT titles and educational books for the international education market.

Macmillan General Books (Eccleston Place address). Managing Director *Ian S. Chapman*. Publishes under **Macmillan, Pan, Picador, Papermac, Sidgwick & Jackson**

Macmillan (FOUNDED 1865) Publisher *Jeremy Trevathan*, Editorial Directors (fiction) *Suzanne Baboneau, Beverley Cousins, Arabella Stein*. *Publishes* novels, detective fiction, sci-fi, fantasy and horror. Editorial Directors (non-fiction) *Georgina Morley, Tanya Stobbs*. *Publishes* autobiography, biography, business and industry, economics, gift books, health and beauty, history, humour, natural history, travel, philosophy, politics and world affairs, psychology, film and theatre, gardening and cookery, encyclopedias, popular science. Editorial Director (reference) *Morven Knowles*. *Publishes* trade reference titles.

Pan (FOUNDED 1947) Publisher *Clare Harington*. *Publishes* fiction: novels, detective fiction, sci-fi, fantasy and horror. Non-fiction: general non-fiction, sports and games, film and theatre, travel, gardening and cookery.

Papermac (FOUNDED 1965) Editorial

Director *Tanya Stobbs*. Serious non-fiction: history, biography, science, political economy, cultural criticism and art history.

Picador (FOUNDED 1972) Publisher *Peter Straus*, Senior Editorial Director *Ursula Doyle*, Deputy Publishing Director *Maria Rejt*. *Publishes* literary international fiction and non-fiction.

Sidgwick & Jackson (FOUNDED 1908) Editorial Director *Gordon Wise*. *Publishes* popular non-fiction with strong personality or marketable identity, from celebrity and showbusiness to ancient mystery, music and true-life adventure to illustrated lifestyle and branded books. Also military history list.

Macmillan Children's Books (Eccleston Place address) Publisher *Kate Wilson*; **Black & White** *Marion Lloyd*; **Full Colour** *Alison Green*. IMPRINTS **Macmillan, Pan, Campbell Books**. *Publishes* novels, board books, picture books, non-fiction (illustrated and non-illustrated), poetry and novelty books in paperback and hardback. No unsolicited material.

Macmillan Reference Ltd (Eccleston Place address) Managing Director *Ian Jacobs*, **Science** *Gina Fullerlove*, **Social Sciences and Humanities** *Sara Lloyd*. *Publishes* works of reference in academic, professional and vocational subjects, dictionaries. TITLES *The New Grove Dictionary of Music and Musicians* ed. Stanley Sadie; and *The Dictionary of Art* ed. Jane Turner.

Boxtree (Eccleston Place address) Managing Director *Adrian Sington*, Editorial Director *Clare Hulton*. *Publishes* books linked to and about television and film; also humour, sport and music. About 150 titles a year. TITLES *Dilbert; Father Ted; Titanic; Elizabeth; Cricket World Cup; Robert Carrier*. **Channel 4 Books** Managing Director *Adrian Sington*, Editorial Director *Ms Charlie Carman*. *Publishes* TV tie-in titles – books that stand on their own merits and not just the 'book of the series'. About 50 titles a year. TITLES *The Codebreakers of Bletchley Park; Heligan: The Complete Works; Frasier; South Park*.

Royalties paid annually or twice-yearly depending on contract.

Authors' Rating In the age of the author friendly publisher Macmillan has come up with AuthorNET, a password protected Website which lists names, telephone numbers and email addresses of everyone in the company a Macmillan author might want to contact. Royalty statements, contracts and marketing plans have been or soon will be added to the stream of communication. There is still the matter of negotiating a minimum terms agreement with the Society of Authors. But nobody is perfect. Disappointment of the year was the failure to buy Cassell which went to Orion. The compensation was the Boxtree five-year rolling deal to publish Channel 4 books.

Julia MacRae
See **Random House UK Ltd**

Mad Jack
See **Funfax Limited**

Madcap
See **André Deutsch Ltd**

Magi Publications
22 Manchester Street, London W1M 5PG
☎0171 486 0925   Fax 0171 486 0926
Publisher *Monty Bhatia*
Editor *Linda Jennings*
Approx. Annual Turnover £2.5 million
Publishes children's picture and novelty books for ages 0–9. No texts over 1200 words. About 24 titles a year. Unsolicited mss, synopses and new ideas welcome, but please telephone first.
Royalties paid annually.

Magic Jewellery
See **Funfax Limited**

Magpie
See **Robinson Publishing Ltd**

Mainstream Publishing Co. (Edinburgh) Ltd
7 Albany Street, Edinburgh EH1 3UG
☎0131 557 2959   Fax 0131 556 8720
Directors *Bill Campbell, Peter MacKenzie*
Approx. Annual Turnover £2.75 million
Publishes art, autobiography/biography, current affairs, health, sport, history, illustrated and fine editions, photography, politics and world affairs, popular paperbacks. Over 80 titles a year. Ideas for books considered, but should be preceded by a letter, synopsis and s.a.e. or return postage.
Royalties paid twice-yearly.
Authors' Rating A Scottish company aiming for a British profile. Keen on finding authors who 'can develop with us'.

Mammoth
See **Egmont Children's Books**

Management Books 2000 Ltd
Cowcombe House, Cowcombe Hill, Chalford, Gloucestershire GL6 8HP
☎01285 760722   Fax 01285 760708
Email: m.b.2000@virgin.net

Website:www.mb2000.com
Managing Director *Nicholas Dale-Harris*
Marketing *Nicholas Murphy*
Approx. Annual Turnover £500,000
FOUNDED 1993 to develop a range of books for executives and managers working in the modern world of business, supplemented with information through other media like seminars, audio and video. *Publishes* business and management and sponsored titles. About 30 titles a year. Unsolicited mss, synopses and ideas for books welcome.

Manchester United Books
See **André Deutsch Ltd**

Manchester University Press
Oxford Road, Manchester M13 9NR
☎0161 273 5539   Fax 0161 274 3346
Email: mup@man.ac.uk
Website:www.man.ac.uk/mup
Publisher/Chief Executive *David Rodgers*
Approx. Annual Turnover £2 million
MUP is Britain's third largest university press, with a list marketed and sold worldwide. Remit consists of occasional trade publications but mainly A-level and undergraduate textbooks and research monographs. *Publishes* in the areas of literature, drama, film, cultural and media studies, history, history of art, design, architecture, politics, international law, economics, modern languages, religion and philosophy. About 120 titles a year, plus journals. Launched a paperback imprint, **Mandolin**, in 1997 for books with mass-market appeal.
    DIVISIONS **Humanities** *Matthew Frost*; **Art History/History/Religion** *Vanessa Graham*; **Politics and Economics** *Nicola Viinikka*. Unsolicited mss welcome.
Royalties paid annually.

Mandolin
See **Manchester University Press**

George Mann Books
PO Box 22, Maidstone, Kent ME14 1AH
☎01622 759591   Fax 01622 209193
Chairman & Managing Director
    George Mann
FOUNDED 1972, originally as library reprint publishers, but has moved on to other things with the collapse of the library market. *Publishes* original non-fiction and selected reprints. Until further notice, not considering new fiction for publication. **Recollections**, an imprint launched in 1992, is for subsidised publication of books of an

autobiographical/biographical nature, for which 'unlimited editorial advice and assistance can be made available'. IMPRINTS **George Mann**; **Arnefold**; **Recollections**. No unsolicited mss; send preliminary letter with synopsis. Material not accompanied by return postage will be neither read nor returned.

Royalties paid twice-yearly.

Mansell
See **Cassell**

Manson Publishing Ltd
73 Corringham Road, London NW11 7DL
☎0181 905 5150   Fax 0181 201 9233
Email: manson@man-pub.demon.co.uk
Chairman/Managing Director
   Michael Manson
Approx. Annual Turnover £600,000

FOUNDED 1992. *Publishes* scientific, technical, medical and veterinary. 20 titles in 1998. No unsolicited mss; synopses and ideas considered.
Royalties paid twice-yearly.

Marc
See **Monarch Publications**

Marshall Pickering
See **HarperCollins Publishers Ltd**

Marston House
Marston House, Marston Magna, Yeovil, Somerset BA22 8DH
☎01935 851331   Fax 01935 851331
Managing Director/Editorial Head
   Anthony Birks-Hay
FOUNDED 1989. Publishing imprint of book packager Alphabet & Image Ltd. *Publishes* fine art, architecture, ceramics. 4 titles a year.
Royalties paid twice-yearly, or flat fee in lieu of royalties.

Kenneth Mason Publications Ltd
Dudley House, 12 North Street, Emsworth, Hampshire PO10 7DQ
☎01243 377977   Fax 01243 379136
Chairman *Kenneth Mason*
Managing Director *Piers Mason*
Approx. Annual Turnover £500,000

FOUNDED 1958. *Publishes* diet, health, fitness, nutrition and nautical. No fiction. About 15 titles a year. Initial approach by letter with synopsis only.
IMPRINT **Boatswain Press**.
Royalties paid twice-yearly (Jun/Dec) in first year, annually (Dec) thereafter.

Kevin Mayhew Publishers
Buxhall, Stowmarket, Suffolk IP14 1HR
☎01449 737978   Fax 01449 737834
Email: kevinmayhewltd@msn.com
Chairman *Kevin Mayhew*
Managing Director *Gordon Carter*
Commissioning Editors *Jonathan Bugden,*
   Helen Elliott
Approx. Annual Turnover £4 million

FOUNDED in 1976. One of the leading sacred music and Christian book publishers in the UK. *Publishes* religious titles – liturgy, sacramental, devotional, also children's books and school resources. 300 titles in 1998. TITLES *Hymns Old & New (Anglican Edition); More Things to do in Children's Worship*. Unsolicited synopses and mss welcome; telephone prior to sending material, please. IMPRINT **Palm Tree Press** *Kevin Mayhew* Bible stories, colouring/activity and puzzle books for children.
Royalties paid annually.

Melrose Press Ltd
St Thomas Place, Ely, Cambridgeshire CB7 4GG
☎01353 646600   Fax 01353 646601
Chairman *Richard A. Kay*
Managing Director *Nicholas S. Law*
Approx. Annual Turnover £2 million

FOUNDED 1960. Took on its present name in 1969. *Publishes* biographical who's who reference only (but not *Who's Who*, which is published by **A. & C. Black**). DIVISION **International Biographical Centre** *Jon Gifford*. TITLES *International Authors and Writers Who's Who; International Who's Who in Music; Who's Who in Australasia and the Pacific Nations*.

Mentor
See **Christian Focus Publications**

Mercat Press
53 South Bridge, Edinburgh EH1 1YS
☎0131 556 6743   Fax 0131 557 8149
Email: enquiries@jthin.co.uk
Chairman/Managing Director
   D. Ainslie Thin
Editorial Heads *Tom Johnstone, Seán Costello*
FOUNDED 1971 as an adjunct to the large Scottish-based bookselling chain of James Thin. Began by publishing reprints of classic Scottish literature but has since expanded into publishing new non-fiction titles. In 1992 the company acquired the bulk of the stock of Aberdeen University Press and the backlist expanded greatly as a result, now standing at around 300

titles. New titles are added regularly. *Publishes* Scottish classics reprints and non-fiction of Scottish interest, mainly historical and literary. TITLES *The Scots Herbal* Tess Darwin; *A History Book for Scots, Selections from Scotichronicon* Walter Bower; *The Scots Kitchen* F. Marian McNeill; *The Handbook to Edinburgh.* Unsolicited synopses of non-fiction Scottish interest books, preferably with sample chapters, are welcome. No new fiction or poetry.
Royalties paid annually.

Merehurst
Ferry House, 51–57 Lacy Road, London SW15 1PR
☎0181 355 1480   Fax 0181 355 1499
CEO/Publisher *Anne Wilson*
Chief Operating Officer *Sharon Miller*
Approx. Annual Turnover £3 million
Owned by Australian media group Murdoch Magazines Pty Ltd. *Publishes* full-colour non-fiction: homes and interiors, gardening, cookery, craft, cake decorating and DIY. About 46 titles a year. Synopses and ideas for books welcome; no unsolicited mss.
Royalties paid twice-yearly.

The Merlin Press Ltd
2 Rendlesham Mews, Rendlesham, Nr Woodbridge, Suffolk IP12 2SZ
☎01394 461313   Fax 01394 461314
Director *Patricia M. Eve*
FOUNDED 1956. *Publishes* economics, history, philosophy, left-wing politics. TITLES *Enemy Within: The Rise and Fall of the British Communist Party* Francis Beckett; *The Romantics: England in a Revolutionary Age* E. P. Thompson. About 20 titles a year. No fiction.
IMPRINT **Seafarer Books** Sailing titles, with an emphasis on the traditional. No unsolicited mss; preliminary letter essential before making any type of submission.
Royalties paid twice-yearly.

Methuen Children's Books
See **Egmont Children's Books**

Methuen Publishing Ltd
215 Vauxhall Bridge Road, London SW1V 1EL
☎0171 828 2838   Fax 0171 233 9827
Email: mearley@methuen.co.uk
Managing Director *Peter Tummons*
Publishing Director *Max Eilenberg*
FOUNDED 1889. Methuen was owned by Reed International until it was bought by Random House in 1997. Purchased by a management buy-out team in 1998 and is now independent. *Publishes* fiction and non-fiction; drama, film, performing arts, humour. 60 titles in 1998.
DIVISIONS **Trade** *Max Eilenberg*; **Drama** *Michael Earley* TITLES *Dancing Away* Deborah Bull; *Monty Python* titles; *Threads of Time* Peter Brook; *Copenhagen* Michael Frayn. No unsolicited mss; synopses and ideas welcome. Prefers to be approached via agents or a letter of inquiry. No first novels, cookery books, personal memoirs, children's titles.
Royalties paid twice-yearly.

Metro Books
Metro Publishing Ltd, 19 Gerrard Street, London W1V 7LA
☎0171 734 1411   Fax 0171 734 1811
Email: metro@metro-books.demon.co.uk
Chairman *Ian Savage*
Managing Director *Susanne McDadd*
Editorial Manager *Mary Remnant*
FOUNDED 1995. *Publishes* general non-fiction – biography, current affairs, popular psychology, health and cookery. 25 titles in 1999. TITLES *Staying Sane* Raj Persaud; *Real Fast Vegetarian Food* Ursula Ferrigno; *Can Reindeer Fly?* Roger Highfield; *Death of a Hero* John Parker.
IMPRINT of Metro Publishing Ltd: **RCB (Richard Cohen Books)** Biographies of Germaine Greer, Siegfried Sasson and C. B. Fry. No unsolicited mss. Send outline, sample chapter, c.v., sales and marketing ideas plus s.a.e. in the first instance.
Royalties paid twice-yearly.

Authors' Rating Author friendly publisher credited with good communications and readiness to involve writers in production decisions.

Michelin Tyre plc
The Edward Hyde Building, 38 Clarendon Road, Watford, Hertfordshire WD1 1SX
☎01923 415000   Fax 01923 415052
Website:www.michelin-travel.com
FOUNDED 1900 as a travel publisher. *Publishes* travel guides, maps and atlases, children's I-Spy books. Travel-related synopses and ideas welcome; no mss.

Midland Publishing Ltd
24 The Hollow, Earl Shilton, Leicester LE9 7NA
☎01455 847256   Fax 01455 841805
Director *N. P. Lewis*
Publishes aviation, military and railways. No

wartime memoirs. No unsolicited mss; synopses and ideas welcome.

Royalties paid quarterly.

Harvey Miller Publishers

K101 Tower Bridge Business Complex, Clements Road, London SE16 4DG
☎0171 252 1531   Fax 0171 252 3510
Editorial Director *Mrs Elly Miller*

FOUNDED 1974. *Publishes* serious studies in the history of art only. Approx. 6 titles a year. No unsolicited mss; synopses and ideas welcome.
Royalties paid annually.

Miller's

See **Octopus Publishing Group**

Mills & Boon

See **Harlequin Mills & Boon Ltd**

Minerva Press Ltd

6th Floor, Canberra House, 315–317 Regent Street, London W1R 7YB
☎0171 580 4114   Fax 0171 580 9256
Email: mail@minerva-press.co.uk
Website:www.minerva-press.co.uk
Managing Directors *A. Anton, K. Davenport*

FOUNDED in 1992, but the imprint dates back to 1792. *Publishes* fiction and non-fiction; biography, poetry, children's and historical. Specialises in new authors. 250 titles in 1998 Unsolicited mss, synopses and ideas for books welcome.
Royalties paid twice-yearly.

Authors' Rating Liable to ask authors to contribute towards costs of publication.

MIRA

See **Harlequin Mills & Boon Ltd**

The MIT Press Ltd

Fitzroy House, 11 Chenies Street, London WC1E 7ET
☎0171 306 0603   Fax 0171 306 0604
Email: info@MUP-MITpress.co.uk
Director *F. Urbanowski*
General Manager *A. Sexsmith*

Part of **The MIT Press**, USA. *Publishes* academic, architecture and design, art history and theory, bibliography, biography, business and industry, cinema and media studies, computer science, cultural studies and critical theory, economics, educational and textbooks, engineering, environment, linguistics, medical, music, natural history, philosophy, photography, physics, politics and world affairs, psychology,

reference, scientific and technical, neurobiology and neuroscience. All mss go to the American office: 5 Cambridge Centre, Cambridge, MA 02142. (See entry under **US Publishers**.)

Mitchell Beazley

See **Octopus Publishing Group**

Mitre

See **Monarch Publications**

Monarch Publications

Broadway House, The Broadway, Crowborough, East Sussex TN6 1HQ
☎01892 652364   Fax 01892 663329
Email: monarch@dial.pipex.com
Directors *Tony & Jane Collins*

Now in association with **Angus Hudson Ltd** (see entry under **UK Packagers**). *Publishes* an independent list of Christian books across a wide range of concerns. About 30 titles a year. In 1994 took on *Renewal* and *Wholeness* magazines and in 1998 launched *Celebrate*, an independent monthly magazine for the Church of England.

IMPRINTS **Monarch** Upmarket, social concern issues list covering a wide range of areas from psychology to future studies, politics, etc., all with a strong Christian dimension; **Marc** Leadership, mission and church growth titles; **Mitre** Creative writing imprint: humour and drama with a Christian dimension. Unsolicited mss, synopses and ideas welcome. 'Regretfully, no poetry or fiction.'

Monitor Press Ltd

Suffolk House, Churchfield Road, Sudbury, Suffolk CO10 6YA
☎01787 378607   Fax 01787 880201
Website:www.monitorpress.co.uk
Managing Director *Mary Ann Bonomo*

Owned by International Business Communications (Holdings) plc. *Publishes* a range of legal, tax, financial, management and business to business newsletters, special reports and books aimed at senior management and professional practices. 34 newsletter titles a year. Unsolicited synopses and ideas welcome. Initial approach in writing.

Mosby International

See **Harcourt Brace and Company Limited**

Motor Racing Publications

Unit 6, The Pilton Estate, 46 Pitlake, Croydon, Surrey CR0 3RY
☎0181 681 3363   Fax 0181 760 5117
Chairman/Editorial Head *John Blunsden*

Approx. Annual Turnover £500,000

FOUNDED soon after the end of World War II to concentrate on motor-racing titles. Fairly dormant in the mid '60s but was reactivated in 1968 by a new shareholding structure. John Blunsden later acquired a majority share and major expansion followed in the '70s. About 10–12 titles a year. *Publishes* motor-sporting history, classic car collection and restoration, road transport, motorcycles, off-road driving and related subjects.

IMPRINTS **Fitzjames Press**; **Motor Racing Publications** TITLES *Grand Prix Cars 1945–65* M. Lawrence; *Jeep CJ to Grand Cherokee* J. Taylor; *MG From A–Z* J. Wood; *Land Rover Discovery* J. Taylor. Unsolicited mss, synopses and ideas in specified subject areas welcome.

Royalties paid twice-yearly.

Mowbray
See **Cassell**

Multi-Sensory Learning Ltd
Earlstrees Court, Earlstrees Road, Corby, Northants NN17 4HH
☎01536 399003   Fax 01536 399012
Email: FirstBest9@aol.com
Senior Editor *Philippa Attwood*

Publishes materials and books related to dyslexia; the multi-sensory learning course for dyslexic pupils needing literacy skills development, plus numerous other items on assessment, reading, maths, music, etc. for dyslexics. Keen to locate authors able to write materials for dyslexic people and for teachers of dyslexics.

John Murray (Publishers) Ltd
50 Albemarle Street, London W1X 4BD
☎0171 493 4361   Fax 0171 499 1792
Chairman *John R. Murray*
Managing Director *Nicholas Perren*

FOUNDED 1768. Independent publisher. *Publishes* general trade books, educational (secondary school and college textbooks) and Success Studybooks.

DIVISIONS **General Books** *Grant McIntyre*; **Educational Books** *Nicholas Perren*. Unsolicited material discouraged.

Royalties paid twice yearly.

Authors' Rating Disappointments in the education market have been more than offset by well-deserved successes with quality general books.

NAG Press Ltd
See **Robert Hale Ltd**

NCVO Publications
Regent's Wharf, 8 All Saints Street, London N1 9RL
☎0171 713 6161   Fax 0171 713 6300
Website:www.ncvo-voc.org.uk
Publications Manager *David Cameron*
Approx. Annual Turnover £140,000

FOUNDED 1928. Publishing imprint of the National Council for Voluntary Organisations, embracing former Bedford Square Press titles and NCVO's many other publications. The list reflects NCVO's role as the representative body for the voluntary sector. *Publishes* directories, management and trustee development, legal, finance and fundraising titles of primary interest to the voluntary sector. TITLES *The Voluntary Agencies Directory; Grants from Europe; The Good Trustee Guide; The Good Campaigns Guide.* No unsolicited mss as all projects are commissioned in-house.

Royalties paid twice-yearly.

Thomas Nelson & Sons Ltd
Nelson House, Mayfield Road, Walton on Thames, Surrey KT12 5PL
☎01932 252211   Fax 01932 246109
Website:www.nelson.co.uk
CEO/Managing Director *Peter McKay*
Approx. Annual Turnover £21.8 million

FOUNDED 1798. Part of the Thomson Corporation. Major educational publisher of printed and electronic product, from pre-school to Higher Education, with emphasis on requirements of National Curriculum, GCSE, A Level, GNVQ and NVQ. Publisher of *The Arden Shakespeare* imprint, and of a range of material for the Caribbean market. TITLES *GAIA: Geography, An Integrated Approach; The Wider World; Nelson English; Nelson Maths; Wellington Square; Route Nationale; Encore Tricolore; Zickzack Neu; World of Sport Examined; New Balanced Science; Bath Science; Foundations of Psychology*

Royalties paid twice-yearly.

Authors' Rating Like all school publishers, Nelson has had problems coping with the vagaries of the market but is banking on new titles to cater for imminent curriculum changes to boost its fortunes.

The New Adventures
See **Virgin Publishing Ltd**

New English Library
See **Hodder Headline plc**

New Holland Publishers (UK) Ltd
24 Nutford Place, London W1H 6DQ
☎0171 724 7773   Fax 0171 724 6184
Email: postmaster@nhpub.co.uk
Chairman *Gerry Struik*
Managing Director *John Beaufoy*
Editorial Heads *Charlotte Parry-Crooke,
Yvonne McFarlane*
Approx. Annual Turnover £5 million
FOUNDED 1956. Relaunched 1987 with new
name and editorial identity. New directions and
rapid expansion transformed the small specialist
imprint into a publisher of illustrated books for
the international market. In 1993, they diversified further with the acquisition of the Charles
Letts Publishing Division list. In 1997, their parent company (New Holland Struik Group, S.
Africa) acquired Southern Book Publishers, and
their sister company (New Holland Australia)
acquired the natural history and lifestyle divisions
of Reed Australia. *Publishes* non-fiction, specialising in natural history, travel, cookery, cake
decorating, crafts, gardening, DIY and outdoor
sports. TITLES *Dive Sites Series; Top Dive Sites of
the World; Climber's Handbook; Globetrotter Travel
Guides and Maps; Bill Oddie's Birds of Britain and
Ireland; Seabirds of the World; Design and Decorate
Series; No-Time Party Cakes; Design Source Books.*
No unsolicited mss; synopses and ideas welcome.
Royalties paid twice-yearly.

Nexus
See **Virgin Publishing Ltd**

Nexus Special Interests
Nexus House, Azalea Drive, Swanley, Kent
BR8 8HY
☎01322 770060   Fax 01322 667633
Manager *Beverly Laughlin*
Publishes aviation, engineering, leisure and
hobbies, modelling, electronics, health, craft,
wine and beer making, woodwork. Send syn-
opses rather than completed mss.
Royalties paid twice-yearly.

NFER-NELSON Publishing Co. Ltd
Darville House, 2 Oxford Road East,
Windsor, Berkshire SL4 1DF
☎01753 858961   Fax 01753 856830
Website:www.nfer-nelson.co.uk
Managing Director *Michael Jackson*
FOUNDED 1981. Jointly owned by the Thomson
Corporation and the National Foundation for
Educational Research. *Publishes* educational and
psychological tests and training materials. Main
interest is in educational, clinical and occu-
pational assessment and training material. Unso-
licited material welcome.
Royalties vary according to each contract.

Nia
See **The X Press**

Nicholson
See **HarperCollins Publishers Ltd**

James Nisbet & Co. Ltd
78 Tilehouse Street, Hitchin, Hertfordshire
SG5 2DY
☎01462 438331   Fax 01462 431528
Chairman *E. M. Mackenzie-Wood*
FOUNDED 1810 as a religious publisher and
expanded into more general areas from around
1850 onwards. The first educational list appeared
in 1926 and the company now specialises in educational material and business studies. About 5
titles a year. No fiction, leisure or religion. No
unsolicited mss; synopses and ideas welcome.
Royalties paid twice-yearly.

NMS Publishing Limited
Royal Museum, Chambers Street, Edinburgh
EH1 1JF
☎0131 247 4026   Fax 0131 247 4012
Website:www.nms.ac.uk
Chairman *Mark Jones*
Director *Helen Kemp*
Approx. Annual Turnover £200,000
FOUNDED 1987 to *publish* non-fiction related to
the National Museums of Scotland collections:
academic and general; children's; archaeology,
history, decorative arts worldwide, history of sci-
ence, technology, natural history and geology,
poetry. 12 titles in 1998. TITLES *Scotland's Past in
Action* series; *The Scottish Home; Domestic Culture
in the Middle East; Agates; Harmony and Contrast:
A Journey Through East Asian Art; Thistle at War;
Precious Cargo; Scots' Lives; Jewellery Moves; Scottish
Coins; Chinese Lacquer.* No unsolicited mss; only
interested in synopses and ideas for books which
are genuinely related to NMS collections and to
Scotland in general.
Royalties paid twice-yearly.

No Exit Press
See **Oldcastle Books Ltd**

Nonesuch Press
See **Reinhardt Books Ltd**

Northcote House Publishers Ltd

Plymbridge House, Estover Road, Plymouth,
Devon PL6 7PY
☎01752 202368   Fax 01752 202330
Managing Director *Brian Hulme*
FOUNDED 1985. Recently launched a new series
of literary critical studies, in association with the
British Council, called *Writers and their Work*.
Publishes education management, literary criticism, educational dance and drama. A new series
of study aids for A-level students and undergraduates in the humanities is in preparation. 25
titles in 1998. 'Well-thought-out proposals,
including contents and sample chapter(s), with
strong marketing arguments welcome.'
    Royalties paid annually.

W. W. Norton & Company Ltd

10 Coptic Street, London WC1A 1PU
☎0171 323 1579   Fax 0171 436 4553
Managing Director *R. A. Cameron*

Owned by US parent company. *Publishes* non-
fiction and academic. No unsolicited material.
Enquiries only in writing.

Nottingham University Press

Manor Farm, Main Street, Thrumpton,
Nottingham NG11 0AX
☎0115 9831011   Fax 0115 9831003
Email: editor@nup.com
Managing Editor *Dr D. J. A. Cole*
Approx. Annual Turnover £150,000

Initially concentrated on agricultural and food
sciences titles but now branching into new
areas including engineering, lifesciences, medicine, law and sport. Sports books published
under subsidiary, Castle Publications. TITLES
*Global 2050; Lung Function Tests; Diet,
Lipoproteins and Coronary Heart Disease; Chinese
Herbs in Animal Nutrition; Progress in Pig Science.*
Castle Publications TITLES *The Mental Game
of Golf; The Natural Sportsman; Rinks to Arenas,
10 Years of British Ice Hockey.*
    Royalties paid twice-yearly.

Oak

See **Omnibus Press**

Oberon Books

521 Caledonian Road, London N7 9RH
☎0171 607 3637   Fax 0171 607 3629
Email: oberon.books@btinternet.com
Publishing Director *James Hogan*
Managing Director *Charles D. Glanville*

Publishes play texts (usually in conjunction with

a production) and theatre books. *Specialises* in
contemporary plays and translations of Euro-
pean classics.
    IMPRINTS **Oberon Books**; **Absolute
Classics**. AUTHORS/TRANSLATORS Rodney
Ackland, Michel Azama, Simon Bent, Steven
Berkoff, Ranjit Bolt, Ken Campbell, Barry
Day, Marguerite Duras, Dario Fo, Jonathan
Gems, Pam Gems, Trevor Griffiths, Sir Peter
Hall, Giles Havergal, Rolf Hochhuth, Michael
Kilgarriff, Robert David MacDonald, Kenneth
McLeish, Adrian Mitchell, Sheridan Morley,
Gregory Motton, Stephen Mulrine, Jimmy
Murphy, Meredith Oakes, Stewart Parker,
David Pownall, Roland Rees, Colin Winslow,
Charles Wood.

Octagon Press Ltd

PO Box 227, London N6 4EW
☎0181 348 9392   Fax 0181 341 5971
Website:www.octagonpress.com
Managing Director *George R. Schrager*
Approx. Annual Turnover £100,000
FOUNDED 1972. *Publishes* philosophy, psychol-
ogy, travel, Eastern religion, translations of
Eastern classics and research monographs in
series. 4–5 titles a year. Unsolicited material
not welcome. Enquiries in writing only.
    Royalties paid annually.

Octopus Publishing Group

2–4 Heron Quays, London E14 4JP
☎0171 531 8400   Fax 0171 531 8650
Website:www.octopus-publishing.co.uk
Chief Executive *Derek Freeman*
Approx. Annual Turnover £45 million
(Group)

A new company formed following a management buyout of Reed Consumer Books from
Reed Elsevier plc in August 1998.

Conran Octopus

Fax 0171 531 8627;
Email: info-co@conran-octopus.co.uk
Website:www.conran-octopus.co.uk
Managing Director *Caroline Proud* Quality illus-
trated lifestyle books, particularly interiors,
design, cookery, gardening and crafts TITLES *East
Meets West* Kelly Hoppen; *The New Office* Francis
Duffy; *Passion for Flavour* Gordon Ramsay; *The
Sensuous Garden* Monty Don.

Hamlyn Octopus

Email: info-ho@hamlyn.co.uk
Website:www.hamlyn.co.uk
Managing Director *Alison Goff* Popular non-
fiction, particularly cookery, gardening, craft,

sport, film tie-ins, rock 'n' roll TITLES *Larousse Gastronomique; Sunday Times Chronicle of Sport; Hamlyn All Colour Cookbook; Hamlyn Book of Gardening; Hamlyn Book of DIY & Decorating.*

Mitchell Beazley/Miller's
Fax 0171 531 8650
Email: info-mb@mitchell-beazley.co.uk
Website:www.mitchell-beazley.co.uk
Managing Director *Jane Aspden* Quality illustrated reference books, particularly wine, gardening, craft, interior design and architecture, antiques, general reference TITLES *Hugh Johnson's Pocket Wine Book; The New Joy of Sex; Miller's Antiques Price Guide.*

Philip's
Fax 0171 531 8460
Email: george.philip@philips-maps.co.uk
Website:www.philips-maps.co.uk
Managing Director *John Gaisford* World atlases, globes, astronomy, road atlases, encyclopaedias, thematic reference TITLES *Philip's Atlas of the World; Philip's Modern School Atlas; Philip's Guide to the Stars and Planets; Ordnance Survey Street Atlas; Philip's Millennium Encyclopaedia; Philip's Atlas of World History.*

Brimax
Fax 0171 531 8607
Email: brimax@brimax.octopus.co.uk
Managing Director *Jacquie Russo* Mass-market board and picture books for children, age groups 1–10.

Bounty
Fax 0171 531 8607
Email: bountybooksinfo-bp@bountybooks.co.uk
Managing Director *Caroline Lake* Bargain and promotional books. New, repackaged and reissued titles.
  Royalties paid twice-yearly/annually, according to contract in all divisions.

Old Forge Gift Collection
See **Anness Publishing Ltd**

Oldcastle Books Ltd
18 Coleswood Road, Harpenden, Hertfordshire AL5 1EQ
☎01582 761264   Fax 01582 712244
Email: info@noxitpress.co.uk
Website:www.noexit.co.uk
Managing Director *Ion S. Mills*
FOUNDED 1985. *Publishes* crime fiction and gambling non-fiction. 20 titles in 1998. *No unsolicited mss;* synopses and ideas for books within the two areas of interest welcome. IMPRINTS **No Exit Press** TITLES *Burglar In the Library* Lawrence Block; *No Beast So Fierce* Eddie Bunker; **Oldcastle Books** TITLES *Little Book of Poker* David Spanier.
  Royalties paid twice-yearly.

Oldie Publications
45/46 Poland Street, London W1V 4AU
☎0171 734 2225   Fax 0171 734 2226
Chairman *Richard Ingrams*
FOUNDED in 1992. Book publishing arm of *The Oldie* magazine. *Publishes* compilations from the magazine, including cartoon books. TITLES *I Once Met; Dictionary For Our Time; The Third Oldie Annual; Jennifer's Diary: By One Fat Lady* Jennifer Paterson.

OM Publishing
See **Paternoster Publishing**

Michael O'Mara Books Ltd
9 Lion Yard, Tremadoc Road, London SW4 7NQ
☎0171 720 8643   Fax 0171 627 8953
Chairman *Michael O'Mara*
Managing Director *Lesley O'Mara*
Approx. Annual Turnover £5 million
FOUNDED 1985. Independent publisher. *Publishes* general non-fiction, royalty, history, humour, anthologies and reference. TITLES *Diana: Her True Story* Andrew Morton; *The Seven Wonders of the World* John Romer; *I Don't Believe It!* Richard Wilson. Unsolicited mss, synopses and ideas for books welcome.
  Royalties paid twice-yearly.

Authors' Rating From Diana to Monica via Morton. The route to riches may look simple enough but plenty of other publishers have lost their way. O'Mara is open to ideas to expand his list. Just bear in mind that he is not likely to stray too far from the mainstream.

Omnibus Press
Book Sales/Music Sales Ltd, 8–9 Frith Street, London W1V 5TZ
☎0171 434 0066   Fax 0171 734 2246
Email: chris.charlesworth@musicsales.co.uk
Editorial Head *Chris Charlesworth*
FOUNDED 1971. Independent publisher of music books, rock and pop biographies, song sheets, educational tutors, cassettes, videos and software IMPRINTS **Amsco; Bobcat; Oak; Omnibus; Wise Publications**. Unsolicited mss, synopses and ideas for books welcome.
  Royalties paid twice-yearly.

Oneworld Publications

185 Banbury Road, Oxford OX2 7AR
☎01865 310597 Fax 01865 310598
Email: oneworld@cix.co.uk
Website:www.oneworld-publications.com

Editorial Director *Juliet Mabey*

FOUNDED 1986. Distributed worldwide by **Penguin Books**. *Publishes* adult non-fiction across a range of subjects from world religions and social issues to psychology and self-help. 25 titles in 1998. A series on world religions was launched in 1994 with authors such as Geoffrey Parrinder, Keith Ward, Klaus Klostermaier. A series of concise encyclopedias has just been launched on world religions and a new series of short histories of countries is planned for 2000. No unsolicited mss; synopses and ideas welcome, but should be accompanied by s.a.e. for return of material and/or notification of receipt. No autobiographies, fiction, poetry or children's.
Royalties paid annually.

Onlywomen Press Ltd

40 St Lawrence Terrace, London W10 5ST
☎0181 960 7122 Fax 0181 960 2817
Email: onlywomen_press@compuserve.com
Website:www.onlywomenpress.com

Editorial Director *Lilian Mohin*

FOUNDED 1974. *Publishes* feminist lesbian books only: literary fiction, genre fiction (crime, sci-fi, romance), non-fiction (feminist theory, psychology, literary criticism) and poetry. Up to 6 titles a year. In 1997/98, published the first title (*Rebellion* by Jay taverner) in **Zest**, a new lesbian historial romance list, original paperbacks set in England. Unsolicited mss, synopses and ideas welcome. Submissions should be accompanied by s.a.e. for response and/or return of material as well as a covering letter 'identifying the author and suggesting reasons to consider publishing her work'.

OPC

See **Ian Allan Publishing Ltd**

Open Gate Press (incorporating Centaur Press 1954)

51 Achilles Road, London NW6 1DZ
☎0171 431 4391 Fax 0171 431 5088
Email: books@opengate.demon.co.uk

Managing Directors *Jeannie Cohen, Elisabeth Petersdorff*

FOUNDED in 1989 to provide a forum for psychoanalytic social and cultural studies. *Publishes* psychoanalysis, philosophy, social sciences, politics, literature, religion, animal rights, environment. SERIES *Psychoanalysis and Society.* Also publishes a journal of psychoanalytic social studies, *New Analysis.*

IMPRINTS **Open Gate Press**; **Centaur Press**; **Linden Press**. Since the acquisition of Centaur Press, Open Gate Press is continuing its work, in particular the *Kinship Library* – a series on the philosophy, politics and application of humane education, with special focus on the subject of animal rights and its relevance to the human condition. Synopses and ideas for books and articles welcome.
Royalties paid twice-yearly.

Open University Press

Celtic Court, 22 Ballmoor, Buckingham, Buckinghamshire MK18 1XW
☎01280 823388 Fax 01280 823233

Managing Director *John Skelton*
Approx. Annual Turnover £3 million

FOUNDED 1977 as an imprint independent of the Open University's course materials. *Publishes* academic and professional books in the fields of education, management, sociology, health studies, politics, psychology, women's studies. No economics or anthropology. Not interested in anything outside the social sciences. About 100 titles a year. No unsolicited mss; enquiries/proposals only.
Royalties paid annually.

Optima Information & Publications

Optima Development Services (Europe) Ltd, Grosvenor House, 112–114 Prince of Wales Road, Norwich, Norfolk NR1 1NZ
☎01603 626808 Fax 01603 663308
Email: optimagroup@compuserve.com

Director *Charles Fik*

FOUNDED 1997. *Publishes* reproducible and other learning resources for public and private sector education and training providers. Business and management are the main areas. Also publishes specialist resources with wider appeal for schools, colleges and universities. Ideas welcome; first approach in writing with outline; no unsolicited mss.
Royalties paid annually.

Orbit

See **Little, Brown & Co. (UK)**

Orchard Books

See **The Watts Publishing Group Ltd**

The Orion Publishing Group Limited

Orion House, 5 Upper St Martin's Lane, London WC2H 9EA
☎0171 240 3444   Fax 0171 240 4822
Chairman *Jean-Louis Lisimachio*
Chief Executive *Anthony Cheetham*
Managing Director *Peter Roche*
Approx. Annual Turnover £40 million
FOUNDED 1992 by Anthony Cheetham, Rosemary Cheetham and Peter Roche. Incorporates Weidenfeld & Nicolson, JM Dent and Chapmans Publishers. Acquired **Cassell** in 1998 (see entry).

DIVISIONS
Orion Managing Director *Malcolm Edwards* Publisher *Rosemary Cheetham* IMPRINTS **Orion** General Publishing Director *Jane Wood* Hardcover fiction/non-fiction; **Orion Business** *Martin Liu* Business books; **Orion Media** Publishing Director *Trevor Dolby* Film and TV; **Orion Children's** Managing Director *Judith Elliott* Children's fiction/non-fiction.
   Weidenfeld & Nicolson Managing Director *Ion Trewin* IMPRINTS **Weidenfeld General** Publishing Director *Rebecca Wilson* General non-fiction, biography and autobiography; **Phoenix House** Publishing Director *Maggie McKernan* Literary fiction; **Weidenfeld Illustrated** Publisher *Michael Dover* Illustrated non-fiction.
   Mass Market Managing Director *Susan Lamb* IMPRINTS **Orion**; **Phoenix**; **Phoenix Illustrated**; **Everyman**.

Authors' Rating Now controlled by Hachette, which has 70 per cent of the equity, Orion has the funds it needs for an ambitious expansion plan. The first move was the takeover of Cassell with its highly prized reference list. Growth in the UK is likely to come from more niche publishing such as the recently launched military list. But all this is a preliminary to the biggest step of all, across the Atlantic, to take Orion and Hachette into the American market.

Osprey Publishing Ltd

Elms Court, Chapel Way, Botley, Oxford OX2 9LP
☎01865 727022   Fax 01865 727017
Email: osprey@osprey-publishing.co.uk
Website:www.osprey-publishing.co.uk
Managing Director *Jonathan Parker*
Editor, Military History *Lee Johnson*
Editor, Automotive & Aviation
   Shaun Barrington

Editor, Aviation *Tony Holmes*
Publishes Illustrated military history, aviation, automotive books. Established thirty years ago, Osprey became independent from **Reed Elsevier** in February 1998. 65 titles in 1998. SERIES *Men-at-Arms; Elite Campaign; New Vanguard; Warrior; Aircraft of the Aces.* TITLES *Combat Aircraft; Stanley Classic Car Year Book; Osprey Companion to Military History.* No unsolicited mss; synopses and ideas welcome.
   Royalties paid twice-yearly.

Peter Owen Ltd

73 Kenway Road, London SW5 0RE
☎0171 373 5628/370 6093
Fax 0171 373 6760
Email: admin@peterowen.u-net.com
Chairman *Peter Owen*
Editorial Director *Antonia Owen*
FOUNDED 1951. *Publishes* biography, general non-fiction, English-language literary fiction and translations, sociology. 'No genre or children's fiction; the company only rarely takes on first novels.' AUTHORS Jane Bowles, Paul Bowles, Shusaku Endo, Anna Kavan, Jean Giono, Anaïs Nin, Jeremy Reed, Peter Vansittart. 35–40 titles a year. Unsolicited synopses welcome for non-fiction material; mss should be preceded by a descriptive letter and synopsis with s.a.e.
   Royalties paid twice-yearly. *Overseas associates* worldwide.

Authors' Rating Peter Owen has been described as 'a publisher of the old and idiosyncratic school'. He has seven Nobel prize-winners on his list.

Oxford Illustrated Press
See **Haynes Publishing**

Oxford University Press

Great Clarendon Street, Oxford OX2 6DP
☎01865 556767   Fax 01865 556646
Email: enquiry@oup.co.uk
Website:www.oup.co.uk
Chief Executive *Henry Reece*
Approx. Annual Turnover £282 million
A department of the university, OUP grew from the university's printing works and developed into a major publishing business in the 19th century. *Publishes* academic books in all categories: student texts, scholarly journals, schoolbooks, ELT material, dictionaries, reference, music, bibles, electronic publishing, as well as paperbacks, general non-fiction and children's books. Around 3000 titles a year.

DIVISIONS **Academic** *I. S. Asquith* Academic and college titles in all disciplines; dictionaries and non-lexical reference, trade books, journals and electronic publishing. TITLES *Concise Oxford Dictionary*; *Birds of the Western Palearctic*; **Educational** *F. E. Clarke* National Curriculum courses; **ELT** *P. R. Mothersole* ELT courses and dictionaries. IMPRINTS **Clarendon Press** Monographs in humanities, science and social science; **Oxford Paperbacks** Trade paperbacks; **Oxford Science Publications**; **Oxford Medical Publications**; **Oxford Electronic Publications**. OUP welcomes first-class academic material in the form of proposals or accepted theses.

Royalties paid twice-yearly. *Overseas subsidiaries* Sister company in USA; also branches in Australia, Canada, East Africa, Hong Kong, India, Japan, New Zealand, Pakistan, Singapore, South Africa. Offices in Argentina, Brazil, France, Germany, Greece, Italy, Mexico, Spain, Taiwan, Thailand, Turkey, Uruguay. Joint companies in Malaysia, Nigeria and Germany.

Authors' Rating Pilloried by the literary establishment for giving up on poetry, OUP, after a disappointing year, had to take some action to balance its commercial interests against the need to satisfy the widest possible range of academic disciplines. Authors are queuing up even though a monograph rarely sells more than 500 copies. As it was said recently in the *Times Literary Supplement*, being published by OUP is like being married to a duchess; the honour is greater than the pleasure. The market leader in dictionaries and English Language Teaching, OUP publishes in 12 countries and has offices and associated companies in 40 others.

Palm Tree Press
See **Kevin Mayhew Ltd**

G. J. Palmer & Sons Ltd
See **Hymns Ancient & Modern Ltd**

Pan Books Ltd
See **Macmillan Publishers Ltd**

Papermac
See **Macmillan Publishers Ltd**

Paragon Press
1A Tower Square, Leeds, West Yorkshire LS1 4HZ
☎0113 2095771   Fax 0113 2095600
Managing Editor *Dorothy James*
FOUNDED 1998. *Publishes* fiction and non-fiction.

SERIES **Paragon Summaries** Short factual series for higher and further education. TITLES *Auguste Comte; Scott Fitzgerald; Sigmund Freud; Charles Darwin*. 70 titles forthcoming. No unsolicited mss; synopses and ideas welcome. Approach in writing but will answer telephone queries.

Paragon Softcover Large Print
See **Chivers Press Ltd**

Partridge Press
See **Transworld Publishers Ltd**

Paternoster Publishing
PO Box 300, Kingstown Broadway, Carlisle, Cumbria CA3 0QS
☎01228 512512   Fax 01228 593388
Publishing Director *Mark Finnie*
Editorial Coordinator *Nancy Lush*
Approx. Annual Turnover £2 million
A division of STL Ltd.

IMPRINTS:
The Paternoster Press FOUNDED 1936. *Publishes* religion and learned/church/life-related journals. Over 60 titles a year. TITLES *Complete Short Works of J. I. Packer; All's Well R. T. Kendall*.

OM Publishing FOUNDED 1966. *Publishes* Christian books on evangelism, discipleship and mission. About 30 titles a year. TITLES *Operation World* Patrick Johnstone; *You Can Change the World* Jill Johnstone; and many titles by Elisabeth Elliot and A. W. Tozer.

Solway FOUNDED 1996. Tackes 'Christianity and Christian art from an original perspective.' About 10 titles a year. TITLES *After Eating the Apricot* John Goldingay; *Learning to Fly* Adrian Plass and Ben Ecclestone. Unsolicited mss, synopses and ideas for books welcome.
Royalties paid twice-yearly.

Pathways
See **How To Books Ltd**

Pavilion Books Ltd
London House, Great Eastern Wharf, Parkgate Road, London SW11 4NQ
☎0171 350 1230   Fax 0171 350 1261
Publisher *Colin Webb*

Acquired by C&B Publishing plc (**Collins & Brown**) in 1997. *Publishes* illustrated books in biography, children's, cookery, gardening, humour, art, sport and travel. Unsolicited ms not welcome. Ideas and synopses for non-fiction titles and children's fiction considered.
Royalties paid twice-yearly.

Payback Press
See **Canongate Books Ltd**

Pearson Education
Edinburgh Gate, Harlow, Essex CM20 2JE
☎01279 623623   Fax 01279 431059
Website:www.awl.co.uk
Contracts & Copyrights Department
   Brenda Gvozdanovic

Formed by a merger in 1998 of Addison Wesley
Longman Ltd and the education divisions of
Simon & Schuster. *Publishes* a range of curriculum subjects, including English language
teaching for students at primary and secondary
school level, college and university. All unsolicited mss should be addressed to the Manager,
Contracts and Copyrights Department.
   Royalties paid twice-yearly. *Overseas associates*
worldwide.

Authors' Rating Now the world's leading
educational publisher. This follows Addison
Wesley Longman's purchase of the education
list of American publisher Simon & Schuster.
Resources are there for product development
particularly in the ELT sector. They must be
doing something right. The Chief Executive of
Pearson was paid more than £1 million in 1998.

Pen & Sword Books Ltd
47 Church Street, Barnsley, South Yorkshire
S70 2AS
☎01226 734734   Fax 01226 734438
Website:www.yorkshire-web.co.uk/ps
Chairman *Sir Nicholas Hewitt*
Chief Executive *Charles Hewitt*

FOUNDED 1990 following the acquisition of
the Leo Cooper imprint from Octopus
Publishing. *Publishes* military history, naval and
aviation history, autobiography and biography.
About 40 titles a year. IMPRINTS **Leo Cooper**;
Wharncliffe Publishing (see entry). Unsolicited synopses and ideas welcome; no unsolicited mss.
   Royalties paid twice-yearly. *Associated company* **Wharncliffe Publishing Ltd**.

Penguin UK
27 Wrights Lane, London W8 5TZ
☎0171 416 3000   Fax 0171 416 3099
Website:www.penguin.co.uk
Chairman *Michael Lynton*
Managing Director *Anthony Forbes Watson*
Approx. Annual Turnover £99.1 million

Owned by Pearson plc. The world's best
known book brand and for more than 60 years
a leading publisher whose adult and children's
lists include fiction, non-fiction, poetry, drama,
classics, reference and special interest areas.
Reprints and new work.

DIVISIONS
Penguin General Books Managing Director
Helen Fraser Adult fiction and non-fiction is
published in hardback under Michael Joseph,
Viking and Hamish Hamilton imprints. Paper-
backs come under the Penguin imprint.
IMPRINTS **Viking/Penguin** Publisher *Juliet
Annan* Publishing Director *Tony Lacey*; **Hamish
Hamilton** Publisher *Simon Prosser*; **Michael
Joseph/Penguin** Publishing Director *Tom
Weldon* Unsolicited mss discouraged.
   Penguin Press Managing Director *Andrew
Rosenheim* Publishing Directors *Alastair Rolfe,
Stuart Proffitt* Academic adult non-fiction, ref-
erence, specialist and classics. IMPRINTS **Allen
Lane**; **Arkana** Mind, body and spirit;
Buildings of England; **Classics**; **Penguin
Books** Approach in writing only.
   Frederick Warne Publisher *Sally Floyer*
Classic children's publishing and merchandising
including *Beatrix Potter™*; *Flower Fairies*; *Orlando*.
Ventura Publisher *Sally Floyer* Producer and
packager of *Spot* titles by Eric Hill.
   Ladybird Books (see entry).
   Penguin Children's Books Managing
Director *Philippa Milnes-Smith* Hardback
IMPRINTS **Hamish Hamilton Children's**;
Viking Children's; Paperback IMPRINT
Puffin Publishers *Penny Morris* (fiction, poetry
and picture books), *Richard Scrivener* (media and
popular non-fiction). Leading children's paper-
back list, publishing in virtually all fields
including fiction, non-fiction, poetry, picture
books, media-related titles. No unsolicited mss;
synopses and ideas welcome.
   Penguin Audiobooks (see entry under
Audio Books).
   Royalties paid twice-yearly. *Overseas associates*
worldwide.

Authors' Rating This most famous of publishers is back on form after a period of radical
restructuring. A brand advertising campaign is
promised.

Pergamon Press
See **Elsevier Science Ltd**

Persephone Books
28 Great Sutton Street, London EC1V 0DS
☎0171 253 5454   Fax 0171 253 5656
Email: sales@persephonebooks.co.uk
Website:www.persephonebooks.co.uk

Managing Director *Nicola Beauman*

FOUNDED 1999. *Publishes* reprint and original fiction and non-fiction, mostly 'by women, for women and about women'. TITLES *William – An Englishman* Cicely Hamilton; *Mariana* Monica Dickens; *Someone at a Distance* Dorothy Whipple. No unsolicited material.

Royalties paid twice-yearly

Petroc Press
See **Librapharm Ltd**

Phaidon Press Limited
Regent's Wharf, All Saints Street, London N1 9PA
☎0171 843 1000   Fax 0171 843 1010
Email: <name>@phaidon.com

Chairman/Publisher *Richard Schlagman*
Managing Director *Andrew Price*
Deputy Publisher *Amanda Renshaw*
Editorial Heads *Karen Stein* (Architecture and Design*)*, *Pat Barylski* (Art and Ideas Series), *Gilda Williams* (Contemporary Art), *Chris Boot* (Photography)
Approx. Annual Turnover £11 million

Publishes quality books on the visual arts, including fine art, art history, architecture, design, photography, decorative arts, music and performing arts. Recently started producing videos. About 100 titles a year. Unsolicited mss welcome but 'only a small amount of unsolicited material gets published'.

Royalties paid twice-yearly.

Authors' Rating One of the fastest growing art book publishers, it seems incredible that it is less than ten years ago that Phaidon had to be bought out of receivership. Now the company is growing at around 10 per cent a year. Much has been achieved by the repackaging of Phaidon's best-known title, Gombrich's *The Story of Art*. Sales are strong in the US, where Phaidon has a subsidiary, and in Europe.

Philip's
See **Octopus Publishing Group**

Phillimore & Co. Ltd
Shopwyke Manor Barn, Chichester, West Sussex PO20 6BG
☎01243 787636   Fax 01243 787639
Email: bookshop@phillimore.co.uk
Website:www.phillimore.co.uk

Chairman *Philip Harris*
Managing Director *Noel Osborne*
Approx. Annual Turnover £1 million

FOUNDED in 1897 by W. P. W. Phillimore, Victorian campaigner for local archive conservation in Chancery Lane, London. Became the country's leading publisher of historical source material and local histories. Somewhat dormant in the 1960s, it was revived by Philip Harris in 1968. *Publishes* British local and family history, including histories of institutions, buildings, villages, towns and counties, plus guides to research and writing in these fields. About 70 titles a year. No unsolicited mss; synopses/ideas welcome for local or family histories. IMPRINT **Phillimore** *Noel Osborne* TITLES *Domesday Book; A History of Essex; Carlisle; The Haberdashers' Company; Channel Island Churches; Bolton Past*.

Royalties paid annually.

Phoenix/Phoenix House/ Phoenix Illustrated
See **The Orion Publishing Group Ltd**

Piatkus Books
5 Windmill Street, London W1P 1HF
☎0171 631 0710   Fax 0171 436 7137
Email: info@piatkus.co.uk

Managing Director *Judy Piatkus*
Approx. Annual Turnover £4.75 million

FOUNDED 1979 by Judy Piatkus. The company is customer-led and is committed to publishing fiction, both commercial and literary, and non-fiction. *Specialises* in publishing books and authors 'who we feel enthusiastic and committed to as we like to build for long-term success as well as short-term!' *Publishes* fiction, biography and autobiography, health, Mind, Body and Spirit, popular psychology, self-help, business and management, cookery 'and other books that tempt us'. In 1996 launched a list of mass-market non-fiction and fiction titles. About 120 titles a year (60 of which are fiction).

DIVISIONS
Non-fiction *Gill Bailey* TITLES *Optimum Nutrition Bible* Patrick Holford; *Detox Yourself* Jane Scrivner; *Clear Your Clutter with Feng Shui* Karen Kingston; *Inside the Foreign Legion* John Parker. **Fiction** *Judy Piatkus* TITLES *Hitched* Zoë Barnes; *Homeport* Nora Roberts; *Mind Games* Hilary Norman; *Only Love* Erich Segal. Piatkus are expanding their range of books and welcome synopses and first three chapters.

Royalties paid twice-yearly.

Authors' Rating Mass market paperback fiction is carrying Piatkus a notch or two up the scale. But in a bold move for a still smallish publisher we find *How to Get Published and Make a Lot of Money* entering the list. It could be that Susan Page (author) and Judy Piatkus know something that has escaped most of us. At least one rejected author has been sent the appropriate order form.

Picador
See **Macmillan Publishers Ltd**

Piccadilly Press
5 Castle Road, London NW1 8PR
☎0171 267 4492   Fax 0171 267 4493
Email: books@piccadillypress.co.uk
Chairman/Managing Director
  Brenda Gardner
Approx. Annual Turnover £600,000
FOUNDED 1983. Independent publisher of children's and parental books. 30 titles in 1998. Welcomes approaches from authors 'but we would like them to know the sort of books we do. It is frustrating to get inappropriate material. They should check in their local libraries or bookshops. We will send a catalogue (please enclose s.a.e.)'. No adult or cartoon-type material.
  Royalties paid twice-yearly.

Pictorial Presentations
See **Souvenir Press Ltd**

Picture Lions
See **HarperCollins Publishers Ltd**

Pimlico
See **Random House UK Ltd**

Pinter
See **Cassell**

Pitkin Unichrome
Healey House, Dene Road, Andover, Hampshire SP10 2AA
☎01264 409200   Fax 01264 334110
Managing Director *Heather Hook*
Pitkin Guides, FOUNDED in 1947, was part of **Reed Books** from 1988 to March 1998 when it merged with Unichrome. *Publishes* illustrated souvenir guides.

Pitman Publishing
See **Financial Times Management**

Plenum Publishing Co. Ltd
New Loom House, 101 Back Church Lane, London E1 1LU
☎0171 264 1910   Fax 0171 264 1919
Email: mail@plenum.co.uk
or Plenum@compuserve.com
Website:www.plenum.co.uk

Managing Director *Dr Ken Derham*
Editor *Joanna Lawrence*
FOUNDED 1966. A division of **Kluwer Academic/Plenum Publishing**, New York. The London office is the editorial base for the company's UK and European operations. *Publishes* postgraduate, professional and research-level scientific, technical and medical textbooks, monographs, conference proceedings and reference books. About 300 titles (worldwide) a year.
  IMPRINTS **Consultants Bureau**; **Kluwer Academic/Plenum Publishers**; **Plenum Medical Company**; **Plenum Press**; **Human Science Press**. Proposals for new publications will be considered, and should be sent to the editor.
  Royalties paid annually.

Pluto Press Ltd
345 Archway Road, London N6 5AA
☎0181 348 2724   Fax 0181 348 9133
Managing Director *Roger Van Zwanenberg*
Publishing Director *Anne Beech*
FOUNDED 1970. Has developed a reputation for innovatory publishing in the field of non-fiction. *Publishes* academic and scholarly books across a range of subjects including cultural studies, politics and world affairs, social sciences and socialist, feminist and Marxist books. About 50–60 titles a year. Synopses and ideas welcome if accompanied by return postage.

Point
See **Scholastic Ltd**

The Policy Press
University of Bristol, 34 Tyndall's Park Road, Bristol BS8 1PY
☎0117 9738797   Fax 0117 9737308
Managing Director *Alison Shaw*
Approx. Annual Turnover £250,000
The Policy Press is a specialist publisher of policy studies. Material published, in the form of books, reports, practice guides and journals, is taken from research findings and provides critical discussion of policy initiatives and their impact, and also recommendations for policy change. 45–50 titles per year. No unsolicited mss; brief synopses and ideas welcome.

Polity Press
65 Bridge Street, Cambridge CB2 1UR
☎01223 324315   Fax 01223 461385
FOUNDED 1984. All books are published in association with **Blackwell Publishers**. *Publishes* archaeology and anthropology, criminology,

economics, feminism, general interest, history, human geography, literature, media and cultural studies, medicine and society, philosophy, politics, psychology, religion and theology, social and political theory, sociology. Unsolicited synopses and ideas for books welcome.
Royalties paid annually.

Polygon
See **Edinburgh University Press**

Pont Books
See **Gomer Press**

Pop Universal
See **Souvenir Press Ltd**

Portland Press Ltd
59 Portland Place, London W1N 3AJ
☎0171 580 5530   Fax 0171 323 1136
Email: edit@portlandpress.co.uk
Website:www.portlandpress.co.uk
Chairman *Professor A. J. Turner*
Managing Director *G. D. Jones*
Editorial Director *Rhonda Oliver*
Approx. Annual Turnover £2.5 million
FOUNDED 1990 to expand the publishing activities of the Biochemical Society (1911). *Publishes* biochemisty and medicine for graduate, postgraduate and research students. Expanding the list to include schools and general readership. 15 titles in 1998. TITLES *Biological Speciment Preparation for Transmission Electron Microscopy; The Impact of Electronic Publishing on the Academic Community; Essays in Biochemistry: The Molecular Biology of the Brain; Engineering Crops for Industrial End Uses.* Unsolicited mss, synopses and ideas welcome. No fiction.
Royalties paid twice-yearly.

T. & A. D. Poyser
See **Harcourt Brace and Company Limited**

Princeton University Press
See **University Presses of California, Columbia & Princeton Ltd**

Prion Books Ltd
Imperial Works, Perren Street, London NW5 3ED
☎0171 482 4248   Fax 0171 482 4203
Managing Director *Barry Winkleman*
Editor *Andrew Goodfellow*
Formerly a packaging operation but began publishing under the Prion imprint in 1987. *Publishes*

non-fiction: humour, popular culture, historical and literary reprints, beauty, food and drink, sex, psychology and health. About 40 titles a year. Unsolicited mss, synopses and ideas welcome.
Royalties paid twice-yearly.

Profile Books
58A Hatton Gardens, London EC1N 8LX
☎0171 404 3001   Fax 0171 404 3003
Email: info@profilebooks.co.uk
Website:www.profilebooks.co.uk
Managing Director *Andrew Franklin*
Approx. Annual Turnover £1 million
FOUNDED 1996. *Publishes* serious nonfiction including current affairs, history, politics, psychology, cultural criticism, business and management. IMPRINTS **Profile Books** *Andrew Franklin*; **Economist Books** *Stephen Brough.* No unsolicited mss.
Royalties paid twice-yearly.

Authors' Rating With Economist Books providing a firm sales base, Profile has expanded its list of other trade titles to 15 a year. All seems set for further expansion of an author-friendly, small non-fiction publisher.

Prowler Press Ltd
See **The Gay Men's Press**

Publishing House
Trinity Place, Barnstaple, Devon EX32 9HJ
☎01271 328892   Fax 01271 328768
Email: publishinghouse@vernoncoleman.com
Website:www.vernoncoleman.com
Managing Director *Vernon Coleman*
Editorial Head *Sue Ward*
Approx. Annual Turnover £500,000
FOUNDED 1989. Self-publisher of fiction, health, humour, animals, politics. 2 titles in 1998. TITLES *Bodycover; Village Cricket Tour; How to Publish Your Own Book* all by Vernon Coleman. No submissions.

Puffin
See **Penguin UK**

Pulp Books
The Depot, 29/31 Brewery Road, London N7 9JQ
☎0171 700 3409
Website:www.pulpfact.demon.co.uk
Specialises in new contemporary British fiction. Currently producing 20–25 titles a year and expanding. TITLES *Go* Simon Lewis; *Serious Time* Joe Ambrose; *Do What You Want* Chris Savage

King. Also **Pulp Faction** (PO Box 12171, London N19 3HB) which produces around two short fiction collections annually with an emphasis on strong, original and sometimes experimental British writing. For upcoming themes, send s.a.e. marked 'Short Story Themes'. Only previously unpublished work considered.

Royalties paid annually.

Pushkin Press Ltd
22 Park Walk, London SW10 0AQ
☎0171 349 9367   Fax 0171 352 8139
Email: pushkinpressltd@compuserve.com
Chairman *Melissa Ulfane*
Editorial Head *Oliver Berggruen*
Approx. Annual Turnover £500,000

Publishes novels, essays and poetry drawn from the best of classic and contemporary European literature. Welcomes unsolicited mss, synopses and ideas for books which come within these areas. No popular/commercial fiction/non-fiction.

Royalties paid twice-yearly.

Putnam Aeronautical Books
See **Brassey's (UK) Ltd**

Quadrille Publishing Ltd
Alhambra House, 27–31 Charing Cross Road, London WC2H 0LS
☎0171 839 7117   Fax 0171 839 7118
Chairman *Sue Thomson*
Managing Director *Alison Cathie*
Publishing Director *Anne Furniss*

FOUNDED in 1994 by four ex-directors of Conran Octopus, with a view to producing a small list of top-quality illustrated books. *Publishes* non-fiction, including cookery, gardening, interior design and decoration, craft, health. 15 titles in 1998. TITLES *Your Place or Mine?* Jean-Christophe Novelli; *Flower Power* Stephen Woodhams; *The Food Bible* Judith Wills; *Titania's Oraqle; House Sensation* Anne McKevitt; *Furniture Facelifts* Liz Wagstaff. No unsolicited mss; synopses and ideas for books welcome. No fiction or children's books.

Royalties paid twice-yearly.

Quantum
See **W. Foulsham & Co.**

Quartet Books
27 Goodge Street, London W1P 2LD
☎0171 636 3992   Fax 0171 637 1866
Chairman *Naim Attallah*
Managing Director *Jeremy Beale*

Publishing Director *Stella Kane*
Approx. Annual Turnover £1 million

FOUNDED 1972. Independent publisher. *Publishes* contemporary literary fiction including translations, popular culture, biography, music, history, politics and some photographic books. Unsolicited mss with return postage welcome; no poetry, romance or science fiction.

Royalties paid twice-yearly.

Queen Anne Press
See **Lennard Associates Ltd**

Quiller Press
46 Lillie Road, London SW6 1TN
☎0171 499 6529   Fax 0171 381 8941
Managing/Editorial Director
  Jeremy Greenwood

Specialises in sponsored books and publications sold through non-book trade channels as well as bookshops. *Publishes* architecture, biography, business and industry, children's, collecting, cookery, DIY, gardening, guidebooks, humour, reference, sports, travel, wine and spirits. About 10 titles a year. TITLES *Running Racing – the Jockey Club Years* John Tyrrel; *Understanding Lloyds* Iain Simpson; *French Entrée Guides* Patricia Fenn; *Eton & Harrow at Lord's* Robert Titchener-Barrett. Most ideas originate in-house – unsolicited mss not welcome unless the author sees some potential for sponsorship or guaranteed sales.

Royalties paid twice-yearly.

Quiz Quest
See **Funfax Limited**

Radcliffe Medical Press Ltd
18 Marcham Road, Abingdon, Oxon OX14 1AA
☎01235 528820   Fax 01235 528830
Email: medical@radpress.win-uk.net
Managing Director *Andrew Bax*
Editorial Director *Gillian Nineham*
Editorial Manager *Jamie Etherington*
Approx. Annual Turnover £1.5 million

FOUNDED 1987. Medical publishers which began by specialising in books for general practice and health service management. *Publishes* clinical, management, health policy books, training materials and CD-ROMs. 80 titles in 1998. Unsolicited mss, synopses and ideas welcome. No non-medical or medical books aimed at lay audience.

Royalties paid twice-yearly.

The Ramsay Head Press

15 Gloucester Place, Edinburgh EH3 6EE
☎0131 225 5646   Fax 0131 225 5646
Managing Directors *Conrad Wilson,*
Mrs Christine Wilson

FOUNDED 1968 by Norman Wilson OBE. A small independent family publisher. *Publishes* biography, cookery, Scottish fiction and non-fiction, plus the bi-annual literary magazine *Books in Scotland*. About 3–4 titles a year. TITLES *Medusa Dozen* Tessa Ransford; *The Happy Land* Howard Denton & Jim C. Wilson. Synopses and ideas for books of Scottish interest welcome.
Royalties paid twice-yearly.

Random House UK Ltd

Random House, 20 Vauxhall Bridge Road, London SW1V 2SA
☎0171 840 8400   Fax 0171 233 6058
Email: enquiries@randomhouse.co.uk
Website:www.randomhouse.co.uk
Chief Executive *Gail Rebuck*
Executive Chairman *Simon Master*

Random's increasing focus on trade publishing, both here and in the US, has been well rewarded, with sales continuing to grow over the last year. Random House UK Ltd is the parent company of three separate publishing divisions following the Group's reorganisation under Gail Rebuck. These are: General Books, the Group's largest publishing division; Children's Books, and Ebury Press Special Books. General Books is subdivided into two operating groups, allowing hardcover editors to see their books through to publication in paperback. The literary imprints Jonathan Cape, Secker & Warburg and Chatto & Windus work side by side with paperback imprints Vintage and Pimlico to form one group; trade imprints Century, William Heinemann and Hutchinson go hand-in-hand with Arrow to form the other group.

IMPRINTS
Jonathan Cape Ltd ☎0171 840 8576 Fax 0171 233 6117 Publishing Director *Dan Franklin* Biography and memoirs, current affairs, fiction, history, photography, poetry, politics and travel. IMPRINT **Yellow Jersey**
    Secker & Warburg ☎0171 840 8649 Fax 0171 233 6117 Editorial Director *Geoff Mulligan* Principally literary fiction with some non-fiction.
    Chatto & Windus Ltd ☎0171 840 8522 Fax 0171 233 6117 Publishing Director *Alison Samuel* Art, belles-lettres, biography and memoirs, current affairs, essays, fiction, history, poetry, politics, philosophy, translations and travel.

Century (including **Business Books**) ☎0171 840 8555 Fax 0171 233 6127 Publisher *Kate Parkin*, Publishing Director Non-fiction *Mark Booth* General fiction and non-fiction, plus business management, advertising, communication, marketing, selling, investment and financial titles.
    William Heinemann ☎0171 840 8400 Fax 0171 233 6127 Publishing Director Fiction *Lynne Drew*, Publishing Director Non-fiction *Ravi Mirchandani* General non-fiction and fiction, especially history, biography, science, crime, thrillers and women's fiction.
    Hutchinson ☎0171 840 8564 Fax 0171 233 7870 Publishing Director *Sue Freestone* General fiction and non-fiction including notably belles-lettres, current affairs, politics, travel and history.
    Arrow ☎0171 840 8516 Fax 0171 233 6127 Publishing Director *Andy McKillop* Mass-market paperback fiction and non-fiction.
    Pimlico ☎0171 840 8630 Fax 0171 233 6117 Publishing Director *Will Sulkin* Large-format quality paperbacks in the fields of history, biography, popular culture and literature.
    Vintage ☎0171 840 8531 Fax 0171 233 6127 Publisher *Caroline Michel* Quality paperback fiction and non-fiction. Vintage was founded in 1990 and has been described as one of the 'greatest literary success stories in recent British publishing'.
    Children's Books ☎0171 840 8400 Fax 0171 233 6058 Managing Director *Debbie Sandford* IMPRINTS **Hutchinson** Publishing Director *Caroline Roberts*; **Jonathan Cape** Publishing Director *Tom Maschler*; **Bodley Head** Publishing Director *Anne McNeil*; **Red Fox** and **Tellastory** Publishing Director *Pilar Jenkins*; **Julia MacRae** Publishing Director *Delia Huddy* Picture books, fiction, non-fiction, novelties and audio cassette (see entry under **Audio Books**).
    Ebury Press Special Books ☎0171 840 8400 Fax 0171 840 8406 Managing Director *Amelia Thorpe*, Publisher *Fiona MacIntyre*, Associate Publisher *Julian Shuckburgh* IMPRINTS **Ebury Press**; **Vermilion**; **Rider**; **Barrie & Jenkins**; **Condé Nast Books**; **Fodor's**. Art, antiques, biography, Buddhism, cookery, gardening, health and beauty, homes and interiors, personal development, spirituality, travel and guides, sport, TV tie-ins. About 150 titles a year. Unsolicited mss, synopses and ideas for books welcome.
Royalties paid twice-yearly for the most part.

Authors' Rating With Random House and Transworld in its portfolio, not to mention Book Club Associates, Germany-based owner

Bertelsmann is a leading force in British and American publishing and on the evidence of recent figures, a highly successful one. Random is seldom out of the bestseller list. On the other hand, proper attention is given to new writers who occupy nearly a third of the fiction frontlist. Newcomers who do not contact a specific editor have their synopses and manuscripts passed on to freelance readers. There is no harm in this – it may even be advantageous – but some correspondents have expressed surprise that this happens.

Ransom Publishing Ltd

Ransom House, 2 High Street, Watlington, Oxfordshire OX9 5PS
☎01491 613711   Fax 01491 613733
Email: ransom@ransompublishing.co.uk
Website:www.ransom.co.uk

Managing Director *Jenny Ertle*

FOUNDED 1995 by ex-McGraw-Hill publisher. Partnerships formed with, among others, Channel 4 and the ICL. *Publishes* educational and consumer multimedia and study packs. Over 20 CD-ROMs, most with educational support packs, and 5 study packs in 1998. TITLES *MIA – The Search for Grandma's Remedy; Whale of a Tale* series, including *Maths, Science, Language and Geography; The History of Life; Castle Under Siege; Brainpower, The Test Book Series; How We Live.* No unsolicited mss. Synopses and ideas for books, as well as multimedia/Internet projects, welcome. Special areas of interest: science, geography, maths, general reference, natural history, education and history.
Royalties paid twice yearly.

Reader's Digest Association Ltd

11 Westferry Circus, Canary Wharf, London E14 4HE
☎0171 715 8000   Fax 0171 715 8181
Website:www.readersdigest.co.uk

Managing Director *Andrew Lynam-Smith*
Editorial Head *Cortina Butler*
Approx. Annual Turnover £170 million

Publishes gardening, natural history, cookery, history, DIY, travel and word books. About 20 titles a year. TITLES *Family Encyclopedia of World History; Know Your Rights; Treasures in Your Home; Foods That Harm, Foods That Heal; Country Walks and Scenic Drives.*

Reaktion BooksLtd

77–79 Farringdon Road, London EC1M 3JY
☎0171 404 9930   Fax 0171 404 9931
Email: reaktionbooks@compuserve.com

Managing Director *Michael R. Leaman*

FOUNDED in Edinburgh in 1985 and moved to its London location in 1988. *Publishes* art history, architecture, Asian studies, cultural studies, design, history, photography and travel. About 20 titles a year. TITLES *Robinson in Space* Patrick Keiller; *Liquid City* Marc Atkins and Iain Sinclair; *The Spoken Image: Photography and Language* Clive Scott; *Tel Aviv: From Dream to City* Joachim Schlör. No unsolicited mss; synopses and ideas welcome.
Royalties paid twice-yearly.

Reardon Publishing

56 Upper Norwood Street, Leckhampton, Cheltenham, Gloucestershire GL53 0DU
☎01242 231800
Website:www.reardon.co.uk

Managing Editor *Nicholas Reardon*

FOUNDED in the mid 1970s. Family-run publishing house specialising in local interest and tourism in the Cotswold area. Member of the **Outdoor Writers Guild**. *Publishes* walking and driving guides, and family history for societies. 10 titles a year. TITLES *The Cotswold Way* (video); *The Cotswold Way Map; Cotswold Walkabout; Cotswold Driveabout; The Donnington Way; The Haunted Cotswolds.* Unsolicited mss, synopses and ideas welcome with return postage only.
Royalties paid twice-yearly.

Rebel Inc.

See **Canongate Books Ltd**

Recollections

See **George Mann Books**

Red Fox

See **Random House UK Ltd**

William Reed Directories

Broadfield Park, Crawley, West Sussex RH11 9RT
☎01293 613400   Fax 01293 610322
Email: directories@william-reed.co.uk
Website:www.foodanddrink.co.uk

Editorial Manager *Ian Tandy*

William Reed Directories, a division of William Reed Publishing, was ESTABLISHED in 1990. Its portfolio includes 13 titles covering the food, drink, non-food, catering, retail and export industries. The titles are produced as directories, market research reports, exhibition catalogues and electronic publishing.

Reed Educational & Professional Publishing

Halley Court, Jordan Hill, Oxford OX2 8EJ
☎01865 311366   Fax 01865 314641
Website:www.repp.co.uk

Chief Executive *John Philbin*

Incorporating Heinemann Educational, Ginn and Butterworth-Heinemann in the UK; Greenwood Heinemann and Rigby in the USA; Rigby Heinemann in Australia.

Heinemann Educational Fax 01865 314140 Managing Director *Bob Osborne*, Primary *Paul Shuter*, Secondary *Kay Symons*. Textbooks/ literature/other educational resources for primary and secondary school and further education. Mss, synopses and ideas welcome.

Ginn & Co Fax 01865 314189 Managing Director *Paul Shuter*, Editorial Director *Jill Duffy*. Textbook/other educational resources for primary and secondary schools.

Butterworth-Heinemann International Linacre House, Jordan Hill, Oxford OX2 8EJ ☎01865 310366 Fax 01865 310898 Managing Director *Philip Shaw*, Engineering & Technology *Neil Warnock-Smith*, Business *Kathryn Grant*, Medical *Geoff Smaldon*. Books and electronic products across business, technical, medical and open-learning fields for students and professionals.

Royalties paid twice-yearly/annually, according to contract in all divisions.

Regency House Publishing Limited

3 Mill Lane, Broxbourne, Hertfordshire EN10 7AZ
☎01992 479988   Fax 01992 479966

Chairman *Brian Trodd*
Managing Director *Nicolette Trodd*
Approx. Annual Turnover £1.3 million

FOUNDED 1991. Publisher and packager of mass-market non-fiction. 20 titles in 1998. No unsolicited mss; synopses and ideas for books welcome. No fiction.

Royalties paid twice-yearly.

Reinhardt Books Ltd

Flat 2, 43 Onslow Square, London SW7 3LR
☎0171 589 3751

Chairman/Managing Director *Max Reinhardt*
Director *Joan Reinhardt*

FOUNDED 1887 as H. F. L. (Publishers), it was acquired by Max Reinhardt in 1947, changing its name in 1987. First publication under the new name was Graham Greene's *The Captain and the Enemy*. Also publishes under the **Nonesuch**

Press imprint. AUTHORS Mitsumasa Anno, Alistair Cooke and Maurice Sendak. New books are no longer considered.

Royalties paid according to contract.

Religious & Moral Educational Press (RMEP)

See **Hymns Ancient & Modern Ltd**

Review

See **Hodder Headline plc**

Richmond House Publishing Company

Douglas House, 3 Richmond Buildings, London W1V 5AE
☎0171 437 9556   Fax 0171 287 3463
Email: sales@rhpco.demon.co.uk

Managing Directors *Gloria Gordon, Spencer Block*

Publishes directories for the theatre and entertainment industries. Synopses and ideas welcome.

Rider

See **Random House UK Ltd**

Robinson Publishing Ltd

7 Kensington Church Court, London W8 4SP
☎0171 938 3830   Fax 0171 938 4214
Email: enquiries@robinsonpublishing.com

Publisher *Nicholas Robinson*
Publishing Director, Robinson *Jan Chamier*
Publishing Director, Magpie
   Nova Jane Heath

FOUNDED 1983. *Publishes* fiction: anthologies; general non-fiction includes, health and self-help, psychology, true crime, puzzles, military history. Children's: anthologies, humour, games. 65 titles in 1997. No unsolicited fiction. Do not send mss; letters/synopses only. No email submissions. IMPRINT **Magpie** Children's books.

Royalties paid twice-yearly.

Authors' Rating Authors tend to be regulars who can turn in acceptable manuscripts to tight deadlines.

Robson Books Ltd

10 Blenheim Court, Brewery Rod, London N7 9NT
☎0171 700 7444   Fax 0171 700 4552

Publisher *Jeremy Robson*
Editorial Head *Kate Mills*

FOUNDED 1973. *Publishes* general non-fiction, including biography, cookery, gardening, guidebooks, health and beauty, humour, travel, sports and games. About 70 titles a year. Unsolicited mss, synopses and ideas for books welcome (s.a.e. essential).

Royalties paid twice-yearly.

Round Hall
See **Sweet & Maxwell Ltd**

Roundhouse Publishing Group
Millstone, Limers Lane, Northam, North Devon EX39 2RG
☎01237 474474   Fax 01237 474774
Email: roundhse@compuserve.com
Editorial Head *Alan Goodworth*

ESTABLISHED 1991. *Publishes* cinema and media-related titles. TITLES *Cinema of Oliver Stone; Cinema of Stanley Kubrick; Shoot the Piano Player; Toms, Coons, Mulattoes, Mammies and Bucks*. Represents and distributes a broad range of non-fiction publishing houses throughout the UK and Europe. No unsolicited mss.

Royalties paid twice-yearly.

Routledge
11 New Fetter Lane, London EC4P 4EE
☎0171 583 9855   Fax 0171 842 2298
Website:www.routledge.com
Managing Director *Roger Horton*
Publishers *Claire L'Enfant, Alan Jarvis, Anna Hodson, Edwina Welham, Phillip Read*
Approx. Annual Turnover (Group) £35.5 million

Routledge was formed in 1987 through an amalgamation of Routledge & Kegan Paul, Methuen & Co., Tavistock Publications, and Croom Helm. Subsequent acquisitions include the Unwin Hyman academic list from **Harper-Collins** (1991), *Who's Who* and historical atlases from **Dent/Orion** (1994), archaeology and ancient history titles from **Batsford** (1996), and the E & FN Spon imprint from ITP Science (1997). In 1998, Routledge became a subsidiary of **Taylor & Francis Group plc** (see entry). *Publishes* academic and professional books and journals in the social sciences, humanities, health sciences and the built environment for the international market. Subjects: addiction, anthropology, archaeology, architecture, Asian studies, biblical studies, the built environment, business and management, civil engineering, classics, heritage, construction, counselling, criminology, development and environment, dictionaries, economics, education, environmental engineering, geography, health, history, Japanese studies, journals, language, leisure studies and leisure management, linguistics, literary criticism, media

and culture, Middle East, nursing, philosophy, politics, political economy, psychiatry, psychology, reference, social administration, social studies and sociology, therapy, theatre and performance studies, women's studies. No poetry, fiction, travel or astrology. About 900 titles a year. Send synopses with sample chapter and c.v. rather than complete mss.

Royalties paid annually and twice-yearly, according to contract.

Ryland Peters and Small Limited
Cavendish House, 51–55 Mortimer Street, London W1N 7TD
☎0171 436 9090   Fax 0171 436 9790
Email: info@rps.co.uk
Managing Director *David Peters*
Publisher *Ane Ryland*

FOUNDED 1996. *Publishes* highly illustrated lifestyle books – gardening, cookery, interior design. No fiction. No unsolicited mss; synopses and ideas welcome.

Royalties paid twice-yearly.

Sage Publications
6 Bonhill Street, London EC2A 4PU
☎0171 374 0645   Fax 0171 374 8741
Website:www.sagepub.co.uk
Managing Director *Stephen Barr*
Editorial Director *Ziyad Marar*

FOUNDED 1971. *Publishes* academic books and journals in humanities and the social sciences. Bought academic and professional books publisher Paul Chapman Publishing Ltd in April 1998.

Royalties paid twice-yearly.

Saint Andrew Press
Board of Communication, Church of Scotland, 121 George Street, Edinburgh EH2 4YN
☎0131 225 5722   Fax 0131 220 3113
Email: cofs.standrew@dial.pipex.com
Website:www.churchnet.org.uk
Publishing Manager *Lesley Ann Taylor*
Approx. Annual Turnover £225,000

FOUNDED in 1954 to publish and promote the 17-volume series *The Daily Study Bible New Testament* by Professor William Barclay. Owned by the Church of Scotland Board of Communication. *Publishes* religious, Scottish local interest and some children's books. No fiction. 17 titles in 1998. No unsolicited mss; synopses and ideas preferred.

Royalties paid annually.

St Paul's Bibliographies
1 Step Terrace, Winchester, Hampshire
SO22 5BW
☎01962 860524
Email: stpauls@stpaulsbib.com
Publishing Director *Robert Cross*
Approx. Annual Turnover £40,000
FOUNDED 1982. *Publishes* bibliographical reference books and works on the history of the book. 2–3 titles a year. TITLES *The Stationers' Company and The Book Trade* ed. Robin Myers and Michael Harris; *The Book Encompassed* ed. Peter Davison; *George Orwell: A Bibliography*. Unsolicited mss, synopses and ideas welcome if relevant to subjects covered. Agent for Oak Knoll Press books.
Royalties paid twice-yearly.

St Pauls Publishers
Morpeth Terrace, London SW1P 1EP
☎0171 828 5582   Fax 0171 828 3329
Email: editions@stpauls.org.uk
Managing Director *Karamvelil Sebastian*
Publishing division of the Society of St Paul. Began publishing in 1914 but activities were fairly limited until around 1948. *Publishes* religious material only: theology, scripture, catechetics, prayer books, children's material and biography. Unsolicited mss, synopses and ideas welcome. About 50 titles a year.

Salamander Books Ltd
8 Blenheim Court, Brewery Road, London N7 9NT
☎0171 700 7799   Fax 0171 700 3572
Managing Director *David Spence*
Editorial Director *Charlotte Davies*
FOUNDED 1973. Part of the Chrysalis Group. *Publishes* colour illustrated books, mainly on collecting, cookery, interiors, gardening, music, crafts, military, aviation, pet care, sport and transport. About 30 titles a year. No unsolicited mss but synopses and ideas for the above subjects welcome.
Royalties outright fee paid instead of royalties.

Sangam Books Ltd
57 London Fruit Exchange, Brushfield Street, London E1 6EP
☎0171 377 6399   Fax 0171 375 1230
Executive Director *Anthony de Souza*
Traditionally an educational publisher of school and college level textbooks. Also *publishes* art, India, medicine, science, technology, social sciences, religion, plus some fiction in paperback.

W. B. Saunders & Co. Ltd/ Saunders Scientific Publications
See **Harcourt Brace and Company Ltd**

SB Publications
c/o 19 Grove Road, Seaford, East Sussex BN25 1TP
☎01323 893498   Fax 01323 893860
Managing Director *Steve Benz*
FOUNDED 1987. *Specialises* in local history, including themes illustrated by old picture postcards and photographs; also travel, guides (town, walking), maritime history and railways. 25 titles a year. IMPRINTS **Historic Military Press** *Benn Gunn*; **Brampton Publications** *Steve Benz* TITLES *Lewes Then and Now; Curiosities of East Sussex; A Dorset Quiz Book*. Also provides marketing and distribution services for local authors.
Royalties paid annually.

Sceptre
See **Hodder Headline plc**

Scholastic Ltd
Villiers House, Clarendon Avenue, Leamington Spa, Warwickshire CV32 5PR
☎01926 887799   Fax 01926 883331
Website:www.scholastic.co.uk
Chairman *M. R. Robinson*
Managing Director *David Kewley*
Approx. Annual Turnover £52 million
FOUNDED 1964. Owned by US parent company. *Publishes* children's fiction and non-fiction and education for primary schools.

DIVISIONS
Scholastic Children's Books *David Fickling* Commonwealth House, 1–19 New Oxford Street, London WC1A 1NU ☎0171 421 9000 Fax 0171 421 9001 IMPRINTS **Scholastic Press** (hardbacks); **Adlib** (12+ fiction); **Hippo** (paperbacks); **Point** (paperbacks) TITLES *Postman Pat; Rosie & Jim; Tots TV; Horrible Histories; Goosebumps; Point Horror*.
  Educational Publishing *Anne Peel* (Villiers House address) Professional books and classroom materials for primary teachers, plus magazines such as *Child Education, Junior Education, Art & Craft, Junior Focus, Infant Projects, Nursery Projects*.
  Red House Book Clubs *David Teale, Victoria Birkett* Cotswold Business Park, Witney, Oxford OX8 5YT ☎01993 774171/771144 Fax 01993 776813 The Book Club group sells to families at home through The Red House Book Club and Book Parties, through Red House School Book Clubs (four different clubs catering

for children from 4–15), and through the Red House International Schools Club.

School Book Fairs *Will Oldham* The Book Fair Division sells directly to children, parents and teachers in schools through 27,000 week-long book events held in schools throughout the UK.

Royalties paid twice-yearly.

Authors' Rating Came out top in a recent Society of Authors survey of author-friendly publishers.

SCM Press Ltd

9–17 St Albans Place, London N1 0NX
☎0171 359 8033   Fax 0171 359 0049
Website:www.taynet.co.uk/users/scp

Managing Director *Rev. Dr John Bowden*
Approx. Annual Turnover £1 million

Publishes religion and theology from an open perspective, with some ethics and philosophy. About 40 titles a year. Relevant unsolicited mss and synopses considered if sent with s.a.e.

Royalties paid annually.

Authors' Rating Leading publisher of religious ideas with well-deserved reputation for fresh thinking. At SCM, 'questioning theology is the norm'.

Scottish Academic Press

22 Hanover Street, Edinburgh EH2 2EP
☎0131 220 6061   Fax 0131 225 3991

Editor *Dr Douglas Grant*

FOUNDED 1969. *Publishes* academic: architecture, biography, education, Gaelic, geology, history, law, literature, philosophy, poetry, social sciences, theology.

Royalties paid annually.

Scribner

See **Simon & Schuster**

Seafarer Books

See **The Merlin Press Ltd**

Search Press Ltd/Burns & Oates

Wellwood, North Farm Road, Tunbridge Wells, Kent TN2 3DR
☎01892 510850   Fax 01892 515903
Email: searchpress@searchpress.com

Managing Director *Martin de la Bédoyère*

FOUNDED 1847. *Publishes* (Search Press) full-colour art, craft, needlecrafts; (Burns & Oates) theology, history, spirituality, reference.

DIVISIONS **Academic** *Paul Burns* TITLES include *Butler's Lives of the Saints*, new full edition, 12 volumes. **Craft** *Rosalind Dace* Books

on papermaking and papercrafts, painting on silk, art techniques and embroidery.

Royalties paid annually.

Secker & Warburg

See **Random House UK Ltd**

Sensation

See **Harlequin Mills & Boon Ltd**

Seren

First Floor, 2 Wyndham Street, Bridgend CF31 1EF
☎01656 663018   Fax 01656 649226

Chairman *Cary Archard*
Managing Director *Mick Feltin*
Approx. Annual Turnover £100,000

FOUNDED 1981 as a specialist poetry publisher but has now moved into general literary publishing with an emphasis on Wales. *Publishes* poetry, fiction, literary criticism, drama, biography, art, history and translations of fiction. 25 titles in 1998. DIVISIONS **Poetry** *Amy Wack* AUTHORS Robert Minhinnick, Tony Curtis, Sheenagh Pugh, Duncan Bush, Deryn Rees-Jones. **Drama** *Brian Mitchell* AUTHORS Edward Thomas, Charles Way, Lucinda Coxon. **Fiction**, **Art**, **Literary Criticism**, **History**, **Translations** *Mick Felton* AUTHORS Christopher Meredith, Leslie Norris, Gwyn Thomas.

IMPRINT **Border Lines Biographies** TITLES *Bruce Chatwin; Dennis Potter; Mary Webb; Wilfred Owen; Raymond Williams.* Unsolicited mss, synopses and ideas for books welcome.

Royalties paid twice yearly.

Serpent's Tail

4 Blackstock Mews, London N4 2BT
☎0171 354 1949   Fax 0171 704 6467
Email: info@serpentstail.com
Website:www.serpentstail.com

Contact *Laurence O'Toole*
Approx. Annual Turnover £650,000

FOUNDED 1986. Won the *Sunday Times* Small Publisher of the Year Award (1989) and the Ralph Lewis Award for new fiction (1992). Serpent's Tail has introduced to British audiences a number of major internationally known writers. Noted for its strong emphasis on design and an eye for the unusual. *Publishes* contemporary fiction, contemporary gay fiction and non-fiction, including works in translation, crime, popular culture and biography. No poetry, romance or fantasy. About 40 titles a year.

IMPRINTS **Serpent's Tail** TITLES *Hero of the Underworld* Jimmy Boyle; *Whatever* Michel

Houellebecq; *Altered State* Matthew Collin. **Five Star** TITLES *Acid Casuals* Nicholas Blincoe; *Always Outnumbered, Always Outgunned* Walter Mosley; *Bombay Talkie* Ameena Meer. Send preliminary letter outlining proposal with a sample chapter. No unsolicited mss. Prospective authors unfamiliar with Serpent's Tail are advised to study the list before submitting anything.
Royalties normally paid annually.

Authors' Rating Take note of the name! Any writer who thinks of this as just another publisher is liable to get stung. Serpent's Tail is dedicated to the literary outsider which means that there is a premium on originality and bold thinking. If anywhere in publishing, the future is here.

Settle Press
10 Boyne Terrace Mews, London W11 3LR
☎0171 243 0695
Chairman/Managing Director *D. Settle*
FOUNDED 1981. *Publishes* guide books. About 10 titles a year. **Travel/Tourist Guides** TITLES *City Breaks Series* (Paris, Rome, Vienna, etc); *Key To Series* (Far East, Indian Ocean, Africa, Florida, etc). Unsolicited synopses accepted but no mss.
Royalties paid by arrangement.

Severn House Publishers
9–15 High Street, Sutton, Surrey SM1 1DF
☎0181 770 3930   Fax 0181 770 3850
Email: info@severnhouse.com
Website:www.severnhouse.com
Chairman *Edwin Buckhalter*
Editorial *Sara Short*
FOUNDED 1974. A leader in library fiction publishing. *Publishes* hardback fiction: romance science fiction, horror, fantasy, crime. About 140 titles a year. No unsolicited material. Synopses/proposals preferred through *bona fide* literary agents only.
Royalties paid twice-yearly. *Overseas associates* Severn House Publishers Inc., New York.

Sheffield Academic Press
Mansion House, 19 Kingfield Road, Sheffield S11 9AS
☎0114 2554433   Fax 0114 2554626
Managing Director *Mrs Jean R.K. Allen*
Approx. Annual Turnover £1.5 million
FOUNDED in 1976 as JSOT Press. Now the leading academic publisher of biblical titles. Recently expanded its list to include archaeology, literary studies, history and culture, languages, scientific, professional, reference. 112 titles in 1998. Unsolicited mss, synopses and ideas welcome. No

fiction. IMPRINTS **Sheffield Academic Press** *Jean Allen*; **Subis**.
Royalties paid annually

Sheldon Press
See **Society for Promoting Christian Knowledge**

Shepheard-Walwyn (Publishers) Ltd
Suite 34, 26 Charing Cross Road, London WC2H 0DH
☎0171 240 5992   Fax 0171 379 5770
Email: shepwalwyn@btinternet.com
Website:
www.craft-fair.co.uk/shepheardwalwyn/
Managing Director *Anthony Werner*
Approx. Annual Turnover £150,000
FOUNDED 1972. 'We regard books as food for the mind and want to offer a wholesome diet of original ideas and fresh approaches to old subjects.' *Publishes* general non-fiction in three main areas: Scottish interest; gift books in calligraphy and/or illustrated; history, political economy, philosophy. About 5 titles a year. Synopses and ideas for books welcome.
Royalties paid twice-yearly.

The Shetland Times Ltd
Prince Alfred Street, Lerwick, Shetland ZE1 0EP
☎01595 693622   Fax 01595 694637
Managing Director *Robert Wishart*
Publications Manager *Charlotte Black*
FOUNDED 1872 as publishers of the local newspaper. Book publishing followed thereafter plus publication of monthly magazine, *Shetland Life*. *Publishes* anything with Shetland connections – local and natural history, music, crafts, maritime. 12 titles in 1998. Prefers material with a Shetland theme/connection.
Royalties paid annually.

Shire Publications Ltd
Cromwell House, Church Street, Princes Risborough, Buckinghamshire HP27 9AA
☎01844 344301   Fax 01844 347080
Website:www.shirebooks.co.uk
Managing Director *John Rotheroe*
FOUNDED 1967. *Publishes* original non-fiction paperbacks. About 25 titles a year. No unsolicited material; send introductory letter with detailed outline of idea.
Royalties paid annually.

Authors' Rating You don't have to live in the country to write books for Shire but it helps.

With titles like *Church Fonts, Haunted Inns* and *Discovering Preserved Railways* there is a distinct rural feel to the list. Another way of putting it, to quote John Rotheroe, Shire specialises in 'small books on all manner of obscure subjects'.

Sidgwick & Jackson
See **Macmillan Publishers Ltd**

Sigma Press
1 South Oak Lane, Wilmslow, Cheshire SK9 6AR
☎01625 531035   Fax 01625 536800
Email: sigma.press@zetnet.co.uk
Website:www.sigmapress.co.uk

Chairman/Managing Director *Graham Beech*

FOUNDED in 1980 as a publisher of technical books. Sigma Press now publishes mainly in the leisure area. *Publishes* outdoor, local heritage, myths and legends, sports, dance and exercise. Recently launched a popular science series. Approx. 45 titles in 1998. No unsolicited mss; synopses and ideas welcome.

DIVISIONS **Sigma Leisure** TITLES *The Celtic Way; Country and Western Line Dancing for Cowgirls and Cowboys; Cone on Cymru – Football in Wales*; **Sigma Press** TITLES *Scrooge's Crypic Carol; Alice in Quantumland.*

Royalties paid twice-yearly.

Signature
See **Hodder Headline plc**

Silhouette Desire
See **Harlequin Mills & Boon Ltd**

Simon & Schuster
Africa House, 64–78 Kingsway, London WC2B 6AH
☎0171 316 1900   Fax 0171 402 0639

Managing Director *Nick Webb*
Editorial Directors *Clare Ledingham, Martin Fletcher, Helen Gummer*

FOUNDED 1986. Offshoot of the leading American publisher. *Publishes* general fiction, including science fiction under its **Earthlight** imprint (Editor *John Jarrold*) and non-fiction in hardback and paperback. Literary fiction and non-fiction is published in trade paperback under the **Scribner** imprint. No academic or technical material.

Royalties paid twice-yearly.

Authors' Rating Following the sale of its US education divisions to Pearson, S&S is free to concentrate on its list of consumer books which grows apace. After the successful Pocket Books

paperback list came the launch of a children's list and a science fiction and fantasy list. Scribner, a new upmarket paperback imprint with the famous US name has just been launched. Hopefully, much of the output will be home-nurtured as opposed to tarted up American imports.

Skoob Books Ltd
11A–15 Sicilian Avenue, Southampton Row, London WC1A 2QH
☎0171 404 3063   Fax 0171 404 4398
Editorial office: 76A Oldfield Road, London N16 0RS   ☎/Fax 0171 275 9811

Managing Director *I. K. Ong*
Editorial *M. Lovell*

Publishes literary guides, cultural studies, esoterica/occult, poetry, new writing from the Orient. No unsolicited mss, synopses or ideas. TITLES *Where We Are* Lucien Stryk; *Skoob Directory of Secondhand Bookshops*; *The Necronomicon* George Hay; *Haunting the Tiger* K. S. Maniam.

Smith Gryphon Ltd
See **Blake Publishing**

Colin Smythe Ltd
PO Box 6, Gerrards Cross, Buckinghamshire SL9 8XA
☎01753 886000   Fax 01753 886469

Managing Director *Colin Smythe*
Approx. Annual Turnover £1.5 million

FOUNDED 1966. *Publishes* Anglo-Irish literature, drama, and criticism, history. About 15 titles a year. No unsolicited mss. Also acts as literary agent for a small list of authors.

Royalties paid annually/twice-yearly.

Society for Promoting Christian Knowledge (SPCK)
Holy Trinity Church, Marylebone Road, London NW1 4DU
☎0171 387 5282   Fax 0171 388 2352

Director of Publishing *Simon Kingston*

FOUNDED 1698, SPCK is the third oldest publisher in the country.

IMPRINTS **SPCK** Editorial Director *Joanna Moriaty* Theology, academic, liturgy, prayer, spirituality, Biblical studies, educational resources, mission, pastoral care, gospel and culture, worldwide. **Sheldon Press** Editorial Director *Joanna Moriarty* Popular medicine, health, self-help, psychology. **Triangle** Editor *Alison Barr* Popular Christian paperbacks. **Lynx** Editor *Robin Keeley* Parish resources, training

and youthwork, textbooks. **Azure** Senior Editor *Alison Barr* General spirituality.
Royalties paid annually.

Authors' Rating Religion with a strong social edge.

Solway
See **Paternoster Publishing**

Souvenir Press Ltd
43 Great Russell Street, London WC1B 3PA
☎0171 580 9307/8 & 637 5711/2/3
Fax 0171 580 5064

Chairman/Managing Director *Ernest Hecht*
Senior Editor *Tessa Harrow*

Independent publishing house. FOUNDED 1951. *Publishes* academic and scholarly, animal care and breeding, antiques and collecting, archaeology, autobiography and biography, business and industry, children's, cookery, crafts and hobbies, crime, educational, fiction, gardening, health and beauty, history and antiquarian, humour, illustrated and fine editions, magic and the occult, medical, military, music, natural history, philosophy, poetry, psychology, religious, sociology, sports, theatre and women's studies. About 55 titles a year. Souvenir's Human Horizons series for the disabled and their carers is one of the most preeminent in its field and recently celebrated 19 years of publishing for the disabled.
IMPRINTS/SERIES **Condor**; **Human Horizons**; **Independent Voices**; **Pictorial Presentations**; **Pop Universal**. TITLES *The Last Barbarians: The Discovery of the Source of the Mekong in Tibet* Michel Peissel; *Yesterdays – The Way We Were, 1919–1939* Eric Midwinter; *Draw Your Own Cartoons with Rolf Harris*; *The Complete Book of Vampires* Leonard R. N. Ashley; *Parkinson's Disease – A Self-Help Guide for Patients and their Families* Marjan Jahanshahi and C. David Marsden; *The Turin Shroud is Genuine* Rodney Hoare; *Politically Incorrect Jokes From the Net* Phillip Adams and Patrice Newell. Unsolicited mss considered but initial letter of enquiry preferred.
Royalties paid twice-yearly.

Authors' Rating If you have a quirky or outrageous idea Souvenir might just go for it.

SPCK
See **Society for Promoting Christian Knowledge**

Neville Spearman
See **The C. W. Daniel Co. Ltd**

Special Edition
See **Harlequin Mills & Boon Ltd**

Spellmount Ltd
The Old Rectory, Staplehurst, Kent
TN12 0AZ
☎01580 893730   Fax 01580 893731
Email: enquiries@spellmount.demon.co.uk

Managing Director *Jamie Wilson*
Approx. Annual Turnover £450,000

FOUNDED 1983. *Publishes* non-fiction in hardcover; primarily history and military history. About 30 titles a year. Synopses/ideas for books in these specialist fields welcome, enclosing return postage.
Royalties paid six-monthly for two years, then annually.

E & FN Spon
See **Routledge**

Springer-Verlag London Limited
Sweetapple House, Catteshall Road,
Godalming, Surrey GU7 3DJ
☎01483 418800   Fax 01483 415144
Email: postmaster@svl.co.uk
Website:www.springer.co.uk

Managing Director *John Watson*
Editorial Director *Beverley Ford*
Approx. Annual Turnover £5 million

The UK subsidiary of **Springer-Verlag GmbH & Co KG** of Germany. *Publishes* science, technical and medical books and journals. About 120 titles a year, plus journals. Specialises in computing, engineering, medicine, mathematics, astronomy and food science. All UK published books are sold through Springer's German and US companies. Not interested in social sciences, fiction or school books but academic and professional science and amateur astronomy mss or synopses welcome.
Royalties paid annually.

Stainer & Bell Ltd
PO Box 110, 23 Gruneisen Road, London
N3 1DZ
☎0181 343 3303   Fax 0181 343 3024

Managing Directors *Carol Y. Wakefield,
Keith M. Wakefield*
Publishing Director *Nicholas Williams*
Approx. Annual Turnover £720,000

FOUNDED 1907 to publish sheet music. *Publishes* music and religious subjects related to hymnody. Unsolicited synopses/ideas for books welcome. Send letter enclosing brief précis.
Royalties paid annually.

Harold Starke Publishers Ltd

Pixey Green, Stradbroke, Near Eye, Suffolk
IP21 5NG
☎01379 388334   Fax 01379 388335
Directors *Harold K. Starke, Naomi Galinski*
Publishes adult non-fiction, medical and reference. No unsolicited mss.
Royalties paid annually.

The Stationery Office Ltd, National Publishing

St Crispins, Duke Street, Norwich, Norfolk
NR3 1PD
☎01603 622211 Fax 01603 694313 (Editorial)
Email: kim.yarwood@theso.co.uk
Website:www.national-publishing.co.uk
Chief Executive *Fred J. Perkins*
Approx. Annual Turnover £250 million
Formerly HMSO, which was FOUNDED 1786.
Became part of the private sector in October 1996. 11,000 new titles each year with 50,000 titles in print. Publisher of material sponsored by Parliament, government departments and other official bodies. Also commercial publishing in the following broad categories: business and professional, environment, transport, education, law and heritage. Unsolicited material may be considered if suitable; s.a.e. with synopsis/samples should be sent in the first instance to *Kim Yarwood*, Editorial Coordinator.

Authors' Rating Not the sexiest name for a publisher – the suggestion of heavy government reports gathering dust is hard to eradicate – but the privatised Stationery Office is working to change its image. Reference is the biggest area of expansion, the recently purchased *Whitaker's Almanac* providing a clutch of spinoffs. Popular illustrated history is also strong.

Patrick Stephens Ltd

See **Haynes Publishing**

Stevens

See **Sweet & Maxwell Ltd**

STL Ltd

See **Paternoster Publishing**

STM

See **Hodder Headline plc**

Straightline Publishing Ltd

29 Main Street, Bothwell, Glasgow G71 8RD
☎01698 853000   Fax 01698 854208
Email: pbellew@straightline.co.uk
Chairman *Frank Docherty*

Editors *B. Taylor, P. Bellew*
Approx. Annual Turnover £300,000
FOUNDED 1989. *Publishes* magazines and directories – trade and technical – books of local interest. 11 titles in 1998. TITLES *Cabletalk; Explosives Engineering*. No unsolicited material.
Royalties paid annually.

Subis

See **Sheffield Academic Press**

Summersdale Publishers

46 West Street, Chichester, West Sussex
PO19 1RP
☎01243 771107   Fax 01243 786300
Email: summersdale@summersdale.com
Directors *Stewart Ferris, Alastair Williams*
Editor *Elizabeth Kershaw*
Approx. Annual Turnover £1 million
FOUNDED 1990. *Publishes* non-fiction: humour, TV/film tie-ins, travel literature, self-help, biography, sport, true crime, gift books, cookery. TITLES *Don't Mention the War; The Romance Book; The Many Faces of Jack the Ripper; The Great British Festival Guide; Chat-up Lines and Put Downs; The Kama Sutra For One*. 50 titles in 1999. No unsolicited mss; synopses and ideas welcome.
Royalties paid.

Susquehanna University Press

See **Golden Cockerel Press**

Sutton Publishing Ltd

Phoenix Mill, Thrupp, Stroud,
Gloucestershire GL5 2BU
☎01453 731114   Fax 01453 731117
Managing Director *David Hogg*
Publishing Director *Peter Clifford*
Approx. Annual Turnover £4.7 million
FOUNDED 1978. Owned by Guiton Group. *Publishes* academic, archaeology, biography, countryside, history, military, regional interest, local history, pocket classics (lesser known novels by classic authors), transport. About 240 titles a year. Send synopsis rather than complete mss.
Royalties paid twice-yearly.

Authors' Rating Recent years have seen a move from local to national history with a balance between serious and popular titles – often on the same subjects. The Pocket Biographies and Pocket Histories point the way for would-be Sutton authors.

Swan Hill Press

See **Airlife Publishing Ltd**

Sweet & Maxwell Ltd

100 Avenue Road, London NW3 3PF
☎0171 393 7000   Fax 0171 393 7010
Email: <name>@smlawpub.co.uk
Website:www.smlawpub.co.uk
Managing Director *Mike Dixon*

FOUNDED 1799. Part of The Thomson Corporation. *Publishes* legal and professional materials in all media, looseleaf works, journals, law reports and on CD-ROM. About 150 book titles a year, with live backlist of over 700 titles, 75 looseleaf services and more than 80 legal periodicals. Not interested in material which is non-legal. The legal and professional list is varied and contains many academic titles, as well as treatises and reference works in the legal and related professional fields.

IMPRINTS **Sweet & Maxwell; Sweet & Maxwell Asia; Stevens; W. Green (Scotland)** General Manager *Martin Redfern*; **Round Hall/Sweet & Maxwell (Ireland)** General Manager *Eleanor McGarry*. Ideas welcome. Writers with legal/professional projects in mind are advised to contact the company at the earliest possible stage in order to lay the groundwork for best design, production and marketing of a project.
Royalties and fees vary according to contract.

Take That Ltd

PO Box 200, Harrogate, North Yorkshire HG1 2YR
☎01423 507545   Fax 01423 526035
Chairman/Managing Director *C. Brown*

FOUNDED 1986. Independent publisher of computing, finance and gambling titles (books and magazines). TITLES *Understand Financial Risk in a Day; Complete Beginner's Guide to the Internet; Successful Spread Betting.* About 10 titles a year. Unsolicited synopses for books welcome; 'no s.a.e., no reply'.
Royalties paid twice-yearly.

Tango Books

See **Sadie Fields Productions Ltd** under **UK Packagers**

I. B. Tauris & Co. Ltd

Victoria House, Bloomsbury Square, London WC1B 4DZ
☎0171 831 9060   Fax 0171 831 9061
Website:www.ibtauris.com
Chairman/Publisher *Iradj Bagherzade*
Managing Director *Jonathan McDonnell*

FOUNDED 1984. Independent publisher. *Publishes* general non-fiction and academic in the fields of international relations, current affairs, history, politics, cultural, media and film studies, Middle East studies. Joint projects with Cambridge University Centre for Middle Eastern Studies, Institute for Latin American Studies and Institute of Ismaili Studies.
Distributes The New Press (New York) outside North America. *Represents* **The Curzon Press** in the UK. IMPRINTS **Tauris Parke Books** Illustrated books on architecture, travel, design and culture. **British Academic Press** Academic monographs. Unsolicited synopses and book proposals welcome.
Royalties paid twice-yearly.

Tavistock Publications

See **Routledge**

Taylor & Francis Group plc

11 New Fetter Lane, London EC4P 4EE
☎0171 583 9855   Fax 0171 842 2298
Website:www.tandf.co.uk
Chairman *Robert Kiernan*
Managing Director *Anthony Selvey*
Approx. Annual Turnover £40.2 million

FOUNDED 1798 with the launch of *Philosophical Magazine* which has been in publication ever since (now a solid state physics journal). The company is privately owned with strong academic connections among the major shareholders. **Falmer Press** (see entry) joined the group in 1979 and it doubled its size in the late '80s with the acquisition of Crane Russak in 1986 and Hemisphere Publishing Co in 1988. In 1995, acquired Lawrence Erlbaum Associates Ltd and Brunner/Mazel in 1997, adding to the growing list of psychology publications. In 1996, UCL Press Ltd was acquired, adding further to its portfolio of publications in science and humanities. In 1997, Garland Publishing Inc. located in New York was acquired. The most recent addition to the Taylor & Francis Group is Routledge Publishing Holdings Ltd, including Carfax Publishing and E & FN Spon. *Publishes* scientific, technical, education titles at university, research and professional levels. About 1600 titles a year.Unsolicited mss, synopses and ideas welcome.
Royalties paid yearly. *Overseas office* Taylor & Francis Inc., Philadelphia, PA and New York.

Authors' Rating Having doubled its size in two years, Taylor & Francis has done it again with the acquisition of Routledge which itself had been growing by acquisition.

Teach Yourself
See **Hodder Headline plc**

Telegraph Books
1 Canada Square, Canary Wharf, London
E14 5DT
☎0171 538 6826   Fax 0171 538 6064
Owner *Telegraph Group Ltd*
Manager *Susannah Charlton*
Approx. Annual Turnover £1.5 million

Concentrates on Telegraph branded books in association/collaboration with other publishers. Also runs Telegraph Books Direct, a direct mail, phone-line bookselling service and off-the-page sales for other publishers' books. *Publishes* general non-fiction: journalism, business and law, cookery, education, gardening, wine, guides, sport, puzzles and games. 44 titles in 1998. Only interested in books if a Telegraph link exists. No unsolicited material.
Royalties paid twice-yearly.

Tellastory
See **Random House UK Ltd**

Temple House Books
See **The Book Guild Ltd**

Thames and Hudson Ltd
181A High Holbron, London WC1V 7QX
☎0171 845 5000   Fax 0171 845 5050
Managing Director *Thomas Neurath*
Editorial Head *Jamie Camplin*
Approx. Annual Turnover £20 million

Publishes art, archaeology, architecture and design, biography, fashion, garden and landscape design, graphics, history, illustrated and fine editions, mythology, music, photography, popular culture, travel and topography. 200 titles a year. SERIES *World of Art; New Horizons; Chic Simple; Celtic Design; World Design; Fashion Memoir; Most Beautiful Villages.* TITLES *The Body; The Book of Kells; Henri Cartier-Bresson; The Complete Pyramids; The Chronicle of Opera; David Hockney's Dog Days; Derek Jarman's Garden; The London Fashion Book; Modern Times, Modern Places; Sensation; The Shock of the New; Website Graphics.* Send preliminary letter and outline before mss.
Royalties paid twice-yearly.

Thomson Learning
Berkshire House, 168–173 High Holborn,
London WC1V 7AA
☎0171 497 1422   Fax 0171 497 1426
Email: info@itpuk.co.uk
Website:www.itpe.com *or* www.itbp.com

CEO (Worldwide) *Bob Christie*
**Managing Director (Europe/Middle East/
   Africa)** *Alan Nelson*
Editorial Head *Julian Thomas*

FOUNDED 1993. Formerly International Thomson Publishing; part of the Thomson Corporation and as such has offices worldwide with the UK office being reported to by Copenhagen (for Europe), Dubai (Middle East) and South Africa. *Publishes* education. 100 titles in 1998. IMPRINT **Business Press** TITLES *Management and Cost Accounting* Drury; *Strategy – Process, Content, Contact* DeWitt and Meyer. Unsolicited material aimed at students is welcome but telephone in the first instance to check out the idea.
Royalties vary according to contract.

Authors' Rating Having disposed of Van Nostrand Reinhold, E & FN Spon and latterly Thomson Science, Thomson has made clear its intention to abandon scientific publishing to concentrate attention on the education and business marketplace. This is further evidenced by the acquisition of Dryden Press which has bolstered International Thomson's Business Press.

Thomson Science & Professional
2–6 Boundary Row, London SE1 8HN
☎0171 865 0066   Fax 0171 522 9623

FOUNDED 1830. Part of International Thomson Publishing. *Publishes* architecture, chemistry, chemical engineering, interior design, civil engineering, electronics, electrical engineering, environmental studies, geography, geology, mathematics, mechanical engineering, medicine, nursing, dentistry, technology.

Stanley Thornes (Publishers) Ltd
Ellenborough House, Wellington Street,
Cheltenham, Gloucestershire GL50 1YW
☎01242 228888   Fax 01242 221914
Managing Director *David Smith*
Approx. Annual Turnover £20 million

FOUNDED 1972. Part of the Wolters-Kluwer Group. *Publishes* secondary school and college curriculum textbooks and primary school resources. About 200 titles a year. Unsolicited mss, synopses and ideas for books welcome if appropriate to specialised list.
IMPRINT **Mary Glasgow Publications** foreign-language teaching materials and teacher support.
Royalties paid annually.

F. A. Thorpe (Publishing) Ltd

The Green, Bradgate Road, Anstey, Leicester LE7 7FU
☎0116 2364325   Fax 0116 2340205
Chairman *David Thorpe*
Group Chief Executive *Robert Thirlby*
Approx. Annual Turnover £500,000

Part of the Ulverscroft Group. *Publishes* fiction and non-fiction large print books. No educational, gardening or books that would not be suitable for large print. 444 titles in 1998. DIVISIONS **Charnwood**; **Ulverscroft**. IMPRINTS **Linford Romance**; **Linford Mystery**; **Linford Western**. No unsolicited material.

Thorsons

See **HarperCollins Publishers Ltd**

Times Books

See **HarperCollins Publishers Ltd**

Titan Books

42–44 Dolben Street, London SE1 0UP
☎0171 620 0200   Fax 0171 620 0032
Email: titanbooks@compuserve.com
Managing Director *Nick Landau*
Editorial Director *Katy Wild*

FOUNDED 1981. Now a leader in the publication of graphic novels and in film and television tie-ins. *Publishes* comic books/graphic novels, film and television titles. About 70–80 titles a year. IMPRINTS **Titan Books** TITLES *Batman; Superman; Alien; Star Trek; Star Wars; The Simpsons; The X Files; The Avengers*. No unsolicited fiction or children's books please. Ideas for film and TV titles considered; send synopsis/outline with sample chapter. Author guidelines available.
Royalties paid twice-yearly.

Tolkien

See **HarperCollins Publishers Ltd**

Tolley Publishing

See **Butterworth Tolley**

Transworld Publishers Ltd

61–63 Uxbridge Road, London W5 5SA
☎0181 579 2652   Fax 0181 579 5479
Managing Director/CEO *Mark Barty-King*
Approx. Annual Turnover £55 million

FOUNDED 1950. A subsidiary of **Random House, Inc.**, New York, which is a wholly-owned subsidiary of Bertelsmann AG, Germany.

Publishes general fiction and non-fiction, children's books, sports and leisure.

DIVISIONS
Adult Trade *Patrick Janson-Smith* **Adult Hardback** *Ursula Mackenzie* **Adult Paperback** *Larry Finlay* IMPRINTS **Anchor** *John Saddler*; **Bantam Press** *Francesca Liversidge*; **Corgi**; **Black Swan** *Bill Scott-Kerr*, **Doubleday** *Marianne Velmans*; **Partridge Press** *Alison Barrow*. AUTHORS Kate Atkinson, Bill Bryson, Catherine Cookson, Jilly Cooper, Nicholas Evans, Frederick Forsyth, Robert Goddard, Germaine Greer, Stephen Hawking, Andy McNab, Terry Pratchett, James Redfield, Gerald Seymour, Danielle Steel, Joanna Trollope, Mary Wesley.

Children's & Young Adult Books *Philippa Dickinson* IMPRINTS **Doubleday** (hardcover); **Picture Corgi**; **Corgi Pups**; **Young Corgi**; **Corgi Yearling**; **Corgi**; **Corgi Freeway**; **Bantam** (paperback). AUTHORS Ian Beck, Malorie Blackman, Anthony Browne, Helen Cooper, Peter Dickinson, Dick King-Smith, Francine Pascal, K. M. Peyton, Terry Pratchett, Philip Pullman, Robert Swindells, Jacqueline Wilson.

Royalties paid twice-yearly. *Overseas associates* Random House Australia Pty Ltd; Random House New Zealand; Random House (Pty) Ltd (South Africa).

Authors' Rating For five years, the number one publisher in the *Guardian*'s bestseller list, and described by *The Economist* as 'the most efficient publisher in the business', Transworld is by far the most profitable of the leading UK trade publishers. There is no secret. Editors are blessed with the talent of knowing what sells and the marketing team knows how to sell it.

Trentham Books Ltd

Westview House, 734 London Road, Stoke on Trent, Staffordshire ST4 5NP
☎01782 745567   Fax 01782 745553
Chairman/Managing Director
    Dr John Eggleston
Editorial Head *Dr Gillian Klein*
Approx. Annual Turnover £1 million

Publishes education (nursery, school and higher), social sciences, intercultural studies and law for professional readers *not* for children and parents. Also academic and professional journals. No fiction, biography or poetry. About 25–30 titles a year. Unsolicited mss, synopses and ideas welcome if relevant to their interests. Material only returned if adequate s.a.e. sent.
Royalties paid annually.

Triangle
See **Society for Promoting Christian Knowledge**

Trident Press Ltd
2–5 Old Bond Street, Mayfair, London
W1X 3TB
☎0171 491 8770   Fax 0171 491 8664
Email: admin@tridentpress.ie
Website:www.tridentpress.com
Managing Director *Peter Vine*
Approx. Annual Turnover £550,000

FOUNDED 1997. *Publishes* TV tie-ins, natural history, travel, geography, underwater/marine life, history, archaeology, culture and fiction. 10 titles in 1998. DIVISIONS **Fiction/General Publishing** *Paula Vine;* **Natural History** *Peter Vine.* TITLES *The Silkweaver; Perspectives on the USA; BBC Wildlife Specials.* No unsolicited mss; synopses and ideas welcome, particularly TV tie-ins. Approach in writing or *brief* communications by email, fax or telephone.
Royalties paid annually.

Trotman & Co. Ltd
2 The Green, Richmond, Surrey TW9 1PL
☎0181 486 1150   Fax 0181 486 1161
Website:www.trotmanpublishing.co.uk
Chairman *Andrew Fiennes Trotman*
Publishing Director *Morfydd Jones*
Approx. Annual Turnover £3 million

Publishes general careers books, higher education guides, teaching support material, employment and training resources. About 50 titles a year. TITLES *Complete Degree Course Offers*; *The Student Book; Students' Money Matters.* Unsolicited material welcome. Also in the educational resources market, producing recruitment brochures.
Royalties paid twice-yearly.

20/20
See **The X Press**

Two-Can Publishing Ltd
346 Old Street, London EC1V 9NQ
☎0171 684 4000   Fax 0171 613 3371
Chairman *Andrew Jarvis*
Marketing Director *Ian Grant*
Creative Director *Sara Lynn*
Approx. Annual Turnover £7 million

FOUNDED 1987 to publish innovative, high-quality material for children. *Publishes* books and magazines. DIVISIONS **Books** *Ian Grant*; **Magazines** *Andrew Jarvis.* No unsolicited mss; send synopses and ideas in the first instance.
Royalties paid twice-yearly.

UCL Press Ltd
See **Taylor & Francis Group**

Ulverscroft
See **F. A. Thorpe (Publishing) Ltd**

University Presses of California, Columbia & Princeton Ltd
1 Oldlands Way, Bognor Regis, West Sussex
PO22 9SA
☎01243 842165   Fax 01243 842167
Email: lois@upccp.demon.co.uk

Publishes academic titles only. US-based editorial offices. Over 200 titles a year. Enquiries only.

Usborne Publishing Ltd
83–85 Saffron Hill, London EC1N 8RT
☎0171 430 2800   Fax 0171 430 1562
Website:www.usborne.com
Managing Director *Peter Usborne*
Editorial Director *Jenny Tyler*
Approx. Annual Turnover £13.3 million

FOUNDED 1973. *Publishes* non-fiction, fiction, puzzle books and music for children and young adults. Some titles for parents. Up to 100 titles a year. Non-fiction books are written in-house to a specific format and therefore unsolicited mss are not normally welcome. Ideas which may be developed in-house are sometimes considered. Fiction for children aged 8+ will be considered. Keen to hear from new illustrators and designers.
Royalties paid twice-yearly.

Authors' Rating Recovering from distribution problems in the US, Usborne's distinctive children's books are popular at home and abroad. Most of the writing is done by in-house editors.

Vallentine Mitchell
See **Frank Cass & Co Ltd**

Ventura
See **Penguin UK**

Vermilion
See **Random House UK Ltd**

Verso
6 Meard Street, London W1V 3HR
☎0171 437 3546   Fax 0171 734 0059
Website:www.versobooks.com
Chairman *George Galfalvi*
Managing Director *Colin Robinson*
Approx. Annual Turnover £2 million

Formerly New Left Books which grew out of

the *New Left Review*. Publishes politics, history, philosophy, economics, cultural studies, sociology, feminism. TITLES *Theatres of Memory* Raphael Samuel; *The Enemy Within* Seumas Milne; *The Missionary Position* Christopher Hitchens; *City of Quartz* Mike Davis; *Year 501* Noam Chomsky; *Ideology* Terry Eagleton; *The Motorcycle Diaries* Ernesto Che Guevara; *The Politics of Friendship* Jacques Derrida. No unsolicited mss; synopses and ideas for books welcome.

Royalties paid annually. *Overseas office* in New York.

Authors' Rating Dubbed by *The Bookseller* as 'one of the most successful small independent publishers'.

Viking/Viking Children's
See **Penguin UK**

Vintage
See **Random House UK Ltd**

Virago Press
Little, Brown & Co. (UK), Brettenham House, Lancaster Place, London WC2E 7EN
☎0171 911 8000   Fax 0171 911 8100
Publisher *Lennie Goodings*
Senior Editor/Publisher, Vs *Sally Abbey*
Editor, Virago Modern Classics
  Imogen Taylor
Approx. Annual Turnover £2.5 million
FOUNDED in 1973 by Carmen Callil, Virago has just passed its quarter century of publishing fiction and non-fiction books of quality by women. Publishing approximately 50 new books a year in the areas of autobiography, biography, fiction, history, politics, psychology and women's issues.

IMPRINTS **Virago Modern Classics** 20th century reprints; **Virago Vs** AUTHORS Margaret Atwood, Maya Angelou, Gail Anderson-Dargatz, Nina Bawden, Jennifer Belle, Sarah Dunant, Marilyn French, Gaby Hauptman, Michele Roberts, Natasha Walter, Sarah Waters. Send synopsis and sample chapter and return postage with all unsolicited material.

Royalties paid twice-yearly.

Virgin Publishing Ltd
Thames Wharf Studios, Rainville Road, London W6 9HT
☎0171 386 3300   Fax 0171 386 3364
Website:www.virgin-books.com
Chairman *Robert Devereux*
Managing Director *Rob Shreeve*
Approx. Annual Turnover £15 million
The Virgin Group's book publishing company.

Publishes non-fiction, reference and large-format illustrated books on entertainment and popular culture, particularly music, TV tie-ins and books about film, showbiz, sport, biography, autobiography and humour. Launched a series of travel guides in 1999. No poetry, short stories, individual novels, children's books.

DIVISIONS/IMPRINTS Non-fiction: **Virgin** Editorial Director *Humphrey Price*; Senior Editor, humour, TV tie-ins and entertainment *Rod Green*; Senior Editor, reference *David Gould*; Senior Editor, music *Ian Gittins*; Music Scout *Stuart Slater*; Senior Editor, sport *Jonathan Taylor*; Editor, biography, popular science *Lorna Russell*.

Illustrated books: Editorial Director *Carolyn Thorne*; Editor *James Bennett*.

Fiction: **Virgin**; **Black Lace** Senior Editor *Kerri Sharp*; **Idol** Editor *Kathleen Bryson*; **Sapphire** Editor *Kathleen Bryson*; **Nexus** Editor *James Marriott*; **The New Adventures**; **Virgin Worlds**. Various branded series of genre fiction.

Royalties paid twice-yearly.

Authors' Rating Erotic fiction has been called 'one of the publishing sensations of the decade' and Black Lace as 'one of the most successful' of the erotic imprints. So it is not surprising that Virgin is intent on what might be described as further penetration of this market. After Black Lace, Nexus and Idol comes Sapphire 'the raunchiest lesbian imprint ever to hit the UK'.

Volcano Press Ltd
PO Box 139, Leicester LE2 2YH
☎0116 2706714   Fax 0116 2706714
Email: asaf@volcano.u-net.com
Chairman *F. Hussain*
Managing Director *A. Hussain*
FOUNDED 1992. *Publishes* academic non-fiction in the following areas: Islam, women's studies, human rights, Middle East, strategic studies and cultural studies. About 15 titles a year. TITLES *Beyond Islamic Fundamentalism; Islam in Britain; Islamic Fundamentalism in Britain; Islam in Everyday Life: An Introduction; Women in the Islamic Struggle*. No unsolicited mss; synopses and ideas welcome. No fiction, poetry or plays.

Royalties paid twice-yearly.

Voyager
See **HarperCollins Publishers Ltd**

University of Wales Press
6 Gwennyth Street, Cathays, Cardiff CF2 4YD
☎01222 231919   Fax 01222 230908
Email: pres@press.wales.ac.uk
Website:www.wales.ac.uk/press

Director *Susan Jenkins*
Deputy Director *Richard Houdmont*
Approx. Annual Turnover £425,000

FOUNDED 1922. *Publishes* academic and scholarly books in English and Welsh in four core areas: history, Welsh and Celtic Studies, European Studies, religion and philosophy. 51 titles in 1998.

IMPRINTS **GPC Books**; **Gwasg Prifysgol Cymru**; **University of Wales Press** TITLES *The Visual Culture of Wales: Industrial Society* Peter Lord; *The Contemporary Challenge of Modernist Theology* Paul Badham; *Editing Women* ed. Anne M. Hutchinson. Unsolicited mss considered. *Royalties* paid annually.

Walker Books Ltd

87 Vauxhall Walk, London SE11 5HJ
☎0171 793 0909   Fax 0171 587 1123

Editors *Vanessa Clarke, Caroline Royds, Sally Christie*
Approx. Annual Turnover £31.7 million

FOUNDED 1979. *Publishes* illustrated children's books, children's fiction and non-fiction. About 300 titles a year. TITLES *Where's Wally?* Martin Handford; *Five Minutes' Peace* Jill Murphy; *Can't You Sleep, Little Bear?* Martin Waddell & Barbara Firth; *Guess How Much I Love You* Sam McBratney & Anita Jeram; *MapHead* Lesley Howarth. Unsolicited mss welcome.
Royalties paid twice-yearly.

Authors' Rating Has some of the best loved titles in contemporary children's fiction but non-fiction has not done so well. There will be fewer titles in this second category and those that do get through will be for the younger age groups.

Ward Lock

See **Cassell**

Ward Lock Educational Co. Ltd

1 Christopher Road, East Grinstead, West Sussex RH19 3BT
☎01342 318980   Fax 01342 410980

Owner Ling Kee (UK) Ltd

FOUNDED 1952. *Publishes* educational books (primary, middle, secondary, teaching manuals) for all subjects, specialising in maths, science, geography, reading and English.

Frederick Warne

See **Penguin UK**

Warner

See **Little, Brown & Co. (UK)**

Warner Chappell Plays Ltd

See entry under **UK Agents**

Waterline Books

See **Airlife Publishing Ltd**

Franklin Watts

See **The Watts Publishing Group Ltd**

The Watts Publishing Group Ltd

96 Leonard Street, London EC2A 4XD
☎0171 739 2929   Fax 0171 739 2318
Email: <name>@wattspub.co.uk

Managing Director *Marlene Johnson*

Part of Groupe Lagardère. *Publishes* children's non-fiction, reference, information, gift, fiction, picture and novelty. About 300 titles a year. IMPRINTS **Franklin Watts** *Philippa Stewart* Non-fiction and information; **Orchard Books** *Francesca Dow* Fiction, picture and novelty books. Unsolicited mss, synopses and ideas for books welcome.
Royalties paid twice-yearly. *Overseas associates* in Australia and New Zealand, US and Canada.

Wayland Publishers Ltd (incorporating Macdonald Young Books)

61 Western Road, Hove, East Sussex BN3 1JD
☎01273 722561   Fax 01273 329314
Website:www.wayland.co.uk

Director & General Manager *Roberta Bailey*
Editorial Director *Stephen White-Thomson*
Approx. Annual Turnover £9.6 million

Part of the Wolters Kluwer Group. FOUNDED 1969. *Publishes* a broad range of subjects for children, mainly colour-illustrated non-fiction and fiction for 5–16-year-olds. About 400 titles a year. No unsolicited mss or synopses as most books are commissioned. Submissions from literary agents considered.
Royalties paid annually. *Overseas associates* Steck-Vaughn Company, USA.

Weidenfeld & Nicolson Ltd

See **The Orion Publishing Group Ltd**

Welsh Academic Press

See **Ashley Drake Publishing Ltd**

West One (Trade) Publishing Ltd

4 Great Portland Street, London W1N 5AA
☎0171 580 6886   Fax 0171 580 9788
Email: sales@west-one.com

Chief Executive *Martin Coleman*

Approx. Annual Turnover £2 million

Publishes travel guides and cartography, including RAC publications. TITLES include *RAC Inspected Hotels Guide to UK and Ireland; France for the Independent Traveller; Europe for the Independent Traveller; Road Atlas Great Britain and Ireland.* Unsolicited synopses and ideas welcome.

Wharncliffe Publishing

47 Church Street, Barnsley, South Yorkshire S70 2AS
☎01226 734222 Fax 01226 734438
Chairman *Sir Nicholas Hewitt*
Chief Executive *C. Hewitt*
Imprint Manager *Mike Parsons*

An imprint of **Pen & Sword Books Ltd**. Wharncliffe is the book and magazine publishing arm of an old-established, independently owned newspaper publishing and printing house. *Publishes* local history throughout the UK, focusing on nostalgia and old photographs. Unsolicited mss, synopses and ideas welcome but return postage must be included with all submissions.
Royalties paid twice-yearly.

Which? Books/
Consumers' Association

2 Marylebone Road, London NW1 4DF
☎0171 830 6000 Fax 0171 830 7660
Director *Sheila McKechnie*
Head of Publishing *Gill Rowley*
FOUNDED 1957. Publishing arm of Consumers' Association, a registered charity. *Publishes* nonfiction: information, reference and how-to books on travel, gardening, health, personal finance, consumer law, food, careers, crafts, DIY. Titles must offer direct value or utility to the UK consumer. 25–30 titles a year.
IMPRINT **Which? Books** *Gill Rowley* TITLES *Good Food Guide; Good Skiing and Snowboarding Guide; The Which? Hotel Guide; The Which? Wine Guide.* No unsolicited mss; send synopses and ideas only.
Royalties, if applicable, paid twice-yearly.

Whittet Books Ltd

Hill Farm, Stonham Road, Cotton, Stowmarket, Suffolk IP14 4RQ
☎01449 781877 Fax 01449 781898
Managing Director *Annabel Whittet*

Publishes natural history, pets, poultry, horses, rural interest. Unsolicited mss, synopses and ideas for books welcome.
Royalties paid twice-yearly.

Whurr Publishers Ltd

19B Compton Terrace, London N1 2UN
☎0171 359 5979 Fax 0171 226 5290
Email: info@whurr.co.uk
Chairman/Managing Director *Colin Whurr*
Approx. Annual Turnover £1 million
FOUNDED in 1987. *Publishes* speech and language therapy, nursing, psychology, psychotherapy, business and management, dyslexia, audiology. No fiction and general trade books. 30 titles in 1998. Unsolicited mss, synopses and ideas in the specialist fields welcome. 'Whurr Publishers believe authors can be best served by a small, specialised company' combining old-fashioned service with the latest publishing technology.
Royalties paid twice-yearly.

Wiley Europe Ltd

Baffins Lane, Chichester, West Sussex PO19 1UD
☎01243 779777 Fax 01243 775878
Website:www.wiley.co.uk
Managing Director *Dr John Jarvis*
Publishing Director *Steven Mair*
Approx. Annual Turnover £56 million
FOUNDED 1807. US parent company. *Publishes* professional, reference trade and text books, scientific, technical and biomedical.
DIVISIONS **Environmental**, **Psychology**, **Business & Healthcare Management** *Sarah Stevens*; **Physical Sciences & Engineering** *Ernest Kirkwood*; **Life/Medical**, **Technology & Stats** *Mike Davis*; **Business & Finance** *David Wilson*; **College Division** *Simon Plumtree.* Unsolicited mss welcome, as are synopses and ideas for books.
Royalties paid annually.

Authors' Rating The academics' favourite. Authors seem to like the way their books are presented and, unusually for this market niche, feel they are fairly treated.

Neil Wilson Publishing Ltd

Suite 303a, The Pentagon Centre,
36 Washington Street, Glasgow G3 8AZ
☎0141 221 1117 Fax 0141 221 5363
Email: nwp@cqm.co.uk
Website:www.nwp.co.uk
Chairman *Gordon Campbell*
Managing Director/Editorial Director
Neil Wilson
Approx. Annual Turnover £300,000
FOUNDED 1992. *Publishes* Scottish interest and history, biography, humour and hillwalking, whisky and beer; also cookery and Irish interest.

About 10 titles a year. Unsolicited mss, synopses and ideas welcome. No fiction, politics, academic or technical.

Royalties paid twice-yearly.

Philip Wilson Publishers Ltd

143–149 Great Portland Street, London W1N 5FB

☎0171 436 4490   Fax 0171 436 4403/4260

Chairman *Philip Wilson*
Managing Director *Antony White*

FOUNDED 1976. *Publishes* art, art history, antiques and collectables. 9 titles in 1998.

DIVISIONS **Philip Wilson Publishers Ltd**; **Flint River Press Ltd** *Philip Wilson*.

Windrow & Greene

See **Compendium Publishing Ltd**

The Windrush Press

Little Window, High Street, Moreton in Marsh, Gloucestershire GL56 0LL

☎01608 652012/652025   Fax 01608 652125
Email: windrushpress@netcomuk.co.uk

Managing Director *Geoffrey Smith*
Editorial Head *Victoria Huxley*

FOUNDED 1987. Independent company. *Publishes* travel guides, biography, history, military history, humour. About 10 titles a year. TITLES *Waterloo: A Near Run Thing; A Traveller's History of China; Key to the Sacred Pattern; Lanzarote: A Windrush Island Guide.* Send synopsis and letter with s.a.e.

Royalties paid twice-yearly.

Windsor Large Print

See **Chivers Press Ltd**

Wise Publications

See **Omnibus Press**

Woburn Press

See **Frank Cass & Co Ltd**

Oswald Wolff Books

See **Berg Publishers**

The Women's Press

34 Great Sutton Street, London EC1V 0LQ

☎0171 251 3007   Fax 0171 608 1938

Managing Director *Elsbeth Lindner*
Approx. Annual Turnover £1 million

Part of the Namara Group. First title 1978. *Publishes* women only: quality fiction and non-fiction. Fiction usually has a female protagonist and a woman-centred theme. International writers and subject matter encouraged. Non-fiction:

subjects of general interest, both practical and theoretical, to women generally; art books, feminist theory, health and psychology, literary criticism. About 50 titles a year. IMPRINTS **Women's Press Crime**; **Women's Press Handbooks Series**; **Livewire Books for Teenagers** Fiction and non-fiction series for young adults. Synopses and ideas for books welcome. No mss without previous letter, synopsis and sample material.

Royalties paid twice-yearly.

Woodhead Publishing Ltd

Abington Hall, Abington, Cambridge CB1 6AH

☎01223 891358   Fax 01223 893694
Email: wp@woodhead-publishing.com
Website:www.woodhead-publishing.com

Chairman *Alan Jessup*
Managing Director *Martin Woodhead*
Approx. Annual Turnover £1.2 million

FOUNDED 1989. *Publishes* engineering, materials technology, finance and investment, food technology, production and management. TITLES *Welding International* (journal); *Reinforced Plastics Durability; Meat Science 6e; Base Metals Handbook; Foreign Exchange Options.* About 40 titles a year. DIVISIONS **Woodhead Publishing** *Martin Woodhead;* **Abington Publishing** (in association with the Welding Institute) *Patricia Morrison.* Unsolicited material welcome.

Royalties paid annually.

Woodstock Books

The School House, South Newington, Banbury, Oxon OX15 4JJ

☎01295 720598   Fax 01295 720717

Chairman/Managing Director *James Price*
Approx. Annual Turnover £150,000

FOUNDED 1989. *Publishes* literary reprints only. Main series: *Revolution and Romanticism, 1789–1834; Hibernia: Literature and Nation in Victorian Ireland.* No unsolicited mss.

Wordsworth Editions Ltd

Cumberland House, Crib Street, Ware, Hertfordshire SG12 9ET

☎01920 465167   Fax 01920 462267
Email: 101512.3577@compuserve.com

Editorial Office: 6 London Street, London W2 1HL

☎0171 706 8822   Fax 0171 706 8833
Email: 100434.276@compuserve.com

Directors *M. C. W. Trayler, E. G. Trayler*
Editorial Director *C. M. Clapham*

Director, Sales & Company Secretary
Clive Reynard
Approx. Annual Turnover £4 million
FOUNDED 1987. *Publishes* reprints of English literature, paperback reference books, poetry, children's classics, classic erotica, military history, American classics. About 75 titles a year. No unsolicited mss.

X Libris
See **Little Brown & Co. (UK)**

The X Press
6 Hoxton Square, London N1 6NU
☎0171 729 1199   Fax 0171 729 1771
Email: vibes@xpress.co.uk
Chairman *Dotun Adebayo*
Managing Director *Steve Pope*
LAUNCHED in 1992 with the cult bestseller *Yardie*, The X Press is the leading publisher of Black-interest fiction in the UK. Also *publishes* general fiction and children's fiction. 28 titles in 1999. IMPRINTS **The X Press** TITLES *Yardie; Baby Father,* **Nia** TITLE *In Search of Satisfaction;* **20/20** TITLE *Curvy Lovebox.* Send mss rather than synopses or ideas (enclose s.a.e.). No poetry.
Royalties paid annually.

Y Ddraig Fach
See **Ashley Drake Publishing Ltd**

Y Lolfa Cyf
Talybont, Ceredigion SY24 5AP
☎01970 832304   Fax 01970 832782
Email: ylolfa@ylolfa.com
Website:www.ylolfa.com/
Managing Director *Robat Gruffudd*
Editor *Lefi Gruffudd*
Approx. Annual Turnover £650,000
FOUNDED 1967. Small company which publishes mainly in Welsh. Handles its own typesetting and printing. *Publishes* Welsh language publications; Celtic language tutors; English language books about Wales for the visitor; nationalism and sociology (English language). 30 titles in 1997. TITLES *Artists in Snowdonia* James Bogle; *The Welsh Learner's Dictionary* Heini Gruffudd. No English language books unless political and Celtic. Write first with synopses or ideas.
Royalties paid twice-yearly.

Yale University Press (London)
23 Pond Street, London NW3 2PN
☎0171 431 4422   Fax 0171 431 3755
Managing Director/Editorial Director
John Nicoll

FOUNDED 1961. Owned by US parent company. *Publishes* academic and humanities. About 200 titles (worldwide) a year. Unsolicited mss and synopses welcome if within specialised subject areas.
Royalties paid annually.

Authors' Rating Yale is not one of the publishers dominated by its American parent. Many of the best ideas originate in this country. Unusually for a university press, the list has much of interest to the general reader.

Roy Yates Books
Smallfields Cottage, Cox Green, Rudgwick, Horsham, West Sussex RH12 3DE
☎01403 822299   Fax 01403 823012
Chairman/Managing Director *Roy Yates*
Approx. Annual Turnover £120,000
FOUNDED 1990. *Publishes* children's books only. No unsolicited material as books are adaptations of existing popular classics suitable for translation into dual-language format.
Royalties paid quarterly.

Yellow Bananas
See **Egmont Children's Books**

Yellow Jersey
See **Random House UK Ltd**

Zastrugi Books
PO Box 2963, Brighton, East Sussex BN1 6AW
☎01273 566369   Fax 01273 566369/562720
Chairman *Ken Singleton*
FOUNDED 1997. *Publishes* English-language teaching books only. No unsolicited mss; synopses and ideas for books welcome.
Royalties paid twice-yearly.

Zed Books Ltd
7 Cynthia Street, London N1 9JF
☎0171 837 4014   Fax 0171 833 3960
Email: hosie@zedbooks.demon.co.uk
Website:www.zedbooks.demon.co.uk
Approx. Annual Turnover £1 million
FOUNDED 1976. *Publishes* international and Third World affairs, development studies, women's studies, environmental studies, cultural studies and specific area studies. No fiction, children's or poetry. About 40 titles a year.
DIVISIONS **Development & Environment** *Robert Molteno;* **Women's Studies, Cultural Studies** *Louise Murray.* TITLES *The Development*

Dictionary ed. Wolfgang Sachs; *Staying Alive* Vandana Shiva; *The Autobiography of Nawal* Nawal El Saadawi. No unsolicited mss; synopses and ideas welcome though.
  Royalties paid annually.

Zest
See **Onlywomen Press Ltd**

Electronic and Internet Publishers

AuthorsOnline
1A Adams Yard, Maidenhead Street, Hertford, Hertfordshire SG14 1DR
☎01992 503151   Fax 01992 535424
Email: theeditor@authorsonline.co.uk
Website:www.authorsonline.co.uk
Owner *Managed Webspace Ltd.*
Chairman/Managing Director *Richard Fitt*
Approx. Annual Turnover £100,000

FOUNDED 1997. Internet publisher whose aim is 'to help authors secure hard-copy contracts and for established authors to re-publish books that are no longer reprinted and on which publishing rights have reverted'. £25 is charged to publish the manuscript on the AuthorsOnline website plus a weekly fee of £1 per week while it remains online. Interested in all types of books; submit mss by post or email. For more information, access the website.

Context Limited
Grand Union House, 20 Kentish Town Road, London NW1 9NR
☎0171 267 8989   Fax 0171 267 1133
Email: postmaster@context.co.uk
Website:www.context.co.uk

FOUNDED 1986. Electronic publisher of UK and European legal and offical information on CD-ROM, on-line and the Internet. TITLE *JUSTIS Cartoons* CD-ROM, developed jointly with **The Centre for the Study of Cartoons and Caricature** at the University of Kent (see entry under **Library Services**), contains over 18,000 political cartoons published in British newspapers from 1912 to 1990. No unsolicited mailshots; enquiries only.

Notting Hill Electronic Publishers
31 Brunswick Gardens, London W8 4AW
☎0171 937 6003   Fax 0171 937 0003
Email: info@nottinghill.com
Website:www.nottinghill.com
  or www.dancer.com
Chairman *Andreas Whittam Smith*
Managing Director *Ben Whittam Smith*

FOUNDED 1994. Award-winning electronic publisher created by Andreas Whittam Smith, founder of *The Independent*. *Publishes* art and popular science on CD-ROMs and websites. TITLES *International Athletics; The Art of Singing; The Evolution of Life; Dancer DNA*.

Online Originals
Priory Cottage, Wordsworth Place, London NW5 4HG
☎0171 267 4244
Email: editor@onlineoriginals.com
Website:www.onlineoriginals.com
Managing Editor *David Gettman*
Commissioning Editor
  Dr Christopher Macann

Publishes book-length works on the Internet only. Acquires global electronic rights (including print-on-demand and digital readings) in literary fiction, intellectual non-fiction, drama, fiction for young readers (ages 8–16). No poetry, fantasy, how-to, self-help, picture books, cookery, hobbies, crafts or local interest. 20 titles in 1998. Unsolicited mss, synopses and ideas for books welcome. *All* communications are by email and authors must have Internet access. Submissions or enquiries on paper will be discarded. Guidelines available from the email address above.
  Royalties paid annually (50% royalties on standard price of £4 or $7).

Authors' Rating One of the handful of publishers determined to make their presence felt on the Internet. Whether authors will make fame and fortune from the enterprise remains to be seen.

Reardon and Rawes
56 Upper Norwood Street, Leckhampton, Cheltenham, Gloucestershire GL53 0DU
☎01242 231800
Editor *Julian Rawes*

FOUNDED 1996. *Publishes* re-issues of out-of-print titles in electronic/multimedia format. Non-fiction historical titles only. TITLES *Picture of Bristol – A Guide* Rev. John Evans; *Proverbs and Family Mottoes* J. A. Mair; *Wessex to Essex* Rosemary Barham. Unsolicited mss welcome.
  Royalties not paid.

Uncle Sam's Satellite

Is Britain losing its identity?
Barry Turner warns of American encroachment

Americanisation continues apace. Almost everyone in the world knows what is happening; even the Americans who, for understandable reasons, prefer to call it globalisation. Only the British remain oblivious. Here, it just happens and no one seems to notice. The media industry is a good example. In any other country it would be a matter of interest, not to say concern, that of the national press, the two foremost opinion leaders, *The Times* and *The Daily Telegraph*, have North American paymasters, that of the twelve top book publishing conglomerates, six are subject to American dictates (HarperCollins, the publishing arm of Rupert Murdoch's American-controlled News Corporation, is the largest consumer book publisher in Britain by a margin of 30 per cent) and that film and television are almost entirely subservient to American interests. But not here. In Britain, while American authors rule the bestseller lists (of the first 25 titles in the *Guardian* list of the 100 top selling paperbacks, 15 are from American authors), Hollywood fills the cinemas, American cop series and sitcoms occupy television prime time and newspapers give more coverage to the States than to all other countries combined, we still kid ourselves that we remain a nation apart, a cultural entity proud of its independence. This is delusion on a grand scale. How? Why is it happening?

The power of language has a lot to do with it. The growing world domination of English (370 million speakers at the last count) reinforces our ignorance of foreigners, including European neighbours, who retain their own way of saying things while drawing us closer to the super power that shares, more or less, our linguistic roots. We accept Americana because it is easy to do so. No subtitles are required.

There are those who choose to believe that the process is two-way; that our cultural influence in America is every bit as great as their impact on us. The evidence rarely extends beyond the Anglophile pages of the *New York Review of Books*. Struck by the bestseller accolade awarded to *Bridget Jones's Diary*, Vicky Ward instructs *Spectator* readers on 'why, in American bookshops, Britannia unexpectedly rules the waves' before conceding that it is dead British authors from Shakespeare to Evelyn Waugh who are heavily promoted on Fifth Avenue. 'Few contemporary British authors are prominently displayed.' Surprise, surprise. Just try buying British in Denver, Colorado. The country wouldn't even show up on the computer screen. Face it, few Americans know or care about Britain.

Not convinced? Then try this. A recent book on the building of the Channel Tunnel (written by an American, of course) tells how the promoters tried to raise money in the States. One finance company asked for a map. It was assumed that their interest was geological. But, no. What they wanted was a map showing where precisely Britain was in relation to the Continent.

Or this. When the CIA decided to share its unrivalled collection of world facts with Internet users, seekers after knowledge on this side of the Atlantic were assured by the intelligence agency that England gained her independence in 1801.

This is not meant to be a sneer at America. The world's only super power has enough to worry about without getting concerned about the fortunes of a way offshore island. Rather, the attack is directed at British pundits who persist in believing that Americans are falling over themselves to do homage to our creative genius.

Cultural jingoism leads only to wishful thinking. When, recently, *The Times* tried to prove that 'UK talent can compete in the toughest TV market' the doubtless indefatigable investigator was reduced to listing American remakes of British series. Even *Fawlty Towers*, unarguably a comedy classic in its own right, has had to be adapted and renamed for CBS. Anyone wanting to view original versions of British-made programmes must resort to the BBC cable network, the popularity of which can be judged by the £7 million loss borne by BBC Worldwide, the commercial setup responsible for launching the service.

The sad fact is that British television, once touted as the world's best, barely registers with the American networks while here it is now impossible to avoid American films and TV programmes. Ten years ago Britain was a net exporter of film and television. Since then, an annual profit of some £100 million has turned into a deficit of £200 million.

The fiction of British culture holding its own against Americana is reinforced by the massed ranks of writers and artists who see Americanisation as a career opportunity. It is surely no coincidence that Martin Amis sets his novel *Night Train* in an unnamed American city, that Peter Ackroyd writes of Milton in America, that Andrew Lloyd Webber transposes his latest musical *Whistle Down the Wind* from the Pennines setting of the original novel to the Louisiana Bible Belt and that British actors galore glad-hand their way round Hollywood in the hope that a producer will see their potential for world stardom. Various explanations are given for the boom–bust history of British cinema except the obvious one that as soon as an actor, director or screenwriter hits the big time in the UK, he applies for his Green Card.

You might think that a government committed to creating an image for Cool Britannia might recognise the danger of becoming over-independent on American culture. But not a bit of it. While the Prime Minister cosies up to his very good friend in the White House, back at home his Culture Minister tells the world that 'during the past few years in Britain we have seen an incredible flowering of the creative industries'. Well, as they say, if you believe that you believe anything. George Walden is closer to the mark when he observes that 'frantically modern Britain is inventing very little; it is selling old lamps as new, and for the moment it is getting away with it'.

When it comes to literature, 'Our most inventive writers adopt a transatlantic style. They do not go out of their way to admit it, but privately they recognise that American writers – Bellow, Updike, De Lillo, Pynchon, Robert Store, Elmore Leonard – represent a more vital literary culture working on a broader canvas and in a language we have lost – an invigorating blend of the demotic and the intellectual.' Walden concludes, 'We used to depend on America for our security. Today we depend on it for our purpose in life.'

George Walden's message, delivered to the University of Chicago last spring, is in fact more upbeat than these selected words imply. He sees a rejuvenated Britain as 'reverting to the kind of country that helped to make America possible in the first place', a self-confident, assertive country born again, but this time in the American image.

Maybe that is the way we must go. But it does suggest ending up like Puerto Rico, the 51st state in all but name, prosperous but culturally defunct. Is there no alternative? Answer comes over a short stretch of water. Europe beckons. One does not have to be a rabid Europhile to regret the cultural opportunities we have lost by standing apart from European integration. Facing the glare from America, our media entrepreneurs have blinded themselves to opportunities closer to home.

As Alan Massie laments, in the twenty-five years since joining the European Community we, as a nation, have become less European. 'We argued fiercely about Sartre and Camus and Existentialism. We read Proust, Gide, de Moutherlant, Malraux. Then a little later we found the most significant writers were German – Günter Grass and Heinrich Böll. All that has gone.'

Quite so. Obsessed as they are by the latest American imports, publishers have all but ignored the wealth of contemporary writing to be found on the Continent. Titles that do manage to transcend the language barrier are drearily translated. In contrast to France and Germany where, quite properly, the translator is seen as a creative artist, in Britain the job is poorly regarded and even more poorly rewarded. What irony that when an exception proves the rule, such as Bernhard Schlink's modern classic *The Reader*, it is an American publisher (in this case, Knopf) who leads the way. The irony is that while the US takes less than 15 per cent of our book exports, over 40 per cent goes to the EU.

The stand-off from Europe has yet more damaging consequences for television. It is not just that we see little of what is produced on the Continent (unless you count the gamble of channel hopping via satellite or cable), we are missing out on an eager market for British programmes. As *The Economist* reminds us, 'When governments on the European mainland started to liberalise their television industries in the 1980s, they created a huge import market. None of the British commercial companies lifted a finger. It took Reg Grundy, an Australian entrepreneur, to see the opportunity, with *Neighbours*. Other Australians followed where he led and now in Germany, the biggest European market, Australians provide nearly a tenth of light entertainment, eight times as much as Britain does.'

It is significant that Australia, another English-speaking nation, does so well in the European entertainment market. For it is a fact of European integration that whatever Britain's political involvement, English will become the Union's *lingua franca*. Already Continental book publishers like Bertelsmann, Holtzbrink, Springer-Verlag, Elsevier and Hachette are among the world's leading producers of English language books. Film and television will follow the same pattern. The evolution of a cultural model that is an alternative to Americanisation but also one that is English-based, is a real possibility. What a tragedy it would be if we are not part of it.

Irish Publishers

An Gúm

44 Sráid Uí Chonaill Uachtarach, Baile Átha
Cliath 1, Republic of Ireland
☎00 353 1 8095034   Fax 00 353 1 8731140
Email: gum@educ.irlgov.ie
Senior Editor *Seosamh Ó Shamráin*
Editors *Antain Mag Shamhráin, Máire
   Nic Mhaoláin*

FOUNDED 1926. The Irish language publications
branch of the Department of Education and
Science. Established to provide general reading,
textbooks and dictionaries in the Irish language.
Publishes educational, children's, music, lexi-
cography and general. Little fiction or poetry.
About 50 titles a year. Unsolicited mss, synopses
and ideas for books welcome. Also welcomes
reading copies of first and second level school
textbooks with a view to translating them into
the Irish language.
Royalties paid annually.

Anvil Books

45 Palmerston Road, Dublin 6, Republic of
Ireland
☎00 353 1 4973628   Fax 00 353 1 4968263
Managing Director *Rena Dardis*

FOUNDED 1964 with the emphasis on Irish history and biography. Expansion of the list followed to include more general interest Irish
material and in 1982 The Children's Press was
established, making Anvil the first Irish publisher
of mass-market children's books of Irish interest.
Publishes illustrated books, history, biography
(particularly 1916–22), folklore and children's
fiction (for ages 8–14). No adult fiction, poetry,
short stories or illustrated books for children
under 8. About 7 titles a year. Only books of
Irish interest considered. No unsolicited mss;
send synopsis only.

DIVISIONS
General TITLES *Guerilla Days in Ireland* Tom
Barry; *The Workhouses of Ireland* John O'Connor;
The Norman Invasion of Ireland Richard Roche.
The Children's Press TITLES *Kids Can Cook*
Sarah Webb; *Drawing Made Easy* Terry Myler;
Riverside Soccer Books Peter Regan.
Royalties paid annually.

Attic Press Ltd

c/o Cork University Press, Crawford Business
Park, Crosses Green, Cork, Co. Cork,
Republic of Ireland
☎00 353 21 321715   Fax 00 353 21 315329
Publisher *Sara Wilbourne*

FOUNDED 1988. Began life in 1984 as a forum
for information on the Irish feminist movement. *Publishes* adult and teenage fiction, and
non-fiction (history, women's studies, politics,
biography). About 10 titles a year.
Royalties paid twice yearly.

Blackwater Press

c/o Folens Publishers, Broomhill Business
Park, Broomhill Road, Tallaght, Dublin 24,
Republic of Ireland
☎00 353 1 4515311   Fax 00 353 1 4520451
Chief Executive *Dirk Folens*
Managing Director *John O'Connor*

Part of Folens Publishers. *Publishes* political,
sports, fiction (*Anna O'Donovan*) and children's
(*Deidre Whelan*). 37 titles in 1998.

Brandon Book Publishers Ltd

See **Mount Eagle Publications Ltd**

Edmund Burke Publisher

Cloonagashel, 27 Priory Drive, Blackrock,
Co. Dublin, Republic of Ireland
☎00 353 1 2882159   Fax 00 353 1 2834080
Email: deburca@indigo.ie
Website: indigo.ie/~deburca/deburca.ie
Chairman *Eamonn De Búrca*
Approx. Annual Turnover £150,000

Small family-run business publishing historical
and topographical and fine limited-edition books
relating to Ireland. TITLES *The Irish Fiants of the
Tudor Sovereigns; Irish Stuart Silver; Irish Names of
Places* Joyce; *History of the Kingdom of Kerry*
Cusack; *Scots Mercenary Forces in Ireland* G. A.
Hayes-McCoy; *The Dean's Friend* Alan Harrison;
Manners and Customs of the Ancient Irish Eugene
O'Curry; *Flowers of Mayo* Nelson and Walsh; *The
Annals of Ulster, A Connacht Man's Ramble*
Costello; *The Three Candles, a Bibliographical
Catalogue* de Búrca. Unsolicited mss welcome.
No synopses or ideas.
Royalties paid annually.

Butterworth Ireland Limited

26 Upper Ormond Quay, Dublin 7,
Republic of Ireland
☎00 353 1 8731555   Fax 00 353 1 8731876

Chairman P. Woods (UK)
General Manager Gerard Coakley
Tax Editor – Managing Susan Keegan
Legal Editor – Managing Louise Leavy

Subsidiary of Butterworth & Co. Publishers, London, (Reed Elsevier is the holding company). *Publishes* solely law and tax books. 6 titles in 1998. Leading publisher of Irish law and tax titles. Unsolicited mss, synopses and ideas welcome for titles within the broadest parameters of tax and law.
Royalties paid twice yearly.

The Children's Press

See **Anvil Books**

Cló Iar-Chonnachta

Indreabhán, Connemara, Galway,
Republic of Ireland
☎00 353 91 593307   Fax 00 353 91 593362

Chairman/Director Micheál Ó Conghaile
Editor Úna Ní Chonchúir
Approx. Annual Turnover 250,000

FOUNDED 1985. *Publishes* fiction, poetry, plays and children's, mostly in Irish, including translations. Also publishes cassettes of writers reading from their own works. TITLES *Aran Song* John Canter; *Facing South* Patrick Gallager; *The Village Sings* Gabriel Fitzmaurice; *Out in the Open* Cathal ó Searcaigh. 15 titles in 1998.
Royalties paid annually.

The Collins Press

West Link Parak, Doughcloyne, Wilton,
Cork, Republic of Ireland
☎00 353 21 347717   Fax 00 353 21 347720

Publisher Con Collins
Editor Maria O'Donovan

FOUNDED 1989. *Publishes* archaeology, biography, fiction, general non-fiction, health, history, spirituality, photography, adventure and travel guides. About 12–15 titles a year. Unsolicited mss, synopses and ideas for books welcome – of Irish interest only.
Royalties paid annually.

The Columba Press

55A Spruce Avenue, Stillorgan Industrial Park,
Blackrock, Co. Dublin, Republic of Ireland
☎00 353 1 2942556   Fax 00 353 1 2942564
Website: www.columba.ie

Chairman Neil Kluepfel

Managing Director Seán O'Boyle
E:mail: sean@columba.ie (editorial) *or*
info@columba.ie (general)
Approx. Annual Turnover £750,000

FOUNDED 1985. Small company committed to growth. *Publishes* religious and land counselling titles. 30 titles in 1998. (Backlist of 225 titles.) TITLES *Passion for the Possible* Daniel J. O'Leary; *The Mystical Imagination of Patrick Kavanagh* Una Agnew. Unsolicited ideas and synopses rather than full mss preferred.
Royalties paid twice yearly.

Cork University Press

Crawford Business Park, Crosses Green, Cork,
Co. Cork, Republic of Ireland
☎00 353 21 902980   Fax 00 353 21 315329
Email: corkunip@ucc.ie
Website: www.ucc.ie/corkunip

Publisher Sara Wilbourne
Editor/Production Manager Eileen O'Carroll

FOUNDED 1925. Relaunched in 1992, the Press *publishes* academic and some trade titles. Plans to publish 26 titles in 1999. Two journals, *Irish Review* (bi-annual), an interdisciplinary cultural review, and *The Irish Journal of Feminist Studies* (bi-annual), are now part of the list. Unsolicited synopses and ideas welcome for textbooks, academic monographs, belles lettres, illustrated histories and journals.
Royalties paid twice yearly.

Drumlin Publications

Nure, Manorhamilton, Co. Leitrim,
Republic of Ireland
☎00 353 72 55237   Fax 00 353 72 56063

Editor Proinnsíos Ó Duigneáin
Director, Marketing & Production
  Betty Duignan

Publishes local, social and family history, any county and biography. Well researched and referenced work only. Ideas welcome; submit specimen chapter or complete ms.

Flyleaf Press

4 Spencer Villas, Glenageary, Co. Dublin,
Republic of Ireland
☎00 353 1 2806228   Fax 00 353 1 8370176
Email: ryanj@biores.irl.ie
Website: www.flyleaf.irish-roots.net/

Managing Director Dr James Ryan

FOUNDED 1981 to publish natural history titles. Now concentrating on family history and Irish history as a background to family history. No fiction. TITLES *Irish Records; Longford and its*

People; Tracing Kerry Ancestors; Tracing Dublin's Ancestors; Tracing Cork Ancestors; Tracing Mayo Ancestors. Unsolicited mss, synopses and ideas for books welcome.

Royalties paid twice yearly.

Four Courts Press Ltd

Fumbally Lane, Dublin 8, Republic of Ireland
☎00 353 1 4534668   Fax 00 353 1 4534672
Email: info@four-courts-press.ie
Website: www.four-courts-press.ie
Chairman/Managing Director *Michael Adams*
Director *Martin Healy*
Approx. Annual Turnover £500,000

FOUNDED 1972. *Publishes* mainly scholarly books in the humanities. About 60 titles a year. Synopses and ideas for books welcome.

Royalties paid annually.

Gill & Macmillan

Goldenbridge, Inchicore, Dublin 8,
Republic of Ireland
☎00 353 1 4531005   Fax 00 353 1 4541688
Managing Director *M. H. Gill*
Approx. Annual Turnover £5.5 million

FOUNDED 1968 when M. H. Gill & Son Ltd and Macmillan Ltd formed a jointly owned publishing company. *Publishes* biography/autobiography, history, current affairs, literary criticism (all mainly of Irish interest), guidebooks, cookery. Also educational textbooks for secondary and tertiary levels. About 100 titles a year. Contacts: *Hubert Mahony* (educational); *Fergal Tobin* (general); *Ailbhe O'Reilly* (tertiary textbooks). IMPRINT **Newleaf** (popular health, psychology, mind, body and spirit). Unsolicited synopses and ideas welcome. Not interested in fiction or poetry.

Royalties paid subject to contract.

Institute of Public Administration

57–61 Lansdowne Road, Dublin 4,
Republic of Ireland
☎00 353 1 2697011   Fax 00 353 1 2698644
Email: SaPes@ipa.ie
Website: www.ipa.ie
Chairman *Michael Quinn*
Director General *John Gallagher*
Acting Publisher *Tony McNamara*
Approx. Annual Turnover £600,000

FOUNDED 1957 by a group of public servants, the Institute of Public Administration is the Irish public sector management development agency. The publishing arm of the organisation is one of its major activities. *Publishes* academic and professional books and periodicals: history,

law, politics, economics and Irish public administration for students and practitioners. 9 titles in 1998. TITLES *Administration Yearbook & Diary; Governance and Accountability; Encounters With Modern Ireland; Irish Social Services.* No unsolicited mss; synopses and ideas welcome. No fiction or children's publishing.

Royalties paid annually.

Irish Academic Press Ltd

44 Northumberland Road, Ballsbridge,
Dublin 4, Republic of Ireland
☎00 353 1 6688244   Fax 00 353 1 6601610
Chairman *Frank Cass (London)*
Managing Editor *Linda Longmore*
Approx. Annual Turnover £250,000

FOUNDED 1974. *Publishes* academic monographs and humanities. 17 titles in 1998. Unsolicited mss, synopses and ideas welcome.

Royalties paid annually.

Irish Management Institute

Sandyford Road, Dublin 16, Republic of Ireland
☎00 353 1 2078400   Fax 00 353 1 2955150
Email: hannawac@imi.ie
Website: www.imi.ie
Chief Executive *Barry Kenny*
Approx. Annual Turnover £8 million

FOUNDED 1952. The Institute is owned by its members (individual and corporate) and its major activities involve management education, training and development. The book publishing arm of the organisation was established in 1970. *Publishes* management practice, interpersonal skills and aspects of national macroeconomics. TITLES *The Economy of Ireland; Practical Finance; Personnel Management; Managing Your Business: A Guidebook for Small Business.* Unsolicited mss welcome given that material is relevant to Irish management practice. Synopses and ideas also welcome.

Royalties paid annually.

The Lilliput Press

62–63 Sitric Road, Arbour Hill, Dublin 7,
Republic of Ireland
☎00 353 1 6711647   Fax 00 353 1 6711233
Email: lilliput@indigo.ie
Website: www.indigo.ie/~lilliput
Chairman *David Dickson*
Managing Director *Antony Farrell*
Approx. Annual Turnover £200,000

FOUNDED 1984. *Publishes* non-fiction: literature, history, autobiography and biography, ecology, essays; criticism; fiction and poetry. About 20 titles a year. TITLES *Ulysses: The Dublin Edition;*

The Growth Illusion (ecology); *Modern Art in Ireland; Nature in Ireland; Visiting Rwanda; A Close Shave with the Devil* (fiction); *The Aran Islands* (photography). Unsolicited mss, synopses and ideas welcome. No children's or sport titles.
Royalties paid annually.

Marino Books
See **Mercier Press Ltd**

Mercier Press Ltd
PO Box No 5, 5 French Church Street, Cork, Co. Cork, Republic of Ireland
☎00 353 21 275040   Fax 00 353 21 274969
Email: (Cork office): books@mercier.ie
(Dublin office): books@marino.ie
Website: www.indigo.ie/mercier
16 Hume Street, Dublin 2
☎00 353 1 661 5299 Fax 00 353 1 661 8583
Chairman *George Eaton*
Managing Director *John F. Spillane*
FOUNDED 1944. One of Ireland's largest publishers with a list of approx 250 Irish interest titles, history, fiction and mind, body, spirit. *Publishes* alternative lifestyle, folklore, women's interest, popular psychology, dual language, children's, cookery, history, politics, poetry and fiction. No academic books.
IMPRINTS **Mercier Press** *Mary Feehan* **Marino Books** *Jo O'Donoghue*. TITLES *Irish High Crosses; Irish Myths & Legends; Durango; The Great Irish Famine; A Short History of Ireland.* Unsolicited mss, synopses and ideas welcome.
Royalties paid annually.

Mount Eagle Publications Ltd
Dingle, Co. Kerry, Republic of Ireland
☎00 353 66 51463   Fax 00 353 66 51234
Publisher *Steve MacDonogh*
Approx. Annual Turnover £350,000
FOUNDED in 1997 when Mount Eagle took over Brandon Book Publishers. Strong Irish fiction and some non-fiction. About 15 titles a year. Not seeking unsolicited mss.

Newleaf
See **Gill & Macmillan**

The O'Brien Press Ltd
20 Victoria Road, Rathgar, Dublin 6
Republic of Ireland
☎00 353 1 4923333   Fax 00 353 1 4922777
Email: books@obrien.ie
Website: www.obrien.ie
Chairman/Managing Director
 Michael O'Brien

Editorial Director *Íde Ní Laoghaire*
FOUNDED 1974 to publish biography and books on the environment. Also *publishes* business, adult fiction, crime, popular biography, music and travel. In recent years the company has become a substantial force in children's publishing, concentrating mainly on juvenile novels. No poetry or academic. About 40 titles a year. Unsolicited mss (with return postage enclosed), synopses and ideas for books welcome.
Royalties paid annually.

Oak Tree Press
Merrion Building, Lower Merrion Street, Dublin 2, Republic of Ireland
☎00 353 1 6761600   Fax 00 353 1 6761644
Email: oaktreep@iol.ie
Website: www.oaktreepress.com
Managing Director *Brian O'Kane*
FOUNDED 1992. Part of Cork Publishing. Specialist publisher of business and professional books: accounting, finance, management and law aimed at students and practitioners in Ireland and the UK. About 25 titles a year. TITLES *The Accountant's Guide to Excel; Winning Business Proposals; The European Handbook of Management Consultancy; Once a Customer, Always a Customer; Working and Living in Ireland.* Unsolicited mss and synopses welcome; send to *David Givens*, General Manager, at the address above.
Royalties paid twice yearly.

On Stream Publications Ltd
Cloghroe, Blarney, Co. Cork, Republic of Ireland
☎00 353 21 385798   Fax 00 353 21 385798
Chairman/Managing Director *Roz Crowley*
Approx. Annual Turnover £200,000
FOUNDED 1992. Formerly Forum Publications. *Publishes* academic, fiction, cookery, wine, general health and fitness, local history, railways, photography and practical guides. About 6 titles a year. TITLES *The Merchants of Ennis; On-Farm Research – The Broad Picture; French Country Roads: A Wine Lovers' Guide to France.* Synopses and ideas welcome. No children's books.
Royalties paid twice yearly.

Poolbeg Press Ltd
123 Baldoyle Industrial Estate, Baldoyle, Dublin 13, Republic of Ireland
☎00 353 1 832 1477   Fax 00 353 1 832 1430
Email: poolbeg@iol.ie
Managing Director *Philip MacDermott*
Editor *Gaye Shortland*
Approx. Annual Turnover £1.5 million+

FOUNDED 1976 to publish the Irish short story and has since diversified to include all areas of fiction (literary and popular), children's fiction and non-fiction, and adult non-fiction: history, biography and topics of public interest. About 70 titles a year. Unsolicited mss, synopses and ideas welcome (mss preferred). No drama.

IMPRINTS **Poolbeg** (paperback and hardback); **Children's Poolbeg**; **Wren**.

Royalties paid bi-annually.

Real Ireland Design Ltd

27 Beechwood Close, Boghall Road, Bray, Co. Wicklow, Republic of Ireland
☎00 353 1 2860799   Fax 00 353 1 2829962

Managing Director *Desmond Leonard*

Producers of calendars, diaries, posters, greetings cards and books, servicing the Irish tourist industry. *Publishes* photography and tourism. About 2 titles a year. No fiction. Unsolicited mss, synopses and ideas welcome.

Royalties paid twice yearly.

Relay Publications

Tyone, Nenagh, Co. Tipperary, Republic of Ireland
☎00 353 67 31734   Fax 00 353 67 31734
Email: relaybooks@tinet.ie

Managing Director *Dònal A. Murphy*

FOUNDED 1980; in abeyance 1985–92. *Publishes* regional history. 4 titles in 1999. Welcomes unsolicited mss, ideas and synopses. No fiction.

Royalties paid twice yearly.

Roberts Rinehart Publishers

Trinity House, Charleston Road, Dublin 6, Republic of Ireland
☎00 353 1 4976860   Fax 00 353 1 4976861

Chairman *Rick Rinehart*
Chief Executive Officer *Jack Van Zandt*

European branch of a US company first established in 1983. Particularly active in the Irish-American market. *Publishes* general non-fiction, particularly arts, environment, nature, Irish interest, photography, politics, history and biography; and colour illustrated children's books, fiction and non-fiction. No adult fiction. About 60 titles a year. TITLES *Literary Ireland; The Troubles; At Home in Ireland; Cats As Cats Can; The People Who Hugged the Trees.*

Royal Dublin Society

Science Section, Ballsbridge, Dublin 4, Republic of Ireland
☎00 353 1 6680866   Fax 00 353 1 6604014
Email: carol.power@rds.ie

Website: www.rds.ie

President *Col. W. A. Ringrose*

FOUNDED 1731 for the promotion of agriculture, science and the arts, and throughout its history has published books and journals towards this end. Publishers hired on contract basis. *Publishes* conference proceedings, biology and the history of Irish science. TITLES *Agricultural Development for the 21st Century; The Right Trees in the Right Places; Agriculture & the Environment; Water of Life; Science, Technology & Realism*; occasional papers in *Irish Science & Technology* series.

Royalties not generally paid.

Royal Irish Academy

19 Dawson Street, Dublin 2, Republic of Ireland
☎00 353 1 6762570   Fax 00 353 1 6762346

Executive Secretary *Patrick Buckley*
Editor of Publications *Rachel McNicholls*
Approx. Annual Turnover £50,000

FOUNDED in 1785, the Academy has been publishing since 1787. Core publications are journals but more books published in last 13 years. *Publishes* academic, Irish interest and Irish language. About 7 titles a year. Welcomes mss, synopses and ideas of an academic standard.

Royalties paid once yearly, where applicable.

Salmon Publishing Ltd

Knockeve, Cliffs of Moher, Co. Clare, Republic of Ireland
☎00 353 65 81941   Fax 00 353 65 81621
Email: salpub@iol.ie
Website: www.salmonpoetry.com

Managing Director *Jessie Lendennie*
Approx. Annual Turnover £50,000

FOUNDED 1982. *Publishes* contemporary Irish and international poetry. 8 titles in 1998. TITLES *Journey Backward* Tom O'Malley; *Iron Mountain Road* Eamonn Wall; *The Knife in the Wave* Mary O'Malley; *Weathering* Ann Zell; *True North* Fred Johnston. Unsolicited mss welcome.

Royalties paid twice yearly.

Tír Eolas

Newtownlynch, Doorus, Kinvara, Co. Galway, Republic of Ireland
☎00 353 91 637452   Fax 00 353 91 637452

Publisher/Managing Director *Anne Korff*
Approx. Annual Turnover £50,000

FOUNDED 1987. *Publishes* books and guides on ecology, archaeology, folklore and culture. TITLES *The Book of the Burren; The Shannon Floodlands; Not a Word of a Lie; The Book of*

Aran; Women of Ireland, A Biographic Dictionary; Kinvara, A Seaport Town on Galway Bay. Unsolicited mss, synopses and ideas for books welcome. No specialist scientific and technical, fiction, plays, school textbooks or philosophy.
Royalties paid annually.

Town House and Country House

Trinity House, Charleston Road, Ranelagh, Dublin 6, Republic of Ireland
☎00 353 1 4972399   Fax 00 353 1 4970927
Email: books@townhouse.ie

Managing Director *Treasa Coady*

FOUNDED 1980. *Publishes* commercial fiction, art and archaeology, biography and environment. About 20 titles a year. TITLES *Love Like Hate Adore* Deirdre Purcell; *Mary, Mary* Julie Parsons; *Now is the Time* Sr. Stanislaus Kennedy; *Wild Wicklow* Richard Nairn and Miriam Crowley. Unsolicited mss, synopses and ideas welcome. No children's books.
Royalties paid twice yearly.

Veritas Publications

7–8 Lower Abbey Street, Dublin 1, Republic of Ireland
☎00 353 1 8788177   Fax 00 353 1 8786507
Email: snmelody@tinet.ie

Chairman *Diarmuid Murray*

Director *Fr Sean Melody*

FOUNDED 1969 to supply religious textbooks to schools and later introduced a more general religious list. Part of the Catholic Communications Institute. *Publishes* religious books only. About 30 titles a year. Unsolicited mss, synopses and ideas for books welcome.
Royalties paid annually.

Wolfhound Press

68 Mountjoy Square, Dublin 1, Republic of Ireland
☎00 353 1 8740354   Fax 00 353 1 8720207

Managing Director *Seamus Cashman*

FOUNDED 1974. Member of **Clé** – the Irish Book Publishers Association. *Publishes* art, biography, children's, fiction, general non-fiction, history, literature, literary studies, audio and gift books. About 30 titles a year. TITLES *Famine; Run With the Wind; Leading Hollywood; Eye Witness Bloody Sunday; Breakfast in Babylon; Father Brown's Titanic Album.* Unsolicited mss (with synopses and s.a.e.) and ideas welcome.
Royalties paid annually.

Wren

See **Poolbeg Press Ltd**

The Future of Crime Fiction

Minette Walters

When Edgar Allen Poe's *The Murders in the Rue Morgue* first appeared in Graham's Lady's and Gentleman's Magazine in 1841, I wonder how many readers recognized that it was the birth of a new literary genre – the detective story. Within a short time the idea had expanded to novel length with Emile Gaboriau's *L'Affaire Lerouge* in France in 1866, Wilkie Collins' *The Moonstone* in England in 1868, Anna Katharine Green's *The Leavenworth Case* in 1878 in America, and Fergus Hume's *The Mystery of a Hansom Cab* in 1886 in Australia.

In a hundred years crime fiction has become one of the most successful of the literary genres, spawning endless sub-genres – most recently: police procedural/forensic science thrillers, legal thrillers, psychological thrillers, and serial-killer thrillers. In addition, many best-selling crime writers of their time are now ranked among the greats of literature – Edgar Allen Poe, Wilkie Collins, Arthur Conan Doyle, G.K. Chesterton, Dorothy L. Sayers, Josephine Tey, Raymond Chandler – with some fictional detectives becoming better known to the public than their creators.

But what of the next hundred years? Will Sherlock Holmes still be a household name at the end of the twenty-first century? Will any of the crime writers of the last three decades be remembered three decades from now? Where can crime fiction go that it hasn't gone already?

The challenge to writers and publishers to keep the genre alive and fresh for another hundred years is a tough one because, across the developed world, reading books as entertainment takes a poor second to watching television, video and computer screens. Indeed a gloomy prediction for the 21st century is that fewer and fewer novels will be published because reading for entertainment will sink below *origami* in popularity. It's already a brave youngster who admits to preferring the loneliness of long-distance reading to the more fashionable, instant gratification of a blockbuster movie where ears, eyes and intellect are stimulated simultaneously and the experience is shared with others.

A happier, and I believe more realistic, prediction is that the public will grow tired of a culture that is governed by what the great and the good consider 'suitable' for mass consumption, and reading fiction will become sexy again. Fashions come and go but the written word has legs. Millions already flock to the uncensored pages of the Internet where ideas can be exchanged freely through a network that doesn't suffer from the heavily regulated approach that pervades the rest of the media. Forty years ago *Lady Chatterley's Lover* broke through the stuffy rules governing tabooed sex words. Today we have the raw, but immensely powerful, language of *Trainspotting*. Twenty years ago it was said that letter-writing had been killed off by the telephone. Today, emails and faxes are the favoured means of communication, particularly across continents where time differences make telephoning difficult.

When I'm asked why I write crime fiction, I always answer that I enjoy playing games. In this I am obviously no different from the majority of the population. The suggestion that parlour games are dead because there's no time for them in modern society is a myth. The format may be different, but the desire to compete is alive and well. *Countdown* is Channel 4's most popular programme with upwards of four million people sitting down every afternoon to try to beat the panellists at television scrabble; and *Who Wants to be a Millionaire?*, ITV's general knowledge quiz, regularly attracts eighteen million viewers who shout at their screens in frustration when contestants don't know the answers to apparently simple questions.

Playing games is as natural to human nature as breathing and reproduction. We like to win ... we like to be right ... we like to demonstrate that we know more than the next man... and the crime novel is custom-made for this side of man's nature. Mystery and suspense are the names of the game for, irrespective of which sub-genre a writer chooses, there is always a question at the heart of the story. Whodunit? Whydunit? Howdunit? Or any imaginative variation on these themes. Even the grittiest and most realistic examples of the genre still demand closure, even if that closure raises further questions in the reader's mind. Just as in real trials, the resolution – a guilty verdict – doesn't necessarily explain why the victim had to die.

Of course it's possible to write a crime story that does not involve murder, but the idea that an individual should see the killing of another as a solution to a problem is a fascinating one. It suggests anything from supreme arrogance to debilitating terror, with the full gamut of emotions in between, yet most of us can only guess at what drives a person to kill, or indeed what it feels like to do it. Nor can we fully understand the awful impact that violent death has on a community unless we've experienced it ourselves. Murder is alien to 99% of the population. It remains the single commandment that most of us have never broken and any treatment of it draws heavily on the author's imagination. How ever much research he does, how ever many murderers he may speak to, one fact remains true: that the dead cannot speak and no murdered victim has ever been able to tell his or her side of the story.

Crime writers are often described as social commentators because detail is important in a crime novel. Not just because readers want a chance to solve the puzzle before the author does, but because fantasy is never so compelling as when it is rooted in a recognisable reality. Would psychological profiling have attracted such world-wide interest so quickly if Thomas Harris hadn't drawn on the wealth of material developed by the FBI's behavioural scientists at Quantaco in order to create Hannibal Lector? Would those of us who have never been to the races know anything about jockeys and their world if Dick Francis hadn't chosen it as the back-drop of his novels?

Agatha Christie, whose reputation has taken something of a battering in recent years from predominately male critics of the hard-boiled school of writing, shines a fascinating spotlight on the dying world of the English middle class pre, during and post the Second World War. In contrast to Dorothy Sayers who was exploring the rarefied atmospheres of the intellectual and aristocratic elite through Lord Peter Wimsey and Oxford, Christie preferred provincial towns and suburban villas where the moderately wealthy were rapidly losing their status as the old world gave way to a new and more dynamic one. Raymond Chandler depicted the mean streets of Los Angeles; Georges Simenon – Paris; Colin Dexter – Oxford; Erle Stanley Gardiner and John Grisham – the court-room; Patricia Cornwell – the Medical Examiner's office in Richmond, Virginia; Val McDermid – Manchester. Others depict society's hidden dangers. Patricia Highsmith, Ruth Rendell, P.D. James and Frances Fyfield have all explored the unpredictable behaviour of social outcasts and loners; I explore the claustrophobic atmosphere of dysfunctional family life where damage is deep, long-lasting and usually kept secret for the sake of respectability.

As one would expect, the style of the genre has gone through various evolutions in one hundred and fifty years. In America it began by adopting the model set by Conan Doyle until Dashiell Hammett and Raymond Chandler introduced the hard-boiled school of writing with its emphasis on tough realism and resolution through action; through Sayers, Christie, Marsh and Allingham in England the development remained truer to Conan Doyle with the emphasis on character analysis and resolution through patient questioning and sifting of evidence. This has led to two distinct voices within the genre, each of which has given rise to different sub-genres. As one example, the serial-killer thriller, with its concentration on the pursuit of an unknown murderer across state boundaries, is a true product of the American evolution; while the psychological thriller, with its concentration on the close portrayal of a limited number of characters in a narrow environment, is a true product of the English evolution.

In an introduction to an anthology of stories in the '30s entitled *Great Short Stories of Detection, Mystery and Horror*, Dorothy L. Sayers wrote: 'Some prefer the intellectual cheerfulness of the detective story; some the uneasy emotions of the ghost-story; but in either case the tale must be about dead bodies ... Death seems to provide the minds of the Anglo-Saxon race with a greater fund of innocent amusement than any other single subject, and when it is occasioned or accompanied by Sin in its more repugnant shapes, the fun grows faster and more furious.' Tough, dark, gritty realism is today's favoured style – closer to Wilkie Collins, ironically, than to Sayers – so 'intellectual cheerfulness', 'innocent amusement' and 'fun' are not the sort of phrases that many contemporary writers would use in connection with their work. Different times, different customs ... but the same fascination with dead bodies.

Whoever wrote Genesis set the pattern. The first two chapters are devoted to God's greatness, the next two to sex and murder. I'd love to think the next millennium will see mankind living in such peace and harmony with itself that words like jealousy, anger and frustration attract the tag archaic in the dictionary and murder stories become as obsolete as medieval Mystery plays, but I can't see it happening. The treatment will change, methods of detection will change but the emotions that drive men to kill will not. We've been at it too long to stop now.

Back to the Bible: three thousand years ago in the tenth century BC, King David ordered the brutal murder of Uriah the Hittite for reasons of sex. He wanted to take Bathsheba, Uriah's wife, into his own bed. Shortly afterwards, one of his sons, Amnon, incestuously raped his sister, Tamar, and was then killed in revenge by his brother Absalom who hated him. In the fifth century BC, Oedipus killed his father in the first recorded incident of road rage when their chariots met at a crossroads and his father refused to give way. *Macbeth* is as compelling now as it was when it was written nearly 500 years ago because the logic at the heart of it – ruthless ambition – is fundamental to the human condition.

Plus ca change, plus c'est la meme chose ...

Minette Walters is the author of The Ice House *(published by Macmillan; winner of the Crime Writers' Association (CWA) John Creasey Award),* The Sculptress *(Macmillan; winner of the Edgar Allen Poe Award),* The Scold's Bridle *(Macmillan; winner of the CWA/Macallan Gold Dagger Award),* The Dark Room, The Echo *and* The Breaker.

Audio Books

Abbey Home Entertainment Group Ltd

Premiere House, Premiere Corner, Queens Park, London W6 3EG

☎0181 930 4484　　　　Fax 0181 930 4463

Managing Director *Anne Miles*

Abbey were the instigators (previously as MSD Holdings) in the development of the spoken word. With over 20 years' experience in recording, marketing and distribution of audio, book and cassette, their catalogue includes major children's story characters such as *Thomas the Tank Engine, Postman Pat, Goosebumps* and *Winnie the Pooh. Specialises* in children's audio cassettes. 50 titles in 1998. Ideas from authors and agents welcome.

BBC Radio Collection

Woodlands, 80 Wood Lane, London W12 0TT

☎0181 576 2230　　　　Fax 0181 576 3851

Owner *BBC Worldwide Ltd*
Publisher *Jan Paterson*
Editorial Director *Mary Kalemkerian*

ESTABLISHED in 1988 as The BBC Radio Collection, BBC Audio now releases material associated with BBC Radio and Television. *Publishes* drama, comedy, science fiction, fiction, non-fiction and sound effects. TITLES *Hancock's Half Hour; Round the Home; Alan Bennett's Diaries; Knowing Me, Knowing You; This Sceptred Isle.* Almost all releases sourced from BBC Radio and Television. Unsolicited work not accepted.

Canongate Audio

See **Canongate Books** under **UK Publishers**

Cavalcade Story Cassettes

See **Chivers Audio Books**

Chivers Audio Books

Windsor Bridge Road, Bath BA2 3AX

☎01225 335336　　　　Fax 01225 310771

Managing Director *Julian Batson*

Part of **Chivers Press Ltd**. *Publishes* a wide range of titles, mainly for library consumption. Fiction, autobiography, children's and crime. 270 titles in 1998. TITLES *Brideshead Revisited* Evelyn Waugh; *Taken on Trust* Terry Waite;

Behind the Scenes at the Museum Kate Atkinson; *The 'Regeneration' Trilogy* Pat Barker; *True Ghost Stories* Terry Deary; *Famous Five Stories* Enid Blyton. IMPRINTS **Chivers Audio Books, Chivers Children's Audio Books, Cavalcade Story Cassettes, Moonlight Romance, Sterling Audio Books, Word for Word Audio Books**.

Corgi Audio

Transworld Publishers Ltd, 61–63 Uxbridge Road, London W5 5SA

☎0181 579 2652　　　　Fax 0181 231 6666

Managing Director *Mark Barty-King*

Part of **Transworld Publishers**. *Publishes* fiction, autobiography, children's and humour. TITLES *Discworld Series* Terry Pratchett; *Notes From a Small Island* Bill Bryson; *A Kentish Lad* Frank Muir; *The Horse Whisperer* Nicholas Evans.

Cover To Cover Cassettes Ltd

PO Box 112, Marlborough, Wiltshire SN8 3UG

☎01672 562255　　　　Fax 01672 564634

E-mail: email@covertocover.co.uk

Managing Director *Helen Nicoll*

Publishes complete and unabridged audio books of classic 19th and 20th century fiction – Jane Austen, Charles Dickens, Anthony Trollope, plus children's titles – *Worst Witch* Jill Murphy; *Sheep-Pig* Dick King-Smith; *Story of Tracy Beaker* Jacqueline Wilson; *In Your Garden* Vita Sackville-West (book/cassette). 26 titles in 1998.

CSA Telltapes Ltd

101 Chamberlayne Road, London NW10 3ND

☎0181 960 8466　　　　Fax 0181 968 0804

E-mail: info@csatelltapes.demon.co.uk

Managing Director *Clive Stanhope*

FOUNDED 1989. *Publishes* fiction, children's, short stories, poetry, travel, biographies. Over 100 titles to-date. Tends to favour quality/classic/nostalgic/timeless literature for the 30+ age group. TITLES *Carry on Jeeves* P. G. Wodehouse; *Great Trials: Oscar Wilde; The Third Man* Graham Greene; *Hideous Kinky* Esther Freud; *England Their England* A. G. Macdonell; *Goodbye Mr Chips* James Hilton; *How Proust Can Change Your Life* Alain de Botton. Ideas for cassettes welcome.

Cult Listening
See **PolyGram Out Loud**

CYP Limited
The Fairway, Bush Fair, Harlow, Essex
CM18 6LY
☎01279 444707   Fax 01279 445570
Joint Managing Directors *Mike Kitson,*
John Bassett
FOUNDED 1978. *Publishes* children's material
for those under 10 years of age; educational,
entertainment, licensed characters (i.e. *Mr Men;*
Little Miss). Ideas for cassettes welcome.

Faber.Penguin Audiobooks
27 Wrights Lane, London W8 5TZ
☎0171 416 3000   Fax 0171 416 3289
3 Queen Square, London WC1N 3AU
☎0171 465 0045   Fax 0171 465 0108
E-mail: audio@penguin.co.uk
Website: http://www.penguin.co.uk
Publishing Manager *Anna Hopkins* (at
Wrights Lane address)
Publishing Director *Joanna Mackle* (at
Queen Square address)

A joint venture between **Penguin Books** and
Faber & Faber. *Publishes* 25–30 titles per year,
drawing on the strength of Faber's authors.
AUTHORS include Wendy Cope, T. S. Eliot,
William Golding, Seamus Heaney, Ted Hughes,
Philip Larkin, Garrison Keillor, Paul Muldoon,
Sylvia Plath.

Golden Days of Radio
See **Hodder Headline Audio Books**

Halsgrove
See entry under **UK Publishers**

HarperCollins AudioBooks
77–85 Fulham Palace Road, London W6 8JB
☎0181 741 7070
Fax 0181 307 4517(adult)/307 4291(children's)
The Collins audio and video company was
acquired in the mid-eighties but the video section was later sold.

DIVISIONS
Adult Managing Director *Adrian Bourne,* Pub-
lisher *Rosalie George. Publishes* a wide range in-
cluding popular and classic fiction, non-fiction,
Shakespeare and poetry. 60 titles in 1998. TITLES
God of Small Things Arundhati Roy; *Angela's*
Ashes Frank McCourt; *Fugitive Pieces* Anne
Michaels; *About a Boy* Nick Hornby; *Cold*

Mountain Charles Frasier; *Memoirs of a Geisha*
Arthur Golden.
   Children's Publishing Director *Gail Penston,*
Senior Editor *Stella Paskins Publishes* picture
books/cassettes and story books/cassettes as well
as single and double tapes for children aged 2–13
years. Fiction, songs, early learning, poetry etc.
60 titles in 1998. AUTHORS C. S. Lewis, Roald
Dahl, Enid Blyton, Robin Jarvis, Colin and
Jacqui Hawkins, Ian Whybrow, Lynne Reid
Banks, Robert Westall, Jean Ure, Nick
Butterworth, Judith Kerr.

Hodder Headline Audio Books
338 Euston Road, London NW1 3BH
☎0171 873 6000   Fax 0171 873 6024
Publisher *Rupert Lancaster*
Editor *Helen Garnons-Williams*
LAUNCHED in 1994 with 50 titles. A strong list,
especially for theatre, vintage radio, film tie-ins,
poetry plus fiction, non-fiction, children's, reli-
gious. Approx 120 titles in 1998. AUTHORS
Louis de Bernières, Enid Blyton, John LeCarré,
Alex Ferguson, Mick Inkpen (*Kipper* books),
Stephen King, Rosamunde Pilcher, Emma
Tennant, Joanna Trollope, Terry Waite, Mary
Wesley. IMPRINT **Golden Days of Radio**
series of classic vintage radio broadcasts.

Isis Audio Books
7 Centremead, Osney Mead, Oxford OX2 0ES
☎01865 250333   Fax 01865 790358
Managing Director *John Durrant*
Editorial Head *Veronica Babington Smith*
Part of **Isis Publishing Ltd**. *Publishes* fiction
and a few non-fiction titles. AUTHORS include
Virginia Andrews, Barbara Taylor Bradford,
Edwina Currie, Leslie Thomas, Douglas Adams,
Terry Pratchett.

Ladybird Books Ltd
Ground Floor, 39 Stoney Street,
Nottingham NG1 1LX
☎0115 9486900   Fax 0115 9486901
Managing Director *Michael Herridge*
Part of the Penguin Group. *Publishes* recordings
of titles which appear on the Ladybird book list
only. 60 titles in 1998. TITLES *The Railway*
Children; Gulliver's Travels; Little Red Riding Hood;
Puss in Boots; Farmyard Stories for Under Fives.

Laughing Stock Productions
81 Charlotte Street, London W1P 1LB
☎0171 637 7943   Fax 0171 436 1646
Managing Director *Colin Collino*

FOUNDED 1991. Issues a wide range of comedy cassettes from family humour to alternative comedy. 12–16 titles per year. TITLES *Red Dwarf; Shirley Valentine* (read by Willy Russell); *Rory Bremner; Peter Cook Anthology; Sean Hughes; John Bird and John Fortune; Eddie Izzard.*

Macmillan Audio Books

25 Eccleston Place, London SW1W 9NF
☎0171 881 8000   Fax 0171 881 8001
Owner *Macmillan Publishers Ltd*
Manager *Alison Muirden*

FOUNDED 1995. *Publishes* adult fiction, non-fiction and autobiography, focusing mainly on lead book titles and releasing audio simultaneously with hard or paperback publication. About 25 titles a year. AUTHORS Wilbur Smith, Ken Follett, Colin Dexter, Clare Francis, Minette Walters, Michael Ondaatje, Richard E. Grant, Helen Fielding, Elizabeth Jane Howard, Martin Cruz Smith, Colin Forbes, James Herbert, Shaun Hutson, Jackie Collins, Kathy Lette, Janet Evanovich, Robin Cook.

MCI Spoken Word

72–74 Dean Street, London W1V 5HB
☎0171 396 8899   Fax 0171 396 8901
Owner *VCI Plc*
Head of Spoken Word *Danny Keene*

Established in 1993 and now a rapidly expanding publisher of a wide range of spoken word titles: comedy, children's, TV programmes. 150 titles to-date. TITLES *Inspector Morse; Thomas the Tank Engine; Eddie Izzard, Cracker; James Bond.*

Moonlight Romance

See **Chivers Audio Books**

Mr Punch Productions

139 Kensington High Street, London W8 6SU
☎0171 368 0088   Fax 0171 368 0051
E-mail: mrpunch@msn.com
Managing Director *Stewart Richards*

FOUNDED 1995. Independent producer of audio books – drama and non-fiction. 10 titles in 1998. SERIES **Classic Journals** and **Hollywood Playhouse**, Oscar-winning films specially adapted for the radio and performed by many of the original stars. TITLES *The Journals of Dorothy Wordsworth; The Letters & Journals of Lord Nelson; Casablanca; All About Eve; Scott of the Antarctic; Tales From the Old Testament.* Ideas for new releases welcome.

Naxos AudioBooks

Unit 4, Wyllyotts Manor, Potters Bar, Hertfordshire EN6 2HN
☎01707 661961   Fax 01707 661971
Email: Naxos_Audiobooks@compuserve.com
Owner *HNH International, Hong Kong*
Managing Director *Nicolas Soames*

FOUNDED 1994. Part of Naxos, the classical budget CD company. *Publishes* classic and modern fiction, non-fiction, children's and junior classics, drama and poetry. TITLES *Paradise Lost* Milton; *Ulysses* Joyce; *Kim* Kipling; *Decline and Fall of the Roman Empire* Gibbon.

Penguin Audiobooks

27 Wrights Lane, London W8 5TZ
☎0171 416 3000   Fax 0171 416 3289
E-mail: audio@penguin.co.uk
Website: http://www.penguin.co.uk
Owner *Penguin Books Ltd*
Publishing Manager *Anna Hopkins*

Launched in November 1993 and has rapidly expanded since then to reflect the diversity of **Penguin Books'** list. *Publishes* mostly fiction, both classical and contemporary, non-fiction, autobiography and an increasing range of children's titles under the **Puffin Audiobooks** imprint. Approx. 90 titles a year. Contemporary AUTHORS include: Paul Theroux, Miss Reed, Dick Francis, Barbara Vine, Michael Ridpath, Anne Fine, Gillian Cross, Stephen King, John Mortimer, Roald Dahl.

PolyGram 'Out Loud'

1 Sussex Place, Hammersmith, London W6 9XS
☎0181 910 5000   Fax 0181 910 5400
Owner *PolyGram*
Product Manager *Alex Mitchison*

One of the oldest players in the Spoken Word industry, dating back to the 1950s with classic recordings including the entire Shakespeare collection (currently being re-released), poetry and many pieces of classic literature. In recent years, PolyGram has worked closely with its video labels, VVL and PVL, to acquire some of the best comedians in the UK. Establishing links with the performers at an early stage in their career has given PolyGram a strong working relationship and link with the comedy circuit. In September 1998, PolyGram 'Spoken Word' was relaunched as PolyGram 'Out Loud' to reflect the changing image of the catalogue. By adding the **Cult Listening** label to the list, PolyGram is giving a clear message of where the industry has its future.

Puffin Audiobooks
See **Penguin Audiobooks**

Random House Audiobooks
20 Vauxhall Bridge Road, London
SW1V 2SA
☎0171 840 8400   Fax 0171 233 6127
Owner *Random House UK Ltd*
Managing Director *Simon King*
Manager *Victoria Williams*

The audiobooks division of Random House started early in 1991. Acquired the Reed Audio list in 1997. *Publishes* fiction, non-fiction and self help. 18 titles in 1998. AUTHORS include John Grisham, Stephen Fry, Charles Handy, Patricia Cornwell, Michael Crichton and Ruth Rendell.

CHILDREN'S DIVISION IMPRINT **Tellastory** AUTHORS include Jane Hissey, Shirley Hughes, David McKee and Michael Palin. About 20 titles in 1998.

Simon & Schuster Audio
Africa House, 64–78 Kingsway, London
WC2B 6AH
☎0171 316 1900   Fax 0171 316 0332
Audio Manager *Darren Nash*

Began by distributing the American parent company's audio products and moved on to repackaging products specifically for the UK market. In 1994 became firmly established in this market with a huge rise in turnover. *Publishes* adult fiction, self help, business, Star Trek titles. TITLES *Mr MacGregor* Alan Titchmarsh; *The Time Machine* H. G. Wells; *Popcorn* Ben Elton; *The 7 Habits of Highly Successful People* Stephen R. Covey; *Deja Dead* Kathy Reichs; *Star Trek IX: Insurrection* J. M. Dillard.

Smith/Doorstop Cassettes
The Poetry Business, The Studio, Byram Arcade, Huddersfield, West Yorkshire
HD1 1ND
☎01484 434840   Fax 01484 426566
Co-directors *Peter Sansom, Janet Fisher*

Publishes poetry, read and introduced by the writer. AUTHORS Simon Armitage, Sujata Bhatt, Carol Ann Duffy, Les Murray, Ian McMillan.

Soundings
Kings Drive, Whitley Bay, Tyne & Wear
NE26 2JT
☎0191 253 4155   Fax 0191 251 0662
Managing Director *John Durrant*

FOUNDED in 1982. *Publishes* fiction and non-fiction; crime, romance, young adults. 192 titles a year. AUTHORS include Angus McVicar, Barbara Cartland, Catherine Cookson;, Olivia Manning, Derek Tangye, Lyn Andrews, Susan Sallis, Mary Jane Staples, Alexander Fullerton, Patrick O'Brian, Pamela Oldfield. Ideas for cassettes welcome.

Sterling Audio Books
See **Chivers Audio Books**

Tellastory
See **Random House Audiobooks**

WALKfree Productions Ltd
56 Upper Norwood Street, Leckhampton, Cheltenham, Gloucestershire GL53 0DU
☎01242 231800
Website: http://www.reardon.co.uk
Publishing/Sales Director *Nicholas Reardon*

FOUNDED 1996. In association with the Ordnance Survey, produces *WALKfree AudioGuides* which 'cultivate a new form of country walking experience in the countryside'. The audio tape is accompanied by a 16-page guide book containing an Ordnance Survey Travelmaster map extract plus outline route maps. Each guide also offers advice on convenient places for refreshment and local contacts. TITLES *The Cotswolds; Peak District; Hadrian's Wall.*

Word for Word Audio Books
See **Chivers Audio Books**

Poetry - A Vigour Verging On Ferocity

Peter Finch

'For an art form often consigned to a quiet corner by those who never read it, poetry displays a vigour verging on ferocity,' said Sean O'Brien in his introduction to *The Firebox*, Picador's splendid new anthology of poetry in Britain and Ireland after 1945. And it's that vigour which is new. No more hiding under cushions, no more relegation to the back of the bookstores, no more ghettos in the midnight reaches of Radio 3. Poetry in the UK has come of age.

You might be forgiven for imagining that things have always been as they are now – more column inches on the Poet Laureate than the Millennium Dome, poetry on the underground, a National Poetry Day, the nation's favourite comic poems in the bestsellers – but go back even ten years and you'll find Britain to have been much more a cultural desert. 'Poetry is best as a sort of Sunday afternoon painting activity,' as one arts official then was heard to say.

Change has been steady – a product, perhaps, of better living standards, increasing literacy, and the distance between us and that post-war image of verse as a sort of prissy, poofterish activity which you engaged in while wearing a pink shirt. Not only can we afford poetry now but the stuff has balls.

The barometer which measures all this is not sales in the market place (for, in terms of profit, poetry remains an indulgence) but the new willingness of our national arts funders to suddenly start sticking substantial sums in the hands of poetry promoters. There are groups up and down the country who have now been given the wherewithal to establish verse venues, small publishing companies, magazines, reading programmes, video projects, web sites and festivals. Finance for this kind of activity has always, to some degree, been available but never so much and across such a wide front as now. Recently the Poetry Society (see **Organisations of Interest to Poets**), our venerable and for most of this century Victorian institution, has taken a terrific turn towards the future. Awarded almost half-a-million by the Lottery the Society has now put poets into places where they've never been seen before: M&S, London Zoo, public parks and gardens, Barnsley Football Club, hospital waiting rooms, the fish and chip shops of Wigan, North Norfolk District Council's refuse department, Worcester Cathedral, the BBC. At the Arts Council of England they have even published a *Policy for Poetry* which suggests that the well-being of both poets and their outlets are of significant importance. 'Poetry is at the root of every culture … poetry matters.'

This might suggest that the poetry gravy train is the one to be on. Just scratch your sonnet onto an envelope back and you're aboard. All poetry is equal and there are magazines everywhere just clamouring to publish it. Last week you spotted a competition in the Sunday papers offering literally thousands in prize money. There was a poetry party on at your local bookshop with 'wine and celebrity guests'. You've watched the fight for the new poet laureate on tv. Fame and fortune are within grasp at last. You borrow the student next door's laptop and turn your envelop back into neat text on white A4. Poetry – the way to glory. Thank god it's not as simple as that.

Beneath the glitz and apparent glamour poetry actually turns out to be somewhat of an overproduced and certainly a significantly underconsumed new millennium fancy. In my annual survey of poetry publishers most welcomed the new recognition of poetry as a vital cultural force but almost all bemoaned the fact that poetry still does not sell. The new poets are out there, desperate for publication, yet most of them still do not put poetry on their weekly shopping lists. Roy Blackman, researching the subject for *Agenda*, came to the conclusion that out of a population of 56 million there were only 20,000 or so regular, active poetry readers. I had a look, again, at the magazine racks at W.H. Smith, just to be sure: lots of *Loaded* and mags about fish-keeping but still no poetry. Could it be that while the odd poem is okay, verse in bulk is off-putting?

What we need here – beyond official recognition that poetry is important – is a way of improving its quality. Less of Ginsberg's 'Best thoughts first thoughts' and more revision, less ignorance of the way poetry today actually is and more reading, less doing it on your own in isolation and more workshopping. We desperately need to move on from a society where the consumers of poetry are by and large its producers. Already the media have begun to use well-made work as cultural fillers – add poignancy to your film by getting the lead to recite some Auden, mark the anniversary by side-barring Sassoon, end the news by reciting Milligan. New poets on the rise (as well as some of the older ones with still open minds) can capitalise here. Be more ambassadorial, only release your best work, encourage others to actually buy poetry, read more yourself. Come to terms with the fact (if you didn't realise it already) that poetry rarely comes down from the clouds like some Blakean ray of light but, rather, it is the result of hard slog. 'If I knew where poems came from, I'd go there,' said Michael Longley. So keep looking.

First Step

Are you up to this? Are you personally convinced that your work is ready? If you are uncertain, then most likely that will be the view of everyone else. Check your text for glips and blips. Rework it. Root out any clichés or archaic poetry expressions such as O, doeth, bewilld'd and the like. Drop any of what Peter Sansom calls 'spirit of the age' poetry words. Do without shards, lozenges, lambent patina, stippled seagulls. If you use rhymes them make them less obvious. Check that any meter you may be using actually works. Try not to clank. If by this time your writing still sounds okay, then go ahead.

Commercial Publishers

Despite the obvious possibilities of making something from poetry in the commercial market place the number of those conglomerate publishers involved is actually pretty limited. Where once there was a plethora of mainstream poetry imprints there are now only three or four. Poetry is increasingly seen today as the quality line which enhances a publisher's list. Rarely there to make profit but more to impart class and fashion to the list. Compared to other lines slim volumes are, with a few exceptions, slow sellers. Their editors are almost always part-time or have other jobs within the company and are never allowed to publish what they would really like.

The obvious exception to this approach is long-term market leader and envy of the whole business **Faber & Faber**. Here editor Paul Keegan, recently moved in from Penguin, along with Jane Feaver, in charge of work for children, preside over a list which continues to be as important to the firm as when T.S. Eliot inaugurated it more than seventy years ago. The best poetry does transcend the limits of the traditional market, they believe. This is the imprint most poets would like to join. The greats of the twentieth century are here – Pound, Eliot, Plath, Hughes, Larkin. Seamus Heaney made half-a-million in sales when he won the Nobel prize. Ted Hughes sold 120,000 of his last book before he died. Wendy Cope regularly sells into five figures. The imprint is built on distinctively designed class and on the roster of contemporary poets are some of the best we have – Simon Armitage, Derek Walcott, Don Paterson, Glyn Maxwell, Andrew Motion, Tom Paulin, Hugo Williams, Paul Muldoon, Douglas Dunn. They have even started a poetry magazine, *First Pressings*, although the marketing for it treats it much more like a book. Faber will read all manuscripts submitted. Send a brief covering letter and a sample of your writing (10-20 poems), not forgetting s.a.e., if you think this is where you'll fit in.

Until recently Faber's leading place was followed closely by the **Oxford University Press** contemporary list of Sean O'Brien, D.J. Enright, Tobias Hill, Penelope Shuttle, Moniza Alvi, Peter Porter, Fleur Adcock and others. But the bottom line talks. The list has been dropped. 'Ninety per cent sell under 200 copies,' reported director Andrew Potter. From now on, apart from contractual obligations, poetry at OUP will only be from the past (although part of the list will continue under the imprint of specialist press Carcanet).

The commercial editor most admired for his taste is still **Cape's** Robin Robertson. His list is by no means all things to all people. Matthew Sweeney, John Burnside, Robert Crawford and Michael Longley are typical. Roberston, himself a fine poet, moved into the editorial chair from **Secker & Warburg**, who abandoned their own poetry list when he went. He produces five to six titles annually – all books, no anthologies and with a number sourced from the other side of the Atlantic. The care taken in their production is obvious – fine design, significant content. Check them out, with their distinctive fold-in flaps these books look worth the money. Worth trying? Yes, but potential contributors should never waste anyone's time by not looking at the list first. Fellow **Random House** imprint, **Chatto & Windus**, was once a major stronghold for poets although, sadly, no longer. A few years ago the poetry list ground to a halt altogether only to be revived again recently because the work on offer 'was too good to turn down'. Bernard O'Donoghue and Gerard Woodward are typical examples. Poetry editor Rebecca Carter expects to publish three or four new titles annually but unless supported by a strong recommendation from an established fellow practitioner does not want to see unsolicited manuscripts. Both Chatto and Cape will preview examples from their lists in the poem for the day section of the new Random House web site at *www.randomhouse.co.uk*

The **Harvill Press** runs one of the smaller commercial poetry lists, publishing one or two new titles annually. Central are the works of Paul Durcan and the late Raymond Carver. They also publish Michael Schmidt's fine anthology *Twentieth Century Poetry In English*. They'll look at new manuscripts but chances are slim. New writers would be better off starting elsewhere.

Among the other commercial houses activity appears to be limited to nominal titles, anthologies or back-list obligations. **Cassell** anthologise the poems from the London Underground (which sell so well you'd think they'd be encouraged to try something else). **Hodder & Stoughton** have anthologies on hope and humour. **Blandford** are in the Celtic mists. **Dent** recycle religion and Irish humanism. **Hutchinson** have Dannie Abse and the inspirational attractions of Helen Steiner Rice. **Methuen** stick to Brecht and John Hegley. Mainstream imprints may once have been the proving grounds for new voices but if recent activity is anything to go on that is certainly no longer the case. Some specialist interests are dealt with at **Lion** (Christian verse) and Oscars (gay) at BM Oscars, London WC1N 3XX – but it isn't a lot.

The Smaller Operators

Not all commercial publishing is vast and conglomerate. Independents still exist and on their lists poetry still occurs. **Payback Press**, an imprint of **Canongate Books**, has published Lemn Sissay's anthology of black British poetry, *The Fire People*. Northern Ireland general publisher, The **Blackstaff Press**, brings out at least one poetry title annually. Carol Rumens, Frank Ormsby and Ruth Carr's anthology of women poets are typical. **Serpent's Tail** keeps sticking its toes in the water with the odd title (but has declared that they do *not* want to see unsolicited new work), Welsh family firm **Gwasg Gomer** produces tidy editions of Brian Morris (Lord Morris of Castle Morris), Nigel Jenkins and Robert Harvard. Former *Sunday Times* Small Publisher of the Year, **Polygon**, (which is an imprint of **Edinburgh University Press**) continues to mix Gaelic with English as part of its 'poetry for the new generation' policy. Jackie Jones and Robert Crawford are editors. The press has at least half a dozen poets on the list including Donny O'Rourke, Rody Gorman, Liz Lochhead and W.N. Herbert.

Check their *The Dream State: The New Scottish Poets*. Send in if you are part of the Scottish renaissance.

Universities

In the UK activity is sparse. OUP down. Reprints and literary studies at **Cambridge**, the same at **Manchester**. At the **University of Wales Press**, who publishes a splendid series of collected works from Welsh poets, you need to be dead. American university presses such as Nebraska, **Chicago**, Pittsburg, Ohio, **Yale**, Duke, Northeastern, **Iowa**, **Syracuse** and **California** along with **W.W. Norton** do an increasing amount of verse but exclusively by Americans. No chances there. In Austria, however, the University of Salzburg Press, now known as Poetry Salzburg (Wolfgang Görtschacher and James Hogg, Universität Salzburg, Institut Für Anglistik und Amerikanistik, A-5020 Salzburg, Austria), has embarked on an extensive programme of substantial poetry volumes from the less commercial. Run by Wolfgang Görtschacher with financial help from its founder, James Hogg, the press output is at least 15 volumes annually. Workmanlike if not brilliantly designed books fill a niche unoccupied by anyone else. Salzburg rescues the neglected as well as spotlights the new. Typical authors include James Kirkup, Peter Russell, Eric Mottram, Alexis Lykiard, Alison Bielski and William Oxley. Hogg and Görtschacher along with Fred Beake also run *The Poet's Voice* magazine and have published a number of anthologies drawn from the little mags including a best of *Ore, Stride* and *Outposts*. Görtschacher's studies of the British Little Mag scene are also Salzburg highlights. Despite its Austrian location the poetry is almost exclusively British in origin

Women

There were days when **Virago** was out front here but no longer. Becoming part of **Little, Brown** clearly means becoming less partisan. In poetry terms the company does little more now than bring out the obvious (Margaret Atwood, Jean Binta Breeze, Merle Collins, Maya Angelou) along with the occasional anthology. At **The Women's Press**, Virago's main competitor, the situation is much the same. Original good intentions sunk into a programme which endlessly publishes Alice Walker, although their anthology of black women's poetry, *Bittersweet*, was an obvious exception. Women poets are better served by the poetry specialists. More of them anon.

The Mass Market Paperback

The cheap and popular end is where many poets imagine the best starting place to be. Paperback houses were founded to publish inexpensive reprints of hard-covered originals and, despite years of innovation and market posturing, to a large extent still fulfil this role. Being neither cheap nor (in sales terms) that popular poetry does not really fit in. Among the carousels at airports you do not see it. Check the empires of **Arrow**, **Corgi**, **Headline** and **Mills & Boon**. If you discount the inspirational, you won't find a book of verse between them. **Vintage**, to their credit, publish the occasional anthology and run reprints of Iain Sinclair but he is also a successful novelist. Elsewhere nothing, although there are two exceptions. At **Penguin**, where things are always different, poetry has a significant role. With a commercial ear ever to the ground the company has correctly assessed the market for contemporary and traditional verse and systematically and successfully filled it. Reprinting important volumes pioneered by poetry presses such as **Anvil**, **Carcanet** and **Bloodaxe**, originating historic and thematic anthologies, reviving classic authors and producing a multitude of translations en route, Penguin continues to provide an almost unrivalled introduction to the world of verse. But appearances aside, this is most certainly no place for the beginner. 'As a large trade publisher, we publish only anthologies plus a handful of famous poets,' publishing director Tony Lacey told me. 'We leave the discovering of poets to the specialists. The smaller presses can take risks; we cannot.' The company acts as main publishers for a select group of sure sellers which includes James Fenton, Geoffrey Hill, Craig Raine, and Roger McGough. The main thrust remains the re-packaging of proven bards such as Simon Armitage, Carol Ann Duffy, U.A. Fanthorpe and Dannie Abse, a good range of modern poets in translation along with larger sets from the likes of Allen Ginsberg and John Ashbery. The *Penguin Modern Poets* series of loosely-connected trios has now reached Volume 13 and represents an excellent cross-section of British and Irish contemporary verse. The company's recent poetry blockbuster and pool of controversy is the Simon Armitage and Robert Crawford edited *British and Irish Poetry Since The War*. Despite these obvious winners Lacey sees the whole market for verse as small, despite the hype.

Penguin's nearest rival, **Picador**, the literary imprint from **Pan Macmillan**, is now exhibiting considerable vigour. Under the commanding eye of successful and non-metropolitan poet Don Paterson it has followed its successful and very non-mainstream anthology of UK outsiders *Conductors of Chaos* with Sean O'Brien's equally important *The Firebox*, a fat anthology of poetry in Britain and Ireland after 1945. The imprint's individual collections have included volumes from proven poets Robin Robertson, Kathleen Jamie and Ruth Sharman, Ciaran Carson, Kate Clanchy, Colette Bryce, Paul Farley and Peter Armstrong. Picador intends to continue an output of four or so titles annually. Worth trying here? 'Certainly: 10 poems better than a full length ms, but establish some track record in the reputable journals first,' advises Paterson.

The Specialists

Despite less than enormous visibility in the commercial arena poetry actually flourishes. Where? With the specialist independents, a host of semi-commercial operations scattered across the country. They are run by genuine poetry enthusiasts whose prime concern is not so much money as the furtherance of their art. Begun as classic small presses which soon outgrew the restraints of back-bedroom offices and under-the-stairs warehousing, they have emerged by stealth. A real force on the poetry scene most now have national representation. These presses have learned well how the business works. You can find them in Waterstones, you can see them in Blackwells and at Ottakars. Most (but not all) receive grant aid, without which their publishing programmes would be sunk. They are models of what poetry publishing should be – active, involving, alert and exciting. They promote their lists through readings, tours, web sites and broadcasts and they involve their authors in the production and sales of their books. Never before have new poets been faced with so many publishing opportunities. And if there is any criticism then this is it. Too many books jamming the market. Just how does the reader see through the flood? By the press's reputation, I guess. Two have emerged well ahead of the pack – Carcanet and Bloodaxe. Along with Faber these two now dominate British poetry publishing.

The larger of the pair is Neil Astley's acclaimed **Bloodaxe Books**. Publishing fifty titles annually the press brings out more poetry books than any other British imprint. Picking up poets dropped by the commercial operators (including a few from the recently sunk OUP), discovering new ones and selling on to the world's anthologists, this is certainly one of poetry's best proving grounds. Based in Newcastle upon Tyne and begun in the early eighties, the press is unhindered by a past catalogue of classical wonders or an overly regional concern. It relentlessly pursues the new. Astley presents the complete service from thematic anthologies, world greats and selecteds to slim volumes by total newcomers. The press has its own range of excellent handbooks to the scene including Paul Hyland's *Getting Into Poetry* and Peter Sansom's *Writing Poems* along with an increasing range of critical volumes. Best poetry sellers are their anthologies: Linda France's *Sixty Women Poets*, Jenni Couzyn's *Contemporary Women Poets*, their decade-framing and still controversial anthology *The New Poetry*. With commendable concern to stay ahead Bloodaxe is pushing *New Blood*, an anthology of poets whose first books were published during the past decade. This plus Maura Dooley's anthology *Making For Planet Alice*, thirty new women poets whose first collections have appeared since 1990. Bloodaxe relishes the chance to publish work from outside the standard English mainstream – Ireland, Scotland, and Wales are all well represented, as are our more traditional UK outsiders such as J.H. Prynne. There is a multi-media thrust – a series of poets on CD and cassette (including a revival of the British Council's recordings of contemporary poets), video productions in conjunction with television and a Bloodaxe web site (*www.bloodaxebooks.demon.co.uk*). Bloodaxe will not go rusty with age. Newcomers are advised to send a sample rather than a full collection. 'If you don't read contemporary poetry we are unlikely to be interested in your work,' comments Astley. Apart from the company's catalogue (which is a sampler in itself) a simple way to taste the imprint's range is to try their anthology *Poetry With An Edge*.

The second, **Carcanet Press**, has been the consistent recipient of critical accolades from the great and the good. Publishing two Nobel Prize-winning authors and four Pulitzers helps. No longer exclusively a publisher of verse (Carcanet began a fiction list in the nineteen eighties), the press still gives poetry pre-eminence and has over 600 titles in print and reps in 42 countries. Managing Director Michael Schmidt agrees with Auden's observation that most people who read verse read it for some reason other than the poetry. He fights the tide with his own mainstream journal *PN Review*. Despite an IRA bombing of his Manchester offices his press continues its policy of serious quality. 'I am strongly aware of the anti-modernist slant in a lot of poetry publishing, and publish to balance this,' he comments. 'Most submissions we receive come from people ignorant of the list to which they are submitting. Nothing is more disheartening than to receive a telephone call asking whether Carcanet publishes poetry.' The press has a four-part editorial programme: to publish new writing, to dust down substantial but neglected figures of this and earlier centuries, to encourage the translation of poetry, and to publish poets' prose and work relating to modern poetry. Typical of their list are John Ash, John Ashbery, Gillian Clarke, Allen Curnow, Edwin Morgan, Les Murray, Sophie Hannah, Miles Champion, Eavan Boland, Andrew Motion and best-seller, Elizabeth Jennings. Their three major millennium projects involve the bringing back into print the entire outputs of Robert Graves, Hugh MacDiarmid and Ford Madox Ford, a total in excess of fifty volumes. Carcanet has an air of purpose about it. 'We avoid the Technicolour and pyrotechnic media razzmatazz,' says Schmidt. Have a look at their web site (*www.carcanet.co.uk*) which is complete with a secure on-line bookselling facility. New poets are welcome to submit but check both your own past performance as well Carcanet's style before you go ahead.

Production standards among other specialists can be equally as good as Carcanet and Bloodaxe (and in the case of Enitharmon, better) although annual output (and as a consequence opportunity for the new poet) is substantially less.

Anvil Press Poetry, under founder Peter Jay, has now done thirty years of independent, alternative publishing and a recent spurt of activity shows the press to be as vigorous as ever. Founded as a small press in 1968 Anvil was an early alternative to the Fabers and OUPs of the poetry scene. Jay still runs his original group of poets – Harry Guest, Peter Levi, Anthony Howell and Heather Buck – although he is adamant about avoiding cliques. If they are right for the imprint new poets will be taken on. Jay has continued his abiding interest in poetry in translation publishing titles from Lip Po, Lorca, Bei Dao, Trakl, Gumilyov and others. Anvil is justly proud of its claim of keeping British poetry open to new work from all over the world. Editions have a quite style with as much attention paid to presentation inside the book as out. Their runaway best-seller is Carol Ann Duffy, with Matthew Sweeney and Ken Smith's anthology, *Beyond Bedlam*, 'poems written out of mental distress' not far behind. The kind of thing Anvil uses can be best sampled in Jay's anthology *The Spaces of Hope*, 'the most memorable work encountered in 30 years of independent publishing'.

Enitharmon Press represents quality, cares about presentation and operates 'at the unfashionable end' of the poetry publishing spectrum. Its books, its splendid poet/artist limited edition collaborations and its occasional pamphlets are produced to the highest of standards. Enitharmon has little interest in fashion. The press is, as Anne Stevenson put it, 'dedicated to a poetry of the human spirit in an age of rampant commercialism'. Owner Stephen Stuart-Smith continues a policy of publishing between eight and ten volumes annually by new, established and unjustly neglected poets. Ruth Pitter's *Collected Poems* sells alongside Kevin Crossley-Holland's *Poems from East Anglia*. Recent books have appeared from David Gascoyne, Nicki Jackowska, Pascale Petit and Myra Schneider. 'It seems unlikely that any new names will be added to the list, as Enitharmon is the only major poetry publisher in Britain which receives no regular subsidy' which is a pity. We need more from publishers like Stuart-Smith.

Seren Books is a Welsh based literary house publishing novels, short fiction, biographies and critical texts. Started by Cary Archard as an offshoot of the magazine *Poetry Wales* the imprint still maintains a solid interest in verse, publishing at least eight new single author volumes annually. In receipt of considerable Arts Council of Wales sponsorship the bias towards work from Wales and the border regions is both admirable and inevitable. Poetry editor Amy Wack reads *everything* submitted but admits that she has only ever accepted one unsolicited manuscript in her entire tenure. Poets should read more, she told me. Editions are quality productions with plenty of attention paid to design inside and out. Typical recent poets include Forward winner Sheenagh Pugh, Deryn Rees-Jones, Paul Henry, Robert Minhinnick and Tony Curtis. Their major best-seller is Dannie Abse's *Twentieth Century Anglo-Welsh Poetry*. A good press sampler is their anthology *Burning The Bracken*. They have also published their own guide to the scene, *The Poetry Business*.

Tony Ward's **Arc Publications**, based in Lancashire, may have declined in output from ten titles annually to eight but commitment is still high on the list. 'We believe in a catholic approach, with an ability to take risks when the work merits,' he remarks. 'Now in its thirtieth year, Arc continues to make available work that would otherwise remain unpublished.' The imprint has David Morley and John Kinsella on board and maintains a backlist of almost 100 titles. Ivor Cutler, John Kinsella and Karl Stead are top sellers. New poets include Conleth O'Connor, Gail Dendy and Andy Brown. Prospective poets should not expect a quick response and most certainly familiarise themselves with the Arc list before sending. 'There are simply too many family/angst/therapy writers believing, without any hint of editing or rewriting, they are god's gift' is the official line. You have been warned.

Rupert Loydell's **Stride** has been gathering reputation as a risk taker for some years now. Based in the south west the press publishes 15 new books annually has a list of well over 200 titles ranging from the totally unknown to the famous. Innovative poetries, 'reinvigorated and re-explored/invented forms' are the backbone although Loydell is certainly no opponent of more formal material. 'Bridging the gap between the avant-garde and the mainstream.' The press runs individual collections, criticism, interviews and a range of excellent, alternative anthologies. Advice to prospective contributors? 'Shape your ms. Consider why you want a book out and who will buy it.' Send for their submission criteria – 'what makes your writing different?' – if you can answer that then send on in. Stride responds to submissions swiftly. Invariably within three weeks and often within three days. Recent successes include Colin Flack, Peter Redgrove, and Pulitzer winner Charles Wright. Check Stride's anthology *Ladder To The Next Floor* for a sampler of how the press got where it is or look at their Web site: *www.madbear.demon.co/stride/*

Peterloo Press, based in Cornwall, represents poetry without frills, without fuss and most definitely without the avant-garde. Run by Harry Chambers the press aims to publish quality work by new and neglected poets, some of them late starters (although if you have been flogging your stuff around the circuit for years and got nowhere then Chambers is unlikely to be your saviour); to co-publish with reputable presses abroad (Goose Lane in Canada, Storyline Press and the University of Pittsburgh in the States and **Cló Iar-Chonnacta** in Ireland); and to establish a Peterloo list of succeeding volumes by a core of poets of proven worth. Chambers avoids anthologies and has finished with magazines and newsletters. The press sticks to books, running an active backlist of nearly two hundred titles. Bestsellers include U.A. Fanthorpe, John Mole with his collections for children, John Whitworth's *From The Sonnet History*, John Latham and Dana Gioia. Recent additions include Anna Crowe and Allison Pryde. The Peterloo Centre in a converted chapel at Calstock, a venture not without its funding difficulties, has now opened. Peterloo, now in its 16th year runs its own poetry competition (£3000 first prize) and insists that prospective contributors to his press have had at least six poems in reputable magazines. Send a full mss accompanied by a stamped envelope large enough to carry your mss back to you. Chambers currently takes a couple of months to reply and is full to the year 2001.

There are other presses with less prodigious outputs but whose editions are still up there with the best of them. In Northumberland, Peter Lewis's **Flambard Press** has continued to grow in stature. Begun in 1991 it now publishes around five titles annually in the Bloodaxe style. With aid from Northern Arts the press is particularly interested in new and neglected poets especially from the North and the Borders. William Scammell, Gerard Benson and Michael Blackburn are typical poets. Gladys Mary Coles has developed her Headland Publications into a regular Peterloo clone. Her interest in Welsh poets is clear – Herbert Williams, Richard Poole, Joseph Clancy top the list. Hertfordshire's Rockingham Press run by David Perman publishes modern Turkish and Persian poetry in translation along with an increasing number of contemporary British poets. Six well-produced volumes plus two chapbooks annually featuring John Greening, Lotte Kramer and others point to the imprint's rising significance. Ken Edwards' **Reality Street Editions** specialises in 'linguistically innovative writing by women and men on both sides of the Atlantic'. Publishing solid single-author volumes, translations, ground-breaking anthologies along with a series of four-poet showcases the press takes the new poetry seriously. One of the few to put such work into trade editions, says Edwards. Typical authors include Barbara Guest, Tony Lopez, Cris Cheek and Denise Riley.

Check their *Out Of Everywhere* anthology of UK and US innovative poetry from women. The press has also published book/CD packages and runs an excellent web site (*www.demon.co.uk/eastfield/reality/*).

At the self-styled poetry capital of Britain, no other place than Huddersfield, Janet Fisher and Peter Sansom run **Smith/Doorstop** the poetry imprint of their enterprising **Poetry Business** (see **Organisations of Interest to Poets**). The press produces a mixture of pamphlets, full-length collections and stylish cassettes. Dorothy Nimbi, Martin Stannard, Jo Haslam, Carcanet Press MD Michael Schmidt and Michael Laskey are typical authors. Simon Armitage, Carol Ann Duffy and Ian McMillan feature in the cassette series. **Slow Dancer Press,** run by detective fiction author John Harvey with the assistance of Sarah Boiling, is one of the few small poetry publishers to take marketing seriously. You can pick up their free *Sampler* at branches of Waterstones. Long in the business of pamphlet production (Peter Sansom, Rebecca Goss, Tamar Yoseloff, Barry MacSweeney, Robert Etty, etc.) Slow Dancer now publishes more substantial works including Lee Harwood, Libby Houston, Ruth Valentine and the late James Schuyler. The press also publishes fiction. A class operation worth checking, if not submitting to. Send for their catalogue or access their web site (*www.mellotone.co.uk*).

Jessie Lendennie runs **Salmon Publishing** from the Cliffs of Moher, Co. Clare. An outgrowth of *The Salmon*, an eighties poetry journal, the press now publishes some of the best designed titles in the West. An Irish connection is pretty useful when trying here although Salmon do look at material from further afield. Typical poets include Adrian Rich, Rita Ann Higgins, Theo Dorgan, Ann Zell, Leland Bardwell and Mary O'Donnell. The press publishes a handbook on creative writing and has an excellent web site (*www.salmonpoetry.com*). And if the poetry is not flowing you can book in to a Salmon residential Creative Writing Workshop – £100 for the weekend.

Peepal Tree is the largest independent publisher of Caribbean, South Asian and black British poetry. Founded in 1986 the press now produces more than ten poetry titles annually. Typical poets include Kwame Dawes, Ralph Thompson, Cyril Dabydeen and Stewart Brown. Check their Kwame Dawes anthology *Wheel and Come Again*. Editors Jeremy Poynting and Hannah Banister read over 1000 submissions annually and are not known for their speedy responses. Send five or six examples of your work along with a biographical note and wait. You can get a Peepal Tree catalogue by e-mail: *hannah@peepal.demon.co.uk*

As technology continues to make life easier for publishers it becomes harder to draw the line between the poetry specialists and the classic small presses. Maybe by now such a division does not exist at all.

The Traditional Outlets

Poetry has a place in our national press, albeit a small one. *The Independent* runs a daily poem, so does *The Express*, *The Guardian* features verse from time to time as do all the serious Sunday heavies. *The Times Literary Supplement* gives over considerable space on a regular basis, whole double page spreads devoted to the work of one poet or to a long single poem are not unusual although the paper does have its favourites. *The London Review Of Books* shows a similar interest although neither appear very keen to use unsolicited work from the mailbox. *The London Magazine*, another stalwart, has the reputation for being the fastest responder in the business (you walk to the post box, mail your poems, then return home to find them rejected and waiting for you on the mat). Auberon Waugh relishes stuffy tradition at *The Literary Review*. Among other weeklies and monthlies the situation is fluid. Poetry gets in when someone on the staff shows an interest. POET GETS JOB AT ZOO and GQ runs a bunch of animal poems. Check your targets along the shelves at W.H. Smith's. Some local newspapers and freesheets devote pages to contributions from readers, mostly dire doggerel and largely unpaid, although it is publication. If your paper hasn't joined in yet try sending your work in the form of a letter to Postbag. Start a trend. Much of this might sound quite reassuring for the poet but the truth is that were poetry to cease to exist overnight, then these publications would continue to operate without a flicker. Who, other than the poets, would notice?

The Regional Anthologies

Running in parallel with the high ground literary approach of much of the poetry world are empires largely unknown to the taste-makers and ignored by the critics. The biggest, Ian and Tracy Walton's **Forward Press** in Peterborough, now turns over a million and a half annually, has almost 3000 titles in print, and reckons to account for around ten per cent of all verse published in the UK. Depressed with 'twenty years of not being able to enjoy poetry' because it was inevitably obscure, the couple have moved from back kitchen to factory unit in the service of 260,000 active British verse scribblers. 'A high proportion of the thousands of letters we receive tell us that many people find poetry over-complex and difficult to understand' runs one of their brochures. For the decade or so since it was founded Forward Press has enthusiastically promoted an 'accessible, sincere poetry which everyone can relate to'. The higher realms are not for them. Publishing under a number of imprints including Poetry Now, Anchor Books, and Triumph House, the operation receives thousands of contributions annually. Poets are sourced through free editorial copy in regional newspapers. The contributors flow in their hundreds. 'It is a bit like amateur dramatics', Ian told me, 'anyone can take part.'

Forward's outstanding success is built on its approachability. The Waltons and their team of exclusively young editors include as many as two hundred and fifty poems in each anthology. Submissions under thirty lines are preferred. Costs are kept down by using in-house printing equipment coupled to serviceable bindings. If you want to see your work in print, and for most contributors this is the whole *raison d'être* for writing, then you have to buy a copy. For many poets this will be their first appearance in book form and chances are they will buy more than a single copy. This is not a traditional vanity operation. No one is actually being ripped off nor are the publishers raking in exorbitant profits. Page for page their titles are no more expensive than those of Cape or Faber and are cheaper than the output of some little presses. However, distribution is patchy – not that many Forward titles make the shelves at Waterstones or Dillons. As for many of the small presses interested parties are encouraged to buy direct. Forward's critics claim that quality is being neglected in exchange for quantity. Reduce your criteria for inclusion, cram the poems in, sell more copies. Undoubtedly the genuine literary achievement of appearing in one of Forward's books is questionable. But in mitigation it must be said that for some people this will be a much-needed beginning and for others the only success they are going to get.

Forward's much criticised royalty payment scheme has been replaced with the *Forward Press Top 100 Awards* which offer a total of £10,000 to the best of the poets published annually in their many anthologies.

In addition to their schools and regional collections Forward runs two magazines, *Poetry Now* and *Triumph Herald* (which specialises in Christian verse), a print and design service for self-publishers, and Poetry Now Introducing – a series of books from single authors. Their Writers' Bookshop imprint publishes a most useful series of guides to the small magazines of Britain, America and Australia along with directories of mainstream publishers and a guide to prizes, grants and bursaries. Forward offers the complete poetry life. If *Season's Delight, Poetic Bond, Happy Days, Cleansing Thoughts* and *Portraits of Life* sound like your scene send for the group's newsletters (Remus House, Coltsfoot Drive, Woodston, Peterborough PE2 9JX), ring them (01733 890099), check their web site (*www.forwardpress.co.uk*) or e-mail your request (*pete@forwardpress.co.uk*). You'll find no dubious accommodation address dealing here but, on the other hand, few literary giants either.

Envious of Forward's success at catching the hearts and minds of most of the UK's poetry hobbyists a good number of rival empire builders have risen in their wake. Regional poetry anthologies, Best of Britain collections, compendiums of English, Scottish, Irish and Welsh verse abound. Contributions are sourced through notices on library walls, local free-sheets, local radio and through direct mail. These operations vary from the glossy to a number of pathetically produced and, one hopes, short-lived incarnations based in the non-metropolitan sticks. No actual rip-off occurs and contributors get in whether they purchase or not. But if you want to see your work then you must buy and the books can cost upwards of twenty pounds. Before agreeing to contribute check the press's output. Do not submit blindly, research their back list. It is what Faber would demand of you. The rule applies to the whole poetry scene.

The Small Press and The Little Magazine

Hobbyist publishing ventures have been with us for quite a long time. Virginia Woolf began the Hogarth Press this way, quite literally on the kitchen table. But it was not until well after the Second War and the rise of the transatlantic mimeo revolution that amateur poetry magazine and pamphlet publication really took off. Recent advances have seen that revolution overturned again. Technologically literate poets are everywhere. Publishing has been stripped of its mystery. Access to laser printers and the computers that drive them are commonplace. Desk-Top Publishing and Word Processing software make it so easy to do. Disposable income has gone up. Poets in growing numbers are able and willing to establish competent one-person publishing operations, turning out neat, professional-looking titles on a considerable scale.

These are the small presses and little magazines. They sell to new and often non-traditional markets rarely finding space on bookshop shelves, where they are regarded as unshiftable nuisances. Professional distribution is still the age-old problem. The Arts Council of England *Policy for Poetry* says that it will look at the problem and not a moment too soon. But for now small mags go hand-to-hand among friends, at slams, readings, concerts, creative writing classes, literary functions, via subscriptions and are liberally exchanged among all those concerned. The network is large. The question remains: is anyone out there not directly concerned with the business of poetry actually reading it? But that is another story.

Statistically, the small presses and the little magazines are the largest publishers of new poetry both in terms of range and circulation. They operate in a bewildering blur of shapes and sizes everywhere from Brighton to Birmingham and Aberystwyth to Aberdeen. Have a look at Derrick Woolf's fine *Poetry Quarterly Review* (Coleridge Cottage, Nether Stowey, Somerset TA5 1NQ) which carries regular reviews, as does Andy Cox's *Zene* (5 Martins Lane, Witcham, Ely, Cambs CB6 2LB) and Gerald England's *New Hope International* (20 Werneth Avenue, Gee Cross, Hyde, Cheshire). There are others.

This country's best poetry magazines all began as classic littles. Between them *PN Review*, *Ambit*, *Agenda*, *Outposts*, *Orbis*, *Poetry Review*, *Rialto*, *Acumen*, *Staple*, *The North*, *Smiths Knoll*, *Envoi* and *Stand* do not come up to even half the circulation of journals like *Shooting Times* and *Practical Fishkeeping* – which says a lot about the way society values its poetry. Nonetheless, taken as a group, they will get to almost everyone who matters. They represent poetry as a whole. Read this group and you will get some idea of where the cutting edge is. In the second division in terms of kudos lie the regional or genre specialists such as *HU* (Irish poetry), *Poetry Scotland*, *The New Welsh Review*, *Poetry Wales*, *Poetry Ireland*, *Queer Words* (the magazine of new lesbian and gay writing), *Psycopoetica* (psychologically based poetry), *Krax* (humorous verse), *Writing Women*, *Christian Poetry Review*, *Snapshots*, *Haiku Magazine* and *Poetry Manchester*. All these magazines are well produced, sometimes with the help of grants, and all represent a specific point of view. In Wales there is *Barddas* for poets using the strict meters and in Scotland *Lallans* for poets working in Lowland Scots. The vast majority of small magazines, however, owe no allegiance and range from fat irregulars like *The Reater* (powered by a Lottery grant), quality general round ups like *Headlock*, *Tears In The Fence*, *Obsessed With Pipework* and *Seam* (small enough to slide up your sleeve), to pamphlets like *The Yellow Crane* (interesting new poems), *The Red Wheelbarrow* (so much depends),

The Interpreter's House (the best prose and verse that the editor can get), *Iota* (recent poetry), *Poetry Monthly* (run by poets for poets), *The Poetry Church* (a magazine of Christian poetry), *Slipstream* (risk-takers welcome) and *Pulsar* (thoughts, comments and observations). *Tabla* has dropped out of the journalistic rat race by becoming an annual book of new verse. Some like *The Penniless Press* are for the poor of pocket and the rich of mind, *Sub Voicive* doesn't like you smoking while *The News That Stays News* is a private affair. If you can't find a magazine that suits you and your style then you can't be writing poetry. On the other hand if you are really sure you are then start your own.

Among the small presses there is a similar range. Maquette dips its toe in the new wave; Bob Cobbing's venerable **Writers Forum** sticks to mainstream experimental; Five Seasons does serious well-printed volumes; **Odyssey**, the side-line of *Poetry Quarterly Review*, based at the aptly named Coleridge Cottage in Somerset mixes the mainstream with the wobbling edge; Dangaroo and **Totem** have third world and ethnic concerns. Staple First Editions insists on the new and unsafe. Prest Roots works with the innovative, as do **Words Worth** and Alfred David Editions. Redbeck follows David Tipton's reliable ear with at least a dozen pamphlets each year. **Y Lolfa** publishes unofficial bards. For the new writer these kinds of presses are the obvious place to try first. Indeed it is where many have. Who put out T.S. Eliot's first? A small publisher. Dannie Abse, Peter Redgrove, James Fenton and Dylan Thomas, the same. R.S. Thomas, Ezra Pound and Edgar Allen Poe didn't even go that far – they published themselves.

Poetry for Children

The thing to remember here is that children rarely buy poetry themselves nor are there poetry magazines aimed at them. On the other hand there are a great number of children's poets out there – McGough, Henri and Patten would be much lesser authors if they'd ignored the under 18s. The schools system regularly pay poets to read to their classes and teach their children. Macmillan, Faber, Penguin, Bellew and a few other publishers run specialist children's poetry lists (*Aliens Stole My Underpants* chosen by Brian Moses is a typical title). But do not imagine this market to be easy nor a place where you can unload your adult failures. Kids do not suffer fools gladly. For more information check with the Poetry Society who publishes a number of poetry in schools checklists along with a handbook.

Cash

A lot of writers new to the business are surprised to learn that their poetry will not make them much money. Being a poet is not really much of an occupation. You get better wages delivering papers. There will be the odd pound from the better heeled magazine, perhaps even as much as £40 or so from those periodicals lucky enough to be in receipt of a grant, but generally it will be free copies of the issues concerned, thank you letters and little more. Those with collections published by a subsidised, specialist publisher can expect a couple of hundred as an advance on royalties. Those using the small presses can look forward to a handful of complimentary copies. The truth is that poetry itself is undervalued. You can earn money writing about it, reviewing it, lecturing on it or certainly by giving public recitations (£100 standard here, £900 or more if you are Roger McGough, several thousand if you are Seamus Heaney). In fact, most things in the poetry business will earn better money than the verse itself. Expect to spend a lot on stamps and a fair bit on sample copies. The majority of the time all you'll get in return is used envelopes.

Readings

Since the great Beat Generation, Albert Hall reading of 1964, there has been an ever-expanding phenomenon of poets on platforms, reading or reciting their stuff to an audience that can be anywhere between raptly attentive and fast asleep. Jaci Stephen, writing in the *Daily Mirror*, reckoned readings to be like jazz. 'Both involve a small group of people making a lot of noise, and then, just when you think it's all over, it carries on.' But I believe there can be a magic in the spoken poem. Not everything, certainly. But when it's good it can be sublime. Yet for some writers the whole thing has devolved so far as to become a branch of the entertainment industry. Whichever way you view it, it is certainly an integral part of the business and one in which the beginner is going to need to engage sooner or later. Begin by attending and see how others manage. Watch out for local events advertised at your local library or ring your local arts board. Poets with heavy reputations can often turn out to be lousy performers while many an amateur can really shake it down. Don't expect to catch every image as you listen. Readings are not places for total comprehension but more for glancing blows. Treat it as fun and it will be. If you are trying things yourself for the first time, make sure you've brought your books along to sell, stand upright, drop the shoulders, gaze at a spot at the back of the hall and blow.

Music

Poetry has also made a number of inroads into the music business. There was a time when this meant Spike Milligan standing up and spouting in front of a jazz band or middle-of-the-road brass run behind John Betjeman reciting his best but no longer. The advent of rap, hip-hop and the ready use of the speech sample as a component part of dancefloor beats has turned the public ear. Dub poets – such as Linton Kwesi Johnson – have long used reggae as a backdrop for their words. Now the likes of Americans Sonja Sohn, Saul Williams and Dana Bryant are softening up the cool crowd with their funk-backed hooks. This is certainly a non-traditional approach well away from poetry's conventional involvement with literature and with books. Scorsese has found space for Sohn in *Bringing Out The Dead*. Check the clubs to hear more and expect what you find to be nothing like what you expected.

Competitions

Poetry competitions have been the vogue for two decades now with the most unlikely organisations sponsoring them. The notion here is that anonymity ensures fairness. Entries are made under pseudonyms so that if your name does happen to be Wislawa Szymborska, then this won't help you much. Results seem to bear this out too. The big competitions run biennially by the **Arvon Foundation** with the help of commercial sponsors and the **Poetry Society** attract an enormous entry and usually throw up quite a number of complete unknowns among the winners. And why do people bother? Cash prizes can be large – thousands of pounds – but it costs at least a pound a poem to enter, and often much more than that. If it is cash you want, then the Lottery scratch-cards are a better bet. And there has been a trend for winners to come from places like Cape Girardeau, Missouri and Tibooburra, Australia. The odds are getting longer. Who won the last Arvon? I don't remember. But if you do fancy a try then it is a pretty innocent activity. You tie up a poem for a few months and you spend a few pounds. Winners' tips include reading the work of the judges to see how they do it, submitting non-controversial middle-of-the-road smiling things, and doing this just before the closing date so you won't have to wait too long. Try two or three of your best. Huge wodges are costly and will only convince the judges of your insecurity. Have a look at *The Ring Of Words* (Sutton Publishing), an excellent anthology of Arvon winners and runners-up. For contests to enter watch the small mags, write to your regional arts board, check out *The New Writer* (one of the best listings around), *Poetry London Newsletter*, *Writer's News* or the listings in *Orbis* magazine, look on the notice board at your local library, or write for the regularly updated list from **The Poetry Library** in London (see **Organisations of Interest to Poets**).

Combining both competition and reading is the Poetry Slam. Here all-comers are given the opportunity to strut their stuff for around three closely-timed minutes before a usually not all that literary crowd. Points are awarded for performance and audience reaction Scatology and street-wise crowd pleasing are more likely to get you through the rounds than closely-honed work. The overall winners get prizes: a slice of the door-take or a donated book. The events, which involve much shouting, can be a lot of fun. Slams have been mounted in places as far apart as Cardiff and Sheffield and the craze is spreading. Even the august **Cheltenham Literary Festival** has put them in its programme.

Radio and TV

The BBC centre most of their efforts on National Poetry Day and their poll to find the Nation's Favourite. This is useful programming focus for the Beeb enabling them to put verse in the mouths of presenters, newscasters and personalities throughout their networks and to actually get an immediate reaction. The public vote by letter, fax and e-mail or through the useful form provided on the BBC's web site. Beyond the star-studded half an hour where the results get revealed there is also a useful spin-off in the form of the BBC-published *The Nation's Favourite Poem* anthology which inevitably hits the best-sellers. Generally, however, coverage is slight. The regular slots are all on radio, naturally enough. It is so hard to make verse visually appealing. Some TV producers have tried, notably Peter Symes who produced both *Poet's News* and *Words On Film* for BBC2. Symes' approach is to avoid the poem illustrated and to concentrate instead on documentary-style collaborations between commissioned poet and film-maker. His great successes have all been with Tony Harrison (who now makes his own films for Channel 4) although projects with Simon Armitage, Jackie Kay, Lemn Sissay, Fred d'Aquiar and others underline his open approach. Poetry can also occasionally be found ladled between the music on MTV but inevitably by the media-promoted bards. On Radio Four, Tim Dee has been active commissioning poets to write pieces with radio in mind. His *Radio Poems* has included Paul Muldoon, Michael Longley, Lavinia Greenlaw, Robert Crawford and others. Mary Sharp looks after the Four's regular Sunday 4.30 strand with *Poetry Please* (a listeners' request show which uses only published material) along with the contemporary series, *Fine Lines,* where two poets (generally an older and a younger) meet to compare notes and read their work. There are also occasional features (such as Lemn Sissay as front man for a piece on British Black poetry.) On Radio Three, Fiona McLean produces *Best Words,* an occasional poetry magazine programme fronted by Michael Rosen. It is also worth listening out for the Sunday feature programme on 3 which includes poetry in its range. Radio 1 puts poetry into some of its evening slots, showcasing poets who have high street-cred. The World Service has Michael Rosen's *Poems By Post* which features listeners' requests. Independent radio are trying verse as fillers. An enlarging but difficult market although the BBC are pretty definite about having no remit to use 'unpublished or amateur verse'. If you are determined to put your verse on air then local radio offers better possibilities. Try sending in self-produced readings on cassette (if you are any good at it) or topical poetry which regional magazine programmes could readily use. Don't expect to be paid much.

Internet

Poetry's appearance on the Internet continues apace. Cyberspace – the place where all this happens – is a mirror of the conventional world. The electronic replicates the real. There are on-line books, magazines, historical and contemporary archives, reference works, and news round-ups. Many dedicate themselves entirely to poetry. They also change almost as fast as the systems they run on. The Internet is enormously volatile. Addresses and providers move here at a much higher rate than they do elsewhere.

Journals – On-line magazines range from those which mirror their print based cousins (and in some cases are simply direct copies) to completely innovative, interactive compilations which mix sound and action with the text. The Net is no static place. It can provide movement, video, sound and user-defined typeface along with actual text. Some mags (e-zines, on-line journals) offer playable recordings of their poets performing, others give space for readers to add criticism. All use the hyper-link, a method of moving instantly from one section of the site to another or off the site altogether. The difference between on-line and print-based magazines becomes more apparent when you discover that what you get when you call them up is not simply the current issue but access to the entire back catalogue. All searchable, storable (put them on your hard drive) and, best of all, free.

Geography dissolves on-line. America is no further and no more costly to access than Britain. One of the great mags, *Isibongo*, is based in South Africa. It's just as easy to read as our own market leader, George Simmers' *Snakeskin* or Mary Buechler's Sacramento *Poetic Express*. In fact, half the time, the user has no idea precisely where the site being accessed is physically based. Place ceases to matter, language takes over.

How do you contribute? Send your poems by e-mail, no s.a.e. needed. A few brave journals will accept work by snail mail from the not yet connected (*New Hope International* insists on this method) although most prefer to deal electronically. On-line mag editors hate re-keying, it goes against the grain. And you'll more than likely get an instant answer. Little waiting around for six weeks before your poems return, rejected, through your letter-box. On-line is quick.

Cyberspace is huge. Some of the sites which list on-line journals, such as *Peter Howard's Poetry Contacts* seems to go on for days. Starting your own mag is easy – frictionless, Microsoft's Bill Gates calls it – and size presents few difficulties. Standards are therefore pretty variable. Not only are the UK's computer literate newbies up there but America, Canada and Australia's too.

Competitions – Naturally there is an on-line variant to the more traditional send five pound and your best work contests. Some actively canvass entries from the unconnected and offer Net publication as the prize. For some poets this will no doubt be sufficient reward. Others accept on-line entries and chose their winners by asking readers to vote – again on-line. Once set up, contemporary software usually allows the entire process to run automatically. The selling point for all these competitions is the enormous audience supposedly sitting around out there in front of their screens. The potential certainly is large – forty or fifty million users already connected and with more joining every day. Yet how many actually bother to access poetry remains debatable. Still, 22,500 visitors to the *Poetic Express* site every quarter is a few more than the number of *Poetry Review* readers (5000 per issue). *Poetic Express*'s competitions are free. Readers vote for the best poem on the site.

Books – If you tire of contributing to the web sites of others then start your own. A whole collection of verse on-line will present relatively little difficulty. Most *ISPs* (Internet Service Providers) now offer an amount of free Web space as part of the subscription. This means that with the aid of some Web authoring software (*HotMetal Pro*, *FrontPage*) or a handbook on *Hyper-Text Mark-Up Language* (html) you can put your work on-line. Hosting your own *home page* is certainly not beyond anyone capable of using conventional computer word processing packages. If you'd like to see the kind of thing that's possible have a look at poet and singer Labi Siffre's home page, or for that matter my own, *The Peter Finch Archive*. If you are reticent get a fan to set up a site devoted to your works. This has happened to David Gascoyne, to J.H. Prynne, John Kinsella, Benjamin Zephaniah and others. Otherwise go to it on your own. If you have a recording of yourself doing your stuff then get one-jump ahead. Put that up there on site too.

Groups – To reduce the poet's traditional feeling of isolation the Net presents a number of opportunities. World-wide poets, once they've got over the stunning breadth of Net facilities, are usually hard to shut up. E-mail provides one vehicle. Here bands of poets circulate their work, their criticisms and their views of world literature. Join a group (no cost, just ask) and you'll find a daily delivery of e-mails in your in-box. Some groups are moderated which means that contributions are filtered by a controlling individual although most are free-for-alls. Discussion can range from the moronic to the stimulating. *The British and Irish Poets Group* established by Ric Caddel and *Cyber Poets* set-up by Peter Howard are two worth looking at.

A variant on e-mail discussion groups are Usenet Newsgroups. Newsgroups run through their own dedicated software (provided by your ISP as part of your subscription) and are open to contributions from anyone anywhere. Articles are delivered to your browser for consumption. If you want to contribute then type it up and it's done. The principle poetry newsgroups, *rec.arts.poems* and *alt.arts.poetry.comments*, offer pretty varied fare. By their world-wide nature they tend to be American dominated and standards of contribution are not always that high. But they are places where you can get an instant reaction to your latest poem. There are also a few masterclasses out there with established poets offering on-line advice. Matthew Sweeney was cyber poet in residence at Chadwyck-Healey for a time. His place more recently has been taken by Eavan Boland.

Tools and resources – The Net offers a multitude of these. There are on-line spell-checkers (in many languages), thesauri, an anagram creator, a rhyming dictionary. The archives of universities (particularly in America) offer the great poetry of the past in comprehensive quantity. Download facsimile editions of *The Germ* (the first ever poetry magazine from 1850) or hear Seamus Heaney recite. Read the complete works of Blake, find out what powered the Beat generation, discover how Hardy worked, check the roots of modern verse. Not only can you find the texts themselves but entire critical apparatuses, historical contexts, biographies, bibliographies, portraits, names of lovers, and shoe sizes for most of the great poets of the world. You can access information on poetry readings or check at the British Council for data on literature festivals. Students seem to revel in posting their dissertations. Archives want their knowledge made available to the everyone. Interested in a particular style? Haiku? Visual poetry? Traditional forms? They've all got their sites.

How to find them – Internet *search engines* are vast, free-to-use, on-line databases which allow users to track down their interests by either key word or subject type. The big ones, such as *Yahoo, InfoSeek, Web Crawler, Excite, AltaVista* and *Lycos* hold billions of records. To use them you need to be specific in your request. I tried keying 'poetry' in to *AltaVista* and got 149,529 results. Much easier is to log on to one of a number of poetry resource sites which run clickable lists of relevant pages. The UK Poetry Society, The Poetry Library and the *Poetry Review*'s 'web watcher' Peter Howard's home page are worth consulting. The *Poetry Web Ring* links poetry pages (and parts of pages) world-wide. Follow it and you'll be up for days stuffing your head with verse. Join the *Internet Poetry Society* (free) and you'll get a regular news update sent to you by e-mail. Ted Slade's *Poetry Kit* provides poetry, competitions, resource lists plus a whole raft of self-help articles.

Where next? – Change on the Net is dynamic. New forms and ideas arrive all the time. trAce, a major on-line writing project set up at Nottingham-Trent University with support from the Arts Council, is signposting many of the ways Net writing can go. The opportunities for poets are as huge as the net itself. Get involved now.

Some Web Addresses For Poets:

British Poets e-mail list	*www.mailbase.ac.uk/lists/british-poets/*
Chadwyck-Healey (poetry database)	*lion.chadwyck.co.uk*
Electronic Poetry Centre	*wings.buffalo.edu/epc*
Internet Poets Society	*www.writing.co.uk*
Isibongo (magazine)	*www.uct.ac.za/projects/poetry/isibongo/isibongo.htm*
New Hope International (magazine)	*www.nhi.clara.net/nhihome.htm*
Peter Finch Archive	*dialspace.dial.pipex.com/peter.finch/*
Peter Howard's Poetry Page	*www.hphoward.demon.co.uk*
Poetic Express (magazine)	*sacramento-news.com/peindex.htm*
Poetry Kit (magazine)	*www.poetrykit.org/*
The Poetry Library	*www.rfh.org.uk/poetry/index.htm*
Poetry On the Web	*www.rfh.org.uk/poetry/index.htm*
The Poetry Society (UK)	*www.rfh.org.uk/poetry/index.htm*
Snakeskin (magazine)	*www.rfh.org.uk/poetry/index.htm*
Trace	*www.rfh.org.uk/poetry/index.htm*

Starting Up

Probably the best place will be locally. Find out through the library or the nearest arts board which writers groups gather in your area and attend. There you will meet others of a like mind, encounter whatever locally produced magazines there might be and get a little direct feedback on your work. 'How am I doing?' is a big question for the emerging poet and although criticism is not all that hard to come by, do not expect it from all sources. Magazine editors, for example, will rarely have the time to offer advice. It is also reasonable to be suspicious of that offered by friends and relations – they will no doubt be only trying to please. Writers groups present the best chance for poets to engage in honest mutual criticism. But if you'd prefer a more detached, written analysis of your efforts and are willing to pay a small sum, then you could apply to *Prescription,* the service operated nationally by the **Poetry Society** (22 Betterton Street, London WC2H 9BU), to the service run by **The Arts Council of Wales** (see **Arts Councils and Regional Arts Boards**) or to those run on an area basis by your local arts board. There are also a number of non-subsidised critical services which you will find advertised in writers' magazines.

If you have made the decision to publish your work – and I don't suppose you'd be reading this if you hadn't – then the first thing to do is some market research. I've already indicated how overstocked the business is with periodicals and publications, yet surprisingly you will not find many of these in your local newsagent. Most new poetry still reaches its public by other routes. However, begin by reading a few newly published mainstream books. Ask at your booksellers for their recommendations. Check Waterstones or Blackwells, who both do a good job. *Waterstone's Guide to Poetry Books* edited by Nick Rennison is a decent map. Most shops these days carry a basic stock, but if you need a specialist then get hold of the Poetry Library's current list of shops with a specific interest in poetry. Enquire at your local library. Try selecting a recent anthology of contemporary verse. To get a broad view of what's going on, not only should you read *Scanning the Century: The Penguin Book of the Twentieth Century in Poetry* edited by Peter Forbes, Simon Armitage and Robert Crawford's Penguin *British and Irish Poetry Since The War,* Sean O'Brien's *The Firebox* (Picador), Hulse, Kennedy and Morley's Bloodaxe *The New Poetry* and *Other: British and Irish Poetry Since 1970* edited by Richard Caddel and Peter Quartermain (Wesleyan), Ian Sinclair's *Conductors of Chaos* (Picador), but Bob Cobbing and Lawrence Upton's *Word Score Utterance Choreography* (Writers Forum), Lemn Sissay's *The Fire People - A Collection of Contemporary Black British Poets* (Payback Press), Jeni Couzyn's *The Bloodaxe Book of Contemporary Women Poets,* Linda France's *Sixty Women Poets* (Bloodaxe), Tony Frazer's *A State Of Independence* (Stride), *From the Other Side of the Century – A New American Poetry 1960–1990* edited by Douglas Messerli (Sun & Moon), and *Postmodern American Poetry,* a really splendid selection edited by Paul Hoover (Norton). These last two might be harder to find but will be worth the effort. Progress to the literary magazine. Write off to a number of the magazine addresses which follow this article and ask the price of sample copies. Enquire about subscriptions. Expect to pay a little but inevitably it will not be a lot. It is important that poets read not only to familiarise themselves with what is currently fashionable and to increase their own facility for self-criticism, but to help support the activity in which they wish to participate. Buy – this is vital for little mags, it is the only way in which they are going to survive. Read; if it's all a mystery to you, try Tony Curtis' *How to Study Modern Poetry* (Macmillan), Matthew Sweeney and John Hartley Williams' *Teach Yourself Writing Poetry*, Peter Sansom's excellent *Writing Poems* (Bloodaxe) or my own *The Poetry Business* (Seren). How real poets actually work can be discovered by reading C. B. McCully's the *Poet's Voice and Craft* (Carcanet) or *How Poets Work* (Seren). After all this, if you still think it's appropriate, try sending in.

How to Do It

Increase your chances of acceptance by following simple, standard procedure:

- Type or print on a single side of the paper, A4 size, single-spacing with double between stanzas, exactly as you'd wish your poem to appear when printed.
- Give the poem a title, clip multi-page works together, include your name and address at the foot of the final sheet. Avoid files, plastic covers, stiffeners and fancy clips of any sort.
- Keep a copy, make a record of what you send where and when, leave a space to note reaction.
- Send in small batches – six is a good number – with a brief covering letter saying who you are. Leave justification, apology and explanation for your writers group.
- Include a self-addressed, stamped envelope of sufficient size for reply and/ or return of your work.
- Be prepared to wait some weeks for a response. Don't pester. Be patient. Most magazines will reply in the end.
- Never send the same poem to two places at the same time.
- Send your best. Work which fails to fully satisfy even the author is unlikely to impress anyone else.

Where?

Try the list which follows. This is by no means the whole UK small press scene but only those where potential contributors might stand a chance. Even here do not expect unrelenting positive responses: magazines get overstocked, editors change, addresses shift, policy alters, operators run out of steam. Be prepared to hunt around and for a lot of your work to come back. You can help improve things by buying copies. Send in an s.a.e. asking how much. The total market is vast and if you want to go further than *The Writer's Handbook* listings then you could consult the following: the *Small Press Guide* (which only covers journals – Writers' Bookshop, Remus

House, Coltsfoot Drive, Woodston, Peterborough PE2 9JX), *Light's List of Literary Magazines* which contains both UK and US addresses (John Light, The Lighthouse, 29 Longfield Road, Tring, Hertfordshire HP23 4DG), and Chantelle Bentley's *Poet's Market* (F&W Publications, Inc.) or Len Fulton's *Directory of Poetry Publishers* (Dustbooks) – the two main American directories.

Scams and Cons

With poetry overpopulated by participants it is not surprising that the con artist should make an appearance. There are plenty of people out there taking money off beginner writers and offering very little in return. The traditional vanity anthology, once the staple of the trickster, is fortunately in retreat. They have been hounded to silence largely by the National Poetry Foundation's Johnathon Clifford (you can read about his campaigns in his self-published *Vanity Press & The Proper Poetry Publishers*). Nonetheless variations and embellishments on the old approach surface steadily. These include offers to put your poetry to music setting you off on the road to stardom, readings of your verse by actors with deep voices to help you break into the local radio market (there isn't one) and further requests for cash to have entries on you appear in leather-bound directories of world poets. Everyone appears, including your uncle. There are bogus competitions where entry fees bear no relation to final prize money and the advertised 'publication of winners in anthology form' often means shelling out more for what will turn out to be a badly printed abomination crammed full of weak work. Poets should look very carefully at anything which offers framed certificates, scrolls or engraved wall hangings. They should also be wary of suggestions that they have come high in the State of Florida's Laureateship Contest (or some such like) and have been awarded a calligraphed testimonial. Presentation usually occurs at a three-day festival held in one of the state's most expensive hotels. To get your bit of paper you need to stay for all three days and it is you who has to settle the bill. If you try your luck at a no-entry-fee, advertised in the Sunday papers international competition don't be too surprised to find you've made it through round one - that happens to everyone. The scam starts with round two when they ask you for money.

How do you spot the tricksters? They change their names and addresses at will. They bill themselves as Foundations, Societies, Libraries, National Associations, Guilds. They sound so plausible. If you have the slightest suspicion then check with the Poetry Society. In the poetry world genuine advertisements for contributions are rare. And if anyone asks you for money then forget it. It is not the way things should be done.

The Next Step

Once you have placed a few poems you may like to consider publishing a booklet. There are as many small presses around as there are magazines. Start with the upmarket professionals by all means – Jonathan Cape, Faber & Faber – but be prepared for compromise. The specialists and the small presses are swifter and more open to new work.

If all else fails you could do it yourself. Blake did, so did Walt Whitman. Modern technology puts the process within the reach of us all and if you can put up a shelf, there is a fair chance you will be able to produce a book to go on it. Read my *How to Publish Yourself* (Allison & Busby), Peter Domanski's *A Practical Guide To Publishing Books Using Your PC* (Domanski-Irvine Books) and Jonathan Zeitlyn's *Print: How You Can Do It Yourself* (Journeyman). Remember that publishing the book may be as hard as writing it but marketing and selling it is quite something else. Check Alison Baverstock's *How To Market Books* (Kogan Page) if you really want to get ahead.

The Listings

None of the lists of addresses which follow are exhaustive. Publishers come and go with amazing frequency. There will always be the brand new press on the look-out for talent and the projected magazine desperate for contributions. For up to the minute information check with some of the **Organisations of Interest to Poets** (see page 139). Poetry has a huge market. It pays to keep your ear to the ground. The magazines and presses listed here have all been active during the past eighteen months and most (although be warned, *not all*) have indicated a willingness to look at new work. Those with a positive disinterest in receiving unsolicited work have been excluded. In all cases check before sending. Ask to see a catalogue or a sample copy. Good luck.

Poetry Presses

Akros Publications *(Publisher of Scottish poetry)* See under **Small Presses**

An Clochan *(Belfast venture on Celtic cultures)* 36 Fruithill Park, Beal Feirste (Belfast) BT11 8GE. ☎01232 293401

Anchor Books *(Poetry – an imprint of the Forward Press Group)* See **Poetry Now** magazine *Heather Killingray,* 1-2 Wainman Road, Woodston, Peterborough PE2 7BU. ☎01733 230746 Fax 01733 230751 Email: pete@forwardpress.co.uk Website:www.forwardpress-co.uk

Anvil Press Poetry *(Contemporary British poetry and poetry in translation)* See under **UK Publishers**

Arc Publications *(Contemporary poetry from new and established writers both in the UK and abroad.* See under **UK Publishers**

Aural Images *(Poetry, philosophy)* See also **Lateral Moves** *Alan White,* 5 Hamilton Street, Astley Bridge, Bolton, Lancs BL1 6RT

BB Books *(Post-Beat poetics and counterculture theoretic. Iconoclastic rants and anarchic psycho-cultural tracts)* See also **Global Tapestry Journal** *Dave Cunliffe,* Spring Bank, Longsight Road, Copster Green, Blackburn, Lancs BB1 9EU. ☎01254 249128

Beyond the Cloister Publications *(Individual poets, theme titles and anthologies) Hugh Hellicar,* Flat 1, 14 Lewes Crescent, Brighton, East Sussex BN2 1FH. ☎01273 676019

Blackwater Press PO Box 5115, Leicester LE2 8ZD ☎0116 2238703

Blaxland Tan *(Publishers of the annual poetry groups register) John Jarrett*, 12 Matthews Road, Taunton, Somerset TA1 4NH. ☎01823 324423

Bloodaxe Books *(Britain's leading publisher of new poetry)* See under **UK Publishers**

Bogle-L'Ouverture Press Ltd *(Promoting an independent voice of the experiences of black people) Jessica Huntley*, 141 Coldershaw Road, Ealing, London W13. ☎0181 579 4920 Fax 0181 579 4920

Carcanet Press *(Major poetry publisher)* See also **PN Review** and under **UK Publishers**

The Celtic Cross Press *(Private press publishing signed and numbered limited editions) Rosemary & Nigel Roberts*, Ovins Well House, Low Street, Lastingham, York YO6 6TJ. ☎01751 417298 Fax 01751 417739 email books@ccpress.ndirect.co.uk Websitehttp://www.praxis.co.uk/ppuk/celtic.htm

Chapman Publishing *(Scottish writing)* See under **UK Publishers**; see also **Chapman** under **Magazines**

Cherrybite Publications *(Poetry)* 45 Burton Road, Little Neston, South Wirral L64 4AE

The Corbie Press *(Scottish and European literature, art, philosophy, some poetry)* See also **Epoch** magazine *Neil Mathers*, 57 Murray Street, Montrose, Angus DD10 8JZ. ☎01674 672625

Crescent Moon *(Poetry, criticism, art, feminism, travel, etc)* See under **Small Presses**, and also **Passion** magazine

Cyhoeddiadau Bardus *(Barddoniaeth Gymreig – Welsh language poetry)* See also **Barddas** magazine *Alan Llwyd*, Pen Rhiw, 71 Fford Pentrepoeth, Treforys, Swansea SA6 6AE. ☎01792 792829

Dagger Press *(32-page pamphlets) Brian Morse*, 70 Dagger Lane, West Bromwich, West Midlands B71 4BS. ☎0121 553 2029

Day Dream Press *Kevin Bailey*, 39 Exmouth Street, Swindon, Wilts SN1 3PU. ☎01793 523927

Diehard Publishers *(Small overworked writer/publishers producing poetry and drama for their friends)* See also **Poetry Scotland** magazine *Ian King & others*, Grindles Bookshop, 3 Spittal Street, Edinburgh EH3 9DY. ☎0131 229 7252

Dionysia Press Ltd *(Poems, short stories, plays, reviews, articles) Denise Smith*, 20a Montgomery Street, Edinburgh EH7 5JS. ☎0131 478 0927 Fax 0131 478 2572

Etruscan Books *(Modernist, sound, visual poetry, US/UK poets) Nicholas Johnson*, 24a Fore Street, Buckfastleigh, South Devon TQ11 0AA

Flambard Press *(Concentrates on poetry but also publishes fiction, especially crime and mystery) Peter Elfed Lewis*, Stable Cottage, East Fourstones, Hexham, Northumberland NE47 5DY. ☎01434 674360 Fax 01434 674178 Email: signatur@dircon.co.uk

Flarestack Publishing *(Considers first collections for A5 stapled pamphlet publication)* See also **Obsessed With Pipework** magazine *Charles Johnson*, Redditch Library, 15 Market Place, Redditch B98 8AE. ☎01527 63291 Fax 01527 68571 Email: flare.stack@virgin.net

Forward Press *(General poetry and short fiction anthologies)* See also **Poetry Now**, **Triumph House** and **Poetry Today** *Ian Walton*, Remus House, Coltsfoot Drive, Woodston, Peterborough PE2 9JX. ☎01733 890099 Fax 01733 313524

The Frogmore Press *(Poetry by new/established writers)* See also **The Frogmore Papers** magazine *Jeremy Page*, 18 Nevill Road, Lewes, E Sussex BN7 1PF

Gomer Press/Gwasg Gomer *(Welsh interest)* See under **UK Publishers**

Greylag Press 7 Moreton Way, Kingsthorpe, Northampton NN2 8PD

Hard Pressed Poetry *(Post-modernist poetry and prose)* See also **The Journal** *Billy Mills*, 37 Grosvenor Court, Templeville Road, Templeogue, Dublin 6 W, Eire

Hilton House (Publishers) *Michael K. Moore*, Hilton House, 39 Long John Hill, Norwich NR1 2JP. ☎/Fax 01603 449845

Hippopotamus Press *(First collections of verse from those with a track record in the magazine)* See also **Outposts Poetry Quarterly** *Roland John*, 22 Whitewell Road, Frome, Somerset BA11 4EL. ☎01373 466653 Fax 01373 466653

Honno *(The Welsh women's press) Gwenllian Dafydd*, Alisa Craig, Heol Y Cawl, Dinas Powys, Bro Morgannwg CF64 4AH. ☎01970 623150 Fax 01970 626765 Email: gol.honno@virgin.net

Ihsan Communication *(Poetry, short stories, social commentaries with emphasis on race, culture & youth)* PO Box 550, Bradford, W. Yorks BD10 0YF

K. T. Publications (Kite Books) *(Poetry)* See also **The Third Half** magazine *Kevin Troop*, 16 Fane Close, Stamford, Lincolnshire PE9 1HG. ☎01780 754193

Katabasis *(English poetry and bilingual editions of Latin American poetry. For humanity against new liberalism)* Dinah Livingstone, 10 St Martin's Close, London NW1 0HR. ☎0171 485 3830 Fax 0171 485 3830

Kernow Press *(Limited small collections from poets)* See also **Links** magazine *Bill Headon*, Bude Haven, 18 Frankfield Rise, Tunbridge Wells, Kent TN2 5LF

Lapwing Publications *(Small first collections in pamphlet form)* Dennis & Rene Greig, 1 Ballysillan Drive, Belfast BT14 8HQ. ☎01232 391240 Fax 01232 391240

Lateral Moves Press *(Poetry)* Ann White, 5 Hamilton Street, Astley Bridge, Bolton, Lancs BL1 6RJ. ☎01204 596369

Y Lolfa *(Welsh language press)* Talybont, Ceredigion SY24 5AP. ☎01970 832304 Fax 01970 832782 Email: ylolfa@ylolfa.com Website:www.ylolfa.com

Luath Press Ltd *(Publishers of Scottish books of all kinds)* See under **Small Presses**

Mango Publishing *(Making the Caribbean voice more widely available)* Diana Birch, PO Box 13378, London SE27 0ZN. ☎0181 480 7771 Fax 0181 480 7771

Mariscat Press *(Currently publishing poetry pamphlets only)* Hamish Whyte & others, 3 Mariscat Road, Glasgow G41 4ND. ☎0141 423 7291

Maypole Editions *(First-time poets' platform; non-profit-making)* See under **Small Presses**

Mo-Saic Imprints PO Box 177, Nottingham NG3 5SU

Mudfog Press *(The best new writers from Teesside)* Andy Croft & others, 11 Limes Road, Linthorpe, Middlesbrough TS5 7QR. ☎012642 864428 Fax 012642 262429 Email: cleveland.arts@onyxnet.co.uk

Oasis Books *(Pamphlets and books of poetry and prose)* See also **Oasis** magazine *Ian Robinson*, 12 Stevenage Road, London SW6 6ES. ☎0171 736 5059

Odyssey Poets *(Poetry/prose; first collections; interim booklets; full collections)* See also **PQR** magazine *Derrick Woolf*, Coleridge Cottage, Nether Stowey, Somerset TA5 1NQ. ☎01278 732662

The Old Style Press *(Fine editions)* Frances & Nicholas McDowell Catchmays Court, Llandogo, Nr Monmouth, Gwent NP45 4TN

The One Time Press *(Poetry of the forties in limited letterpress editions. Illustrated)* Peter Wells, Model Farm, Linstead Magna, Halesworth, Suffolk IP19 0DT. ☎01986 785422

The Other Press *(Experimental poetry by women)* Frances Presley 19 Marriott Road, London N4 3QN. ☎0171 272 9023 Email: fpresley@compuserve.com

Partners in Poetry Ian Deal, 289 Elmwood Avenue, Feltham, Middlesex TW13 7QB. ☎0181 751 8652

Peepal Tree Press *(Best in Caribbean and South Asian writing from around the world)* Jeremy Poynting, 18 King's Avenue, Leeds, W. Yorks LS6 1QS. ☎0113 2451703 Fax 0113 2468368 Email: hannah@peepal.demon.co.uk

Peterloo Poets Harry Chambers, The Old Chapel, Sand Lane, Calstock, Cornwall PL18 9QU. ☎01822 833473

The Poetry Business Peter Sansom & others, 51 Byram Arcade, Westgate, Huddersfield, W. Yorks HD1 1ND

Poetry Monthly Press See also **Poetry Monthly** magazine Martin Holroyd, 39 Cavendish Road, Long Eaton, Nottingham NG10 4HY. ☎0115 9461267 Email: martinholroyd@compuserve.com

Poetry Now *(Includes **Poetry Now Young Writers**)* Andrew Head, Remus House, Coltsfoot Drive, Woodston, Peterborough PE2 9JX. ☎01733 890099 Fax 01733 313524 Email: forward_press@ compuserve. com Website: www.forwardpress–co.uk

Poetry Today *(Part of Forward Press group)* Remus House, Coltsfoot Drive, Woodston, Peterborough PE2 9JX. ☎01733 890099 Fax 01733 313524 Email: forward_press@compuserve.com Website:www.forwardpress.co.uk

Polygon Books *(Prize-winning independent literary publisher specialising in new fiction and poetry)* See under **UK Publishers** Marion Sinclair, **Edinburgh University Press**, 22 George Square, Edinburgh EH8 9LF. ☎0131 650 8436 Fax 0131 662 0053 Email: polygon@eup.ed.ac.uk Website:www.eup.ed.ac.uk

Psychopoetica Publications *(Psychologically-based poetry)* See also **Psychopoetica** magazine Geoff Lowe, Dept of Psychology, University of Hull, Hull HU6 7RX Fax 01482 465599 Website: www.fernhse. demon.co.uk/ eastword/psycho

Reality Street Editions *(New poetry from Britain and Europe)* Ken Edwards & others, 4 Howard Court, Peckham Rye, London SE15 3PH

Red Candle Press *('Traditionalist poetry is our great interest.')* See also **Candelabrum Poetry Magazine** *Michael Leonard McCarthy,* 9 Milner Road, Wisbech, Cambridgeshire PE13 2LR. ☎01945 581067

Rive Gauche Publishing *(Poetry by women writing and performing in Bristol in the 1990s)* *P.V.T West,* 69 Lower Redland Road, Bristol BS6 6SP. ☎0117 9745106

Salmon Poetry See under **Irish Publishers** *Jessie Lendennie,* Knockeve, Cliffs of Moher, Co Clare, Eire. ☎00 353 658 1941 Email: salpub@iol.ie Website:www.salmonpoetry.com

Seren Books *(Poetry, fiction, lit. crit., biography, essays)* See under **UK Publishers** and also **Poetry Wales** magazine

Slow Dancer Press *(Contemporary poetry publishers; no unsolicited mss considered)* John Harvey, 59 Parliament Hill, London NW3 2TB Email: john@mellotone.co.uk Website:www.mellotone.co.uk

SMH Books *(Real-life books, including poetry and memoirs)* Sandra M. H. Saer, Pear Tree Cottage, Watersfield, Pulborough, West Sussex RG20 1NG. ☎01798 831260 Fax 01798 831906 Email: smhpublishing services@ukbusiness.co

Smith/Doorstop Books *(Contemporary poetry books, pamphlets and cassettes)* See also **The North** magazine *Peter Sansom & others,* The Studio, Byram Arcade, Westgate, Huddersfield, W. Yorks HD1 1ND. ☎01484 434840 Fax 01484 426566 Email: poetbus@pop3.poptel.org.uk

Spoon Editions *(New writing)* See also **The Big Spoon** magazine *Martin Crawford,* 32 Salisbury Court, Belfast BT7 1DD. ☎01232 232353 Fax 01232 232650 Email: martin@fortnite.dnet.co.uk

Starborn Books *(Children's books, song books, poetry, local interest)* Phil Forder, Glanrhydwilym, Llandissilio, Clinderwen, Pembrokeshire SA66 7QH. ☎01437 563562 Fax 01239 613754

Stride Publications *(Innovative poetry, fiction, anthologies, essays and interviews)* See under **Small Presses** *Rupert Loydell,* 11 Sylvan Road, Exeter, Devon EX4 6EW Email: rml@madbear.demon.co.uk W'site: www.madbear.demon.co.uk/ stride/

Swansea Poetry Workshop *Nigel Jenkins,* 124 Overland Road, Mumbles, Swansea SA3 4EU

Tabla *(Publisher of the annual Tabla Book of New Verse)* Stephen James, University of Bristol, Dept of English, 3-5 Woodland Road, Bristol BS8 1TB ☎0117 9288132

Tarantula Publications *(Collections of poetry)* See also **Brando's Hat** magazine *Sean Body,* 14 Vine Street, Salford, Manchester M7 3PG. ☎0161 792 4593 Fax 0161 792 4593

Totem *(Publishers of contemporary literature and art)* Fiifi Annobil, 60 Swinley House, Redhill Street, Regent's Park, London NW1 4BB. ☎0171 387 7216

Triumph House *(An imprint of the Forward Press)* Ian Walton, Remus House, Coltsfoot Drive, Woodston, Peterborough PE2 9JX

Underground Press *(Matters relating to art and language)* John Evans, 9 Laneley Terrace, Maesycoed, Pontypridd, Mid Glamorgan CF37 1ER

Ventus Books *(Publisher of plays, scores and poems by Tony Breeze)* Tony Breeze, 70 Nottingham Road, Burton Joyce, Notts NG14 5AL. ☎0115 9313356

The Windows Project See also **Smoke** magazine *David Ward,* First Floor, Liver House, 96 Bold Street, Liverpool L1 4HY. ☎0151 709 3688

Words Worth Books *(Innovative literary, visual & performance work; formerly Zimmer Press)* See also **Words Worth** magazine *Alaric Sumner,* BM Box 4515, London WC1N 3XX Email: a.sumner@dartington.ac.uk

Writers Forum *(Innovative language and visual poetries)* See also **And** magazine *Bob Cobbing,* 89a Petherton Road, London N5 2QT. ☎0171 226 2657

Writers' Own Publications See also **Writers' Own Magazine** *Mrs E. M. Pickering,* 121 Highbury Grove, Clapham, Bedford MK41 6DU. ☎01234 365982

Yorkshire Art Circus Ltd *(Community publisher)* See under **Small Presses**

Zum Zum Books *(Wild, brilliant, deep, sensuous, philosophical poetry)* Neil Oram, Goshem, Bunlight, Drumnadrochit, Inverness-shire IV3 6AH. ☎01456 450402

Poetry Magazines

Many poetry magazines have links with or are produced by companies listed in **Poetry Presses**

AABye *(Contemporary international poetry journal open to all genres) Gerald England,* 20 Werneth Avenue, Gee Cross, Hyde, Cheshire SK14 5NL. ☎0161 351 1878 Email: aabye@geocities.com Website: www.geocities.com/Athens/café/9091

Acid Angel *(The re-incarnation of **Dada Dance**; grown older and slicker but still as subversive) Dee Rimbaud,* 35 Falkland Street, Glasgow G12 9QZ. ☎0141 221 1223 Email: acidangel@acidity.globalnet.co.uk

Acumen *(Good poetry, intelligent articles and wide-ranging reviews) See also* **Long Poem Group Newsletter** *Patricia Oxley,* 6 The Mount, Higher Furzeham, Brixham, Devon TQ5 8QY. ☎01803 851098 Fax 01803 851098

The Affectionate Punch *(New and experienced writers with something to write about) Andrew Tutty,* 35 Brundage Road, Manchester M22 0BY. ☎0161 499 9943

Agenda *(Quarterly poetry magazine, founded in 1959) William Cookson,* 5 Cranbourne Court, Albert Bridge Road, London SW11 4PE. ☎0171 228 0700 Fax 0171 228 0700

Aireings *(Poetry – 40 pages – published since 1980 – leans towards women's work) Jean Barker,* 3/24 Brudenell Road, Leeds, W. Yorks LS6 1BD

Alien Skull *(Poetry, fiction, sf, fortean matters, literary topics, cultural flotsam) Adrian Hodges,* Flat 3, 43 Park Street, Cheltenham, Glos GL50 3NG Website: www.daffy007.dircon.co.uk

Ambit *(Poetry, fiction, graphics, arts, reviews) Martin Bax,* 17 Priory Gardens, London N6 5QY Website:www.ambit.co.uk

And *(Visual and linguistically innovative poems) See also* **Writers Forum** press *Bob Cobbing & Adrian Clarke,* 89a Petherton Road, London N5 2QT. ☎0171 226 2657

Apostrophe/Mr Pillows Press *(Bi-annual of new poetry from unknown and established poets) Diana Andersson,* Orton House, 41 Canute Road, Faversham, Kent ME13 8SH. ☎01795 536185

The Arcadian *(Poetry) Mike Boland,* 11 Boxtree Lane, Harrow Weald, Middlesex HA3 6JU

Areopagus *(A Christian-based arena for creative writers) Julian Barritt,* 101 May Tree Close, Badger Farm, Winchester SO22 4JF

Bad-Breakfast All Day *(Short fiction, poetry, graphic stories, cartoons, opinion and comment) Philip Boxall,* 43 Kingsdown House, Amhurst Road, London E8 2AS. ☎0033 235 403326 Fax 0033 235 403326

Bad Poetry Quarterly *(Weekly mag of poetry/illustrations – "the Viz of poetry") Gordon Smith,* PO Box 6319, London E11 2EP

Barddas *(Barddoniaeth Gymreig – Welsh language poetry – especially in the strict meters) See also* **Cyhoeddiadau Barddas** *Alan Llwyd,* Pen Rhiw, 71 Fford Pentrepoeth, Treforys, Swansea SA6 6AE. ☎01792 792829

The Big Spoon *(New writing, culture, photography and the visual arts) See also* **Spoon Editions** *Martin Crawford,* 32 Salisbury Court, Belfast BT7 1DD. ☎01232 232353 Fax 01232 232650 Email: martin@fortnite.dnet.co.uk

Billy Liar *(State of the nation through fiction, journalism, poetry, visual art and reviews) Paul Summers & others,* 235 Rothbury Terrace, Heaton, Newcastle upon Tyne NE6 5DD. ☎0191 240 2131 Fax 0191 2402131

Blade *(A mag on the cutting edge of poetry) Jane Holland,* Maynrys, Glen Chass, Port St Mary, Isle of Man IM9 5PN

The Bloody Quill *(Vampire poetry) J. Rogerson,* West Lodge, Higher Lane, Liverpool L9 7AB

Borderlines *(Journal of the Anglo-Welsh Poetry Society) Dave Bingham,* Nant Y Brithyll, Llangynyw, Welshpool, Powys SY21 0JS. ☎01938 810263

Brando's Hat *(Poetry) See also* **Tarantula Publications** *Sean Body,* 14 Vine Street, Salford, Manchester M7 3PG. ☎0161 792 4593 Fax 0161 792 4593

Brangle *(Essays, reviews and poetry from N. Ireland and beyond) Carol Rumens,* 100a Tunis Road, London W12 7EY. ☎0181 740 0660

Braquemard *(Forty pages of excellent poetry, prose and artwork) David Allenby,* 20 Terry Street, Hull HU3 1UD

Brass Butterfly *(Poetry)* 17a Edward Road, Dorchester, Dorset DT1 2HL

Cadmium Blue Literary Journal *(Traditional romantic and lyrical poetry)* Peter Geoffrey Paul Thompson, 71 Harrow Crescent, Romford, Essex RM3 7BJ

Candelabrum Poetry Magazine *(Twice-yearly poetry, mostly traditional)* See also **Red Candle Press** Michael Leonard McCarthy, 9 Milner Road, Wisbech, Cambs PE13 2LR. ☎01945 581067

Chapman *(The best in Scottish and international writing, well-established writers)* See under **Magazines** and also **Chapman Press**

Christian Poetry Review *(A platform for Christians writing poetry in today's world)* F. T. Lewis, Grendon House, 67 Walsall Road, Lichfield, Staffs WS13 8AD. ☎01543 411015 Fax 01543 411015

The Collective Seasonal *(Work from the Abergavenny Collective)* John Jones, Penlanlas Farm, Abergavenny NP7 7HN Email: peaks3pr@aol.com

Connections *(Encourages new writing, carries information, stories, poems, articles)* Narissa Knights, 13 Wave Crest, Whitstable, Kent CT5 1EH

Corpses and Clarinets *(Poetry and prose)* Simon Jennor, 51 Waterloo Street, Hove, East Sussex BN3 1AH

Cyphers *(Irish literary magazine: poetry, prose, reviews)* Eilean NcChuilleanain, 3 Selskar Terrace, Ranelagh, Dublin 6, Eire Fax 00 353 1 497 8866

The David Jones Journal *(Articles, information, reviews and inspired works)* Anne Price-Owen, The David Jones Society, 48 Sylvan Way, Sketty, Swansea SA2 9JB. ☎01792 206144 Fax 01792 205305 Email: jstapleton@sihe.ac.uk

Dial 174 *(Poetry and poetry-orientated articles, travelogues, etc.)* Joseph Hemmings, 21 Mill Road, Watlington, King's Lynn, Norfolk PE33 0HH Email: apoet@globalnet.co.uk Website:users.global.co.uk/apoet

Dream Catcher Paul Sutherland, 4 St John Street, York YO3 7QT. ☎01904 628138

Eastern Rainbow *(Focuses on 20th century culture via poetry, prose and art)* See also **Peace and Freedom** magazine Paul Rance, 17 Farrow Road, Whaplode Drove, Spalding, Lincs PE12 0TS

Ecorche *(The more extreme realms of the avant garde)* Ian Taylor, 17 Eastfields, Thornford, Sherborne, Dorset DT9 6PU

Ecto 1 *(Poetry, pics, paranormal, news clippings, feminism and futurism)* Michelle Oliver, 4 Pen Y Cwm, Pentyrch, Cardiff CF4 8PS

Edinburgh Review See under **Magazines** and also **Polygon Books**

Envoi *(Poetry, sequences, features, reviews, competitions)* Roger Elkin, 44 Rudyard Road, Biddulph Moor, Stoke-on-Trent, Staffs ST8 7JN

Epoch Magazine *(Scottish and European literature, art, philosophy, some poetry)* Neil Mathers, 57 Murray Street, Montrose, Angus DD10 8JZ. ☎01674 672625

Erran Publishing *(Poetry)* See also **Poetic Hours** magazine Nick Clark, 8 Dale Road, Carlton, Notts NG4 1GT

Federation *(Magazine of the Federation of Workers Writers & Community Publishers)* Tim Diggles, 67 The Boulevard, Tunstall, Stoke-on-Trent ST6 6HD. ☎01792 8222327 Fax 01792 8222327 Email: fwwcp@cwcom.net Website:www.fwwcp.mcmail.com

Fire *(Poetry: alternative, unfashionable, experimental, spiritual, demotic)* Jeremy Hilton, Field Cottage, Old White Hill, Tackley, Kidlington, Oxon OX5 3AB

First Time *(New poets)* Josephine Austin, 4 Burdett Place, George Street, Hastings, East Sussex TN34 3ED

Flaming Arrows *(Mystical insights through original writing, graphics, photography, poetry)* Leo Regan, County Sligo V.E.C., Riverside, Sligo, Eire

For Poets PO Box 1009, Storrington, Pulborough RH20 3YT. ☎01903 747224 Fax 01903 746238

The Frogmore Papers See also **The Frogmore Press** Jeremy Page, 18 Nevill Road, Lewes, East Sussex BN7 1PF

Gairm *(All-Gaelic literary quarterly)* Derek Thomson, 29 Waterloo Street, Glasgow G2 6BZ

Galloway Poets *(Focusing on Scotland and abroad)* See also **Markings** magazine John Hudson & Anne Darling, 77 High Street, Kirkcudbright DG6 4JW. ☎01557 331557 Fax 01557 331557 Email: j.hudson@btinternet.com

Glasshouse Electric *(Experimental poetry and word art)* J. Rogerson, West Lodge, Highlane, Liverpool L9 7AB

Global Tapestry Journal *(Global Bohemia, post-Beat and counterculture orientation)* See also **BB Books** Dave Cunliffe, Spring Bank, Longsight Road, Copster Green, Blackburn, Lancs BB1 9EU. ☎01254 249128

Headlock *(Wall-to-wall poetry) Tony Charles,* The Old Zion Chapel, The Triangle, Somerton, Somerset TA11 6QP

How Do I Love Thee? *(The magazine for love poetry) Adrian Bishop,* 1 Blue Ball Corner, Water Lane, Winchester, Hants SO23 0ER. Email: adrian.bishop@virgin.net Website:freespace.virgin.net/poetry.life

HQ Poetry Magazine (Haiku Quarterly) *(General poetry mag with slight bias towards impeistic/haikuesque work)* See also **Day Dream Press** *Kevin Bailey,* 39 Exmouth Street, Swindon, Wiltshire SN1 3PU. ☎01793 523927

HU – The Honest Ulsterman *(Ireland's premier journal for new poems, prose, articles) Tom Clyde,* 49 Main Street, Greyabbey, Co. Down BT22 2NF

Hybrid *(Poetry)* 42 Christchurch Place, Peterlee, Co. Durham SR8 2NR

Interchange *Richard Marggraf Turley,* Dept. of English, U.C.W. Aberystwyth, Aberystwyth, Ceredigion SY23 3DY Fax 01970 622530 Email: rcm@aber.ac.uk

The Interpreter's House *(Poems and stories up to 2500 words, new and established writers) Merryn Williams,* 10 Farrell Road, Wootton, Bedfordshire MK43 9DU. ☎01234 766579

Intimacy *(Communication experienced as nakedness) Adam McKeown,* 11c, Elizabeth House, Alexandra Street, Maidstone, Kent ME14 2BX. ☎01622 672628

Iota *(Poetry – no political, philosophical or religious hobby-horses) David Holliday,* 67 Hady Crescent, Chesterfield, Derbyshire S41 0EB. ☎01246 276532

Journal of Contemporary Anglo-Scandinavian Poetry *(Scandinavian, Nordic and European poems in translation alongside poetry written in English) Sam Smith,* 11 Heatherton Park, Bradford-on-Tone, Taunton, Somerset TA4 1EV. ☎01823 461725

The Journal *(Post-modernist poetry and prose)* See also **Hard Pressed Poetry** *Billy Mills & Catherine Walsh,* 37 Grosvenor Court, Templeville Road, Templeogue, Dublin 6 W, Eire

Konfluence *(Local West Country material)* Bath House, Bath Road, Nailsworth, Glos GL6 0JB

Krax *(Light-hearted, contemporary poetry, short fiction and graphics) Andy Robson,* 63 Dixon Lane, Wortley, Leeds, W. Yorks LS12 4RR

Kunapipi *(Journal of post-colonial writing)* PO Box 20, Hebden Bridge, W Yorks HX7 5QZ Email: kunapipi@english.novell. leeds.ac.uk

Lallans *(The magazine for writing in Scots) Neil MacCullum,* 18 Redford Avenue, Edinburgh EH13 0BU. ☎0131 441 3724

Lateral Moves *(Poems, stories, articles, humour, listings, letters, interviews, how-tos)* See also **Aural Images** *Ann White,* 5 Hamilton Street, Astley Bridge, Bolton, Lancs BL1 6RJ. ☎01204 596369 Website: basil.acs. boltonac.uk/~plu1/ai/ index.htm

Links *(Poetry magazine committed to quality writing and reviews)* See also **Kernow Press** *Bill Headdon,* Bude Haven, 18 Frankfield Rise, Tunbridge Wells, Kent TN2 5LF

Literary Review See under **Magazines**

London Magazine – See under **Magazines**

The Long Poem Group Newsletter *William Oxley,* 6 The Mount, Higher Furzeham, Brixham, S Devon TQ5 8QY. ☎01803 851098 Fax 01803 851098

The Magazine *(Poetry and short fiction sponsored by the critical writing programme, University of Warwick) Sally Russell,* Open Studies, Dept of Continuing Education, University of Warwick, Coventry, Warwickshire CV4 7AL. ☎01203 523831

Magma *(New poetry plus poetry reviews and interviews) David Boll,* The Stukely Press, 43 Keslake Road, London NW6 6DH. ☎0181 537 6263 Email: magma@dcd.gmw.ac.uk Website: www.dcs.qmw.ac.uk/ ~timk/magma

The Magpie's Nest *(Quarterly literary magazine – poems and short stories by new writers and poets) Bal Saini,* 176 Stoney Lane, Sparkhill, Birmingham B12 8AN Email: bal.saini@virgin.net

Markings *(Poems, stories, art and criticism focusing on Scotland and abroad)* See also **Galloway Poets** *John Hudson & Anne Darling,* 77 High Street, Kirkcudbright DG6 4JW. ☎01557 331557 Fax 01557 331557 Email: j.hudson@btinternet.com

Metre *(International poetry and critical prose) David Wheatley,* Dept of English, Trinity College, Dublin 2, Eire

Micropress Midlands Poetry *(Advice service and magazine) Geoff Stevens,* 25 Gutter Road, West Bromwich B71 2EH

Moonstone *(Pagan/antheistic poetry) Talitha Clare,* SOS, The Old Station Yard, Settle N. Yorks BD24 9RP

Mslexia *(For women who write)* PO Box 656, Newcastle upon Tyne NE99 2XD. ☎0191 281 9772 0191 281 9445 Email: postbag@mslexia.demon.co.uk

Nasty Piece of Work *(Quarterly mag of morbid, sick and macabre horror fiction and poetry)* David A. Green, 20 Drum Mead, Petersfield, Hants GU22 3AQ

The New Shetlander See under **Magazines**

New Welsh Review *(Wales's leading literary quarterly in English: articles, poems, etc.)* See under **Magazines**

The New Writer (incorporating **Acclaim** & **Quartos**) *(Advice magazine which includes poetry)* See under **Magazines**

Night Dreams *(Horror, poetry, artwork)* Anthony Barker, 52 Denman Lane, Huncote, Leicester LE9 3BS

Nomad *(Poetry and creative writing by survivors of the mental health system, of abuse or addictions)* Gerry Loose, Survivors Press, 30 Cranworth Street, Glasgow G12 8AG. ☎0141 357 6838 Fax 0141 357 6939 Email: sps@gisp.net

The North See also **Smith/Doorstop Books** *(Contemporary poetry, some fiction and graphics, extensive reviews)* Peter Sansom & Janet Fisher, The Studio, Byram Arcade, Westgate, Huddersfield, W. Yorks HD1 1ND. ☎01484 434840 Fax 01484 426566 Email: poetbus@pop3.poptel.org.uk

Northwords *(Poetry and short fiction, focusing on the North)* Angus Dunn, The Stable, Long Road, Avoch, Ross-shire IV9 8QR. ☎01381 621561 Email: stable@cali.co.uk

Oasis *(Poetry, short fiction, essays, reviews, etc.)* See also **Oasis Books** Ian Robinson, 12 Stevenage Road, Fulham, London SW6 6ES. ☎0171 736 5059

Obsessed With Pipework *(Open quarterly 'poetry to surprise and delight with a high-wire aspect')* See also **Flarestack Publishing** Charles Johnson, Redditch Library, 15 Market Place, Redditch B98 8AR. ☎01527 63291 Fax 01527 68571 Email: flare.stack@virgin.net

Orbis *(An independent international quarterly of poetry and prose with many reader-friendly features)* Mike Shields, 27 Valley View, Primrose, Jarrow, Tyne & Wear NE32 5QT. ☎0191 489 7055 Fax 0191 430 1297

Other Poetry *(Poems, reviews and interviews)* Evangeline Paterson, 105 Osborne Court, Osborne Avenue, Newcastle upon Tyne NE2 1LE. ☎0191 281 9474

Outposts *(Longest surviving independent poetry magazine in the UK)* See also **Hippopotamus Press** Roland John, 22 Whitewell Road, Frome, Somerset BA11 4EL. ☎01373 466653 Fax 01373 466653

Outreach *(Free quarterly for the housebound, elderly and disabled)* Rev. M. J. Kirby, 7 Grayson Close, Stockbridge, Sheffield, S. Yorks S36 5BJ. ☎0114 2885346 Fax 0114 2884903

Pagan America *(Bi-annual journal of new American poetry)* See also **Crescent Moon** and **Passion** Jeremy Robinson, PO Box 393, Maidstone, Kent ME14 5XU. ☎01622 728593

Passion *(Poetry, fiction, arts, criticism, philosophy)* See also **Crescent Moon** and **Pagan America** Jeremy Robinson, PO Box 393, Maidstone, Kent ME14 5XU. ☎01622 728593

Passport *(Short fiction, poetry and articles)* Carol Gordon, The Writer's Co-operative, 6 Chaplin Grove, Crownhill, Milton Keynes MK8 0DG

Pause *(Magazine of the National Poetry Foundation)* Helen Robinson, 27 Mill Road, Fareham, Hants PO16 0TH

Peace and Freedom *(Humanitarian/ecologically-minded arts mag)* See also **Eastern Rainbow** Paul Rance, 17 Farrow Road, Whaplode Drove, Spalding, Lincs PE12 0TS

Peer Poetry Magazine *(Poets who have not yet succeeded in making a name)* Paul Amphlett, 26 Arlington House, Bath Street, Bath BA1 1QN. ☎01225 445298

The Penniless Press *(Quarterly for the poor pocket and the rich mind. Poetry, fiction, essays)* Alan Dent, 100 Waterloo Road, Ashton, Preston, Lancs PR2 1EP. ☎01772 736421

Pennine Platform *(Poetry magazine which combines modern sensibility with respect for traditional craft)* Dr K. E. Smith, 7 Cockley Hill Lane, Kirkheaton, Huddersfield, W. Yorks HD5 0HH. ☎01484 516804

Planet *(The Welsh Internationalist – current affairs, arts, environment)* John Barnie, PO Box 44, Aberystwyth SY23 3ZZ. ☎01970 611255 Fax 01970 611197

Planet Prozac *(Sf, fantasy, poetry, gothic horror, humour)* Literally Literary, 8 Marlborough Gardens, Wordsley, Stourbridge, West Midlands DY8 5EE

Plume *(Anglo-French literary mag – poetry, prose and illustrations)* Jan Bentley, 15 Bolehill Park, Hove Edge, Brighouse HD6 2RS. ☎01484 717808 Email: plumelit@aol.com

PN Review See **Carcanet Press** under **UK Publishers**

The Poet's Voice (Published with Univ. of Salzburg) *Fred Beake & others*, 12 Dartmouth Avenue, Bath BA2 1AT Email: wolfgang.goertschacher@sbg.ac.at

Poetic Hours *(Non-profit supporter of Third world charities)* See also **Erran Publishing** magazine *Nick Clark*, 8 Dale Road, Carlton, Notts NG4 1GT

Poetic Licence *(New poetry, rotating editorial team, fresh perspectives) Peter L. Evans*, 70 Aveling Close, Purley, Surrey CR8 4DW. ☎0181 645 9956

Poetry and Audience *(Poems, articles, reviews, short stories, essays, letters, art work) Jessica Gardner*, School of English, University of Leeds, Leeds, W. Yorks LS2 9JT. ☎0113 2431751 Fax 0113 2334774 Email: engpanda@english.novel.leeds.ac.uk Website: www.leeds.ac.uk/english/ $general/pla.html

The Poetry Church *(Free distribution)* See also **Feather Books** under **Small Presses** *Rev J. Waddington Feather*, Fair View, Old Coppice, Lyth Bank, Shrewbury, Shropshire SY3 0BW. ☎01743 872177 Fax 01743 872177 Email: john@feather.icom-web.com Website: www.feather.icom-web.com

Poetry Ireland Review/Eigse Eireann *(Quarterly journal of poetry and reviews) Niamn Morris*, Bermingham Tower, Upper Yard, Dublin Castle, Dublin 2, Eire. ☎00 353 1 671 4632 Fax 00 353 1 671 4634 Email: poetry@iol.ie

Poetry Life Magazine *(A magazine to explore the rich and booming UK poetry scene)* See also **How Do I Love Thee?** *Adrian Bishop*, 1 Blue Ball Corner, Water Lane, Winchester, Hants SO23 0ER. Email: adrian.bishop@virgin.net Website: freespace.virgin.net/poetry.life

Poetry London Newsletter *(Poetry, listings, information) P. Daniels*, 35 Bethnal Road, London E16 7AR Website: www.rmple. co.uk/eduweb/sites/poetry.index.html

Poetry Manchester *Sean Boustead*, 13 Napier Street, Swinton, Manchester M27 0JQ

Poetry Monthly *(Poems, articles, comment – new and experienced poets) Martin Holroyd*, 39 Cavendish Road, Long Eaton, Nottingham NG10 4HY. ☎0115 9461267 Email: martinholroyd@compuserve.com Website: ourworld.compuserve. com/homepage/martinholroyd

Poetry Nottingham International *(Poetry, articles, letters, features, reviews, 44 pages, quarterly) Cathy Grindrod & others*, 71 Saxton Avenue, Heanor, Derbyshire DE75 7PZ

Poetry Now *(48-page poetry magazine with articles, workshop, letters and news) Andrew Head*, Remus House, Coltsfoot Drive, Woodston, Peterborough, Cambs PE2 9JX. ☎01733 890099 Fax 01733 313524 Website: www.forwardpress-co.uk

Poetry Review *(Quarterly forum on the state of poetry) Peter Forbes*, Poetry Society, 22 Betterton Street, London WC2H 9BU. ☎0171 420 9883 Fax 0171 240 4818 Email: poetrysoc@dial.pipex.com Website: www.poetrysoc.com

Poetry Scotland *(Quarterly broadsheet 'forty poems by twenty poets')* See also **Diehard Publishers** *Sally Evans*, Grindles Bookshop, 3 Spittal Street, Edinburgh EH3 9DY. ☎0131 229 7252

Poetry Wales *(Focuses on new and established poets from Wales plus translations)* See also **Seren Books** under **UK Publishers** *Robert Minhinnick*, First Floor, 2 Wyndham Street, Bridgend CF31 1EF. ☎01656 767834 Fax 01656 767834

PQR – Poetry Quarterly Review *(Reviews)* See also **Odyssey Poets** press *Derrick Woolf*, Coleridge Cottage, Nether Stowey, Somerset TA5 1NQ

Presence *(Haiku, senryu, tanka, renku and related poetry in English) Martin Lucas*, 12 Grovehall Avenue, Leeds, W. Yorks LS11 7EX Email:: stuart@newmind.co.uk Website: www.newmind.co.uk/ myriadgrasses/

Prop *(Poetry, short fiction plus related essays, reviews and interviews) Stephen Blythe & Chris Hart*, 31 Central Avenue, Farnworth, Bolton, Lancs BL4 0AU

Psychopoetica *(A magazine of psychologically-based poetry)* See also **Psychopoetica Publications** *Geoff Lowe*, Dept of Psychology, University of Hull, Hull HU6 7RX Fax 01482 465599 Website:fernhse.demon.co.uk/eastword/ psycho

Pulsar *(Hard hitting/inspirational poetry – quarterly) David Pike*, 34 Lineacre, Grangepark, Swindon, Wilts SN5 6DA. ☎01793 875941 Fax 01793 875941 Email: david.pike@virgin.net Website:www.i-way.co.uk/~swindonlink/ poetry.html

Pussy Poetry *(Women's poetry) Erica*, 6 Rookery Close, Keddington Park, Louth, Lincolnshire LN11 0GF

Quantum Leap *(Poetry from new and established writers)* 81 Breval Crescent, Hardgate, Clydebank G81 6LS

Queer Words *(Paperback mag of new lesbian and gay writing)* Michael Nobbs, PO Box 23, Aberystwyth, Dyfed SY23 1AA

The Reater *(No flowers, just blunt chiselled poetry)* Shane Rhodes, Wrecking Ball Press, 18 Church Street, Northcave, Brough, E. Yorks HU15 2LW. ☎01430 424346

The Red Kite/Y Bacud Coch *(Independent, radical political mag for Wales; global and local issues)* Kate Baillie, Brynmadog, Gwernogle, Carmarthen SA32 7RN. ☎01267 202375 Fax 01267 202471 Email: redkite@democraticleft.org.uk Website: www.democraticleft.org.uk

The Rialto *(Deliberately eclectic, dedicated to excellence, 'love poetry, love life')* Michael Mackmin, PO Box 309, Aylsham, Norwich, Norfolk NR11 6LN

A Riot of Emotions *(Art/poetry fanzine with small press and music reviews)* Andrew Cocker, Dark Diamonds Pubs, PO Box HK 31, Leeds, West Yorks LS11 9XN

Roisin Dubh Free Poetry Zine *(Poetry)* 3 Irvine Road, Newmilns, Ayrshire KA15 9JB

Rustic Rub (formerly **And What of Tomorrow**) *(Poetry and art magazine – international mix of styles – likes to take chances)* Jay Woodman, 33 Meadow Walk, Fleet, Hants GU13 8BA. ☎01252 628538

Saccade *(Bizarre and fantastic fiction – non-fiction, poetry, artwork – any style – horror, sf, fantasy)* Robert Gill, 93 Green Lane, Dronfield, Sheffield S18 6FG

Salopoet *(Journal of the Salopian Poetry Society)* 5 Squires Close, The Fairways, Madeley, Telford TF7 5RU

Saltburn Scene *(Science, rock music, poetry, folk and fairy lore, history – local and otherwise)* Mark Beevers, Glenside Cottage, Glenside Terrace, Saltburn, Cleveland TR12 1SS

Scintilla *(Journal of the Usk Valley Vaughan Association)* Anne Cluysenaar, Little Wentwood Farm, Llantrisant, Usk, Monmouthshire NP5 1ND. ☎01291 673797

Scriptor *(Poetry, short stories, essays from the South East)* John & Lesley Dench, 22 Plough Lane, Swalecliffe, Whitstable, Kent CT5 2NZ. ☎01227 793819

Seam *(New poetry)* Maggie Freeman & others, PO Box 3684, Danbury, Chelmsford, Essex CM3 4GP

Seshat *(Cross-cultural perspectives in poetry and philosophy)* Terence Duquesne & others, PO Box 9313, London E17 8XL

Slacker *(Poetry, short stories and cartoons)* David Brewster, Flat 1/L, 3 MacIntyre Place, Paisley PA2 6EE

Slipstream *(Poetry, fiction, writing)* Cathy Cullis, 4 Crossways, Crookham Village, Fleet, Hampshire GU13 0TA

Smiths Knoll *(New poems and nothing but poems)* Roy Blackman & others 49 Church Road, Little Glemham, Woodbridge, Suffolk IP13 0BJ

Smoke *(Poetry, graphics, short prose – 24pp – bi-annual)* Dave Ward, The Windows Project, 1st Floor, Liver House, 96 Bold Street, Liverpool L1 4HY. ☎0151 709 3688

Snapshots *(Haiku)* John Barlow, PO Box 35, Sefton Park, Liverpool L17 3EG

Sol Poetry Magazine *(Poetry, fiction, reviews, artwork)* Malcolm E. Wright, 24 Fowler Close, Southchurch, Southend-on-Sea, Essex SS1 2RD

South (incorporating **Doors**) *(Poetry for the southern counties)* Michael Fealty, 61 West Borough, Wimborne, Dorset BH21 1LX. ☎01202 889669 Fax 01202 881061 Email: wordandaction@wanda.demon.co.uk

Southfields *(Poetry, essays, reviews. A Scottish little mag with wide ranging concerns)* Richard Price, 8 Richmond Road, Staines TW18 2AB

The Spotted Rhubard Zene *(Art, poetry, music, reviews)* Krystian Taylor, 102 Old Church Road, Nailsea, Bristol BS19 2ND

Stand *(Quarterly magazine of poetry and new writing)* Michael Hulse and John Kinsella, School of English, University of Leeds, Leeds LS2 9JT Email: jk20@hermes.cam.ac.uk

Staple New Writing *(Mainstream poetry and fiction magazine, established in 1982, not a closed shop)* Bob Windsor & Don Mesham, Tor Cottage, 81 Cavendish Road, Matlock, Derbyshire DE4 3HD. ☎01629 582764

Still *(Literary journal with a Zen approach to haiku and short verse)* Al Li, 49 Englands Lane, London NW3 4YD Email: still@into.demon.co.uk Website: www.into.demon.co.uk

Super-Trouper *(The small press mag on tape – songs, poetry, reviews, music)* Andrew Savage, 35 Kearsley Road, Sheffield S2 4TE

Swagmag *(Mag of Swansea's writers and artists)* Peter Thabit Jones, Dan-y-Bryn, 74 Cwm Level Road, Brynhyfred, Swansea SA5 9DY. ☎01792 774070

The Swansea Review *(Magazine of poetry, criticism and prose) Glyn Pursglove*, Dept of English, University College Swansea, Singleton Park, Swansea SA2 8PP

Symtex & Grimmer *(Experimental and mainstream poetry – English German and visual) Chris Jones*, Clatto Bothy, 2 Sunnybraes, Boarhills, Fife KY16 8PU Email: csj2@st-andrews.ac.uk

Tandem *(Poetry, some prose, reviews. Encourages young writers. Annual) Michael J. Woods*, 13 Stephenson Road, Barbourne, Worcester WR1 3EB. ☎01905 28002 Email: mjw@tandem-poetry.demon.co.uk Website:www.tandem-poetry.demon.co.uk

Tangled Hair *(Tanka) John Barlow*, Snapshot Press, PO Box 35, Sefton Park, Liverpool L17 3EG

Target *(Poetry and comment) Bryn Fortey*, 212 Caerleon Road, Newport NP9 7GQ

Tears In The Fence *(Magazine looking for the unusual, perceptive, risk-taking, lived and visionary literature) David Caddy*, 38 Hod View, Stourpaine, Nr Blandford Forum, Dorset DT11 8TN. ☎01258 456803 Email: poets@in2it.co.uk

10th Muse *(A5, stapled, nonist, poems and reviews, neither matter no spirit but sexy) Andrew Jordan*, 33 Hartington Road, Southampton SO14 0EW

Terrible Work *(Magazine of new poetry, texts, art and articles) Tim Allen*, 21 Overston Gardens, Mannamead, Plymouth, Devon PL3 5BX

The Text *(Loose-leaf magazine for fiction and experimental writing) Keith Jafrate*, The Word Hoard, 46-47 Byram Arcade, Westgate, Huddersfield HD1 1ND. ☎01484 452070 Fax 01484 455049 Email: hoard@zoo.co.uk

The Third Alternative *(Quality speculative and slipstream writing – fiction, poetry, comment)* See also **ZENE** under **Magazines** *Andy Cox*, 5 St Martin's Lane, Witcham, Ely, Cambs CB6 2LB

The Third Half *(Looking for a good script – do you have one?)* See also **K. T. Publications** *Kevin Troop*, 16 Fane Close, Stamford, Lincs PE9 1HG. ☎01780 754193

This Is *(Quarterly, themed, writing with an edge, b&w art and photography) Carol Cornish*, Writing Space Publications, PO Box 16185, London NW1 8ZH. ☎0171 586 0244 Fax 0171 586 5666 Email: writingspace@btinternet.com Website:www.btinternet.com/ ~writingspace/thisis/

Thumbscrew *(International journal of poetry and poetry-related criticism) Tim Kendall* PO Box 657, Oxford OX2 6PH Email: tim.kendall@bristol.ac.uk

Time Haiku *(Established and new writers of haiku, tanka, short poems) Dr Erica Facey*, 105 Kings Head Hill, London E4 7JG. ☎0181 529 6478

Triumph Herald *(Christian writers' magazine with poetry, stories and articles written by subscribers) Chris Walton*, Remus House, Coltsfoot Drive, Woodston, Peterborough, Cambs PE2 9JX. ☎01733 890099 Fax 01733 323524

Upstart *(Literary magazine) Carol Barac*, 19 Cawarden, Stantonbury, Milton Keynes MK14 6AH. ☎01908 317535

Urthona *(Bringing together the Western arts and Buddhism) Ratnagarbha Shantigarbha*, 3 Coral Park, Henley Road, Cambridge CB1 3EA. ☎01223 566567 Fax 01223 566568 Email: windhorset@aol.com

Various Artists *(Poetry and graphics)* 34 Northleaze, Long Ashton, Bristol BS41 9HT

Voice and Verse 7 Pincott Place, London SE4 2ER

Voyage *(Space stations) John Dunne*, Regent Chambers, 40 Lichfield Street, Wolverhampton WV1 1DG

Wasafiri *(Black writing in English) Susheila Nasta*, Dept. of English, Queen Mary and Westfield College, Mile End Road, London E1 4SN Email: wasafiri@qmw.ac.uk Website:www.qmw.ac.uk~english/ Wasafiri.html

Wavelength *(Good poetry) Susan Ashby*, 235 Cedar Road, Camphill Estate, Nuneaton, Warwickshire CV10 9DG

West Coast Magazine *(Stories, poems, reviews) Joe Murray*, Top Floor, 15 Hope Street, Glasgow G2 6AB

Words Worth Language Arts *(Irregular journal publishing linguistically innovative, visual and performance writings)* See also **Words Worth Books** *Alaric Sumner*, BM Box 4515, London WC1N 3XX Email: a.sumner@dartington.ac.uk

Wordshare *(Creative writing from disabled people) John Wilkinson*, 8 Bodmin Moor Close, North Hykham, Lincoln LN6 9BB

Writers' Own Magazine *(Short stories, poetry, articles, competitions, reviews, letters) Mrs E.M. Pickering*, 121 Highbury Grove, Clapham, Bedford MK41 6DU. ☎01234 365982

Writing Women *(Poetry, short stories by women. Three a year) Linda Anderson &*

others, PO Box 111, Newcastle upon Tyne NE3 1WF

The Yellow Crane *(Interesting new poems from South Wales and beyond …)* Jonathan Brookes Flat 6, 23 Richmond Crescent, Roath, Cardiff CF2 3AH

Zed 2 0 *(Annual poetry, prose and articles on literature and the arts)* See also **Akros Publications** Duncan Glen, 33 Lady Nairn Avenue, Kirkcaldy, Fife KY1 2AW. ☎01592 651522

Organisations of Interest to Poets

A survey of some of the societies, groups and other bodies in the UK which may be of interest to practising poets. Organisations not listed should send details to The Editor, *The Writer's Handbook*, 34 Ufton Road, London N1 5BX for inclusion in future editions.

Academi Literature Promotion

3rd Floor, Mount Stuart House, Mount Stuart Square, Cardiff Bay, Cardiff CF1 6DQ
☎01222 492025   Fax 01222 492930
Email: academi@dial.pipex.com
Website: dspace.dial.pipex.com/academi

Chief Executive *Peter Finch*

The writers' organisation of Wales with special responsibility for literary activity, writers' residencies, writers on tour, festivals, writers' groups, readings, tours, exchanges and other development work. **Yr Academi Gymreig/The Welsh Academy** won the 1998 Arts Council of Wales franchise for Wales-wide literature development. It has offices in Cardiff and fieldworkers based in North and West Wales. *Publishes* the Lottery-funded *Encyclopedia of Wales*, the Welsh-medium literary magazine *Taliesin*, the *Academi English– Welsh Dictionary* and co-publishes *The New Welsh Review* along with a number of other projects. The Academi sponsors a number of annual contests including the prestigious **Cardiff International Poetry Competition**. Publishes *A470* a bimonthly literary information magazine.

Apples & Snakes

Unit 7, Theatre Place, 489a New Cross Road, London SE14 6TQ
☎0181 692 0393   Fax 0181 692 4551
Email: apples@snakes.demon.co.uk

Contacts *Geraldine Collinge, Roger Robinson, Malika Booker*

A unique, independent promotional organisation for poetry and poets - furthering poetry as an innovative and popular medium and cross-cultural activity. A&S organises an annual programme of over 150 events (including their London season which actively pushes new voices), tours, residencies and festivals as well as operating a Poets-in-Education Scheme and a non-profit booking agency for relevant poets.

Arts Councils and Regional Arts Boards

For a full list of addresses see **Arts Councils and Regional Arts Boards**

The Arvon Foundation

See entry under **Professional Associations**

The British Haiku Society

35 Downs Park West, Westbury Park, Bristol BS6 7QH
☎0117 962 1035
Website:dspace.dial.pipex.com/town/place/xst19/index.htm

Secretary *Alan J Summers*

Formed in 1990. Promotes the appreciation and writing within the British Isles of haiku, senyru, tanka, and renga by way of tutorials, workshops, exchange of poems, critical comment and information. The society runs a haiku library and administers the annual James W. Hackett Award. *Publishes The Haiku Kit* teaching pack and the quarterly journal, *Blithe Spirit*.

The Eight Hand Gang

5 Cross Farm, Station Road, Padgate, Warrington WA2 0QG

Secretary *John F. Haines*

An association of British SF poets. *Publishes Handshake*, a single-sheet newsletter of SF poetry and information available free in exchange for an s.a.e.

The Little Magazine Collection, Poetry Store and Alternative Press Collections

University College London, Gower Street, London WC1E 6BT

☎0171 380 7796   Fax 0171 380 7727

Website: www.ucl.ac.uk/library/special-coll

Librarian *Gillian Furlong*

Housed at University College London Library, these are the fruits of Geoffrey Soar and David Miller's interest in UK and US alternative publishing, with a strong emphasis on poetry. The Little Magazines Collection runs to over 3600 titles mainly in the more experimental and avant-garde areas. The Poetry Store consists of over 12,200 small press items, mainly from the '60s onwards, again with some stress on experimental work. In addition, there are reprints of classic earlier little magazines, from Symbolism through to the present. Anyone who is interested can consult the collections, and it helps if you have some idea of what you want to see. Bring evidence of identity for a smooth ride. The collections can be accessed by visiting the Manuscripts and Rare Books Room at University College at the above address between 10.00am and 5.00pm on weekdays. Most items are available on inter-library loans.

The National Small Press Centre

BM Bozo, London WC1N 3XX

Director *John Nicholson*

Press Officer *Cecilia Boggis*

Liaison Officers *John & Lesley Dench*

Treasurer *Andy Hopton*

A point of focus for small, self and independent publishers. Offers advice surgeries, book ordering services, publicity, help with origination and design, mounts exhibitions and workshops, holds a comprehensive reference library. Publishes *News From The Centre* (bi-monthly) and *Small Press Listings* (quarterly). Joint annual subscription to these publications is £12. The Centre's *Handbook* is available at £12.00 (plus £1.50 postage). An outgrowth of the former Small Press Group, the Centre was originally housed at Middlesex University but is currently relocating. Contact the liaison officers for more information.

The Northern Poetry Library

Central Library, The Willows, Morpeth, Northumberland NE61 1TA

☎01670 534524/534514   Fax 01670 534513

Email: amenities@northumberland.gov.uk

Membership available to everyone in Cleveland, Cumbria, Durham, Northumberland and Tyne and Wear. Associate membership available for all outside the region. Over 13,000 books and magazines for loan including virtually all poetry published in the UK since 1968. Access to English Poetry, the full text database of all English Poetry from 600 - 1900. Postal lending available too. In association with MidNag publishes *Red Herring*, a poetry magazine.

The Poetry Book Society

Book House, 45 East Hill, London SW18 2QZ

☎0181 870 8403   Fax 0181 877 1615

Website: poetrybooks.co.uk

Director *Clare Brown*

For readers, writers, students and teachers of poetry. Founded in 1953 by T. S. Eliot and funded by the Arts Council, the PBS is a unique membership organisation providing up-to-date and comprehensive information about poetry from publishers in the UK and Ireland. Members receive the quarterly *PBS Bulletin* packed with articles by poets, poems, news, listings and access to discounts of at least 25% off featured titles. These range from classics to contemporary works. There are three membership packages – two of which include a number of new books specially selected by the Society's panel of experts. Subscriptions start at £10. The PBS also runs the annual **T. S. Eliot Prize** for the best collection of new poetry.

The Poetry Business

The Studio, Byram Arcade, Westgate, Huddersfield, West Yorkshire HD1 1ND

☎01484 434840   Fax 01484 426566

Email: poetbus@pop3.poptel.org.uk

Administrators *Peter Sansom, Janet Fisher*

Founded in 1986, the Business publishes *The North* magazine and books, pamphlets and cassettes under the **Smith/Doorstop** imprint. It runs an annual competition and organises monthly writing Saturdays. Send an s.a.e. for full details.

Poetry Ireland/Eigse Eireann

Bermingham Tower, Upper Yard, Dublin Castle, Dublin, Republic of Ireland

☎00 353 1 6714632   Fax 00 353 1 6714634

E-mail: poetry@iol.ie

Director *Theo Dorgan*

General Manager *Niamh Morris*

The national poetry organisation for Ireland, supported by Arts Councils both sides of the border. Publishes a quarterly magazine *Poetry Ireland Review* and a bi-monthly newsletter of upcoming events and competitions, as well as organising tours and readings by Irish and foreign poets and the National Poetry Competition of the Year, open to poets working in both Irish and English. Administers the Austin Clarke Library, a collection of over 6000 volumes and is Irish partner in the European Poetry Translation Network.

The Poetry Library

Royal Festival Hall, Level 5, London SE1 8XX
☎0171 921 0943/0664/0940
Fax 0171 921 0939
Email poetrylibrary@rfh.org.uk
Website: www.poetrylibrary.org.uk

Librarian *Mary Enright*

Founded by the Arts Council in 1953. A collection of 45,000 titles of modern poetry since 1912, from Georgian to Rap, representing all English-speaking countries and including translations into English by contemporary poets. Two copies of each title are held, one for loan and one for reference. A wide range of poetry magazines and ephemera from all over the world are kept along with cassettes, records and videos for consultation, with many available for loan.

There is a children's poetry section with a teacher's resource collection. An information service compiles lists of poetry magazines, competitions, publishers, groups and workshops, which are available from the Library on receipt of a large s.a.e. or direct from the library's Website. It also has a noticeboard for lost quotations, through which it tries to identify lines or fragments of poetry which have been sent in by other readers.

General enquiry service available. Membership is free, proof of identity and address are essential to join. Open 11.00am to 8.00pm, Tuesday to Sunday. The Library's Website is one of the best poetry resources on the Net.

Beside the Library is *The Voice Box*, a performance space especially for literature. For details of current programme ring 0171 921 0906.

Poetry London Newsletter

35 Benthal Road, London N16 7AR
Email: pdaniels@easynet.co.uk

Contacts *Peter Daniels* (listings & subscriptions), *Katherine Gallagher* (promotions), *Pascale Petit* (poetry editor), *Scott Verner* (reviews).

Published three times a year, *PLN* includes poetry by new and established writers, reviews of recent collections and anthologies, features

on issues relating to poetry, and an encyclopaedic listings section of virtually everything to do with poetry in the capital and the South East. The magazine also carries a limited coverage of events elsewhere.

The Poetry School

130c Evering Road, London N16 7BD
☎0181 985 0090

Co-ordinator Mimi Khalvati

Funded by the London Arts Board the School offers a core programme of tuition in reading and writing poetry through a series of workshops, courses, masterclasses and seminars. Tutors include Don Paterson, Jo Shapcott, Jane Duran and Alison Fell. The School also provides a forum for practitioners to share experiences, develop skills and extend appreciation of the traditional and innovative aspects of their art.

The Poetry Society

22 Betterton Street, London WC2H 9BU
☎0171 240 4810   Fax 0171 240 4818
Email: poetrysoc@dial.pipex.com
Website: www.poetrysoc.com

Chair *Mary Enright*
Director *Chris Meade*

Founded in 1909, which ought to make it venerable, the Society exists to help poets and poetry thrive in Britain. At one time notoriously strife-ridden, it has been undergoing a renaissance lately, reaching out from its Covent Garden base to promote the national health of poetry in a range of imaginative ways. Membership costs £32 for individuals. Friends membership is £15. Current activities include:

- A quarterly, recently redesigned magazine of new verse, views and criticism, *Poetry Review*, edited by Peter Forbes.
- A quarterly newsletter, *Poetry News*.
- Promotions, events and co-operation with Britain's many literature festivals, poetry venues and poetry publishers.
- Competitions and awards including the annual **National Poetry Competition** with a substantial first prize.
- A mss diagnosis service, *The Poetry Prescription*, which gives detailed reports on submissions. Reduced rates for members.
- Seminars, fact sheets, training courses, ideas packs.
- Provides information and advice. Publishes books, posters and resources for schools and libraries. Education membership costs £45

Recently published *The Young Poetry Pack*, a colourful guide to reading, writing and performing poetry, along with colourful poetry posters for Keystages 2 & 3. Many of Britain's most popular poets - including Michael Rosen, Roger McGough and Jackie Kay – contribute, offering advice and inspiration.

- The Poetry Café serving snacks & drink to members, friends and guests, part of *The Poetry Place*, a venue for many poetry activities – readings, poetry clinic, workshops and poetry launches.

Current developments at the Society include *Poetry Places*, a national programme of residencies, placements and projects.

Point

Apdo 119, E-03590 Altea, Spain
☎00 34 6 584 2350   Fax 00 34 6 584 2350

Brusselsesteenweg 356, B-9402 Ninove, Belgium
☎00 32 54 32 4748   Fax 00 32 54 32 4660
Email: elpoeta@point-editions.com
Website: www.point-editions.com

Director *Germain Droogenbroodt*

Founded as Poetry International in 1984, Point has offices in Spain and Belgium. A multilingual publisher of contemporary verse from established poets, the organisation has brought out more than 60 titles in at least eight languages, including English. Editions run the original work alongside a verse translation into Dutch made in co-operation with the poet. The organisation's Website is highly developed and features much English language verse. Point also co-organises an annual international poetry festival.

Regional Arts Boards
See **Arts Councils and Regional Arts Boards**

Scottish Poetry Library

Tweeddale Court, 14 High Street, Edinburgh EH1 1TE
☎0131-557 2876
Email: spl/queries@presence.co.uk

Librarian *Penny Duce*

A comprehensive reference and lending collection of work by Scottish poets in Gaelic, Scots and English and of international poets, including books, tapes, videos, news cuttings and magazines. Borrowing is free to all. Services include: a postal lending scheme, for which there is a small fee, a mobile library which can visit schools and other centres by arrangement, exhibitions, bibliographies, publications, information and promotion in the field of poetry. There is an online catalogue and computer index to poetry and poetry periodicals and a membership scheme costing £10 annually. Members receive a newsletter and support the library.

Survivors' Poetry

Diorama Arts Centre, 34 Osnaburgh Street, London NW1 3ND
☎0171 916 5317   Fax 0171 916 0830
Email survivor@survivorspoetry.org.uk

Director *Victoria Field*
Administration *Clare Douglas*
Outreach *Alison Smith*

A unique national literature organisation promoting poetry by survivors of mental distress through workshops, readings, performances and publications. *Surviving the Millennium*, a three-year project supported by the National Lottery includes the following activities:

- programming survivor poets at mainstream literature festivals;
- creative writing courses specifically targeted at young survivors and survivors from Black and Asian communities;
- facilitator training courses;
- seminars with art health and education professionals;
- translation and publication of work by survivor poets from other countries.

Tŷ Newydd

Llanystumdwy, Cricieth, Gwynedd LL52 0LW
☎01766 522811   Fax 01766 523095
Email: tynewydd@dial.pipex.com
Director *Sally Baker*

Run by the Taliesin Trust, an independent, Arvon-style residential writers centre established in the one-time home of Lloyd George in North Wales. The programme (which runs in both Welsh and English) has a regular poetry content. Fees start at £100 for weekends and £275 for week-long courses. Among the many tutors to-date have been: Gillian Clarke, Wendy Cope, Roger McGough, Carol Ann Duffy, Liz Lochhead, Peter Finch and Paul Henry. Send for the centre's descriptive leaflets and a copy of the newsletter.

Going It Alone:
The Self-Publishing Alternative

Vanity publishing is when you pay someone else to publish
your book. Self-publishing is more like running your
own business, with all the attendant risks – and rewards.
Graham King explains.

Despite its reputation as a shameful, last-ditch alternative to having your work
bought for real money by a conventional publisher, the practice of self-publishing
has a long and honourable history. Self-publishing was common up to the nineteenth century. But when the publishing trade began to exert a monopoly on
printing and distributing books – at the same time removing a multitude of messy
chores from the author's care – the author/publisher virtually faded from sight,
appearing only as the response to dire and desperate circumstances, like rejection.

It is hardly surprising that William Blake never found a publisher. An innocent,
a visionary, a self-taught poet whose work consisted of transcribing his commu-
nion with the spiritual universe, he must have seemed half-mad to most publishers
of his day. Blake had no alternative but to go it alone, self-publishing his first book,
which was a disaster. His second, *Songs of Innocence*, was completed six years later,
in 1789, a tiny volume of verse – 4³/₄ by 3 inches – with 25 hand-engraved illustrations. Always poor and on the verge of bankruptcy, Blake continued to bring
out his books, acting as author, artist, engraver, printer, bookbinder and publisher,
even inventing a novel process for printing his designs and grinding his own inks
and colours – everything except make the paper. Today, those little books of
Blake's are treasured more and, inch for square inch are probably worth more,
than any other example of the printed word.

For a century after Blake's death in 1827, the conservatism of British publishing
ensured a steady stream of self-publishers: Samuel Butler, Charles Reade, Lawrence
and Joyce and even, surprisingly, William Makepeace Thackeray among them.
Although his great novel, *Vanity Fair* appeared in *Colburn's Magazine*, Thackeray
failed to find a London publisher interested in bringing it out as a book, so he published it himself, complete with his own illustrations. It took so long for English
publishers to appreciate Thackeray's earlier work that American pirate publishers
often beat them to it.

The situation in America was hardly different but there in the land of self-
help, the heartbeat of self-publishing was much stronger. One of the most
notable 'go-it-alone' achievements was Mary Baker Eddy's *Science and Health*.
She could not find a single publisher who shared her faith in her religious and
metaphysical views, so she turned to her helpers at a small Christian Science

Home in Massachusetts. A first edition printing of 1000 copies appeared in 1875 – crudely printed and bound and even more shoddily written. Despite a lot of adverse publicity (which included a blistering attack from Mark Twain), Mrs Eddy knew she was on to a good thing and fresh editions appeared at regular intervals; by the time *Science and Health* had reached its 16th edition in the 1890s – the faithful were exhorted to buy the latest editions – it was earning the author just under $20,000 a year.

Kate Douglas Wiggin is best remembered for her children's classic, *Rebecca of Sunnybrook Farm*, which came out in 1903 and is still in print. Yet her beginning as an author was quite humble and her first book, *The Story of Patsy*, was written and printed in 1882 to raise money for a San Francisco kindergarten. Wiggin continued to publish her own books until her fame spread to New York and she was signed up by Houghton Mifflin. (Beatrix Potter in England had a similar experience; after her *The Tale of Peter Rabbit* was refused by Frederick Warne and six other publishers, she paid for its publication herself. Sales were so good that Warne recanted, bought the rights and proceeded to make a fortune.)

Who was Archibald Clavering Gunter? Although little remembered now, Gunter was, for almost a decade, the most popular novelist in America and no account of self-publishing would be complete without his story. An English-born-jack-of-all-trades, Gunter turned to writing in the 1880s and produced a brash and lively novel called *Mr Barnes of New York*. After having it rejected by every publisher he approached, Gunter and his wife founded their own Home Publishing Co in 1887 to bring it out and *Mr Barnes of New York* eventually hit one million sales in the US alone. Without the problem of finding publishers, the author ground out no less than 39 more novels which were described by Gunter, a talented publicist, as 'The most successful novels ever published'.

Still found on library shelves is *Bartlett's Familiar Quotations*, which isn't bad for a tome that first appeared in 1855. It was the work of a university book store clerk in Cambridge, Massachusetts, John Bartlett, who compiled it as a kind of commonplace book of quotes from the Bible, Shakespeare and famous authors and poets. Finding little interest in it outside of university precincts he self-published a paperbound edition which, because people liked to include such quotations in their own writing, rapidly caught on. So did the novelty of quotation-dropping and Bartlett published two more editions until Little, Brown realised the book's potential and bought it in 1863. Bartlett himself accompanied the book as editor, a post he held until his death in 1905.

A less benign climate faced the Baltimore-born journalist and novelist Upton Sinclair at the beginning of this century. Supporting himself by hack journalism, Sinclair offered his first novel, *Springtime and Harvest*, for publication, only to have it resoundingly rejected. Borrowing money from an uncle, he self-published a cheaply produced edition of 1000, of which, after some years, only 200 were sold. In later years, after the author's career was established, and retitled *King Midas*, the same book was a critical success but before this, nearly two decades were to pass during which Sinclair was unremittingly dogged by rejection.

At about the same time as Sinclair was battling for recognition, an Ohio dentist named Zane Grey moved to New York and in his spare time wrote an historical novel called *Better Zane*, only to come up against publisher indifference. Being a resourceful countryman he raised some money, hired a printer and within a few weeks was holding the finished book in his hands. He never forgot the elation he felt. But it took seven years of rejection and self-publishing before he hit on the winning Western formula which was to make him a household name. He became the first American to make a million dollars from writing.

One of the most courageous self-publishing efforts was that of Anaïs Nin, subsequently famous for her ubiquitous diaries. Nin emigrated to the US in 1939 and brought with her a copy of *Winter of Artifice*, which had been published in France, and the manuscript of *Under a Glass Bell*, the former having earned the praise of fellow writers Henry Miller, Lawrence Durrell and Rebecca West. New York publishers, however, did not share their opinion and they were rejected. 'I did not accept the verdict,' Nin wrote later, 'and decided to print my own books.' She bought a small secondhand treadle press for $75 and $100 worth of type, borrowing money from friends to do so. 'It took me months to typeset *Under a Glass Bell* and *Winter of Artifice*. Then there were the printed pages to be placed between blotters and later cut, put together for the binder and gathered into signatures. Then the type had to be redistributed in the boxes.' Nin did not repeat the experience and was grateful when she did find a publisher who found her writing sufficiently commercial.

Nin's do-it-yourself response to rejection is not uncommon among poets and writers of radical/intellectual/experimental leanings. The granddaddy of this bunch is probably Walt Whitman who, in 1855, set the type himself for the 95 pages of *Leaves of Grass* in Brooklyn, helped to run off a thousand copies and wrote most of the highly favourable reviews himself. Unfortunately the bookselling trade found many of the poems rather too sexually – and homosexually – explicit, so Whitman was driven to hawking his books around in a basket. Hearing of the poet's poverty and neglect, Rossetti and Swinburne took up his cause and praised his poetry, which then began to attract worldwide attention. But Whitman was still self-publishing *Leaves of Grass* to the end of his life.

So far we have dealt with writers who've had the self-publishing option forced upon them, or who have decided their particular product would never succeed with a commercial publishing house anyway. But there are other authors who know they have a marketable book but for whom self-publishing is their first choice. Why let a publisher in on the profits? is their line of thinking. One of the big sensations of the sixties was an off-the-wall book called *In Praise of Older Women*, a first novel by Hungarian Stephen Vizinczey who, after fighting in the Hungarian Revolution in 1956 escaped and fled to Canada. Like Vladimir Nabokov, who wrote a similar erotic classic two years later, Vizinczey had a serendipitous way with the English language and a deep conviction about his gifts as a novel writer. This conviction extended to an estimate of his worth, which wasn't matched by those of the publishers he approached with *In Praise of*

Older Women. A confirmed all-rounder, Vizinczey left his job, borrowed money and published it himself, persuading literary celebrities to endorse it, charming editors into writing about it, and all the while closely attending to its distribution, often carrying bundles of books himself to the bookstores.

Within two months *In Praise of Older Women* hit the Canadian bestseller list and from there it went on to an eventual worldwide sale of 2.5 million copies in 11 languages. It was a self-publishing grand slam. More recently, several established writers, notably Susan Hill, Jill Paton Walsh and Timothy Mo, have opted for self-publishing but without saying how they have made out.

One who makes no secret of his success is Richard Binns, perhaps the only writer to take a book from a gleam in the eye right through to the customer sale. Binns' speciality is holding the hands of travellers through France via ingenious and fiendishly detailed guidebooks. His career as a self-publisher started in 1980 after he had submitted some sample pages to Pan and received an instant response: no. Octopus never bothered to answer. Mitchell Beazley offered him a deal he easily refused: one per cent of gross sales. Suddenly he was in the publishing business.

French Leave, his guide to good hotels sold well – so well, in fact, that it hit the No. 1 spot on *The Sunday Times* bestseller list ahead of Arthur C. Clarke, David Attenborough and James Herriott. Despite this, though, he still had to pulp an unsold batch of 6000 copies from the edition of 29,000; he was still learning the publishing game. A second, revised and updated edition went better and also sold to a book club.

Binns' second book, *France a la Carte*, attracted attention on both sides of the Atlantic and one article by its food critic featuring the book in the *New York Times* pulled 2000 orders. By now Binns had established close links with his readers and every day brought letters of appreciation, advice and admonishment, much of which was incorporated into the books. By the time his third book came out – *Hidden France* – he was issuing new versions of the earlier books only to discover what the publishers of similar guidebooks had known for decades: that people do not necessarily buy updated editions each year but only every three or four years. He narrowly avoided a financial setback by selling off customised editions to travel and ferry companies.

By the time his fourth title appeared in 1986 – *En Route*, which is a guide to services at 300 Autoroute exits – Binns realised his distribution resources were hopelessly inadequate and he bowed to the inevitable. The title of No. 1 One-Man Band Publisher, which he had held for five years, passed to other hands. Corgi happily picked up the sure-fire winner and now all four titles are published by Transworld.

The hard truth about self-publishing was also discovered by Hunter Davies. 'I woke up one morning,' he said, and decided 'this time I'll publish it myself. I hadn't fallen out with any of them [his publishers] and I could easily have got one of them to do this particular book, but I thought no, I'll just see if I can do it myself.' And Davies became one of the 21,000 publishers in the UK.

The book he had in mind was an idiosyncratic guide to the Lake District, which he knew intimately. In advance of writing it he drew up its specifications: a narrow format paperback of about 200 pages, to sell at a popular £2.95 to the tourists and backpackers (1984 prices). The typesetting, printing and binding would be done in Cumbria, he decided and he asked four local firms to provide estimates for an edition of 10,000 copies: 'Three of the firms estimated £6000 and one estimated £6700. I chose the latter but I said, look here, the other three are quoting much cheaper, so he brought his estimate down to £6000. He seemed the keenest, the most enterprising and liveliest and I thought I would get on with him best. Nothing very logical. But when you're a one-man firm, spending your own money, you decide on whims.' The partnership worked well and two months after receiving Davies' manuscript the books were delivered.

Davies came to an arrangement with Century to distribute the guide and after receiving the encouraging news that 9000 advance orders had come in, also received the biggest shock of his publishing career, which was the size of the margins taken by the trade. 'Out of the notional return of £30,000, £26,000 goes in discounts to booksellers, distribution and printing. As publisher I take just £4000 for all my work and enterprise – and that's without paying myself anything at all as an author.'

Davies at least succeeds in making out a good case for the commercial publishers! On the other hand, if a book continues to sell for many years, a self-publisher can make good profits from the reprints. That was certainly the case with John Muir's *How to Keep Your Volkswagen Alive* in the US, whicn over several years chalked up sales of over 800,000. And yet another mundane title, *The Factory Outlet Shopping Guide*, a 32-page pamphlet first self-published by Joan Bird in 1971, is now a substantial network of guides published in eight east coast states. Specialist, non-mainstream subjects will always entice budding self-publishers to chance their arms.

The phenomenon of self-publishing is, as we have seen from the recent rush of 'I'll publish and damn 'em anyway!' books, far from extinct. With the availability of loan capital and affordable desktop publishing techniques, it is a particularly attractive option for niche books to command wider notice among commercial publishers. If a book succeeds in a limited market then it offers a reduced-risk proposition to mainstream publishers. The author benefits because, with some of the risk removed, the publisher is prepared to pay more.

This has been a growing practice in the US for at least a couple of decades, where the self-publisher can cooperate with other self-publishers, with small specialised presses, or with publishing cooperatives, taking advantage of marketing experience and having access to at least some semblance of national distribution. Perhaps the most popular option – because it has scored some remarkable successes – is for an author to subsidise a small press to bring out a limited edition of his book; the market is sampled and, if sales are satisfactory, copies of the book together with its sales performance are sent to likely commercial publishers. One notable success was a job-hunting manual, *What Colour is Your*

Parachute? by Richard Bolles. It was first published by the author then republished by a small Californian outfit called Ten Speed Press before ultimately reaching the *New York Times'* bestseller list via a commercial publisher, where it stayed for four years and sold over three million copies.

An even more astonishing and longer lasting success was achieved by the Klutz Press, the invention of three Stanford University graduates who saw a market niche occupied by klutzes – stumblers and fumblers and butter-fingers who wanted to improve their coordination. With a borrowed $7000 they published *Juggling for the Complete Klutz*, complete with three small bean-bags. The gimmick caught on with both bookstores and novelty shops stocking it. This encouraged other packaged titles for the reflex disadvantaged: jumping (with skipping rope); boomerang throwing; and *Playing a Blues Harmonica for the Musically Hopeless*. Perhaps Klutz should add a new title: *Self-publishing for the Complete Klutz*.

Further reading: How to Publish Your Own Book *by Vernon Coleman (Blue Books, Publishing House, Trinity Place, Barnstaple, Devon EX32 9HJ, £14.95)*

Small Presses

Aard Press

c/o Aardverx, 31 Mountearl Gardens, London SW16 2NL

Managing Editor D. Jarvis, Dawn Redwood

FOUNDED 1971. *Publishes* artists' bookworks, experimental/visual poetry, 'zines, eonist literature, topographics, ephemera and international mail-art documentation. AUTHORS/ARTISTS: Dawn Redwood, Petal Jeffery, Phaedra Kelly, Barry Edgar Pilcher (Eire), D. Jarvis, Harry Fox, Y. Kumykov (Russia). Very small editions. No unsolicited material or proposals.

Royalties not paid. No sale-or-return deals.

Abbey Press

Abbey Grammar School, Courtenay Hill, Newry, Co. Down BT34 2ED
☎01693 63142   Fax 01693 62514
Also at: 24 Martello Park, Old Seahill, Craigavad, Co. Down BT18 0DG
☎ 01232 422209   Fax 01232 422209

Editor Adrian Rice

FOUNDED in 1997, Abbey Press is a fast growing literary publisher with a strong poetry list. Also *publishes* biography, memoirs, fiction, history, politics, Irish language and academic. 6 titles in 1998. Send synopsis, sample of work, biographical note and s.a.e.

ABCD

See **Allardyce, Barnett, Publishers**

Agneau 2

See **Allardyce, Barnett, Publishers**

AK Press/AKA Books

PO Box 12766, Edinburgh EH8 9YE
☎0131 555 5165   Fax 0131 555 5215

Managing Editor Alexis McKay

AK Press grew out of the activities of AK Distribution which distributes a wide range of radical (anarchist, feminist, etc.) literature (books, pamphlets, periodicals, magazines), both fiction and non-fiction. *Publishes* politics, history, situationist work, occasional fiction in both book and pamphlet form. About 12 titles a year. Proposals and synopses welcome if they fall within AK's specific areas of interest.

Royalties paid.

Akros Publications

33 Lady Nairn Avenue, Kirkcaldy, Fife KY1 2AW
☎01592 651522

Publisher Duncan Glen

FOUNDED 1965. *Publishes* poetry collections, pamphlets and anthologies; literary essays and studies; travel books with a literary slant; local histories and memoirs. About 10 titles a year. Ideas for books welcomed; no unsolicited mss.

Royalties paid twice-yearly.

The Alembic Press

Hyde Farm House, Marcham, Abingdon, Oxon OX13 6NX
☎01865 391391   Fax 01865 391322
Email: AlembicPrs@aol.com

Owner Claire Bolton

FOUNDED 1976. Publisher of hand-produced books by traditional letterpress methods. Short print-runs. *Publishes* bibliography, book arts and printing, miniatures and occasional poetry. Book design and production service to like-minded authors wishing to publish in this manner. No unsolicited mss.

Allardyce, Barnett, Publishers

14 Mount Street, Lewes, East Sussex BN7 1HL
☎01273 479393   Fax 01273 479393

Publisher Fiona Allardyce
Managing Editor Anthony Barnett

FOUNDED 1981. *Publishes* art, literature and music, with past emphasis on contemporary English poets. About 3 titles a year. IMPRINTS **Agneau 2**, **ABCD**, **Allardyce Books**. Unsolicited mss and synopses cannot be considered.

Anglo-Saxon Books

Frithgarth, Thetford Forest Park, Hockwold cum Wilton, Norfolk IP26 4NQ
☎01842 828430   Fax 01842 828332
Email: asbooks@englisc.demon.co.uk
Website: www.englisc.demon.co.uk

Managing Editor Tony Linsell

FOUNDED 1990 to promote a greater awareness of and interest in early English history and culture. Originally concentrated on Old English texts but now also publishes less academic, more popular titles. Seeking titles for all periods of

English history. *Publishes* English history, culture, language and society. About 5–10 titles a year. Unsolicited synopses welcome but return postage necessary.

Royalties standard rate.

AVERT
AIDS Education and Research Trust, 4 Brighton Road, Horsham, West Sussex RH13 5BA
☎01403 210202   Fax 01403 211001
Email: avert@dial.pipex.com
Website: www.avert.org

Managing Editor *Annabel Kanabus*

Publishing arm of the AIDS Education and Research Trust, a national registered charity established 1986. *Publishes* books and leaflets about HIV infection and AIDS. About 3 titles a year. Unsolicited mss, synopses and ideas welcome.

Royalties paid accordingly.

M. & M. Baldwin
24 High Street, Cleobury Mortimer, Kidderminster DY14 8BY
☎01299 270110   Fax 01299 270110

Managing Editor *Dr Mark Baldwin*

FOUNDED 1978. *Publishes* local interest/history, WW2 codebreaking and inland waterways books. Up to 5 titles a year. Unsolicited mss, synopses and ideas for books welcome (not general fiction).

Royalties paid.

Bardon Enterprises
20 Queens Keep, Palmerston Road, Southsea, Hampshire PO5 3NX
☎01705 874900   Fax 01705 874900
Email: info@bardonia.softnet.co.uk
Website: www.soft.net.uk/bardonia

Managing Director *W. B. Henshaw*

FOUNDED 1996. *Publishes* music, art, biographies, poetry, academic books and sheet music. 6 titles in 1998. Unsolicited mss, synopses and ideas welcome. No pictorial books.

Barnworks Publishing
Asbury, Roydon Road, Launceston, Cornwall PL15 8DN
☎01566 777303   Fax 01566 777303

Managing Editor *Hazel Kelly*

Publishes interesting lives. 'We accept mss for full and part vanity publishing, offering individual, tailored advice, editing, format suggestions and aid with distribution.' Telephone in the first instance.

Royalties paid.

BB Books
See under **Poetry Presses**

Between the Lines
9 Woodstock Road, London N4 3ET
☎0171 272 8719   Fax 0181 374 5736
Email: philiphoy@aol.com
Website: www.pbk.co.uk/btl/

Editorial Board *Peter Dale, Ian Hamilton, Philip Hoy*

FOUNDED 1998. *Publishes* extended interviews with leading contemporary poets. By mid-2000, it is planned to have seven volumes in print, featuring W.D. Snodgrass, Michael Hamburger, Anthony Thwaite, Anthony Hecht, Donald Hall, Richard Wilbur and Hans Magnus Enzensberger. Each volume features a career sketch, comprehensive bibliography and a representative selection of quotations from the poets' critics and reviewers.

Black Cat Books
See **Neil Miller Publications**

The Bonaventura Press
Bagpath, Tetbury, Gloucestershire GL8 8YG
☎01453 860827   Fax 01453 860487
Email: Janet@Bonaventura.free-online.co.uk
Website: www.bonaventura.co.uk

Managing Editor *Janet Sloss*

FOUNDED 1995 as a self-publishing venture. Synopses and ideas concerning the British connection with Menorca welcome.

The Book Castle
12 Church Street, Dunstable, Bedfordshire LU5 4RU
☎01582 605670   Fax 01582 662431

Managing Editor *Paul Bowes*

FOUNDED 1986. *Publishes* non-fiction of local interest (Bedfordshire, Hertfordshire, Buckinghamshire, Oxfordshire, Northamptonshire, the Chilterns). 6+ titles a year. About 50 titles in print. Unsolicited mss, synopses and ideas for books welcome.

Royalties paid.

The Book Gallery
Bedford Road, St. Ives, Cornwall TR26 1SP
☎01736 793545

Directors *David & Tina Wilkinson*

FOUNDED 1991. *Publishes* limited edition monographs by and about writers/painters associated with the so-called Newlyn and St Ives schools of painting. Topics include Sven Berlin, Kit Barker,

Arthur Caddick, Guido Morris, Leach Pottery. Ideas welcome.

Royalties not paid; flat fee.

Book-in-Hand Ltd
20 Shepherds Hill, London N6 5AH
☎0181 341 7650   Fax 0181 341 7650
Email: books@book-in-hand.demon.co.uk

Contact *Ann Kritzinger*

Print production service for self-publishers. Includes design and editing advice to give customers a greater chance of selling in the open market.

Bookmarque Publishing
26 Cotswold Close, Minster Lovell, Oxfordshire OX8 5SX
☎01993 775179

Managing Editor *John Rose*

FOUNDED 1987. Publishing business with aim of filling gaps in motoring history of which it is said 'there are many!' *Publishes* motoring history, motor sport and 'general' titles. About 8 titles a year (increasing). All design and typesetting of books done in-house. Unsolicited mss, synopses and ideas welcome on transport titles. S.a.e. required for reply or return of material or for advice on publishing your work.

Royalties paid.

Bozo
BM Bozo, London WC1N 3XX
Managing Editors *John & Cecilia Nicholson*

FOUNDED 1981. Began by producing tiny pamphlets (*Patriotic English Tracts*) and has gained a reputation as 'one of England's foremost pamphleteers'. *Publishes* historical analyses, apocalyptic rants, wry/savage humour and political 'filth'. Considerable expansion of titles is underway. No unsolicited mss, synopses or ideas.

Royalties not paid.

Brantwood Books
PO Box 144, Orpington, Kent BR6 6LZ
☎01689 897520   Fax 01689 897520
Email: brantwood@planxty.com
Website: www.planxty.com/brantwood

Publishing Director *Philip Turner*

Publishes highly illustrated, limited edition print runs of specialist cinema titles, ranging from Russian cinema architecture to 32-page illustrated guides to British and North American cinema circuit histories. 3 titles in 1998.

DIVISIONS **Brantwood Books** and **Outline Publications** UK/US cinema circuit and film studio histories; **Brantwood Biographical** Biographies of movie moguls, producers and directors; **Brantwood Miniature Life** Series of outline biographies of popular movie stars; **Brantwood Technical** Screen, film and camera/projector topics. Ideas which can be adapted to a 32-page format are welcome.

Brilliant Publications
The Old School Yard, Leighton Road, Northall, Dunstable, Bedfordshire LU6 2HA
☎01525 222844   Fax 01525 221250

Publisher *Priscilla Hannaford*

FOUNDED 1993. *Publishes* books for teachers, parents and others working with 0–13-year-olds. About 10–15 titles a year. SERIES *How to Dazzle at ...* (9–13-year-olds with special needs); *How to be Brilliant at ...* (7–11-year-olds); *Hot to Sparkle at ...* (5–7-year-olds); *Activities* (3–5-year-olds). Submit synopsis and sample pages in the first instance.

Royalties paid twice yearly.

Brinnoven
9 Thomson Green, Livingston, West Lothian EH54 8TA
☎01506 442846   Fax 01506 431060

Proprietor *William Murray*

FOUNDED 1991. *Publishes* Scottish interest titles specialising in local history, dialects, languages and traditional/folk music. About 3–5 titles a year. Unsolicited mss, synopses and ideas welcome but return postage must be included.

Royalties and fees paid.

Business Innovations Research
Tregeraint House, Zennor, St Ives, Cornwall TR26 3DB
☎01736 797061   Fax 01736 797061

Managing Director *John T. Wilson*

Publishes business books and newsletters, home study courses, and guidebooks. Production service available to self-publishers.

Businesslike Publishing
'Bluepool', Strathoykel, Ardgay, Inverness-shire IV24 3DP
☎01549 441211
Website: www.dorian.blue@btinternet.com

Managing Editor *Iain R. McIntyre*

FOUNDED 1989. Provides a printing and publishing service for members of the **Society of Civil Service Authors**. *Publishes* magazines, collections of poetry, short stories (not individual poems or short stories) and Scottish history.

About 6 titles a year. Ideas/synopses accepted. No unsolicited mss.
Royalties generally not paid but negotiable in some circumstances.

Cartmel Press Associates
Old Orchard, Barber Green, Grange-over-Sands, Cumbria LA11 6HU
☎015395   36390
Email: dguthrie@ndirect.co.uk
Managing Editor *D. M. Guthrie*
FOUNDED in 1983 to publish art monographs and now publishing full-length biographies. No unsolicited mss; synopses and ideas welcome.
Royalties paid.

Chameleon HH Publishing
The Quarry House, East End, Witney, Oxfordshire OX8 6QA
☎01993 880223   Fax 01993 880236
Email: chameleon.hh@virgin.net
and sales@chameleonhh.co.u
Website: www.chameleonhh.co.uk
Directors *David Hall, Marion Hazzledine*
FOUNDED 1997. CD-ROM and Web publishers on behalf of commercial publishers, institutes, associations and government bodies. No marketing or distribution department so no unsolicited mss but all enquiries welcome. Full editorial services also offered.

Chapter Two
13 Plum Lane, Plumstead Common, London SE18 3AF
☎0181 316 5389   Fax 0181 854 5963
Managing Editor *E. N. Cross*
FOUNDED 1976. Chapter Two's chief activity is the propagation of the Christian faith through the printed page. *Publishes* exclusively on Plymouth Brethren. About 12 titles a year. No unsolicited mss, synopses or ideas. Enquiries only.
Royalties not paid.

Charlewood Press
7 Weavers Place, Chandlers Ford, Eastleigh, Hampshire SO53 1TU
☎01703 261192   Email: gponting@clara.net
Website: www.home.clara.net/gponting/
Managing Editors *Gerald Ponting, Anthony Light*
FOUNDED 1987. Publishes local history books on the Fordingbridge area, researched and written by the two partners and leaflets on local walks. No unsolicited mss.
Royalties not paid.

The Cheverell Press
Manor Studios, Manningford Abbots, Pewsey, Wiltshire SN9 6HS
☎01672 563163   Fax 01672 564301
Managing Editor *Sarah de Larrinaga*
Publishes careers, media and performing arts. No fiction.
IMPRINTS **The Cheverell Press, First Hand Books.** Currently using researchers/ writers on a fee basis, rather than royalties. No unsolicited mss. Started as a self–publisher and has produced a self–publishers information pack. Write for details.

Chrysalis Press
7 Lower Ladyes Hills, Kenilworth, Warwickshire CV8 2GN
☎01926 855223   Fax 01926 856611
Managing Editor *Brian Boyd*
FOUNDED 1994. *Publishes* fiction, literary criticism and biography. No unsolicited mss.
Royalties paid.

CNP Publications
The Roseland Institute, Gorran, St Austell, Cornwall
☎01726 843501   Fax 01726 843501
Managing Editor *Dr James Whetter*
FOUNDED 1975. *Publishes* poetry, political essays, local Cornish interest/biography and Celtic design. 1–2 titles a year. Cornish history published under the **Lyfrow Trelyspen** imprint. Unsolicited mss, synopses and ideas welcome.
Royalties not paid.

Codex Books
PO Box 148, Hove, East Sussex BN3 3DQ
☎01273 722201   Fax 01273 205502
Email: codex@overground.co.uk
Website: www.overground.co.uk/codex.htm
Managing Editor *Hayley Ann*
FOUNDED 1994. Originally part of a small indie/punk record label, Codex has a history of working with musicians, releasing author performance CD-ROMS of Kathy Acker, Alan Moore and Iain Banks. *Publishes* cult/transgressive/alternative underground fiction, journalism and non-fiction. Cyber punk, pulp, psychedelic, queercore, music-connected titles. 6 titles planned for 1999. Prefers to receive sample (approx. 50pp) with brief synopsis and author info, following introductory phone call.
Royalties paid.

Condor Books
1 Green Lane, Coventry, West Midlands
CV3 6DH
☎01203 413685
Email: ingaro@globalnet.co.uk
Contact *Alvaro Graña*

Condor Books was created by pan-pipes expert Alvaro Graña to publish his book *How to Make and Play Pan-Pipes*.

Copperfield Books
Hillbrook House, Lyncombe Vale Road, Bath
BA2 4LS
☎01225 442835   Fax 01225 319755
Managing Director *John Brushfield*

Publishes paperback fiction and general non-fiction. No unsolicited mss; 'we only commission books to our own specification'.

Corvus Press
See **ignotus press**

The Cosmic Elk
68 Elsham Crescent, Lincoln LN6 3YS
☎01522 820922
Email: HevHobden@aol.com
Managing Editor *Heather Hobden*

FOUNDED 1988. For academic, specialised and local interests, in science, history and the history of science. Books, leaflets, posters, handbooks, booklets to accompany exhibitions, videos, CD-ROMs, websites, tutorial notes, etc. A4 card and comb bindings. Illustrations and colour. Future paperbacks planned. Enquiries welcome; phone or email.

Crescent Moon Publishing and Joe's Press
PO Box 393, Maidstone, Kent ME14 5XU
Managing Editor *Jeremy Robinson*

FOUNDED 1988 to publish critical studies of figures such as D. H. Lawrence, Thomas Hardy, André Gide, Walt Disney, Rilke, Leonardo da Vinci, Mark Rothko, C. P. Cavafy and Hélène Cixous. *Publishes* literature, criticism, media, art, feminism, painting, poetry, travel, guidebooks, cinema and some fiction. Literary magazine, *Passion*, launched February 1994. Quarterly. Twice-yearly anthology of American poetry, *Pagan America*. About 15–20 titles per year. Unsolicited mss, synopses and ideas welcome but approach in writing first and send an s.a.e.
    Royalties negotiable.

Daniels Medica
Zetland House, Cley Next The Sea, Norfolk
NR25 7RS
☎01263 740230   Fax 01263 740343
Email: daniels@breathe.co.uk
Publisher *Dr Victor G. Daniels*

Educational materials and training packs for the pharmaceutical industry.

Dionysia Press
See under **Poetry Presses**

Dog House Publications
18 Marlow Avenue, Eastbourne, East Sussex
BN22 8SJ
☎01323 729214
Email: doghouse@rapport.softnet.co.uk
Website: www.soft.net.uk/rapport/
Managing Editor *Silvia Kent*

FOUNDED 1990. Publishes books and booklets on dog training and behaviour. 'We no longer accept unsolicited mss. Following a major restructuring in 1997, we have reduced the range of our titles to concentrate on new editions of our best sellers.' Free training and dog care booklets available to charities on request.
    Royalties paid.

Dragon's Head Press
PO Box 3369, London SW6 6JN
Managing Editor *Ade Dimmick*

Founded 1993. Independent small press publishing project, specialising in dragon-lore and related themes. Member of the **Association of Little Presses**. Unsolicited mss welcome 'in keeping with the editorial spirit'.

The Dragonby Press
15 High Street, Dragonby, Scunthorpe, North Lincolnshire DN15 0BE
☎01724   840645
Email: rah.williams@virgin.net
Managing Editor *Richard Williams*

FOUNDED 1987 to publish affordable bibliography for reader, collector and dealer. About 3 titles a year. Unsolicited mss, synopses and ideas welcome for bibliographical projects only.
    Royalties paid.

Dramatic Lines
PO Box 201, Twickenham TW2 5RQ
☎0181 296 9502   Fax 0181 296 9503
Managing Editor *John Nicholas*

Founded to promote drama for young people. Publications with a wide variety of theatrical

applications including classroom use and school assemblies, drama examinations, auditions, festivals and theatre group performance. Unsolicited drama related mss, proposals and synopses welcome.
Royalties paid.

Education Now Publishing Cooperative Ltd
113 Arundel Drive, Bramcote Hills, Nottingham NG9 3FQ
☎0115 9257261   Fax 0115 9257261
Website: www.gn.apc.org/edheretics
Managing Editors *Dr Roland Meighan, Philip Toogood*

A non-profit research and writing group set up in reaction to 'the totalitarian tendencies of the 1988 Education Act'. Its aim is to widen the terms of the debate about education and its choices. *Publishes* reports on positive educational initiatives such as flexi-schooling, mini-schooling, small schooling, home-based education and democratic schooling. 4–5 titles a year. No unsolicited mss or ideas. Enquiries only.
Royalties generally not paid.

Educational Heretics Press
113 Arundel Drive, Bramcote Hills, Nottingham NG9 3FQ
☎0115 9257261   Fax 0115 9257261
Website: www.gn.apc.org/edheretics
Directors *Janet & Roland Meighan*

Non-profit venture which aims to question the dogmas of schooling in particular and education in general and establishing the logistics of the next learning system. No unsolicited material. Enquiries only.
Royalties not paid but under review.

EKO Fund
Wedgwood Memorial College, Barlaston, Staffs ST12 9DG
☎01782 372105   Fax 01782 372393
Managing Editor *Brian W. Burnett*

FOUNDED January 1996 to publish modern, lively books and magazines in and about Esperanto. Unsolicited mss, synopses and ideas welcome.
Royalties paid.

Enable Enterprises
Coventry University Technocentre, Puma Way, Coventry CV1 2TT
☎070 209 21158   Fax 0870 164 0607
Email: enquiries@enableenterprises.co.uk
Website: www.enableenterprises.co.uk

Contact *Simon Stevens*

Enable Enterprises provides accessibilty awareness publications and other services to a wide range of organisations. It welcomes unsolicited material related to accessibility and disability issues.

estamp
204 St Albans Avenue, London W4 5JU
☎0181 994 2379   Fax 0181 994 2379
Email: st@estamp.demon.co.uk
Contact *Silvie Turner*

Independent publisher of fine art books on printmaking, papermaking and artists' book–making. Books are designed and written for artists, craftspeople and designers. Approach in writing in first instance.

Feasac Publications
See **ignotus press**

Feather Books
Fair View, Old Coppice, Lyth Bank, Shrewsbury, Shropshire SY3 0BW
☎01743 872177   Fax 01743 872177
Email: john@feather-books.com
Website: www.feather-books.com
Managing Director *Rev. John Waddington-Feather*

FOUNDED 1980 to publish writers' group work. All material has a strong Christian ethos. *Publishes* poetry (mainly, but not exclusively, religious). 20 titles a year. Produces poetry, drama and music CD/cassettes. No unsolicited mss, synopses or ideas. All correspondence to include s.a.e. please.

Fern House
19 High Street, Haddenham, Ely, Cambridgeshire CB6 3XA
☎01353 740222   Fax 01353 741987
Email: on45@dial.pipex.com
Website: www.fernhouse.com
Managing Editor *Rodney Dale*

FOUNDED 1995. *Publishes* non-fiction with a bias towards biography, reference and technology. 3 titles in 1998. Unsolicited synopses and ideas welcome. Preliminary approach by letter, telephone or the website preferred.
Royalties paid.

Ferry Publications Ltd
PO Box 9, Narberth, Pembrokeshire SA68 0YT
☎01834 891460   Fax 01834 891463
Managing Editor *Miles Cowsill*

FOUNDED 1987 to publish ferry and shipping books. 3–4 titles a year. Also publishes *European Ferry Scene* - 4 issues per year. Unsolicited mss, synopses and ideas welcome.
Royalties paid.

First Hand Books
See **The Cheverell Press**

First Rank Publishing
23 Ditchling Rise, Brighton, East Sussex BN1 4QL
☎01273 279934   Fax 01273 297128
Contact *Byron Jacobs, Andrew Kinsman*
FOUNDED 1996. Packagers and publishers of sports, games and leisure books. 12–15 titles a year. Also providers of editorial, production and typesetting services. No unsolicited mss but ideas and synopses welcome.
Fees paid.

Five Leaves Publications
PO Box 81, Nottingham NG5 4ER
☎0115 9693597
Contact *Ross Bradshaw*
FOUNDED 1995 (taking over the publishing programme of Mushroom Bookshop), producing 6–8 titles a year. *Publishes* fiction, poetry, politics and Jewish Interest. Publisher of several books by Michael Rosen. No unsolicited mss; titles normally commissioned.
Royalties and fees paid.

Forth Naturalist & Historian
University of Stirling, Stirling FK9 4LA
☎01259 215091   Fax 01786 464994
Email: Lindsay.Corbett@stir.ac.uk
Website: www.stir.ac.uk/theuni/forthnat/
Also at: 30 Dunmar Drive, Alloa, Clackmannanshire FK10 2EH
Honorary Editors *Lindsay Corbett, Neville Dix*
FOUNDED 1975 by the collaboration of Stirling University members and the Central Regional Council to promote interests and publications on central Scotland. Aims to provide a 'valuable local studies educational resource for mid-Scotland schools, libraries and people'. Runs an annual symposium: Man and the Landscape. *Publishes* naturalist, historical and environmental studies and maps, including 1890s maps 25" to the mile - 24 of Central Scotland areas/places with historical notes. Over 20 selected papers from the annual *The Forth Naturalist & Historian from 1976* are published in pamphlet form. Welcomes papers, mss and ideas relevant to central Scotland. Promotes annual environment/

heritage symposia – 1999 will be the 25th year.
Royalties not paid.

The Frogmore Press
See under **Poetry Presses**

Frontier Publishing
Windetts, Kirstead, Norfolk NR15 1BR
☎01508 558174   Fax 01508 550194
Managing Editor *John Black*
FOUNDED 1983. *Publishes* travel, photography and literature. 2–3 titles a year. No unsolicited mss; synopses and ideas welcome.
Royalties paid.

Galactic Central Publications
Imladris, 25A Copgrove Road, Leeds, West Yorkshire LS8 2SP
Email: philsp@compuserve.com
Managing Editor *Phil Stephensen-Payne*
FOUNDED 1982 in the US. *Publishes* science fiction bibliographies. About 4 titles a year. All new publications originate in the UK. Unsolicited mss, synopses and ideas welcome.

The Gargoyle's Head
Chatham House, Gosshill Road, Chislehurst, Kent BR7 5NS
☎0181 467 8475   Fax 0181 295 1967
Managing Editor *Jennie Gray*
FOUNDED 1990. *Publishes* a six-monthly magazine and newsletter plus books and supplements on Gothic and macabre subjects. History, literary criticism, reprints of forgotten texts, biography, architecture, art etc., usually with a gloomy and black-hued flavour. About 4 titles a year. Synopses and ideas welcome.
Flat fee paid.

Geological Society Publishing House
Unit 7, Brassmill Enterprise Centre, Brassmill Lane, Bath BA1 3JN
☎01225 445046   Fax 01225 442836
Website: www.geolsoc.org.uk
Managing Editor *Mike Collins*
Publishing arm of the Geological Society which was founded in 1807. *Publishes* undergraduate and postgraduate texts in the earth sciences. 25 titles a year. Unsolicited mss, synopses and ideas welcome.
Royalties not paid.

Global Books
See **Neil Miller Publications**

Glosa

PO Box 18, Richmond, Surrey TW9 2AU
☎0181 948 8417

Managing Editors *Wendy Ashby, Ronald Clark*

FOUNDED 1981. *Publishes* textbooks, dictionaries and translations for the teaching, speaking and promotion of Glosa (an international, auxiliary language); also a newsletter and journal. Rapid growth in the last couple of years. In 1994 launched *Sko-Glosa*, a publication for and by younger students of Glosa to be distributed to schools in different countries. Also in 1994 published several fairy stories and activity pages for school children who are learning Glosa in school. Unsolicited mss and ideas for Glosa books welcome.

Gothic Press

PO Box 542, Highgate, London N6 6BG
Managing Editor *Robin Crisp*

Specialist publisher of Gothic titles in quality, case editions. Mostly non-fiction at present (*Carmel: Authentic Sequel to Bram Stoker's Dracula* is a notable exception). *Publishes* mysticism, supernatural, history, biography, Gothic novels. No unsolicited mss; synopses and ideas might be welcome.
Flat fee paid.

Grant Books

The Coach House, New Road, Cutnall Green, Droitwich, Worcestershire WR9 0PQ
☎01299 851588   Fax 01299 851446
Email: golf@grantbooks.co.uk
Website: www.grantbooks.co.uk

Managing Editor *H. R. J. Grant*

FOUNDED 1978. *Publishes* golf-related titles only: course architecture, history, biography, etc., but no instructional material. New titles and old, plus limited editions. About 6 titles a year. Unsolicited mss, synopses and ideas welcome.
Royalties paid.

Grevatt & Grevatt

9 Rectory Drive, Newcastle upon Tyne NE3 1XT
Chairman/Editorial Head *Dr S. Y. Killingley*

FOUNDED 1981. Alternative publisher of works not normally commercially viable. Three books have appeared with financial backing from professional bodies. *Publishes* academic titles and conference reports, particularly language, linguistics and religious studies. Some poetry also. No unsolicited mss. Synopses and ideas should be accompanied by s.a.e.
Royalties paid annually (after first 500 copies).

GRM Publications

PO Box 213, Leeds LS6 4YQ
☎0113 2752456   Fax 0113 2752456

Managing Editors *Graham Wade, Elizabeth Wade*

FOUNDED 1996. Publishes monographs on classical music and musicians.

GSSE

11 Malford Grove, Gilwern, Abergavenny, Monmouthshire NP7 0RN
☎01873   830872
Email: GSSE@zoo.co.uk

Owner/Manager *David P. Bosworth*

Publishes newsletters and booklets describing classroom practice (at all levels of education and training). Ideas welcome – particularly from practising teachers, lecturers and trainers describing how they use technology in their teaching.
Royalties paid by arrangement.

Happy House

3b Castledown Avenue, Hastings, East Sussex TN34 3RJ
☎01424 434778

FOUNDED 1992 as a self-publishing venture for Dave Arnold/Martin Honeysett collaboration of poetry and cartoons.

Haunted Library

Flat 1, 36 Hamilton Street, Hoole, Chester, Cheshire CH2 3JQ
☎01244 313685   Fax 01244 313685
Email: pardos@globalnet.co.uk
Website: www.users.globalnet.co.uk/
          pardos/GS.html

Managing Editor *Rosemary Pardoe*

FOUNDED 1979. *Publishes* a twice-yearly ghost story magazine in the antiquarian tradition of M. R. James. The magazine publishes stories, news and articles. No unsolicited mss.
Royalties not paid.

Heart of Albion Press

2 Cross Hill Close, Wymeswold, Loughborough, Leicestershire LE12 6UJ
☎01509 880725
Email: albion@gmtnet.co.uk
Website: www.gmtnet.co.uk/albion/

Managing Editor *R. N. Trubshaw*

FOUNDED 1990 to publish books and booklets on the East Midlands area. *Publishes* mostly local history. Future publications on CD-ROM only. No unsolicited mss.
Royalties negotiable.

Hilmarton Manor Press

Calne, Wiltshire SN11 8SB
☎01249 760208   Fax 01249 760379
Email: hilmartonpress@lineone.net

Chairman/Managing Director *Charles Baile de Laperriere*

Publishes fine art reference only.
Royalties paid.

Horseshoe Publications

PO Box 37, Kingsley, Warrington, Cheshire WA6 8DR
☎01928 787477 (Afternoons and evenings)

Managing Editor *John C. Hibbert*

FOUNDED in 1994, initially to publish work of Cheshire writers. Poetry, short stories and own writing. Shared cost publishing considered in certain circumstances. Reading fee on full mss £25. Unsolicited mss, synopses and ideas in the realm of commercial fiction welcome. S.a.e. for return.

ignotus press

BCM-Writer, 27 Old Gloucester Street, London WC1X 3XX

Publisher *Suzanne Ruthven*

Specialises in full length esoteric non-fiction and fiction of all traditions although writers are advised to send s.a.e. for authors' guidelines before submitting material for consideration. All mss are checked for accuracy and knowledge of subject by specialists who will reject sword-n-sorcery and idealistic New Age material. Also *publishes Comhairle*, the official journal of the Comhairli Cairde. The articles and features published in the quarterly magazine illustrate the range of material sought by any of the ignotus press imprints. Sample copies available priced £3 from the publisher.

IMPRINTS **Corvus Press** *Christine Sempers* Non-fiction paperbacks and booklets relating to self-help, healing, herb lore and primitive native traditions. **Feasac Publications** *Frances Denton* Non-fiction paperbacks and booklets on indigenous craft and arts/craft covering Anglo Saxon, Nordic and Celtic traditions.
Royalties paid.

Intellect Books

E.F.A.E., Earl Richards Road North, Exeter, Devon EX2 6AS
☎01392 475110   Fax 01392 475110
Email: books@intellect-net.com
Website: www.intellect-net.com

Publisher *Masoud Yazdani*
Assistant Publisher *Robin Beecroft*

A multidisciplinary publisher for both individual and institutional readers. Tracks newest developments in digital creative media – art, film, television, design, etc. – and examines distinct theories in education, language, gender study and international culture through scholarly articles. Also publishes in AI, computer science and human–computer interaction in books, journals and website.
Royalties paid.

Iolo

38 Chaucer Road, Bedford MK40 2AJ
☎01234 270175   Fax 01234 270175

Managing Director *Dedwydd Jones*

Publishes Welsh theatre-related material and campaigns for a Welsh National Theatre. Ideas on Welsh themes welcome; approach in writing.

JAC Publications

28 Bellomonte Crescent, Drayton, Norwich, Norfolk NR8 6EJ
☎01603 861339

Managing Editor *John James Vasco*

Publishes World War II Luftwaffe history only. Unsolicited mss welcome. No synopses or ideas.
Royalties paid.

The Jupiter Press

Oracle House, 1–3 Gospel End Road, Sedgley, Dudley, West Midlands DY3 3LT
☎01902 665477   Fax 01902 678655

Managing Editor *Gordon Drury*

FOUNDED 1995. Looking for niche market and information publications, particularly sport orientated (golf and soccer), also quiz, puzzles and games content. Also interested in clairvoyance, esoteric subjects. Synopses and ideas for books welcome.
Royalties paid.

Katabasis

See under **Poetry Presses**

Richard Kay Publications

80 Sleaford Road, Boston, Lincolnshire PE21 8EU
☎01205 353231

Managing Editor *Richard Kay*

FOUNDED 1970. Non-profit motivated publisher of local interest (Lincolnshire) material: dialect, history, autobiography and biography, philosophy, medico-political and contemporary dissent on current affairs. About 6 titles a year. No unsolicited mss; synopses and ideas welcome.
Royalties paid if appropriate.

Kittiwake

3 Glantwymyn Village Workshops, Nr.
Machynlleth, Montgomeryshire SY20 8LY
☎01650 511314 Fax 01650 511602
Email: PerroCarto@aol.com
Website: www.owg.uk/dvid.perrott
Managing Editor *David Perrott*

FOUNDED 1986. *Publishes* guidebooks only, with
an emphasis on careful design/production.
Unsolicited mss, synopses and ideas for guidebooks welcome. Specialist cartographic and electronic publishing services available.
Royalties paid.

Lily Publications

PO Box 9, Narberth, Pembrokeshire
SA68 0YT
☎01834 891461 Fax 01834 891463
Managing Editor *Miles Cowsill*

FOUNDED 1991. *Publishes* holiday guides and
specialist books. Publishers of *Flagship®* for
P&O European Ferries, UK. Unsolicited mss,
synopses and ideas welcome. Sister company
Lily Publications (Isle of Man) Ltd., PO Box 1,
Portland House, Ballasalla, Isle of Man. Tel/fax
01624 823848.
Royalties paid.

The Lindsey Press

Unitarian Headquarters, 1–6 Essex Street,
Strand, London WC2R 3HY
☎0171 240 2384 Fax 0171 240 3089
Email: ga@unitarian.org.uk
Convenor *Kate Taylor*

Established at the end of the 18th century as a
vehicle for disseminating liberal religion. Adop-
ted the name of The Lindsey Press at the beginning of the 20th century (after Theophilus
Lindsey, the great Unitarian Theologian). *Publishes* books reflecting liberal religious thought or
Unitarian denominational history. Also worship
material – hymn books, collections of prayers
etc. No unsolicited mss; synopses and ideas welcome.
Royalties not paid.

Logaston Press

Logaston, Woonton, Almeley, Herefordshire
HR3 6QH
☎01544 327344
Managing Editors *Andy Johnson, Ron Shoesmith*

FOUNDED 1885. *Publishes* guides, archaeology,
social history, rural issues and local history for
Wales, the Welsh Border and West Midlands.

6–8 titles a year. Unsolicited mss, synopses and
ideas welcome. Return postage appreciated.
Royalties paid.

Luath Press Ltd

543/2 Castlehill, The Royal Mile, Edinburgh
EH1 2ND
☎0131 225 4326 Fax 0131 225 4324
Email: gavin.macdougall@luath.co.uk
Website: www.luath.co.uk
Managing Editor *G. H. MacDougall*

FOUNDED 1981. *Publishes* mainly books with a
Scottish connection. About 15–20 titles a year.
Unsolicited mss, synopses and ideas welcome;
committed to publishing well-written books
worth reading.
Royalties paid.

Lyfrow Trelyspen
See **CNP Publications**

Madison Publishing Ltd

Fairway House, 27 Comyn Road, London
SW11 1QB
☎0370 873399 Fax 0171 585 0079
Managing Director *Nathan Andrew Iyer*

FOUNDED 1995. *Publishes* British fiction. No
unsolicited mss. Synopses (no more than 2pp)
and ideas welcome.

Marine Day Publishers

64 Cotterill Road, Surbiton, Surrey KT6 7UN
☎0181 399 7625
Managing Editor *Anthony G. Durrant*

FOUNDED 1990. Part of The Marine Press Ltd.
Publishes local history.
Royalties not paid.

Matching Press

1 Watermans End, Matching Green, Harlow,
Essex CM17 0RQ
☎01279 731308
Publisher *Patrick Streeter*

FOUNDED 1993. *Publishes* biography, autobiography, social history and fiction. Enquiries welcome.
Royalties paid.

Maypole Editions

22 Mayfair Avenue, Ilford, Essex IG1 3DQ
☎0181 252 3937
Contact *Barry Taylor*

Publisher of plays and poetry in the main. 2–3
titles a year. Unsolicited mss welcome provided
return postage is included. Poetry always

welcome for collected anthologies. Poems should be approximately 30 lines long, broadly covering social concerns, ethnic minorities, feminist issues, romance, travel, lyric rhyming verse. No politics. The annual collected anthology is designed as a small press platform for first-time poets who might not otherwise get into print, and a permanent showcase for those already published who want to break into the mainstream. Catalogue £1, plus s.a.e. 'Please be patient when sending work because of the huge volume of submissions.' Exempt Charity Status.

Meadow Books

22 Church Meadow, Milton under Wychwood, Chipping Norton, Oxfordshire OX7 6JG
☎01993 831338

Managing Director *C. O'Neill*

FOUNDED 1990. Published a social history of hospitals.

Mercia Cinema Society

19 Pinder's Grove, Wakefield, West Yorkshire WF1 4AH
☎01924 372748

Managing Editor *Brian Hornsey*

FOUNDED 1980 to foster research into the history of picture houses. *Publishes* books and booklets on the subject, including cinema circuits and chains. Books are often tied in with specific geographical areas. Unsolicited mss, synopses and ideas.
  Royalties not paid.

Meridian Books

40 Hadzor Road, Oldbury, West Midlands B68 9LA
☎0121 429 4397

Managing Editor *Peter Groves*

FOUNDED 1985 as a small home-based enterprise following the acquisition of titles from Tetradon Publications Ltd. *Publishes* local history, walking and regional guides. 4–5 titles a year. Unsolicited mss, synopses and ideas welcome if relevant. Send s.a.e. if mss is to be returned.
  Royalties paid.

Merton Priory Press Ltd

67 Merthyr Road, Whitchurch, Cardiff CF4 1DD
☎01222 521956   Fax 01222 623599

Managing Director *Philip Riden*

FOUNDED 1993. *Publishes* academic and mid-market history, especially local and industrial history; also distributes for small publishers working in the same field. About 6 titles a year. Full catalogue available.
  Royalties paid twice yearly.

Neil Miller Publications

Mount Cottage, Grange Road, Saint Michael's, Tenterden, Kent TN30 6EE

Managing Editor *Neil Miller*

FOUNDED 1994. *Publishes* tales with a twist, comedy, suspense, mystery, fantasy, science fiction, horror and the bizarre under the **Black Cat Books** imprint. **Global Books** romance tales. Also *publishes* paperbacks: classics, rare tales, tales of the unexpected. New authors always welcome. Evaluation and critique service available for large mss. 'We seek short story writers, in any genre. No unsolicited mss, please. In the first instance, send £3.75 and large s.a.e. for author's package, which includes free book. We have published 131 new authors since 1994. We will help and advise on anything well written and researched.'

Millers Dale Publishers

7 Weavers Place, Chandlers Ford, Eastleigh, Hampshire SO53 1TU
☎01703   261192
Email: gponting@clara.net
Website: www.home.clara.net/gponting/

Managing Editor *Gerald Ponting*

FOUNDED 1990. *Publishes* booklets related to slide presentations by Gerald Ponting. Also books on local history related to central Hampshire. Ideas for local history books on Hampshire considered.

Minority Rights Group

379 Brixton Road, London SW9 7DE
☎0171 978 9498   Fax 0171 738 6265
Email: minority.rights@mrgmail.org
Website: www.minorityrights.org

Deputy Head of Communications
  Angela Warren

FOUNDED in the late 1960s, MRG works to raise awareness of minority issues worldwide. *Publishes* books, reports and educational material on minority rights. 8–10 titles a year.

Morton Publishing

PO Box 23, Gosport, Hampshire PO12 2XD

Managing Editor *Nik Morton*

FOUNDED 1994. *Publishes* fiction – genre novellas (eg crime, science fiction, fantasy, horror, western), max. 20,000 words; short

story anthologies – max. 4000 words per story. Unsolicited synopses and ideas for books welcome. Also offers literary agent service of guidance and advice (fees on applications)
Royalties paid annually.

Need2Know
Remus House, Coltsfoot Drive, Woodston, Peterborough PE2 9JX
☎01733 898103   Fax 01733 313524
Managing Editor *Anne Sandys*

FOUNDED 1995 'to fill a gap in the market for self-help books'. Need2Know is an imprint of Forward Press (see under **Poetry Presses**). *Publishes* self-help, reference guides for people in difficult situations. Mss, synopses and ideas for books welcome with return postage. It is important to ensure the project fits in with the series and that the subject is not already covered; contact for guidelines.
Payment Advance plus 15% royalties.

New Millennium
292 Kennington Road, London SE11 4LD
☎0171 582 1477   Fax 0171 582 4084
Managing Editor *Tom Deegan*

New Millennium is the imprint of the Professional Authors' & Publishers' Association (see entry under **Professional Associations**), established in 1993 'to provide self-publishing writers with an alternative to the vanity trade'. *Publishes* general fiction and non-fiction. 85 titles in 1998.

Nimbus Press
18 Guilford Road, Leicester LE2 2RB
☎0116 2706318   Fax 0116 2706318
Email: clifford.sharp@nimbuspress.demon.co.uk
Managing Editor *Clifford Sharp*
Assistant Editor *Justin Moulder*

FOUNDED in 1991 to encourage churches to use drama in worship. *Publishes* Christian drama, humour and short books on Christian themes. Plays of not more than 30 minutes' length and suitable for production by church drama groups welcome. Other short works on Christian themes or books of prayers or graces also considered.
Royalties paid.

Norvik Press Ltd
School of Modern Languages & European Studies, University of East Anglia, Norwich, Norfolk NR4 7TJ
☎01603 593356   Fax 01603 250599
Email: norvik.pres@uea.ac.uk

Website: www.uea.ac./eur/norvik_press/button.htm
Managing Editors *James McFarlane, Janet Garton, Michael Robinson*

Small academic press. *Publishes* the journal *Scandinavica* and books related to Scandinavian literature. About 4 titles a year. Interested in synopses and ideas for books within its *Literary History and Criticism* series. No unsolicited mss.
Royalties paid.

Nyala Publishing
4 Christian Fields, London SW16 3JZ
☎0181 764 6292
Fax 0181 764 6292/0115 9819418
Email: nyala.publish@geo-group.demon.co.uk
Editorial Head *J. F. J. Douglas*

FOUNDED 1996. Publishing arm of Geo Group. *Publishes* biography, travel and general non-fiction. No unsolicited mss; synopses and ideas considered. Also offers a wide range of publishing services.
Royalties paid twice-yearly.

Orpheus Publishing House
4 Dunsborough Park, Ripley Green, Ripley, Guildford, Surrey GU23 6AL
☎01483 225777   Fax 01483 225776
Email: orpheuspubl.ho@btinternet.com
Managing Editors *J. S. Gordon, S. H. Francke*

FOUNDED 1996. *Publishes* 'well-researched and properly argued' books in the fields of occult science, esotericism and comparative philosophy/religion. 'Keen to encourage good (but sensible) new authors.' In the first instance, send maximum 3-page synopsis with s.a.e.
Royalties by agreement.

Outline Publications
See **Brantwood Books**

Palladour Books
Hirwaun House, Aberporth, Nr. Cardigan, Ceredigion SA43 2EU
☎01239 811658   Fax 01239 811658
Managing Editors *Jeremy Powell/Anne Powell*

FOUNDED 1986. Started with a twice-yearly issue of catalogues on the literature and poetry of World War I. Occasional catalogues on World War II poetry have also been issued. No unsolicited mss.
Royalties not paid.

Pandora
See **Rivers Oram Press**

Parapress Ltd
Magpie Shaw, Barden Road, Speldhurst, Kent
TN3 0LE
☎01892 863123   Fax 01892 863123
Managing Editor *Elizabeth Imlay*
FOUNDED 1993. *Publishes* autobiography, biography, diaries, journals of military personnel,
composers and sportsmen. Also books on local
history. About 12 titles a year. Largely self-
publishing.

Parthian Books
53 Colum Road, Cardiff CF1 3EF
☎01222 341314   Fax 01222 341314
Chairman *Gillian Griffiths*
Publisher *Richard Davies*
Approx. Annual Turnover £25,000
FOUNDED in 1993. *Publishes* contemporary
Welsh drama in English, also translations of
Welsh language fiction. Parthian runs *The
Cambrensis Initiative*, a 3-year year, Arts for All
supported, programme of publications. No
unsolicited mss; synopses with sample chapters
and ideas welcome.
Royalties paid annually.

Partizan Press
816–818 London Road, Leigh on Sea, Essex
SS9 3NH
☎01702 473986   Fax 01702 473986
Website: wwww.caliverbooks.demon.co.uk
Managing Editor *David Ryan*
Caters for the growing re-enactment and war-
gaming market. *Publishes* military history, with
particular regard to the 17th and 18th centuries; also *Odyssey*, a science fiction and fantasy short-story magazine. Copies and author's
notes available.
Royalties paid.

Paupers' Press
27 Melbourne Road, West Bridgford,
Nottingham NG2 5DJ
☎0115 9815063   Fax 0115 9815063
Email: stan2727uk@aol.com
Website: members.aol.com/stan2727uk/
pauper.htm
Managing Editor *Colin Stanley*
FOUNDED 1983. *Publishes* extended essays in
booklet form (about 15,000 words) on literary
criticism and philosophy. About 6 titles a year.
Limited hardback editions of bestselling titles.

No unsolicited mss but synopses and ideas for
books welcome.
Royalties paid.

Peepal Tree Press Ltd
17 King's Avenue, Leeds, West Yorkshire
LS6 1QS
☎0113 2451703   Fax 0113 2459616
Email: hannah@peepal.demon.co.uk
Managing Editor *Jeremy Poynting*
FOUNDED 1985. *Publishes* fiction, poetry,
drama and academic studies. *Specialises* in
Caribbean, Black British and South Asian wri-
ting. About 18 titles a year. In-house printing
and finishing facilities. AUTHORS Kamau
Brathwaite, Cyril Dabydeen, Beryl Gilroy,
Velma Pollard, Jan Shinebourne and **Forward
Poetry Prize** winner Kwame Dawes. 'Please
send an A5 s.a.e. with a 38p stamp for a copy of
our submission guidelines.' Write or 'phone for
a free catalogue.
Royalties paid.

The Penniless Press
100 Waterloo Road, Ashton, Preston,
Lancashire PR2 1EP
Managing Editor *Alan Dent*
Publishes quarterly magazine with literary, philosophical, artistic and political content, including
reviews of poetry, fiction, non-fiction and
drama. Prose of up to 3000 words welcome. No
mss returned without s.a.e.
Payment Free copy of magazine.

Pentaxion Ltd
180 Newbridge Street, Newcastle upon Tyne
NE1 2TE
☎0191 232 6189   Fax 0191 232 6190
Email: pentaxion@pentaxion.force9.co.uk
Managing Editor *Adrian Spooner*
Publishes academic, educational, medical, arts
and professional studies. 7 titles in 1998. No
unsolicited mss; synopses and ideas welcome.
'Under certain circumstances we will enter
into joint ventures with authors.'
Royalties paid.

Pexa Publications
5 Grove Road, Whetstone, Leicestershire
LE8 6LN
☎0116 2750472/3   Fax 0116 2750472
Email: pexapub.freeserve.co.uk
Managing Editor *Ian Dench*
Founded 1997. *Publishes* workbooks for children
aged between 6–12. No fiction. 6 titles in 1998.

No unsolicited mss; synopses and ideas for books welcome. Approach by fax in the first instance.
Royalties paid twice yearly.

Pipers' Ash Ltd
'Pipers' Ash', Church Road, Christian Malford, Chippenham, Wiltshire SN15 4BW
☎01249 720563   Fax 0870 0568916
Email: pipersash@supamasu.demon.co.uk
Website: www.supamasu.demon.co.uk
Managing Editor *Mr A. Tyson*

FOUNDED 1976 to publish technical manuals for computer-controlled systems. Later broadened the company's publishing activities to include individual collections of contemporary short stories, science fiction short stories, poetry, short novels, local histories, children's fiction, philosophy, biographies, translations and general non-fiction. 65 titles in 1998. No unsolicited mss. Synopses and ideas welcome; 'new authors with potential will be actively encouraged'.
Royalties paid annually.

Planet
PO Box 44, Aberystwyth, Ceredigion SY23 5ZZ
☎01970 611255   Fax 01970 611197
Managing Editor *John Barnie*

FOUNDED 1985 as publishers of the arts and current affairs magazine *Planet: The Welsh Internationalist* and branched out into book publishing in 1995. All books so far have been commissioned. Unsolicited synopses and ideas welcome.
Royalties paid.

Playwrights Publishing Co.
70 Nottingham Road, Burton Joyce, Nottinghamshire NG14 5AL
☎0115 9313356
Managing Editors *Liz Breeze, Tony Breeze*

FOUNDED 1990. *Publishes* one-act and full-length plays. Unsolicited scripts welcome. No synopses or ideas. Reading fees: £15 one act; £30 full length.
Royalties paid.

Pomegranate Press
Church Cottage, Lewes Road, Westmeston, Hassocks, Sussex BN6 8RH
☎01273 846743   Fax 01273 846743
Email: 106461.1316@compuserve.com
Website:ourworld.compuserve.com/
    PomegranatePress

Managing Editor *David Arscott*

FOUNDED in 1992 by writer/broadcaster David Arscott, who also administers the **Sussex Book Club**. *Specialises* in books about Sussex.
    IMPRINT **Pomegranate Practicals** how-to books. No unsolicited mss; synopses and ideas for books welcome.
Royalties paid twice yearly.

David Porteous Editions
PO Box 5, Chudleigh, Newton Abbot, Devon TQ13 0YZ
☎01626 853310   Fax 01626 853663
Publisher *David Porteous*

FOUNDED 1992 to produce high quality colour illustrated books on hobbies and leisure for the UK and international markets. *Publishes* crafts, hobbies, art techniques and needlecrafts. No poetry or fiction. 3–4 titles a year. Unsolicited mss, synopses and ideas welcome if return postage included.
Royalties paid twice yearly.

Power Publications
1 Clayford Avenue, Ferndown, Dorset BH22 9PQ
☎01202 875223   Fax 01202 875223
Contact *Mike Power*

FOUNDED 1989. *Publishes* local interest, pub walk guides and mountain bike guides. 2–3 titles a year. Unsolicited mss/synopses/ideas welcome.
Royalties paid.

Praxis Books
Sheridan, Broomers Hill Lane, Pulborough, West Sussex RH20 2DU
☎01798   873504
Email: 100543.3270@compuserve.com
Website: www.beckysmith.demon.co.uk
Proprietor *Rebecca Smith*

FOUNDED 1992. *Publishes* reissues of Victorian fiction, general interest. 14 titles to date. Unsolicited mss accepted with s.a.e. No fiction or humour. Editing service available. Shared funding, shared proceeds. 'I am most likely to accept work with a clearly identifiable market.'

Previous Parrot Press
The Foundry, Church Hanborough, Nr. Witney, Oxford OX8 8AB
☎01993 881260   Fax 01993 883080
Managing Editor *Dennis Hall*

Publishes limited editions with a strong emphasis on illustration. About 2 titles a year.

Primrose Hill Press Ltd

58 Carey Street, London WC2A 2JB
☎0171 405 7484   Fax 0171 405 7459
Email: php@hill-pub.com
Managing Director *Brian H. W. Hill*

FOUNDED in 1997, having taken over the stock
and projects in progress of Silent Books Ltd.
Publishes general art titles, wood engraving,
poetry and books for the gift market, 'all high
quality productions'. No fiction. About 12 titles
a year. Unsolicited mss, synopses and ideas welcome.

Prism Press Book Publishers Ltd

The Thatched Cottage, Partway Lane,
Hazelbury Bryan, Sturminster Newton,
Dorset DT10 2DP
☎01258 817164   Fax 01258 817635
Managing Director *Julian King*

FOUNDED 1974. *Publishes* alternative medicine,
conservation, environment, psychology, health,
mysticism, philosophy, politics and cookery.
About 6 titles a year. Synopses and ideas welcome.
    Royalties paid twice-yearly. *Overseas associates*
Prism Press USA.

Pulp Faction

See **Pulp Books** under **UK Publishers**

QED of York

1 Straylands Grove, York YO31 1EB
☎01904 424242   Fax 01904 424381
Email: qed@enterprise.net
Managing Editor *John Bibby*

Publishes and *distributes* resource guides and
learning aids, including laminated posters, for
mathematics and science. Synopses (3pp) and
ideas for books welcome. QED arranges publicity for other small presses and has many contacts overseas. Also provides publishing services
for other publishers and arranges exhibitions at
Frankfurt, LIBF, educational conferences etc.
    Royalties by agreement.

QueenSpark Books

49 Grand Parade, Brighton, East Sussex
BN2 2QA
☎01273 571710   Fax 01273 571710

A community writing and publishing group
run mainly by volunteers who work together
to write and produce books. Since the early
1970s they have published 60 titles: local autobiographies, humour, poetry, history and politics. Free writing workshops and groups held
on a regular basis. New members welcome.

Redstone Press

7A St Lawrence Terrace, London W10 5SU
☎0171 352 1594   Fax 0171 352 8749
Email: redstone.press@virgin.net
Managing Editor *Julian Rothenstein*

FOUNDED 1987. *Publishes* art and literature.
About 5 titles a year. No unsolicited mss; syn-
opses and ideas welcome but familiarity with
Redstone's list advised in the first instance.
    Royalties paid.

Rivers Oram Press

144 Hemingford Road, London N1 1DE
☎0171 607 0823   Fax 0171 609 2776
Email: ro@riversoram.demon.co.uk
Managing Director *Elizabeth Fidlon*
Editorial *Katharine Bright-Holmes*

FOUNDED 1990. *Publishes* radical political and
social sciences: social history, sociology, politics, gender studies, women's studies.
    IMPRINT **Pandora** *Katharine Bright-Holmes*
Feminist titles – general non-fiction: biography, arts, media, health, current affairs, reference and sexual politics. No fiction, children's
or cookery.
    Royalties paid annually.

The Robinswood Press

30 South Avenue, Stourbridge, West
Midlands DY8 3XY
☎01384 397475   Fax 01384 440443
Email: robinswoodpress@cwcom.net
Website: www.robinswoodpress.mcmail.com
Managing Editor *Christopher J. Marshall*

FOUNDED 1985. *Publishes* education, particularly
teacher resources, SEN and Waldorf. About 3–5
titles a year. Unsolicited mss, synopses and ideas
welcome.
    Royalties paid.

Romer Publications

Smith Yard, Unit 5, 29A Spelman Street,
London E1 6LQ
Also at: PO Box 10120, NL–1001 EC,
Amsterdam, The Netherlands
☎/Fax 00 31 20 6769442
Managing Editor *Hubert de Brouwer*

FOUNDED 1986. *Publishes* children's books but
main tenet remains critical reflection on origins
and legitimacy of established institutions.
Specialises in history, education and law. Will
consider sound, coherent and quality mss, synopses or ideas appropriate to its list.
    Royalties paid.

Scottish Cultural Press

Unit 14, Leith Walk Business Centre,
130 Leith Walk, Edinburgh EH6 5DT
☎0131 555 5950   Fax 0131 555 5018
Email: scp@sol.co.uk
Chair/Managing Editor *Jill Dick*
Children's Press Administrator *Avril Gray*
FOUNDED 1992. Began publishing in 1993.
Publishes Scottish interest titles, including cultural, literature, poetry, archaeology, local history, children's fiction and non-fiction.
IMPRINTS **Scottish Cultural Press**,
Scottish Children's Press. Unsolicited mss,
synopses and ideas welcome provided return
postage is included.
Royalties paid.

Serif

47 Strahan Road, London E3 5DA
☎0181 981 3990   Fax 0181 981 3990
Email: stephen@serif.demon.co.uk
Website: www.serif.demon.co.uk/
Managing Editor *Stephen Hayward*
FOUNDED 1994. *Publishes* cookery, Irish and
African studies and modern history; no fiction.
Ideas and synopses welcome; no unsolicited mss.
Royalties paid.

Sherlock Publications

6 Bramham Moor, Hill Head, Fareham,
Hampshire PO14 3RU
☎01329 667325
Managing Editor *Philip Weller*
FOUNDED to supply publishing support to a
number of Sherlock Holmes societes. *Publishes*
Sherlock Holmes and other Conan Doyle studies only. About 14 titles a year. No unsolicited
mss; synopses and ideas welcome.
Royalties not paid.

Silver Link Publishing Ltd

The Trundle, Ringstead Road, Great
Addington, Kettering, Northamptonshire
NN14 4BW
☎01536 330588   Fax 01536 330588
Website: www.slinkp-p.demon.co.uk
Managing Editor *Peter Townsend*
FOUNDED 1985 in Lancashire, changed hands in
1990 and now based in Northamptonshire. Small
independent company specialising in nostalgia
titles including illustrated books on railways,
trams, ships and other transport subjects, also,
under the Past and Present Publishing imprint,
post-war nostalgia on all aspects of social history.
Fees paid.

Spacelink Books

115 Hollybush Lane, Hampton, Middlesex
TW12 2QY
☎0181 979 3148
Managing Director *Lionel Beer*
FOUNDED 1986. Named after a UFO magazine
published in the 1960/70s. *Publishes* nonfiction titles connected with UFOs, Fortean
phenomena and paranormal events. No unsolicited mss; send synopses and ideas. Publishers
of *TEMS News* for the Travel and Earth
Mysteries Society. Distributor of wide range of
related titles and magazines.
Royalties and fees paid according to contract.

Springboard

See **Yorkshire Art Circus Ltd**

Stenlake Publishing

Ochiltree Sawmill, The Lade, Ochiltree,
Ayrshire KA18 2NX
☎01290 423114   Fax 01290 423114
Publishes local history, transport, Scottish and
industrial. 38 titles in 1998. Unsolicited mss,
synopses and ideas welcome if accompanied by
s.a.e.
Royalties or fixed fee paid.

Stone Flower Limited

9 The Drive, Ilford, Essex IG1 3EY
Managing Editor *L. G. Norman*
FOUNDED 1989. *Publishes* biography, law,
humour and general fiction. Currently developing a new-style series of legal and general
textbooks. Will consider mss only if acommpanied by £100 reading fee, or synopses and
ideas sent with s.a.e. or IRC. Approach in
writing in the first instance.

Stride

11 Sylvan Road, Exeter, Devon EX4 6EW
Email: RML@madbear.demon.co.uk
Website: www.madbear.demon.co.uk/stride/
Managing Editor *Rupert Loydell*
FOUNDED in 1982 as a magazine and booklet
series. Since the mid-1980s, the press has published paperback editions of imaginative new
writing. *Publishes* poetry, experimental fiction,
criticism, reviews, interviews, arts (particularly
experimental music). 22 titles in 1998. Unsolicited mss preferred to synopses. Ideas for future
books welcome. Approach in writing only (with
s.a.e.).
Royalties 'sometimes paid; free copies usually.'

T.C.L. Publications
8 Hywel Way, Pembroke SA71 4EF
☎01646 685637

Managing Editor *Duncan Haws*

FOUNDED 1966 as Travel Creatours Limited (TCL). *Publishes* nautical books only – the *Merchant Fleet* series (33 vols.). 2 titles in 1998. Unsolicited mss welcome, 'provided they are in our standard format and subject matters'. No unsolicited synopses or ideas.
Royalties paid.

Tamarind Ltd
PO Box 52, Northwood, Middlesex HA6 1UN
☎0181 866 8808   Fax 0181 866 5627
Email: TamrindLTD@aol.com

Managing Editor *Verna Wilkins*

FOUNDED 1987 to publish picture books which give Black children a high, unselfconscious, positive profile. Won Gold Award for Best Product, Nursery & Creche Exhibition, 1994. All titles sold into both trade and educational markets. Age range: 2–12.

Tarquin Publications
Stradbroke, Diss, Norfolk IP21 5JP
☎01379 384218   Fax 01379 384289

Managing Editor *Gerald Jenkins*

FOUNDED 1970 as a hobby which gradually grew and now *publishes* mathematical, cut-out models, teaching and pop-up books. Other topics covered if they involve some kind of paper cutting or pop-up scenes. 7 titles in 1999. No unsolicited mss; letter with 1–2 page synopses welcome.
Royalties paid.

Tarragon Press
Moss Park, Ravenstone, Whithorn DG8 8DR
☎01988 850368
Fax 01988 850304
Email: dsumner@mpravenstone.freeserve.co.uk

Director/Editorial Head *David Sumner*

FOUNDED 1987. *Publishes* medical and scientific for the layperson. About 3 titles a year. Unsolicited mss, synopses and ideas for books welcome.
Royalties paid annually.

Tartarus Press
5 Birch Terrace, Hangingbirch Lane, Horam, East Sussex TN21 0PA
☎01435 813224
Email: tartarus@pavilion.co.uk
Website: freepages.pavilion.net/users/tartarus

Managing Director *Raymond Russell*

FOUNDED 1987. *Publishes* fiction, short stories, essays and local history. Also books by and about Arthur Machen. About 12 titles a year. 'Please do not send submissions. We cater to a small, collectable market; we solicit the fiction we publish.'

Thames Publishing
14 Barlby Road, London W10 6AR
☎0181 969 3579

Publishing Manager *John Bishop*

FOUNDED 1970. *Publishes* music, and books about English music and musicians, particularly of this century but not pop. About 4 titles a year. No unsolicited mss; send synopses and ideas in first instance.

Tredegar Press
PO Box 4830, London SW11 4XQ
☎0171 223 6364   Fax 0171 738 9328
Website: www.stripguide.com

Managing Editor *David Allsop*

FOUNDED 1995. *Publishes* humorous pocket books and guides. Unsolicited mss, synopses and ideas welcome. Approach in writing in the first instance with s.a.e. for return of material.
Royalties negotiable.

Tuckwell Press Ltd
The Mill House, Phantassie, East Linton, East Lothian EH40 3DG
☎01620 860164   Fax 01620 860164
Email: tuckwellpress@sol.co.uk
Website: www.tuckwellpress.co.uk

Managing Director *John Tuckwell*

FOUNDED 1995. *Publishes* literature, ethnology, biography, architecture, gardening history, genealogy, palaeography, with a bias towards Scottish and academic texts, also north of England. 85 titles in print. No unsolicited mss but synopses and ideas welcome if relevant to subjects covered.
Royalties paid annually.

Two Heads Publishing
9 Whitehall Park, London N19 3TS
☎0171 561 1606   Fax 0171 561 1607

Contact *Charles Frewin*

Independent publisher of sport, particularly football and cricket. Synopses and ideas welcome; write in the first instance.
Royalties paid quarterly.

UNKN

Highfields, Brynymor Road, Aberystwyth,
Ceredigion SY23 2HX
☎01970 627337   Fax 01970 627337
Managing Editor *Niall Quinn*
Publisher *Siobhán O'Rourke*

FOUNDED 1995 originally to promote the work
of writers (primarily poets) engaged in the production of experimental and marginal text – its
core commitment.

Wakefield Historical Publications

19 Pinder's Grove, Wakefield, West Yorkshire
WF1 4AH
☎01924 372748
Managing Editor *Kate Taylor*

FOUNDED 1977 by the Wakefield Historical
Society to publish well-researched, scholarly
works of regional (namely West Riding) historical significance. 1–2 titles a year. Unsolicited
mss, synopses and ideas for books welcome.
Royalties not paid.

Paul Watkins Publishing

18 Adelaide Street, Stamford, Lincolnshire
PE9 2EN
☎01780 756793   Fax 01780 756793
Proprietor *Shaun Tyas*

Publishes non-fiction – medieval, academic,
biography, nautical, local history. No fiction.
Distributor for the English Place-Name Society
and the Richard III and Yorkist History Trust. 9
titles in 1998. Unsolicited mss, synopses and
ideas for books welcome.
Royalties paid twice yearly.

Whittles Publishing

Roseleigh House, Latheronwheel, Caithness
KW5 6DW
☎01593 741240   Fax 01593 741360
Email: whittl@globalnet.co.uk
Website: www.users.globalnet.co.uk/~whittl
Managing Editor *Dr Keith Whittles*

FOUNDED 1986 to offer freelance commissioning
and consulting. Started publishing a few years
ago in the field of civil engineering and surveying. Also general books with a marine/Scottish
theme. 7 titles in 1998. Unsolicited mss, synopses
and ideas welcome on appropriate themes.
Royalties paid annually.

Whyld Publishing Co-op

Moorland House, Kelsey Road, Caistor,
Lincolnshire LN7 6SF
☎01472 851374   Fax 01472 851374
Managing Editor *Janie Whyld*

Having taken over former ILEA titles on anti-
sexist work with boys which would otherwise
have vanished, Janie Whyld has gone on to
publish a specialist list of educational materials
for teachers, trainers and students, with an
emphasis on equal opportunities and interpersonal skills. Would welcome being taken
over by anyone/organisation interested in
preserving the list.
Royalties nominal.

Witan Books & Publishing Services

Cherry Tree House, 8 Nelson Crescent, Cotes
Heath, via Stafford ST21 6ST
☎01782 791673
Managing Editor *Jeff Kent*

FOUNDED in 1980 for self-publishing and commenced publishing other writers in 1991.
Publishes general books, including biography,
education, environment, geography, history,
politics, popular music and sport. 2 titles in
1998. Witan Publishing Services, which began
as an offshoot to help writers get their work
into print, offers guidance, editing, proofreading etc. Unsolicited mss, synopses and ideas
welcome (include s.a.e.).
Royalties paid.

Writers' Bookshop

Remus House, Coltsfoot Drive, Woodston,
Peterborough PE2 9JX
☎01733 898103   Fax 01733 313524
Managing Editor *Anne Sandys*

Writers' Bookshop is an imprint of Forward
Press (see under **Poetry Presses**). *Publishes*
writers' aids in the form of directories and
how-to guides. Best-known annual title is the
Small Press Guide.
Payment Advance plus 15% royalties.

Xavier Music Ltd

PO Box 17, Abergavenny NP8 1XA
☎01874 730897   Fax 01874 730897
Email: xavier@so-strong.com
Website: www.so-strong.com
Managing Editor *Peter Lloyd*

Opened the books division in 1993 to publish
poetry and works by Labi Siffre. *Publishes*
poetry and one-act plays. No unsolicited
material.
Royalties not paid.

Yorkshire Art Circus Ltd

School Lane, Glasshoughton, Castleford,
West Yorkshire WF10 4QH
☎01977 550401   Fax 01977 512819
Email: admin@artcircus.org.uk
Website: www.artcircus.org.uk

Books Coordinator *Ian Daley*

FOUNDED 1986. *Specialises* in new writing by first-time authors. *Publishes* autobiography, community books, fiction (novels and short stories) and local interest (Yorkshire/Humberside). No local history, children's, poetry, reference, nostalgia. Unsolicited mss discouraged; send for fact sheet first. **Springboard** fiction IMPRINT launched 1993 mainly for Yorkshire/Humberside-based writers. Free catalogue available. *Royalties* paid.

UK Packagers

The Albion Press Ltd
Spring Hill, Idbury, Oxfordshire OX7 6RU
☎01993 831094   Fax 01993 831982
Chairman/Managing Director
Emma Bradford

FOUNDED 1984 to produce high-quality illustrated titles. *Commissions* illustrated trade titles, particularly children's. About 4 titles a year. TITLES *From a Distance* Jane Ray and Julie Gold; *The Little Mermaid and other Fairy Stories* Isabelle Brent. Unsolicited synopses and ideas for books not welcome.

Royalties paid; fees paid for introductions and partial contributions.

Alphabet & Image Ltd
See **Marston House** under **UK Publishers**

Andromeda Oxford Ltd
9–13 The Vineyard, Abingdon, Oxfordshire OX14 3PX
☎01235 550296   Fax 01235 550330
Managing Director *Michael Holyoak*

FOUNDED 1986. *Commissions* adult and junior international illustrated reference, both single volume and series.

DIVISIONS **Adult Books** *Graham Bateman* Editorial Director; **Children's Books** *Nick Leggett* Editorial Director; TITLES *Encyclopedia of World Geography; Cultural Atlases; Science Encyclopedia; Atlas of World History; Factfiles.* Approach by letter in the first instance.

Archival Facsimiles Limited
The Old Bakery, 52 Crown Street, Banham, Norwich, Norfolk NR16 2HW
☎01953 887277   Fax 01953 888361
Email: erskpres@aol.com
Chief Executive *Crispin de Boos*

FOUNDED 1986. Specialist private publishers for individuals and organisations. Produces scholarly reprints and limited editions for academic/business organisations in Europe and the USA, ranging from leather-bound folios of period print reproductions to small illustrated booklets. Under the **Erskine Press** imprint publishes books on Antarctic exploration, general interest autobiographies and medical related 'Patient's Guides' (*Hip & Knee Replacement; Chronic Fatigue Syndrome*). No unsolicited mss. Ideas welcome.

Royalties paid twice yearly.

AS Publishing
73 Montpelier Rise, London NW11 9DU
☎0181 458 3552   Fax 0181 458 0618
Managing Director *Angela Sheehan*

FOUNDED 1987. *Commissions* children's illustrated non-fiction. No unsolicited synopses or ideas for books, but approaches welcome from experienced authors, editors and illustrators in this field.

Fees paid.

BCS Publishing Ltd
1 Bignell Park Barns, Kirtlington Road, Chesterton, Bicester, Oxon OX6 8TD
☎01869 324423   Fax 01869 324385
Managing Director *Steve McCurdy*
Approx. Annual Turnover £350,000

Commissions general interest non-fiction for international co-edition market.

Belitha Press Ltd
London House, Great Eastern Wharf, Parkgate Road, London SW11 4NQ
☎0171 978 6330   Fax 0171 223 4936
Publishing Director *Chester Fisher*
Editorial Director *Mary-Jane Wilkins*

FOUNDED 1980. *Commissions* children's non-fiction in all curriculum areas. About 50 titles a year. All titles are expected to sell in at least four co-editions. TITLES *World Cities; The Other Half of History; Life in Victorian Times; Our Earth; Future Tech; Speedy Machines; Building Works; Looking at Animals; The Human Machine; Measuring Up.* No unsolicited mss. Synopses and ideas for books welcome from experienced children's writers.

Bellew Publishing Co. Ltd
See entry under **UK Publishers**

Bender Richardson White
PO Box 266, Uxbridge, Middlesex UB9 5BD
☎01895 832444   Fax 01895 835213
Email: brw@brw.co.uk

Partners *Lionel Bender, Kim Richardson, Ben White*

FOUNDED 1990 to produce illustrated non-fiction for children aged 7–14 for publishers in the UK and abroad. 20 titles in 1998. Unsolicited material not welcome.

Fees paid.

David Bennett Books Ltd

15 High Street, St Albans, Hertfordshire AL3 4ED

☎01727 855878   Fax 01727 864085

Creative Director *David Bennett*

FOUNDED 1989. Producer of children's books: picture and novelty books, interactive and board books, baby gifts and non-fiction for babies and toddlers. Synopses and ideas for books welcome. Unsolicited mss may not be returned. No fiction or poetry.

Payment Both fees and royalties.

Book Packaging and Marketing

3 Murswell Lane, Silverstone, Towcester, Northamptonshire NN12 8UT

☎01327 858380   Fax 01327 858380

Contact *Martin F. Marix Evans*

FOUNDED 1989. Essentially a project management service, handling books demanding close designer/editor teamwork or complicated multi-contributor administration, for publishers, business 'or anyone who needs one'. Mainly illustrated adult non-fiction including military, travel, historical, home reference and coffee-table books. No fiction or poetry. 5–8 titles a year. Proposals considered; and additional writers are sometimes required for projects in development. TITLES *Canals of England; Contemporary Photographers*, 3rd ed.; *Michelin's Paris in Your Pocket; The Battles of the Somme 1916–18; The Military Heritage of Britain and Ireland; Passchendale and the Battle of Ypres; The Boer War.*

Payment Authors contract direct with client publishers; fees paid on first print usually and royalties on reprint but this depends on publisher.

Breslich & Foss Ltd

20 Wells Mews, London W1P 3FJ

☎0171 580 8774   Fax 0171 580 8784

Email: sales@breslichfoss.com

Directors *Paula Breslich, K. B. Dunning*

Approx. Annual Turnover £1.5 million

Packagers of non-fiction titles only, including art, children's, crafts, gardening and health.

Unsolicited mss welcome but synopses preferred. Include s.a.e. with all submissions.

Royalties paid twice yearly.

Brown Wells and Jacobs Ltd

Forresters Hall, 25–27 Westow Street, London SE19 3RY

☎0181 771 5115   Fax 0181 771 9994

Email: pastmaster@popking.demon.co.uk

Website: www.bwj.org

Managing Director *Graham Brown*

FOUNDED 1979. *Commissions* non-fiction, novelty, pre-school and first readers, natural history and science. About 40 titles a year. Unsolicited synopses and ideas for books welcome.

Fees paid.

Calmann & King Ltd

71 Great Russell Street, London WC1B 3BN

☎0171 831 6351   Fax 0171 831 8356

Email: enquiries@calmann-king.co.uk

Website: www.calman-king.com

Chairman *Robin Hyman*

Managing Director *Laurence King*

FOUNDED 1976. *Commissions* books on art, the decorative arts, design, architecture, graphic design, carpets and textiles. About 40 titles a year. Unsolicited synopses and ideas for books welcome.

Royalties paid twice yearly.

Cameron Books (Production) Ltd

PO Box 1, Moffat, Dumfriesshire DG10 9SU

☎01683 220808   Fax 01683 220012

Website: www.cameronbooks.co.uk

Directors *Ian A. Cameron, Jill Hollis*

Approx. Annual Turnover £350,000

Commissions contemporary art, including environmental art, film, design, collectors' reference, educational reference, conservation, natural history, social history, decorative arts, esoteric gardening and cookery. About 6 titles a year. Unsolicited synopses and ideas for books welcome.

Payment varies with each contract.

Chancerel International Publishers Ltd

120 Long Acre, London WC2E 9PA

☎0171 240 2811   Fax 0171 836 4186

Managing Director *W. D. B. Prowse*

FOUNDED 1976. *Commissions* educational books, and *publishes* language-teaching materials in most languages. Language teachers/writers often required as authors/consultants, especially native speakers other than English.

Payment generally by flat fee but royalties sometimes.

Roger Coote Publishing

Gissing's Farm, Fressingfield, Eye, Suffolk IP21 5SH
☎01379 588044   Fax 01379 588055
Director *Roger Goddard-Coote*

FOUNDED 1993. Packager of high-quality children's and adult non-fiction for trade, school and library markets. About 24 titles a year. No fiction. Include s.a.e. for return.

Fees paid; no royalties.

Diagram Visual Information Ltd

195 Kentish Town Road, London NW5 2JU
☎0171 482 3633   Fax 0171 482 4932
Managing Director *Bruce Robertson*

FOUNDED 1967. Producer of library, school, academic and trade reference books. About 10 titles a year. Unsolicited synopses and ideas for books welcome.

Fees paid; no payment for sample material/submissions for consideration.

Direct Image Publishing

8 Sharpes Mill, White Cross, Lancaster LA1 4XQ
☎01524 840880
Fax 01524 840990
Email:enquiries@directimageprod.
    demon.co.uk
Website: www.directimageprod.co.uk
Co-directors *Chris Ware, Elaine Ware*

A sub-division of **Direct Image Productions Ltd**. FOUNDED in 1992 to support video training programmes. *Publishes* outdoor pursuits, outdoor education titles and teachers' resource material, usually as part of a video and book package. Developing an outdoor leisure series and launching an outdoor magazine, *Challenge*, with the Association for Outdoor Learning. No unsolicited mss; approach with letter and outline of idea in the first instance.

Payment One-off fee paid.

Dorling Kindersley Ltd

See entry under **UK Publishers**

Duncan Petersen Publishing Limited

See entry under **UK Publishers**

Eddison Sadd Editions

St Chad's House, 148 King's Cross Road, London WC1X 9DH
☎0171 837 1968   Fax 0171 837 2025
Managing Director *Nick Eddison*
Editorial Director *Ian Jackson*
Approx. Annual Turnover £3.5 million

FOUNDED 1982. Produces a wide range of popular illustrated non-fiction, with books published in 25 countries. Ideas and synopses are welcome but titles must have international appeal.

Royalties paid twice yearly; flat fees paid when appropriate.

Erskine Press

See **Archival Facsimiles Limited**

Expert Publications Ltd

Sloe House, Halstead, Essex CO9 1PA
☎01787 474744   Fax 01787 474700
Email: expert@lineone.net
Chairman *Dr. D. G. Hessayon*

FOUNDED 1993. Produces the Expert series of books by Dr. D. G. Hessayon. Currently 18 titles in the series, including *The NEW Flower Expert; The Evergreen Expert; The NEW Vegetable & Herb Expert; The Flowering Shrub Expert; The Container Expert*. No unsolicited material.

First Rank Publishing

See entry under **Small Presses**

Geddes & Grosset Ltd

See entry under **UK Publishers**

Angus Hudson Ltd

Concorde House, Grenville Place, Mill Hill, London NW7 3SA
☎0181 959 3668   Fax 0181 959 3678
Managing Director *Nicholas Jones*
Approx. Annual Turnover £3.5 million

FOUNDED 1977. Management buyout from Maxwell Communications in 1989. Leading packager of religious co-editions. *Commissions* Christian books for all ages and co-editioning throughout the world. About 150 titles in 1998. Publishes under **Candle Books**; **Gazelle Books** and **Monarch Books** imprints. Prototype dummies complete with illustrations welcome for consideration. Synopses for text books welcome; no unsolicited mss, please.

Royalties paid.

Lexus Ltd

13 Newton Terrace, Glasgow G3 7PJ
☎0141 221 5266   Fax 0141 226 3139
Email: pt@lexus.win-uk.net

Managing/Editorial Director *P. M. Terrell*

FOUNDED 1980. Compiles bilingual reference, language and phrase books. About 20 titles a year. TITLES *Rough Guide Phrasebooks; Collins Italian Concise Dictionary; Harrap Study Aids; Hugo's Phrase Books; Harrap Shorter French Dictionary* (revised); *Impact Specialist Bilingual Glossaries; Oxford Student's Japanese Learner*. No unsolicited material. Books are mostly commissioned. Freelance contributors employed for a wide range of languages.

Payment generally flat fee.

Lionheart Books

10 Chelmsford Square, London NW10 3AR
☎0181 459 0453   Fax 0181 451 3681

Senior Partner *Lionel Bender*
Partner *Madeleine Samuel*
Designer *Ben White*
Approx. Annual Turnover £250,000

A design/editorial packaging team. Titles are primarily commissioned from publishers. Highly illustrated non-fiction for children aged 8–14, mostly natural history, history and general science. About 20 titles a year.

Payment generally flat fee.

Market House Books Ltd

2 Market House, Market Square, Aylesbury, Buckinghamshire HP20 1TN
☎01296 84911   Fax 01296 437073
Email: mhb_aylesbury@compuserve.com

Directors *Dr Alan Isaacs, Dr John Daintith, Peter Sapsed*

FOUNDED 1970. Formerly Laurence Urdang Associates. *Commissions* dictionaries, encyclopedias and reference. About 15 titles a year. TITLES *Concise Medical Dictionary; Brewer's 20th Century Phrase and Fable; Oxford Dictionary for Science Writers and Editors; Oxford Dictionary of Accounting; Bloomsbury Thesaurus; Larousse Thematica* (6 volume encyclopedia); *Collins English Dictionary; The Macmillan Encyclopedia; Grolier Bibliographical Encyclopedia of Scientists* (10 vols); *Oxford Paperback Encyclopedia; Oxford International Business Dictionary; Penguin Biographical Dictionary of Women; Penguin Shakespeare Dictionary; Penguin Dictionary of Plant Sciences*. Unsolicited material not welcome as most books are compiled in-house.

Fees paid.

Marshall Editions Ltd

The Orangery, 161 New Bond Street, London W1Y 9PA
☎0171 291 8222   Fax 0171 291 8233

Publisher *Barbara Anderson*
Editorial Director (adult titles)
  Ellen Dupont
Editorial Director (children's)
  Cindy O'Brien

FOUNDED 1977. *Commissions* non-fiction, including health, gardening, lifestyle, self-improvement, leisure, popular science and visual information for children.

MM Productions Ltd

33 Warner Road, Ware, Hertfordshire SG12 9JL
☎01920 466003   Fax 01920 466003

Chairman/Managing Director *Mike Moran*

Packager and publisher. TITLES *MM Publisher Database; MM Printer Database* (available in UK, European and international editions).

Oyster Books Ltd

Unit 4, Kirklea Farm, Badgworth, Axbridge, Somerset BS26 2QH
☎01934 732251   Fax 01934 732514

Managing Director *Jenny Wood*

FOUNDED 1985. Packagers of quality books and book/toy/gift items for children of pre-school age to ten years. About 20 titles a year. Most material is created in-house.

Payment usually fees.

Parke Sutton Ltd

Orchard House, Grange Farm, Ashwellthorpe, Norfolk NR16 1ET
☎01508 489212   Fax 01508 489212

Director *Ian S. McIntyre*

FOUNDED 1982. Packages books for publishers. Unsolicited synopses and ideas for books welcome. S.a.e. essential. Also publishing consultant.

Royalties paid twice yearly; fees sometimes paid rather than royalties.

Playne Books Limited

Chapel House, Trefin, Haverfordwest, Pembrokeshire SA62 5AU
☎01348 837073   Fax 01348 837063
Email: playne.books@virgin.net

Director *Gill Davies*
Design & Production *David Playne*

FOUNDED 1987. *Commissions* early learning titles for young children – fun ideas with an educational slant and novelty books. Also highly illustrated and practical books on any subject. Unsolicited synopses and ideas for books welcome.

Royalties paid 'on payment from publishers'. Fees sometimes paid instead of royalties.

Mathew Price Ltd
The Old Glove Factory, Bristol Road, Sherborne, Dorset DT9 4HP
☎01935 816010   Fax 01935 816310
Email: mathewp@mathew-price.com
Chairman/Managing Director
Mathew Price
Approx. Annual Turnover £1 million

Commissions high-quality, full-colour novelty picture books and fiction for young children plus children's non-fiction for all ages.

Fees sometimes paid instead of royalties.

Quarto Publishing
The Old Brewery, 6 Blundell Street, London N7 9BH
☎0171 700 6700/333 0000
Fax 0171 700 4191/700 0077
Chairman *Laurence Orbach*

FOUNDED 1976. Britain's largest book packager. *Commissions* illustrated non-fiction, including painting, graphic design, visual arts, history, cookery, gardening, crafts. *Publishes* under the Apple imprint. Unsolicited synopses/ ideas for books welcome.

Payment Flat fees paid.

Reader's Digest Children's Publishing Ltd
King's Court, Parsonage Lane, Bath BA1 1ER
☎01225 463401   Fax 01225 460942
Email: paul.stuart@readersdigest.co.uk
Website: www.childrens-books.com
Managing Director *Paul Stuart*
Approx. Annual Turnover £9 million

Part of the Reader's Digest Group. *Commissions* children's projects in novelty or interactive formats – acetate, pop-up, toy add-ons. Also religious list. About 100 titles a year.

Royalties or flat fee according to contract.

Regency House Publishing Limited
See entry under **UK Publishers**

Sadie Fields Productions Ltd
4C/D West Point, 36–37 Warple Way, London W3 0RG
☎0181 746 1171   Fax 0181 746 1170
Directors *David Fielder, Sheri Safran*

FOUNDED 1981. Quality children's books with international co-edition potential: pop-ups, three-dimensional, novelty, picture and board books, 1500 words maximum. About 30 titles a year. Approach with preliminary letter and sample material in the first instance. *Publishes* in the UK under the Tango Books imprint.

Royalties based on a per-copy-sold rate and paid in stages.

Salariya Book Company Ltd
25 Marlborough Place, Brighton, East Sussex BN1 1UB
☎01273 603306   Fax 01273 693857
Email: salariya@fastnet.co.uk
Managing Director *David Salariya*

FOUNDED 1989. Children's information books – fiction, history, art, music, science, architecture, education and picture books.

Payment by arrangement.

Savitri Books Ltd
115J Cleveland Street, London W1P 5PN
☎0171 436 9932   Fax 0171 580 6330
Managing Director *Mrinalini S. Srivastava*
Approx. Annual Turnover £200,000

FOUNDED 1983 and since 1998, Savitri Books has also become a publisher in its own right (textile crafts). Keen to work 'very closely with authors/illustrators and try to establish long-term relationships with them, doing more books with the same team of people'. *Commissions* high-quality, illustrated non-fiction, crafts, New Age and nature. About 7 titles a year. Unsolicited synopses and ideas for books 'very welcome'.

Royalties 10–15% of the total price paid by the publisher.

Sheldrake Press
188 Cavendish Road, London SW12 0DA
☎0181 675 1767   Fax 0181 675 7736
Email: mail@sheldrakepress.demon.co.uk
Website: www.sheldrakepress.demon.co.uk
Publisher *Simon Rigge*
Approx. Annual Turnover £250,000

Commissions illustrated non-fiction: history, travel, style, cookery and stationery. TITLES *The Victorian House Book; The Shorter Mrs Beeton; The Power of Steam; The Railway Heritage of Britain; Wild Britain; Wild France; Wild Spain; Wild Italy; Wild Ireland; Amsterdam: Portrait of a City; The Kate Greenaway Baby Book.* Synopses and ideas for books welcome, but not interested in fiction.

Fees or royalties paid.

Stonecastle Graphics Ltd/ Touchstone

Old Chapel Studio, Plain Road, Marden, Tonbridge, Kent TN12 9LS
☎01622 832590   Fax 01622 832592
Email: touchstone@touchstone.ndirect.co.uk
Partners *Paul Turner, Sue Pressley*
Editorial Head *Sue Pressley*
Approx. Annual Turnover £300,000

FOUNDED 1976. Formed additional design/ packaging partnership, Touchstone, in 1983. *Commissions* high-quality, illustrated non-fiction general books – motoring, health, sport, leisure, home interest and popular culture. 20 titles in 1998. TITLES *Aston Martin, The Legend; Creating a Home; The Concise Encyclopedia of Fishing; Essential Health for Women.* Unsolicited synopses and ideas for books welcome.
Fees paid.

Templar Publishing

Pippbrook Mill, London Road, Dorking, Surrey RH4 1JE
☎01306 876361   Fax 01306 889097
Managing Director/Editorial Head
Amanda Wood
Approx. Annual Turnover £5 million

FOUNDED 1981. A division of The Templar Company plc. *Commissions* novelty and gift books, children's illustrated non-fiction, educational and story books, children's illustrated non-fiction. 100 titles a year. Synopses and ideas for books welcome.
Royalties by arrangement.

Toucan Books Ltd

Fourth Floor, 32–38 Saffron Hill, London EC1N 8BS
☎0171 404 8181   Fax 0171 404 8282
Managing Director *Robert Sackville-West*
Approx. Annual Turnover £1,600,000

FOUNDED 1985. Specialises in international co-editions and fee-based editorial, design and production services to film. *Commissions* illustrated non-fiction only. About 20 titles a year. TITLES *The Eventful Century; The Earth, Its Wonders, Its Secrets; Leith's Cookery Bible; Charles II; The Complete Photography Course; Journeys into the Past* series. Unsolicited synopses and ideas for books welcome. No fiction or non-illustrated titles.
Royalties paid twice-yearly; fees paid in addition to or instead of royalties.

Touchstone

See **Stonecastle Graphics Ltd**

Touchstone Publishing Ltd

Gissing's Farm, Fressingfield, Eye, Suffolk IP21 5SH
☎01379 588044   Fax 01379 588055
Chairman/Managing Director
Roger Goddard-Coote
Editorial Director *Edwina Conner*

FOUNDED 1989. Packager of children's non-fiction for trade, school and library markets. About 8 titles a year. No fiction, textbooks or adult material. Synopses and ideas welcome. Include s.a.e. for return.
Fees paid; no royalties.

Wordwright Books

25 Oakford Road, London NW5 1AJ
☎0171 284 0056   Fax 0171 284 0041
Contact *Charles Perkins*

FOUNDED by ex-editorial people 'so good writing always has a chance with us'. *Commissions* illustrated non-fiction: social history and comment, military history, women's issues, sport. *Specialises* in military and social history, natural history, science, art, cookery, and gardening. 4–6 titles a year. Unsolicited synopses/ ideas (a paragraph or so) welcome for illustrated non-fiction.
Payment usually fees but royalties (twice-yearly) paid for sales above a specified number of copies.

Working Partners Ltd

11a Dunraven Road, London W12 7QY
☎0181 735 0888   Fax 0181 749 5013
Email: working.partners@btinternet.com
Contact *Ben Baglio, Rod Ritchie*

Specialises in children's mass-market series fiction books. Creators of *Animal Ark; Puppy Patrol; Internet Detectives; Mystery Club; Sheltie, Stacy & Friends and Survive!.* No unsolicited mss.
Payment fees and royalties by arrangement.

Zöe Books Ltd

15 Worthy Lane, Winchester, Hampshire SO23 7AB
☎01962 851318   Fax 01962 843015
Managing Director *Imogen Dawson*
Director *Bob Davidson*

FOUNDED 1990. *Specialises* in full-colour information and reference books for schools and libraries worldwide. *Publishes* about 30 titles a year. Tends to generate own ideas but happy to hear from experienced freelance writers and editors of information books. Does *not* publish picture books or fiction.
Fees paid.

Popular Fiction for Women

Elizabeth Buchan

It seems invidious to talk about 'women's fiction' for just a quick glance at any bestseller lists reveals that the authors and their novels which ride high on them, year in and year out, are, clearly, read by both sexes. *Captain Corelli's Mandolin, Miss Smilla's Feeling for Snow, Enduring Love, Birdsong...* this is a tiny clutch of the many titles whose power and reach is effortlessly cross-gender.

Nevertheless, women authors and readers have exerted a strong influence on the writing and publishing of popular fiction and publishers expend huge sums of money on feeding a section of the market which is predominantly female. Women, it seems, are a good, faithful and hungry audience. This is, perhaps, not surprising. Until recently, women have been confined to a domestic area and reading was an area where they were free to express a choice, indulge an escapism, give reign to their fantasies and, quite simply, to enjoy themselves.

So what is women's fiction? What do women seek and find in the pages of Catherine Cookson, Mary Wesley, Joanna Trollope and Helen Fielding? Traditionally, women are the articulate sex. They use words to manoeuvre relationships, to orchestrate a multi-layered life, to absorb the nexus of emotion and to make connections. They have a devouring interest in lives, gossip, minutia – which is precisely what novels are about. Virginia Woolf placed her bony, elegant finger on it in her short story, *Memoirs of a Novelist*: 'George Eliot and Charlotte Bronte between them must share the parentage of many novels...' she writes, 'for they disclosed the secret that the precious stuff of which books are made lies all about one, in drawing-rooms and kitchens where women live, and accumulates with every tick of the clock'.

Exactly. Pinning down life – comic, tragic, full of love, passion, hatred, spoilt ungrateful children, grieving orphans, gardens, debt, linen cupboards, the death of the family cat, the profound and important shift in emotion or spirit as it is experienced while peeling the potatoes is the bedrock of fiction. And what fictions there are from which to choose – from traditional romances to the young, sassy, smart comedies, the tougher, abrasive slices of life in the big cities, the gentler, often bitter-sweet reflective stories of rites of passage and, of course, the great epic fireworks which take the reader to the edge of physical and mental frontiers. Yet, and this one of the more delightful conclusions to have arrived at, a significant characteristic of these novels is not only their emphasis on narrative and a good story but the subversion which runs through them, sometimes surfacing in a great eruption, sometimes quietly simmering under the text. How many Victorian women secretly identified with and applauded George Eliot's portrait of the gifted Dorothea who longs to break out of her domestic prison in order to do something worthwhile or thrilled to Jane Eyre's great reverberating cry of affirmation in Charlotte Bronte's eponymous novel: 'I have fully as much heart and soul as you'? Daphne du Maurier's *Rebecca* is not only a romance noir but also a power struggle between the young, ignorant, nameless heroine and her sophisticated bridegroom in which the balance eventually swings in the former's favour – at a price, of course. (This – unconscious – fictional tendency to tame the beast of man by mutilating him either physically or psychologically, beginning with Mr Rochester's blindness, is one of the more obvious retaliations open to women.) Examine Mary Wesley's novels and what becomes apparent are the forces at work against conventional ways of behaving. In *Not That Sort of Girl*, Rose is respectably married but conducts a passionate and lifelong affair with Mylo. In *Harnessing Peacocks*, Hebe earns the money to educate her son privately with stylish and elegant prostitution.

Popular novels are as prey to fashion as anything else. From the doctor and nurse romances of the Second World War battlefield, 'the great husband hunt' of the fifties, the restless but still polite novel of the sixties, to the emergence of the bonkbuster and glitzy novels of the seventies and eighties, and the Aga Saga of the nineties. With the possible exception of the strongly regionally-based clogs-and-shawl sagas, and the one or two outstanding historical novelists such as the bold and supple-prosed Philippa Gregory, historical fiction appears to have fallen on hard times unless, as is the case with Barbara Erskine and her time-travel plots, there is a strong alternative marketing handle. Whereas, paradoxically, the more literary writers are beginning to revivify the genre. Rose Tremain's *Restoration*, Hilary Mantel's massive evocation of the French Revolution *A Place of Greater Safety* and Jane Smiley's *The All-True Travels and Adventures of Lidie Newton* have injected a fire, wit, erudition and singing prose into an area where the jibes about maidens swooning over codpieces have been – sometimes – justified.

A genre which has displayed a remarkable sticking power in the face of continual pillorying is the Aga Saga which specialises in novels of domestic upheaval mostly set in the shires. Something about the notion of quiet (and occasionally dull and badly-written) frustrations of middle-class housewives longing for a fling or coping with truculent teenagers as they stack china on their dressers seems to engender a savagery in the literary critic's breast which he or she does not direct at the equally dull and badly contrived conventions of a crime or science-fiction novel. Sexual politics die hard and the question must be posed: is this the residue from the bad old days when the areas of legitimate female interest were held in contempt?

But critics make a mistake. The novels of Joanna Trollope, *The Rector's Wife* for example, are sharp, subtle, truthful. Their concern, to render accessible what Anthony Trollope termed 'the daily lacerations of the spirit' bridge the gap between the nineteenth-century concerns of morality and sensibility with the more critical and plural viewpoints that we have today and do so in a manner which speaks to hundreds and thousands of readers.

For the cultural historian, women's popular fiction is a treasure house. From Jane Austen and Mrs Gaskell through to Jane Green's *Jemima J*, it is possible to trace the flickering voice of the female: her aspirations, her delights, hers tragedies and her shortfalls. Mrs Gaskell's Molly Gibson, the heroine of *Wives and Daughters* is the rosy maiden whose duty is to marry and become the embodiment of womanly virtues. Helen Fielding's calorie-crunching, weepy, smoke-wreathed Bridget Jones is also searching for Mr Right – but Mr Right will have to respect her, be a dab hand at nappies, give her personal space and be prepared to prop up a wobbling psyche. This is romance dressed up to the nineties, but the hollow sound of the ticking biological clock, an on-going battle with the weighting scales, confusion of roles and a fear of loneliness is cruelly revealing of a thirty-something girl who, two generations back would have been safely married and matroned by twenty-one. And for those women who do have their men, the scenario seems just as bleak. The shoulder-padded, bejewelled boardroom-strutting dominatrices of Barbara Taylor Bradford, Judith Kranz and Shirley Conran have collapsed into the exhausted, gym-lashed, vitamin-rattling, designer-watered heroines of Maeve Haran's novel who ask: can we have it all?

But what is sauce for the goose is also sauce for the gander. Heroes can no longer count on the dumb adoring blonde hanging on their arm and we have bidden a regretful farewell to proud Mr Darcy, the dashing, blockade-running Rhett Butler, the bad-tempered, impeccably-dressed aristocrats of the delicious Georgette Heyer novel and the Gucci-loafered rats slinking between the pages of glitzy sagas. These days, heroes have a tough time for they are obliged to carry forward enough of the macho sexual brutishness of the bad old days and combine it with New Man. In the hands of less-talented writers this can be an excruciating reading experience.

Is there a discernible trend in the fiction that women read? As bookshops have sharpened up their image, literary pages have become less lofty and academic and the media expend more space on authors, reading tastes have become increasingly sophisticated. The days of the formulaic offering are in abeyance – new, harsh market conditions have seen to that – and onto the bookshelves have sprung writers of the first rank: Margaret Atwood, Jane Hamilton and Anne Tyler – coincidentally all from North America but whose fictions tackle huge epic themes as well as a mapping of individual sensibility. *Memoirs of A Geisha* by Arthur Golden, *Your Blue-Eyed Boy* by Helen Dunmore, Madeleine St John's honied, acerbic forays into the nature of modern love, Margaret Forster's translucently truthful novels, including *Lady's Maid*, and Elizabeth Jane Howard's bestselling Cazelet quartet offer a diversity of subject, settings, techniques and voices, plus the best of prose styles, building the bridge between what is considered commercial and up-market and, in this respect, making a nonsense of the perceived division.

In all this plurality of content and genre the one unifying factor is the continuing female interest and concern in dramatising and exploring feelings and relationships. 'Woman are hungry for emotion,' wrote the acute Stendhal, 'anytime and anywhere.' Naturally, love in its manifestations – comic, tragic, mental, spiritual, physical and mystical – has been mined endlessly for its fictional riches. Radcliffe Hall's *The Well of Loneliness*, Nancy Mitford's *The Pursuit of Love*, Kathryn Hume's

The Nun's Story, Colleen McCulloch's *The Thorn Birds* and Rosamunde Pilcher's *The Shell Seekers* are titles extrapolated at random from a large and varied corpus of novels that have made their mark in defining one aspect of it or another.

It is not, necessarily, love at any price. In 1847 Jane Eyre demanded equality for her heart and soul. Over a hundred and fifty years later, the widowed Anna Bouverie in *The Rector's Wife* declares that she is delighted to take a lover but is 'desperate for a rest from marriage'. Women have been busy taming the predatory, plundering male in the pages of a novel since Samuel Richardson wrote *Clarissa* and *Pamela* and it is a highly significant process, at whatever level is it tackled. Perhaps, this is the best way to sum up the tastes, concerns and voting powers of women readers. They are willing to read through the gamut of comedy, tragedy, satire and polemic because, sensible and intuitive creatures as they are, they know that the novel has provided during the space of one millennium a glorious and, in some cases, peerless education in the workings of the human heart – and it will be no different in the next.

Elizabeth Buchan is the author of Daughters of the Storm, Light of the Moon, Consider the Lily, Perfect Love *and* Against Her Nature. *For* Consider the Lily *she won the Romantic Novelists' Association Award for Romantic Novel of the Year and in 1997 she was both chairman of the Betty Trask Award and a judge for the Whitbread Prize.*

Book Clubs

David Arscott's Sussex Book Club
Church Cottage, Westmeston, Hassocks,
Sussex BN6 8RH
☎01273 846743   Fax 01273 846743
Email: 106461@compuserve.com
FOUNDED January 1998. Specialises in books
about the county of Sussex. Represents all the
major publishers of Sussex books and offers a
wide range of titles.

Artists' Choice
PO Box 3, Huntingdon, Cambridgeshire
PE18 0QX
☎01832 710201   Fax 01832 710488
Specialises in books for the amateur artist at all
levels of ability.

BCA (Book Club Associates)
87 Newman Street, London W1P 4EN
☎0171 637 0341   Fax 0171 291 3525
With two million members, BCA is Britain's
largest book club organisation. Consists of 21
book clubs, catering for general and specific in-
terests: Ancient & Medieval History Book Club,
The Arts Guild, The Book Club of Ireland, Book
of the Month Club, The Christian Book Club,
Discovery The Book Club for Children, The
English Book Club, Ergo, Escape, The Travel
Book Club, Executive World, Fantasy and
Science Fiction, History Guild, Home Software
World, The Literary Guild, Military and Aviation
Book Society, Mind, Body & Spirit, Mystery and
Thriller Guild, The New Home & Garden
Guild, Quality Paperbacks Direct, Railway Book
Club, World Books.

Bookmarks Club
1 Bloomsbury Street, London WC1B 3QE
☎0171 637 1848   Fax 0171 637 3416
New and recent books of interest to Socialists at
discount prices. Write, phone or fax for latest list.

Books for Children (Time–Life Entertainment Group Ltd)
Brettenham House, Lancaster Place, London
WC2E 7RL
☎0171 322 1400   Fax 0171 322 1488
Editor *Sian Hardy*
Editorial Director *Shelagh Casebourne*
Hardcover and paperback books for children

from newly-born to teenage. Also occasional
adult fiction and non-fiction – cookery, family
interest, parenting guides.

The Bookworm Club
Heffers Booksellers, 20 Trinity Street,
Cambridge CB2 1TY
☎01223 568650   Fax 01223 354936
Email: club@heffers.co.uk
Website: www.heffers.co.uk
Sells paperback books for children through
schools.

Citron Press Book Club
Suite 155, The Business Design Centre,
52 Upper Street, London N1 0QH
☎0171 288 6024   Fax 0171 288 6196
Website: www.citronpress.co.uk
Dedicated to new fiction 'offering a highly individual alternative in reading'. Every Citron
book includes critique cards for readers' reviews.
See also **Citron Press** under **UK Publishers**

Cygnus Book Club
PO Box 15, Llandeilo, Carmarthenshire
SA19 6YX
☎01550 777701   Fax 01550 777569
Email: enquiries@cygnus-books.co.uk
'Books which make people think.' Books on
spirituality, complementary healthcare, environmental issues, plus some management and education titles.

The Folio Society
44 Eagle Street, London WC1R 4FS
☎0171 400 4222   Fax 0171 400 4242
Fine editions of classic titles and reference; also
some children's classics.

Letterbox Library
Children's Book Cooperative, Unit 2D/2nd
Floor, Leroy House, 436 Essex Road, London
N1 3QP
☎0171 226 1633   Fax 0171 226 1768
Hard and softcover, non-sexist and multi-
cultural books for children from one to teenage.

Poetry Book Society
See entry under **Organisations
of Interest to Poets**

Readers Union Ltd

Brunel House, Newton Abbot, Devon
TQ12 2DW
☎01626 323200   Fax 01626 323318

Has nine book clubs, all dealing with specific interests: Country Review, The Craft Club, Craftsman Society, Equestrian Society, The Gardeners Society, Life Matters, Needlecrafts with Cross Stitch, Focal Point, Ramblers & Climbers Society.

Red House Book Clubs

See **Scholastic Ltd** under **UK Publishers**

The Softback Preview
(Time-Life UK)

Brettenham House, Lancaster Place, London
WC2E 7RL
☎0171 322 1427   Fax 0171 322 1488

Senior Editor *Sarah Willis*

Publishing Director *Shelagh Casebourne*

Mainly serious non-fiction.

The Women's Press Book Club

The Women's Press, 34 Great Sutton Street, London EC1V 0DX
☎0171 251 3007   Fax 0171 608 1938
Email: jas@interbooks.com
Website: www.the-womens-press.com

'Best women writers from more than 70 publishers.' Fiction, biography and autobiography; popular mind, body and spirit; health and self-help; also a collection of women's studies, social issues and current affairs.

Writers Book Society

PO Box 4, Nairn IV12 4HU
☎01667 454441   Fax 01667 454401

Specialises in books for writers.

Doing the Business

A good agent is one who understands publishing. This statement of the obvious is consistently ignored. The fault starts with the agents themselves. A number of them are attracted to the occupation by the simplicity of setting up in business. No formal qualifications are needed. Overheads are limited to a telephone, headed notepaper and a small ad in one of the literary journals. Then it is just a case of waiting for the manuscripts to pour in.

And pour they do. There are thousands of aspiring writers who are convinced that all it takes to put them into the big time is an honest broker to represent their interests. Some of them – maybe – are right but they do themselves no great service by hitching on to an incompetent however well meaning. For the trouble with many agents is that they never bother to learn the market – to find out what will sell as opposed to pushing what they think ought to sell. Their clients hang on more in desperation than in hope until the day when the letter arrives with the news that the mastermind in whom they had put their faith has decided to pack up agenting in favour of running a B&B in the West Country.

All of which begs the question. How can the best-selling or even a middle-range-selling author in the making, find the right person to exercise marketing and negotiating skills on his behalf?

To get on the list of one of the hundred best agencies, the fledgling writer must be able to show that he is capable of paying his way. He can do this by coming up with the big idea (Carole Blake of Blake Friedmann discovered Michael Ridpath's thriller *Free to Trade* on her slush pile, a chance find that made Mr Ridpath's fortune) or, more probably, by showing a body of work in evidence of talent that is bursting to take off. Neither the one-book writer nor the occasional writer ('I like to keep my hand in') is welcome.

It works both ways. If it is economically unsound for an agent to sign up a writer who is unable or unwilling to aim high, it makes even less sense for an author to give up part of a modest income when he could just as easily handle his own affairs. It would be like hiring a top lawyer to negotiate a simple letter of agreement. For this reason, few agents are interested in academic, technical or educational works.

While most agents actively seek new writers few do so by a close study of unsolicited manuscripts. More often they exercise their skills in talent spotting by reading first novels, literary magazines and review sections of the national press, or rely on word of mouth recommendations from social and professional contacts.

This fact of life often goes unrecognised by budding authors. Unsolicited manuscripts clog the agent's post. An average intake is thirty to fifty packages a month but two agents are in the eighty to a hundred category and one agent tops 150. Of these submissions, less than two per cent showed real promise. An agent who receives twenty to thirty unsolicited manuscripts a month reports 'less than five strong leads in fourteen years'.

When it comes to opening the daily post, agents much prefer to see synopses rather than completed manuscripts or at most, synopses with sample chapters. Constructive criticism is reserved for submissions that hint at potential or, as one agent concedes, 'when the writer is a friend of an existing client'.

Over the years, *The Writer's Handbook* has petitioned agents for a few lines of best advice to writers in search of representation. Here is a selection:

■ When referring to *The Writer's Handbook*, make sure you read the agent's entry carefully. Some agents don't handle certain literary material such as poetry, short stories and original dramatic works. Remember, no reputable agent charges a reading fee and authors should never agree to pay one. This system allows agents to react as briefly or as fully to new work as they like. So don't expect a detailed report as a matter of course.

■ If you want detailed criticism go to those who specialise in editorial advice such as The Literary Consultancy (see page 559).

■ Present material clearly and neatly. Submit only what is asked for. Know who your market may be (especially in non-fiction). Only ever submit a finished piece, be it a story, synopsis or sample chapter, *never* a draft.

■ Don't alienate oversubscribed agents with boastful or gimmicky letters. Make sure your opening and first chapter are as good as you can make them and send a few pages with your synopsis. When asked to send several more chapters, send consecutive ones and *not* picked from here and there (unless it is a practical non-fiction book).

■ Write – don't telephone – to one agent at a time, sending a brief covering letter to the agent concerned. Too often authors send photocopies addressed 'Dear Sir/Madam' so it is obvious all the agents in this book are being approached at the same time. These go straight into the agent's bin.

■ First-time writers should ensure that their submissions to agents include a full c.v. The completed manuscript must be typed, double-spaced and properly formatted (especially important with illustrated and children's books). Do not try to submit to publishers first and then decide to use an agent without admitting to rejections. Either write direct to publishers or use an agent from the outset. Some market research on overlap with other books is always useful.

■ Always send return postage – preferably a stamped envelope - and a stamped card if you want an acknowledgement. Agents cannot be expected to subsidise a service they give for free.

■ *Always* keep a copy of any material submitted – don't use registered post or recorded delivery as this can entail collection from a distant post office – and allow at least a month for a response.

■ It's always worth attempting to get things published in literary magazines or read on the radio and entering respected writing competitions. Anything published should be mentioned in the covering letter.

■ To those who think they can jump on the band-wagon of such subjects as political thrillers, horror, or whatever happens to be in vogue, don't do it. Write about something that matters to you and on subjects that you genuinely care about.

■ Study the market – talk to booksellers, libraries – look at catalogues, go to trade fairs. Persist, persist, persist.

It is a mistake to assume, as many do, that the strength of an agent should be judged purely on his ability to negotiate huge advances. There are agents famed for their mega-deals but like those who never feature in the headlines, they really prove their worth in knowing the pitfalls of a publishing contract and helping his client to avoid them.

The good agent understands the small print and, to greater advantage, spots the omissions – such as the failure to allow for higher royalties beyond a certain minimum sale. The agented author has a say on bookclub deals, promotion budgets, cover design, the timing of publication, print number and on subsidiary rights – the latter capable of attracting earnings long after the book is out of print. The sheer range of potential subsidiary rights is mind-boggling – overseas publication (the publisher will try for world rights but when an agent is acting, US and translation rights are nearly always reserved to the ultimate benefit of the author), film and television adaptations, audio cassettes, video, information retrieval – to mention only the most obvious. Above all, the good agent keeps a watching brief after the contract has been signed, always ready to challenge the publisher to do better on behalf of his author.

There are authors who have a natural talent for wheeler-dealing and prefer to remain unagented. Others would dearly like to be represented but for the life of them cannot find an agent to suit their personality or are rejected because the agent of their choice is already overloaded with clients. Fortunately, there is a way of breaking the impasse and that is to join the **Society of Authors**. There is always someone there to advise - on a contract and to run a cynical eye over the more abstruse clauses.

There are writers and publishers who swear by the **Association of Authors' Agents**. To qualify, an agent must have been in business for three or more years and bring in average commissions totalling not less than £25,000 a year. The Association's code of practice rules that all monies due to clients should be paid within 21 days of cheques being cleared.

Agents who specialise in representing playwrights and screenwriters (not to mention directors, producers and actors) are likely to belong to the **Personal Managers' Association**. Where a client's interests overlap (a playwright may turn to novel writing, or a novelist may become a top-flight television dramatist), two or more specialist agencies may cooperate on a shared-commission basis. These interlocked deals are on the increase.

Advice frequently given by the agented to the agentless is to seek out the opinion of authors who have been through the mill and learn from their experiences. Writers' circles and seminars organised by the Society of Authors and the **Writers' Guild** are fruitful sources of gossip.

It is useful to know from the start what agents charge for their services. Ten per cent is standard but an increasing number go for 15 per cent and a few pitch as high as 17½ or 20 per cent – plus VAT. A VATable author can reclaim the tax. Others must add 17½ per cent to the commission to calculate the agent's deduction from earnings. Some agents invoice certain administrative costs such as photocopying.

Do not be disappointed if an agent, or even several agents, gives the thumbs down. They may be overloaded with clients. But even if this is not so, remember that all writing is in the realm of value judgement. Where one agent fails to see talent, another may be more perceptive. The best advice is to keep trying.

A good agent combines the skills of a salesman, an accountant and a lawyer. If asked to provide his own job definition, he would probably call himself a professional adviser. But never a teacher. On one thing all agents agree. They do not expect to tell anyone how to write.

The Society of Authors, 84 Drayton Gardens, London SW10 9SB. ☎*0171 373 6642; Fax 0171 373 5768*

The Writers' Guild of Great Britain, 430 Edgware Road, London W2 1EH. ☎*0171 723 8074; Fax 0171 706 2413*

Association of Authors' Agents, c/o Sheil Land Associates Ltd, 43 Doughty Street, London WC1N 2LF. ☎ *0171 405 9351; Fax 0171 831 2127*

Personal Managers' Association Ltd, 1 Summer Road, East Molesey, Surrey KT8 9LX. ☎*/Fax 0181 398 9796*

UK Agents

★ = Members of the **Association of Authors' Agents**

The Agency (London) Ltd★
24 Pottery Lane, Holland Park, London
W11 4LZ
☎0171 727 1346   Fax 0171 727 9037
Email: info@theagency.co.uk

Contact *Stephen Durbridge, Leah Schmidt,
Sebastian Born, Julia Kreitman, Bethan Evans,
Hilary Delamere, Katie Haines*

FOUNDED 1995. *Handles* children's fiction, TV,
film, theatre, radio scripts. No adult fiction or
non-fiction. Unsolicited TV, film and radio
scripts welcome. Send letter with s.a.e. No
reading fee. CLIENTS include William Boyd,
Andrew Davies, Jimmy McGovern, Lucy
Gannon. *Commission* Home 10%; US various.

Gillon Aitken Associates Ltd★
29 Fernshaw Road, London SW10 0TG
☎0171 351 7561   Fax 0171 376 3594

Contact *Gillon Aitken, Antony Harwood,
Emma Parry, Clare Alexander*

FOUNDED 1984. *Handles* fiction and non-fiction.
No plays or scripts unless by existing clients.
Send preliminary letter, with synopsis and return
postage, in the first instance. No reading fee.
CLIENTS include Pat Barker, Agatha Christie,
Sebastian Faulks, Helen Fielding, Germaine
Greer, Alan Hollinghurst, Susan Howatch, A. L.
Kennedy, Douglas Kennedy, Pauline Melville,
V. S. Naipul, Tim Parks, Caryl Phillips, Piers
Paul Read. *Commission* Home 10%; US 15%;
Translation 20%.

Michael Alcock Management
5–7 Young Street, London W8 5EH
☎0171 937 5277   Fax 0171 937 2833
Email: michaelalcock@compuserve.com

Contact *Michael Alcock*

FOUNDED 1997. *Handles* general non-fiction
including current affairs, biography and memoirs, history, lifestyle, health and personal
development, media; and literary and commercial mainstream fiction. No poetry or plays. No
unsolicited mss; approach in writing in the first
instance giving details of writing and other
media experience, plus synopsis and s.a.e. (for
fiction send first three chapters as well). No
reading fee. CLIENTS include Michael Brunson,

James Burke, Tom Dixon, Philip Dunn, Kevin
Gould, Mark Griffiths, Katherine Marsden,
Manuela Dunn Mascetti, Lynne Robinson,
Philip Weller. *Commission* Home 15%; US and
Translation 20%.

Jacintha Alexander Associates
See **Lucas Alexander Whitley**

Darley Anderson Literary, TV & Film Agency★
Estelle House, 11 Eustace Road, London
SW6 1JB
☎0171 385 6652   Fax 0171 386 5571
Email: DAnder6652@aol.com

Contact *Darley Anderson, Kerith Biggs*
(Crime/Foreign Rights), *Gabi Chase*
(Film/TV Scripts), *Elizabeth Wright*
(Women's Fiction/Love Stories/'Tear
jerkers'), *Petra Sluka* (Non-Fiction)

Run by an ex-publisher with a sympathetic
touch and a knack for spotting and encouraging talent who is known to have negotiated
over £1,000,000 in advances and a Hollywood
film deal for for one first-time novelist and a
£350,000 UK advance for another first-time
novelist. *Handles* commercial fiction & non-
fiction; also scripts for film, TV and radio. No
academic books or poetry. *Special interests*
Fiction: all types of thrillers and all types of
women's and young male fiction including
contemporary, 20th-century romantic sagas,
women in jeopardy; also crime (American/
hard-boiled/cosy/historical), horror, comedy,
all types of American and Irish novels. Non-
fiction: celebrity autobiographies, biographies,
'true life' women in jeopardy, relevatory history and science, popular psychology, self-
improvement, diet, health, beauty and fashion,
humour/cartoons, gardening, cookery, inspirational and religious. Send letter and outline
with first three chapters; return postage/s.a.e.
essential. CLIENTS Gyles Brandreth, Paul
Carson, Lee Child, Martina Cole, John
Connolly, Joseph Corvo, Jane English, Peter
Guttridge, Joan Jonker, Beryl Kingston, Frank
Lean, Deborah McKinlay, Lesley Pearse, Allan
Pease, Adrian Plass, Ben Richards, Fred
Secombe, Peter Sheridan, Julia Stephenson.
Commission Home 15%; US & Translation

20%; TV/Film/Radio 20%. *Overseas associates* Renaissance-Swanson Film/Book Agency (LA/Hollywood); and leading foreign agents throughout the world.

Anubis Literary Agency
79 Charles Gardner Road, Leamington Spa, Warwickshire CV31 3BG
☎01926 832644   Fax 01926 311607

Contact *Steve Calcutt, Maggie Heavey*

FOUNDED 1994. *Handles* mainstream adult fiction, especially historical, horror, crime and women's. Also literary fiction. No children's books, poetry, short stories, journalism, academic or non-fiction. No unsolicited mss; send a covering letter and brief (one-page) synopsis (s.a.e. essential). No telephone calls. No reading fee. *Commission* Home 15%; US & Translation 20%.

Author Literary Agents
53 Talbot Road, Highgate, London N6 4QX
☎0181 341 0442   Fax 0181 341 0442
Email: author@dial.pipex.com
Website: www.authors.co.uk

Contact *John Ridley Havergal*

'Agile agenting, all genres and media.' New writers welcome. For details, contact via email.

Yvonne Baker Associates
8 Temple Fortune Lane, London NW11 7UD
☎0181 455 8687   Fax 0181 458 3143

Contact *Yvonne Baker*

FOUNDED 1987. *Handles* scripts for TV, theatre, film and radio. Books extremely rarely. No poetry. Approach by letter giving as much detail as possible, including s.a.e. No reading fee. *Commission* Home 10%; US & Translation 20%.

Blake Friedmann Literary Agency Ltd*
122 Arlington Road, London NW1 7HP
☎0171 284 0408   Fax 0171 284 0422

Contact *Carole Blake* (books), *Julian Friedmann* (film/TV), *Conrad Williams* (original scripts/radio), *Isobel Dixon* (books)

FOUNDED 1977. *Handles* all kinds of fiction from genre to literary; a varied range of specialised and general non-fiction, plus scripts for TV, radio and film. No poetry, juvenile, science fiction or short stories (unless from existing clients). *Special interests* commercial women's fiction, literary fiction, upmarket non-fiction. Unsolicited mss welcome but initial letter with synopsis and first

two chapters preferred. Letters should contain as much information as possible on previous writing experience, aims for the future, etc. No reading fee. CLIENTS include Ted Allbeury, Jane Asher, Joanna Briscoe, Elizabeth Chadwick, Teresa Crane, Barbara Erskine, Maeve Haran, John Harvey, Ken Hom, Juliet Mead, Glenn Meade, Lawrence Norfolk, Joseph O'Connor, Eve Pollard, Michael Ridpath, Tim Sebastian. *Commission* Books: Home 15%; US & Translation 20%. Radio/TV/Film: 15%. *Overseas associates* throughout Europe, Asia and the US.

David Bolt Associates
12 Heath Drive, Send, Surrey GU23 7EP
☎01483 721118   Fax 01483 721118

Contact *David Bolt*

FOUNDED 1983. *Handles* fiction and general non-fiction. No books for small children or verse (except in special circumstances). No scripts. *Special interests* fiction, African writers, biography, history, military, theology. Preliminary letter with s.a.e. essential. Reading fee for unpublished writers. Terms on application. CLIENTS include Chinua Achebe, David Bret, Eilis Dillon, James Purdy, Joseph Rhymer, Colin Wilson. *Commission* Home 10%; US & Translation 19%.

BookBlast Ltd
21 Chesterton Road, London W10 5LY
☎0181 968 3089   Fax 0181 932 4087

Director *G. Chamberet*

HANDLES traditional and underground literature. No poetry, plays, light romance, science fiction, horror, travel, fantasy, children's, cookery, gardening, health. No reading fee. No unsolicited mss. Will suggest revisions. Preliminary letter, biographical information and s.a.e. essential, also names of agents and publishers previously contacted. *Commission* Home 10%; US 20%; Translation 20%.

Alan Brodie Representation Ltd
(incorporating **Michael Imison Playwrights Ltd**)
211 Piccadilly, London W1V 9LD
☎0171 917 2871   Fax 0171 917 2872
Email: alanbrodie@aol.com

Contact *Alan Brodie, Sarah McNair*

FOUNDED 1989. *Handles* theatre, film and TV scripts. No books. Preliminary letter plus professional recommendation and c.v. essential. No reading fee but s.a.e. required. *Commission* Home 10%; Overseas 15%.

Rosemary Bromley Literary Agency

Avington, Near Winchester, Hampshire
SO21 1DB
☎01962 779656   Fax 01962 779656
Contact *Rosemary Bromley*

FOUNDED 1981. *Handles* non-fiction. Also scripts
for TV and radio. No poetry or short stories.
Special interests natural history, leisure, biography
and cookery. No unsolicited mss. Send preliminary letter with full details. Enquiries unaccompanied by return postage will not be answered.
CLIENTS include Elisabeth Beresford, Linda
Birch, Gwen Cherrell, Teresa Collard, estate
of Fanny Cradock, Cécile Curtis, Glenn
Hamilton, Jacynth Hope-Simpson, David Rees,
Keith West, Ron Wilson, John Wingate.
Commission Home 10%; US 15%; Translation
20%; Illustration 20%.

Felicity Bryan★

2A North Parade, Banbury Road, Oxford
OX2 6LX
☎01865 513816   Fax 01865 310055
Contact *Felicity Bryan*

FOUNDED 1988. *Handles* fiction of various types
and non-fiction with emphasis on history, biog-
raphy, science and current affairs. No scripts for
TV, radio or theatre. No crafts, how-to, science
fiction or light romance. No unsolicited mss.
Best approach by letter. No reading fee.
CLIENTS include John Charmley, Liza Cody,
John Julius Norwich, Rosamunde Pilcher,
Miriam Stoppard, Roy Strong. *Commission*
Home 10%; US & Translation 20%. *Overseas
associates* Sane Toregard, Scandinavia; Andrew
Nurnberg, Europe; **Curtis Brown Ltd**, US.

Peter Bryant (Writers)

94 Adelaide Avenue, London SE4 1YR
☎0181 691 9085   Fax 0181 692 9107
Contact *Peter Bryant*

FOUNDED 1980. *Special interests* animation,
children's fiction and TV sitcoms. Also *handles*
drama scripts for theatre, radio, film and TV.
No reading fee for these categories but return
postage essential for all submissions. CLIENTS
include Isabelle Amyes, Roy Apps, Joe Boyle,
Andrew Brenner, Jimmy Hibbert, Jan Page,
Allan Plenderleith, Ruth Silvestre, Peter
Symonds, George Tarry. *Commission* 10%.
Overseas associates Hartmann & Stauffacher,
Germany.

Juliet Burton Literary Agency

2 Clifton Avenue, London W12 9DR
☎0181 762 0148   Fax 0181 743 8765
Contact *Juliet Burton*

FOUNDED 1999. *Handles* fiction and non-fiction.
Special interests crime and women's fiction. No
plays, film scripts, articles, poetry or academic
material. No reading fee. Approach in writing in
the first instance; send synopsis and two sample
chapters with s.a.e. No unsolicited mss.
Commission Home 10%; US & Translation 20%.

Campbell Thomson & McLaughlin Ltd★

1 King's Mews, London WC1N 2JA
☎0171 242 0958   Fax 0171 242 2408
Contact *John McLaughlin, Charlotte Bruton*

FOUNDED 1931. *Handles* fiction and general
non-fiction, excluding children's. No plays,
film/TV scripts, articles, short stories or poetry.
No unsolicited mss or synopses. Preliminary letter with s.a.e. essential. No reading fee. *Overseas
associates* Fox Chase Agency, Pennsylvania;
Raines & Raines, New York.

Casarotto Ramsay Ltd

National House, 60–66 Wardour Street,
London W1V 3HP
☎0171 287 4450   Fax 0171 287 9128
Email: agents@casarotto.uk.com
Film/TV/Radio *Jenne Casarotto,*
   Tracey Smith, Rachel Swann, Charlotte Kelly
Stage *Tom Erhardt, Mel Kenyon*
(Books *Handled by* **Lutyens and Rubinstein)**

Took over the agency responsibilities of
Margaret Ramsay Ltd in 1992, incorporating a
strong client list, with names like Alan
Ayckbourn, Caryl Churchill, Willy Russell and
Muriel Spark. *Handles* scripts for TV, theatre,
film and radio, plus general fiction and non-
fiction. No poetry or books for children. No
unsolicited material without preliminary letter.
CLIENTS include J. G. Ballard, Edward Bond,
Simon Callow, David Hare, Terry Jones, Neil
Jordan, Willy Russell, David Yallop. *Commission*
Home 10%; US & Translation 20%. *Overseas
associates* worldwide.

Celia Catchpole

56 Gilpin Avenue, London SW14 8QY
☎0181 255 7200   Fax 0181 288 0653
Contact *Celia Catchpole*

FOUNDED 1996. *Handles* children's books –
artists and writers. No TV, film, radio or theatre

scripts. No unsolicited mss. *Commission* Home 10% (writers) 15% (artists); US & Translation 20%. Works with associate agents abroad.

Chapman & Vincent
The Mount, Sun Hill, Royston, Hertfordshire SG8 9ATZ
☎01763 247474   Fax 01763 243033
Contact *Jennifer Chapman, Gilly Vincent*

A small agency whose clients come mainly from personal recommendation and write original non-fiction and quality fiction. Since the agency aims to look after only a small number of writers, it is not actively seeking clients but 'we are enthusiasts who are happy to consider really original work'. No poetry, children's, romantic fiction, science fiction, film scripts or avant-garde prose. No reading fee but in the case of non-fiction a fully-developed idea is required for consideration together with confirmation that a ms is 50% complete; for fiction, send a synopsis and two sample chapters. Write, please do not telephone, and enclose s.a.e. Do not send complete ms in the first instance. CLIENTS include Leslie Geddes-Brown, Sara George, Rowley Leigh, Dorit Peleg. *Commission* Home 15%; US & Europe 20%.

Mic Cheetham Literary Agency
11–12 Dover Street, London W1X 3PH
☎0171 495 2002   Fax 0171 495 5777
Contact *Mic Cheetham*

ESTABLISHED 1994. *Handles* general and literary fiction, crime and science fiction, and non-fiction. No film/TV scripts apart from existing clients. No children's, illustrated books or poetry. No unsolicited mss. Approach in writing with publishing history, first two chapters and return postage. No reading fee. CLIENTS include Iain Banks, Anita Burgh, Laurie Graham, Janette Turner Hospital, Toby Litt, Antony Sher. *Commission* Home 10%; US & Translation 20%. Works with **The Marsh Agency** for all translation rights.

Judith Chilcote Agency★
8 Wentworth Mansions, Keats Grove, London NW3 2RL
☎0171 794 3717   Fax 0171 794 7431
Email: Judybks@aol.com
Contact *Judith Chilcote*

FOUNDED 1990. *Handles* commercial fiction, TV tie-ins, health and nutrition, sport, cinema, self-help, popular psychology, biography and autobiography, cookery and current affairs. No

academic, science fiction, children's, short stories or poetry. No approaches by email; no unsolicited mss. Send letter with c.v., synopsis, three chapters and s.a.e. for return. No reading fee. CLIENTS include Jane Alexander, Richard Barber, Roger Golten, Fiona Harrold, Paul Kilduff, Brigid McConville, Douglas Thompson. *Commission* Home 15%; Overseas 20–25%.

Teresa Chris Literary Agency
43 Musard Road, London W6 8NR
☎0171 386 0633
Contact *Teresa Chris*

FOUNDED 1989. *Handles* crime, lifestyle, general, women's, commercial and literary fiction, and non-fiction: health, travel, cookery, sport and fitness, gardening etc. *Specialises* in crime fiction and commercial women's fiction. No scripts. Film and TV rights handled by co-agent. No poetry, short stories, fantasy, science fiction or horror. Unsolicited mss welcome. Send query letter with first two chapters plus two-page synopsis (*s.a.e. essential*) in the first instance. No reading fee. CLIENTS include J. Wallis Martin, Joan Marysmith, Marguerite Patten. *Commission* Home 10%; US 15%; Translation 20%. *Overseas associates* Thompson & Chris Literary Agency, USA; representatives in most other countries.

Serafina Clarke★
98 Tunis Road, London W12 7EY
☎0181 749 6979   Fax 0181 740 6862
Contact *Serafina Clarke*

FOUNDED 1980. *Handles* fiction: romance, horror, thrillers, literary; and non-fiction: travel, cookery, gardening and biography. No unsolicited approaches or mss; taking on no new authors at present.

Mary Clemmey Literary Agency★
6 Dunollie Road, London NW5 2XP
☎0171 267 1290   Fax 0171 267 1290
Contact *Mary Clemmey*

FOUNDED 1992. *Handles* fiction and non-fiction – high-quality work with an international market. No science fiction, fantasy or children's books. TV, film, radio and theatre scripts from existing clients only. No unsolicited mss. Approach by letter giving a description of the work in the first instance. S.a.e. essential. No reading fee. CLIENTS include Paul Gilroy, Sheila Kitzinger, Ray Shell, Elaine Showalter, Prof. David Wiggins; US & Canadian clients: The Bukowski Agency, **Frederick Hill Associates**,

Lynn C. Franklin Associates Ltd, The Miller Agency, Roslyn Targ Literary Agency Inc. *Commission* Home 10%; US & Translation 20%. *Overseas Associate* Elaine Markson Literary Agency, New York.

Jonathan Clowes Ltd★
10 Iron Bridge House, Bridge Approach, London NW1 8BD
☎0171 722 7674   Fax 0171 722 7677
Contact *Brie Burkeman, Lisa Whadcock*
FOUNDED 1960. Pronounced 'clewes'. Now one of the biggest fish in the pond, and not really for the untried unless they are true high-flyers. Fiction and non-fiction, plus scripts. No textbooks or children's. *Special interests* situation comedy, film and television rights. No unsolicited mss; authors come by recommendation or by successful follow-ups to preliminary letters. CLIENTS include David Bellamy, Michael Cooney, Len Deighton, Elizabeth Jane Howard, Doris Lessing, David Nobbs, and the estate of Kingsley Amis. *Commission* Home & US 15%; Translation 19%. *Overseas associates* **Andrew Nurnberg Associates**; Sane Töregard Agency.

Elspeth Cochrane Agency
11–13 Orlando Road, London SW4 0LE
☎0171 622 0314/4279   Fax 0171 622 5815
Contact *Elspeth Cochrane*
FOUNDED 1960. *Handles* fiction, non-fiction, biographies, screenplays. Subjects have included Marlon Brando, Sean Connery, Clint Eastwood, Lord Olivier. Also scripts for all media, with special interest in drama. No unsolicited mss. Preliminary letter, synopsis and s.a.e. is essential in the first instance. CLIENTS include Royce Ryton, Robert Tanitch. *Commission* 12½% ('but this can change; the percentage is negotiable, as is the sum paid to the writer').

Rosica Colin Ltd
1 Clareville Grove Mews, London SW7 5AH
☎0171 370 1080   Fax 0171 244 6441
Contact *Joanna Marston*
FOUNDED 1949. *Handles* all full-length mss, plus theatre, film, television and sound broadcasting. Preliminary letter with return postage essential; writers should outline their writing credits and whether their mss have previously been submitted elsewhere. May take 3–4 months to consider full mss; synopsis preferred in the first instance. No reading fee. *Commission* Home 10%; US 15%; Translation 20%.

Combrógos Literary Agency
10 Heol Don, Whitchurch, Cardiff CF4 2AU
☎01222 623359   Fax 01222 529202
Contact *Meic Stephens*
FOUNDED 1990. *Specialises* in books about Wales or by Welsh authors, including novels, short stories, poetry, biography and general. Good contacts in Wales and London. Also editorial services, arts and media research. No unsolicited mss; preliminary letter (s.a.e. essential). *Commission* 10%.

Jane Conway-Gordon★
1 Old Compton Street, London W1V 5PH
☎0171 494 0148   Fax 0171 287 9264
Contact *Jane Conway-Gordon*
FOUNDED 1982. Works in association with **Andrew Mann Ltd**. *Handles* fiction and general non-fiction, plus occasional scripts for TV/radio/theatre. No poetry or science fiction. Unsolicited mss welcome; preliminary letter and return postage essential. No reading fee. *Commission* Home 10%; US & Translation 20%. *Overseas associates* **McIntosh & Otis, Inc.**, New York; plus agencies throughout Europe and Japan.

Rupert Crew Ltd★
1A King's Mews, London WC1N 2JA
☎0171 242 8586
Fax 0171 831 7914
Email: (correspondence only)
    rupertcrew@compuserve.com
Contact *Doreen Montgomery,*
    Caroline Montgomery
FOUNDED 1927. International representation, handling volume and subsidiary rights in fiction and non-fiction properties. No plays or poetry, journalism or short stories. Preliminary letter and return postage essential. No reading fee. *Commission* Home 15%; Elsewhere 20%.

The Croft Agency
13 Croft Road, Caister–on–Sea, Great Yarmouth, Norfolk NR30 5EJ
☎01493 721919
Contact *John Laity*
FOUNDED 1995. *Handles* general fiction including crime, suspense and drama, murder mysteries, adventure, thrillers and novels with 'social issues'. No poetry, children's, science fiction, occult, supernatural, cookbooks or picture books. 'The agency is always interested in hearing from new and previously unpublished authors.' *No unsolicited mss or part mss. Initial*

enquiry by letter only (no phone calls) and s.a.e. for agency conditions and free copy of 'helpful hints' for new authors. All mss will be read; minor revisions suggested free of charge. Reading/critique fee from £10, refunded from commission. May charge admin/submission fee. CLIENTS John Collins, Catherine Hill, B. M. Rogers, Jonathan Sparkes. *Commission* Home 10%; US 15%; Translation 20%.

Curtis Brown Group Ltd★
Haymarket House, 28/29 Haymarket, London SW1Y 4SP
☎0171 396 6600   Fax 0171 396 0110
Chairman *Paul Scherer*
Group Managing Director *Jonathan Lloyd*
Directors *Jane Bradish-Ellames, Mark*
  Collingbourne (Finance), Tim Curnow
  (Australia), Sue Freathy, Jonny Geller, Giles
  Gordon, Diana Mackay, Nick Marston (MD,
  Media Division), Anthea Morton-Saner, Peter
  Murphy, Peter Robinson, Vivienne Schuster,
  Michael Shaw, Elizabeth Stevens

Long-established literary agency, whose first sales were made in 1899. Merged with John Farquharson, forming the Curtis Brown Group Ltd in 1989. *Handles* a wide range of subjects including fiction, general non-fiction, children's and specialist, scripts for film, TV, theatre and radio. Send synopsis with covering letter and c.v. rather than complete mss. No reading fee. *Commission* Home 10%; US & Translation 20%. *Overseas associates* in Australia, Canada and the US.

Judy Daish Associates Ltd
2 St Charles Place, London W10 6EG
☎0181 964 8811   Fax 0181 964 8966
Contact *Judy Daish, Sara Stroud,*
  Deborah Harwood

FOUNDED 1978. Theatrical literary agent. *Handles* scripts for film, TV, theatre and radio. No books. Preliminary letter essential. No unsolicited mss.

Caroline Davidson
Literary Agency
5 Queen Anne's Gardens, London W4 1TU
☎0181 995 5768   Fax 0181 994 2770
Contact *Caroline Davidson, Alice Hunt*

FOUNDED 1988. *Handles* fiction and non-fiction, including archaeology, architecture, art, astronomy, biography, cookery, crafts, design, fitness, gardening, history, investigative journalism, medicine, music, natural history, photography, reference, science, self-help and

how-to, TV tie-ins. Many highly illustrated books. Finished first novels positively welcomed. No occult, short stories, plays or poetry. Writers should telephone or send an initial letter giving details of the project together with c.v. and s.a.e. CLIENTS Susan Aldridge, Robert Baldock, Nigel Barlow, John Brackenbury, Elizabeth Bradley, Stuart Clark, Andrew Dalby, Emma Donoghue, Robert Feather, Anissa Helou, Paul Hillyard, Tom Jaine, Adrian Lyttelton, Huon Mallalieu, Simon Nolan, Diane Purkiss, S4C (the Welsh Channel Four). *Commission* US, Home, Commonwealth, Translation 12½%; occasionally more (20%) if sub-agents have to be used.

Merric Davidson Literary Agency
12 Priors Heath, Goudhurst, Cranbrook, Kent TN17 2RE
☎01580 212041   Fax 01580 212041
Contact *Merric Davidson, Wendy Suffield*

FOUNDED 1990. *Handles* fiction, general non-fiction and children's books. No scripts. No academic, short stories or articles. Particularly keen on contemporary fiction. No unsolicited mss. Send preliminary letter with synopsis and biographical details. S.a.e. essential for response. No reading fee. CLIENTS include Valerie Blumenthal, Francesca Clementis, Murray Davies, Louise Doughty, Harold Elletson, Elizabeth Harris, Alison Habens, Alison MacLeod, Frankie Park, Mark Pepper, Luke Sutherland. *Commission* Home 10%; US 15%; Translation 20%.

Felix de Wolfe
Manfield House, 1 Southampton Street, London WC2R 0LR
☎0171 379 5767   Fax 0171 836 0337
Contact *Felix de Wolfe*

FOUNDED 1938. *Handles* quality fiction only, and scripts. No non-fiction or children's. No unsolicited mss. No reading fee. CLIENTS include Jan Butlin, Robert Cogo-Fawcett, Brian Glover, Sheila Goff, Jennifer Johnston, John Kershaw, Bill MacIlwraith, Angus Mackay, Gerard McLarnon, Braham Murray, Julian Slade, Malcolm Taylor, David Thompson, Paul Todd, Dolores Walshe. *Commission* Home 12½%; US 20%.

Dorian Literary Agency (DLA)
Upper Thornehill, 27 Church Road, St Marychurch, Torquay, Devon TQ1 4QY
☎01803 312095   Fax 01803 312095
Contact *Dorothy Lumley*

FOUNDED 1986. *Handles* mainstream and commercial full-length adult fiction; specialities are women's (including contemporary and sagas), crime and thrillers; horror, science fiction and fantasy. Also, limited non-fiction: primarily self-help and media-related subjects; plus scripts for TV and radio. No poetry, children's, theatrical scripts, short stories, academic or technical. Introductory letter with synopsis/outline and first chapter (with return postage) only please. Equiries or submissions by fax or email will not be acceptable. No reading fee. CLIENTS include Stephen Jones, Brian Lumley, Amy Myers, Dee Williams. *Commission* Home 10%; US 15%; Translation 20–25%. Works with agents in most countries for translation.

Anne Drexl
8 Roland Gardens, London SW7 3PH
☎0171 244 9645
Contact *Anne Drexl*

FOUNDED 1988. *Handles* commercially orientated full-length mss for women's fiction, general, family sagas and crime. Ideas welcome for business-related books, how-to, DIY, hobbies and collecting. Strong interest too in juvenile fiction, including children's games and activity books. Writers should approach with preliminary letter and synopsis (including s.a.e.). No reading fee but may ask for a contribution to admin. costs. *Commission* Home 12½%; US & Translation 20% (but varies depending on agent used).

Toby Eady Associates Ltd
9 Orme Court, London W2 4RL
☎0171 792 0092   Fax 0171 792 0879
Contact *Toby Eady: toby@tobyeady.demon. co.uk;*
Alexandra Pringle: alexandra@tobyeady.
demon.co.uk;
Victoria Hobbs: victoria@tobyeady.demon.co.uk

Handles fiction, and non-fiction. No scripts. No unsolicited mss. Approach by letter first. No reading fee. CLIENTS include Nuha Al-Radi, Elspeth Barker, Sister Wendy Beckett, Ronan Bennett, Julia Blackburn, John Carey, Jung Chang, Bernard Cornwell, Nell Dunn, Patricia Duncker, Geoff Dyer, Lucy Ellmann, Amanda Foreman, Esther Freud, Kuki Gallmann, Tobias Hill, Michael Hofmann, Tim Jeal, Rana Kabbani, Que Lei Lei, Karl Miller, Tim Pears, Sun Shuyun, Amir Taheri, Barbara Trapido, Hong Ying. *Commission* Home 10%; US & Translation 20%. *Overseas associates* La Nouvelle Agence; Mohr Books; The English Agency, Tokyo; Jan Michael; Rosemarie Buckman.

Eddison Pearson Ltd
3rd Floor, 22 Upper Grosvenor Street,
London W1X 9PB
☎0171 629 2414   Fax 0171 629 7181
Email: box1@eddisonpearson.com
Contact *Clare Pearson*

FOUNDED 1995. *Handles* literary fiction and non-fiction, contemporary fiction, poetry for the literary market, children's books; also feature screenplays, stage plays, TV and radio scripts. Unsolicited mss with return postage welcome. Advisable to send sample chapters in the first instance. No reading fee. 'Please do not email submissions.' *Commission* Home 10%; US & Translation 15%.

Edwards Fuglewicz
49 Great Ormond Street, London WC1N 3HZ
☎0171 405 6725   Fax 0171 405 6726
Contact *Ros Edwards, Helenka Fuglewicz*

FOUNDED 1996. *Handles* fiction (literary and commercial); non-fiction: biography, current affairs, business books, music and film. No scripts. Unsolicited mss welcome; approach in writing in the first instance with covering letter giving brief c.v., up to three chapters and a synopsis (enclose s.a.e. for return of mss; disks and email submissions not acceptable). No reading fee. *Commission* Home 10%; US & Translation 20%.

Faith Evans Associates*
27 Park Avenue North, London N8 7RU
☎0181 340 9920   Fax 0181 340 9410
Contact *Faith Evans*

FOUNDED 1987. Small agency. *Handles* fiction and non-fiction. New clients by recommendation only; no unsolicited mss or phone calls, please. CLIENTS include Melissa Benn, Eleanor Bron, Caroline Conran, Helen Falconer, Midge Gillies, Saeed Jaffrey, Helena Kennedy, Cleo Laine, Seumas Milne, Christine Purkis, Sheila Rowbotham, Lorna Sage, Hwee Hwee Tan, Marion Urch, Harriet Walter, Elizabeth Wilson, Andrea Weiss. *Commission* Home 15%; US & Translation 20%. *Overseas associates* worldwide.

Lisa Eveleigh Literary Agency
26A Rochester Square, London NW1 9SA
☎0171 482 5331   Fax 0171 482 5338
Email: eveleigh@dial.pipex.com
Contact *Lisa Eveleigh*

FOUNDED 1996. *Handles* literary and commercial fiction and non-fiction. No scripts, science fiction or historical fiction. *Specialises* in rock biography, health and astrology. Unsolicited mss welcome; preliminary letter with synopsis (plus three chapters for fiction) and return postage required. No reading fee. CLIENTS include Philip Casey, Mary Flanagan, Paul Heiney, Sophie Packin, Libby Purves, Grace Wynne-Jones. *Commission* Home 10%; US & Translation 20%. *Associates* Translation: **Gillon Aitken Associates Ltd**; US: Scovil Chichak Galen.

John Farquharson*
See **Curtis Brown Group Ltd**

Film Rights Ltd
See **Laurence Fitch Ltd**

Laurence Fitch Ltd
483 Southbank House, Black Prince Road, Albert Embankment, London SE1 7SJ
☎0171 735 8171

Contact *Brendan Davis*

FOUNDED 1952, incorporating the London Play Company (1922) and in association with Film Rights Ltd (1932). *Handles* scripts for theatre, film, TV and radio only. No unsolicited mss. Send synopsis with sample scene(s) in the first instance. No reading fee. CLIENTS include Carlo Ardito, Hindi Brooks, John Chapman & Ray Cooney, John Graham, Glyn Robbins, Gene Stone, the estate of Dodie Smith, Edward Taylor. *Commission* UK 10%; Overseas 15%. *Overseas associates* worldwide.

Jill Foster Ltd
9 Barb Mews, Brook Green, London W6 7PA
☎0171 602 1263   Fax 0171 602 9336

Contact *Jill Foster, Alison Finch, Ann Foster, Kim Dockrey*

FOUNDED 1976. *Handles* scripts for TV, drama and comedy. No fiction, short stories or poetry. No unsolicited mss; approach by letter in the first instance. No reading fee. CLIENTS include Colin Bostock-Smith, Jan Etherington and Gavin Petrie, Phil Ford, Rob Gittins, Julia Jones, Peter Tilbury, Peter Tinniswood, Susan Wilkins. *Commission* Home 12½%; US & Translation 15%.

Fox & Howard Literary Agency
4 Bramerton Street, London SW3 5JX
☎0171 352 8691   Fax 0171 352 8691

Contact *Chelsey Fox, Charlotte Howard*

FOUNDED 1992. A small agency, specialising in non-fiction, that prides itself on 'working closely with its authors'. *Handles* biography, popular history, current affairs, reference, business, gardening, mind, body and spirit, self-help, health. No scripts. No poetry, plays, short stories, children's, science fiction, fantasy and horror. No unsolicited mss; send letter, synopsis and sample chapter with s.a.e. for response. No reading fee. CLIENTS Sarah Bartlett, Sir Rhodes Boyson, Simon Collin, Professor Bruce King, Bill Laws, Tony Clayton Lea, Jane Struthers. *Commission* Home 10–15%; US & Translation 20%.

French's
9 Elgin Mews South, London W9 1JZ
☎0171 266 3321   Fax 0171 286 6716

Contact *Mark Taylor*

FOUNDED 1973. *Handles* fiction and non-fiction; and scripts for all media. No religious or medical books. No unsolicited mss. 'For unpublished authors we offer a reading service at £60 per ms, exclusive of postage.' Interested authors should write in the first instance. *Commission* Home 10%.

Vernon Futerman Associates*
159A Goldhurst Terrace, London NW6 3EU
☎0171 625 9601   Fax 0171 625 9601
Email: grose17@aol.com

All submissions to: 17 Deanhill Road, London SW14 7DQ
☎0181 286 4860
Fax 0181 286 4861

Academic/Politics/Current Affairs
  Vernon Futerman
Music/Art *Alexandra Groom*
Fiction/Show Business/TV & Film Scripts *Guy Rose*
Theatre Scripts *Christopher Oxford*

FOUNDED 1984. *Handles* fiction and non-fiction, including music, art, biography, politics, current affairs, show business; also scripts for film, TV and theatre. No short stories, science fiction, crafts or hobbies. No unsolicited mss; send preliminary letter with a brief resumé, detailed synopsis and s.a.e. No reading fee. CLIENTS include Lorraine Chase, Valerie Grosvenor Myer, Sir Martin Ewans, Susan George, Ernie Wise, Nigel St John Groom, Lorraine Chase, Hon. Kingsley Fielding, Angus Graham-Campbell, Victor Serebriakoff, Prince Mangal Kapoor, Angela Meredith, Sue Lenier, Joseph Miller, Aubrey Dillon-Malone, Russell Warren Howe, Judy Upton, Simon Woodham, Peter King, Dapo Odesanya, Professor Wu Ningkun, Adam Shaw, Brian Milton.

Commission Literature: Home 12½%; Overseas: 17½%. Drama/Screenplays: Home 15%; Overseas 20%; Translation 20%. *Overseas associates* USA, South Africa, France (Lora Fountain), Germany/Austria/Switzerland (Brigitte Axter).

Jüri Gabriel

35 Camberwell Grove, London SE5 8JA
☎0171 703 6186   Fax 0171 703 6186
Contact *Jüri Gabriel*

Handles quality fiction, non-fiction and (almost exclusively for existing clients) film, TV and radio rights/scripts. Jüri Gabriel worked in television, wrote books for 20 years and is chairman of **Dedalus** publishers. No short stories, articles, verse or books for children. Unsolicited mss ('Two-page synopsis and three sample chapters in first instance, please') welcome if accompanied by return postage and letter giving sufficient information about author's writing experience, aims etc. CLIENTS Nigel Cawthorne, Diana Constance, Stephen Dunn, Miriam Dunne, Pat Gray, James Hawes, Robert Irwin, Mark Lloyd, David Madsen, David Miller, Prof. Cedric Mims, John Outram, Dr Stefan Szymanski, Dr Terence White, John Wyatt, Dr Robert Youngson. *Commission* Home 10%; US & Translation 20%.

Eric Glass Ltd

28 Berkeley Square, London W1X 6HD
☎0171 629 7162   Fax 0171 499 6780
Contact *Janet Glass*

FOUNDED 1934. *Handles* fiction, non-fiction and scripts for publication or production in all media. No poetry or short stories. No unsolicited mss. No reading fee. CLIENTS include Marc Camoletti, Charles Dyer, Jack Popplewell and the estates of Rodney Ackland, Jean Cocteau, Philip King, Wolf Mankowitz, Robin Maugham, Beverley Nichols, Jean-Paul Sartre. *Commission* Home 10%; US & Translation 20% (to include sub-agent's fee). *Overseas associates* in the US, Australia, France, Germany, Greece, Holland, Italy, Japan, Poland, Scandinavia, South Africa, Spain.

David Godwin Associates

14 Goodwins Court, Covent Garden, London WC2N 4LL
☎0171 240 9992   Fax 0171 240 3007
Contact *David Godwin, Penny Jones*

FOUNDED 1996. *Handles* literary and general fiction, non-fiction, biography. No scripts, science fiction or children's. No reading fee. Send

covering letter with first three chapters. *Commission* Home 10%; Overseas 20%.

Annette Green Authors' Agent

6 Montem Street, London N4 3BE
☎0171 281 0009   Fax 0171 686 5884
Email: annettegreen@cableinet.co.uk
Contact *Material should be addressed to the Company*

FOUNDED 1998. *Handles* literary and general fiction and non-fiction, upmarket popular culture, biography and memoirs. No dramatic scripts or poetry. Preliminary letter and s.a.e. essential. No reading fee. CLIENTS include Bill Broady, Ian Marchant, Mick Barlay. *Commission* Home 15%; US & Translation 20%.

Christine Green Authors' Agent★

40 Doughty Street, London WC1N 2LF
☎0171 831 4956   Fax 0171 405 3935
Contact *Christine Green*

FOUNDED 1984. *Handles* fiction (general and literary) and general non-fiction. No scripts, poetry or children's. No unsolicited mss; initial letter and synopsis preferred. No reading fee but return postage essential. *Commission* Home 10%; US & Translation 20%.

Greene & Heaton Ltd★

37 Goldhawk Road, London W12 8QQ
☎0181 749 0315   Fax 0181 749 0318
Contact *Carol Heaton, Judith Murray, Antony Topping*

A small agency with a varied list of clients. *Handles* fiction (no science fiction, fantasy or children's books) and general non-fiction. No original scripts for theatre, film or TV. No reply to unsolicited submissions without s.a.e. and/or return postage. CLIENTS include Geraldine Bedell, Bill Bryson, Kate Charles, Jan Dalley, Colin Forbes, P. D. James, Mary Morrissy, Conor Cruise O'Brien and William Shawcross. *Commission* Home 10%; US & Translation 20%.

Gregory & Radice Authors' Agents★

3 Barb Mews, London W6 7PA
☎0171 610 4676   Fax 0171 610 4686
Contact *Jane Gregory, Dr Lisanne Radice (Editorial)*

FOUNDED 1987. *Handles* full-length fiction and non-fiction. *Special interest* crime, suspense, thrillers, literary and commercial fiction, politics. 'We are particularly successful in selling foreign rights.' No original plays, film or TV scripts (only published books are sold to film and TV). No science fiction, fantasy, poetry, academic or children's books. No reading fee. Editorial advice given to new authors. No unsolicited mss; send a preliminary letter with synopsis and first three chapters (plus return postage). No submissions by fax or email. *Commission* Home 15%; Newspapers 20%; US & Translation 20%; Radio/TV/Film 15%. Is well represented throughout Europe, Asia and USA.

David Grossman Literary Agency Ltd
118b Holland Park Avenue, London W11 4UA
☎0171 221 2770   Fax 0171 221 1445
Contact *Material should be addressed to the Company*

FOUNDED 1976. *Handles* full-length fiction and general non-fiction – good writing of all kinds and anything healthily controversial. No verse or technical books for students. No original screenplays or teleplays (only works existing in volume form are sold for performance rights). Generally works with published writers of fiction only but 'truly original, well-written novels from beginners' will be considered. Best approach by preliminary letter giving full description of the work. All material must be accompanied by return postage. No approaches or submissions by fax. No unsolicited mss. No reading fee. *Commission* Rates vary for different markets. *Overseas associates* throughout Europe, Asia, Brazil and the US.

Richard Hamilton Literary Agency
PO Box 476, Northumberland Street, Huddersfield, West Yorkshire HD1 4XY
Contact *Charlotte Smith*

FOUNDED 1997. *Handles* fiction, non-fiction, children's, poetry, TV, film and theatre scripts. No science fiction. No unsolicited mss; approach in writing with synopsis and s.a.e. in the first instance. A reading fee is charged in some instances. *Commission* Home 15%; US 20%.

Margaret Hanbury Literary Agency★
27 Walcot Square, London SE11 4UB
☎0171 735 7680   Fax 0171 793 0316
Email: mhanbury@mhanbury.demon.co.uk
Contact *Margaret Hanbury, Lisa Darnell*

Personally-run agency representing quality fiction and non-fiction. No plays, scripts, poetry,

children's books, fantasy, horror. No unsolicited mss; preliminary letter with s.a.e. essential. *Commission* Home 15%; Overseas 20%.

Roger Hancock Ltd
4 Water Lane, London NW1 8NZ
☎0171 267 4418   Fax 0171 267 0705
Contact *Material should be addressed to the Company*

FOUNDED 1961. *Special interests* drama and light entertainment. Scripts only. No books. Unsolicited mss not welcome. Initial phone call required. No reading fee. *Commission* 10%.

A. M. Heath & Co. Ltd★
79 St Martin's Lane, London WC2N 4AA
☎0171 836 4271   Fax 0171 497 2561
Contact *Bill Hamilton, Sara Fisher, Sarah Molloy*

FOUNDED 1919. *Handles* fiction, general non-fiction and children's. No dramatic scripts, poetry or short stories. Preliminary letter and synopsis essential. No reading fee. CLIENTS Joan Aiken, Christopher Andrew, Anita Brookner, Helen Cresswell, Katie Fforde, Lesley Glaister, Graham Hancock, Hilary Mantel, Hilary Norman, Susan Price, Adam Thorpe. *Commission* Home 10–15%; US & Translation 20%; Film & TV 15%. *Overseas associates* in the US, Europe, South America, Japan and the Far East.

Hermes *The Literary Agency*
5 Thames House, Manor House Lane, Datchet, Berkshire SL3 9EB
☎01753 582941
Contact *Susan Wells*

FOUNDED 1993. *Handles* full-length fiction, *specialising* in the high-concept thriller genre – manuscripts and screenplays. Unsolicited, fully revised mss accepted with return postage (also for acknowledgement), c.v., one-page synopsis, telephone numbers, and copies of all rejections. No reading fee. No telephone calls. CLIENTS include Sam Christopher, Vaughan Kent-Payne. *Commission* Home 10–15%; US & Translation 20%; Motion Picture 20%.

David Higham Associates Ltd★
5–8 Lower John Street, Golden Square, London W1R 4HA
☎0171 437 7888   Fax 0171 437 1072
Scripts *Elizabeth Cree, Nicky Lund, Georgina Ruffhead, Gemma Hirst*
Books *Bruce Hunter, Jacqueline Korn, Anthony Goff, Sara Menguc, Caroline Walsh, Daniela Bernardelle*

FOUNDED 1935. *Handles* fiction and general non-fiction: biography, history, current affairs, etc. Also scripts. Preliminary letter with synopsis essential in first instance. No reading fee. CLIENTS include John le Carré, Stephen Fry, Jane Green, James Herbert, Jeremy Paxman. *Commission* Home 10%; US & Translation 20%.

Vanessa Holt Ltd★
59 Crescent Road, Leigh-on-Sea, Essex SS9 2PF
☎01702 473787   Fax 01702 471890
Contact *Brenda White*
FOUNDED 1989. *Handles* general adult fiction and non-fiction. No scripts, poetry, academic or technical. *Specialises* in commercial and crime fiction. No unsolicited mss. Approach by letter in first instance, 'although taking on few new clients at present'; s.a.e. essential. No reading fee. *Commission* Home 10%; US & Translation 20%; Radio/TV/Film 15%.
Overseas associates in the US, Europe, South America and Japan.

Valerie Hoskins
20 Charlotte Street, London W1P 1HJ
☎0171 637 4490   Fax 0171 637 4493
Email: ValerieHoskinsAss@compuserve.com
Contact *Valerie Hoskins, Rebecca Watson*
FOUNDED 1983. *Handles* scripts for film, TV and radio. *Special interests* feature films, animation and TV. No unsolicited scripts; preliminary letter of introduction essential. No reading fee. *Commission* Home 12½%; US 20% (maximum).

Tanja Howarth Literary Agency★
19 New Row, London WC2N 4LA
☎0171 240 5553/836 4142
Fax 0171 379 0969
Email: tanja.howarth@virgin.net
Contact *Tanja Howarth*
FOUNDED 1970. Interested in taking on both fiction and non-fiction from British writers. No children's books, plays or poetry, but all other subjects considered providing the treatment is intelligent. *No unsolicited mss.* Preliminary letter preferred. No reading fee. Also an established agent for foreign literature, particularly from the German language. *Commission* Home 15%; Translation 20%.

ICM
Oxford House, 76 Oxford Street, London W1N 0AX
☎0171 636 6565   Fax 0171 323 0101
Contact *Greg Hunt, Cathy King, Michael McCoy, Alan Radcliffe, Sue Rodgers, Jessica Sykes*
FOUNDED 1973. *Handles* film, TV and theatre scripts. No books. No unsolicited mss. Preliminary letter essential. No reading fee. *Commission* 10%. *Overseas associates* ICM, New York/Los Angeles.

IMG
Pier House, Strand on the Green, Chiswick, London W4 3NN
☎0181 233 5000   Fax 0181 233 5001
Contact *Sarah Wooldridge (London), Carolyn Krupp, David Chalfant (New York)*
Part of the Mark McCormack Group. Offices in New York. *Handles* celebrity books, sports-related books, commercial fiction (New York), non-fiction, how-to business books. No TV, film, radio, theatre, children's books, poetry and academic. No unsolicited mss; send letter with c.v., synopsis, three chapters and s.a.e. CLIENTS include Tony Buzan, Pat Conroy, Mark McCormack, professional sports stars, classical musicians, broadcasting personalities. *Commission* Home & US 20%; Translation 25%.

Michael Imison Playwrights Ltd
See **Alan Brodie Representation Ltd**

Intercontinental Literary Agency
The Chambers (5th Floor), Chelsea Harbour, London SW10 0XF
☎0171 351 4763   Fax 0171 351 4809
Contact *Anthony Guest Gornall, Nicki Kennedy, Jessica Buckman*
FOUNDED 1965. *Handles* translation rights only for, among others, the authors of **Peters Fraser & Dunlop**, London; Lucci Alexander Whitley, London; Harold Matson Co. Inc., New York.

International Copyright Bureau Ltd
22A Aubrey House, Maida Avenue, London W2 1TQ
☎0171 724 8034   Fax 0171 724 7662
Contact *Joy Westendarp*
FOUNDED 1905. *Handles* scripts for TV, theatre, film and radio. Now mainly represent-

ing authors' estates and not taking on new clients. *Commission* Home 10%; US & Translation 19%. *Overseas agents* in New York and most foreign countries.

International Scripts
1 Norland Square, London W11 4PX
☎0171 229 0736   Fax 0171 792 3287
Contact *Bob Tanner, Pat Hornsey, Jill Lawson*

FOUNDED 1979 by Bob Tanner. *Handles* most types of books (non-fiction and fiction) and scripts for most media. No poetry, articles or short stories. Preliminary letter plus s.a.e. required. CLIENTS include Simon Clark, Paul Devereux, Ed Gorman, Peter Haining, Julie Harris, Robert A. Heinlein, Anna Jacobs, Richard Laymon, Nick Oldham, Mary Ryan, John and Anne Spencer, Jerry Sykes, **Barrons** (USA), **Masquerade Books** (USA). *Commission* Home 15%; US & Translation 20%. *Overseas associates* include Ralph Vicinanza, USA; Thomas Schlück, Germany; Yanez, Spain; Eliane Benisti, France.

Heather Jeeves Literary Agency
9 Kingsfield Crescent, Witney, Oxfordshire OX8 6JB
☎01993 700253   Fax 01993 700253
Contact *Heather Jeeves*

FOUNDED 1989. *Handles* general trade, specialising in crime and cookery. Scripts for TV, film, and theatre are handled through **Casarotto Ramsay Ltd**. Not interested in academic, fantasy, science fiction, romances, poetry, short stories, sports, military history or freelance journalism. *No* unsolicited mss. First approach in writing, describing the project and professional experience. Return postage essential. No reading fee. CLIENTS include Debbie Bliss, Lindsey Davis, estates of H. M. Bateman and Elspeth Huxley, Susan Kay, Mark Timlin. *Commission* Home 10%; US 15–20%; Translation 20%. *Overseas associates* throughout Europe, USA and Japan.

John Johnson (Authors' Agent) Limited★
Clerkenwell House, 45/47 Clerkenwell Green, London EC1R 0HT
☎0171 251 0125   Fax 0171 251 2172
Contact *Andrew Hewson, Margaret Hewson, Elizabeth Fairbairn*

FOUNDED 1956. *Handles* general fiction and non-fiction. No science fiction, technical or academic material. Scripts from existing clients only. No unsolicited mss; send a preliminary letter and s.a.e. in the first instance. No reading fee. *Commission* Home 10%; US 15–20%; Translation 20%.

Jane Judd Literary Agency★
18 Belitha Villas, London N1 1PD
☎0171 607 0273   Fax 0171 607 0623
Contact *Jane Judd*

FOUNDED 1986. *Handles* general fiction and non-fiction: women's fiction, crime, thrillers, literary fiction, humour, biography, investigative journalism, health, women's interests and travel. 'Looking for good contemporary women's fiction but not Mills & Boon-type.' No scripts, academic, gardening or DIY. Approach with letter, including synopsis, first chapter and return postage. Initial telephone call helpful in the case of non-fiction. CLIENTS include Patrick Anthony, John Brunner, Jillie Collings, Andy Dougan, Jill Mansell, Jonathon Porritt, Rosie Rushton, Manda Scott. *Commission* Home 10%; US & Translation 20%.

Juvenilia
Avington, Near Winchester, Hampshire SO21 1DB
☎01962 779656   Fax 01962 779656
Contact *Rosemary Bromley*

FOUNDED 1973. *Handles* young/teen fiction and picture books; non-fiction and scripts for TV and radio. No poetry or short stories unless part of a collection or picture book material. No unsolicited mss. Send preliminary letter with full details of work and biographical outline in first instance. Preliminary letters unaccompanied by return postage will not be answered. No enquiries by phone or fax. CLIENTS include Paul Aston, Elisabeth Beresford, Linda Birch, Denis Bond, Terry Deary, Steve Donald, Ann Evans, Gaye Hicyilmaz, Tom Holt, Phil McMylor, Elizabeth Pewsey, Saviour Pirotta, Eira Reeves, Kelvin Reynolds, James Riordan, Peter Riley, Malcolm Rose, Cathy Simpson, Margaret Stuart Barry, Keith West. *Commission* Home 10%; US 15%; Translation 20%.

Michelle Kass Associates★
36–38 Glasshouse Street, London W1R 5RH
☎0171 439 1624   Fax 0171 734 3394
Contact *Michelle Kass, Tishna Molla*

FOUNDED 1991. *Handles* fiction, TV, film, radio and theatre scripts. Approach with telephone call/explanatory letter in the first instance. No reading fee. *Commission* Home 10%; US & Translation 15–20%.

Frances Kelly*

111 Clifton Road, Kingston upon Thames,
Surrey KT2 6PL
☎0181 549 7830   Fax 0181 547 0051
Contact *Frances Kelly*
FOUNDED 1978. *Handles* non-fiction, including
illustrated: biography, history, art, self-help, food
& wine, complementary medicine and therapies,
New Age; and academic non-fiction in all disciplines. No scripts except for existing clients. No
unsolicited mss. Approach by letter with brief
description of work or synopsis, together with
c.v. and return postage. *Commission* Home 10%;
US & Translation 20%.

Paul Kiernan

PO Box 120, London SW3 4LU
☎0171 352 5562   Fax 0171 351 5986
Contact *Paul Kiernan*
FOUNDED 1990. *Handles* fiction and non-fiction, including autobiography and biography,
plus specialist writers like cookery or gardening.
Also scripts for TV, film, radio and theatre (TV
and film scripts from book-writing clients only).
No unsolicited mss. Preferred approach is by
letter or personal introduction. Letters should
include synopsis and brief biography. No reading fee. CLIENTS include K. Banta, Lord
Chalfont, Ambassador Walter J. P. Curley, Sir
Paul Fox. *Commission* Home 15%; US 20%.

Knight Features

20 Crescent Grove, London SW4 7AH
☎0171 622 1467   Fax 0171 622 1522
Contact *Peter Knight, Gaby Martin, Ann King-
Hall, Andrew Knight*
FOUNDED 1985. *Handles* motor sports, cartoon
books, puzzles, business, history, factual and biographical material. No poetry, science fiction or
cookery. No unsolicited mss. Send letter accompanied by c.v. and s.a.e. with synopsis of proposed work. CLIENTS include Frank Dickens,
Christopher Hilton, Gray Jolliffe, Angus McGill,
Barbara Minto, Frederic Mullally. *Commission*
dependent upon authors and territories. *Overseas
associates* United Media, US; Auspac Media,
Australia.

Labour and Management Limited (tricia sumner – literary agency)

Milton House, Milton Street, Waltham
Abbey, Essex EN9 1EZ
☎01992 711511   Fax 01992 711511
Email: TriciaSumner@classic.msn.com

Contact *Tricia Sumner*
FOUNDED 1995. *Specialises* in literary fiction,
biography, general non-fiction, theatre, TV,
radio and film. *Special interests* in multi-cultural,
gay, feminist and anti-establishment writing.
No unsolicited mss. Covering letter and brief
synopsis and sample chapters essential, together
with return postage. No reading fee. CLIENTS
Marion Baraitser, John R. Gordon, Catherine
Muschamp, Olusola Oyeleye. *Commission* Home
12½%; Overseas 20%.

Cat Ledger Literary Agency*

33 Percy Street, London W1P 9FG
☎0171 436 5030   Fax 0171 631 4273
Contact *Cat Ledger*
FOUNDED 1996. *Handles* non-fiction: popular
culture – film, music, sport, travel, humour,
biography, politics; investigative journalism;
fiction (non-genre). No scripts. No children's,
poetry, fantasy, science fiction, romance. No
unsolicited mss; approach with preliminary
letter, synopsis and s.a.e. No reading fee.
Commission Home 10%; US & Translation
20%.

Barbara Levy Literary Agency*

64 Greenhill, Hampstead High Street, London
NW3 5TZ
☎0171 435 9046   Fax 0171 431 2063
Contact *Barbara Levy, John Selby*
FOUNDED 1986. *Handles* general fiction, non-
fiction and scripts for TV and radio. No unsolicited mss. Send detailed preliminary letter in
the first instance. No reading fee. *Commission*
Home 10%; US 20%; Translation by arrangement, in conjunction with **The Marsh
Agency**. *US associate* Arcadia Ltd, New York.

Limelight Management*

33 Newman Street, London W1P 3PD
☎0171 637 2529   Fax 0171 637 2538
Contact *Fiona Lindsay, Linda Shanks*
FOUNDED 1991. *Handles* general non-fiction and
fiction books; cookery, gardening, wine, art and
crafts, health, historical and romantic. No TV,
film, radio or theatre. Not interested in science
fiction, short stories, plays, children's. *Specialises*
in illustrated books. Unsolicited mss welcome;
send preliminary letter (s.a.e. essential). No reading fee. *Commission* Home 12½%; US &
Translation 20%.

Litopia™

186 Bickenhall Mansions, Bickenhall Street,
London W1H 3DE
☎0171 224 1748   Fax 0171 224 1802
Email: enquiries@litopia.com
Website: www.litopia.com

Managing Director *Peter Cox*

FOUNDED in 1993 by author Peter Cox to manage a restricted number of clients. 'We are prepared to consider any author, known or unknown, with major international potential.' Sells directly to key overseas markets with particular emphasis on the USA. 'Litopia personnel visit New York once a month.' No radio or theatre scripts. No unsolicited mss; initial contact should be by email for a brochure and submission guidelines. No reading fee. CLIENTS Stephen Twigg, Michelle Paver, Dr Danny Penman, Isidore Rosmarin, Marnie Inskip, Peggy Brusseau. *Commission* by negotiation.

The Christopher Little
Literary Agency (1979)*

10 Eel Brook Studios, 125 Moore Park Road,
London SW6 4PS
☎0171 736 4455   Fax 0171 736 4490
Email: christopher@clittle.demon.co.uk *or*
    pwalsh@clittle.demon.co.uk

Fiction/Non-fiction *Christopher Little,*
    Patrick Walsh
Office Manager *Emma Schlesinger*

FOUNDED 1979. *Handles* commercial and literary full-length fiction, non-fiction, and film/TV scripts. *Special interests* crime, thrillers, autobiography, popular science and narrative, and investigative non-fiction. No reading fee. Send detailed letter ('giving a summary of present and future intentions together with track record, if any'), synopsis and/or first two chapters and s.a.e. in first instance. CLIENTS include Felice Arena, Simon Beckett, Marcus Berkmann, Colin Cameron, Harriet Castor, Linford Christie, Michael Cordy, Mike Dash, John Gordon Davis, Frankie Dettori, Ginny Elliot, Penny Faith, Simon Gandolfi, Janet Gleeson, Brian Hall, Paula Hamilton, Damon Hill, Tom Holland, Vivien Kelly, Alastair MacNeill, Robert Mawson, Marcus Palliser, Ruriko Pilgrim, A. J. Quinnell, Alvin Rakoff, Rebbecca Ray, Patrick Redmond, Candace Robb, Peter Rosenberg, J. K. Rowling, Simon Singh, Alan Smith, Frank Tallis, Laura Thompson, John Watson, James Whitaker, John Wilson. *Commission* Home 15%; US, Canada, Translation, Motion Picture 20%.

London Independent Books

26 Chalcot Crescent, London NW1 8YD
☎0171 706 0486   Fax 0171 724 3122

Proprietor *Carolyn Whitaker*

FOUNDED 1971. A self-styled 'small and idiosyncratic' agency. *Handles* fiction and non-fiction reflecting the tastes of the proprietors. All subjects considered (except computer books and young children's), providing the treatment is strong and saleable. Scripts handled only if by existing clients. *Special interests* boats, travel, travelogues, commercial fiction. No unsolicited mss; letter, synopsis and first two chapters with return postage the best approach. No reading fee. *Commission* Home 15%; US & Translation 20%.

The Andrew Lownie
Literary Agency*

17 Sutherland Street, London SW1V 4JU
☎0171 828 1274   Fax 0171 828 7608
Email:lownie@globalnet.co.uk
Website:www.andrewlownie.co.uk

Contact *Andrew Lownie*

FOUNDED 1988 *Specialises* in non-fiction, especially history, biography, current affairs, military history, UFOs, reference and packaging celebrities and journalists for the book market. Formerly a journalist, publisher and himself the author of 12 non-fiction books, Andrew Lownie's CLIENTS include Norma Major, Gloria Hunniford, Patrick MacNee, the Marquess of Bath, Ken Bates, Jeremy Thorpe, Sir John Mills, Juliet Barker, Timothy Good, Nick Pope. Approach with letter, synopsis, sample chapter and s.a.e. Translation rights handled by **The Marsh Agency**. *Commission* Worldwide 15%.

Lucas Alexander Whitley*
(incorporating Jacintha Alexander Associates)

14 Vernon Street, London W14 0RJ
☎0171 471 7900   Fax 0171 471 7910
Email: law@lawagency.co.uk

Contact *Mark Lucas, Julian Alexander,*
    Araminta Whitley, Roger Houghton, Sally
    Hughes, Celia Hayley, Lucinda Cook

FOUNDED 1996. *Handles* full-length general and literary fiction and non-fiction. No plays, poetry, textbooks, children's books or fantasy. Film and TV scripts handled for established clients only. Preliminary letter with s.a.e. essential. *Commission* Home 15%; US & Translation 20%. *Overseas associates* worldwide.

Lutyens and Rubinstein*

231 Westbourne Park Road, London
W11 1EB
☎0171 792 4855   Fax 0171 792 4833
Partners *Sarah Lutyens, Felicity Rubinstein*
Submissions *Susannah Godman*
FOUNDED 1993. *Handles* adult fiction and non-fiction books. No TV, film, radio or theatre scripts. Unsolicited mss accepted; send introductory letter, c.v., two chapters and return postage for all material submitted. No reading fee. *Commission* Home 10%; US & Translation 20%.

Duncan McAra

28 Beresford Gardens, Edinburgh EH5 3ES
☎0131 552 1558   Fax 0131 552 1558
Contact *Duncan McAra*
FOUNDED 1988. *Handles* fiction (literary fiction) and non-fiction, including art, architecture, archaeology, biography, military, travel and books of Scottish interest. Preliminary letter, synopsis and sample chapter (including return postage) essential. No reading fee. *Commission* Home 10%; Overseas by arrangement.

Bill McLean Personal Management

23B Deodar Road, London SW15 2NP
☎0181 789 8191
Contact *Bill McLean*
FOUNDED 1972. *Handles* scripts for all media. No books. No unsolicited mss. Phone call or introductory letter essential. No reading fee. CLIENTS include Dwynwen Berry, Graham Carlisle, Jane Galletly, Patrick Jones, Lynn Robertson Hay, Tony Jordan, Bill Lyons, John Maynard, Michael McStay, Les Miller, Ian Rowlands, Jeffrey Segal, Ronnie Smith, Barry Thomas, Frank Vickery, Mark Wheatley. *Commission* Home 10%.

McLean and Slora Agency

20A Eildon Street, Edinburgh EH3 5JU
☎0131 556 3368   Fax 0131 624 4029
Also at: 25 Colinton Road, Edinburgh
EH10 5DR
☎0131 447 8001
Contact *Barbara McLean, Annie Slora*
FOUNDED 1996. *Handles* literary fiction; some non-fiction including biography and cookery. *Specialises* in books of Scottish interest. No science fiction or scripts. No unsolicited mss. Send preliminary letter, synopsis, sample chapter(s); s.a.e. essential. No initial reading fee. CLIENTS

Tom Bryan, John Herdman, Ruari McLean. *Commission* Home 15%; US & Translation 25%.

Eunice McMullen Children's Literary Agent Ltd

38 Clewer Hill Road, Windsor, Berkshire
SL4 4BW
☎01753 830348   Fax 01753 833459
Contact *Eunice McMullen*
FOUNDED 1992. *Handles* all types of children's material from picture books to teenage fiction. Particularly interested in younger children's fiction and illustrated texts. Has 'an excellent' list of picture book illustrators. In need of strong picture book texts to pair with existing illustrators who don't write themselves. Authors with track record in this area preferred. No unsolicited scripts. CLIENTS include Wayne Anderson, Reg Cartwright, Richard Fowler, Charles Fuge, Adrian Henri, Simon James, Susie Jenkin-Pearce, Angela McAllister, Graham Oakley, Sue Porter, Susan Winter, David Wood. *Commission* Home 10%; US 15%; Translation 20%.

Andrew Mann Ltd*

1 Old Compton Street, London W1V 5PH
☎0171 734 4751   Fax 0171 287 9264
Email: manuscript@compuserve.com
Contact *Anne Dewe, Tina Betts*
In association with **Jane Conway-Gordon**.
FOUNDED 1975. *Handles* fiction, general non-fiction and film, TV, theatre, radio scripts. No unsolicited mss. Preliminary letter, synopsis and s.a.e. essential. No reading fee. *Commission* Home 15%; US & Translation 20%. *Overseas associates* various.

Manuscript ReSearch

PO Box 33, Bicester, Oxfordshire OX6 7PP
☎01869 323447   Fax 01869 324096
Contact *Graham Jenkins*
FOUNDED 1988. Principally *handles* scripts suitable for film/TV outlets. Will only consider book submissions from established clients. Preferred first approach from new contacts is by letter with brief outline and s.a.e. *Commission* Home 10%; Overseas 20%.

Marjacq Scripts Ltd

34 Devonshire Place, London W1N 1PE
☎0171 935 9499   Fax 0171 935 9115
Email: enquiries@marjacq.com
Website: www.marjacq.com
Contact *Mark Hayward*

HANDLES general fiction and non-fiction, and screenplays. Special interest in crime, sagas and science fiction. No poetry, children's books or plays. Send synopsis and three chapters; will suggest revision for promising mss. No reading fee. *Commission* Home 10%; Overseas 20%.

The Marsh Agency*
11/12 Dover Street, London W1X 3PH
☎0171 399 2800   Fax 0171 399 2801
Email: enquiries@marsh-agency.co.uk
Website: www.marsh-agency.co.uk

Contact *Paul Marsh, Susanna Nicklin*

FOUNDED 1994. *Handles* translation rights only. No TV, film, radio or theatre. No unsolicited mss. CLIENTS include several British and American agencies and publishers. *Commission* 10%.

Martinez Literary Agency
60 Oakwood Avenue, Southgate, London N14 6QL
☎0181 886 5829

Contact *Mary Martinez, Francoise Budd*

FOUNDED 1988. *Handles* high-quality fiction, children's books, arts and crafts, interior design, alternative health/complementary medicine, autobiography, biography, popular music, sport and memorabilia books. No unsolicited mss. Phone call in the first instance before sending letter with synopsis; s.a.e. essential. (Possible change of address; telephone first before sending submissions.) No reading fee but may charge an admin. fee where appropriate. DTP service available. *Commission* Home 15%; US, Overseas & Translation 20%; Performance Rights 20%. *Overseas associates* various.

MBA Literary Agents Ltd*
62 Grafton Way, London W1P 5LD
☎0171 387 2076   Fax 0171 387 2042
Email: agent@mbalit.co.uk

Contact *Diana Tyler, John Richard Parker, Meg Davis, Ruth Needham, Laura Longrigg, Gil McNeil (Foreign Rights)*

FOUNDED 1971. *Handles* fiction and non-fiction. No poetry. Works in conjunction with agents in most countries. Also UK representative for **Writers House**, the Donald Maass Agency and the **Susan Schulman Agency**. No unsolicited mss. CLIENTS include Campbell Armstrong, A. L. Barker, Harry Bowling, Jeffrey Caine, Glenn Chandler, Andrew Cowan, Patricia Finney, Maggie Furey, Sue Gee, the estate of B. S. Johnson, Paul J. McAuley, Anne McCaffrey, Sir Roger Penrose, Susan Oudot, Anne Perry, Iain Sinclair, E. V. Thompson, Mark Wallington, Douglas Watkinson, Valerie Windsor. *Commission* Home 10%; Overseas 20%; Theatre/TV/Radio 10%; Film 10–20%.

Midland Exposure
4 Victoria Court, Oadby, Leicestershire LE2 4AF
☎0116 271 8332   Fax 0116 281 2188
Email: midexp@gleebody.freeserve.co.uk

Partners *Cari Crook, Lesley Gleeson*

FOUNDED 1996. *Handles* short fiction for magazines only. *Specialises* in women's, teenage and children's magazine fiction. No books. 'Keen to encourage new writers.' Unsolicited mss welcome. Reading fee of £5 per script. *Commission* Home 15–25%; US 20%.

Richard Milne Ltd
15 Summerlee Gardens, London N2 9QN
☎0181 883 3987   Fax 0181 883 0323

Contact *R. M. Sharples, K. N. Sharples*

FOUNDED 1956. *Specialises* in drama and comedy scripts for radio, film and television. Not presently in the market for new clients as 'fully committed handling work by authors we already represent'. No unsolicited mss. *Commission* Home 10%; US 15%; Translation 25%.

Jay Morris & Co., Authors' Agents
Suite 112, 91 Western Road, Brighton, East Sussex BN1 2NW
☎01273 727337   Fax 01273 775452

Directors *Jay Morris (Managing), Professor Phillida Kanta (Children's Dept)*
Assistant Directors *Toby Tillyard-Burrows, Zoë Wasson*

FOUNDED 1994. 'Selective. Aims to target fresh, real talent.' *Handles* full-length mainstream commercial adult fiction: racy sagas, gay erotica, horror, children's fantasy, women in power (not women's issues), thrillers and crime. Reading fee dependent on length of ms and publishing history of author. S.a.e. for all material essential. No faxes. Approach by letter enclosing synopsis in the first instance. CLIENTS include Lord Douglas, Piers de Villias, Elika Rise, Randet Singh, Hon. Dolores Denning. *Commission* Home 15%; Overseas 20%.

William Morris Agency UK Ltd*
1 Stratton Street, London W1X 6HB
☎0171 355 8500   Fax 0171 355 8600

Film/TV/Stage *Tanya Cohen, Jim Crabbe, Simone Ireland*
Books *Stephanie Cabot*

FOUNDED 1965. Worldwide theatrical and literary agency with offices in New York, Beverly Hills and Nashville and associates in Sydney. *Handles* film, TV, stage scripts; fiction and general non-fiction. No unsolicited film, TV or stage material *at all*. Mss for books with preliminary letter. No reading fee. *Commission* Film/TV/Theatre/UK Books 10%; US Books & Translation 20%.

Michael Motley Ltd
42 Craven Hill Gardens, London W2 3EA
☎0171 723 2973   Fax 0171 262 4566
Contact *Michael Motley*
FOUNDED 1973. *Handles* all subjects, except science fiction, horror, short mss (e.g. journalism), poetry and original dramatic material. No unsolicited mss. No reading fee. CLIENTS include Simon Brett, Richard Denny, K. M. Peyton, Annette Roome, Barry Turner. *Commission* Home 10%; US 15%; Translation 20%. *Overseas associates* in all publishing centres.

William Neill-Hall Ltd
Loganholm, Tiscott Hill, Stibb, Nr Bude, Cornwall EX23 9HL
☎01288 355335   Fax 01288 355335
Email: wneill-hall@msn.com
Contact *William Neill-Hall*
FOUNDED 1995. *Handles* general non-fiction, religion. No TV, film, theatre or radio scripts; no fiction or poetry. *Specialises* in religion, sport, history and current affairs. No unsolicited mss. Approach by phone or letter. Enclose return postage. No reading fee. CLIENTS include Mary Batchelor, Mark Bryant, Archbishop of Canterbury (George Carey), Richard Foster, Jennifer Rees Larcombe, Heather Pinchen, David Pytches, Mary Pytches. *Commission* Home 10%; US 15%; Translation 20%.

New Authors Showcase
See entry under **Miscellany**

The Maggie Noach Literary Agency★
21 Redan Street, London W14 0AB
☎0171 602 2451   Fax 0171 603 4712
Email: m-noach@dircon.co.uk
Contact *Maggie Noach*
FOUNDED 1982. Pronounced 'no-ack'. *Handles* a wide range of well-written books including general non-fiction, especially biography, commercial fiction and non-illustrated children's books for ages 7–12. No scientific, academic or specialist non-fiction. No poetry, plays, short stories or books for the very young. Recommended for promising young writers but *very* few new clients taken on as it is considered vital to give individual attention to each author's work. Unsolicited mss not welcome. Approach by letter (*not by telephone*), giving a brief description of the book and enclosing a few sample pages. Return postage essential. No reading fee. *Commission* Home 15%; US & Translation 20%.

Northern Writes
4 Pilton Road, Pilton Park, Westerhope Village, Tyne and Wear NE5 4PP
☎0191 214 5449   Fax 0191 243 4910
Email: N.Write@cableinet.co.uk
Contact *Carole Wilkinson*
FOUNDED 1997. *Handles* adult fiction (particularly reflecting contemporary life), children's fiction and humour (illustrated or otherwise; intelligent and satirical). TV, theatre, radio and film scripts also handled. No erotic, violent, science fiction, technical, non-fiction or poetry. In the first instance send synopsis and covering letter including s.a.e. 'without which there is no guarantee of a reply. Please do not telephone or fax, the first contact should always be by post.' A reading fee of £25 may be charged on acceptance of full manuscript. *Commission* Home 10%; US & Translation 20%.

Andrew Nurnberg Associates Ltd★
Clerkenwell House, 45–47 Clerkenwell Green, London EC1R 0HT
☎0171 417 8800   Fax 0171 417 8812
Email: all@nurnberg.co.uk
Directors *Andrew Nurnberg, Klaasje Mul, Sarah Nundy*
FOUNDED in the mid-1970s. *Specialises* in foreign rights, representing leading authors and agents. Branches in Moscow, Bucharest, Budapest, Prague, Sofia, Warsaw and Riga. *Commission* Home 15%; US & Translation 20%.

Alexandra Nye
44 Braemar Avenue, Dunblane, Perthshire FK15 9EB
☎01786 825114
Contact *Alexandra Nye*
FOUNDED 1991. *Handles* fiction and topical non-fiction. *Special interests* literary fiction, historicals, thrillers. Unsolicited mss welcome (s.a.e. essential

for return). Preliminary approach by letter, with synopsis, preferred. Reading fee for supply of detailed report. CLIENTS include Dr Tom Gallagher, Harry Mehta, Robin Jenkins. *Commission* Home 10%; US 20%; Translation 15%.

David O'Leary Literary Agents
10 Lansdowne Court, Lansdowne Rise, London W11 2NR
☎0171 229 1623   Fax 0171 727 9624
Contact *David O'Leary*
FOUNDED 1988. *Handles* fiction, both popular and literary, and non-fiction. Areas of interest include thrillers, history, popular science, Russia and Ireland (history and fiction). No poetry, science fiction or children's. No unsolicited mss but happy to discuss a proposal. Ring or write in the first instance. No reading fee. CLIENTS include James Barwick, David Crackanthorpe, James Kennedy, Jim Lusby, Gretta Mulrooney. *Commission* Home 10%; US 10%. *Overseas associates* Lennart Sane, Scandinavia/Spain/South America; Tuttle Mori, Japan.

Deborah Owen Ltd★
78 Narrow Street, Limehouse, London E14 8BP
☎0171 987 5119/5441   Fax 0171 538 4004
Contact *Deborah Owen, Dawn Fozard*
FOUNDED 1971. Small agency specialising in representing authors direct around the world. *Handles* international fiction and non-fiction (books which can be translated into a number of languages). No scripts, poetry, science fiction, children's or short stories. No unsolicited mss. No new authors at present. CLIENTS include Penelope Farmer, Amos Oz, Ellis Peters, Charlie Ross, Delia Smith. *Commission* Home 10%; US & Translation 15%.

Owen Robinson Literary Agents
16 Manor Close, Baston, Peterborough PE6 9PH
☎01778 560511   Fax 01778 560511
Contact *Justin Robinson*
FOUNDED 1998. *Handles* fiction, non-fiction, poetry, TV, film, theatre and radio scripts. Unsolicited mss welcome; approach in writing with s.a.e. in the first instance; send synopsis and sample pages subsequently. £75 reading fee (for full ms only; refundable upon acceptance by publisher). *Commission* Home 10%; US 15%.

Mark Paterson & Associates★
10 Brook Street, Wivenhoe, Colchester, Essex CO7 9DS
☎01206 825433   Fax 01206 822990
Email: markpaterson@compuserve.com
Contact *Mark Paterson, Mary Swinney, Penny Tyndale-Hardy*
FOUNDED 1961. World rights representatives of authors and publishers handling many subjects, with specialisation in psychoanalysis and psychotherapy. CLIENTS range from Balint, Bion, Casement and Ferenczi, through to Freud and Winnicott; plus Hugh Brogan, Peter Moss and the estates of Sir Arthur Evans, Hugh Schonfield and Dorothy Richardson. No scripts, poetry, children's, articles, short stories or 'unsaleable mediocrity'. No unsolicited mss, but preliminary letter and synopsis with s.a.e. welcome. *Commission* 20% (including sub-agent's commission).

John Pawsey
60 High Street, Tarring, Worthing, West Sussex BN14 7NR
☎01903 205167   Fax 01903 205167
Contact *John Pawsey*
FOUNDED 1981. Experience in the publishing business has helped to attract some top names here, but the door remains open for bright, new talent. *Handles* non-fiction: biography, politics, current affairs, show business, gardening, travel, sport, business and music; and fiction; will consider any well-written novel except science fiction, fantasy and horror. *Special interests* sport, current affairs and popular fiction. No drama scripts, poetry, short stories, journalism or academic. Preliminary letter with s.a.e. essential. No reading fee. CLIENTS include Jonathan Agnew, Dr David Lewis, David Rayvern Allen, Patricia Hall, Elwyn Hartley Edwards, Peter Hobday, Jon Silverman. *Commission* Home 10–15%; US & Translation 19%. *Overseas associates* in the US, Japan, South America and throughout Europe.

Maggie Pearlstine Associates Ltd★
31 Ashley Gardens, Ambrosden Avenue, London SW1P 1QE
☎0171 828 4212   Fax 0171 834 5546
Contact *Maggie Pearlstine*
FOUNDED 1989. Small, selective agency. *Handles* general and illustrated non-fiction and commercial fiction. Special interest: history, current affairs, biography and health. Only deals with children's, poetry or short stories by existing clients. Seldom takes on new authors. No un-

solicited mss. No preliminary letters by fax, email, from abroad or without s.a.e. No reading fee. CLIENTS Debbie Beckerman, John Biffen, Matthew Baylis, Kate Bingham, Menzies Campbell, Uri Geller, Prof Roger Gosden, Roy Hattersley, Prof Lisa Jardine, Charles Kennedy, Mark Leonard, Prof Nicholas Lowe, Dr Raj Persaud, Prof Lesley Regan, Jackie Rowley, Henrietta Spencer-Churchill, Dr Alan Stewart, Jack Straw, Dr Tonmoy Sharma, Dr Thomas Stuttaford, Maureen Waller, Prof Robert Winston, Shaun Woodward. Translation rights handled by **Gillon Aitken Associates Ltd**. *Commission* Home 12½% (fiction), 10% (non-fiction); US & Translation 20%; TV, Film & Journalism 20%.

Pelican Literary Agency

17 Ned Lane, Slaithwaite, Huddersfield, West Yorkshire HD7 5HQ
☎01484 846125/Mobile: 07979 226077

Contact *Mike Austin, Jessie Martin*

FOUNDED 1998. *Handles* fiction and general non-fiction – memoirs, autobiography, biography, erotica, travel and children's stories. No poetry, scripts, academic, manuals, cookery and crafts. No unsolicited mss. Send synopsis with one sample chapter with return postage. No reading fee. *Commission* Home 10%; US & Translation 15%.

Peninsula Literary Agency

'Woodbank', 17 Manesty View, Keswick, Cumbria CA12 4JF
☎017687 74880/01634 271326
Fax 017687 74880/01634 271326
Email: Peninlit@aol.com

Contact *Colin J. Wright, Lynn V. Hardley*

FOUNDED 1998. *Handles* fiction – all genres, adult and children's, poetry, short stories, general non-fiction including biography, autobiography. No scripts. Send sample chapters rather than complete mss. Contact by phone or in writing in the first instance. S.a.e. essential. No reading fee. CLIENTS Neil MacNeil, Kenneth Stephen, Marion Harris, Rory Kilalea. *Commission* Home 10%; US 15%.

Peters Fraser & Dunlop Group Ltd★

503–504 The Chambers, Chelsea Harbour, Lots Road, London SW10 0XF
☎0171 344 1000Fax 0171 352 7356/351 1756
Email: rscoular@pfd.co.uk
Website: www.pfd.co.uk

Joint Chairmen *Michael Sissons, Anthony Jones*
Managing Director *Anthony Baring*

Books *Michael Sissons, Pat Kavanagh, Caroline Dawnay, Sarah Leigh, Robert Kirby, Charles Walker, Rosemary Canter*
Serial *Pat Kavanagh, Carol MacArthur*
Film/TV *Anthony Jones, Tim Corrie, Norman North, Charles Walker, Vanessa Jones, St. John Donald, Rosemary Scoular, Natasha Galloway*
Actors *Maureen Vincent, Ginette Chalmers, Dallas Smith, Lindy King*
Theatre *Kenneth Ewing, St John Donald, Nicki Stoddart*
Children's *Rosemary Canter*
Multimedia *Rosemary Scoular*

FOUNDED 1988 as a result of the merger of A. D. Peters & Co. Ltd and Fraser & Dunlop, and was later joined by the June Hall Literary Agency. *Handles* all sorts of books including fiction and children's, plus scripts for film, theatre, radio and TV material. No third-rate DIY. No unsolicited mss. Prospective clients should write 'a full letter, with an account of what he/she has done and wants to do'. Enclose s.a.e. No reading fee. CLIENTS include Julian Barnes, Alan Bennett, A. S. Byatt, Alan Clark, Margaret Drabble, Nick Hornby, Clive James, John Mortimer, Douglas Reeman, Ruth Rendell, Anthony Sampson, Gerald Seymour, Tom Stoppard, Joanna Trollope, the estate of Evelyn Waugh. *Commission* Home 10%; US & Translation 20%.

Charles Pick Consultancy Ltd★

3/3 Bryanston Place, London W1H 7FN
☎0171 402 8043   Fax 0171 724 5990
Email: 100551.3554@compuserve.com

Contact *Martin Pick, Sandra Sljivic*

FOUNDED 1985. *Handles* Fiction and non-fiction general books. Deals only with scripts by existing clients. No unsolicited mss. Pefers an approach to be made on the recommendation of someone qualified in their field. Send letter with a short description/synopsis. CLIENTS include Wilbur Smith, Peter O'Toole, Deirdre Purcell, Julie Parsons. *Commission* Home 15%; US & Translation 20%; Film 20%.

Laurence Pollinger Limited

18 Maddox Street, London W1R 0EU
☎0171 629 9761
Fax 0171 629 9765
Email:LaurencePollinger@compuserve.com
  or 106225.3645@compuserve.com
Website:ourworld.compuserve.com/
  homepages/LaurencePollinger

Contact *Gerald J. Pollinger*
Children's Books *Lesley Hadcroft*

Foreign Rights *Heather Chalcroft*
Website: ourworld.compuserve.com/
   homepages/LaurencePollinger/
FOUNDED 1958. A successor of Pearn, Pollinger & Higham. *Handles* all types of books, including children's, except for pure science, academic or technological. Good for crime and romantic fiction. CLIENTS include Nigel Colborn, Michael Coleman, Philip Gross, Laura Kalpakian, Gene Kemp, Maureen Lee, Barbara Nadel, Gary Paulsen, Nicholas Rhea, Wendy Robertson. Also the estates of H. E. Bates, Erskine Caldwell, W. Heath Robinson, William Saroyan, Llewellyn Powys, D. H. Lawrence and other notables. Unsolicited mss welcome if preceded by letter. A contribution of £20 is requested towards editorial costs. *Commission* Home & US 15%; Translation 20%.

Shelley Power Literary Agency Ltd★

Le Montaud, 24220 Berbiguières, France
☎00 33 55329 6252   Fax 00 33 55329 6254
Email: puissant@easynet.fr
Contact *Shelley Power*
FOUNDED 1976. Shelley Power works between London and France. This is an English agency with London-based administration/accounts office and the editorial office in France. *Handles* general commercial fiction, quality fiction, business books, self-help, true crime, investigative exposés, film and entertainment. No scripts, short stories, children's or poetry. Preliminary letter with brief outline of project (plus return postage as from UK or France) essential. 'We do not consider submissions by email.' No reading fee. *Commission* Home 10%; US & Translation 19%.

PVA Management Limited

Hallow Park, Worcester WR2 6PG
☎01905 640663   Fax 01905 641842
Email: pvamanltd@aol.com
Managing Director *Paul Vaughan*
FOUNDED 1978. *Handles* non-fiction only. Please send synopsis and sample chapters together with return postage. *Commission* 15%.

Radala & Associates

17 Avenue Mansions, Finchley Road, London NW3 7AX
☎0171 794 4495   Fax 0171 431 7636
Contact *Richard Gollner, Neil Hornick, Anna Swan, Andy Marino*
FOUNDED 1970. *Handles* quality fiction, non-fiction, drama, performing and popular arts, psy-chotherapy, writing from Eastern Europe. Also provides editorial services, initiates in-house projects and can recommend independent professional readers if unable to read or comment on submissions. No poetry or screenplays. Prospective clients should send a shortish letter plus synopsis (maximum 2pp), first two chapters (double-spaced, numbered pages) and s.a.e. for return. *Commission* Home 10%; US 15–20%; Translation 20%. *Overseas associates* **Writers House, Inc.** (Al Zuckerman), New York; plus agents throughout Europe.

Rogers, Coleridge & White Ltd★

20 Powis Mews, London W11 1JN
☎0171 221 3717   Fax 0171 229 9084
Contacts *Deborah Rogers, Gill Coleridge, Patricia White, David Miller*
Foreign Rights *Ann Warnford-Davis*
FOUNDED 1967. *Handles* fiction, non-fiction and children's books. No poetry, plays or technical books. No unsolicited mss, please and no submissions by fax or email. Rights representative in UK and translation for several New York agents. *Commission* Home 10%; US 15%; Translation 20%. *Overseas associates* ICM, New York.

Hilary Rubinstein Books

32 Ladbroke Grove, London W11 3BQ
☎0171 792 4282   Fax 0171 221 5291
Contact *Hilary Rubinstein*
FOUNDED 1992. *Handles* fiction and non-fiction. No poetry or drama. Approach in writing in the first instance. No reading fee but return postage, please. CLIENTS include Lucy Irvine, Eric Lomax, Donna Williams. *Commission* Home 10%; US & Translation 20%. *Overseas associates* **Ellen Levine Literary Agency** New York; **Andrew Nurnberg Associates** (European rights).

Uli Rushby-Smith Literary Agency

72 Plimsoll Road, London N4 2EE
☎0171 354 2718   Fax 0171 354 2718
Contacts *Uli Rushby-Smith*
FOUNDED 1993. *Handles* fiction and non-fiction, commercial and literary, both adult and children's. Film and TV rights handled in conjunction with a sub-agent. No plays, poetry, science fiction or fantasy. Approach with an outline, two or three sample chapters and explanatory letter in the first instance (s.a.e. essential). No reading fee. *Commission* Home 10%; US & Translation 20%. Represents UK rights for **Curtis Brown**, New

York (children's) and 2.13.61 in the USA, Penguin (Canada) and the Alice Toledo Agency (NL).

Rosemary Sandberg Ltd
6 Bayley Street, London WC1B 3HB
☎0171 304 4110   Fax 0171 304 4109
Contact *Rosemary Sandberg*
FOUNDED 1991. In association with **Ed Victor Ltd.** *Handles* children's picture books and novels; women's interests e.g. cookery. *Specialises* in children's writers and illustrators. No unsolicited mss as client list is currently full. *Commission* 10–15%.

Tessa Sayle Agency★
11 Jubilee Place, London SW3 3TE
☎0171 823 3883   Fax 0171 823 3363
Books *Rachel Calder*
Film/TV *Jane Villiers, Matthew Bates*
Handles fiction: literary novels rather than category fiction; non-fiction: current affairs, social issues, travel, biographies, historical; TV/film: contemporary social issues or drama with comedy, rather than broad comedy. No poetry, children's, textbooks, science fiction, fantasy, horror or musicals. No unsolicited mss. Preliminary letter essential, including a brief biographical note and a synopsis. No reading fee. CLIENTS Books: Stephen Amidon, Peter Benson, Pete Davies, Margaret Forster, Georgina Hammick, Paul Hogarth, Andy Kershaw, Phillip Knightley, Rory MacLean, Denise Mina, Ann Oakley, Kate Pullinger, Ronald Searle, Gitta Sereny, William Styron, Chris Wallace, Mary Wesley. Drama: William Corlett, Shelagh Delaney, Marc Evans, John Forte, Stuart Hepburn, David Hilton, Chris Monger, Ken Russell, Sue Townsend. *Commission* Home 10%; US & Translation 20%. *Overseas associates* in the US, Japan and throughout Europe.

Seifert Dench Associates
24 D'Arblay Street, London W1V 3FH
☎0171 437 4551   Fax 0171 439 1355
Website: www.seifert-dench.co.uk
Contact *Linda Seifert, Elizabeth Dench, Michelle Arnold*
FOUNDED 1972. *Handles* scripts for TV and film. Unsolicited mss will be read, but a letter with sample of work and c.v. (plus s.a.e.) is preferred. CLIENTS include Peter Chelsom, Tony Grisoni, Stephen Volk. *Commission* Home 12½–15%. *Overseas associates* include: William Morris/Sanford Gross and C.A.A., Los Angeles.

The Sharland Organisation Ltd
9 Marlborough Crescent, London W4 1HE
☎0181 742 1919   Fax 0181 995 7688
Contact *Mike Sharland, Alice Sharland*
FOUNDED 1988. *Specialises* in national and international film and TV negotiations. Also negotiates multimedia, interactive TV deals and computer game contracts. *Handles* scripts for film, TV, radio and theatre; also non-fiction. Markets books for film and handles stage, radio, film and TV rights for authors. No scientific, technical or poetry. No unsolicited mss. Preliminary enquiry by letter or phone essential. *Commission* Home 15%; US & Translation 20%. *Overseas associates* various.

Vincent Shaw Associates Ltd
20 Jay Mews, Kensington Gore, London SW7 2EP
☎0171 581 8215   Fax 0171 225 1079
Email: vincentshaw@clara.net
Contact *Vincent Shaw*
FOUNDED 1954. *Handles* TV, radio, film and theatre scripts. Unsolicited mss welcome. Approach in writing enclosing s.a.e. No phone calls. *Commission* Home 10%; US & Translation by negotiation. *Overseas associates* Herman Chessid, New York.

Sheil Land Associates Ltd★
43 Doughty Street, London WC1N 2LF
☎0171 405 9351   Fax 0171 831 2127
Agents, UK & US *Sonia Land, Luigi Bonomi, Vivien Green, Anthony Sheil, Simon Trewin, John Rush (film/drama/TV)*
Foreign & US *Amelia Cummins, Chi Ann Rajah*
FOUNDED 1962. (Incorporates Richard Scott Simon Ltd 1971 and Christy & Moore 1912.) *Handles* full-length general, commercial and literary fiction and non-fiction, including: biography, travel, cookery and humour, UK and foreign estates. Also theatre, film, radio and TV scripts. One of the UK's more dynamic agencies, Sheil Land represents over 300 established clients and welcomes approaches from new clients looking either to start or to develop their careers. Known to negotiate sophisticated contracts with publishers. Preliminary letter with s.a.e. essential. No reading fee. CLIENTS include Peter Ackroyd, Melvyn Bragg, John Banville, Stephanie Calman, Nicky Clarke, Catherine Cookson, Josephine Cox, Seamus Deane, Alan Drury, John Fowles, Alan Garner, Susan Hill, HRH The Prince of Wales, John Humphries, John Keegan, Bernard Kops, Charlotte Lamb,

Richard Mabey, Colin McDowell, David Mellor, Andrew Miller, Van Morrison, Esther Rantzen, Pam Rhodes, Martin Riley, Colin Shindler, Tom Sharpe, Brian Sibley, Alan Titchmarsh, Rose Tremain, Sally Ward, John Wilsher, Paul Wilson. *Commission* Home 10–15%; US & Translation 20%. *Overseas associates* Georges Borchardt, Inc. (Richard Scott Simon). UK representatives for **Farrar, Straus & Giroux, Inc**. US Film and TV representation: CAA, H.N. Swanson, and others.

Caroline Sheldon Literary Agency★
71 Hillgate Place, London W8 7SS
☎0171 727 9102
Contact *Caroline Sheldon*

FOUNDED 1985. *Handles* adult fiction, in particular women's, both commercial and literary novels. Also full-length children's fiction. No TV/film scripts unless by book-writing clients. Send letter with all relevant details of ambitions and four chapters of proposed book (enclose large s.a.e.). No reading fee. *Commission* Home 10%; US & Translation 20%.

Silent Partners Ltd
c/o D.J. Harper International Ltd,
18 Redwood Road, Yew Tree Estate,
Walsall, West Midlands
☎0411 320949
Contact *Jonathan Stuart-Brown*

Handles full-length screenplays with particular interest in pieces about the lives of Catholic Saints. No unsolicited mss; send a letter in the first instance. 'Completely unsolicited material goes into the bin unread or even the shredder but everyone who phones gets a call back and a chance to state your case.'

Jeffrey Simmons
10 Lowndes Square, London SW1X 9HA
☎0171 235 8852   Fax 0171 235 9733
Contact *Jeffrey Simmons*

FOUNDED 1978. *Handles* biography and autobiography, cinema and theatre, fiction (both quality and commercial), history, law and crime, politics and world affairs, parapsychology and sport (but not exclusively). No science fiction/fantasy, children's books, cookery, crafts, hobbies or gardening. Film scripts handled only if by book-writing clients. *Special interests* personality books of all sorts and fiction from young writers (i.e. under 40) with a future. Writers become clients by personal introduction or by letter, enclosing a synopsis if possible, a brief biography, a note of any previously published books,

plus a list of any publishers and agents who have already seen the mss. *Commission* Home 10–15%; US 15%; Translation 20%.

Simpson Fox Associates
52 Shaftesbury Avenue, London W1V 7DE
☎0171 434 9167   Fax 0171 494 2887
Contact *Georgina Capel*

ESTABLISHED 1973. *Handles* literary and commercial fiction, general non-fiction, and film/play scripts. No children's books. Approach with synopsis and sample chapter, with s.a.e., in the first instance. CLIENTS include Julie Burchill, Andrew Greig, Henry Porter, Andrew Roberts. *Commission* Home, US & Translation 15%.

Robert Smith Literary Agency
12 Bridge Wharf, 156 Caledonian Road,
London N1 9UU
☎0171 278 2444   Fax 0171 833 5680
Contact *Robert Smith*

FOUNDED 1997. *Handles* mainly non-fiction; biography, lifestyle, showbusiness and true crime. No scripts, literary fiction, poetry, academic or children's books. No unsolicited mss. Send a letter and synopsis in the first instance. No reading fee. CLIENTS Liz Brewer, James Haspiel, Christine Keeler, Norman Parker, Mike Reid. *Commission* Home 15%; US & Translation 20%. *Overseas associates* Frédérique Poretta Literary Agency (France); Thomas Schlück Literary Agency (Germany).

Elaine Steel
110 Gloucester Avenue, London NW1 8HX
☎0181 348 0918/0171 483 2681
Fax 0181 341 9807
Contact *Elaine Steel*

FOUNDED 1986. *Handles* scripts and screenplays. No technical or academic. Initial phone call preferred. CLIENTS include Les Blair, Anna Campion, Michael Eaton, Brian Keenan, Troy Kennedy Martin, Rob Ritchie. *Commission* Home 10%; US & Translation 15–20%.

Abner Stein★
10 Roland Gardens, London SW7 3PH
☎0171 373 0456   Fax 0171 370 6316
Contact *Abner Stein*

FOUNDED 1971. Mainly represents US agents and authors but *handles* some full-length fiction and general non-fiction. No scientific, technical, etc. No scripts. Send letter and outline in the first instance rather than unsolicited mss. *Commission* Home 10%; US & Translation 20%.

Micheline Steinberg
Playwrights' Agent
409 Triumph House, 187–191 Regent Street,
London W1R 7WF
☎0171 287 4383   Fax 0171 287 4384
Contact *Micheline Steinberg*

FOUNDED 1988. *Specialises* in plays for stage,
TV, radio and film. Best approach by preliminary letter (with s.a.e.). Dramatic associate for
Laurence Pollinger Limited. *Commission*
Home 10%; Elsewhere 15%.

tricia sumner – literary agency
See **Labour and Management Limited**

The Susijn Agency
820 Harrow Road, London NW10 5JU
☎0181 968 7435   Fax 0181 354 0415
Email: LSusijn@aol.com
Contact *Laura Susijn*

FOUNDED April 1998. *Specialises* in selling
rights worldwide in literary fiction and non-
fiction. Preliminary letter, synopsis and first
two chapters preferred. No reading fee. Also
represents non-English language authors and
publishers for UK, US and translation rights
worldwide. *Commission* Home 15%; US &
Translation 15–20%.

J. M. Thurley Management
30 Cambridge Road, Teddington, Middlesex
TW11 8DR
☎0181 977 3176   Fax 0181 943 2678
Email: JMThurley@aol.com
Contact *Jon Thurley*

FOUNDED 1976. *Handles* full-length fiction,
non-fiction, TV and films. Particularly interested in strong commercial and literary fiction.
Will provide creative and editorial assistance to
promising writers. No unsolicited mss;
approach by letter in the first instance with
synopsis and first three chapters plus return
postage. No reading fee. *Commission* Home
15%; US & Translation 15%.

Lavinia Trevor Agency★
7 The Glasshouse, 49A Goldhawk Road,
London W12 8QP
☎0181 749 8481   Fax 0181 749 7377
Contact *Lavinia Trevor*

FOUNDED 1993. *Handles* general fiction and
non-fiction, including popular science. No
poetry, academic or technical work. No TV,
film, radio, theatre scripts. Approach with a
preliminary letter, a brief autobiography and

first 50–100 typewritten pages. S.a.e. essential.
No reading fee. *Commission* Rate by agreement
with author.

Jane Turnbull★
13 Wendell Road, London W12 9RS
☎0181 743 9580   Fax 0181 749 6079
Contact *Jane Turnbull*

FOUNDED 1986. *Handles* fiction and non-
fiction. No science fiction, sagas or romantic
fiction. *Specialises* in biography, history, current
affairs, health and diet. No unsolicited mss.
Approach with letter in the first instance. No
reading fee. CLIENTS include Penny Junor,
Kevin McCloud, Monty Roberts, Judith Wills.
Translation rights handled by **Gillon Aitken
Associates Ltd**. *Commission* Home 10%; US
15%; Translation 20%.

Utopia Media Associates
22c Belfort Road, London SE15 2JD
☎0171 639 7981   Fax 0171 252 9309
Email: utopiamedia@btinternet.com
Contact *Christopher Norris*

FOUNDED 1998. *Handles* adult fiction and non-
fiction (trade), children's books, TV, film,
radio and theatre scripts. No poetry. *Specialises*
in subjects with potential for sale in many different media; 'Utopia Media is "story-led", not
"medium-led".' No unsolicited mss. Authors
by referral. No reading fee. *Commission* Home
& US 15%; Translation 20%.

Ed Victor Ltd★
6 Bayley Street, Bedford Square, London
WC1B 3HB
☎0171 304 4100   Fax 0171 304 4111
Contact *Ed Victor, Graham Greene,
Maggie Phillips, Sophie Hicks*

FOUNDED 1976. *Handles* a broad range of material from Iris Murdoch to Jack Higgins, Erich
Segal to Erica Jong. Leans towards the more
commercial ends of the fiction and non-fiction
spectrums. No scripts, no academic. Takes on
very few new writers. After trying his hand at
book publishing and literary magazines, Ed
Victor, an ebullient American, found his true
vocation. Strong opinions, very pushy and works
hard for those whose intelligence he respects.
Loves nothing more than a good title auction.
Please telephone in the first instance. No unsolicited mss. CLIENTS include Douglas Adams,
Michael Dobbs, Frederick Forsyth, Josephine
Hart, Jack Higgins, Erica Jong, Kathy Lette, Iris
Murdoch, Erich Segal, Lisa St Aubin de Terán
and the estates of Raymond Chandler, Sir

Stephen Spender and Irving Wallace. *Commission* Home 15%; US 15%; Translation 20%.

Cecily Ware Literary Agents
19C John Spencer Square, London N1 2LZ
☎0171 359 3787   Fax 0171 226 9828
Contact *Cecily Ware, Gilly Schuster, Warren Sherman*

FOUNDED 1972. Primarily a film and TV script agency representing work in all areas: drama, children's, series/serials, adaptations, comedies, etc. Also radio and occasional general fiction. No unsolicited mss or phone calls. Approach in writing only. No reading fee. *Commission* Home 10%; US 10–20% by arrangement.

Warner Chappell Plays Ltd
Griffin House, 161 Hammersmith Road, London W6 8BS
☎0181 563 5888   Fax 0181 563 5801
Contact *Michael Callahan*

Formerly the English Theatre Guild, Warner Chappell are now both agents and publishers of scripts for the theatre. No unsolicited mss; introductory letter essential. No reading fee. CLIENTS include Ray Cooney, John Godber, Peter Gordon, Debbie Isitt, Arthur Miller, Sam Shepard, John Steinbeck. *Overseas representatives* in the US, Canada, Australia, New Zealand, India, South Africa and Zimbabwe.

Watson, Little Ltd★
Capo Di Monte, Windmill Hill, London NW3 6RJ
☎0171 431 0770   Fax 0171 431 7225
Email: sz@watlit.demon.co.uk
Contact *Sheila Watson, Mandy Little, Sugra Zaman*

Handles fiction and non-fiction. *Special interests* history, popular science, psychology, self-help and business books. No scripts. Not interested in authors who wish to be purely academic writers. Send preliminary ('intelligent') letter with synopsis. *Commission* Home 10%; US 24%; Translation 19%. *Overseas associates* worldwide.

A. P. Watt Ltd★
20 John Street, London WC1N 2DR
☎0171 405 6774   Fax 0171 831 2154
Email: hpw@hpwatt.co.uk
Directors *Caradoc King, Linda Shaughnessy, Derek Johns, Joanna Frank, Sam North*

FOUNDED 1875. The oldest-established literary agency in the world. *Handles* full-length typescripts, including children's books, screenplays

for film and TV, and plays. No poetry, academic or specialist works. No unsolicited mss accepted. CLIENTS include Quentin Blake, Marika Cobbold, Helen Dunmore, Nicholas Evans, Giles Foden, Janice Galloway, Martin Gilbert, Nadine Gordimer, Linda Grant, Colin and Jacqui Hawkins, Michael Holroyd, Michael Ignatieff, Mick Jackson, Philip Kerr, John Lanchester, Alison Lurie, Jan Morris, Andrew O'Hagan, Graham Swift, Colm Toibin and the estates of Wodehouse, Graves and Maugham. *Commission* Home 10%; US & Translation 20%.

John Welch, Literary Consultant & Agent
Milton House, Milton, Cambridge CB4 6AD
☎01223 860641   Fax 01223 440575
Contact *John Welch*

FOUNDED 1992. *Handles* military history, aviation, history, biography and sport. No poetry, children's books or scripts for radio, TV, film or theatre. Already has a full hand of authors so no new authors being considered at present. CLIENTS include Alexander Baron, Michael Calvert, Paul Clifford, Norman Scarfe, Jason Woolgar, David Wragg. *Commission* Home 10%.

Dinah Wiener Ltd★
12 Cornwall Grove, Chiswick, London W4 2LB
☎0181 994 6011   Fax 0181 994 6044
Email: dinahwiener@enterprise.net
Contact *Dinah Wiener*

FOUNDED 1985. *Handles* fiction and general non-fiction: auto/biography, popular science, cookery. No scripts, children's or poetry. Approach with preliminary letter in first instance, giving full but brief c.v. of past work and future plans. Mss submitted must include s.a.e. and be typed in double-spacing. CLIENTS include Catherine Alliott, T. J. Armstrong, Christiaan Barnard, Joy Berthoud, Malcolm Billings, Alison Brodie, Hugh Brune, Guy Burt, Victoria Corby, David Deutsch, Robin Gardiner, Daemon Goodhope, Phillip Hall, Stuart Harrison, Jenny Hobbs, Mark Jeffery, Tania Kindersley, Mary Long, Daniel Snowman, Peta Tayler, Marcia Willett. *Commission* Home 15%; US & Translation 20%.

Michael Woodward Creations Ltd
Parlington Hall, Aberford, West Yorkshire LS25 3EG
☎0113 2813913   Fax 0113 2813911
Email: art@mwc.uk.com
Contact *Michael Woodward, Janet Woodward*

FOUNDED 1979. International licensing company with own in-house studio. Worldwide representation for artists and illustrators. Current properties include *Rambling Ted, Teddy Tum Tum, Railway Children, Kit 'n' Kin, Bad Taste Bears, Robots in Big Boots*. New artists should forward full-concept synopses with sample illustrations. Scripts or stories not accepted without illustration/design or concept mock-ups. No standard commission rate; varies according to contract.

Writing Children's Fiction: or You Cannot Be Serious

Philip Pullman

Children's fiction is no different from adult fiction except for the ways in which it's not the same. For one thing, the forms you use are identical with those employed by people whose work is read only by grown-ups. A novel is a novel, a short story is a short story, whether it's by William Boyd or William Mayne, Bernard Malamud or Bernard Ashley. It can deal with any subject matter you like, but you still have to make it in the same way: you have to think of some interesting incidents, find out what connects them together, put them in the best order, and discover a voice and a point of view from which you can narrate the whole thing most effectively. The storyteller on the Palaeolithic savannahs did exactly that, and so did Marcel Proust.

Next, the process of writing itself is exactly the same, whether your readers are children or adults or both, whether you use a pencil and paper or a typewriter or a computer. It consists of sitting in one place for several hours every day and groaning immoderately while you make marks of one colour on a surface of another. Inspiration has precious little to do with it and brutal toil a great deal.

Third, the business of getting your work in front of readers happens no differently. You have to find a publisher, whose job is to take you to lunch and agree to spend money on making your words available to the public. A good agent will help you do so and get a reasonable agreement; and a good editor will help you do the difficult and vital business of seeing your work for the first time through innocent eyes. And just like the people who write books that children don't read, you will probably feel when the book is finally out that your publishers aren't spending enough on advertising, send out no review copies, have laid off all their reps, and have a long-standing feud with every single bookshop in the country, resulting in a nationwide boycott of your work. This feeling sometimes becomes a conviction that there's a secret clause in your contract, which says that instead of publishing your book on such-and-such a date, they will from that day on actively attempt to conceal its existence.

If you feel that, relax: everything's going as it should. You and your friend who writes for grown-ups are both in business. Poverty, paranoia, and the puzzled sense that everyone's getting rich and famous except you are the common fare of authors, and have been since William Caxton drew up his first contract.

But while in every other way writing for children is exactly like writing for grown-ups, there are a few minor differences between the public life of your books and that of your friend's. I've never seen this better exemplified than it was recently in the *New York Review of Books*, in a piece by the novelist Robert Stone. Writing about Philip Roth's latest book, Stone opened by praising Roth for his great achievements in the past thirty years, the authority of his voice, his manic but modulated virtuosity, his energy, and so forth. And then he went on to say that Roth was – I quote him exactly – 'an author so serious he makes most of his contemporaries seem like children's writers.' So that's what those of us who write children's books are: we are an example of what is not serious. And he doesn't mean funny, of course; he means trivial. There are several things that result from this.

For one thing, you won't see a review for weeks, if you see one at all. Review space in the newspapers for children's books is minute compared to the yards given to the latest literary biography or Booker Prize candidate. There are a few exceptions (the *Guardian* has a *Children's Book of the Week* spot, which is a treasure; though it isn't on the book pages, where the general reader might be interested in glancing at it, but in the Education supplement, where it will only be seen by specialists), but the general picture is dismal. Ask literary editors why, and they invoke that secret concealment clause in your contract: children's publishers don't spend much on advertising, apparently, so they don't get the editorial space. Personally, I don't believe it. I think it's due to the contempt that pretty well anything to do with children evokes in this country. Look at the way we pay teachers.

Then there are prizes. Children's books can win awards, just like serious books, but don't give up the day job. If you're lucky enough to win the Whitbread Children's Book of the Year award, for example, you take home a cheque for £10,000. The author of the Whitbread (adult) Book of the Year wins £21,000. Don't be surprised: you can't be trusted with a large amount of money, because you're not serious, and you'd probably spend it all on sweets.

But there's an opportunity in this.

It's simply stated: if we're not taken seriously, we can do exactly what we like. We can get away with all kinds of stuff that *they* don't notice. *They*, of course, are the literary commentators, the guardians of our culture, the inspectors of our children's moral welfare. We can write books that entertain the reader while dealing with the questions that *they* might not approve of: we can bring speculation about profound philosophical matters into books that look and behave like rattling good yarns; we can combine hard-hitting political analysis with powerful adventure; we can explore the furthest reaches of moral sensibility while telling a story of the most technically challenging kind – the kind that looks as if it's simple.

For the evidence of this, read Jan Mark, Anne Fine, Janni Howker, Peter Dickinson, Henrietta Branford, Susan Price, Alan Garner, and dozens of others. Look at the pictures and then watch how they work on the text in books by Quentin Blake, John Burningham, Shirley Hughes. And dozens of others.

Nor is that the only advantage of not being serious. There's also the way those of us whose writing is labelled 'for children' are free to move from one genre to another, from short books to long ones, from tragic to comic, from crime to fantasy to contemporary psychological fiction, and take our readers with us. Watch the way adult readers choose books, and you'll see an intractable conservatism: they go for the same kinds of books; the same shelves in the library; another one like the one they had last time. Children are more adventurous: if they like the cover, they'll try anything. And publishers of children's books are more open, in my experience, to the idea that an author might try something different next time. We have a freedom that adult writers don't have.

So far, so good. But don't we have to think about reading difficulty and levels of literacy and sentence length and all that sort of thing?

Not a bit of it. The only thing we have to remember about our readers is that they don't know as much about the world as we do. That's all. They're not less intellectually curious than grown-ups, or more stupid, or less aware that the world is complicated, or more frightened of long words, or less willing to try out new ideas; they're just not as well informed about the way things work. We have to explain a little more fully.

And what about the strange thing known as attention span? Adults who conspicuously know very little themselves are fond of saying that, of course, because of television and video games, children's attention span is now very short, so we have to give them very short pieces of story in the style of screen drama with its short scenes and rapid cuts. That's twaddle; take no notice of it. A child's attention span is as long as the story we're telling, provided that it's a good story in the first place and we know how to tell it.

But I maintain that the best attitude to this invisibility of ours is that of satisfaction. Nobody knows what we're doing. We can move about and do our work unsuspected, like secret agents. There's not even any risk of their finding out from this article, because I guarantee that no one who has any importance in the adult world will read this paragraph: the word Children at the top will make it invisible.

And there are other compensations. There's the game of watching for the subtle change in the expression of the stranger you meet at a party, and who has learned that you write books, when they find out that you write children's books. That never fails to entertain. A good way of countering it, if you want to, is to refer innocently to children's books simply as books, and to books for adults as adult books. That will make them sound like adult films or adult magazines, and we all know what that means.

In short, children's books are a place where we can be free to do proper writing that's interesting for us and nourishing for our readers, and where no one interferes. And as we work we can enjoy the company of the most enterprising and courageous publishers, like David Fickling of Scholastic; the finest designers, like Ian Butterworth of Transworld; the most efficient and persuasive publicists, like Clare Hall-Craggs of Random House; the most gifted and helpful editors (too many to mention), the most energetic sales teams, the most supportive booksellers, the best-informed librarians, and the most enthusiastic, generous, and rewarding readers in the world. In fact, writing for children is too good to share with the serious people. I think we ought to keep it a secret.

Philip Pullman writes books that are read by both children and adults. They include Northern Lights, The Subtle Knife *(both published by Scholastic), and* I Was A Rat! *(Transworld).*

National Newspapers

Departmental e-mail addresses are too numerous to include in this listing. They can be obtained from the newspaper's main switchboard or the department in question

Daily Mail
Northcliffe House, 2 Derry Street, Kensington, London W8 5TT
☎0171 938 6000   Fax 0171 937 4463
Owner *Associated Newspapers/Lord Rothermere*
Editor *Paul Dacre*
Circulation 2.34 million

In-house feature writers and regular columnists provide much of the material. Photo-stories and crusading features often appear; it's essential to hit the right note to be a successful *Mail* writer. Close scrutiny of the paper is strongly advised. Not a good bet for the unseasoned. Accepts news on savings, building societies, insurance, unit trusts, legal rights and tax.

  News Editor *Ian MacGregor*
  Business/Financial Editor *Michael Walters*
  Political Editor *David Hughes*
  Education Editor *Tony Halpin*
  Diary Editor *Nigel Dempster*
  Features Editor *Veronica Wadley*
  Literary Editor *Jane Mays*
  Sports Editor *Bryan Cooney*

Femail Jackie Annesley

Weekend: Saturday supplement **Editor** *Gillian Rowe*

Daily Record
Anderston Quay, Glasgow G3 8DA
☎0141 248 7000   Fax 0141 242 3340
Website:www.record-mail.co.uk
Owner *Mirror Group Newspapers*
Editor-in-Chief *Martin Clarke*
Circulation 685,536

Mass-market Scottish tabloid. Freelance material is generally welcome.

  News Editor *Gordon Hay*
  Features Editor *Mandy Appleyard*
  Assistant Editor (Features) *Jane Johnson*
  Financial Editor *Bill Caven*
  Education *Jamie McCaskill*
  Political Editor *Tom Brown*
  Sports Editor *James Traynor*
  Women's Page *Roz Paterson*
  Magazine Editor *Lorna Frame*

Daily Sport
19 Great Ancoats Street, Manchester M60 4BT
☎0161 236 4466   Fax 0161 236 4535
Website: www.dailysport.co.uk
Owner *Sport Newspapers Ltd*
Editor *Jeff McGowan*
Circulation 235,000

Tabloid catering for young male readership. Unsolicited material welcome; send to News Editor.

  News Editor *Simon Dean*
  Sports Editor *Marc Smith*

Daily Star
Ludgate House, 245 Blackfriars Road, London SE1 9UX
☎0171 928 8000   Fax 0171 922 7960
Website: www.megastar.co.uk
Owner *United News & Media*
Editor *Peter Hill*
Circulation 517,546

In competition with *The Sun* for off-the-wall news and features. Freelance opportunities available.

  Executive Editor *Henry Macrory*
  Deputy Editor *Hugh Whittow*
  Features Editor *Dawn Neesom*
  Sports Editor *Jim Mansell*

The Daily Telegraph
1 Canada Square, Canary Wharf, London E14 5DT
☎0171 538 5000   Fax 0171 513 2506
Website: www.telegraph.co.uk
Owner *Conrad Black*
Editor *Charles Moore*
Circulation 1.05 million

Unsolicited mss not generally welcome – 'all are carefully read and considered, but only about one in a thousand is accepted for publication'. As they receive about 20 weekly, this means about one a year. Contenders should approach the paper in writing, making clear their authority for writing on that subject. No fiction.

News Editor *Richard Spencer* Tip-offs or news reports from *bona fide* journalists. Must phone the news desk in first instance. Maximum 200 words. *Payment* minimum £10 (tip).

Arts Editor *Sarah Crompton*
Business Editor *Roland Gribben*
Political Editor *George Jones*
Diary Editor *Simon Davis* Always interested in diary pieces; contact *Peterborough* (Diary column).
Education *John Clare*
Environment *Charles Clover*
Features Editor *Richard Preston* Most material supplied by commission from established contributors. New writers are tried out by arrangement with the features editor. Approach in writing. Maximum 1500 words.
Literary Editor *John Coldstream*
Sports Editor *David Welch* Occasional opportunities for specialised items.
Style/Wellbeing Editor *Jane Taylor*
Payment by arrangement.

Daily Telegraph Weekend: Saturday colour supplement. **Editor** *Eric Bailey*. *T2*: Saturday tabloid for under-16s. **Editor** *Kitty Melrose*. Website: www.t2online.com

The Express/
The Express on Sunday
Ludgate House, 245 Blackfriars Road, London SE1 9UX
☎0171 928 8000   Fax 0171 620 1654
Website: www.expressnewspapers.co.uk
Owner *United News and Media*
Editor *Rosie Boycott*
Circulation 1.10 million (Express)/ 988,720 (Express on Sunday)

Now being run as a seven-day publication with *The Express* published Monday to Friday, *The Express on Saturday* and *The Express on Sunday*, with all editors working for each publication. The general rule of thumb is to approach in writing with an idea; all departments are prepared to look at an outline without commitment. Ideas welcome but already receives many which are 'too numerous to count'.

News Editor (Express) *Sean Rayment*
News Editor (Sunday Express)
   Simon Young
Diary Editor *John McEntee (William Hickey)*
Features Editor *Albert Read*
Business Editor *Steven Day*
Political Editor *Tony Bevins*
Financial Editor *Robert Miller*
Education Editor *Dorothy Lepkowska*
Literary Editor *Maggie Pringle*

Sports Editor *Mike Allen*
Planning Editor (News Desk) should be circulated with copies of official reports, press releases, etc., to ensure news desk cover at all times.

Saturday magazine **Editor** *Catherine Ostler*

Express on Sunday Magazine: colour supplement. **Editor** *Helen Birch*. No unsolicited mss. All contributions are commissioned. Ideas in writing only.
Payment negotiable.

Financial Times
1 Southwark Bridge, London SE1 9HL
☎0171 873 3000   Fax 0171 873 3076
Website: www.ft.com
Owner *Pearson*
Editor *Richard Lambert*
Circulation 380,581

FOUNDED 1888. Business and finance-orientated certainly, but by no means as featureless as some suppose. All feature ideas must be discussed with the department's editor in advance. Not snowed under with unsolicited contributions – they get less than any other national newspaper. Approach in writing with ideas in the first instance.

News Editor *Lionel Barber*
Features Editor *John Parker*
Arts Editor *Peter Aspden*
Financial Editor *Jonathan Guthrie*
Literary Editor *Jan Dalley*
Diary Editor *Michael Cassell*
Education *Simon Targett*
Environment *Vanessa Houlder*
Political Editor *Robert Peston*
Small Businesses *Katherine Campbell*
Sports Editor *Patrick Harverson*
Women's Interest *Edwina Ings-Chambers*

The Guardian
119 Farringdon Road, London EC1R 3ER
☎0171 278 2332   Fax 0171 837 2114
Website: www.guardian.co.uk
Owner *The Scott Trust*
Editor *Alan Rusbridger*
Circulation 402,182

Of all the nationals *The Guardian* probably offers the greatest opportunities for freelance writers, if only because it has the greatest number of specialised pages which use freelance work. But mss must be directed at a specific slot.

News Editor *Clare Margetson* No opportunities except in those regions where there is presently no local contact for news stories.

Arts/Literary Editor *Claire Armitstead*
Financial Editor *Alex Brummer*
Business Editor *Steve Bosfield*
On Line *Bill O'Neill* Science, computing and technology. A major part of Thursday's paper, almost all written by freelancers. Expertise essential – but not a trade page; written for 'the interested man in the street' and from the user's point of view. Computing/ communications (Internet) articles should be addressed to *Jack Schofield*; science articles to *Tim Radford*. Mss on disk or by email (online@ guardian.co.uk).
Diary Editor *Matthew Norman*
Education Editor *John Carvel* Expert pieces on modern education welcome. Maximum 1000 words.
Environment *John Vidal*
Features Editor *Ian Katz* Receives up to 50 unsolicited mss a day; these are passed on to relevant page editors.
Guardian Society *Malcolm Dean* Focuses on social change in the '90s – the forces affecting us, from environment to government policies. Top journalists and outside commentators on nine editorial pages.
Media Editor *Kamal Ahmed* Approximately six pieces a week, plus diary. Outside contributions are considered. All aspects of modern media, advertising and PR. Background insight important. Best approach is a note, followed by phone call.
Political Editor *Mike White*
Sports Editor *Mike Averis*
Women's Page *Becky Gardiner* Now runs three days a week. Unsolicited ideas used if they show an appreciation of the page in question. Maximum 800–1000 words.

The Guardian Weekend Saturday issue. **Editor** *Katherine Viner*. *The Guide* *Ben Olins*.

The Herald (Glasgow)

195 Albion Street, Glasgow G1 1QP
☎0141 552 6255   Fax 0141 553 3335
Website: www.theherald.co.uk
Owner *Scottish Media Group*
Editor *Harry Reid*
Circulation 101,079

The oldest national newspaper in the English-speaking world, The Herald, which dropped its 'Glasgow' prefix in February 1992, was bought by Scottish Television in 1996. Lively, quality, national Scottish daily broadsheet. Approach with ideas in writing or by phone in first instance.

News Editor *Bill McDowall*
Arts Editor *Keith Bruce*
Business Editor *Robert Powell*
Diary *Tom Shields*
Education/Environment *Liz Buie*
Sports Editor *Iain Scott*
Herald Magazine *Cate Devine*

The Independent

1 Canada Square, Canary Wharf, London E14 5DL
☎0171 293 2000   Fax 0171 293 2435
Website:www.independent.co.uk
Owner *Independent Newspapers*
Editor *Simon Kelner*
Circulation 224,494

FOUNDED October 1986. *The Independent* and *The Independent on Sunday* were acquired by Irish tycoon Tony O'Reilly's Independent Newspapers from Mirror Group Newspapers in March 1998. Particularly strong on its arts/ media coverage, with a high proportion of feature material. Theoretically, opportunities for freelancers are good. However, unsolicited mss are not welcome; most pieces originate in-house or from known and trusted outsiders. Ideas should be submitted in writing.

News Editor *Jason Burt*
Features/Financial Editor *Nick Coleman*
Arts Editor *Ian Irvine*
Business Editor *Jeremy Warner*
Education *Judith Judd*
Environment *Michael McCarthy*
Literary Editor *Boyd Tonkin*
Political Editor *Paul Waugh*
Sports Editor *Chris Maume*
Travel Editor *Simon Calder*

The Independent Magazine: Saturday supplement. **Editor** *Sue Matthias*. *The Information* **Editor** *Debbie Gordon*.

Independent on Sunday

1 Canada Square, Canary Wharf, London E14 5DL
☎0171 293 2000   Fax 0171 293 2027
Website:www.independent.co.uk/sindy/ sindy.html
Owner *Independent Newspapers*
Editor *Kim Fletcher*
Circulation 251,409

FOUNDED 1986. Regular columnists contribute most material but feature opportunites exist. Approach with ideas in first instance.

News Editor *Adam Leigh*
Features Editor *Ruth Metzstein*

Arts Editor *Jenny Turner*
Commissioning Editor, Features
  Caroline Roux
Business/City Editor *Peter Koenig*
Education Editor *Judith Judd*
Literary Editor *Suzi Feay*
Environment *Geoffrey Lean*
Political Editor *Rachel Sylvester*
Sports Editor *Neil Morton*

Review supplement. **Editor** *Kate Summerscale.*

International Herald Tribune
181 avenue Charles de Gaulle, 92200 Neuilly-
sur-Seine, France
☎0033 1 4143 9300   Fax 0033 1 4143 9338
Website: www.iht.com

Editor *Michael Getler*
Circulation 227,700

Published in France, Monday to Saturday, and
circulated in Europe, the Middle East, North
Africa, the Far East and the USA. General news,
business and financial, arts and leisure. Uses regular freelance contributors. Query letter to Features Editor in first instance.

Features Editor *Katherine Knorr*
Managing Editor *Walter Wells*

The Mail on Sunday
Northcliffe House, 2 Derry Street,
Kensington, London W8 5TS
☎0171 938 6000   Fax 0171 937 3829
Owner *Associated Newspapers/Lord Rothermere*
Editor *Peter Wright*
Circulation 2.22 million

Sunday paper with a high proportion of newsy
features and articles. Experience and judgement
required to break into its band of regular feature
writers.

News Editor *(Miss) Ray Clancy*
Financial Editor *Russell Hotton*
Business Editor *Ruth Sunderland*
Diary Editor *Nigel Dempster*
Features Editor/Women's Page
  Sian James
Literary Editor *Jane Adams*
Education Editor *Rosie Waterhouse*
Industrial/Environment Editor
  Christopher Leake
Political Editor *Joe Murphy*
Sports Editor *Daniel Evans*
Night & Day: review supplement. **Editor**
  Christena Appleyard

You – The Mail on Sunday Magazine: colour
supplement. Many feature articles, supplied
entirely by freelance writers. **Editor** *Dee Nolan*
Features Editor *Victoria Hinton*

The Mirror
1 Canada Square, Canary Wharf, London
E14 5AP
☎0171 293 3000   Fax 0171 293 3409
Website: www.mirror.co.uk

Owner *Mirror Group Newspapers*
Editor *Piers Morgan*
Circulation 2.33 million

No freelance opportunities for the inexperi-
enced, but strong writers who understand what
the tabloid market demands are always needed.

News Editor *David Leigh*
Features Editor *Mark Thomas*
Political Editor *Kevin Maguire*
Business Editor *Clinton Manning*
Education Editor *Richard Garner*
Showbusiness Diary Editor *Richard Wallace*
Sports Editor *Tony Cornell*
Women's Page *Lisa Collins*

Morning Star
1–3 Ardleigh Road, London N1 4HS
☎0171 254 0033   Fax 0171 254 5950
Email: morsta@geo2.poptel.org.uk

Owner *Peoples Press Printing Society*
Editor *John Haylett*
Circulation 9,000

Not to be confused with the *Daily Star*, the
Morning Star is the farthest left national daily.
Those with a penchant for a Marxist reading
of events and ideas can try their luck, though
feature space is as competitive here as in the
other nationals.

Business/City Editor *Brian Denny*
News/Features/Education/Women's
  Page *Chris Kasrils*
Literary Editor *Mike Parker*
Political Editor *Mike Ambrose*
Sports Editor *Amanda Kendal*

The News of the World
1 Virginia Street, London E1 9XR
☎0171 782 4000   Fax 0171 583 9504
Website: www.lineone.net

Owner *News International plc/Rupert Murdoch*
Editor *Phil Hall*
Circulation 4.18 million

Highest circulation Sunday paper. Freelance
contributions welcome. Features Department
welcomes tips and ideas. Approach by fax in
first instance with follow-up phone call.

Assistant Editor (News) *Greg Miskiw*
Assistant Editor (Features) *Gary Thompson*
Business/City Editor *Peter Prendergast*

Political/Environment Editor *Eben Black*
Sports Editor *Mike Dunn*

Sunday Magazine: colour supplement. **Editor** *Judy McGuire*. Showbiz interviews and strong human-interest features make up most of the content, but there are no strict rules about what is "interesting'. Unsolicited mss and ideas welcome.

The Observer

119 Farringdon Road, London EC1R 3ER
☎0171 278 2332   Fax 0171 713 4250
Email: editor@observer.co.uk
Website: www.observer.co.uk

Owner *Guardian Newspapers Ltd*
Editor *Roger Alton*
Circulation 402,484

FOUNDED 1791. Acquired by Guardian Newspapers from Lonrho in May 1993. Occupies the middle ground of Sunday newspaper politics. Unsolicited material is not generally welcome, 'except from distinguished, established writers'. Receives far too many unsolicited offerings already. No news, fiction or special page opportunities. The newspaper runs annual competitions which change from year to year. Details are advertised in the newspaper.

  Home News Editor *Andy Malone*
  Features Editor *Lisa O'Kelly*
  Arts Editor *Jane Ferguson*
  Political Editor *Patrick Wintour*
  Business News Editor *Andy Beven*
  City Editor *Paul Farrelly*
  Education Correspondent *Martin Bright*
  Environment Editor *John Arlidge*
  Literary Editor *Robert McCrum*
  Sports Editor *Brian Oliver*

Life: arts and lifestyle supplement. **Editor** *Sheryl Garratt*.

Scotland on Sunday

20 North Bridge, Edinburgh EH1 1YT
☎0131 225 2468   Fax 0131 220 2443
Website: www.scotsman.com

Owner *Scotsman Publications Ltd*
Editor *John McGurk*
Circulation 125,321

Scotland's top-selling quality broadsheet. Welcomes ideas rather than finished articles.
  News Editor *Ian Stewart*
  Political Editor *Iain Martin*

Scotland on Sunday Magazine: colour supplement. **Editor** *Margot Wilson*. Features on personalities, etc.

The Scotsman

20 North Bridge, Edinburgh EH1 1YT
☎0131 225 2468   Fax 0131 226 7420
Website: www.scotsman.com

Owner *Scotsman Publications Ltd*
Editor *Alan Ruddock*
Circulation 79,930

Scotland's national newspaper. Many unsolicited mss come in, and stand a good chance of being read, although a small army of regulars supply much of the feature material not written in-house.
  News Editor *Magnus Llewellin*
  City/Financial Editor *Martin Flanagan*
  Education *Tom Little*
  Environment *Christopher Cairn*
  Features Editor *Aileen Easton*
  Book Reviews *Catherine Lockerbie*

Weekend **Editor** *Nicola McCormack* Travel articles, etc.

The Sun

1 Virginia Street, London E1 9BD
☎0171 782 4000   Fax 0171 782 4108
Website: www.the-sun.co.uk

Owner *News International plc/Rupert Murdoch*
Editor *David Yelland*
Circulation 3.75 million

Highest circulation daily with a populist outlook; very keen on gossip, pop stars, TV soap, scandals and exposés of all kinds. No room for non-professional feature writers; 'investigative journalism' of a certain hue is always in demand, however.
  News Editor *Glenn Goodey*
  Features Editor *Sam Carlisle*
  Political Editor *Trevor Kavanagh*
  Sports Editor *Ted Chadwick*
  Literary Editor/Women's Page
    Vicki Grimshaw

Sunday Business

200 Gray's Inn Road, London WC1X 8XR
☎0171 418 9601   Fax 0171 418 9605

Owner *Press Holdings*
Editor *Jeff Randall*
Circulation 56,065

LAUNCHED April 1996 and 'relaunched' February 1998. National newspaper dedicated to business, finance and politics.
  Deputy Editor *Richard Northedge*
  News Editor *Frank Kane*
  Features Editor *Vivien Goldsmith*
  City Editor *Nils Pratley*
  Political Editor *Sebastian Hamilton*

Sunday Herald

195 Albion Street, Glasgow G1 1QP
☎0141 302 7800   Fax 0141 302 7809
Website: www.sundayherald.co.uk
Owner *Scottish Media Group*
Editor *Andrew Jaspan*
Circulation 50,000

LAUNCHED February 1999. New Scottish seven-section broadsheet aimed at the 20–45 age group.
  Deputy Editor *Rob Brown*
  News Editor *David Milne*
  Features Editor *Barry Didcock*
  Political Editor *Torquil Crichton*
  Sports Editor *Donald Cowey*
  Magazine Editor *Charlotte Ross*

Sunday Life

124–144 Royal Avenue, Belfast BT1 1EB
☎01232 264300   Fax 01232 554507
Owner *Trinity International Holdings plc*
Editor *Martin Lindsay*
Circulation 101,210

Deputy Editor *Dave Culbert*
  Features Editor *Sue Corbett*
  Sports Editor *Jim Gracey*

Sunday Mail

Anderston Quay, Glasgow G3 8DA
☎0141 248 7000   Fax 0141 242 3587
Website: www.record-mail.co.uk
Owner *Mirror Group Newspapers*
Editor *Jim Cassidy*
Circulation 847,776

Popular Scottish Sunday tabloid.
  News Editor *Alan Crow*
  Features Editor *Rob Bruce*
  Women's Page *Melanie Reid*

XS: weekly supplement. **Editor** *Rob Bruce*.

Sunday Mirror

1 Canada Square, Canary Wharf, London
E14 5AP
☎0171 293 3000   Fax 0171 293 3939
Website: www.sundaymirror.co.uk
Owner *Mirror Group Newspapers*
Editor *Colin Myler*
Circulation 1.96 million

Receives anything up to 100 unsolicited mss weekly. In general terms, these are welcome, though the paper patiently points out it has more time for contributors who have taken the trouble to study the market. Initial contact in writing preferred, except for live news situations. No fiction.

News Editor *Matthew Bell* The news desk is very much in the market for tip-offs and inside information. Contributors would be expected to work with staff writers on news stories.
  City/Financial Editor *Joy Shillingford*
  Features Editor *Deborah Sherwood* 'Anyone who has obviously studied the market will be dealt with constructively and courteously.' Cherishes its record as a breeding ground for new talent.
  Sports Editor *Steve McKenlay*

Personal: colour supplement. **Editor** *Siona Wingett*.

Sunday People

1 Canada Square, Canary Wharf, London
E14 5AP
☎0171 293 3000   Fax 0171 293 3810
Website: www.people.co.uk
Owner *Mirror Group Newspapers*
Editor *Neil Wallis*
Circulation 1.65 million

Slightly up-market version of *The News of the World*. Keen on exposés and big-name gossip. Interested in ideas for investigative articles. Phone in first instance.
  News Editor *David Wooding*
  City Editor *Cathy Gunn*
  Features Editor *Helen Carroll*
  Political Editor *Nigel Nelson*
  Sports Editor *Ed Barry*
  Travel Editor *Neil Wallis*

The People Magazine. **Editor** *Amanda Cable*. Approach by phone with ideas in first instance.

Sunday Post

2 Albert Square, Dundee DD1 9QJ
☎01382 223131   Fax 01382 201064
Email: post@dcthomson.co.uk
Website: www.sundaypost.com
Owner *D. C. Thomson & Co. Ltd*
Editor *Russell Reid*
Circulation 738,848

Contributions should be addressed to the editor.

Sunday Post Magazine: monthly colour supplement. **Editor** *Maggie Dun*.

Sunday Sport

19 Great Ancoats Street, Manchester
M60 4BT
☎0161 236 4466   Fax 0161 236 4535
Website: www.sundaysport.co.uk
Owner *David Sullivan*
Editor *Mark Harris*

Circulation 217,668

FOUNDED 1986. Sunday tabloid catering for a particular sector of the male 15–35 readership. As concerned with 'glamour' (for which, read: 'page 3') as with human interest, news, features and sport. Unsolicited mss are welcome; receives about 90 a week. Approach should be made by phone in the case of news and sports items, by letter for features. All material should be addressed to the news editor.

News Editor *Simon Dean* Off-beat news, human interest, preferably with photographs.

Features Editor *Sarah Stephens* Regular items: glamour, showbiz and television, as well as general interest.

Sports Editor *Marc Smith* Hard-hitting sports stories on major soccer clubs and their personalities, plus leading clubs/people in other sports. Strong quotations to back up the news angle essential.

Payment negotiable and on publication.

Sunday Telegraph

1 Canada Square, Canary Wharf, London E14 5DT
☎0171 538 5000   Fax 0171 538 6242
Website: www.telegraph.co.uk

Owner *Conrad Black*
Editor *Dominic Lawson*
Circulation 825,678

Right-of-centre quality Sunday paper which, although traditionally formal, has pepped up its image to attract a younger readership. Unsolicited material from untried writers is rarely ever used. Contact with idea and details of track record.

  News Editor *Jonathan Petre*
  Features Editor *Sandy Mitchell*
  City Editor *Neil Bennett*
  Political Editor *Tom Baldwin*
  Education Editor *Martin Bentham*
  Arts Editor *John Preston*
  Environment Editor *Greg Neale*
  Literary Editor *Miriam Gross*
  Diary Editor *Adam Helliker*
  Sports Editor *Colin Gibson*
  Women's Page *Annie Shaw*

Sunday Telegraph Magazine **Editor** *Lucy Tuck*

The Sunday Times

1 Pennington Street, London E1 9XW
☎0171 782 5000   Fax 0171 782 5731
Website: www.sunday-times.co.uk

Owner *News International plc/Rupert Murdoch*

Editor *John Witherow*
Circulation 1.40 million

FOUNDED 1820. Tendency to be anti-establishment, with a strong crusading investigative tradition. Approach the relevant editor with an idea in writing. Close scrutiny of the style of each section of the paper is strongly advised before sending mss. No fiction. All fees by negotiation.

News Editor *Charles Hymas* Opportunities are very rare.

News Review Editor *Sarah Baxter* Submissions are always welcome, but the paper commissions its own, uses staff writers or works with literary agents, by and large. The features sections where most opportunities exist are *Style* and *The Culture*.

  Arts Editor *Helen Hawkins*
  Business Editor *Andrew Lorenz*
  City Editor *Kirstie Hamilton*
  Education *Judith O'Reilly*
  Environment *Jonathan Leake*
  Literary Editor *Geordie Greig*
  Sports Editor *Alex Butler*
  Style Editor *Jeremy Langmead*

Sunday Times Magazine: colour supplement. **Editor** *Robin Morgan*. No unsolicited material. Write with ideas in first instance.

The Times

1 Pennington Street, London E1 9XN
☎0171 782 5000   Fax 0171 488 3242
Website: www.the-times.co.uk

Owner *News International plc/Rupert Murdoch*
Editor *Peter Stothard*
Circulation 744,490

Generally right (though features can range in tone from diehard to libertarian). *The Times* receives a great many unsolicited offerings. Writers with feature ideas should approach by letter in the first instance. No fiction.

  News Editor *John Wellman*
  Features Editor *Sandra Parsons*
  Associate Editor *Brian MacArthur*
  City/Financial Editor *Patience Wheatcroft*
  Diary Editor *Jasper Gerrard*
  Arts Editor *Richard Morrison*
  Education *John O'Leary*
  Environment *Nick Nuttall*
  Literary Editor *Erica Wagner*
  Political Editor *Phil Webster*
  Sports Editor *David Chappell*

Weekend Times **Editor** *Gill Morgan*

The Times Magazine: Saturday supplement.
Editor *Nicholas Wapshott*
  Features Editor *Sandra Parsons*

Wales on Sunday

Thomson House, Havelock Street, Cardiff
CF1 1WR
☎01222 223333   Fax 01222 583725
Owner *Trinity International Holdings plc*
Editor *Alan Edmunds*

Circulation 62,286

LAUNCHED 1989. Tabloid with sports supplement. Does not welcome unsolicited mss.
News Editor *Ceri Gould*
Features/Women's Page *Mike Smith*
Sports Editor *Paul Abbandonato*

Freelance Rates – Newspapers

Freelance rates vary enormously. The following minimum rates, negotiated by the **National Union of Journalists**, should be treated as guidelines. Most work can command higher fees from employers whether or not they have NUJ agreements. It is up to freelancers to negotiate the best deal they can.

National Newspapers
(Including *The Herald, Sunday Herald, Daily Record, Sunday Mail, The Scotsman, Scotland on Sunday, Evening Standard*)

Features (including reviews, obituaries, etc)
Broadsheet rates start at under £210 per 1000 words but sums of over £500 are common. Payment of less than £210 is not acceptable. Tabloids often pay considerably more than broadsheets though items are usually shorter.

News
News may be paid for per 1000 words or by the day. When payment is by the word, the absolute minimum should be £210 per 1000 words or pro rata. (Applies to all areas of news reporting, including sport.)

Day Rates
£115 lowest minimum, but preferably £125 or more. Accept day rates only if required to be in the office for the day.

Exclusives
These can command very high fees, depending on how much the newspaper wants the story. A prominent position for the piece should command £530 or more. A guaranteed minimum of at least £265 should be negotiated in case it appears further down the page in a shorter form.

Colour Supplements
Seek payment of double all the rates given above.

Cartoons
Cartoon size: 1 column b&w £100, thereafter subject to individual negotiation. For a colour cartoon charge double the above rate. (All rates quoted are for one British use.)

Crosswords
15 × 15 squares and under: at least £110; 15x15 squares and over: at least £140.

Regional & Provincial Newspapers (England and Wales)

Features
Minimum Rate (for features submitted on spec) Weekly newspapers: £2 for up to and including 10 lines; 20p per line thereafter. Daily, evening and Sunday newspapers: £3.40 for up to and including 10 lines; 34p per line thereafter.

News
Minimum Lineage (usually 4 words) Rate Weekly newspapers: £1.80 for up to and including 10 lines; 18p per line thereafter. Daily, evening and Sunday newspapers: £3.10 for up to and including 10 lines; 31p per line thereafter.

Cartoons
Single Frame: at least £55
Feature Strip (up to 4 frames): £102

Crosswords
At least £64.

Regional Newspapers

Regional newspapers are listed in alphabetical order under town.
Thus the *Evening Standard* appears under 'L' for London;
the *Lancashire Evening Post* under 'P' for Preston.

Aberdeen

Evening Express (Aberdeen)
PO Box 43, Lang Stracht, Mastrick, Aberdeen
AB15 6DF
☎01224 690222   Fax 01224 699575
Owner *Northcliffe Newspapers Group Ltd*
Editor *Donald Martin*
Circulation 68,191

Circulates in Aberdeen and the Grampian region. Local, national and international news and pictures, family finance and property news. Unsolicited mss welcome 'if on a controlled basis'.
News Editor *Sally McDonald* Freelance news contributors welcome.
Payment £30-60.

The Press and Journal
PO Box 43, Lang Stracht, Mastrick, Aberdeen
AB9 8AF
☎01224 690222   Fax 01224 663575
Owner *Northcliffe Newspapers Group Ltd*
Editor *Derek Tucker*
Circulation 104,548

Circulates in Aberdeen, Grampians, Highlands, Tayside, Orkney, Shetland and the Western Isles. A well-established regional daily which is said to receive more unsolicited mss a week than the *Sunday Mirror*. Unsolicited mss are nevertheless welcome; approach in writing with ideas. No fiction.
News Editor *David Knight* Wide variety of hard or off-beat news and features relating especially, but not exclusively, to the North of Scotland.
Sports Editor *Jim Dolan*
Women's Page *Susan Mansfield*
Payment by arrangement.

Barrow in Furness

North West Evening Mail
Abbey Road, Barrow in Furness, Cumbria
LA14 5QS
☎01229 821835   Fax 01229 840164
Owner *CN Group Ltd*

Editor *Sara Hadwin*
Circulation 20,068

All editorial material should be addressed to the editor.
Assistant Editor (Production) *Bill Myers*
Assistant Editor (Mail) *R. A. Herbert*
Sports Editor *Leo Clarke*

Basildon

Evening Echo
Newspaper House, Chester Hall Lane,
Basildon, Essex SS14 3BL
☎01268 522792   Fax 01268 282884
Owner *Newsquest Media Group*
Editor *Martin McNeill*
Circulation 47,000

Relies almost entirely on staff and regular outside contributors, but will very occasionally consider material sent on spec. Approach the editor in writing with ideas. Although the paper is Basildon-based, its largest circulation is in the Southend area.

Bath

The Bath Chronicle
Windsor House, Windsor Bridge Road, Bath
BA2 3AU
☎01225 322322   Fax 01225 322291
Owner *BUP Plc*
Editor *David Gledhill*
Circulation 16,781

Local news and features especially welcomed.
Deputy Editor *John McCready*
News Editor *Paul Wiltshire*
Features Editor *Andrew Knight*
Sports Editor *Neville Smith*

Belfast

Belfast Telegraph
Royal Avenue, Belfast BT1 1EB
☎01232 264000   Fax 01232 554506/554540
Owner *Trinity International Holdings Plc*
Editor *Edmund Curran*

Circulation 124,530

Weekly business supplement.
   Deputy Editor *Jim Flanagan*
   News Editor *Paul Connolly*
   Features Editor *John Caruth*
   Sports Editor *John Laverty*
   Business Editor *Frances McDonnell*

The Irish News

113/117 Donegall Street, Belfast BT1 2GE
☎01232 322226   Fax 01232 337505

Owner *Irish News Ltd*
Editor *Noel Doran*
Circulation 50,334

All material to appropriate editor (phone to
check), or to the news desk.
   Head of Content *Fiona McGarry*
   Arts Editor *Tim Brannigan*
   Sports Editor *John Haughey*
   Women's Page *Ann Molloy*

Ulster News Letter

46-56 Boucher Crescent, Belfast BT12 6QY
☎01232 680000   Fax 01232 664412

Owner *Century Newspapers Ltd*
Editor *Geoff Martin*
Circulation 33,853

Supplements: *Farming Life* (weekly); *Belfast
Newsletter; North Down News; East Belfast News.*
   Deputy Editor *Mike Chapman*
   News Editor *Ric Clark/Steven Moore*
   Features Editor *Geoff Hill*
   Sports Editor *Brian Millar*
   Fashion & Lifestyle/Property Editor
      Sandra Chapman
   Business Editor *Adrienne McGill*
   Agricultural Editor *David McCoy*

Birmingham

Birmingham Evening Mail

28 Colmore Circus, Queensway, Birmingham
B4 6AX
☎0121 236 3366   Fax 0121 233 0271

Owner *Mirror Group Plc*
Editor *Ian Dowell*
Circulation 187,598

Freelance contributions are welcome, particularly topics of interest to the West Midlands
and Women's Page pieces offering original and
lively comment.
   News Editor *Steve Dyson*
   Features Editor *Paul Cole*
   Women's Page *Bryony Jones*

Birmingham Post

28 Colmore Circus, Queensway, Birmingham
B4 6AX
☎0121 236 3366   Fax 0121 625 1105

Owner *Midland Independent Newspapers Plc*
Editor *Nigel Hastilow*
Circulation 27,050

One of the country's leading regional news-
papers. Freelance contributions are welcome.
Topics of interest to the West Midlands and
pieces offering lively, original comment are
particularly welcome.
   News Editor *Chris Russon*
   Features Editor *Peter Bacon*
   Women's Page *Ros Dodd*

Sunday Mercury (Birmingham)

28 Colmore Circus, Queensway, Birmingham
B4 6AZ
☎0121 236 3366   Fax 0121 234 5877
Email: SundayMercury@mrn.co.uk

Owner *Birmingham Post & Mail Ltd*
Editor *Fiona Alexander*
Circulation 149,639
   Assistant Editor (News & Features)
      James Windle
   Assistant Editor (Sport) *Lee Gibson*

Blackburn

Lancashire Evening Telegraph

Newspaper House, High Street, Blackburn,
Lancashire BB1 1HT
☎01254 678678   Fax 01254 680429

Owner *Newsquest Media Group Ltd*
Editor *Peter Butterfield*
Circulation 43,753

News stories and feature material with an East
Lancashire flavour (a local angle, or written by
local people) welcome. Approach in writing
with an idea in the first instance. No fiction.
   News/Features/Women's Page Editor
      Nick Nunn

Blackpool

The Gazette (Blackpool)

PO Box 20, Avroe House, Avroe Crescent,
Blackpool, Lancashire FY4 2DP
☎01253 400888   Fax 01253 361870

Owner *RIM*
Managing Director *Philip Welsh*
Editor *Gerard Henderson*
Circulation 40,002

Unsolicited mss welcome in theory. Approach in writing with an idea. Supplements: *Eve* (women, Tuesday); *Wheels* (motoring, Weds); *Property* (Thurs); *Big Weekend* (entertainment, Fri); *Sevendays* (entertainment & leisure, Sat).
   Sports Editor *Jonathan Lee*

Bolton
Bolton Evening News
Newspaper House, Churchgate, Bolton, Lancashire BL1 1DE
☎01204 522345   Fax 01204 365068
Email: ben_editorial@newsquest.co.uk
Website: www.thisislancashire.co.uk
Owner *Newsquest Media Group Ltd*
Editor *Mark Rossiter*
Circulation 42,035

Business, children's page, travel, local services, motoring, fashion and cookery.
   News Editor *Melvyn Horrocks*
   Features Editor/Women's Page
   Angela Kelly

Bournemouth
Daily Echo
Richmond Hill, Bournemouth, Dorset BH2 6HH
☎01202 554601   Fax 01202 292115
Owner *Newscom Plc*
Managing Editor *Ian Murray*
Editor *Neal Butterworth*
Circulation 45,090

FOUNDED 1900. Has a strong features content and invites specialist articles, particularly on unusual and contemporary subjects but only with a local angle. Supplements: business, education, homes and gardens, motoring, what's on, *Weekender*. Regular features on weddings, property, books, local history, green issues, the Channel coast. All editorial material should be addressed to the **News Editor** *Andy Martin*.
   Payment on publication.

Bradford
Telegraph & Argus (Bradford)
Hall Ings, Bradford, West Yorkshire BD1 1JR
☎01274 729511   Fax 01274 723634
Owner *Newsquest Media Group Ltd*
Editor *Perry Austin-Clarke*
Circulation 51,838

No unsolicited mss – approach in writing with samples of work. No fiction.

News Editor *Jan Brierley* Local features and general interest. Showbiz pieces. 600–1000 words (maximum 1500).
   Sports Editor *Alan Birkinshaw*
   Features Editor *Lynn Ashwell*

Brighton
Evening Argus
Argus House, Crowhurst Road, Hollingbury, Brighton, East Sussex BN1 8AR
☎01273 544544   Fax 01273 505703
Email: simonb@argus-btn.co.uk
Website: www.thisisbrighton.co.uk
Owner *Newsquest (Sussex) Ltd*
Circulation 51,405
Editor-in-Chief *Simon Bradshaw*
News Editor *Claire Byrd*
Sports Editor *Chris Giles*

Bristol
Evening Post
Temple Way, Bristol BS99 7HD
☎0117 9343000   Fax 0117 9343575
Owner *Bristol United Press plc*
Editor *Mike Lowe*
Circulation 79,346
News Editor *Kevan Blackadder*
Features Editor *Matthew Shelley*
Sports Editor *Chris Bartlett*

Western Daily Press
Temple Way, Bristol BS99 7HD
☎0117 9343000   Fax 0117 9343574
Owner *Bristol Evening Post & Press Ltd*
Editor *Ian Beales*
Circulation 60,139
Contents Editor *Roger Tavener*
Features Editor *Jane Riddiford*
Sports Editor *Bill Beckett*
Women's Page *Lynda Cleasby*

Burton upon Trent
Burton Mail
65-68 High Street, Burton upon Trent, Staffordshire DE14 1LE
☎01283 512345   Fax 01283 515351
Owner *Burton Daily Mail Ltd*
Editor *Brian Vertigen*
Circulation 18,456

Fashion, health, wildlife, environment, nostalgia, financial/money (Monday); consumer, motoring (Tuesday); women's world, rock (Wednesday);

property (Thursday); motoring, farming, what's on (Friday); what's on, leisure (Saturday).

News/Features Editor *Andrew Parker*
Sports Editor *Rex Page*
Women's Page *Bill Pritchard*

Cambridge

Cambridge Evening News

Winship Road, Milton, Cambridge CB4 6PP
☎01223 434434   Fax 01223 434415

Owner *Cambridge Newspapers Ltd*
Editor *Colin Grant*
Circulation 42,503
News Editor *Helen Montgomery*
Business Editor *Jenny Chapman*
Sports Editor *Cyrus Pundole*
Women's Page *Angela Singer*

Cardiff

South Wales Echo

Thomson House, Havelock Street, Cardiff CF1 1XR
☎01222 223333   Fax 01222 583624
Website: www.totalwales.com

Owner *Trinity Plc*
Editor *Robin Fletcher*
Circulation 75,959

Circulates in South and Mid Glamorgan and Gwent.

Head of News *Mark Walden*
Head of Features *Judith Halliday*
Head of Sport *Richard Williams*

The Western Mail

Thomson House, Havelock Street, Cardiff CF1 1WR
☎01222 223333   Fax 01222 583652

Owner *Trinity Plc*
Editor *Neil Fowler*
Circulation 64,172

Circulates in Cardiff, Merthyr Tydfil, Newport, Swansea and towns and villages throughout Wales. Mss welcome if of a topical nature, and preferably of Welsh interest. No short stories or travel. Approach in writing to the editor. 'Usual subjects already well covered, e.g. motoring, travel, books, gardening. We look for the unusual.' Maximum 1000 words. Opportunities also on women's page. Supplements: Saturday Magazine; Welsh Homes; Country and Farming; Business; Sport, Motoring.

Deputy Editor *Simon Farrington*
Assistant Editor *Alastair Milburn*

Head of Content *Lee Wenham*
Sports Editor *Mark Tattersall*

Carlisle

News & Star

Newspaper House, Dalston Road, Carlisle, Cumbria CA2 5UA
☎01228 612600   Fax 01228 612601

Owner *Cumbrian Newspaper Group Ltd*
Editor *Keith Sutton*
Circulation 25,375
News Editor *Nick Turner*
Head of Content *Steve Johnston*
Sports Editor *John Reynolds*
Women's Page *Jane Loughran*

Chatham

Kent Today

395 High Street, Chatham, Kent ME4 4PQ
☎01634 830600   Fax 01634 829484

Owner *Kent Messenger Group*
Editor *Ron Green*
Circulation 21,567
Assistant Editor (Production) *Neil Webber*
Business Editor *Trevor Sturgess*
Community Editor *David Jones*
Sports Editor *Mike Rees*

Cheltenham

Gloucestershire Echo

1 Clarence Parade, Cheltenham, Gloucestershire GL50 3NZ
☎01242 271900   Fax 01242 271848

Owner *Northcliffe Newspapers Group Ltd*
Editor *Anita Syvret*
Circulation 25,426

All material, other than news, should be addressed to the editor.

News Editor *Owen Jones*

Chester

Chronicle Newspapers (Chester & North Wales)

Chronicle House, Commonhall Street, Chester CH1 2BJ
☎01244 340151   Fax 01244 340165
Email: B.Adams@chron8.demon.co.uk
Website: www.cheshirenews.co.uk

Owner *Trinity Plc*
Editor-in-Chief *Bob Adams*

All unsolicited feature material will be considered.

Colchester

Evening Gazette (Colchester)

Oriel House, 43-44 North Hill, Colchester,
Essex CO1 1TZ
☎01206 506000   Fax 01206 508274
Email: irene_kettle@essex-news.co.uk
Website: www.thisisessex.co.uk
Owner *Newsquest (Essex)*
Editor *Irene Kettle*
Circulation 28,206

Monday-Friday daily newspaper servicing
north and mid-Essex including Colchester,
Harwich, Clacton, Braintree, Witham, Maldon
and Chelmsford. Unsolicited mss not generally
used. Relies heavily on regular contributors.
  Features Editor *Iris Clapp*

Coventry

Coventry Evening Telegraph

Corporation Street, Coventry CV1 1FP
☎01203 633633   Fax 01203 550869
Owner *Mirror Group*
Editor *Alan Kirby*
Circulation 82,417

Unsolicited mss are read, but few are published.
Approach in writing with an idea. No fiction.
All unsolicited material should be addressed to
the editor. Maximum 600 words for features.
  News Editor *John West*
  Features Editor *Paul Simoniti*
  Sports Editor *Roger Draper*
  Women's Page *Barbara Argument*
  Payment negotiable.

Darlington

The Northern Echo

Priestgate, Darlington, Co. Durham DL1 1NF
☎01325 381313   Fax 01325 380539
Owner *North of England Newspapers*
Editor *Peter Baron*
Circulation 70,358

FOUNDED 1870. Freelance pieces welcome but
telephone first to discuss submission.
  News Editor *Sarah Andrews* Interested in
reports involving the North-East or North
Yorkshire. Preferably phoned in.
  Features Editor *Chris Lloyd* Background
pieces to topical news stories relevant to the
area. Must be arranged with the features editor
before submission of any material.
  Business Editor *Colin Tapping*
  Sports Editor *Nick Loughlan*
  Payment and length by arrangement.

Derby

Derby Evening Telegraph

Northcliffe House, Meadow Road, Derby
DE1 2DW
☎01332 291111   Fax 01332 253027
Owner *Northcliffe Newspapers Group Ltd*
Editor *Keith Perch*
Circulation 60,691

Weekly business supplement.
  News Editor *Andy Wright*
  Features Editor/Women's Page
    Nigel Poulson
  Sports Editor *Steve Nicholson*
  Motoring Editor *Bob Maddox*

Doncaster

The Doncaster Star

40 Duke Street, Doncaster, South Yorkshire
DN1 3EA
☎01302 344001   Fax 01302 329072
Owner *Sheffield Newspapers Ltd*
Editor/News Editor *Graham Walker*
Circulation 9,716

Address all editorial material to the editor.
  Deputy News Editor *Jane Cartledge*
  Sports Editor *Steve Hossack*
  Women's Page *Jane Stapleton*

Dundee

The Courier and Advertiser

80 Kingsway East, Dundee DD4 8SL
☎01382 223131   Fax 01382 454590
Email: courier@dcthomson.co.uk
Website: www.thecourier.co.uk
Owner *D. C. Thomson & Co. Ltd*
Editor *Adrian Arthur*
Circulation 95,508

Circulates in East Central Scotland. Features
occasionally accepted on a wide range of subjects, particularly local/Scottish interest – including finance, insurance, agriculture, motoring,
modern homes, lifestyle and fitness. Maximum
length, 500 words.
  News Editor *Arliss Rhind*
  Features Editor/Women's Page
    Shona Lorimer
  Sports Editor *Graham Dey*

Evening Telegraph & Post

80 Kingsway East, Dundee DD4 8SL
☎01382 223131   Fax 01382 454590
Owner *D. C. Thomson & Co. Ltd*
Editor *Alan Proctor*

Circulation 33,304

Circulates in Tayside, Dundee and Fife. All material should be addressed to the editor.

East Anglia

East Anglian Daily Times
See under *Ipswich*

Eastern Daily Press
See under *Norwich*

Edinburgh

Evening News
20 North Bridge, Edinburgh EH1 1YT
☎0131 225 2468   Fax 0131 225 7302

Owner *European Press Holdings Ltd*
Editor *John C. McLellan*
Circulation 90,000

FOUNDED 1873. Circulates in Edinburgh, Fife, Central and Lothian. Coverage includes: entertainment, gardening, motoring, shopping, fashion, health and lifestyle, showbusiness. Occasional platform pieces, features of topical interest and/or local interest. Unsolicited feature material welcome. Approach the appropriate editor by telephone.

    Associate Editor (News) *David Lee*
    Associate Editor (Features) *Helen Martin*
    Sports Editor *Andrew Baillie*
    Payment NUJ/house rates.

Exeter

Express & Echo
Heron Road, Sowton, Exeter, Devon EX2 7NF
☎01392 442211
Fax 01392 442294/442287 (editorial)
Email: echo@mail.eurobell.co.uk

Owner *Westcountry Publications Limited*
Editor *Steve Hall*
Circulation 30,978

Weekly supplements: *Business Week; Property Echo; Wheels; Weekend Echo.*

    News Editor *Chris Styles*
    Features Editor/Women's Page *Sue Kemp*
    Sports Editor *Jerry Charge*

Glasgow

Evening Times
195 Albion Street, Glasgow G1 1QP
☎0141 552 6255   Fax 0141 553 1355

Owner *Scottish Media Newspapers Ltd*

Editor *John D. Scott*
Circulation 117,650

Circulates in Glasgow and the west of Scotland. Supplements: *Job Search; Home Front; Woman; Time Out* (leisure); *Go* (weekend preview).

    News Editor *Joe Donnelly*
    Features Editor *Russell Kyle*
    Sports Editor *David Stirling*
    Women's Editor *Agnes Stevenson*

The Herald (Glasgow)
See **National Newspapers**

Gloucester

The Citizen
St John's Lane, Gloucester GL1 2AY
☎01452 424442   Fax 01452 307238

Owner *Northcliffe Newspapers Group Ltd*
Editor *Spencer Feeney*
Circulation 25,426

All editorial material to be addressed to the **News Editor** *Gavin Curry*.

Gloucestershire Echo
See under *Cheltenham*

Greenock

Greenock Telegraph
2 Crawfurd Street, Greenock PA15 1LH
☎01475 726511   Fax 01475 783734

Owner *Clyde & Forth Press Ltd*
Editor *Ian Wilson*
Circulation 19,872

Circulates in Greenock, Port Glasgow, Gourock, Kilmacolm, Langbank, Bridge of Weir, Inverkip, Wemyss Bay, Skelmorlie, Largs. Unsolicited mss considered 'if they relate to the newspaper's general interests'. No fiction. All material to be addressed to the editor.

Grimsby

Grimsby Evening Telegraph
80 Cleethorpe Road, Grimsby, N. E. Lincs DN31 3EH
☎01472 360360   Fax 01472 372257

Owner *Northcliffe Newspapers Group Ltd*
Editor *Peter Moore*
Circulation 71,167

Sister paper of the *Scunthorpe Evening Telegraph*. Unsolicited mss generally welcome. Approach in writing. No fiction. Monthly supplement: *Business Telegraph*. All material to be addressed

to the **News Editor** *S. P. Richards*. Particularly welcome hard news stories – approach in haste by telephone.
   Special Publications Editor *B. Farnsworth*

Guernsey

Guernsey Evening Press & Star

Braye Road, Vale, Guernsey, Channel Islands
GY1 3BW
☎01481 45866   Fax 01481 48972
Email: newsroom@guernsey-press.com
Website: www.guernsey-press.com
Owner *Guernsey Press Co. Ltd*
Editor *Nick Machon*
Circulation 15,908

Special pages include children's and women's interest, gardening and fashion.
   News Editor *James Falla*
   Sports Editor *Rob Batiste*
   Women's Page *Kay Leslie*

Halifax

Evening Courier

PO Box 19, Halifax, West Yorkshire
HX1 2SF
☎01422 260200   Fax 01422 260341
Owner *Johnston Press Plc*
Editor *Edward Riley*
Circulation 29,000
News Editor *John Kenealy*
Features Editor *William Marshall*
Sports Editor *Ian Rushworth*
Women's Page *Diane Crabtree*

Hartlepool

Mail (Hartlepool)

New Clarence House, Wesley Square,
Hartlepool TS24 8BX
☎01429 274441   Fax 01429 869024
Owner *Northeast Press Ltd*
Acting Editor *Harry Blackwood*
Circulation 25,705
News Editor *Neil Hunter*
Features Editor *Bernice Saltzer*
Sports Editor *Roy Kelly*

Huddersfield

Huddersfield Daily Examiner

Queen Street South, Huddersfield, West
Yorkshire HD1 2TD
☎01484 430000   Fax 01484 437789
Owner *Trinity International Holdings plc*

Editor *John Williams*
Circulation 35,218

Home improvement, home heating, weddings, dining out, motoring, fashion, services to trade and industry.
   Deputy Editor *Melvyn Briggs*
   Assistant Editor *John Bird*
   News Editor *Neil Atkinson*
   Features Editor *Andrew Flynn*
   Sports Editor *John Gledhill*
   Women's Page *Hilarie Stelfox*

Hull

Hull Daily Mail

Blundell's Corner, Beverley Road, Hull,
North Humberside HU3 1XS
☎01482 327111   Fax 01482 584353
Owner *Northcliffe Newspapers Group Ltd*
Editor *John Meehan*
Circulation 88,000
Head of News *Marc Astley*
Head of Content *Mark Woodward*
Production Editor *Chris Harvey*
Women's Page *Jo Davison*

Ipswich

East Anglian Daily Times

30 Lower Brook Street, Ipswich, Suffolk
IP4 1AN
☎01473 230023   Fax 01473 211391
Owner *Eastern Counties Newspapers Group Ltd*
Editor *Terry Hunt*
Circulation 46,008

FOUNDED 1874. Unsolicited mss generally not welcome; three or four received a week and almost none are used. Approach in writing in the first instance. No fiction. Supplements: Sport; Young Readers' section (Monday); Community News (Tuesday); Essex Free Ads (Tuesday, Essex edition); Job Quest (Wednesday); Business (Wednesday); Property (Thursday); Motoring (Friday); Magazine (Saturday).
   News Editor *Mark Hindle* Hard news stories involving East Anglia (Suffolk, Essex particularly) or individuals resident in the area are always of interest.
   Features *Steve Hughes* (**Deputy Editor**) Mostly in-house, but will occasionally buy in if the subject is of strong Suffolk/East Anglian interest. Photofeatures preferred (extra payment). Special advertisement features are run regularly: some opportunities here. Max. 1000 words.
   Sports Editor *Nick Garnham*
   Women's Page *Victoria Hawkins*

Evening Star

30 Lower Brook Street, Ipswich, Suffolk
IP4 1AN
☎01473 230023   Fax 01473 225296
Owner *Eastern Counties Newspaper Group*
Editor *Nigel Pickover*
Circulation 30,391
Deputy Editor (News) *Russell Cook*
Sports Editor *Mike Horne*

Jersey

Jersey Evening Post

PO Box 582, Jersey, Channel Islands JE4 8XQ
☎01534 611611   Fax 01534 611622
Email: jepdaily@itl.net
Owner *Jersey Evening Post Ltd*
Editor *Chris Bright*
Circulation 23,070

Special pages: gardening, motoring, property, boating, technology, young person's (16–25), women, food and drink, personal finance, rock reviews, health, business.
  News Editor *Sue Le Ruez*
  Features Editor *Richard Pedley*
  Sports Editor *Ron Felton*

Kent

Kent Messenger

See under *Maidstone*

Kent Today

See under *Chatham*

Kettering

Evening Telegraph

Newspaper House, Ise Park, Rothwell Road, Kettering, Northamptonshire NN16 8GA
☎01536 506100   Fax 01536 506195
Owner *Johnston Press Plc*
Editor-in-Chief *David Rowell*
Circulation 33,346

Northamptonshire Business Guide (weekly); *Guide* supplement (Thursday/Saturday), featuring TV, gardening, videos, films, eating out; and a monthly supplement, *Home & Garden*.
  News Editor *Helen O'Neill*
  Sports Editor *Ian Davidson*

Lancashire

Lancashire Evening Post

See under *Preston*

Lancashire Evening Telegraph

See under *Blackburn*

Leamington Spa

Leamington Spa Courier

32 Hamilton Terrace, Leamington Spa, Warwickshire CV32 4LY
☎01926 888222   Fax 01926 339960
Owner *Central Counties Newspapers*
Editor *Martin Lawson*
Circulation 13,410

One of the Leamington Spa Courier Series which also includes the *Warwick Courier* and *Kenilworth Weekly News*. Unsolicited feature articles considered, particularly matter with a local angle. Telephone with idea first.
  News Editor *Joan Hewitt*

Leeds

Yorkshire Evening Post

Wellington Street, Leeds, West Yorkshire
LS1 1RF
☎0113 2432701   Fax 0113 2388536
Owner *Regional Independent Media*
Editor *Neil Hodgkinson*
Circulation 100,596

Evening sister of the *Yorkshire Post*.
  News Editor *David Helliwell*
  Features Editor *Anne Pickles*
  Sports Editor *Stephen White*
  Women's Page *Carmen Bruegmann*

Yorkshire Post

Wellington Street, Leeds, West Yorkshire
LS1 1RF
☎0113 2432701   Fax 0113 2388537
Owner *Regional Independent Media*
Editor *Tony Watson*
Circulation 75,836

A serious-minded, quality regional daily with a generally conservative outlook. Three or four unsolicited mss arrive each day; all will be considered but initial approach in writing preferred. All submissions should be addressed to the editor. No fiction, poetry or family histories.
  Head of Content *John Furbisher*
  Features Editor *Mick Hickling* Open to suggestions in all fields (though ordinarily commissioned from specialist writers).
  Sports Editor *Bill Bridge*
  Women's Page *Jill Armstrong*

Leicester

Leicester Mercury

St George Street, Leicester LE1 9FQ
☎0116 2512512   Fax 0116 2530645
Owner *Northcliffe Newspapers Group Ltd*
Editor *Nick Carter*
Circulation 108,793
News Editor *Simon Orrell*
  Acting Features Editor *Alex Dawon*

Lincoln

Lincolnshire Echo

Brayford Wharf East, Lincoln LN5 7AT
☎01522 525252   Fax 01522 545759
Email: editorecho@dial.pipex.com
Owner *Northcliffe Newspapers Group Ltd*
Editor *Brian Aitken*
Circulation 29,206

Best buys, holidays, motoring, dial-a-service, restaurants, sport, leisure, home improvement, record reviews, gardening corner, stars. All editorial material to be addressed to the **Assistant Editor** *Mike Gubbins*.

Liverpool

Daily Post

PO Box 48, Old Hall Street, Liverpool L69 3EB
☎0151 227 2000   Fax 0151 236 4682
Email: online@day-post.u-net.com
Owner *Liverpool Daily Post and Echo Ltd*
Editor *Alastair Machray*
Circulation 72,776

Unsolicited mss welcome. Receives about six a day. Approach in writing with an idea. No fiction. Local, national/international news, current affairs, profiles – with pictures. Maximum 800–1000 words.
  Features Editor *Andrew Forgrave*
  News Editor *Ian Lang*
  Sports Editor *Simon Jones*
  Women's Page *Margaret Kitchen*

Liverpool Echo

PO Box 48, Old Hall Street, Liverpool L69 3EB
☎0151 227 2000   Fax 0151 236 4682
Owner *Liverpool Daily Post & Echo Ltd*
Editor *John Griffith*
Circulation 157,999

One of the country's major regional dailies. Unsolicited mss welcome; initial approach with ideas in writing preferred.
  News Editor *Andrew Edwards*
  Features Editor *Mark Davies*
  Sports Editor *Ken Rogers*
  Women's Editor *Susan Lee*

London

Evening Standard

Northcliffe House, 2 Derry Street, London W8 5EE
☎0171 938 6000   Fax 0171 937 2648
Owner *Associated Newspapers/Lord Rothermere*
Editor *Max Hastings*
Circulation 450,000

Long-established evening paper, serving Londoners with both news and feature material. Genuine opportunities for London-based features. Produces a weekly colour supplement, *ES The Evening Standard Magazine*, a weekly listings magazine *Hot Tickets* and regular weekly supplements: *Just the Job* (Monday) and *Homes & Property* (Wednesday).
  Deputy Editor *Andrew Bordiss*
  Associate Editor (Features) *Nicola Jeal*
  News Editor *Stephen Clackson*
  Features Editor *Bernice Davison*
  Sports Editor *Simon Greenberg*
  Editor, ES *Louise Chunn*
  Editor, Hot Tickets *Miles Chapman*

Maidstone

Kent Messenger

6 & 7 Middle Row, Maidstone, Kent ME14 1TG
☎01622 695666   Fax 01622 757227
Owner *Kent Messenger Group*
Editor *Simon Irwin*
Circulation 45,048

Very little freelance work is commissioned.

Manchester

Manchester Evening News

164 Deansgate, Manchester M60 2RD
☎0161 832 7200   Fax 0161 834 3814
Owner *Manchester Evening News Ltd*
Editor *Paul Horrocks*
Circulation 173,446

One of the country's major regional dailies. Initial approach in writing preferred. No fiction. *Property* (Tuesday); *holiday feature* (Saturday); *Lifestyle* (Friday/Saturday).
  News Editor *Lisa Roland*

Features Editor *Maggie Henfield* Regional news features, personality pieces and showbiz profiles considered. Maximum 1200 words.
Sports Editor *Peter Spencer*
Women's Page *Diane Cooke*
Payment based on house agreement rates.

Middlesbrough
Evening Gazette
Borough Road, Middlesbrough, Cleveland TS1 3AZ
☎01642 234242   Fax 01642 249843
Owner *Trinity International Holdings plc*
Editor *Ranald Allan*
Circulation 69,000

Special pages: business, motoring, home, computing.
News Editor *Tony Beck*
Features Editor/Women's Page *Kathryn Armstrong*
Sports Editor *Allan Boughey*
Consumer *Karen Bell*
Health *Amanda Todd*
Councils *Sandy McKenzie*

Mold
Evening Leader
Mold Business Park, Wrexham Road, Mold, Clwyd CH7 1XY
☎01352 707707   Fax 01352 752180
Owner *North Wales Newspapers*
Editor *Reg Herbert*
Circulation 30,976

Circulates in Wrexham, Flintshire, Rhyl, Deeside and Chester. Special pages/features: motoring, travel, arts, women's, children's, photography, local housing, information and news for the disabled, music and entertainment.
Features Page *Debra Greenhouse*
News Editor *Joanne Shone* (Welsh edition); *Nick Bourne* (Chester); *Steve Rogers* (Rhyl)
Women's Page *Gail Cooper*
Sports Editor *Allister Syme*

Newcastle upon Tyne
Evening Chronicle
Thomson House, Groat Market, Newcastle upon Tyne, Tyne and Wear NE1 1ED
☎0191 232 7500   Fax 0191 232 2256
Owner *Trinity PLC*
Editor *Alison Hastings*
Circulation 109,685

Receives a lot of unsolicited material, much of which is not used. Family issues, gardening, pop, fashion, cooking, consumer, films and entertainment guide, home improvements, motoring, property, angling, sport and holidays. Approach in writing with ideas.
News Editor *Mark Smith*
Features Editor *Richard Ord* Limited opportunities due to full-time feature staff. Maximum 1000 words.
Sports Editor *Paul New*
Women's Interests *Kay Jordan*

The Journal
Thomson House, Groat Market, Newcastle upon Tyne, Tyne & Wear NE1 1ED
☎0191 232 7500
Fax 0191 232 2256/0191 201 6044
Email: jnl.newsdesk@ncjmedia.co.uk
Website: www.the-journal.co.uk
Owner *Trinity Plc*
Editor *Mark Dickinson*
Circulation 51,936

Daily platforms include farming and business. Monthly full-colour business supplement: *The Journal Northern Business Magazine*.
Deputy Editor *Paul Robertson*
Sports Editor *Nick Crockford*
Arts & Entertainment Editor *David Whetstone*
Environmental Editor *Tony Henderson*
Business Editor *Justin Strong*

Sunday Sun
Thomson House, Groat Market, Newcastle upon Tyne, Tyne & Wear NE1 1ED
☎0191 201 6330   Fax 0191 230 0238
Owner *Trinity Plc*
Editor *Peter Montellier*
Circulation 112,918

All material should be addressed to the appropriate editor (phone to check), or to the editor.
Sports Editor *Dylan Younger*

Newport
South Wales Argus
Cardiff Road, Maesglas, Newport, Gwent NP9 1QW
☎01633 810000   Fax 01633 462202
Owner *Newscom Plc*
Editor *Gerry Keighley*
Circulation 30,644

Circulates in Newport, Gwent and surrounding areas.
News Editor *Nicole Garnon*

Features Editor/Women's Page
Lesley Williams
Sports Editor *Rob Freeman*

Northampton
Chronicle and Echo
Upper Mounts, Northampton NN1 3HR
☎01604 231122   Fax 01604 233000
Owner *Northamptonshire Newspapers*
Editor *Mark Edwards*
Circulation 27,778

Unsolicited mss are 'not necessarily unwelcome but opportunities to use them are rare'. Some three or four arrive weekly. Approach in writing with an idea. No fiction. Supplements: *Sports Chronicle* (Monday); *Property Week* (Wednesday); *What's On Guide* (Thursday); *Weekend Motors* (Friday).
News Editor *Steve Scoles*
Features Editor/Women's Page
Jessica Pilkington
Sports Editor *Steve Pitts*

Northern Ireland
Belfast Telegraph
See under *Belfast*

The Irish News
See under *Belfast*

Sunday Life (Belfast)
See **National Newspapers**

Norwich
Eastern Daily Press
Prospect House, Rouen Road, Norwich,
Norfolk NR1 1RE
☎01603 628311   Fax 01603 612930
Website: www.ech.co.uk
Owner *Eastern Counties Newspapers*
Editor *Peter Franzen*
Circulation 78,647

Most pieces by commission only. Supplements: what's on (daily); motoring, business, property pages, women's interests, agriculture (all weekly); employment (twice-weekly); arts focus (monthly); plus horse and rider, boating, golf and wildlife; Saturday full colour magazine.
News Editor *Paul Durrant*
Features Editor *Rebecca Holmes*
Sports Editor *David Thorpe*
Magazine Editor *Peter Waters*

Evening News
Prospect House, Rouen Road, Norwich,
Norfolk NR1 1RE
☎01603 628311   Fax 01603 219060
Owner *Eastern Counties Newspapers*
Editor *Bob Crawley*
Circulation 36,458

Includes special pages on local property, motoring, children's page, pop, fashion, arts, entertainments and TV, gardening, local music scene, home and family.
Assistant Editor *Roy Strowger*
Deputy Editor *Celia Sutton*
Features Editor *Derek James*

Nottingham
Evening Post Nottingham
Castle Wharf House, Nottingham NG1 7EU
☎0115 9482000   Fax 0115 9644032
Owner *Northcliffe Newspapers Group Ltd*
Editor *Graham Glen*
Circulation 97,000

Unsolicited mss welcome. Good local interest only. Maximum 800 words. No fiction. Send ideas in writing. Supplements: motoring, business, holidays and travel supplements; financial, employment and consumer pages.
News Editor *Neil White*
Deputy Editor *Jon Grubb*
Sports Editor *Kevin Pick*

Oldham
Evening Chronicle
PO Box 47, Union Street, Oldham,
Lancashire OL1 1EQ
☎0161 633 2121   Fax 0161 652 2111
Email: oec@compuserve.com
Owner *Hirst Kidd & Rennie Ltd*
Editor *Philip Hirst*
Circulation 32,206

Motoring, food and wine, women's page, business page.
News Editor *Mike Attenborough*
Women's Page *Ralph Badham*

Oxford
Oxford Mail
Osney Mead, Oxford OX2 0EJ
☎01865 425262   Fax 01865 425554
Owner *Newsquest (Oxfordshire) Ltd*
Editor *Chris Cowley*

Circulation 35,000

Unsolicited mss are considered but a great many unsuitable offerings are received. Approach in writing with an idea, rather than by phone. No fiction. All fees negotiable.

Head of Content *Anne Harrison*

Paisley

Paisley Daily Express

14 New Street, Paisley PA1 1YA
☎0141 887 7911   Fax 0141 887 6254

Owner *Scottish & Universal Newspapers Ltd*
Editor *Norman Macdonald*
Circulation 9,067

Circulates in Paisley, Linwood, Renfrew, Johnstone, Elderslie, Neilston and Barrhead. Unsolicited mss welcome only if of genuine local (Paisley) interest. The paper does not commission work, and will consider submitted material. Maximum 1000-1500 words. All submissions to the editor.

News Editor *Anne Dalrymple*
Sports Editor *Matthew Vallance*

Plymouth

Evening Herald

17 Brest Road, Derriford Business Park, Derriford, Plymouth, Devon PL6 5AA
☎01752 765500   Fax 01752 765527

Owner *Northcliffe Newspapers Group Ltd*
Editor *Rachael Campey*
Circulation 53,626

All editorial material to be addressed to the editor or the **News Editor** *Bill Martin*.

Sunday Independent

Burrington Way, Plymouth, Devon PL5 3LN
☎01752 206600   Fax 01752 206164

Owner *Newscom Plc*
Deputy Editor *Anna Jenkins*
Circulation 38,958

Tabloid Sunday covering the whole of the West Country from Bristol to Weymouth and Land's End. News stories/tips, news features. All editorial should be addressed to the editor. Payment by arrangement.

Western Morning News

17 Brest Road, Derriford Business Park, Derriford, Plymouth, Devon PL6 5AA
☎01752 765500   Fax 01752 765535

Owner *Northcliffe Newspapers Group Ltd*

Editor *Barrie Williams*
Circulation 51,823

Unsolicited mss welcome, but must be of topical and local interest and addressed to the **News Editor**, *Jason Clark*.

Sports Editor *Rick Cowdery*

Portsmouth

The News

The News Centre, Hilsea, Portsmouth, Hampshire PO2 9SX
☎01705 664488   Fax 01705 673363
Email: newsdesk@thenews.co.uk
Website: www.thenews.co.uk

Owner *Portsmouth Printing & Publishing Ltd*
Editor *Geoffrey Elliott*
Circulation 71,843

Unsolicited mss not generally accepted. Approach by letter.

News Editor *Mary Williams*
Features Editor *Rachel Hughes* General subjects of S. E. Hants interest. Maximum 600 words. No fiction.
Sports Editor *Dave King* Sports background features. Maximum 600 words.
Woman's Page *Seren Boyd*

Preston

Lancashire Evening Post

Olivers Place, Eastway, Fulwood, Preston, Lancashire PR2 9ZA
☎01772 254841   Fax 01772 880173
Website: www.lep.co.uk

Owner *Regional Independent Media*
Editor *Roger Borrell*
Circulation 48,831

Unsolicited mss are not generally welcome; many are received and not used. All ideas in writing to the editor.

Reading

Reading Evening Post

8 Tessa Road, Reading, Berkshire RG1 8NS
☎0118 9575833   Fax 0118 9599363

Owner *Guardian Media Group*
Editor *Andy Murrill*
Circulation 23,802

Unsolicited mss welcome; one or two received every day. Fiction rarely used. Interested in local news features, human interest, well-researched investigations. Special sections include holidays & travel (Monday); food page (Tuesday); children's page (Tuesday); style page (Wednesday); business (Wednesday & Friday); motoring and motorcycling; gardening; rock music (Friday).

Scarborough

Scarborough Evening News
17-23 Aberdeen Walk, Scarborough, North Yorkshire YO11 1BB
☎01723 363636   Fax 01723 383825
Email: editor@scarborough-news.demon.co.uk
Owner *Yorkshire Regional Newspapers Ltd*
Editor *David Penman*
Circulation 17,154

Special pages include property (Monday); motoring (Tuesday/Friday).
   News Editor *Damian Holmes*
   Motoring *Dennis Sissons*
   Sports Editor *Charles Place*
All other material should be addressed to the editor.

Scotland

Daily Record (Glasgow)
See **National Newspapers**

Scotland on Sunday (Edinburgh)
See **National Newspapers**

The Scotsman (Edinburgh)
See **National Newspapers**

Sunday Herald (Glasgow)
See **National Newspapers**

Sunday Mail (Glasgow)
See **National Newspapers**

Sunday Post (Dundee)
See **National Newspapers**

Scunthorpe

Scunthorpe Evening Telegraph
Doncaster Road, Scunthorpe, N. E. Lincs DN15 7RQ
☎01724 273273   Fax 01724 273101
Owner *Northcliffe Newspapers Group Ltd*
Editor *P. L. Moore*
Circulation 24,292

All correspondence should go to the **News Editor** *Jane Manning.*

Sheffield

The Star
York Street, Sheffield, South Yorkshire S1 1PU
☎0114 2767676   Fax 0114 2725978
Owner *Sheffield Newspapers Ltd*
Editor *Peter Charlton*
Circulation 102,749

Unsolicited mss not welcome, unless topical and local.
   News Editor *Bob Westerdale* Contributions only accepted from freelance news reporters if they relate to the area.
   Features Editor *Jim Collins* Rarely require outside features, unless on specialised subject.
   Sports Editor *Martin Smith*
   Women's Page *Fiona Firth*
   Payment negotiable.

Shropshire

Shropshire Star
See under **Telford**

South Shields

Gazette
Chapter Row, South Shields, Tyne & Wear NE33 1BL
☎0191 455 4661   Fax 0191 456 8270
Website: www.shields-gazette.co.uk
Owner *Northeast Press Ltd*
Editor *Rob Lawson*
Circulation 23,332
News Editor *Huw Lewis*
Sports Editor *John Cornforth*
Women's Page *Joy Yates*

Southampton

The Southern Daily Echo
Newspaper House, Test Lane, Redbridge, Southampton, Hampshire SO16 9JX
☎01703 424777   Fax 01703 424770
Owner *Newscom Plc*
Editor *Ian Murray*
Circulation 60,343

Unsolicited mss 'tolerated'. Approach the editor in writing with strong ideas; staff supply almost all the material.

Stoke on Trent
The Sentinel
Sentinel House, Etruria, Stoke on Trent,
Staffordshire ST1 5SS
☎01782 602525   Fax 01782 280781
Owner *Staffordshire Sentinel Newspapers Ltd*
Editor *Sean Dooley*
Circulation 90,368

Weekly sports final supplement. All material
should be sent to the **Head of Content** *Michael
Wood.*

Sunderland
Sunderland Echo
Echo House, Pennywell, Sunderland, Tyne &
Wear SR4 9ER
☎0191 501 5800   Fax 0191 534 5975
Owner *North East Press Ltd*
Group Editorial Director *Andrew Smith*
Circulation 57,327

All editorial material to be addressed to the
News Editor *Patrick Lavell.*

Swansea
South Wales Evening Post
Adelaide Street, Swansea, West Glamorgan
SA1 1QT
☎01792 510000   Fax 01792 514697
Owner *Northcliffe Newspapers Group Ltd*
Editor *George Edwards*
Circulation 63,856

Circulates throughout south west Wales.
   News Editor *Jonathan Isaacs*
   Features Editor *Andy Pearson*
   Sports Editor *David Evans*

Swindon
Evening Advertiser
100 Victoria Road, Swindon, Wiltshire
SN1 3BE
☎01793 528144   Fax 01793 542434
Website: www.thisiswiltshire.co.uk
Owner *Newsquest (Wiltshire) Ltd*
Editor *Simon O'Neill*
Circulation 26,343

Copy and ideas invited. 'All material must be
strongly related or relevant to Swindon or the
county of Wiltshire.' Little scope for freelance
work. Fees vary depending on material.
   Deputy Editor *Pauline Leighton*
   Sports Editor *Alan Johnson*

Telford
Shropshire Star
Ketley, Telford, Shropshire TF1 4HU
☎01952 242424   Fax 01952 254605
Owner *Shropshire Newspapers Ltd*
Editor *Adrian Faber*
Circulation 89,619

No unsolicited mss; approach the editor with
ideas in writing in the first instance. No news or
fiction.
   News Editor *Sarah-Jane Smith*
   Head of Supplements *Sharon Walters* Limited opportunities; uses mostly in-house or syn-
dicated material. Maximum 1200 words.
   Sports Editor *Keith Harrison*

Torquay
Herald Express
Harmsworth House, Barton Hill Road,
Torquay, Devon TQ2 8JN
☎01803 676000   Fax 01803 676299/676228
Owner *Northcliffe Newspapers Group Ltd*
Editor *J. C. Mitchell*
Circulation 30,174

Drive scene, property guide, What's On Now –
leisure guide, Monday sports, special pages, rail
trail, Saturday surgery, nature and conservation
column. Supplements: *Gardening* (quarterly);
Visitors Guide and *Antiques & Collectables* (fortnightly); *Devon Days Out* (every Saturday in
summer and at Easter and May Bank Holidays).
Unsolicited mss generally not welcome. All editorial material should be addressed to the editor
in writing.

Wales
South Wales Argus
See under *Newport*

South Wales Echo
See under *Cardiff*

South Wales Evening Post
See under *Swansea*

Wales on Sunday
See **National Newspapers**

Western Mail
See under *Cardiff*

West of England

Express & Echo
See under *Exeter*

Western Daily Press
See under *Bristol*

Western Morning News
See under *Plymouth*

Weymouth

Dorset Evening Echo
57 St Thomas Street, Weymouth, Dorset
DT4 8EU
☎01305 784804   Fax 01305 760387

Owner *Newscom Plc*
Editor *David Murdock*
Circulation 20,430

Farming, by-gone days, films, arts, showbiz, brides, children's page, motoring, property, weekend leisure and entertainment including computers and gardening.
News Editor *Paul Thomas*
Sports Editor *Jack Wyllie*

Wolverhampton

Express & Star
Queen Street, Wolverhampton,
West Midlands WV1 3BU
☎01902 313131   Fax 01902 319721

Owner *Midlands News Association*
Editor *Warren Wilson*
Circulation 186,969
Deputy Editor *Richard Ewels*
News Editor *John Bray*
Features Editor *Garry Copeland*
Sports Editor *Steve Gordos*
Women's Page *Shirley Tart*

Worcester

Evening News
Berrow's House, Hylton Road, Worcester
WR2 5JX
☎01905 748200   Fax 01905 748009

Owner *Newsquest (Midlands South) Ltd*
Editor *Andrew Martin*
Circulation 23,102

Local events (Tuesday); property (Thursday); showbiz/what's on, motoring/Pulse pop page (Friday); holidays/what's on (Saturday).
News Editor *Tina Faulkner*
Features Editor/Women's Page
    Mark Higgitt
Sports Editor *Paul Ricketts*

York

Evening Press
PO Box 29, 76–86 Walmgate, York YO1 9YN
☎01904 653051   Fax 01904 612853

Owner *Newsquest Media Group*
Editor *Elizabeth Page*
Circulation 42,074

Unsolicited mss not generally welcome, unless submitted by journalists of proven ability. *Business Press Pages* (Tuesday); *Property Press* (Thursday); *Friday Night Fever* what's on supplement (Friday); *8 Days* TV supplement (Saturday).
News Editor *Fran Clee*
Picture Editor *Martin Oates*
Sports Editor *Martin Jarred*
Payment negotiable.

Yorkshire

Yorkshire Evening Post
See under *Leeds*

Yorkshire Post
See under *Leeds*

Whose Rights?

Copyright is a hazy notion. It is difficult and, on occasion, almost impossible to enforce. Just think what can be done with the new technology.

Nicholas Negroponte, the media guru at Massachusetts Institute of Technology, predicts the end to all constraints on the copying of material.

'When I read something on the Internet and, like a clipping from a newspaper, wish to send a copy of it to somebody else or to a mailing list of people, this seems harmless. But, with less than a dozen keystrokes, I could redeliver that material to literally thousands of people all over the world.'

Duplication is not only efficient, it is incredibly cheap which is why, after initial enthusiasm, few publishers are making money from the Internet. Even if this changes and some rational economic model is laid on top of the Internet, it may cost a penny or two to distribute a million bits to a million people. It certainly will not cost anything like postage. Negroponte concludes: 'Copyright law is totally out of date. It is a Gutenberg artefact. Since it is a reactive process, it will probably have to break down completely before it is corrected.'

There is no shortage of statistics to underline his message. In the Far East it is reckoned that over 90 per cent of all videocassettes sold are pirated. Unauthorised printing of books in China, Russia and a motley of smaller nations is said to be depriving British publishers and their authors of £200 million a year. As for the photocopier, it is now responsible for some 300 billion pages of illegally reproduced material.

What is to be done?

In endeavouring to enforce their rights copyright holders have legislation on their side. Until recently, British copyright lasted for 50 years beyond the author's death. Now, courtesy of the European Community, it is 70 years. There is support too for efforts to secure a decent return from those who would readily exploit an author's work without paying for it. Photocopying used to be a licence to save money. Hardly anyone thought twice before reproducing articles, chapters from books or even a whole book without reference to the copyright holder. Today, the **Authors' Licensing and Collecting Society** (ALCS) has forged agreements with education and commerce on a licensing scheme for reprographic rights. Whether or not a similar scheme can be applied to electronic rights depends on developing an effective policing system. If Negroponte is right in believing that the superhighway is also a freeway, then a large area of copyright will be unenforceable. But reports are already filtering through the technological grapevine of new metering systems which will allow publishers to monitor and record the use of its information on the Internet and other networks. In 1997, the World Intellectual Property Organisation, the UN's agency responsible for administering copyright conventions, required member states to outlaw devices aimed at bypassing technical measures to prevent unauthorised copying.

Meanwhile, there is much that the individual writer can do to guard against the free use of what is, or what might turn out to be, a valuable property. Start with a check on the small print of a contract.

Any publisher who offers a deal that is dependent on exclusive rights must be regarded with suspicion. It is likely that he has no intention of paying the author a single penny beyond a basic fee or royalty. This is what happens to contributors to academic and specialist journals who are invariably asked to assign their copyright as a condition of publication. Even those who make a living out of writing and are skilled in the devious ways of publishing can lose out simply by ignoring the subsidiary clauses of a contract or, if reading them, by not realising the long term implications.

Once surrendered, copyright cannot be retrieved. As Nicola Solomon warns, 'an assignment of copyright is binding ... it is not contingent on an agreed fee or royalties being paid. If a publisher fails to pay, your only remedy ... is to sue for the unpaid debt but you will not be able to regain copyright.'

Never say never. There must be occasions when the surrender of copyright is justified. A writer who works to order, adapting material provided for a company training course, say, or a sponsored history to be used as a promotional tool, would be pushing his luck to argue for more than a set fee.

Another moot point arises when it is not altogether clear who it is that has first claim to copyright. The most obvious example is the journalist – say, a columnist whose by-line appears twice weekly in a national newspaper. If he is on the payroll, with all the rights and responsibilities of an employee, then copyright on his articles is assumed to belong to his employer – 'unless otherwise agreed'. In other words, if the journalist is a self-assertive type who is ready to bargain with his editor he may well emerge with a contract which secures his copyright beyond the first printing. A scribe with less muscle might prefer to rely on his editor's sense of decency in handing over a share of any supplementary fees. It does happen on most national papers, but over the rest of the printed media those who commission work invariably demand exclusive copyright, including syndication rights. This applies to freelancers who, technically speaking, are entitled to copyright, as well as to regular employees. The journalists' unions urge members to resist but the need to make a living in a highly competitive market weakens the resolve of all but the star turns.

Film and Television

In late 1992 the European Commission's Rental and Lending Directive declared the 'author' of a film to have the right to '"equitable" remuneration'. But who is the 'author'? Under British law, he is generally assumed to be the producer, an interpretation which naturally offends writers and directors. The European

Community, on the other hand, takes its lead from France where the primary author of a film is the director while others, including the scriptwriter, can be named as co-authors. Producers have tried to frustrate the change, threatening expensive legal action but in 1996 Parliament gave the go-ahead for scriptwriters and authors whose work has been filmed or broadcast to receive payments for the rental of their works. Checking who owes what to whom is made easier by signing up with the ALCS which acts as a collecting agency on behalf of its members.

Problems remain, however. Lending is horrendously difficult to control. It has been known for years that the loss of income attributed to domestic sound and video recorders runs into billions. With the advance of technology, the problem is bound to worsen. Before long we will have video on demand, an almost limitless choice of programming available to any home at a push of the remote control. Imagine what that will do to undermine copyright.

Extent of Copyright

In most books a copyright notice appears on one of the front pages. In its simplest form this is the symbol © followed by the name of the copyright owner and the year of first publication. The assertion of copyright may be emphasised by the phrase 'All rights reserved', and in case there are any lingering doubts the reader may be warned that 'No part of this publication may be reproduced or transmitted in any form or by any means without permission'.

But this is to overstate the case. In principle, a quotation of a 'substantial' extract from a copyright work or for any quotation of copyright material, however short, for an anthology must be approved by the publishers of the original work.

But there is no fixed rule on what constitutes a substantial extract. In any case, even a lengthy quotation from a copyright work may not be an infringement if it is 'fair dealing ... for purposes of criticism or review'. Much depends on the standing of the writer being quoted. If he is a world famous author he or his heirs are liable to take a tougher line than, say, the copyright holder of an esoteric work on relative density. The families of literary giants are notoriously stingy. In granting permission to quote they are liable to charge hefty fees or, if the applicant is at all suspect, a biographer who is liable to do the dirt on a revered memory, for example, to refuse to cooperate in any way. For this, if for no other reason, an author who needs permission to quote should deal with the matter at an early stage in his work. Last minute requests just before a book goes to press can lead to crisis if fees are too high or if permission is refused.

A contract must specify the territory permissions will cover. The difference between British Commonwealth and the World can be a yawning gap in costs. Some publishers have a standard letter for clearing permissions which may help to speed up negotiations. But rights departments are notoriously slow in responding to requests from individuals who are unclear as to what they want or who give the impression of writing in on spec.

Difficulties can arise when the identity of a copyright holder is unclear. The publisher of the relevant book may have gone out of business or been absorbed into a conglomerate, leaving no records of the original imprint. Detective work can be yet more convoluted when it comes to unpublished works. When copyright holders are hard to trace, the likeliest source of help is the **Writers and their Copyright Holders** project, otherwise known as W.A.T.C.H. A joint enterprise of the universities of Texas and Reading, W.A.T.C.H. has created a database of English language authors whose papers are housed in archives and manuscript repositories. The database is available free of charge on the Internet.

If, despite best efforts, a copyright owner cannot be traced, there are two options; either to cut the extract or to press ahead with publication in the hope that if the copyright holder does find out he will not demand an outrageous fee. The risk can be minimised by open acknowledgement that every effort to satisfy the law has been made.

Anthology and Quotation Rates

Prose
The rate suggested by the **Society of Authors** and the **Publishers Association** is £95–115 per 1,000 words for world rights. The rate for the UK and Commonwealth or the USA alone is usually half of the world rate. For an individual country: one quarter of the world rate. Where an extract is complete in itself (e.g. a chapter or short story) publishers sometimes charge an additional fee at half the rate applicable for 1,000 words. This scale generally covers one edition only. An additional fee may be payable if the material is used in a reset or offset edition or in a new format or new binding (e.g. a paperback edition) and will certainly be required if the publisher of an anthology sub-licenses publication rights to another publisher.

Fees vary according to the importance of the author quoted, the proportion of the original work that the user intends to quote and its value to the author/publisher requesting permission. The expected size of the print-run should also be taken into consideration. Fees for quotations in scholarly works with print-runs of under 1,000 copies are usually charged at half the normal rate.

Poetry
For anthology publication in the UK and Commonwealth a minimum fee of £36 should be charged for the first 10 lines; thereafter £1.80 per line for the next 20 lines and £1.20 a line subsequently but the rates for established poets may well be significantly higher.

Moral Rights

With the 1988 Copyright Designs and Patents Act, the European concept of 'moral rights' was introduced into British law. The most basic is the right of paternity which entitles authors to be credited as the creators of their work.

However, paternity must be asserted in writing and is not retrospective. No right of paternity attaches to authors of computer programs or to writers who create works as part of their employment or journalists or as contributors to a 'collective work' such as an encyclopedia, dictionary or year book.

A second moral right is that of integrity. In theory, this opens the way to forceful objections to any 'derogatory treatment' if derogatory amounts to 'distortion or mutilation ... or is otherwise prejudicial to the honour or reputation of the author'. But mis-correction of grammar by an illiterate editor does not qualify and in the absence of test cases it seems that a book would have to be savaged beyond recognition for an injunction to be granted.

Those most likely to have their right of integrity infringed are film directors (specifically mentioned in the 1988 Act) and visual artists who might, for example, suffer the attentions of an airbrusher. For those in the writing trade, the Society of Authors urges 'locking the stable door before the horse bolts by ensuring that your contract does not permit the publishers to make significant editorial changes without your agreement' though with the virtual abandonment of hard copy in favour of disks, changes can be introduced without the author noticing – until it is too late.

Moral rights may 'be waived by written agreement or with the consent of the author'. There are cases where the concession is justified. For example, a ghost writer who has chosen to be anonymous may reasonably be expected to waive moral rights.

Titles and Trademarks

Technically, there is no copyright in a title. But where a title is inseparable from the work of a particular author, proceedings for 'passing off' are likely to be successful. Everything depends on the nature of the rival works, the methods by which they are exploited and the extent to which the title is essentially distinctive.

The risks of causing offence multiply when a unique image is involved. Mickey Mouse, Thomas the Tank Engine, and the *Mr Men* characters created by Roger Hargreaves (60 million books sold to date) are examples of registered trademarks that protect against literary and other predators. The interesting feature of trademarks is that unlike copyright, they go on for ever. The Coca-Cola and Kodak marks, for example, are well over 100 years old.

In theory it should be easier to preserve copyright in fictional characters than on titles. But in broadcasting, a frequent source of dispute is the lifting of characters from one series to another when there are two or more writers involved. Sometimes royalties are paid; other times, not. Production companies are liable to take possession of fictional characters unless their originators make a fuss.

The Singularity of Letters

The copyright status of a letter is something of a curiosity. The actual document belongs to the recipient, but the copyright remains with the writer and after death, to the writer's estate. This has caused difficulty for some biographers who have assumed that it is the owners of letters who are empowered to give permission to quote from them. This only applies if the writer has assigned copyright. Even then, the way may not be smooth. Witness the frustration of Eric Jacobs, the biographer of Sir Kingsley Amis, who found himself unable to quote from letters written by the novelist because the Bodleian Library, which has the bulk of the Amis papers, would not concede any part of the copyright Sir Kingsley has invested in them. The matter was resolved only when the letter writer himself requested permission to quote from his own correspondence.

Copyright in Lectures and Speeches

Even if a speaker talks without notes, copyright exists in a lecture as soon as it is recorded (in writing or otherwise) but not until then. The copyright belongs to the person who spoke the words, whether or not the recording was made with the permission of the speaker. There is one important exception: when a record of spoken words is made to report current events.

Copyright on Ideas

Writers trying to sell ideas should start on the assumption that it is almost impossible to stake an exclusive claim. So much unsolicited material comes the way of publishers and script departments, the duplication of ideas is inevitable.

Frequent complaints of plagiarism have led publishers and production companies to point out the risks whenever they acknowledge an unsolicited synopsis or script, warning correspondents, 'it is often the case that we are currently considering or have already considered ideas that may be similar to your own'.

In America the studios are now so worried about being sued that any writer offering an idea or script must sign a document waiving rights.

A writer who is nervous of the attention of rivals is best advised to maintain a certain reticence in dealings with the media. He should, for example, resist the urge to give out all his best ideas at an expensive lunch or in a brain-storming session with an ever so friendly producer. It is flattering to be invited to hold forth but the experience can be costly unless there is an up front fee.

At the same time, remember that there is no such thing as an entirely original plot. To succeed in an action for infringement of copyright on an idea or on the bare bones of a plot, the copying of 'a combination or series of dramatic events' must be very close indeed. Proceedings have failed because incidents common to two works have been stock incidents or revolving around stock characters common to many works.

Last year a Californian judge threw out a $100 million copyright infringement suit filed by two New Zealand playwrights against the producers of *The Full Monty*. The playwrights claimed the film closely resembled their 10-year-old play, *Ladies Night*. The late Hughie Green unsuccessfully fought a court battle to stop New Zealand producers making a show he claimed was a version of *Opportunity Knocks*. Since little of his original idea was ever committed to paper his claim was too difficult to prove.

For queries on British copyright contact: The Copyright Directorate, The Patent Office, Harmsworth H ouse, 13–15 Bouverie Street, London EC4Y 8DP. ☎0171 596 6513; Fax 0171 596 6526; Email: copyright@patent.gov.uk

Magazines

Abraxas
57 Eastbourne Road, St Austell, Cornwall
PL25 4SU
☎01726 64975   Fax 01726 64975
Owner *Paul Newman*
Editors *Paul Newman, Pamela Smith-Rawnsley*
FOUNDED 1991. QUARTERLY incorporating the *Colin Wilson Newsletter*. Unsolicited mss welcome after a study of the magazine – initial approach by phone or letter preferred.
Features Essays, translations and reviews. Issues have had Colin Wilson remembering R.D. Laing and appraising the work of Jacques Derrida and Michel Foucault. Welcomes provocative, lively articles on little-known literary figures (e.g. David Lindsay/E.H. Visiak/ Laura Del Rivo) and new slants on psychology, existentialism and ideas. Maximum length 2000 words. *Payment nominal if at all.*
Fiction One story per issue. Favours compact, obsessional stories – think of writers like Kafka, Borges or Wolfgang Borchert – of not more than 2000 words.
Poetry Double-page spread – slight penchant for the surreal but open to most styles – has published D. M. Thomas, Zofia Ilinksa, Kenneth Steven and John Ellison.
Payment free copy of magazine.

Acclaim
See **The New Writer**

Accountancy
40 Bernard Street, London WC1N 1LD
☎0171 833 3291   Fax 0171 833 2085
Owner *Institute of Chartered Accountants in England and Wales*
Editor *Brian Singleton-Green*
Circulation 68,377
FOUNDED 1889. MONTHLY. Written ideas welcome. **Features** *Brian Singleton-Green* Accounting/tax/business-related articles of high technical content aimed at professional/managerial readers. Maximum 2000 words.
Payment by arrangement.

Accountancy Age
32–34 Broadwick Street, London W1A 2HG
☎0171 316 9000/Features: 0171 316 9611
Fax 0171 316 9250
Email: accountancy_age@vnu.co.uk
Website: www.vnu.co.uk
Owner *VNU Business Publications*
Editor *Douglas Broom*
News Editor *Damian Wild (0171 316 9237)*
Circulation 76,650
FOUNDED 1969. WEEKLY. Unsolicited mss welcome. Ideas may be suggested in writing provided they are clearly thought out.
Features *Liz Loxton* Topics right across the accountancy, business and financial world. Maximum 2000 words.
Payment negotiable.

Active Life
Lexicon, 1st Floor, 1–5 Clerkenwell Road, London EC1M 5PA
☎0171 253 5775   Fax 0171 253 5676
Email: activelife@aspenplc.co.uk
Owner *Lexicon Publishing*
Editor *Helene Hodge*
Assistant to Editor *Claire Selsby*
FOUNDED 1990. BI-MONTHLY magazine aimed at over 50s. General consumer interests including travel, finance, property and leisure. Opportunities for freelancers in all departments, including fiction. Approach in writing with synopsis of ideas. Authors' notes available on receipt of s.a.e.

Acumen
See under **Poetry Magazines**

African Affairs
Dept of Historical & Cultural Studies, Goldsmiths College, University of London, New Cross, London SE14 6NW
☎0171 919 7486   Fax 0171 919 7398
Email: afraf@compuserve.com
Owner *Royal African Society*
Editors *David Killingray, Stephen Ellis*
Circulation 2250
FOUNDED 1901. QUARTERLY learned journal publishing articles on recent political, social and economic developments in sub-Saharan countries. Also included are historical studies that illuminate current events in the continent. Unsolicited mss welcome. Maximum 8000 words.
No payment.

Air International

PO Box 100, Stamford, Lincolnshire
PE9 1XQ
☎01780 755131   Fax 01780 757261
Email: English@keymags.demon.co.uk
Owner *Key Publishing Ltd*
Editor *Malcolm English*

FOUNDED 1971. MONTHLY. Civil and military aircraft magazine. Unsolicited mss welcome but initial approach by phone or in writing preferred.

AirForces Monthly

PO Box 100, Stamford, Lincolnshire PE9 1XQ
☎01780 755131   Fax 01780 757261
Email: edafm@keymags.demon.co.uk
Owner *Key Publishing Ltd*
Editor *Alan Warnes*
Circulation 24,749

FOUNDED 1988. MONTHLY. Modern military aircraft magazine. Unsolicited mss welcome but initial approach by phone or in writing preferred.

Amateur Gardening

Westover House, West Quay Road, Poole,
Dorset BH15 1JG
☎01202 440840   Fax 01202 440860
Website: www.ipc.co.uk/pubs/amgarden.htm
Owner *IPC Magazines Ltd*
Editor *Adrian Bishop*
Circulation 48,782

FOUNDED 1884. WEEKLY. New contributions are welcome especially if they are topical and informative. All articles/news items should be supported by colour pictures (which may or may not be supplied by the author).
Features Topical and practical gardening articles. Maximum 1000 words.
News Compiled and edited in-house generally.
Payment negotiable.

Amateur Photographer

King's Reach Tower, Stamford Street,
London SE1 9LS
☎0171 261 5100   Fax 0171 261 5404
Website: www.ipc.co.uk/pubs/amphotog.htm
Owner *IPC Magazines Ltd*
Editor *Garry Coward-Williams*
Circulation 28,709

FOUNDED 1884. WEEKLY. For the competent amateur with a technical interest. Freelancers are used but writers should be aware that there is ordinarily no use for words without pictures.

Amateur Stage

Hampden House, 2 Weymouth Street,
London W1N 3FD
☎0171 636 4343   Fax 0171 636 2323
Email: cvtheatre@aol.com
Owner *Platform Publications Ltd*
Editor *Charles Vance*

Some opportunity here for outside contributions. Topics of interest include amateur premières, technical developments within the amateur forum and items relating to landmarks or anniversaries in the history of amateur societies. Approach in writing only (include s.a.e. for return of mss).
No payment.

Ambit

See under **Poetry Magazines**

Amiga Format

30 Monmouth Street, Bath BA1 2AP
☎01225 442244   Fax 01225 732275
Email: amformat@futurenet.co.uk
Owner *Future Publishing*
Editor *Nick Veitch*
Circulation 19,220

FOUNDED 1988. MONTHLY. Specialist computer magazine dedicated to Commodore Amiga home computers, offering reviews, features and product information of specific interest to Amiga users. Unsolicited material welcome. Contact by phone with ideas.
News *Ben Vost* Amiga-specific exclusives and product information. Length 500–1000 words.
Features *Nick Veitch* Computer-related features (i.e. CD-ROMs, games, virtual reality) with Amiga-specific value. Maximum 10,000 words.
Special Pages *Ben Vost* Hardware and software reviews. Maximum 3000 words.
Payment £100 per 1000 words.

Ancient: The Bimonthly Magazine of Antiquity

18 Springfield Road, Brighton, East Sussex
BN1 6DA
☎01273 508150   Fax 01273 556641
Owner *Agora Publications Ltd*
Editor *Ward Rutherford*
Circulation 5000

FOUNDED 1987. BI-MONTHLY magazine devoted to the distant past from the Palaeolithic through to the Anglo-Saxon era. 'Ancient is a specialist magazine and many of our contributors are academics or specialists of some kind. It is therefore

better to approach us by letter, phone or fax before submitting material.' No highly speculative articles or those with a New Age or occult slant unless fully supported by evidence. No fiction. Maximum length for features: 1500–2000 words.
Payment £25 per 1000 words.

Animal Action
Causeway, Horsham, West Sussex RH12 1HG
☎01403 264181   Fax 01403 241048
Email: publications@rspca.org.uk
Website: www.rspca.org.uk
Owner *RSPCA*
Editor *Michaela Miller*
Circulation 80,000

BI-MONTHLY. RSPCA youth membership magazine. Articles (pet care, etc.) are written in-house. Good-quality animal photographs welcome.

The Antique Dealer and Collectors' Guide
PO Box 805, Greenwich, London SE10 8TD
☎0181 691 4820   Fax 0181 691 2489
Owner *Statuscourt Ltd*
Publisher *Philip Bartlam*
Circulation 12,500

FOUNDED 1946. MONTHLY. Covers all aspects of the antiques and fine art worlds. Unsolicited mss welcome.

Features Practical but readable articles on the history, design, authenticity, restoration and market aspects of antiques and fine art. Maximum 2000 words. *Payment £76 per 1000 words.*

News *Philip Bartlam* Items on events, sales, museums, exhibitions, antique fairs and markets. Maximum 300 words.

Antique Interiors International
162 Parkington Street, Islington, London N1 8RA
☎0171 359 6011   Fax 0171 359 6025
Owner *Antique Publications*
Editor-in-Chief *Alistair Hicks*
Managing Editor *Steven Pryke*
Circulation 22,000

FOUNDED 1986. QUARTERLY. Amusing coverage of antiques, art and interiors. Unsolicited mss not welcome. Approach by phone or in writing

in the first instance. Interested in freelance contributions on international art news items.

Antiques & Art Independent
PO Box 1945, Comely Bank, Edinburgh EH4 1AB
☎07000 765263   Fax 0131 332 4481
Owner *Antiques & Art Independent Ltd*
Publisher/Editor *Tony Keniston*
Circulation 20,000

FOUNDED 1997. BI-MONTHLY. Up-to-date information for the British antiques and art trade, circulated to dealers and collectors throughout the UK. News, photographs, gossip and controversial views on all aspects of the fine art and antiques world welcome. Articles on antiques and fine arts themselves are not featured. Approach in writing with ideas.

Apollo Magazine
1 Castle Lane, London SW1E 6DR
☎0171 233 6640   Fax 0171 630 7791
Email: editorial@apollomag.com
Owner *Paul Z. Josefowitz*
Editor *David Ekserdjian*

FOUNDED 1925. MONTHLY. Specialist articles on art and antiques, exhibition and book reviews, exhibition diary, information on dealers and auction houses. Unsolicited mss welcome. Interested in specialist, usually new research in fine arts, architecture and antiques. Approach in writing. Not interested in crafts or practical art, photography or art after 1945.

Aquarist & Pondkeeper
20 High Street, Charing, Kent TN27 0HX
☎01233 713188   Fax 01233 714288
Owner *M. J. Publications Ltd*
Editor *Dick Mills*
Circulation 20,000

FOUNDED 1924. MONTHLY. Covers all aspects of aquarium and pondkeeping: conservation, herpetology (study of reptiles and amphibians), news, reviews and aquatic plant culture. Unsolicited mss welcome. Ideas should be submitted in writing first.

Features Good opportunities for writers on any of the above topics or related areas. 1500 words (maximum 2500), plus illustrations. 'We have stocks in hand for up to two years, but new material and commissioned features will be published as and when relevant.' Average lead-in 4–6 months.

News Very few opportunities.

Architects' Journal

151 Rosebery Avenue, London EC1R 4GB
☎0171 505 6700   Fax 0171 505 6701
Owner *EMAP Construct*
Editor *Paul Finch*
Circulation 18,000

WEEKLY trade magazine dealing with all aspects of the industry. No unsolicited mss. Approach in writing with ideas.

Architectural Design

42 Leinster Gardens, London W2 3AN
☎0171 262 5097   Fax 0171 262 5093
Owner *Academy Group Ltd*
Editor *Maggie Toy*
Circulation 12,000

FOUNDED 1930. BI-MONTHLY. Theoretical architectural magazine. Unsolicited mss not generally welcome. Copy tends to come from experts in the field.

The Architectural Review

151 Rosebery Avenue, London EC1R 4GB
☎0171 505 6725   Fax 0171 505 6701
Owner *EMAP Construct*
Editor *Peter Davey*
Circulation 24,116

MONTHLY professional magazine dealing with architecture and all aspects of design. No unsolicited mss. Approach in writing with ideas.

Arena

Block A, Exmouth House, Pine Street,
London EC1R 0JL
☎0171 689 9999   Fax 0171 698 0901
Owner *Wagadon Ltd/Condé Nast Publications*
Editor *Ekow Eshun*
Circulation 86,922

Style and general interest magazine for men. Intelligent feature articles and profiles, plus occasional fiction.
　　Features Fashion, lifestyle, film, television, politics, business, music, media, design, art, architecture and sport.
　　Payment £200–250 per 1000 words.

Art & Craft

Villiers House, Clarendon Avenue,
Leamington Spa, Warwickshire CV32 5PR
☎01926 887799   Fax 01926 883331
Owner *Scholastic Ltd*
Editor *Sian Morgan*
Circulation 15,000

FOUNDED 1936. MONTHLY aimed at a specialist market – the needs of primary school teachers,

art coordinators and pupils. Ideas and synopses considered for commission.
　　Features The majority of contributors are primary school teachers with good art and craft skills and familiar with the curriculum.
　　News Handled by in-house staff. No opportunities.

Art Monthly

Suite 17, 26 Charing Cross Road, London
WC2H 0DG
☎0171 240 0389   Fax 0171 497 0726
Email: artmonthly@compuserve.com
Owner *Brittania Art Publications*
Editor *Patricia Bickers*
Circulation 5000

FOUNDED 1976. TEN ISSUES YEARLY. News and features of relevance to those interested in modern and contemporary visual art. Unsolicited mss welcome. Contributions should be addressed to the editor, accompanied by an s.a.e.
　　Features Alongside exhibition reviews: usually 750–1000 words and almost always commissioned. Interviews and articles of up to 1500 words on art theory, individual artists, contemporary art history and issues affecting the arts (e.g. funding and arts education). Book reviews of 750–1000 words.
　　News Brief reports (250–300 words) on art issues.
　　Payment negotiable.

The Art Newspaper

27-29 Vauxhall Grove, London SW8 1SY
☎0171 735 3331   Fax 0171 735 3332
Owner *Umberto Allemandi & Co. Publishing*
Editor *Anna Somers Cocks*
Circulation 22,000

FOUNDED 1990. Eleven issues per year. Tabloid format with hard news on the international art market, news, museums, exhibitions, archaeology, conservation, books and current debate topics. Length 250–2000 words. No unsolicited mss. Approach with ideas in writing. Commissions only.
　　Payment £120 per 1000 words.

The Artist

Caxton House, 63–65 High Street,
Tenterden, Kent TN30 6BD
☎0158076 3673   Fax 0158076 5411
Owner/Editor *Sally Bulgin*
Circulation 18,200

FOUNDED 1931. MONTHLY. Art journalists, artists, art tutors and writers with a good knowledge of art materials are invited to write to the editor with ideas for practical and informative features about art, materials, techniques and artists.

Artscene
Dean Clough Industrial Park, Halifax,
West Yorkshire HX3 5AX
☎01422 322527   Fax 01422 322518
Owner *Yorkshire and Humberside Arts*
Editor *Victor Allen*
Circulation 25,000

FOUNDED 1973. MONTHLY. Listings magazine for Yorkshire and Humberside. No unsolicited mss. Approach by phone with ideas.

Features Profiles of artists (all media) and associated venues/organisers of events of interest. Topical relevance vital. Maximum length 1500 words. *Payment* £100 per 1000 words.

News Artscene strives to bring journalistic values to arts coverage – all arts 'scoops' in the region are of interest. Maximum length 500 words. *Payment* £100 per 1000 words.

Asian Times
148 Cambridge Heath Road, London E1 5QJ
☎0171 702 8012   Fax 0171 702 7937
Owner *Ethnic Media Group*
Editor *Siddartha Shivdasani*
Circulation 33,000

FOUNDED 1983. WEEKLY community paper for the Asian community in Britain. Interested in relevant general, local and international issues. Approach in writing with ideas for submission.

Attitude
Northern & Shell Tower, City Harbour,
London E14 9GL
☎0171 308 5090   Fax 0171 308 5075
Owner *Northern & Shell plc*
Editor *Adam Mattera*
Circulation 50,000

FOUNDED 1994. MONTHLY. Style magazine aimed primarily, but not exclusively, at gay men. Celebrity, fashion and cultural coverage. Brief summaries of proposed features, together with details of previously published work, should be sent by post or fax only. 'It sounds obvious, but anyone wanting to contribute to the magazine should read it first.

The Author
84 Drayton Gardens, London SW10 9SB
☎0171 373 6642
Owner *The Society of Authors*
Editor *Derek Parker*
Manager *Kate Pool*

Circulation 7,500

FOUNDED 1890. QUARTERLY journal of **The Society of Authors**. Most articles are commissioned.

Autocar
60 Waldegrave Road, Teddington, Middlesex
TW11 8LG
☎0181 943 5630   Fax 0181 943 5759
Email: autocar@compuserve.com
Owner *Haymarket Magazines Ltd*
Editor *Patrick Fuller*
Circulation 77,403

FOUNDED 1895. WEEKLY. All news stories, features, interviews, scoops, ideas, tip-offs and photographs welcome.

Features *Hugo Andreae*
News *Chris Rosamond*
Payment from £200 per 1000 words/negotiable.

Baby Magazine
WV Publications, 57–59 Rochester Place,
London N1 9JY
☎0171 226 2222   Fax 0171 359 5225
Email: danbrom@hotmail.com
Owner *Highbury House Communications*
Editor *Dan Bromage*
Circulation 79,000

MONTHLY. For parents-to-be and parents of children up to two years old. No unsolicited mss.

Features Send synopsis of feature with covering letter in the first instance. Unsolicited material is not returned.

Baby's Best Buys
WV Publications, 57–59 Rochester Place,
London N1 9JY
☎0171 226 2222   Fax 0171 359 5225
Email: danbrom@hotmail.com
Owner *Highbury House Communications*
Editor *Dan Bromage*

QUARTERLY. Comprehensive product testing for parenting equipment and maternity wear.

Babycare and Pregnancy
D. C. Thomson & Co. Ltd, 80 Kingsway East,
Dundee DD4 8SL
☎01382 223131   Fax 01382 452491
Email: baby@dcthomson.co.uk/mags/baby
Website: www.dcthomson.co.uk/mags/baby
Owner *D. C. Thomson & Co. Ltd*
Editor *Irene K. Duncan*
Circulation 27,000

FOUNDED 1994. MONTHLY magagine on

pregnancy, birth and babycare. Unsolicited mss on these topics welcome. Not interested in material relating to children over three years of age. Approach in writing or by phone.

Back Brain Recluse (BBR)
PO Box 625, Sheffield S1 3GY
Website: www.bbr-online.com/magazine
Owner/Editor *Chris Reed*
Circulation 3000

Award-winning British fiction magazine which actively seeks new fiction that ignores genre pigeonholes. 'We tread the thin line between experimental speculative fiction and avant garde literary fiction. We strongly recommend familiarity with our guidelines for contributors, and with recent issues of *BBR*, before any material is submitted.' All correspondence must be accompanied by s.a.e. or international reply coupons; US$1 is an acceptable alternative to IRCs. If a response by email is wanted, send disposable copy and no return postage.
Payment £10 per 1000 words.

Badminton
Connect Sports, 14 Woking Road, Cheadle Hulme, Cheshire SK8 6NZ
☎0161 486 6159   Fax 0161 488 4505
Owner *Mrs S. Ashton*
Editor *William Kings*

BI-MONTHLY. Specialist badminton magazine, with news, views, product information, equipment reviews, etc. Unsolicited material will be considered. Approach the editor by phone with an idea.
Features *William Kings/Sue Ashton* Open to approaches and likes to discuss ideas in the first instance. Interested in badminton-related articles on health, fitness, psychology, clothing, accessories, etc.
Payment £60.

The Badminton Times
PO Box 3250, Wokingham, Berkshire RG40 4FR
☎0118 973 7744

Editor *Mr R. Richardson*

FOUNDED 1980. QUARTERLY. Events, players, fashion and footwear, rackets, facilities, technique and tactics.

Balance
British Diabetic Association, 10 Queen Anne Street, London W1M 0BD
☎0171 323 1531   Fax 0171 637 3644
Email: balance@diabetes.org.uk

Owner *British Diabetic Association*
Editor *John Isitt*
Circulation 200,000

FOUNDED 1935. BI-MONTHLY. Unsolicited mss are not accepted. Writers may submit a brief proposal in writing. Only topics relevant to diabetes will be considered.
Features *John Isitt* Medical, diet and lifestyle features written by people with diabetes or with an interest and expert knowledge in the field. General features are mostly based on experience or personal observation. Maximum 1500 words. *Payment* NUJ rates.
News *John Isitt* Short pieces about activities relating to diabetes and the lifestyle of diabetics. Maximum 150 words.
Young Balance Any kind of article written by those under 18 and with personal experience of diabetes.
Payment varies.

The Banker
149 Tottenham Court Road, London W1P 9LL
☎0171 896 2507   Fax 0171 896 2586
Website:www.bbcworldwide.com/
Owner *Financial Times Business*
Editor *Stephen Timewell*
Circulation 14,155

FOUNDED 1926. MONTHLY. News and features on banking, finance and capital markets worldwide and technology.

BBC Gardeners' World Magazine
Woodlands, 80 Wood Lane, London W12 0TT
☎0181 576 3959   Fax 0181 576 3986
Website:www.bbcworldwide.com/
Owner *BBC Worldwide Publishing Ltd*
Editor *Adam Pasco*
Circulation 375,138

FOUNDED 1991. MONTHLY. Gardening advice, ideas and inspiration. No unsolicited mss: phone or write in with ideas – interested in features about exceptional small gardens.

BBC Good Food
Woodlands, 80 Wood Lane, London W12 0TT
☎0181 576 2000   Fax 0181 576 3931
Website:www.bbcworldwide.com/
Owner *BBC Worldwide Publishing Ltd*
Editor *Orlando Murrin*
Circulation 303,457

FOUNDED 1989. MONTHLY food and drink magazine with television and radio links. No unsolicited mss.

BBC Homes & Antiques

Woodlands, 80 Wood Lane, London W12 0TT
☎0181 576 3490   Fax 0181 576 3867
Website:www.bbcworldwide.com/
Owner *BBC Worldwide Publishing Ltd*
Editor *Judith Hall*
Circulation 213,671

FOUNDED 1993. MONTHLY traditional home interest magazine with a strong bias towards antiques and collectables. Opportunities for freelancers are limited; most features are commissioned from regular stable of contributors. No fiction, health and beauty, fashion or general showbusiness. Approach with ideas by phone or in writing.

Features *Caroline Wheater* At-home features: inspirational houses – people-led items. Pieces commissioned on recce shots and cuttings. Guidelines available on request. Celebrity features: 'at homes or favourite things' – send cuttings of relevant work published. Maximum 1500 words.

Special Pages Regular feature on memories of childhood homes. Maximum 800 words.

Payment negotiable.

BBC Music Magazine

Room A1004, Woodlands, 80 Wood Lane, London W12 0TT
☎0181 576 3283/3693   Fax 0181 576 3292
Email: music.magazine@bbc.co.uk
Website: www.bbcworldwide.com/
    musicmagazine
Owner *BBC Worldwide Publishing Ltd*
Editor *Helen Wallace*
Circulation 68,652 (UK edition)

FOUNDED 1992. MONTHLY. All areas of classical music. Not interested in unsolicited material. Approach with ideas only, by fax or in writing.

BBC Top Gear Magazine

Woodlands, 80 Wood Lane, London W12 0TT
☎0181 576 3716   Fax 0181 576 3754
Website:www.bbcworldwide.com/
Owner *BBC Worldwide Publishing Ltd*
Editor *Kevin Blick*
Circulation 184,000

FOUNDED 1993. MONTHLY companion magazine to the popular TV series. No unsolicited material as most features are commissioned.

BBC Vegetarian Good Food

Room AG175, Woodlands, 80 Wood Lane, London W12 0TT
☎0181 576 3767   Fax 0181 576 3825
Website:www.bbcworldwide.com/

Owner *BBC Worldwide Publishing Ltd*
Editor *Gilly Cubitt*
Circulation 70,962

FOUNDED 1992. MONTHLY magazine containing recipes, health and environment features. Unsolicited mss not welcome. Approach in writing with ideas.

BBC Wildlife Magazine

Broadcasting House, Whiteladies Road, Bristol BS8 2LR
☎0117 973 8402   Fax 0117 946 7075
Website:www.bbcworldwide.com/
Owner *BBC Worldwide Publishing Ltd*
Editor *Rosamund Kidman Cox*
Circulation 116,537

FOUNDED 1963 (formerly *Wildlife*, née *Animals*). MONTHLY. Unsolicited mss generally not welcome.

Features Most features commissioned from writers with expert knowledge of wildlife or conservation subjects. Maximum 3500 words. *Payment* £120–350.

News Most news stories commissioned from known freelancers. Maximum 800 words. *Payment* £40–100.

Bee World

18 North Road, Cardiff CF1 3DY
☎01222 372409   Fax 01222 665522
Email: ibra@cf.ac.uk
Website: www.cf.ack.uk/ibra/
Owner *International Bee Research Association*
Editor *Dr P. A. Munn*
Circulation 1700

FOUNDED 1919. QUARTERLY. High-quality factual journal, including peer-reviewed articles, with international readership. Features on apicultural science and technology. Unsolicited mss welcome but authors should write to the Editor for guidelines before submitting mss.

Bella

H. Bauer Publishing, Shirley House, 25–27 Camden Road, London NW1 9LL
☎0171 241 8000   Fax 0171 241 8056

Owner *H. Bauer Publishing*
Editor-in-Chief *Jackie Highe*
Circulation 661,807

FOUNDED 1987. WEEKLY. Women's magazine specialising in real-life, human interest stories.

Features *Sue Ricketts* Contributions welcome for some sections of the magazine: readers' letters, 'Precious Moments', 'Blush with Bella' and 'Bella Rat'.

Fiction *Linda O'Byrne* Maximum 1200–2000 words. Send s.a.e. for guidelines.

Best

197 Marsh Wall, London E14 9SG
☎0171 519 5500   Fax 0171 519 5516
Owner *G & J (UK)*
Editor *Louise Court*
Circulation 511,841

FOUNDED 1987. WEEKLY women's magazine and stablemate of *Prima*. Multiple features, news, short stories on all topics of interest to women. Important for would-be contributors to study the magazine's style which differs from many other women's weeklies. Approach in writing with s.a.e.

Features Maximum 1500 words. No unsolicited mss.

Fiction Short story slot; unsolicited mss accepted. Maximum 1000 words.

Payment negotiable.

Best of British

CMS Publishing, Rock House, Scotgate, Stamford, Lincolnshire PE9 2YQ
☎01780 763063   Fax 01780 765788
Email: mail@cmspublishing.co.uk
Owner *CMS Publishing*
Editor *Peter Kelly*

FOUNDED 1994. MONTHLY magazine celebrating all things British, both past and present. Study of the magazine is advised in the first instance. All preliminary approaches should be made in writing. No telephone calls, please.

Best Solutions

38 Broad Street, Earls Barton, Northamptonshire NN6 0ND
☎01635 522488   Fax 01635 522212
Owner *Grahame White*
Editor *Geoff Ellis*
Circulation 300,000

FOUNDED 1996. QUARTERLY business to business consultancy magazine. No unsolicited mss. 'Interested in articles (1000 words) for heads of substantial consultancy practices.' Approach in writing.

The Big Issue

236–240 Pentonville Road, London N1 9JY
☎0171 526 3200   Fax 0171 526 3201

Editor-in-Chief *A. John Bird*
Editor *Matthew Collin*
Deputy Editor *Andrew Davies*

Circulation 127,033

FOUNDED 1991. WEEKLY. An award-winning campaigning and street-wise general interest magazine sold in London, the Midlands, the North East and South of England. Separate regional editions sold in Manchester, Scotland, Wales, the South West and Ireland.

Features *Andrew Davies* Interviews, campaigns, comment, opinion and social issues reflecting a varied and informed audience. Balance includes social issues but mixed with arts and cultural features. Freelance writers used each week – commissioned from a variety of writers. Best approach is to fax or post synopses to features editor with examples of work in the first instance. Maximum 1500 words. *Payment* £150 for 1000 words.

News *Jane Cassidy* Hard-hitting exclusive stories with emphasis on social injustice aimed at national leaders.

Arts *Tina Jackson* Interested in comment, interviews and analysis ideas. Reviews written in-house. Send synopses to arts editor.

BIG!

Mappin House, 4 Winsley Street, London W1N 7AR
☎0171 436 1515   Fax 0171 312 8246
Email: big@ecm.emap.com
Owner *EMAP Metro*
Editor *Frances Sheen*
Circulation 206,116

FOUNDED 1990. FORTNIGHTLY celebrity/entertainment magazine for teenage girls. Interested in interviews with celebrities from the worlds of pop, film and television. 1500 words maximum; approach by phone in the first instance.

Bird Life Magazine

RSPB, The Lodge, Sandy, Bedfordshire SG19 2DL
☎01767 680551   Fax 01767 683262
Owner *Royal Society for the Protection of Birds*
Editor *Derek Niemann*
Circulation 90,000

FOUNDED 1965. BI-MONTHLY. Bird, wildlife and nature conservation for 8–12-year-olds (Young Ornithologist Club members). No unsolicited mss. No 'captive/animal welfare' articles.

Features *Derek Niemann* Unsolicited material rarely used. 'Good transparencies to accompany articles help success.'

News *Derek Niemann* News releases welcome but news stories must relate to YOC members. Approach in writing in the first instance.

Birds

The Lodge, Sandy, Bedfordshire SG19 2DL
☎01767 680551　　　　Fax 01767 683262
Owner *Royal Society for the Protection of Birds*
Editor *R. A. Hume*
Circulation 1 million

QUARTERLY magazine which covers not only wild birds but also wildlife and related conservation topics. No interest in features on pet birds or 'rescued' sick/injured/orphaned ones. Mss or ideas welcome. 'No captive birds, please.'

Birdwatch

3D/F Leroy House, 436 Essex Road, London N1 3QP
☎0171 704 9495　　　　Fax 0171 704 2767
Website: www.birdwatch.co.uk
Owner *Solo Publishing*
Editor *Dominic Mitchell*
Circulation 16,500

FOUNDED 1992. MONTHLY high-quality magazine featuring illustrated articles on all aspects of birds and birdwatching, especially in Britain. No unsolicited mss. Approach in writing with synopsis of 100 words maximum. Annual **Birdwatch Bird Book of the Year** award (see entry under **Prizes**).

Features *Dominic Mitchell* Unusual angles/personal accounts, if well-written. Articles of an educative or practical nature suited to the readership. Maximum 2000–3000 words.

Fiction *Dominic Mitchell* Very little opportunity although occasional short story published. Maximum 1500 words.

News *Tim Harris* Very rarely use external material.

Payment £40 per 1000 words.

Bizarre

John Brown Publishing, The New Boathouse, 136–142 Bramley Road, London W10 6SR
☎0171 565 3000　　　　Fax 0171 565 3055
Email: bizarre@johnbrown.co.uk
Website: www.bizarremag.com
Owner *John Brown Publishing*
Editor *Fiona Jerome*
Circulation 98,000

FOUNDED 1997. MONTHLY magazine featuring amazing stories and images from around the world. No fiction, poetry, illustrations, short snippets.

Features *Fiona Jerome* Particularly interested in global stories and celebrity interviews. Maximum 2,500 words. Approach in writing

Payment £120 per 1000 words.

Black Beauty & Hair

Hawker Consumer Publications Ltd, 13 Park House, 140 Battersea Park Road, London SW11 4NB
☎0171 720 2108　　　　Fax 0171 498 3023
Owner *Hawker Consumer Publications Ltd*
Editor *Irene Shelley*
Circulation 22,017

BI-MONTHLY with one annual special: *The Hairstyle Book* in October; and a *Bridal Supplement* in the April/May issue. Black hair and beauty magazine with emphasis on authoritative articles relating to hair, beauty, fashion, health and lifestyle. Unsolicited contributions welcome.

Features Beauty and fashion pieces welcome from writers with a sound knowledge of the Afro-Caribbean beauty scene plus bridal features. Minimum 1000 words.

Payment £95 per 1000 words.

Bliss Magazine

Endeavour House, 189 Shaftesbury Avenue, London WC2H 8JG
☎0171 208 3478　　　　Fax 0171 208 3591
Email: alice.davies@ecm.emap.com
Owner *EMAP plc*
Editor *Kerry Parnell*
Circulation 337,188

FOUNDED 1995. MONTHLY teenage lifestyle magazine for girls. No unsolicited mss; 'call the deputy editor with an idea and then send it in.'

News *Peter Hart* Worldwide teenage news. Maximum 200 words. *Payment* £50–100.

Features *Maria Coole* Real life teenage stories with subjects willing to be photographed. Reports on teenage issues. Maximum 2000 words. *Payment* £350.

Boat International

5–7 Kingston Hill, Kingston upon Thames, Surrey KT2 7PW
☎0181 547 2662　　　　Fax 0181 547 9731
Owner *Edisea Ltd*
Editor *Amanda McCracken*
Circulation 32,000

FOUNDED 1983. MONTHLY. Unsolicited mss welcome. Approach with ideas in writing and s.a.e.

Features Maximum 2000 words.
News Maximum 300 words.

Book and Magazine Collector

43–45 St. Mary's Road, London W5 5RQ
☎0181 579 1082　　　　Fax 0181 566 2024
Owner *John Dean*

Editor *Crispin Jackson*
Circulation 12,000

FOUNDED 1984. MONTHLY. Contains articles about collectable authors/publications/subjects. Unsolicited mss welcome, but write first with ideas. Must be bibliographical and include a full bibliography and price guide; not interested in purely biographical features.
Features Maximum length 4000 words.
Payment £30 per 1000 words.

The Book Collector

PO Box 12426, London W11 3GW
☎0171 792 3492   Fax 0171 792 3492
Owner *The Collector Ltd*
Editor *Nicolas J. Barker*

FOUNDED 1950. QUARTERLY magazine on bibliography and the history of books, book-collecting, libraries and the book trade.

The Book Directory

'Ambleside', 52 Heaton Street, Brampton, Chesterfield, Derbyshire S40 3AQ
☎01246 230408
Owner/Editor *Ron Mihaly*

FOUNDED 1997. QUARTERLY. Contains articles on all bibliographical subjects, with list of book fairs for a particular quarter. Unsolicited mss and ideas welcome – but write first, please. Maximum 2000 words.
Payment Commissions: £15 per 1000 words.

Book World Magazine

2 Caversham Street, London SW3 4AH
☎0171 351 4995   Fax 0171 351 4995
Owner *Christchurch Publishers Ltd*
Editor *James Hughes*
Circulation 5,500

FOUNDED 1980. MONTHLY news and reviews for serious book collectors, librarians, antiquarian and other booksellers. No unsolicited mss. Interested in material relevant to literature, art and book collecting. Send letter in the first instance.

Bookdealer

Suite 34, 26 Charing Cross Road, London WC2H 0DH
☎0171 240 5890   Fax 0171 379 5770
Editor *Barry Shaw*

WEEKLY trade paper which acts almost exclusively as a platform for people wishing to buy or sell rare/out-of-print books. Twelve-page editorial only; occasional articles and book reviews by regular freelance writers.

Books

39 Store Street, London WC1F 7DB
☎0171 692 2900   Fax 0171 419 2111
Editor *Liz Thomson*
Circulation 115,000

Formerly *Books and Bookmen*. Consumer magazine dealing chiefly with features about authors and reviews of books. Carries few commissioned pieces.
Payment negotiable.

The Bookseller

12 Dyott Street, London WC1A 1DF
☎0171 420 6000 (Editorial)
Fax 0171 420 6103

Website:www.theBookseller.com
Owner *J. Whitaker & Sons Ltd*
Editor *Nicholas Clee*

Trade journal of the publishing and book trade – the essential guide to what is being done to whom. Trade news and features, including special features, company news, publishing trends, etc. Unsolicited mss rarely used as most writing is either done in-house or commissioned from experts within the trade. Approach in writing first.
Features *Jenny Bell*
News *Ms Danuta Kean*

Boxing Monthly

40 Morpeth Road, London E9 7LD
☎0181 986 4141   Fax 0181 986 4145
Email: bm@boxing-monthly.demon.co.uk
Owner *Topwave Ltd*
Editor *Glyn Leach*
Circulation 30,000

FOUNDED 1989. MONTHLY. International coverage of professional boxing; previews, reports and interviews. Unsolicited material welcome. Interested in small hall shows and grass-roots knowledge. No big fight reports. Approach in writing in the first instance.

Boyz

72 Holloway Road, London N7 8NZ
☎0171 296 6230   Fax 0171 296 0026
Editor *David Hudson*
Circulation 55,000

FOUNDED 1994. WEEKLY Entertainment and features magazine aimed at a gay readership covering clubs, fashion, TV, films, music, theatre, celebrities and the UK gay scene in general. Unsolicited mss are looked at but not often used.

Brides and Setting Up Home

Vogue House, Hanover Square, London
W1R 0AD
☎0171 499 9080 Fax 0171 460 6369
Owner *Condé Nast Publications Ltd*
Editor *Sandra Boler*
Circulation 63,543

BI-MONTHLY. Much of the magazine is produced in-house, but a good, relevant feature on
cakes, jewellery, music, flowers, etc. is always
welcome. Maximum 1000 words. Prospective
contributors should telephone with an idea in
the first instance.

British Birds

Fountains, Park Lane, Blunham, Bedford
MK44 3NJ
☎01767 640025 Fax 01767 640025
Owner *British Birds Ltd*
Editor *Dr J. T. R. Sharrock*
Circulation 10,000

FOUNDED 1907. MONTHLY ornithological
journal. Features annual *Reports on Rare Birds in
Great Britain*, bird news from official national
correspondents throughout Europe and sponsored competitions for Bird Photograph of the
Year, Bird Illustrator of the Year and Young
Ornithologists of the Year. Unsolicited mss
welcome from ornithologists only.
     Features Well-researched, original material
relating to Western Palearctic birds welcome.
Maximum 6000 words.
     News *Bob Scott/Wendy Dickson* Items ranging
from conservation to humour. Maximum 200
words.
     Payment only for photographs, drawings and
paintings.

British Chess Magazine

The Chess Shop, 69 Masbro Road, London
W14 0LS
☎0171 603 2877 Fax 0171 371 1477
Owner/Editor *Murray Chandler*

FOUNDED 1881. MONTHLY. Emphasis on tour-
naments, the history of chess and chess-related
literature. Approach in writing with ideas.
Unsolicited mss not welcome unless from qualified chess experts and players.

British Medical Journal

BMA House, Tavistock Square, London
WC1H 9JR
☎0171 387 4499 Fax 0171 383 6418
Email: editor@bmj.com
Website: www.bmj.com

Owner *British Medical Association*
Editor *Professor Richard Smith*

British Philatelic Bulletin

Royal Mail National, Royal London House,
22 Finsbury Square, London EC2A 1NL
☎0171 614 7029 Fax 0171 614 7209
Owner *Royal Mail*
Editor *John Holman*
Circulation 30,000

FOUNDED 1963. MONTHLY bulletin giving
details of forthcoming British stamps, features on
older stamps and postal history, and book
reviews. Welcomes photographs of interesting,
unusual or historic letter boxes.
     Features Articles on all aspects of British
philately. Maximum 1500 words.
     News Reports on exhibitions and philatelic
events. Maximum 500 words. Approach in
writing in the first instance.
     Payment £45 per 1000 words.

British Railway Modelling

The Maltings, West Street, Bourne,
Lincolnshire PE10 9PH
☎01778 391167 Fax 01778 393668
Owner *Warners Group Publications Plc*
Editor *David Brown*
Assistant Editor *Jarrod Cotter*
Circulation 17,594

FOUNDED 1993. MONTHLY. A general magazine
for the practising modeller. No unsolicited mss
but ideas are welcome. Interested in features on
quality models, from individual items to complete layouts. Approach in writing.
     Features Articles on practical elements of
the hobby, e.g. locomotive construction, kit
conversions etc. Layout features and articles on
individual items which represent high standards
of the railway modelling art. Maximum length
6000 words (single feature). *Payment* up to £50
per published page.
     News and reviews containing the model rail-
way trade, new products etc. Max. length 1000
words. *Payment* up to £50 per published page.

Broadcast

33-39 Bowling Green Lane, London
EC1R 0DA
☎0171 505 8014 Fax 0171 505 8050
Owner *EMAP Business Communications*
Editor *Steve Clarke*
Circulation 13,556

FOUNDED 1960. WEEKLY. Opportunities for
freelance contributions. Write to the relevant
editor in the first instance.

Features *Lucy Rouse* Any broadcasting issue. Maximum 1500 words.

News *Tabitha Cole* Broadcasting news. Maximum 350 words.

Payment £200 per 1000 words.

Brownie
17–19 Buckingham Palace Road, London SW1W 0PT
☎0171 834 6242   Fax 0171 828 8317
Email: chq@guides.org.uk
Website: www.guides.org.uk
Owner *The Guide Association*
Editor *Marion Thompson*
Circulation 30,000

FOUNDED 1962. MONTHLY. Aimed at Brownie members aged 7–10.

Articles Crafts and simple make-it-yourself items using inexpensive or scrap materials.

Fiction Brownie content an advantage. No adventures involving unaccompanied children in dangerous situations – day or night. Maximum 600 words.

Payment £50 per 1000 words pro rata.

The Burlington Magazine
14–16 Duke's Road, London WC1H 9AD
☎0171 388 1228   Fax 0171 388 1230
Owner *The Burlington Magazine Publications Ltd*
Editor *Caroline Elam*

FOUNDED 1903. MONTHLY. Unsolicited contributions welcome on the subject of art history provided they are previously unpublished. All preliminary approaches should be made in writing.

Exhibition Reviews Usually commissioned, but occasionally unsolicited reviews are published if appropriate. Maximum 1000 words.

Articles Maximum 4500 words. *Payment* £100 (maximum).

Shorter Notices Maximum 2000 words. *Payment* £50 (maximum).

Business Brief
PO Box 582, Five Oaks, St Saviour, Jersey JE4 8XQ
☎01534 611600   Fax 01534 611610
Owner *MSP Publishing*
Editor *Debbie Binding*
Circulation 5,000

FOUNDED 1989. MONTHLY magazine covering business developments in the Channel Islands and how they affect the local market. Interested in business-orientated articles only – 800 words maximum.

Payment £8 per 100 words.

Business Life
Haymarket House, 1 Oxendon Street, London SW1Y 4EE
☎0171 925 2544   Fax 0171 839 4508
Owner *Premier Magazines*
Editor *Sandra Harris*
Assistant Editor *Catherine Flanagan*
Circulation 193,000

TEN ISSUES YEARLY plus two double issues. Glossy business travel magazine with few opportunities for freelancers. Distributed on BA European routes, TAT and Deutsche BA only. Unsolicited mss not welcome. Approach with ideas in writing only.

Business Traveller
Russell Square House, 10–12 Russell Square, London WC1B 5ED
☎0171 580 9898   Fax 0171 580 6676
Owner *Perry Publications*
Editor-in-Chief *Julia Brookes*
Circulation 38,760

MONTHLY Consumer publication. Opportunities exist for freelance writers but unsolicited contributions tend to be 'irrelevant to our market'. Would-be contributors are advised to study the magazine first. Approach in writing with ideas.

Payment varies.

Camcorder User
57–59 Rochester Place, London NW1 9JU
☎0171 331 1000   Fax 0171 331 1242
Email: CamUserEd@AOL.com
Owner *W. V. Publications*
Editor *Adrian Justins*
Circulation 21,797

FOUNDED 1988. MONTHLY magazine dedicated to camcorders, with features on creative technique, shooting advice, new equipment, accessory round-ups and interesting applications on location. Unsolicited mss, illustrations and pictures welcome. *Payment* negotiable.

Campaign
174 Hammersmith Road, London W6 7JP
☎0181 267 4656   Fax 0181 267 4914
Owner *Haymarket Publishing Ltd*
Editor *Stefano Hatfield*
Circulation 17,700

FOUNDED 1968. WEEKLY. Lively magazine serving the advertising and related industries. Freelance contributors are best advised to write in the first instance.

Features Articles of 1500–2000 words.

News Relevant news stories of up to 300 words.
Payment negotiable.

Camping and Caravanning
Greenfields House, Westwood Way,
Coventry, Warwickshire CV4 8JH
☎01203 694995   Fax 01203 694886
Owner *Camping and Caravanning Club*
Editor *Peter Frost*
Circulation 147,296

FOUNDED 1901. MONTHLY. Interested in journalists with camping and caravanning knowledge. Write with ideas for features in the first instance.

Features Outdoor pieces in general, plus items on specific regions of Britain. Maximum 1200 words. Illustrations to support text essential.

Camping Magazine
Star Brewery, Castle Ditch Lane, Lewes, East Sussex BN7 1YJ
☎01273 477421   Fax 01273 477421
Owner *Garnett Dickinson Publishing*
Editor *John Lloyd*

FOUNDED 1961. MONTHLY magazine with features on camping. Aims to reflect this enjoyment by encouraging readers to appreciate the outdoors and to pursue an active camping holiday, whether as a family in a frame tent or as a lightweight backpacker. Articles that have the flavour of the camping lifestyle without being necessarily expeditional or arduous are always welcome. Study of the magazine is advised in the first instance. Ideas welcome. Contact editor by phone before sending mss.
Payment negotiable.

Canal and Riverboat
Inter Regional House, 9 Thorpe Road,
Norwich, Norfolk NR1 1EP
☎01603 623856   Fax 01603 623856
Email: chris@canalandriverboat.co.uk
Website: www.canalandriverboat.co.uk
Owner *A. E. Morgan Publications Ltd*
Editor *Chris Cattrall*
Circulation 26,000

Covers all aspects of waterways, narrow boats and cruisers. Contributions welcome. Make initial approach in writing.

Features *Chris Cattrall* Waterways, narrow boats and motor cruisers, cruising reports, practical advice, etc. Unusual ideas and personal comments are particularly welcome. Maximum 2000 words. Articles should be supplied in PC Windows format disk. *Payment* around £50 per page.

News *Chris Cattrall* Items of up to 300 words welcome on the Inland Waterways System, plus photographs if possible. *Payment* £15.

Car Mechanics
Kelsey Publishing, Cudham Tithe Barn, Bottom Burn Farm, Cudham, Kent TN16 3AG
☎01959 541444   Fax 01959 541400
Owner *Kelsey Publishing*
Editor *Peter Simpson*
Circulation 35,000

MONTHLY. Practical guide to maintenance and repair of post–1978 cars for DIY and the motor trade. Unsolicited mss, with good-quality colour prints or transparencies, 'at sender's risk'. Ideas preferred. Initial approach by letter or phone welcome and strongly recommended, 'but please read a recent copy first for style'.

Features Good, technical, entertaining and well-researched material welcome, especially anything presenting complex matters clearly and simply.
Payment by arrangement ('but generous for the right material').

Caravan Life
Warners Group Publications plc,
The Maltings, West Street, Bourne,
Lincolnshire PH10 9PH
☎01778 391027   Fax 01778 423063
Editor *Nick Harding*
Circulation 16,119

FOUNDED 1987. Magazine for experienced caravanners and enthusiasts providing practical and useful information and product evaluation. Opportunities for caravanning, relevant touring and travel material with good-quality colour photographs.

Caravan Magazine
Link House, Dingwall Avenue, Croydon,
Surrey CR9 2TA
☎0181 686 2599   Fax 0181 781 6044
Website: www.linkhouse.co.uk/caravan.html
Owner *IPC Magazines Ltd*
Editor *Rob McCabe*
Circulation 21,002

FOUNDED 1933. MONTHLY. Unsolicited mss welcome. Approach in writing with ideas. All correspondence should go direct to the editor.

Features Touring with strong caravan bias, technical/DIY features and how-to section. Maximum 1500 words.
Payment by arrangement.

Caribbean Times

148 Cambridge Heath Road, London E1 5QJ
☎0171 702 8012   Fax 0171 702 7937
Owner *Ethnic Media Group*
Editor *Michael Eboda*
Circulation 22,500

FOUNDED 1981. WEEKLY community paper for the African and Caribbean communities in Britain. Interested in general, local and international issues relevant to these communities. Approach in writing with ideas for submission.

Carmarthenshire Life

Swan House Publishing, Swan House, Bridge Street, Newcastle Emlyn, Carmarthenshire SA38 9DX
☎01239 710632
Owner *Swan House Publishing*
Editor *David Fielding*

FOUNDED 1995. MONTHLY county magazine with articles on local history, issues, characters, off-beat stories with good colour or b&w photographs. No country diaries, short stories or poems. Most articles are commissioned from known freelancers but 'always prepared to consider ideas from new writers'. No mss. Send cuttings of previous work (published or not) and synopsis to the editor.

Cars and Car Conversions Magazine

Link House, Dingwall Avenue, Croydon, Surrey CR9 2TA
☎0181 686 2599   Fax 0181 781 1159
Website: www.ipc.co.uk/pubs/car.htm
Owner *IPC Magazines Ltd*
Editor *Steve Bennett*
Circulation 34,928

FOUNDED 1963. MONTHLY. Unsolicited mss welcome but prospective contributors are advised to make initial contact by telephone.
Features Technical articles on current motorsport and unusual sport-orientated road cars. Length by arrangement.
Payment negotiable.

Cat World

Avalon Court, Star Road, Partridge Green, West Sussex RH13 8RY
☎01403 711511   Fax 01403 711521
Owner *Ashdown Publishing Ltd*
Editor *Lisa Lidderdale*
Circulation 19,000

FOUNDED 1981. MONTHLY. Unsolicited mss welcome but initial approach in writing preferred.
Features Lively, first-hand experience features on every aspect of the cat. Breeding features and veterinary articles by acknowledged experts only. Maximum 1800 words.
News Short, concise, factual or humorous items concerning cats. Maximum 100 words.
Submit on disk (MS Word) if possible, with accompanying hard copy and s.a.e. for return.

Catholic Herald

Lamb's Passage, Bunhill Row, London EC1Y 8TQ
☎0171 588 3101   Fax 0171 256 9728
Email: catholic@atlas.co.uk
Editor *Dr William Oddie*
Deputy Editor *Joe Jenkins*
Literary Editor *Damian Thompson*
Circulation 22,000

WEEKLY. Interested mainly in straight Catholic issues but also in general humanitarian matters, social policies, the Third World, the arts and books.
Payment by arrangement.

The Celtic Field

Celtic Publications, Glendoo Cottage, Glen Road, Ballaugh, Isle of Man IM7 5JB
☎01624 897263   Fax 01624 897263
Owner/Editor *Robert Watson*
Circulation 5000

FOUNDED 1996. QUARTERLY Celtic magazine featuring anything to do with Scotland, Ireland, Wales, Cornwall, Isle of Man, Brittany and other Celtic countries. Unsolicited mss welcome on Celtic/Gaelic subjects; ancient or modern history; fiction and book reviews welcome if on a Celtic theme – maximum 2000 words for fiction.
Payment negotiable/free magazine for news items.

Challenge

50 Loxwood Avenue, Worthing, West Sussex BN14 7RA
☎01903 824174   Fax 01903 824376
Owner *Challenge Publishing*
Editor *Donald Banks*
Circulation 70,000

FOUNDED 1958. MONTHLY Christian newspaper which welcomes contributions. No fiction. Send for sample copy of writers' guidelines in the first instance.
News Items of up to 500 words (preferably

with pictures) 'showing God at work', and human interest photo stories. 'Churchy' items not wanted. Stories of professional sportsmen and musicians who are Christians always wanted but check first to see if their story has already been used.

Women's Page Relevant items of interest welcome.

Payment negotiable.

Chapman

4 Broughton Place, Edinburgh EH1 3RX
☎0131 557 2207   Fax 0131 556 9565
Email: chapman_pub@ndirect.co.uk
Website: www.airstrip-one.ndirect.
co.uk/chapman

Owner/Editor *Joy M. Hendry*
Circulation 2000

FOUNDED 1970. QUARTERLY. Scotland's quality literary magazine. Features poetry, short works of fiction, criticism, reviews and articles on theatre, politics, language and the arts. Unsolicited material welcome if accompanied by s.a.e. Approach in writing unless discussion is needed. Priority is given to full-time writers.

Features Topics of literary interest, especially Scottish literature, theatre, culture or politics. Maximum 5000 words.

Fiction Short stories, occasionally novel extracts if self-contained. Maximum 6000 words. *Payment* copies.

Special Pages Poetry, both UK and non-UK in translation (mainly, but not necessarily, European). *Payment* by negotiation.

Chapter One

See **Alliance of Literary Societies** under **Professional Associations**

Chat

King's Reach Tower, Stamford Street,
London SE1 9LS
☎0171 261 6565   Fax 0171 261 6534
Website: www.ipc.co.uk/pubs/chat.htm

Owner *IPC Magazines Ltd*
Editor-in-Chief *Iris Burton*
Editor *Keith Kendrick*
Circulation 497,731

FOUNDED 1985. WEEKLY general interest women's magazine. Unsolicited mss considered; approach in writing with ideas. Not interested in contributors 'who have never bothered to read *Chat* and therefore don't know what type of magazine it is'.

Features *Paula Lockey* Human interest and humour. Maximum 1000 words. *Payment* up to £600 maximum.

Fiction *Olwen Rice* Maximum 1000 words.

Cheshire Life

2nd Floor, Oyston Mill, Strand Road,
Preston, Lancashire PR1 8UR
☎01772 722022   Fax 01772 760905

Owner *Life Magazines*
Editor *Patrick O'Neill*
Circulation 15,000

FOUNDED 1934. MONTHLY. Homes, gardens, personalities, business, farming, conservation, property, heritage, books, fashion, arts, science – anything which has a Cheshire connection somewhere.

Child Education

Villiers House, Clarendon Avenue,
Leamington Spa, Warwickshire CV32 5PR
☎01926 887799   Fax 01926 883331

Owner *Scholastic Ltd*
Editor *Gill Moore*
Circulation 56,791

FOUNDED 1923. MONTHLY magazine aimed at nursery, pre-school playgroup, infant and first teachers. Articles from teachers, relating to education for 4–7-year age group, are welcome. Maximum 1200 words. Approach in writing with synopsis. No unsolicited mss.

Choice

Apex House, Oundle Road, Peterborough,
Cambridgeshire PE2 9NP
☎01733 555123   Fax 01733 898487
Email: choice@ecm.emap.com
Website: www.choicemagazine.com

Owner *EMAP/Bayard Presse*
Editor *Sue Dobson*
Circulation 100,000

MONTHLY full-colour, lively and informative magazine for people aged 50 plus which helps them get the most out of their lives, time and money after full-time work.

Features Real-life stories, hobbies, interesting (older) people, British heritage and countryside, involving activities for active bodies and minds, health, relationships, book/entertainment reviews. Unsolicited mss read (s.a.e. for return of material); write with ideas and copies of cuttings if new contributor. No phone calls, please.

Rights/Money All items affecting the magazine's readership are written by experts. Areas of interest include pensions, state benefits, health, finance, property, legal.

Payment by arrangement.

Christian Herald

96 Dominion Road, Worthing, West Sussex
BN14 8JP
☎01903 821082   Fax 01903 821081
Email: news@christianherald.org.uk
Website: www.christianherald.org.uk

Owner *Christian Media Centre Ltd*
Editor *Russ Bravo*
Circulation 18,000

WEEKLY evangelical, interdenominational Christian newspaper aimed at committed Christians. News, bible-based comment and incisive features. No poetry. Contributors' guidelines available.

Payment Christian Media rates.

Church Music Quarterly

151 Mount View Road, London N4 4JT
☎0181 341 6408   Fax 0181 340 0021
Email: cmqeditor@aol.com

Owner *Royal School of Church Music*
Editor *Trevor Ford*
Associate Editor *Marianne Barton*
Circulation 13,700

QUARTERLY. Contributions welcome. Telephone in the first instance.

Features *Trevor Ford* Articles on church music or related subjects considered. Maximum 2000 words.

Payment £60 per page.

Church of England Newspaper

10 Little College Street, London SW1P 3SH
☎0171 878 1545   Fax 0171 976 0783

Owner *Parliamentary Communications Ltd*
Editor *Colin Blakely*
Circulation 9,200

FOUNDED 1828. WEEKLY. Almost all material is commissioned but unsolicited mss are considered.

Features *Claire Shelley* Preliminary enquiry essential. Maximum 1200 words.

News *Andrew Carey* Items must be sent promptly and should have a church/Christian relevance. Maximum 200–400 words.

Payment negotiable.

Church Times

33 Upper Street, London N1 0PN
☎0171 359 4570   Fax 0171 226 3073

Owner *Hymns Ancient & Modern*
Editor *Paul Handley*
Circulation 38,000

FOUNDED 1863. WEEKLY. Unsolicited mss considered.

Features *Paul Handley* Articles and pictures (any format) on religious topics. Maximum 1600 words. *Payment* £100 per 1000 words.

News *Paul Handley* Occasional reports (commissions only) and up-to-date photographs. *Payment* by arrangement.

Classic Boat

Link House, Dingwall Avenue, Croydon, Surrey CR9 2TA
☎0181 686 2599   Fax 0181 781 6535
Email: cb@lhm.co.uk
Website: www.classicboat.co.uk

Owner *IPC Magazines Ltd*
Editor *Nic Compton*
Circulation 19,138

FOUNDED 1987. MONTHLY. Traditional boats and classic yachts old and new; maritime history. Unsolicited mss, particularly if supported by good photos, are welcome. Sail and power boat pieces considered. Approach in writing with ideas. Interested in well-researched stories on all nautical matters. News reports welcome. Contributor's notes available (s.a.e.).

Features Boatbuilding, boat history and design, events, yachts and working boats. Material must be well-informed and supported where possible by good-quality or historic photos. Maximum 3000 words. Classic is defined by excellence of design and construction – the boat need not be old and wooden! *Payment* £75-100 per published page.

News New boats, restorations, events, boatbuilders, etc. Maximum 500 words. *Payment* according to merit.

Classic Cars

EMAP Active, Homenene House, Orton Centre, Peterborough PE2 5UW
☎01733 237111   Fax 01733 465857
Website: www.classiccarsworld.co.uk

Owner *EMAP National Publications*
Editor *John Westlake*
International Editor *Robert Coucher*
Circulation 86,177

FOUNDED 1973. MONTHLY international classic car magazine containing entertaining and informative articles about classic cars, events and associated personalities.

Classical Guitar

1 & 2 Vance Court, Trans Britannia Enterprise Park, Blaydon on Tyne NE21 5NH
☎0191 414 9000   Fax 0191 414 9001
Email: classicalguitar@ashleymark.co.uk
Website: www.ashleymark.co.uk/

Owner *Ashley Mark Publishing Co.*
Editor *Colin Cooper*
FOUNDED 1982. MONTHLY.
  Features *Colin Cooper* Usually written by staff writers. Maximum 1500 words. *Payment* by arrangement.
  News *Thérèse Wassily Saba* Small paragraphs and festival concert reports welcome. *No payment.*
  Reviews *Chris Kilvington* Concert reviews of up to 250 words are usually written by staff reviewers.

Classical Music

241 Shaftesbury Avenue, London
WC2H 8EH
☎0171 333 1742   Fax 0171 333 1769
Email: classical.music@rhinegold.co.uk
Owner *Rhinegold Publishing Ltd*
Editor *Keith Clarke*
FOUNDED 1976. FORTNIGHTLY. A specialist magazine using precisely targeted news and feature articles aimed at the music business. Most material is commissioned but professionally written unsolicited mss are occasionally published. Freelance contributors may approach in writing with an idea but should familiarise themselves beforehand with the style and market of the magazine.
  Payment negotiable.

Classics

Berwick House, 8–10 Knoll Rise, Orpington, Kent BR6 0PS
☎01689 887200   Fax 01689 838844
Email: classics@splgroup.demon.co.uk
Owner *SPL*
Editor *Andrew Noakes*
FOUNDED 1997. MONTHLY how-to magazine for classic car owners, featuring everything from repairing and restoring to buying, selling and enjoying all types of cars from the '50s to '80s. Includes vehicle comparison tests, price guide, practical advice and technical know-how from experts and owners, plus hundreds of readers' free ads.
  Features Illustrated features on classic car maintenance, repair and restoration with strong technical content and emphasis on DIY.
  News All classic car related news stories and topical photos.

Climber

PO Box 28, Altrincham, Cheshire WA14 2FG
☎0161 928 3480   Fax 0161 941 6897
Owner *Myatt McFarlane plc*

Editor *Bernard Newman*
FOUNDED 1962. MONTHLY. Unsolicited mss welcome (they receive about ten a day). Ideas welcome.
  Features Freelance features (accompanied by photographs) are accepted on climbing and mountaineering in the UK and abroad, but the standard of writing must be extremely high. Maximum 2000 words. *Payment* negotiable.
  News No freelance opportunities as all items are handled in-house.

Club Guide

PO Box 6160, Birmingham B16 8XA
☎0121 643 1575   Fax 0121 643 4450
Managing Editor *Sam Allen*
Editor *S. Howard*
Circulation 30,000
FOUNDED 1990. QUARTERLY Club features and listings. Interested in receiving items for club listings; approach in writing. No unsolicited mss.

Club International

2 Archer Street, London W1V 8JJ
☎0171 292 8000   Fax 0171 734 5030
Email: club@pr-org.co.uk
Owner *Paul Raymond*
Editor *Robert Swift*
Circulation 180,000
FOUNDED 1972. MONTHLY. Features and short humorous items aimed at young male readership aged 18–30.
  Features Maximum 1000 words.
  Shorts 200–750 words.
  Payment negotiable.

Coin News

Token Publishing Ltd, PO Box 14, Honiton, Devon EX14 9YP
☎01404 46972   Fax 01404 831895
Email: info@coin-news.com
Website: www.coin-news.com
Owners *J. W. Mussell and Carol Hartman*
Editor *J. W. Mussell*
Circulation 10,000
FOUNDED 1964. MONTHLY. Contributions welcome. Approach by phone in the first instance.
  Features Opportunity exists for well-informed authors 'who know the subject and do their homework'. Maximum 2500 words.
  Payment £20 per 1000 words.

Comhairle

See **ignotus press** under **Small Presses**

Commerce Magazine

Station House, Station Road, Newport
Pagnell, Milton Keynes MK16 0AG
☎01908 614477   Fax 01908 616441
Owner *Holcot Press Group*
Group Editor *Steve Brennan*
Circulation 25,000

MONTHLY. Ideas welcome. Approach by
phone or in writing first.

Features By-lined articles frequently used.
Generally 750–800 words with photos.

News Handled in-house.

Special Pages Throughout the year –
media and marketing; building and construction; finance and professional; office update.

No payment.

Company

National Magazine House, 72 Broadwick
Street, London W1V 2BP
☎0171 439 5000   Fax 0171 439 5117
Owner *National Magazine Co. Ltd*
Editor *Sam Baker*
Circulation 290,402

MONTHLY. Glossy women's magazine appealing to the independent and intelligent young
woman. A good market for freelancers: 'We
look for great newsy features relevant to young
British women'. Keen to encourage bright,
new, young talent, but uncommissioned material is rarely accepted. Feature outlines are the
only sensible approach in the first instance.
Maximum 1500–2000 words. Features to *Celia
Duncan*, Features Editor.

Payment £250 per 1000 words.

Company Clothing Magazine

7 Holbrook Road, Leicester LE2 3LG
☎0116 270 4075   Fax 0116 270 0136
Owner *Company Clothing Information Services Ltd*
Editor *Leonie Barrie*
Circulation 13,000

Only UK magazine dedicated to the corporate
clothing industry. Unsolicited mss welcome on
any aspect of business clothing and workwear.

Compass Sport

Ballencrieff Cottage, Ballencrieff Toll,
Bathgate, West Lothian EH48 4LD
☎01506 632728   Fax 01506 635444
Email: pages@clara.net
Website: home.clara.net/pages
Owner *Pages Editorial & Publishing Services*
Editor *Suse Coon*

BI-MONTHLY orienteering magazine covering
all disciplines of the sport including mountain
marathons, mountain bike O, ski O and trail
O. Includes profiles and articles on relevant
topics, with subsections on fixtures, junior
news and mountain marathons which are compiled by sub-editors. Letters, puzzles and competition. Phone or email to discuss content and
timing.

Payment by arrangement.

Computer Weekly

Quadrant House, The Quadrant, Sutton,
Surrey SM2 5AS
☎0181 652 3122   Fax 0181 652 8979
Email: computer.weekly@rbi.co.uk
Owner *Reed Business Information*
Editor *Karl Schneider*
Circulation 150,000

FOUNDED 1966. Freelance contributions welcome.

Features *Ian Mitchell* Always looking for
good new writers with specialised industry
knowledge. Previews and show features on
industry events welcome. Maximum 1500
words.

News *Hooman Bassirian* Some openings for
regional or foreign news items. Maximum 300
words.

Payment Up to £50 for stories/tips.

Computing, The IT Newspaper

32–34 Broadwick Street, London
W1A 2HG
☎0171 316 9000   Fax 0171 316 9160
Website: www.vnu.co.uk
Owner *VNU Business Publications Ltd*
Editor *Douglas Hayward*
Circulation 114,000

FOUNDED 1973. WEEKLY newspaper for IT
professionals.

Features/Associate Editor *Ian Stobie*
News *Tim Stammers*
Unsolicited technical articles welcome.
Please enclose s.a.e. for return.

Payment negotiable.

Condé Nast Traveller

Vogue House, Hanover Square, London
W1R 0AD
☎0171 499 9080   Fax 0171 493 3758
Email: traveller@msmail.condenast.co.uk
Website:www.cntraveller.co.uk
Owner *Condé Nast Publications*
Editor *Sarah Miller*
Circulation 70,000

FOUNDED 1997. Monthly travel magazine.

Proposals rather than completed mss preferred. Approach in writing in the first instance.

Contemporary Review

Cheam Business Centre, 14 Upper Mulgrave Road, Cheam, Surrey SM2 7AZ
☎0181 643 4846   Fax 0181 241 7507
Owner *Contemporary Review Co. Ltd*
Editor *Dr Richard Mullen*

FOUNDED 1866. MONTHLY. One of the first periodicals to devote considerable space to the arts. Covers a wide spectrum of interests, including international affairs and politics, literature and the arts, history, travel and religion. No fiction. Maximum 3000 words.

Literary Editor *Dr James Munson* Monthly book section with reviews which are always commissioned.

Payment £5 per page.

Cosmopolitan

National Magazine House, 72 Broadwick Street, London W1V 2BP
☎0171 439 5000   Fax 0171 439 5016
Owner *National Magazine Co. Ltd*
Editor-in-Chief *Mandi Norwood*
Circulation 476,288

MONTHLY. Designed to appeal to the mid-twenties, modern-minded female. Popular mix of articles, with emphasis on relationships and careers, and hard news. Known to have a policy of not considering unsolicited mss but always on the look-out for 'new writers with original and relevant ideas and a strong voice'. Send short synopsis of idea. All would-be writers should be familiar with the magazine.

Payment about £250 per 1000 words.

Cotswold Life

Treaford House, 54 Lansdown Road, Cheltenham, Gloucestershire GL51 6QB
☎01242 255334   Fax 01242 255116
Owner *Loyalty & Conquest Communications Ltd*
Managing Editor *David MacDonald*
Circulation 10,000

FOUNDED 1968. MONTHLY. News and features on life in the Cotswolds. Contributions welcome.

Features Interesting places and people, reminiscences of Cotswold life in years gone by, and historical features on any aspect of Cotswold life. Approach in writing in the first instance. Maximum 1500–2000 words.

Payment by negotiation after publication.

Counselling at Work

Association for Counselling at Work, Eastlands Court, St Peter's Road, Rugby, Warwickshire CV21 3QP
☎01788 335617   Fax 01788 335618
Email: ACWoffice@compuserve.com
Owner *British Association for Counselling*
Editor *David Kinchin (d.kinchin@ukonline.co.uk)*
Circulation 1600

FOUNDED 1993. QUARTERLY official journal of the Association for Counselling at Work, a division of B.A.C. Looking for well-researched articles (500–1600 words) about *any* aspect of workplace counselling. Mss from those employed as counsellors or in welfare posts are particularly welcome. Photographs not accepted at present but that may change in the near future. No fiction or poetry. Send A4 s.a.e. for writer's guidelines and sample copy of the journal.

No payment.

Country

Shuttleworth, Old Warden Park, Biggleswade, Bedfordshire SG18 9EA
☎01767 626242   Fax 01767 627158
Owner *The Country Gentlemen's Association*
Chief Executive *Christopher Page*
Circulation 25,000

FOUNDED 1893. Subscription MONTHLY. News and features covering rural events, countryside, leisure, heritage, homes and gardens. Some outside contributors. Approach in writing in the first instance.

Payment by arrangement.

Country Homes and Interiors

King's Reach Tower, Stamford Street, London SE1 9LS
☎0171 261 6451   Fax 0171 261 6895
Website: www.ipc.co.uk/pubs/counthom.htm
Owner *IPC Magazines Ltd*
Editor *Katherine Hadley*
Circulation 110,855

FOUNDED 1986. MONTHLY. The best approach for prospective contributors is with an idea in writing as unsolicited mss are not welcome.

Features *Jean Carr* Monthly personality interviews of interest to an intelligent, affluent readership (women and men), aged 25–44. Maximum 1200 words. Also hotel reviews, leisure pursuits and weekending pieces in England and abroad. Length 750 words.

Houses *Sarah Whelan* Country-style homes with excellent design ideas. Length 1000 words.

Payment negotiable.

Country Life

King's Reach Tower, Stamford Street,
London SE1 9LS
☎0171 261 7058   Fax 0171 261 5139
Website: www.countrylife.co.uk

Owner *IPC Magazines*
Editor *Clive Aslet*
Circulation 44,774

ESTABLISHED 1897. WEEKLY. Features articles
which relate to architecture, countryside, wildlife, rural events, sports, arts, exhibitions,
current events, property and news articles of
interest to town and country dwellers. Strong
informed material rather than amateur enthusiasm. 'We regret we cannot be liable for the safe
custody or return of any solicited or unsolicited
materials.'
   Payment variable, depending on word length
and picture size.

Country Living

National Magazine House, 72 Broadwick
Street, London W1V 2BP
☎0171 439 5000   Fax 0171 439 5093

Owner *National Magazine Co. Ltd*
Editor *Susy Smith*
Circulation 181,090

Magazine aimed at country dwellers and town
dwellers who love the countryside. Covers
people, conservation, wildlife, houses (gardens
and interiors) and country businesses. No
unsolicited mss.
   Payment negotiable.

Country Smallholding

Broad Leys Publishing Company, Buriton
House, Station Road, Newport, Saffron
Walden, Essex CB11 3PL
☎01799 540922   Fax 01799 541367

Owner *D. and K. Thear*
Editor *Helen Sears*
Circulation 21,000

FOUNDED 1975. MONTHLY journal dealing
with practical country living. Unsolicited mss
welcome; around 30 are received each week.
Articles should be detailed and practical, based
on first-hand knowledge and experience of
smallholding.

Country Sports

The Old Town Hall 367 Kennington Road,
London SE1 4PT
☎0171 582 5432   Fax 0171 793 8484

Owner *Countryside Alliance*
Editor *Graham Downing*

Circulation 60,000

FOUNDED 1996. QUARTERLY magazine on
country sports and conservation issues. No
unsolicited mss.

Country Walking

Apex House, Oundle Road, Peterborough,
Cambridgeshire PE2 9NP
☎01733 898100   Fax 01733 465070

Owner *EMAP Plc*
Editor *Lynne Maxwell*
Circulation 51,203

FOUNDED 1987. MONTHLY magazine containing walks, features related to walking and
things you see, country crafts, history, nature,
photography etc., plus pull-out walks guide
containing 25+ routes every month. Very few
unsolicited mss accepted. An original approach
to subjects welcomed. Not interested in book
or gear reviews, news cuttings or poor-quality
pictures. Approach by phone with ideas.
   Features *Vincent Crump* Reader's story
(maximum 800 words). Practical (200–600
words).
   Special Pages 'Down your way' section
walks. Accurately and recently researched walk
and fact file. Points of interest along the way
and pictures to illustrate. Please contact for
guidelines (unsolicited submissions not often
accepted for this section).
   Payment not negotiable.

Country-Side

BNA, 48 Russell Way, Higham Ferrers,
Northamptonshire NN10 8EJ
☎01933 314672   Fax 01933 314672

Owner *British Naturalists' Association*
Editor *Dr D. Applin*

FOUNDED 1905. BI-ANNUAL. 'In-house' conservation and natural history magazine. Unsolicited mss and ideas for features welcome on
conservation, environmental and natural history topics. Approach in writing with ideas.
Maximum 1400 words.
   Payment £50 (with pictures).

The Countryman

King's Reach Tower, Stamford Street,
London SE1 9LS
☎0171 261 5000
Website: www.ipc.co.uk/pubs/countman.htm

Owner *IPC Magazines Ltd*
Editor *Tom Quinn*
Circulation 36,471

FOUNDED 1927. EIGHT ISSUES YEARLY. Unsolicited mss with s.a.e. welcome; about 120 received each week. Contributors are strongly advised to study the magazine's content and character in the first instance. Articles supplied with top quality illustrations (colour transparencies, archive b&w prints and line drawings) are far more likely to be used. No fiction. Maximum article length 1500 words.

The Countryman's Weekly
(incorporating **Gamekeeper and Sporting Dog**)
Yelverton, Devon PL20 7PE
☎01822 855281   Fax 01822 855372
Publisher *Vic Gardner*
Features Editor *Kelly Gardner*
FOUNDED 1895. WEEKLY. Unsolicited material welcome.
   Features On any country sports topic. Maximum 1000 words.
Payment rates available on request.

County
PO Box 2486, Cane End, Reading,
Berkshire RG4 6YA
☎0118 972 4800   Fax 0118 972 4900
Owners *Mr and Mrs Watts*
Editor *Mrs Ashlyn Watts*
Circulation 50,000
FOUNDED 1986. QUARTERLY lifestyle magazine featuring homes, interiors, gardening, fashion and beauty, motoring, leisure and dining. Welcomes unsolicited mss. All initial approaches should be made in writing.

The Cricketer International
Third Street, Langton Green, Tunbridge Wells, Kent TN3 0EN
☎01892 862551   Fax 01892 863755
Email: editorial@cricketer.co.uk
Owner *Ben G. Brocklehurst*
Editor *Peter Perchard*
Circulation 40,000
FOUNDED 1921. MONTHLY. Unsolicited mss considered. Ideas in writing only. No initial discussions by phone. All correspondence should be addressed to the editor.

Crimewave
5 Martins Lane, Witcham, Ely,
Cambridgeshire CB6 2LB
☎01353 777931
Email: ttapress@aol.com
Website: purl.oclc.org/net/ttaonline/index.html
Owner *TTA Press*

Editor *Mat Coward*
FOUNDED 1998. QUARTERLY B5 colour magazine of crime fiction. 'The UK's only magazine specialising in crime short stories publishing the very best from across the spectrum.' Every issue contains stories by authors who are household names in the crime fiction world but room is found for lesser known and unknown writers. Submissions welcome (not via email) with appropriate return postage. Potential contributors are advised to study the magazine. Contracts exchanged upon acceptance; payment on publication.

Cumbria and Lake District Magazine
Dalesman Publishing Co. Ltd, Stable Courtyard, Broughton Hall, Skipton, North Yorkshire BD23 3AE
☎01756 701381   Fax 01756 701326
Email: editorial@dalesman.co.uk
Owner *Dalesman Publishing Co. Ltd*
Editor *Terry Fletcher*
Circulation 16,100
FOUNDED 1951. MONTHLY. County magazine of strong regional and countryside interest, focusing on the Lake District. Unsolicited mss welcome. Maximum 1500 words. Approach in writing or by phone with feature ideas.

Cycle Sport
King's Reach Tower, Stamford Street,
London SE1 9LS
☎0171 261 5588   Fax 0171 261 5758
Website: www.ipc.co.uk/pubs/cyclsprt.htm
Owner *IPC Magazines Ltd*
Editor *Luke Edwardes-Evans*
Circulation 23,299
FOUNDED 1993. MONTHLY magazine dedicated to professional cycle racing. Unsolicited ideas for features welcome.

Cycling Weekly
King's Reach Tower, Stamford Street,
London SE1 9LS
☎0171 261 5588   Fax 0171 261 5758
Website: www.ipc.co.uk/pubs/cyclweek.htm
Owner *IPC Magazines Ltd*
Editor *Robert Garbutt*
Circulation 31,735
FOUNDED 1891. WEEKLY. All aspects of cycle sport covered. Unsolicited mss and ideas for features welcome. Approach in writing with ideas. Fiction rarely used.

Features Cycle racing, technical material and related areas. Maximum 2000 words. Most work commissioned but interested in seeing new work. *Payment* around £60–100 per 1000 words (quality permitting).

News Short news pieces, local news, etc. Maximum 300 words. *Payment* £15 per story.

The Dalesman
Stable Courtyard, Broughton Hall, Skipton, North Yorkshire BD23 3AE
☎01756 701381   Fax 01756 701326
Email: editorial@dalesman.co.uk
Owner *Dalesman Publishing Co. Ltd*
Editor *Terry Fletcher*
Circulation 51,000

FOUNDED 1939. Now the biggest-selling regional publication of its kind in the country. MONTHLY with articles of specific Yorkshire interest. Unsolicited mss welcome; receives approximately ten per day. Initial approach in writing or by phone. Maximum 1500 words. *Payment* negotiable.

Dance Theatre Journal
Laban Centre London, Laurie Grove, London SE14 6NH
☎0181 692 4070   Fax 0181 694 8749
Owner *Laban Centre London*
Editor *Ian Bramley*
Circulation 2000

FOUNDED 1982. THRICE-YEARLY. Interested in features on every aspect of the contemporary dance scene, particularly issues such as the funding policy for dance, critical assessments of choreographers' work and the latest developments in the various schools of contemporary dance. Unsolicited mss welcome. Length 1000–3000 words. *Payment* varies 'according to age and experience'.

The Dancing Times
Clerkenwell House, 45–47 Clerkenwell Green, London EC1R 0EB
☎0171 250 3006   Fax 0171 253 6679
Email: dancing_times@compuserve.com
Owner *The Dancing Times Ltd*
Editor *Mary Clarke*

FOUNDED 1910. MONTHLY. Freelance suggestions welcome from specialist dance writers and photographers only. Approach in writing.

Darts World
28 Arrol Road, Beckenham, Kent BR3 4PA
☎0181 650 6580   Fax 0181 654 4343
Owner *World Magazines Ltd*

Editor *A. J. Wood*
Circulation 24,500

Features Single articles or series on technique and instruction. Max. 1200 words.

Fiction Short stories with darts theme of no more than 1000 words.

News Tournament reports and general or personality news required. Max. 800 words.
Payment negotiable.

Dateline Magazine
25 Abingdon Road, London W8 6AL
☎01869 351525   Fax 01869 351526
Owner *Columbus Group plc*
Editors *Peter Bennett, Nicky Boult*
Circulation 10,000

FOUNDED 1976. MONTHLY magazine for single people. Unsolicited mss welcome.

Features Anything of interest to, or directly concerning, single people. Max. 2500 words.

News Items required at least six weeks ahead. Max. 2500 words.
Payment from £45 per 1000 words; £10 per illustration/picture used.

Day by Day
Woolacombe House, 141 Woolacombe Road, Blackheath, London SE3 8QP
☎0181 856 6249
Owner *Loverseed Press*
Editor *Patrick Richards*
Circulation 24,000

FOUNDED 1963. MONTHLY. News commentary and digest of national and international affairs, with reviews of the arts (books, plays, art exhibitions, films, opera, musicals) and county cricket and Test reports among regular slots. Unsolicited mss welcome (s.a.e. essential). Approach in writing with ideas. Contributors are advised to study the magazine in the first instance. (Specimen copy 90p.)

News *Ronald Mallone* Interested in themes connected with non-violence and social justice only. Max. 600 words.

Features No scope for freelance contribution.

Fiction *Michael Gibson* Very rarely published.

Poems *Michael Gibson* Short poems in line with editorial principles considered, max. 20 lines.
Payment negotiable.

Dazed & Confused
112 Old Street, London EC1V 1BD
☎0171 336 0766   Fax 0171 336 0966
Email: dazed@confused.co.uk
Website: www.confused.co.uk

Owner *Waddell Ltd*
Editor *Jefferson Hack*
Circulation 80,000

FOUNDED 1992. MONTHLY. Cutting edge fashion, music, art interviews and features. No unsolicited material. Approach in writing with ideas in the first instance.

Decanter

583 Fulham Road, London SW6 5UA
☎0171 610 3929   Fax 0171 381 5282
Email: editorial@decanter.com
Website: www.decantermagazine.com

Editor *Susan Keevil*
Circulation 35,000

FOUNDED 1975. Glossy wines and spirits magazine. Unsolicited material welcome but an advance telephone call or faxed outline appreciated. No fiction.

News/Features All items and articles should concern wines, spirits, food and related subjects.

Derbyshire Life and Countryside

Heritage House, Lodge Lane, Derby DE1 3HE
☎01332 347087   Fax 01332 290688
Owner *B. C. Wood*
Editor *Vivienne Irish*
Circulation 12,243

FOUNDED 1931. MONTHLY county magazine for Derbyshire. Unsolicited mss and photographs of Derbyshire welcome, but written approach with ideas preferred.

Descent

51 Timbers Square, Roath, Cardiff CF2 3SH
☎01222 486557   Fax 01222 486557
Email: descent@wildpp.globalnet.co.uk
Owner *Wild Places Publishing*
Editor *Chris Howes*
Assistant Editor *Judith Calford*

FOUNDED 1969. BI-MONTHLY magazine for cavers and mine enthusiasts. Submissions welcome from freelance contributors who can write accurately and knowledgeably on any aspect of caves, mines or underground structures.

Features General interest articles of under 1000 words welcome, as well as short foreign news reports, especially if supported by photographs/illustrations. Suitable topics include exploration (particularly British, both historical and modern), expeditions, equipment, techniques and regional British news. Maximum 2000 words.

Payment on publication according to page area filled.

Desire

192 Clapham High Street, London SW4 7UD
☎0171 627 5155   Fax 0171 627 5808
Owner *Moondance Media Ltd*
Editor *Ian Jackson*

FOUNDED 1994. SIX ISSUES YEARLY. Britain's first erotic magazine for both women and men, celebrating sex and sensuality with a mix of articles, columns, features, reviews, interviews, fantasy and poetry (1000–2500 words).

For sample copy of magazine plus contributors' guidelines and rates, please enclose four first class stamps.

Director

116 Pall Mall, London SW1Y 5ED
☎0171 766 8950   Fax 0171 766 8840
Editor *Tom Nash*
Managing Editor *Jo Higgins*
Circulation 46,000

1991 Business Magazine of the Year. Published by The Director Publications Ltd. for the members of the Institute of Directors. Wide range of features from political and business profiles and management thinking to employment and financial issues. Also book reviews. Regular contributors used. Send letter with synopsis/published samples rather than unsolicited mss. Strictly no 'lifestyle' writing.

Payment negotiable.

Dirt Bike Rider (DBR)

PO Box 100, Stamford, Lincolnshire PE9 1XQ
☎01780 755131   Fax 01780 757261
Email: dbr@keymags.demon.co.uk
Owner *Key Publishing Ltd*
Editor *Tony Carter*
Circulation 19,836

FOUNDED 1981. MONTHLY. Off-road dirt bikes (motocross, enduro and trials).

Disability Now

6 Market Road, London N7 9PW
☎0171 619 7323   Fax 0171 619 7331
Publisher *SCOPE* (Formerly The Spastics Society)
Editor *Mary Wilkinson*
Circulation 30,000

FOUNDED 1984. MONTHLY. Leading publication for the disabled in the UK, reaching people with a wide range of physical disabilities, as well as their families, carers and relevant professionals. No unsolicited material but freelance contributions welcome. Approach in writing.

Features Covering new initiatives and services, personal experiences and general issues of interest to a wide national readership. Max. 1200 words. Disabled contributors welcome.
News Max. 300 words.
Special Pages Possible openings for cartoonists.
Payment by arrangement.

Disabled Driver
DDMC, Cottingham Way, Thrapston, Northamptonshire NN14 4PL
☎01832 734724   Fax 01832 733816
Email: ddme@ukonline.co.uk
Website: www.ukonline.co.uk/ddmc
Owner *Disabled Drivers' Motor Club*
Editor *Lesley Browne*
Circulation 14,500 plus

BI-MONTHLY publication of the Disabled Drivers' Motor Club, an organisation which aims to promote and protect the interests and welfare of disabled people and help and encourage them in gaining increased mobility. Various discounts available for members; membership costs £8 p.a. (single), £12 (joint). The magazine includes information for members plus members' letters. Approach in writing with ideas. Unsolicited mss welcome.

Diva, lesbian life and style
Worldwide House, 116–134 Bayham Street, London NW1 0BA
☎0171 482 2576   Fax 0171 284 0329
Email: diva@gaytimes.co.uk
Owner *Millivres Ltd*
Editor *Gillian Rodgerson*

FOUNDED 1994. MONTHLY journal of lesbian news and culture. Welcomes news, features, short fiction and photographs. No poetry. Contact *Vicky Powell* with news items and *Gillian Rodgerson* with features, fiction and photographs. Approach in writing in the first instance.

Dog World
Somerfield House, Wotton Road, Ashford, Kent TN23 6LW
☎01233 621877   Fax 01233 645669
Owner *Dog World Ltd*
Editor *Simon Parsons*
Circulation 28,252

FOUNDED 1902. WEEKLY newspaper for people who are seriously interested in pedigree dogs. Unsolicited mss occasionally considered but initial approach in writing preferred.
Features Well-researched historical items or items of unusual interest concerning dogs. Maximum 1000 words. Photographs of unusual 'doggy' situations occasionally of interest. *Payment* up to £50; photos £15.
News Freelance reports welcome on court cases and local government issues involving dogs.

Eastern Eye
148 Cambridge Heath Road, London E1 5QJ
☎0171 702 8012   Fax 0171 702 7937
Owner *Ethnic Media Group*
Editor *Sarwar Ahmed*
Circulation 40,000

WEEKLY community paper for the Asian community in Britain. Interested in relevant general, local and international issues. Approach in writing with ideas for submission.

The Ecologist
Unit 18, Chelsea Wharf, 15 Lots Road, London SW10 0QJ
☎0171 351 3578   Fax 0171 351 3617
Email: ecologist@gn.apc.org
Owner *Ecosystems Ltd*
Co-Editors *Edward Goldsmith, Zac Goldsmith*
Circulation 10000

FOUNDED 1970. MONTHLY. Unsolicited mss welcome but best approach is in writing to the editors, outlining experience and background, and summarizing suggested article. Writers should study the magazine for style.
Features Radical approach to political, economic, social and environmental issues, with an emphasis on rethinking the basic assumptions that underpin modern society. Articles of 500–4000 words should be fully referenced.
Payment £100 per 1000 words.

Economist
25 St James's Street, London SW1A 1HG
☎0171 830 7000   Fax 0171 839 2968
Website: www.economist.com
Owner *Pearson/individual shareholders*
Editor *Bill Emmott*
Circulation 696,000

FOUNDED 1843. WEEKLY. Worldwide circulation. Approaches should be made in writing to the editor. No unsolicited mss.

The Edge
65 Guinness Buildings, Fulham Palace Road, London W6 8BD
☎0171 460 9444
Editor *Graham Evans*

BI-MONTHLY magazine. Looking for articles on

film (non-Hollywood/mainstream), modern fiction, TV, popular culture. Film reviewers wanted. Contact the editor (enclose s.a.e.). 'Always reading for modern science fiction/ horror and imaginative fiction.' Sample copy £2.75, cheques payable to The Edge. Writers' guidelines available on request. Send s.a.e.

Payment £20 per 1000 words, fiction; £20–50, articles; £150+, interviews.

Edinburgh Review
22 George Square, Edinburgh EH8 9LF
☎0131 650 4218   Fax 0131 662 0053
Website: www.eup.ed.ac.uk
Owner *Edinburgh University Press*
Circulation 750

FOUNDED 1969. BI-ANNUAL. Articles and fiction on Scottish and international literary, cultural and philosophical themes. Unsolicited contributions are welcome (1600 are received each year), but prospective contributors are strongly advised to study the magazine first. Allow up to six months for a reply.

Features Interest will be shown in accessible articles on philosophy and its relationship to literature or visual art.

Fiction Scottish and international. Maximum 6000 words.

Electrical Times
Quadrant House, The Quadrant, Sutton, Surrey SM2 5AS
☎0181 652 3115   Fax 0181 652 8972
Owner *Reed Business Information*
Editor *Christopher Bennett*
Circulation 12,900

FOUNDED 1891. MONTHLY. Aimed at electrical contractors, designers and installers. Unsolicited mss welcome but initial approach preferred.

Elle
Endeavour House, 189 Shaftesbury Avenue, London WC2H 8JG
☎0171 437 9011   Fax 0171 208 3599
Owner *EMAP Elan Publications*
Editor *Fiona McIntosh*
Circulation 200,436

FOUNDED 1985. MONTHLY fashion glossy. Prospective contributors should approach the relevant editor in writing in the first instance, including cuttings.

Features Maximum 2000 words.

News/Insight Short articles on current/ cultural events with an emphasis on national, not London-based, readership. Max. 500 words.

Payment about £250 per 1000 words.

Empire
Mappin House, 4 Winsley Street, London W1N 7AR
☎0171 436 1515   Fax 0171 312 8249
Website: www.empireonline.co.uk
Owner *EMAP Metro Publications*
Editor *Ian Nathan*
Circulation 165,778

FOUNDED 1989. Launched at the Cannes Film Festival. MONTHLY guide to the movies which aims to cover the world of films in a 'comprehensive, adult, intelligent and witty package'. Although most of *Empire* is devoted to films and the people behind them, it also looks at the developments and technology behind television and video plus music, multimedia and books. Wide selection of in-depth features and stories on all the main releases of the month, and reviews of over 100 films and videos. Contributions welcome but must approach in writing first.

Features Behind-the-scenes features on films.

Payment by agreement.

The Engineer
City Reach, 5 Greenwich View Place, Millharbour, London E14 9NN
☎0171 861 6118   Fax 0171 861 6229
Owner *Miller Freeman*
Editor *Paul Carslake*
Circulation 38,000

FOUNDED 1856. News magazine for the UK manufacturing industry.

Features Most outside contributions are commissioned but good ideas are always welcome. Max. 2000 words.

News Scope for specialist regional freelancers, and for tip-offs. Max. 500 words.

Techscan Technology news from specialists, and tip-offs. Max. 500 words.

Payment by arrangement.

The English Garden
Romsey Publishing Ltd, Glen House, Stag Place, London SW1E 5AQ
☎0171 233 9191   Fax 0171 630 8084
Owner *Romsey Publishing Ltd*
Editor *Vanessa Berridge*
Circulation 100,867

FOUNDED 1996. MONTHLY. Features on beautiful gardens with practical ideas on design and planting. No unsolicited mss.

Features *Julia Watson/Caroline Jowett* Maximum 1000–1200 words. Approach in writing in the first instance; send synopsis of 150 words with strong design and planting ideas, or sets of photographs of interesting gardens. 'No stately home or estate gardens with teams of gardeners.'

English Nature

English Nature, Northminster House, Peterborough, Cambridgeshire PE1 1UA
☎01733 455193   Fax 01733 455188
Email: press@english-nature.org.uk
Website: www.english-nature.org.uk

Owner *English Nature*
Editor *Martin Tither*
Circulation 16,000

FOUNDED 1992. BI-MONTHLY magazine which explains the work of English Nature, the government adviser on wildlife policies. No unsolicited material.

Enigmatic Tales

1 Gibbs Field, Bishops Stortford, Hertfordshire CM23 4EY
Email: michael@micksims.force9.co.uk
Website: www.epress.force9.co.uk
Editors *Mick Sims, Len Maynard*

QUARTERLY illustrated anthology of supernatural stories and novellas of any length. Ghost stories, horror, psychological, traditional and modern. New writers and rare fiction from the past. Prefers submissions on disk, accompanied by hard copy. Enclose s.a.e. for any enquiries requiring a response. Full details and guidelines on the website. Also publishes *Enigmatic Novellas*, a quarterly publication for longer pieces.
Payment free copy of relevant issue.

The Erotic Review

EPS, 4th Floor, 5–7 Carnaby Street, London W1V 1PG
☎0171 437 8887
Email: eros@eps.org.uk
Owner *Erotic Print Society*
Editor *Rowan Pelling*
Circulation 30,000

FOUNDED 1997. MONTHLY erotic literary magazine containing articles, humour, fiction, poetry and art work. Unsolicited material welcome. No pornography. Approach in writing in the first instance enclosing a brief sample of work and s.a.e.
Features Esoteric, humorous or real-life experiences. Max. 2000 words. *Payment* £40–100. **Fiction** Erotic short stories. Max. 2000 words. *Payment* £50–100.

ES (Evening Standard magazine)

See entry under **Regional Newspapers**

Esquire

National Magazine House, 72 Broadwick Street, London W1V 2BP
☎0171 439 5000   Fax 0171 312 3920

Owner *National Magazine Co. Ltd*
Editor *Peter Howarth*
Circulation 112,166

FOUNDED 1991. MONTHLY. Quality men's general interest magazine. No unsolicited mss or short stories.

Essentials

King's Reach Tower, Stamford Street, London SE1 9LS
☎0171 261 6970   Fax 0171 261 5262
Website: www.ipc.co.uk/pubs/essentl.htm

Owner *IPC Magazines*
Editor *Karen Livermore*
Circulation 296,904

FOUNDED 1988. MONTHLY women's interest magazine. Unsolicited mss (not originals) welcome if accompanied by s.a.e. Initial approach in writing preferred. Prospective contributors should study the magazine thoroughly before submitting anything. No fiction.
Features Maximum 2000 words (double-spaced on A4).
Payment negotiable, but minimum £100 per 1000 words.

Essex Countryside

Griggs Farm, West Street, Coggeshall, Essex CO6 1NT
☎01376 563994   Fax 01376 562581
Email: andy@countryside.demon.co.uk
Owner *Market Link Publishing Ltd*
Editor *Sue Corner*
Circulation 17,000

FOUNDED 1952. MONTHLY. Welcomes unsolicited material of Essex interest. No general interest material.
Features Countryside, culture and crafts in Essex. Maximum 1500 words.
Payment £40.

European Medical Journal

Publishing House, Trinity Place, Barnstaple, Devon EX32 9HJ
☎01271 328892   Fax 01271 328768
Email: emj@vernoncoleman.com
Website: www.vernoncoleman.com

Owner/Editor *Dr Vernon Coleman*
Circulation 21,000

FOUNDED 1991. MONTHLY critical medical review.

Eventing
See **Horse and Hound**

Evergreen
PO Box 52, Cheltenham, Gloucestershire GL50 1YQ
☎01242 577775 Fax 01242 222034
Editor R. *Faiers*
Circulation 75,000

FOUNDED 1985. QUARTERLY magazine featuring articles and poems about Britain. Unsolicited contributions welcome.

Features Britain's natural beauty, towns and villages, nostalgia, wildlife, traditions, odd customs, legends, folklore, crafts, etc. Length 250–2000 words.

Payment £15 per 1000 words; poems £4.

Executive Woman
2 Chantry Place, Harrow, Middlesex HA3 6NY
☎0181 420 1210 Fax 0181 420 1691
Owner *Saleworld*
Editor *Angela Giveon*
Circulation 75,000

FOUNDED 1987. BI-MONTHLY magazine for female executives in the corporate field and female entrepreneurs. Unsolicited material welcome. Initial approach by phone or in writing.

Features New and interesting business issues and 'Women to Watch'. Health and fitness, beauty, fashion, training and arts items. Maximum 850–1600 words.

Legal/Financial Opportunities for lawyers/accountants to write on issues in their field. Maximum 850 words.

Payment negotiable.

Express on Sunday Magazine
See under **National Newspapers (Express on Sunday)**

The Face
3rd Floor, Block A, Exmouth House, Pine Street, London EC1R 0JL
☎0171 689 9999 Fax 0171 689 0300
Owner *Wagadon Ltd*
Editor *Adam Higginbotham*
Fashion Editor *Karina Givargisoff*
Circulation 100,744

FOUNDED 1980. Magazine of the style generation, concerned with who's what and what's cool. Profiles, interviews and stories. No fiction. Acquaintance with the 'voice' of *The Face*

is essential before sending mss on spec.

Features *Craig McLean* New contributors should write to the features editor with their ideas. Maximum 3000 words. *Payment* £250 per 1000 words.

Diary No news stories.

Family Circle
King's Reach Tower, Stamford Street, London SE1 9LS
☎0171 261 5000 Fax 0171 261 5929
Website: www.ipc.co.uk/pubs/famcircl.htm
Owner *IPC Magazines Ltd*
Editor *Tba*
Circulation 280,687

FOUNDED 1964. THIRTEEN ISSUES YEARLY. Little scope for freelancers as most material is produced in-house. Unsolicited material is rarely used, but it is considered. Prospective contributors are best advised to send written ideas to the relevant editor.

Style *Amanda Cooke*
Food and Wine *Jane Curran*
Features *Sara Harris* Very little outside work commissioned.

Fiction *Dee Remmington* Short stories of 1000–1500 words.

Home *Lucy Searle*
Payment by arrangement.

Family Tree Magazine
61 Great Whyte, Ramsey, Huntingdon, Cambridgeshire PE17 1HL
☎01487 814050 Fax 01487 711361
Owner *Armstrong Boon & Marriott (Publishing)*
Editorial Director *J.M. Armstrong*
Circulation 39,000

FOUNDED 1984. MONTHLY. News and features on matters of genealogy. Not interested in own family histories. Approach in writing with ideas. All material should be addressed to *Avril Cross*.

Features Any genealogically related subject. Maximum 2500 words. No puzzles or fictional articles.

Payment £35 per 1000 words (news and features).

Farmers Weekly
Quadrant House, Sutton, Surrey SM2 5AS
☎0181 652 4911 Fax 0181 652 4005
Email: farmers.weekly@rbi.co.uk
Website: www.fwi.co.uk
Owner *Reed Business Information*
Editor *Stephen Howe*
Circulation 98,268

WEEKLY. 1996 Business Magazine of the Year.

For practising farmers. Unsolicited mss considered.

Features A wide range of material relating to farmers' problems and interests: specific sections on arable and livestock farming, farm life, practical and general interest, machinery and business.

News General farming news.
Payment negotiable.

Farming News

Miller Freeman House, Sovereign Way, Tonbridge, Kent TN9 1RW
☎01732 364422   Fax 01732 377675
Owner *Miller Freeman plc*
Editor *Donald Taylor*
Circulation 74,000

News of direct concern to farmers and the agricultural supply trade.

Fast Car

Berwick House, 8–10 Knoll Rise, Orpington, Kent BR6 0PS
☎01689 887200   Fax 01689 838844
Email: fastcar@splgroup.demon.co.uk
Owner *SPL*
Editor *Ian Strachan*
Circulation 85,000

FOUNDED 1987. 13 ISSUES A YEAR. Lad's magazine about perfomance tuning and modifying cars. Covers all aspects of this youth culture including the latest street styles and music. Features cars and their owners, product tests and in-car entertainment. Also includes a free reader ads section.

Features Innovative ideas in line with the above and in the *Fast Car* writing style. Generally four pages in length. No Kit-car features, race reports or road test reports of standard cars. Copy should be as concise as possible. *Payment* negotiable.

News Any item in line with the above.

FHM

Mappin House, 4 Winsley Street, London W1N 7AR
☎0171 436 1515   Fax 0171 312 8191
Website: www.fhm.co.uk
Owner *EMAP Metro*
Editor *Anthony Noguera*
Circulation 751,431

FOUNDED in 1986 as a free fashion magazine, FHM evolved to become more male oriented but without much public acclaim until EMAP bought the title in 1994. Since then it has become the best-selling men's magazine in the UK covering all areas of men's lifestyle. Published MONTHLY. Unsolicited mss welcome; send to the Editor.

The Field

King's Reach Tower, Stamford Street, London SE1 9LS
☎0171 261 5198   Fax 0171 261 5358
Website: www.thefield.co.uk
Owner *IPC Magazines*
Editor *Jonathan Young*
Circulation 32,860

FOUNDED 1853. MONTHLY magazine for those who are serious about the British countryside and its pleasures. Unsolicited mss (and transparencies) welcome but initial approach should be made in writing.

Features Exceptional work on any subject concerning the countryside. Most work tends to be commissioned.
Payment varies.

Film and Video Maker

Church House, 1st Floor, 102 Pendlebury Road, Swinton, Manchester M27 4BF
☎0161 794 8282   Fax 0161 793 9696
Owner *Film Maker Publications*
Editor *Mrs Liz Donlan*
Circulation 2400

FOUNDED in the 1930s. BI-MONTHLY magazine of the Institute of Amateur Cinematographers. Reports, news and views of the Institute. Unsolicited mss welcome but all contributions are unpaid.

Film Review

Visual Imagination Ltd, 9 Blades Court, Deodar Road, London SW15 2NU
☎0181 875 1520   Fax 0181 875 1588
Owner *Visual Imagination Ltd*
Editor *Neil Corry*
Circulation 50,000

MONTHLY. Reviews, profiles, interviews and special reports on films. Unsolicited material considered.
Payment negotiable.

First Down

7–9 Rathbone Street, London W1P 1AF
☎0171 323 1988   Fax 0171 637 0862
Owner *Independent Magazines (UK)Ltd*
Editor *Keith Webster*
Circulation 15,000

FOUNDED 1986. WEEKLY American football

tabloid paper. Features and news. Welcomes contributions; approach in writing.

The First Word Bulletin
Calle Domingo Fernandez 5, Box 500, 28036 Madrid Spain
☎00 34 1 359 6418   Fax 00 34 1 320 8961
Email: gw83@correo.interlink.es
Website: www.interlink.es/peraso/first
Owner *The First Word Bulletin Associates*
Publisher/Editor *G. W. Amick*
Circulation 5000

FOUNDED 1995. QUARTERLY international magazine, printed in Madrid and distributed to the English speaking community worldwide. Welcomes articles on self-improvement, both mental and physical, also environmental problems and cures. Human interest, alternative medicine, fiction and non-fiction, nature stories, young adult and senior citizen retirement articles. 'No smut, pornography, love stories, detective stories, science fiction or horror.' 400 words maximum. Approach in writing with s.a.e. and IRCs. Disk submissions accepted; no submissions by email. Contributors' guidelines not sent by email. *Payment* £30 maximum.

Fishkeeping Answers
See **Practical Fishkeeping**

Flight International
Quadrant House, The Quadrant, Sutton, Surrey SM2 5AS
☎0181 652 3882   Fax 0181 652 3840
Email: flight.international@rbi.co.uk
Owner *Reed Business Information*
Editor *Carol Reed*
Circulation 65,000

FOUNDED 1909. WEEKLY. International trade magazine for the aerospace industry, including civil, military and space. Unsolicited mss considered. Commissions preferred – phone with ideas and follow up with letter. Email, modem and disk submissions encouraged.
Features *Carole Reed* Technically informed articles and pieces on specific geographical areas with international appeal. Analytical, indepth coverage required, preferably supported by interviews. Maximum 1800 words.
News *Andrew Chuter* Opportunities exist for news pieces from particular geographical areas on specific technical developments. Maximum 350 words.
Payment NUJ rates.

Flora International
The Fishing Lodge Studio, 77 Bulbridge Road, Wilton, Salisbury, Wiltshire SP2 0LE
☎01722 743207   Fax 01722 743207
Owner/Publisher *Maureen Foster*
Editor *Judith Blacklock*
Circulation 16,000

FOUNDED 1974. BI-MONTHLY magazine for flower arrangers and florists. Unsolicited mss welcome. Approach in writing with ideas. Not interested in general gardening articles.
Features Fully illustrated, preferably with b&w photos or illustrations/colour transparencies. Flower arranging, flower gardens and flowers. Floristry items written with practical knowledge and well illustrated are particularly welcome. Max. 2000 words.
Profiles/Reviews Personality profiles and book reviews.
Payment £40 per 1000 words.

FlyPast
PO Box 100, Stamford, Lincolnshire PE9 1XQ
☎01780 755131   Fax 01780 757261
Owner *Key Publishing Ltd*
Editor *Ken Ellis*
Circulation 47,000

FOUNDED 1981. MONTHLY. Historic aviation, mainly military, Second World War period up to c.1970. Unsolicited mss welcome.

Focus
See **British Science Fiction Association** under **Professional Associations**

Folk Roots
PO Box 337, London N4 1TW
☎0181 340 9651   Fax 0181 348 5626
Owner *Southern Rag Ltd*
Editor *Ian A. Anderson*
Circulation 14,000

FOUNDED 1979. MONTHLY. Features on folk and roots music, and musicians. Max. 3000 words.

For Women
Fantasy Publications, 4 Selsdon Way, London E14 9EL
☎0171 308 5090   Fax 0171 308 5075
Editor *To be appointed*
Circulation 60,000

FOUNDED 1992. MONTHLY magazine of erotic and sex interest for women – celebrity interviews, beauty, health and sex, erotic fiction and erotic photography. No homes and gardens articles. Approach in writing in the first instance.

Features Relationships and sex. Max. 2500 words. *Payment* £150 per 1000 words.

Fiction *Elizabeth Coldwell* Erotic short stories. Max. 2000 words. *Payment* £125 total.

Fortean Times: The Journal of Strange Phenomena

PO Box 2409, London NW5 4NP
☎0171 485 5002   Fax 0171 485 5002
Email: sieveking@forteantimes.com
Website: www.forteantimes.com
Owners/Editors *Bob Rickard/Paul Sieveking*
Circulation 50,000

FOUNDED 1973. MONTHLY. Accounts of strange phenomena and experiences, curiosities, mysteries, prodigies and portents. Unsolicited mss welcome. Approach in writing with ideas. No fiction, poetry, rehashes or politics.

Features Well-researched and referenced material on current or historical mysteries, or first-hand accounts of oddities. Maximum 3000 words, preferably with good relevant photos/ illustrations.

News Concise copy with full source references essential.

Payment negotiable.

Foundation: The International Review of Science Fiction

c/o Dept. of History, University of Reading, Whiteknights, Reading, Berkshire RG6 6AA
☎0118 9263047   Fax 0118 9316440
Owner *Science Fiction Foundation*
Editor *Professor Edward James*

THRICE-YEARLY publication devoted to the critical study of science fiction.

Payment None.

France Magazine

Dormer House, Digbeth Street, Stow-on-the-Wold, Gloucestershire GL54 1BN
☎01451 833210   Fax 01451 833234
Owner *Centralhaven*
Editor *Philip Faiers*
Circulation 61,000

FOUNDED 1989. QUARTERLY magazine containing all things of interest to Francophiles – in English. Approach in writing in the first instance.

Freelance Market News

Sevendale House, 7 Dale Street, Manchester M1 1JB
☎0161 228 2362   Fax 0161 228 3533
Editor *Angela Cox*
Circulation 4000

MONTHLY. News and information on the free-lance writers' market, both inland and overseas. Includes market information on competitions, seminars, courses, overseas openings, etc. Short articles (700 words max.). Unsolicited contributions welcome.

Payment £35 per 1000 words

The Freelance

NUJ, Acorn House, 314 Gray's Inn Road, London WC1X 8DP
☎0171 843 3706   Fax 0171 278 1812

BI-MONTHLY published by the **National Union of Journalists**.

Garden Answers (incorporating Practical Gardening)

Apex House, Oundle Road, Peterborough, Cambridgeshire PE2 9NP
☎01733 898100   Fax 01733 898433
Owner *EMAP Apex Publications Ltd*
Editor *Jim Ward*
Circulation 192,000

FOUNDED 1982. MONTHLY. 'It is unlikely that unsolicited manuscripts will be used, as articles are usually commissioned and must be in the magazine style.' Prospective contributors should approach the editor in writing. Interested in hearing from gardening writers on any subject, whether flowers, fruit, vegetables, houseplants or greenhouse gardening.

Garden News

Apex House, Oundle Road, Peterborough, Cambridgeshire PE2 9NP
☎01733 898100   Fax 01733 898433
Owner *EMAP Active Publications Ltd*
Editor *Sarah Page*
Circulation 86,967

FOUNDED 1958. Britain's biggest-selling, full-colour gardening WEEKLY. News and advice on growing flowers, fruit and vegetables, plus colourful features on all aspects of gardening especially for the committed gardener. News and features welcome, especially if accompanied by top-quality photos or illustrations. Contact the editor before submitting any material.

The Garden, Journal of the Royal Horticultural Society

Apex House, Oundle Road, Peterborough, Cambridgeshire PE2 9NP
☎01733 898100   Fax 01733 341895
Email: thegarden@rhs.org.uk
Website: www.rhs.org.uk

Owner *The Royal Horticultural Society*
Editor *Ian Hodgson*
Circulation 250,000

FOUNDED 1866. MONTHLY journal of the Royal Horticultural Society. Covers all aspects of the art, science and practice of horticulture and garden making. 'Articles must have depth and substance'; approach by letter with a synopsis in the first instance. Max. 2500 words.

Gardens Illustrated

John Brown Publishing Ltd, The New Boathouse, 136–142 Bramley Road, London W10 6SR
☎0171 565 3000   Fax 0171 565 3056
Owner *John Brown Publishing Ltd*
Editor *Rosie Atkins*
Circulation 50,588

FOUNDED 1993. TEN ISSUES YEARLY. 'Britain's fastest growing garden magazine' with a worldwide readership. The focus is on garden design, with a strong international flavour. Unsolicited mss are rarely used and it is best that prospective contributors approach the editor with ideas in writing, supported by photographs.

Gargoyle Magazine

152 Harringay Road, London N15 3HL
☎0181 292 7350   Fax 0171 401 2055
Email: gargoyle@ursarum.demon.co.uk
Owner *Paycock Press*
London Editor *Maja Prausnitz*
US Editors *Richard Peabody, Lucinda Ebersole*
Circulation 5000

FOUNDED 1976. BI-ANNUAL literary magazine dedicated to championing work by new poets and fiction writers alongside the more established, and aiming to bridge the American and European literary worlds. Unsolicited mss welcome, though some knowledge of *Gargoyle* is recommended before submission.
Payment one copy of relevant issue.

Gay Times

Worldwide House, 116–134 Bayham Street, London NW1 0BA
☎0171 482 2576   Fax 0171 284 0329
Owner *Millivres Ltd*
Editor *David Smith*
Circulation 57,000

Covers all aspects of gay life, plus general interest likely to appeal to the gay community, art reviews and news. Regular freelance writers used. Unsolicited contributions welcome.
Payment negotiable.

Gibbons Stamp Monthly

Stanley Gibbons, 5 Parkside, Ringwood, Hampshire BH24 3SH
☎01425 472363   Fax 01425 470247
Owner *Stanley Gibbons Ltd*
Editor *Hugh Jefferies*
Circulation 22,000

FOUNDED 1890. MONTHLY. News and features. Unsolicited mss welcome. Make initial approach in writing or by telephone to avoid disappointment.
Features *Hugh Jefferies* Unsolicited material of specialised nature and general stamp features welcome. Max. 3000 words but longer pieces can be serialised. *Payment* £20–50 per 1000 words.
News *Michael Briggs* Any philatelic news item. Max. 500 words. *No payment.*

Girl About Town

9 Rathbone Street, London W1P 1AF
☎0171 636 6651   Fax 0171 255 2352
Owner *Independent Magazines*
Editor-in-Chief *Bill Williamson*
News/Style Pages *Dee Pilgrim*
Circulation 85,000

FOUNDED 1972. Free WEEKLY magazine for women aged 16 to 26. Unsolicited mss may be considered. No fiction.
Features Standards are 'exacting'. Commissions only. Some chance of unknown writers being commissioned. Max. 1500 words.
Payment negotiable.

Golf Monthly

King's Reach Tower, Stamford Street, London SE1 9LS
☎0171 261 7237   Fax 0171 261 7240
Website: www.ipc.co.uk/pubs/golfmnth.htm
Owner *IPC Magazines Ltd*
Editor *Colin Callander*
Circulation 72,905

FOUNDED 1911. MONTHLY. Player profiles, golf instruction, general golf features and columns. Not interested in instruction material from outside contributors. Unsolicited mss welcome. Approach in writing with ideas.
Features Max. 1500–2000 words.
Payment by arrangement.

Golf Weekly

Bretton Court, Bretton, Peterborough, Cambridgeshire PE3 8DZ
☎01733 264666   Fax 01733 465221
Owner *EMAP Active Ltd*
Managing Editor *Bob Warters*

Circulation 20,000

FOUNDED 1890. WEEKLY. Unsolicited material welcome from full-time journalists only. For features, approach in writing in first instance; for news, fax or phone.

Features Maximum 1500 words.
News Maximum 300 words.
Payment negotiable.

Golf World

Angel House, 338–346 Goswell Road, London EC1V 7QP
☎01733 264666   Fax 0171 477 7274

Owner *EMAP Active Ltd*
Editor *David Clarke*
Circulation 85,181

FOUNDED 1962. MONTHLY. No unsolicited mss. Approach in writing with ideas.

Good Food Retailing

PO Box 1525, Gillingham, Dorset SP8 5TA
☎01963 371271   Fax 01963 371270
Email: bobfarrand@btinternet.com

Owner/Editor *Robert Farrand*
Circulation 4200

FOUNDED 1980. TEN ISSUES YEARLY. Serves the speciality food retail trade. Small budget for freelance material.

Good Health Magazine

Shadwell House, 65 Lower Green Road, Rusthall, Tunbridge Wells, Kent TN4 8TW
☎01892 535300   Fax 01892 535311

Owner *Good Health Publications Ltd*
Publisher *Jack Hay*

FOUNDED 1997. MONTHLY. Aimed primarily at women and their families, covering all aspects of maintaining a healthy lifestyle, featuring health expert writers and professional practitioners. The magazine gives advice on all aspects of family health, including allergies, diet, emotions, fitness, hair, skin and body care, with emphasis on real-life experiences. Features and casebooks: variable length – average article 1200 words.
Payment negotiable.

Good Holiday Magazine

3A High Street, Esher, Surrey KT10 9RP
☎01372 468140   Fax 01372 470765
Email: goodholiday@btinternet.com

Editor *John Hill*
Circulation 100,000

FOUNDED 1985. QUARTERLY aimed at better-off holiday-makers rather than travellers.

Worldwide destinations including Europe and domestic. Any queries regarding work/commissioning must be in writing. Copy must be precise and well-researched – the price of everything from coffee and tea to major purchases are included along with exchange rates, etc.
Payment negotiable.

Good Housekeeping

National Magazine House, 72 Broadwick Street, London W1V 2BP
☎0171 439 5000   Fax 0171 439 5591

Owner *National Magazine Co. Ltd*
Editor-in-Chief *Pat Roberts Cairns*
Circulation 400,063

FOUNDED 1922. MONTHLY glossy. No unsolicited mss. Write with ideas in the first instance to the appropriate editor.

Features *Marilyn Warnick* Most work is commissioned but original ideas are always welcome. No ideas are discussed on the telephone. Send short synopsis, plus relevant cuttings, showing previous examples of work published. No unsolicited mss.

Fiction *Marilyn Warnick* No unsolicited mss.

Entertainment *Kerry Packer* Reviews and previews on film, television, theatre and art.

Good Motoring

Station Road, Forest Row, East Sussex RH18 5EN
☎01342 825676   Fax 01342 824847

Owner *Guild of Experienced Motorists*
Editor *Derek Hainge*
Deputy Editor *John Taylor*
Circulation 50,000

FOUNDED 1932. QUARTERLY motoring, road safety and travel magazine. Occasional general features. 1500 words maximum. Prospective contributors should approach in writing only.

Good Ski Guide

3A High Street, Esher, Surrey KT10 9RP
☎01372 468140   Fax 01372 470765
Email: goodskiguide@btinternet.com
Website: www.goodskiguide.com

Editor *John Hill*
Circulation 79,654

FOUNDED 1976. QUARTERLY. Unsolicited mss welcome from writers with a knowledge of skiing and ski resorts. Prospective contributors are best advised to make initial contact in writing as ideas and work need to be seen before any discussion can take place.
Payment negotiable.

The Goodlife Magazine

28 Coleherne Mews, London SW10 9EA
☎0171 373 7282   Fax 0171 373 3215
Owner/Editor *Eileen Spence-Moncrieff*
Circulation 50,000

FOUNDED 1988. QUARTERLY. Features on fashion, interiors, restaurants, theatre, health and beauty. No unsolicited mss.

GQ

Vogue House, Hanover Square, London W1R 0AD
☎0171 499 9080   Fax 0171 629 2093
Website:www.gq-magazine.co.uk
Owner *Condé Nast Publications Ltd*
Editor *Dylan Jones*
Circulation 129,294

FOUNDED 1988. MONTHLY. Men's style magazine. No unsolicited material. Write or fax with an idea in the first instance.

Granta

2–3 Hanover Yard, Noel Road, London N1 8BE
☎0171 704 9776   Fax 0171 704 0474
Editor *Ian Jack*
Deputy Editor *Liz Jobey*

QUARTERLY magazine of new writing, including fiction, autobiography, politics, history and reportage published in paperback book form. Highbrow, diverse and contemporary, with a thematic approach. Unsolicited mss (including fiction) considered. A lot of material is commissioned. Important to read the magazine first to appreciate its very particular fusion of cultural and political interests. No reviews. No poetry.
Payment negotiable.

The Great Outdoors

See **TGO**

Guardian Weekend

See under **National Newspapers (The Guardian)**

Guiding

17–19 Buckingham Palace Road, London SW1W 0PT
☎0171 834 6242   Fax 0171 828 8317
Owner *The Guide Association*
Editor *Jan Clampett*
Circulation 28,000

FOUNDED 1914. MONTHLY. Unsolicited mss welcome provided topics relate to the Movement and/or women's role in society. Ideas in writing appreciated in first instance.
Features Topics that can be useful in the Guide programme. Maximum 1200 words.
News Guide activities. Maximum 100–150 words.
Payment £70 per 1000 words.

Hair

King's Reach Tower, Stamford Street, London SE1 9LS
☎0171 261 6975   Fax 0171 261 7382
Website: www.ipc.co.uk/pubs/hair.htm
Owner *IPC Magazines Ltd*
Editor *Carol Ramsey*
Circulation 152,602

FOUNDED 1977. BI-MONTHLY hair and beauty magazine. No unsolicited mss, but always interested in good photographs. Approach with ideas in writing.
Features *Georgia Goodall* Fashion pieces on hair trends and styling advice. Maximum 1000 words.
Payment negotiable.

Hairflair

Kimber House, 134–136 King Street, Hammersmith, London W6 0QU
☎0181 563 2266   Fax 0181 563 2299
Owner *James Kimber Publishing Ltd*
Editor *Rebecca Barnes*
Circulation 100,000

FOUNDED 1982. BI-MONTHLY. Original and interesting hair and beauty-related features written in a young, lively style to appeal to a readership aged 16–35 years. Unsolicited mss not welcome, although freelancers are used occasionally.
Features Hair and beauty. Maximum 1500 words.
Payment negotiable.

Harpers & Queen

National Magazine House, 72 Broadwick Street, London W1V 2BP
☎0171 439 5000   Fax 0171 439 5506
Owner *National Magazine Co. Ltd*
Editor *Fiona Macpherson*
Circulation 93,863

MONTHLY. Up-market glossy combining the stylish and the streetwise. Approach in writing (not phone) with ideas.
Features *Lydia Slater/Anthony Gardner* Ideas only in the first instance.
News Snippets welcome if very original.
Payment negotiable.

Health & Fitness Magazine

Nexus Media, Nexus House, Azalea Drive,
Swanley, Kent BR8 8HY
☎01322 660070   Fax 01322 615636
Website: 4231999
Owner *Nexus Media*
Editor *Mary Comber*
Circulation 65,000
FOUNDED 1983. MONTHLY. Will consider ideas;
approach in writing in the first instance.

Health Education

MCB University Press, 60–62 Toller Lane,
Bradford, West Yorkshire BD8 9BY
☎01274 777700   Fax 01274 785200/785201
Owner *MCB University Press*
Editor *Sharon Kingman*
Circulation 2000
FOUNDED 1992. SIX ISSUES YEARLY. Health education magazine with an emphasis on schools and
young people. Professional readership. Most
work is commissioned but ideas are welcome.

Heat

Mappin House, 4 Winsley Street, London
W1N 7AR
☎0171 436 1515   Fax 0171 817 8847
Owner *EMAP Metro*
Editor *Mark Frith*
Circulation 100,000 (first two issues)
FOUNDED January 1999. WEEKLEY entertainment magazine dealing with TV, film and radio
information and features, with an emphasis on
celebrity interviews and news. Targets 18–40-
year-old readership, male and female. Articles
written both in-house and by trusted freelancers.
No unsolicited mss.

Hello!

Wellington House, 69–71 Upper Ground,
London SE1 9PQ
☎0171 667 8700   Fax 0171 667 8716
Owner *Hola!* (Spain)
Editor *Maggie Koumi*
Circulation 506,027
WEEKLY. Owned by a Madrid-based publishing
family, *Hello!* has grown faster than any other
British magazine since its launch here in 1988
and continues to grow despite the recession.
The magazine is printed in Madrid, with editorial offices both there and in London. Major
colour features plus regular news pages.
Although much of the material is provided by
regulars, good proposals do stand a chance.

Approach with ideas in the first instance. No
unsolicited mss.
   Features Interested in celebrity based features
with a newsy angle, and exclusive interviews
from generally unapproachable personalities.
Payment by arrangement.

Here's Health

Endeavour House, 189 Shaftesbury Avenue,
London WC2H 8JG
☎0171 437 9011   Fax 0171 208 3583
Owner *EMAP Elan Publications*
Editor *Elaine Griffiths*
Circulation 37,502
FOUNDED 1956. MONTHLY. Full-colour magazine dealing with alternative medicine, nutrition, natural health, wholefoods, supplements,
organics and the environment. Prospective
contributors should bear in mind that this is a
specialist magazine with a pronounced bias
towards alternative/complementary medicine,
using expert contributors on the whole.
Payment negotiable.

Heritage

4 The Courtyard, Denmark Street,
Wokingham, Berkshire RG40 2AZ
☎01189 771677   Fax 01189 772903
Owner *Bulldog Magazines*
Editor *Sian Ellis*
Circulation 71,000
FOUNDED 1984. BI-MONTHLY. Interested in
complete packages of written features with high-
quality transparencies – words or pictures on
their own also accepted. Not interested in
poetry, fiction or non-British themes. Approach
in writing with ideas.
   Features British villages, tours, towns, castles,
gardens, traditions, crafts, historical themes and
people. Max. length 1200 words. *Payment*
approx. £100 per 1000 words.
   News Small pieces – usually picture stories in
Diary section. Limited use. Max. length 100–150
words. *Payment* £20.

Heritage Scotland

5 Charlotte Square, Edinburgh EH2 4DU
☎0131 243 9387   Fax 0131 243 9309
Owner *National Trust for Scotland*
Editor *Myra Sanderson*
Circulation 137,668
FOUNDED 1983. QUARTERLY magazine containing heritage/conservation features. No
unsolicited mss.

Hi-Fi News & Record Review

Link House, Dingwall Avenue, Croydon,
Surrey CR9 2TA
☎0181 686 2599   Fax 0181 781 6046
Website: www.ipc.co.uk/pubs/hifi.htm
Owner *IPC Magazines Ltd*
Editor *Steve Harris*
Circulation 21,196

FOUNDED 1956. MONTHLY. Write in the first
instance with suggestions based on knowledge
of the magazine's style and subject. All articles
must be written from an informed technical or
enthusiast viewpoint.
   Payment negotiable, according to technical
content.

High Life

Haymarket House, 1 Oxendon Street,
London SW1Y 4EE
☎0171 925 2544   Fax 0171 839 4508
Owner *Premier Magazines*
Editor *Mark Jones*
Circulation 295,000

FOUNDED 1973. MONTHLY glossy. British Airways in-flight magazine. Almost all the content is
commissioned. No unsolicited mss. Few opportunities for freelancers.

Home & Country

104 New Kings Road, London SW6 4LY
☎0171 731 5777   Fax 0171 736 4061
Owner *National Federation of Women's Institutes*
Editor *Susan Seager*
Circulation 62,000

FOUNDED 1919. MONTHLY. Official full-colour
journal of the Federation of Women's Institutes, containing articles on a wide range of
subjects of interest to women. Strong environmental country slant with crafts and cookery
plus gardening appearing every month. Unsolicited mss, photos and illustrations welcome.
   Payment by arrangement.

Home & Family

Mary Sumner House, 24 Tufton Street,
London SW1P 3RB
☎0171 222 5533   Fax 0171 222 1591
Owner *MU Enterprises Ltd*
Editor *Jill Worth*
Circulation 75,000

FOUNDED 1976. QUARTERLY. Unsolicited mss
considered. No fiction or poetry. **Features**
Family life, social problems, marriage, Christian
faith, etc. Maximum 1000 words.
   Payment 'modest'.

Home Wine and Beer Maker

East Side Offices, South Mezzanine Floor,
King's Cross Station, London N1 9AP
Owner *Railnews Ltd*
Publisher *Alan Marshall*
Editor *Andy Milne*
Circulation 150,000

FOUNDED 1986. QUARTERLY. Articles on all
aspects of home wine and beer making and the
use of homemade wine in cooking, etc. Unsolicited mss welcome.

Homes & Gardens

King's Reach Tower, Stamford Street,
London SE1 9LS
☎0171 261 5000   Fax 0171 261 6247
Website: www.ipc.co.uk/pubs/hgardens.htm
Owner *IPC Magazines Ltd*
Editor *Matthew Line*
Circulation 171,556

FOUNDED 1919. MONTHLY. Almost all published articles are specially commissioned. No
fiction or poetry. Best to approach in writing
with an idea, enclosing snapshots if appropriate.

Homes & Ideas

King's Reach Tower, Stamford Street,
London SE1 9LS
☎0171 261 7494   Fax 0171 261 7495
Website: www.ipc.co.uk/pubs/homeidea.htm
Owner *IPC Magazines Ltd*
Editor *Debbie Djordjevic*
Circulation 192,127

FOUNDED 1993. MONTHLY magazine for
homeowners looking for new styles and decorating techniques. No unsolicited mss; all work
is commissioned.

Horse & Pony Magazine

Apex House, Oundle Road, Peterborough,
Cambridgeshire PE2 9NP
☎01733 898100   Fax 01733 315984
Owner *EMAP Active Publications*
Acting Editor *Sarah Gaydon*
Circulation 54,260

Magazine for young (aged 10–16) owners and
'addicts' of the horse. Features include pony care,
riding articles and celebrity pieces. Some interest
in freelancers but most feature material is produced by staff writers.

Horse and Hound

King's Reach Tower, Stamford Street,
London SE1 9LS
☎0171 261 6315   Fax 0171 261 5429

Email: jenny_sims@ipc.co.uk
Website: www.ipc.co.uk/pubs/hhound.htm
Owner *IPC Magazines Ltd*
Editor *Arnold Garvey*
Circulation 66,898

FOUNDED 1884. WEEKLY. The oldest equestrian magazine on the market, now re-launched with modern make-up and colour pictures throughout. Contains regular veterinary advice and instructional articles, as well as authoritative news and comment on fox hunting, international and national showjumping, horse trials, dressage, driving and endurance riding. Also weekly racing and point-to-points, breeding reports and articles. Regular books and art reviews, and humorous articles and cartoons are frequently published. Plenty of opportunities for freelancers. Unsolicited contributions welcome.

Also publishes a sister monthly publication, *Eventing*, which covers the sport of horse trials comprehensively.

Payment NUJ rates.

Horse and Rider

Haslemere House, Lower Street, Haslemere, Surrey GU27 2PE
☎01428 651551   Fax 01428 653888
Owner *D. J. Murphy (Publishers) Ltd*
Editor *Alison Bridge*
Assistant Editor *Sarah Muir*
Circulation 46,000

FOUNDED 1949. MONTHLY. Adult readership, largely horse-owning. News and instructional features, which make up the bulk of the magazine, are almost all commissioned. New contributors and unsolicited mss are occasionally used. Approach the editor in writing with ideas.

Horticulture Week

174 Hammersmith Road, London W6 7JP
☎0171 413 4595   Fax 0171 413 4518
Owner *Haymarket Magazines Ltd*
Editor *Vicky Browning*
Circulation 11,200

FOUNDED 1841. WEEKLY. Specialist magazine involved in the supply of business-type information. No unsolicited mss. Approach in writing in first instance.

Features No submissions without prior discussion. *Payment* negotiable.

News *Maja Pawinska* Information about horticultural businesses – nurseries, garden centres, landscapers and parks departments in the various regions of the UK. No gardening stories.

House & Garden

Vogue House, Hanover Square, London W1R 0AD
☎0171 499 9080   Fax 0171 629 2907
Website:www.houseandgarden.co.uk/index.html
Owner *Condé Nast Publications Ltd*
Editor *Susan Crewe*
Circulation 163,313

FOUNDED 1947. MONTHLY. Most feature material is produced in-house but occasional specialist features are commissioned from qualified freelancers, mainly for the interiors, wine and food sections and travel.

Features *Liz Elliot* Suggestions for features, preferably in the form of brief outlines of proposed subjects, will be considered.

House Beautiful

National Magazine House, 72 Broadwick Street, London W1V 2BP
☎0171 439 5000   Fax 0171 439 5595
Owner *National Magazine Co. Ltd*
Editor *Caroline Atkins*
Circulation 288,452

FOUNDED 1989. MONTHLY. Lively magazine offering sound, practical information and plenty of inspiration for those who want to make the most of where they live. Over 100 pages of easy-reading editorial. Regular features about decoration, DIY and home finance. Approach in writing with synopses or ideas in the first instance.

i-D Magazine

Universal House, 251–255 Tottenham Court Road, London W1P 0AE
☎0171 813 6170   Fax 0171 813 6179
Email: editor@i-Dmagazine.co.uk
Owner *Levelprint*
Editor *Avril Mair*
Circulation 45,000

FOUNDED 1980. MONTHLY lifestyle magazine for both sexes with a fashion bias. International. Very hip. Does not accept unsolicited contributions but welcomes new ideas from the fields of fashion, music, clubs, art, film, technology, books, sport, etc. No fiction or poetry. 'We are always looking for freelance non-fiction writers with new or unusual ideas.' A different theme each issue – past themes include Green politics, taste, films, sex, love and loud dance music – means it is advisable to discuss feature ideas in the first instance.

Ideal Home
King's Reach Tower, Stamford Street,
London SE1 9LS
☎0171 261 6474   Fax 0171 261 6697
Website: www.ipc.co.uk/pubs/idealhom.htm
Owner *IPC Magazines Ltd*
Editor-in-Chief *Isobel McKenzie-Price*
Circulation 200,070

FOUNDED 1920. MONTHLY glossy. Unsolicited feature articles are welcome if appropriate to the magazine. Prospective contributors wishing to submit ideas should do so in writing to the editor. No fiction.

Features Furnishing and decoration of houses, kitchens or bathrooms; interior design, soft furnishings, furniture and home improvements, lifestyle, travel, etc. Length to be discussed with editor.
Payment negotiable.

The Illustrated London News
20 Upper Ground, London SE1 9PF
☎0171 805 5562   Fax 0171 805 5911
Owner *James Sherwood*
Editor *Alison Booth*
Circulation 47,547

FOUNDED 1842. BI-ANNUAL: the Christmas and Summer issues, plus the occasional special issue to coincide with particular events. Although the *ILN* covers issues concerning the whole of the UK, its emphasis remains on the capital and its life. Travel, wine, restaurants, events, cultural and current affairs are all covered. There are few opportunities for freelancers but all unsolicited mss are read (receives about 20 a week). The best approach is with an idea in writing. Particularly interested in articles relating to events and developments in contemporary London, and about people working in the capital. All features are illustrated, so ideas with picture opportunities are particularly welcome.

Image Magazine
Upper Mounts, Northampton NN1 3HR
☎01604 231122   Fax 01604 233000
Owner *Northamptonshire Newspapers Ltd*
Editor *Ruth Supple*
Circulation 12,000

FOUNDED 1905. MONTHLY general interest regional magazine. No unsolicited mss. Approach by phone or in writing with ideas. No fiction.

Features Local issues, personalities, businesses, etc., of Northamptonshire, Bedfordshire,

Buckinghamshire interest. Max. 500 words. *Payment* negotiable.

News No hard news as such, just monthly diary column.

Other Regulars on motoring, fashion, beauty, lifestyle, travel and horoscopes. Maximum 500 words.

In Britain
Haymarket House, 1 Oxendon Street,
London SW1Y 4EE
☎0171 925 2544   Fax 0171 976 1088
Email: in_britain@premiermags.co.uk
Owner *Premier Magazines*
Editor *Andrea Spain*
Circulation 40,000

MONTHLY. Travel magazine of the British Tourist Authority. Articles vary from 1000 to 1500 words. Approach in writing with ideas and samples – not much opportunity for unsolicited work.

Independent Magazine
See under **National Newspapers (The Independent)**

Interzone: Science Fiction & Fantasy
217 Preston Drove, Brighton, East Sussex
BN1 6FL
☎01273 504710
Owner/Editor *David Pringle*
Circulation 10,000

FOUNDED 1982. MONTHLY magazine of science fiction and fantasy. Unsolicited mss are welcome 'from writers who have a knowledge of the magazine and its contents'. S.a.e. essential for return.

Fiction 2000–6000 words. *Payment* £30 per 1000 words.

Features Book/film reviews, interviews with writers and occasional short articles. Length by arrangement. *Payment* negotiable.

Investors Chronicle
Maple House, 149 Tottenham Court Road,
London W1P 9LL
☎0171 896 2525   Fax 0171 896 2054
Owner *Pearson*
Editor *Ceri Jones*
Surveys Editor *Stephen Moore*
Circulation 63,000

FOUNDED 1860. WEEKLY. Opportunities for freelance contributors in the survey section only. All approaches should be made in writing. Over forty surveys are published each year on a wide variety of subjects, generally with a financial, business or investment emphasis. Copies of survey list and synopses of individual surveys are obtainable from the surveys editor.

Payment negotiable.

J17
Endeavour House, 189 Shaftesbury Avenue, London WC2H 8JG
☎0171 208 3408   Fax 0171 208 3590
Owner *EMAP Elan Publications*
Editor *Ally Oliver*
Circulation 242,016

FOUNDED 1983. MONTHLY. News, articles and quizzes of interest to girls aged 13–17. Ideas are sought in all areas. Prospective contributors should send ideas to the deputy editor.
   Beauty *Lara Williamson*
   Features *Caroline Orme*
   Music/News *Sarra Manning*
   Payment by arrangement.

Jane's Defence Weekly
Sentinel House, 163 Brighton Road, Coulsdon, Surrey CR5 2YH
☎0181 700 3700   Fax 0181 763 1007
Owner *Jane's Information Group*
Publishing Director *Alan Condron*
Editor *Clifford Beal*
Circulation 25,492

FOUNDED 1984. WEEKLY. No unsolicited mss. Approach in writing with ideas in the first instance.
   Features Current defence topics (politics, strategy, equipment, industry) of worldwide interest. No history pieces. Max. 2000 words.

Jazz Journal International
1–5 Clerkenwell Road, London EC1M 5PA
☎0171 608 1348   Fax 0171 608 1292
Owner *Jazz Journal Ltd*
Editor-in-Chief *Eddie Cook*
Circulation 10,000+

FOUNDED 1948. MONTHLY. A specialised jazz magazine, mainly for record collectors, principally using expert contributors whose work is known to the editor. Unsolicited mss not welcome, with the exception of news material (for which no payment is made). It is not a gig guide, nor a free reference source for students.

Jersey Now
PO Box 582, Five Oaks, St Saviour, Jersey, Channel Islands JE4 8XQ
☎01534 611600   Fax 01534 611610
Owner *MSP Publishing*

Managing Editor *Peter Body*
Production Manager *Simon Petulla*
Circulation 10,000

FOUNDED 1984. SEASONAL lifestyle magazine with features on homes, leisure, motoring, fashion, beauty, health, local issues and travel. No fiction. No unsolicited mss. Approach by phone in the first instance.

Jewish Chronicle
25 Furnival Street, London EC4A 1JT
☎0171 415 1500   Fax 0171 405 9040
Email: jconline@jchron.co.uk
Owner *Kessler Foundation*
Editor *Edward J. Temko*
Circulation 50,000

WEEKLY. Unsolicited mss welcome if 'the specific interests of our readership are borne in mind by writers'. Approach in writing, except for urgent current news items. No fiction. Max. 1500 words for all material.
   Features *Gerald Jacobs*
   Leisure/Lifestyle *Alan Montague*
   Home News *Barry Toberman*
   Foreign News *Joseph Millis*
   Supplements *Angela Kiverstein*
   Payment negotiable.

Jewish Quarterly
PO Box 2078, London W1A 1JR
☎0171 629 5004   Fax 0171 629 5110
Publisher *Jewish Literary Trust Ltd*
Editor *Matthew Reisz*

FOUNDED 1953. QUARTERLY illustrated magazine featuring Jewish literature and fiction, politics, art, music, film, poetry, history, dance, community, autobiography, Hebrew, Yiddish, Israel and the Middle East, Judaism, interviews, Zionism, philosophy and holocaust studies. Features a major books and arts section. Unsolicited mss welcome but letter or phone call preferred in first instance.

Jewish Telegraph
Jewish Telegraph Group of Newspapers, 11 Park Hill, Bury Old Road, Prestwich, Manchester M25 0HH
☎0161 740 9321   Fax 0161 740 9325
Email: telegraph@jaytel.demon.co.uk
Editor *Paul Harris*
Circulation 16,000

FOUNDED 1950. WEEKLY publication with local, national and international news and features. (Separate editions published for Manchester, Leeds, Liverpool and Glasgow.) Unsolicited features on Jewish humour and history welcome.

The Journal Magazines (Norfolk, Suffolk, Cambridgeshire)

The Old County School, Northgate Street, Bury St Edmunds, Suffolk IP33 1HP
☎01284 701190   Fax 01284 701680

Owner *Hawksmere plc*
Editor *Pippa Bastin*
Circulation 9000 each

FOUNDED 1990. MONTHLY magazines covering items of local interest – history, people, conservation, business, places, food and wine, fashion, homes and sport.
    Features 750 words max., plus pictures. Approach the deputy editor by phone with ideas in the first instance.

Judaism Today: An Independent Journal of Jewish Thought

PO Box 16096, London N3 3WG
☎0181 346 1668   Fax 0181 346 1776
Email: colsh@today.u-net.com

Owner *The Judaism Today Trust Limited*
Editor *Dr Colin Shindler*

FOUNDED 1994, the magazine aims to meet the need for an independent and open discussion of contemporary Jewish religious issues in a non-partisan forum that is reasoned, enlightened and tolerant. Unsolicited mss welcome but a letter or telephone call beforehand is preferred.

Just Seventeen

See **J17**

Kennel Gazette

15 Knightsbridge Green, London SW1X 7QL
☎0171 584 8200   Fax 0171 581 2865

Owner *Kennel Club*
Editor *Charles Colborn*
Circulation 10,000

FOUNDED 1873. MONTHLY concerning dogs and their breeding. Unsolicited mss welcome.
    Features Maximum 2500 words.
    News Maximum 500 words.
    Payment £70 per 1000 words.

Kent Life

Datateam Publishing, Fairmeadow, Maidstone, Kent ME14 1NG
☎01622 687031   Fax 01622 757646

Publisher *Datateam Publishing*
Editor *Roderick Cooper*
Circulation 10,000

FOUNDED 1962. MONTHLY. Strong Kent interest plus fashion, food, books, wildlife, motoring, property, sport, interiors with local links. Unsolicited mss welcome. Interested in anything with a genuine Kent connection. No fiction or non-Kentish subjects. Approach in writing with ideas. Maximum length 1500 words.
    Payment negotiable.

The Lady

39–40 Bedford Street, Strand, London WC2E 9ER
☎0171 379 4717   Fax 0171 497 2137

Owner *T. G. A. Bowles*
Editor *Arline Usden*
Circulation 49,006

FOUNDED 1885. WEEKLY. Unsolicited mss are accepted provided they are not on the subject of politics or religion, or on topics covered by staff writers, i.e. fashion and beauty, health, cookery, household, gardening, finance and shopping.
    Features Well-researched pieces on British and foreign travel, historical subjects or events; interviews and profiles and other general interest topics. Maximum 1000 words for illustrated articles; 900 words for one-page features; 450 words for first-person 'Viewpoint' pieces. All material should be addressed to the editor. Photographs supporting features may be supplied as colour transparencies or b&w prints.

Lakeland Walker

Cromwell Court, New Road, St Ives, Cambridgeshire PE17 4BG

Owner *Raven Marketing Group*
Editor *David Ogle*

FOUNDED 1996. QUARTERLY. News and features relating to the Lake District and walking in the area – wildlife, local history, places to visit, local transport. Maximum 1000–1500 words. Unsolicited material welcome.

Land Rover World

Link House, Dingwall Road, Croydon, Surrey CR9 2TA
☎0181 686 2599   Fax 0181 781 6042
Website: www.ipc.co.uk/pubs/rover.htm

Owner *Link House Magazines Ltd*
Editor *John Carroll*
Circulation 30,000

FOUNDED 1994. MONTHLY. Incorporates *Practical Land Rover World*. Unsolicited material welcome, especially if supported by high-quality illustrations. 'Editorial policy is to encourage and support unknown writers and beginners wherever possible.'

Features All articles with a Land Rover theme of interest. Potential contributors are strongly advised to examine previous issues before starting work.
Payment negotiable.

Leisure Vehicle Times

Golden Boot Chambers, 27 Gabriels Hill, Maidstone, Kent ME15 6HX
☎01634 574951   Fax 01634 574952
Owner *Déésse Media*
Editor *Dave Randle*
Circulation 85,000

FOUNDED 1997. Colour magazine for leisure motorists. 'More scope for freelancers as title becomes established.' Approach by 'phone or letter/fax with ideas.

Lexikon

PO Box 754, Stoke-on-Trent, Staffordshire ST1 4BU
☎01782 205060   Fax 01782 285331
Email: lexikon@anderson.karoo.co.uk
Website: www.karoo.net/lexikon/index.htm
Editors *Francis Anderson, Alan Barrett, Roger Bradley, Rosemary Munden*

'Sharp, discerning prose, giving writers in the UK and abroad the opportunity to share their work and exchange new ideas.' Poetry, short stories, critical articles, book reviews plus regular competitions with cash prizes. Maxi. of 2000 words for short stories; maximum of 60 lines for poetry. Please enclose s.a.e. with all submissions. Subscription: £8 for 4 issues available in print, disk (ASCII/WP), email and (for the blind and visually impaired only) on audiocassette. *Payment* complimentary copies.

Life&Soul Magazine

PO Box 119, Chipping Norton OX7 6GR
☎01993 832578   Fax 01993 832578
Email: editor@lifeandsoul.com
Website: www.lifeandsoul.com
Publisher *Karma Publishing Ltd*
Editor *Roy Stemman*
Circulation 3000

QUARTERLY. The only magazine in the world dealing with all aspects of reincarnation – from people who claim to recall their past lives spontaneously to those who have been regressed. It also examines other evidence for immortality, including near-death experiences and spirit communication.

Lincolnshire Life

County Life Ltd, PO Box 81, Lincoln LN1 1HD
☎01522 527127   Fax 01522 560035
Email: editorial@lincolnshirelife.co.uk
Website: www.lincolnshirelife.co.uk
Publisher *A. L. Robinson*
Executive Editor *Pam Mallender*
Circulation 10,000

FOUNDED 1961. MONTHLY county magazine featuring geographically relevant articles. Max. 1000–1500 words. Contributions supported by three or four good-quality photographs are always welcome. Approach in writing.
Payment varies.

The List

14 High Street, Edinburgh EH1 1TE
☎0131 558 1191   Fax 0131 557 8500
Email: editor@list.co.uk
Owner *The List Ltd*
Publisher *Robin Hodge*
Editor *Alan Morrison*
Circulation 16,500

FOUNDED 1985. FORTNIGHTLY. Events guide covering Glasgow and Edinburgh. Interviews and profiles of people working in film, theatre, music and the arts. Max. 1200 words. No unsolicited mss. Phone with ideas. News material tends to be handled in-house.
Payment £100.

Literary Review

44 Lexington Street, London W1R 3LH
☎0171 437 9392   Fax 0171 734 1844
Owner *Namara Group*
Editor *Auberon Waugh*
Circulation 15,000

FOUNDED 1979. MONTHLY. Publishes book reviews (commissioned), features and articles on literary subjects. Prospective contributors are best advised to contact the editor in writing. Unsolicited mss not welcome. Runs a monthly competition, the Literary Review Grand Poetry Competition, on a given theme. Open to subscribers only. Details published in the magazine.
Payment varies.

Living France

The Picture House, 79 High Street, Olney, Buckinghamshire MK46 4EF
☎01234 713203   Fax 01234 711507
Email: livingfrance@easynet.co.uk
Website: www.livingfrance.com
Editor *Trevor Yorke*

FOUNDED 1989. TEN ISSUES YEARLY. A Francophile magazine catering for those with a passion for France, French culture and lifestyle. Editorial covers all aspects of holidaying, living and working in France. Property section for those owning or wishing to buy a property in France. No unsolicited mss; approach in writing with an idea.

Loaded

King's Reach Tower, Stamford Street,
London SE1 9LS
☎0171 261 5562   Fax 0171 261 5557
Email: kate-jacobs@ipc.co.uk
Website: www.ipc.co.uk/pubs/loaded.htm

Owner *IPC Magazines*
Editor *Tim Southwell*
Circulation 457,318

FOUNDED 1994. MONTHLY men's lifestyle magazine featuring music, sport, sex, humour, travel, fashion, hard news and popular culture. Will consider material which comes into these categories; approach in writing in the first instance. No fiction, poetry or articles on relationships.

Logos

5 Beechwood Drive, Marlow,
Buckinghamshire SL7 2DH
☎01628 477577   Fax 01628 477577

Owner *Whurr Publishers Ltd*
Editor *Gordon Graham*
Associate Editor *Betty Graham*

FOUNDED 1990. QUARTERLY. Aims to 'deal in depth with issues which unite, divide, excite and concern the world of books,' with an international perspective. Each issue contains 6–8 articles of between 3500–7000 words. Hopes to establish itself as a forum for contrasting views. Suggestions and ideas for contributions are welcome, and should be addressed to the editor. 'Guidelines for Contributors' available. Contributors write from their experience as authors, publishers, booksellers, librarians, etc. *No payment.*

London Magazine

30 Thurloe Place, London SW7 2HQ
☎0171 589 0618

Owner/Editor *Alan Ross*
Deputy Editor *Jane Rye*
Circulation 4500

FOUNDED 1954. BI-MONTHLY paperback journal providing an eclectic forum for literary talent, thanks to the dedication of Alan Ross. *The Times* once said that '*London Magazine* is far and away the most readable and level-headed, not to mention best value for money, of the literary magazines'. Today it boasts the publication of early works by the likes of William Boyd, Graham Swift and Ben Okri among others. The broad spectrum of interests includes art, memoirs, travel, poetry, criticism, theatre, music, cinema, short stories and essays, and book reviews. Unsolicited mss welcome; s.a.e. essential. About 150–200 unsolicited mss are received weekly.

Fiction Maximum 5000 words.
Payment £100 maximum.
Annual Subscription £28.50 or $67.

London Review of Books

28 Little Russell Street, London WC1A 2HN
☎0171 209 1101   Fax 0171 209 1102

Owner *LRB Ltd*
Editor *Mary-Kay Wilmers*
Circulation 25,585

FOUNDED 1979. FORTNIGHTLY. Reviews, essays and articles on political, literary, cultural and scientific subjects. Also poetry. Unsolicited contributions welcome (approximately 50 received each week). No pieces under 2000 words. Contact the editor in writing. Please include s.a.e.

Payment 150 per 1000 words; poems £50.

Looking Good

Upper Mounts, Northampton NN1 3HR
☎01604 231122   Fax 01604 233000

Owner *Northamptonshire Newspapers Ltd*
Editor *Ruth Supple*
Circulation 6000

FOUNDED 1984. QUARTERLY county lifestyle magazine of Northamptonshire. Contributions occasionally considered but majority of work is done in-house.

Looks

Endeavour House, 189 Shaftesbury Avenue,
London WC2H 8JG
☎0171 437 9011   Fax 0171 208 3586

Owner *EMAP Elan Publications*
Editor *Eleni Kyriacou*
Circulation 138,340

MONTHLY celebrity-led magazine for young women aged 16–24, with fashion, beauty and hair, as well as general interest features, interviews, giveaways, etc. Freelance writers are occasionally used in all areas of the magazine. Contact the editor with ideas.

Payment varies.

Loving Holiday Special

PO Box 435A, Surbiton, Surrey KT6 6YT
Owner *Perfectly Formed Publishing Ltd*
Editor *Jo Pink*
Circulation 40,000

ANNUAL. Unclichéd summer love stories for women under 30. Story lengths 1000–4000 words. Write with an s.a.e. for a style guide (December/January/February only) before putting pen to paper.

M & E Design

Quadrant House, The Quadrant, Sutton, Surrey SM2 5AS
☎0181 652 3115   Fax 0181 652 8951
Email: richard.simmonds@rbi.co.uk
Owner *Reed Business Information*
Deputy Editor *Richard Simmonds*
Circulation 8,000

FOUNDED 1996. MONTHLY. Aimed at mechanical and electrical consulting engineers and designers. Would-be contributors should submit a 300-word synopsis via email to the Deputy Editor.

Machine Knitting Monthly

PO Box 1479, Maidenhead, Berkshire SL6 8YX
☎01628 783080   Fax 01628 633250
Owner *RPA Publishing Ltd*
Editor *Anne Smith*

FOUNDED 1986. MONTHLY. Unsolicited mss considered 'as long as they are applicable to this specialist publication. We have our own regular contributors each month but we're always willing to look at new ideas from other writers.' Approach in writing in first instance.

Management Today

174 Hammersmith Road, London W6 7JP
☎0171 413 4566
Email: management.today@haynet.com
Owner *Haymarket Business Publications Ltd*
Editor *Rufus Olins*
Circulation 89,414

General business topics and features. Ideas welcome. Send brief synopsis to the editor.
Payment about £300 per 1000 words.

marie claire

2 Hatfields, London SE1 9PG
☎0171 261 5240   Fax 0171 261 5277
Website: www.ipc.co.uk/pubs/marie.htm
Owner *European Magazines Ltd*
Acting Editor *Elsa McAlonan*

Circulation 445,289

FOUNDED 1988. MONTHLY. An intelligent glossy magazine for women, with strong international features and fashion. No unsolicited mss. Approach with ideas in writing. No fiction.
Features *Helen Johnston* Detailed proposals for feature ideas should be accompanied by samples of previous work.

Market Newsletter

Focus House, 497 Green Lanes, London N13 4BP
☎0181 882 3315   Fax 0181 886 5174
Owner *Bureau of Freelance Photographers*
Editor *John Tracy*
Deputy Editor *Stewart Gibson*
Circulation 7,000

FOUNDED 1965. MONTHLY. News of current markets – magazines, books, cards, calendars, etc – and the type of submissions (mainly photographs) they are currently looking for. Includes details of new magazine launches, publication revamps etc. Also profiles of particular markets and photographers. Circulated to members of the Bureau of Freelance Photographers (annual membership fee: £40 UK; £55 Overseas). Limited scope for non-members to contribute.

Marketing Week

12–26 Lexington Street, London W1R 4HQ
☎0171 970 4000   Fax 0171 970 6721
Website: www.marketing-week.co.uk
Owner *Centaur Communications*
Editor *Stuart Smith*
Circulation 39,000

WEEKLY trade magazine of the marketing industry. Features on all aspects of the business, written in a newsy and up-to-the-minute style. Approach with ideas in the first instance.
Features *Joanne Flack*
Payment negotiable.

Match

Bretton Court, Bretton, Peterborough, Cambridgeshire PE3 8DZ
☎01733 260333   Fax 01733 465206
Website: www.matchfacts.co.uk
Owner *EMAP Active Ltd*
Editor *Chris Hunt*
Circulation 145,749

FOUNDED 1979. Popular WEEKLY football magazine aimed at 10–15-year-olds. Most material is generated in-house by a strong news and features team. Some freelance material used if suitable. No submissions without prior consultation with editor, either by phone or in writing. Work experience placements often given to trainee journalists and students.

Features/News Good and original material is always considered. Maximum 500 words.

Payment negotiable.

Matrix
See **British Science Fiction Association** under **Professional Associations**

Maxim
19 Bolsover Street, London W1P 7HJ
☎0171 631 1433   Fax 0171 917 7663
Owner *Dennis Publishing*
Editor *Chris Maillard*
Circulation 300,786

ESTABLISHED 1995. MONTHLY glossy men's lifestyle magazine featuring sex, travel, health, finance, motoring and fashion. No fiction or poetry. Approach in writing in the first instance, sending outlines of ideas only together with examples of published work. Some scope for first-person accounts.

Mayfair
2 Archer Street, Piccadilly Circus, London W1V 8JJ
☎0171 292 8000   Fax 0171 734 5030
Owner *Paul Raymond Publications*
Editor *Steve Shields*
Circulation 331,760

FOUNDED 1966. THIRTEEN ISSUES YEARLY. Unsolicited material accepted if suitable to the magazine. Interested in features and humour aimed at men aged 20–30. For style, length, etc., writers are advised to study the magazine. 'No more romantic fiction, we beseech you!'

Mayfair Times
102 Mount Street, London W1X 5HF
☎0171 629 3378   Fax 0171 629 9303
Owner *Mayfair Times Ltd*
Editor *Stephen Goringe*
Circulation 20,000

FOUNDED 1985. MONTHLY. Features on Mayfair of interest to both residential and commercial readers. Unsolicited mss welcome.

Medal News
Token Publishing Ltd, PO Box 14, Honiton, Devon EX14 9YP
☎01404 46972   Fax 01404 831895
Email: info@medal-news.com
Website: www.medal-news.com
Owners *J. W. Mussell, Carol Hartman*

Editor *John Sly*
Circulation 4500

FOUNDED 1989. MONTHLY. Unsolicited material welcome but initial approach by phone or in writing preferred.

Features Only interested in articles from well-informed authors 'who know the subject and do their homework'. Max. 2500 words.

Payment £20 per 1000 words.

Media Week
Quantum House, 19 Scarbrook Road, Croydon, Surrey CR9 1LX
☎0181 565 4200   Fax 0181 565 4394
Email: mweeked@qpp.co.uk
Website: www.mediaweek.co.uk
Owner *Quantam*
Editor *Patrick Barrett*
Circulation 13,944

FOUNDED 1986. WEEKLY trade magazine. UK and international coverage on all aspects of commercial media. No unsolicited mss. Approach in writing with ideas.

Maker
26th Floor, King's Reach Tower, Stamford Street, London SE1 9LS
☎0171 261 6229   Fax 0171 261 6706
Website: www.ipc.co.uk/pubs/melomake.htm
Owner *IPC Magazines Ltd*
Editor *Mark Sutherland*
Circulation 40,349

FOUNDED 1926. WEEKLY. Freelance contributors used on this tabloid magazine competitor of the *NME*. Opportunities exist in reviewing and features.

Features *Ian Watson* A large in-house team, plus around six regulars, produce most feature material.

Reviews *Sharon O'Connell* (Live), *Neil Mason* (Albums) Sample reviews, whether published or not, welcome on pop, rock, soul, funk, etc.

Payment negotiable.

Men's Health
7–10 Chandos Street, London W1M 0AD
☎0171 291 6000   Fax 0171 291 6060
Owner *Rodale Press*
Editor *Simon Geller*
Circulation 245,900

FOUNDED 1994. MONTHLY men's healthy lifestyle magazine covering health, fitness, nutrition, stress and sex issues. No unsolicited mss; will consider ideas and synopses tailored to men's health. No fiction, celebrities, sportsmen or extreme sports. Approach in writing in the first instance.

MiniWorld Magazine

Link House, Dingwall Road, Croydon, Surrey
CR9 2TA
☎0181 774 0645   Fax 0181 781 6042
Email: MiniWorld@LHM.co.uk

Owner *Link House Magazines Ltd*
Editor *Monty Watkins*
Circulation 37,082

FOUNDED 1991. MONTHLY car magazine devoted to the Mini. Unsolicited material welcome but prospective contributors are advised
to make initial contact by phone.

Features Restoration, tuning tips, technical
advice and sporting events. Readers' cars and
product news. Length by arrangement.
Payment negotiable.

Minx

Endeavour House, 189 Shaftesbury Avenue,
London WC2H 8JG
☎0171 208 3428   Fax 0171 208 3323

Owner *EMAP*
Editor *Vanessa Thompson*
Circulation 160,708

FOUNDED 1996. MONTHLY lifestyle magazine
for young women. Interested in receiving ideas
for features; approach in writing in the first
instance. No fiction.

Mizz

King's Reach Tower, Stamford Street,
London SE1 9LS
☎0171 261 6319   Fax 0171 261 6032
Website: www.ipc.co.uk/pubs/mizz.htm

Owner *IPC Magazines Ltd*
Editor *Lucie Tobin*
Circulation 130,254

FOUNDED 1985. FORTNIGHTLY magazine for
the 11–14-year-old girl. Freelance articles welcome on real life, human interest stories and
emotional issues. Also quizzes. All material
should be addressed to the features editor.

Features *Julie Burniston* Approach in writing, with synopsis, for feature copy; send sample writing with letter for general approach.
Fiction Max. 1000 words.

Model Railway Enthusiast

PO Box 199, Scarborough, North Yorkshire
YO11 3GT
☎01723 506326   Fax 01723 506326
Email: pehammond@aol.com

Owner *Garnett Dickinson Publishing*
Editor *Pat Hammond*
Circulation 20,000

FOUNDED 1993. MONTHLY magazine, the only
national model railway magazine in the UK
catering specifically for model railway collectors
as well as average railway modellers. Articles with
good photographs or drawings on the subject of
collecting or modelling are welcome but ideas
should be discussed first with the editor.
Payment £40 per 1000 words; £5 per picture published.

Mojo

Mappin House, 4 Winsley Street, London
W1N 7AR
☎0171 436 1515   Fax 0171 312 8296
Email: mojo@ecm.emap.com

Owner *EMAP-Metro*
Editor *Mat Snow*
Circulation 75,365

FOUNDED 1993. MONTHLY magazine containing
features, reviews and news stories about rock
music and its influences. Receives about five mss
per day. No poetry, pieces on dead rock stars or
similar fan worship.

Features Amateur writers discouraged
except as providers of source material, contacts,
etc. *Payment* negotiable.

News All verifiable, relevant stories considered. *Payment* approx. £150 per 1000 words.

Reviews Write to Reviews Editor with relevant specimen material. *Payment* approx. £150
per 1000 words.

Moneywise

RD Publications Ltd, 11 Westferry Circus,
Canary Wharf, London E14 4HE
☎0171 715 8465   Fax 0171 715 8725
Website: www.moneywise.co.uk

Owner *Reader's Digest Association*
Editor *Matthew Vincent*
Circulation 105,000

FOUNDED 1990. MONTHLY. Unsolicited mss
with s.a.e. welcome but initial approach in writing preferred.

More!

Endeavour House, 189 Shaftesbury Avenue,
London WC2H 8JG
☎0171 208 3165   Fax 0171 208 3595

Owner *EMAP Elan Publications*
Editor *Marina Gask*
Features Director *Julian Linley*
Associate Editor/Features *Nigel May*
Editorial Enquiries *Alice Butler*
Circulation 293,369

FOUNDED 1988. FORTNIGHTLY women's magazine aimed at the working woman aged 18–24.

Features on sex and relationships plus news. Most items are commissioned; approach features editor with idea. Prospective contributors are strongly advised to study the magazine's style before submitting anything.

Mother and Baby

Endeavour House, 189 Shaftesbury Avenue, London WC2H 8JG
☎0171 208 3234   Fax 0171 208 3584
Owner *EMAP Elan Publications*
Editor *Melanie Deeprose*
Circulation 88,096

FOUNDED 1956. MONTHLY. Unsolicited synopses welcome, about practical pregnancy, birth, baby and childcare subjects. Approaches may be made by telephone or in writing to the Features Editor *Tina Gough.*

Motor Boat and Yachting

King's Reach Tower, Stamford Street, London SE1 9LS
☎0171 261 5333   Fax 0171 261 5419
Email: mby@ipc.co.uk
Website: www.mby.com
Owner *IPC Magazines Ltd*
Editor *Alan Harper*
Circulation 19,625

FOUNDED 1904. MONTHLY for those interested in motor boats and motor cruising.

Features *Alan Harper* Cruising features and practical features especially welcome. Illustrations/photographs (mostly colour) are just as important as text. Max. 3000 words. *Payment* £100 per 1000 words or by arrangement.

News *Tom Isitt* Factual pieces. Max. 200 words. *Payment* up to £50 per item.

Motorcaravan Motorhome Monthly (MMM)

PO Box 44, Totnes, Devon TQ9 5XB
Owner *Sanglier Publications Ltd*
Editor *Mike Jago*
Circulation 24,730

FOUNDED 1966. MONTHLY. 'There's no money in motorcaravan journalism but for those wishing to cut their first teeth...' Unsolicited mss welcome if relevant, but ideas in writing preferred in first instance.

Features Caravan site reports. Maximum 500 words.

Travel Motorcaravanning trips (home and overseas). Maximum 2000 words.

News Short news items for miscellaneous pages. Maximum 200 words.

Fiction Must be motorcaravan-related and

include artwork/photos if possible. Maximum 2000 words.

Special pages DIY – modifications to motorcaravans. Maximum 1500 words.

Owner Reports Contributions welcome from motorcaravan owners. Contact the Editor for requirements. Maximum 2000 words. *Payment* varies.

Motorgliding International

281 Queen Edith's Way, Cambridge CB1 9NH
☎01223 247725   Fax 01223 413793
Email: bryce.smith@virgin.net
Owner *British Gliding Association/Soaring Society of America*
Editor *Gillian Bryce-Smith*

FOUNDED November 1998 for an international market concentrating entirely on motorgliding. Few opportunities for freelance writers. *No payment.*

Ms London

7–9 Rathbone Street, London W1P 1AF
☎0171 636 6651
Owner *Independent Magazines*
Editor-in-Chief *Bill Williamson*
Editor *Cathy Howes*
Circulation 85,000

FOUNDED 1968. WEEKLY. Aimed at working women in London, aged 18–35. Unsolicited mss must be accompanied by s.a.e.

Features Content is varied and topical, ranging from celebrity interviews to news issues, fashion, health, careers, relationships and homebuying. Approach in writing only with ideas in the first instance and enclose sample of published writing. Material should be London-angled, sharp or humorous and fairly sophisticated in content. Max. 1500 words. *Payment* about £130 per 1000 words on publication.

News Handled in-house but follow-up feature ideas welcome.

Mslexia (For Women Who Write)

PO Box 656, Newcastle upon Tyne NE99 2XD
☎0191 281 9772   Fax 0191 281 9445
Email: postbag@mslexia.demon.co.uk
Website: www.mslexia.co.uk
Owner *Mslexia Publications Limited*
Editor *Debbie Taylor*
Circulation 5000

FOUNDED 1997. QUARTERLY. Articles, advice, reviews, interviews, events for women writers plus new poetry and prose. Will consider fiction, poetry, features and letters but contributors *must* send for guidelines first. Approach in writing.

Music Week

8 Montague Close, London SE1 9UR
☎0171 620 3636   Fax 0171 401 8035
Owner *Miller Freeman Entertainment*
Editor-in-Chief *Steve Redmond*
Editor *Ajax Scott*
Circulation 13,900

Britain's only WEEKLY music business magazine also includes dance industry title *Record Mirror*. No unsolicited mss. Approach in writing with ideas.

Features *Ajax Scott* Analysis of specific music business events and trends.

News Music industry news only.

Musical Opinion

2 Princes Road, St Leonards on Sea, East Sussex TN37 6EL
☎01424 715167   Fax 01424 712214
Owner *Musical Opinion Ltd*
Editor *Denby Richards*
Circulation 5000

FOUNDED 1877. QUARTERLY with eight free supplements in intervening months. Classical music content, with topical features on music, musicians, festivals, etc., and reviews (concerts, festivals, opera, ballet, jazz, CDs, CD-ROMs, videos, books and printed music). International readership. No unsolicited mss; commissions only. Ideas always welcome though; approach by phone or fax, giving 'phone number. It should be noted that topical material has to be submitted six months prior to events. Not interested in review material, which is already handled by the magazine's own regular team of contributors.
Payment negotiable.

Musical Times

☎0171 482 5697   Fax 0171 482 5697
Owner *The Musical Times Publications Ltd*
Editor *Nicholas Williams*

FOUNDED 1844. Scholarly journal with a practical approach to its subject. All material is commissioned.

My Weekly

80 Kingsway East, Dundee DD4 8SL
☎01382 223131   Fax 01382 452491
Owner *D. C. Thomson & Co. Ltd*
Editor *Harrison Watson*
Circulation 376,146

Traditional women's WEEKLY. D. C. Thomson

has long had a policy of encouragement and help to new writers of promise. Ideas welcome. Approach in writing.

Features Particularly interested in human interest pieces (1000–1500 words) which by their very nature appeal to all age groups.

Fiction Three stories a week, ranging in content from the emotional to the off-beat and unexpected. 1500–4000 words. Also serials.
Payment negotiable.

The National Trust Magazine

36 Queen Anne's Gate, London SW1H 9AS
☎0171 222 9251   Fax 0171 222 5097
Owner *The National Trust*
Editor *Gina Guarnieri*
Circulation 2.6 million

FOUNDED 1968. THRICE-YEARLY. Conservation of historic houses, coast and countryside in England, Northern Ireland and Wales. No unsolicited mss. Approach in writing with ideas.

Natural World

Victory House, 14 Leicester Place, London WC2H 7QH
☎0171 306 0304   Fax 0171 306 0314
Owner *River Publishing Ltd*
Editor *Sarah-Jane Forder*
Circulation 178,000

FOUNDED 1981. THRICE-YEARLY. Unsolicited mss not accepted. Ideas in writing preferred. No poetry.

Features Popular but accurate articles on British wildlife and the countryside, particularly projects associated with the local wildlife trusts. Maximum 1500 words.

News Interested in national wildlife conservation issues, particularly those involving local nature conservation or wildlife trusts. Maximum 300 words.
Payment negotiable.

The Naturalist

c/o University of Bradford, Bradford, West Yorkshire BD7 1DP
☎01274 234212   Fax 01274 234231
Email: m.r.d.seaward@bradford.ac.uk
Owner *Yorkshire Naturalists' Union*
Editor *Prof. M. R. D. Seaward*
Circulation 5000

FOUNDED 1875. QUARTERLY. Natural history, biological and environmental sciences for a professional and amateur readership. Unsolicited mss and b&w illustrations welcome. Particularly interested in material – scientific papers – relating to the north of England. *No payment.*

Nature

Porters South, 4–6 Crinan Street, London
N1 9XW
☎0171 833 4000

Owner *Macmillan Magazines Ltd*
Editor *Philip Campbell*
Circulation 57,897

Covers all fields of science, with articles and news on science policy only. No features. Little scope for freelance writers.

Needlecraft

30 Monmouth Street, Bath BA1 2BW
☎01225 442244   Fax 01225 732398

Owner *Future Publishing*
Editor *Katriel Costello*
Circulation 35,000

FOUNDED 1991. MONTHLY. Needlework projects with full instructions covering cross-stitch, needlepoint, embroidery, patchwork quilting and lace. Will consider ideas or sketches for projects covering any of the magazine's topics. Initial approaches should be made in writing.

Features on the needlecraft theme. Discuss ideas before sending complete mss. Maximum 1000 words.

Technical pages on 'how to' stitch, use different threads, etc. Only suitable for experienced writers.

Payment negotiable.

New Beacon

224 Great Portland Street, London W1N 6AA
☎0171 388 1266   Fax 0171 388 0945

Owner *Royal National Institute for the Blind*
Editor *Ann Lee*
Circulation 6000

FOUNDED 1917. MONTHLY (except August). Published in print, braille and on tape and disk. Unsolicited mss welcome. Approach with ideas in writing. Personal experiences by writers who have a visual impairment (partial sight or blindness), and authoritative items by professionals or volunteers working in the field of visual impairment welcome. Maximum 1500 words.

Payment negotiable

New Humanist

Bradlaugh House, 47 Theobald's Road, London WC1X 8SP
☎0171 430 1371
Fax 0171 430 1271
Email: jim.rpa@humanism.org.uk

Owner *Rationalist Press Association*
Editor *Jim Herrick*

Circulation 1500

FOUNDED 1885. QUARTERLY. Unsolicited mss welcome. No fiction.

Features Articles with a humanist perspective welcome in the following fields: religion (critical), humanism, human rights, philosophy, current events, literature, history and science. 2000–4000 words. *Payment* nominal, but negotiable.

Book reviews 750–1000 words, by arrangement with the editor.

New Impact

Anser House, Courtyard Offices,
3 High Street, Marlow, Bucks SL7 1AX
☎01628 475570   Fax 01628 475570

Owner *D. E. Sihera*
Editor *Elaine Sihera*
Features Editor *Daphne Bullock*
Circulation 10,000

FOUNDED 1993. BI-MONTHLY. Celebrates diversity, enterprise and achievement from a minority ethnic perspective. Unsolicited mss welcome. Interested in training, arts, features, personal achievement, small business features, profiles of personalities especially for a multicultural audience. Promotes the British Diversity Awards each November and the Windrush Awards each June, the Diversity Associates Register (DIVAS) and the Register of Diversity Managers among employers.

News Local training/business features – some opportunities. Maximum length 250 words. *Payment* negotiable.

Features Original, interesting pieces with a deliberate multicultural/diversity focus. Personal/professional successes and achievements welcome. Maximum length 1500 words. *Payment* negotiable.

Fiction Short stories, poems – especially from minority writers. Not interested in romantic/sexual narratives. Maximum length 1500 words. *Payment* negotiable.

Special Pages Interviews with personalities – especially Asian, African Caribbean. Maximum length 1200 words. *Payment* negotiable.

New Internationalist

55 Rectory Road, Oxford OX4 1BW
☎01865 728181   Fax 01865 793152
Email: ni@newint.org
Website: www.newint.org/

Owner *New Internationalist Trust*
Co-Editors *Vanessa Baird, Chris Brazier, David Ransom, Nikki van der Gaag*
Circulation 70,000

Radical and broadly leftist in approach, but unaligned. Concerned with world poverty and global issues of peace and politics, feminism and environmentalism, with emphasis on the Third World. Difficult to use unsolicited material as they work to a theme each month and features are commissioned by the editor on that basis. The way in is to send examples of published or unpublished work; writers of interest are taken up. Unsolicited material for shorter articles could be used in the magazine's regular *Update* section.

New Musical Express

King's Reach Tower, Stamford Street, London SE1 9LS
☎0171 261 6472   Fax 0171 261 5185
Website: www.nme.com
Owner *IPC Magazines Ltd*
Editor *Steve Sutherland*
Circulation 100,093

Britain's best-selling musical WEEKLY. Freelancers used, but always for reviews in the first instance. Specialisation in areas of music (or film, which is also covered) is a help.
    Reviews: Books/Film *Gavin Martin* **LPs** *John Robinson* **Live** *James Oldham.* Send in examples of work, either published or specially written samples.

New Nation

148 Cambridge Heath Road, London E1 5QJ
☎0171 702 8012   Fax 0171 702 7937
Owner *Ethnic Media Group*
Editor *Michael Eboda*
Circulation 30,000

FOUNDED 1996. WEEKLY community paper for the Black community in Britain. Interested in relevant general, local and international issues. Approach in writing with ideas for submission.

New Scientist

1st Floor, 151 Wardour Street, London W1V 4BN
☎0171 331 2701   Fax 0171 331 2777
Owner *Reed Business Information Ltd*
Editor *Dr Alun Anderson*
Circulation 130,994

FOUNDED 1956. WEEKLY. No unsolicited mss. Approach with ideas – one A4-page synopsis – by fax.
    Features *Jeremy Webb* Commissions only, but good ideas welcome. Maximum 3500 words.
    News *Peter Aldhous* Mostly commissions, but ideas for specialist news welcome. Maximum 1000 words.
    Reviews *Maggie McDonald* Reviews are commissioned.

Forum *Richard Fifield* Unsolicited material welcome if of general/humorous interest and related to science. Maximum 1000 words.
    Payment negotiable.

The New Shetlander

11 Mounthooly Street, Lerwick, Shetland ZE1 0BJ
☎01595 693816   Fax 01595 696787
Owner *Shetland Council of Social Service*
Editors *Alex Cluness, John Hunter*
Circulation 1750

FOUNDED 1947. QUARTERLY literary magazine containing short stories, essays, poetry, historical articles, literary criticism, political comment, arts and books. The magazine has two editors and an editorial committee who all look at submitted material. Interested in considering short stories, poetry, historical articles with a northern Scottish or Scandinavian flavour, literary pieces and articles on Shetland. As a rough guide, items should be between 1000 and 2000 words although longer mss are considered. Initial approach in writing, please.
    Payment complimentary copy.

New Statesman

Victoria Station House, 191 Victoria Street, London SW1E 5NE
☎0171 828 1232   Fax 0171 828 1881
Publisher *Spence Neal*
Editor *Peter Wilby*
Deputy Editor *Christina Odone*
Circulation 26,000

WEEKLY magazine, the result of a merger (1988) of *New Statesman* and *New Society.* Coverage of news, book reviews, arts, current affairs, politics and social reportage. Unsolicited contributions with s.a.e. will be considered. No short stories.
    Books *Jason Cowley*
    Arts *David Gibbons*

New Welsh Review

Chapter Arts Centre, Market Road, Cardiff CF5 1QE
☎01222 665529   Fax 01222 665529
Owner *New Welsh Review Ltd*
Editor *Robin Reeves*
Circulation 1000

FOUNDED 1988. QUARTERLY Welsh literary magazine in the English language. Welcomes material of literary and cultural interest to Welsh readers and those with an interest in Wales. Approach in writing in the first instance.

Features Max. 3000 words. *Payment £25 per 1000 words.*
Fiction Max. 5000 words. *Payment £40–80 average.*
News Max. 400 words. *Payment £10–£30.*

New Woman
Endeavour House, 189 Shaftesbury Avenue, London WC2H 8JG
☎0171 437 9011   Fax 0171 930 7246
Website: www.newwomanonline.co.uk
Owner *Hachette/EMAP Elan Ltd*
Editor *Jo Elvin*
Circulation 281,681

MONTHLY women's interest magazine. Winner of the PPA 'Magazine of the Year' award in 1998. Aimed at women aged 25–35. An 'entertaining, informative and intelligent' read. Main topics of interest include men, sex, love, health, careers, beauty and fashion. Uses mainly established freelancers but unsolicited ideas submitted in synopsis form will be considered. Welcomes ideas from male writers for humorous 'men's opinion' pieces.

Features/News *Margi Conklin* Articles must be original and look at subjects or issues from a new or unusual perspective.

Fashion *Corinna Kitchen*

The New Writer
PO Box 60, Cranbrook, Kent TN17 2ZR
☎01580 212626   Fax 01580 212041
Publisher *Merric Davidson*
Editor *Suzanne Ruthven*
Poetry Editor *Abi Hughes-Edwards*

FOUNDED 1996. Published MONTHLY following the merger between *Acclaim* and *Quartos* magazines. TNW continues to offer practical 'nuts and bolts' advice on poetry and prose but with the emphasis on *forward-looking* articles and features on all aspects of the written word that demonstrate the writer's grasp of contemporary writing and current editorial/publishing policies. Plenty of news, views, competitions, reviews and regional gossip in the Newsletter section; writers' guidelines available with s.a.e.

Features Unsolicited mss welcome. Interested in lively, original articles on writing in its broadest sense. Approach with ideas in writing in the first instance. No material is returned unless accompanied by s.a.e. *Payment £20 per 1000 words.*

Fiction Publishes short-listed entries from the **Ian St James Awards** and subscriber-only submissions. *Payment £10 per story.*

Poetry Unsolicited poetry welcome: both short and long unpublished poems, provided they are original and interesting. *Payment £3 per poem.*

Newcastle Life
See **North East Times**

19
King's Reach Tower, Stamford Street, London SE1 9LS
☎0171 261 6410   Fax 0171 261 7634
Website: www.ipc.co.uk/pubs/19.htm
Owner *IPC Magazines Ltd*
Editor *Lee Kynaston*
Circulation 173,244

FOUNDED 1968. MONTHLY women's magazine aimed at 16–20-year-olds. A little different from the usual teen magazine mix: *19* is now aiming for a 50/50 balance between fashion/lifestyle aspects and newsier, meatier material, e.g. women in prison, boys, abortion, etc. 40% of the magazine's feature material is commissioned, ordinarily from established freelancers. 'But we're always keen to see bold, original, vigorous writing from people just starting out.'

Features Approach in writing with ideas.

North East Times
Tattler House, Beech Avenue, Fawdon, Newcastle upon Tyne NE3 4LA
☎0191 284 4495   Fax 0191 285 9606
Owner *Chris Robinson (Publishing) Ltd*
Editor *Chris Robinson*
Circulation 10,000

MONTHLY county magazine incorporating *Newcastle Life*. No unsolicited mss. Approach with ideas in writing. Not interested in any material that is not applicable to ABC1 readers.

The North
See **Poetry Magazines**

Now
King's Reach Tower, Stamford Street, London SE1 9LS
☎0171 261 6274
Website: www.ipc.co.uk/pubs/now.htm
Owner *IPC Magazines Ltd*
Editor *Jane Ennis*
Circulation 350,000

FOUNDED 1996. WEEKLY magazine with celebrity gossip, news and topical features aimed at the working woman. Unlikely to use freelance contributions due to specialist content – e.g.

exclusive showbiz interviews – but ideas will be considered. Approach in writing; no faxes.

Nursing Times
Greater London House, Hampstead Road, London NW1 7EJ
☎0171 874 0500   Fax 0171 874 0505
Owner *EMAP Healthcare*
Editor *Tricia Reid*
Circulation 80,670

A large proportion of *Nursing Times'* feature content is from unsolicited contributions sent on spec. Pieces on all aspects of nursing and health care, both practical and theoretical, written in a lively and contemporary way, are welcome. Commissions also.

Payment varies/NUJ rates apply to commissioned material from union members only.

OK! Magazine
The Northern & Shell Tower, City Harbour, London E14 9GL
☎0171 308 5091   Fax 0171 301 5082
Owner *Richard Desmond*
Editor *Martin Townsend*
Circulation 226,504

FOUNDED 1996. WEEKLY celebrity-based magazine. Welcomes interviews and pictures on well known personalities, and ideas for general features. Approach by phone or fax in the first instance.

The Oldie
45–46 Poland Street, London W1V 4AU
☎0171 734 2225   Fax 0171 734 2226
Email: theoldie@theoldie.demon.co.uk
Website: www.theoldie.co.uk
Owner *Oldie Publications Ltd*
Editor *Richard Ingrams*
Circulation 45,000

FOUNDED 1992. MONTHLY general interest magazine with a strong humorous slant for the older person. Submissions welcome; enclose s.a.e.

OLS (Open Learning Systems) News
11 Malford Grove, Gilwern, Abergavenny, Monmouthshire NP7 0RN
☎01873 830872   Fax 01873 830872
Email: GSSE@zoo.co.uk
Owner/Editor *David P. Bosworth*
Circulation 800

FOUNDED 1980. QUARTERLY dealing with the application of open, flexible, distance learning and supported self-study at all educational/training levels. Interested in open-access learning and the application of educational technology to learning situations. Case studies particularly welcome. Not interested in theory of education alone, the emphasis is strictly on applied policies and trends.

Features Learning programmes (how they are organised); student/learner-eye views of educational and training programmes with an open-access approach. Sections on teleworking and lifelong learning. Approach the editor by email or in writing.

No payment for 'news' items. Focus items will negotiate.

On the Ball
Moondance Publications, The Design Works, William Street, Gateshead, Tyne and Wear NE10 0JP
☎0191 420 8383   Fax 0191 420 4950
Owner *Moondance Publications Ltd*
Editor *Jennifer O'Neill*
Circulation 30,000

FOUNDED 1996. BI-MONTHLY. The only magazine for women football players. Contributions welcome.

Features *Jennifer O'Neill* International reports, player and team profiles, diet, health and fitness, tactics, training advice, fund-raising, play improvement. 1500 words maximum.

News *Wilf Frith* Match reports, team news, transfers, injuries, results and fixtures. 600 words maximum.

Payment negotiable.

Opera
1A Mountgrove Road, London N5 2LU
☎0171 359 1037   Fax 0171 354 2700
Email: operamag@clara.co.uk
Website: www.opera.co.uk
Owner *Opera Magazine Ltd*
Editor *Rodney Milnes*
Circulation 11,500

FOUNDED 1950. MONTHLY review of the current opera scene. Almost all articles are commissioned and unsolicited mss are not welcome. All approaches should be made in writing.

Opera Now
241 Shaftesbury Avenue, London WC2H 8EH
☎0171 333 1740   Fax 0171 333 1769
Publisher *Rhinegold Publishing Ltd*

Editor-in-Chief *Ashutosh Khandekar*
Deputy Editor *Antonia Couling*
Assistant Editor *Matthew Peacock*
FOUNDED 1989. BI-MONTHLY. News, features and reviews aimed at those involved as well as those interested in opera. No unsolicited mss. All work is commissioned. Approach with ideas in writing.

Orbis

See under **Poetry, Little Magazines**

Organic Gardening

PO Box 29, Minehead, Somerset TA24 6YY
☎01984 641212   Fax 01984 641212
Editor *Gaby Bartai Bevan*
Circulation 20,000
FOUNDED 1988. MONTHLY. Articles and features on all aspects of gardening based on organic methods, with special emphasis on old varieties and conservation. Unsolicited material welcome, maximum 600–2000 words for features and 100–300 for news items. Prefers 'hands-on' accounts of projects, problems, challenges and how they are dealt with. Approach by phone or in writing.
Payment by arrangement.

OS (Office Secretary) Magazine

Brookmead House, Thorney Leys Business Park, Witney, Oxfordshire OX8 7GE
☎01993 775545   Fax 01993 778884
Owner *Peebles Publishing Group*
Editor *Elizabeth Toppin*
Circulation 50,000
FOUNDED 1986. QUARTERLY. Features articles of interest to secretaries and personal assistants aged 25–60. No unsolicited mss.
Features Informative pieces on technology and practices, office and employment-related topics. Length 1000 words.
Payment by negotiation.

Palmtop Magazine

Palmtop Publications, PO Box 188, Bicester, Oxfordshire OX6 0GP
☎01869 249287   Fax 01869 246043
Email: editor@palmtop.co.uk
Website: www.palmtop.co.uk
Owner *Mr S. Clack/Miss R. A. Rolfe*
Editor *Mr S. Clack*
Circulation 12,000
FOUNDED 1994. BI-MONTHLY users' magazine for Psion hand-held computers. No unsolicited mss; approach by 'phone or email in the first instance.

Parents

Endeavour House, 189 Shaftesbury Avenue, London WC2H 8JG
☎0171 437 9011   Fax 0171 208 3584
Owner *EMAP Elan Publications Ltd*
Editor *Ruth Beattie*
Circulation 36,336
FOUNDED 1976. MONTHLY. Features commissioned from outside contributors. No unsolicited mss. Approach with ideas in the first instance. Age span: from pregnancy to four years.

PC Format

Future Publishing, 30 Monmouth Street, Bath BA1 2BW
☎01225 442244   Fax 01225 732275
Email: pcfmail@futurenet.co.uk
Website: www.futurenet.co.uk
Owner *Future Publishing*
Editor *Richard Longhurst*
Circulation 110,227
FOUNDED 1991. FOUR-WEEKLY magazine covering everything for the consumer PC – games, hardware, Internet creativity. Welcomes feature ideas in the first instance; approach by telephone or in writing.

PC Week

32–34 Broadwick Street, London W1A 2HG
☎0171 316 9000   Fax 0171 316 9355
Email: pcweek@vnu.co.uk
Website: www.vnu.co.uk
Owner *VNU Business Publications*
Editor *Fiona Harvey*
Circulation 50,000
FOUNDED 1986. WEEKLY news, analysis and opinion on the corporate IT market. Welcomes reviews of PC software and hardware products; brief synopsis in the first instance. Approach by email, fax or in writing.
Features Most articles are commissioned. Max. 2000 words.
News Max. 800 words.

Peak and Pennine

33 Park Road, Bakewell, Derbyshire DE45 1AX
☎01629 812034   Fax 01629 812034
Email: rolysmith@compuserve.com
Owner *Dalesman Publishing Co. Ltd*
Editor *Roly Smith*
FOUNDED 1997. MONTHLY. Predominantly outdoors, natural history and heritage, serving the Peak District National Park and South Pennines. Unsolicited material considered but telephone first. Max. 1500 words.

Pembrokeshire Life

Swan House Publishing, Bridge Street, Newcastle Emlyn, Carmarthenshire SA38 9DX
☎01239 710632

Owner *Swan House Publishing*
Editor *David Fielding*

FOUNDED 1989. MONTHLY county magazine with articles on local history, issues, characters, off-beat stories with good colour or b&w photographs. No country diaries, short stories, poems. Most articles are commissioned from known freelancers but 'always prepared to consider ideas from new writers'. No mss. Send cuttings of previous work (published or not) and synopsis to the editor.

People Management

Personnel Publications Limited, 17 Britton Street, London EC1M 5TP
☎0171 880 6200   Fax 0171 336 7635
Email: editorial@peoplemanagement.co.uk
Website: www.peoplemanagement.co.uk

Editor *Rob MacLachlan*
Circulation 90,000

FORTNIGHTLY magazine on human resources. industrial relations, employment issues, etc. Welcomes submissions but apply for 'Guidelines for Contributors' in the first instance; approach in writing. **Features** *Jane Pickard* **News** *Jennie Walsh* **Law at Work** *Jill Evans*.

The People's Friend

80 Kingsway East, Dundee DD4 8SL
☎01382 462276/223131   Fax 01382 452491

Owner *D. C. Thomson & Co. Ltd*
Editor *Sinclair Matheson*
Circulation 449,595

The *Friend* is basically a fiction magazine, with two serials and several short stories each week. FOUNDED in 1869, it has always prided itself on providing 'a good read for all the family'. All stories should be about ordinary, identifiable characters with the kind of problems the average reader can understand and sympathise with. 'We look for the romantic and emotional developments of characters, rather than an over-complicated or contrived plot. We regularly use period serials and, occasionally, mystery/adventure.' Guidelines on request with s.a.e.

Short Stories Can vary in length from 1000 words or less to as many as 4000.

Serials Long-run serials of 10–15 instalments or more preferred. Occasionally shorter.

Articles Short fillers welcome.

Payment on acceptance.

Period Living & Traditional Homes

Endeavour House, 189 Shaftesbury Avenue, London WC2H 8JG
☎0171 208 3507   Fax 0171 208 3597

Owner *EMAP Elan Ltd*
Editor *Sue Garland*
Circulation 93,084

FOUNDED 1992. Formed from the merger of *Period Living* and *Traditional Homes*. Covers interior decoration in a period style, period house profiles, traditional crafts, renovation of period properties.

Features *Pamela Shipkey*
Payment varies according to length/type of article.

Personal

See under **National Newspapers (Sunday Mirror)**

Personal Finance

Arnold House, 36–41 Holywell Lane, London EC2A 3SF
☎0171 827 5454   Fax 0171 827 0567

Owner *Charterhouse Communications plc*
Editor *Juliet Oxborrow*
Circulation 50,000

ESTABLISHED 1994. MONTHLY finance magazine.

Features All issues relating to personal finance, particularly investment, insurance, banking, mortgages, savings, borrowing, health care and pensions. No corporate articles or personnel issues. Write to the editor with ideas in the first instance. No unsolicited mss.

Payment £150–175.

News All items written in-house.

The Philosopher

4 Wellington Road, Ilkley, West Yorkshire LS29 8HR

Owner *The Philosophical Society*
Editor *Martin Cohen*
Website: www.rmplc.co.uk/eduweb/sites/
  cite/staff/philosopher/

FOUNDED 1913. BI-ANNUAL journal of the Philosophical Society of Great Britain with an international readership made up of members, libraries and specialist booksellers. Wide range of interests, but leaning towards articles that present philosophical investigation which is relevant to the individual and to society in our modern era. Accessible to the non-specialist. Will consider articles and book reviews. Notes for Contributors available; send s.a.e. or see website.

As well as short philosophical papers, will accept:

News about lectures, conventions, philosophy groups. Ethical issues in the news. Maximum 1000 words.

Reviews of philosophy books (maximum 600 words); discussion articles of individual philosophers and their published works (maximum 2000 words)

Miscellaneous items, including graphics, of philosophical interest and/or merit.

Payment free copies.

Piano
241 Shaftesbury Avenue, London WC2H 8EH
☎0171 333 1724   Fax 0171 333 1769
Owner *Rhinegold Publishing*
Editor *Jeremy Siepmann*
Circulation 11,000
FOUNDED 1993. BI-MONTHLY magazine containing features, profiles, technical information, news, reviews of interest to those with a serious amateur or professional concern with pianos or their playing. No unsolicited material. Approach with ideas in writing only.

Picture Postcard Monthly
15 Debdale Lane, Keyworth, Nottingham NG12 5HT
☎0115 9374079   Fax 0115 9376197
Email: reflections@argonet.co.uk
Owners *Brian & Mary Lund*
Editor *Brian Lund*
Circulation 4000
FOUNDED 1978. MONTHLY. News, views, clubs, diary of fairs, sales, auctions, and well-researched postcard-related articles. Might be interested in general articles supported by postcards. Unsolicited mss welcome. Approach by phone or in writing with ideas.

Pilot
The Clock House, 28 Old Town, Clapham, London SW4 0LB
☎0171 498 2506   Fax 0171 498 6920
Email: pilotmagazine@compuserve.com
Website: www.hiway.co.uk/pilot
Owner/Editor *James Gilbert*
Circulation 29,358
FOUNDED 1968. MONTHLY magazine for private plane pilots. No staff writers; the entire magazine is written by freelancers – mostly regulars. Unsolicited mss welcome but ideas in writing preferred. Perusal of any issue of the magazine will reveal the type of material bought. 700 words of 'Advice to would-be contributors' sent on receipt of s.a.e. (mark envelope 'Advice').

Features *James Gilbert* Many articles are unsolicited personal experiences/travel accounts from pilots of private planes; good photo coverage is very important. Maximum 5000 words. *Payment* £100–700 (first rights). Photos £26 each.

News *Mike Jerram* Contributions need to be as short as possible. See *Pilot Notes* in the magazine.

Pink Paper
72 Holloway Road, London N7 8NZ
☎0171 296 6210   Fax 0171 957 0046
Email: editorial@pinkpaper.co.uk
Owner *Chronos Group*
Executive Editor *David Bridle*
Circulation 56,783
FOUNDED 1987. WEEKLY. Only national newspaper for lesbians and gay men covering politics, social issues, health, the arts and all areas of concern to lesbian/gay people. Unsolicited mss welcome. Initial approach by phone with an idea preferred. Interested in profiles, reviews, in-depth features and short news pieces.

News Maximum 300 words.
Payment by arrangement.

Planet: The Welsh Internationalist
See **Planet** under **Small Presses**

Plays and Players Applause
Northway House, 1379 High Road, London N20 9LP
☎0181 343 9977   Fax 0181 343 7831
Owner *Mineco Designs*
Editor *Sandra Rennie*
Circulation 10,000
Theatre MONTHLY which publishes a mixture of news, reviews, reports and features on all the performing arts. Rarely uses unsolicited material but writers of talent are taken up. Almost all material is commissioned.

PN Review
See under **Poetry Magazines**

Poetry Ireland Review
See under **Poetry Magazines**

Poetry Review
See under **Poetry Magazines**

Poetry Scotland
See under **Poetry Magazines**

Poetry Wales
See under **Poetry Magazines**

Ponies Today

TP Publications Ltd, Barn Acre House, Saxtead Green, Suffolk IP13 9QJ
☎01354 741538   Fax 01728 685842

Owner *Today Magazines*
Editor *Charlotte Jarvis*

FOUNDED 1998. Magazine for adults who ride, show, breed and drive ponies, with the emphasis on native ponies. All topics relating to ponies covered with the slant on ponies not horses. Veterinary, breeding and driving articles welcome. Prize pony spot. Length 500–100 words; photos welcomed (and returned). Send for free sample copy; phone/write with ideas.
Payment 'modest at present'.

Pony

D.J. Murphy (Publishers) Ltd, Haslemere House, Lower Street, Haslemere, Surrey GU27 2PE
☎01428 651551   Fax 01428 653888

Owner *D. J. Murphy (Publishers) Ltd*
Editor *Janet Rising*
Assistant Editor *Nicky Moffatt*
Circulation 36,288

FOUNDED 1948. Lively MONTHLY aimed at 10–16-year-olds. News, instruction on riding, stable management, veterinary care, interviews. Approach in writing with an idea.
Features welcome. Maximum 900 words.
News Written in-house. Photographs and illustrations (serious/cartoon) welcome.
Payment £65 per 1000 words.

Popular Crafts

Azalea Drive, Swanley, Kent BR8 8HL
☎01322 660070   Fax 01322 616319

Owner *Nexus Special Interests*
Editor *Debbie Moss*
Circulation 32,000

FOUNDED 1980. MONTHLY. Covers crafts of all kinds. Freelance contributions welcome – copy needs to be lively and interesting. Approach in writing with an outline of idea and photographs.
Features Project-based under the headings: Homecraft; Needlecraft; Popular Craft; Kidscraft; News and Columns. Any craft-related material including projects to make, with full instructions/patterns supplied in all cases; profiles of crafts people and news of craft group activities or successes by individual persons; articles on collecting crafts; personal experiences and anecdotes.
Payment on publication.

PR Week

174 Hammersmith Road, London W6 7JP
☎0171 413 4520   Fax 0171 413 4509

Owner *Haymarket Business Publications Ltd*
Editor *Kate Nicholas*
Circulation 17,000

FOUNDED 1984. WEEKLY. Contributions accepted from experienced journalists. Approach in writing with an idea.
Features *Maja Pawinska*
News *Juliette Garside*
Payment negotiable.

Practical Boat Owner

Westover House, West Quay Road, Poole, Dorset BH15 1JG
☎01202 440820   Fax 01202 440850
Website: www.ipc.co.uk/pubs/pracboat.htm

Owner *IPC Magazines Ltd*
Editor *Rodger Witt*
Circulation 54,819

FOUNDED 1967. MONTHLY magazine of practical information for cruising boat owners. Receives about 1500 mss per year. Interested in hard facts about gear, equipment, pilotage and renovation, etc. from experienced yachtsmen.
Features Technical articles about maintenance, restoration, modifications to cruising boats, power and sail up to 45ft, or reader reports on gear and equipment. European pilotage articles and cruising guides. Approach in writing with synopsis in the first instance.
Payment negotiable.

Practical Caravan

60 Waldegrave Road, Teddington, Middlesex TW11 8LG
☎0181 943 5629   Fax 0181 943 5777
Email: practicalcaravan@dial.pipex.com

Owner *Haymarket Magazines Ltd*
Editor *Rob McCabe*
Senior Staff Writer *Michael Le Caplain*
Circulation 47,037

FOUNDED 1967. MONTHLY. Contains caravan reviews, travel features, investigations, products, park reviews. Unsolicited mss welcome on travel relevant only to caravanning/touring vans. No motorcaravan or static van stories. Approach with ideas by phone or letter.
Features *Rob McCabe* Must refer to caravanning or towing and be written in friendly, chatty manner. Features with pictures/transparencies welcome but not essential. Maximum length 2000 words. *Payment* negotiable (usually £120 per 1000 words).

Practical Fishkeeping (incorporating **Fishkeeping Answers**)
Apex House, Oundle Road, Peterborough, Cambridgeshire PE2 9NP
☎01733 898100   Fax 01733 898487
Owner *EMAP Apex Publications Ltd*
Managing Editor *Steve Windsor*
Circulation 30,000

MONTHLY. Practical articles on all aspects of fishkeeping. Unsolicited mss welcome. Approach in writing with ideas. Quality photographs of fish always welcome. No fiction or verse.

Practical Gardening
See **Garden Answers**

Practical Parenting
King's Reach Tower, Stamford Street, London SE1 9LS
☎0171 261 5058   Fax 0171 261 6542
Website: www.ipc.co.uk/pubs/pracpare.htm
Owner *IPC Magazines Ltd*
Editor-in-Chief *Jayne Marsden*
Circulation 76,554

FOUNDED 1987. MONTHLY. Practical advice on pregnancy, birth, babycare and childcare up to five years. Submit ideas in writing with synopsis or send mss on spec. Interested in feature articles of up to 3000 words in length, and in readers' experiences/personal viewpoint pieces of 750–1000 words. All material must be written for the magazine's specifically targeted audience and in-house style.
Payment negotiable.

Practical Photography
Apex House, Oundle Road, Peterborough, Cambridgeshire PE2 9NP
☎01733 898100   Fax 01733 894472
Owner *EMAP Active Publications Ltd*
Editor *William Cheung*
Circulation 77,654

MONTHLY. All types of photography, particularly technique-orientated pictures. No unsolicited mss. Preliminary approach may be made by telephone. Always interested in new ideas.
Features Anything relevant to the world of photography, but not 'the sort of feature produced by staff writers'. Features on technology and humour are two areas worth exploring. Bear in mind that there is a three-month lead-in time. Max. 2000 words.
News Only 'hot' news applicable to a monthly magazine. Max. 400 words.
Payment varies.

Practical Wireless
Arrowsmith Court, Station Approach, Broadstone, Dorset BH18 8PW
☎01202 659910   Fax 01202 659950
Email: <name>@pwpublishing.ltd.uk
Website: www.pwpublishing.ltd.uk
Owner *P.W. Publishing*
Editor *Rob Mannion*
Circulation 27,000

FOUNDED 1932. MONTHLY. News and features relating to amateur radio, radio construction and radio communications. Unsolicited mss welcome. Author's guidelines available (send s.a.e.). Approach by phone with ideas in the first instance. Copy should be supported where possible by artwork, either illustrations, diagrams or photographs.
Payment £54–70 per page.

Practical Woodworking
Nexus Media, Nexus House, Azalea Drive, Swanley, Kent BR8 8HU
☎01322 660070   Fax 01332 667633
Owner *Nexus Media Ltd*
Editor *Mark Chisholm*
Circulation 23,479 (1997)

FOUNDED 1965. FOUR-WEEKLY. Contains articles relating to woodworking – projects, techniques, new products, tips, letters, etc. Unsolicited mss welcome. No fiction. Approach with ideas in writing or by phone.
News Anything related to woodworking.
Payment £60 per published page.
Features Projects, techniques etc. *Payment* £60–75 per published page.

Prediction
Link House, Dingwall Avenue, Croydon, Surrey CR9 2TA
☎0181 686 2599   Fax 0181 781 6044
Owner *Link House Magazines Ltd*
Editor *Jo Logan*
Circulation 35,000

FOUNDED 1936. MONTHLY. Covering astrology and occult-related topics. Unsolicited material in these areas welcome (200–300 mss received every year). Writers' guidelines available on request.
Astrology Pieces, of either 750 words or 1500–2000 words, depending on number of charts, should be practical and of general interest. Charts and astro data should accompany them, especially if profiles.
Features *Jo Logan* Articles on mysteries of the earth, alternative medicine, psychical/occult

experiences and phenomena are considered. 800–2000 words. *Payment £25–100 and over.*

News & Views Items of interest to readership welcome. Max. 300 words. *No payment.*

Pregnancy Magazine
WV Publications, 57–59 Rochester Place, London N1 9JY
☎0171 226 2222   Fax 0171 359 5225
Email: danbrom@hotmail.com
Owner *Highbury House Communications*
Editor *Dan Bromage*

QUARTERLY magazine for parents-to-be.

Press Gazette
Quantum House, 19 Scarbrook Road, Croydon, Surrey CR9 1LX
☎0181 565 4200   Fax 0181 565 4395
Email: pged@qpp.co.uk
Owner *Quantum*
Editor *Philippa Kennedy*
Deputy Editor *Jon Slattery*
Circulation 9,500

WEEKLY magazine for all journalists – in regional and national newspapers, magazines, broadcasting and online – containing news, features and analysis of all areas of journalism, print and broadcasting. Unsolicited mss welcome; interested in profiles of magazines, broadcasting companies and news agencies, personality profiles, technical and current affairs relating to the world of journalism. Approach with ideas by phone, email, fax or in writing.

Pride
Hamilton House, 55 Battersea Bridge Road, London SW11 3AX
☎0171 228 3110   Fax 0171 228 3129
Email: pridemagazine.com
Owner *Carl Cushnie Junior*
Editor *Dionne St Hill*
Circulation 36,000

FOUNDED 1991. MONTHLY lifestyle magazine for black women with features, beauty, arts and fashion. No unsolicited material; approach in writing with ideas.

Features *Dionne St Hill* Issues pertaining to the black community. 'Ideas and solicited mss are welcomed from new freelancers.' Max. 2000 words. *Payment £200.* **Fiction** *Diana Evans* Publishes the occasional short story. Unsolicited mss welcome. Max. 3000 words. *No payment.* **Beauty** *Sherry Dixon* Freelancers used for short features. Max. 1000 words. *Payment 10 pence per word.*

Prima
197 Marsh Wall, London E14 9SG
☎0171 519 5500   Fax 0171 519 5514
Owner *Gruner & Jahr (UK)*
Editor *Lindsay Nicholson*
Circulation 510,142

FOUNDED 1986. MONTHLY women's magazine.

Features Coordinator *Verity Watkins* Mostly practical and written by specialists, or commissioned from known freelancers. Unsolicited mss not welcome.

Private Eye
6 Carlisle Street, London W1V 5RG
☎0171 437 4017   Fax 0171 437 0705
Owner *Pressdram*
Editor *Ian Hislop*
Circulation 190,000

FOUNDED 1961. FORTNIGHTLY satirical and investigative magazine. Prospective contributors are best advised to approach the editor in writing. News stories and feature ideas are always welcome, as are cartoons. All jokes written in-house.

Payment in all cases is 'not great', and length of piece varies as appropriate.

Prospect
4 Bedford Square, London WC1B 3RA
☎0171 255 1281   Fax 0171 255 1279
Email: prospect-magazine@compuserve.com
Website: www.prospect-magazine.co.uk
Owner *Prospect Publishing Limited*
Editor *David Goodhart*
Circulation 20,000

FOUNDED 1995. MONTHLY. Essays, reviews and research on current/international affairs and cultural issues. No news features. No unsolicited mss. Approach in writing with ideas in the first instance.

Psychic News
Clock Cottage, Stansted Hall, Stansted, Essex CM24 8UD
☎01279 817050   Fax 01279 817051
Owner *Psychic Press 1995 Ltd*
Editor *Lyn Guest de Swarte*
Circulation 40,000

FOUNDED 1932. *Psychic News* is the world's only WEEKLY spiritualist newspaper. It covers subjects such as psychic research, hauntings, ghosts, poltergeists, spiritual healing, survival after death, and paranormal gifts. Unsolicited material considered.

Publishing News

39 Store Street, London WC1E 7DB
☎0171 692 2900   Fax 0171 419 2111
Email: mailbox@publishingnews.co.uk
Website: www.publishingnews.co.uk

Editor *Rodney Burbeck*

WEEKLY newspaper of the book trade. Hardback and paperback reviews and extensive listings of new paperbacks and hardbacks. Interviews with leading personalities in the trade, authors, agents and features on specialist book areas.

Punch

Trevor House, 100 Brompton Road, London SW3 1ER
☎0171 225 6716   Fax 0171 225 6766
Email: edit@punch.co.uk
Website: www.punch.co.uk

Owner *Liberty Publishing*
Editor *James Steen*

FOUNDED in 1841 and RELAUNCHED in 1996. BI-WEEKLY investigative and gossip magazine. Ideas are welcome; approach in writing in the first instance.
Payment negotiable.

Q

Mappin House, 4 Winsley Street, London W1N 7AR
☎0171 436 1515   Fax 0171 312 8247
Website: www.qonline.co.uk

Owner *EMAP Metro Publications*
Editor *Andy Pemberton*
Circulation 203,865

FOUNDED 1986. MONTHLY. Glossy aimed at educated popular music enthusiasts of all ages. Few opportunities for freelance writers. Unsolicited mss are strongly discouraged. Prospective contributors should approach in writing only.

Quartos Magazine

See **The New Writer**

QWF Magazine

71 Bucknill Crescent, Hillmorton, Rugby CV21 4HE
☎01788 560972   Fax 01788 560972

Editor *Jo Good*

BI-MONTHLY small press magazine. FOUNDED in 1994, as a showcase for the best in women's short story writing – original and thought-provoking. Only considers stories that are previously unpublished and of less than 4000 words; articles must be less than 1000 words and of interest to the writer. Include covering letter, s.a.e. and brief biography with mss. Also runs script appraisal service and regular short story competitions. For further information and detailed guidelines for contributors, contact the editor at the address above.

Racing Post (incorporating The Sporting Life)

1 Canada Square, Canary Wharf, London E14 5AP
☎0171 293 3000
Email: info@racingpost.co.uk
Website: www.racingpost.co.uk

Owner *Mirror Group Newspapers Ltd*
Editor *Alan Byrne*

FOUNDED 1986. DAILY horse racing paper with some general sport. In 1998, following an agreement between the owners of *The Sporting Life* and the *Racing Post*, the two papers merged with the latter becoming the senior partner.

Radio Times

80 Wood Lane, London W12 0TT
☎0181 576 3999   Fax 0181 576 3160
Email: radio.times@bbc.co.uk
Website: www.radiotimes.beeb.com

Owner *BBC Worldwide Limited*
Editor *Sue Robinson*
Deputy Editor *Liz Vercoe*
Circulation 1,406,152

WEEKLY. UK's leading broadcast listings magazine. The majority of material is provided by freelance and retained writers, but the topicality of the pieces means close consultation with editors is essential. Very unlikely to use unsolicited material. Detailed BBC, ITV, Channel 4, Channel 5 and satellite television and radio listings are accompanied by feature material relevant to the week's output. *Payment* by arrangement.

RAIL

Apex House, Oundle Road, Peterborough, Cambridgeshire PE2 9NP
☎01733 898100   Fax 01733 894472

Owner *EMAP Active Ltd*
Managing Editor *Nigel Harris*
Circulation 33,811

FOUNDED 1981. FORTNIGHTLY magazine dedicated to modern railway. News and features, and topical newsworthy events. Unsolicited mss welcome. Approach by phone with ideas. Not interested in personal journey reminiscences. No fiction.
Features By arrangement with the editor. All modern railway British subjects considered.

Max. 2000 words. *Payment* varies/negotiable.

News Any news item welcomed. Max. 500 words. *Payment* varies (up to £100 per 1000 words).

The Railway Magazine
King's Reach Tower, Stamford Street, London SE1 9LS
☎0171 261 5533/5821   Fax 0171 261 5269
Email: railway@ipc.co.uk
Website: www.ipc.co.uk/pubs/railway.htm
Owner *IPC Magazines Ltd*
Editor *Nick Pigott*
Circulation 33,132

FOUNDED 1897. MONTHLY. Articles, photos and short news stories of a topical nature, covering modern railways, steam preservation and railway history, welcome. Max. 2000 words, with sketch maps of routes, etc., where appropriate. Unsolicited mss welcome. *Payment* negotiable.

Rambling Today
1–5 Wandsworth Road, London SW8 2XX
☎0171 339 8500   Fax 0171 339 8501
Email: ramblers@london.ramblers.org.uk
Owner *Ramblers' Association*
Editor *Maggie Paterson*
Circulation 125,000

QUARTERLY. Official magazine of the Ramblers' Association, available to members only. Unsolicited mss welcome. S.a.e. required for return.

Features Freelance features are invited on any aspect of walking in Britain and abroad. Length 800–1300 words, preferably with good photographs. No general travel articles.

Reader's Digest
11 Westferry Circus, Canary Wharf, London E14 4HE
☎0171 715 8000   Fax 0171 715 8716
Website: www.readersdigest.co.uk
Owner *Reader's Digest Association Ltd*
Editor-in-Chief *Russell Twisk*
Circulation 1.4 million

In theory, a good market for general interest features of around 2500 words. However, 'a tiny proportion' comes from freelance writers, all of which are specially commissioned. Toughening up its image with a move into investigative journalism. Opportunities exist for short humorous contributions to regular features – 'Life's Like That', 'Humour in Uniform'. Issues a helpful booklet called 'Writing for Reader's Digest' available by post at £4.50. *Payment* up to £200.

Record Collector
43–45 St Mary's Road, Ealing, London W5 5RQ
☎0181 579 1082   Fax 0181 566 2024
Owner *Johnny Dean*
Editor *Peter Doggett*

FOUNDED 1979. MONTHLY. Detailed, well-researched articles welcome on any aspect of record collecting or any collectable artist in the field of popular music (1950s–90s), with complete discographies where appropriate. Unsolicited mss welcome. Approach with ideas by phone.
Payment negotiable.

Record Mirror
See **Music Week**

Red
Endeavour House, 189 Shaftesbury Avenue, London WC2H 8JG
☎0171 437 9011   Fax 0171 208 3218
Owner *EMAP Elan Publications*
Editor *Kathryn Brown*
Circulation 175,000

FOUNDED 1998. MONTHLY magazine aimed at the 30-something woman. Will consider material sent in 'on spec' but tends to rely regular contributors.

Report
ATL, 7 Northumberland Street, London WC2N 5DA
☎0171 930 6441   Fax 0171 925 0529
Owner *Association of Teachers and Lecturers*
Editor *Heather Pinnell*
Circulation 160,000

FOUNDED 1978. EIGHT ISSUES YEARLY during academic terms. Contributions welcome. All submissions should go directly to the editor. Articles should be no more than 800 words and must be of practical interest to the classroom teacher and F. E. lecturers.

Resident Abroad
4th Floor, 149 Tottenham Court Road, London W1P 9LL
☎0171 896 2500   Fax 0171 896 2229
Owner *Financial Times Business*
Editor *Cristina Nordenstahl*
Circulation 16,577

FOUNDED 1979. MONTHLY magazine aimed at British expatriates. Unsolicited mss considered, if suitable to the interests of the readership.

Features Up to 1200 words on finance, property, employment opportunities and other topics likely to appeal to readership, such as living conditions in countries with substantial British expatriate populations. No 'lighthearted looks' at anything.

Fiction Rarely published, but exceptional, relevant stories (no longer than 1000 words) might be considered.

Payment negotiable.

Riding

Suite D, Barber House, Storeys Bar Road, Fengate, Peterborough, Cambridgeshire PE1 5YS

☎01733 555830   Fax 01733 555831

Owner *GreenShires Creative Colour Ltd*
Editor *Steve Moore*

Aimed at an adult, horse-owning audience. Most of the writers on *Riding* are freelance with the emphasis on non-practical and lifestyle-orientated features. New and authoritative writers always welcome.

Payment negotiable.

Right Now!

BCM Right, London WC1N 3XX

☎0181 692 7099   Fax 0181 692 7099
Email: rightnow@compuserve.com
Website: www.right-now.org

Owner *Right Now!*
Editor *Derek Turner*
Circulation 2450

FOUNDED 1993. QUARTERLY right-wing conservative commentary. Welcomes well-documented disputations, news stories and elegiac features about British heritage ('the more politically incorrect, the better!'). No fiction and poems, although exceptions may be made. Approach in writing in the first instance.

No payment.

Rugby News

7–9 Rathbone Street, London W1P 1AF

☎0171 323 1944   Fax 0171 323 1943

Owner *Independent Magazines Ltd*
Editor *Graeme Gillespie*
Circulation 44,000

FOUNDED 1987. Contains news, views and features on the UK and the world rugby scene, with special emphasis on clubs, schools, fitness and coaching. Welcomes unsolicited material.

Rugby World

23rd Floor, King's Reach Tower, Stamford Street, London SE1 9LS

☎0171 261 6830   Fax 0171 261 5419
Website: www.ipc.co.uk/pubs/rugbywld.htm

Owner *IPC Magazines Ltd*
Editor *Paul Morgan*
Circulation 36,915

FOUNDED 1960. MONTHLY. Features of special rugby interest only. Unsolicited contributions welcome but s.a.e. essential for return of material. Prior approach by phone or in writing preferred.

Runner's World

7–10 Chandos Street, London W1M 0AD

☎0171 291 6000   Fax 0171 291 6080

Owner *Rodale Press*
Editor *Steven Seaton*
Circulation 44,604

FOUNDED 1979. MONTHLY magazine giving practical advice on all areas of distance running including products and training, travel features, up-to-date athlete profiles and news. Personal running-related articles, famous people who run or off-beat travel articles are welcome. No elite athlete or training articles. Approach in writing in the first instance.

Saga Magazine

The Saga Building, Middelburg Square, Folkestone, Kent CT20 1AZ

☎01303 771523   Fax 01303 776699

Owner *Saga Publishing Ltd*
Editor *Paul Bach*
Circulation 889,385

FOUNDED 1984. MONTHLY. '*Saga Magazine* sets out to celebrate the role of older people in society. It reflects their achievements, promotes their skills, protects their interests, and campaigns on their behalf. A warm personal approach, addressing the readership in an upbeat and positive manner, required.' It has a hard core of celebrated commentators/writers (e.g. Clement Freud, Keith Waterhouse) as regular contributors. Articles mostly commissioned or written in-house but exclusive celebrity interviews welcome if appropriate/relevant. Length 1000–1200 words (max. 1600).

Sailing Today

30 Monmouth Street, Bath BA1 2BW

☎01225 442244   Fax 01225 732248

Owner *Future Publishing*
Editor *Digby Fox*
Deputy Editor *Rupert Holmes*
Boat Editor *Keith Colwell*

FOUNDED 1997. MONTHLY practical magazine for cruising sailors. *Sailing Today* covers owning and buying a boat, equipment and products for sailing and is about improving readers' skills, boat maintenance and product tests. Most articles are commissioned but will consider practical features and cruise stories with photos. Approach by telephone or in writing in the first instance.

Sailplane and Gliding
PO Box 2039, Pulborough, West Sussex
RH20 2FN
☎01798   87483
Email: le@blot.co.uk
Owner *British Gliding Association*
Editor *Le Forbes*
Circulation 6500

FOUNDED 1930. BI-MONTHLY for gliding enthusiasts. A specialist magazine with very few opportunities for freelancers.
No payment.

Sainsbury's The Magazine
20 Upper Ground, London SE1 9PD
☎0171 633 0266   Fax 0171 401 9423
Owner *New Crane Publishing*
Editor *Michael Wynn Jones*
Consultant Food Editor *Delia Smith*
Circulation 410,767

FOUNDED 1993. MONTHLY featuring a main core of food and cookery, features, health, beauty, fashion, home, gardening and news. No unsolicited mss. Approach in writing with ideas only in the first instance.

The Salisbury Review
33 Canonbury Park South, London N1 2JW
☎0171 226 7791   Fax 0171 354 0383
Email: salisbury-review@easynet.co.uk
Website: easyweb.easynet.co.uk/
    ~salisbury-review
Owner *Claridge Press*
Editor *Roger Scruton*
Managing Editor *Merrie Cave*
Circulation 1700

FOUNDED 1982. QUARTERLY magazine of conservative thought. Editorials and features from a right-wing viewpoint. Unsolicited material welcome.
    Features Maximum 4000 words.
    Reviews Maximum 1000 words.
    No payment.

Sci-Fright
Springbeach Press, 11 Vernon Close, Eastbourne, East Sussex BN23 6AN
Email: sian@springbeachpress.freeserve.co.uk
Owner *Springbeach Press*
Editor *Sian Ross*

Circulation 3000

FOUNDED 1999. BI-MONTHLY magazine with fiction, features and some poetry in the following genres: science fiction, horror, fantasy, humour. No mainstream. Interested in fiction, poetry, features and b&w artwork. No poems over 40 lines, colour artwork or 'tea-break' fiction. Send ideas by email or post; no full submissions by email.
    Payment copy of magazine.

Scotland on Sunday Magazine
See under **National Newspapers (Scotland on Sunday)**

The Scots Magazine
2 Albert Square, Dundee DD1 9QJ
☎01382 223131   Fax 01382 322214
Owner *D. C. Thomson & Co. Ltd*
Editor *John Methven*
Circulation 63,000

FOUNDED 1739. MONTHLY. Covers a wide field of Scottish interests ranging from personalities to wildlife, climbing, reminiscence, history and folklore. Outside contributions welcome; 'staff delighted to discuss in advance by letter'.

The Scottish Farmer
Caledonian Magazines Ltd, 6th Floor, 195 Albion Street, Glasgow G1 1QQ
☎0141 302 7700   Fax 0141 302 7799
Email: info@calmags.co.uk
Owner *Caledonian Magazines Ltd*
Editor *Alasdair Fletcher*
Circulation 23,000

FOUNDED 1893. WEEKLY. Farmer's magazine covering most aspects of Scottish agriculture. Unsolicited mss welcome. Approach with ideas in writing.
    Features *Alasdair Fletcher* Technical articles on agriculture or farming units. 1000–2000 words.
    News *John Duckworth* Factual news about farming developments, political, personal and technological. Maximum 800 words.
    Weekend Family Pages Rural and craft topics.

Scottish Field
Special Publications, Royston House, Caroline Park, Edinburgh EH5 1QJ
☎0131 551 2942   Fax 0131 551 2938
Owner *Oban Times*
Editor *Archie Mackenzie*
FOUNDED 1903. MONTHLY. Scotland's quality lifestyle magazine. Unsolicited mss welcome but writers should study the magazine first.

Features Articles of general interest on Scotland and Scots abroad with good photographs or, preferably, colour slides. Approx 1000 words. *Payment* negotiable.

Scottish Golfer
c/o The Scottish Golf Union, Drumoig, Leuchars, St Andrews, Fife KY16 0BE
☎01382 549500   Fax 01382 549510
Owner *Scottish Golf Union*
Editor *Martin Dempster*
Circulation 30,000

FOUNDED mid-1980s. MONTHLY. Features and results, in particular the men's events. No unsolicited mss. Approach in writing with ideas.

Scottish Home & Country
42A Heriot Row, Edinburgh EH3 6ES
☎0131 225 1934   Fax 0131 225 8129
Owner *Scottish Women's Rural Institutes*
Editor *Stella Roberts*
Circulation 14,000

FOUNDED 1924. MONTHLY. Scottish or rural-related issues. Unsolicited mss welcome but reading time may be from 2–3 months. Commissions are rare and tend to go to established contributors only.

Scottish Rugby Magazine
11 Dock Place, Leith, Edinburgh EH6 6LU
☎0131 554 0540   Fax 0131 554 0482
Email: scottish.rugby@virgin.net
Editor *David Ferguson*
Circulation 19,200

FOUNDED 1990. MONTHLY. Features, club profiles, etc. Approach in writing with ideas.

Scouting Magazine
Baden Powell House, Queen's Gate, London SW7 5JS
☎0171 584 7030   Fax 0171 590 5124
Owner *The Scout Association*
Editor *Ron Crabb*
Circulation 30,000

MONTHLY magazine for adults connected to or interested in the Scouting movement. Interested in Scouting-related features only. No fiction. *Payment* by negotiation.

Screen
Gilmorehill Centre for Theatre, Film and Television, University of Glasgow, Glasgow G12 8QQ
☎0141 330 5035   Fax 0141 330 3515
Email: screen@arts.gla.ac.uk

Publisher *Oxford University Press*
Editors *Annette Kuhn, John Caughie, Simon Frith, Norman King, Karen Lury, Jackie Stacey*
Editorial Assistant *Caroline Beven*
Circulation 1500

QUARTERLY refereed academic journal of film and television studies for a readership ranging from undergraduates to screen studies academics and media professionals. There are no specific qualifications for acceptance of articles. Straightforward film reviews are not normally published. Check the magazine's style and market in the first instance.

Screen International
33–39 Bowling Green Lane, London EC1R 0DA
☎0171 505 8056   Fax 0171 505 8117
Owner *EMAP Business Communications*
Managing Editor *Denis Seguin*

International trade paper of the film, video and television industries. Expert freelance writers are occasionally used in all areas. No unsolicited mss. Approach with ideas in writing. **Features** *Leo Barraclough* *Payment* negotiable on NUJ basis.

Sea Breezes
Units 28–30, Spring Valley Industrial Estate, Braddan, Isle of Man IM2 2QS
☎01624 626018   Fax 01624 661655
Owner *Print Centres*
Editor *Captain A. C. Douglas*
Circulation 14,500

FOUNDED 1919. MONTHLY. Covers virtually everything relating to ships and seamen. Unsolicited mss welcome; they should be thoroughly researched and accompanied by relevant photographs. No fiction, poetry, or anything which 'smacks of the romance of the sea'.

Features Factual tales of ships, seamen and the sea, Royal or Merchant Navy, sail or power, nautical history, shipping company histories, epic voyages, etc. Length 1000–4000 words. 'The most readily acceptable work will be that which shows it is clearly the result of first-hand experience or the product of extensive and accurate research.'

Payment £7 per page (about 500 words).

She Magazine
National Magazine House, 72 Broadwick Street, London W1V 2BP
☎0171 439 5000   Fax 0171 439 5350
Owner *National Magazine Co. Ltd*
Editor *Alison Pylkkanen*

Circulation 226,079

Glossy MONTHLY for the thirtysomething woman, addressing her needs as an individual, a partner and a parent. Talks to its readers in an intelligent, humorous and sympathetic way. Features should be about 1500 words long. Approach with ideas in writing. No unsolicited material.

Payment NUJ rates.

Ships Monthly

Link House Magazines Ltd, 222 Brandon Road, Burton-upon-Trent, Staffs DE14 3BT
☎01283 542721   Fax 01283 546436

Owner *IPC Country & Leisure Media Ltd*
Editor *Robert Shopland*
Circulation 22,000

FOUNDED 1966. MONTHLY magazine for ship enthusiasts. News, photographs and illustrated articles on all kinds of ships – mercantile and naval, sail and steam, past and present. No yachting. Most articles are commissioned; prospective contributors should telephone in the first instance.

Shoot Magazine

King's Reach Tower, Stamford Street, London SE1 9LS
☎0171 261 6287   Fax 0171 261 6019
Website: www.ipc.co.uk/pubs/shoot.htm

Owner *IPC Magazines Ltd*
Editor *Andy Winter*
Circulation 71,352

FOUNDED 1969. WEEKLY football magazine. No unsolicited mss. Present ideas for news, features or colour photo-features to the editor by telephone.

Features Hard-hitting, topical and off-beat.

News Items welcome, especially exclusive gossip and transfer speculation.

Payment negotiable.

Shooting and Conservation (BASC)

Marford Mill, Rossett, Wrexham, Clwyd LL12 0HL
☎01244 573000   Fax 01244 571678

Owner *The British Association for Shooting and Conservation (BASC)*
Editor *Jeffrey Olstead*
Circulation 120,000

FOUR ISSUES PER YEAR. Good articles and stories on shooting, conservation and related areas are always sought although most material used is commissioned. Maximum 1500 words.

Payment negotiable.

Shooting Times & Country Magazine

King's Reach Tower, Stamford Street, London SE1 9LS
☎0171 261 6180   Fax 0171 261 7179
Website: www.ipc.co.uk/pubs/shootime.htm

Owner *IPC Magazines Ltd*
Editor *Mark Hedges*
Circulation 27,435

FOUNDED 1882. WEEKLY. Covers shooting, fishing and related countryside topics. Unsolicited mss considered. *Payment* negotiable.

Shout!

PO Box YR46, Leeds, West Yorkshire LS9 6XG
☎0113 2485700   Fax 0113 2956076
Email: editor@shoutmag.demon.co.uk
Website: www.shoutmag.demon.co.uk

Owner/Editor *Mark Michalowski*
Circulation 7000

FOUNDED 1995. MONTHLY lesbian/gay and bisexual news, views, arts and scene for Yorkshire; lgb health and politics. Interested in reviews of Yorkshire lgb events, happenings, news, analysis – 300 to max. 1000 words. No fiction, fashion or items with no reasonable relevance to Yorkshire and the north.

Payment £30 per 1000 words.

Shropshire Magazine

77 Wyle Cop, Shrewsbury, Shropshire SY1 1UT
☎01743 362175

Owner *Shropshire Newspapers Ltd*
Editor *Keith Parker*

FOUNDED 1950. MONTHLY. Unsolicited mss welcome but ideas in writing preferred.

Features Personalities, topical items, historical (e.g. family) of Shropshire; also general interest: homes, weddings, antiques, etc. Max. 1000 words.

Payment negotiable 'but modest'.

Sight & Sound

British Film Institute, 21 Stephen Street, London W1P 2LN
☎0171 255 1444   Fax 0171 436 2327
www.bfi.org.uk/s&s/default.htm

Owner *British Film Institute*
Editor *Nick James*

FOUNDED 1932. MONTHLY. Topical and critical articles on international cinema, with regular columns from the USA and Europe. Length 1000–5000 words. Relevant photographs appreciated. Also book, film and video release reviews. Unsolicited material welcome. Approach in writing with ideas.

Payment by arrangement.

The Sign
See **Hymns Ancient & Modern Ltd** under **UK Publishers**

Ski and Board
The White House, 57–63 Church Road, Wimbledon, London SW19 5SB
☎0181 410 2000   Fax 0181 410 2001
Email: s&b@skiclub.co.uk
Website: www.skiclub.co.uk
Owner *Ski Club of Great Britain*
Editor *Gill Williams*
Circulation 19,675

FOUNDED 1903. FIVE ISSUES YEARLY. Features from established ski writers only.

The Skier and The Snowboarder Magazine
1st Floor, Squires House, 205 High Street, West Wickham, Kent BR4 0PH
☎0181 777 4426   Fax 0181 777 8789
Owner *Mountain Marketing Ltd*
Editor *Frank Baldwin*
Circulation 20,000

Official magazine to the World Ski and Snowboard Association, UK. SEASONAL. From September to May. FIVE ISSUES YEARLY. Outside contributions welcome.

Features Various topics covered, including race reports, resort reports, fashion, equipment update, dry slope, school news, new products, health and safety. Crisp, tight, informative copy of 1000 words or less preferred.

News All aspects of skiing news covered.

Payment negotiable.

Slimming
Endeavour House, 189 Shaftesbury Avenue, London WC2H 8JG
☎0171 437 9011   Fax 0171 434 0656
Owner *EMAP Elan Publications*
Editor *Juliette Kellow*
Circulation 105,780

FOUNDED 1969. ELEVEN ISSUES YEARLY. Leading magazine about slimming, diet and health. Opportunities for freelance contributions on general health (diet-related); psychology related to health and fitness; celebrity interviews. It is best to approach with an idea in writing.

Payment negotiable.

Smallholder
Hook House, Wimblington March, Cambridgeshire PE15 0QL
☎01354 741182   Fax 01354 741182
Owner *News Com, West Country Magazines*
Editor *Liz Wright*
Circulation 20,000

FOUNDED 1982. MONTHLY. Outside contributions welcome. Send for sample magazine and editorial schedule before submitting anything. Follow up with samples of work to the editor so that style can be assessed for suitability. No poetry or humorous but unfocused personal tales.

Features New writers always welcome, but must have high level of technical expertise – 'not textbook stuff'. Illustrations and photos welcomed and paid for. Length 750–1500 words.

News All agricultural and rural news welcome. Length 200–500 words.

Payment negotiable ('but modest').

Smash Hits
Mappin House, Winsley Street, London W1N 7AR
☎0171 436 1515   Fax 0171 636 5792
Owner *EMAP Metro Publications*
Editor *Gavin Reeve*
Circulation 434,525

FOUNDED 1979. FORTNIGHTLY. Top of themid-teen market. Unsolicited mss are not accepted, but prospective contributors may approach in writing with ideas.

Snooker Scene
Cavalier House, 202 Hagley Road, Edgbaston, Birmingham B16 9PQ
☎0121 454 2931   Fax 0121 452 1822
Owner *Everton's News Agency*
Editor *Clive Everton*
Circulation 16,000

FOUNDED 1971. MONTHLY. No unsolicited mss. Approach in writing with an idea.

Somerset Magazine
23 Market Street, Crewkerne, Somerset TA18 7JU
☎01460 78000   Fax 01460 76718
Owner *Smart Print Publications Ltd*
Editor *Roy Smart*
Circulation 6500

FOUNDED 1991. MONTHLY magazine with features on any subject of interest (historical, geographical, arts, crafts) to people living in Somerset. Length 1000–1500 words, preferably with illustrations. Unsolicited mss welcome but initial approach in writing preferred.

Payment negotiable.

The Spectator

56 Doughty Street, London WC1N 2LL
☎0171 405 1706   Fax 0171 242 0603
Email: editor@spectator.co.uk
Website: www.spectator.co.uk

Owner *The Spectator (1828) Ltd*
Editor *Frank Johnson*
Circulation 56,705

FOUNDED 1828. WEEKLY political and literary magazine. Prospective contributors should write in the first instance to the relevant editor. Unsolicited mss welcome, but no 'follow up' phone calls, please.

Deputy Editor *Petronella Wyatt*
Assistant Editor *Edward Heathcoat Amory*
Books *Mark Amory*
Payment nominal.

The Sporting Life

See **Racing Post**

Sports in the Sky

Freestyle Publications, Alexander House, Ling Road, Tower Park, Poole, Dorset BH12 4NZ
☎01202 735090   Fax 01202 733969
Email: sportssky@freepubs.co.uk
Website: www.freepubs.co.uk

Owner *Mark Nuttall*
Editor *Gethin James*

FOUNDED 1996. MONTHLY magazine highlighting the excitement of aerial sports such as sky-diving, paragliding, hang-gliding, ballooning and microlighting. Features, equipment reviews, profiles and flight guides. Unsolicited material welcome; approach in writing first. Not interested in 'my first parachute jump' stories.

Springboard – Writing To Succeed

30 Orange Hill Road, Prestwich,
Manchester M25 1LS
☎0161 773 5911
Email: leobrooks@rammy.com

Owner/Editor *Leo Brooks*
Circulation 200

FOUNDED 1990. QUARTERLY. *Springboard* is not a market for writers but a forum from which they can find encouragement and help. Provides articles, news, market information, competition/folio news directed at helping writers to achieve success. Free to subscribers: a copy of *The Curate's Egg* – a collection of poetry submitted.

The Squash Times

PO Box 3250, Wokingham, Berkshire
RG40 4FR
☎0118 9737744

Editor *Mr R. Richardson*

FOUNDED 1980. QUARTERLY. Events, players, news, fashion and footwear, rackets, facilities, technique and tactics.

Staffordshire Life

The Publishing Centre, Derby Street, Stafford
ST16 2DT
☎01785 257700   Fax 01785 253287

Owner *The Staffordshire Newsletter*
Editor *Philip Thurlow-Craig*
Circulation 20,000

FOUNDED 1982. TEN ISSUES YEARLY. Full-colour county magazine devoted to Staffordshire, its surroundings and people. Contributions welcome. Approach in writing with ideas.

Features Maximum 1200 words.

Fashion Copy must be supported by photographs.
Payment NUJ rates.

The Stage (incorporating Television Today)

47 Bermondsey Street, London SE1 3XT
☎0171 403 1818   Fax 0171 357 9287

Owner *The Stage Newspaper Ltd*
Editor *Brian Attwood*
Circulation 40,000

FOUNDED 1880. WEEKLY. No unsolicited mss. Prospective contributors should write with ideas in the first instance.

Features Preference for middle-market, tabloid-style articles. 'Puff pieces', PR plugs and extended production notes will not be considered. Max. 800 words.

News News stories from outside London are always welcome. Max. 300 words.
Payment £100 per 1000 words.

Stand Magazine

See under **Poetry Magazines**

Staple New Writing

See under **Poetry Magazines**

The Strad

7 St. John's Road, Harrow, Middlesex
HA1 2EE
☎0181 863 2020   Fax 0181 863 2444
Website: www.orphpl.com

Owner *Orpheus Publications Ltd*

Editor *Joanna Pieters*
Circulation 16,000
FOUNDED 1890. MONTHLY for classical string musicians, makers and enthusiasts. Unsolicited mss welcome 'though acknowledgement/return not guaranteed'.
    Features Profiles of string players, teachers, luthiers and musical instruments, also relevant research. Maximum 2000 words.
    Reviews *Juliette Barber.*
    Payment £100 per 1000 words.

Student Guide

PO Box 6160, Birmingham B16 8XA
☎0121 643 1575   Fax 0121 643 4450
Managing Editor *Sam Allen*
Editor *Sally Howard*
Circulation 30,000
FOUNDED 1990. Published each semester. Student listings and lifestyle. Interested in receiving features and listings items; approach in writing. No unsolicited mss.

Suffolk and Norfolk Life

Barn Acre House, Saxtead Green, Suffolk IP13 9QJ
☎01728 685832   Fax 01728 685842
Owner *Today Magazines Ltd*
Editor *Kevin Davis*
Circulation 17,000
FOUNDED 1989. MONTHLY. General interest, local stories, historical, personalities, wine, travel, food. Unsolicited mss welcome. Approach by phone or in writing with ideas. Not interested in anything which does not relate specifically to East Anglia.
    Features *Kevin Davis* Maximum 1500 words, with photos.
    News *Kevin Davis* Maximum 1000 words, with photos.
    Special Pages *William Locks* Study the magazine for guidelines. Maximum 1500 words.
    Payment £25 (news); £30 (other).

Sugar Magazine

17 Berners Street, London W1P 3DD
☎0171 664 6440   Fax 0171 636 5055
Editor *Sarah Pyper*
Circulation 451,690
FOUNDED 1994. MONTHLY. Everything that might interest the teenage girl. No unsolicited mss. Will consider ideas or contacts for real-life features. No fiction. Approach in writing in the first instance.

Sunday Magazine

See under **National Newspapers**
(The News of the World)

Sunday Post Magazine

See under **National Newspapers**
(Sunday Post, Glasgow)

Sunday Times Magazine

See under **National Newspapers**
(The Sunday Times)

Superbike Magazine

Link House, Dingwall Avenue, Croydon, Surrey CR9 2TA
☎0181 686 2599   Fax 0181 781 1164
Publisher *Alan Morgan*
Editor *Grant Leonard*
Circulation 70,483
FOUNDED 1977. MONTHLY. Dedicated to all that is best and most exciting in the world of high-performance motorcycling. Unsolicited mss, synopses and ideas welcome.

Surrey County

Datateam Publishing, Fairmeadow, Maidstone, Kent ME14 1NG
☎01622 687031   Fax 01622 757646
Owner *Datateam Publishing*
Editor *Roderick Cooper*
Circulation 10,000
FOUNDED 1970. MONTHLY. Strong Surrey interest plus fashion, food, books, wildlife, motoring, property, sport, interiors with local links. Unsolicited mss welcome. Interested in anything with a genuine Surrey connection. No fiction or non-Surrey subjects. Approach in writing with ideas. Maximum length 1500 words. *Payment* negotiable.

Sussex Life

Baskerville Place, 28 Teville Road, Worthing, West Sussex BN11 1UG
☎01903 218719   Fax 01903 820193
Owner *Sussex Life Ltd*
Editor *Trudi Linscer*
Circulation 70,000
FOUNDED 1965. MONTHLY. Sussex and general interest magazine. Regular supplements on education, fashion, homes and gardens. Interested in investigative, journalistic pieces relevant to the area and celebrity profiles. Unsolicited mss, synopses and ideas in writing welcome. Minimum 500 words. *Payment* £15 per 500 words and picture.

Swimming Times
18 Derby Square, Loughborough,
Leicestershire LE11 5AL
☎01509 618743   Fax 01509 618746
Owner *Amateur Swimming Association*
Editor *P. Hassall*
Circulation 20,000

FOUNDED 1923. MONTHLY about competitive
swimming and associated subjects. Unsolicited
mss welcome.
    Features Technical articles on swimming,
water polo, diving or synchronised swimming.
Length and payment negotiable.

The Tablet
1 King Street Cloisters, Clifton Walk, London
W6 0QZ
☎0181 748 8484   Fax 0181 748 1550
Email: TheTablet@compuserve.com
Owner *The Tablet Publishing Co Ltd*
Editor *John Wilkins*
Circulation 20,000

FOUNDED 1840. WEEKLY. Quality international
Roman Catholic magazine featuring articles –
political, social, cultural, theological or spiritual –
of interest to concerned Christian laity and
clergy. Unsolicited material welcome (1500
words) if relevant to magazine's style and market.
All approaches should be made in writing.
    Payment from about £75.

Take a Break
Shirley House, 25–27 Camden Road, London
NW1 9LL
☎0171 284 0909
Owner *H. Bauer*
Editor *John Dale*
Circulation 1.3 million

FOUNDED 1990. WEEKLY. True-life feature
magazine. Approach with ideas in writing.
    News/Features Always on the look-out for
good, true-life stories. Maximum 1200 words.
Payment negotiable.
    Fiction Sharp, succinct stories which are
well told and often with a twist at the end. All
categories, provided it is relevant to the magazine's style and market. Maximum 1000 words.
Payment negotiable.

Taste of Wales
Cardiff Business Technology Centre,
Senghennydd Road, Cardiff CF2 4AY
☎01222 640456   Fax 01222 640048
Owner *Welsh Food Promotions Ltd*
Editor *Sandra Williams*

Circulation 30,000

FOUNDED 1991. QUARTERLY. Welsh national
food magazine. Features on Welsh food and
drink, food-related tourist attractions and events,
interesting people in the food and hospitality
industries, new product reviews and recipes.
Articles on Welsh food welcome. Maximum
1000 words. Contact the editor by phone in the
first instance. *Payment* negotiable.

The Tatler
Vogue House, Hanover Square, London
W1R 0AD
☎0171 499 9080   `Fax 0171 409 0451
Website: www.tatler.co.uk
Owner *Condé Nast Publications Ltd*
Editor *Jane Procter*
Circulation 85,673

Up-market glossy from the Condé Nast stable.
New writers should send in copies of either
published work or unpublished material; writers of promise will be taken up. The magazine
works largely on a commission basis: they are
unlikely to publish unsolicited features, but will
ask writers to work to specific projects.
    Features *Lucy Yeomans*

Telegraph Magazine
See under **National Newspapers**
(The Daily Telegraph)

The Tennis Times
PO Box 3250, Wokingham, Berkshire
RG40 4FR
☎0118 9737744
Editor *Mr R. Richardson*

FOUNDED 1980. QUARTERLY. Events, players,
news, fashion and footwear, rackets, facilities,
technique and tactics.

TGO (The Great Outdoors)
195 Albion Street, Glasgow G1 1QP
☎0141 302 7700   Fax 0141 302 7799
Owner *Caledonian Magazines Ltd*
Editor *Cameron McNeish*
Circulation 22,000

FOUNDED 1978. MONTHLY. Deals with walking, backpacking and wild country topics.
Unsolicited mss are welcome.
    Features Well-written and illustrated items
on relevant topics. Maximum 2500 words. Colour photographs only please.
    News Short topical items (or photographs).
Maximum 300 words.
    Payment £200–300 for features; £10–20 for
news.

that's life!
2nd Floor, 1–5 Maple Place, London W1P 5FX
☎0171 462 4700   Fax 0171 462 4741
Owner H. Bauer Publishing Ltd
Editor Janice Turner
Circulation 500,000

FOUNDED 1995. WEEKLY. True-life stories, puzzles, fashion, cookery and fun. Interested in considering true-life stories. Approach by phone or in writing in the first instance.
Features Karen Jones Maximum 1600 words. Payment £650.
Fiction Emma Fabian 1200 words. Payment £200–300.

Theologia Cambrensis
Church in Wales Centre, Woodland Place, Penarth, Cardiff CF64 2YQ
☎01222 705278   Fax 01222 712413
Owner The Church in Wales
Editor Rev. Nigel John

FOUNDED 1988. THRICE YEARLY. Concerned exclusively with theology and news of theological interest. Includes religious poetry, letters and book reviews (provided they have a scholarly bias). No secular material. Unsolicited mss welcome. Approach in writing with ideas.

The Third Alternative
5 Martins Lane, Witcham, Ely, Cambridgeshire CB6 2LB
☎01353 777931
Email: ttapress@aol.com
Website: purl.oclc.org/net/ttaonline/index.html
Owner TTA Press
Editor Andy Cox

FOUNDED 1993. Quarterly A4 colour magazine of horror, fantasy, science fiction and slipstream fiction, plus interviews, profiles, comment, cinema, travel and artwork. Publishes talented newcomers alongside famous authors. Unsolicited mss welcome if accompanied by s.a.e. or International Reply Coupons (no length restriction, but no novels or serialisations). Queries and letters welcome via email but submissions as hard copy only. Potential contributors are advised to study the magazine. Contracts are exchanged upon acceptance; payment is upon publication. Winner of British Fantasy Awards. The magazine is supported by **Eastern Arts**.

This England
PO Box 52, Cheltenham, Gloucestershire GL50 1YQ
☎01242 577775   Fax 01242 222034
Owner This England Ltd

Editor Roy Faiers
Circulation 200,000

FOUNDED 1968. QUARTERLY, with a strong overseas readership. Celebration of England and all things English: famous people, natural beauty, towns and villages, history, traditions, customs and legends, crafts, etc. Generally a rural basis, with the 'Forgetmenots' section publishing readers' recollections and nostalgia. Up to one hundred unsolicited pieces received each week. Unsolicited mss/ideas welcome. Length 250–2000 words. Payment £25 per 1000 words.

Time
Brettenham House, Lancaster Place, London WC2E 7TL
☎0171 499 4080   Fax 0171 322 1230
Owner Time Warner, Inc.
Editor (Europe, Middle East, Africa)
    Christopher Redman
Circulation 5.46 million

FOUNDED 1923. WEEKLY current affairs and news magazine. There are few opportunities for freelancers on Time as almost all the magazine's content is written by staff members from various bureaux around the world. No unsolicited mss.

Time Out
Universal House, 251 Tottenham Court Road, London W1P 0AB
☎0171 813 3000   Fax 0171 813 6001
Publisher Tony Elliott
Editor Vicky Mayer
Circulation 98,839

FOUNDED 1968. WEEKLY magazine of news and entertainment in London.
Features Elaine Paterson 'Usually written by staff writers or commissioned, but it's always worth submitting an idea by phone if particularly apt to the magazine.' Maximum 2500 words.
News Ruth Bloomfield Despite having a permanent team of staff news writers, sometimes willing to accept contributions from new journalists 'should their material be relevant to the issue'.
Payment £164 per 1000 words.

The Times Educational Supplement
Admiral House, 66–68 East Smithfield, London E1 9XY
☎0171 782 3000   Fax 0171 782 3200
Email: editor@tes.co.uk or copy@tes.co.uk
Website: www.tes.co.uk

Owner *News International*
Editor *Caroline St John-Brooks*
Circulation 145,735

FOUNDED 1910. WEEKLY. New contributors are welcome and should fax ideas on one sheet of A4 for news, features or reviews.

Opinion *Jeremy Sutcliffe* 'Platform': a weekly slot for a well-informed and cogently argued viewpoint. Maximum 1200 words. 'Another Voice': a shorter comment on an issue of the day by non-education professionals. Maximum 700 words.

School Management *Neil Levis*/**Governors** *Victoria Neumark* Weekly pages on practical issues for school governors and managers. Max. 800 words.

Further Education *Ian Nash* Includes training, college management and lifelong learning.

Friday A weekly magazine with *The TES* which includes:

Features *Sarah Bayliss* Unsolicited features are rarely accepted but ideas are welcome accompanied by cuttings and/or c.v. Length 1000– 2000 words.

Arts *Heather Neill*
Books *Geraldine Brennan*
Curriculum Materials *Mary Cruickshank*
Resources, TV and Health *Janette Wolf*
Primary *Diane Hofkins*
Secondary *Brendan O'Malley*
Subject of the Week *Joyce Arnold* Subjects covered include: science, music, modern languages, history, geography, mathematics, environmental education, design and technology (includes food, textiles, graphics), special needs. Articles should relate to current educational practice. Age range covered is primary to sixth form. Maximum 1000–1300 words.

Talkback *Jill Craven* Short, first-person pieces, maximum 650 words, are welcome for consideration. Humour from teachers is encouraged, especially for the 'Thank God it's Friday' column.

Primary *Diane Hofkins* A monthly glossy magazine with *The TES*.

Online (Computers in Education) *Merlin John* A magazine devoted to information technology appearing with *The TES* nine times a year.

Special Needs *Virginia Makins* A magazine on special education needs appearing with *The TES* three times a year.

Special Issues Occasional pull-outs on topics including school management (*Neil Levis*), first appointments (*Joyce Arnold*), business links (*Ian Nash*), school visits – *Going Places* – (*Joyce Arnold*).

The Times Educational Supplement Scotland

Scott House, 10 South St Andrew Street, Edinburgh EH2 2AZ
☎0131 557 1133   Fax 0131 558 1155
Email: editor@timsup4.demon.co.uk
Website: www.tes.co.uk

Owner *Times Supplements Ltd*
Editor *Willis Pickard*
Circulation 9000

FOUNDED 1965. WEEKLY. Unsolicited mss welcome.

Features Articles on education in Scotland. Maximum 1000 words.

News Items on education in Scotland. Maximum 600 words.

The Times Higher Education Supplement

Admiral House, 66–68 East Smithfield, London E1 9XY
☎0171 782 3000   Fax 0171 782 3300
Email: editor@thes.co.uk
Website: www.thes.co.uk

Owner *News International*
Editor *Auriol Stevens*
Circulation 28,300

FOUNDED 1971. WEEKLY. Unsolicited mss are welcome but most articles and *all* book reviews are commissioned. 'In most cases it is better to write, but in the case of news stories it is all right to phone.'

Books *Andrew Robinson*
Features *Sian Griffiths* Most articles are commissioned from academics in higher education.
News *Claire Sanders-Smith* Freelance opportunities very occasionally.
Science *Kam Patel, Julia Hinde*
Science Books *Andrew Robinson*
Foreign *David Jobbins*
Payment by negotiation.

The Times Literary Supplement

Admiral House, 66–68 East Smithfield, London E1 9XY
☎0171 782 3000   Fax 0171 782 3100
Website: www.the-tls.co.uk

Owner *Times Supplements*
Editor *Ferdinand Mount*
Circulation 34,500

FOUNDED 1902. WEEKLY review of literature. Contributors should approach in writing and be familiar with the general level of writing in the *TLS*.

Literary Discoveries *Alan Jenkins*
Poems *Mick Imlah*
News *Ferdinand Mount* News stories and general articles concerned with literature, publishing and new intellectual developments anywhere in the world. Length by arrangement.
Payment by arrangement.

Titbits
2 Caversham Street, London SW3 4AH
☎0171 351 4995   Fax 0171 351 4995
Owner *Sport Newspapers Ltd*
Editor *James Hughes*
Circulation 150,000

FOUNDED 1895. MONTHLY. Consumer magazine for men covering show business and general interests. Unsolicited mss and ideas in writing welcome. Maximum 3000 words. News, features, particularly photofeatures (colour), and fiction.
Payment negotiable.

Today's Golfer
Bretton Court, Bretton, Peterborough, Cambridgeshire PE3 8DZ
☎01733 264666   Fax 01733 465248
Owner *EMAP Active Ltd*
Editor *Neil Pope*
Deputy Editor *John McKenzie*
Circulation 65,000

FOUNDED 1988. MONTHLY. Golf instruction, features, player profiles and news. Most features written in-house but unsolicited mss will be considered. Approach in writing with ideas. Not interested in instruction material from outside contributors.
Features/News *Kevin Brown* Opinion, player profiles and general golf-related features.

Today's Runner
Apex House, Oundle Road, Peterborough, Cambridgeshire PE2 9NP
☎01733 898100   Fax 01733 465070
Owner *EMAP Pursuit Publishing Ltd*
Editor *Paul Larkins*
Circulation 26,075

FOUNDED 1985. MONTHLY. Instructional articles on running, fitness, and lifestyle, plus running-related activities and health.
Features Specialist knowledge an advantage. Opportunities are wide, but approach with ideas in first instance.
News Opportunities for people stories, especially if backed up by photographs.

Top of the Pops Magazine
Room A1136, Woodlands, 80 Wood Lane, London W12 0TT
☎0181 576 3910   Fax 0181 576 2694
Website: www.bbc.worldwide.com
Owner *BBC Worldwide Publishing*
Editor *Ian McLeish*
Circulation 437,090

FOUNDED 1995. MONTHLY teenage pop music magazine with a lighthearted and humorous approach. No unsolicited material apart from pop star interviews.

Total Football
30 Monmouth Street, Bath BA1 2BW
☎01225 442244   Fax 01225 732248
Email: richard.jones@futurenet.co.uk
Owner *Future Publishing*
Editor *Richard Jones*
Circulation 34,791

FOUNDED 1995. MONTHLY. News, features and reviews covering all aspects of domestic and international football. Contributions welcome.
Features *Richard Jones/Alex Murphy* New and interesting angles; particularly funny pieces and fan-based articles. 2000 words maximum. *Payment* negotiable.
News *Richard Jones/Alex Murphy* Unusual stories from all areas of the game – tabloid style. 500 words max. *Payment* £75 per 500 words.

Total Style
57–59 Rochester Place, London NW1 9JU
☎0171 331 1265   Fax 0171 331 1241
Owner *WV Publications*
Editor *Christine Davies*

FOUNDED 1998. BI-MONTHLY. Welcomes informative features on beauty, hair and fashion, aimed at women aged 25–45. 1200–2000 words. *Payment* approximately £225 per feature, depending on length. Also, celebrity 'style' features and interviews. No fiction. Approach in writing in the first instance.

Town and Country Post
Bridge House, Blackden Lane, Goostrey, Cheshire CW4 8PZ
☎01477 534440   Fax 01477 535756
Email: post2001@aol.com
Owner *Town and Country Post Ltd*
Editor *John Williams*
Circulation 28,000

FOUNDED 1981. MONTHLY. Local news and features on mid-Cheshire. Very little freelance material is used. No unsolicited mss. Approach by telephone in the first instance.

Traditional Woodworking

The Well House, High Street, Burton on Trent, Staffordshire DE14 1JQ
☎01283 742950   Fax 01283 561077
Owner *Waterways World*
Editor *Helen Adkins*

FOUNDED 1988. MONTHLY. Features workshop projects, techniques, reviews of the latest woodworking tools and equipment, general articles on woodworking and furniture making.
    Features Technical features and furniture projects welcome. The latter must include drawings and cutting lists. A photograph of the piece is required before commissioning. *Payment* negotiable. Approach in writing in the first instance.

Trail

Apex House, Oundle Road, Peterborough, Cambridgeshire PE2 9NP
☎01733 898100   Fax 01733 341895
Owner *EMAP Active Publishing Ltd*
Editor *Victoria Tebbs*
Circulation 35,172

FOUNDED 1990. MONTHLY. Gear reports, where to walk and practical advice for the hillwalker and long distance walker. Inspirational reads on people and outdoor/walking issues. Health, fitness and injury prevention for high level walkers and outdoor lovers. Approach by phone or in writing in the first instance.
    Features *Victoria Tebbs* Very limited requirement for overseas articles, 'written to our style'. Ask for guidelines. Max. 2000 words.
    Limited requirement for guided walks articles. Specialist writers only. Ask for guidelines. Max. 750–2000 words (depending on subject).
    Payment £80 per 1000 words.

Traveller

45–49 Brompton Road, London SW3 1DE
☎0171 581 0500   Fax 0171 581 1357
Owner *I. M. Wilson*
Editor *Jonathan Lorie*
Circulation 35,359

FOUNDED 1970. QUARTERLY.
    Features Six colour features per issue – copy must be accompanied by good-quality colour transparencies. Articles welcome on off-beat cultural or anthropological subjects and unusual journeys. Western Europe rarely covered. Maximum 2000 words.
    Payment £150 per 1000 words.

Trout Fisherman

EMAP Active Ltd, Bushfield House, Orton Centre, Peterborough, Cambridgeshire PE2 5UN
☎01733 237111   Fax 01733 465658
Owner *EMAP Active Ltd*
Editor *Chris Dawn*
Circulation 42,220

FOUNDED 1977. MONTHLY instructive magazine on trout fishing. Most of the articles are commissioned, but unsolicited mss and quality colour transparencies welcome.
    Features Maximum 2500 words.
    Payment varies.

Turkeys

PO Box 18, Bishopsdale, Leyburn DL8 3YY
☎01969 663764   Fax 01969 663764
Owner *Fancy Fowl Publications Ltd*
Editor *Shirley Murdoch*
Circulation 2000

BI-MONTHLY publication aiming to deal with all aspects of turkey breeding, growing, processing and marketing at an international level. Specialist technical information from qualified contributors will always be considered. Length by arrangement. No unsolicited mss. Approach in writing with ideas, or by phone. *Payment* £70 per 1000 words.

TVTimes

King's Reach Tower, Stamford Street, London SE1 9LS
☎0171 261 7000   Fax 0171 261 7777
Website: www.ipc.co.uk/pubs/tvtimes.htm
Owner *IPC Magazines*
Editor *Peter Genower*
Circulation 850,282

FOUNDED 1955. WEEKLY magazine of listings and features serving the viewers of independent television, BBC, satellite and radio. Almost no freelance contributions used, except where the writer is known and trusted by the magazine. No unsolicited contributions.

Twinkle

2 Albert Square, Dundee DD1 2QJ
☎01382 223131   Fax 01382 322214
Owner *D. C. Thomson & Co. Ltd*
Editor *David Robertson*
Circulation 45,000

FOUNDED 1968. WEEKLY magazine for 5–7-year-olds. Mainly picture stories but some text-based pieces.

Ulster Tatler
39 Boucher Road, Belfast BT12 6UT
☎01232 681371 Fax 01232 381915
Email: ulstertat@aol.com
Website: www.ulstertatler.com
Owner/Editor *Richard Sherry*
Circulation 15,000

FOUNDED 1965. MONTHLY. Articles of local interest and social functions appealing to Northern Ireland's ABC1 population. Welcomes unsolicited material; approach by phone or in writing in the first instance.
Features *Noreen Dorman* Maximum 1500 words. *Payment* £50.
Fiction *Richard Sherry* Maximum 3000 words. *Payment* £150.

The Universe
St James's Buildings, Oxford Street, Manchester M1 6FP
☎0161 236 8856 Fax 0161 236 8892
Owner *Gabriel Communications Ltd*
Editor *Joe Kelly*
Circulation 80,000

Occasional use of new writers, but a substantial network of regular contributors already exists. Interested in a very wide range of material: all subjects which might bear on Christian life. Fiction not normally accepted. *Payment* negotiable.

Vector
See **British Science Fiction Association** under **Professional Associations**

The Vegan
Donald Watson House, 7 Battle Road, St Leonards on Sea, East Sussex TN37 7AA
☎01424 427393 Fax 01424 717064
Email: richard@vegansociety.com
Website: www.vegansociety.com
Owner *Vegan Society*
Editor *Richard Farhall*
Circulation 5000

FOUNDED 1944. QUARTERLY. Deals with the ecological, ethical and health aspects of veganism. Unsolicited mss welcome. Maximum 2000 words. *Payment* negotiable.

Verbatim: The Language Quarterly
PO Box 156, Chearsley, Aylesbury, Buckinghamshire HP18 0DQ
☎01844 208474
Email: verbatim.uk@tesco.net
Website: www.verbatimmag.com
Owner *Word, Inc.*
Editor *Erin McKean*

FOUNDED 1974. QUARTERLY journal devoted to what is amusing, interesting and engaging about the English language and languages in general. Will consider unsolicited material but write for writer's guidelines in the first instance. For a sample copy of the magazine, send 50p (stamp or IRC).
Payment ranges from £20–300, 'depending on length, wit and other merit'.

Veteran Car
Jessamine Court, 15 High Street, Ashwell, Hertfordshire SG7 5NL
☎01462 742818 Fax 01462 742997
Owner *The Veteran Car Club of Great Britain*
Editor *Elizabeth Bennett*
Circulation 1600

FOUNDED 1938. BI-MONTHLY magazine which exists primarily for the benefit of members of The Veteran Car Club of Great Britain. It is concerned with all aspects of the old vehicle hobby – events, restoration, history, current world news, legislation, etc., relating to pre-1919 motor cars. Most professional writers who contribute to the magazine are Club members. No budget for paid contributions.

Vintage Times
PhD Publishing, Navestock Hall, Navestock, Essex RM4 1HA
☎01708 370053
Owner *PhD Publishing*
Editor *David Hoppit*
Circulation 60,000

FOUNDED 1994. QUARTERLY lifestyle magazine 'for over-40s who have not quite given up hope of winning Wimbledon'. Preliminary approach by phone or in writing with ideas.

Vogue
Vogue House, Hanover Square, London W1R 0AD
☎0171 499 9080 Fax 0171 408 0559
Website: www.vogue.co.uk
Owner *Condé Nast Publications Ltd*
Editor *Alexandra Shulman*
Circulation 202,265

Condé Nast Magazines tend to use known writers and commission what's needed, rather than using unsolicited mss. Contacts are useful.
Features *Justine Picardie* Upmarket general interest rather than 'women's'. Good proportion

of highbrow art and literary articles, as well as travel, gardens, food, home interest and reviews. No fiction.

Voyage

Regent Chambers, 40 Lichfield Street, Wolverhampton WV1 1DG
☎01902 423353   Fax 01902 423353
Owner *JGD Publishing*
Editor *John Dunne*
Circulation 5000

FOUNDED 1998. BI-MONTHLY of fiction, poetry and features. Unsolicited mss welcome but writers need to see at least one copy to get an idea of what material is required. S.a.e. essential. 'Reasons for rejection given.'
    Fiction Maximum 6000 words; **Poetry** Up to 60 lines; **Features** Maximum 5000 words.
    Payment 'dependent on quality, not length'.

Voyager

Mediamark Publishing International, 11 Kingsway, London WC2B 6PH
☎0171 212 9000   Fax 0171 212 9001
Email: info@mediamark.co.uk
Owner *Mediamark/British Midland Airways*
Editor *Howard Rombough*
Circulation 54,191

TEN ISSUES PER YEAR. In-flight magazine of British Midland Airways. European lifestyle features and profiles, plus British Midland information. No unsolicited mss. Approach in writing with ideas in the first instance. No destination travel articles.

The War Cry

101 Queen Victoria Street, London EC4P 4EP
☎0171 332 0022   Fax 0171 236 3491
Owner *The Salvation Army*
Editor *Captain Charles King*
Circulation 80,000

FOUNDED 1879. WEEKLY magazine containing Christian comments on current issues. Unsolicited mss welcome if appropriate to contents. No fiction or poetry. Approach by phone with ideas.
    News relating to Christian Church or social issues. Maximum length 500 words. *Payment* £20 per article.
    Features Magazine-style articles of interest to the 'man/woman-in-the-street'. Maximum length 500 words. *Payment* £20 per article.

The Water Gardener

Somerfield House, Wotton Road, Ashford, Kent TN23 6LW
☎01233 621877   Fax 01233 645669
Owner *Dog World Publishing*
Editor *Yvonne Rees*
Circulation 23,568

FOUNDED 1994. MONTHLY. Everything relevant to water gardening. Will consider photonews items and features on aspects of the subject; write with idea in the first instance. Maximum 2000 words.
    Payment by negotiation.

Waterways World

The Well House, High Street, Burton on Trent, Staffordshire DE14 1JQ
☎01283 742950   Fax 01283 742957
Email: ww@wellhouse.easynet.co.uk
Owner *Waterways World Ltd*
Editor *Hugh Potter*
Circulation 22,408

FOUNDED 1972. MONTHLY magazine for inland waterway enthusiasts. Unsolicited mss welcome, provided the writer has a good knowledge of the subject. No fiction.
    Features *Hugh Potter* Articles (preferably illustrated) are published on all aspects of inland waterways in Britain and abroad, including recreational and commercial boating on rivers and canals.
    News *Regan Milnes* Maximum 500 words.
    Payment £37 per 1000 words.

Waymark

Woodlands, West Lane, Sutton in Craven, Keighley, West Yorkshire BD20 7AS
☎01535 637957   Fax 01535 637576
Email: waymark@bigfoot.com
Editor *Stephen Jenkinson*
Circulation 1000

FOUNDED 1986. QUARTERLY journal of the Institute of Public Rights of Way Officers. Glossy, spot colour magazine for countryside access managers in England and Wales, employed throughout the public and private sectors. Available to non-members by subscription. Read by politicians, landowners, environmental lobbyists and countryside access users.
    News Most produced in-house but some opportunities for original/off-beat items. Maximum 500 words.
    Features Ideas welcome on any topic broadly relating to the British countryside and public access to it. Controversial, thought

provoking pieces readily considered. Maximum 1750 words.

Special Pages Cartoons or brief humorous items on an access or countryside/environmental theme welcome. Send ideas in writing with s.a.e. initially.

Payment negotiable, up to £35.

Wedding and Home

King's Reach Tower, Stamford Street, London SE1 9LS
☎0171 261 7471   Fax 0171 261 7459
Email: weddingandhome@ipc.co.uk
Website: www.ipc.co.uk/pubs/weddhome.htm
Owner *IPC Magazines Ltd*
Editor *Christine Prunty*
Circulation 44,269

FOUNDED 1985. BI-MONTHLY offering ideas and inspiration for women planning their wedding. Most features are written in-house or commissioned from known freelancers. Unsolicited mss are not welcome, but approaches may be made in writing.

Weekly News

Albert Square, Dundee DD1 9QJ
☎01382 223131   Fax 01382 201390
Owner *D. C. Thomson & Co. Ltd*
Editor *David Hishmurgh*
Circulation 206,302

FOUNDED 1855. WEEKLY. Newsy, family-orientated magazine designed to appeal to the busy housewife. 'We get a lot of unsolicited stuff and there is great loss of life among them.' Usually commissions, but writers of promise will be taken up. Series include showbiz, royals and television. No fiction.

Payment negotiable.

West Lothian Life

Ballencrieff Cottage, Ballencrieff Toll, Bathgate, West Lothian EH48 4LD
☎01506 632728   Fax 01506 635444
Email: pages@clara.net
Website: home.clara.net/pages
Owner *Pages Editorial & Publishing Services*
Editor *Susan Coon*

QUARTERLY county magazine for people who live, work or have an interest in West Lothian. Includes three or four major features (1500 words) on successful people, businesses or initiatives. A local walk takes up the centre spread. Regular articles by experts on collectables, property, interior design, cookery and local gardening, plus news items, letters and a com-

petition. Freelance writers used exclusively for main features. Phone first to discuss content and timing.

Payment by arrangement.

What Car?

60 Waldegrave Road, Teddington, Middlesex TW11 8LG
☎0181 943 5000   Fax 0181 943 5750
Owner *Haymarket Motoring Publications Ltd*
Editor *Julian Rendell*
Circulation 153,164

MONTHLY. The car buyer's bible, *What Car?* concentrates on road test comparisons of new cars, news and buying advice on used cars, as well as a strong consumer section. Some scope for freelancers. Testing is only offered to the few, and general articles on aspects of driving are only accepted from writers known and trusted by the magazine. No unsolicited mss.

Payment negotiable.

What Hi-Fi?

38–42 Hampton Road, Teddington, Middlesex TW11 0JE
☎0181 943 5000   Fax 0181 943 5019
Owner *Haymarket Magazines Ltd*
Publisher *Nicole Levesconte*
Publishing Director *Kevin Costello*
Editor *Andy Clough*
Circulation 75,000

FOUNDED 1976. MONTHLY. Features on hi-fi and new technology. No unsolicited contributions. Prior consultation with the editor essential.

Features General or more specific on hi-fi and new technology pertinent to the consumer electronics market.

Reviews Specific product reviews. All material is now generated by in-house staff. Freelance writing no longer accepted.

What Investment

Arnold House, 36–41 Holywell Lane, London EC2A 3SF
☎0171 827 5454   Fax 0171 827 0567
Owner *Charterhouse Communications*
Editor *Iain Yule*
Circulation 37,000

FOUNDED 1983. MONTHLY. Features articles on a variety of savings and investment matters. All approaches should be made in writing.

Features Length 1200–1500 words (maximum 2000).

Payment NUJ rates minimum.

What Mortgage
Arnold House, 36–41 Holywell Lane, London EC2A 3SF
Owner *Charterhouse Communications*
Editor *Lizzie Sparrow*
Circulation 35,000

FOUNDED 1982. MONTHLY magazine on property purchase, choice and finance. No unsolicited material; prospective contributors may make initial contact with ideas either by telephone or in writing.
Features Up to 1500 words on related topics are considered. Particularly welcome are new angles, ideas or specialities relevant to mortgages.
Payment £150 per 1000 words.

What Satellite TV
WV Publications, 57–59 Rochester Place, London NW1 9JU
☎0171 331 1000   Fax 0171 331 1241
Email: wvwhatsat@AOL.com
Website: www.wofsat.com
Owner *WV Publications*
Editor *Geoff Bains*
Circulation 65,000

FOUNDED 1986. MONTHLY including news, technical information, equipment tests, programme background, listings. Contributions welcome – phone first.
Features *Geoff Bains* Unusual installations and users. In-depth guides to popular/cult shows. Technical tutorials.
News *Mark Newman* Industry and programming. 250 words maximum.

What's New in Building
City Reach, 5 Greenwich View Place, Millharbour, London E14 9NN
☎0181 861 6309   Fax 0181 861 6241
Owner *Miller Freeman plc*
Editor *Mark Pennington*
Circulation 31,496

MONTHLY. Specialist magazine covering new products for building. Unsolicited mss not generally welcome. The only freelance work available is rewriting press release material. This is offered on a monthly basis of 25–50 items of about 150 words each.
Payment £5.25 per item.

What's On in London
180–182 Pentonville Road, London N1 9LB
☎0171 278 4393   Fax 0171 837 5838
Owner *E. G. Shaw*

Editor *Michael Darvell*
Circulation 40,000

FOUNDED 1935. WEEKLY entertainment-based guide and information magazine. Features, listings and reviews. Always interested in well-thought-out and well-presented mss. Articles should have London/Home Counties connection, except during the summer when they can be of much wider tourist/historic interest, relating to unusual traditions and events. Phone the editor in the first instance.
Features *Graham Hassell*
Art *Rosanna Negrotti*
Cinema *Neil Smith*
Pop Music *Danny Scott*
Classical Music *Michael Darvell*
Theatre *Sam Marlowe*
Events *Roger Foss*
Payment by arrangement.

Wine
Quest Magazines Ltd., 6–8 Underwood Street, London N1 7JQ
☎0171 549 2572   Fax 0171 549 2550
Owner *Wilmington Publishing*
Editor *Susan Vumback Low*
Circulation 35,000

FOUNDED 1983. MONTHLY. No unsolicited mss.
News/Features Wine, food and food/wine-related travel stories. Prospective contributors should approach in writing.

Wisden Cricket Monthly
25 Down Road, Merrow, Guildford, Surrey GU1 2PY
☎01483 570358   Fax 01483 533153
Owner *Wisden Cricket Magazines Ltd*
Editor *Tim de Lisle*
Circulation 20,000

FOUNDED 1979. MONTHLY. Very few uncommissioned articles are used, but would-be contributors are not discouraged. Approach in writing. *Payment* varies.

Woman
King's Reach Tower, Stamford Street, London SE1 9LS
☎0171 261 5000   Fax 0171 261 5997
Website: www.ipc.co.uk/pubs/woman.htm
Owner *IPC Magazines Ltd*
Editor *Carole Russell*
Circulation 711,133

FOUNDED 1937. WEEKLY Long-running, popular women's magazine which boasts a readership of over 2.5 million. No unsolicited mss. Most work commissioned. Approach with ideas in writing.

Features *Kate Corr* Maximum 1250 words.
Books *Gillian Carter*

Woman and Home

King's Reach Tower, Stamford Street,
London SE1 9LS
☎0171 261 5000   Fax 0171 261 7346
Website: www.ipc.co.uk/pubs/womhome.htm

Owner *IPC Magazines Ltd*
Editor *Jan Henderson*
Circulation 330,001

FOUNDED 1926. MONTHLY. No unsolicited mss. Prospective contributors are advised to write with ideas, including photocopies of other published work or details of magazines to which they have contributed. S.a.e. essential for return of material. Most freelance work is specially commissioned.

Woman's Journal

King's Reach Tower, Stamford Street,
London SE1 9LS
☎0171 261 6622   Fax 0171 261 7061
Website: www.ipc.co.uk/pubs/journal.htm

Owner *IPC Magazines Ltd*
Editor *Elsa McAlonan*
Circulation 110,762

FOUNDED 1927. MONTHLY. Original feature ideas on 35+ women and their lives welcome, with samples of previous work. Major features are generally commissioned.
Payment negotiable.

Woman's Own

King's Reach Tower, Stamford Street,
London SE1 9LS
☎0171 261 5474   Fax 0171 261 5346
Website: www.ipc.co.uk/pubs/womanown.htm

Owner *IPC Magazines Ltd*
Editor *Ms Terry Tavner*
Circulation 654,473

FOUNDED 1932. WEEKLY. Prospective contributors should contact the features editor *in writing* in the first instance before making a submission. No unsolicited fiction.

Woman's Realm

King's Reach Tower, Stamford Street,
London SE1 9LS
☎0171 261 5000
Fax 0171 261 5326/261 7678 (Features)
Website: www.ipc.co.uk/pubs/womrealm.htm

Owner *IPC Magazines Ltd*

Editor *Mary Frances*
Deputy Editor *Linda Belcher*
Circulation 197,313

FOUNDED 1958. WEEKLY. Some scope here for freelancers. Write to the appropriate editor.

Features *Liz Jarvis* General, real-life and human interest. Unsolicited mss not accepted.

Fiction Two short stories used every week, a one-pager (up to 1000 words), plus a longer one (2000 words). Unsolicited mss not accepted.

Woman's Weekly

King's Reach Tower, Stamford Street,
London SE1 9LS
☎0171 261 5393   Fax 0171 261 6322
Website: www.ipc.co.uk/pubs/womweek.htm

Owner *IPC Magazines Ltd*
Editor *Gilly Sinclair*
Assistant Editor *Frances Quinn*
Circulation 594,680

FOUNDED 1911. Mass-market women's WEEKLY.
Features Inspiring, positive human interest stories, especially first-hand experiences, of up to 1200 words. Freelancers used regularly but tend to be experienced magazine journalists. Synopses and ideas should be submitted in writing.

Fiction *Gaynor Davies* Short stories 1000–2500 words; serials 12,000–30,000 words. Guidelines for serials: 'a strong emotional theme with a conflict not resolved until the end'; short stories should have warmth and originality.

Women's Health

WV Publications, 57–59 Rochester Place,
London NW1 9JU
☎0171 331 1000   Fax 0171 331 1242
Email: wvmags@compuserve.com

Owner *Highbury House Communications*
Editor *Christine Morgan*
Circulation 100,000

FOUNDED 1998. MONTHLY lifestyle magazine with a health twist, taking an irrelevant approach. Aimed at ABC1 women of 25–45. No unsolicited mss. Interested in ideas for items with an unconventional angle on fitness, fashion and beauty. No alternative health articles. Approach in writing in the first instance.

Woodworker

Azalea Drive, Swanley, Kent BR8 8HU
☎01322 660070   Fax 01322 667633

Owner *Nexus Special Interests*
Editor *Mark Ramuz*
Circulation 45,000

FOUNDED 1901. MONTHLY. Contributions

welcome; approach with ideas in writing.

Features Articles on woodworking with good photo support appreciated. Maximum 2000 words. *Payment £40–60 per page.*

News Stories and photos (b&w) welcome. Max. 300 words. *Payment £10–25 per story.*

World Fishing

Nexus House, Swanley, Kent BR8 8HY
☎01322 660070   Fax 01322 666408
Owner *Nexus Media Ltd*
Editor *Mark Say*
Circulation 6,700

FOUNDED 1952. MONTHLY. Unsolicited mss welcome; approach by phone or in writing with an idea.

News/Features of a technical or commercial nature relating to the commercial fishing and fish processing industries worldwide. Max. 1000 words.

Payment by arrangement.

The World of Embroidery

PO Box 42B, East Molesley, Surrey KT8 9BB
☎0181 943 1229   Fax 0181 977 9882
Email: magsmag@compuserve.com
Website: hiraeth.com/world–emb
Owner *Embroiderers' Guild*
Editor *Maggie Grey*
Circulation 14,500

FOUNDED 1933. BI-MONTHLY. Features articles on embroidery techniques, historical and foreign embroidery, and contemporary artists' work with illustrations. Also reviews. Unsolicited mss welcome. Maximum 1000 words.

Payment negotiable.

The World of Interiors

Vogue House, Hanover Square, London W1R 0AD
☎0171 499 9080   Fax 0171 493 4013
Website: www.worldofinteriors.co.uk
Owner *Condé Nast Publications Ltd*
Editor *Min Hogg*
Circulation 70,128

FOUNDED 1981. MONTHLY. Best approach by fax or letter with an idea, preferably with reference snaps or guidebooks.

Features *Sarah Howell* Most feature material is commissioned. 'Subjects tend to be found by us, but we are delighted to receive suggestions of interiors, archives, little-known museums, collections, etc. unpublished elsewhere, and would love to find new writers.'

World Soccer

King's Reach Tower, Stamford Street, London SE1 9LS
☎0171 261 5737   Fax 0171 261 7474
Website: www.ipc.co.uk/pubs/worldsoc.htm
Owner *IPC Magazines Ltd*
Editor *Gavin Hamilton*
Circulation 63,211

FOUNDED 1960. MONTHLY. Unsolicited material welcome but initial approach by phone or in writing preferred. News and features on world soccer.

Writers News/Writing Magazine

PO Box 4, Nairn IV12 4HU
☎01667 454441   Fax 01667 454401
Owner *David St John Thomas*
Editor *Richard Bell*
Circulation 18,500(WN)/35,000(WM)

FOUNDED 1989. MONTHLY/BI-MONTHLY magazines containing news and advice for writers. *Writers News* is exclusive to mail-order members who also receive *Writing Magazine* which is available on newsstands. No poetry or general items on 'how to become a writer'. Receive 1000 mss each year. Approach in writing.

News *Carolyn Stowe* Exclusive news stories of interest to writers. Maximum 350 words.

Features *Richard Bell* How-to articles of interest to professional writers. Maximum 2000 words.

Yachting Monthly

King's Reach Tower, Stamford Street, London SE1 9LS
☎0171 261 6040   Fax 0171 261 7555
Website: www.ipc.co.uk/pubs/yachtmth.htm
Owner *IPC Magazines Ltd*
Editor *Sarah Norbury*
Circulation 37,083

FOUNDED 1906. MONTHLY magazine for yachting enthusiasts. Unsolicited mss welcome, but many are received and not used. Prospective contributors should make initial contact in writing.

Features *Paul Gelder* A wide range of features concerned with maritime subjects and cruising under sail; well-researched and innovative material always welcome, especially if accompanied by colour transparencies. Maximum 2750 words.

Payment £90–110 per 1000 words.

Yachting World

King's Reach Tower, Stamford Street, London SE1 9LS
☎0171 261 6800   Fax 0171 261 6818

Email: yachting_world@ipc.co.uk
Website: www.yachting-world.com
Owner *IPC Magazines Ltd*
Editor *Andrew Bray*
Circulation 34,316

FOUNDED 1894. MONTHLY with international coverage of yacht racing, cruising and yachting events. Will consider well researched and written sailing stories. Preliminary approaches should be by phone for news stories and in writing for features.
Payment by arrangement.

You – The Mail on Sunday Magazine

See under **National Newspapers (The Mail on Sunday)**

You and Your Wedding

Silver House, 31–35 Beak Street, London W1R 3LD
☎0171 437 2998 (editorial)Fax 0171 287 8655
Owner *AIM Publications Ltd*
Editor *Carole Hamilton*
Circulation 58,000

FOUNDED 1985. BI-MONTHLY. Anything relating to weddings, setting up home, and honeymoons. No unsolicited mss. Ideas may be submitted in writing only, especially travel features. No phone calls.

Young Writer

Glebe House, Weobley, Hereford HR4 8SD
☎01544 318901   Fax 01544 318901
Email: youngwriter@entertprise.net
Website: www.mystworld.com/youngwriter
Editor *Kate Jones*

Describing itself as 'The Magazine for Children with Something to Say', *Young Writer* is issued three times a year, at the back-to-school times of September, January and April. A forum for young people's writing – fiction and non-fiction, prose and poetry – the magazine is an introduction to independent writing for young writers.
Payment from £20 to 100 for freelance commissioned articles.

Your Cat Magazine

Roebuck House, 33 Broad Street, Stamford, Lincolnshire PE9 1RB
☎01780 766199   Fax 01780 766416
Owner *EMAP Apex*
Editor *Sue Parslow*

FOUNDED 1994. MONTHLY magazine giving practical information on the care of cats and kittens, pedigree and non-pedigree, plus a wide range of general interest items on cats. Will consider 'true life' cat stories (maximum 900 words) and quality fiction. Send synopsis in the first instance. 'No articles written as though by a cat.'

Your Garden Magazine

IPC Magazines Ltd., Westover House, West Quay Road, Poole, Dorset BH15 1JG
☎01202 440870   Fax 01202 440860
Email: yourgarden@ipc.co.uk
Website: www.ipc.co.uk/pubs/yrgarden.htm
Owner *IPC Magazines Ltd*
Editor *Michael Pilcher*
Circulation 57,260

FOUNDED 1993. MONTHLY full colour glossy for all gardeners. Welcomes good, solid gardening advice that is well written and fun. Receives approx 50 mss per month but only five per cent are accepted. Always approach in writing in the first instance.
Features Good leisure gardening features, preferably with a new slant. Small gardens only. Maximum 1000 words. Photographs welcome.
Payment negotiable – all rights preferred.

Yours Magazine

Apex House, Oundle Road, Peterborough, Cambridgeshire PE2 9NP
☎01733 555123   Fax 01733 898487
Owner *Choice Publications - Bayard Presse*
Editor *Neil Patrick*
Circulation 271,210

FOUNDED 1973. MONTHLY plus four seasonal specials. Aimed at a readership aged 55 and over.
Features Best approach by letter with outline in first instance. Maximum 1000 words.
News Short, newsy items of interest to readership welcome. Length 300–500 words.
Fiction One or two short stories used in each issue.
Payment negotiable.

ZENE

5 Martins Lane, Witcham, Ely, Cambridgeshire CB6 2LB
☎01353 777931
Email: ttapress@aol.com
Website: purl.oclc.org/net/ttaonline/index.html
Owner *TTA Press*
Editor *Andy Cox*

FOUNDED 1994. Features detailed contributors' guidelines of international small press and semi-professional publications, plus varied articles, news, views, reviews and interviews.

Features Unsolicited articles welcome on any aspect of small press publishing: market information, writing, editing, illustrating, interviews and reviews. All genres. Submissions should include adequate return postage. 'Please study the magazine: this will greatly enhance your chances of acceptance.'

The Zone

13 Hazely Combe, Arreton, Isle of Wight
PO30 3AJ
☎01983 865668

Publisher *Pigasus Press*
Editor *Tony Lee*

FOUNDED 1994. BI-ANNUAL science fiction magazine. Unsolicited mss welcome but writers are advised to study recent issues and be familiar with the content before sending material. Contributors' guidelines and mail order details available. (All correspondence must be accompanied by an s.a.e. or IRC.)

Fiction Original, imaginative science fiction and fantasy (no supernatural horror), 1000–5000 words. Prose-poems, 60–70 lines; genre verse also appears in the SF poetry showcase, but by invitation only.

Features Interviews with prominent SF authors. Critical articles and essays on any aspect or theme related to SF/fantasy scene, whether topical or retrospective, will be considered. Length 1000–10,000 words. Approach in writing with ideas in the first instance.

Reviews Books, cinema, video and TV. Reviews are usually commissioned but will consider reviews of new SF and non-fiction books. Length 300–500 words.

Payment Token £5 for stories and non-fiction of over 2000 words; otherwise payment in copy only.

Freelance Rates – Magazines

Freelance rates vary enormously. The following minimum rates, negotiated by the **National Union of Journalists**, should be treated as guidelines. Most work can command higher fees from employers whether or not they have NUJ agreements. It is up to freelancers to negotiate the best deal they can.

Examples of NUJ categories for magazines:

Group A (over £13,000 per page of advertising)
Cosmopolitan, Hello!, Radio Times, TV Times, Woman, Woman's Own.

Group B (between £7000 and £13,000 per page of advertising)
The Economist, GQ, Loaded, marie claire, Q, Vanity Fair.

Group C (between £2500 and £7000 per page of advertising)
Architect's Journal, The British Medical Journal, Music Week, The Spectator, Time Out.

Group D (less than £2500 per page of advertising)
Accountancy Age, Nursing Times.

The following figures are the minimum rates which should be paid by magazines in the above groups for first use only:

Features (per 1000 words)
Group A	£400
Group B	£275
Group C	£225
Group D	£160

Cartoons (b&w)

	Group A	Group B & C	Group D
Minimum fee	£100	£80	£64
Feature strip (up to 4 frames)	£123	£107	£100

For colour, charge at least double these rates.

Crosswords

	Group A	Group B & C	Group D
15 × 15 squares and under	£160	£85	£64
Over 15 × 15 squares	£210	£125	£85

News Agencies

AP–Dow Jones News Service
10 Fleet Place, London EC4M 7RB
☎0171 832 9000   Fax 0171 832 9101

A real-time financial and business newswire operated by The Associated Press, the US news agency, and Dow Jones & Co., publishers of *The Wall Street Journal*. No unsolicited material.

Associated Press News Agency
12 Norwich Street, London EC4A 1BP
☎0171 353 1515
Fax 0171 353 8118 (Newsdesk)

Material is either generated in-house or by regulars. Hires the occasional stringer. No unsolicited mss.

National News Press and Photo Agency
109 Clifton Street, London EC2A 4LD
☎0171 684 3000   Fax 0171 684 3030

All press releases welcome. Most work is ordered or commissioned. Coverage includes courts, tribunals, conferences, general news, etc. – words and pictures – as well as PR.

Press Association Ltd
292 Vauxhall Bridge Road, London SW1V 1AE
☎0171 963 7107
Fax 0171 963 7192 (24-hr Newsdesk)
Email: newsdesk@pa.press.net
Website: www.pa.press.net

No unsolicited material. Most items are produced in-house though occasional outsiders may be used. A phone call to discuss specific material may lead somewhere 'but this is rare'.

Reuters Ltd
85 Fleet Street, London EC4P 4AJ
☎0171 250 1122
No unsolicited mss.

Solo Syndication Ltd
49-53 Kensington High Street, London W8 5ED
☎0171 376 2166   Fax 0171 938 3165

FOUNDED 1978. *Specialises* in worldwide newspaper syndication of photos, features and cartoons. Professional contributors only.

South Yorkshire Sport
6 Sharman Walk, Apperknowle, Sheffield, South Yorkshire S18 4BJ
☎01246 414767/07970 284848 (mobile)
Fax 01246 414767
Email: Nicksport1@aol.com

Provides written/broadcast coverage of sport in the South Yorkshire area.

Worldwide Media Limited
PO Box 3821, London NW2 4DQ
☎0181 452 6241   Fax 0181 452 7258

FOUNDED 1995. Supplies magazines around the world with well-written feature articles, most of which focus on women's interests and health topics. Commissions a large proportion of the features it syndicates. 'Often looking for freelance writers to research and write specific pieces.'

The Ever Interesting Topic –
Writers and Their Earnings

This article is accompanied by a health warning. It can lead to dizziness, confusion and violent changes of mood from elation to utter despondency. The subject, of course, is money.

Writers are often thought to be unworldly characters who renounce the profit motive. But even those high on ideals have to live. And for the rest, as the sage observed, money isn't everything but what it isn't it can buy.

There are no set rules to paying writers. The **Society of Authors**, the **Writers' Guild** and the **National Union of Journalists** make a good stab at establishing minimum terms. For radio, television and hard print journalism they specify figures. (See pages 227, 329 and 358 for more on this.) A first play of 60 minutes for the BBC, for example, should gather in £4551 while a feature for a big newspaper might attract £500 for 1000 words. But the operative words are 'should' and 'might'. As the writers' organisations are the first to concede, there is much that goes on in the media that is beyond their remit. An independent production company will not necessarily follow the example of pay and conditions set by the BBC. A magazine or newspaper with a regular team of well-rewarded freelancers may mete our inferior treatment to occasional contributors.

It is yet more of a guessing game for books. The Society of Authors has negotiated minimum terms with most of the top publishers but the only figures mentioned in these agreements are percentages such as the royalties an author can expect on hardback and softcover sales at home and abroad. But even these guidelines are open to interpretation.

Old hands remember the days when it was standard for a publisher to offer 10 per cent on hardback and 7½ per cent on paperback with built-in increases tied to volume of sales. No longer. High pressure marketing now requires a more flexible approach. Concessions to powerful booksellers by way of increased discounts have to be paid for and it can well be that the writer is asked to take a lower royalty so that his book may be sold more aggressively. Fair or unfair? Who is to say until the cheque arrives in the post and the author jumps for joy or rings the Samaritans.

Electronic rights complicate matters still further. The Society of Authors supports a 80:20 division of the proceeds in the writer's favour. Publishers are inclined to switch the advantage or compromise on a 50:50 split. Exports are another contentious area. Contracts usually provide for royalties to be based not on the UK published price but on the price or net receipts received by the publishers. It is not at all unusual for an author to hear good news – that a container load of his books has joined the export drive – followed by the bad news – the deal was done at such a cheap rate that earnings will be derisory.

When it comes to the advances on royalties, the money that kick-starts a book, an author (or his agent) needs to have a realistic view of his value in the marketplace. Big names get big advances. The six- or seven-figure deal is a regular item of literary news. Early in the year, Nick Hornby moved from Gollancz to Penguin in a two-book contract worth £2 million.

The big names may be great writers. But then again, they may not. For every Nick Hornby there is a name famous for anything but writing – a royal, a Hollywood star, a maverick businessman – famous, perhaps, for just being famous, who will be inspired by a publisher waving a large cheque. You can understand the reasoning. A personality who is regularly in the headlines is more likely to attract the bookshop passing trade than an unknown – however talented the latter and however bovine the former.

There are exceptions that prove the rule. Barely a week passes without a trumpeted discovery of a bestseller in the making, plucked from obscurity by a sharp-eyed publisher or agent. But million dollar deals can prove as ephemeral as the newspapers which give them prominence. Publishers quote astronomical sums to beat up public interest; they neglect to mention that six figure advance is often conditional on the sale of rights, be they paperback, foreign, film or television. If the deals do not come through, neither does the money. One young innocent given the star treatment reappeared in the news a year later. She was spotted on the dole queue.

Needless to say, flash Harry publishing does not extend to authors judged to be respectable but not mega-sellers. The best they can hope for is a sum equivalent to 60 per cent of projected royalties on a first edition, split three ways, part on signature of contract, part on delivery of manuscript and part on publication. Marketing people, who tend towards a low view of public taste, are squeezing the sales estimates of books that might be described as 'literary' with the inevitable result that advances too are tighter. They don't always get it right. For *Birdsong*, Sebastian Faulkes was paid a measly £25,000 advance. The book turned into one of the most popular novels of the decade with more than 500,000 copies sold. Insiders suggested re-titling the book *Going For a Song*.

There are other examples of quality authors selling in large numbers – Roddy Doyle, Helen Fielding, Bill Bryson, Minette Walters, Robert Harris, to take names at random – but the fact remains that publishers are ever more reluctant to take chances. It is not simply that advances are down (a novelist starting out on a writing career is lucky to get more than £2000 up front) but fewer titles are being published. 1997 saw a drop of 244 fiction titles on the previous year's total. The upside is that more books are being bought than ever before. There are fortunes to be made but by whom and for what remains a tantalising mystery.

Television and Radio

BBC TV and Radio
Website: www.bbc.co.uk

Following restructuring, network television and radio were brought together as bi-media departments under BBC Production and BBC Broadcast. The Broadcast Directorate is responsible for the commissioning, scheduling and broadcasting of programmes on television and radio. BBC Production includes all the BBC drama producers (television, radio and World Service) in England, as well as education, entertainment, music, arts and factual areas. The bi-media divisions within BBC Production are BBC Arts and Classical Music, BBC Children's Programmes, BBC Documentaries and History, BBC Drama Production, BBC Education Production, BBC Entertainment, BBC Features and Events, BBC Music Entertainment, BBC Religion, BBC Science and BBC Sport.

TELEVISION
Director, Television *Alan Yentob*
Chief Executive, BBC Broadcast *Will Wyatt*
Chief Executive, BBC Production
 Matthew Bannister
Controller, BBC1 *Peter Salmon*
Controller, BBC2 *Jane Root*

RADIO
Director of Radio/Controller, Radio 1
 Andy Parfitt
Controller, Radio 2 *James Moir*
Controller, Radio 3 *Roger Wright*
Controller, Radio 4 *James Boyle*
Controller, Radio 5 Live *Roger Mosey*

Radio 1 is the popular music-based station; Radio 2 broadcasts popular light entertainment with celebrity presenters; Radio 3 is devoted to classical and contemporary music; Radio 4 is the main news and current affairs station while broadcasting a wide range of other programmes such as consumer matters, wildlife, science, gardening, etc. It also produces the bulk of drama, comedy, serials and readings. Radio 5 Live is the 24-hour news and sport station.

BBC News
BBC Television Centre, Wood Lane, London
W12 7RJ
☎0181 743 8000
Website: www.bbc.co.uk/news

BBC News is the world's largest newsgathering organisation, with 2000 journalists, 250 foreign correspondents and 50 bureaux around the world. BBC News serves: BBC1, BBC2, Radios 1, 2, 3, 4 and 5 Live, BBC News 24, BBC Parliament, BBC World, BBC World Service, BBC Online, Ceefax.

Chief Executive, BBC News *Tony Hall*
Deputy Chief Executive *Richard Ayre*
Head of News Gathering
 Richard Sambrook
Head of News Programmes
 Richard Clemmow
Head of Current Affairs and Business Programmes *Helen Boaden*
Head of Political Programmes
 Mark Damazer

NEWS PROGRAMMES/CONTINUOUS NEWS
Executive Editor, Radio Daily Current Affairs *Anne Koch*
Executive Editor, TV Daily Current Affairs *Jon Barton*
Commissioning Editor *Richard Clark*
Editor, The Today Programme *Rod Liddle*
Editor, The World at One/World This Weekend/PM/Broadcasting House
 Kevin Marsh
Editor, Radio 1 News Programmes
 Colin Hancock
The World Tonight, Editors *Pru Keely, Jenni Russell*
Editor, One O'Clock News *Jay Hunt*
Editor, Six O'Clock News *Mark Popescu*
Editor, Nine O'Clock News
 Jonathan Baker
Editor, Newsnight *Sian Kevill*
Editor, Breakfast News *Andrew Thompson*
Breakfast With Frost, Editor *Barney Jones*
CONTINUOUS NEWS
Acting Director, Continuous News
 Roger Mosey
Controller, TV News Channels *Tim Orchard*
Controller, Radio 5 Live *Roger Mosey*
Managing Editor, News 24 *Chris Birkett*
Managing Editor, BBC World
 Peter Knowles
Managing Editor, BBC Parliament
 Nigel Charters
UK News Editor, News Online *Pete Clifton*
Acting Editor, Ceefax *Paul Brannan*

Ceefax
Room 7013, BBC Television Centre,
Wood Lane, London W12 7RJ
☎0181 576 1801

Subtitling
Room 1468, BBC White City, Wood Lane,
London W12 7RJ
☎0181 752 7054/0141 339 8844 ext. 2128
A rapidly expanding service available via Ceefax
page 888. Units based in London and Glasgow.

BBC Arts and Classical Music
EM07 East Tower, BBC Television Centre,
Wood Lane, London W12 9RJ
☎0181 895 6770/6500   Fax 0181 895 6586

Head of BBC Arts and Classical Music
  Kim Evans
Head of Classical Music (Radio)
  Dr John Evans
Head of Classical Music (Television)
  Peter Maniura
Editor, Arts Features *Keith Alexander*
Series Editor, Omnibus *Basil Comely*
Series Editor, Arena *Anthony Wall*
Editor, Close Up, Late Review *Michael Poole*
Editor, Radio *John Boundy*
Editor, World Service *Jenny Bowen*

Television, radio and World Service production of Arts programmes such as *Omnibus*; *Arena*; *Late Review*; *Night Waves* and *Meridian*.

BBC Children's Programes
BBC Television Centre, Wood Lane, London
W12 7RJ
☎0181 743 8000

Head of BBC Children's Programmes
  Lorraine Heggessey
Executive Producer, Children's Acquisitions *Theresa Plummer-Andrews*
Executive Producer, Children's Drama
  Elaine Sperber
Executive Producer, Entertainment
  Chris Bellinger
Executive Producer, News and Factual Programmes *Roy Milani*
Editor, Blue Peter *Steve Hocking*
Producer, Grange Hill *Jo Ward*
Editor, Live & Kicking *Angela Sharp*

BBC Documentaries and History
BBC White City: 201 Wood Lane, London
W12 7TS
☎0181 752 6354   Fax 0181 752 6060

Head of BBC Documentaries and History, Television *Paul Hamann*

Editor, Inside Story *Olivia Lichtenstein*
Editor, Modern Times *Alex Holmes*
Editor, Reputations *Janice Hadlow*
Editor, Timewatch *Laurence Rees*

BBC Drama Production
TV: BBC Television Centre, Wood Lane,
London W12 7RJ
☎0181 743 8000

Controller, BBC Drama *Colin Adams*
Head of Serials, BBC1 *Jane Tranter*
Head of Serials, BBC2 *Hilary Salmon*
Head of Series *Mal Young*
Head of Single Drama & Films *David Thompson*
Head of Development, Serials *Pippa Harris*
Head of Development, Series *Patrick Spence*
Head of Development, Single Drama & Films *Tracey Scoffield*

RADIO: Broadcasting House, London
W1A 1AA
☎0171 580 4468

Head of Radio Drama *Kate Rowland*
Executive Producer *Jeremy Mortimer*
Executive Producer *David Hunter*
Executive Producer (Manchester)
  Sue Roberts
Executive Producer (Birmingham)/Editor, The Archers
  Vanessa Whitburn
Executive Producer (World Service Drama) *Gordon House*

BBC Drama's New Writing Initiative develops and nurtures new writing talent across BBC TV and Radio Drama and handles unsolicited scripts for Single TV dramas and radio drama. To be considered for one of the schemes run by the New Writing Initiative please send a sample full length drama script to: New Writing Initiative, Room 6059, BBC Broadcasting House, Portland Place, London W1A 1AA. For guidelines on unsolicited scripts please send a large s.a.e. to the same address.
  BBC Drama Coordinator, New Writing Initiative *Lucy Hannah*

BBC Education Production
BBC White City, 201 Wood Lane, London
W12 7TS
☎0181 752 5252

Head of BBC Education Production
  Marilyn Wheatcroft
Executive Producers, Schools *Clare Elstow, Geoff Marshall-Taylor, Sue Nott*

Executive Producer, Languages *David Wilson*
Managing Editor, World Service *David Thomas*
Executive Producer, Radio *Clare McGinn*
Executive Producer, Learning *Tina Fletcher*

BBC OPEN UNIVERSITY PRODUCTION CENTRE
Walton Hall, Milton Keynes, MK7 6BH
☎01908 655544   Fax 01908 376324
Head of Production *Ian Rosenbloom*

Television and radio production of schools and college programmes, language courses, education for adults, plus multimedia and audiovisual material in partnership with the Open University. The Learning Zone broadcasts education, training and information programmes on BBC2 from midnight during the week.

BBC Entertainment

BBC Television Centre, Wood Lane, London W12 7RJ
☎0181 743 8000
Controller, BBC Entertainment *Paul Jackson*
Head of Light Entertainment, Television *David Young*
Head of Comedy *Geoffrey Perkins*
Script Executive *Bill Dare*
Head of Comedy Entertainment *Jon Plowman*
Producer, The News Huddlines *Carol Smith*

Programmes produced by BBC Entertainment range from *Shooting Stars* and *Jonathan Creek* on television to *Just a Minute*; *I'm Sorry I Haven't a Clue* and *The News Quiz* on Radio 4. Virtually every comic talent in Britain got their first break writing one-liners for topical comedy weeklies like Radio 2's *The News Huddlines* (currently paying about £10 for a 'quickie' – one- or two-liners). Ideas welcome; send to Broadcasting House, London W1A 1AA.

BBC Features and Events

Room 4360, BBC White City Wood Lane, London W12 7TS
☎0181 752 5906   Fax 0181 752 5915
Head of BBC Features and Events *Anne Morrison*
Executive Editor, Radio *Graham Ellis*
Executive Producer, Crimewatch *Seetha Kumar*

Covers consumer affairs, major national events and informal education, producing television and radio progammes such as *Crimewatch*; *Watchdog*; *You and Yours*; *Holiday* and *Woman's Hour*.

BBC Music Entertainment

Room 213, Western House, 99 Great Portland Street, London W1A 1AA
☎0171 765 5407
Head of BBC Music Entertainment *Trevor Dann*

Pop music production for television, radio and video with programmes such as *Top of the Pops*, *Later With Jools* and coverage of the Country Music Awards.

BBC Religion

New Broadcasting House, Oxford Road, Manchester M60 1SJ
☎0161 200 2020   Fax 0161 244 3183
Head of Religious Broadcasting *Rev. Ernest Rea*
Managing Editor, Religious Programmes *Helen Alexander*

Regular programmes for television include *Songs of Praise*; *Everyman*; *Heart of the Matter*. Radio output includes *Good Morning Sunday*; *Sunday Half Hour*; *Choral Evensong*; *The Brains Trust*.

BBC Science

BBC White City, 201 Wood Lane, London W12 7TS
☎0181 752 5252
Head of BBC Science *Glenwyn Benson*
Editor, Tomorrow's World *Saul Nasse*
Editor, Horizon *John Lynch*
Editor, QED *Michael Mosley*

Produces programmes such as *Animal Hospital* and *Tomorrow's World* for television and radio.

BBC Sport

Broadcasting House, London W1A 1AA
☎0171 765 5050
Acting Head of BBC Sport *Bob Shennan*
Deputy Head of Sport, Executive Editor, Football *Niall Sloane*

Sports news and commentaries across television and Radios 1, 4 and 5 Live, with the majority of output on Radio 5 Live. Regular programmes include *Sportsnight*; *Sports News*; *Sports on Five* and *Littlejohn* (presented by Richard Littlejohn).

BBC Birmingham

Broadcasting Centre, Pebble Mill Road, Birmingham B5 7QQ
☎0121 414 8888   Fax 0121 414 8634
Head of Regional and Local Programmes *Laura Dalgleish*
Editor, Newsgathering *Rod Beards*

Producers, Midlands Today
Charles Watkins, Naomi Bishop
Producers, The Midlands Report
David Nelson, Sarah Eglin

Home of the Pebble Mill Studio. Output for the network includes: *The Clothes Show; Telly Addicts; Top Gear; The Really Useful Show; Style Challenge; Call My Bluff; Gardener's World; Kilroy.* Openings exist for well-researched topical or local material.

BBC Birmingham serves opt-out stations in Nottingham and Norwich:

BBC East Midlands (Nottingham)
East Midlands Broadcasting Centre, York House, Mansfield Road, Nottingham NG1 3JA
☎0115 9550500

Head of Regional and Local Programmes
Richard Lucas
Head of Newsgathering *Emma Agnew*
Producers, East Midlands Today
Kevin Hill, Liz Howell

BBC East (Norwich)
St Catherine's Close, All Saint's Green, Norwich, Norfolk NR1 3ND
☎01603 619331

Head of Regional and Local Programmes
David Holdsworth
Head of Newsgathering *Tim Bishop*
Poducers, Look East *Ian Kings, Roger Farrant*
Producers, Matter of Fact *Dick Meadows, Martin Friend, Diana Hare*

BBC Bristol
Broadcasting House, Whiteladies Road, Bristol BS8 2LR
☎0117 9732211

Head of Features *Jeremy Gibson* (bi-media)
Head of Natural History Unit *Keith Scholey* (bi-media)

BBC Bristol is the home of the BBC's Natural History Unit, producing programmes such as *Wildlife on One; The Natural World; The Life of Birds;* and *The Really Wild Show* for BBC1 and BBC2. It also produces natural history programmes for Radio 4 and Radio 5 Live. The Features department produces a wide range of television programmes, including *999; Antiques Roadshow; 10x10; Picture This; Vets in Practice; War Walks* and *Under the Sun* in addition to radio programmes specialising in history, travel, literature and human interest features for Radio 4.

BBC Northern Ireland
Broadcasting House, Ormeau Avenue, Belfast BT2 8HQ
☎01232 338000
Website: www.bbc.co.uk/northernireland

Controller *Patrick Loughrey*
Head of Broadcasting *Anna Carragher*
Head of Production *Paul Evans*
Head of News & Current Affairs
Andrew Colman
Head of Drama *Robert Cooper*
Chief Producer, Sport *Terry Smyth*
Chief Producer, Music & Arts *David Byers*
Chief Producer, Youth & Community
Fedelma Harkin
Chief Producer, Education *Michael McGowan*
Chief Producer, Topical Programmes
Bruce Batten
Chief Producer, Religion *Bert Tosh*

Regular television programmes include *Newsline 6.30; Hearts and Minds* and *Country Times.* Radio stations: BBC Radio Foyle and BBC Radio Ulster (see entries).

BBC Scotland
Broadcasting House, Queen Margaret Drive, Glasgow G12 8DG
☎0141 338 2000
Website: www.bbc.co.uk/scotland

Controller *John McCormick*
Head of Production *Colin Cameron*
Head of Broadcast *Ken MacQuarrie*
Head of Drama *Barbara McKissack*
Head of News and Current Affairs *Kenneth Cargill*
Head of Children's and Features *Liz Scott*
Head of Arts & Entertainment *Mike Bolland*
Head of Education and Religious Broadcasting *Andrew Barr*
Head of Sport *Neil Fraser*
Head of Programmes, North *Andrew Jones*
Head of Gaelic *Donalda MacKinnon*

Headquarters of BBC Scotland with centres in Aberdeen, Dundee, Edinburgh and Inverness. Regular programmes include *Reporting Scotland* and *Sportscene* on television and *Good Morning Scotland; Fred Macaulay* and *Storyline* on radio.

Aberdeen
Broadcasting House, Beechgrove Terrace, Aberdeen AB9 2ZT
☎01224 625233

News, plus some features, including the regular *Beechgrove Garden.* Second TV centre, also with regular radio broadcasting.

Dundee
Nethergate Centre, 66 Nethergate, Dundee
DD1 4ER
☎ 01382 202481
News base only; contributors' studio.

Edinburgh
Broadcasting House, Queen Street, Edinburgh
EH2 1JF
☎0131 225 3131
Religious, arts and science programming base.
Bi-media news operation.

Inverness
7 Culduthel Road, Inverness 1V2 4AD
☎01463 720720
News features for Radio Scotland. HQ for Radio
Nan Gaidheal, the Gaelic radio service serving
most of Scotland (**Editor** *Ishbel MacLennan*).

BBC North/BBC North West/ BBC North East & Cumbria

The regional centres at Leeds, Manchester and
Newcastle make their own programmes on a
bi-media approach, each centre having its own
head of regional and local programmes.

BBC North (Leeds)
Broadcasting Centre, Woodhouse Lane,
Leeds, West Yorkshire LS2 9PX
☎0113 2441188
Head of Regional and Local Programmes
Colin Philpott
Editor, Newsgathering *Kate Watkins*
Producer, North of Westminster *Rod Jones*
Producer, Close Up North *Ian Cundall*
Producers, Look North *Denise Wallace,
Paul Greenan*

BBC North West (Manchester)
New Broadcasting House, Oxford Road,
Manchester M60 1SJ
☎0161 200 2020
Head of Regional and Local Programmes
Martin Brooks
Editor, Newsgathering *Mike Briscoe*
Producers, Northwest Tonight *Tamsin
O'Brien, Jim Clark*
Producer, Close Up North *Deborah van Bishop*
Producer, Northwestminster *Liam Fogarty*

**BBC North East & Cumbria (Newcastle
upon Tyne)**
Broadcasting Centre, Barrack Road,
Newcastle Upon Tyne NE99 2NE
☎0191 232 1313

Head of Regional and Local Programmes
Olwyn Hocking
Editor, Newsgathering *To be appointed*
Producers, Look North *Iain Williams,
Andrew Lambert*
Producer, North of Westminster *Michael
Wild*
Producers, Close Up North *Dave Morrison,
Michael Wild*

BBC Wales
Broadcasting House, Llandaff, Cardiff
CF5 2YQ
☎01222 322000   Fax 01222 552973
Website: www.bbc.co.uk/wales
Controller *Geraint Talfan Davies*
Head of Production *John Geraint*
Head of Programmes (Welsh Language)
Gwynn Pritchard
Head of Programmes (English Language)
Dai Smith
Head of News & Current Affairs *Aled Eurig*
Head of Drama *Pedr James*
Series Editor, Pobol y Cwm *William Gwyn*

Headquarters of BBC Wales, with regional centres in Wrexham, Bangor and Swansea. BBC
Wales television produces up to 12 hours of
English language programmes a week, 10 hours
in Welsh for transmission on **S4C** and an
increasing number of hours on network services.
Regular programmes include *Wales Today; Wales
on Saturday* and *Pobol y Cwm* (Welsh-language
soap) on television and *Good Morning Wales;
Good Evening Wales; Post Cyntaf* and *Post
Prynhawn* on radio.

Bangor
Broadcasting House, Meirion Road, Bangor,
Gwynedd LL57 2BY
☎01248 370880   Fax 01248 351443
Head of Centre *Marian Wyn Jones*

BBC West/BBC South/BBC South West/BBC South East

The four regional television stations, BBC
West, BBC South, BBC South West and BBC
South East produce more than 1100 hours of
television each year, including the nightly news
magazine programmes, as well as regular 30-
minute local current affairs programmes and
parliamentary programmes. The leisure programme *Out + About* is also produced regionally. The region operates a comprehensive local
radio service. The four stations all have a 'bi-
media' approach – which means that both
radio and television share their resources – as

well as a range of correspondents specialising in health, education, business, local government, home affairs and the environment.

BBC West (Bristol)
Broadcasting House, Whiteladies Road,
Bristol BS8 2LR
☎0117 9732211

Head of Regional and Local Programmes
Leo Devine (BBC West, BBC Radio Bristol, BBC Somerset Sound, BBC Radio Gloucestershire and BBC Wiltshire Sound)
Editor, Newsgathering *Ian Cameron*
Series Producer, Close Up West
James MacAlpine

BBC South (Southampton)
Broadcasting House, Havelock Road,
Southampton, Hampshire SO14 7PU
☎01703 226201

Head of Regional and Local Programmes
Andy Griffee (BBC South, BBC Solent and BBC Southern Counties Radio)
Editors, Newsgathering *Mia Costello, Lee Desty*
Series Producer, Southern Eye *Peter Pitt*

BBC South West (Plymouth)
Broadcasting House, Seymour Road,
Mannamead, Plymouth, Devon PL3 5BD
☎01752 229201

Head of Regional and Local Programmes
Eve Turner (BBC South West, BBC Radio Devon, BBC Radio Cornwall, BBC Radio Guernsey and BBC Radio Jersey)
Editor, Newsgathering *Roger Clark*
Editor, Current Affairs *Simon Willis*

BBC South East (Elstree)
Elstree Centre, Clarendon Road,
Borehamwood, Hertfordshire WD6 1JF
☎0181 953 6100

Head of Regional and Local Programmes
Jane Mote (Responsible for BBC South East, BBC Radio Kent, BBC Thames Valley FM and BBC GLR)
Editor, Newsgathering *Peter Solomons*
Executive Producer, First Sight
John Samson

BBC World Service
PO Box 76, Bush House, Strand, London
WC2B 4PH
☎0171 240 3456   Fax 0171 557 1900
Website: www.bbc.co.uk/worldservice

Chief Executive *Mark Byford*
Director, World Service News & Programme Commissioning *Bob Jobbins*

The World Service broadcasts in English and 43 other languages. The English service is round-the-clock, with news and current affairs as the main component. With around 140 million listeners, excluding countries where research is not possible, it reaches a bigger audience than its five closest competitors combined. The World Service is increasingly available throughout the world on local FM stations, via satellite and on-line as well as through short-wave frequencies. Coverage includes world business, politics, people/events/opinions, development issues, the international scene, developments in science and technology, sport, religion, music, drama, the arts. BBC World Service broadcasting is financed by a grant-in-aid voted by Parliament amounting to £165.9 million for 1999/2000.

If you have an idea for a feature programme or series, please direct your enquiry to: Radio News Features on 0171 257 2203.

BBC Local Radio
Henry Wood House, 3 & 6 Langham Place,
London W1A 1AA
☎0171 580 4468
Website: www.bbc.co/england

There are 39 local BBC radio stations in England transmitting on FM and medium wave. These present local news, information and entertainment to local audiences and reflect the life of the communities they serve. Each has its own newsroom which supplies local bulletins and national news service. Many have specialist producers. A comprehensive list of programmes for each is unavailable and would soon be out of date. For general information on programming, contact the relevant station direct.

BBC Asian Network
BBC Pebble Mill, Birmingham B5 7SH
☎0121 432 8558   Fax 0121 432 8185
Email: asian.network@bbc.co.uk
Website: www.bbc.co.uk/england/asiannetwork

Also at: Epic House, Charles Street, Leicester
LE1 3SH
☎0116 2516688   Fax 0116 2532004
Managing Editor *Vijay Sharma*

Commenced broadcasting in November 1996 to a Midlands audience with programmes in English, Bengali, Gujerati, Hindi, Punjabi and Urdu.

BBC Radio Bristol

PO Box 194, Bristol BS99 7QT
☎0117 9741111   Fax 0117 9732549
Email: radio.bristol@bbc.co.uk
Website: www.bbc.co.uk/england/radiobristol
Managing Editor *Jenny Lacey*
Wide range of feature material used.

BBC Radio Cambridgeshire

PO Box 96, 104 Hills Road, Cambridge
CB2 1LD
☎01223 259696   Fax 01223 460832
Email: Cambs@bbc.co.uk
Website: www.bbc.co.uk/england/
   radiocambridgeshire
Editor *Andrew Wilson*

Short stories are broadcast occasionally.

BBC Radio Cleveland

Broadcasting House, PO Box 95FM,
Middlesbrough, Cleveland TS1 5DG
☎01642 225211   Fax 01642 211356
Email: radio.cleveland@bbc.co.uk
Website: www.bbc.co.uk/england/
   radiocleveland

Managing Editor *David Peel*

Material used is almost exclusively local to
Cleveland, Co. Durham and North Yorkshire,
and written by local writers. Contributions welcome for *House Call* (Sundays 5–6 pm, presented
by Bill Hunter). Poetry and the occasional short
story are included.

BBC Radio Cornwall

Phoenix Wharf, Truro, Cornwall TR1 1UA
☎01872 275421   Fax 01872 275045
Email: radio.cornwall@bbc.co.uk
Website: www.bbc.co.uk/england/
   radiocornwall

Senior Broadcast Journalists *Pauline Causey,*
Lidia Rapecki, Andy Farrant, Daphne Skinnard

On air from 1983 serving Cornwall and the Isles
of Scilly. The station broadcasts a news/talk
format 18 hours a day on 103.9/95.2 FM. Chris
Blount's afternoon programme includes interviews with local authors and arts-related features
on Cornish themes.

BBC Coventry & Warwickshire

Holt Court, Greyfriars Road, Coventry
CV1 2WR
☎01203 860086   Fax 01203 570100
Email: coventry.warwickshire@bbc.co.uk
Website: www.bbc.co.uk/england/
   coventrywarwickshire

Managing Editor *David Robey*
Senior Editor *Stuart Linnell*

News, current affairs, public service information and community involvement, relevant to
its broadcast area: Coventry and Warwickshire.
Occasionally uses the work of local writers,
though cannot handle large volumes of unsolicited material. Any material commissioned
will need to be strong in local interest and
properly geared to broadcasting.

BBC Radio Cumbria

Annetwell Street, Carlisle, Cumbria CA3 8BB
☎01228 592444   Fax 01228 511195
Email: radio.cumbria@bbc.co.uk
Website: www.bbc.co.uk/england/
   radiocumbria

Editor *Nigel Dyson*

Occasional opportunities for plays and short
stories are advertised on-air. No outlet for literary material with the exception of *Write*
Now, a weekly 30-minute local writing programme broadcast on Sundays at 17.30.

BBC Radio Cymru

Broadcasting House, Llandaff, Cardiff
CF5 2YQ
☎01222 322000   Fax 01222 322473
Email: radio.cymru@bbc.co.uk
Website: www.bbc.co.uk/cymru/radio/
   index.shtml

Editor *Aled Glynne Davies*
Editor, Radio Cymru News *Wil Morgan*

Welsh and English-language programmes,
including *Post Cyntaf; Jonsi a Nia; Chwaraeon*
and *Gwyndaf Roberts*.

BBC Radio Derby

PO Box 269, Derby DE1 3HL
☎01332 361111   Fax 01332 290794
Email: radio.derby@bbc.co.uk
Website: www.bbc.co.uk/england/radioderby

Managing Editor *Mike Bettison*

News and information (the backbone of the
station's output), local sports coverage, daily
magazine and phone-ins, minority interest,
Asian and West Indian weekly programmes.

BBC Radio Devon

PO Box 5, Broadcasting House, Seymour
Road, Plymouth, Devon PL3 5YQ
☎01752 260323   Fax 01752 234599
Email: radio.devon@bbc.co.uk
Website: www.bbc.co.uk/england/radiodevon

Managing Editor *John Lilley*

Short stories – up to 1000 words from local authors only – used weekly on the Sunday afternoon show (2.05–3.30 pm). Contact *Becky Newell*.

BBC Essex

198 New London Road, Chelmsford, Essex CM2 9XB
☎01245 262393   Fax 01245 492983
Email: essex@bbc.co.uk
Website: www.bbc.co.uk/england/essex

Editor *Margaret Hyde*

Provides no regular outlets for writers but mounts special projects from time to time; these are well publicised on the air.

BBC Radio Foyle

8 Northland Road, Londonderry BT48 7JD
☎01504 262244   Fax 01504 378666

Manager *Ana Leddy*
News Producers *Felicity McCall, Paul McFadden*
Arts/Book Reviews *Frank Galligan, Colum Arbuckle*
Features *Michael Bradley*

Radio Foyle broadcasts about seven hours of original material a day, seven days a week to the north west of Northern Ireland. Other programmes are transmitted simultaneously with Radio Ulster. The output ranges from news, sport, and current affairs to live music recordings and arts reviews.

BBC Radio Gloucestershire

London Road, Gloucester GL1 1SW
☎01452 308585   Fax 01452 306541
Email: radio.gloucestershire@bbc.co.uk
Website: www.bbc.co.uk/england/radiogloucestershire

Managing Editor *Bob Lloyd-Smith*

News and information covering the large variety of interests and concerns in Gloucestershire. Leisure, sport and music, plus African-Caribbean and Asian interests. Regular book reviews and interviews with local authors.

BBC GLR

PO Box 94.9, 35c Marylebone High Street, London W1A 4LG
☎0171 224 2424   Fax 0171 935 1779
Email: glr@bbc.co.uk
Website: www.bbc.co.uk/ england/glr

Managing Editor *Steve Panton*
Assistant Editor (News) *Martin Shaw*

Assistant Editor (General Programmes) *Suzanne Gilfillan*

Greater London Radio was launched in 1988. It broadcasts news, information, travel bulletins, sport and rock music to Greater London and the Home Counties.

BBC GMR

PO Box 951, Manchester M60 1SD
☎0161 200 2000   Fax 0161 236 5804
Email: gmr@bbc.co.uk
Website: www.bbc.co.uk/england/gmr

Editor *Karen Hannah*

BBC Radio Guernsey

Commerce House, Les Banques, St Peter Port, Guernsey, Channel Islands GY1 2HS
☎01481 728977   Fax 01481 713557
Email: radio.guernsey@bbc.co.uk
Website: www.bbc.co.uk/england/radioguernsey

Managing Editor *Denzil Dudley*

BBC Hereford & Worcester

Hylton Road, Worcester WR2 5WW
☎01905 748485   Fax 01905 748006
Also at: 43 Broad Street, Hereford HR4 9HH
☎01432 355252   Fax 01432 356446
Email: BBC.Hereford.Worcs@bbc.co.uk
Website: www.bbc.co.uk/england/herefordworcester

Managing Editor *James Coghill*

Holds competitions on an occasional basis for short stories, plays or dramatised documentaries with a local flavour.

BBC Radio Humberside

9 Chapel Street, Hull, North Humberside HU1 3NU
☎01482 323232   Fax 01482 621403
Email: radio.humberside@bbc.co.uk
Website: www.bbc.co.uk/england/radiohumberside

Editor *Barrie Stephenson*

Occasionally broadcasts short stories by local writers and holds competitions for local amateur authors and playwrights.

BBC Radio Jersey

18 Parade Road, St Helier, Jersey, Channel Islands JE2 3PL
☎01534 870000   Fax 01534 32569
Email: radio.jersey@bbc.co.uk
Website: www.bbc.co.uk/england/radiojersey

Managing Editor *Denzil Dudley*
Senior Producer *Claire Stanley*
Local news, current affairs and community items.

BBC Radio Kent
Sun Pier, Chatham, Kent ME4 4EZ
☎01634 830505   Fax 01634 830573
Email: radio.kent@bbc.co.uk
Website: www.bbc.co.uk/england/radiokent
Editor, Local Services *David Farwig*
Occasional commissions are made for local interest documentaries and other one-off programmes.

BBC Radio Lancashire
Darwen Street, Blackburn, Lancashire BB2 2EA
☎01254 262411   Fax 01254 680821
Email: radio.lancashire@bbc.co.uk
Website: www.bbc.co.uk/england/
   radiolancashire
Editor *Steve Taylor*
Journalism-based radio station, interested in interviews with local writers. Also *Write Now*, a weekly half-hour regional local writing programme, shared with BBC Radio Cumbria and BBC Radio Merseyside (see BBC Radio Merseyside).

BBC Radio Leeds
Broadcasting House, Woodhouse Lane, Leeds, West Yorkshire LS2 9PN
☎0113 2442131   Fax 0113 2420652
Email: radio.leeds@bbc.co.uk
Website: www.bbc.co.uk/england/radioleeds
Managing Editor *Ashley Peatfield*
One of the country's biggest local radio stations, BBC Radio Leeds was also one of the first, coming on air in the 1960s as something of an experimental venture. The station is 'all talk', with a comprehensive news, sport and information service as the backbone of its daily output. BBC Radio Leeds has been a regular finalist for the title of Sony Regional Station of the Year. Has also won two Gold Sonys for best presentation. For the past six years, it has won the National Award for best speech-based religious affairs programmes.

BBC Radio Leicester
Epic House, Charles Street, Leicester LE1 3SH
☎0116 2516688
Fax 0116 2513632/2511463 (News)
Email: radio.leicester@bbc.co.uk

Website: www.bbc.co.uk/england/radioleicester
Managing Editor *Liam McCarthy*
The first local station in Britain. Concentrates on speech-based programmes in the morning and on a music/speech mix in the afternoon.

BBC Radio Lincolnshire
PO Box 219, Newport, Lincoln LN1 3XY
☎01522 511411   Fax 01522 511726
Email: radio.lincolnshire@bbc.co.uk
Website: www.bbc.co.uk/england/
   radiolincolnshire
Managing Editor *David Wilkinson*
Unsolicited material considered only if locally relevant. Maximum 1000 words: straight narrative preferred, ideally with a topical content.

BBC Radio Manchester
See **BBC GMR**

BBC Radio Merseyside
55 Paradise Street, Liverpool L1 3BP
☎0151 708 5500   Fax 0151 794 0988
Email: radio.merseyside@bbc.co.uk
Website: www.bbc.co.uk/england/
   radiomerseyside
Editor *Mick Ord*
Write Now, a weekly 25-minute regional writers' programme, is produced at Radio Merseyside and also broadcast on BBC Radio Cumbria and BBC Radio Lancashire. Short stories (maximum 1200 words), plus poetry and features on writing. Contact *Jenny Collins* by post at the address above.

BBC Radio Newcastle
Broadcasting Centre, Barrack Road, Newcastle upon Tyne NE99 1RN
☎0191 232 4141
Email: radio.newcastle@bbc.co.uk
Website: www.bbc.co.uk/england/
   radionewcastle
Editor *Tony Fish*
Senior Producer (Programmes) *Jon Harte*

BBC Radio Norfolk
Norfolk Tower, Surrey Street, Norwich, Norfolk NR1 3PA
☎01603 617411   Fax 01603 633692
Email: norfolk@bbc.co.uk
Website: www.bbc.co.uk/england/radionorfolk
Editor *David Clayton*
Good local material welcome for features/documentaries, but must relate directly to Norfolk.

BBC Radio Northampton

Broadcasting House, Abington Street,
Northampton NN1 2BH
☎01604 239100   Fax 01604 230709
Email: northampton@bbc.co.uk
Website: www.bbc.co.uk/england/
   radionorthampton

Editor, Local Services *Mike Day*
Senior Broadcast Journalists *Sarah Foster,*
Jim Hawkins, Matthew Price

Books of local interest are regularly featured.
Authors and poets are interviewed on merit.
Poems and short stories are reviewed occasion-
ally, but not broadcast.

BBC Radio Nottingham

London Road, Nottingham NG2 4UU
☎0115 9550500   Fax 0115 9021983
Email: radio.nottingham@bbc.co.uk
Website: www.bbc.co.uk/england/
   radionottingham

Editor *Kate Squire*

Rarely broadcasts scripted pieces of any kind
but interviews with authors form a regular part
of the station's output.

BBC Radio Scotland (Dumfries)

Elmbank, Lover's Walk, Dumfries DG1 1NZ
☎01387 268008   Fax 01387 252568
Senior Producer *Glenn Cooksley*
News Editor *Willie Johnston*

Previously Radio Solway. The station mainly
outputs news bulletins (four daily). Changes have
seen the station become more of a production
centre with programmes being made for Radio
Scotland as well as BBC Radio 2 and 5 Live.
Freelancers of a high standard, familiar with
Radio Scotland, should contact the producer.

BBC Radio Scotland (Orkney)

Castle Street, Kirkwall, Orkney KW15 1DF
☎01856 873939   Fax 01856 872908
Senior Producer *John Fergusson*

Regular programmes include *Around Orkney*
(weekday news programme); *Bruck* (magazine
programme); *Yesterday's Yarns* (local archive
material).

BBC Radio Scotland (Selkirk)

Municipal Buildings, High Street, Selkirk
TD7 4JX
☎01750 21884   Fax 01750 22400
Senior Producer *Carol Wightman*

Formerly BBC Radio Tweed. Produces weekly

international travel and holiday programme, *The
Case for Packing*.

BBC Radio Scotland (Shetland)

Brentham House, Lerwick, Shetland
ZE1 0LR
☎01595 694747   Fax 01595 694307
Senior Producer *Mary Blance*

Regular programmes include *Good Evening
Shetland*. An occasional books programme highlights the activities of local writers and writers'
groups.

BBC Radio Sheffield

60 Westbourne Road, Sheffield S10 2QU
☎0114 2686185   Fax 0114 2664375
Email: radio.sheffield@bbc.co.uk
Website: www.bbc.co.uk/england/radiosheffield

Editor *Barry Stockdale*

Weekly feature, *Write On* (Tuesday, 10.30 to
11.00 am).

BBC Radio Shropshire

2–4 Boscobel Drive, Shrewsbury, Shropshire
SY1 3TT
☎01743 248484   Fax 01743 271702
Email: radio.shropshire@bbc.co.uk
Website: www.bbc.co.uk/england/
   radioshropshire

Editor *Barbara Taylor*

Unsolicited literary material very rarely used,
and then only if locally relevant.

BBC Radio Solent

Broadcasting House, Havelock Road,
Southampton, Hampshire SO14 7PW
☎01703 631311   Fax 01703 339648
2Email: radio.solent@bbc.co.uk
Website: www.bbc.co.uk/england/radiosolent

Managing Editor *Chris Van Schaick*

BBC Somerset Sound

14 Paul Street, Taunton, Somerset TA1 3PF
☎01823 252437   Fax 01823 332539
Email: richard.austin@bbc.co.uk
Website: www.bbc.co.uk/england/
   radiobristol/history.shtml

Senior Producer *Richard Austin*

Informal, speech-based programming, with
strong news and current affairs output and
regular local-interest features, including local
writing. Poetry and short stories on the *Adam
Thomas Programme*.

BBC Southern Counties Radio

Broadcasting Centre, Guildford, Surrey
GU2 5AP
☎01483 306306   Fax 01483 304952
Email: southern.counties.radio@bbc.co.uk
Website: www.bbc.co.uk/england/
southerncounties

Managing Editor *Mike Hapgood*

Formerly known as BBC Radio Sussex and
Surrey. Regular programmes include three
individual breakfast shows: *Breakfast Live in
Brighton with Jo Anne Good/in Surrey with Adrian
Love/in Sussex with John Radford.*

BBC Radio Stoke

Cheapside, Hanley, Stoke on Trent,
Staffordshire ST1 1JJ
☎01782 208080   Fax 01782 289115
Email: radio.stoke@bbc.co.uk
Website: www.bbc.co.uk/england/radiostoke

Managing Editor *Mark Hurrell*

Emphasis on news, current affairs and local
topics. Music represents one fifth of total output. Unsolicited material of local interest is
welcome – send to managing editor.

BBC Radio Suffolk

Broadcasting House, St Matthews Street,
Ipswich, Suffolk IP1 3EP
☎01473 250000   Fax 01473 210887
Email: suffolk@bbc.co.uk
Website: www.bbc.co.uk/england/radiosuffolk

Managing Editor *Keith Beech*

Strongly speech-based, dealing with news, current affairs, community issues, the arts, agriculture, commerce, travel, sport and leisure.
Programmes often carry interviews with writers.

BBC Thames Valley

269 Banbury Road, Oxford OX2 7DW
☎0645 311444   Fax 0645 311555
Email: thames.valley@bbc.co.uk
Website: www.bbc.co.uk/england/thamesvalley

Programme Editor *David Clargo*

The station has introduced local programmes for
Berkshire and Oxfordshire at peak times. No
opportunities at present as the outlet for short
stories has been discontinued for the time being
though the station frequently carries interviews
with authors and offers books as prizes.

BBC Three Counties Radio

PO Box 3CR, Hastings Street, Luton,
Bedfordshire LU1 5XL
☎01582 441000   Fax 01582 401467
Email: 3cr@bbc.co.uk

Website: www.bbc.co.uk/england/threecounties

Managing Editor *Mark Norman*

Encourages freelance contributions from the
community across a wide range of radio output, including interview and feature material.
The station *very* occasionally broadcasts drama.
Stringent local criteria are applied in selection.
Particularly interested in historical topics (five
minutes maximum).

BBC Radio Ulster

Broadcasting House, Ormeau Avenue, Belfast
BT2 8HQ
☎01232 338000   Fax 01232 338800

Head of Broadcasting *Anna Carragher*
Head of Production *Paul Evans*

Programmes broadcast from 6.30 am – midnight
weekdays and from 7.55 am – midnight at weekends. Radio Ulster has won seven Sony awards
in recent years. Programmes include: *Good
Morning Ulster; John Bennett; Gerry Anderson; Talk
Back; Newsbreak; Just Jones; Evening Extra* and
Across the Line.

BBC Radio Wales

Broadcasting House, Llandaff, Cardiff
CF5 2YQ
☎01222 322000   Fax 01222 322960
Email: radio.wales@bbc.co.uk
Website: www.bbc.co.uk/wales/radio

Editor *Daniel Jones*
Editor, Radio Wales News *Geoff Williams*

Broadcasts regular news bulletins Monday to
Friday and until lunchtime on Saturday.
Programmes include *Good Morning Wales; Wales
at One; Adam Walton* and *The Weekenders.*

BBC Wiltshire Sound

Broadcasting House, Prospect Place, Swindon,
Wiltshire SN1 3RW
☎01793 513626   Fax 01793 513650
Email: wiltshire.sound@bbc.co.uk
Website: www.bbc.co.uk/england/
wiltshiresound

Editor *Sandy Milne*

Regular programmes include: *Salisbury Today;
Saturday Matinee; Wiltshire Today; Wiltshire at One.*

BBC Radio WM

PO Box 206, Birmingham B5 7SD
☎0121 432 9000   Fax 0121 472 3174
Email: radio.wm@bbc.co.uk
Website: www.bbc.co.uk/england/radiowm

Managing Editor *David Robey*

News and current affairs station.

BBC Radio York

20 Bootham Row, York YO30 7BR
☎01904 641351   Fax 01904 610937
Email: radio.york@bbc.co.uk
Website: www.bbc.co.uk/england/radioyork

Editor *Jane Sampson*
Senior Broadcast Journalist *Martin Cooper*

A regular outlet for short stories of up to 10
minutes' duration. They must be locally written or based (i.e. North Yorkshire).

Independent Television

Anglia Television

Anglia House, Norwich, Norfolk NR1 3JG
☎01603 615151   Fax 01603 631032

London office: 48 Leicester Square, London
WC2H 7FB
☎0171 389 8555   Fax 0171 930 8499

Email: angliatv@angliatv.co.uk
Website: www.anglia.tv.co.uk

Managing Director *Graham Creelman*
Director of Programmes *Malcolm Allsop*
Controller of News *Guy Adams*

Anglia Television is a major producer of programmes for the ITV network, including *Tricia,
Sunday Morning* and *Survival*. Network dramas
for 1998 included: *Where the Heart Is* and
Touching Evil.

Border Television plc

Television Centre, Durranhill, Carlisle,
Cumbria CA1 3NT
☎01228 525101   Fax 01228 541384
Website: http:www.border-tv.com

Chairman *James Graham OBE*
Head of Programmes *Neil Robinson*

Border's programming concentrates on documentaries rather than drama. Most scripts are
supplied in-house but occasionally there are
commissions. Apart from notes, writers should
not submit written work until their ideas have
been fully discussed.

Carlton Television

101 St Martin's Lane, London WC2N 4AZ
☎0171 240 4000   Fax 0171 240 4171
Website: www.carltontv.co.uk

Chairman *Nigel Walmsley*
Chief Executive *Clive Jones*
Director of Programmes *Steve Hewlett*

Carlton Television comprises: Carlton Broadcasting which is responsible for the ITV licence

for London and the South East, plus **Central
Broadcasting** and **Westcountry** (see entries);
Carlton Productions (see entry under **Film,
TV and Video Production Companies**);
Carlton Sales which sells airtime and sponsor-
ship. Also runs two facilities operations: Carlton
Studios in Nottingham, supplying studios and
related services and Carlton 021, the largest com-
mercial operator of Outside Broadcast Services in
Europe.

Central Broadcasting

Central Court, Gas Street, Birmingham B1 2JT
☎0121 643 9898   Fax 0121 634 4957
Website: www.carltontv.co.uk

Managing Director *Ian Squires*

Part of **Carlton Television**. Responsible for the
ITV licence for East, West and South Midlands.
Ideas for programmes should be addressed to
Carlton Productions (see entry under **Film,
TV and Video Production Companies**).
Regular regional programmes include *Central
Weekend; Asian Eye; Heart of the Country; Back to
the Present*. Network drama includes *Peak Practice*
and *Picking up the Pieces*.

Channel 4

124 Horseferry Road, London SW1P 2TX
☎0171 396 4444   Fax 0171 306 8356
Website: www.channel4.com

Director of Programmes *Tim Gardam*
Deputy Director of Programmes
   Karen Brown
Head of Film *Paul Webster*
Head of Entertainment *Kevin Lygo*

COMMISSIONING EDITORS
Independent Film & Video *Adam Barker*
Arts *Janey Walker*
Head of Drama and Animation *Gub Neal*
Entertainment *Caroline Leddy*
Documentaries *Peter Dale*
News & Current Affairs *David Lloyd*
Sport *Mike Sharman*
Multicultural Programmes *Yasmin Anwar*
Religion & Features *Peter Grimsdale*
Controller of Acquisition *June Dromgoole*

When Channel 4 started broadcasting as a
national channel in November 1982, it was the
first new TV service to be launched in Britain
for 18 years. Under the 1981 Broadcasting Act
it was required to cater for tastes and audiences
not previously served by the other broadcast
channels, and to provide a suitable proportion
of educational programmes. Channel 4 does not
make any of its own programmes; they are
commissioned from independent production

companies, from the ITV sector, or co-produced with other organisations. The role of the commissioning editors is to sift through proposals for programmes and see interesting projects through to broadcast. Regulated by the ITC.

Channel 5
22 Long Acre, London WC2E 9LY
☎0171 550 5555 Fax 0171 497 5222
Chief Executive David Elstein
Director of Programmes Dawn Airey
Controller of Children's Programmes
Nick Wilson
Controller of Features and Arts
Michael Attwell
Controller of News, Current Affairs &
Documentaries Chris Shaw
Controller of Drama Corinne Hollingworth

Channel 5 Broadcasting Ltd, led by Greg Dyke of Pearson TV, won the franchise for Britain's third commercial terrestrial television station in 1995 and came on air at the end of March 1997. Regular programmes include *Family Affairs* (Monday to Friday soap opera) and *Good Afternoon* (daytime magazine show), plus documentaries, drama, films, children's programmes, sport and entertainment.

Channel Television
The Television Centre, La Pouquelaye, St Helier, Jersey, Channel Islands JE1 3ZD
☎01534 816816 Fax 01534 816817
Also at: Television House, Bulwer Avenue, St Sampsons, Guernsey, Channel Islands GY2 4LA
☎01481 41888 Fax 01481 41878
Website: www.channeltv.co.uk
Chief Executive John Henwood
Managing Director Michael Lucas
Head of Programmes Karen Rankine
Head of Sales Gordon De Ste Croix
Head of Transmission & Resources
Tim Ringsdore

Channel Television is the Independent Television broadcaster to the Channel Islands. The station has been broadcasting for 35 years and with its remit to serve 143,000 residents, most of whom live on the main islands, Jersey, Guernsey, Alderney and Sark, Channel Television has pushed forward the frontiers of community television on ITV. The station has a weekly reach of more than 94% with local programmes (in the region of 6 hours each week) at the heart of the ITV service to the islands. Produced two series of the soap, *Island*, for CITV.

In 1997 Channel Television began transmitting a subtitling service for some of the station's local programmes including the weekday daily flagship news magazine, *Channel Report*.

GMTV
The London Television Centre, Upper Ground, London SE1 9TT
☎0171 827 7000 Fax 0171 827 7001
Managing Director Christopher Stoddart
Director of Programmes Peter McHugh
Managing Editor John Scammell

Winner of the national breakfast television franchise. Jointly owned by Scottish Television, Carlton, Granada, The Guardian and Disney. GMTV took over from TV-AM on 1 January 1993, with live programming from 6 am to 9.25 am. Regular news headlines, current affairs, topical features, showbiz and lifestyle, sports and business, quizzes and competitions, travel and weather reports.

Grampian Television Limited
Queen's Cross, Aberdeen AB15 4XJ
☎01224 846846 Fax 01224 846800
Website: www.scottishmediagroup.com
Controller Derrick Thomson
Head of News Bert Ovenstone
Head of Current Affairs Alan Cowie

Extensive regional news and reports including farming, fishing and sports, interviews and leisure features, various light entertainment, Gaelic and religious programmes, and live coverage of the Scottish political, economic and industrial scene. Serves the area stretching from Fife to Shetland. Regular programmes include *North Tonight; Scotland's Larder* and *Telefios.*

Granada Television
Quay Street, Manchester M60 9EA
☎0161 832 7211 Fax 0161 953 0283
Website: www.granadatv.co.uk
Director of Programmes Simon Shaps
Director of Production Max Graesser
Director of Channel Programming,
GTP/Controller of Lifestyle
Programmes, GTV James Hunt
Controller of Drama Simon Lewis
Controller of Factual Programmes
Charles Tremayme
Controller of Comedy Andy Harries
Controller of Entertainment Duncan Gray

Opportunities for freelance writers are not great but mss from professional writers will be considered. All mss should be addressed to the head of scripts. Regular programmes include *Coronation Street; World in Action* and *This Morning.*

HTV Wales

Television Centre, Culverhouse Cross, Cardiff
CF5 6XJ
☎01222 590590   Fax 01222 597183
Website: http:www.htv.co.uk

Managing Director *Menna Richards*

HTV (West)

Television Centre, Bath Road, Bristol BS4 3HG
☎0117 9722722   Fax 0117 9722400

Managing Director *Jeremy Payne*
Controller of Children's Programmes
   Dan Maddicott
Controller of Factual Programmes
   Tom Archer
Director of Programmes, Partridge Films
   Michael Rosenberg

Drama, children's, factual and natural history
programming is produced for national and
international markets. Programmes include
Wycliffe; *The Famous Five* and *The Slow Norris*.
Now part of the UNM Group (United News
and Media).

ITN (Independent Television News Ltd)

200 Gray's Inn Road, London WC1X 8XZ
☎0171 833 3000
Website: www.itn.co.uk

Chief Executive *Stewart Purvis*
Editor-in-Chief *Richard Tait*
Editor, ITN News for ITV *Nigel Dacre*
Editor, Channel 4 News *Jim Gray*
Editor, Channel 5 News *Gary Rogers*

Provider of the main national and international
news for ITV, Channel 4 and Channel 5 and
radio news for IRN. Programmes on ITV:
*Lunchtime News; Evening News; Nightly News;
ITN Morning News*, plus regular news summaries,
and three programmes a day at weekends. Programmes on Channel 4: in-depth news analysis
programmes, including *Channel 4 News* and *The
Big Breakfast*. Programmes on Channel 5: *5 News
Early; 5 News at Noon; 5 News* plus regular
updates. ITN also provides the World News, for
Public Television in the USA, and has operating
control of Euronews, Europe's only pan-European broadcaster.

LWT (London Weekend Television)

The London Television Centre, Upper
Ground, London SE1 9LT
☎0171 620 1620
Website: www.lwt.co.uk

Chief Operating Officer *Charles Allen*
Managing Director *Liam Hamilton*

Director of Programmes *Marcus Plantin*
Controller of Entertainment *Nigel Lythgoe*
Controller of Drama *Jo Wright*
Controller of Arts *Melvyn Bragg*
Controller of Factual Programmes *Jim Allen*

Makers of current affairs, entertainment and
drama series such as *Blind Date; Surprise Surprise;
The Knock; London's Burning* also *The South Bank
Show* and *Jonathan Dimbleby*. Provides a large
proportion of ITV's drama and light entertainment, and also for BSkyB and Channel 4.

Meridian Broadcasting

Television Centre, Southampton, Hampshire
SO14 0PZ
☎01703 222555   Fax 01703 335050
London office: Ludgate House, 245 Blackfriars
Road, London SE1 9UY
☎0171 921 5000
Email: dutyoffice@meridiantv.com
Website: www.meridian.tv.co.uk

Managing Director *Mary McAnally*
Director of Broadcasting *Richard Platt*
Director of Programmes *Richard Simons*
Director of News Strategy *Jim Raven*

Meridian's newly refurbished studios in Southampton provide a base for network and regional
productions. Regular regional programmes
include the award-winning news service,
Meridian Tonight; Countryways and *The Pier*.

S4C

Parc Ty Glas, Llanishen, Cardiff CF4 5DU
☎01222 747444   Fax 01222 754444
Website: www.s4c.co.uk

Chief Executive *Huw Jones*
Director of Production *Huw Eirug*

The Welsh 4th Channel, established by the
Broadcasting Act 1980, is responsible for a
schedule of Welsh and English programmes on
the Fourth Channel in Wales. Known as S4C,
the service is made up of about 30 hours per
week of Welsh language programmes and more
than 85 hours of English language output from
Channel 4. Ten hours a week of the Welsh programmes are provided by the BBC; the remain-
der are purchased from HTV and independent
producers. Drama, comedy and documentary are
all part of S4C's programming.

Scottish Television Ltd

Cowcaddens, Glasgow G2 3PR
☎0141 300 3000   Fax 0141 300 3030
London office: 20 Lincoln's Inn Field, London
WC2A 3ED
☎0171 446 7000   Fax 0171 446 7021

Website: www.stv.co.uk
Chief Executive *Andrew Flanagan*
Managing Director, Broadcasting
Donald Emslie
Controller, Regional Programming
Sandy Ross
Controller, Scottish Television
Scott Ferguson
Controller of Drama *Philip Hinchcliffe*
Head of Features & Entertainment
Agnes Wilkie
Senior News Producer *Paul McKinney*
Head of Sport & General Factual
Programmes *Denis Mooney*

An increasing number of STV programmes such as *Taggart* and *McCallum* are now networked nationally. Programme coverage includes drama, religion, news, sport, outside broadcasts, special features, entertainment and the arts, education and Gaelic programmes. Produces many one-offs for ITV and Channel 4.

Teletext Ltd

101 Farm Lane, Fulham, London SW6 1QJ
☎0171 386 5000   Fax 0171 386 5002
Website: www.teletext.co.uk
Managing Director *Mike Stewart*
Editor-in-Chief *Graham Lovelace*

On 1 January 1993, Teletext Ltd took over the electronic publishing service for both ITV and Channel 4. Transmits a wide range of news pages and features, including current affairs, sport, TV listings, weather, travel, holidays, finance, games, competitions, etc. Provides a regional service to each of the ITV regions.

Tyne Tees Television

Television Centre, Newcastle upon Tyne
NE1 2AL
☎0191 261 0181   Fax 0191 261 2302
Email: tyne.tees@granadamedia.com
Website: www.granadamedia.com
Managing Director *Margaret Fay*
Director of Broadcasting and Controller of
News & Current Affairs *Graeme Thompson*
Head of Network Features *Malcolm Wright*
Head of Young People's Programmes
Lesley Oakden
Head of Training & Community Affairs
Annie Wood
Head of Sport *Roger Tames*

Programming covers religion, politics, news and current affairs, regional documentaries, business, entertainment, sport and arts. Regular programmes include *North East Tonight with Mike Neville* and *Around the House* (politics).

UTV (Ulster Television)

Havelock House, Ormeau Road, Belfast
BT7 1EB
☎01232 328122   Fax 01232 246695
Website: www.utvlive.com
Controller of Programming *Alan Bremner*
Head of News & Current Affairs
Rob Morrison
Head of General Programmes *Philip Morrow*

Regular programmes on news and current affairs, politics, sport, education, music, light entertainment, arts, health and local culture.

Westcountry Television

Langage Science Park, Western Wood Way,
Plymouth, Devon PL7 5BG
☎01752 333333   Fax 01752 333444
Website: www.westcountry.co.uk/index1.html
Managing Director *Mark Haskell*
Director of Programmes *Jane McCloskey*
Director of News & Current Affairs
Brad Higgins

Part of **Carlton Television**. Came on air in January 1993. News, current affairs, documentary and religious programming. Regular programmes include *Westcountry Live; Westcountry Focus; Westcountry Showcase*.

Yorkshire Television

The Television Centre, Leeds, West Yorkshire
LS3 1JS
☎0113 2438283   Fax 0113 2445107
London office: Global House, 96–108 Great Suffolk Street, London SE1 0BE
☎0171 578 4304   Fax 0171 578 4320
Website: www.granadamedia.com
Chairman *Charles Allen*
Managing Director *Richard Gregory*
Controller of Drama, YTV *Carolyn Reynolds*
Controller of Drama, Yorkshire Tyne
Tees Productions *Keith Richardson*
Controller of Comedy Drama and Drama
Features *David Reynolds*
Controller of Factual Programmes
Chris Bryer
Head of News & Current Affairs
Clare Morrow
Deputy Controller of Children's, Granada
Media Group *Patrick Titley*

Part of Granada Media Group. Drama series, situation comedies, film productions and long-running series like *Emmerdale* and *Heartbeat*. Always looking for strong writing in these areas, but prefers to find it through an agent. Documentary/current affairs material tends to be supplied by producers; opportunities in these areas are rare but adaptations of published work as a documentary subject are considered. In theory, opportunity exists within series, episode material. Best approach is through a good agent.

Cable and Satellite Television

Asianet
PO Box 38, Greenford, Middlesex UB3 7SP
☎0181 566 9000   Fax 0181 810 5555

Chief Executive Dr Banad Viswanath
Managing Director Deepak Viswanath
Broadcasting since September 1994, Asianet transmits entertainment to the Asian community 24 hours a day in English, Hindi, Gujarati, Punjabi, Bengali and Urdu.

British Sky Broadcasting Ltd (BSkyB)
Grant Way, Isleworth, Middlesex TW7 5QD
☎0171 705 3000   Fax 0171 705 3030
Website: www.sky.co.uk

Managing Director, Sky Networks
  Elisabeth Murdoch
Managing Director, Sky Entertainment
  Ian West
Head of Programming James Baker
General Manager, Broadcasting
  Bruce Steinberg
Chief Executive, British Interactive
  Broadcasting James Ackerman

BSkyB programming is distributed via cable and DTH satellite to 6.88 million homes in the UK and Eire. Launched in 1989, Sky operates 13 wholly-owned channels and 10 joint venture channels. With the launch of SkyDigital in 1998, opportunities increased for many of the joint venture channels to expand hours of transmission.

WHOLLY-OWNED SKY CHANNELS:

Sky Premier
Blockbusting action, comedy and romance, featuring recent box office hits.

Sky MovieMax
Contemporary hit movies, embracing all genres, from Hollywood's major studios.

Sky Cinema
Classic and popular movies from 70 years of cinema, including seasons and retrospectives.

Sky News
Award winning 24-hours news service with hourly bulletins and expert comment.

Sky One
The most frequently watched Sky channel with the accent on family entertainment.

Sky Soap
Romance every weekday afternoon with a mix of classic and contemporary soap operas.

Sky Sports 1/Sky Sports 2/Sky Sports 3
Over 1000 hours of sport a month, much of it exclusively live, across three channels including FA Carling Premiership football, England internationals, Rugby Union and golf.

Sky Travel
Magazine shows and documentaries.

.tv
Entertaining, informative and educational programming for experts and beginners.

PREMIUM CHANNELS
Sky Movies Screen 1, Sky Movies Screen 2, Sky Sports 1, Sky Sports 2.

PREMIUM BONUS CHANNELS
Sky Movies Gold, The Disney Channel – available when you subscribe to both Sky Movies Screen 1 and Sky Movies Screen 2. Sky Sports 3 – available when you subscribe to Sky Sports 1.

THE SKY MULTI-CHANNELS PACKAGE
Sky One; Sky News; The Discovery Channel; The National Geographic Channel; MTV; VH-1; The History Channel; The Sci-Fi Channel; Nickelodeon; Fox Kids Network; The Children's Channel; The Computer Channel; UK Gold; Sky Soap; Sky Travel; UK Living; Granada Good Life; Granada Plus; Granada Men & Motors; The Paramount Comedy Channel; CNBC; EBN; Bravo; Sky Scottish; Challenge TV; CMT; Discovery Home & Leisure; QVC.

CNBC
10 Fleet Place, London EC4M 7QS
☎0171 653 9300   Fax 0171 653 9333
Email: feedback@cnbceurope.com
Website: www.cnbceurope.com

Managing Director Marga McNally

A service of NBC and Dow Jones. 24-hour European financial and corporate news broadcasting. Programmes include Europe Today; Europe This Week; The Tonight Show With Jay Leno.

Cable News Network International
CNN House, 19–22 Rathbone Place, London W1P 1DF
☎0171 637 6800   Fax 0171 637 6868
Website: www.cnn.com

Bureau Chief *Tom Mintier*
Managing Director CNN Financial News
  Europe *Bill Baggitt*

LAUNCHED in 1985 as the international sister network to CNN. Wholly-owned subsidiary of Time Warner Inc. Distributes 24-hour news to more than 149 million households in more than 210 countries and territories. Nearly six hours of programming are originated and produced daily in London: *World News; World Business Today; Inside Europe; Artclub; Pinnacle Europe*, plus 14 two-minute business news updates.

L!VE TV

24th Floor, One Canada Square, Canary Wharf, London E14 5DJ
☎0171 293 3900   Fax 0171 293 3820
Website: www.livetv.co.uk
Managing Director *Mark Cullen*
Director of Programming *Mark Murphy*

24-hour cable channel with an emphasis on upbeat and lively entertainment and information programming. Owned by Mirror Group plc.

Living

160 Great Portland Street, London W1N 5TB
☎0171 299 5000   Fax 0171 299 6000
Website: www.livingtv.co.uk
Head of Programming *Emma Tennant*

Living broadcasts from 6.00 am to midnight daily. Women's magazine programmes, talk shows (including the *Jerry Springer Show*), soaps and films.

MTV Networks Europe Inc

Hawley Crescent, London NW1 8TT
☎0171 284 7777   Fax 0171 284 7788
Website: www.mtv.com
President & Chief Executive *Brent Hansen*

ESTABLISHED 1987. Europe's 24-hour music and youth entertainment channel, available on cable and via satellite. Transmitted from London in English across Europe.

NBC Europe

Unit 1/1, Harbour Yard, Chelsea Harbour, London SW10 0XD
☎0171 352 9205   Fax 0171 352 9628
Chairman *Patrick Cox*
Director of Programming *Bernhard Bertram*

24-hour European broad-based news, information and entertainment service in English, with additional programmes in German and occasional advertisements in Dutch and German.

Travel (Landmark Travel Channel)

66 Newman Street, London W1P 3LA
☎0171 636 5401   Fax 0171 636 6424
Website: www.travelchannel.co.uk

Launched in February 1994. Broadcasts programmes and information on the world of travel. Destinations reports, lifestyle programmes plus food and drink, sport and leisure pursuits.

National Commercial Radio

Classic FM

7 Swallow Place, London W1R 7AA
☎0171 343 9000   Fax 0171 344 2700
Website: www.classicfm.co.uk
Chief Executive *Ralph Bernard*
Programme Director *Steve Orchard*
Head of News *Darren Henley*

Britain's first independent national commercial radio station, it started broadcasting in September 1992. Plays accessible classical music 24 hours a day and broadcasts news, weather, travel, business information, charts, music and book event guides, political/celebrity/general interest talks, features and interviews. Classic has gone well beyond its expectations, attracting 5.14 million listeners a week.

Talk Radio UK

76 Oxford Street, London W1N 0TR
☎0171 636 1089   Fax 0171 636 1053
Website: www.talk-radio.co.uk
C.E.O. *Kelvin MacKenzie*
Programme Director *Bill Ridley*

LAUNCHED in February 1995, Talk Radio is the third national commercial radio station. Broadcasts 24 hours a day with a mix of news, opinions, entertainment, weather, traffic and sport based on studio interviews, celebrity chat and 'the views of the Great British listening audience'.

Virgin Radio

1 Golden Square, London W1R 4DJ
☎0171 434 1215   Fax 0171 434 1197
Website: www.virginradio.com
Chief Executive *John Pearson*
Programme Director *Geoff Holland*

Classic tracks and the best of today's music aimed at an audience of 25–45 year-olds. Acquired by Chris Evans' Ginger Media Group in December 1997, Virgin has seen its audience figures rocket to around 7 million, making it the most successful commercial radio station in the UK.

Independent Local Radio

96.3 Aire FM/Magic 828
PO Box 2000, 51 Burley Road, Leeds, West Yorkshire LS3 1LR
☎0113 2835500   Fax 0113 2835501
Websites: www.airefm.com
  and www.magic828.com
Programme Director *John O'Hara*

Music-based programming. 96.3 Aire FM caters for the 15–34–year–old listener while Magic 828 aims at the 25–44 age group with classic oldies.

Beacon FM/WABC
267 Tettenhall Road, Wolverhampton, West Midlands WV6 0DQ
☎01902 757211   Fax 01902 838266
Website: www.beaconfm.com
Programme Director *Steve Martin*

Part of the GWR Group plc. No outlets for unsolicited literary material at present.

Radio Borders
Tweedside Park, Tweedbank, Galashiels TD1 3TD
☎01896 759444   Fax 01896 759494
Website: www.radioborders.co.uk
Programme Controller *Danny Gallagher*
Head of News *Gordon Brown*

Music-based station with local and national news.

The Breeze
See **Essex FM**

BRMB-FM 96.4/1152 Capital Gold
Radio House, Aston Road North, Birmingham B6 4BZ
☎0121 359 4481   Fax 0121 359 1117
Website: http:www.brmb.co.uk
Programme Controller *Paul Jackson*
News Editor *Gordon Davidson*

Music-based stations; no outlets for writers.

Broadland 102/Classic Gold Amber
St Georges Plain, 47–49 Colegate, Norwich, Norfolk NR3 1DB
☎01603 630621   Fax 01603 666252
Website: www.BROADLAND102.co.uk
Programme Controller *Dave Brown*

Part of GWR Group plc. Popular music programmes and local news only.

1152 Capital Gold
See **BRMB-FM 96.4/1152 Capital Gold**

Capital Radio
30 Leicester Square, London WC2H 7LA
☎0171 766 6000   Fax 0171 766 6100
Website: www.capitalfm.com
Group Programme Director *Richard Park*

Europe's largest commercial radio station. Main outlet is news and showbiz programme each weekday at 7.30 pm called *Drivetime Showtime*. This covers current affairs, showbiz, features and pop news, aimed at a young audience. The vast majority of material is generated in-house.

107.5 CAT FM
Regent Arcade, Cheltenham, Gloucestershire GL50 1JZ
☎01242 699555   Fax 01242 699666
Website: www.catfm.co.uk
Programme Controller *Huw James*

Music-based programmes, broadcasting 24 hours a day.

Central FM Ltd
201–203 High Street, Falkirk FK1 1DU
☎01324 611164   Fax 01324 611168
Managing Director *Sheena Borthwick*
Programme Controller *David Bain*

Broadcasts music, sport and local news to Central Scotland 24 hours a day.

Century Radio
Century House, PO Box 100, Church Street, Gateshead NE8 2YY
☎0191 477 6666   Fax 0191 477 5660
Programme Controller *John Caine*

Music, talk, news and interviews, 24 hours a day.

CFM
PO Box 964, Carlisle, Cumbria CA1 3NG
☎01228 818964   Fax 01228 819444
Programme Controller *Simon Monk*
Head of Commercial Production
  Peter White
News Editor *Gill Garston*

Music, news and information station.

Channel 103 FM
6 Tunnell Street, St Helier, Jersey, Channel Islands JE2 4LU
☎01534 888103   Fax 01534 887799
Email: chan103@itl.net
Website: www.103fm.itl.net
Station Manager *Richard Johnson*

Music programmes, 24 hours a day.

Classic Gold GEM AM
See **96 TRENT FM/Classic Gold GEM AM**

Radio Clyde/Clyde 1 FM/Clyde 2
Clydebank Business Park, Clydebank
G81 2RX
☎0141 565 2200   Fax 0141 565 2265
Website: www.radioclyde.co.uk
Director *Alex Dickson, OBE,AE,FRSA,FIMgt*
Programmes usually originate in-house or by
commission. All documentary material is made
in-house. Good local news items always con-
sidered.

Cool FM
See **Downtown Radio**

Downtown Radio/Cool FM
Newtownards, Co. Down, Northern Ireland
BT23 4ES
☎01247 815555   Fax 01247 815252
Email: programmes@downtown.co.uk
Website: www.downtown.co.uk
Programme Head *John Rosborough*
Downtown Radio first ran a highly successful
short story competition in 1988, attracting over
400 stories. The competition is now an annual
event and writers living within the station's
transmission area are asked to submit material
during the winter and early spring. The com-
petition is promoted in association with Eason
Shops. For further information, write to *Derek
Ray* at the station.

Essex FM/The Breeze
Radio House, Clifftown Road, Southend on
Sea, Essex SS1 1SX
☎01702 333711   Fax 01702 345224
Website: www.essexradio.co.uk
Programme Director *Paul Chantler*
Music-based stations. No real opportunities for
writers' work as such, but will occasionally inter-
view local authors of published books. Contact
Heather Bridge (Programming Secretary) in the
first instance.

Fame 1521 AM
See **Mercury FM 102.7/Fame 1521 AM**

Forth AM/Forth FM
Forth House, Forth Street, Edinburgh
EH1 3LF
☎0131 556 9255   Fax 0131 558 3277
Website: www.scottwilson.com
Director of Programming *Tom Steele*

News Editor *David Johnston*
News stories welcome from freelancers. Music-
based programming.

FOX FM
Brush House, Pony Road, Cowley, Oxford
OX4 2XR
☎01865 871000   Fax 01865 871037 (news)
Managing Director *Lyn Long*
Head of News *Karen Thorpe*
Backed by an impressive list of shareholders
including the Blackwell Group of Companies
and Capital Radio Plc. No outlet for creative
writing.

Galaxy 101
Millennium House, 26 Baldwin Street, Bristol
BS1 1SE
☎0117 9010101   Fax 0117 9014666/
Fax 0117 9014555 (news & programmes)
Email: newsdesk@galaxy101.co.uk
Programme Controller *John Dash*
Dance music, 24 hours a day. Occasionally
features books about local places. Contact the
Programme Controller in the first instance.

Galaxy 102.2
1 The Square, 111 Broad Street, Birmingham
B15 1AS
☎0121 695 0000   Fax 0121 695 0055
Email: mail@galaxy1022.co.uk
Managing Director *Paul Fairburn*
Programme Controller *Neil Greenslade*
Commenced broadcasting in January 1995 (as
Choice FM) and re-branded Galaxy in January
1999. Today's dance and soul, news and infor-
mation.

Gemini Radio FM/Westward Radio
Hawthorn House, Exeter Business Park,
Exeter, Devon EX1 3QS
☎01392 444444   Fax 01392 444433
Programme Controller (FM) *Kevin Kane*
Programme Controller (AM) *Colin Slade*
Took over the franchise previously held by
DevonAir Radio in January 1995. Part of
Orchard Media Group. Occasional outlets for
poetry and short stories on the AM wave-
length. Contact *Colin Slade*.

GWR FM (West)/Classic Gold 1260
GWR FM (West): PO Box 2000/Classic
Gold: PO Box 2020, Bristol BS99 7SN
☎0117 9843200   Fax 0117 9843202
Website: www.gwrfm.musicradio.com

Programme Controller, GWR FM (West)
Mark Beaver
**Programme Controller, Classic Gold
1260** *Paul Robey*

Very few opportunities. Almost all material
originates in-house. Part of the GWR Group
plc.

Hallam FM/Magic AM
Radio House, 900 Herries Road, Sheffield
S6 1RH
☎0114 2853333   Fax 0114 2853159
Website: www.hallamfm.co.uk
Programme Director *Tony McKenzie*

Music, news and features, 24 hours a day.

100.7 Heart FM
1 The Square, 111 Broad Street, Birmingham
B15 1AS
☎0121 695 0000   Fax 0121 695 0055
Email: mail@heartfm.co.uk
Managing Director *Phil Riley*
Programme Controller *Paul Fairburn*
Programme Director *Alan Carruthers*

Commenced broadcasting in September 1994.
Music, regional news and information.

Heartbeat 1521 AM
Carn Business Park, Craigavon, Co. Armagh
BT63 5RH
☎01762 330033   Fax 01762 391896
Managing Director *Kenny James*

Commenced broadcasting in April 1996 as
Radio 1521 AM and was relaunched as Heartbeat in November 1997. Predominantly music-
based programmes.

102.7 Hereward FM/Classic Gold 1332 AM
PO Box 225, Queensgate Centre,
Peterborough, Cambridgeshire PE1 1XJ
☎01733 460460   Fax 01733 281445
Programme Controller *Chris Pegg*

Part of GWR Group plc. Not usually any
openings offered to writers as all material is
compiled and presented by in-house staff.

FM 103 Horizon
Broadcast Centre, Crownhill, Milton Keynes,
Buckinghamshire MK8 0AB
☎01908 269111   Fax 01908 564893
Website: www.mkweb.co.uk
Programme Controller *Trevor Marshall*

Part of the GWR Group plc. Music and news.

Invicta FM/Capital Gold
PO Box 100, Whitstable, Kent CT5 3QX
☎01227 772004   Fax 01227 771558
Website: www.invictafm.com
Programme Controller *Andrew Phillips*

Music-based station, serving listeners in Kent.

Island FM
12 Westerbrook, St Sampsons, Guernsey,
Channel Islands GY2 4QQ
☎01481 242000   Fax 01481 249676
Website: www.islandfm.guernsey.net
Managing Director *Kevin Stewart*

Music-based programming.

Isle of Wight Radio
Dodnor Park, Newport, Isle of Wight
PO30 5XE
☎01983 822557   Fax 01983 821690
Email: news@iwradio.co.uk
Website: www.iwradio.co.uk
Managing Director *Andy Shier*
Programme Director *Stuart McGinley*

Part of the Local Radio Company, Isle of
Wight Radio is the island's only radio station
broadcasting local news, music and general
entertainment.

Key 103
See **Piccadilly 1152**

LBC 1152 AM
See **News Direct 97.3 FM**

105.4 FM Leicester Sound
Granville House, Granville Road, Leicester
LE1 7RW
☎0116 2561300   Fax 0116 2561305
Station Director *Carlton Dale*
Programme Controller *Steve Marsh*
News Editor *Peter Bearne*

Part of GWR Group plc. Predominantly a
music station. Very occasionally, unsolicited
material of local interest – 'targeted at our particular audience' – may be broadcast.

1458 Lite AM
PO Box 1458, Quay West, Trafford Park,
Manchester M17 1FL
☎0161 872 1458   Fax 0161 872 0206
Head of Programming *Kris Burford*
Head of Music *Paul Fairclough*

Music-based programmes, 24 hours a day.

Magic 1152AM
See **Metro FM/Magic 1152AM**

Magic 1161
See **Viking FM**

Magic 1548
See **Radio City Ltd**

Magic 828
See **96.3 Aire FM**

Magic AM
See **Hallam FM**

Marcher Gold
Marcher Sound Ltd., The Studios, Mold Road, Wrexham LL11 4AF
☎01978 752202   Fax 01978 759701
Email: kevin.howard@mfmradio.co.uk
Website: www.marchergold.co.uk
Programme Controller *Kevin Howard*

Occasional features and advisory programmes. Hour-long Welsh language broadcasts are aired weekdays at 6.00 pm.

Medway FM
Berkeley House, 186 High Street, Rochester, Kent ME1 1EY
☎01634 841111   Fax 01634 841122
Website: www.medwayfm.com
Managing Director *Nick Jenkins*
Programme Director *Bob Le-Roi*

A wide range of music programming plus news, views and local interest.

Mercia FM/Mercia Classic Gold
Mercia Sound Ltd., Hertford Place, Coventry CV1 3TT
☎01203 868200   Fax 01203 868202
Managing Director *Ian Rufus*
Programme Controller *Dave Myatt*

Music-based station.

Mercury FM 102.7/Fame 1521 AM
The Stanley Centre, Kelvin Way, Manor Royal, Crawley, West Sussex RH10 2SE
☎01293 519161   Fax 01293 560927
Website: www.mercuryfm.co.uk
Programme Director *Paul Chantler*

Mercury FM plays contemporary music targeting 25–44 years. Fame 1521 plays hits from the '60s to '90s, targeting 35 years-plus. Both services carry local, national and international news.

Metro FM/Magic 1152AM
Swalwell, Newcastle upon Tyne NE99 1BB
☎0191 420 0971 (Metro)/420 3040 (Magic)
Fax 520191 488 0933
Website: www.metrofm.co.uk
Programme Director *Sean Marley*

Very few opportunities for writers, but phone-in programmes may interview relevant authors.

Minster FM
PO Box 123, Dunnington, York YO1 5ZX
☎01904 488888   Fax 01904 488811
Website: www.minsterfm.demon.co.uk
Managing Director *Lynn Bell*

Music, local news and sport.

Moray Firth Radio
PO Box 271, Scorguie Place, Inverness IV3 8UJ
☎01463 224433   Fax 01463 243224
Email: MFR@mfr.cuk.com
Managing Director/Programme Controller *Thomas Prag*
Programme Organiser *Ray Atkinson*
Book Reviews *May Marshall*

Book reviews every Monday afternoon at 2.20 pm.

New Chiltern FM/Classic Gold 828
Chiltern Road, Dunstable, Bedfordshire LU6 1HQ
☎01582 676200   Fax 01582 676241
Programme Controller, FM *Trevor James*
Programme Controller, Classic Gold 828 *Don Douglas*

Part of the GWR Group plc. Music-based programmes, broadcasting 24 hours a day.

New Wyvern FM
5–6 Barbourne Terrace, Worcester WR1 3JZ
☎01905 612212/611788 (newsroom)
Fax 01905 21580
Managing Director *Rhian Garbett-Edwards*
Programme Controller *Sasha French*

Part of the GWR Group plc since spring 1997. Music-based programming.

News Direct 97.3 FM/ LBC 1152 AM
200 Gray's Inn Road, London WC1X 8XZ
☎0171 973 1152   Fax 0171 312 8470
(FM)/8565 (AM)
Websites: www.newsdirect.co.uk
and www.lbc.co.uk

Programme Director *John Simons*

News Direct 97.3 FM – 24-hour rolling news station; LBC 1152 AM – news, views and entertainment for London.

Northants 96FM/Classic Gold 1557
19–21 St Edmunds Road, Northampton NN1 5DY
Tel 01604 795600   Fax 01604 795601
Email: reception@northants96.musicradio.com
Programme Controller *Mark Jeeves*
Music and news, 24 hours a day.

NorthSound Radio
45 King's Gate, Aberdeen AB15 4EL
☎01224 337000   Fax 01224 400003
Programme Controller *Rod Webster*
Features and music programmes 24 hours a day.

Ocean Radio Group
Radio House, Whittle Avenue, Segensworth West, Fareham, Hampshire PO15 5SH
☎01489 589911   Fax 01489 589453
Email: info@oceanradio.co.uk
Programme Controller *Mark Sadler*
Head of News *Jamie Stephenson*
Music-based programming only.

Orchard FM
Haygrove House, Shoreditch, Taunton, Somerset TA3 7BT
☎01823 338448   Fax 01823 321611
Email: bob@orchardfm.co.uk
Website: http:www.orchardfm.co.uk
Programme Director *Bob McCreadie*
News Editor *Alan Jennings*.
Music-based programming only.

Piccadilly 1152/Key 103
Castlequay, Castlefield, Manchester M15 4NJ
☎0161 288 5000   Fax 0161 288 5001
Website: www.key103fm.com
Programme Director *Dave Shearer*
Music-based programming with some opportunities for comedy writers.

Plymouth Sound FM/AM
Earl's Acre, Alma Road, Plymouth, Devon PL3 4HX
☎01752 227272   Fax 01752 670730
Website: www.plymouthsouth.com
Programme Controller *Peter Greig*
Music-based station. No outlets for writers.

Premier Radio
Glen House, Stag Place, London SW1E 5AG
Tel 0171 316 1300   Fax 0171 233 6706
Email: premier@premier.org.uk
Website: www.premier.org.uk
Managing Director *Peter Kerridge*
Broadcasts programmes that reflect the beliefs and values of the Christian faith, 24 hours a day.

Q103.FM
PO Box 103, Vision Park, Chivers Way, Histon, Cambridge CB4 4WW
☎01223 235255   Fax 01223 235161
Website: www.q103fm.com
Managing Director *Alistair Wayne*
Part of GWR Group plc. Music and news.

96.3 QFM
PO Box 96.3, Paisley PA1 2LG
☎0141 887 9630   Fax 0141 887 0963
Email: classichits@q-fm.demon.co.uk
Managing Director *John Collins*
Programme Director *Mike Arthur*
Music-based programming plus local information and news.

Radio City Ltd/Magic 1548
8–10 Stanley Street, Liverpool L1 6AF
☎0151 227 5100   Fax 0151 471 0330
Website: www.radiocity967.com
Managing Director *Tom Hunter*
Programme Director *Paul Jordan*
Opportunities for writers are very few and far between as this is predominantly a music station.

RAM FM
Market Place, Derby DE1 3AA
☎01332 292945   Fax 01332 205588
Email: ramfm@musicradio.com
Programme Controller *Rob Wagstaff*
Part of the GWR Group plc. Music-based programming only.

Red Dragon FM/Touch Radio
Radio House, West Canal Wharf, Cardiff CF1 5XL
☎01222 384041   Fax 01222 384014
Website: www.rdfm.co.uk
Programme Controller *Andy Johnson*
News Editor *Andrew Jones*
Music-based programming only.

Red Rose 999 AM/Rock FM

PO Box 301, St Paul's Square, Preston,
Lancashire PR1 1YE
☎01772 556301   Fax 01772 201917
Website: www.redrose.demon.co.uk

Programme Director *Mark Matthews*

Music-based stations. No outlets for writers.

Sabras Sound

Radio House, 63 Melton Road, Leicester
LE4 6PN
☎0116 2610666   Fax 0116 2667776
Email: dk@sabrasradio.com
Website: www.sabrasradio.com

Programme Controller *Don Kotak*

Programmes for the Asian community, broadcasting 24 hours a day.

SCOT FM

Number 1 Albert Quay, Leith, Edinburgh
EH6 7DN
☎0131 554 6677   Fax 0131 554 2266
Managing Director *Mike Bawden*
Programme Controller *Donny Hughes*

Commenced broadcasting in September 1994
to the central Scottish region. Music and conversation.

Severn Sound FM/Classic Gold 774

Old Talbot House, Southgate Street,
Gloucester GL1 2DQ
☎01452 313200   Fax 01452 313213
Managing Director *Penny Holton*

Part of the GWR Group plc. Music and news.

SGR FM 97.1/96.4

Alpha Business Park, Whitehouse Road,
Ipswich, Suffolk IP1 5LT
☎01473 461000   Fax 01473 741200
Website: www.sgrfm.co.uk
Managing Director *Mike Stewart*
Programme Controller *Mark Pryke*
Features Producer *Nigel Rennie*

Music-based programming.

Signal FM

Regent House, 1st Floor, Heaton Lane,
Stockport, Cheshire SK4 1BX
☎0161 285 4545   Fax 0161 285 1010
Email: signal@1049.com
Website: www.signalradio.com

Programme Controller *Mark Chivers*

Strong local flavour to programmes. Part of the
Signal Network.

Signal One/Signal Two/ Signal Stafford

Stoke Road, Shelton, Stoke on Trent,
Staffordshire ST4 2SR
☎01782 747047   Fax 01782 744110/747777
Programme Director *John Evington*
Head of News *Paul Sheldon*

Music-based station. No outlets for writers.
Part of the Radio Partnership.

Southern FM

PO Box 2000, Brighton, East Sussex BN41 2SS
☎01273 430111   Fax 01273 430098
Website: www.southernfm.com

Programme Controller *Danny Pike*
News Manager *Laurence King*

Music, news, entertainment and competitions.

Spectrum Radio

204–206 Queenstown Road, Battersea,
London SW8 3NR
☎0171 627 4433   Fax 0171 627 3409
Email: spectrum@spectrum558am.co.uk
Website: www.spectrum558am.co.uk

Managing Director *Wolfgang Bucci*

Programmes for a broad spectrum of ethnic
groups in London.

Spire FM

City Hall Studios, Malthouse Lane, Salisbury,
Wiltshire SP2 7QQ
☎01722 416644   Fax 01722 415102
Website: www.spirefm.co.uk

Station Director *Gary Haberfield*

Music, news current affairs, quizzes and sport.
Won the Sony Award for the best local radio
station in 1994.

Sun FM 103.4

PO Box 1034, Sunderland, Tyne & Wear
SR1 3YZ
☎0191 548 1034   Fax 0191 548 7171
Managing Director *Brian Lister*
Programme Controller *Ricky Durkin*

Music-based programmes only.

Sunrise FM

Sunrise House, 30 Chapel Street, Bradford,
West Yorkshire BD1 5DN
☎01274 735043   Fax 01274 728534

**Programme Controller, Chief Executive
   & Chairman** *Usha Parmar*

Programmes for the Asian community in
Bradford. Part of the Sunrise Radio Group.

Sunshine 855

South Shropshire Communications Ltd.,
Sunshine House, Waterside, Ludlow,
Shropshire SY8 1GS
☎01584 873795   Fax 01584 875900

Operations Director *Austin Powell*
Programme Controller *Mark Edwards*

Music, news and information broadcast 24
hours a day.

Swansea Sound 1170 MW

Victoria Road, Gowerton, Swansea
SA4 3AB
☎01792 511170   Fax 01792 511171
Email: admin@swanseasound.co.uk
Website: www.swanseasound.co.uk

Managing Director *Esther Morton*
Head of News *Lynn Courtney*

Interested in a wide variety of material, though
news items must be of local relevance. An
explanatory letter, in the first instance, is advisable.

Tay FM/Radio Tay AM

Radio Tay Ltd., PO Box 123, Dundee
DD1 9UF
☎01382 200800   Fax 01382 423252
Email: tayfm@frh.co.uk
  and tayam@frh.co.uk

Managing Director *Sandy Wilkie*
Programme Director *Ally Ballingall*

Wholly-owned subsidiary of Scottish Radio
Holdings. Carries a 20-minute book pro-
gramme every Sunday evening, presented by
Mabel Adams. Unsolicited material is assessed.
Short stories and book reviews of local interest
are welcome. Send to the programme director.

107.8FM Thames Radio

Brentham House, 45c High Street, Hampton
Wick, Kingston upon Thames, Surrey
KT1 4DG
☎0181 288 1300   Fax 0181 288 1312
Website: www.thamesradio.co.uk

Station Manager *Martin Mumford*
Programme Controller *Mark Walker*

Music-based programmes of current hits and
classic pop.

Touch Radio

See **Red Dragon FM**

96 Trent FM/Classic Gold GEM AM

29–31 Castlegate, Nottingham NG1 7AP
☎0115 9527000   Fax 0115 9129302
Email: admin@trentfm.musicradio.com
Managing Director *Chris Hughes*

Part of the GWR Group plc.

2CR-FM (Two Counties Radio)

5–7 Southcote Road, Bournemouth, Dorset
BH1 3LR
☎01202 259259   Fax 01202 255244
Website: www.2crfm.co.uk

Programme Controller *Steve Woods*

Wholly-owned subsidiary of the GWR Group
plc. Serves Dorset and Hampshire. All reviews/
topicality/press releases to the Programme
Controller, 2CRFM at the address above.

2-Ten FM/Classic Gold

PO Box 2020, Reading, Berkshire RG31 7FG
Tel 0118 454400   Fax 0118 9288456
Website: www.2-tenfm.co.uk

Programme Controller *To be appointed*

A subsidiary of the GWR Group plc. Music-
based programming.

Viking FM/Magic 1161

Commercial Road, Hull, North Humberside
HU1 2SG
☎01482 325141   Fax 01482 587067
Websites: www.vikingfm.co.uk
  and www.magic1161.co.uk

Managing Director *Mel Booth*
Programme Controller *Andrew Robson*
News Co-ordinator *Shirley Renwick*

Music-based programming.

WABC

See **Beacon Radio**

The Wave

Victoria Road, Gowerton, Swansea SA4 3AB
☎01792 511964   Fax 01792 511965
Email: admin@thewave.co.uk
Website: www.thewave.co.uk

Managing Director *Esther Morton*
Head of News *Lynn Courtney*

Wessex FM

Radio House, Trinity Street, Dorchester,
Dorset DT1 1DJ
☎01305 250333   Fax 01305 250052
Website: www.wessexfm.co.uk

Programme Manager *Phil Miles*

Music, local news, information and features.

These include motoring, cooking, reviews of theatre, cinema, books, videos, local music. Expert phone-ins on gardening, antiques, pets, legal matters, DIY and medical issues.

West Sound FM/West FM

Radio House, 54 Holmston Road, Ayr
KA7 3BE
☎01292 283662
Fax 01292 283665/262607 (news)
Website: www.westfm.mcmail.com

Programme Controller *Gordon McArthur*

Music-based broadcasting.

Westward Radio

See **Gemini Radio FM**

102.4 Wish FM

Orrell Road, Wigan WN5 8HJ
☎01942 761024   Fax 01942 777694
Website: www.wishfm.net

Programme Director *Steve Collins*

Music-based programming plus news and sport.

Radio XL 1296 AM

KMS House, Bradford Street, Birmingham
B12 0JD
☎0121 753 5353   Fax 0121 753 3111

Station Manager *Barry Curtis*

Asian broadcasting for the West Midlands, 24 hours a day. Broadcasts *Love Express* featuring love stories and poems. Writers should send material to *Priya Kular*.

Freelance Rates – Broadcasting

Freelance rates vary enormously. The following minimum rates should be treated as guidelines. Most work can command higher fees from employers. It is up to freelancers to negotiate the best deal they can.

BBC Guidelines for Freelance Minimum Rates

BBC – Published Material
(Negotiated by **The Publishers Association** and **The Society of Authors**)

Domestic Radio

Plays/prose (per minute)	£12.52
Prose for dramatisation (per minute)	£9.77
Poems (per half-minute)	£12.52
Prose translation (per minute)	£8.34

World Service Radio (English)

Plays/prose (per minute)	£6.27
Prose for dramatisation (per minute)	£4.89
Poems (per half-minute)	£6.27
Prose translation (per minute)	£4.18

Television

Prose (per minute)	£18.97
Poems (per half-minute)	£22.02

BBC Radio Drama
(negotiated by **The Society of Authors** and **The Writers' Guild**)
A beginner in radio drama should receive at least £41.49 per minute for a 60-minute script. For an established writer – one who has three or more plays to his credit – the minimum rate per minute is £63.16.

An attendance payment of £37.15 per production is paid to established writers. The rate per script for *The Archers* is £640.

The Daily Morning Serial agreement has a three-model approach:
1) Where the storyline, characters, format, etc. are provided, the minimum fee is £510;
2) Where the overall format and structure are provided but the writer provides the storyline, some characters, etc. the minimum fee is £675;
3) Where the format, characters and original idea are provided by the writer, the fee is subject to individual negotiation but shall not be less than the equivalent rate per episode under the Radio Drama Agreement. (All fees cover one origination and one repeat.)

BBC Interviews and Talks
Interviews of up to 5 minutes: £50; *5–8 minutes:* £55; *8–10 minutes:* £66.50.
Linked interviews: one interview £82; two interviews £107.
Illustrated talks: £15.40 per minute.

Features/documentaries
Up to 7 minutes: £178.50; £25.50 per minute thereafter.

Independent Radio

News reports: £22.14 for the first 2 minutes; £7.38 per minute thereafter
(NUJ/CRCA agreement).
News copy: £8.21 per item.
Day Rates: Exclusive engagement of a freelance journalist: £77.10 per day;
£38.54 per half day.

Research
TV organisations which hire freelancers to research programme items should
pay on a day rate which reflects the value of the work and the importance of the
programme concerned.

Presentation
In all broadcast media, presenters command higher fees than news journalists.
There is considerable variation in what is paid for presenting programmes and
videos, according to their audience and importance. Day rates with television
companies are usually about £140–160 a day.

Television Drama

For a 60 minute teleplay, the BBC will pay an established writer £7170 and a
beginner £4551. The corresponding figures for ITV are £9245 for the established writer and £6568 for a writer new to television but with a solid reputation in other literary areas. ITV also has a 'beginner' category with a payment
of £6296 for a 60 minute teleplay.

Day rates for attendance at read-throughs and rehearsals is £65 for the BBC
and £74.40 for ITV.

(*NB* ITV rates currently under negotiation)

Feature Films

An agreement between **The Writers' Guild** and **PACT** allows for a minimum
guaranteed payment to the writer of £31,200 on a feature film with a budget in
excess of £2 million; £19,000 on a budget from £750,000 to £2 million;
£14,000 on a budget below £750,000.

Film, TV and Video Production Companies

Aardman
Gas Ferry Road, Bristol BS1 6UN
☎0117 9848485   Fax 0117 9848486
Website: www.aardman.com
Head of Film & TV *Michael Rose*

FOUNDED 1972. Award-winning animation studio producing films, television series, videos and commercials. OUTPUT includes: *Rex the Runt; Morph Files; Creature Comforts; Wallace and Gromit.* Welcomes ideas; send one-page synopsis.

Absolutely Productions Ltd
8th Floor, Alhambra House, 27–31 Charing Cross Road, London WC2H 0AU
☎0171 930 3113   Fax 0171 930 4114
Email: info@absolutely-uk.com
Website: www.absolutely-uk.com
Executive Producer *Miles Bullough*
Development Executive *Alex Jackson-Long*

TV and radio production company specialising in comedy and entertainment. OUTPUT *mr don and mr george* (Ch4); *Absolutely* series 1–4 (Ch4); *Squawkietalkie* (Ch4); *The Preventers* (ITV); *Scotland v England* (Ch4); *Barry Welsh is Coming* (HTV); *The Jack Docherty Show* (Ch5); *The Morwenna Banks Show* (Ch5); *Stressed Eric* (BBC2); *Armstrong & Miller* (Paramount/Ch4); *The Creatives* (BBC2); *Trigger Happy* (Ch4).

Abstract Images
117 Willoughby House, Barbican, London EC2Y 8BL
☎0171 638 5123
Email: productions@abstract-images.co.uk
Contact *Howard Ross*

Television documentary and drama programming. OUTPUT includes *Bent* (drama); *God: For & Against* (documentary); *This Is a Man* (drama/doc). Encourages new writers; send synopsis in the first instance.

Acacia Productions Ltd
80 Weston Park, London N8 9Tb
☎0181 341 9392   Fax 0181 341 4879
Email: acacia@dial.pipex.com
Website: www.greenindex.co.uk
Contact *J. Edward Milner*

Producer of television and video documentaries; also corporates and programmes for educational charities. No unsolicited mss. OUTPUT includes a documentary series in association with TVE, London and NHK, Japan entitled *Last Plant Standing; A Farm in Uganda; Montserrat: Under the Volcano; Biodiversity: Wealth or Wilderness.*

Acrobat Television
Vector House, Battersea Road, Heaton Mersey, Stockport, Cheshire SK4 3EA
☎0161 442 9999   Fax 0161 442 8888
Email: acrobattelevision@btinternet.com
Contact *Annabel Maudsley, Sarah Hunter*

Corporate video producer. OUTPUT includes instructional video for the British Association of Ski Instructors; corporate videos for Sunworld Sailing, Hepworth Building Products, The Simon Group and First Choice Ski. No unsolicited mss.

Action Time Ltd
Wrendal House, 2 Whitworth Street West, Manchester M1 5WX
☎0161 236 8999   Fax 0161 236 8845
Joint Managing Directors *Stephen Leahy, Trish Kinane*

Major producer and licenser of TV quiz and game entertainment shows such as *Catchphrase; Here's One I Made Earlier; Wipeout; Mr & Mrs; Men for Sale.* Action Time has co-production partners in Spain, Sweden, Denmark, Norway, Ireland and India.

Alomo Productions
1 Stephen Street, London W1P 1PJ
☎0171 691 6000   Fax 0171 691 6081

Part of the Pearson Group since 1996. Major producer of television drama and comedy. OUTPUT *Goodnight Sweetheart; Birds of a Feather; Love Hurts; The New Statesman; Grown Ups; Unfinished Business; Cry Wolf.* Scripts not welcome unless via agents but new writing is encouraged.

Anglo/Fortunato Films Ltd
170 Popes Lane, London W5 4NJ
☎0181 932 7676   Fax 0181 932 7491
Contact *Luciano Celentino*

Film, television and video producer of action comedy and psych-thriller drama. No unsolicited mss.

Antelope (UK) Ltd

29b Montague Street, London WC1B 5BH
☎0171 209 0099   Fax 0171 209 0098
Managing Director *Mick Csáky*
Head of Non-Fiction *Krishan Arora*

Film, television and video productions for drama, documentary and corporate material. OUTPUT *Cyberspace* (ITV); *Brunch* (Ch5); *The Pier* (weekly arts and entertainment programme); *Placido Domingo* (ITV); *Baden Powell – The Boy Man; Howard Hughes – The Naked Emperor* (Ch4 'Secret Lives' series); *Hiroshima*. No unsolicited mss – 'we are not reading any new material at present'.

Apex Television
Production & Facilities Ltd

Button End Studios, Harston, Cambridge CB2 5NX
☎01223 872900   Fax 01223 873092
Contact *Bernard Mulhern*

Video producer: drama, documentary, commercials and corporate. Largely corporate production for a wide range of international companies. Many drama-based training programmes and current-affairs orientated TV work. No scripts. All work is commissioned against a particular project.

Arena Films Ltd

2 Pelham Road, London SW19 1SX
☎0181 543 3990   Fax 0181 540 3992
Producer *David Conroy*

Film and TV drama. Scripts with some sort of European connection or tie-in particularly welcome. Open-minded with regard to new writing.

Argus Video Productions

52 Church Street, Briston, Melton Constable, Norfolk NR24 2LE
☎01263 861152   Fax 01263 740025
Contact *Siri Taylor*

Producer of corporate, documentary and educational videos. OUTPUT includes *View & Do* series on leisure and hobby interests; *The Chainsaw Safety* and *Relaxation* series; and *Moving Postcard Series on East Anglia*. No unsolicited mss.

Ariel Productions Ltd

Ealing Studios, Ealing Green, London W5 5EP
☎0181 567 6655   Fax 0181 758 8658
Producer *Otto Plaschkes*

Feature film and television producer. OUTPUT includes *Georgy Girl; Hopscotch; In Celebration; Butley; Doggin' Around*. Encourages new writers through involvement with the **National Film and Television School** and Screen Laboratory. No unsolicited mss.

Arlington Productions Limited

Pinewood Studios, Iver Heath, Buckinghamshire SL0 0NH
☎01753 651700   Fax 01753 656050
Contact *Kevin Francis, Gillian Garrow*

Television drama. OUTPUT *The Masks of Death* (TVM); *Murder Elite* (TVM); *A One-Way Ticket to Hollywood* (entertainment documentary). Prefers to see synopsis in the first instance. 'We try to encourage new writers.'

The Ashford Entertainment
Corporation Ltd

20 The Chase, Coulsdon, Surrey CR5 2EG
☎0181 763 2558   Fax 0181 763 2558
Email: frazer_ashford@compuserve.com
Managing Director *Frazer Ashford*

FOUNDED in 1996 by award-winning film and TV producer Frazer Ashford whose credits include *Great Little Trains* (Mainline Television for Westcountry/Ch4, starring the late Willie Rushton); *Street Life* and *Make Yourself at Home* (both for WTV). Produces theatrical films and television – drama, lifestyle and documentaries. Happy to receive ideas for dramas and documentaries but submit a one-page synopsis only in the first instance, enclosing s.a.e. 'Be patient, allow up to four weeks for a reply. Be precise with the idea; specific details rather than vague thoughts. Attach a back-up sheet with credentials and supporting evidence, ie, can you ensure that your idea is feasible?'

Assembly Film and Television Ltd

Riverside Studios, Crisp Road, London W6 9RL
☎0181 237 1075   Fax 0181 237 1071
Email: 100256.2376@compuserve.com
Contact *William Burdett-Coutts, Judith Murrell*

Television documentary producer. OUTPUT includes the Prudential Awards for the Arts, the London Comedy Festival, Ch4's Black Season and *In Exile: Sitcom*. Runs the Ch4 Sitcom Festival in conjunction with the Channel. Welcomes unsolicited mss; 'We are always interested in looking at new writers.'

Associated Press Television News
The Interchange, Oval Road, London
NW1 7DZ
☎0171 410 5200   Fax 0171 413 8302
Contact *Tim Sparke*

Video and TV: documentary, news, features, sport and entertainment. OUTPUT *Love Me For A Reason* (2 x 1hr documentary series); *Flightline* (aviation magazine series); *Animal Tracks* (children's wildlife series); *Top Secret* (3 x 1 hour documentary series); *Animal X* (animal mysteries); plus many one-off specials. Unsolicited material welcome.

Astomedia
Astra House, 140 Benhill Road, Sutton,
Surrey SM1 3SA
☎0181 641 6264   Fax 0181 641 6274
Email: gill@atomedia.com
Contact *Paul Fahey, Gill Arney*

Television producer of drama, documentary and corporate material. OUTPUT includes promotional, information and training videos for selected clients. Also audio, Internet design and publishing.

Avalon Films
1 Rook's Farm Road, Yelland, Barnstaple,
North Devon EX31 3EQ
☎01271 860294   Fax 01271 860294
Joint Managing Directors *Robin Price,*
 Andrew Vincent
Senior Script Executive *Dennis Price*

Rapidly expanding producer of feature films, television, drama and documentaries with over sixty projects in active development. Unsolicited material always welcome and given serious consideration. 'We work closely to help new writers develop their talents and are sometimes able to help them place material elsewhere if it doesn't fit our requirements.' Projects in development include nine feature films, adaptations of several Wilkie Collins novels, and a new Sherlock Holmes series for TV and several documentaries, including *Sleep With the Devil; Wedgwood; Strangers in the Night.*

Bamboo Film & TV Productions Ltd
15 Rochester Square, London NW1 9SA
☎0171 916 9353   Fax 0171 485 4692
Contact *Rosemary Forgan, Natasha Sweeney*

Television documentary producer. OUTPUT includes *The Lost Gardens of Heligan; There's Something About a Covent Girl; Mushroom Magic.*

No unsolicited mss; 'We do *not* do fiction/drama.'

Steve Barron
30 Oval Road, Camden, London NW1 7DE
Email: steve@bogo.co.uk

Film and TV drama. Director of *Teenage Mutant Ninja Turtles; Coneheads; The Adventures of Pinocchio; Merlin; Arabian Nights* and executive producer on *While You Were Sleeping* and *The Specialist.* Welcomes unsolicited scripts.

Bazal
See **GMG Endemol Entertainment plc**

Beckmann Productions Ltd
Meadow Court, West Street, Ramsey, Isle of
Man IM8 1AE
☎01624 816585   Fax 01624 816589
Email: beckmann@enterprise.net
Contact *Stuart Semark*

Isle of Man-based company. Video and television documentary. OUTPUT *Practical Guide to Europe* (travel series); *Maestro* (12-part series on classical composers); *Ivory Orphans; A Question of Guilt; Ages in History.*

Paul Berriff Productions Ltd
Cedar House, 53 Heads Lane, Hessle, East
Yorkshire HU13 0JH
☎01482 641158   Fax 01482 649692
Email: pberriff@aol.com
Contact *Paul Berriff*

Television documentary. OUTPUT *Rescue* (13-part documentary for ITV); *M25: The Magic Roundabout* ('First Tuesday'); *Animal Squad Undercover* (Ch4); *Evidence of Abuse* (BBC1 'Inside Story'); *Lessons of Darkness* (BBC2 'Fine Cut'); *The Nick* (Ch4 series); *Confrontation on E Wing* (BBC 'Everyman'); *Astronauts* (Ch4 series); *Passport Control* ('Cutting Edge').

BFI Production
21 Stephen Street, London W1P 2LN
☎0171 255 1444   Fax 0171 580 9456
Email: production@bfi.org.uk
Website: www.bfi.org.uk
Head of Production *Roger Shannon*

Part of the **British Film Institute**. Develops and produces a range of projects from short films and videos to feature-length films, acting as executive producer and co-investor. Cooperates with film organisations across the country to identify new film-making and writing talent. OUTPUT includes *Under the Skin; Love Is the Devil;*

Anthrakitis; Beautiful People; I Could Read the Sky. Runs New Directors scheme with Film Four Lab (advertised annually).

Black Coral Productions Ltd

PO Box 333, Woodford Green, Essex
IG9 6DB
☎0181 281 0401   Fax 0181 504 3338
Email: black.coral@virgin.net
Website: www.script-city.com
Contact *Lazell Daley*

Producer of drama and documentary film and television. Committed to the development of new writing with a particular interest in short and feature-length dramas. Offers a script consultancy service for which a fee is payable. Runs courses – see **Black Coral Training** under **Writers' Courses, Circles and Workshops**.

Blackbird Productions

Suite 115, The Plaza, 535 Kings Road, Chelsea, London SW10 0SZ
☎0171 352 4882   Fax 0171 351 3728
Contact *Sally Bell*

Television and video producer of documentary, corporate work; also commercials and sitcoms. OUTPUT includes *Wild Bunch* (sitcom). No unsolicited mss but will consider 2–3-page synopsis with 2–3 pages of script. 'Always enclose s.a.e., please.'

Blackstone Pictures Ltd

12 Avondale Park Road, London W11 4HL
☎0171 243 3565   Fax 0171 243 3564
Email: mail@blaxpix.demon.co.uk
Contact *Christopher Davis*

Film, television and video documentary producer. OUTPUT includes *Rwanda, the Betrayal* (Ch4) and *Charles Manson, The Man Who Killed the Sixties*. No unsolicited mss.

Blackwatch Productions Limited

29 Otago Street, Kelvinbridge, Glasgow
G12 8JJ
☎0141 341 0044   Fax 0141 341 0055
Email: blackwatch@cqm.co.uk
Company Director *Nicola Black*
Development Officer *Paul Gallagher*

Film, television, video producer of drama and documentary programmes. OUTPUT incudes *Lightbox* (film drama) and, for Ch4: *Mirrorball* (music video series); *Documentary Lab* (documentary series); *Carry On Darkly* (documentary); *Post Mortem* (drama-doc series). Currently working

with five new writers but does not welcome unsolicited mss.

Blue Heaven Productions Ltd

116 Great Portland Street, London W1N 5PG
☎0171 436 5552   Fax 0171 436 0888
Contact *Graham Benson, Christine Benson*

Film and television drama and occasional documentary. OUTPUT *The Ruth Rendell Mysteries; Crime Story: Dear Roy, Love Gillian; Ready When You Are/Screen Challenge* (three series for Meridian Regional); *The Man who Made Husbands Jealous* (Anglia Television Entertainment/Blue Heaven). Scripts considered but treatments or ideas preferred in the first instance. New writing encouraged.

Bond Clarkson Russell Ltd

16 Trinity Churchyard, Guildford, Surrey
GU1 3RR
☎01483 594000   Fax 01483 302732
Email: bcr@bcr-marketing.co.uk
Contact *Peter Bond, Simon Kozak*

Corporate literature, contract magazine publisher and film, video and multi-media producer of a wide variety of material, including conference videos, for blue-chip companies in the main. No scripts. All work is commissioned.

Box Clever Productions

The Maples Centre, 144 Liverpool Road, London N1 1LA
☎0171 619 0606   Fax 0171 700 2248
Contact *Claire Walmsley*

Broadcast TV, film and video documentaries, specialising in social and current affairs. Sister company of Boxclever Communication Training, specialising in media interview skills, presentation and communication skills. OUTPUT documentaries for BBC and Ch4; corporate videos for the European Commission, public sector and voluntary organisations. No unsolicited scripts; outlines and proposals only.

British Lion Screen Entertainment Ltd

Pinewood Studios, Iver, Buckinghamshire
SL0 0NH
☎01753 651700   Fax 01753 656391
Chief Executive *Peter R. E. Snell*

Film production. OUTPUT has included *A Man for All Seasons; Treasure Island; A Prayer for the Dying; Lady Jane; The Crucifer of Blood; Death Train.* No unsolicited mss. Send synopses only.

Broadcast Communications
See **GMG Endemol Entertainment plc**

Bronco Films Ltd
The Producers Centre, 61 Holland Street, Glasgow G2 4NJ
☎0141 287 6817   Fax 0141 287 6815
Email: broncofilm@btinternet.com
Contact *Peter Broughan*

Film, television and video drama. OUTPUT includes *Rob Roy* (feature film) and *Young Person's Guide to Becoming a Rock Star* (TV series). No unsolicited mss.

Buccaneer Films
5 Rainbow Court, Oxhey, Hertfordshire WD1 4RP
☎01923 254000   Fax 01923 254000
Contact *Michael Gosling*

Corporate video production and still photography specialists in education and sport. No unsolicited mss.

Bumper Films Ltd
Unit 15, Bridgwater Court, Weston-super-Mare BS24 9AY
☎01934 418961   Fax 01934 624494
Email: bumper@ibm.net
Contact *John Walker*

Producer of children's model animations. OUTPUT includes, for BBC1: *Fireman Sam; Joshua Jones; Star Hill Ponies* and *Rocky Hollow* for TVAM/S4C. Welcomes unsolicited mss; 'We are always looking for new projects in pre-school area.'

Can Television & Marketing
Smitham House, 127 Brighton Road, Coulsdon, Surrey CR5 2NJ
☎0181 763 9444   Fax 0181 763 0762
Contact *Philip Saben*

Television and video producer of corporate programmes and commercials for clients such as London Electricity and NatWest. No unsolicited mss.

Caravel Film Techniques Ltd
The Great Barn Studios, Cippenham Lane, Slough, Berkshire SL1 5AU
☎01753 534828   Fax 01753 571383
Contact *Denis Statham*

Film, video and TV: documentary, commercials and corporate. OUTPUT Promos for commercial TV, documentaries for BBC & ITV, sales and training material for corporate blue chip companies. No unsolicited scripts. Prepared to review mostly serious new writing.

Carey St. Productions
Unit 8, Utopia Village, 7 Chalcot Road, London NW1 8LH
☎0171 722 8225   Fax 0171 722 8254
Email: utopia@compuserve.com
Contact *Charlie Hamp, Eben Foggitt, Genevieve Christie*

Film, television and video documentaries. OUTPUT includes drama-documentaries for the Discovery Channel. No unsolicited mss.

Carlton Productions
35–38 Portman Square, London W1H 0NU
☎0171 486 6688   Fax 0171 486 1132
Director of Programmes *Steve Hewlett*
Director of Drama & Co-production *Jonathan Powell*
Controller of Entertainment *Mike Wells*
Controller of Factual Programmes *Polly Bide*
Controller of Comedy *Nick Symons*

Makers of independently produced TV drama for ITV. OUTPUT *She's Out; Kavanagh QC; Morse; Boon; Gone to the Dogs; The Guilty; Tanamera; Soldier, Soldier; Seekers; Sharpe; Peak Practice; Cadfael; Faith*. 'We try to use new writers on established long-running series.' Scripts welcome from experienced writers and agents only.

Carnival (Films & Theatre) Ltd
12 Raddington Road, Ladbroke Grove, London W10 5TG
☎0181 968 0968/1818/1717
Fax 0181 968 0155/0177
Email: (name)@carnival-films.co.uk
Contact *Brian Eastman*

Film, TV and theatre producer. OUTPUT Film: *The Mill on the Floss* (BBC); *Firelight* (Hollywood Pictures/Wind Dancer Productions); *Up on the Roof* (Rank/Granada); *Shadowlands* (Savoy/Spelling); *In Hitler's Shadow* (Home Box Office); *Under Suspicion* (Columbia/Rank/LWT); *Wilt* (Rank/LWT); *Whoops Apocalypse* (ITC). Television: *Every Woman Knows a Secret* and *Oktober* (both for ITV Network Centre); *The Fragile Heart* (Ch4); *Crime Traveller* (BBC); *Poirot 1–6* (LWT); *Bugs 1–4* (BBC); *Anna Lee* (LWT); *All or Nothing At All* (LWT); *Head Over Heels* (Carlton); *The Big Battalions* (Ch4); *Jeeves & Wooster I–IV* (Granada); *Traffik* (Ch4); *Forever Green 1–3* (LWT); *Porterhouse Blue* (Ch4); *Blott on the Landscape* (BBC). Theatre: *Juno & the Paycock; Murder is Easy; Misery; Ghost Train; What a Performance; Map of the Heart; Up on the Roof*.

Cartwn Cymru

Screen Centre, Llantrisant Road, Cardiff
CF5 2PU
☎01222 575999   Fax 01222 575919
Contact *Naomi Jones*

Animation production company. OUTPUT *Toucan 'Tecs* (YTV/S4C); *Turandot: Operavox* and *Funnybones* (both S4C/BBC); *Testament: The Bible in Animation* (BBC2/S4C); *The Jesus Story* – working title (S4C/BBC/British Screen/Icon Entertainment International).

CCC Wadlow

3rd Floor South, Harling House, 47–51 Great Suffolk Street, London SE1 0BL
☎0171 450 4720   Fax 0171 450 4734
Head of Productions *Nicholas Crean*

Film and video, multimedia and graphic design: corporate and commercials. CLIENTS include Bovis; Camelot; De La Rue plc; Del Monte Foods International; East Midlands Electricity; Hill & Norton; Knowlton; Lloyds of London; Nationwide Building Society; P&O; M&C Saatchi; Samaritans. 'We are very keen to hear from new writers, but please send c.v.s rather than scripts.'

Celtic Films Ltd

1–2 Bromley Place, London W1P 5HB
☎0171 637 7651   Fax 0171 436 5387
Email: celticfilms@compuserve.com
Contact *Muir Sutherland*

Film and television drama producer. OUTPUT includes 14 feature-length *Sharpe* TV films for Carlton and *A Life for a Life – The True Story of Stefan Kiszko* TV film for ITV. Supports new writing and welcomes unsolicited mss.

Central Office of Information Film & Video

Hercules Road, London SE1 7DU
☎0171 261 8667   Fax 0171 261 8776
Email: graison@coi.gov.uk
Contact *Geoff Raison*

Film, video and TV: drama, documentary, commercials, corporate and public information films. OUTPUT includes government commercials and corporate information. No scripts. New writing commissioned as required.

Chain Production Limited

2 Clanricarde Gardens, London W2 4NA
☎0171 229 4277   Fax 0171 229 0861
Contact *Garwin Davison*

Theatrical feature and televison films. OUTPUT

includes *Senso Unico* (feature, co-production with India and Italy); *The Protagonists* (feature). 'Actively looking for drama action thrillers for TV movie production with international partners.' Send treatments rather than complete mss.

Chameleon Television Ltd

Television House, 104 Kirkstall Road, Leeds, West Yorkshire LS3 1JS
☎0113 2444486   Fax 0113 2431267
Email: allen@chamtv.demon.co.uk
Contact *Allen Jewhurst, Kevin Sim, Anna Hall*

Film and television drama and documentary producer. OUTPUT includes *The Reckoning* (USA/Ch4); *Dunblane* (ITV); *Foul Play* (Ch5); *St Hildas* and *Rules of the Game* (both for Ch4); *Divorces From Hell* and *New Voices* (both for ITV). 'We have produced four dramas written by new writers within the Granada–Tyne Tees–Yorkshire TV initiative *New Voices*.'

Channel X Communications Ltd

22 Stephenson Way, London NW1 2HD
☎0171 387 3874   Fax 0171 387 0738
Email: mail@channelx.co.uk
Contact *Alan Marke*

FOUNDED 1986 by Jonathan Ross and Alan Marke to develop Ross's first series *The Last Resort*. Now producing comedy series and documentary. Actively developing narrative comedy and game shows. OUTPUT *XYZ; Jo Brand – Through The Cakehole; Sean's Show; The Smell of Reeves & Mortimer; Fantastic Facts; One for the Road; Funny Business; Shooting Stars; Barking; Food Fight; Johnny Vaughan Meets Madonna; Families at War; Leftfield; The Cooler.*

Chatsworth Television Limited

97–99 Dean Street, London W1V 5RA
☎0171 734 4302   Fax 0171 437 3301
Email: television@chatsworth-tv.co.uk
Managing Director *Malcolm Heyworth*

Drama, factual and entertainment television producer. Interested in contemporary and factually based series.

The Children's Film & Television Foundation Ltd

The John Maxwell Building, Elstree Film Studios, Shenley Road, Borehamwood, Hertfordshire WD6 1JG
☎0181 953 0844   Fax 0181 207 0860
Email: annahome@cftf.onyxnet.co.uk
Chief Executive *Stanley T Taylor, FCIS*

Film and tv drama. Unsolicited mss welcome.

Chromatose Films

9 Camberwell Grove, London SE5 8JA
☎0171 207 6413   Fax 0171 207 6413
Email: E9COOOL@aol.com

Film and video producer of pop promos and 'shorts'. Unsolicited mss welcome.

Cinécosse

Riversfield Studios, Ellon, Aberdeenshire
AB41 9EY
☎01358 722150   Fax 01358 720053
Email: admin@cinecosse.co.uk
Website: www.cinecosse.co.uk
Contact *Michael Marshall*

Television and video documentary and corporate productions. OUTPUT includes *Scotland's Larder* (Scottish/Grampian TV); safety and training videos for industry; tourism promotional and sales information. All scripts are commissioned; no unsolicited mss.

Cinema Verity Productions Ltd

11 Addison Avenue, London W11 4QS
☎0171 460 2777   Fax 0171 371 3329
Contact *Verity Lambert*

Leading television drama producer whose credits include *She's Out* by Lynda la Plante; *Class Act* by Michael Aitkens; *May to December* (BBC series); *Running Late* by Simon Gray (Screen 1). No unsolicited mss.

Circus Films

See **Elstree (Production) Co. Ltd.**

Claverdon Films Ltd

28 Narrow Street, London E14 8DQ
☎0171 702 8700   Fax 0171 702 8701
Contact *Tony Palmer, Michela Antonello*

Film and TV: drama and documentary. OUTPUT *Menuhin; Maria Callas; Testimony; In From the Cold; Pushkin; England, My England* (by John Osborne); *Kipling*. Unsolicited material is read, but please send a written outline first.

Cleveland Productions

5 Rainbow Court, Oxhey, Near Watford, Hertfordshire WD1 4RP
☎01923 254000   Fax 01923 254000
Contact *Michael Gosling*

Communications in sound and vision A/V production and still photography specialists in education and sport. No unsolicited mss.

Collingwood & Convergence Productions Ltd

10–14 Crown Street, Acton, London
W3 8SB
☎0181 993 3666   Fax 0181 993 9595
Email: info@crownstreet.co.uk
Producers *Christopher O'Hare, Terence Clegg, Tony Collingwood*
Head of Development *Helen Stroud*

Film and TV. Convergence Productions produces live action, drama documentaries; Tony Collingwood Productions specialises in children's animation. OUTPUT **Convergence**: *Pierrepoint* (6-part film drama series); *Plastic Fantastic* (UK cosmetic surgery techniques, Ch5) and *David Starkey's Henry VIII* (Ch4 historical documentary). **Collingwood**: *RARG* (award-winning animated film); 26 episodes of *Captain Zed and the Zee Zone* (ITV); *Daisy-Head Mayzie* (Dr Seuss animated series for Turner Network and Hanna-Barbera); *Animal Stories* (52 x 5 minute animated poems, ITV network). Unsolicited mss not welcome 'as a general rule as we do not have the capacity to process the sheer weight of submissions this creates. We therefore tend to review material from individuals recommended to us through personal contact with agents or other industry professionals. We like to encourage new writing and have worked with new writers but our ability to do so is limited by our capacity for development. We can usually only consider taking on one project each year, as development/finance takes several years to put in place.'

Convergence Productions Ltd

See **Collingwood & Convergence Productions Ltd**

Cosgrove Hall Films

8 Albany Road, Chorlton–cum–Hardy, Manchester M21 0AW
☎0161 882 2500   Fax 0161 882 2556
Email: ANIMATION@chf.co.uk
Contact *Mark Hall, Iain Pelling*

Children's animation producer; film video and television. OUTPUT includes *Noddy* (BBC); *Lavender Castle* by Gerry Anderson and *The Fox Busters* (both for children's ITV); Terry Pratchett's *Discworld* (Ch4). 'We try to select writers on a project-by-project basis.' Hosted the **Writers' Guild** workshop in 1998.

Judy Counihan Films

See **Dakota Films Ltd**

Creative Channel Ltd
Channel TV, Television Centre, La Pouquelaye, St Helier, Jersey, Channel Islands JE1 3ZD
☎01534 816873   Fax 01534 816889
Head of Creative Channel *Tim Ringsdore*
Production Manager *David Evans*

Part of the Channel Television Group. Producer of TV commercials and corporate material: information, promotional, sales, training and events coverage. OUTPUT *Exploring Guernsey* and *This is Jersey* (video souvenir travel guides); promotional videos for all types of businesses in the Channel Islands and throughout Europe; plus over 300 commercials a year. No unsolicited mss; new writing/scripts commissioned as required. Interested in hearing from local writers resident in the Channel Islands.

Creative Film Makers Ltd
Pottery Lane House, 34A Pottery Lane, London W11 4LZ
☎0171 229 5131   Fax 0171 229 4999
Contact *Michael Seligman, Nicholas Seligman*

Corporate and sports documentaries, commercials and television programmes. OUTPUT *The World's Greatest Golfers*, plus various corporate and sports programmes for clients like Nestlé, Benson & Hedges, Wimpey, Bouygues. 'Always open to suggestions but have hardly ever received unsolicited material of any value.' Keen nevertheless to encourage new writers.

The Creative Partnership
13 Bateman Street, London W1V 5TB
☎0171   439   7762
Email: creative@sohocp.co.uk
Contact *Christopher Fowler, Jim Sturgeon*

'Europe's largest "one-stop shop" for advertising and marketing campaigns for the film and television industries.' Clients include most major and independent film companies. No scripts. 'We train new writers in-house, and find them from submitted c.v.s. All applicants must have previous commercial writing experience.' Freelance writers employed for special projects.

Cricket Ltd
23A Great Queen Street, London WC2B 5BB
☎0171 287 4848   Fax 0171 413 0654
Creative Director *Andrew Davies*
Head of Production (Film & Video)
  Jonathan Freer

Film and video, live events and conferences, print and design, and business television.

'Communications solutions for business clients wishing to influence targeted external and internal audiences.'

Croft Television Ltd
Croft House, Progress Business Centre, Whittle Parkway, Slough SL1 6DQ
☎01628 668735   Fax 01628 668791
Contact *Keith Jones, Terry Adlam*

Producer of video and TV for drama, documentary, commercials, corporate, training and children's educational programmes. Also any form of visual communication and entertainment.

Cromdale Films Ltd
12 St Paul's Road, London N1 2QN
☎0171 226 0178
Contact *Ian Lloyd*

Film, video and TV: drama and documentary. OUTPUT *The Face of Darkness* (feature film); *Drift to Dawn* (rock music drama); *The Overdue Treatment* (documentary); *Russia, The Last Red Summer* (documentary). Initial phone call advised before submission of scripts.

Crown Business Communications Ltd
United House, 9 Pembridge Road, London W11 3JY
☎0171 727 7272   Fax 0171 727 9940
Email: samowens@crownbc.com
Website: www.crownbc.com
Contact *Sam Owens*

Leading producer of video, live events, digital and Internet communication for business. Interested in talented scriptwriters with experience in any of these areas, especially Internet.

Cutting Edge Productions Ltd
27 Erpingham Road, Putney, London SW15 1BE
☎0181 780 1476   Fax 0181 780 0102
Email: norridge@globalnet.co.uk
Contact *Julian Norridge*

Corporate and documentary video and tv. OUTPUT includes US series on evangelicalism, 'Dispatches' on US tobacco and government videos. No unsolicited mss; 'we commission all our writing to order but are open to ideas.'

Cwmni'r Castell Ltd
12 Carlton Road, Colwyn Bay, Conwy LL29 8RS
☎01492 533148   Fax 01492 531126
Email: castell@enterprise.net

Contact *Elwyn Vaughan Williams*

Television light entertainment and corporate video producer. OUTPUT includes four series with Welsh comedians and *Bob yn Ddau* ('Two by Two') – a daily quiz. Welcomes material from new comedy writers.

Dakota Films Ltd
12A Newburgh Street, London W1V 1LG
☎0171 287 4329   Fax 0171 287 2303
Head of Development *Lila Rawlings*
Managing Director *Judy Counihan*

Film and television drama. Feature films include: *Let Him Have It; Othello.* Judy Counihan Films: *Before the Rain; Antonia's Line.* Currently developing a John Sayles script as well as a number of projects by new writers. Welcomes unsolicited mss; 'Our policy is to encourage and work with new writers who show screenwriting talent.'

Dareks Production House
58 Wickham Road, Beckenham, Kent BR3 6RQ
☎0181 658 2012   Fax 0181 325 0629
Email: dareks@dircon.co.uk
Contact *David Crossman*

Independent producer of corporate and broadcast television. 'We are interested in *short* (10–15 minute) narrative scripts.'

D
ifferent Film Ideas Ltd
6 Haycroft Gardens, London NW10 3BN
☎0181 965 8493   Fax 01253 400601
Contact *Paul Woods, Kevan Van Thompson, Andrew Woods*

Film, television and video; drama, corporate and commercials. Currently developing three feature film scripts, two television series, one television film and three videos. No unsolicited mss; 'we prefer a treatment intially and will request a script if we are interested'.

Direct Image Productions Ltd
8 Sharpes Mill, White Cross, Lancaster LA1 4XQ
☎01524 840880   Fax 01524 840990
Email: enquiries@directimageprod.
   demon.co.uk
Website: www.directimageprod.co.uk
Co-directors *Chris Ware, Elaine Ware*

An independent broadcast and video production company FOUNDED over 25 years ago. Produces outdoor adventure and outdoor education video and book packages with its publishing arm, **Direct Image Publishing** (see entry under **UK Packagers**). Ideas for programmes for outdoor education and/or training welcome. Send letter and outline in the first instance.

Diverse Production Limited
Gorleston Street, London W14 8XS
☎0171 603 4567   Fax 0171 603 2148
Contact *Roy Ackerman, Narinder Minhas*

Broadcast television production with experience in popular prime-time formats, strong documentaries (one-offs and series), investigative journalism, science, business and history films, travel series, arts and music, talk shows, schools and education. 'We have always been committed to editorial and visual originality.' Recent OUTPUT includes *Secret Lives; Omnibus; Cutting Edge; Equinox; Modern Times; Dispatches; Without Walls; Panorama; The Big Idea; Empires and Emperors* and the *Little Picture Show.*

DMS Films Ltd
369 Burnt Oak Broadway, Edgware, Middlesex HA8 5XZ
☎0181 951 6060   Fax 0181 951 6050
Producer *Daniel San*

Film drama producer. OUTPUT includes *Understanding Jane; Hard Edge.* Welcomes unsolicited mss.

Double-Band Films
Crescent Arts Centre, 2–4 University Road, Belfast BT7 1NH
☎01232 243331   Fax 01232 236980
Email: info@dbfilms.dnet.coluk
Contact *Michael Hewitt, Dermot Lavery*

Documentary and drama programmes for film and television. Has specialised in documentary production for the past ten years (programmes include *Escobar's Own Goal* for Ch4) but moved into drama production with the short film *Still Life* in 1998. Wecomes unsolicited mss.

Dragon Pictures
23 Golden Square, London W1R 3PA
☎0171 734 6307   Fax 0171 734 6202
Email: info@dragonpictures.demon.co.uk
Contact *Katie Goodson, Lucy Guaro, Graham Broadbent*

Feature films, including *Welcome to Sarajevo; Gridlock'd; The Debt Collector; Splendor; A Texas*

Funeral. Likes to encourage young talent but cannot consider unsolicited mss.

Drake A-V Video Ltd
89 St Fagans Road, Fairwater, Cardiff
CF5 3AE
☎01222 560333   Fax 01222 554909
Website: www.drakegroup.co.uk
Contact *Ian Lewis*

Corporate A-V film and video, mostly promotional, training or educational. Scripts in these fields welcome. Other work includes interactive multimedia and CD-ROM production.

The Drama House Ltd
1 Hertford Place, London W1P 5RS
☎0171 388 9140   Fax 0171 388 3511
Contact *Jack Emery*

Film and television producer. OUTPUT *Little White Lies* (BBC1); *Witness Against Hitler* (BBC1); *Suffer the Little Children* (BBC2 'Stages'). Scripts (synopses preferred) welcome but only read and returned if accompanied by full postage. Interested in developing contacts with new and established writers.

Charles Dunstan Communications Ltd
42 Wolseley Gardens, London W4 3LS
☎0181 994 2328   Fax 0181 994 2328
Contact *Charles Dunstan*

Producer of film, video and TV for documentary and corporate material. OUTPUT *Renewable Energy* for broadcast worldwide in *Inside Britain* series; National Power Annual Report video *The Electric Environment*. No unsolicited scripts.

Ealing Films Limited
Unit 8, Utopia Village, 7 Chalcot Road, London NW1 8LH
☎0171 586 4433   Fax 0171 722 8254
Email: utopia8@compuserve.com
Managing Director *Eben Foggitt*
Head of Development *Tori Bramah*

Film and television drama producer. Unsolicited mss welcome;'we encourage new writers'.

East Anglian Productions
Studio House, 21–23 Walton Road, Frinton on Sea, Essex CO13 0AA
☎01255 676252   Fax 01255 850528
Contact *Ray Anderson*

Film, video and TV: drama and documentary, children's television, comedy, commercials and corporate.

Eden Productions Ltd
24 Belsize Lane, London NW3 5AB
☎0171 435 3242   Fax 0171 794 1519
Email: jancis@cix.co.uk
Contact *Nicholas Lander, Jancis Robinson*

Producer of *Jancis Robinson's Wine Course; Vintners' Tales with Jancis Robinson; Taste with Jancis Robinson* and wine training videos for British Airways. No unsolicited mss.

Edinburgh Film & Video Productions
Nine Mile Burn, by Penicuik, Midlothian EH26 9LT
☎01968 672131   Fax 01968 672685
Contact *R. Crichton*

Film, TV drama and documentary. OUTPUT *Sara; Moonacre; Torch; Silent Mouse; The Curious Case of Santa Claus; The Stamp of Greatness*. No unsolicited scripts at present.

Elstree (Production) Co. Ltd
Shepperton Studios, Studios Road, Shepperton, Middlesex TW17 0QD
☎01932 572680/1   Fax 01932 572682
Contact *Greg Smith*

Produces feature films and TV drama. OUTPUT *Othello* (BBC); *Great Expectations* (Disney Channel); *Porgy & Bess* (with Trevor Nunn); *Old Curiosity Shop* (Disney Channel/RHI); *Animal Farm* and *David Copperfield* (both for Hallmark/TNT). Co-owner of Circus Films with Trevor Nunn for feature film projects.

Enigma Productions Ltd
29A Tufton Street, London SW1P 3QL
☎0171 222 5757   Fax 0171 222 5858
Chairman *Lord Puttnam of Queensgate*

Backed by Warner Bros. OUTPUT *Memphis Belle; Meeting Venus; Being Human; War of the Buttons; Le Confessional* by Robert Lepage. Enigma has no plans for production in the near future. 'Lord Puttnam is currently concentrating on his role as a working Peer. We are not accepting *any* submissions.'

Excalibur Productions
13–15 Northgate, Heptonstall, West Yorkshire HX7 7ND
☎01422 843871   Fax 01422 843871
Contact *Jay Jones*

Most recent productions are medical documentaries such as an investigation into diabetes control sponsored by Bayer Diagnostics, collaborative literary and cultural projects such as *The Boys From Savoy* with David Glass, and corporates for clients such as South Yorkshire Supertram and Datacolor International. Interested in ideas, scripts and possible joint development for broadcast, sell-through and experimental arts.

Fairline Productions Ltd
15 Royal Terrace, Glasgow G3 7NY
☎0141 331 0077   Fax 0141 331 0066
Email: fairprods@aol.com
Contact *Mandi Cragg*

Television and video producer of documentary and corporate programmes and commercials. OUTPUT includes *Hooked*, a 15-part angling series, Discovery Channel, plus training and instructional videos for Forbo-Nairn Ltd, Royal Bank of Scotland, and Health & Safety Executive. Welcomes unsolicited mss; 'however, it is reasonably difficult for small independent production companies to gain commissions, so the quality of writing should be high.'

Farnham Film Company Ltd
34 Burnt Hill Road, Lower Bourne, Farnham, Surrey GU10 3LZ
☎01252 710313   Fax 01252 725855
Website: www.farnfilm.demon.co.uk
Contact *Ian Lewis*

Television and film: children's drama and documentaries. Unsolicited mss usually welcome. Check website for current needs.

Farrant Partnership
91 Knatchbull Road, London SE5 9QU
☎0171 733 0711   Fax 0171 738 5224
Email: farrant.stern@dial.pipex.com
Contact *James Farrant*

Corporate video productions.

Feelgood Fiction
49 Goldhawk Road, London W12 8QP
☎0181 746 2535   Fax 0181 740 6177
Email: fiction_@msn.com
Contact *Laurence Bowen*

Producer of film and TV drama. Recent OUTPUT includes: *The Hello Girls; Stone, Scissors, Paper; Dual Balls* and *Painted Angels*.

Festival Film and Television Ltd
Festival House, Tranquil Passage, Blackheath, London SE3 0BJ
☎0181 297 9999   Fax 0181 297 1155
Contact *Ray Marshall*

Film and television drama. Production credits include: Catherine Cookson's *Colour Blind* and *The Gambling Man*. Has produced 16 Cookson mini-series in the last nine years but 'our interests go beyond costume drama'. New writing is welcome as long as it is aimed at a particular audience and is realistic about expectations. Manuscripts must be presented professionally.

Film and General Productions Ltd
10 Pembridge Place, London W2 4XB
☎0171 221 1141   Fax 0171 792 1167
Contact *Clive Parsons*

Film and television drama. Feature films include *True Blue* and *Tea with Mussolini*. Also *Seesaw* (ITV drama) and *The Queen's Nose* (children's series for BBC). Interested in considering new writing but subject to prior telephone conversation.

Firehouse Productions
42 Glasshouse Street, London W1R 5RH
☎0171 439 2220   Fax 0171 439 2210
Email: firehousefilm@demon.co.uk
Contact *Julie-anne Edwards, Gavin Knight*

Corporate film and video programmes plus commercials and pop promos. OUTPUT includes corporate film for Conoco; British Airways in-flight commercial; The Divine Comedy 'National Express' pop promo. No unsolicited mss.

First Creative Group Ltd
Belgrave Court, Caxton Road, Fulwood, Preston, Lancashire PR2 9PL
☎01772 651555   Fax 01772 651777
Contact *M. Mulvihill*
Email: mail@firstcreative.com

Film, video and TV productions for documentary, corporate and multimedia material. Unsolicited scripts welcome. Open to new writing.

Fitting Images Ltd
Alfred House, 127A Oatlands Drive, Weybridge, Surrey KT13 9LB
☎01932 840056   Fax 01932 858075
Email: fitting_images@compuserve.com
Managing Director *Sue Fleetwood*

Promotional, training, medical/pharmaceutical; contacts from experienced writers of drama and comedy welcome. 'We are also interested in broadcast projects.'

Flashback Communication Ltd
25 Greenhead Street, Glasgow G40 1ES
☎0141 554 6868   Fax 0141 554 6869
Contact *Chris Attkins*

Video and TV producer: drama, documentary, corporate, training and education, and sell-throughs. OUTPUT includes dramatised training videos and TV programmes or inserts for the ITV network, BBC and stations worldwide. Proposals considered; no scripts. New talent encouraged. Interested in fresh ideas and effective style.

Flashback Television Limited

11 Bowling Green Lane, London EC1R 0BD
☎0171 490 8996　　Fax 0171 490 5610
Email: mailbox@flashbacktv.co.uk

Contact *Timothy Ball*

Producer of television documentaries such as *Garden Doctors* (Ch4); *Duel in the Desert* and *Battle of the Clans* (A&E). Welcomes ideas and treatments; no unsolicited mss.

Flicks Films Ltd

101 Wardour Street, London W1V 3TD
☎0171 734 4892　　Fax 0171 287 2307

Managing Director/Producer *Terry Ward*

Film and video: children's animated series and specials. OUTPUT *The Mr Men; Little Miss; Bananaman; The Pondles; Nellie the Elephant; See How They Work With Dig and Dug; Timbuctoo.* Scripts specific to their needs will be considered. 'Always willing to read relevant material.'

Focus Films Ltd

The Rotunda Studios, Rear of 116–118
Finchley Road, London NW3 5HT
☎0171 435 9004/5　　Fax 0171 431 3562
Email: focus@pupix.demon.co.uk

Contact *David Pupkewitz, Lisa Disler, Malcolm Kohll (Head of Development)*

Film and TV producer. Drama OUTPUT *CrimeTime* (medium-budget feature thriller); *Diary of a Sane Man* (experimental feature for Ch4); *Othello* (Ch4 drama). Projects in development include *The 51st State; Camden Girls; Secret Society; Sandmother; Cut and Paste; Barry.* No unsolicited scripts.

Mark Forstater Productions Ltd

27 Lonsdale Road, London NW6 6RA
☎0171 624 1123　　Fax 0171 624 1124

Production *Mark Forstater*

Active in the selection, development and production of material for film and TV. OUTPUT *Monty Python and the Holy Grail; The Odd Job; The Grass is Singing; Xtro; Forbidden; Separation; The Fantasist; Shalom Joan Collins; The Silent Touch; Grushko; The Wolves of Willoughby Chase; Between the Devil and the Deep Blue Sea; Doing Rude Things.* No unsolicited mss.

Friday Productions Ltd

23a St. Leonards Terrace, London SW3 4QG
☎0171 730 0608　　Fax 0171 730 0608

Contact *Georgina Abrahams*

Film and TV productions for drama material. OUTPUT *Goggle Eyes; Harnessing Peacocks; The December Rose.* No unsolicited scripts. New writing encouraged especially from under-represented groups.

Full Moon Productions

16 Westbourne Gardens, Glasgow G12 9PB
☎0141 334 3591　　Fax 0141 334 3591

Contact *Barry C. Paton, BSc*

Documentary and corporate videos. 'We are keen to explore drama production.' No unsolicited mss; initial contact should be by letter. 'Interested in creative/commercial (i.e. broadcast) ideas that are new and innovative.'

Gabriela Productions Limited

51 Goldsmith Avenue, London W3 6HR
☎0181 993 3158　　Fax 0181 993 8216
Email: witold01@globalnet.co.uk

Contact *W. Starecki*

Film and television drama and documentary productions, including *Blooming Youth* and *Dog Eat Dog* for Ch4 and *Spider's Web* for Polish TV. Welcomes unsolicited mss.

Gaia Communications

Sanctuary House, 35 Harding Avenue,
Eastbourne, East Sussex BN22 8PL
☎01323 734809/727183　Fax 01323 734809
Email: gaiavc@globalnet.co.uk
Website: www.users.globalnet.co.uk/~gaiavc

Producer *Robert Armstrong*
Script Editor *Loni Webb*

ESTABLISHED 1987. Video and TV corporate and documentary. OUTPUT *Discovering* (south east regional tourist and local knowledge series); *Holistic* (therapies and general information). 'Submissions must relate to our field of production, synopsis only on first contact.'

Gala International Ltd

25 Stamford Brook Road, London W6 0XJ
☎0181 741 4200　　Fax 0181 741 2323

Producer *David Lindsay*

TV commercials, promos, film and TV documentaries.

John Gau Productions
24 The Quadrangle, 49 Atalanta Street,
London SW6 6PR
☎0171 381 8182   Fax 0171 610 1466
Contact *John Gau*

Documentaries and series for TV, plus corporate video. OUTPUT includes *The Great Sell-Off*; *Reaching for the Skies*; *The Power and The Glory*; *The Team – A Season With McLaren* (all for BBC2); *Korea* series (BBC1); *Voyager* (Central); *The Great Outdoors*; *The Triumph of the Nerds*; *Glory of the Geeks* (all for Ch4); *Lights, Camera, Action!: A Century of the Cinema* (ITV network). Open to ideas from writers.

Noel Gay Television
1 Albion Court, Hammersmith, London
W6 0QT
☎0181 600 5200   Fax 0181 600 5222
Contact *Anne Mensah*

The association with Noel Gay (agency/management, film production and music publishing) makes this one of the most securely financed independents in the business. OUTPUT: *Hububb – Series 2 & 3* (BBC); *I-Camcorder* (Ch4); *Frank Stubbs Promotes* (Carlton/ ITV); *10%ers – Series 2* (Carlton/ ITV); *Call Up the Stars* (BBC1); *Smeg Outs* (BBC video); *Les Bubb* (BBC Scotland); *Red Dwarf – Series 8*; *Making of Red Dwarf* (BBC video); *Dave Allen* (ITV); *Windrush* (BBC2). Joint ventures and companies include a partnership with Odyssey, a leading Indian commercials, film and TV producer, and the Noel Gay Motion Picture Company, whose credits include *Virtual Sexuality*; *Trainspotting* (with Ch4 and Figment Films), and *Killer Tongue*, a co-production with Iberoamericana. Other associate NGTV companies are Grant Naylor Productions, Rose Bay Film Productions (see entry), Pepper Productions and Brazen Husky. NGTV is willing to accept unsolicited material from writers but 1–2-page treatments only. No scripts, please.

GMG Endemol Entertainment plc
46/47 Bedford Square, London WC1B 3DP
☎0171 462 9000   Fax 0171 462 9001
Chief Executive *Tom Barnicoat*
Creative Director *Peter Bazalgette*
Managing Director – Initial *Malcolm Gerrie*
Managing Director – Bazal *Nikki Cheetham*
Managing Director – Gem *Peter Christiansen*

GMG Endemol Entertainment (formerly known as Broadcast Communications) is joint owned by the Guardian Media Group and Dutch producer Endemol Entertainment. One of Britain's largest independent producers, GMG Endemol Entertainment is responsible for over 1000 hours of programming for all the UK's terrestrial networks as well as cable and satellite. It has two production companies: Bazal, specialising in leisure and lifestyle entertainment programming and Initial, specialising in music, live event and entertainment programming. Gem is the distribution arm of the company, handling full exploitation of rights and brands.

GMT Productions Ltd
The Old Courthouse, 26A Church Street,
Bishop's Stortford, Hertfordshire CM23 2LY
Fax 01279 501644
Email: pwpprods@aol.com
Contact *Patrick Wallis, Barney Broom*

Film, television and video: drama, documentary, corporate and commercials. No unsolicited mss.

Goldcrest Films International Ltd
65–66 Dean Street, London W1V 6PL
☎0171 437 8696   Fax 0171 437 4448
Chairman *John Quested*
Contact *Ekatarina Mosesson*

FOUNDED in the late '70s. Formerly part of the Brent Walker Leisure Group but independent since 1990 following management buy-out led by John Quested. The company's core activities are film production and worldwide distribution. Scripts via agents only.

The Good Film Company
2nd Floor, 14–15 D'Arblay Street, London
W1V 3FP
☎0171 734 1331   Fax 0171 734 2997
Contact *Yanina Barry*

Commercials and pop videos. CLIENTS include Hugo Boss, Cadbury's, Wella, National Express Coaches, Camel Cigarettes, Tunisian Tourist Board. No unsolicited mss.

Granada Film
The London Television Centre, Upper Ground, South Bank, London SE1 9LT
☎0171 737 8681   Fax 0171 737 8682
Contact *Pippa Cross, Janette Day, Rebecca Hodgson*

Films and TV films. OUTPUT *My Left Foot*; *Jack & Sarah*; *Misadventures of Margaret*; *Girls Night*; *Rogue Trader*. No unsolicited scripts. Supportive of new writing but often hard to offer real help as Granada are developing mainstream commercial projects which usually requires some status in talent areas.

Granite Film & Television Productions Ltd

5 Hanover Yard, Noel Road, London N1 8BE
☎0171 354 3232   Fax 0171 354 0205
Email: Research@Granite.co.uk
Contact Simon Welfare

Producer of television documentary programmes such as *Nicholas & Alexandra; Victoria & Albert* and *Arthur C. Clarke's Mysterious Universe*. No unsolicited mss.

Grasshopper Productions Ltd

50 Peel Street, London W8 7PD
☎0171 229 1181   Fax 0171 229 2070
Contact Joy Whitby

Children's programmes and adult drama. No unsolicited mss.

Green Umbrella Ltd

The Production House, 147a St Michael's Hill, Bristol BS2 8DB
☎0117 9731729   Fax 0117 9467432
Website: www.umbrella.co.uk

Television documentary maker and children's drama producer. OUTPUT includes episodes for *The Natural World, Wildlife on One* and original series such as *Living Europe* and *Triumph of Life*. Unsolicited treatments relating to natural history and science subjects are welcome.

Greenwich Films Ltd

Studio 2B1, The Old Seager Distillery, Brookmill Road, London SE8 4FT
☎0181 694 2211   Fax 0181 694 2971
Contact Liza Brown, Development Dept.

Film, television and video: drama. 'We welcome new writers, though as a small outfit we prefer to meet them through personal contacts as we do not have the resources to deal with too many enquiries. No unsolicited mss, just outlines, please.'

Hammer Film Productions Ltd

Elstree Film Studios, Borehamwood, Hertfordshire WD6 1JG
☎0181 207 4011   Fax 0181 905 1127
Contact Roy Skeggs, Graham Skeggs

Television and feature films. No unsolicited scripts.

Hammerwood Film Productions

110 Trafalgar Road, Portslade, East Sussex BN41 1GS
☎01273 277333   Fax 01273 705451
Contact Ralph Harvey, Petra Ginman

Film, video and TV drama. OUTPUT *Sacre Bleu; Operation Pandora* (on-going TV series, episodes are invited); *Boadicea – Queen of the Iceni* (co-production with Pan-European Film Productions). 1999 projects: *The Ghosthunter; A Symphony of Spies* (true stories of World War 2 espionage and resistance required); *Can You Kill a Dead Man?*. Most material is written in-house. 'We do not have the time to read scripts but will always read 2–3-page synopses/plot outlines. Anything of interest will be followed up and then script requested.' Hammerwood are also distributors with a stock of 5000 movies and TV programmes.

Hand Pict Productions Ltd

4 Picardy Place, Edinburgh EH1 3JT
☎0131 558 1543   Fax 0131 556 0792
Contact George Cathro

Mostly television documentary material. OUTPUT *The Ken Fine Show* (6-part series for Scottish Television); *Face Value* (Ch4); *Et in Stadia Ego* ('Without Walls', Ch4); *Blood Ties* (arts documentary for BBC Wales); *Blackfish* (current affairs for Ch4); *The Boat Band* (BBC). No unsolicited mss.

HandMade Films Ltd

19 Beak Street, London W1R 3LB
☎0171 434 3132   Fax 0171 434 3143

Feature films. OUTPUT has included *The Life of Brian; Withnail and I; Mona Lisa; The Missionary; Time Bandits; The Lonely Passion of Judith Hearne; The Raggedy Rawney; Long Good Friday; A Private Function; How To Get Ahead in Advertising; Nuns on the Run; Intimate Relations; Sweet Angel Mine; The Wrong Guy; The Assistant; The James Gang; Dinner at Fred's*. Films in post-production/completed: *The Man With Rain in His Shoes; The Secret Laughter of Women; Lock, Stock and Two Smoking Barrels*. No unsolicited mss at present.

Hartswood Films Ltd

Twickenham Studios, The Barons, St Margarets, Middlesex TW1 2AW
☎0181 607 8736   Fax 0181 607 8744
Contact Elaine Cameron

Film and TV production for drama and light entertainment. OUTPUT *Men Behaving Badly* (BBC, previously Thames); *Is It Legal?* (Ch4);

The English Wife (Meridian); *A Woman's Guide to Adultery* (Carlton); *Wonderful You* (ITV, 4x documentaries).

Hat Trick Productions Ltd
10 Livonia Street, London W1V 3PH
☎0171 434 2451   Fax 0171 287 9791
Contact *Denise O'Donoghue*

Television programmes. OUTPUT includes *Clive Anderson All Talk; Confessions; Drop the Dead Donkey; Father Ted; Game On; Have I Got News For You; If I Ruled the World; Room 101; The Best Show in the World...Probably; The Peter Principle; Whatever You Want; Whose Line is it Anyway?* The company's drama output includes: *A Very Open Prison; Boyz Unlimited; Crossing the Floor; Eleven Men Against Eleven; Gobble; Lord of Misrule; Mr White Goes to Westminster; Underworld.*

Head to Head Communication Ltd
The Hook, Plane Tree Crescent, Feltham, Middlesex TW13 7AQ
☎0181 893 7766   Fax 0181 893 2777
Email: enquiries @hthc.co.uk
Contact *Bob Carson*

Producer of business and corporate communication programmes and events.

Healthcare Productions Limited
Unit 301, Blackfriars Foundry, 156 Blackfriars Road, London SE10 0JL
☎0171 721 7150   Fax 0171 721 7151
Email: penny@healthcareprod.co.uk
Contact *Penny Webb*

Television and video: corporate and documentary. Produces training and educational material, both text and video, mostly health-related, social care issues, law and marriage. No unsolicited mss.

Jim Henson Productions Ltd
30 Oval Road, Camden, London NW1 7DE
☎0171 428 4000   Fax 0171 428 4001
Contact *Angus Fletcher*

Feature films and TV: family entertainment and children's. OUTPUT *Gulliver's Travels; Buddy; Muppet Treasure Island; The Muppet Christmas Carol; Labyrinth; The Witches* (films); *Dinosaurs* (ABC); *Muppet Tonight* (BBC/Sky); *The Muppet Show* (ITV); *The Storyteller* (Ch4); *Dr Seuss; The Secret Life of Toys* (BBC); *The Animal Show* (BBC); *Mopatop's Shop* (ITV); *Brats of the Lost Nebula* (WB); *Farscape* (Sci-Fi/USA); *Bear in the Big Blue House* (Disney Channel). Scripts via agents only.

Hightimes Productions Ltd
19 Ailsa Road, St Margaret's, Twickenham TW1 1QJ
☎0181 892 2724   Fax 0181 744 9382
Contact *A. C. Mitchell*

Television comedies. OUTPUT *Trouble in Mind* (sitcom, 9 episodes, LWT); *Me & My Girl* (sitcom, 5 series, LWT package); *The Zodiac Game* (game show, 2 series, Anglia package); *Guys 'n' Dolls* (light entertainment, 13 episodes, BSkyB).

Holmes Associates
38–42 Whitfield Street, London W1P 5RF
☎0171 813 4333   Fax 0171 637 9024
Contact *Andrew Holmes*

Prolific originator, producer and packager of documentary, drama and music television and films. OUTPUT has included *Prometheus* (Ch4 'Film on 4'); *The Shadow of Hiroshima* (Ch4 'Witness'); *The House of Bernarda Alba* (Ch4/ WNET/Amaya); *Piece of Cake* (drama mini-series for LWT); *The Cormorant* (BBC/Screen 2); *John Gielgud Looks Back; Rock Steady; Well Being; Signals; Ideal Home?* (all Ch4); *Timeline* (with MPT, TVE Spain & TRT Turkey); *Seven Canticles of St Francis* (BBC2). Unsolicited drama/film scripts will be considered but may take some time for response.

Hourglass Pictures Ltd
117 Merton Road, Wimbledon, London SW19 1ED
☎0181 540 8786   Fax 0181 542 6598
Email: pictures@hourglass.co.uk
Website: www.hourglass.co.uk
Director *Martin Chilcott*

Film and video: documentary, drama and commercials. OUTPUT includes television science documentaries and educational programming. Also health and social issues for the World Health Organisation and product information for pharmaceutical companies. Open to new writing.

Hourglass Productions Limited
4 The Heights, London SE7 8JH
☎0181 858 6870   Fax 0181 858 6870
Producer/Director *John Walsh, MD*
Producer/Head of Finance *David Walsh, ACA*
Producer/Head of Development *Maura Walsh*

Award-winning producer of drama and documentaries. OUTPUT *Monarch* (major feature film marking the 450th anniversary of the death of King Henry VIII); *Ray Harryhausen: Movement Into Life*; *The Comedy Store*; *Spiritual World*; *Sceptic & The Psychic*; *The Sleeper*. 'We prefer to receive mss through agents but do consider unsolicited material.' Current productions include *Boyz & Girlz*, a 15-part half-hour factual series for Ch5 and *Cowboyz & Cowgirlz*, a US sequel to the first hit series. Feature films in development include *Otto Palindrome* and *Snatch*.

Hungry Horse Pictures Ltd
16 Golden Square, London W1R 3AG
☎0171 734 7979   Fax 0171 434 4588
Email: hungryhorse@compuserve.com
Contact *John Deery*

Producer of film drama, including *Conspiracy of Silence*, and *County Kilburn* (comedy-drama TV series). Unsolicited mss welcome; wants to work 'with *all* writers, new or established'.

Icon Films
4 West End, Somerset Street, Bristol BS2 8NE
☎0117 9248535   Fax 0117 9420386
Contact *Harry Marshall*

Film and TV documentaries. OUTPUT *The Elephant Men* (WNET/Ch4); *The Living Edens – Bhutan, The Last Shangri La* (ABC/Kane); *Joanna Lumley in the Kingdom of the Thunder Dragon* (BBC); *Lost Civilisations – Tibet* (Time Life for NBC). Specialises in documentaries. Open-minded to new filmmakers. Proposals welcome.

Ideal Image Ltd
Cherrywood House, Crawley Down Road, Felbridge, Surrey RH19 2PP
☎01342 300566   Fax 01342 312566
Contact *Alan Frost*

Producer of documentary and drama for film, video, TV and corporate clients. OUTPUT *Just Another Friday* (corporate drama); *Living in a Box; The Future for Rupert*. No unsolicited scripts.

Illuminations Films
19–20 Rheidol Mews, Rheidol Terrace, London N1 8NU
☎0171 288 8400   Fax 0171 359 1151
Email: griff@illumin.co.uk
Website: www.illumin.co.uk
Contact *Keith Griffiths*

Film and TV drama. OUTPUT includes projects with directors like Jan Svankmajer, the Brothers Quay, G. F. Newman, Chris Petit and Patrick Keiller. 'We try to promote new talent and develop work by young writers new to the screen and experienced writers looking for new and imaginative ways to express their ideas.'

Initial
See **GMG Endemol Entertainment plc**

Interesting Television Ltd
Oakslade Studios, Station Road, Hatton, Warwickshire CV35 7LH
☎01926 844044   Fax 01926 844045
Senior Producer *John Pluck*

Producer of broadcast television documentaries and feature series on film and video for ITV and BBC TV. Currently looking towards cable, satellite and home video to broaden its output. Ideas for television documentaries particularly welcome. Send a treatment in the first instance, particularly if the subject is 'outside our area of current interest'. OUTPUT has included television programmes on heritage, antiques, gardening, science and industry; also projects on heritage, health and sports for the home video front.

Isis Productions
106 Hammersmith Grove, London W6 7HB
☎0181 748 3042   Fax 0181 748 3046
Directors *Nick de Grunwald, Jamie Rugge-Price*
Production coordinator *Catriona Lawless*

Formed in 1991 and maintaining an earlier link with **Oxford University Press**, Isis Productions focuses on the production of music and documentary programmes, and co-produces children's programmes under its Rocking Horse banner. Current: *Classic Albums* (major international series on the making of the greatest records in rock history, including films on Grateful Dead, Stevie Wonder, Jimi Hendrix, Paul Simon, The Band. Co-produced with Daniel Television, BBC, NCRV, VH-1 and Castle Communications); *Energize! –* kids-in-sport magazine series for Westcountry TV (Rocking Horse). OUTPUT *Behind the Reporting Line* (behind-the-scenes look at foreign news gathering with Foreign Editor John Simpson for BBC2); *Dido and Aeneas* (film of Purcell's opera for BBC2/Thirteen WNET/ZDF-Arte/NVC Arts); *The Score* (classical music magazine series, co-produced with After Image for BBC2); *The Making of Sgt Pepper* (60-min film for Buena Vista International/LWT – winner of Grand Prix at MIDEM); *Mine Eyes Have Seen the Glory* (3-part documentary series for Ch4, co-produced with Cutting Edge/WTTW Chicago).

JAM Pictures and Jane Walmsley Productions

8 Hanover Street, London W1R 9HF
☎0171 290 2676   Fax 0171 290 2677

Contact *Jane Walmsley, Michael Braham*

JAM Pictures was FOUNDED in 1996 to produce drama for film, TV and stage. Projects include *Breakthrough* (feature co-production with Viacom Productions, Inc. for the ABC Television network, starring Ted Danson); *One More Kiss* (feature, directed by Vadim Jean); *Bad Blood* (UK theatre tour); *Chalet Girls* (ITV sitcom). Jane Walmsley Productions, formed in 1985 by TV producer, writer and broadcaster, Jane Walmsley, has completed award-winning documentaries and features such as *Hot House People* (Ch4). No unsolicited mss. 'Letters can be sent to us, asking if we wish to see mss; we are very interested in quality material.'

Kaje Limited

Breck Lodge, Kniveton, Ashbourne, Derbyshire DE6 1JF
☎01335 343536   Fax 01135 345634
Email: sales@unkajed.com
Website: www.unkajed.com

Contact *Jamie Avery*

Television and video; documentary, commercials, corporate programming plus news and sport shorts for the cable TV channel – The Local Channel. No unsolicited mss. 'We like and encourage new writing from many sources for use in the fields we work in.'

KEO Films

Studio 2B, 151–157 City Road, London EC1V 1JH
☎0171 490 3580   Fax 0171 490 8419
Email: KeoFilms@compuserve.com

Contact *Alethea Palmer*

Television documentaries and factual entertainment. OUTPUT includes BBC's 'QED': *The Maggot Mogul* and *Sleeping it Off*; plus *A Cook on the Wild Side; TV Dinners; Beast of the Amazon* ('Ends of the Earth' series) and *Big Snake*, all for Ch4. No unsolicited mss.

King Rollo Films Ltd

Dolphin Court, High Street, Honiton, Devon EX14 8LS
☎01404 45218   Fax 01404 45328
Email: admin@kingrollofilms.co.uk

Contact *Clive Juster*

Film, video and TV: children's animated series. OUTPUT *Surprise, Surprise; It's My Birthday;*

Badger's Bring Something Party; How Many Days to My Birthday?; The Trouble With Jack; Bear's Birthday; Elephant Pie; Good Night, Sleep Tight; Go to Sleep; Get into Bed; I'm not Sleepy; Good Night Everyone; Little Princess Bedtime; Bedtime Story; Dad, I Can't Sleep; Spot and His Grandparents Visit the Carnival; Spot's Magical Christmas; Maisy; Philipp; Jakob. Generally works from existing published material 'although there will always be the odd exception'. Proposals or phone calls in the first instance. No scripts.

Kingfisher Television Productions Ltd

Carlton Studios, Lenton Lane, Nottingham NG7 2NA
☎0115 9645262   Fax 0115 9645263

Contact *Tony Francis*

Broadcast television production.

Kismet Film Company

27–29 Berwick Street, London W1V 3RF
☎0171 734 9878   Fax 0171 734 9871
Email: kismetfilms@dial.pipex.com

Production Assistant *Rosie Bridge*

Feature films. OUTPUT includes *Photographing Fairies; This Year's Love* and *Untitled Love Story*. Welcomes screenplay mss. 'We are very supportive of new writing. The three films produced by Kismet have all been written by first-time feature film writers and we have several projects in development with exciting new playwrights and screenwriters.' Involved in workshops such as PAL Writer's Workshop, **Equinoxe Screenwriting Workshops** and North by Northwest.

Kudos Productions Limited

65 Great Portland Street, London W1N 5DH
☎0171 580 8686   Fax 0171 580 8787
Email: sally.woodward@kudosproductions.co.uk

Contact *Sally Woodward Gentle*

Film and television; drama and documentaries such as *Among Giants* (feature) and *Psychos* (Ch4 series). No unsolicited mss.

Lagan Pictures Ltd

21 Tullaghbrown, Tullaghgarley, Ballymena, Co Antrim BT42 2LY
☎01232 639479/0498 528797 (mobile)
Fax 01232 639479

Producer/Director *Stephen Butcher*
Producer *Alison Grundle*

Film, video and TV: drama, documentary and

corporate. OUTPUT *A Force Under Fire* (Ulster TV). In development: *Smallholdings* (one-off drama); *Into the Bright Light of Day* (drama-doc); *The £10 Float* (feature film). 'We are always interested in hearing from writers originating from or based in Northern Ireland or anyone with, preferably unstereotypical, projects relevant to Northern Ireland. We do not have the resources to deal with unsolicited mss, so please phone or write with a brief treatment/synopsis in the first instance.'

Lamancha Productions Ltd
Northumberland House, 230 High Street, Bromley, Kent BR1 1PQ
☎0181 466 0700　　　Fax 0181 313 9682
Email: ken@lamancha.demon.co.uk
Contact *Ken Maliphant*

Television and video documentary. OUTPUT includes *Battlefield* (series of documentaries on World War 2 battles); *Science of War* (series for The Learning Channel). No unsolicited mss.

Landseer Film and Television Productions Ltd
140 Royal College Street, London NW1 0TA
☎0171 485 7333　　　Fax 0171 485 7573
Email: landseerfilms@msn.com
Contact *Claire Mills*

Film and video production: documentary, drama, music and arts, children's and current affairs. OUTPUT *Sunny Stories* – Enid Blyton (Bookmark); *J. R. R. Tolkien* (Tolkien Partnership); *Should Accidentally Fall* (BBC/Arts Council); *Nobody's Fool* ('South Bank Show' on Danny Kaye for LWT); *Gounod's Faust* (Ch4); *Swinger* (BBC2/Arts Council); *Auld Lang Syne* (BBC Scotland); *Nureyev Unzipped* (Ch4); *Retying the Knot – The Incredible String Band* (BBC Scotland); *Benjamin Zander* ('The Works', BBC2); *Zeffirelli* ('The South Bank Show', LWT); *The Judas Tree* (Ch4); *Death of a Legend – Frank Sinatra* ('South Bank Show' special); *Petula Clark* ('South Bank Show').

Lightarama Ltd
12a Wellfield Avenue, London N10 2EA
☎0181 444 8315　　　Fax 0181 444 8315
Contact *Alexis Key*

Video and TV production for commercials and corporate material and also special effects. No unsolicited scripts but c.v.s welcome. Interested in new and creative ideas.

Lilyville Productions Ltd
7 Lilyville Road, London SW6 5DP
☎0171 371 5940　　　Fax 0171 736 9431
Email: tonycash@msn.com
Contact *Tony Cash*

Drama and documentaries for TV. OUTPUT *Poetry in Motion* (series for Ch4); 'South Bank Show': *Ben Elton* and *Vanessa Redgrave*; *Musique Enquête* (drama-based French language series, Ch4); *Landscape and Memory* (arts documentary series for the BBC); Jonathan Miller's production of the *St Matthew Passion* for the BBC; major documentary on the BeeGees for the *South Bank Show*. Scripts with an obvious application to TV may be considered. Interested in new writing for documentary programmes.

Limelight Entertainment
33 Newman Street, London W1P 3PD
☎0171 637 2529　　　Fax 0171 637 2538
Email: limelight.management@virgin.net
Contact *Linda Shanks, Frances Whitaker, Fiona Lindsay*

Television and video lifestyle programming. OUTPUT includes a 13-part cookery series for Carlton Food Network entitled *First Taste*. No unsolicited mss.

Little Dancer Ltd
Avonway, Naseby Road, London SE19 3JJ
☎0181 653 9343　　　Fax 0181 653 9343
Contact *Robert Smith, Sue Townsend*

Television and cinema, both shorts and full-length features.

London Broadcast Ltd
Premier House, 77 Oxford Street, London W1R 1RB
☎0171 439 1188　　　Fax 0171 734 8367
Chairman *Eric Peters*
Head of Development & Programming *Michael Jacobs*

Television and radio producer. Specialises in light entertainment, especially the talk show format. Producer of the St Patrick's Day Concert for worldwide television distribution. Also operates a training school for radio and television. Always on the lookout for new talent. Format ideas should be sent to Head of Programming.

London Scientific Films Ltd
Suckling's Yard, Church Street, Ware, Hertfordshire SG12 9EN
☎01920 486602　　　Fax 01920 462206
Email: lsf@compuserve.com

Contact *Mike Cockburn*

Film and video documentary and corporate programming. No unsolicited mss.

Lucida Productions

Studio 1A, 14 Havelock Walk, London
SE23 3HG
☎0181 699 5070   Fax 0181 693 8002

Contact *Paul Joyce*

Television and cinema: arts, adventure, current affairs, documentary, drama and music. OUTPUT has included *Motion and Emotion: The Films of Wim Wenders; Dirk Bogarde – By Myself; Sam Peckinpah – Man of Iron; Kris Kristofferson – Pilgrim; Wild One: Marlon Brando; Stanley Kubrick: 'The Invisible Man'*. Currently in development for documentary and drama projects.

Main Communications

City House, 16 City Road, Winchester,
Hampshire SO23 8SD
☎01962 870680   Fax 01962 870699
Email: main@main.co.uk

Contact *Eben Wilson*

Multimedia marketing, communications, electronic and publishing company for film, video and TV: drama, documentary and commercials. OUTPUT includes marketing communications, educational, professional and managerial distance learning, documentary programmes for broadcast TV and children's material. Interested in proposals for television programmes, and in ideas for video sell-throughs, interactive multimedia and business information texts and programming.

Malone Gill Productions Ltd

9–15 Neal Street, London WC2H 9PU
☎0171 460 4683/4   Fax 0171 460 4679
Email: ikonic@compuserve.com

Contact *Georgina Denison*

Mainly documentary but also some drama. OUTPUT includes *The Face of Russia* (PBS); *Vermeer* ('South Bank Show'); *Highlanders* (ITV); *Storm Chasers* (Ch4); *Nature Perfected* (Ch4); *The Feast of Christmas* (Ch4); *The Buried Mirror: Reflections on Spain and the New World* by Carlos Fuentes (BBC2/Discovery Channel). Approach by letter with proposal in the first instance.

Mike Mansfield Television Ltd

41–42 Berners Street, London W1P 3AA
☎0171 580 2581   Fax 0171 580 2582

Contact *Mr Hilary McLaren*

Television for BBC, ITV, Ch4 and Ch5.

OUTPUT includes *Viva Diva!* (Shirley Bassey music special).

Mars Productions Ltd

8 Clanricarde Gardens, London W2 4NA
☎0171 243 2750   Fax 0171 792 8584
Email: mars.prod@virgin.net

Contact *Robert Marshall*

Television and video: history, arts and social documentaries. Robert Marshall teaches writing for television at BBC TV Training. 'Sometimes' welcomes unsolicited mss.

Bill Mason Films Ltd

Orchard House, Dell Quay, Chichester,
West Sussex PO20 7EE
☎01243   783558
Email: bill.mason@argonet.co.uk

Contact *Bill Mason*

Film and video: documentaries only. OUTPUT *Racing Mercedes; The History of Motor Racing; The History of the Motor Car*. No need for outside writing; all material is written in-house. The emphasis is on automotive history.

Maverick Television

The Custard Factory, Gibb Street,
Birmingham B9 4AA
☎0121 771 1812   Fax 0121 771 1550

Contact *Clare Welch*

FOUNDED 1994. High quality and innovative DVC programming in both documentary and drama. Expanding into light entertainment and more popular drama. OUTPUT includes *Trade Secrets* (BBC2); *Picture This: Accidental Hero* (BBC2); *Motherless Daughters, Highland Bollywood: Black Bag* and *Health Alert: My Teenage Menopause* (all for Ch4).

Maya Vision Ltd

43 New Oxford Street, London
WC1A 1BH
☎0171 836 1113   Fax 0171 836 5169

Contact *John Cranmer*

Film and TV: drama and documentary. OUTPUT *Saddam's Killing Fields* (for 'Viewpoint', Central TV); *3 Steps to Heaven* and *A Bit of Scarlet* (feature films for BFI/Ch4); *A Place in the Sun* and *North of Vortex* (drama for Ch4/Arts Council); *The Real History Show* (Ch4); *In the Footsteps of Alexander the Great* (BBC1 documentary); *Out* (several pieces for Ch4's lesbian and gay series). No unsolicited material; commissions only.

MBP TV

Saucelands Barn, Coolham, Horsham, West Sussex RH13 8QG
☎01403 741620   Fax 01403 741647
Email: info@mbptv.com
Contact *Mark Jennings*

Maker of film and video specialising in programmes covering equestrianism and the countryside. No unsolicited scripts, but always looking for new writers who are fully acquainted with the subject.

MediSciHealthcare Communications

Stoke Grange, Fir Tree Avenue, Stoke Poges, Buckinghamshire SL2 4NN
☎01753 516644   Fax 01753 516965
Email: kerry@medsci.co.uk
Contact *Peter Fogarty, Kerry Williams*

Corporate: medical programmes and training packages for health care professionals. Health care ideas welcome. No unsolicited mss.

Melendez Films

1–17 Shaftesbury Avenue, London W1V 7RL
☎0171 434 0220   Fax 0171 434 3131
Contact *Steven Melendez, Graeme Spurway*

Independent producers working with TV stations. Animated films aimed mainly at a family audience, produced largely for the American market, and prime-time network broadcasting. Also develops and produces feature films (eight so far). OUTPUT has included *Peanuts* (half-hour TV specials); *The Lion, the Witch and the Wardrobe; Babar the Elephant* (TV specials); *Dick Deadeye or Duty Done*, a rock musical based on Gilbert & Sullivan operettas. Synopses only, please. Enclose s.a.e. for return.

Mersey Television Company Ltd

Campus Manor, Childwall Abbey Road, Liverpool L16 0JP
☎0151 722 9122   Fax 0151 722 1969
Chairman *Prof. Phil Redmond*

The best known of the independents in the North of England. Makers of television drama. OUTPUT *Brookside; Hollyoaks* (both for Ch4).

Moonstone Films Ltd

6 Drayton Road, London W13 0LD
☎0181 998 6016   Fax 0181 998 6664
Email: moonstone@connect-2.co.uk
Contact *Tony Stark, Ingrid Geser*

Television documentaries such as *Arafat's*

Authority, a critical look at the Palestinian authority in the West Bank and Gaza for the BBC. Unsolicited mss welcome.

Alan More Films

Suite 205–206, Pinewood Studios, Pinewood Road, Iver, Buckinghamshire SL0 0NH
☎01753 656789   Fax 01753 656844
Contact *Alan More, Judith More*

Film, video and TV: documentary, commercials and corporate. No scripts. No need of outside writers

Max Morgan-Witts Productions Ltd

26 Woodsford Square, London W14 8DP
☎0171 602 0657   Fax 0171 602 8556
Contact *Max Morgan-Witts*

Film, video and TV: drama, documentary, corporate and sell-through videos. Literary: joint-author 10 non-fiction books including re-published *Voyage of the Damned; Enola Gay; Guernica*. M.D., Scandinavia Connection, specialist in books and videos.

The Morrison Company

302 Clive Court, Maida Vale, London W9 1SF
☎0171 289 7976   Fax 0171 289 7976
Email: don@morrisonco.com
Website: www.morrisonco.com
Contact *Don Morrison*

Film and video: drama, documentary and multimedia. Unsolicited mss welcome.

MW Entertainments Ltd

48 Dean Street, London W1V 5HL
☎0171 734 7707   Fax 0171 734 7727
Email: mw@mwents.demon.co.uk
Contact *Michael White*

High-output company whose credits include *Widow's Peak; White Mischief; Nuns on the Run* (co-production with **HandMade Films Ltd**); *The Comic Strip Series*. Also theatre projects, including *Fame; Me and Mamie O'Rourke; She Loves Me; Crazy for You*. Contributions are passed by Michael White to a script reader for consideration.

Newgate Company

13 Dafford Street, Larkhall, Bath, Somerset BA1 6SW
☎01225 318335
Contact *Jo Anderson*

A commonwealth of established actors, directors and playwrights, Newgate originally concerned itself solely with theatre writing (at the Bush, Stratford, Roundhouse, etc.) However, in the course of development, several productions fed into a list of ongoing drama for BBC TV/Ch4. Now looking to develop this co-production strand for film, television and radio projects with other 'Indies'.

Northlight Productions Ltd

The Media Village, Grampian Television, Queen's Cross, Aberdeen AB15 4XJ
☎01224 646460   Fax 01224 646450
Email: tv@northlight.co.uk
Website: www.northlight.co.uk
Contact *Robert Sproul-Cran*

Film, video and TV: drama, documentary and corporate work. OUTPUT ranges from high-end corporate fund-raising videos for the National Museum of Scotland to *Anything But Temptation*, a feature film currently in development; *Calcutta Chronicles* (5-part documentary series for Ch4) and two schools series for Ch4. Scripts welcome. Has links with EAVE (European Audio-Visual Entrepreneurs) and Media

ONtv (Oxford Network Television)

Larkhill House, PO Box 400, Abingdon, Oxford OX14 1FD
☎01235 537400
Email: ontv@oxfordnetwork.co.uk
Contact *Ms Martine Benoit*

An independent production company FOUNDED in 1985 to produce high-quality factual programming, including science, current affairs, series, authored documentaries for television, as well as for corporates and heritage markets. OUTPUT Ch4's *Equinox*, *Dispatches* and *Short Stories*, plus BBC2's *Horizon*.

Open Media

Ground Floor, 9 Leamington Road Villas, London W11 1HS
☎0171 229 5416   Fax 0171 221 4842
Contact *Alice Kramers Pawsey, Sebastian Cody*

Broadcast television: OUTPUT *After Dark*; *The Secret Cabaret*; *James Randi Psychic Investigator*; *Opinions*; *Is This Your Life?*; *Don't Quote Me*; *Brave New World*; *The Talking Show*; *Natural Causes*; *Equinox*; *Dispatches*.

Open Mind Productions

6 Newburgh Street, London W1V 1LH
☎0171 437 0624   Fax 0171 434 9256
Directors *Chris Ellis, Roland Tongue*

Video and TV production, including documen-

tary and educational. OUTPUT *Investigating Britain* (BBC); *Living Proof* (Ch4); *The Geography Programme: Images of the Earth* (for BBC Schools TV); *Eureka: The Earth in Space; Geography, Start Here: The Local Network; Rat-a-tat-tat; The Number Crew* series 1 & 2 (for Ch4 Schools). No unsolicited material. Currently developing children's drama series. 'We are a small company interested in programmes that reflect our name. We want to produce more drama and multi-media resources.' Chris Ellis, a writer himself, is a guest lecturer on scriptwriting with BBC TV Training and the London Media Workshop.

Orlando TV Productions

Up-the-Steps, Little Tew, Chipping Norton, Oxfordshire OX7 4JB
☎01608 683218   Fax 01608 683364
Email: orlando.tv@btinternet.com
Contact *Mike Tomlinson*

Producer of TV documentaries, with science subjects as a specialisation. OUTPUT includes programmes for *Horizon* and *QED* (BBC). Approaches by established writers/journalists to discuss proposals for collaboration are welcome.

Orpheus Productions

6 Amyand Park Gardens, Twickenham, Middlesex TW1 3HS
☎0181 892 3172   Fax 0181 892 4821
Contact *Richard Taylor*

Television documentaries and corporate work. OUTPUT has included programmes for BBC Current Affairs, Music and Arts, and the African-Caribbean Unit as well as documentaries for the Shell Film Unit and Video Arts. Unsolicited scripts are welcomed with caution. 'We have a preference for visually stirring documentaries with quality writing of the more personal and idiosyncratic kind, not straight reportage.'

Outcast Production

474 Upper Richmond Road, London SW15 5JG
☎0181 878 9486
Email: 100613.3445@compuserve.com
Contact *Andreas Wisniewski*

Low-budget feature films. No unsolicited mss; send synopsis or treatment only. 'We are actively searching for and encouraging new writing.'

Ovation Productions

One Prince of Wales Passage, 117 Hampstead Road, London NW1 3EF
☎0171 387 2342   Fax 0171 380 0404
Contact *John Plews*

Corporate video and conference scripts. Unsolicited mss not welcome. 'We talk to new writers from time to time.' Ovation also runs the fringe theatre, 'Upstairs at the Gatehouse' in Highgate, north London, and welcomes new plays.

Oxford Scientific Films Ltd

Lower Road, Long Hanborough, Oxfordshire OX8 8LL
☎01993 881881   Fax 01993 882808
Commercials Division: 45–49 Mortimer Street, London W1N 7TD
☎0171 323 0061   Fax 0171 323 0161
Email: enquiries@osf.uk.com
Website: www.osf.uk.com
Managing Director *Karen Goldie-Morrison*

Established media company with specialist knowledge and expertise in award-winning natural history films and science-based programmes. Film, video and TV: documentaries, TV commercials, multimedia, and educational films. Scripts welcome. Operates an extensive stills and film footage library specialising in wildlife and special effects (see **Picture Libraries**).

Pace Productions Ltd

12 The Green, Newport Pagnell, Buckinghamshire MK16 0JW
☎01908 618767   Fax 01908 617641
Email: chris@paceproductions.com
Website: www.paceproductions.com
Contact *Chris Pettit*

Film and video: corporate and commercials.

Paladin Pictures Ltd

500 Chiswick High Road, London W4 5RG
☎0181 740 1811   Fax 0181 740 7220
Contact *Clive Syddall*

Film and television: drama and documentary programmes such as *Plague Wars* (mini series on biological warfare, BBC1); *Dance Ballerina Dance* with Deborah Bull (BBC2); *Purple Secret* (Ch4's 'Secret History'). No unsolicited mss; 'send a letter with 1-page outline of the book to see if we are interested.' Works with writers before their books are published to enable TV tie-in.

Barry Palin Associates Ltd

143 Charing Cross Road, London WC2H 0EE
☎0171 478 4680   Fax 0171 478 4788
Email: info@eurocentergroup.com
Contact *Barry Palin*

Film, video and TV production for drama, documentary, commercials and corporate material. OUTPUT *Harmfulness of Tobacco* Anton Chekhov short story – BAFTA Best Short Film Award-winner (Ch4); Corporate: Kraft Jacobs Suchard. Unsolicited scripts welcome. New writing encouraged.

Panther Pictures Ltd

53 Montpelier Walk, London SW7 1JH
☎0976 256610   Fax 0171 589 1663
Email: rsutton@lineone.net
Contact *Robert Sutton*

Feature films, including *Inside/Out*, a US/UK/Canada/France co-production. Welcomes unsolicited mss; 'originality is the key – the idea is all.'

Paper Moon Productions

Wychwood House, Burchetts Green Lane, Littlewick Green, Nr. Maidenhead, Berkshire SL6 3QW
☎01628 829819   Fax 01628 825949
Email: david@paper-moon.co.uk
Contact *David Haggas*

Television and video: medical and health education documentaries. OUTPUT includes *Shamans and Science*, a medical documentary examining the balance between drugs discovered in nature and those synthesised in laboratories. Unsolicited scripts welcome. Interested in new writing 'from people who really understand television programme-making'.

Parallax Pictures Ltd

7 Denmark Street, London WC2H 8LS
☎0171 836 1478   Fax 0171 497 8062
Contact *Sally Hibbin*

Feature films/television drama. OUTPUT *Riff-Raff; Bad Behaviour; Raining Stones; Ladybird, Ladybird; I.D.; Land and Freedom; The Englishman Who Went up a Hill But Came Down a Mountain; Bliss; Jump the Gun; Carla's Song; The Governess; My Name Is Joe; Stand and Deliver.*

Passion Pictures

25–27 Riding House Street, London W1P 7PB
☎0171 323 9933   Fax 0171 323 9030
Email: (name)@pashpics.demon.co.uk
Managing Director *Andrew Ruhemann*
Producer *Sophie Byrne*

Television commercials: Dairylea, Levi's and, for the BBC, the 3-minute *Future Generations*. Unsolicited mss welcome.

Pathé Pictures

14–17 Kent House, Market Place, London
W1N 8AR
☎0171 323 5151   Fax 0171 631 3568

Development Executive *Ruth McGance*
Development Assistant *Vicki Patterson*

Produces 4–6 theatrical feature films each year.
Together with partners, Orange, Pathé Pictures
has launched a screenwriting and promotion
award aimed specifically at new writing talent
(see entry under **Prizes**). 'We are pleased to
consider all material that has representation
from an agent or production company.'

PBF Motion Pictures

The Little Pickenhanger, Tuckey Grove,
Ripley, Surrey GU23 6JG
☎01483 225179   Fax 01483 224118
Email: peter@pbf.co.uk

Contact *Peter B. Fairbrass*

Film, video and TV: drama, documentary,
commercials and corporate. Also televised
chess series and chess videos. OUTPUT
Grandmaster Chess (in association with Thames
TV); *Glue Sniffing; RN Special Services;
Nightfrights* (night-time TV chiller series).
CLIENTS include GEC-Marconi, Coca Cola,
MoD, Marks & Spencer, various government
departments, British Consulate. No scripts;
send one-page synopsis only in the first
instance. 'Good scripts which relate to current
projects will be followed up, otherwise not, as
PBF do not have the time to reply to proposals
which do not interest them. Only good writing
stands a chance.'

Pearson Television Ltd

1 Stephen Street, London W1P 1PJ
☎0171 691 6000

Chief Executive *Greg Dyke*
Chief Executive, UK Production *Alan Boyd*
Head of Entertainment *Richard Holloway*
Head of Comedy *Tony Charles*

UK's largest independent production and distri-
bution company. OUTPUT includes *The Bill;
Birds Of A Feather; Goodnight Sweetheart; This is
Your Life; Wing and a Prayer; Unfinished Business;
Mosley; Neighbours; Wish You Were Here ...?*

Pelicula Films

59 Holland Street, Glasgow G2 4NJ
☎0141 287 9522   Fax 0141 287 9504

Contact *Mike Alexander*

Television producer. Makers of drama documentaries and music programmes for the BBC

and Ch4. OUTPUT *As an Eilean (From the
Island); The Trans-Atlantic Sessions 1 & 2; Nanci
Griffith, Other Voices 2; Follow the Moonstone.*

Penumbra Productions Ltd

80 Brondesbury Road, London NW6 6RX
☎0171 328 4550   Fax 0171 328 3844

Contact *H. O. Nazareth*

Film, video, TV and radio: drama, documentary and information videos on health, housing,
arts and political documentaries. OUTPUT
includes *Fugitive Pieces* (Radio 3 play); *Stories
My Country Told Me* (BBC2, 'Arena'); *Repomen*
(Ch4, 'Cutting Edge'). Film treatments, drama
proposals and documentary synopses welcome.
Keen to assist in the development of new writing but only interested in social issue-based
material.

Photoplay Productions Ltd

21 Princess Road, London NW1 8JR
☎0171 722 2500   Fax 0171 722 6662
Email: photoplay@compuserve.com

Contact *Patrick Stanbury*

Documentaries for film, television and video
plus restoration of silent films and their theatrical presentation. OUTPUT includes *Cinema
Europe: The Other Hollywood; Universal Horror;
D. W. Griffith: Father of Film* and the 'Channel
4 Silents' series of silent film restoration,
including *The Wedding March*. No unsolicited
mss; 'we tend to create and write all our own
programmes.'

Picardy Television

1 Park Circus, Glasgow G3 6AX
☎0141 333 1200   Fax 0141 332 6002

Senior Producer *John Rocchiccioli*

Television and video: arts documentaries,
training and promotional videos, education
projects, multi-media productions, and TV and
cinema commercials. Unsolicited mss welcome; 'keen to encourage new writing.'

Picture Palace Films Ltd

19 Edis Street, London NW1 8LE
☎0171 586 8763   Fax 0171 586 9048
Email: 100444.2737@compuserve.com

Contact *Malcolm Craddock*

FOUNDED 1971. Leading independent producer of TV drama. OUTPUT *A Life for A Life*
(1 x 2-hour film for ITV); *Sharpe's Rifles* (14 x
2-hour films for Carlton TV); *Little Napoleons*
(4-part comedy drama for Ch4); *The Orchid
House* (4-part drama serial for Ch4); plus

episodes of *Eurocops; Tandoori Nights; 4 Minutes; When Love Dies; Ping Pong* (feature film). Material will only be considered if submitted through an agent.

Phil Pilley Productions

Ferryside, Felix Lane, Shepperton, Middlesex TW17 8NG
☎01932 702916   Fax 01932 702916

Programmes for TV and video, mainly sports, including documentaries for the BBC, ITV, Ch4 and the US. Also books, newspapers and magazine features, mainly sports.

Planet 24 Ltd

The Planet Building, Thames Quay, 195 Marsh Wall, London E14 9SG
☎0171 345 2424   Fax 0171 345 9400
Executive Producer/Managing Director
Charles Parsons

Television and radio producer of light entertainment, comedy, music and features. Bought by Carlton Communications in March 1999. OUTPUT TV: *The Big Breakfast; The Word; The Messiah* (live recording); *Hotel Babylon; Gaytime TV; Delicious; Extra Time, Nothing But the Truth; Watercolour Challenge; Rock Parties.* Radio: *Entertainment Superhighway; Straight Up; Rock Wives; Pulp; Planet A-List; Arthur Smith's Amusing Bits.*

Plantagenet Films Limited

Ard-Daraich Studio B, Ardgour, Nr Fort William, Inverness-shire PH33 7AB
☎01855   841248
Email: plantagenet@amumby.globalnet.co.uk
Contact *Norrie Maclaren*

Film and television: documentary and drama programming such as *Dig* (gardening series for Ch4); various 'Dispatches' for Ch4 and 'Omnibus' for BBC. Keen to encourage and promote new writing; unsolicited mss welcome.

Platinum Film & TV Production Ltd

1B Murray Street, London NW1 9RE
☎0171 916 9091   Fax 0171 916 5238
Email: terry@plat-tv.demon.co.uk
Contact *Terry Kelleher*

Television documentaries, including drama-documentary. OUTPUT *South Africa's Black Economy* (Ch4); *Murder at the Farm* (Thames TV); *The Biggest Robbery in the World* (major investigative true-crime drama-documentary for Carlton TV); *Dead Line* (original drama by Chilean-exiled writer, Ariel Dorfman for Ch4). Scripts and format treatments welcome.

Portman Productions

167 Wardour Street, London W1V 3TA
☎0171 468 3400   Fax 0171 468 3499

Television drama. OUTPUT includes: *Gravy Train* and *Gravy Train Goes East; Downwardly Mobile; Famous Five Series; Rebecca; Coming Home; Nancherro.* Synopses in the first instance, please.

Portobello Pictures

14–15 D'Arblay Street, London W1V 3FP
☎0171 379 5566   Fax 0171 379 5599
Email: portopics@aol.com
Contact *Ed Whitmore, Andrea Lawrence*

Film drama, including *Mojo,* director, Jez Butterworth; *Kolya,* Jan Sverak; *The War Zone,* Tim Roth, plus BBC1's *Dalziel and Pascoe* (series 1–3). Welcomes unsolicited mss; 'we will always read and comment.'

Premiere Productions Ltd

3 Colville Place, London W1P 1HN
☎0171 255 1650
Contact *Henrietta Fudakowski*

Film and television. Currently looking for feature film or TV drama scripts, with a preference for stories with humour. No horror or sci fi. Return postage and list of credits essential.

Gavin Prime Television

Christmas House, 213 Chester Road, Castle Bromwich, Solihull, West Midlands B36 0ET
☎0121 749 7147
Contact *Gavin Prime*

Film and television: documentary, commercials, entertainment and animation. Welcomes unsolicited mss, 'depending on type.'

Primetime plc

Seymour Mews House, Seymour Mews, Wigmore Street, London W1H 9PE
☎0171 935 9000   Fax 0171 935 1992
Contact *Richard Price, Simon Willock*

Television distribution and packaging, plus international co-productions. OUTPUT *An Evening with Sir Peter Ustinov; Porgy and Bess* (BBC, Homevale, Greg Smith); *Re:Joyce* (BBC); *The CIA* (BBC/A&E/NRK); *José Carreras – A Life* (LWT); *Othello* (BBC); *Ustinov on the Orient Express* (A&E/CBC/NOB/JMP); *Ethan Frome* (American Playhouse). Works closely with associated US company, Primetime Entertainment and in the music and arts area through Anglo-

German company Euro-Arts-Primetime. OUT-PUT *Who could ask for anything more?* (Ira Gershwin tribute); *The Gold and Silver Gala* (a celebration of Placido Domingo's 25th anniversary and 50th anniversary of the Royal Opera House company); *Neville's Island 90* (comedy, ITV). No unsolicited scripts.

Prospect Pictures
Prospect House, 150 Great Portland Street, London W1N 6BB
☎0171 636 1234   Fax 0171 636 1236
Contact *Kirsten Parker*

Drama, documentary and corporate video and TV. Actively looking for projects from new writers; 'using our development fund for new drama'. Welcomes treatments and synopses of scripts.

Red Lion Multimedia
1–5 Poland Street, London W1V 3DG
☎0171 734 5364   Fax 0171 734 0322
Contact *Mike Kilcooley*

Multimedia producers: commercials, training and corporate work, including product launch videos, in-house training, open learning and CBT.

Red Rooster Film and Television Entertainment
14/15 D'Arblay Street, London W1V 3FP
☎0171 439 6969   Fax 0171 439 6767
Contact *Joanna Anderson, Mervyn Watson, Sam King*

Film and TV drama. OUTPUT *Trust; The Alchemists; Deadly Summer; Beyond Fear; The Sculptress; Wilderness; Crocodile Shoes; Body & Soul.* No unsolicited scripts. Encourages new writers; 'recommend that they find an agent'.

Reel Movies Ltd
49/51 Rathbone Street, London W1P 1AN
☎0171 637 0087   Fax 0171 637 0117
Contact *Matthew Wakefield, Debby Mendoza, John Hayes*
Email: dnm@mendoza.demon.com
or hayes@mendoza.demon.com

Commercials, title sequences (e.g. Alan Bleasdale's *G.B.H.*); party political broadcasts. Currently in pre-production on a feature-length comedy film. Unsolicited mss welcome but 'we'd rather receive work from experienced writers'. Material will not be returned without s.a.e. Involved with the **London Screenwriters' Workshop**.

Renaissance Films
34–35 Berwick Street, London W1V 3RF
☎0171 287 5190   Fax 0171 287 5191
Producer *Stephen Evans*
Head of Development *Caroline Wood*

Feature films: *The Wings of the Dove; The Madness of King George* (as Close Call Films); *Twelfth Night; Much Ado About Nothing; Peter's Friends; Henry V.* No unsolicited mss.

Renaissance Vision
15 Capitol House, Heigham Street, Norwich, Norfolk NR2 4TE
☎01603 767272   Fax 01603 768163
Contact *B. Gardner*

Video: full range of corporate work (training, sales, promotional, etc.). Producers of educational and special-interest video publications. Willing to consider good ideas and proposals.

Richmond Films & Television Ltd
5 Dean Street, London W1V 5RN
☎0171 734 9313   Fax 0171 287 2058
Contact *Sandra Hastie*

Film and TV: drama and comedy. OUTPUT *Press Gang; The Lodge; The Office; Wavelength.* 'We will accept *two pages only* consisting of a brief treatment of your project (either screenplay or TV series) which includes its genre and its demographics. Please tell us also where the project has been submitted previously and what response you have had. *No unsolicited scripts.*

Rocking Horse
See **Isis Productions**

Rose Bay Film Productions
1 Albion Court, Albion Place, London W6 0QT
☎0181 600 5200   Fax 0181 600 5222
Email: rosebay@msn.com
Contact *Matthew Steiner, Simon Usiskin*

Associate company of **Noel Gay Television**. Film and TV production: entertainment and comedy. Unsolicited scripts welcome.

Rough Sea Productions
47 Laet Street, North Shields NE29 6NN
☎0191 259 1184   Fax 0191 259 1184
Email: uktvprodco@compuserve.com
Also at: 52 Leyden Mansions, Warltersville Road, London N19 3AW
Contact *Mark Lavender*

Film, television and video: drama, documentary, corporate and commercials. Documentaries include: *Shooting the Albatross* and *Moving Mountains* (both for ITV). Encourages new writers; unsolicited mss welcome.

Brenda Rowe Productions
42 Wellington Park, Clifton, Bristol
BS9 2NW
☎0117 9730390　　　　Fax 0117 9738254
Email: brenda@roweprod.demon.co.uk
Contact *Brenda Rowe*

Produces observational, investigative, current affairs TV documentaries, and training and promotional videos for business organisations. Open to new work; unsolicited mss welcome.

Sands Films
119 Rotherhithe Street, London SE16 4NF
☎0171 231 2209　　　　Fax 0171 231 2119
Contact *Richard Goodwin, Christine Edzard, Olivier Stockman*

Film and TV drama. OUTPUT *Little Dorrit; The Fool; As You Like It; A Dangerous Man; The Long Day Closes; A Passage to India; The Kiss; Swan Princess; Berlioz; The Nutcracker; Seven Years in Tibet*. In development: *Buddenbrooks*. No unsolicited scripts.

Scala Productions Ltd
15 Frith Street, London W1V 5TS
☎0171 734 7060　　　　Fax 0171 437 3248
Email: scalaproductions@aol.com
Contact *Stephen Woolley, Nik Powell, Rachel Wood*

Production company set up by ex-Palace Productions Nik Powell and Stephen Woolley, who have an impressive list of credits including *Company of Wolves; Absolute Beginners; Mona Lisa; Scandal; Crying Game; Backbeat; Hollow Reed; Neon Bible*. Productions include: *B. Monkey; 24:7; Little Voice; Divorcing Jack; Dead Heart* (now known as *Welcome to Woop Woop*); *The Lost Son*. In development: *St Agnes' Stand; Skintight; Jonathan Wild; Mort; Wise Children; Money; The Last Yellow; Fanny and Elvis; The Last September; History is Made at Night.*

Science Pictures Limited
See **Science Footage Limited** under **Picture Libraries**

Scope Productions Ltd
Keppie House, 147 Blythswood Street, Glasgow G2 4EN
☎0141 332 7720　　　　Fax 0141 332 1049
TV Commercials *Sharon Fullarton*

Corporate *Bill Gordon*

Corporate film and video; broadcast documentaries and sport; TV commercials. Unsolicited, realistic scripts/ideas welcome.

Screen First Ltd
The Studios, Funnells Farm, Down Street, Nutley, East Sussex TN22 3LG
☎01825 712034　　　　Fax 01825 713511
Email: info@screenfirst.co.uk
Contact *M. Thomas, P. Madden*

Television dramas, documentaries, arts and animation programmes. Developing major drama series, feature films, animated specials and series. No unsolicited scripts.

Screen Ventures Ltd
49 Goodge Street, London W1P 1FB
☎0171 580 7448　　　　Fax 0171 631 1265
Email: sales@screenventures.com
Contact *Christopher Mould, Caroline Furness*

Film and TV sales and production: documentary, music videos and drama. OUTPUT *Woodstock Diary; Vanessa Redgrave* (LWT 'South Bank Show'); *Mojo Working; Burma: Dying for Democracy* (Ch4); *Genet* (LWT 'South Bank Show'); *Dani Dares* (Ch4 series on strong women); *Pagad* (Ch4 news report).

Screenhouse Productions Ltd
378 Meanwood Road, Leeds, West Yorkshire LS7 2JF
☎0113 2392292　　　　Fax 0113 2392293
Email: info@screenhouse.co.uk
Website: www.screenhouse.co.uk/screenhouse
Contact *Paul Bader, Lisa Holdsworth*

Television documentary producer. OUTPUT includes five series of *Local Heroes*, factual programmes about the greats of science and two series of *Hart-Davis on History*, a magazine series about local history and how to become involved in historical research (both for BBC2). Welcomes unsolicited mss; 'we take each case on its merits'.

September Films
35 Beak Street, London W1R 3LD
☎0171 494 1884　　　　Fax 0171 439 1194
Email: september@tcp.co.uk
Head of Production *Elaine Day*
Head of Development *Kate Thompson*

Film and television drama and documentary programming. OUTPUT includes *Solomon & Gaenor* (feature film, co-production, Ch4/S4C); *Teen Spirit; The Truth About Men; Desperately Seeking*

Stardom; The Truth About Sex Appeal; Office Affairs; The Truth About Women (all for ITV/ITEL); *American Lifestyles* (BSkyB/ITEL); *The Truth About Soaps* (ITV/Meridian). 'We are interested in developing a small number of projects with new writing talent.' Unsolicited mss welcome, 'in most instances'.

Serendipity Picture Company
Avoncliff House, 24–30 Hotwell Road, Bristol BS8 4UD
☎0117 9290417   Fax 0117 9292520
Contact *Tony Yeadon, Nick Dance*

Television and video; corporate and documentary programming. Encourages new writing and will consider scripts.

Seventh House Films
1 Hall Farm Place, Bawburgh, Norwich, Norfolk NR9 3LW
☎01603 749068   Fax 01603 749069
Contact *Clive Dunn, Angela Rule*

Documentary for film, video and TV. on subjects ranging from arts to history and science to social affairs. OUTPUT *Dark Miracle* (an investigation into a near nuclear disaster in East Anglia); *A Pleasant Terror* (life and ghosts of M. R. James); *Piano Pieces* (musical excursion exploring different aspects of the piano); *Rockin' the Boat* (memories of pirate radio); *White Knuckles* (on the road with a travelling funfair); *King Romance* (life of Henry Rider Haggard); *A Drift of Angels* (three women and the price of art); *Bare Heaven* (the life and fiction of L. P. Hartley); *A Swell of the Soil* (life of Alfred Munnings); *Light Out of the Sky* (the art and life of Edward Seago). 'We welcome programme proposals with a view to collaborative co-production. Always interested in original and refreshing expressions for visual media.'

Sianco Cyf
7 Ffordd Segontiwm, Caernarfon, Gwynedd LL55 2LL
☎01286 673436   Fax 01286 673436
Email: sian@treannedd.demon.co.uk
Contact *Siân Teifi*

Children's, youth and education programmes and children's drama.

Signals, Media Arts
Victoria Chambers, St Runwald Street, Colchester, Essex
☎01206 560255   Fax 01206 369086
Email: admin@signals.org.uk
Website: www.signals.org.uk

Director *Audrey Droisen*

Promotion and documentary work for the voluntary and arts sectors. Specialists in media education projects. Film, video and multimedia facilities. No unsolicited mss.

Silent/Sound Films Ltd
Cambridge Court, Cambridge Road, Frinton on Sea, Essex CO13 9HN
☎01255 676381   Fax 01255 676381
Contact *Timothy Foster*

Active in European film co-production with mainstream connections in the USA. Special interest in developing new projects for live orchestral accompaniment. Also film musicals and documentaries on the arts. No unsolicited material.

Siriol Productions
3 Mount Stuart Square, Butetown, Cardiff CF1 6RW
☎01222 488400   Fax 01222 485962
Contact *Andrew Offiler*

Animated series, mainly for children. OUTPUT includes *The Hurricanes; Tales of the Toothfairies; Billy the Cat; The Blobs*, as well as the feature films, *Under Milkwood* and *The Princess and the Goblin*. Write with ideas and sample script in the first instance.

Skyline Productions
10 Scotland Street, Edinburgh EH3 6PS
☎0131 557 4580   Fax 0131 556 4377
Email: producer@skyline1.win-uk.net
Contact *Leslie Hills*

Film and television drama and documentary programmes such as *Hamish McBeth* for BBC1 and *Bombay Blue* for Ch4. Skyline's policy is to work with new writers but telephone first before sending material.

Specific Films
25 Rathbone Street, London W1P 1AG
☎0171 580 7476   Fax 0171 494 2676
Email: specificfilms@compuserve.com
Contact *Michael Hamlyn, Christian Routh*

FOUNDED 1991. OUTPUT includes *Mr Reliable* (feature film co-produced by PolyGram and the AFFC); *The Adventures of Priscilla, Queen of the Desert*, full-length feature film co-produced with Latent Image (Australia) and financed by PolyGram and AFFC; *U2 Rattle and Hum* (full-length feature – part concert film/part cinema verité documentary); *Paws* (executive producer); *The Last Seduction 2* (Polygram); and numerous pop promos for major international artists. First-Look deal with PolyGram Filmed Entertainment.

Spectel Productions Ltd

1 Trethorns Court, Ludgvan, Penzance, Cornwall TR20 8HE
☎01736 740989   Fax 01736 740989
Email: Davidwebster@msn.com

Contact *David Webster*

Film and video: documentary and corporate; also video publishing. No unsolicited scripts.

Spellbound Productions Ltd

90 Cowdenbeath Path, Islington, London N1 0LG
☎0171 278 0052   Fax 0171 278 0052

Contact *Paul Harris*

Specialises in film and television drama. Keen to support and encourage new writing. 'Please send scripts only, in the correct format, with s.a.e. otherwise material will not be considered.'

'Spoken' Image Ltd

The Design Centre, 44 Canal Street, Manchester M1 3WD
☎0161 236 7522   Fax 0161 236 0020

Contact *Geoff Allman, Steve Foster, Phil Griffin*

Film, video and TV production for documentary and corporate material. Specialising in high-quality brochures and reports, CD-ROMs, exhibitions, conferences, film and video production for broadcast, industry and commerce. Unsolicited scripts welcome. Interested in educational, and historical new writing, mainly for broadcast programmes.

Stirling Film & TV Productions Limited

137 University Street, Belfast BT7 1HP
☎01232 333848   Fax 01232 438644
Email: Astirling@btinternet.com

Contact *Anne Stirling*

Television and video producer for corporate, documentary and entertainment. Welcomes unsolicited mss; 'will look over any material that comes our way.'

Storm Film Productions Ltd

32–34 Great Marlborough Street, London W1V 1HA
☎0171 439 1616   Fax 0171 439 4477

Contact *Nic Auerbach*

Producer of commercials for clients such as

British Airways and Shell. Unsolicited mss welcome.

Straight Forward Film & Television Productions Ltd

Ground Floor, Crescent House, 14 High Street, Holywood, Co. Down BT18 9AZ
☎01232 426298   Fax 01232 423384

Contact *John Nicholson, Ian Kennedy*

Northern Ireland-based production company specialising in documentary, feature and lifestyle series. Unsolicited mss welcome. New work in drama and documentary fields welcome, particularly those with a strong Irish theme, contemporary or historical. OUTPUT *Close to Home* (Ch4 documentary on abortion laws in N. Ireland); *Greenfingers* (BBC/RTE gardening series); *Places Apart* (BBC Northern Ireland series); *The Last Colony* (Ch4 documentary on the Troubles); *Adventure Ireland* (BBC N. Ireland holiday series). In production: *Just Jones* (BBC Radio Ulster daily show); *Missing* (BBC N. Ireland documentary); *Awash With Colour* (10-part painting series, BBC N. Ireland/BBC Daytime).

Strawberry Productions Ltd

36 Priory Avenue, London W4 1TY
☎0181 994 4494   Fax 0181 742 7675

Contact *John Black*

Film, video and TV: drama and documentary; corporate and video publishing.

Sunset & Vine plc

30 Sackville Street, London W1X 1DB
☎0171 478 7300   Fax 0171 478 7403

Sports, children's and music programmes for television. No unsolicited mss. 'We hire free-lancers only upon receipt of a commission.'

Swanlind Communication

The Wharf, Bridge Street, Birmingham B1 2JR
☎0121 616 1701   Fax 0121 616 1520
Email: comms@swanlind.co.uk
Website: www.swanlind.co.uk

Chief Executive *Peter Stack*

Producer of business television, internal communication strategies, multimedia and conferences.

Sweetheart Films

15 Quennel Mansions, Weir Road, London SW12 0NQ
☎0181 673 3855

Producer *Karel Bata*

Low-to-medium budget feature films. No unsolicited mss; 'an introductory letter with, perhaps, a short sample of work would certainly receive consideration. We are constantly on the look-out for talent, whether new or not so new.'

Table Top Productions
1 The Orchard, Chiswick, London W4 1JZ
☎0181 742 0507   Fax 0181 742 0507
Email: arakoff@aol.com
Contact *Alvin Rakoff*

TV and film. OUTPUT *Paradise Postponed* (TV mini-series); *A Voyage Round My Father; The First Olympics 1896; Dirty Tricks; A Dance to the Music of Time.* No unsolicited mss. Also Dancetime Ltd.

Talisman Films Limited
5 Addison Place, London W11 4RJ
☎0171 603 7474   Fax 0171 602 7422
Email: email@talismanfilms.com
Contact *Richard Jackson*

Drama for film and TV: developing the full range of drama – TV series, serials and single films, as well as theatric features. 'We will only consider material submitted via literary agents.' Interested in supporting and encouraging new writing.

TalkBack Productions
36 Percy Street, London W1P 0LN
☎0171 323 9777   Fax 0171 637 5105
Managing Director *Peter Fincham*

Independent TV production company set up in 1981 by Mel Smith and Griff Rhys Jones. Specialises in comedy, comedy drama and drama; also feature lifestyle programmes, corporate and training films. OUTPUT *Smith and Jones; Murder Most Horrid; Bonjour la Classe; Demob; The Day Today; Paris; Knowing Me Knowing You with Alan Patridge; Milner; Loose Talk; In Search of Happiness; They Think It's All Over; Never Mind the Buzzcocks; Brass Eye; House Doctor; She's Gotta Have It; Grand Designs.*

Tandem TV & Film Ltd
10 Bargrove Avenue, Hemel Hempstead, Hertfordshire HP1 1QP
☎01442 261576   Fax 01442 219250
Email: info@tandemtv.com
Website: www.tandemtv.com
Contact *Barbara Page*

Produces training videos, especially health and safety; construction and civil engineering documentaries; drama-doc life stories for satellite

television; Christian church and charity documentary, training and promotional programmes. Welcomes unsolicited mss.

Teamwork Productions
Gate House, Walderton, Chichester, West Sussex PO18 9ED
☎01705 631384/0410 483149
Contact *Rob Widdows*

Video and TV producer of documentary, corporate and commercial work. OUTPUT includes motor racing coverage, motor sport productions and corporate motor sport videos. Good ideas will always be considered. No scripts.

Telemagination Ltd
41 Buckingham Palace Road, London SW1W 0PP
☎0171 828 5331   Fax 0171 828 7631
Email: mail@tmation.co.uk
Website: www.telemagination.co.uk
Contact *John M. Mills*

Producer of television animation. OUTPUT includes *The Animals of Farthing Wood; Noah's Island; Wiggly Park.* 'New writing welcome although please ask for a submissions letter before presenting any work.'

Televideo Productions
The Riverside, Furnival Road, Sheffield, South Yorkshire S4 7YH
☎0114 2491500   Fax 0114 2491505
Contact *Graham King*

Video and television: TV news and sports coverage, documentary and corporate work; sell-through videos (distributed on own label). OUTPUT includes *The Premier Collection* (football club videos); varied sports coverage for cable, satellite and terrestrial broadcasters plus a wide range of corporate work from drama-based material to documentary.

Teliesyn
26 Mortimer Street, Cardiff CF1 9JZ
☎01222 300876   Fax 01222 300877
Contact *Chris Davies*

Film and video: produces drama, documentary, music and social action in English and Welsh. Celtic Film Festival, BAFTA Cymru, Grierson and Indie award winner. OUTPUT *Branwen* (90 minute feature film for S4C); *Reel Truth* (drama doc series on the history of early film for S4C and Ch4); *Subway Cops and the Mole Kings*

(Ch4); *Dragon's Song* (music series for schools, Ch4); *Codi Clawr Hanes II* (a second drama-documentary series on women's history for S4C). Will consider unsolicited mss only if accompanied by synopsis and c.v. Encourages new writing wherever possible, in close association with a producer.

Tern Television Productions Ltd
73 Crown Street, Aberdeen AB11 6EX
☎01224 211123   Fax 01224 211199
Email: office@terntv.u-net.com
Website: www.terntv.u-net.com

Contact *David Strachan, Gwyneth Hardy, Nick Ibbotson*

Broadcast, video, corporate and training. Specialises in factual entertainment. Currently developing drama. Unsolicited mss welcome.

Theatre of Comedy Co.
See **Theatre Producers**

Tiger Aspect Productions Ltd
5 Soho Square, London W1V 5DE
☎0171 434 0672   Fax 0171 287 1448
Email: general@tigeraspect.co.uk

Contact *Charles Brand*

Television producer for comedy, drama, documentary and entertainment. OUTPUT *Births, Marriages & Deaths; Bloody Foreigners; Cop Shop; Country House; Gimme Gimme Gimme; Harry Enfield & Chums; Howard Goodalls' Choir Works; Playing the Field I & II; Streetmate; The Thin Blue Line; The Vicar of Dibley*. Only considers material submitted via an agent or from writers with a known track record.

Tonfedd
Uned 33, Cibyn, Caernarfon, Gwynedd LL55 2BD
☎01286 676800   Fax 01286 676466
Email: tonfedd@aol.com

Contact *Hefin Elis*

Light entertainment and music.

Alan Torjussen Productions Ltd
17 Heol Wen, Cardiff CF4 6EG
☎01222 624669   Fax 01222 624667
Contact *Alan Torjussen*

Film, video and TV production for drama, documentary, commercials and corporate material. Particularly interested in all types of documentary, education, schools and drama. Background includes work in the Welsh language. Unsolicited scripts welcome, particu-larly if about Wales by Welsh writers (includes Welsh language scripts). Also original ideas for comedy and documentary/dramas.

Touch Productions Ltd
The Malt House Studios, Donhead St Mary, Dorset SP7 9DN
☎01747 828030   Fax 01747 828004
Email: touch.productions@virgin.net

Contact *Erica Wolfe-Murray, Malcolm Brinkworth*

Television documentaries such as *Simon Weston V; Flying Soldiers; Siege Doctors* (all for BBC); *The Good Life; The Surgery; Coast of Dreams; A French Affair; Watching the Detectives* (all for Ch4); *Bionic Woman* (BBC1's 'QED'); *Dreamtown* (Meridian). Unsolicited mss welcome.

Transatlantic Films Production and Distribution Company
Studio One, 3 Brackbury Road, London W6 0BE
☎0181 735 0505   Fax 0181 735 0605
Executive Producer *Revel Guest*

Producer of TV documentaries. OUTPUT *Horse Tales* (Discovery Channel); *History's Turning Points* (26x30-mins programmes on decisive moments in world history, The Learning Channel); *Greek Fire* (10 x 30 mins on Greek culture, Ch4); *Four American Composers* (4x1 hour, Ch4); *The Horse in Sport* (8 x 1 hour, Ch4); *A Year in the Life of Placido Domingo*. No unsolicited scripts. Interested in new writers to write 'the book of the series', e.g. for *Greek Fire* and *The Horse in Sport*, but not usually drama script writers.

TV Choice Ltd
22 Charing Cross Road, London WC2H 0HR
☎0171 379 0873   Fax 0171 379 0263
Email: 101367.2325@compuserve.com
Website: ourworld.compuserve.com/
    homepages/tvchoice

Contact *Norman Thomas*

Produces a range of educational videos for schools and colleges on subjects such as history, geography, business studies and economics. No unsolicited mss; send proposals only.

Twentieth Century Fox Film Co
Twentieth Century House, 31–32 Soho Square, London W1V 6AP
☎0171 437 7766   Fax 0171 434 2170
London office of the American giant.

Two Four Productions Limited
Quay West Studios, Old Newnham,
Plymouth, Devon PL7 5BH
☎01752 345424   Fax 01752 344224
Email: enq@twofour.co.uk
Website: www.twofour.co.uk
Managing Director *Charles Wace*
Broadcast Director *Jill Lourie*

Video and television: drama, documentary,
commercials and corporate. OUTPUT includes
current productions: *Collectors' Lot* (116 x 30 min,
Ch4); *Monet's Garden* (5 x 10 min, BBC); *Submarine* (6 x 30 min, Westcountry); and *Royal
Horticultural Society Shows 1999* for Ch4.
Corporate clients include British Heart Foundation and Audi(UK).

UBA Ltd
21 Alderville Road, London SW6 2EE
☎01984 623619   Fax 01984 623733
Contact *Peter Shaw*

Quality feature films and TV for an international
market. OUTPUT *Windprints; The Lonely Passion
of Judith Hearne* (co-production with **Hand-
Made Films Ltd**); *Taffin; Castaway; Turtle
Diary; Sweeney Todd; Keep the Aspidistra Flying*. In
development: *Kinder Garden; Rebel Magic; No
Man's Land*. Prepared to commission new writing whether adapted from another medium or
based on a short outline/treatment. Concerned
with the quality of the script (*Turtle Diary* was
written by Harold Pinter) and breadth of appeal.
'Exploitation material' not welcome.

Umbrella Productions Ltd
The Production Centre, 19 Marine Crescent,
Glasgow G51 1HD
☎0141 429 1750/01505 872041
Fax 0141 429 1751
Contact *David Muir*

Feature films and TV drama. OUTPUT includes
The Acid House (feature film distributed by
Ch4) and *Clean* (drama for Ch4). Unsolicited
mss welcome. 'New writers should submit
story outlines first with some sample dialogue.'

United Film and Television Productions
48 Leicester Square, London WC2H 7FB
☎0171 389 8555   Fax 0171 930 8499
Managing Director *John Willis*
Controller of Drama *Michele Buck*
Head of Drama Development *Tim Vaughan*

Television drama. OUTPUT *Hornblower* (4 x
120 min); *Walking on the Moon* by Martin
Sadofski (drama–doc); *Touching Evil* (4 x 60 min,
series III); *Where the Heart Is* (14 x 60 min, series
III).

United Media Ltd
68 Berwick Street, London W1V 3PE
☎0171 287 2396   Fax 0171 287 2398
Email: umedia@globalnet.co.uk
Contact *L. Patterson*

Film, video and TV: drama. OUTPUT *To the
Lighthouse* (TV movie with BBC); *Jamaica Inn*
(HTV mini-series); *The Krays* (feature film
with Fugitive/Rank). Unsolicited scripts welcome but synopses preferred in the first
instance. 'We encourage new writing if we see
commercially orientated talent.'

Vanson Productions
PO Box 16926, London SW18 3ZP
☎0181 874 4241   Fax 0181 874 4241
Contact *Yvette Vanson*

OUTPUT *The Stephen Lawrence Story* (winner of
CRE 'Best Documentary 1998') and *Hoping for a
Miracle* (Ch4); *Doomwatch* by John Howlett and
Ian McDonald (science drama with **Working
Title Films** for Ch5); *The Murder of Stephen
Lawrence* by Paul Greengrass (a film with Granada
for ITV). In development, amongst others,
Cowboys & Angels by Ian McDonald; *Web of
Belonging* adapt. by Alan Plater from a novel by
Stevie Davies. Moving into movies in 1999 with
The Fanmaker by Alex Williams; *Wired to the
Moon* by Kerry Crabbe, based on plays by
Christina Reid.

Video Enterprises
12 Barbers Wood Road, High Wycombe,
Buckinghamshire HP12 4EP
☎01494 534144 (mobile: 0831 875216)
Fax 01494 534144
Email: maurice@vident.u–net.com
Website: www.vident.u–net.com
Contact *Maurice R. Fleisher*

Video and TV, mainly corporate: business and
industrial training, promotional material and
conferences. No unsolicited material 'but
always ready to try out good new writers'.

Video Presentations
PO Box 281, Wimbledon, London
SW19 3DD
☎0181 542 7721   Fax 0181 543 0855
Email: jhvp@btinternet.com
Contact *John Holloway*

Corporate video. CLIENTS include the Post

Office, IBM, British Gas, Freemans, Eastern Electricity.

Videocraft Media Productions Ltd
1 Lower Bar, Newport, Shropshire
TF10 7BE
☎01952 814567   Fax 01952 825715
Contact *Robin Ware*

Corporate videos. No unsolicited mss.

The Visual Connection
1 Rostrevor Mews, London SW6 5AZ
☎0171 731 6300   Fax 0171 736 9462
Email: info@tvc.co.uk
Website: www.tvc.co.uk
Contact *Linda Tenger, Stuart Blake*

Corporate film and video; visitor attractions at museums and exhibitions such as the Macau Pavilion at Lisbon Expo '98 and 11 programmes on the Singapore Discovery Centre. No unsolicited mss.

W.O.W. Productions
26A Fordwych Road, London NW2 3TG
☎0181 830 5978   Fax 0181 830 5978
Email: wow@dircon.co.uk
Contact *Carl Schonfeld, Dom Rotheroe*

Film and television drama and documentary programming. OUTPUT includes *A Sarajevo Diary* (documentary) and *My Brother Rob* (feature). Welcomes unsolicited mss.

Brian Waddell Productions Ltd
Strand Studios, 5/7 Shore Road, Holywood, Co. Down BT18 9HX
☎01232 427646   Fax 01232 427922
Contacts *Brian Waddell*

Producer of a wide range of television programmes in leisure activities, the arts, music, children's, comedy, travel/adventure and documentaries. Currently developing several drama projects.

Wall to Wall Television
8–9 Spring Place, London NW5 3ER
☎0171 485 7424   Fax 0171 267 5292
Contact *Alex Graham*

Documentaries, features and drama. OUTPUT includes *Plotlands; It's Not Unusual; Nightmare: The Birth of Horror* (BBC); *Baby It's You; A Taste of the Times; Weekly Planet* (Ch4); *Our Boy* (BBC); *A Rather English Marriage* (BBC). Material is produced in-house; occasional outside ideas accepted. Continued expansion of drama production means more opportunities for writers.

The Walnut Partnership
Crown House, Armley Road, Leeds, West Yorkshire LS12 2EJ
☎0113 2456913   Fax 0113 2439614
Email: info@walpart.co.uk
Contact *Geoff Penn*

A film and video production company specialising in business communication.

Warner Sisters Film & TV Ltd
The Cottage, Pall Mall Deposit, 124 Barlby Road, London W10 6BL
☎0181 960 3550   Fax 0181 960 3880
Email: Sisters@WarnerCine.com
Chief Executives *Lavinia Warner, Jane Wellesley, Anne-Marie Casey, Dorothy Viljoen*

FOUNDED 1984. Drama and comedy. TV and feature films. OUTPUT includes *Selling Hitler; Rides; Life's a Gas; She-Play; A Village Affair; Dangerous Lady; Dressing for Breakfast; The Spy that Caught a Cold; The Bite; Jilting Joe; The Jump.* Developing a wide range of projects including *Mad Mary* (feature film).

Paul Weiland Film Company
14 Newburgh Street, London W1V 1LF
☎0171 287 6900   Fax 0171 434 0146
Email: weiland@easynet.co.uk
Contact *Mary Francis*

Television commercials and pop promos. Unsolicited mss sometimes welcome; 'we encourage new writing.'

Wessex Films Ltd
57 Abbots Park, London Road, Borehamwood, Hertfordshire AL1 1TP
☎01727 852879   Fax 01727 845775
Email: darylbristow@mcmail.com
Contact *Daryl Bristow, Peter Doman*

Film and TV drama. OUTPUT includes *Zoe's Lighthouse; Lionheart; Ever Upright; O'Hara's Road; No Publicity.* Unsolicited mss welcome; 'provided they have commercial theatrical (wide) release potential, if film, or mainstream TV channel release potential if TV drama (i.e. not arthouse material).'

Western Eye Business Television
Easton Business Centre, Felix Road, Easton, Bristol BS5 0HE
☎0117 9415854   Fax 0117 9415851
Contact *Steve Spencer*

Corporate video production for Royal Mail, Re-Solv, NACAB, Water Aid, BT. Looking for experienced writers in the above field.

Michael White Productions Ltd
See **MW Entertainments Ltd**

Windrush Productions Ltd
7 Woodlands Road, Moseley, Birmingham B13 4EH
☎0121 449 6439   Fax 0121 449 6439
Contact *Pogus Caesar, Shawn Caesar*

Television documentaries including a multi-cultural series for Carlton TV (*Xpress and Respect*); *The A-Force* (BBC); *I'm Black in Britain* (Central TV). Also produces *Windrush E. Smith Show* (comedy, BBC Radio Pebble Mill). Encourages new writing, especially from the regions. 'We try to seek scripts from writers interested in developing new Black fiction/comedy.' Runs courses for writers in conjunction with Birmingham Education Dept.

WitzEnd Productions
1 Stephen Street, London W1P 1PJ
☎0171 691 6000   Fax 0171 691 6082

Bought by Pearson in 1996. Producer of television comedy (sitcoms, sketch shows, etc.). OUTPUT *Pie in the Sky; Lovejoy; Tracey Ullman: A Class Act; We Know Where You Live.* Scripts not welcome unless via agents.

Working Title Films Ltd
Oxford House, 76 Oxford Street, London W1N 9FD
☎0171 307 3000   Fax 0171 307 3001/2/3
Co-Chairmen (Films) *Tim Bevan, Eric Fellner*
Head of Development (Films) *Debra Hayward*
Development Executive (Films) *Natascha Wharton*
Television *Simon Wright*

Feature films, TV drama; also family/children's entertainment and TV comedy. OUTPUT Films: *Notting Hill; Elizabeth; Hi Lo Country; Plunkett & Macleane; Bean; The Borrowers; The Matchmaker; Fargo; Dead Man Walking; French Kiss; Four Weddings and a Funeral; The Hudsucker Proxy; The Tall Guy; A World Apart; Wish You Were Here; My Beautiful Laundrette.* Television: *More Tales of the City; Lano and Woodley; The Borrowers I & II; Armisted Maupin's Tales of the City; News Hounds; Echoes.* No unsolicited mss at present, but keen to encourage new writing nevertheless via New Writers Scheme - contact Natascha Wharton.

Worldview Pictures
Unit 10, Cameron House, 12 Castlehaven Road, London NW1 8QW
☎0171 916 4696   Fax 0171 916 1091
Email: anyone@worldviewpictures.co.uk
Contact *Stephen Trombley, Bruce Eadie*

Documentaries and series for television, plus theatrical. OUTPUT *A Death in the Family; Project X* (Dixcovery); *War and Civilization* (8 x 60min for The Learning Channel); *Nuremberg* (Discovery/Ch4); *Raising Hell: The Life of A. J. Bannister; The Execution Protocol* (both for Discovery/BBC/France 2); *Drancy: A Concentration Camp in Paris; The Lynchburg Story* (both for Discovery/Ch4/France 2).

Worthwhile Productions Ltd
4 Park Square Mews, Upper Harley Street, London NW1 4PP
☎0171 224 2446   Fax 0171 224 2446
Contact *Jeremy Wootliff*

Feature films, video; documentary, corporate and commercials. Unsolicited mss welcome.

Wortman Productions UK
48 Chiswick Staithe, London W4 3TP
☎0181 994 8886
Producer *Neville Wortman*

Film, video and TV production for drama, documentary, commercials and corporate material. OUTPUT *House in the Country* John Julius Norwich (ITV series); *Ellington* (jazz series); *Theatre Celebration Theatre Company for the Young – The Winter's Tale.* Open to new writing but preferably from agents; single page outline and couple of pages of dialogue.

Wot Films & Television Ltd
Suite 3, 44 Mortimer Street, London W1N 7DG
☎0171 323 5901/2   Fax 0171 323 5903
Contact *Jackie Thomas, Nick Fleming*

Television and video drama plus a film in development. Welcomes unsolicited mss.

The Writers Studio c/o Screen Production Associates Ltd
21A Parkhill Road, London NW3 2YH
☎0171 586 7315   Fax 0171 586 7315
Contact *Piers Jackson*

Feature films. OUTPUT *The 4th Man; The Truth Game; The Late 20th; Black Badge.* No unsolicited mss. Send preliminary letter outlining project (only movie screenplays) and c.v.

X-Dream International Limited

The Coach House, Ashford Lodge, Halstead, Essex CO9 3RR
☎01787 479000
Email: xdream@xdream.co.uk

Contact *Alistair Gosling*

Film, television and video; drama and documentary. Unsolicited mss welcome.

Yoda Productions Ltd

36 Steers Mead, Mitcham, Surrey CR4 3JU
☎0181 715 9278   Fax 0181 241 2516
Email: 100770.473@compuserve.com

Contact *Gail Lowe*

Medical, scientific, technical marketing and promotional, training videos and multimedia. No unsolicited mss.

Yoyo Films

79 Dean Street, London W1V 5HA
☎0171 642 8954   Fax 0171 737 3901
Email: yoyofilms@compuserve.com

Contact *Laurens Postma*

Film, television and video; drama and documentary. Unsolicited mss welcome; 'looking for new writing all the time.'

Zenith Entertainment plc

43–45 Dorset Street, London W1H 4AB
☎0171 224 2440   Fax 0171 224 3194

Script Executive *Ming Ho*

Feature films and TV drama. OUTPUT Films: Todd Haynes' *Velvet Goldmine; Wisdom of Crocodiles*; Nicole Holofcener's *Walking and Talking*. Television: *Hamish Macbeth; Rhodes; Bodyguards; The Uninvited*. No unsolicited scripts.

Theatre Producers

Actors Touring Company

Alford House, Aveline Street, London
SE11 5DQ
☎0171 735 8311Fax 0171 735 1031 attn ATC
Email: atc@cwcom.net

Artistic Director *Nick Philippou*

'Actors Touring Company takes old stories and works with living writers to produce new theatre.' Collaborations with writers are based on adaptation and/or translation work and unsolicited mss will only be considered in this category. 'We endeavour to read mss but do not have the resources to do so quickly.' As a small-scale company, all plays must have a cast of six or less.

Almeida Theatre Company

Almeida Street, Islington, London N1 1TA
☎0171 226 7432   Fax 0171 704 9581
Website: www.almeida.co.uk

Artistic Directors *Ian McDiarmid, Jonathan Kent*

FOUNDED 1980. Now in its tenth year as a full-time producing theatre, presenting a year-round theatre and music programme in which international writers, composers, performers, directors and designers are invited to work with British artists on challenging new and classical works. Previous productions: *Butterfly Kiss; The Rules of the Game; Medea; No Man's Land; The Rehearsal; Bajazet; Galileo; Moonlight; The School for Wives; Hamlet; Tartuffe; Who's Afraid of Virginia Woolf; Ivanov; The Government Inspector; Naked; The Judas Kiss; The Iceman Cometh.* No unsolicited mss: 'our producing programme is very limited and linked to individual directors and actors'.

Alternative Theatre Company Ltd

Bush Theatre, Shepherds Bush Green, London W12 8QD
☎0171 602 3703   Fax 0171 602 7614
Email: thebush@dircon.co.uk

Literary Manager *Tim Fountain*

FOUNDED 1972. Trading as The Bush Theatre. Produces nine new plays a year (principally British) including up to four visiting companies also producing new work: 'we are a writer's theatre'. Previous productions: *Kiss of the Spiderwoman* Manuel Puig; *Raping the Gold* Lucy Gannon; *The Wexford Trilogy* Billy Roche; *Love and Understanding* Joe Penhall; *This Limetree Bower* Conor McPherson; *Discopigs* Enda Walsh; *The Pitchfork Disney* Philip Ridley; *Caravan* Helen Blakeman; *Beautiful Thing* Jonathan Harvey; *Killer Joe* Tracy Letts; *Shang-a-Lang* Catherine Johnson. Scripts are read by a team of associates, then discussed with the management, a process which takes about three months. The theatre offers a small number of commissions, recommissions to ensure further drafts on promising plays, and a guarantee against royalties so writers are not financially penalised even though the plays are produced in a small house. Writers should send scripts with small s.a.e. for acknowledgement and large s.a.e. for return of script.

Yvonne Arnaud Theatre

Millbrook, Guildford, Surrey GU1 3UX
☎01483 440077   Fax 01483 564071

Contact *James Barber*

Credits include: *Alarms and Excursions* Michael Frayn; *Tom and Clem* Stephen Churchett; *Life Support* Simon Gray; *Equally Divided* Ronald Harwood; *Things We Do For Love* Alan Ayckbourn; *Laughter on the 23rd Floor* Neil Simon; *A Passionate Woman* Kay Mellor; *Indian Ink* Tom Stoppard; *Home* David Storey; *Cellmates* Simon Gray; *Letter of Resignation* Hugh Whitemore.

Birmingham Repertory Theatre

Broad Street, Birmingham B1 2EP
☎0121 236 6771   Fax 0121 236 7883

Artistic Director *Bill Alexander*
Associate Director *Tony Clark*
Literary Manager *Ben Payne*
Literary Officer *Liz Ingrams*

The Birmingham Repertory Theatre aims to provide a platform for the best work from new writers from both within and beyond the West Midlands region along with a programme which also includes classics and 'discovery' plays. The Rep is committed to a policy of integrated casting and to the production of new work which reflects the diversity of contemporary experience. The commissioning of new plays takes place across the full range of the theatre's activities: in the Main House, The Door (which is a dedicated new writing space) and on tour to community venues in the region. 'Writers are advised that the Rep is very unlikely to produce an unsolicited script. We usually assess unsolicited submissions on the basis of whether it indicates a writer with whom the theatre may be interested in working. The theatre runs a programme of writers' attachments every year in addition to its commissioning policy and maintains close links with *Stagecoach* (the regional writers' training agency) and the **MA in Playwriting Studies** at the University of Birmingham.' For more information contact the Literary Officer.

Black Theatre Co-op

Unit 3P Leroy House, 436 Essex Road,
London N1 3QP
☎0171 226 1225   Fax 0171 226 0223
Email: olivia.btc@virgin.net
Artistic Director *Felix Cross*

FOUNDED 1978. Plays to a mixed audience, approximately 65% female. Usually tours nationally twice a year. 'Committed in the first instance to new writing by Black British writers and work which relates to the Black culture and experience throughout the Diaspora, although anything considered.' Unsolicited mss welcome.

Bootleg Theatre Company

23 Burgess Green, Bishopdown, Salisbury,
Wiltshire SP1 3El
☎01722 421476
Contact *Colin Burden*

FOUNDED 1984. Tries to encompass as wide an audience as possible and has a tendency towards plays with socially relevant themes. A good bet for new writing since unsolicited mss are very welcome. 'Our policy is to produce new and/or rarely seen plays and anything received is given the most serious consideration.' Actively seeks to obtain grants to commission new writers for the company. *Hanging Hanratty* by Michael Burnham is due for a London run before a film version in 2000; *The Boys Are Back in Town* by Trevor Suthers was premièred in 1998. Future productions: *Titanic Wakes* and *Savagely Yours.*

Borderline Theatre Company

Darlington New Church, North Harbour
Street, Ayr KA8 8AA
☎01292 281010   Fax 01292 263825
Artistic Director *Leslie Finlay*
Chief Executive *Eddie Jackson*

FOUNDED 1974. Borderline is one of Scotland's leading touring companies. Committed to new writing, it tours a programme of new plays and radical adaptations/translations of classic texts in an accessible and entertaining style. Tours to main-house theatres across Scotland and small venues in outlying districts. Shows are premièred at the Edinburgh Festival and in London. Productions include: British première of *Kevin's Bed* by Bernard Farrell; *Sabina!*, a revival of the award-winning romantic comedy by Chris Dolan; *The Misanthrope*, a new version by Martin Crimp. Under commission: *The Angels' Share* by Chris Dolan; *Indian Summer* by A. L. Kennedy. 'We are committed to touring new writing for young people' – *Broken Angel* by Lin Coghlan and *The Prince and the Pilot* by Anita Sullivan. Past tours have included works by Dario Fo, A. L. Kennedy, Liz Lochhead, Roald Dahl and Carl MacDougal. Synopsis with cast size preferred in the first instance.

Bright Ltd

1–2 Henrietta Street, London WC2E 8PS
☎0171 379 7474   Fax 0171 379 8484
Email: chapman@dircon.co.uk
Contacts *Guy Chapman, Paul Spyker*

Performs to young audiences with innovative, experimental theatre. Productions include: *Shopping and Fucking*; *Love Upon the Throne*; *Crave*; *Disco Pigs.* Welcomes unsolicited mss; interested in modern issues, exciting boundary-pushing work.

Bristol Express Theatre Company

24 Well's House Road, East Acton, London
NW10 6EE
☎0181 838 4482   Fax 0181 838 4482
Director *Andy Jordan*

A non-funded, professional, sometimes middle-scale national touring company which has a continuing commitment to the discovery, development and encouragement of new writing, principally through its research and development programme *The Play's The Thing!* This consists of public/private staged and rehearsed readings; workshops and full-scale productions. Previous productions: *Child's Play* Jonathan Wolfman; *Winter Darkness* Allan Cubitt; *Prophets in the Black Sky* John Matshikiza; *Lunatic & Lover* Michael Meyer; *Heaven* Sarah Aicher; *Syme* Michael Bourdages; *Gangster Apparel* Richard Vetere. 'We look for plays that are socially/emotionally/theatrically/politically significant, analytical and challenging. The company is keen to produce work which attempts to mix genres (and create new ones!), is eloquent and honest, while remaining accessible and entertaining.'

Bristol Old Vic Company

Theatre Royal, King Street, Bristol BS1 4ED
☎0117 9493993   Fax 0117 9493996

Bristol Old Vic is committed to the commissioning and production of new writing in the Theatre Royal (650 seats). Plays must have enough popular appeal to attract an audience of significant size. The theatre will read and report on unsolicited scripts, and asks for a fee of £15 per script to cover the payments to readers.'We also seek to attract emerging talent to the Basement, a profit-share venue (50 seats) committed to producing one-act plays by un-proven writers. Plays for the Basement will be read free of charge although no report can be provided. At present we rarely produce in the New Vic Studio (150 seats) but often receive productions of new plays from visiting companies.'

Bush Theatre

See **Alternative Theatre Company Ltd**

Carnival (Films & Theatre) Ltd

See entry under **Film, TV and Video Production Companies**

Chester Gateway Theatre Trust Ltd

Hamilton Place, Chester, Cheshire CH1 2BH
☎01244 344238   Fax 01244 317277

Artistic Director *Deborah Shaw*

FOUNDED 1968. Plays to a broad audience across a wide range of work, classical to contemporary, including Shakespeare, John Godber, Tennessee Williams, Alan Ayckbourn, Arthur Miller, Pinter, etc. An emphasis on new writing with 14 world premières in the last four years. Small-cast material, children's and young people, large-scale youth theatre, people with learning difficulties, plays by women and adaptations of novels. Anything with a cast of over eight is unlikely to reach production. Scripts welcome but reading will take some time. Please send synopsis first. Winner of *The Stage* Award for Special Achievement in Regional Theatre in 1996.

Citizens Theatre

Gorbals, Glasgow G5 9DS
☎0141 429 5561   Fax 0141 429 7374

Artistic Director *Giles Havergal*

No formal new play policy. The theatre has a play reader but opportunities to do new work are limited.

Clwyd Theatr Cymru

Mold, Flintshire CH7 1YA
☎01352 756331   Fax 01352 758323
Email: drama@celtic.co.uk
Website: www.theatr-clwyd-cymru.co.uk

Literary Manager *William James*

Theatre of the Year 1998–99 (Barclays/TMA), Clwyd Theatr Cymru produces a season of plays each year performed in repertoire by a resident company, along with tours throughout Wales (in English and Welsh). Plays are a mix of classics, revivals, contemporary drama and new writing. Recent new writing includes: *The Journey of Mary Kelly* Sian Evans; *Rape of the Fair Country* and *Hosts of Rebecca* both by Alexander Cordell, adapt. Manon Eames; *The Changelings* Gregg Cullen; *Celf* by Yasmina Reza, translated into Welsh by Manon Eames. Unsolicited plays by Welsh writers or with Welsh themes will be considered.

Michael Codron Plays Ltd

Aldwych Theatre Offices, Aldwych, London WC2B 4DF
☎0171 240 8291   Fax 0171 240 8467

General Manager *Paul O'Leary*

Michael Codron Plays Ltd manages the Aldwych Theatre in London's West End. The plays it produces don't necessarily go into the Aldwych, but always tend to be big-time West End fare. Previous productions: *Hapgood; Uncle Vanya; The Sneeze; Rise and Fall of Little Voice; Arcadia; Dead Funny*. No particular rule of thumb on subject matter or treatment. The acid test is whether 'something appeals to Michael'. Straight plays rather than musicals.

Colchester Mercury Theatre Limited

Balkerne Gate, Colchester, Essex CO1 1PT
☎01206 577006   Fax 01206 769607
Email: mercury.theatre@virgin.net

Artistic Producer *Gregory Floy*
Associate Director *Adrian Stokes*

Producing theatre with a wide-ranging audience. Unsolicited scripts welcome. The theatre has a free playwright's group for adults with a serious commitment to writing plays.

The Coliseum, Oldham

Fairbottom Street, Oldham, Lancashire OL1 3SW
☎0161 624 1731   Fax 0161 624 5318

Chief Executive *Kenneth Alan Taylor*

The policy of the Coliseum is to present high

quality work that is unashamedly 'popular'. Has a special interest in new work that has a Northern flavour, however this does not rule out other plays. Unsolicited scripts are all read but will only be returned if a s.a.e. is included.

Communicado Theatre Company
See **Theatre Archipelago**

Contact Theatre Company
Oxford Road, Manchester M15 6JA
☎0161 274 3434   Fax 0161 273 6286
Contact *Artistic Director*

FOUNDED 1972. Plays to a young audience (up to 25). New productions have included: *Rupert Street Lonely Hearts Club* Jonathan Harvey; *Tell Me* Matthew Dunster (both world premières). NB Future policy on submissions uncertain at the time of going to press as a new artistic director was in the process of being appointed.

Crucible Theatre
55 Norfolk Street, Sheffield S1 1DA
☎0114 2760621   Fax 0114 2701532
Artistic Director *Deborah Paige*

'Our priorities are towards new emerging writers and established writers from whom *we* seek ideas for development. However, all unsolicited scripts are seen by a reader and will be returned if accompanied by s.a.e.'

Cwmni Theatr Gwynedd
Deiniol Road, Bangor, Gwynedd LL57 2TL
☎01248 351707   Fax 01248 351915
Artistic Director *Siân Summers*

FOUNDED 1984. A mainstream company, performing in major theatres on the Welsh circuit. Welsh-language work only at present. Classic Welsh plays, translations of European repertoire and new work, including adaptations from novels. New Welsh work always welcome; works in English considered if appropriate for translation (i.e. dealing with issues relevant to Wales). 'We are keen to discuss projects with established writers and offer commissions where possible.'

Derby Playhouse
Eagle Centre, Derby DE1 2NF
☎01332 363271   Fax 01332 294412
Website: www.derbyplayhouse.demon.co.uk
Artistic Director *Mark Clements*

Derby Playhouse is interested in new work and has produced several world premières over the last year. 'We have a discrete commissioning budget but already have several projects under way. Due to the amount of scripts we receive, we now ask writers to send a letter accompanied by a synopsis of the play, a résumé of writing experience and any ten pages of the script they wish to submit. We will then determine whether we think it is suitable for the Playhouse, in which case we will ask for a full script.' Writers are welcome to send details of rehearsed readings and productions as an alternative means of introducing the theatre to their work.

Druid Theatre Company
Druid Lane, Galway, Republic of Ireland
☎00 353 91 568660   Fax 00 353 91 563109
Contact *Literary Manager*

FOUNDED 1975. Plays to a wide-ranging audience, urban and rural, from young adults to the elderly. National and international theatre with an emphasis on new Irish work, though contemporary European theatre is commonplace in the repertoire. Currently has six writers under commission and is commissioning more. Enclose s.a.e. for return of scripts.

The Dukes Playhouse Ltd
Moor Lane, Lancaster LA1 1QE
☎01524 67461
Administrative Director *Amanda Belcham*

FOUNDED 1971. The only producing house in Lancashire. Wide target market for cinema and theatre. Plays in a 320-seater end-on auditorium and in a 198-seater in-the-round studio. In the summer months open-air promenade performances are held in Williamson Park. Also, community based Youth Arts Centre.

Dundee Repertory Theatre
Tay Square, Dundee DD1 1PB
☎01382 227684   Fax 01382 228609
Artistic Director *Hamish Glen*

FOUNDED 1939. Plays to a varied audience. Translations and adaptations of classics, and new local plays. Most new work is commissioned. Interested in contemporary plays in translation and in new Scottish writing. No scripts except by prior arrangement.

Eastern Angles Theatre Company
Sir John Mills Theatre, Gatacre Road, Ipswich, Suffolk IP1 2LQ
☎01473 218202   Fax 01473 250954
Contact *Ivan Cutting*

FOUNDED 1982. Plays to a rural audience for the most part. New work only: some commissioned, some devised by the company, some researched documentaries. Unsolicited mss welcome from regional writers. 'We are always keen to develop and produce new writing, especially that which is germane to a rural area.'

Edinburgh Royal Lyceum Theatre
See **Royal Lyceum Theatre Company**

English Stage Company Ltd
See **Royal Court Theatre**

English Touring Theatre
New Century Building, Hill Street, Crewe CW1 2BX
☎01270 501800   Fax 01270 501888
Email: admin@englishtouringtheatre.co.uk
Artistic Director *Stephen Unwin*

FOUNDED 1993. National touring company visiting middle-scale receiving houses and arts centres throughout England. Mostly mainstream. Largely classical programme, but with increasing interest to tour one modern English play per year. Strong commitment to Education and Community Outreach work. No unsolicited mss.

Everyman Theatre
5–9 Hope Street, Liverpool L1 9BH
☎0151 708 0338   Fax 0151 709 0398
Contact *Literary Manager*

Currently offers a script-reading service and commissions new work.

Robert Fox Ltd
6 Beauchamp Place, London SW3 1NG
☎0171 584 6855   Fax 0171 225 1638
Contact *Robert Fox*

Producers and co-producers of work suitable for West End production. Previous productions: *Another Country; Chess; Lettice and Lovage; Burn This; When She Danced; The Ride Down Mount Morgan; The Importance of Being Earnest; The Seagull; Goosepimples; Vita & Virginia; The Weekend; Three Tall Women; Skylight; Who's Afraid of Virginia Woolf; Masterclass; A Delicate Balance; Amy's View; Closer.* Scripts, while usually by established playwrights, are always read.

Gate Theatre Company Ltd
11 Pembridge Road, London W11 3HQ
☎0171 229 5387   Fax 0171 221 6055
Literary Manager *Philip Crispin*

FOUNDED 1979. Plays to a mixed, London-wide audience, depending on production. Aims to produce British premières of plays which originate from abroad and translations of neglected classics. Most work is with translators. Recent productions: *Une Tempête* by Aimé Césaire; *Volunteers* by Brian Friel. Positively encourages writers from abroad to send in scripts or translations. All such unsolicited scripts are read but as it is unlikely that new British, Irish or North American plays will have any future at the theatre due to emphasis on plays originating from abroad, the Gate does not welcome primary anglophone material and will not read these plays. Always enclose s.a.e. if play needs returning.

Graeae Theatre Company
Interchange Studios, Dalby Street, London NW5 3NQ
☎0171 267 1959   Fax 0171 267 2703
Minicom 0171 267 3164
Artistic Director *Jenny Sealey*
Administrative Director *Kevin Dunn*

Europe's premier theatre company of disabled people, the company tours nationally and internationally with innovative theatre productions highlighting both historical and contemporary disabled experience. Graeae also runs Forum Theatre and educational programmes available to schools, youth clubs and day centres nationally, provides vocational training in theatre arts (including playwriting). Unsolicited scripts – from disabled writers - welcome. New work examining disability issues is commissioned.

Hampstead Theatre
Swiss Cottage Centre, Avenue Road, London NW3 3EX
☎0171 722 9224   Fax 0171 722 3860
Literary Manager Ben Jancovich

Produces new plays and the occasional modern classic. Scripts are intially assessed by a team of script readers and their responses are shared with management in monthly script meetings. The literary manager and/or artistic director then read and consider many submsissions in more detail. It can therefore take 2–3 months to reach a decision. Writers produced in the past ten years include: Marguerite Duras, Terry Eagleton, Brad Fraser, Michael Frayn, Brian Friel, William Gaminara, Beth Henley, Stephen Jeffreys, Terry Johnson, Tony Kushner, Doug Lucie, Frank McGuinness, Rona Munro, Jennifer Phillips, Stephen Poliakoff, Philip Ridley, Martin Sherman, Shelagh Stephenson and Timberlake Wertenbaker.

Harrogate Theatre Company

Oxford Street, Harrogate, North Yorkshire
HG1 1QF
☎01423 502710   Fax 01423 563205
Contact *Artistic Director/Executive Director*
FOUNDED 1950. Describes its audience as 'eclectic, all ages and looking for innovation'. Previous productions: *The Marriage of Figaro* (commissioned adaptation of Beaumarchais, Mozart, Da Ponte); *Barber of Seville* (commissioned translation and adaptation of Beaumarchais, Rossini and Sterbini); *School for Wives*; *The Baltimore Waltz* Paula Vogel (European première); *Hot 'n' Throbbing* Paula Vogel (European première); *My Children! My Africa!*; *Wings* (Kopit, Lunden & Perlman European première); new adaptations of *The Government Inspector* and *The Turn of the Screw*; *Marisol* Jose Rivera; *Lulu* Angela Carter world première; *Skylight* David Hare. Always struggling to produce new work. The studio theatre was reopened in 1998 for small-scale productions including *White Lies* and *Mercy Killing* by Robert Shearman.

The Hiss & Boo Company

1 Nyes Hill, Wineham Lane, Bolney, West Sussex RH17 5SD   Fax 01444 882057
Email: hissboo@msn.com
Website: www.hissboo.co.uk
Contact *Ian Liston*
Particularly interested in new thrillers, comedy thrillers, comedy and melodrama – must be commercial full-length plays. Also interested in plays/plays with music for children. No one-acts. Previous productions: *Sleighrider; Beauty and the Beast; An Ideal Husband; Mr Men's Magical Island; Mr Men and the Space Pirates; Nunsense; Corpse!; Groucho: A Life in Revue; See How They Run; Christmas Cat and the Pudding Pirates; Pinocchio*. No unsolicited scripts; no telephone calls. Send synopsis and introductory letter in the first instance.

Hull Truck Theatre Company

Spring Street, Hull HU2 8RW
☎01482 224800   Fax 01482 581182
Executive Director *Simon Stallworthy*
John Godber, of *Teechers, Bouncers, Up 'n' Under* fame, the artistic director of this high-profile Northern company since 1984, has very much dominated the scene in the past with his own successful plays. The emphasis is still on new writing but Godber's work continues to be toured extensively. Most new plays are commissioned. Previous productions: *Dead Fish* Gordon Steel; *Off Out* Gill Adams; *Fish and Leather* Gill Adams; *Happy Families* John Godber. The company now reads all unsolicited scripts and aims to respond within three months. Bear in mind the artistic policy of Hull Truck, which is 'accessibility and popularity'. In general they are not interested in musicals, or in plays with casts of more than eight.

Pola Jones Associates Ltd

14 Dean Street, London W1V 5AH
☎0171 439 1165   Fax 0171 437 3994
Contact *André Ptaszynski*
FOUNDED 1982. Comedy, musicals and sitcoms preferred. Previous productions have included: *Neville's Island; The Nerd; Tommy; Crazy For You; Me and My Girl; Return To The Forbidden Planet; Chicago; West Side Story; From A Jack To A King*. Also produces comedy for TV: *Tygo Road; Joking Apart; Chalk*. Unsolicited scripts welcome.

Stephen Joseph Theatre

Westborough, Scarborough, North Yorkshire
YO11 1JW
☎01723 370540   Fax 01723 360506
Artistic Director *Alan Ayckbourn*
Literary Manager *Laura Harvey*
A two-auditoria complex housing a 165-seat end stage theatre/cinema (the McCarthy) and a 400-seat theatre-in-the-round (the Round). Positive policy on new work. For obvious reasons, Alan Ayckbourn's work features quite strongly but with a new writing programme now in place, plays from other sources are actively encouraged. Previous première productions include: *Woman in Black* (adapt. Stephen Mallatratt); *The Ballroom* Peter King; *Neville's Island* and *The End of the Food Chain* Tim Firth; *Penny Blue* Vanessa Brooks; *Fool To Yourself* Robert Shearman; *All Things Considered* Ben Brown; *Perfect Pitch* John Godber. Plays should have a strong narrative and be accessible. Submit to Laura Harvey enclosing an s.a.e. for return of mss.

Bill Kenwright Ltd

Warwick House, 106 Harrow Road,
London W2 1XD
☎0171 446 6200   Fax 0171 446 6222
Contact *Bill Kenwright*
Presents both revivals and new shows for West End and touring theatres. Although new work tends to be by established playwrights, this does not preclude or prejudice new plays from new playwrights. Scripts should be addressed to Bill

Kenwright with a covering letter and s.a.e. 'We have enormous amounts of scripts sent to us although we very rarely produce unsolicited work. Scripts are read systematically. Please do not phone; the return of your script or contact with you will take place in time.'

King's Head Theatre
115 Upper Street, London N1 1QN
☎0171 226 8561   Fax 0171 226 8507

The first pub theatre since Shakespearean times and the first venue in the UK for dinner theatre, the King's Head produces some strong work, including previously neglected work by playwrights such as Terence Rattigan and Vivian Ellis. Noël Coward's work also has a strong presence; the company is committed to its contribution to the reappraisal of his work and in 1995 toured *Cavalcade*. Previous productions: *Noël and Gertie*; *The Famous Five*; *Philadelphia, Here I Come!*; *Accapulco*; *Elegies for Angels, Punks and Raging Queens*; *A Day in the Death of Joe Egg*; *Journey's End*. Recent productions which have transferred to the West End include *The Boys in the Band* and *Burning Blue*. The King's Head is also committed to new work and has a new writing programme called 'Ninety/Nine/Moves'.

Komedia
Gardner Street, North Lane, Brighton, East Sussex BN1 1UN
☎01273 647101   Fax 01273 647102
Website: www.komedia.dircon.co.uk

Contact *David Lavender*

FOUNDED in 1994, Komedia promotes, produces and presents new work. Mss of new plays welcome.

Leeds Playhouse
See **West Yorkshire Playhouse**

Leicester Haymarket Theatre
Belgrave Gate, Leicester LE1 3YQ
☎0116 2530021   Fax 0116 2513310

Artistic Director *Paul Kerryson*

'We aim for a balanced programme of original and established works.' Recent productions include: *Edward II* with Eddie Izzard and *King Lear* with Kathryn Hunter as Lear. A script-reading panel has been established, and new writing is welcome. An Asian initiative has been set up to promote Asian work and Asian practitioners. Future productions include a new commission for Clare McIntyre, a new play by David Greer, the British première of Sondheim's *Sunday in the Park with George* and the première of *Airport*

2000. There is also a full studio season and programme of activity for the outreach and education department, including youth theatre and community tours.

Library Theatre Company
St Peter's Square, Manchester M2 5PD
☎0161 234 1913   Fax 0161 228 6481
Website: www.libtheatreco.org.uk

Artistic Director *Christopher Honer*

Produces new and contemporary work, as well as occasional classics. No unsolicited mss. Send outline of the nature of the script first. Encourages new writing through the commissioning of new plays and through a programme of rehearsed readings to help writers' development.

Live Theatre Company
7–8 Trinity Chare, Newcastle upon Tyne NE1 3DF
☎0191 261 2694   Fax 0191 232 2224

Artistic Director *Max Roberts*
General Manager *Jane Tarr*

FOUNDED 1973. Produces shows at its newly refurbished 200-seat venue, The Live Theatre, and also tours regionally and nationally. Company policy is to produce work that is rooted in the culture of the region, particularly for those who do not normally get involved in the arts. The company is particularly interested in promoting new writing. As well as full-scale productions the company organises workshops, rehearsed readings and other new writing activities. The company also enjoys a close relationship with New Writing North. Productions include: *Blow Your House Down* Sarah Daniels; *The Grass House* Pauline Hadaway; *Your Home in the West* Rod Wooden; *Seafarers* Tom Hadaway; *Up and Running* Phil Woods; *Buffalo Girls* by Karin Young; *Two* Jim Cartwright; *Cabaret*, and an ambitious cycle of plays – *Twelve Tales of Tyneside* – which involved 12 writers.

Liverpool Everyman
See **Everyman Theatre**

London Bubble Theatre Company
3–5 Elephant Lane, London SE16 4JD
☎0171 237 4434   Fax 0171 231 2366
Email: peth@londonbubble.org.uk

Artistic Director *Jonathan Petherbridge*

Produces workshops, plays and events for a mixed audience of theatregoers and non-theatregoers, wide-ranging in terms of age, culture and class. Previous productions: *Dealing*

With Feelings; The Lower Depths; Ali Baba and the Forty Thieves. Unsolicited mss welcome but 'our reading service is extremely limited and there can be a considerable wait before we can give a response'. Produces at least one new show a year which is invariably commissioned.

Lyric Theatre Hammersmith
King Street, London W6 0QL
☎0181 741 0824   Fax 0181 741 7694
Chief Executive *Sue Storr*
Artistic Director *Neil Bartlett*
Administrative Producer *Simon Mellor*

The main theatre stages an eclectic programme of new and revived classics with a particular interest in music theatre. Interested in developing projects with writers, translators and adaptors. Treatments, synopses and c.v.s only. No longer able to produce in its 110-seat studio owing to reduced funding but the venue continues to host work, including new, by some of the best touring companies in the country.

MAC - The Centre for Birmingham
Cannon Hill Park, Birmingham B12 9QH
☎0121 440 4221   Fax 0121 446 4372
Director *Dorothy Wilson*

MAC is a theatre and music-theatre producer, commissioning 3–5 scripts each year and presenting new writing. Home of the Geese Theatre Company, Sampad South Asian Arts, Stan's Café Theatre Company and a host of other arts/performance-related organisations based in Birmingham. Details on Geese available from the Centre.

Cameron Mackintosh
1 Bedford Square, London WC1B 3RA
☎0171 637 8866   Fax 0171 436 2683

Musical producer. His productions include *Oliver!; Little Shop of Horrors; Side by Side by Sondheim; Cats; Les Misérables; Phantom of the Opera; Miss Saigon.* Unsolicited scripts are read and considered (there is no literary manager, however) but new projects are rarely taken on.

Made In Wales
Chapter, Market Road, Canton, Cardiff CF5 1QE
☎01222 344737   Fax 01222 344738
Email: madein.wales@virgin.net
Artistic Director *Jeff Teare*
Associate Director *Rebecca Gould*

FOUNDED 1982. Made In Wales is Wales' leading new writing development and production company. It has produced nearly 50 new plays, recently not only in Wales but also Ireland and England with a prospective Australian production in development. Runs various development programmes and workshops and offers a free script-reading service. Three recently produced scripts have been published by Parthian Books under the title, *New Welsh Drama.* 'Made In Wales is particularly concerned to develop and present work reflecting our multicultural society.'

Man in the Moon Theatre Ltd
392 Kings Road, Chelsea, London SW3 5UZ
☎0171 351 5701   Fax 0171 351 1873
Email: manmoon@netcomuk.co.uk
Executive Director *Leigh Shine*
Literary Manager *Diana Hillier*
General Manager *Pete Staves*

FOUNDED 1982. Fringe theatre. In 1996, awarded the Guinness Ingenuity Award for creativity and innovation. Often tries to fit new plays into seasons such as 'Nationalism' and 'Family Values' and very keen to do rehearsed readings. Unsolicited scripts welcome; 'interested in submissions from first-time writers or writers in the initial stages of their career'. Particularly keen to consider plays which challenge the relationship between performer and audience. No unfinished scripts or treatments.

Manchester Library Theatre
See **Library Theatre Company**

Method & Madness
25 Short Street, London SE1 8LJ
☎0171 450 1990   Fax 0171 450 1991
Artistic Director *Mike Alfreds*

Method & Madness tends to form long-term relationships with authors and is 'unlikely to be in a position to produce another writer's new work until the year 2000'. Limited script-reading facilities. Unsolicited mss will not be read. Letters welcome; scripts only returned with s.a.e.

Midland Arts Centre
See **MAC - The Centre for Birmingham**

N.T.C. Touring Theatre Company
The Playhouse, Bondgate Without, Alnwick, Northumberland NE66 1PQ
☎01665 602586   Fax 01665 605837
Contact *Gillian Hambleton*
Administrator *Anna Flood*

FOUNDED 1978. Formerly Northumberland

Theatre Company. Winner of one of only two drama production franchises in the Northern region. Predominantly rural, small-scale touring company, playing to village halls and community centres throughout the Northern region, the Scottish Borders and countrywide. Productions range from established classics to new work and popular comedies, but must be appropriate to their audience. Unsolicited scripts welcome but are unlikely to be produced. All scripts are read and returned with constructive criticism within six months. Writers whose style is of interest may then be commissioned. The company encourages new writing and commissions when possible. Financial constraints restrict casting to a *maximum* of five.

New Victoria Theatre
Etruria Road, Newcastle under Lyme, Staffordshire ST5 0JG
☎01782 717954   Fax 01782 712885
Artistic Director *Gwenda Hughes*

The New Vic is a purpose-built theatre-in-the-round. Plays to a fairly broad-based audience which tends to vary from one production to another. A high proportion are not regular theatre-goers and new writing has been one of the main ways of contacting new audiences. Synopses preferred to unsolicited scripts.

Newpalm Productions
26 Cavendish Avenue, London N3 3QN
☎0181 349 0802   Fax 0181 346 8257
Contact *Phil Compton*

Rarely produces new plays (*As Is* by William M. Hoffman, which came from Broadway to the Half Moon Theatre, was an exception to this). National tours of productions such as *Peter Pan (The Musical); Noises Off, Seven Brides for Seven Brothers* and *Rebecca*, at regional repertory theatres, are more typical examples of Newpalm's work. Unsolicited mss, both plays and musicals, are, however, welcome; scripts are preferable to synopses.

Northampton Royal Theatre
See **Royal Theatre**

Northcott Theatre
Stocker Road, Exeter, Devon EX4 4QB
☎01392 256182   Fax 01392 499641
Artistic Director *Ben Crocker*

FOUNDED 1967. The Northcott is the Southwest's principal subsidised repertory theatre, situated on the University of Exeter campus. Describes its audience as 'geographically diverse,

conservative in taste, with a core audience of AB1s (40–60 age range)'. Continually looking to broaden the base of its audience profile, targeting younger and/or non-mainstream theatregoers in the 16–35 age range. Aims to develop, promote and produce quality new writing which reflects the life of the region and addresses the audience it serves. Generally works on a commission basis but occasionally options existing new work. Unsolicited mss welcome – current turnaround on script reading service approx. three months and no mss can be returned unless a correct value s.a.e. is included with the original submission.

Northern Stage
Newcastle Playhouse, Barras Bridge, Newcastle upon Tyne NE1 7RH
☎0191 232 3366   Fax 0191 261 8093
Artistic Director *Alan Lyddiard*

A contemporary performance company whose trademarks are a strongly visual and physical style, international influences, appeal to young people and strongly linked programmes of community work. As likely to produce devised work as conventional new writing. Before submitting unsolicited scripts, please contact *Ed Robson*, Associate Director.

Norwich Puppet Theatre
St James, Whitefriars, Norwich, Norfolk NR3 1TN
☎01603 615564   Fax 01603 617578
Artistic Director *Luis Boy*
General Manager *Ian Woods*

Plays to a young audience (aged 3–12) but developing shows for adult audiences interested in puppetry. All year round programme plus tours to schools and arts venues. Unsolicited mss welcome if relevant.

Nottingham Playhouse
Nottingham Theatre Trust, Wellington Circus, Nottingham NG1 5AF
☎0115 9474361   Fax 0115 9475759
Artistic Director *Giles Croft*

Aims to make innovation popular, and present the best of world theatre, working closely with the communities of Nottingham and Nottinghamshire. Unsolicited mss will be read. It normally takes about six months, however, and 'we have never yet produced an unsolicited script. All our plays have to achieve a minimum of 60 per cent audiences in a 732-seat theatre. We have no studio.' Also see **Roundabout** – the Nottingham Playhouse's theatre-in-education company.

Nuffield Theatre

University Road, Southampton, Hampshire
SO17 1TR
☎01703 315500   Fax 01703 315511
Artistic Director *Patrick Sandford*
Script Executive *Penny Gold*

Well-known as a good bet for new playwrights, the Nuffield gets an awful lot of scripts. They do a couple of new main stage plays every season. Previous productions: *Exchange* by Yri Trifonov (trans. Michael Frayn) which transferred to the Vaudeville Theatre; *The Floating Light Bulb* Woody Allen (British première); new plays by Claire Luckham: *Dogspot; The Dramatic Attitudes of Miss Fanny Kemble;* and by Claire Tomalin: *The Winter Wife.* Open-minded about subject and style, producing musicals as well as straight plays. Also opportunities for some small-scale fringe work. Scripts preferred to synopses in the case of writers new to theatre. All will, eventually, be read 'but please be patient. We do not have a large team of paid readers. We read everything ourselves.'

Octagon Theatre Trust Ltd

Howell Croft South, Bolton, Lancashire
BL1 1SB
☎01204 529407   Fax 01204 380110
Artistic Director *Lawrence Till*
Administrative Director *Amanda Belcham*

FOUNDED 1967. The Octagon Theatre has pursued a dynamic policy of commissioning new plays in recent years. These have been by both established writers such as Paul Abbott, Tom Elliott, Henry Livings and Les Smith as well as new and emerging writers through partnerships with organisations such as **North West Playwrights**, **Pearson Television** and the national new writing company **Paines Plough**. Whilst there is no prescriptive 'house style' at The Octagon, the theatre is nevertheless keen to encourage the development of writers from the North West region, telling stories that will resonate with the local audience. Unfortunately, the theatre does not have a resident literary manager or readers and is therefore unable to read and respond to unsolicited scripts.

Orange Tree Theatre

1 Clarence Street, Richmond, Surrey
TW9 2SA
☎0181 940 0141   Fax 0181 332 0369
Email: orangetree@enterprise.net
Website: www.enterprise.net/orangetreetheatre

Artistic Director *Sam Walters*

One of those theatre venues just out of London which are good for new writing, both full-scale productions and rehearsed readings (although these usually take place in The Room, above the Orange Tree pub). Main house productions: *A Wife Without a Smile* Arthur Pinero; *Sperm Wars* David Lewis; *The House Among the Stars* Michel Tremblay; *Lips Together, Teeth Apart* Terrence McNally; *The Way of the World* William Congreve; *Low Flying Aircraft* Jane Coles; *The Last Thrash* David Cregan; *The Cassilis Engagement* St John Hankin. The Room: *Dissident, goes without saying* Michael Vinaver; *Bad Faith* David Lewis; *The Girlz* Judy Upton; *The Stringless Marionette* Nicholas McInerny; *The Second Cosmic Hair Gallery* Deborah Catesby; *Jinx* Matt Parker; *Survivors* Amrit Wilson. Unsolicited mss are read, but patience (and s.a.e.) required.

Orchard Theatre

108 Newport Road, Barnstaple, Devon
EX32 9BA
☎01271 371475   Fax 01271 371825
Email: OrchardTheatre@compuserve.com
Website: ourworld.compuserve.com/
    homepages/OrchardTheatre
Artistic Director *Bill Buffery*

FOUNDED 1969. Plays appealing to a wide age range, which tour some 60 or 70 cities, towns and villages throughout Devon, Cornwall, Dorset, Somerset and Gloucestershire. Programme includes classics, new adaptations, outstanding modern work and newly commissioned plays. OUTPUT *A Doll's House; East o' the Sun and West o' the Moon; Halfway to Paradise; La Ronde; An Enemy of the People.*

Out of Joint

20–24 Eden Grove, London N7 8EA
☎0171 609 0207   Fax 0171 609 0203
Email: ojo@outofjoint.demon.co.uk
Director *Max Stafford-Clark*
Producer *Graham Cowley*
Literary Manager *Lee White*

FOUNDED 1993. Award-winning theatre company with new writing central to its policy. Produces new plays which reflect society and its concerns, placing an emphasis on education activity to attract young audiences. Welcomes unsolicited mss. Productions include: *Blue Heart* Caryl Churchill; *Our Lady of Sligo* and *The Steward of Christendom* Sebastian Barry; *Shopping and Fucking* Mark Ravenhill.

Oxford Stage Company

131 High Street, Oxford OX1 4DH
☎01865 723238   Fax 01865 790625
Artistic Director *Dominic Dromgoole*

A middle-scale touring company producing
established and new plays. At least one new
play or new adaptation a year. Due to forthcoming projects not considering unsolicited
scripts at present.

Paines Plough – New Writing New Theatre

4th Floor, 43 Aldwych, London WC2B 4DA
☎0171 240 4533   Fax 0171 240 4534
Email: paines.plough@dial.pipex.com
Artistic Director *Vicky Featherstone*
Literary Manager *Jessica Dromgoole*

Tours new plays nationally. Works with writers to develop their skills and voices through
courses, workshops, free script-reading service
and surgeries. Encourages writers to bridge the
gap between arthouse and commercial plays
with entertaining and provocative work for
audiences beyond the London fringe and West
End. Welcomes new scripts from writers. For
script-reading service send two s.a.e.s for
acknowledgement and return of script.

Palace Theatre, Watford

Clarendon Road, Watford, Hertfordshire
WD1 1JZ
☎01923 235455   Fax 01923 819664
Contact *Artistic Director*

An important point of policy is the active com-
missioning of new plays. Previous productions:
Diplomatic Wives Louise Page; *Over A Barrel*
Stephen Bill; *The Marriage of Figaro*; *The Barber of
Seville* (adapt. Ranjit Bolt); Jon Canter's *The
Baby*; *Borders of Paradise* by Sharman Macdonald;
Elton John's Glasses by David Farr (winner of the
1997 **Writers' Guild** Best Regional Play
award); *The Talented Mr Ripley* by Phyllis Nagy;
The Dark by Jonathan Holloway and *The Late
Middle Classes* by Simon Gray. Also supports
local writers via Education Department
(☎01923 810307).

Perth Repertory Theatre Ltd

185 High Street, Perth PH1 5UW
☎01738 472700   Fax 01738 624576
Email: theatre@perth.org.uk
Website: www.perth.org.uk/perth/theatre.htm
Artistic Director *Michael Winter*
General Manager *Paul Hackett*

FOUNDED 1935. Combination of three- and
four-weekly repertoire of plays and musicals,
incoming tours, studio productions and local
out-touring. Unsolicited mss are read when
time permits, but the timetable for return of
scripts is lengthy. New plays staged by the
company are invariably commissioned under
the SAC scheme.

Plymouth Theatre Royal

See **Theatre Royal**

Polka Theatre for Children

240 The Broadway, Wimbledon, London
SW19 1SB
☎0181 542 4258   Fax 0181 542 7723
Email: polkatheatre@dial.pipex.com
Website: www.polkatheatre.com
Artistic Director *Vicky Ireland*
Administrator *Stephen Midlane*

FOUNDED in 1967 and moved into its
Wimbledon base in 1979. Leading children's
theatre committed to commissioning and producing new plays. Programmes are planned two
years ahead and at least three new plays are commissioned each year. 'Because of our specialist
needs and fixed budgets, all our scripts are commissioned from established writers with whom
we work very closely. Writers are selected via
recommendation and previous work. We do not
perform unsolicited scripts. Potential new writers' work is read and discussed on a regular basis;
thus we constantly add to our pool of interesting
and interested writers.'

Praxis Theatre Company Ltd

24 Wykeham Road, London NW4 2SU
☎0181 203 1916   Fax 0181 203 1916
Email: praxisco@globalnet.co.uk
Website: www.users.globalnet.co.uk/~praxisco
Artistic Director *Sharon Kennet*

FOUNDED 1993. Performs to a mixed European
audience, 'crossing the divide between text-
based theatre and visual theatre'. No unsolicited
mss. Previous productions: *Seed*; *My Brother
Whom I Love*.

Queen's Theatre, Hornchurch

Billet Lane, Hornchurch, Essex RM11 1QT
☎01708 456118   Fax 01708 452348
Email: queens@globalnet.co.uk
Artistic Director *Bob Carlton*

The Queen's Theatre is a 500-seat producing
theatre in the London Borough of Havering
and within the M25. Established in 1953, the
theatre has been located in its present building
since 1975 and produces up to nine in-house

productions per year, including pantomime. The Queen's has re-established a permanent core company of actor/musicians under the new artistic leadership of Bob Carlton. Aims to produce distinctive and accessible performances in an identifiable house style focused upon actor/musician shows but, in addition, embraces straight plays, classics and comedies. 'New play/musical submissions are welcome and will be read and given a report.' Each year there is a large-scale community play commissioned from a local writer culminating in a summer event beside the theatre.

The Questors Theatre
12 Mattock Lane, Ealing, London W5 5BQ
☎0181 567 0011   Fax 0181 567 8736
Email: smtp production@questors.org.uk
Artistic Directors *Anne Gilmour, Brian Ingram*
Theatre Manager *Paul Maurel*
Production Secretary *Kris Collier*

FOUNDED 1929. Attracts an intelligent, discerning, wide age range audience looking for something different, innovative, daring. Recent productions include: *A Doll's House* Ibsen; *The Rose Tattoo* Tennessee Williams; *Accidental Death of an Anarchist* Dario Fo; *Andromache* Racine. Unsolicited mss welcome. All new plays are carefully assessed. Scripts received are acknowledged and all writers receive a written response to their work. Occasionally, unsolicited plays receive productions, others rehearsed readings.

The Really Useful Group Ltd
20 Tower Street, London WC2H 9NS
☎0171 240 0880   Fax 0171 240 1204

Commercial/West End theatre producers whose output has included *Jesus Christ Superstar; Sunset Boulevard; Joseph and the Amazing Technicolor Dreamcoat; Cats; Phantom of the Opera; Starlight Express; Daisy Pulls It Off; Lend Me a Tenor; Arturo Ui* and *Aspects of Love.*

Red Ladder Theatre Company
3 St Peter's Buildings, York Street, Leeds, West Yorkshire LS9 8AJ
☎0113 2455311   Fax 0113 2455351
Email: red-ladder@geo2.poptel.org.uk
Artistic Director/Literary Manager *Wendy Harris*
Administrator *Janis Smyth*

FOUNDED 1968. Commissioning company touring 2–3 shows a year with a strong commitment to new work and new writers. Aimed at an audience of young people aged between 14–25 years who have little or no access to theatre. Performances held in youth clubs and similar venues where young people choose to meet. Recent productions: 1998: *Crush* Rosy Fordham; *Wise Guys* by Philip Osment, a co-production with Theatre Centre. The company has scripts in development with John Binnie, Mike Kenny, Maya Chowdhry, Rosy Fordham and Noël Greig. While unsolicited scripts are not discouraged, the company is particularly keen to enter into a dialogue with writers with regard to creating new work for young people.'

Red Shift Theatre Company
9 The Leathermarket, Weston Street, London SE1 3ER
☎0171 378 9787   Fax 0171 378 9789
Contact *Jonathan Holloway, Artistic Director*
General Manager *Sophie Elliott*

FOUNDED 1982. Small-scale touring company which plays to a theatre-literate audience. Unlikely to produce an unsolicited script as most work is commissioned. Welcomes contact with writers – 'we try to see their work' – and receipt of c.v.s and treatments. Occasionally runs workshops bringing new scripts, writers and actors together. These can develop links with a reservoir of writers who may feed the company. Interested in new plays with subject matter which is accessible to a broad audience and concerns issues of importance; also new translations and adaptations. 1999 production: *Hamlet: First Cut*, a new version of the First Folio 'Hamlet'.

Ridiculusmus
10F Owen O'Cork Mill, Beersbridge Road, Belfast BT5 5DX
☎01232 460630   Fax 01232 460620
Email: Ridiculusmus@altavista.net
Artistic Directors *Jon Hough, David Woods*

FOUNDED 1992. Touring company which plays to a wide range of audiences. Productions have included adaptations of *Three Men In a Boat; The Third Policeman; At Swim Two Birds* and two new works: *All About H. Hatterr* and *The Exhibitionists.* Unsolicited scripts welcome but not political drama.

Roundabout Theatre in Education
Nottingham Playhouse, Wellington Circus, Nottingham NG1 5AF
☎0115 9474361   Fax 0115 9539055
Contact *Kitty Parker*

FOUNDED 1973. Theatre-in-Education company of the **Nottingham Playhouse**. Plays to a young audience aged 5–18 years of age. Some programmes are devised or adapted in-house, many are commissioned. Unable to resource the adequate response required for unsolicited scripts. 'We are committed to the encouragement of new writing as and when resources permit.'

Royal Court Theatre/English Stage Company Ltd

St Martin's Lane, London WC2N 4BG
☎0171 565 5050   Fax 0171 565 5002
Literary Manager *Graham Whybrow*

The English Stage Company was founded by George Devine in 1956 to put on new plays. John Osborne, John Arden, Arnold Wesker, Edward Bond, Caryl Churchill, Howard Barker and Michael Hastings are all writers this theatre has discovered. Christopher Hampton and David Hare have worked here in the literary department. 'The aim of the Royal Court is to develop and perform the best in new writing for the theatre, encouraging writers from all sections of society to address the problems and possibilities of our times.' (The company is due to move back to its refurbished theatre in Sloane Square, SW1 in the autumn of '99.)

Royal Exchange Theatre Company

St Ann's Square, Manchester M2 7DH
☎0161 833 9333   Fax 0161 832 0881
Literary Manager *Sarah Frankcom*

FOUNDED 1976. The Royal Exchange has developed a new writing policy which it finds is attracting a younger audience to the theatre. The company has produced new plays by Shelagh Stephenson, Brad Fraser, Simon Burke, Michael Wall, Rod Wooden, and Alex Finlayson. Also English and foreign classics, modern classics, adaptations and new musicals. The Royal Exchange receives 500–2000 scripts a year. These are read by Sarah Frankcom and a team of experienced readers. Only a tiny percentage is suitable, but a number of plays are commissioned each year.

Royal Lyceum Theatre Company

Grindlay Street, Edinburgh EH3 9AX
☎0131 248 4800   Fax 0131 228 3955
Artistic Director *Kenny Ireland*
Administration Manager *Ruth Dick*

FOUNDED 1965. Repertory theatre which plays to a mixed urban Scottish audience. Produces classic, contemporary and new plays. Would like to stage more new plays, especially Scottish.

No full-time literary staff to provide reports on submitted scripts.

Royal National Theatre

South Bank, London SE1 9PX
☎0171 452 3333   Fax 0171 452 3344
Website: www.nt-online.org
Literary Manager *Jack Bradley*

The majority of the National's new plays come about as a result of direct commission or from existing contacts with playwrights. There is no quota for new work, though so far more than a third of plays presented have been the work of living playwrights. Writers new to the theatre would need to be of exceptional talent to be successful with a script here, though the Royal National Theatre Studio helps a limited number of playwrights, through readings, workshops and discussions. In some cases a new play is presented for a shorter-than-usual run in the Cottesloe Theatre. Scripts considered (send s.a.e).

Royal Shakespeare Company

Literary Office, Barbican Centre, London EC2Y 8BQ
☎0171 382 2303   Fax 0171 382 2320
Website: www.rsc.org.uk/
Artistic Director *Adrian Noble*
Literary Manager *Simon Reade*

The RSC is a classical theatre company based in Stratford upon Avon, bringing its repertoire into London at the Barbican Theatre for six months of the year, and with residencies in Newcastle and Plymouth. It also tours extensively – nationally and internationally. As well as Shakespeare, English classics and foreign classics in translation, new plays counterpoint the RSC's repertory, especially those which celebrate language. 'The literary department is proactive rather than reactive and seeks out the plays and playwrights it wishes to commission. It will read all translations of classic foreign works submitted, or of contemporary works where the original writer and/or translator is known. It is unable to read unsolicited work from less established writers. It can only return scripts if an s.a.e. is enclosed with submission.'

Royal Theatre

15 Guildhall Road, Northampton NN1 1EA
☎01604 638343   Fax 01604 602408
Artistic Director *Michael Napier Brown*

Describes its audience as 'wide-ranging in terms of taste, with a growing population which is encouraging a more adventurous and innovative programme'. Produces at least three new works each year. The studio theatre, theatre-in-education, community touring and youth theatre tend to produce the majority of new work, but there are normally two main-house premières each year. Previous productions: *Oleanna; An Old Man's Love; Mail Order Bride; Keely and Du; The Winter's Tale; Top Girls; Shaken not Stirred.* Unsolicited scripts welcome and always read, 'but be patient!'.

7:84 Theatre Company Scotland

333 Woodlands Road, Glasgow G3 6NG
☎0141 334 6686   Fax 0141 334 3369
Email: 7.84-theatre@btinternet.com
Artistic Director *Iain Reekie*
Administrator *Tessa Rennie*

FOUNDED 1973. One of Scotland's foremost touring theatre companies committed to producing work that addresses current social, cultural and political issues. Recent productions include commissions by Scottish playwrights such as Stephen Greenhorn, (*Dissent*); David Greig (*Caledonia Dreaming*) and the Scottish premières of Tony Kushner's *Angels in America* and Athol Fugard's *Valley Song.* 'The company is committed to a new writing policy that encourages and develops writers at every level of experience, to get new voices and strong messages on to the stage.' Although happy to read unsolicited mss, 'it would be impossible to respond in detail to everything that we receive ... we simply do not have the resources to make this possible'. New writing development has always been central to 7:84's core activity and has included Summer Schools and the 7:84 Writers Group. The company continues to be committed to this work and its development.

Shared Experience Theatre

The Soho Laundry, 9 Dufours Place, London W1V 1FE
☎0171 434 9248   Fax 0171 287 8763
Email: 106250.1562@compuserve.com
Artistic Director *Nancy Meckler*
Associate Director *Polly Teale*

FOUNDED 1975. Varied audience depending on venue, since this is a touring company. Recent productions have included: *The Birthday Party* Harold Pinter; *Sweet Sessions* Paul Godfrey; *Anna Karenina* (adapt. Helen Edmundson); *Trilby & Svengali* (adapt. David Fielder); *Mill on the Floss* (adapt. Helen Edmundson); *The Danube* Maria Irene Fornes; *Desire Under the Elms* Eugene O'Neill; *War and Peace* (adapt. Helen Edmundson); *The Tempest*

William Shakespeare; *Jane Eyre* (adapt. Polly Teale); *I Am Yours* Judith Thompson. No unsolicited mss. Primarily not a new writing company but 'we are interested in innovative new scripts'.

Sherman Theatre Company

Senghennydd Road, Cardiff CF2 4YE
☎01222 396844   Fax 01222 665581
Artistic Director *Phil Clark*

FOUNDED 1973. Theatre for Young People, with main house and studio. Encourages new writing; has produced 70 new plays in the last six years. Previous productions: *Erogenous Zones, Roots & Wings* Frank Vickery; *Fern Hill, A Long Time Ago* Mike Kenny; *A Spell of Cold Weather* Charles Way; *101 Dalmations* adapt. Glyn Robbins; *Under the Bed* Brendan Murray; *Break, My Heart* Arnold Wesker. In 1997, the company presented six new plays live on stage and broadcast on BBC Radio Wales, and a new series of one-act lunchtime plays on stage and then filmed for HTV Wales. Priority will be given to Wales-based writers.

Show of Strength

Hebron House, Sion Road, Bedminster, Bristol BS3 3BD
☎0117 9021356   Fax 0117 9021330
Artistic Director *Sheila Hannon*

FOUNDED 1986. Plays to an informal, younger than average audience. Aims to stage at least one new play each season with a preference for work from Bristol and the South West. Will read unsolicited scripts but a lack of funding means they are unable to provide written reports. Interested in full-length stage plays; 'we are undeterred by large casts'. OUTPUT *A Busy Day* Fanny Burney; *A Man and Some Women* Githa Sowerby; *Blue Murder* Peter Nichols and *Rough Music* James Wilson (both world premières). Also, three rehearsed readings of new work each season.

Snap People's Theatre Trust

Unit A, 2 The Causeway, Bishop's Stortford, Hertfordshire CM23 2Ej
☎01279 836200   Fax 01279 501472
Contact *Andy Graham, Mike Wood*

FOUNDED 1979. Plays to young people in four age groups (5–7; 7–11; 11–14; 15–21), and to the thirty-something age group. Classic adaptations and new writing. Writers should make an appointment to discuss possibilities rather than submit unsolicited material. New writing encouraged. 'Projects should reflect the writer's own beliefs, be thought-provoking, challenging and accessible.'

Soho Theatre Company

21 Dean Street, London W1V 6NE
☎0171 287 5060   Fax 0171 287 5061
Email: mail@sohotheatre.com
Artistic Director *Abigail Morris*
Literary Manager *Paul Sirett*

Soho Theatre Company is dedicated to new writing. Having bought 21 Dean Street in 1997 with the help of Lottery money, work is underway to transform it into a new theatre and writers centre, due to open at the end of 1999. The company has an extensive research and development programme consisting of a free script reading service, workshops and readings. Also runs many courses for new writers. The company produces around four plays a year. Previous productions include: *Saints and Angels* Jessica Townsend, joint winnter of the 1998 Peggy Ramsay Award; *Gabriel* Moira Buffini, winner of the 1996 LWT Award; *Brothers of the Brush* Jimmy Murphy; *Kindertransporte* Diane Samuels. Runs the **Verity Bargate Award**, a biennial competition (see entry under **Prizes**).

Sphinx Theatre Company

25 Short Street, London SE1 8LJ
☎0171 401 9993   Fax 0171 401 9995
Artistic Director *Sue Parrish*

FOUNDED 1973. Tours new plays by women nationally to studio theatres and arts centres. Synopses and ideas are welcome.

The Steam Industry

Finborough Theatre, 118 Finborough Road, London SW10 9ED
☎0171 244 7439   Fax 0171 835 1853
Artistic Director *Phil Willmott*
Literary Manager *Gill Foreman*

Since June 1994, the Finborough Theatre has been a base for The Steam Industry who produce in and out of the building. Their output is diverse and prolific and includes a high percentage of new writing alongside radical adaptations of classics and musicals. The space is also available for a number of hires per year and the hire fee is sometimes negotiable to encourage innovative work. Unsolicited scripts are welcome but due to minimal resources it can take up to six months to respond. Send s.a.e. with material. The company regularly workshops new scripts at Monday-night play-readings and has developed new work by writers such as

Anthony Neilson, Naomi Wallace, Conor McPherson, Tony Marchant, Diane Samuels and Mark Ravenhill.

Stoll Moss Theatres Ltd

Manor House, 21 Soho Square, London W1V 5FD
☎0171 494 5200   Fax 0171 434 1217
Contact *Nica Burns*

Influential theatrical empire, with ten theatres under its umbrella: Apollo; Cambridge; Duchess; Garrick; Gielgud; Her Majesty's; London Palladium; Lyric Shaftesbury Avenue; Queen's and Theatre Royal Drury Lane.

Swan Theatre

The Moors, Worcester WR1 3EF
☎01905 726969   Fax 01905 723738
Artistic Director *Jenny Stephens*

Repertory company producing a wide range of plays to a mixed audience coming largely from the City of Worcester and the county of Hereford and Worcester. A writing group meets at the theatre. Unsolicited scripts discouraged.

Swansea Little Theatre Ltd

Dylan Thomas Theatre, Maritime Quarter, Gloucester Place, Swansea, West Glamorgan SA1 1TY
☎01792 473238
Contact *Annalie Williams (Chair, Artistic Committee)*

A wide variety of plays, from pantomime to the classics. New writing encouraged. New plays considered by the Artistic Committee.

Talawa Theatre Company Ltd

23/25 Great Sutton Street, London EC1V 0DN
☎0171 251 6644   Fax 0171 251 5969
Email: hq@talawa.com
Website: www.talawa.com
Artistic Director *Yvonne Brewster*
General Manager *Anthony Corriette*

FOUNDED 1985. Plays to an ABC audience of 60% black, 40% white across a wide age range depending upon the nature of productions and targeting. Previous productions include all-black performances of *The Importance of Being Earnest* and *Antony and Cleopatra*; plus Jamaican pantomime *Arawak Gold; The Gods Are Not to Blame; The Road* Wole Soyinka; *Beef, No Chicken* Derek Walcott; *Flying West* Pearl Cleage; *Othello* William Shakespeare. Restricted to new work from Black writers only. Occasional commissions, though these tend to go to established writers. 'Interested in the innovative, the modern classic with special reference to the African diasporic experience.' Runs a Black script development project. Talawa is funded by the **London Arts Board** (for three years).

Theatre Absolute

Office 5, 61 Corporation Street, Coventry CV1
☎01203 257380

Producer *Julia Negus*

FOUNDED 1992. Commissions, produces and tours new writing for performance in studio and small-scale venues. Productions have included: *She's Electric; Big Burger Chronicles; Violent Times; Car.* Launched 'The Writing House' in 1998, a scheme funded by the National Lottery and run in collaboration with the Belgrade Theatre. Its aims are to work with writers in workshop/laboratory situations, developing ideas, scripts and relationships togwards future commissions and production.

Theatre Archipelago

2 Hill Street, Edinburgh EH2 3JZ
☎0131 624 4040   Fax 0131 624 4041

Artistic Director *Helena Kaut-Howson*

FOUNDED in 1982 as Communicado and changed its name to Theatre Archipelago in 1999. Scottish touring company which aims to present dynamic and challenging theatre to the widest range of audience in Scotland and internationally. 'We encourage new writing, especially, but not exclusively, of Scots origin. Unfortunately there are no facilities for dealing with unsolicited scripts.' Productions have included: *Mary Queen of Scots Got Her Head Chopped Off* Liz Lochhead; *Cyrano de Bergerac* trans. Edwin Morgan; *Sacred Hearts* Sue Glover; *Tall Tales for Cold Dark Nights; Tales of the Arabian Nights* both by Gerard Mulgrew.

Theatre of Comedy Company

210 Shaftesbury Avenue, London
WC2H 8DP
☎0171 379 3345   Fax 0171 836 8181

Contact *Andrew Leigh (Chief Executive)*

FOUNDED 1983 to produce new work as well as classics and revivals. Interested in strong comedy in the widest sense – Chekhov comes under the definition as does farce. Also has a light entertainment division, developing new scripts for television, namely situation comedy and series. Not reading unsolicited scripts in 1999/2000.

Theatre Royal, Plymouth

Royal Parade, Plymouth, Devon PL1 2TR
☎01752 668282   Fax 01752 671179

Contact *Liz Turgeon, Simon Stokes*

Stages small-, middle- and large-scale drama including musicals and music theatre. Commissions and produces new plays. Unsolicited scripts are read and reported on.

Theatre Royal Stratford East

Gerry Raffles Square, London E15 1BN
☎0181 534 7374   Fax 0181 534 8381

Associate Director *Kerry Michael*

Lively East London theatre, catering for a very mixed audience, both local and London-wide. Produces plays, musicals, youth theatre and local community plays/events, all of which is new work. Special interest in Asian and Black British work. New initiatives include developing contemporary British musicals. Unsolicited scripts which are fully completed and have never been produced are welcome.

Theatre Royal Windsor

Windsor, Berkshire SL4 1PS
☎01753 863444   Fax 01753 831673

Executive Producer *Bill Kenwright*
Executive Director *Mark Piper*

Plays to a middle-class, West End-type audience. Produces thirteen plays a year and 'would be disappointed to do fewer than two new plays in a year; always hope to do half a dozen'. Modern classics, thrillers, comedy and farce. Only interested in scripts along these lines.

Theatre Workshop Edinburgh

34 Hamilton Place, Edinburgh EH3 5AX
☎0131 225 7942   Fax 0131 220 0112

Artistic Director *Robert Rae*

Plays to a young, broad-based audience with much of the work targeted towards particular groups or communities. OUTPUT has included adaptations of Gogol's *The Nose* and Aharon Appelfeld's *Badenheim 1939* – two community performance projects. Particularly interested in new work for children and young people. Frequently engages writers for collaborative/devised projects. Commissions a significant amount of new writing for a wide range of contexts, from large-cast community plays to small-scale professional tours. Favours writers based in Scotland, producing material relevant to a contemporary Scottish audience. Member of Scottish Script Centre to whom it refers senders of unsolicited scripts.

Tiebreak Touring Theatre

Heartsease High School, Marryat Road,
Norwich, Norfolk NR7 9DF
☎01603 435209   Fax 01603 435184
Email: tie.break@virgin.net
Artistic Director *David Farmer*

FOUNDED 1981. Specialises in high-quality
theatre for children and young people, touring
schools, youth centres, museums and festivals.
Productions: *Fast Eddy; Breaking the Rules; George
Speaks; Frog and Toad; Love Bites; Singing in the
Rainforest; Boadicea – The Movie; Dinosaurs on Ice;
The Invisible Boy; My Friend Willy; The Ugly
Duckling; Almost Human.* New writing encouraged. Interested in low-budget, small-cast material only. School, educational and socially relevant material of special interest. Scripts welcome.

Torch Theatre

St Peter's Road, Milford Haven,
Pembrokeshire SA73 2BU
☎01646 694192   Fax 01646 698919
Artistic Director *Peter Doran*

FOUNDED 1976. Plays to a mixed audience hard
to attract to new work on the whole. Committed to new work but financing has become
somewhat prohibitive. Small–cast pieces with
broad appeal welcome. Previous productions:
*Frankie and Tommy; School for Wives; Tess of
the d'Urbervilles.* The repertoire runs from
Ayckbourn to Friel. Scripts sometimes welcome.

Traverse Theatre

Cambridge Street, Edinburgh EH1 2ED
☎0131 228 3223   Fax 0131 229 8443
Email: john@traverse.co.uk
Website: www.traverse.co.uk
Artistic Director *Philip Howard*
Literary Director *John Tiffany*
Literary Assistant *Hannah Rye*

The Traverse is the best-known theatre in Scotland for new writing; it has a policy of putting on
nothing but new work by new writers. Also has
a strong international programme of work in
translation and visiting companies. Previous productions: *Kill the Old, Torture their Young* David
Harrower; *Perfect Days* Liz Lochhead; *Heritage*
Nicola McCartney; *Passing Places* Stephen
Greenhorn. No unsolicited scripts. Writers welcome to make contact by phone or in writing.

Trestle Theatre Company

Birch Centre, Hill End Lane, St Albans,
Hertfordshire AL4 0RA
☎01727 850950   Fax 01727 855558
Artistic Directors *Joff Chafer, Toby Wilsher*

FOUNDED 1981. Physical, mask theatre for
mostly student-based audiences (18–36 years).
All work is devised by the company. Scripts
which have the company's special brand of theatre in mind will be considered. No non-physi-
cal-based material. New writing welcome.

Tricycle Theatre

269 Kilburn High Road, London NW6 7JR
☎0171 372 6611   Fax 0171 328 0795
Artistic Director *Nicolas Kent*

FOUNDED 1980. Plays to a very mixed audience,
in terms of both culture and class. Previous pro-
ductions: *Two Trains Running* August Wilson;
The Day the Bronx Died Michael Henry Brown;
Half the Picture Richard Norton-Taylor and John
McGrath; *Nativity* Nigel Williams; *Playboy of the
West Indies* Mustapha Matura; *Joe Turner's Come
and Gone* and *The Piano Lesson* August Wilson;
Pecong Steve Carter; *A Love Song for Ulster* Bill
Morrison; *Three Hotels* Jon Robin Baitz;
Nuremberg adapt. from transcripts of the trials by
Richard Norton-Taylor; *Srebrenica* adapt.
Nicolas Kent. New writing welcome from
women and ethnic minorities (particularly Black,
Asian and Irish). Looks for a strong narrative
drive with popular appeal, not 'studio' plays. Can
only return scripts if postage coupons or s.a.e. are
enclosed with original submission.

Tron Theatre Company

63 Trongate, Glasgow G1 5HB
☎0141 552 3748   Fax 0141 552 6657
Email: neil@tron.co.uk
Website: www.tron.co.uk
Artistic Director *Irina Brown*

FOUNDED 1981. Plays to a broad cross-section of
Glasgow and beyond, including international
tours (Toronto 1990 & 1996; New York 1991;
Montreal 1992). Recent productions: *Sea Urchins*
Sharman Macdonald; *Mate in Three* Vittorio
Franceschi; *The Trick is to Keep Breathing* Janice
Galloway/Michael Boyd; *Endgame* Beckett;
Good C. P. Taylor; *Macbeth; Lavochkin-5 (La Funf
in der Luft)* Alexei Shipenko, trans. Iain Heggie/
Irina Brown. Interested in ambitious plays by
UK and international writers. No unsolicited
mss.

The Unearthly Theatre Company

150 Havelock Street, Preston, Lancashire
PR1 7NJ
☎01772 886003   Fax 01772 886003
Email: moship@msn.com

Contact *James Miley, Gary Nixon, Michael Moss*
FOUNDED 1997. A new company operating
from the University of Central Lancashire.
Produces three plays a year, both contemporary
and period. OUTPUT includes a new adaption of
Dracula, a contemporary play, *Delirium* for World
Aids Day 1998, and a highly successful production of *Our Boys*. Unsolicited material is not welcome; initial approach should be made in writing, enclosing an s.a.e. to ensure a response.

Unicorn Theatre for Children

St Mark's Studios, Chillingworth Road,
London N7 8QJ
☎0171 700 0702   Fax 0171 700 3870
Artistic Director *Tony Graham*
FOUNDED 1947 as a touring company, and was
resident at the Arts Theatre from 1967 until
April 1999 when it moved its base to the
Pleasance Theatre in north London. Plays mainly
to children between the ages of 4–12. Previous
productions: *The Lost Child* by Mike Kenny;
Cinderella, Hansel and Gretel by Stuart Paterson;
Jemima Puddleduck and her Friends adapt. by
Adrian Mitchell; *Something Beginning With ...* by
Brendan Murray; *Fairytaleheart* by Philip Ridley.

Upstairs at the Gatehouse

See **Ovation Productions** under **Film, TV
and Video Production Companies**

Charles Vance Productions

Hampden House, 2 Weymouth Street,
London W1N 3FD
☎0171 636 4343   Fax 0171 636 2323
Email: cvtheatre@aol.com
Contact *Charles Vance, Jill Streatfeild*
In the market for medium-scale touring productions and summer-season plays. Hardly any
new work and no commissions but writing of
promise stands a good chance of being passed
on to someone who might be interested in it.
Occasional try-outs for new work in the
Sidmouth repertory theatre. Send s.a.e. for
return of mss.

Warehouse Theatre, Croydon

Dingwall Road, Croydon CR0 2NF
☎0181 681 1257   Fax 0181 688 6699
Email: warehous@dircon.co.uk
Website: www.uk-live.co.uk/
   warehouse_theatre
Artistic Director *Ted Craig*
South London's new writing theatre (adjacent

to East Croydon railway station) seats 100–120
and produces up to six new plays a year. Also
co-produces with, and hosts, selected touring
companies who share the theatre's commitment
to new work. Continually building upon a tradition of discovering and nurturing new writers, with activities including a monthly writers'
workshop and the annual **International
Playwriting Festival**. Also hosts youth theatre
workshops and Saturday morning children's
theatre. A new purpose-built theatre is in the
final states of planning. Previous productions:
Iona Rain by Peter Moffat and *Fat Janet is Dead*
by Simon Smith (both past winners of the
International Playwriting Festival); *The Blue
Garden* Peter Moffat; *Coming Up* James Martin
Charlton and M. G. 'Monk' Lewis; *The Castle
Spectre* edited by Phil Willmott. Unsolicited
scripts welcome but it is more advisable to submit plays through the theatre's International
Playwriting Festival.

Watford Palace Theatre

See **Palace Theatre**

West Yorkshire Playhouse

Playhouse Square, Leeds, West Yorkshire
LS2 7UP
☎0113 2137800   Fax 0113 2137250
Committed to programming new writing as part
of its overall policy. Before sending an unso-
licited script please phone or write. The Play-
house does readings and workshops on new plays
with writers from all over Britain and also has
strong links with local writers and Yorkshire
Playwrights. The theatre has writers-in-residence.
Premières include: *A Passionate Woman* Kay
Mellor; *Fathers Day* Maureen Lawrence; *The
Beatification of Area Boy* Wole Soyinka; *The
Winter Guest* Sharman Macdonald; *You'll Have
Had Your Hole* Irvine Welsh.

Whirligig Theatre

14 Belvedere Drive, Wimbledon, London
SW19 7BY
☎0181 947 1732   Fax 0181 879 7648
Contact *David Wood*
One play a year in major theatre venues, usually
a musical for primary school audiences and
weekend family groups. Interested in scripts
which exploit the theatrical nature of children's
tastes. Previous productions: *The See-Saw Tree;
The Selfish Shellfish; The Gingerbread Man; The
Old Man of Lochnagar; The Ideal Gnome
Expedition; Save the Human; Dreams of Anne
Frank; Babe, the Sheep-Pig*.

Michael White Productions Ltd
See **MW Entertainments Ltd** under **Film, TV and Video Production Companies**

White Bear Theatre Club
138 Kennington Park Road,
London SE11 4DJ

Administration: 3 Dante Road, Kennington, London SE11 4RB
☎0171 793 9193   Fax 0171 277 0526

Contact *Michael Kingsbury*
Administrator *Kelly Maglia*

FOUNDED 1988. OUTPUT primarily new work for an audience aged 20–35. Unsolicited scripts welcome, particularly new work with a keen eye on contemporary issues, though not agitprop. Holds readings throughout the year. A recent production, *Absolution* by Robert Sherwood was nominated by the Writers' Guild for 'Best Fringe Play'. **The Writers' Guild**, sponsored by the Mackintosh Foundation, are leading writer workshops and readings throughout the year.

Windsor Theatre Royal
See **Theatre Royal Windsor**

York Theatre Royal
St Leonard's Place, York YO1 2HD
☎01904 658162   Fax 01904 611534

Artistic Director *Damian Cruden*

Not a new writing theatre in the main. Previous productions: *Into the Woods; Macbeth; Tom Jones* (musical version adapted by John Doyle). Send synopses only.

The Young Vic
66 The Cut, London SE1 8LZ
☎0171 633 0133   Fax 0171 928 1585

Artistic Director *Tim Supple*

FOUNDED 1970. The Young Vic produces adventurous and demanding work for an audience with a youthful spirit. The main house is one of London's most exciting spaces and seats up to 500. In addition, a smaller, entirely flexible space, The Young Vic Studio, seats 100 and is used for experiment, performance, rehearsals and installations. 'We are not able to produce many new scripts at the moment; nor are we able to develop or read unsolicited scripts with the care they deserve. However, we are always happy to receive work.'

Freelance Rates –
Subsidised Repertory Theatres
(excluding Scotland)

The following minimum rates were negotiated by **The Writers' Guild** and Theatrical Management Association and are set out under the TMA/Writers Agreement.

Theatres are graded by a 'middle range salary level' (MRSL), worked out by dividing the 'total basic salaries' paid by the total number of 'actor weeks' in the year.

	MRSL 1	MRSL 2	MRSL 3
Commissioned Play			
Commission payment	£3,215	£2,630	£2,046
Delivery payment	£1,462	£1,168	£1,168
Acceptance payment	£1,462	£1,168	£1,168
Total payment	*£6,139*	*£4,966*	*£4,382*
Non-Commissioned Play			
Delivery payment	£4,677	£3,798	£3,214
Acceptance payment	£1,462	£1,168	£1,168
Total payment	*£6,139*	*£4,966*	*£4,382*
Rehearsal Attendance	£43.14	£37.84	£34.88

Options

UK (excluding West End)	£1,824
West End/USA	£3,040
Rest of the World (English speaking productions)	£2,432

Festivals

Aberystwyth International Poetry Festival & Summer School
Aberystwyth Arts Centre, Penglais,
Aberystwyth SY23 3DE
☎01970　　　　　　　　　622889/622883
Email: lla@aber.ac.uk

FOUNDED 1996. Annual week-long festival held in June. The 1999 Festival, which was sponsored by **Bloodaxe Books** and *Western Mail*, featured guest writers Jack Mapanje, Jo Shapcott and Menna Elfyn. Also Summer School courses 'for anyone who enjoys writing – young or old, from published poets to beginners'.

Aldeburgh Poetry Festival
Reading Room Yard, The Street, Brockdish,
Diss, Norfolk IP21 4JZ
☎01379 668345　　　　　Fax 01379 668844
Contact *Michael Laskey*

Now in its twelfth year, an annual international festival of contemporary poetry held over one weekend each November in Aldeburgh and attracting large audiences. Regular features include a four-week residency leading up to the festival, poetry readings, children's event, workshops, public masterclass, lecture, performance spot and the festival prize for the year's best first collection (see entry under **Prizes**).

Arundel Festival
The Arundel Festival Society Ltd, The Mary Gate, Arundel, West Sussex BN18 9AT
☎01903 883690　　　　　Fax 01903 884243
Email: arundel.festival@argonet.co.uk
Website: www.argonet.co.uk/arundel.festival
Coordinator *Victoria Moles*

Annual ten-day summer festival (27 August – 5 September in 1999). Events include small-scale theatre, open-air theatre in Arundel Castle, concerts with internationally known artists, jazz, visual arts and active fringe.

Aspects Literature Festival
North Down Borough Council, Tower House, 34 Quay Street, Bangor BT20 5ED
☎01247 278032　　　　　Fax 01247 467744
Festival Director *Kenneth Irvine*
Administrator *Paula Clamp*

FOUNDED 1992. 'Ireland's Premier Literary Festival' is held at the end of September and celebrates the richness and diversity of living Irish writers with occasional special features on past generations. It draws upon all disciplines – fiction (of all types), poetry, theatre, non-fiction, cinema, song-writing, etc. It also includes a day of writing for young readers and sends writers to visit local schools during the festival. Highlights of recent festivals include appearances by Bernard MacLaverty, Marion Keyes, Alice Taylor, Frank Delaney, Seamus Heaney, Brian Keenan, Fergal Keane.

Bath Fringe Festival
The Bell, 103 Walcot Street, Bath BA1 5BW
☎01225 480079　　　　　Fax 01225 427441
Chair *David Stevenson*

FOUNDED 1981 to complement the international music festival, the Fringe presents theatre, poetry, jazz, blues, comedy, cabaret, street performance and more in venues, parks and streets of Bath during late May and early June.

Belfast Festival at Queen's
Festival House, 25 College Gardens, Belfast BT9 6BS
☎01232 667687　　　　　Fax 01232 663733
Executive Director *Robert Agnew*

FOUNDED 1964. Annual three-week festival held in the autumn (29 October – 14 November in 1999). Organised by Queen's University in association with the **Arts Council of Northern Ireland**, the festival covers a wide variety of events, including literature. Programme available in September.

Between the Lines – The Belfast Literary Festival
Crescent Arts Centre, 2–4 University Road, Belfast BT7 1NH
☎01232 242338　　　　　Fax 01232 246748

FOUNDED 1998. Annual 7–10-day international event held in March. Features readings, workshops, open platforms, quizzes and performance. All genres covered: playwriting, prose, poetry, screenwriting, etc. and special events for children. Previous guest: A. L. Kennedy, Troy Kennedy Martin, Ariel Dorfman, Will Self, James Kelman, Lavinia Greenlaw, Hugo Hamilton. Telephone to join free mailing list.

Beyond the Border International Storytelling Festival

St Donats Arts Centre, St Donats Castle, Vale of Glamorgan CF61 1WF
☎01446 794848   Fax 01446 794711
Festival Directors *David Ambrose, Ben Haggarty*
FOUNDED 1993. Annual event held over the first weekend in July when storytellers from around the world gather in the grounds of a medieval cliff-top castle. Features formal and informal story sessions, ballad singing, story-walks, folk and world music, dance and a full programme of events for children.

Birmingham Readers and Writers Festival

Festival Office, Central Library, Chamberlain Square, Birmingham B3 3HQ
☎0121 303 4244   Fax 0121 233 9702
Festival Director *Helen Cross*
FOUNDED 1983. Annual ten-day festival held in November in arts venues and libraries in Birmingham. Concerned with all aspects of contemporary reading and writing, with visiting authors, workshops, performances, cabaret, conferences and special programmes for young people.

Book Now!

Langholm Lodge, 146 Petersham Road, Richmond, Surrey TW10 6UX
☎0181 831 6138   Fax 0181 940 7568
Email: leisure@richmond.gov.uk
Website: www.richmond.gov.uk/leisure
Director *Nigel Cutting*
FOUNDED 1992. Annual festival which runs throughout the month of November, administered by the Arts Section of Richmond Council. Principal focus is on poetry and serious fiction, but events also cover biography, writing for theatre, children's writing. Programme includes readings, discussions, workshops, debates, exhibitions, schools events. Writers to appear at past festivals include A. S. Byatt, Penelope Lively, Benjamin Zephaniah, Sir Dirk Bogarde, Roger McGough, Rose Tremain, John Mortimer and Sean Hughes.

Bradford Festival

Provincial House, Centenary Square, Bradford, West Yorkshire BD1 1NH
☎01274 309199   Fax 01274 724213
Email: info@bradfordfestival.yorks.com
Website: www.bradfordfestival.yorks.com
Director *Mark Fielding*
FOUNDED 1987. June/July; two weeks. The 'largest, award-winning annual community arts festival in the country'. Includes the Mela ('bazaar' or 'fair' in Urdu) reflecting the city's cultural mix, and Cafe Bradford in Centenary Square with music, street theatre, food, drink and spectacle.

Brighton Festival

Festival Office, 21–22 Old Steine, Brighton, East Sussex BN1 1EL
☎01273 292950   Fax 01273 622453
Email: info@brighton-festival.org.uk
Website: www.brighton-festival.org.uk
Contact *General Manager*
FOUNDED 1967. For 24 days every May, Brighton hosts England's largest mixed arts festival. Music, dance, theatre, film, opera, literature, comedy and exhibitions. Literary enquiries will be passed to the literature officer. Deadline October for following May.

Bristol Poetry Festival

The Poetry Can, Unit 11, 20–22 Hepburn Road, Bristol BS2 8UD
☎0117 9426976   Fax 0117 9441478
Festival Director *Hester Cockcroft*
FOUNDED 1996. Annual festival taking place across the city throughout October. A celebration of the best in contemporary poetry, from readings and performances to cabaret and multimedia. Local, national and international poetry is showcased and explored in all its manifestations, with events for adults and children including masterclasses, workshops, debates and competitions. Telephone for further details.

Broadstairs Dickens Festival

8 Stone Road, Broadstairs, Kent CT10 1DY
☎01843 601364
Organiser *Priscilla Foot*
FOUNDED 1937 to commemorate the 100th anniversary of Charles Dickens' first visit to Broadstairs in 1837, which he continued to visit until 1859. The Festival lasts for eight days and events include an opening gala entertainment of words and music, a parade, a performance of a Dickens play (*Oliver Twist* in 1999), a garden party, duels, melodramas, Dickens readings, a Victorian cricket match, Victorian sea bathing, talks, music hall, two-day Victorian country fair. Costumed Dickensian ladies in crinolines with top-hatted escorts promenade during the week.

Bury St Edmunds Festival

Borough Offices, Angel Hill, Bury St
Edmunds, Suffolk IP33 1XB
☎01284 756933/756933/4
Fax 01284 756932
Email: kevin.appleby@burybo.stedsbc.gov.uk
Website: www.stedmundsbury.gov.uk/buryfest

Contact *Kevin Appleby, Festival Manager*

FOUNDED 1986. ANNUAL 17-day spring festival
in various venues throughout this historic East
Anglian town and outlying areas. Programme
features orchestral concerts, chamber music, jazz,
world music, drama, dance, comedy and exhibitions. 1999 highlights were Vladimir Ashkenazy,
The Philharmonia Orchestra, City of London
Sinfonia, John Surman, Fascinating Aida, The
Black Dyke Band and Magnus Magnusson.

Buxton Festival

1 Crescent View, Hall Bank, Buxton,
Derbyshire SK17 6EN
☎01298 70395   Fax 01298 72289

Contact *General Manager*

FOUNDED 1979. Annual two-week festival
held in July. Rarely performed operas are
staged in Buxton Opera House and the programme is complemented by a wide variety of
other musical events, including recitals, Young
Artists series, festival masses, chamber music
and cabarets. Also, the Buxton Jazz Festival.

Canterbury Festival

Christ Church Gate, The Precincts,
Canterbury, Kent CT1 2EE
☎01227 452853   Fax 01227 781830

Festival Director *Mark Deller*

FOUNDED 1984. Annual two-week festival held
in October. A mixed programme of events
including talks by visiting authors, readings and
storytelling, walks, concerts in the cathedral, jazz,
masterclasses, drama, visual arts, opera, film,
cabaret and dance.

Champion Women Festival

96 Hurst Road, Eastbourne, East Sussex
BN21 2PW
☎01323 639554   Fax 01323 639554

Contact *Molly Bartlett*

FOUNDED in 1995, this annual mixed arts festival
is held in Eastbourne for ten days in mid-June. It
celebrates women's achievements in every arena
by providing something for everyone – arts, films
walks, talks and workshops. The programme
includes many literature-based events – readings,
discussions, writing competitions. Previous

guests have included Germaine Greer, Joanna
Trollope, Victoria Glendinning, Nina Bawden,
Lisa St Aubin de Teran, Sally Cline.

The Cheltenham Festival of Literature

Town Hall, Imperial Square, Cheltenham,
Gloucestershire GL50 1QA
☎01242 521621   Fax 01242 256457
Email: sarahsm@cheltenham.gov.uk
Website: www.cheltenhamfestivals.co.uk

Festival Organiser *Sarah Smyth*

FOUNDED 1949. Annual festival held in
October. The first purely literary festival of its
kind, this festival has over the past decade
developed from an essentially local event into
the largest and most popular in Europe. A wide
range of events including talks and lectures,
poetry readings, novelists in conversation,
exhibitions, discussions and a large bookshop.

Chester Literature Festival

8 Abbey Square, Chester CH1 2HU
☎01244 319985   Fax 01244 341200

Chairman *John Elsley*

FOUNDED 1989. Annual festival always held in
early October (2 – 17 October in 1999). Events
include international and nationally known writers, as well as events by local literary groups.
There is a Literary Lunch, events for children,
workshops, competitions, etc. Free mailing list.

Chichester Festivities

Canon Gate House, South Street, Chichester,
West Sussex PO19 1PU
☎01243 785718   Fax 01243 528356

Festival Administrator *Amanda Sharp*

FOUNDED in 1975 to celebrate the 900th
anniversary of Chichester Cathedral, which
remains the principal venue for concerts (classical
and jazz) and lectures. Subsequently became an
annual event, now in its 25th year. Events also
include chamber recitals, literary talks, comedy,
exhibitions, films, theatre and outdoor events in
other venues, notably Crookwood House and
Racecourse, the latter the setting for a military
tattoo and fireworks spectacular.

City Voice – a festival of words

Library HQ, 32 York Road, Leeds, West
Yorkshire LS9 8TD
☎0113 2143337   Fax 0113 2143339
Email: jane.stubbs@leeds.gov.uk

Festival Director *Jane Stubbs*

FOUNDED in 1997 by the Leeds Word Arena and

Leeds Library & Information Services, City Voice focuses on new writing and reading and is held at the beginning of June. Strongly, but not exclusively, features commissioned new writing by Leeds-based writers. Previous events have included a commissioned sculpture based on readings, workshops for writing tutors and open spots in libraries. Visiting authors to-date include Jean Binta Breeze, Patricia Duncker and Courttia Newland. Call to join free mailing list.

Dartington Literary Festival
See **Ways With Words**

Dorchester Festival
Dorchester Arts Centre, School Lane, The Grove, Dorchester, Dorset DT1 1XR
☎01305 266926   Fax 01305 261589
Contact *Artistic Director*
FOUNDED 1996. A biennial four-day festival over early May Bank Holiday weekend which includes performing, media and visual arts, with associated educational and community projects in the three weeks around the Festival. Includes a wide range of events, in many venues, for all age groups, including some literature and poetry. Next festival planned for April/early May 2000.

The Festival of Dover
Dover District Council, White Cliffs Business Park, Dover, Kent CT16 3PD
☎01304 872058   Fax 01304 872062
Festival Organiser *Lisa Webb*
In 1999, the annual community arts celebration presented a week of workshops, exhibitions, processions, street and showcase events in the performing and visual arts, including Dancing Times, Music Lab, Beside the Seaside, Open Stages, Teddy Bears Fairy Tale Picnic.

Dublin Writers' Festival
Irish Writers' Centre, 19 Parnell Square, Dublin 1
☎00 353 1 8721302

Biennial festival held in September. Features conference sessions, public interviews, debates, readings and exhibitions, with some of the world's leading authors in attendance.

Dumfries and Galloway Arts Festival
Gracefield Arts Centre, 28 Edinburgh Road, Dumfries DG1 1JQ
☎01387 260447
Festival Organiser *Beryl Jago*

FOUNDED 1980. Annual week-long festival held at the end of May with a variety of events including classical and folk music, theatre, dance, literary events and exhibitions.

Durham Literary Festival
Durham City Arts, Byland Lodge, Hawthorn Terrace, Durham City DH1 4TD
☎0191 386 6111 ext. 338 Fax 0191 386 0625
Contact *The Director*
FOUNDED 1989. Annual 2–3-week festival held in June at various locations in the city. Workshops, plus performances, cabaret, and other events.

Edinburgh International Book Festival
Scottish Book Centre, 137 Dundee Street, Edinburgh EH11 1BG
☎0131 228 5444   Fax 0131 228 4333
Email: admin@edbookfest.co.uk
Director *Faith Liddell*
FOUNDED 1983. Europe's largest and liveliest public book event, now taking place on an annual basis. Held during the first fortnight of the Edinburgh International Festival, it presents an extensive programme for both adults and children including discussions, readings, lectures, demonstrations and workshops.

Exeter Festival
Festival Office, Civic Centre, Exeter, Devon EX1 1JN
☎01392 265200   Fax 01392 265366
Festival Organiser *Lesley Maynard*
FOUNDED 1980. Annual two-week festival with a variety of events including concerts, theatre, dance and exhibitions.

Grayshott and Hindhead Literary Festival
Little Nutcombe, Portsmouth Road, Hindhead, Surrey GU26 6AQ
☎01428 606689   Fax 01428 605665
Festival Organiser *Denise McCulloch*
FOUNDED 1995. Annual festival which runs over a weekend in mid-September. The programme features a mix of workshops, lectures and presentations covering classic and contemporary literature and poetry, travel, comedy, creative and script writing and children's/family events. Previous guests include: Deborah Moggach, Roger McGough, U. A. Fanthorpe, Michael Nicholson, Simon Brett. Also writing workshops and competitions throughout the year.

Greenwich & Docklands International Festival

6 College Approach, London SE10 9HY
☎0181 305 1818   Fax 0181 305 1188
Email: greendock@globalnet.co.uk
Director *Bradley Hemmings*
FOUNDED 1970. Annual summer festival. Features a wide variety of events, including world music, theatre, dance, classical music, jazz, comedy, art, literature and free open-air events.

Guildford Book Festival

c/o Arts Office, University of Surrey, Guildford, Surrey GU2 5XH
☎01483 259167   Fax 01483 300803
Book Festival Organiser *Patricia Grayburn*
FOUNDED 1990. A ten-day celebration of books and writing held annually, during the autumn half-term, throughout the town. Programme includes literary lunches, poetry readings, a writer-in-residence, children's events, writing workshops and competitions, the Annual University Poetry Lecture, and bookshop events.

Hallam Literature Festival and Book Fair

School of Cultural Studies, Sheffield Hallam University, 32 Colegiate Crescent Campus, Sheffield S10 2BP
☎0114 225 2228   Fax 0114 2254403
Festival Coordinator *E. A. Markham*
FOUNDED 1997. The second festival, held in March 1999, featured critics and literary journalists reflecting the range of the university's Creative Writing programme, book launches, stage readings of new plays, poetry readings, discussions on the short story and televised debates between writers.

Haringey Literature Festival

Haringey Arts Council, The Chocolate Factory, Unit 104 Building B, Clarendon Road, London N22 6XJ
☎0181 365 7500   Fax 0181 365 8686
Festival Organiser *Dana Captainino*
FOUNDED 1995. Annual festival which runs from March to October. The programme is a mixture of poetry and literature in the form of readings, discussions, workshops and masterclasses. Writers who have appeared at past festivals include: Fay Weldon, Louis de Bernières, Nick Hornby, Blake Morrison, Bernice Rubens, James Kelman, Jean Binta Breeze, Beryl Bainbridge and Matthew Sweeney.

Harrogate International Festival

1 Victoria Avenue, Harrogate, North Yorkshire HG1 1EQ
☎01423 562303   Fax 01423 521264
Email: info@harrogate-festival.org.uk
Website: www.harrogate-festival.org.uk
Festival Director *William Culver Dodds*
Administrator *Fiona Goh*
FOUNDED 1966. Annual two-week festival at the end of July and beginning of August. Events include international symphony orchestras, chamber concerts, ballet, celebrity recitals, contemporary dance, opera, drama, jazz, comedy plus an international street theatre festival.

Hastings International Poetry Festival

Burdett Cottage, 4 Burdett Place, George Street, Old Town, Hastings, East Sussex TN34 3ED
Contact *Josephine Austin*
FOUNDED 1968. Annual weekend poetry festival held in November in the Marina Pavilion in St Leonards-on-Sea. Runs the Hastings National Poetry Competition; entry forms available from the address above.

Hay Children's Festival of the Arts

15 Knowle Avenue, Burley, Leeds, West Yorkshire LS4 2PQ
☎0113 2304661   Fax 0113 2304661
Festival Director *Caroline Wylie*
FOUNDED 1994. Annual three-day festival of the arts in Hay-on-Wye for primary school-aged children presenting a unique programme of arts workshops, visiting best-selling authors and children's theatre. Brochure/booking form available mid-April.

The Hay Festival

See **The Sunday Times Hay Festival**

Huddersfield Poetry Festival

The Word Hoard, Kirklees Media Centre, 7 Northumberland Street, Huddersfield, West Yorkshire HD1 1RL
☎01484 452070   Fax 01484 455049
Email: hoard@zoo.co.uk

Twice-yearly event consisting of a spring season in March/April of around four/six events combined with a participatory multi-arts collaborative project; and four days of writing workshops and performances in October exploring particular themes. Also occasional one-off events. Though very interested in local writers, the festival has a cosmopolitan outlook and features related performing arts including music, theatre and the visual arts.

Hull Literature Festival

City Arts, Central Library, Albion Street, Kingston upon Hull HU1 3TF
☎01482 616875/6   Fax 01482 616827
Contact *City Arts Unit*
FOUNDED 1992. Annual festival running in November.

Ilkley Literature Festival

Festival Office, Manor House Museum, Ilkley, West Yorkshire LS29 9DT
☎01943 601210
Director *David Porter*
FOUNDED 1973. Major literature festival in the north with events running throughout the year. Large-scale festival in autumn each year. Runs an open poetry competition. Telephone to join free mailing list.

The International Festival of Mountaineering Literature

Bretton Hall College of the University of Leeds, West Bretton, Wakefield, West Yorkshire WF4 4LG
☎01924 830261   Fax 01924 832006
Director *Terry Gifford*
FOUNDED 1987. Annual one-day festival held at the end of November celebrating recent books, commissioning new writing, overviews of national literatures, debates of issues, discussion with Chair of Judges of the adjudication of the annual **Boardman Tasker Award** for the best mountaineering book of the year. Announces the winner of the festival writing competition run in conjunction with *High* magazine. Write to join free mailing list.

International Playwriting Festival

Warehouse Theatre, Dingwall Road, Croydon CR0 2NF
☎0181 681 1257   Fax 0181 688 6699
Email: warehous@dircon.co.uk
Website: www.uk-live.co.uk/
   warehouse_theatre
FOUNDED 1985. Annual competition for full-length unperformed plays, judged by a panel of theatre professionals. Finalists given rehearsed readings during the festival week in November. Entries welcome from all parts of the world. Scripts plus two s.a.e.s (one script-sized) should reach the theatre by the end of the first week of July, accompanied by an entry form (available

from the theatre). Previous winners produced at the theatre include: Kevin Hood *Beached*; Ellen Fox *Conversations with George Sandburgh After a Solo Flight Across the Atlantic*; Guy Jenkin *Fighting for the Dunghill*; James Martin Charlton *Fat Souls*; Peter Moffat *Iona Rain*; Dino Mahoney *YoYo*; Simon Smith *Fat Janet is Dead*; Dominic McHale *The Resurrectionists*. Shares plays with its partner festival in Italy, the Premio Candoni Arta Terme.

Kent Literature Festival

The Metropole Arts Centre, The Leas, Folkestone, Kent CT20 2LS
☎01303 255070
Festival Director *Ann Fearey*
FOUNDED 1980. Annual week-long festival held at the end of September which aims to bring the best in modern writing to a large audience. Visiting authors and dramatic presentations are a regular feature along with creative writing workshops, seminars, discussions and children's/family events. Also runs the **Kent Short Story Competition**.

King's Lynn, The Fiction Festival

19 Tuesday Market Place, King's Lynn, Norfolk PE30 1JW
☎01553 691661 (office hours) or 761919
Fax 01553 691779
Contact *Anthony Ellis*
FOUNDED 1989. Annual weekend festival held in March. Over the weekend there are readings and discussions, attended by guest writers of which there are usually eight. Previous guests have included Beryl Bainbridge, Malcolm Bradbury, Marina Warner, William Golding, Hilary Mantel, Elizabeth Jane Howard.

King's Lynn, The Poetry Festival

19 Tuesday Market Place, King's Lynn, Norfolk PE30 1JW
☎01553 691661 (office hours) or 761919
Fax 01553 691779
Contact *Anthony Ellis*
FOUNDED 1985. Annual weekend festival held at the end of September (24th– 26th in 1999), with guest poets (usually eight). Previous guests have included Carol Ann Duffy, Paul Durcan, Gavin Ewart, Peter Porter, Stephen Spender. Events include readings and discussion panels.

Lancaster LitFest

Sun Street Studios, 23–29 Sun Street, Lancaster LA1 1ET
☎01524 62166   Fax 01524 841216
Email: all@lancslitfest.demon.co.uk

Website: www.folly.co.uk/litfest

FOUNDED 1978. A regional Literature Development Agency which organises workshops, readings, residencies and publications. It has a year-round programme of literature-based events and annual festival in October featuring a wide range of writers from the UK and overseas. Organises annual poetry competition with winners receiving cash prizes and anthology publication.

Ledbury Poetry Festival

Town Council Offices, Church Lane, Ledbury, Herefordshire HR8 1DH
☎01531 634156
Email: Blanca@ledburypoetryfestival. freeserve.co.uk
Website: www.ledburypoetfest.org.uk

Contact *Blanca Rey Surman*

FOUNDED 1997. Annual ten-day festival held in July. Includes readings, discussions, workshops, exhibitions, music and walks. There are also writers in residence at local schools and residential homes, a national poetry competition and the Town Party. Past guests have included Andrew Motion, Benjamin Zephaniah, Simon Armitage, Roger McGough, John Hegley and Germaine Greer. Full programme available in May.

City of London Festival

230 Bishopsgate, London EC2M 4HW
☎0171 377 0540   Fax 0171 377 1972
Email: cityfest@dircon.co.uk
Website: www.city-of-london-festival.org.uk

Director *Michael MacLeod*

FOUNDED 1962. Annual three-week festival held in June and July. Features over fifty classical and popular music events alongside poetry and prose readings, street theatre and open-air extravaganzas, in some of the most outstanding performance spaces in the world.

The London Festival of Literature

See **The Word – The London Festival of Literature**

London New Play Festival

Diorama Arts Centre, 34 Osnabrook Street, London NW1 3ND
☎0171 209 2326
Email: lnpf@reverb.co.uk
Website: come.to/lnpf

Artistic Director *Phil Setren*
Education Director *Christopher Preston*
Literary Manager *David Prescott*

FOUNDED 1989. Annual festival of new writing.

The 1998 season featured four full productions and six rehearsed readings at the Riverside Studios, collaborative and visiting new drama at the Diorama Arts Centre and a West End Platform Season at the Apollo Theatre, Shaftesbury Avenue. Open to full-length and one-act plays which are assessed for originality, form, etc by a reading committee. Deadline for scripts according to festival dates – call for information. LNPF Writing School - one-day workshops, courses and dramaturgy sessions held throughout the year. For full details check the Website. Script reading service – scripts read and critique supplied by Festival Reading Committee year round for a set fee of £25. Call for details.

Ludlow Festival

Castle Square, Ludlow, Shropshire SY8 1AY
☎01584 875070   Fax 01584 877673

Contact *Festival Administrator*

FOUNDED 1959. Annual two-week festival held in the last week of June and first week of July with an open-air Shakespeare production held at Ludlow Castle and a varied programme of events including recitals, opera, dance, popular and classical concerts, literary and historical lectures.

Manchester Festival of Writing

Manchester Central Library, St Peter's Square, Manchester M2 5PD
☎0161 234 1981

Contact *Jane Mathieson*

FOUNDED 1990. An annual event organised by Manchester Libraries and Commonword community publishers. It consists of a programme of practical writing workshops on specific themes/genres run by well-known writers. Attendance at all workshops is free to Manchester residents.

Manchester Poetry Festival

2nd Floor, Enterprise House, 15 Whitworth Street West, Manchester M1 5WG
☎0161 907 0031

Contact *Richard Michael*

Held in November, the Festival aims to bring the world's best poets to Manchester and promote Manchester poets to the rest of the world. Includes workshops and events for children.

Mole Valley Literature and Media Festival

Mole Valley Leisure Services, Pippbrook, Dorking, Surrey RH4 1SJ
☎01273 478943   Fax 01273 478943
Email: jo_king@compuserve.com

Contact *Joan König*

A festival which celebrates literary talent both past and present throughout the Mole Valley. Includes film fair, a programme of readings, workshops, exhibitions, storytelling, performance poetry, children's and young people's events. Dedicated to encouraging, promoting and developing literature in its broadest sense. Initiates sustainable literary projects for all the community.

National Eisteddfod of Wales

4th Floor, Brackla House, Brackla Road, Bridgend CF31 1BZ
☎01656 659898/01222 763777
Fax 01656 660789/01222 763737
Email: eleri.twynog@btinternet.com

The National Eisteddfod, held in August, is the largest arts festival in Wales, attracting over 170,000 visitors during the week-long celebration of more than 800 years of tradition. Competitions, bardic ceremonies and concerts

National Student Drama Festival

See **University College, Scarborough** under **Writers' Courses**

Norfolk and Norwich Festival

42–58 St George's Street, Norwich, Norfolk NR3 1AB
☎01603 614921   Fax 01603 632303
Email: info@nnfest.eastern-arts.co.uk

Festival Director *Marcus Davey*

FOUNDED 1772, this performing arts festival is the second oldest in the UK. Held annually in October (1–17th in 1999), the festival includes talks by writers along with poetry and storytelling events.

North East Lincolnshire Literature Festival

Arts Development, North East Lincolnshire Council, Knoll Street, Cleethorpes, Lincolnshire DN35 8LN
☎01472 323000   Fax 01472 323005

Festival Programmer *Lynne Conlan*

FOUNDED 1997. Annual themed festival held in February/March. Reflecting the heritage of the area, the festival aims to make literature accessible to all ages and abilities through a varied and unusual programme. In 1999 the Festival was entitled 'Life is an Open Book'. Guests included Barnsley Football Club's Poet in Residence Ian McMillan and Bill Oddie. Events featured poetry readings, storytelling and children's events.

Northern Children's Book Festival

Information North, Bolbec Hall, Westgate Road, Newcastle upon Tyne NE1 1SE
☎0191 232 0877   Fax 0191 232 0804
Email: ce24@dial.pipex.com

FOUNDED 1984. Annual two-week festival held in November. Events in schools and libraries for children in the North East region. One Saturday during the festival sees the staging of a large book event hosted by one of the local authorities involved. Publications include books on holding your own book week such as: *Celebrating the North East*; *Getting the Show On the Road* and *Read On, Write On*.

Off the Shelf Literature Festival

Central Library, Surrey Street, Sheffield S1 1XZ
☎0114 2734716/4400   Fax 0114 2735009

Festival Organisers *Maria de Souza, Susan Walker*

FOUNDED 1992. Annual two-week festival held during the last fortnight in October. Lively and diverse mix of readings, workshops, children's events, storytelling and competitions. Previous guests have included Bill Bryson, Irvine Welsh, Benjamin Zephaniah, Terry Pratchett and Wendy Cope.

Oxford Literary Festival

301 Woodstock Road, Oxford OX2 7NY
☎01865 514149   Fax 01865 514804

Directors *Sally Dunsmore, Angela Prysor-Jones*

FOUNDED 1997. Annual three-day festival held in March (two weekends prior to Easter). Authors speaking about their books, covering a wide variety of writing: fiction, poetry, biography, travel, food, gardening, children's art. Previous guests have included William Boyd, Andrew Motion, Candia McWilliam, Beryl Bainbridge, Sophie Grigson, Jamie McKendrick, Bernard O'Donoghue, Philip Pullman and Korky Paul.

The Round Festival

c/o Word And Action (Dorset), 61 West Borough, Wimborne, Dorset BH12 1LX
☎01202 883197   Fax 01202 881061

Contact *Kate Wood*

FOUNDED 1990. International Festival of theatre-in-the-round offering a variety of workshops and performances celebrating and exploring the form. Programme includes poetry performances and playreading in the round.

Royal Court Young Writers Programme

Royal Court Theatre, Sloane Square, London
SW1W 8AS
☎0171 565 5050   Fax 0171 565 5001
Associate Director *Ola Animashawin*

Open to young people up to the age of 26. The
festival focuses on the process of playwriting and
is open to young writers all over the country.
Intensive work on the final draft of plays pre-
cedes production at the Royal Court Theatre
Upstairs.

Rye Festival

PO Box 33, Rye, East Sussex TN31 7YB
☎01797 222552
Artistic Director *David Willison*

FOUNDED 1972. Annual two-week September
event, plus short winter series. Variety of events
with strong emphasis on literature (1998 nomination by *Harpers & Queen* as one of six best
British Literary Festivals), classical and modern
music, visual arts, workshops and masterclasses.
Write or phone to join free mailing list.

Salisbury Festival

Festival Office, 75 New Street, Salisbury,
Wiltshire SP1 2PH
☎01722 323883   Fax 01722 410552
Director *Helen Marriage*

FOUNDED 1972. Annual festival held late May/
early June. The 1999 festival included classical
music, theatre, jazz, exhibitions.

Scottish Young Playwrights Festival

6th Floor, Gordon Chambers, 90 Mitchell
Street, Glasgow G1 3NQ
☎0141 221 5127   Fax 0141 221 9123
Email: sy001@post.almac.co.uk
Artistic Director *Mary McCluskey*

The Scottish Young Playwrights project operates
throughout Scotland. In every region an experienced theatre practitioner runs regular young
writers' workshops aimed at developing the best
possible scripts from initial ideas. A representative
selection of scripts is then selected to form a
showcase. The festival is mounted in conjunction with the Royal Scottish Academy of Music
and Drama. Scripts will be workshopped, revised
and developed culminating in an evening presentation. Scripts are welcome throughout the
year from young people aged 15–25 who are
native Scots and/or resident in Scotland; synopses of unfinished scripts also considered. No
restriction on style, content or intended media,
but work must be original and unperformed.
Further details from address above.

Shorelines

Gosport Borough Council, Town Hall, High
Street, Gosport, Hampshire PO12 1EB
☎01705 529129   Fax 01705 511856
Also at: Fareham Borough Council, Civic
Offices, Civic Way, Fareham, Hampshire
PO16 7PR
☎01329 236100   Fax 01329 822732
Arts Development Officers *Helen Payne
(Gosport), Julia Mayo (Fareham)*

FOUNDED 1998. A joint initiative of Gosport
and Fareham Borough Councils. Shorelines
aims to present a literary programme of depth
and substance, promoting literature to a wider
audience. Workshops, performances, exhibitions, talks and book signings.

Stratford–upon–Avon Poetry Festival

The Shakespeare Centre, Henley Street,
Stratford–upon–Avon, Warwickshire
CV37 6QW
☎01789 204016   Fax 01789 296083
Email: director@shakespeare.org.uk
Festival Director *Roger Pringle*

FOUNDED 1953. Annual festival held on Sunday
evenings during July and August. Readings by
poets and professional actors.

The Sunday Times Hay Festival

Festival Office, Hay-on-Wye HR3 5BX
☎01497 821217   Fax 01497 821066
Website: www.litfest.co.uk
Festival Director *Peter Florence*

FOUNDED 1988. Annual May festival sponsored
by *The Sunday Times*. Guests have included
Salman Rushdie, Toni Morrison, Stephen Fry,
Joseph Heller, Carlos Fuentes, Maya Angelou,
Amos Oz, Arthur Miller.

Swansea Festivals

Dylan Thomas Centre, Somerset Place,
Swansea SA1 1RR
☎01792 463980   Fax 01792 463993
Email: dylan.thomas@cableol.uk
Website: www.dylanthomas.org
Contact *David Woolley*

September 12–25 1999: Swansea Literature
Prom, fifth annual festival of literature, music and
film; October 4–9: Wordplay, fifth annual festival of literature and arts for young people. The
Dylan Thomas Celebration in July/August 1999

saw three weeks of performances, talks, lectures, films, music, poetry, exhibitions and celebrity guests.

Warwick & Leamington Festival

Warwick Arts Society, Northgate, Warwick CV34 4JL
☎01926 410747   Fax 01926 407606
Festival Director *Richard Phillips*
FOUNDED 1980. Annual festival lasting 12 days in the first half of July. Basically a chamber and early music festival, with some open-air, large-scale concerts in Warwick Castle, the Festival also promotes plays by Shakespeare in historical settings. Large-scale education programme. Interested in increasing its literary content, both in performances and workshops.

Ways with Words

Droridge Farm, Dartington, Totnes, Devon TQ9 6JQ
☎01803 867311   Fax 01803 863688
Email: wwwords@globalnet.co.uk
Website:www.users.globalnet.co.uk/~wwwords
Festival Director *Kay Dunbar*
Ways with Words runs a major literature festival at Dartington Hall in south Devon in July each year. Features over 200 writers giving lectures, readings, interviews, discussions, performances, masterclasses and workshops.
    Ways with Words also runs literary weekends in Southwold, Bury St Edmunds (Suffolk) and York plus writing, reading and painting courses in the UK and abroad.

Wellington Literary Festival

Civic Offices, Tan Bank, Wellington, Telford, Shropshire TF1 1LX
☎01952 222935   Fax 01952 222936
Contact *Derrick Drew*
FOUNDED 1997. Annual festival held throughout October. Events include story telling, writers' forum, 'Pints and Poetry', children's poetry competition, story competition, theatre review and guest speakers.

Wells Festival of Literature

Tower House, St Andrew Street, Wells, Somerset BA5 2UN
☎01749 673385
Contact *Pamela Egan*
FOUNDED 1992. Annual weekend-plus festival held at the end of October. Main venue is the historic, moated Bishop's Palace. A wide range of speakers caters for different tastes in reading,

previous guests: Douglas Hurd, Iris Murdoch, Elizabeth Jennings, P. D. James, Simon Jenkins, Barbara Trapido. Short story and poetry competitions are run in conjunction with the Festival.

Wimborne Poetry Festival

Word And Action (Dorset), 61 West Borough, Wimborne, Dorset BT2 1LX
☎01202 883197   Fax 01202 881061
Email: wordandaction@wanda.demon.co.uk
Contact *Kate Wood*
Bi-annual festival of poetry readings, performances and workshops. Culminates in an open-air poetry fair with guest poets, stalls and quizzes. Events vary each festival and aim to involve the whole community both on a local scale and nationally.

The Word – The London Festival of Literature

245 St John Street, London EC1V 4NB
☎0171 837 2555   Fax 0171 278 0480
Email: admin@theword.org.uk
Website: www.theword.org.uk
Director *Peter Florence*
FOUNDED 1999. Annual ten-day carnival celebration of the written and spoken word, featuring the best contemporary writing in every medium. Campaign and programme of competitions, conversations, debates, fairs, films, lectures, masterclasses, plays, readings, receptions, workshops feature hundreds of writers, musicians and artists. Guest writers at the first Festival (held in March): Margaret Atwood, Chinua Achebe, Joseph Heller, Shirley Hughes, Hanif Kureishi, Doris Lessing, Armistead Maupin, Ian McEwan, Terry Pratchett, Edward Said, Wole Soyinka, Derek Walcott and Benjamin Zephaniah.

Wordplay

See **Swansea Festivals**

Writearound

Cleveland Arts, Gurney House, Gurney Street, Middlesbrough, Cleveland TS1 1JL
☎01642   262424
Email: Cleveland.Arts@onyxnet.co.uk
Contact *Bob Beagrie, Andy Croft*
FOUNDED 1989. Annual festival with a commitment to local writers. Held during October, featuring workshops and readings, plus guest writers and opportunities for new writers. Publishes anthologies of poetry by local children. Contact address above for further information. Programmes available in August.

European Publishers

Austria

Springer-Verlag KG
PO Box 89, 1200 Vienna
☎00 43 1 3302415   Fax 00 43 1 3302426
FOUNDED 1924. *Publishes* anthropology, architecture, art, business, chemistry, computer science, economics, education, interior design, environmental studies, engineering, law, maths, dentistry, medicine, nursing, philosophy, physics, psychology, technology and general science.

Verlag Carl Ueberreuter
Postfach 306, A-1091 Vienna
☎00 43 1 404440   Fax 00 43 1 404445
FOUNDED 1548. *Publishes* fiction and general non-fiction: art, government, history, economics, political science, general science, science fiction, fantasy, music and dance.

Paul Zsolnay Verlag GmbH
Postfach 142, A-1041 Vienna
☎00 43 1 50576610   Fax 00 43 1 50576610
FOUNDED 1923. *Publishes* biography, fiction, general non-fiction, history, poetry.

Belgium

Brepols NV
Steenweg op Tielen 68, 2300 Turnhout
☎00 32 14 402500   Fax 00 32 14 428919
FOUNDED 1796. *Publishes* art, architecture, interior design, history, religion.

Facet NV
Willem Linnigstr 13, 2060 Antwerp
☎00 32 3 2274028   Fax 00 32 3 2273792
FOUNDED 1976. *Publishes* children's books.

Uitgeverij Lannoo NV
Kasteelstr 97, B-8700 Tielt
☎00 32 51 424211   Fax 00 32 51 401152
FOUNDED 1909. *Publishes* general non-fiction, art, biography, economics, gardening, health, history, management, nutrition, photography, poetry, government, political science, religion, travel.

Standaard Uitgeverij
Belgiëlei 147a, 2018 Antwerp
☎00 32 3 2857200   Fax 00 32 3 2857299
FOUNDED 1919. *Publishes* education, fiction, humour.

Denmark

Forlaget Apostrof ApS
Postboks 2580, DK-2100 Copenhagen
☎00 45 39 208420   Fax 00 45 39 208453
FOUNDED 1980. *Publishes* essays, fiction, humour, literature, literary criticism, general non-fiction, psychology, psychiatry.

Aschehoug Fakta
PO Box 2179, DK-1017 Copenhagen K
☎00 45 33 305522   Fax 00 45 33 305825
FOUNDED 1977. *Publishes* cookery, health, how-to, maritime and nutrition.

Borgens Forlag A/S
Valbygardsvej 33, DK-2500 Valby
☎00 45 36 462100   Fax 00 45 36 441488
FOUNDED 1948. *Publishes* fiction, literature, literary criticism, science fiction, general non-fiction, art, crafts, education, environmental studies, essays, games, gay and lesbian, hobbies, health, nutrition, music, dance, philosophy, poetry, psychology, psychiatry, religion.

Egmont Wangel AS
Gerdasgade 37, 2500 Valby
☎00 45 36 156600   Fax 00 45 36 441162
FOUNDED 1946. *Publishes* fiction and management.

Forum Publishers
Snaregade 4, DK-1205 Copenhagen K
☎00 45 33 147714   Fax 00 45 33 147791
FOUNDED 1940. *Publishes* fiction and mysteries.

GEC Gads Forlags Aktieselskab
Vimmelskaftet 32, DK-1161 Copenhagen K
☎00 45 33 150558   Fax 00 45 33 110800
FOUNDED 1855. *Publishes* general non-fiction, biological sciences, cookery, crafts, games, economics, education, English as a second language,

environmental studies, gardening, history, mathematics, natural history, physics, plants, travel.

Gyldendalske Boghandel-Nordisk Forlag A/S
Klareboderne 3, DK-1001 Copenhagen K
☎00 45 33 110775   Fax 00 45 33 110323
FOUNDED 1770. *Publishes* fiction, art, biography, dance, dentistry, education, history, how-to, medicine, music, poetry, nursing, philosophy, psychology, psychiatry, general and social sciences, sociology.

Hekla Forlag
Valbygaardsvej 33, DK-2500 Valby
☎00 45 36 462100   Fax 00 45 36 441488
FOUNDED 1979. *Publishes* general fiction and non-fiction.

Høst & Søns Publishers Ltd
PO Box 2212, DK-1018 Copenhagen
☎00 45 33 153031   Fax 00 45 33 155155
FOUNDED 1836. *Publishes* fiction, crafts, environmental studies, games, hobbies, regional interests, travel.

Egmont Lademann A/S
Gerdasgade 37, 2500 Valby
☎00 45 361 56600   Fax 00 45 361 44162
FOUNDED 1954. *Publishes* general non-fiction.

Lindhardt og Ringhof
Kristianiagade 14, DK-2100 Copenhagen
☎00 45 33 695000   Fax 00 45 33 436520
FOUNDED 1971. *Publishes* fiction and general non-fiction.

Munksgaard International Publishers & Booksellers Ltd
PO Box 2148, DK-1370 Copenhagen K
☎00 45 77 333333   Fax 00 45 77 333377
Email: direct@munksgaarddirect.dk
Website: www.munksgaard.dk
FOUNDED 1917. *Publishes* fiction, general non-fiction, education, dentistry, medicine, nursing, psychology, psychiatry, general science, social sciences, sociology.

Nyt Nordisk Forlag Arnold Busck A/S
Købmagergade 49, DK-1150 Copenhagen K
☎00 45 33 111103   Fax 00 45 33 934490
FOUNDED 1896. *Publishes* fiction, art, biography, dance, dentistry, history, how-to, music, philosophy, religion, medicine, nursing, psy-

chology, psychiatry, general and social sciences, sociology.

Politikens Forlag A/S
Vestergade 26, DK-1456 Copenhagen K
☎00 45 33 470707   Fax 00 45 33 470708
FOUNDED 1946. *Publishes* general non-fiction, art, crafts, dance, history, games, hobbies, how-to, music, natural history, sport, travel.

Samlerens Forlag A/S
Pilestraede 51, DK-1001 Copenhagen K
☎00 45 33 131023   Fax 00 45 33 144314
FOUNDED 1942. *Publishes* essays, fiction, government, history, literature, literary criticism, political science.

Det Schønbergske Forlag
Landemaerket 5, DK-1119 Copenhagen K
☎00 45 33 113066   Fax 00 45 33 330045
FOUNDED 1857. *Publishes* art, biography, fiction, history, humour, philosophy, poetry, psychology, psychiatry, travel

Spektrum Forlagsaktieselskab
4 Snaregade, DK-1205 Copenhagen K
☎00 45 33 147714   Fax 00 45 33 147791
FOUNDED 1990. *Publishes* general non-fiction.

Tiderne Skifter Forlag A/S
Pilestraede 51/5, DK-1001 Copenhagen K
☎00 45 33 325772   Fax 00 45 33 144205
FOUNDED 1979. *Publishes* fiction, literature and literary criticism, essays, ethnology, photography, behavioural sciences.

Finland

Gummerus Publishers
PO Box 2, SF-00131 Helsinki
☎00 358 9 584301   Fax 00 358 9 58430200
FOUNDED 1872. *Publishes* fiction and general non-fiction.

Karisto Oy
PO Box 102, SF-13101 Hämeenlinna
☎00 358 3 6161551   Fax 00 358 3 6161565
FOUNDED 1900. *Publishes* fiction and general non-fiction.

Kirjayhtymä Oy
Urho Kekkosen Katu 4–6E, SF-00100 Helsinki
☎00 358 9 6937641   Fax 00 358 9 69376366
FOUNDED 1958. *Publishes* fiction and general non-fiction.

Otava Kustannusosakeyhtiö
PO Box 134, 00121 Helsinki
☎00 358 9 19961   Fax 00 358 9 643136
FOUNDED 1890. *Publishes* fiction, general non-fiction, how-to.

Werner Söderström
Osakeyhtiö (WSOY)
PO Box 222, 00121 Helsinki
☎00 358 9 61681   Fax 00 358 9 6168405
FOUNDED 1878. *Publishes* fiction, general non-fiction, education.

Tammi Publishers
PO Box 410, 00101 Helsinki
☎00 358 9 6937621   Fax 00 358 9 69376266
FOUNDED 1943. *Publishes* fiction, general non-fiction.

France

Editions Arthaud SA
26 rue Racine, F–75278 Paris Cedex 06
☎00 33 1 4051 3100   Fax 00 33 1 4329 2148
FOUNDED 1890. Imprint of **Flammarion SA**.
Publishes art, history, literature, literary criticism, essays, sport, travel.

Editions Belfond
12 avenue d'Italie, 75627 Paris
☎00 33 1 4416 0500   Fax 00 33 1 4416 0506
FOUNDED 1963. *Publishes* fiction, literature, literary criticism, essays, mysteries, romance, poetry, general non-fiction, art, biography, dance, health, history, how-to, music, nutrition.

Editions Bordas
21 rue du Montparnasse BP50, 75283 Paris
Cedex 06
☎00 33 1 4439 4400   Fax 00 33 1 4439 4107
FOUNDED 1946. *Publishes* education and general non-fiction.

Editions Calmann-Lévy SA
3 rue Auber, 75009 Paris
☎00 33 1 4742 3833   Fax 00 33 1 4742 7781
FOUNDED 1836. *Publishes* fiction, science fiction, fantasy, biography, history, humour, philosophy, psychology, psychiatry, social sciences, sociology, sport, economics.

Editions Denoël Sàrl
9 rue du Cherche-Midi, 75006 Paris
☎00 33 1 4439 7373   Fax 00 33 1 4439 7390
FOUNDED 1932. *Publishes* art, economics, fiction, science fiction, fantasy, government, history, philosophy, general science, political science, psychology, psychiatry, sport.

Librairie Arthème Fayard
75 rue des Saints-Pères, F-75278 Paris Cedex 06
☎00 33 1 4549 8200   Fax 00 33 1 4222 4017
FOUNDED 1854. *Publishes* biography, fiction, history, dance, music, philosophy, religion, social sciences, sociology, general science, technology.

Flammarion SA
26 rue Racine, F–75278 Paris Cedex 06
☎00 33 1 4051 3100   Fax 00 33 1 4329 2148
FOUNDED 1875. *Publishes* general fiction and non-fiction, art, architecture, gardening, plants, interior design, literature, literary criticism, essays, medicine, nursing, dentistry, wine and spirits.

Editions Gallimard
5 rue Sébastien-Bottin, 75007 Paris Cedex 07
☎00 33 1 4054 1457   Fax 00 33 1 4954 1451
FOUNDED 1911. *Publishes* fiction, poetry, art, biography, dance, history, music, philosophy.

Société des Editions
Grasset et Fasquelle
61 rue des Saints-Pères, 75006 Paris
☎00 33 1 4439 2200   Fax 00 33 1 4222 6418
FOUNDED 1907. *Publishes* fiction and general non-fiction, essays, literature, literary criticism, philosophy.

Hachette Groupe Livre
43 quai de Grenelle, 75905 Paris Cedex 15
☎00 33 1 4392 3000   Fax 00 33 1 4392 3030
FOUNDED 1826. *Publishes* fiction and general non-fiction, architecture and interior design, art, economics, education, general engineering, government, history, language and linguistics, political science, philosophy, general science, self-help, social sciences, sociology, sport, travel.

Editions Robert Laffont Fixot,
Seghers, Julliard
24 ave Marceau, 75008 Paris Cedex 08
☎00 33 1 5367 1400   Fax 00 33 1 5367 1490
FOUNDED 1941. *Publishes* fiction and non-fiction.

Librairie Larousse
17 rue de Montparnasse, 75298 Paris Cedex 06
☎00 33 1 4439 4400   Fax 00 33 1 4439 4107
FOUNDED 1852. *Publishes* general and social

sciences, sociology, language arts, linguistics, technology.

Editions Jean-Claude Lattès

17 rue Jacob, F–75006 Paris
☎00 33 1 4441 7400   Fax 00 33 1 4325 3047

FOUNDED 1968. *Publishes* fiction and general non-fiction, biography, religion.

Les Editions Magnard Sàrl

20 rue Berbier-du-Mets, 75013 Paris
☎00 33 1 4408 4930   Fax 00 33 1 4408 4939

FOUNDED 1933. *Publishes* education.

Michelin et Cie
(Services de Tourisme)

46 ave de Breteuil, F–75324 Paris Cedex 07
☎00 33 1 4566 1234   Fax 00 33 1 4566 1163

FOUNDED 1900. *Publishes* travel.

Les Editions de Minuit SA

7 rue Bernard-Palissy, 75006 Paris
☎00 33 1 4439 3920   Fax 00 33 1 4544 8236

FOUNDED 1942. *Publishes* fiction, essays, literature, literary criticism, philosophy, social science, sociology.

Fernand Nathan

9 rue Méchain, 75676 Paris
☎00 33 1 4587 5000   Fax 00 33 1 4331 2169

FOUNDED 1881. *Publishes* education, history, philosophy, psychology, psychiatry, general and social sciences, sociology.

Presses de la Cité

12 ave d'Italie, 75627 Paris
☎00 33 1 4416 0500   Fax 00 33 1 4416 0505

FOUNDED 1947. *Publishes* literature, literary criticism, essays, science fiction, fantasy, anthropology, biography, history, how-to, military science, travel.

Presses Universitaires
de France (PUF)

12 rue Jean-de-Beauvais, 75005 Paris 06
☎00 33 1 4326 2216   Fax 00 33 1 4354 2633

FOUNDED 1921. *Publishes* art, biography, dance, dentistry, geography, geology, government, general engineering, history, law, medicine, music, nursing, philosophy, psychology, psychiatry, religion, political and social sciences, sociology.

Editions du Seuil

27 rue Jacob, 75261 Paris Cedex 06
☎00 33 1 4046 5050   Fax 00 33 1 4329 0829

FOUNDED 1935. *Publishes* fiction, literature, literary criticism, essays, poetry, art, biography, dance, government, history, how-to, music, photography, philosophy, psychology, psychiatry, religion, general and social sciences, sociology.

Les Editions de la Table Ronde

7 rue Corneille, 75006 Paris
☎00 33 1 4046 7070   Fax 00 33 1 4046 7101

FOUNDED 1944. *Publishes* fiction and general non-fiction, biography, history, psychology, psychiatry, religion.

Librairie Vuibert SA

20 rue Berbier-du-Mets, 75013 Paris
☎00 33 1 6608 6900   Fax 00 33 1 6608 6929

FOUNDED 1877. *Publishes* biological and earth sciences, chemistry, chemical engineering, economics, law, mathematics, physics.

Germany

Verlag C. H. Beck (OHG)

Wilhelmstr 9, 80801 Munich
☎00 49 89 381890   Fax 00 49 89 38189398

FOUNDED 1763. *Publishes* general non-fiction, anthropology, archaeology, art, dance, economics, essays, history, language, law, linguistics, literature, literary criticism, music, philosophy, social sciences, sociology, theology.

Bertelsmann Lexikon Verlag GmbH

Postfach 800360, 81603 Munich
☎00 49 431890   Fax 00 49 43189743

Publishes fiction and non-fiction, anthropology, art, biography, business, career development, economics, film, history, how-to, law, management, marketing, medicine, dentistry, nursing, radio, television, video, technology, travel.

Carlsen Verlag GmbH

Postfach 500380, 22703 Hamburg
☎00 49 40 3910090   Fax 00 49 40 39100962

FOUNDED 1953. *Publishes* humour and general non-fiction.

Deutscher Taschenbuch Verlag
GmbH & Co. KG (dtv)

Postfach 400422, 80704 Munich
☎00 49 89 38167-0   Fax 00 49 89 346428

FOUNDED 1961. *Publishes* fiction and general non-fiction; art, astronomy, biography, child care and development, cookery, computer science, dance, education, government, history, how-to, music, poetry, psychiatry, psychology, philosophy, political science, religion, medicine, dentistry, nursing, social sciences, literature, literary criticism, essays, humour, travel.

Droemersche Verlagsanstalt Th. Knaur Nachfolger
Rauchstr 9–11, 81679 Munich
☎00 49 89 92710   Fax 00 49 89 9271168
FOUNDED 1901. *Publishes* fiction, general non-fiction, cookery, how-to, self-help, travel and general science.

Econ-Verlag GmbH
Postfach 300321, 40403 Düsseldorf
☎00 49 211 43596   Fax 00 49 211 4359768
FOUNDED 1950. *Publishes* general non-fiction and fiction, economics, general science.

Falken-Verlag GmbH
Postfach 1120, 65521 Niederhausen
☎00 49 6127 7020   Fax 00 49 6127 702133
FOUNDED 1923. *Publishes* crafts, cookery, education, games, gardening, health, history, hobbies, how-to, humour, nutrition, photography, sport.

S Fischer Verlag GmbH
Postfach 700355, 60553 Frankfurt am Main
☎00 49 69 60620   Fax 00 49 69 6062214
FOUNDED 1886. *Publishes* fiction, general non-fiction, essays, literature, literary criticism.

Carl Hanser Verlag
Postfach 860420, 81631 Munich
☎00 49 89 998300   Fax 00 49 89 984809
FOUNDED 1928. *Publishes* general non-fiction, poetry, computer science, economics, electronics, electrical, mechanical and general engineering, environmental studies, management, mathematics, medicine, nursing, dentistry, philosophy, physics.

Wilhelm Heyne Verlag
Türkenstr 5–7, 80333 Munich
☎00 49 89 286350   Fax 00 49 89 2800943
FOUNDED 1934. *Publishes* fiction, mystery, romance, humour, science fiction, fantasy, astrology, biography, cookery, film, history, how-to, occult, psychology, psychiatry, video.

Hoffmann und Campe Verlag
Postfach 130444, 20139 Hamburg
☎00 49 40 441880   Fax 00 49 40 44188-290
FOUNDED 1781. *Publishes* fiction and general non-fiction; art, biography, dance, history,

music, poetry, philosophy, psychology, psychiatry, general science, social sciences, sociology.

Ernst Klett Verlag GmbH
Postfach 106016, 70049 Stuttgart
☎00 49 711 66720   Fax 00 49 711 628053
FOUNDED 1897. *Publishes* education, career development, geography, geology.

Gustav Lübbe Verlag GmbH
Postfach 200127, 51431 Bergisch Gladbach
☎00 49 2202 1210   Fax 00 49 2202 121708
FOUNDED 1963. *Publishes* fiction and general non-fiction, archaeology, biography, history, how-to.

Mosaik Verlag GmbH
Postfach 800360, 81673 Munich 80
☎00 49 89 431890   Fax 00 49 89 43189743
Publishes animals, antiques, architecture and interior design, child care and development, cookery, crafts, economics, finance, career development, film, gardening, games, hobbies, health, house and home, human relations, nutrition, pets, self-help, sport, video, wine and spirits, women's studies.

Pestalozzi-Verlag Graphische Gesellschaft mbH
Am Pestalozziring 14, 91058 Erlangen
☎00 49 9131 60600   Fax 00 49 9131 773090
FOUNDED 1844. *Publishes* crafts, games, hobbies.

Rowohlt Taschenbuch Verlag GmbH
Postfach 1349, 21465 Reinbeck
☎00 49 40 72720   Fax 00 49 40 7272319
FOUNDED 1953. *Publishes* fiction and general non-fiction; archaeology, art, computer science, crafts, education, essays, games and hobbies, gay and lesbian, government, history, literature, literary criticism, philosophy, psychology, psychiatry, religion, general science, social sciences, sociology.

Springer-Verlag GmbH & Co KG
Postfach 311340, 10643 Berlin
☎00 49 30 827870   Fax 00 49 30 8214091
FOUNDED 1842. *Publishes* agriculture, architecture and interior design, astronomy, behavioural sciences, business, biological sciences, chemical engineering, chemistry, civil engineering, computer science, dentistry, economics, finance, geography, geology, health, nutrition, library and information sciences, management, market-

ing, mechanical engineering, electronics, electrical engineering, general engineering, physical sciences, earth sciences, environmental studies, law, mathematics, medicine, nursing, psychology, psychiatry, physics, general science, technology.

Suhrkamp Verlag
Postfach 101945, 60019 Frankfurt am Main
☎00 49 69 756010   Fax 00 49 69 75601522
FOUNDED 1950. *Publishes* biography, fiction, philosophy, poetry, psychology, psychiatry, general science.

SV-Hüthig Fachinformation GmbH
Sendlingerstr 8, 80331 Munich
☎00 49 89 2183620   Fax 00 49 89 21838490
Formed by the merger of Süddeutscher Verlag and Hüthig in 1998, this is Germany's fourth largest professional publisher.

K. Thienemanns Verlag
Blumenstr 36, 70182 Stuttgart
☎00 49 711 210550   Fax 00 49 711 2105539
FOUNDED 1849. *Publishes* fiction and general non-fiction.

Ullstein Buchverlage GmbH & Co KG
Charlottenstr 13, 10969 Berlin
☎00 49 30 25913500
Fax 00 49 30 25913590
FOUNDED 1903. *Publishes* fiction and general non-fiction, romance, mysteries, architecture and interior design, art, biography, dance, film, video, education, essays, ethnology, geography, geology, government, health, history, how-to, humour, literature, literary criticism, maritime, military science, music, nutrition, poetry, political science, general science, social sciences, sociology, travel.

Weka Firmengruppe GmbH & Co KG
Postfach 1180, 86425 Kissing
☎00 49 8233 230   Fax 00 49 8233 23195
FOUNDED 1973. Germany's largest professional publisher. *Publishes* architecture and interior design, business, career development, civil engineering, general engineering, how-to, electronics, energy, outdoor recreation, communications, management, mechanical engineering, medicine, nursing and dentistry, law, technology, environmental studies, behavioural sciences.

Italy

Adelphi Edizioni SpA
Via S. Giovanni sul Muro 14, 20121 Milan
☎00 39 02 72000975   Fax 00 39 02 89010337
FOUNDED 1962. *Publishes* fiction, art, biography, dance, music, philosophy, psychology, psychiatry, religion, general science.

Bompiana
Via Mecenate 91, 20138 Milan
☎00 39 02 50951   Fax 00 39 02 50952058
FOUNDED 1929. *Publishes* fiction and general non-fiction, art, drama, theatre and general science.

Bulzoni Editore SRL (Le Edizioni Universitarie d'Italia)
Via Dei Liburni 14, 00185 Rome
☎00 39 06 4455207   Fax 00 39 06 4450355
FOUNDED 1969. *Publishes* fiction, literature, literary criticism, essays, art, drama, general engineering, film, law, language, linguistics, philosophy, general science, social sciences, sociology, theatre, video.

Nuova Casa Editrice Licinio Cappelli GEM srl
Via Farini 14, 40124 Bologna
☎00 39 051 239060   Fax 00 39 051 239286
FOUNDED 1851. *Publishes* fiction, art, biography, drama, film, government, history, music and dance, medicine, nursing, dentistry, philosophy, poetry, political science, psychology, psychiatry, religion, general science, social sciences, sociology, theatre, video.

Garzanti Editore
Via Newton 18A, 20148 Milan
☎00 39 02 487941   Fax 00 39 02 76009233
FOUNDED 1861. *Publishes* fiction, literature, literary criticism, essays, art, biography, history, poetry, government, political science.

Giunti Publishing Group
Via Bolognese 165, 50139 Florence
☎00 39 055 66791   Fax 00 39 055 6679298
FOUNDED 1840. *Publishes* fiction, literature, literary criticism, essays, art, chemistry, chemical engineering, education, history, how-to, language arts, linguistics, mathematics, psychology, psychiatry, general science. Italian publishers of National Geographical Society books.

Gremese Editore SRL
Via Agnelli 88, 00151 Rome
☎00 39 06 65740507 Fax 00 39 06 65740509

FOUNDED 1978. *Publishes* fiction and non-fiction; art, astrology, cookery, crafts, dance, drama, environmental studies, fashion, games, hobbies, essays, literature, literary criticism, music, occult, parapsychology, photography, sport, travel, theatre, film, video, radio.

Istituto Geografico de Agostini SpA
Via Giovanni da Verrazzano 15, 28100 Novara
☎00 39 0321 471830 Fax 00 39 0321 471286

Publishes education, geography, geology, history and general science.

Longanesi & C
Corso Italia 13, 20122 Milan
☎00 39 02 8692640   Fax 00 39 02 72000306

FOUNDED 1946. *Publishes* fiction, art, biography, dance, history, how-to, medicine, nursing, dentistry, music, philosophy, psychology, psychiatry, religion, general and social sciences, sociology.

Arnoldo Mondadori Editore SpA
Via Mondadori, 20090 Segrate (Milan)
☎00 39 02 75421   Fax 00 39 02 75422886

FOUNDED 1907. *Publishes* fiction, mystery, romance, art, biography, dance, dentistry, history, how-to, medicine, music, poetry, philosophy, psychology, psychiatry, religion, nursing, general science, education.

Società Editrice Il Mulino
Str Maggiore 37, 40125 Bologna
☎00 39 051 256011   Fax 00 39 051 256034

FOUNDED 1954. *Publishes* dance, drama, economics, government, history, law, language, linguistics, music, philosophy, political science, psychology, psychiatry, social sciences, sociology, theatre.

Gruppo Ugo Mursia Editore SpA
Via Tadino 29, 20124 Milan
☎00 39 02 29403030 Fax 00 39 02 29525557

FOUNDED 1922. *Publishes* fiction, poetry, art, biography, education, history, maritime, philosophy, religion, sport, general and social sciences, sociology.

RCS Libri SpA
Via Mecenate 91, 20138 Milan
☎00 39 02 50952918 Fax 00 39 02 50952638

FOUNDED 1945. *Publishes* art, crafts, dance,

environmental studies, games, hobbies, history, music, medicine, nursing, dentistry, outdoor recreation, general science.

Societa Editrice Internazionale – SEI
Corso Regina Margherita 176, 10152 Turin
☎00 39 011 52271   Fax 00 39 011 5211320

FOUNDED 1908. *Publishes* literature, literary criticism, essays, education, geography, geology, history, mathematics, philosophy, physics, religion, psychology, psychiatry.

Sonzogno
Via Mecenate 91, 20138 Milan
☎00 39 02 50951   Fax 00 39 02 5065361

FOUNDED 1818. *Publishes* fiction, mysteries, and general non-fiction.

Sperling e Kupfer Editori SpA
Via Borgonuovo 24, 20121 Milan
☎00 39 02 290341   Fax 00 39 02 6590290

FOUNDED 1899. *Publishes* fiction and general non-fiction, biography, economics, health, how-to, management, nutrition, general science, sport, travel.

Sugarco Edizioni SRL
Via Fermi 9, 21040 Carnago (Varese)
☎00 39 0331 985511 Fax 00 39 0331 985385

FOUNDED 1956. *Publishes* fiction, biography, history, how-to, philosophy.

Todariana Editrice
Via Gardone 29, 20139 Milan
☎00 39 02 8812953   Fax 00 39 02 55213405

FOUNDED 1967. *Publishes* fiction, poetry, science fiction, fantasy, literature, literary criticism, essays, language arts, linguistics, psychology, psychiatry, social sciences, sociology, travel.

The Netherlands

Addison Wesley Longman Publishers BV
Concertgebouwplein 25, 1071 LM Amsterdam
☎00 31 20 575 5800   Fax 00 31 20 664 5334

FOUNDED 1942. *Publishes* education, business, computer science, economics, management, technology.

A.W. Bruna Uitgevers BV
Postbus 8411, 3503 RK Utrecht
☎00 31 30 2470411   Fax 00 31 30 2410018

FOUNDED 1868. *Publishes* fiction and general

non-fiction; computer science, history, philosophy, psychology, psychiatry, general and social science, sociology.

Uitgeverij BZZTÔH
Laan van Meerdervoort 10, 2517 AJ Gravenhage
☎00 31 70 3632934   Fax 00 31 70 3631932
FOUNDED 1970. *Publishes* fiction, mysteries, general non-fiction, animals, astrology, biography, cookery, dance, humour, music, occult, pets, religion (Buddhist), romance, travel.

Elsevier Science BV
PO Box 2400, 1000 CK Amsterdam
☎00 31 20 4853911   Fax 00 31 20 4852457
FOUNDED 1946. Parent company – Reed Elsevier. *Publishes* sciences (all fields), management and professional, medicine, nursing, dentistry, economics, engineering (computer, chemical and general), mathematics, physics, technology.

Uitgeverij Hollandia BV
Postbus 70, 3740 AB Baarn
☎00 31 35 5418941   Fax 00 31 35 5421917
FOUNDED 1899. *Publishes* fiction, maritime, travel.

Uitgeversmaatschappij J. H. Kok BV
PO Box 130, 8260 AC Kampen
☎00 31 38 3392555   Fax 00 31 38 3327331
FOUNDED 1894. *Publishes* fiction, poetry, art, biography, crafts, education, environmental studies, games, history, hobbies, how-to, psychology, psychiatry, religion, general and social sciences, sociology, medicine, nursing, dentistry.

M & P Publishing House
Postbus 170, 3990 DD Houten
☎00 31 30 6377736   Fax 00 31 30 6377764
FOUNDED 1974. *Publishes* general non-fiction.

Meulenhoff & Co BV
Prins Hendriklaan 56, 1075 BE Amsterdam
☎00 31 20 5244310   Fax 00 31 20 6387376
FOUNDED 1895. *Publishes* international co-productions, fiction and general non-fiction. Specialises in Dutch and translated literature.

Uitgeverij Het Spectrum BV
Postbus 2073, 3500 GB Utrecht
☎00 31 30 2650650   Fax 00 31 30 2620850
FOUNDED 1935. *Publishes* science fiction, fantasy, literature, literary criticism, essays, mystery, crime, general non-fiction, computer sci-

ence, history, astrology, occult, management, environmental studies, travel.

Time-Life Books BV
Ottho Heldringstr 5, 1066 AZ Amsterdam
☎00 31 20 5104371   Fax 00 31 20 6176594
Publishes art, cookery, gardening, plants, history, how-to, health and nutrition, house and home, mystery.

Unieboek BV
Postbus 170, 3995 DB Houten
☎00 31 30 6377660   Fax 00 31 30 6377600
FOUNDED 1891. *Publishes* fiction, general non-fiction, architecture and interior design, government, political science, literature, literary criticism, essays, archaeology, cookery, history.

Uniepers BV
Postbus 69, 1390 AB Abcoude
☎00 31 294 285111   Fax 00 31 294 283013
FOUNDED 1961. *Publishes* (mostly in co-editions) antiques, anthropology, archaeology, architecture and interior design, art, culture, dance, history, music, nature, natural history.

Veen Uitgevers Group
Postbus 14095, 3508 SC Utrecht
☎00 31 30 2349211   Fax 00 31 20 2349208
FOUNDED 1887. Part of Wolters Kluwer Trade Publishing. *Publishes* general non-fiction, fiction, essays, Dutch and foreign literature, literary criticism, travel, business,

Wolters Kluwer NV
PO Box 818, 1000 AV Amsterdam
☎00 31 20 6070400   Fax 00 31 20 6070490
FOUNDED 1889. *Publishes* education, medical, technical encyclopedias, trade books and journals, law and taxation, periodicals.

Norway

H. Aschehoug & Co (W. Nygaard) A/S
Postboks 363, 0102 Sentrum, Oslo
☎00 47 22 400400   Fax 00 47 22 206395
FOUNDED 1872. *Publishes* fiction and general non-fiction, general and social science, sociology.

J. W. Cappelens Forlag A/S
Postboks 350, 0101 Sentrum, Oslo
☎00 47 22 365000   Fax 00 47 22 365040
FOUNDED 1829. *Publishes* fiction, general non-fiction, religion.

N. W. Damm og Søn A/S
Postboks 1755, Vika, 0122 Oslo
☎00 47 22 471100   Fax 00 47 22 360874
FOUNDED 1845. *Publishes* fiction and general non-fiction.

Ex Libris Forlag A/S
Postboks 2130 Grünerløkka, 0505 Oslo
☎00 47 22 384450   Fax 00 47 22 385160
FOUNDED 1982. *Publishes* cookery, health, nutrition, humour, human relations, publishing and book trade reference.

Gyldendal Norsk Forlag A/S
Postboks 6860, 0130 St Olaf, Oslo
☎00 47 22 034100   Fax 00 47 22 034105
FOUNDED 1925. *Publishes* fiction, science fiction, fantasy, art, dance, biography, government, political science, history, how-to, music, social sciences, sociology, poetry, philosophy, psychology, psychiatry, religion.

Hjemmets Bokforlag AS
Postboks 1755, Vika, N-0055 Oslo
☎00 47 22 471000   Fax 00 47 22 471098
FOUNDED 1969. *Publishes* fiction and general non-fiction.

NKS-Forlaget
Postboks 5853, 0308 Oslo
☎00 47 22 596000   Fax 00 47 22 596300
FOUNDED 1971. *Publishes* accountancy, childcare and development, English as a second language, health, nutrition, mathematics, natural history, general and social sciences, sociology.

Tiden Norsk Forlag
PO Box 8813, Youngstorget, 0028 Oslo
☎00 47 22 007100   Fax 00 46 22 426458
FOUNDED 1933. *Publishes* fiction, general non-fiction; essays, literature, literary criticism, science fiction, fantasy, management.

Portugal

Bertrand Editora Lda
Rua Anchieta 29 – 1d90, 1200 Lisbon
☎00 351 1 3420084   Fax 00 351 1 3479728
FOUNDED 1727. *Publishes* art, essays, literature, literary criticism, social sciences, sociology.

Editorial Caminho SARL
Al Santo Antonio dos Capuchos 6B, 1150 Lisbon
☎00 351 1 3152683   Fax 00 351 1 534346
FOUNDED 1977. *Publishes* fiction, government, political science.

Livraria Civilizacão (Américo Fraga Lamares & Ca Lda)
Rua Alberto Aires de Gouveia 27, 4050 Porto
☎00 351 2 6062286   Fax 00 351 2 6066557
FOUNDED 1921. *Publishes* fiction, art, economics, history, social and political science, government, sociology.

Publicações Dom Quixote Lda
Rua Luciano Cordeiro 116-2, 1050 Lisbon
☎00 351 1 3158079   Fax 00 351 1 3574595
FOUNDED 1965. *Publishes* fiction, poetry, education, history, philosophy, general and social sciences, sociology.

Publicações Europa-America Lda
Apdo 8, Estrada Lisbon-Sintra Km 14, 2726 Mem Martins Cedex
☎00 351 1 9211461   Fax 00 351 1 9217846
FOUNDED 1945. *Publishes* fiction, poetry, art, biography, dance, education, general engineering, history, how-to, music, philosophy, medicine, nursing, dentistry, psychology, psychiatry, general and social sciences, sociology, technology.

Gradiva – Publicações Lda
Rua Almeida e Sousa 21–r/c Esq, 1350 Lisbon
☎00 351 1 3974067   Fax 00 351 1 3953471
FOUNDED 1981. *Publishes* fiction, science fiction, fantasy, education, history, human relations, philosophy, general science.

Livros Horizonte Lda
Rua Chagas 17 - 1 Dto, 1200 Lisbon
☎00 351 1 3466917   Fax 00 351 1 3426921
FOUNDED 1953. *Publishes* art, education, history, psychology, psychiatry, social sciences, sociology.

Editorial Verbo SA
Av Antón 10 Augusto de Aguiar 148–6, 1050 Lisbon
☎00 351 1 3801100   Fax 00 351 1 3865396
FOUNDED 1959. *Publishes* education, history, general science.

Spain

Editorial Alhambra SA
Fernandez de la Hoz 9, 28010 Madrid
☎00 349 1 5940020   Fax 00 349 1 5941280
FOUNDED 1942. *Publishes* art, education, history, language arts, linguistics, medicine and nursing, dentistry, general science, psychology, psychiatry, philosophy.

Alianza Editorial SA
Juan Ignacio Luca de Tena 15,
28027 Madrid
☎00 349 1 7416600   Fax 00 349 1 3207480
FOUNDED 1965. *Publishes* fiction, poetry, art,
history, mathematics, dance, music, philosophy, government, political and social sciences,
sociology, general science.

Ediciones Anaya SA
Juan Ignacio Luca de Tena 15,
28027 Madrid
☎00 349 1 3938800   Fax 00 349 1 7426631
FOUNDED 1959. *Publishes* education.

Editorial Don Quijote
Compãs del Porvenir 6, 41013 Seville
☎00 349 5 4235080
FOUNDED 1981. *Publishes* fiction, literature, literary criticism, poetry, essays, drama, theatre,
history.

EDHASA (Editora y Distribuidora Hispano – Americana SA)
Av Diagonal 519, 08029 Barcelona
☎00 349 3 4949720   Fax 00 349 3 4194584
FOUNDED 1946. *Publishes* fiction, literature, literary criticism, essays, history.

Editorial Espasa-Calpe SA
Apdo 547, Carretera de Irún Km 12, 200,
28080 Madrid
☎00 349 1 358 9689   Fax 00 349 1 358 9364
FOUNDED 1925. *Publishes* fiction, science fiction, fantasy, English as a second language,
general non-fiction, art, child care and development, cookery, biography, essays, history,
literature, literary criticism, self-help, social sciences, sociology.

Ediciones Grijalbo SA
Aragò 385, 08013 Barcelona
☎00 349 3 4587000   Fax 00 349 3 4580495
FOUNDED 1942. *Publishes* fiction, general non-fiction, art, biography, history, government,
political science, philosophy, psychology, psychiatry, religion, social sciences, sociology, technology.

Grijalbo Mondadori SA
Aragó 385, 08013 Barcelona
☎00 349 3 4767100   Fax 00 349 3 4767116
FOUNDED 1962. *Publishes* fiction, general non-fiction, archaeology, economy, essays, history,
human relations, literature, literary criticism.

Grupo Editorial CEAC SA
C/Peru 164, 08020 Barcelona
☎00 349 3 3075004   Fax 00 349 3 2660067
Publishes education, technology, science fiction,
fantasy.

Ediciones Hiperión SL
Calle Salustiano Olózaga 14, 28001 Madrid
☎00 349 1 5576015   Fax 00 349 1 4358690
FOUNDED 1976. *Publishes* literature, literary
criticism, essays, poetry, religions (Islamic and
Jewish).

Editorial Luis Vives (Edelvives)
C/Xaudaró 25, 28034 Madrid
☎00 349 1 3344883   Fax 00 349 1 3344893
FOUNDED 1890. *Publishes* education.

Editorial Molino
Calabria 166 baixos, 08015 Barcelona
☎00 349 3 2260625   Fax 00 349 3 2266998
FOUNDED 1933. *Publishes* cookery, education,
sport, fiction.

Editorial Planeta SA
Córsega 273–279, 08008 Barcelona
☎00 349 3 4154100   Fax 00 349 3 2173850
FOUNDED 1952. *Publishes* fiction and general
non-fiction.

Plaza y Janés SA
Enrique Granados 86–88, 08008 Barcelona
☎00 349 3 4151100   Fax 00 349 3 4156976
FOUNDED 1959. *Publishes* fiction and general
non-fiction.

Santillana SA
Elfo 32, 28027 Madrid
☎00 349 1 3224500   Fax 00 349 1 3224475
FOUNDED 1964. *Publishes* fiction, essays, literature, literary criticism, travel.

Editorial Seix Barral SA
Córsega 270, Apdo 4, 08008 Barcelona
☎00 349 3 2186400   Fax 00 349 3 2184773
FOUNDED 1945. *Publishes* fiction, poetry,
drama, theatre.

Tusquets Editores
Cesare Cantù 8, 08023 Barcelona
☎00 349 3 2530400   Fax 00 349 3 4176703
FOUNDED 1969. *Publishes* fiction, biography,
essays, literature, literary criticism, general
science.

Ediciones Versal SA
Calabria 108, 08015 Barcelona
☎00 349 3 3257404   Fax 00 349 3 4236898
FOUNDED 1984. *Publishes* general non-fiction, biography, literature, literary criticism, essays.

Sweden

Albert Bonniers Förlag AB
Box 3159, Sveavägen 56, S-103 63 Stockholm
☎00 46 8 6968000   Fax 00 46 8 6968359
FOUNDED 1837. *Publishes* fiction and general non-fiction.

Bokförlaget Bra Böcker AB
Södra Vägen, S-26380 Höganäs
☎00 46 42 339000   Fax 00 46 42 330504
FOUNDED 1965. *Publishes* fiction, geography, geology, history.

Brombergs Bokförlag AB
Box 12886, Industrigaton 4A,
S-112 98 Stockholm
☎00 46 8 6503390   Fax 00 46 8 56262085
FOUNDED 1973. *Publishes* fiction, general non-fiction, government, political science, general science.

Bokförlaget Forum AB
PO Box 70321, Gamla Brogatan 26,
Riddargatan 23A, S-107 23 Stockholm
☎00 46 8 6968440   Fax 00 46 8 6968368
FOUNDED 1944. *Publishes* fiction and general non-fiction.

Bokförlaget Natur och Kultur
Box 27323, Karlavägen 31,
S-102 54 Stockholm
☎00 46 8 4538600   Fax 00 46 8 4538790
FOUNDED 1922. *Publishes* fiction and general non-fiction, biography, history, psychology, psychiatry, general science.

Norstedts Förlag AB
Box 2052, Tryckerigatan 4, S-103 12 Stockholm
☎00 46 8 7893000   Fax 00 46 8 7893038
FOUNDED 1823. *Publishes* fiction and general non-fiction.

AB Rabén och Sjögren Bokförlag
PO Box 45022, Kungstengatan 49,
S-104 30 Stockholm
☎00 46 8 4570300   Fax 00 46 8 4570331
FOUNDED 1942. *Publishes* fiction and general non-fiction.

Richters Förlag AB
Ostra Förstadsgatan 46, 205 75 Malmö
☎00 46 40 380600   Fax 00 46 40 933708
FOUNDED 1942. *Publishes* fiction.

B Wählströms Bokförlag AB
Box 30022, S-104 25 Stockholm
☎00 46 8 6198600   Fax 00 46 8 6189761
FOUNDED 1911. *Publishes* fiction and general non-fiction.

Switzerland

**Arche Verlag AG,
Raabe und Vitali**
Postfach 8030, CH-8030 Zurich
☎00 41 1 2522410   Fax 00 41 1 2611115
FOUNDED 1944. *Publishes* literature and literary criticism, essays, biography, fiction, poetry, music, dance, travel.

Artemis Verlags AG
Munstergasse 9, CH-8001 Zurich
☎00 41 1 2521100   Fax 00 41 1 2624792
FOUNDED 1943. *Publishes* art, architecture and interior design, biography, history, philosophy, political science, government, travel.

Diogenes Verlag AG
Sprecherstr 8, CH-8032 Zurich
☎00 41 1 2548511   Fax 00 41 1 2528407
FOUNDED 1952. *Publishes* fiction, essays, literature, literary criticism, mysteries, art, drama, theatre, philosophy.

Langenscheidt AG Zürich-Zug
Postfach 326, CH-8021 Zurich
☎00 41 1 2115000   Fax 00 41 1 2122149
Part of Langenscheidt Group, Germany. *Publishes* language arts and linguistics.

Larousse (Suisse) SA
3 Route du Grand-Mont,
CH-1052 Le Mont-sur-Lausanne
☎00 41 22 369140
Publishes dictionaries, reference and textbooks.

Neptun-Verlag
Fidlerstr, Postfach 171,
CH-8272 Ermatingen
☎00 41 72 642020   Fax 00 41 72 642023
FOUNDED 1946. *Publishes* history and travel.

Orell Füssli Verlag

Dietzingerstrasse 3, CH-8036 Zurich

☎00 41 1 2113630   Fax 00 41 1 4667412

FOUNDED 1519. *Publishes* art, biography, economics, education, geography, geology, history, how-to.

Editions Payot Lausanne

18 ave de la Gare, CP 529, CH-1001 Lausanne

☎00 41 21 3290264   Fax 00 41 21 3290266

FOUNDED 1875. *Publishes* general non-fiction, anthropology, dance, education, history, law, medicine, nursing, dentistry, music, literature, literary criticism, essays, general science.

Sauerländer AG

Laurenzenvorstadt 89, CH-5001 Aarau

☎00 41 62 8368626   Fax 00 41 62 8245780

FOUNDED 1807. *Publishes* biography, education, history, poetry, medicine, nursing, dentistry, general science, social sciences, sociology.

Scherz Verlag AG

Theaterplatz 4–6, CH-3000 Berne 7

☎00 41 31 3277117   Fax 00 41 31 3277171

FOUNDED 1939. *Publishes* fiction and general non-fiction; biography, history, psychology, psychiatry, philosophy, parapsychology.

European Television Companies

Austria

ORF (Österreichisher Rundfunk)
Würzburggasse 30, A–1136 Vienna
☎00 43 1 87 8780   Fax 00 43 1 87 8783766
Website:www.orf.at

Belgium

Vlaamse Radio en Televisieomroep (VRT)
Auguste Reyerslaan 52, B–1043 Brussels
☎00 32 2 741 3111   Fax 00 32 2 736 5786
Website:www.vrt.be

Vlaamse Televisie Maatschappij (VTM) (cable)
Medialaan 1, B–1800 Vilvoorde
☎00 32 2 255 3211   Fax 00 32 2 252 5141

Radio-Télévision Belge de la Communauté Française (RTBF)
Boulevard Auguste Reyers 52,
B–1044 Brussels
☎00 32 2 737 2560   Fax 00 32 2 737 2556
Website:www.rtbf.be

Denmark

Danmarks Radio–TV
TV Byen, DK–2860 Søborg
☎00 45 35 20 3040   Fax 00 45 35 20 3023
Website:www.dr.dk

TV–2 Danmark
Rugaardsvej 25, DK–5100 Odense C
☎00 45 65 91 1244   Fax 00 45 65 91 3322
Website:www.tv2.dk

TV Danmark
Indiakaj 12, DK–2100 Copenhagen 0
☎00 45 35 43 0522   Fax 00 45 35 43 0655

Finland

MTV3 Finland
Ilmalantori 2, SF–00240 Helsinki
☎00 358 9 15001   Fax 00 358 9 1500707
Website:www.mtv3.fi

Yleisradio Oy (YLE)
PO Box 00024 Yleisradio, SF–00240 Helsinki
☎00 358 9 14801   Fax 00 358 9 14803391
Website:www.yle.fi

France

France Television (France 2/ France 3)
7 Esplanade Henri de France, Paris Cedex 15
France 2: ☎00 33 1 56 22 42 42
France 3: ☎00 33 1 56 22 30 30
Website:www.france2.fr and france3.fr

La Sept/Arte (cable & satellite)
8 rue Marceau, 92785 Issy les Moulineaux Cedex 9
☎00 33 1 55 00 77 77Fax 00 33 1 55 00 77 00
Website:www.lasept-arte.fr

Canal + (pay TV)
85–89 quai André Citroën, 75711 Paris Cedex 15
☎00 33 1 44 25 10 00Fax 00 33 1 44 25 12 34
Website:www.cplus.fr

La Cinquième
18 rue Horace-Vernet,
92136 Issey Les Moulineaux
☎00 33 1 41 46 55 55
Fax 00 33 1 41 08 02 22
Website:www.lacenquieme.fr

RFO (Radio Télévision Française d'Outre-mer)
5 ave du Recteur Poincaré, 75782 Paris
☎00 33 1 42 15 71 00
Fax 00 33 1 42 15 74 37
Website:www.rfo.fr

TF1
1 quai du Pont du Jour, 92656 Boulogne
☎00 33 1 41 41 12 34
Fax 00 33 1 41 41 28 40
Website:www.tf1.fr

Germany

ARD – Das Erste
ARD Büro, Bertramstr 8,
60320 Frankfurt am Main
☎00 49 69 59 0607   Fax 00 49 69 15 52075
Website:www.ard.de

ZDF (Zweites Deutsches Fernsehen)
ZDF-Strasse 1, 55100 Mainz
☎00 49 61 31 70 2060
Fax 00 49 61 31 70 6822
Website:www.zdf.de

Ireland

Radio Telefis Éireann (RTE – RTE 1)
Donnybrook, Dublin 4
☎00 353 1 208 3111   Fax 00 353 1 208 3080

Teilefis na Gaelige
Baile na hAbhann, Co Na Gaillimhe
☎00 353 91 505050   Fax 00 353 91 505021

Italy

RAI (RadioTelevisione Italiana)
Viale Mazzini 14, 00195 Rome
☎00 39 06 38781   Fax 00 39 06 3226070

Tele piu' (pay TV)
Via Piranesi 44/a, 20137 Milan
☎00 39 02 700 271   Fax 00 39 02 700 27201

The Netherlands

AVRO (Algemene Omroep Vereniging)
Postbus 2, 1200 JA Hilversum
☎00 31 35 671 79 11 Fax 00 31 35 671 74 39
Website:www.omroep.nl/avro

IKON
Postbus 10009, 1201 EA Hilversum
☎00 31 35 672 72 72
Fax 00 31 35 621 51 00
Website:www.omroep.nl/ikon

NCRV (Nederlandse Christelijke Radio Vereniging)
Postbus 25000, 1202 HBC Hilversum
☎00 31 35 671 99 11
Fax 00 31 35 671 92 85
Website:www.ncrv.nl

NOS (Nederlandse Omroep Stichting)
Postbus 26600, 1202 JT Hilversum
☎00 31 35 677 92 22 Fax 00 31 35 624 20 23
Website:www.omroep.nl/nos

NPS (Nederlandse Programma Stichting)
Postbus 29000, 1202 MA Hilversum
☎00 31 35 677 93 33
Fax 00 31 35 677 4959
Website:www.omroep.nl/nps

TROS (Televisie en Radio Omroep Stichting)
Postbus 28450, 1202 LL Hilversum
☎00 31 35 671 57 15
Fax 00 31 35 671 52 36
Website:www.omroep.nl/tros

VARA
Postbus 175, 1200 AD Hilversum
☎00 31 35 671 19 11
Fax 00 31 35 671 13 33
Website:www.omroep.nl/vara

VPRO
Postbus 11, 1200 JC Hilversum
☎00 31 35 671 29 11
Fax 00 31 35 671 22 54

Norway

NRK (Norsk Rikskringkasting)
Bjørnstjerne Bjørnsons Plass 1, N–0340 Oslo
☎00 47 23 04 7000
Website:www.nrk.no

TVNorge
Sagveien 17, 0459–Oslo 4
☎00 47 22 38 7800   Fax 00 47 22 35 1000

TV2
Postboks 2, N–5002 Bergen
☎00 47 55 90 8070   Fax 00 47 55 90 8090

Portugal

Radiotelevisâo Portuguesa (RTP)
Av 5 de Outubro 197, 1000 Lisbon
☎00 35 11 793 1774   Fax 00 35 11 796 6227

SIC (Sociedade Independente de Comunicaçâo
Estrada da Outurela 119, 2796 Carnaxide
☎00 35 11 417 9550   Fax 00 35 11 417 3118

TVI (Televisâo Independente)
Rua Márió Castelhano 40, Queluz de Baixo, 2745 Barcarena
☎00 35 11 434 7500   Fax 00 35 11 435 5076

Spain

RTVE (Radiotelevision Espaola)
Edificio Prado del Rey, E–28223 Madrid
☎00 349 1 581 5404   Fax 00 349 1 581 5412

TVE (Televisión Espaola, SA)
O'Donnell 77, 28007 Madrid
☎00 349 1 346 8723   Fax 00 349 1 346 9777

Sweden

Sveriges Television
Oxenstiernsgatan 26–34, S–10510 Stockholm
☎00 46 8 784 0000   Fax 00 46 8 784 1500
Website:www.svt.se

TV4
Storangskroken 10, S–11579 Stockholm
☎00 46 8 459 4000   Fax 00 46 8 459 4444
Website:www.tv4.se

Switzerland

SBC (Swiss Broadcasting Corp.)
Giacomettistr 3, CH-3000 Bern 15
☎00 41 31 350 91 11
Fax 00 41 31 350 92 56

Schweizer Fernsehen DRS
(German TV)
Fernsehenstrasse 1–4, CH–8052 Zurich
☎00 41 1 305 66 11   Fax 00 41 1 305 56 60

TSR (Télévision Suisse Romande)
Quai Ernest Ansermet 20,
CH–1211 Geneva 8
☎00 41 22 708 99 11 Fax 00 41 22 708 98 00

RTSI (Radiotelevisione svizzera di lingua Italiana)
Casella postale, CH–6903 Lugarno
☎00 41 91 803 51 11 Fax 00 41 91 803 91 50

US Publishers

International Reply Coupons (IRCs)
For return postage, send IRCs, available from post offices. Letters, 60 pence; mss according to weight.

ABC–Clio, Inc.

Suite 350, 501 South Cherry Street, Denver CO 80246
☎001 303 333 3003   Fax 001 303 333 4037
Website: www.abc-clio.com

Vice-President/Publisher *Rolf A Janke*

FOUNDED 1955. *Publishes* non-fiction: reference, including mythology, government and politics, history, current world issues, social sciences, humanities, literature, cultural anthropology, sport, multimedia. No unsolicited mss; synopses and ideas welcome.
Royalties paid annually. *UK subsidiary* **ABC-Clio Ltd**, Oxford.

Abingdon Press

201 Eighth Avenue South, Box 801, Nashville TN 37202–0801
☎001 615 749 6404   Fax 001 615 749 6512

Editorial Director *Harriett Jane Olson*

Publishes non-fiction: religious (lay and professional), children's religious and academic texts. About 100 titles a year. Approach in writing only with synopsis and samples. IRCs essential.

Harry N. Abrams, Inc.

100 Fifth Avenue, New York NY 10011
☎001 212 206 7715   Fax 001 212 645 8437

CEO/President/Editor-in-chief
 Paul Gottlieb

FOUNDED 1950. *Publishes* illustrated books: art, architecture, nature, entertainment and children's. No fiction. Submit completed mss (no dot matrix), together with sample illustrations.

Academy Chicago Publishers

363 W. Erie Street, Chicago IL 60610
☎001 312 751 7300   Fax 001 312 751 7306
Website: www.academychicago.com

Senior Editor *Anita Miller*

FOUNDED 1975. *Publishes* mainstream fiction; non-fiction: history, women's studies. No romance, children's, young adult, religious, sexist or avant-garde.

IMPRINT **Cassandra Editions** ('Lost' Women Writers). Send first three chapters only, accompanied by IRCs; no synopses or ideas.
Royalties paid twice-yearly. *Distributed* in the UK and Europe by Gazelle, Lancaster.

Ace Science Fiction & Fantasy
See **Berkley Publishing Group**

Adams Media Corporation

260 Center Street, Holbrook MA 02343
☎001 781 767 8100   Fax 001 781 767 0994
Website: www.adamsmedia.com

Editor-in-Chief *Edward Walters*

FOUNDED 1980. *Publishes* general non-fiction: careers, business, personal finance, relationships, parenting and maternity, self-improvement, reference, cooking, sports, games and humour. Ideas welcome but publisher will not respond to or return unsolicited material unless interested.

Addison Wesley Longman, Inc

One Jacob Way, Reading, MA 01867–3999
☎001 781 944 3700   Fax 001 781 944 9338
Website: www.awl.com

Chairman/CEO *Peter Jovanovich*

Acquired by Pearson plc in 1998, AWL is one of the world's largest educational publishers of books, multimedia and learning programmes.

University of Alabama Press

Box 870380, Tuscaloosa AL 35487
☎001 205 348 5180   Fax 001 205 348 9201

Director *Nicole Mitchell*

FOUNDED 1945. *Publishes* academic books in the fields of American history, American literature, history of science and technology, linguistics, archaeology, rhetoric and speech communication, Judaic studies, political science and public administration, with special emphasis on Southern regional studies. About 40 titles a year.

Aladdin Books
See **Simon & Schuster Children's Publishing Division**

University of Alaska Press
1st Floor, Gruening Building, PO Box 756240, University of Alaska, Fairbanks AK 99775–6240
☎001 907 474 5831   Fax 001 907 474 5502
Email: fypres@uaf.edu
Website: www.uaf.edu/uapress
Manager *Debbie Gonzalez*
Managing Editor *Carla Helfferich*
Acquisitions *Pam Odom*

Traces its origins back to 1927 but was relatively dormant until the early 1980s. *Publishes* scholarly works about Alaska and the North Pacific rim, with a special emphasis on circumpolar regions. 5–10 titles a year. No fiction or poetry.

DIVISIONS **Ramuson Library Historical Translation Series** *Marvin Falk*; **Monograph Series** *Carla Helfferich*; **Oral Biography Series** *William Schneider;* **Classic Reprint Series** *Terrence Cole;* **Lanternlight Library** Informal non-fiction covering Northern interest. Unsolicited mss, synopses and ideas welcome.

AMACOM Books
1601 Broadway, New York NY 10019–7406
☎001 212 586 8100   Fax 001 212 903 8083
Publisher *Harold V. Kennedy*

Owned by American Management Association. *Publishes* business books only, including general management, business communications, sales and marketing, finance, computers and information systems, human resource management and training, career/personal growth skills, research development, project management and manufacturing, quality/customer service titles. 65–70 titles a year. Proposals welcome. *Royalties* paid twice-yearly.

Anchor Books
See **Bantam Doubleday Dell Publishing Group, Inc.**

Anvil
See **Krieger Publishing Co., Inc.**

Archway
See **Pocket Books**

University of Arizona Press
1230 North Park Avenue, Suite 102, Tucson AZ 85719–4140
☎001 520 621 1441   Fax 001 520 621 8899
Website: www.uapress.arizona.edu
Interim Director *Christine Szuter*

FOUNDED 1959. *Publishes* academic non-fiction, particularly with a regional/cultural link, plus Native-American and Hispanic literature. About 50 titles a year.

University of Arkansas Press
McIlroy House, 201 Ozark Avenue, Fayetteville AR 72701
☎001 501 575 3246   Fax 001 501 575 6044
Director *John Coghlan*

FOUNDED 1980. *Publishes* scholarly monographs, poetry and general trade including biography, etc. Particularly interested at present in scholarly works in history, politics and literary criticism. About 30 titles a year. *Royalties* paid annually.

Aspect
See **Warner Books Inc.**

Atheneum Books for Young Readers
See **Simon & Schuster Children's Publishing Division**

Atlantic Monthly Press
See **Grove/Atlantic Inc**

AUP (Associated University Presses)
AUP New Jersey titles are handled in the UK by **Golden Cockerel Press** (see entry under **UK Publishers**).

Avery Publishing Group, Inc.
120 Old Broadway, Garden City Park, New York NY 11040
☎001 516 741 2155   Fax 001 516 742 1892
Website: www.averypublishing.com
Publisher *Rudy Shur*

FOUNDED 1976. *Publishes* adult trade non-fiction, specialising in childbirth, childcare, alternative health, self-help, New Age and natural cooking. About 50 titles a year. No unsolicited mss; synopses and ideas welcome if accompanied by s.a.e. *Royalties* paid twice-yearly.

Avon Books
1350 Avenue of the Americas, New York NY 10019
☎001 212 261 6800   Fax 001 212 261 6895
Senior Vice President/Publisher *Lou Aronica*

FOUNDED 1941. A division of the Hearst Corporation. *Publishes* hardcover, trade and mass-market paperbacks. Fiction: contemporary and historical romance, literary fiction, science fiction and fantasy, mystery and suspense thrillers, commercial fiction, and young adult. Non-fiction: history, health, sports, humour, film, parenting and childcare, gay and lesbian studies, music, self-help, psychology, true crime, science, current events, business, nature, inspirational and literary non-fiction. Submit query letter and sample chapter.

Back Bay Books
See **Little, Brown & Company, Inc.**

Badboy
See **Masquerade Books**

Baker Book House
PO Box 6287, Grand Rapids MI 49516–6287
☎001 616 676 9185   Fax 001 616 676 9573
Website: www.bakerbooks.com
President *Dwight Baker*
Director of Publications *Allan Fisher*
FOUNDED 1939. Began life as a used-book store and began publishing in earnest in the 1950s, primarily serving the evangelical Christian market. About 165 titles a year. Additional information for authors on Website.

DIVISIONS/IMPRINTS
Baker Books *Publishes* religious non-fiction and fiction, Bible reference, professional (pastors and church leaders) books, children's books. About 80 titles a year. Proposals welcome (request guidelines, specifying non-fiction, fiction, professional or children's).

Baker Academic *Jim Weaver Publishes* college/seminary textbooks, religious reference books, biblical studies monographs. About 30 titles a year. Proposals welcome (guidelines available on request). No unsolicited mss. **Fleming H. Revell** *Linda Holland* FOUNDED 1870. A family-owned business until 1978, Revell was one of the first Christian publishers to take the step into secular publishing. Joined Baker Book House in 1992. *Publishes* adult fiction and non-fiction for evangelical Christians. About 45 titles a year. Synopses and ideas welcome.

Chosen Books *Jane Campbell* FOUNDED 1971; joined Baker Book House in 1992. *Publishes* charismatic adult non-fiction for evangelical Christians. About 10 titles a year. Synopses or ideas welcome.

Royalties paid twice-yearly.

The Ballantine Publishing Group (Ballantine/Del Rey/Fawcett/House of Collectibles/Ivy/One World)
201 East 50th Street, New York NY 10022
☎001 212 572 2713   Fax 001 212 572 4912
Website: www.randomhouse.com
Group President *Linda Grey*

Snr. Div. VP/Publisher, Ballantine
Judith Curr
Div. VP/Executive Editor, One World
Cheryl Woodruff
FOUNDED 1952. Division of **Random House, Inc.** *Publishes* fiction and non-fiction, science fiction. IMPRINTS **Ballantine Books**; **Del Rey**; **Fawcett Columbine**; **Fawcett Crest**; **Fawcett Gold Medal**; **Fawcett Juniper**; **Ivy**; **House of Collectibles**; **One World**.

Banner Books
See **University Press of Mississippi**

Bantam Doubleday Dell Publishing Group, Inc.
1540 Broadway, New York NY 10036
☎001 212 354 6500   Fax 001 212 302 7985
Website: www.bdd.com
Chairman *Jack Hoeft*
President/CEO *Erik Engstrom*
Group Snr. VP/Publisher,
   Bantam Books *Irwyn Applebaum*
President/Publisher, Doubleday
   Stephen Rubin
Group Snr. VP/Publisher, Dell
   Publishing *Carole Baron*
President/Publisher BDD Audio
   Publishing *Jenny Kuntz Frost*
President/Publisher, Books for Young
   Readers *Craig Virden*

Owned by Bertelsmann, the international media company which bought **Random House, Inc.** in March 1998. *Publishes* general commercial fiction and non-fiction, young readers and children's.

DIVISIONS/IMPRINTS **Bantam Books**; **Doubleday**; **Dell Publishing**; **Broadway Books**; **Delacorte Books for Young Readers**; **BBD Audio Publishing**; **Anchor Books**; **Currency**; **DD Equestrian Library**; **Delta Books**; **Dial Press**; **Dolphin Books**; **Double D Western**; **Foundation Books**; **Image Books**; **Island Books**; **Laurel Leaf**; **Loveswept**; **New Age Books**; **New Sciences**; **Peacock Press**; **Skylark**; **Spectra**; **Starfire**; **Sweet Dreams**; **Nan A. Talese Books**; **Yearling Books**. Most work comes through agents. No unsolicited mss.

Barron's Educational Series
250 Wireless Boulevard, Hauppauge NY 11788
☎001 516 434 3311   Fax 001 516 434 3723
Chairman/President *Manuel H. Barron*
Managing Editor *Grace Freedson*

FOUNDED 1942. *Publishes* adult non-fiction, children's fiction and non-fiction, test preparation materials and language materials/tapes, cookbooks, gardening, pets, business, art and painting. No adult fiction. 200 titles a year. Unsolicited mss, synopses and ideas for books welcome. *Royalties* paid twice-yearly.

Basic Books
See **HarperCollins Publishers, Inc.**

Beacon Press
25 Beacon Street, Boston MA 02108
☎001 617 742 2110   Fax 001 617 723 3097
Website: www.beacon.org

Director *Helene Atwan*

Publishes general non-fiction. About 50 titles a year. Does not accept unsolicited mss. For further information, refer to Website page.

Bedford Books
See **St Martin's Press, Inc.**

Beech Tree Books
See **William Morrow & Co., Inc.**

Berkley Publishing Group
200 Madison Avenue, New York NY 10016
☎001 212 951 8800   Fax 001 212 213 6706
Website: http:/www.penguinputnam.com

President *David Shanks*
Executive Editor *Hillary Cige*

FOUNDED 1954. Subsidiary of **Penguin Putnam Inc**. *Publishes* paperbacks: general interest fiction and non-fiction. About 700 titles a year. IMPRINTS **Ace Science Fiction & Fantasy** Submit synopsis and first three chapters; **Berkley Books**; **Berkley Prime Crime**; **Berkley Boulevard Books**; **Jove**. *Royalties* paid twice-yearly.

H. & R. Block
See **Simon & Schuster Trade Division**

Boyds Mills Press
815 Church Street, Honesdale PA 18431
☎001 570 253 1164   Fax 001 570 253 0179

Publisher *Kent Brown Jr*
Editorial Director *Larry Rosler*

A subsidiary of Highlights for Children, Inc. FOUNDED 1990 as a publisher of children's trade books. *Publishes* children's fiction, non-fiction and poetry. About 50 titles a year. Unsolicited mss, synopses and ideas for books welcome. No romance or fantasy novels. *Royalties* paid twice-yearly.

Bradford Books
See **The MIT Press**

Brassey's, (an imprint of Batsford Brassey Inc.)
4380 MacArthur Blvd., NW, 2nd Floor, Washington DC 20007
☎001 202 333 2500   Fax 001 202 333 5100
Email: brasseys@aol.com

President *Ron Davis*
Editorial Director *Don McKeon*

FOUNDED 1983. Associated with **Brassey's** and Batsford Communications Plc of London. *Publishes* non-fiction titles on defence and military affairs, national and international, current affairs, foreign policy, history, biography, intelligence and sports. About 30 titles a year. No unsolicited mss; synopses and ideas welcome. *Royalties* paid annually.

Broadway Books
See **Bantam Doubleday Dell Publishing Group, Inc.**

Browndeer Press
See **Harcourt Brace Children's Books Division**

Bulfinch Press
See **Little, Brown & Company, Inc.**

Bullseye Books
See **Random House, Inc.**

University of California Press
2120 Berkeley Way, Berkeley CA 94720
☎001 510 642 4247   Fax 001 510 643 7127

Director *James H. Clark*

Publishes scholarly and scientific non-fiction; some fiction and poetry in translation. Preliminary letter with outline preferred.

Carol Publishing Group
120 Enterprise Avenue, Secaucus NJ 07094
☎001 201 866 0490   Fax 001 201 866 8159

Publisher *Steven Schragis*

FOUNDED 1989. *Publishes* some fiction but mostly non-fiction: biography and autobiography, history, science, humour, how-to, illustrated and self-help.

Carolrhoda Books, Inc.
241 First Avenue North, Minneapolis MN 55401
☎001 612 332 3344   Fax 001 612 332 7615

Submissions Editor *Rebecca Poole*

Publishes children's: nature, biography, history, beginners' readers, world cultures, photo essays and historical fiction. Please send s.a.e. for author guidelines, making sure guideline requests are clearly marked on the envelope or they will be returned. 'We are *only* accepting submissions twice a year – from March 1–31 and October 1–31. Submissions postmarked with other dates will be returned unopened. Also, only submissions with s.a.e. will receive a response.'

Cassandra Editions
See **Academy Chicago Publishers**

Chapters
See **Houghton Mifflin Co.**

Charlesbridge Publishing
85 Main Street, Watertown MA 02472
☎001 617 926 0329   Fax 001 617 926 5720
Email: books@charlesbridge.com
Website: www.charlesbridge.com
Chairman *Brent Farmer*
Managing Editor *Elena Dworkin Wright*
FOUNDED 1980 as an educational publisher focusing on teaching thinking processes. *Publishes* children's educational programmes, non-fiction picture books and multicultural fiction for 3- to 12-year-olds. Also publishes mathematical stories, *Maths Adventures*, as well as other trade fiction, in picture-book format. Complete mss or proposals welcome with self-addressed envelope and IRCs. Mss should be paged, with suggested illustrations described for each page.

University of Chicago Press
5801 South Ellis Avenue, Chicago IL 60637–1496
☎001 773 702 7700   Fax 001 773 702 9756

FOUNDED 1891. *Publishes* academic non-fiction only. 277 titles in 1998.

Children's Press
See **Grolier, Incorporated**

Chosen Books
See **Baker Book House**

Chronicle Books
85 Second Street, Sixth Floor, San Francisco CA 94105
☎001 415 537 3730   Fax 001 800 858 7787
Website: chroniclebooks.com
Publisher *Jack Jensen*
Publishing Director *Caroline Herter*
FOUNDED 1966. Division of Chronicle Publish-

ing Co. *Publishes* fiction and non-fiction and children's books. Also stationery and gift items. About 200 titles a year.

DIVISIONS **Children's** *Victoria Rock*; **Fiction** *Jay Schaefer* **Chronicle Gift** *Caroline Herter*. Query or submit outline/synopsis and sample chapters and artwork.

Royalties paid twice-yearly.

Clarion Books
See **Houghton Mifflin Co.**

Clarkson Potter
See **The Crown Publishing Group**

Classic Reprint
See **University of Alaska Press**

Copper Beech Books
See **The Millbrook Press, Inc.**

Crescent
See **Random House, Inc.**

The Crown Publishing Group
201 East 50th Street, New York NY 10022
☎001 212 572 2409   Fax 001 212 940 7408
Website: www.randomhouse.com
President/Publisher *Chip Gibson*
FOUNDED 1933. Division of **Random House, Inc.** *Publishes* popular trade fiction and non-fiction. 333 titles in 1998. IMPRINTS **Clarkson Potter** *Lauren Shakely*; **Harmony** *Doug Pepper*; **Living Languages**; *Lisa Alpert* **Three Rivers Press** *Steve Magnuson*; **Crown** *Steve Ross*.

Currency
See **Bantam Doubleday Dell Publishing Group, Inc.**

Da Capo Press
See **Kluwer Academic/Plenum Publishers**

DAW Books, Inc.
375 Hudson Street, 3rd Floor, New York NY 10014–3658
☎001 212 366 2096/Submissions: 366 2095
Fax 001 212 366 2090
Publishers *Elizabeth R. Wollheim,*
  Sheila E. Gilbert
Submissions Editor *Peter Stampfel*
FOUNDED 1971 by Donald and Elsie Wollheim as the first mass-market publisher devoted to science fiction and fantasy. *Publishes* science fiction/fantasy, and some horror. No short stories, anthology ideas or non-fiction. Unsolicited mss,

synopses and ideas for books welcome. About 36 titles a year.

Royalties paid twice-yearly.

DD Equestrian Library
See **Bantam Doubleday Dell Publishing Group, Inc.**

Dearborn Financial Publishing, Inc., A Kaplan Professional Company
155 N. Wacker Drive, Chicago
IL 60606–1719
☎001 312 836 4400   Fax 001 312 836 1021
President *Dennis Blitz*
Vice President *Carol Luitjens* (Textbook),
Dan Tromblay (Course);
Mark Emmons (Training-Securities)

A niche publisher serving the financial services industries. Formerly part of Longman. *Publishes* real estate, insurance, financial planning, securities, commodities, investments, banking, professional education, motivation and reference titles, investment reference and how-to books for the consumer (personal finance, real estate) and small business owner. About 150 titles a year.

DIVISIONS/IMPRINTS**Trade/Professional** *Cynthia Zigmund*; **Textbook: Real Estate Education Company** *Carol Luitjens*; **Insurance** *Dan Trombley*; **Securities Training** *Mark Emmons*; **Upstart Publishing Company** *Robin Nominelli*; **Commodity Trend Service** *Dennis Blitz*. Unsolicited mss, synopses and ideas welcome.

Royalties paid twice-yearly.

Del Rey
See **The Ballantine Publishing Group**

Delacorte Books for Young Readers
See **Bantam Doubleday Dell Publishing Group, Inc.**

Dell Publishing
See **Bantam Doubleday Dell Publishing Group, Inc.**

Delta Books
See **Bantam Doubleday Dell Publishing Group, Inc.**

Derrydale
See **Random House, Inc.**

Michael di Capua Books
See **HarperCollins Publishers**

Dial Books for Young Readers
345 Hudson Street, New York
NY 10014–3657
☎001 212 366 2800   Fax 001 212 404 3394
Queries *Submissions Coordinator*

FOUNDED 1961. A division of Penguin Putnam Books for Young Readers. *Publishes* children's books, including picture books, beginning readers, fiction and non-fiction for middle grade and young adults. 70 titles a year.

IMPRINTS Hardcover only: **Dial Books for Young Readers**; **Dial Books**; hardcover and paperback editions: **Dial Easy-to-Read**. No unsolicited mss accepted; query letters with return postage only. *Royalties* paid twice-yearly.

Dial Press
See **Bantam Doubleday Dell Publishing Group, Inc.**

Dolphin Books
See **Bantam Doubleday Dell Publishing Group, Inc.**

Double D Western
See **Bantam Doubleday Dell Publishing Group, Inc.**

Doubleday
See **Bantam Doubleday Dell Publishing Group, Inc.**

Dragonfly Books
See **Random House, Inc.**

Lisa Drew Books
See **Simon & Schuster Trade Division**

Thomas Dunne Books
See **St Martin's Press, Inc.**

Sanford J. Durst Publications
11 Clinton Avenue, Rockville Centre, New York NY 11570
☎001 516 766 4444   Fax 001 516 766 4520
Owner *Sanford J. Durst*

FOUNDED 1975. *Publishes* non-fiction: numismatic and related, philatelic, legal and art. Also children's books. About 12 titles a year.

Royalties paid twice-yearly.

Dushkin/McGraw-Hill
See **The McGraw-Hill Companies**

Dutton Children's Books
See **Penguin Putnam Inc**

Eaglebrook
See **William Morrow & Co., Inc.**

Edge Books
See **Henry Holt & Co Inc.**

William B. Eerdmans Publishing Co.
255 Jefferson Avenue SE, Grand Rapids MI 49503
☎001 616 459 4591   Fax 001 616 459 6540
Email: sales@eerdmans.com
President *William B. Eerdmans Jr*
Vice President/Editor-in-Chief *Jon Pott*
FOUNDED 1911 as a theological and reference publisher. Gradually began publishing in other genres with authors like C. S. Lewis, Dorothy Sayers and Malcolm Muggeridge on its lists. *Publishes* religious: theology, biblical studies, ethical and social concern, social criticism and children's. 120 titles in 1998.
    DIVISIONS **Children's** *Judy Zylstra*; **Other** *Jon Pott.* Unsolicited mss, synopses and ideas welcome. *Royalties* paid twice-yearly.

M. Evans & Co., Inc.
216 East 49th Street, New York NY 10017
☎001 212 688 2810   Fax 001 212 486 4544
Email: mevans@sprynet.com
President *George C. de Kay*
FOUNDED 1954 as a packager. Began publishing in 1962. Best known for its popular psychology and health books, with titles like *Body Language, Open Marriage, Pain Erasure* and *Aerobics. Publishes* general non-fiction and fiction. About 40 titles a year. No unsolicited mss; query first. Synopses and ideas welcome.
    Royalties paid twice-yearly.

Everyman's Library
See **Alfred A. Knopf, Inc.**

Faber & Faber, Inc.
19 Union Square West, New York NY 1003
☎001 212 741 6900   Fax 001 212 633 9385
Chairman *Thomas Kelleher*
A division of **Farrar, Straus & Giroux, Inc.** *Publishes* fiction and non-fiction for adults. About 100 titles a year. No unsolicited mss.
    Royalties paid twice-yearly.

Facts On File, Inc.
11 Penn Plaza, New York NY 10001
☎001 212 967 8800   Fax 001 212 967 9196
President *Mark McDonnell*

Publisher *Laurie E. Likoff*
Started life in the early 1940s with News Digest subscription series to libraries. Began publishing on specific subjects with the Checkmark Books series and developed its current reference and trade book programme in the 1970s. *Publishes* general trade, young adult trade and academic reference for the school and library markets. *Specialises* in single subject encyclopedias. About 135 titles a year. No fiction, cookery or popular non-fiction.
    DIVISIONS **General Reference** *Laurie Likoff*; **Academic Reference** *Eleanora Von Dehsen*; **Adult Trade** *James Chambers*; **Young Adult** *Nicole Bowen*; **Electronic Publishing** *Antonio Gomez.* Unsolicited synopses and ideas welcome; no mss. Send query letter in the first instance.
    Royalties paid twice-yearly.

Farrar, Straus & Giroux, Inc.
19 Union Square West, New York NY 10003
☎001 212 741 6900   Fax 001 212 741 6973
President/CEO *Roger W. Straus III*
Snr Vice-President/Editor-in-Chief *Jonathan Galassi*
FOUNDED 1946. *Publishes* general fiction, non-fiction, juveniles. About 190 titles a year.
    DIVISIONS **Children's Books** *Margaret Ferguson Publishes* fiction and non-fiction, books and novels for children and young adults. Approximately 100 titles a year. Submit synopsis and sample chapters (copies of artwork/photographs as part of package). **Hill & Wang** *Elisabeth Sifton*
    IMPRINTS **MIRASOL Libros Juveniles**; **Noonday Press** *Elisabeth Dyssegaard*; **North Point Press**; **Sunburst Books**.

Fawcett
See **The Ballantine Publishing Group**

Fireside
See **Simon & Schuster Trade Division**

Fodor's Travel Publications
See **Random House, Inc.**

Forge
See **St Martin's Press, Inc.**

Foundation Books
See **Bantam Doubleday Dell Publishing Group, Inc.**

The Free Press
See **Simon & Schuster Trade Division**

Samuel French, Inc.
45 West 25th Street, New York NY 10010
☎001 212 206 8990   Fax 001 212 206 1429
Senior Editor *William Talbot*
FOUNDED 1830. *Publishes* plays in paperback:
Broadway and off-Broadway hits, light comedies, mysteries, one-act plays and plays for
young audiences. Unsolicited mss welcome.
No synopses.
   Royalties paid annually (books); twice-yearly
(amateur productions); monthly (professional
productions). *Overseas associates* in London,
Toronto and Sydney.

The Globe Pequot Press
PO Box 833, 6 Business Park Road, Old
Saybrook CT 06475
☎001 860 395 0440   Fax 001 860 395 1418
President *Linda Kennedy*
Associate Publisher *Michael K. Urban*

Publishes regional and international travel, how-
to, personal finance, and outdoor recreation.
Also publishes the *Recommended Country Inns*
guides. About 200 titles a year. Unsolicited mss,
synopses and ideas welcome, particularly for
travel and outdoor recreation books.
   Royalties paid.

Grammercy
See **Random House, Inc.**

Greenwillow Books
See **William Morrow & Co., Inc.**

Griffin Trade Paperbacks
See **St Martin's Press**

Grolier, Incorporated
90 Sherman Turnpike, Danbury CT 06816
☎001 203 797 3500   Fax 001 203 797 3197
Chairman/CEO *Arnaud Lagardere*
FOUNDED 1895. *Publishes* juvenile non-fiction,
encyclopedias, speciality reference sets, children's fiction and picture books. Aout 600
titles a year. DIVISIONS **Children's Press**;
Grolier Educational; **Grolier Reference**;
Orchard Books; **Franklin Watts** (see entry).

Grosset & Dunlap
See **Penguin Putnam Inc**

Grove/Atlantic Inc.
841 Broadway, New York NY 10003–4793
☎001 212 614 7850   Fax 001 212 614 7886
President/Publisher *Morgan Entrekin*
Senior Editor *Anton Mueller*

FOUNDED 1952. *Publishes* general fiction and
non-fiction. IMPRINTS **Atlantic Monthly
Press**; **Grove Press**.

Gulliver Books
See **Harcourt Brace Children's Books
Division**

Harcourt Brace Children's Books Division
525 B Street, Suite 1900, San Diego
CA 92101–4495
☎001 619 231 6616   Fax 001 619 699 6777
Vice President/Publisher *Louise Pelan*

A division of Harcourt Brace & Company.
Publishes fiction, poetry and non-fiction cover-
ing a wide range of subjects: biography, en-
vironment and ecology, history, travel, science
and current affairs for children and young adults.
About 175 titles a year.
   IMPRINTS **Browndeer Press**; **Gulliver
Books**; **Gulliver Green® Books** Ecology and
environment; **Harcourt Brace Children's
Books**; **Harcourt Brace Paperbacks**;
Odyssey Paperbacks Novels; **Red Wagon
Books** For ages 6 months to 3 years; **Voyager
Paperbacks** Picture books; **Silver Whistle**.
No unsolicited mss.

Hard Candy
See **Masquerade Books**

Harlequin Historicals
See **Silhouette Books**

Harmony
See **The Crown Publishing Group**

HarperCollins Publishers, Inc.
10 East 53rd Street, New York NY 10022
☎001 212 207 7000   Fax 001 212 207 7797
Website: www.harpercollins.com
President/Chief Executive Officer
   Jane Friedman
FOUNDED 1817. Owned by News Corpor-
ation. *Publishes* general fiction, non-fiction and
college textbooks in hardcover, trade paper-
back and mass-market formats.
   DIVISIONS/IMPRINTS **Adult Trade** *Lawrence
Ashmead* VP/Executive Editor; **Harper
Reference** *Linda Cunningham* Vice President/
Publishing Director; **HarperCollins Children's
Books** *Susan Katz* President/Publisher; **Harper
Paperbacks** *Marjorie Braman* Snr VP/Publishing
Director; **Harper Audio/Caedmon** *Linda
Cunningham* Vice President/Publishing Director;

Harper Prism *John Douglas* Executive Editor; **Michael di Capua Books** *Michael di Capua* Vice President/Publisher; **Regan Books** *Judith Regan* President/Publisher; **Basic Books**.

SUBSIDIARY **Zondervan Publishing House** (see entry).

Harvard University Press

79 Garden Street, Cambridge MA 02138
☎001 617 495 2611   Fax 001 617 496 4677

Editor-in-Chief *Aida D. Donald*

Publishes scholarly non-fiction only: general interest, literature, science and behaviour, social science, history, humanities, psychology, political science, sociology, economics, law, business, classics, religion, cultural studies, philosophy. 130 new titles a year and 80–90 paperbacks. Free book catalogue available.

Hearst Books/Hearst Marine Books

See **William Morrow & Co., Inc.**

Hill & Wang

See **Farrar, Straus & Giroux, Inc**

Hippocrene Books, Inc.

171 Madison Avenue, New York NY 10016
☎001 212 685 4371   Fax 001 212 779 9338

President/Editorial Director
  George Blagowidow

FOUNDED 1971. *Publishes* general non-fiction and reference books. Particularly strong on foreign language dictionaries, language studies, military history and international cookbooks. No fiction. Send brief summary, table of contents and one chapter for appraisal. S.a.e. essential for response. For manuscript return include sufficient postage cover (IRCs).

Holiday House, Inc.

425 Madison Avenue, New York NY 10017
☎001 212 688 0085   Fax 001 212 421 6134

Vice President/Editor-in-Chief *Regina Griffin*

Publishes children's general fiction and non-fiction (pre-school to secondary). About 50 titles a year. Submit synopsis and three sample chapters for novels and chapter books; complete mss (without artwork) for picture books. Mss will not be returned without return postage.

Henry Holt & Co Inc.

115 West 18th Street, New York NY 10011
☎001 212 886 9200   Fax 001 212 633 0748

Senior Editor, Adult Trade *Ray Roberts*
Managing Editor, Books for
  Young Readers *George Wen*

FOUNDED in 1866, Henry Holt is one of the oldest publishers in the United States. *Publishes* fiction, by both American and international authors, biographies, and books on history and politics, ecology and psychology. IMPRINTS **Edge Books**; **John Macrae Books**; **Bill Martin Jr Books**; **Metropolitan Books** *Sara Bershtel*; **Owl Books** Tracy Brown; **Red Feather Books**.

Houghton Mifflin Co.

222 Berkeley Street, Boston MA 02116
☎001 617 351 5000

Contact *Submissions Editor*

FOUNDED 1832. *Publishes* literary fiction and general non-fiction, including autobiography, biography and history. Also school and college textbooks; children's fiction and non-fiction. Average 100 titles a year. Queries only for adult material; synopsis, outline and sample chapters for children's non-fiction; complete mss for children's fiction. IRCs required with all submissions/queries.

DIVISIONS **Clarion Books** (children's and young adult); **Mariner Books** (trade paperback imprint); **Chapters** (cookbooks) .

House of Collectibles

See **The Ballantine Publishing Group**

Hudson River Editions

See **Simon & Schuster Trade Division**

University of Illinois Press

1325 South Oak Street, Champaign
IL 61820–6903
☎001 217 333 0950   Fax 001 217 244 8082
Email: uipress@uillinois.edu
Website: www.press.uillinois.edu

Editorial Director *Willis Regier*

Publishes non-fiction, scholarly and general, with special interest in Americana, women's studies, African–American studies, American music and regional books. About 110–120 titles a year.

Image Books

See **Bantam Doubleday Dell Publishing Group, Inc.**

Indiana University Press

601 North Morton Street, Bloomington
IN 42404–3797
☎001 812 855 4203   Fax 001 812 855 7931

Director *John Gallman*

Publishes scholarly non-fiction in the following subject areas: African studies, anthropology,

Asian studies, Afro-American studies, environment and ecology, film, folklore, history, Jewish studies, literary criticism, medical ethics, Middle East studies, military, music, paleontology, philanthropy, philosophy, politics, religion, semiotics, Russian and East European studies, Victorian studies, women's studies, a few fiction reprints. Query in writing in first instance.

Insight Books
See **Kluwer Academic/Plenum Publishers**

University of Iowa Press
Kuhl House, 119 West Park Road, Iowa City IA 52242
☎001 319 335 2000   Fax 001 319 335 2055
Interim Director *Holly Carver*
FOUNDED 1969 as a small scholarly press publishing about five books a year. Now publishing about 35 a year in a variety of scholarly fields, plus local interest, short stories, autobiography and poetry. No unsolicited mss; query first. Unsolicited ideas and synopses welcome.
Royalties paid annually.

Iowa State University Press
2121 South State Avenue, Ames IA 50010
☎001 515 292 0140   Fax 001 515 292 3348
Email: vanhouten@isupress.edu
Website: www.isupress.edu
Director *Linda Speth*
Editor-in-Chief *Gretchen Van Houten*
FOUNDED 1934 as an offshoot of the university's journalism department. *Publishes* scholarly books and textbooks, agriculture, aeronautics, environmental studies, regional history, journalism, and veterinary medicine.
Royalties paid annually; sometimes twice-yearly.

Irwin/McGraw-Hill
See **The McGraw-Hill Companies**

Island Books
See **Bantam Doubleday Dell Publishing Group, Inc.**

Ivy
See **The Ballantine Publishing Group**

Jellybean Books
See **Random House, Inc.**

Jove
See **Berkley Publishing Group**

University Press of Kansas
2501 West 15th Street, Lawrence KS 66049–3905
☎001 785 864 4154   Fax 001 785 864 4586
Email: mail@newpress.upress.ukans.edu
Director *Fred M. Woodward*
FOUNDED 1946. Became the publishing arm for all six state universities in Kansas in 1976. *Publishes* scholarly books in American history, women's studies, presidential studies, social and political philosophy, political science, military history and environmental. About 50 titles a year. Proposals welcome.
Royalties paid annually.

Jean Karl Books
See **Simon & Schuster Children's Publishing Division**

Kent State University Press
Kent OH 44242–0001
☎001 330 672 7913   Fax 001 330 672 3104
Director *John T. Hubbell*
Editor-in-Chief *Julia Morton*
FOUNDED 1965. *Publishes* scholarly works in history and biography, literary studies and general non-fiction. 25–30 titles a year. Queries welcome; no mss. *Royalties* paid annually.

Kluwer Academic/Plenum Publishers
233 Spring Street, New York NY 10013–1578
☎001 212 620 8000   Fax 001 212 463 0742
Email: info@plenum.com
Website: www.plenum.com
Acquisitions Editors *Ken Howell* (chemistry/geology), *Tom Cohn* (computer science/mathematics), *Michael Hennelly* (life sciences), *Mariclaire Cloutier* (medical/behavioural sciences), *Amelia McNamara* (physics/materials science/engineering), *Eliot Werner* (social/behavioural sciences)
FOUNDED 1946. *Publishes* scholarly scientific books and journals. Over 300 titles a year. Queries only. IMPRINTS **Plenum Press** Scientific, technical, medical books. **Insight Books** Personal health, psychology, education. **Da Capo Press** Paperback non-fiction reprints.

Alfred A. Knopf, Inc.
201 East 50th Street, New York NY 10022
☎001 212 751 2600   Fax 001 212 572 2593
President/Editor-in-Chief *Sonny Mehta*
FOUNDED 1915. Subsidiary of **Random**

House, Inc. *Publishes* fiction and non-fiction, poetry, juvenile. IMPRINT **Everyman's Library**.

Krieger Publishing Co., Inc.
PO Box 9542, Melbourne FL 32902–9542
☎001 407 724 9542   Fax 001 407 951 3671
Email: info@krieger-pub.com
Website: www.web4u.com/krieger-publishing/
Chairman *Robert E. Krieger*
President *Donald E. Krieger*
Editorial Head *Mary Roberts*

FOUNDED 1970. *Publishes* education and communications, history, medical science, psychology, chemistry, physical and natural sciences, reference, space sciences, technology and engineering.

IMPRINTS **Anvil; Exploring Community History Series; Open Forum; Orbit; Professional Practices in Adult Education and Human Resource Development; Public History.** Unsolicited mss welcome. Not interested in synopses/ideas or trade type titles.

Royalties paid yearly.

LA Weekly Books
See **St Martin's Press, Inc.**

Lanternlight Library
See **University of Alaska Press**

Laurel Leaf
See **Bantam Doubleday Dell Publishing Group, Inc.**

Lehigh University Press
See **Golden Cockerel Press** under **UK Publishers**

Lerner Publications Co. (A Division of the Lerner Publishing Group)
241 First Avenue North, Minneapolis MN 55401
☎001 612 332 3344   Fax 001 612 332 7615
Website: www.lernerbooks.com

Submissions Editor *Jennifer Martin*

Publishes primarily non-fiction for readers of all grade levels. List includes titles encompassing nature, geography, natural and physical science, current events, ancient and modern history, world art, special interest, sports, world cultures and numerous biography series. Some young adult and middle grade fiction. No alphabet, puzzle, song or text books, religious subject matter or plays. Submissions are accepted in the months of March and October *only*. Work received in any other month will be returned unopened. S.a.e. required for authors who wish to have their material returned. Please allow 2–6 months for a response. No phone calls.

Little Simon
See **Simon & Schuster Children's Publishing Division**

Little, Brown and Company, Inc.
3 Center Plaza, Boston MA 02108-2084
☎001 617 227 0730
Website: www.littlebrown.com
Vice-President/Publisher, Trade
  Sarah Crichton

Division of Time Warner Trade Publishing. FOUNDED 1837. *Publishes* contemporary popular fiction and literary fiction. Also non-fiction: cookbooks, biographies, drama, history, mysteries, poetry, art, photography, reference, science, sport, travel and juvenile.

IMPRINTS **Back Bay Books; Bulfinch Press.** No unsolicited mss. Query letter in the first instance.

Living Languages
See **The Crown Publishing Group**

Llewellyn Publications
PO Box 64383, St Paul MN 55164–0383
☎001 612 291 1970   Fax 001 612 291 1908
President/Publisher *Carl L. Weschcke*
Acquisitions Manager *Nancy J. Mostad*

Division of Llewellyn Worldwide Ltd. FOUNDED 1901. *Publishes* self-help and how-to: astrology, alternative health, tantra, Fortean studies, tarot, yoga, Santeria, dream studies, metaphysics, magic, witchcraft, herbalism, shamanism, organic gardening, women's spirituality, graphology, palmistry, parapsychology. Also fiction with an authentic magical or metaphysical theme. About 100 titles a year. Unsolicited mss welcome; proposals preferred. IRCs essential in all cases. Books are distributed in the UK by Airlift Book Co.

Lothrop, Lee & Shepard
See **William Morrow and Co., Inc.**

Louisiana State University Press
Baton Rouge LA 70893
☎001 504 388 6295   Fax 001 504 388 6461
Director *L. E. Phillabaum*

Publishes non-fiction: Southern history, American history, Southern literary criticism,

American literary criticism, biography, political science, music (jazz) and Latin American studies. About 70 titles a year. Send IRCs for mss guidelines.

Love Inspired
See **Silhouette Books**

Loveswept
See **Bantam Doubleday Dell Publishing Group, Inc.**

The Lyons Press
123 West 18th Street, New York NY 10011
☎001 212 620 9580   Fax 001 212 929 1836
Managing Director *Tony Lyons*
Editor-in-Chief *Bryan Oettel*

Publishes outdoor, nature, sports, gardening and angling titles, plus cookery, woodwork and art. About 120 titles a year. No unsolicited mss; synopses and ideas welcome.
Royalties paid twice-yearly.

Margaret K. McElderry Books
See **Simon & Schuster Children's Publishing Division**

McFarland & Company, Inc., Publishers
PO Box 611, Jefferson NC 28640
☎001 336 246 4460   Fax 001 336 246 5018
Email: mcfarland@fastransit.net
Website: www.mcfarlandpub.com
President/Editor-in-Chief *Robert Franklin*
Vice President *Rhonda Herman*
Senior Editor *Steve Wilson*
Editors *Virginia Tobiassen, Marty McGee*

FOUNDED 1979. A library reference and upper-end speciality market press publishing scholarly books in many fields: international studies, performing arts, popular culture, sports, women's studies, music and fine arts, chess, history, war memoirs and librarianship. *Specialises* in general reference. Especially strong in cinema studies. No fiction, poetry, children's, New Age or inspirational/devotional works. About 150 titles a year. No unsolicited mss; send query letter first. Synopses and ideas welcome.
Royalties paid annually.

The McGraw-Hill Companies
1221 Avenue of the Americas, New York NY 10020
☎001 212 512 2000
President/CEO *Harold McGraw III*
Contact *Submissions Editor*

FOUNDED 1873. US parent of the UK-based **McGraw-Hill Book Co. Europe**. *Publishes* a wide range of educational, professional, business, science, engineering and computing books.

DIVISIONS **Educational & Professional Publishing Group; Professional Publishing Group; Business & General Reference Group; Electronic Publishing; Science, Technology & Medical Group; McGraw-Hill Higher Education; Dushkin/McGraw-Hill; Irwin/McGraw-Hill; Osborne/McGraw-Hill; WCB/McGraw-Hill.**

John Macrae Books
See **Henry Holt & Co Inc.**

Magic Attic Press
See **The Millbrook Press, Inc.**

Mariner Books
See **Houghton Mifflin Co.**

Bill Martin Jr Books
See **Henry Holt & Co Inc.**

Masquerade Books
801 Second Avenue, New York NY 10017
☎001 212 661 7878   Fax 001 212 986 7355
Website: www.masqueradebooks.com
Publisher *Richard Kasak*

FOUNDED 1989. *Publishes* erotic fiction and sexual commentary. IMPRINTS **Badboy; Hard Candy; Rhinoceros; Masquerade; Rosebud**.

University of Massachusetts Press
PO Box 429, Amherst MA 01004–0429
☎001 413 545 2217   Fax 001 413 545 1226
Website: www.umass.edu/umpress
Director *Bruce Wilcox*
Senior Editor *Clark Dougan*

FOUNDED 1964. *Publishes* scholarly, general interest, African-American, ethnic, women's and gender studies, cultural criticism, architecture and environmental design, literary criticism, poetry, philosophy, biography, history, sociology. Unsolicited mss considered but query letter preferred in the first instance. Synopses and ideas welcome. 40 titles in 1998.
Royalties paid annually.

Margaret K. McElderry Books
See **Simon & Schuster Children's Publishing Division**

Metropolitan Books
See **Henry Holt & Co Inc.**

The University of Michigan Press
PO Box 1104, 839 Greene Street, Ann Arbor
MI 48106
☎001 734 764 4388   Fax 001 734 615 1540
Email: um.press@umich.edu
Website: www.press.umich.edu/
Director *Colin Day*
FOUNDED 1930. *Publishes* non-fiction, text-
books, literary criticism, theatre, economics,
political science, history, classics, anthropology,
law studies, women's studies, English as a sec-
ond language.
Royalties paid twice-yearly.

The Millbrook Press, Inc.
2 Old New Milford Road, PO Box 335,
Brookfield CT 06804
☎001 203 740 2220   Fax 001 203 775 5643
School/Library Publisher *Jean Reynolds*
Trade Publisher *Judy Korman*
Managing Editor *Colleen Seibert*
FOUNDED 1989. *Publishes* mainly non-fiction,
children's and young adult, for trade, school
and public library. About 120 titles a year.
IMPRINTS **Copper Beech Books**;
Twenty-First Century Books; **Magic Attic
Press**.
Royalties paid twice-yearly.

Minstrel Books
See **Pocket Books**

MIRASOL Libros Juveniles
See **Farrar, Straus & Giroux, Inc**

University Press of Mississippi
3825 Ridgewood Road, Jackson
MS 39211–6492
☎001 601 982 6205   Fax 001 601 982 6217
Email: press@ihl.state.ms.us
Website: www.upress.state.ms.us
Director/Editor-in-Chief *Seetha Srinivasan*
FOUNDED 1970. The non-profit book publisher partially supported by the eight State universities. *Publishes* scholarly and trade titles in
literature, history, American culture, Southern
culture, African-American, women's studies,
popular culture, folklife, ethnic, performance,
art and photography, and other liberal arts.
About 50 titles a year.
IMPRINTS **Muscadine Books** *Craig Gill*
Regional trade titles. **Banner Books** Paperback

reprints of significant fiction and non-fiction.
Send letter of enquiry, prospectus, table of con-
tents and sample chapter prior to submission of
full mss.
Royalties paid annually. *Represented* worldwide.
UK representatives: **Roundhouse Publishing
Ltd**.

University of Missouri Press
2910 LeMone Boulevard, Columbia
MO 65201–8227
☎001 573 882 7641   Fax 001 573 884 4498
Website: www.system.missoouri.edu/upress
Director/Editor-in-Chief *Beverly Jarrett*
Publishes academic: history, literary criticism,
intellectual history and related humanities disciplines and short stories – usually four volumes
a year. Best approach is by letter. Send one
short story for consideration, and synopses for
academic work. About 55 titles a year.

The MIT Press
5 Cambridge Ctr., Cambridge MA 02142
☎001 617 253 5646   Fax 001 617 258 6779
Editor-in-Chief *Laurence Cohen*
FOUNDED 1961. *Publishes* scholarly and professional, technologically sophisticated books,
including computer science and artificial intelligence, economics, architecture, cognitive
science, neuroscience, environmental studies,
linguistics and philosophy. IMPRINT **Bradford
Books**.

The Modern Library
See **Random House, Inc.**

Monograph Series
See **University of Alaska Press**

William Morrow & Co., Inc.
1350 Avenue of the Americas, New York
NY 10019
☎001 212 261 6500   Fax 001 212 261 6595
Editor-in-Chief *Betty Kelly*
Executive Editors *Henry Ferris, Claire Wachtel*
FOUNDED 1926. *Publishes* fiction, biography and
general non-fiction. Approach in writing only.
No unsolicited mss or proposals for adult books.
Proposals read only if submitted through a liter-
ary agent. About 600 titles a year.
IMPRINTS **Hearst Books/Hearst Marine
Books** *Jacqueline Deval* VP/Publisher, *Elizabeth
Rice* Editorial Director; **Quill Trade Paper-
backs** *Toni Sciarra* Executive Editor; **Morrow
Junior Books** *Barbara Lalicki* Snr. VP/Publisher,
Rosemary Brosnan Executive Editor, *Meredith*

Charpentier Executive Editor; **Lothrop, Lee & Shepard** *Susan Pearson* VP/Editor-in-Chief; **Greenwillow Books** *Susan Hirschman* Snr. VP/Editor-in-Chief, *Virginia Duncan* Executive Editor; **Eaglebrook** *Joann Davis*; **Mulberry Books/Beech Tree Books** (trade paperbacks) *Paulette Kaufmann* VP/Editor-in-Chief; **Rob Weisbach Books** *Rob Weisbach.*

MTV Books
See **Pocket Books**

Mulberry Books
See **William Morrow and Co., Inc.**

Muscadine Books
See **University Press of Mississippi**

Mysterious Press
See **Warner Books Inc.**

University of Nevada Press
MS 166, Reno NV 89557–0076
☎001 775 784 6573   Fax 001 775 784 6200

Director *Ronald Latimer*
Editor-in-Chief *Margaret Dalrymple*
FOUNDED 1960. *Publishes* serious fiction, Native American studies, natural history, Western Americana, Basque studies and regional studies. About 40 titles a year including reprints. Unsolicited material welcome if it fits in with areas published, or offers a 'new and exciting' direction. *Royalties* paid twice-yearly.

New Age Books
See **Bantam Doubleday Dell Publishing Group, Inc.**

University Press of New England
23 South Main Street, Hanover
NH 03755–2048
☎001 603 643 7100   Fax 001 603 643 1540
Website: www.dartmouth.edu/acad-inst/upne/

Director & Acquisitions Editor
  Richard Abel
Managing Director *Philip Pochoda*
FOUNDED 1970. A scholarly book publisher sponsored by six institutions of higher education in the region: Brandeis, Dartmouth, Middlebury, Tufts, Wesleyan and the University of New Hampshire. *Publishes* general and scholarly non-fiction; plus poetry through the Wesleyan Poetry Series and Hardscrabble Books fiction of New England. About 75 titles a year.
  IMPRINT **Wesleyan University Press** Interdisciplinary studies, history, literature,

women's studies, government and public issues, biography, poetry, natural history and environment. Unsolicited material welcome.
  Royalties paid annually. *Overseas associates:* UK – University Presses Marketing; Europe – Trevor Brown Associates.

University of New Mexico Press
1720 Lomas Boulevard NE, Albuquerque
NM 87131–1591
☎001 505 277 2346   Fax 001 505 277 9270

Director *Elizabeth C. Hadas*
Editor *Larry Durwood Ball*
Publishes scholarly and regional books. No fiction, how-to, children's, humour, self-help, technical or textbooks. 60 titles in 1998.

New Sciences
See **Bantam Doubleday Dell Publishing Group, Inc.**

Noonday Press
See **Farrar, Straus & Giroux, Inc**

North Point Press
See **Farrar, Straus & Giroux, Inc**

University of North Texas Press
PO Box 311336, Denton TX 76203–1336
☎001 940 565 2142   Fax 001 940 565 4590
Website: www.unt.edu/untpress

Director *Frances B. Vick (Email: vick@unt.edu)*
Associate Director/Editorial Director
  Charlotte M. Wright (Email: cwright@unt.edu)
FOUNDED 1987. *Publishes* folklore, regional interest, contemporary, social issues, history, military, women's issues, writing and publishing reference. Publishes the Vassar Miller Poetry Prize winner each year. About 14 titles a year. No unsolicited mss. Approach by letter in the first instance. Synopses and ideas welcome.
  Royalties paid annually.

W. W. Norton & Company
500 Fifth Avenue, New York NY 10110
☎001 212 354 5500   Fax 001 212 869 0856

FOUNDED 1923. *Publishes* quality fiction, poetry and non-fiction, college textbooks, professional and medical books. About 300 titles a year.

NTC/Contemporary Publishing Group
4255 West Touhy Avenue, Lincolnwood
IL 60646–1975
☎001 847 679 5500   Fax 001 847 679 2494

Editorial Director *John Nolan*

FOUNDED 1947. *Publishes* general adult non-fiction and adult education books. 800 titles in 1998. Submissions require s.a.e. for response.

Odyssey Paperbacks
See **Harcourt Brace Children's Books Division**

University of Oklahoma Press
1005 Asp Avenue, Norman OK 73019–6051
☎001 405 325 5111   Fax 001 405 325 4000
Website: www.ou.edu/oupress

Director *John N. Drayton*

FOUNDED 1928. *Publishes* general scholarly non-fiction only: American Indian studies, history of American West, classical studies, literary theory and criticism, anthropology, archaeology, natural history, political science and women's studies. About 100 titles a year.

One World
See **The Ballantine Publishing Group**

Open Forum
See **Krieger Publishing Co., Inc.**

Orbit
See **Krieger Publishing Co., Inc.**

Orchard Books
See **Grolier, Incorporated**

Osborne/McGraw Hill
See **The McGraw-Hill Companies**

Owl Books
See **Henry Holt & Co Inc.**

Paragon House
2700 University Avenue, Suite 200, St Paul MN 55114–1016
☎001 651 644 3087   Fax 001 651 644 0997
Email: paragon@paragonhouse.com
Website: www.paragonhouse.com

Executive Director *Gordon L. Anderson*

FOUNDED 1982. *Publishes* non-fiction: reference and academic. Subjects include history, religion, philosophy, New Age, Jewish interest, self-help, political science, international relations, psychology.
Royalties paid twice-yearly.

Peacock Press
See **Bantam Doubleday Dell Publishing Group, Inc.**

Pelican Publishing Company
Box 3110, Gretna LA 70054–3110
☎001 504 368 1175

Editor-in-Chief *Nina Kooij*

Publishes general non-fiction: popular history, cookbooks, travel, art, business, children's, editorial cartoon, architecture, golf, Scottish interest, and motivational. About 90 titles a year. Initial enquiries required for all submissions.

Pelion Press
See **Rosen Publishing Group, Inc.**

Penguin Putnam Inc
375 Hudson Street, New York NY 10014
☎001 212 366 2000   Fax 001 212 366 2666
Email: webmaster@penguinputnam.com
Website: www.penguin.com

Chairman/CEO, The Penguin Group
   Michael Lynton
President *Phyllis Grann*

Penguin Putnam is a division of the Penguin Group, which is owned by Pearson plc. The group is the second-largest trade book publisher in the world. *Publishes* fiction and non-fiction in hardback and paperback; adult and children's.

DIVISIONS/IMPRINTS/SUBSIDIARY COMPANIES include **Penguin Putnam Books for Young Readers**; **Dial Books for Young Readers** (see entry); **Dutton Children's Books** *Susan Van Metre* Snr. Acquisitions Editor; **Grosset & Dunlap** *Catherine Daly-Weir* Snr. Editor; **Puffin Books** *Gerard Mancini* Managing Editor/Assoc. Publisher; **Berkley Publishing Group** (see entry); **DAW Books Inc.** (see entry); **G. P. Putnam's Sons** (see entry); **The Viking Press/Viking Children's Books**; **Perigee Books** *John Duff* Publisher; **Penguin Audio**; **Rough Guides**; **Riverhead Books** *Wendy Carlton* Editor; **Price Stern Sloan** *Lara Rice Bergen* Editorial Director; **Jeremy P. Tarcher** *Jeremy P. Tarcher* President; **Frederick Warne**.
Royalties paid twice-yearly.

University of Pennsylvania Press
4200 Pine Street, Philadelphia
PA 19104–4011
☎001 215 898 6271   Fax 001 215 898 0404
Website: www.upenn.edu/pennpress

Director *Eric Halpern*

FOUNDED 1896. *Publishes* serious non-fiction: scholarly, reference, professional, textbooks and semi-popular trade. No original fiction or poetry. About 75 titles a year. No unsolicited mss but synopses and ideas for books welcome.
Royalties paid annually.

Perigee Books
See **Penguin Putnam Inc**

Picador USA
See **St Martin's Press, Inc.**

Players Press
PO Box 1132, Studio City CA 91614-0132
☎001 818 789 4980

Chairman *William-Alan Landes*
Managing Director *David Cole*

FOUNDED 1965 as a publisher of plays; now publishes across the entire range of performing arts: plays, musicals, theatre, film, cinema, television, costume, puppetry, plus technical theatre and cinema material. 60 titles in 1998. No unsolicited mss; synopses/ideas welcome. Send query letter.
Royalties paid twice-yearly. *Overseas subsidiaries* in Canada, Australia and the UK.

Plenum Press
See **Kluwer Academic/Plenum Publishers**

Pocket Books
1230 Avenue of the Americas, New York NY 10020
☎001 212 698 7000   Fax 001 212 698 7439

President/Publisher *Gina Centrello*

FOUNDED 1939. A division of Simon & Schuster Consumer Group. *Publishes* trade paperbacks and hardcovers; mass-market, reprints and originals. IMPRINTS **Archway**; **Minstrel Books**; **Pocket Star Books**; **Washington Square Press**; **MTV Books**.

PowerKids Press
See **Rosen Publishing Group, Inc.**

Price Stern Sloan
See **Penguin Putnam Inc**

Public History
See **Krieger Publishing Co., Inc.**

Puffin Books
See **Penguin Putnam Inc**

G. P. Putnam's Sons
345 Hudson Street, New York NY 10014
☎001 212 414 3600

President/Publisher *Nancy Paulsen*
Senior Editor *Kathy Dawson*

A children's book division of Penguin Putnam Books for Young Readers, a member of **Penguin Putnam Inc**. *Publishes* picture books, middle-grade fiction and young adult fiction.

Quill Trade Paperbacks
See **William Morrow and Co., Inc.**

Rand McNally
8255 North Central Park Avenue, Skokie IL 60076
☎001 847 329 8100   Fax 001 847 673 0539

Executive Editor *Jon Leverenz*

FOUNDED 1856. *Publishes* world atlases and maps, road atlases of North America and Europe, city and state maps of the United States and Canada, educational wall maps, atlases and globes, plus children's products. Includes electronic multimedia products.

Random House, Inc.
201 East 50th Street, New York NY 10022
☎001 212 751 2600   Fax 001 212 572 8700
Website: www.randomhouse.com

Chairman/Chief Executive Officer
Alberto Vitale

FOUNDED 1925. The world's largest English-language general trade book publisher. Owned by Advance Publications Inc. until it was bought by the German media company, Bertelsmann, in 1998. Submissions via agents preferred.

DIVISIONS/IMPRINTS
Random House Trade Publishing Group; **Random House AudioBooks**; **Random House Adult Trade Books** AUTHORS Truman Capote, Gore Vidal, Maya Angelou, Norman Mailer, General Colin Powell; **Villard Books** AUTHORS Robert Fulghum, Roxanne Pulitzer, Whitney Otto; **The Modern Library**; **Times Books** (see entry); **Random House Reference & Information Publishing** *Publishes* reference works in both book and electronic formats. TITLES *Random House Webster's College Dictionary; Random House Webster's College Thesaurus.*
Alfred A. Knopf, Inc. (see entry). **The Crown Publishing Group** (see entry). **The Ballantine Publishing Group** (see entry).
Random House Children's Publishing Group AUTHORS Roald Dahl, Theodore Geisel (*Dr Seuss*), Leo Lionni. IMPRINTS **Dragonfly Books**; **Knopf Paperbacks**; **Bullseye Books**; **Children's Media** CD-ROMs and videos; **Random House Entertainment**.
Random House Value Publishing General interest books across a wide range of categories. IMPRINTS **Wings**; **Crescent**; **Grammercy**; **Children's Classics**; **Jellybean Books**; **Derrydale**.
Fodor's Travel Publications Travel guides in both book and electronic format.
Royalties paid twice-yearly.

Rawson Associates
See **Simon & Schuster Trade Division**

Reader's Digest Association, Inc
Reader's Digest Road, Pleasantville,
NY 10570–7000
☎001 914 238 1000   Fax 001 914 238 4559
Website: www.readersdigest.com
Chairman/CEO *Thomas Ryder*

Publishes cooking, DIY, health, gardeing, children's books; videos and magazines.

Red Feather Books
See **Henry Holt & Co Inc.**

Red Wagon Books
See **Harcourt Brace Children's Books
Division**

Regan Books
See **HarperCollins Publishers, Inc.**

Fleming H. Revell
See **Baker Book House**

Rhinoceros
See **Masquerade Books**

Riverhead Books
See **Penguin Putnam Inc**

Rosebud
See **Masquerade Books**

The Rosen Publishing Group, Inc.
29 East 21st Street, New York NY 10010
☎001 212 777 3017   Fax 001 212 253 6915
President *Roger Rosen*
**PowerKids Press, Editorial Division
Leader** *Kristin Ward*
Editors, Young Adult *Sean Dolan, Amy
Gelman Haugesag*
Editor, Reference *Michael Isaac*

Publishes non-fiction books (supplementary to the curriculum, reference and self-help) for a young adult audience. Reading levels are years 7–12, 4–6 (books for teens with literacy problems), and 5–9. Areas of interest include health, religion, careers, self-esteem, sexuality, drug abuse prevention, personal safety, science, health, sport, African studies, Holocaust studies and a wide variety of other multicultural titles. About 180 titles a year.
IMPRINTS **Pelion Press** Music titles;
PowerKids Press *Heather Feldman, Sarah Silbert*
Non-fiction books for Reception up to Year 4

that are supplementary to the curriculum. Subjects include conflict resolution, character building, health, safety, drug abuse prevention, history, self-help, religion and multicultural titles. 144 titles a year. For all imprints, write with outline and sample chapters.

Rough Guides
See **Penguin Putnam Inc**

Rutgers University Press
100 Joyce Kilmer Avenue, Piscataway
NJ 08854–8099
☎001 732 445 7762   Fax 001 732 445 7039
Editor-in-Chief *Leslie Mitchner*

FOUNDED 1936. *Publishes* scholarly books, regional and social sciences. Unsolicited mss, synopses and ideas for books welcome. No original fiction or poetry. About 75 titles a year. *Royalties* paid annually.

St Martin's Press, Inc.
175 Fifth Avenue, New York NY 10010
☎001 212 674 5151   Fax 001 212 420 9314
Chairman/Chief Executive *John Sargent*
President/Publisher (Trade Division)
Sally Richardson

FOUNDED 1952. A subsidiary of **Macmillan Publishers** (UK), St Martin's Press made its name and fortune by importing raw talent from the UK to the States and has continued to buy heavily in the UK. *Publishes* general fiction, especially mysteries and crime; and adult non-fiction: history, self-help, political science, travel, biography, scholarly, popular reference, college textbooks.
IMPRINTS **Picador USA**; **Griffin Trade Paperbacks**; **St Martin's Paperbacks (Mass)**; **Thomas Dunne Books**; **Tor**; **Forge**; **Bedford Books**; **LA Weekly Books**.

Scarecrow Press, Inc.
4720 Boston Way, Lanham Maryland 20706
☎001 301 459 3366   Fax 001 301 459 2118
Website: www.scarecrowpress.com
Associate Publisher *Shirley Lambert*

FOUNDED 1950 as a short-run publisher of library reference books. Acquired by **University Press of America, Inc.** in 1995 which is now part of Rowman and Littlefield Publishers, Inc. *Publishes* reference, scholarly and monographs (all levels) for libraries. Reference books in all areas except sciences, specialising in the performing arts, music, cinema and library science. About 165 titles a year. Publisher for the Society of American Archivists, Children's Literature Association, Institute of Jazz

Studies of Rutgers – the State University of New Jersey, the American Theological Library Association. Also publisher of *VOYA* (Voice of Youth Advocates); six issues a year. Unsolicited mss welcome but material will not be returned unless requested and accompanied by return postage. Unsolicited synopses and ideas for books welcome. Send submissions to Katie Regen, Assistant Editor (email: kregen@scarecrowpress. com) *Royalties* paid annually.

Scholastic, Inc.

555 Broadway, New York NY 10012
☎001 212 343 6100   Fax 001 212 343 6390
Website: www.scholastic.com/

Executive Vice President *Barbara Marcus*
Senior Vice-President/Publisher *Jean Feiwel*

FOUNDED 1920. The world's largest publisher and distributor of children's books in the English language. *Publishes* picture books and fiction for middle grade (8–12-year-olds) and young adults: family, friendship, humour, fantasy, mystery and school stories. Also nonfiction: biography, reference and multicultural subjects. About 500 titles a year. Does not accept unsolicited mss.

Anne Schwartz Books

See **Simon & Schuster Children's Publishing Division**

Scott Foresman

1900 E Lake Avenue, Glenview
IL 60025–2086
☎001 847 729 3000   Fax 001 847 486 3999
President, Scott Foresman *Paul McFall*

FOUNDED 1896. *Publishes* elementary and secondary education materials.

Scribner

See **Simon & Schuster Trade Division**

Silhouette Books

300 East 42nd Street, New York NY 10017
☎001 212 682 6080   Fax 001 212 682 4539
Editorial Director *Tara Gavin*

FOUNDED 1979 as an imprint of **Simon & Schuster** and was acquired by a wholly owned subsidiary of Toronto-based Harlequin Enterprises Ltd in 1984. *Publishes* category, contemporary romance fiction and historical romance fiction only. Over 360 titles a year across a number of imprints.

IMPRINTS
Silhouette Romance *Mary Theresa Hussey;*

Silhouette Desire *Joan Marlow Golan;* **Silhouette Special Edition** *Karen Taylor Richman;* **Silhouette Intimate Moments** *Leslie Wainger,* **Harlequin Historicals** *Tracy Farrell;* **Steeple Hill** *Tracy Farrell.* New imprint, launched in 1997, **Love Inspired** publishes a line of inspirational contemporary romances with stories designed to 'lift readers' spirits and gladden their hearts'. No unsolicited mss. Submit query letter in the first instance or write for detailed submission guidelines/tip sheets.

Royalties paid twice-yearly. *Overseas associates* worldwide.

Silver Whistle

See **Harcourt Brace Children's Books Division**

Simon & Schuster Children's Publishing Division

1230 Avenue of the Americas, New York NY 10020
☎001 212 698 7200
President and Publisher *Rick Richter*

A division of the Simon & Schuster Consumer Group. *Publishes* pre-school to young adult, picture books, hardcover and paperback fiction, non-fiction, trade, library and mass-market titles.

IMPRINTS
Aladdin Books *Ellen Krieger* Picture books, paperback fiction and non-fiction reprints and originals, and limited series for ages pre-school to young adult; **Atheneum Books for Young Readers** *Jonathan Lanman* Picture books, hardcover fiction and non-fiction books across all genres for ages 3 to young adult. Two lines within this imprint are **Jean Karl Books** quality fantasy-fiction and **Anne Schwartz Books** distinct picture books and high-quality fiction; **Little Simon** *Alison Weir* Mass-market novelty books (pop-ups, board books, colouring & activity) and merchandise (book and audiocassette) for ages birth through 8; **Margaret K. McElderry Books** *Emma Dryden* Picture books, hardcover fiction and non-fiction trade books for children ages 3 to young adult; **Simon & Schuster Books for Young Readers** *Stephanie Owens Lurie* Picture books, hardcover fiction and non-fiction for children ages 3 to young adult. **Simon Spotlight** *Jennifer Koch* New imprint devoted exclusively to children's media tie-ins and licensed properties.

For submissions to all imprints: send envelope (US size 10) for guidelines, attention: *Manuscript Submissions Guidelines.*

Simon & Schuster Trade Division (Division of Simon & Schuster Consumer Group)

1230 Avenue of the Americas, New York NY 10020

☎001 212 698 7000   Fax 001 212 698 7007

President/Publisher *Carolyn K. Reidy*

Publishes fiction and non-fiction.

DIVISIONS **The Free Press** *Paula Barker Duffy* VP & Publisher, *Elizabeth Maguire* VP & Editorial Director; **Fireside/Touchstone** *Mark Gompertz* VP & Publisher, *Trish Todd* VP & Editor-in-Chief; **Scribner** *Susan Moldow* VP & Publisher, *Nan Graham* VP & Editor-in-Chief; **Simon and Schuster** *David Rosenthal* VP & Publisher, *Michael V. Korda* Senior VP & Editor-in-Chief; **Trade Paperbacks** *Mark Gompertz* VP & Publisher, *Trish Todd* VP & Editor-in-Chief.

IMPRINTS **H. & R. Block**; **Lisa Drew Books**; **Fireside**; **The Free Press**; **Free Press Paperbacks**; **Hudson River Editions**; **Rawson Associates**; **Scribner**; **Scribner Classics**; **Scribner Paperback Fiction**; **S&S Libros eñ Espanol**; **Simon & Schuster**; **Touchstone**. No unsolicited mss.

Royalties paid twice-yearly.

Simon Spotlight

See **Simon & Schuster Children's Publishing Division**

Skylark

See **Bantam Doubleday Dell Publishing Group, Inc.**

Southern Illinois University Press

PO Box 3697, Carbondale IL 62902–3697

☎001 618 453 2281   Fax 001 618 453 1221

Director *John F. Stetter*

FOUNDED 1956. *Publishes* scholarly and general interest non-fiction books and educational materials. 50 titles a year.

Royalties paid annually.

Sovereign Publications

128 East Reynold Road, Lexington KY 40517

☎001 606 971 0080   Fax 001 606 971 9190

Chairman *Dorothy Deering*
Managing Director *B. Richardson*

FOUNDED 1996. *Publishes* fiction and non-fiction, cookbooks and children's books. Unsolicited mss, synopses and ideas for books welcome. No pornography.

Royalties paid twice-yearly.

Spectra

See **Bantam Doubleday Dell Publishing Group, Inc.**

Stackpole Books

5067 Ritter Road, Mechanicsburg PA 17055

☎001 717 796 0411   Fax 001 717 796 0412

Email: sales@stackpolebooks.com

Website: www.stackpolebooks.com

President *David Ritter*
Vice President/Editorial Director *Judith Schnell*

FOUNDED 1933. *Publishes* outdoor sports, fishing, nature, photography, military reference, history, PA Books. 75 titles in 1998.

Royalties paid twice-yearly.

Stanford University Press

Stanford CA 94305-2235

☎001 650 723 9434   Fax 001 650 725 3457

Director *Norris Pope*

Publishes non-fiction: scholarly works in all areas of the humanities, social sciences, natural sciences, history and literature. About 120 titles a year. No unsolicited mss; query in writing first.

Starfire

See **Bantam Doubleday Dell Publishing Group, Inc.**

Steeple Hill

See **Silhouette Books**

Sterling Publishing Co. Inc.

387 Park Avenue South, 5th Floor, New York NY 10016–8810

☎001 212 532 7160   Fax 001 212 213 2495

President *Lincoln Boehm*
Executive Vice-President/Editorial Director *Charles Nurnberg*
Contact *Sheila Anne Barry*

FOUNDED 1949. *Publishes* non-fiction: reference and information books, science, nature, arts and crafts, architecture, home improvement, history, photography, children's humour, complementary health, wine and food, social sciences, sports, music, psychology, New Age, occult, woodworking, pets, hobbies, gardening, puzzles and games. 700 titles in 1998.

Sunburst Books

See **Farrar, Straus & Giroux, Inc**

Susquehanna University Press

See **Golden Cockerel Press** under **UK Publishers**

Sweet Dreams
See **Bantam Doubleday Dell Publishing Group, Inc.**

Syracuse University Press
621 Skytop Road, Syracuse NY 13244–5290
☎001 315 443 5534   Fax 001 315 443 5545
Director *Robert Mandel*
FOUNDED 1943. *Publishes* scholarly books in the following areas: contemporary Middle East studies, international affairs, Irish studies, Iroquois studies, women and religion, Jewish studies, peace studies. About 70 titles a year. Also co-publishes with a number of organisations such as the American University of Beirut. No unsolicited mss. Send query letter with IRCs.
Royalties paid annually.

Nan A. Talese Books
See **Bantam Doubleday Dell Publishing Group, Inc.**

Jeremy P. Tarcher
See **Penguin Putnam Inc**

Temple University Press
1601 N. Broad Street, 083–42, Philadelphia PA 19122–6099
☎001 215 204 8787   Fax 001 215 204 4719
Email: tempress@astro.ocis.temple.edu
Editor-in-Chief *Janet M. Francendese*
FOUNDED 1969. *Publishes* scholarly non-fiction: American history, Latin American studies, gay and lesbian studies, ethnic studies, psychology, Asian American studies, anthropology, law, cultural studies, sociology, women's studies, health care and disability, philosophy, public policy, labour studies, urban and environmental studies, photography and Black studies. About 60 titles a year. Authors generally academics. Write in first instance.

University of Tennessee Press
293 Communications Building, Knoxville TN 37996
☎001 423 974 3321   Fax 001 423 974 3724
Managing Editor *Stan Ivestor*
FOUNDED in 1940. *Publishes* scholarly and regional non-fiction. *Royalties* paid twice-yearly.

University of Texas Press
PO Box 7819, Austin TX 78713-7819
☎001 512 471 7233/Editorial: 471 4278
Fax 001 512 320 0668
Website: www.utexas.edu/utpress/
Director *Joanna Hitchcock*

**Assistant Director/
Executive Editor** *Theresa J. May*
Publishes scholarly non-fiction: anthropology, archaeology, cultural geography, Latin/Mexican/Native American studies, politics, biology and earth sciences, environmental, American/Texan urban studies, Texana, women's, film, cultural, media studies, Middle Eastern studies, regional cookbooks, natural history, Latin American/Middle Eastern literature in translation, art and architecture, classics. Unsolicited material welcome in above subject areas only. About 90 titles a year and 12 journals.
Royalties paid annually.

Three Rivers Press
See **The Crown Publishing Group**

Time-Life Inc.
2000 Duke Street, Alexandria VA 22314
☎001 703 838 7000   Fax 001 703 838 7225
President/Chief Executive/Chairman
George Artandi
FOUNDED 1961. Subsidiary of Time Warner Inc. *Publishes* non-fiction: cooking, food, gardening, health, history, home maintenance, nature, science. No unsolicited mss. About 300 titles a year. DIVISIONS/IMPRINTS **Time-Life Books**; **Time-Life Custom Publishing; Time-Life Education; Time-Life International; Time-Life Music; Time-Life Video & Television**.

Times Books
201 East 50th Street, New York NY 10022
☎001 212 572 2170   Fax 001 212 940 7464
Publisher *Peter Bernstein*
FOUNDED 1959. A division of **Random House, Inc.** *Publishes* general non-fiction and consumer reference. Unsolicited mss not considered. Letter essential.

Tor
See **St Martin's Press, Inc.**

Touchstone
See **Simon & Schuster Trade Division**

Twenty-First Century Books
See **The Millbrook Press, Inc.**

Tyndale House Publishers, Inc.
351 Executive Drive, Carol Stream IL 60188
☎001 630 668 8300   Fax 001 630 668 8311
Chairman *Kenneth N. Taylor*
President *Mark D. Taylor*
FOUNDED 1962 by Kenneth Taylor. Non-

denominational religious publisher of around 100–150 titles a year for the evangelical Christian market. Books cover a wide range of categories from home and family to inspirational, theology, doctrine, Bibles, general reference and fiction. Also produces video material, calendars and audio books for the same market. No poetry. No unsolicited mss; they will be returned unread. Synopses and ideas considered. Send query letter summarising contents of books and length. Include a brief biography, detailed outline and sample chapters. IRCs essential for response or return of material. No audio cassettes, disks or video tapes in lieu of mss. Response time around 6–12 weeks. No phone calls. Send s.a.e. for free catalogue and full submission guidelines.
Royalties paid annually.

University Press of America, Inc.
4720 Boston Way, Lanham MD 20706
☎001 301 459 3366   Fax 001 301 459 2118
Publisher *James E. Lyons*

FOUNDED 1974. *Publishes* scholarly monographs, college and graduate level textbooks. No children's, elementary or high school. About 450 titles a year. Submit outline or request proposal questionnaire. *Royalties* paid annually. Distributed by Oxford Publicity Partners, Oxford.

Upstart Publishing Company
See **Dearborn Financial Publishing, Inc.**

Van Nostrand Reinhold
See **John Wiley & Sons Inc.**

The Viking Press/Viking Children's Books
See **Penguin Putnam Inc**

Villard Books
See **Random House, Inc.**

Voyager Paperbacks
See **Harcourt Brace Children's Books Division**

J. Weston Walch, Publisher
321 Valley Street, PO Box 658, Portland ME 04104-0658
☎001 207 772 2846   Fax 001 207 772 3105
Website: www.walch.com
President *Suzanne Sanborn Austin*
Editor-in-Chief *Lisa French*
Acquisitions Editor *Kate O'Halloran*

FOUNDED 1927. *Publishes* supplementary educational materials for secondary schools across a wide range of subjects, including art, business, technology, careers, literacy, mathematics, science, music, social studies, special needs, etc. Always interested in ideas from secondary school teachers who develop materials in the classroom. Unsolicited mss, synopses and ideas welcome.
Royalties paid twice-yearly.

Walker & Co.
435 Hudson Street, New York NY 10014
☎001 212 727 8300   Fax 001 212 727 0984
Contact *Submissions Editor*

FOUNDED 1959. *Publishes* mystery, childrens and non-fiction. Please contact the following editors in advance before sending any material to be sure of their interest, then follow up as instructed:
Mystery *Michael Seidman* 60–70,000 words. Send first three chapters and 3–5 page synopsis. **Trade non-fiction** *George Gibson* Permission and documentation must be available with mss. Submit prospectus first, with sample chapters and marketing analysis. **Books for Young Readers** *Emily Easton* Fiction and non-fiction. Query before sending non-fiction proposals. Especially interested in young science, historical and picture books and contemporary fiction for middle grades and young adults.

Frederick Warne
See **Penguin Putnam Inc**

Warner Books Inc.
1271 Avenue of the Americas, New York NY 10020
☎001 212 522 7200   Fax 001 212 522 7991
Chief Executive Officer *Laurence J. Kirshbaum*
VP/Executive Editor *Rick Horgan*

FOUNDED 1961. *Publishes* fiction and non-fiction, audio books, gift books.
IMPRINTS **Aspect** *Betsy Mitchell*; **Mysterious Press** *William Malloy*; **Warner Audio Books**; **Warner Vision**. Query or submit outline with sample chapters and letter.

Washington Square Press
See **Pocket Books**

Washington State University Press
PO Box 645910, Pullman WA 99164-5910
☎001 509 335 3518   Fax 001 509 335 8568
Website: www.publications.wsu.edu/wsupress
Director *Thomas H. Sanders*

FOUNDED 1928. Revitalised in 1984 to publish hardcover originals, trade paperbacks and reprints. *Publishes* mainly on the history, prehistory and culture of the Northwest United States (Washington, Idaho, Oregon, Montana, Alaska) and British Columbia, but works that focus on national topics or other regions may also be considered. 8–10 titles a year. Unsolicited mss and queries welcome.

Royalties paid annually.

Franklin Watts Inc. (A Division of Grolier Publishing)

90 Sherman Turnpike, Danbury CT 06816
☎001 203 797 3500   Fax 001 203 797 6986

Vice President/Publisher *John W. Selfridge*
Executive Editor *Mark Friedman*

FOUNDED 1942 and acquired by **Grolier** in 1975. *Publishes* non-fiction: curriculum-based material for ages 5–18 across a wide range of subjects, including history, social sciences, natural and physical sciences, health and medicine, biography. Over 100 titles a year. No unsolicited mss. Synopses and ideas considered. Address samples to 'Submissions' and include IRCs if response required. Be prepared for a three-month turnaround.

Royalties paid twice-yearly.

WCB/McGraw-Hill
See **The McGraw-Hill Companies**

Rob Weisbach Books
See **William Morrow & Co., Inc.**

Wesleyan University Press
See **University Press of New England**

John Wiley & Sons Inc.

605 Third Avenue, New York NY 10158
☎001 212 254 3232   Fax 001 212 850 6142
Website: www.wiley.com

Chief Executive Officer *William J. Pesce*

FOUNDED 1848. Formerly Van Nostrand Reinhold. *Publishes* professional and reference in the following fields: culinary arts and hospitality, architecture/design, environmental and occupational health and safety, business technology.

Wings
See **Random House, Inc.**

Yearling Books
See **Bantam Doubleday Dell Publishing Group, Inc.**

Zondervan Publishing House

5300 Patterson Avenue SE, Grand Rapids MI 49530
☎001 616 698 6900   Fax 001 616 698 3421

President/Chief Executive *Bruce E. Ryskamp*

FOUNDED 1931. Subsidiary of **HarperCollins Publishers, Inc.** *Publishes* Protestant religion, Bibles, books, audio & video, computer software, calendars and speciality items.

US Agents

★ = Members of the **Association of Authors' Representatives, Inc.**

Adler & Robin Books, Inc.
3000 Connecticut Avenue, Suite 317,
Washington DC 20008
☎001 202 986 9275   Fax 001 202 986 9485
Email: adlerbooks@adlerbooks.com
President/Agent *Bill Adler Jr*
Senior Agent *Martha K. Anitay, Laura Bett,
Djana Pearson Morris*

FOUNDED 1988. *Handles* popular adult fiction
and non-fiction. Unsolicited synopses and
queries welcome. Send letter with outline or
proposal and sample chapters if possible.
Electronic submissions accepted. No reading
fee. CLIENTS H. Michael Frase, Richard
Laermer, Arthur J. Magida. *Commission* Home
15%; UK 20%.

The Ahearn Agency, Inc.
2021 Pine Street, New Orleans LA 70118
☎001 504 861 8395   Fax 001 504 866 6434
Email: pahearn@aol.com
President *Pamela G. Ahearn*

FOUNDED 1992. *Handles* general and genre fiction, and non-fiction. Particularly interested in
women's fiction, suspense fiction and historical
romance. No children's books, poetry, autobiography, plays, screenplays or short fiction.
Reading fee charged to unpublished authors.
Send brief query letter with s.a.e. for reply in
the first instance. CLIENTS include John Ames,
Meagan McKinney, Laura Joh Rowland, Marc
Vargo. *Commission* Home 15%; Translation
and UK 20%. *Overseas associates* in Europe and
Latin America.

Marcia Amsterdam Agency
Suite 9A, 41 West 82nd Street, New York
NY 10024
☎001 212 873 4945
Contact *Marcia Amsterdam*

FOUNDED 1969. *Specialises* in mainstream fic-
tion, horror, suspense, humour, young adult,
TV and film scripts. No poetry, books for the
8–10 age group or how-to. No unsolicited mss.
First approach by letter only and enclose IRCs.
No reading fee for outlines and synopses.
CLIENTS include Jenna Bruce, L. E. Hawes,
Christopher Hinz, Ruby Jean Jensen, Robert
Leininger, William H. Lovejoy, Isaac Millman,

L. J. Schneiderman. *Commission* Home 15%;
Dramatic 10%; Foreign 20%.

Bart Andrews & Associates Inc
7510 Sunset Boulevard, Suite 100, Los
Angeles CA 90046–3418
☎001 310 271 9916
Contact *Bart Andrews*

FOUNDED 1982. General non-fiction: show
business, biography and autobiography, film
books, trivia, TV and nostalgia. No scripts. No
fiction, poetry, children's or science. No books
of less than major commercial potential.
Specialises in working with celebrities on autobiographies. No unsolicited mss. 'Send a brilliant
letter (with IRCs for response) extolling your
manuscript's virtues. Sell me!' CLIENTS include J.
Randy Taraborrelli, Wayne Newton, Bart
Andrews. No reading fee. *Commission* Home &
Translation 15%. *Overseas associates* **Abner Stein**,
London.

Joseph Anthony Agency
15 Locust Court Road, 20 Mays Landing,
New Jersey NJ 08330
☎001 609 625 7608
Contact *Joseph Anthony*

FOUNDED 1964. *Handles* all types of novel and
scripts for TV: 2-hour mini-series, screenplays
and ½-hour sitcoms. No poetry, short stories or
pornography. *Specialises* in action, romance and
detective novels. Last sale to **Silhouette Books**
by writer Karen Alaire. Unsolicited mss welcome. Enclose return postage (US money order
or US cheque). Send query first. Reading fee
charged to new writers: novels $85; screenplays
$100. CLIENTS include Ed Adair, Robert Long,
Joseph McCullough, Sandi Wether. Signatory of
the Writer's Guild of America. *Commission*
Home 15%; Dramatic & Translation 20%.

The Artists Group
10100 Santa Monica Boulevard, Suite 2490,
Los Angeles CA 90067
☎001 310 552 1100   Fax 001 213 277 9513
Contact *Robert Malcolm, Hal Stalmaster*

FOUNDED 1978. Screenplays and plays for film
and TV. No unsolicited mss. Write with list of
credits, if any. No reading fee. *Commission* 10%.

Malaga Baldi Literary Agency

2112 Broadway, Suite 403, New York
NY 10023
☎001 212 579 5075
Contact *Malaga Baldi*

FOUNDED 1986. *Handles* quality fiction and non-fiction. No scripts. No westerns, men's adventure, science fiction/fantasy, romance, how-to, young adult or children's. Writers of fiction should send mss with covering letter, including IRCs for return of mss and stamped addressed postcard for notification of receipt. Allow ten weeks *minimum* for response. For non-fiction, approach in writing with a proposal, table of contents and two sample chapters. No reading fee. CLIENTS include Margaret Erhart, Daniel Harris, Felice Picano, David J. Skal. *Commission* 15%. *Overseas associates* **Abner Stein**, **Marsh & Sheil Ltd**, UK; Japan Uni.

The Balkin Agency, Inc.*

PO Box 222, Amherst MA 01004
☎001 413 548 9835   Fax 001 413 548 9836
Contact *Richard Balkin*

FOUNDED 1973. *Handles* adult non-fiction only. No reading fee for outlines and synopses. *Commission* Home 15%; Foreign 20%.

Maximilian Becker Agency

See **Aleta M. Daley**

Meredith Bernstein Literary Agency, Inc.*

2112 Broadway, Suite 503A, New York
NY 10023
☎001 212 799 1007   Fax 001 212 799 1145
Contact *Meredith Bernstein, Elizabeth Cavanaugh*

FOUNDED 1981. *Handles* fiction (women's and men's), mysteries, romance, and non-fiction (women's issues, personal memoirs, parenting, psychology, business, spirituality, science, travel, fashion, inspiration and humour). 'Always interested in new ideas, voices and other original projects. We are looking for mainstream fiction, psychological suspense, medical thrillers, love stories (but not romances).' Not taking on any unpublished romance writers at present. *Commission* Home & Dramatic 15%; Translation 20%. *Overseas associates* **Abner Stein**, UK; Lennart Sane, Holland, Scandinavia and Spanish language; Thomas Schluck, Germany; Bardon Chinese Media Agency; William Miller, Japan; Frederique Porretta, France; Agenzia Letteraria, Italy.

Reid Boates Literary Agency

PO Box 328, 69 Cooks Crossroad, Pittstown
NJ 08867-0328
☎001 908 730 8523   Fax 001 908 730 8931
Email: rboatesla@aol.com
Contact *Reid Boates*

FOUNDED 1985. *Handles* general fiction and non-fiction. *Specialises* in journalism and media, serious self-help, biography and autobiography, true crime and adventure, popular science, current affairs, trade reference and quality fiction. No scripts. No science fiction, fantasy, romance, western, gothic, personal memoirs, children's or young adult. Enquire by letter with IRCs in first instance. No reading fee. CLIENTS include Dr James Rippe, Stephen Singular, Jon Winokur and the estate of Ava Gardner. *Commission* Home & Dramatic 15%; Translation 20%. *Overseas associates* Michael Meller, UK & Germany; Kyoshi Asano, Japan; Raquel de la Concha, Spanish languages; Eliane Baristi, France.

Georges Borchardt, Inc.*

136 East 57th Street, New York NY 10022
☎001 212 753 5785   Fax 001 212 838 6518

FOUNDED 1967. Works mostly with established/published authors. *Specialises* in fiction, biography, and general non-fiction of unusual interest. Unsolicited mss not read. *Commission* Home, UK, Dramatic 15%; Translation 20%. *UK associates* **Sheil Land Associates Ltd** (Richard Scott Simon), London.

Brandt & Brandt Literary Agents, Inc.*

1501 Broadway, New York NY 10036
☎001 212 840 5760   Fax 001 212 840 5776
Contact *Carl D. Brandt, Gail Hochman, Marianne Merola, Charles Schlessiger*

FOUNDED 1914. *Handles* non-fiction and fiction. No poetry or children's books. No unsolicited mss. Approach by letter describing background and ambitions. No reading fee. *Commission* Home & Dramatic 15%; Foreign 20%. *UK associates* **A. M. Heath & Co. Ltd**.

Pema Browne Ltd

Pine Road, HCR Box 104B, Neversink
NY 12765
☎001 914 985 2936   Fax 001 914 985 7635
Contact *Pema Browne, Perry Browne*

FOUNDED 1966. ('Pema rhymes with Emma.') *Handles* mass-market mainstream and hardcover fiction: romance, men's adventure, business, humour, children's picture books and young adult; non-fiction: how-to and reference. No unsolicited mss; send query letter with IRCs. No fax queries. Also handles illustrators' work. CLIENTS include Linda Cargill, Gary J. Grappo, Miriam Moore. *Commission* Home 15%; Translation 20%; Dramatic 10%; Overseas authors 20%.

Sheree Bykofsky Associates, Inc.★
16 West 36th Street, 13th Floor, New York NY 10018
☎001 212 308 1253
Contact *Sheree Bykofsky*
FOUNDED 1985. *Handles* adult fiction and non-fiction. No scripts. No children's, young adult, horror, science fiction, romance, westerns, occult or supernatural. *Specialises* in popular reference, self-help, psychology, biography and highly commercial or highly literary fiction. No unsolicited mss. Send query letter first with brief synopsis or outline and writing sample (1–3 pp) for fiction. IRCs essential for reply or return of material. No phone calls. No reading fee. CLIENTS include Richard Carlson & Benjamin Shield, Martin Edelston, Glenn Ellenbogen, Merrill Furman, Don Gabor, Bruce Jacobs, Alan Lakein, Nancy Mair, Roshumba Williams. *Commission* Home 15%; UK (including sub-agent's fee) 25%.

Maria Carvainis Agency, Inc.★
235 West End Avenue, New York NY 10023
☎001 212 580 1559   Fax 001 212 877 3486
Contact *Maria Carvainis*
FOUNDED 1977. *Handles* fiction: literary and mainstream, contemporary women's, mystery, suspense, fantasy, historical, children's and young adult novels; non-fiction: business, finance, women's issues, political and film biography, medicine, psychology and popular science. No film scripts unless from writers with established credits. No science fiction. No unsolicited mss; they will be returned unread. Queries only, with IRCs for response. No reading fee. *Commission* Domestic & Dramatic 15%; Translation 20%.

Martha Casselman, Literary Agent★
PO Box 342, Calistoga CA 94515-0342
☎001 707 942 4341
Contact *Martha Casselman*
FOUNDED 1979. *Handles* all types of non-fiction. No fiction at present. Main interests: food/cookery, biography, current affairs, popular sociology. No scripts, textbooks, poetry, coming-of-age fiction or science fiction. Especially interested in

cookery with an appeal to the American market for possible co-publication in UK. Send queries and brief summary, with return postage. No mss. If you do not wish return of material, please state so. Also include, where applicable, any material on previous publications, reviews, brief biography. No proposals via fax. No reading fee. *Commission* Home 15%.

The Catalog Literary Agency
PO Box 2964, Vancouver WA 98668
☎001 360 694 8531
Contact *Douglas Storey*
FOUNDED 1986. *Handles* popular, professional and textbook material in all subjects, especially business, health, money, science, technology, computers, electronics and women's interests; also how-to, self-help, mainstream fiction and children's non-fiction. No genre fiction. No scripts, articles, screenplays, plays, poetry or short stories. No reading fee. No unsolicited mss. Query with an outline and sample chapters and include IRCs. CLIENTS include Don Brown, Malcolm S. Foster, Deborah Wallace. *Commission* 15%.

The Linda Chester Literary Agency
Rockefeller Center, 630 Fifth Avenue, New York NY 10111
☎001 212 218 3350   Fax 001 212 218 3343
Contact *Joanna Pulcini*
FOUNDED 1978. *Handles* literary and commercial fiction and non-fiction in all subjects. No scripts, children's or textbooks. No unsolicited mss. No reading fee for solicited material. *Commission* Home & Dramatic 15%; Translation 25%.

Clausen, Mays & Tahan Literary Agency
249 West 34th Street, Suite 605, New York NY 10001
☎001 212 239 4343   Fax 001 212 239 5248
Contact *Stedman Mays, Mary M. Tahan*
Handles non-fiction work such as memoirs, biography, true crime, true stories, how-to, psychology, spirituality, relationships, style, health/nutrition, fashion/beauty, women's issues, humour and cookbooks. No fiction. Books include *The Rules* Ellen Fein & Sherrie Schneider; Quentin Crisp's *Resident Alien; A Flat Stomach ASAP* Ellington Darden; *Ageless Beauty* Dayle Hadden; *I Was a Better Mother Before I Had Kids* Lori Borgman. Send query letter only. Include s.a.e. *UK associates* **David Grossman Literary Agency Ltd**.

Hy Cohen Literary Agency Ltd
PO Box 43770, Up. Montclair NJ 07043
☎001 973 783 9494 Fax 001 973 783 9867
Email: cogency@home.com
President *Hy Cohen*
FOUNDED 1975. Fiction and non-fiction. No
scripts. Unsolicited mss welcome, but synopsis
with sample 100 pp preferred. IRCs essential.
No reading fee. *Commission* Home & Dramatic
10%; Foreign 20%. *Overseas associates* **Abner
Stein**, UK.

Ruth Cohen, Inc.★
Box 7626, Menlo Park CA 94025
☎001 650 854 2054
President *Ruth Cohen*
FOUNDED 1982. Works mostly with estab-
lished/published authors but will consider new
writers. *Specialises* in high-quality mystery and
women's fiction, plus historical romance. No
poetry, short stories or film scripts. No unsolicited mss. Send opening 10 pp with synopsis. Include enough IRCs for return postage or materials *will not be returned*. No reading fee. *Commission*
Home & Dramatic 15%; Foreign 20%.

Frances Collin Literary Agent★
PO Box 33, Wayne PA 19087–0033
☎001 610 254 0555 Fax 001 610 254 5029
Contact *Frances Collin*
FOUNDED 1948. Successor to Marie Rodell.
Handles general fiction and non-fiction. No
scripts. No unsolicited mss. Send query letter
only, with IRCs for reply, for the attention of
Marsha Kear. No reading fee. Rarely accepts
non-professional writers or writers not represented in the UK. *Overseas associates* worldwide.

Don Congdon Associates, Inc.★
156 Fifth Avenue, Suite 625, New York NY
10010–7002
☎001 212 645 1229 Fax 001 212 727 2688
Contact *Don Congdon, Michael Congdon,
Susan Ramer*
FOUNDED 1983. *Handles* fiction and non-fiction.
No academic, technical, romantic fiction, or
scripts. No unsolicited mss. Approach by letter in
the first instance. No reading fee. *Commission*
Home 10%; UK & Translation 19%. *Overseas
associates* **The Marsh Agency** (Italy, Germany,
Spain, Portugal, Latin America), **Abner Stein**
(UK), Michelle Lapautre (France), Tuttle Mori
Agency (Japan), **Andrew Nurnberg** (Eastern
Europe), Lennart Sane (Scandinavia and The
Netherlands).

The Connor Literary Agency
2911 West 71st Street, Richfield MN 55423
☎001 612 866 1486 Fax 001 612 869 4074
Contact *Marlene Connor, John Lynch*
FOUNDED 1985. *Handles* general non-fiction,
contemporary women's fiction, popular fiction, Black fiction and non-fiction, how-to,
mysteries and crafts. Particularly interested in
illustrated books. No unsolicited mss; send
query letter in the first instance. Previously
published authors preferred. CLIENTS include
Simplicity Pattern Company, *Essence Magazine*,
Bonnie Allen, Ron Elmore, Nadezda
Obradovic. *Commission* Home 15%; UK &
Translation 25%. *Overseas associates* in England,
Spain, Japan, France and Germany.

Richard Curtis Associates, Inc.★
171 East 74th Street, Second Floor, New
York NY 10021
☎001 212 772 7363 Fax 001 212 772 7393
Email: rcurtis@curtisagency.com
Website: www.e-rights.com
Contact *Richard Curtis*
FOUNDED 1969. *Handles* genre and mainstream
fiction, plus commercial non-fiction. Scripts
rarely. *Specialises* in electronic rights and multimedia.

Curtis Brown Ltd★
10 Astor Place, New York NY 10003
☎001 212 473 5400
Book Rights *Laura Blake Peterson, Ellen Geiger,
Peter L. Ginsberg, Emilie Jacobson, Ginger
Knowlton, Perry Knowlton, Marilyn E. Marlow,
Andrew Pope, Clyde Taylor, Maureen Walters,
Mitchell Walters*
Film, TV, Audio Rights *Timothy Knowlton,
Edwin Wintle*
Translation *Dave Barbor*
FOUNDED 1914. *Handles* general fiction and
non-fiction. Also some scripts for film, TV and
theatre. No unsolicited mss; queries only, with
IRCs for reply. No reading fee. *Overseas associates*
Representatives in all major foreign countries.

Aleta M. Daley/Maximilian Becker Agency
444 East 82nd Street, New York NY 10028
☎001 212 744 1453 Fax 001 212 249 2088
1021 Budapest, Széher lit 72, Hungary
☎/fax 00 36 1 200 3148
Contact *Aleta M. Daley*
FOUNDED 1950. *Handles* non-fiction and fic-

tion; also scripts for film and TV. No unsolicited mss. Send query letter in the first instance with sample chapters or a proposal. No reading fee, but handling fee is charged to cover postage, telephone, etc. *Commission* Home 15%; UK 20%.

Joan Daves Agency

21 West 26th Street, New York
NY 10010–1003
☎001 212 685 2663   Fax 001 212 685 1781
Director *Jennifer Lyons*
FOUNDED 1952. Literary fiction and nonfiction. No romance or textbooks. No scripts. Send query letter in the first instance. 'A detailed synopsis seems valuable only for non-fiction work. Material submitted should specify the author's background, publishing credits and similar pertinent information.' No reading fee. CLIENTS include Frederick Franck, Frank Browning, Suzy McKee Charnas, John Maclean, Elizabeth Holtzman, Melvin Jules Buklet, April Reynolds, Ted Perl, Christina Shea, Roger Shattack, Leora Tannenbaum and the estates of Isaac Babel, Heinrich Böll, Christina Stead, Frank O'Connor. *Commission* Home 15%; Dramatic 10–25%; Foreign 20%.

Sandra Dijkstra Literary Agency★

1155 Camino del Mar, Suite 515–C, Del Mar
CA 92014
☎001 619 755 3115
Contact *Sandra Zane*
FOUNDED 1981. *Handles* quality and commercial non-fiction and fiction, including some genre fiction. No scripts. No westerns, contemporary romance or poetry. Willing to look at children's projects. *Specialises* in quality fiction, mystery/thrillers, psychology, self-help, science, health, business, memoirs, biography. Dedicated to promoting new and original voices and ideas. For fiction: send brief synopsis (1 page) and first 50 pages; for non-fiction: send proposal with overview, chapter outline, author biog. and two sample chapters. All submissions should be accompanied by IRCs. No reading fee. *Commission* Home 15%; Translation 20%. *Overseas associates* **Abner Stein**, UK; Ursula Bender, Agence Hoffman, Germany; Monica Heyum, Scandinavia; Luigi Bernabo, Italy; M. Casanovas, Spain; Caroline Van Gelderen, Netherlands; M. Kling (La Nouvelle Agence), France; William Miller, The English Agency, Japan.

Jane Dystel Literary Management★

One Union Square West, Suite 904, New
York NY 10003
☎001 212 627 9100   Fax 001 212 627 9313
Website: www.dystel.com
Contact *Jane Dystel, Miriam Goderich, Todd Keithley, Jessica Jones*
FOUNDED 1991. *Handles* non-fiction and fiction. *Specialises* in politics, history, biography, cookbooks, current affairs, celebrities, commercial and literary fiction. No reading fee. CLIENTS include Lorene Cary, Thomas French, Dan Gearino, Lynne Rossetto Kasper, Gus Lee, Alice Medrich, Thomas Moran, Barack Obama, Mary Russell, Elaine St James, 'Judge Judy' Sheindlin, Michael Tucker.

Educational Design Services, Inc.

PO Box 253, Wantagh NY 11793
☎001 718 539 4107/516 221 0995
Email: linder.eds@juno.com
President *Bertram Linder*
Vice President *Edwin Selzer*
FOUNDED 1979. *Specialises* in educational material and textbooks for sale to school markets. IRCs must accompany submissions. *Commission* Home 15%; Foreign 25%.

Elek International Rights Agents

457 Broome Street, New York NY 10013
☎001 212 431 9368   Fax 001 212 966 5768
Website: www.theliteraryagency.com
Contact *Lauren Mactas*
FOUNDED 1979. *Handles* adult non-fiction and children's picture books. No scripts, fiction, psychology, New Age, poetry, short stories or autobiography. No unsolicited mss; send letter of enquiry with IRCs for reply; include résumé, credentials, brief synopsis. No reading fee. CLIENTS Tedd Arnold, Dr Robert Ballard, Patrick Brogan, Robert Bateman, Laura Cornell, Chris Dodd, Dan Drexler, Tracy Harrast, Sally Placksin, Betsy Treitler. *Commission* Home 15%; Dramatic & Foreign 20%. Through wholly-owned subsidiary The Content Company Inc., licenses and manages clients' intellectual property for development into electronic formats – CD-ROM/CD-I/DVD/On-Line/CD-Plus, etc. 'We manage our own website where clients' projects are promoted. Additionally, we feature their published works and provide links to Amazon.com for consumer purchases.'

Ann Elmo Agency, Inc.*

60 East 42nd Street, New York NY 10165
☎001 212 661 2880/1 Fax 001 212 661 2883

Contact *Lettie Lee, Mari Cronin, Andree Abecassis*

FOUNDED in the 1940s. *Handles* literary and romantic fiction, mysteries and mainstream; also non-fiction in all subjects, including biography and self-help. Some children's (8-12-year-olds). Query letter with outline of project in the first instance. No reading fee. *Commission* Home 15–20%. *Overseas associates* **John Johnson Ltd**, UK.

Frieda Fishbein Associates

PO Box 723, Bedford NY 10506
☎001 914 234 7232   Fax 001 914 234 4196

President *Janice Fishbein*
Associates *Heidi Carlson, Douglas Michael*

FOUNDED 1925. Eager to work with new/unpublished writers. *Specialises* in TV, theatre, plays, screenplays and young adult books. No poetry, magazine articles, short stories or young children's. First approach with query letter. No reading fee for outlines at our request or for published authors working in the same genre. *Commission* Home & Dramatic 10%; Foreign 20%.

ForthWrite Literary Agency & Speakers Bureau

28990 Pacific Coast Highway, Suite 106, Malibu CA 90265
☎001 310 457 5785   Fax 001 310 457 9785

Contact *Wendy Keller*

FOUNDED 1988. *Specialises* in non-fiction: biography, business (marketing, finance, management and sales), alternative health, cookery, gardening, nature, popular psychology, history, self-help, home and health, crafts, computer, how-to, animal care. Handles electronic, foreign (translation and distribution) and resale rights for previously published books. Send query letter with IRCs. No reading fee. *Commission* Foreign 20%.

Robert A. Freedman Dramatic Agency, Inc.*

Suite 2310, 1501 Broadway, New York NY 10036
☎001 212 840 5760

President *Robert A. Freedman*
Vice President *Selma Luttinger*

FOUNDED 1928 as Brandt & Brandt Dramatic

Department, Inc. Took its present name in 1984. Works mostly with established authors. *Specialises* in plays, film and TV scripts. Unsolicited mss not read. *Commission* Dramatic 10%.

Max Gartenberg, Literary Agent

521 Fifth Avenue, Suite 1700, New York NY 10175
☎001 212 860 8451   Fax 001 973 535 5033

Contact *Max Gartenberg*

FOUNDED 1954. Works mostly with established/published authors. *Specialises* in non-fiction and trade fiction. Query first. CLIENTS include Linda Davis, Ralph Hickok, Charles Little, Howard Owen, David Roberts, Ralph Sawyer. *Commission* Home & Dramatic 10%; 15% on initial sale, 10% thereafter; Foreign 15/20%.

Gelfman Schneider Literary Agents, Inc.*

250 West 57th Street, Suite 2515, New York NY 10107
☎001 212 245 1993   Fax 001 212 245 8678

Contact *Deborah Schneider, Jane Gelfman*

FOUNDED 1919 (London), 1980 (New York). Formerly John Farquharson Ltd. Works mostly with established/published authors. *Specialises* in general trade fiction and non-fiction. No poetry, short stories or screenplays. No reading fee for outlines. Submissions must be accompanied by IRCs. *Commission* Home 15%; Dramatic 15%; Foreign 20%. *Overseas associates* **Curtis Brown Group Ltd**, UK.

Goldberg Literary Agents, Inc.

255 West 84th Street, New York NY 10024
☎001 212 799 1260

Editorial Director *Kathrine Butler*

FOUNDED 1974. *Handles* fiction and non-fiction. No unsolicited mss. Send query letter (enclose IRCs) describing work in the first instance. *Commission* Home 10%; UK 20%. *Overseas associate* Peter Knight, UK.

Sanford J. Greenburger Associates, Inc.*

15th Floor, 55 Fifth Avenue, New York NY 10003
☎001 212 206 5600   Fax 001 212 463 8718

Contact *Heide Lange, Faith Hamlin, Beth Vesel, Theresa Park*

Handles fiction and non-fiction. No unsolicited mss. First approach with query letter, sample chapter and synopsis. No reading fee.

The Charlotte Gusay Literary Agency

10532 Blythe Avenue, Los Angeles CA 90064
☎001 310 559 0831   Fax 001 310 559 2639
Contact *Charlotte Gusay*
FOUNDED 1988. *Handles* fiction, both literary and commercial, plus non-fiction: children's and adult humour, parenting, gardening, women's and men's issues, feminism, psychology, memoirs, biography, travel. No science fiction, horror, short pieces or collections of stories. No unsolicited mss; send query letter first, then if your material is requested, send succinct outline and first three sample chapters for fiction, or proposal for non-fiction. No response without IRCs. No reading fee. *Commission* Home 15%; Dramatic 10%; Translation & Foreign 25%.

Joy Harris Literary Agency, Inc.★

156 Fifth Avenue, Suite 617, New York NY 10010
☎001 212 924 6269   Fax 001 212 924 6609
Contact *Joy Harris, Kassandra Duane, Leslie Daniels*
Handles adult non-fiction and fiction. No unsolicited mss. Query letter in the first instance. No reading fee. *Commission* Home & Dramatic 15%; Foreign 20%. *Overseas associates* Michael Meller, Germany; **Abner Stein**, UK; The English Agency, Japan.

John Hawkins & Associates, Inc.★

71 West 23rd Street, Suite 1600, New York NY 10010
☎001 212 807 7040   Fax 001 212 807 9555
Contact *John Hawkins, William Reiss*
FOUNDED 1893. *Handles* film and TV rights and software. No unsolicited mss; send queries with 1–3 page outline and 1 page c.v. IRCs necessary for response. No reading fee. *Commission* Apply for rates.

The Jeff Herman Agency, LLC★

332 Bleecker Street, Suite 6–31, New York NY 10014
☎001 212 941 0540   Fax 001 212 941 0614
Contact *Jeffrey H. Herman*
Handles all areas of non-fiction, textbooks and reference and commercial fiction. No scripts. No unsolicited mss. Query letter with IRCs in the first instance. No reading fee. Jeff Herman publishes a useful reference guide to the book trade called *The Writer's Guide to Book Editors, Publishers & Literary Agents* (Prima). *Commission* Home 15%; Translation 10%.

Susan Herner Rights Agency, Inc.

PO Box 303, Scarsdale NY 10583
☎001 914 725 8967   Fax 001 914 725 8969
Contact *Susan N. Herner, Sue P. Yuen*
FOUNDED 1987. Adult fiction and non-fiction in all areas. No children's books. *Handles* film and TV rights and software. Send query letter with outline and sample chapters. No reading fee. *Commission* Home 15%; Dramatic & Translation 20%. *Overseas associates* **David Grossman Literary Agency Ltd**, UK.

Frederick Hill Associates

1842 Union Street, San Francisco CA 94123
☎001 415 921 2910   Fax 001 415 921 2802
Contact *Fred Hill, Bonnie Nadell, Irene Moore*
FOUNDED 1979. General fiction and non-fiction. No scripts. Send query letter detailing past publishing history if any. IRCs required. CLIENTS Katherine Neville, Richard North Patterson, David Foster Wallace. *Commission* Home & Dramatic 15%; Foreign 20%. *Overseas associates* **Mary Clemmey Literary Agency**, UK.

Hull House Literary Agency

240 East 82nd Street, New York NY 10028
☎001 212 988 0725   Fax 001 212 794 8758
President *David Stewart Hull*
Associate *Lydia Mortimer*
FOUNDED 1987. *Handles* commercial fiction, mystery, biography, military history. No scripts, poetry, short stories, romance, science fiction and fantasy, children's or young adult. No unsolicited mss; send single-page letter describing project briefly, together with short biographical note and list of previous publications if any. IRCs essential. No reading fee. *Commission* Home 15%; Translation 20%.

IMG Literary

22 East 71st Street, New York NY 10021–4911
☎001 212 772 8900   Fax 001 212 772 2617
Contact *David Chalfant (Vice President)*
FOUNDED 1986. A wholly-owned subsidiary of IMG, The Mark McCormack Group of Companies. *Handles* non-fiction and fiction. No science fiction, fantasy, poetry or photography. No scripts. Query first. Submissions should include brief synopsis (typed), sample chapters (50 pp maximum), publishing history, etc. CLIENTS include Pat Conroy, Jan Morris, Arnold Palmer, Malachy McCourt, Brian Hall, Muhammed Ali. *Commission* Home & Dramatic 15%; Foreign 20%. *Overseas associates* worldwide.

Kidde, Hoyt & Picard Literary Agency★

333 East 51st Street, New York NY 10022
☎001 212 755 9461/9465
Fax 001 212 223 2501

Chief Associate *Katharine Kidde*
Associate *Laura Langlie*

FOUNDED 1981. *Specialises* in mainstream and literary fiction, romantic fiction (historical and contemporary), and quality non-fiction in humanities and social sciences (biography, history, current affairs, the arts). No reading fee. Query first, include s.a.e. CLIENTS include Michael Cadnum, Bethany Campbell, Jim Oliver, Patricia Robinson. *Commission* 15%.

Kirchoff/Wohlberg, Inc.★

866 United Nations Plaza, Suite 525, New York NY 10017
☎001 212 644 2020   Fax 001 212 223 4387

Authors' Representative *Elizabeth Pulitzer-Voges*

FOUNDED 1930. *Handles* books for children and young adults, specialising in children's picture books. No adult material. No scripts for TV, radio, film or theatre. Send letter of enquiry with synopsis or outline and IRCs for reply or return. No reading fee.

Paul Kohner, Inc.

9300 Wilshire Boulevard, Suite 555, Beverly Hills CA 90212
☎001 310 550 1060   Fax 001 310 276 1083

Contact *Gary Salt, Stephen Moore, Deborah Obad*

FOUNDED 1938. *Handles* a broad range of books for subsidiary rights sales to film and TV. Few direct placements with publishers as film and TV scripts are the major part of the business. *Specialises* in true crime, biography and history. Non-fiction preferred to fiction for the TV market but anything 'we feel has strong potential' will be considered. No short stories, poetry, science fiction or gothic. Unsolicited material will be returned unread, if accompanied by s.a.e. Approach via a third-party reference or send query letter with professional résumé. No reading fee. CLIENTS Ed McBain, Tony Huston, John Katzenbach, Charles Marowitz, Alan Sharp, Donald Westlake. *Commission* Home & Dramatic 10%; Publishing 15%.

Barbara S. Kouts, Literary Agent★

PO Box 560, Bellport NY 11713
☎001 516 286 1278   Fax 001 516 286 1538

Contact *Barbara S. Kouts*

FOUNDED 1980. *Handles* fiction, non-fiction and children's. No romance, science fiction or scripts. No unsolicited mss. Query letter in the first instance. No reading fee. CLIENTS include Hal Gieseking, Nancy Mairs, Robert San Souci. *Commission* Home 10%; Foreign 20%.

Peter Lampack Agency, Inc.

551 Fifth Avenue, Suite 1613, New York NY 10176
☎001 212 687 9106   Fax 001 212 687 9109

Contact *Loren Soeiro*

FOUNDED in 1977. *Handles* commercial fiction: male action and adventure, contemporary relationships, historical, mysteries and suspense, literary fiction; also non-fiction from recognised experts in a given field, plus auto/biographies. Also handles theatrical, motion picture, and TV rights from book properties. No original scripts or screenplays, series or episodic material. Approach by letter in first instance. No reply without s.a.e. 'We will respond within three weeks and invite the submission of manuscripts we would like to examine.' No reading fee. No unsolicited mss. CLIENTS J. M. Coetzee, Clive Cussler, Martha Grimes, Judith Kelman, Johanna Kingsley, Jessica March, Doris Mortman, Gerry Spence, Fred Mustard Stewart. *Commission* Home & Dramatic 15%; Translation & UK 20%.

The Lazear Agency, Inc.

326 South Broadway, Suite 214, Wayzata MN 55391
☎001 612 249 1500   Fax 001 612 249 1460

Contact *Christi Cardenas, Jonathon Lazear, Wendy Lazear, Neil Ross, Anne Blackstone*

FOUNDED 1984. *Handles* fiction: mysteries, suspense, young adult and literary; also true crime, addiction recovery, biography, travel, business, and scripts for film and TV, CD-ROM, broad band interactive television. Children's books from previously published writers. No poetry or stage plays. Approach by letter, with description of mss, short autobiography and IRCs. No reading fee. CLIENTS include Noah Adams, Andrei Codrescu, Al Franken, Jane Goodall, Julius Lester, Harvey Mackay, The Pillsbury Co., B. Smith, Ray Suarez, Bailey White. *Commission* Home & Dramatic 15%; Translation 20%.

Ellen Levine, Literary Agency, Inc.★

Suite 1801, 15 East 26th Street, New York NY 10010-1505
☎001 212 899 0620   Fax 001 212 725 4501

Contact *Diana Finch, Elizabeth Kaplan, Louise Quayle, Ellen Levine*

FOUNDED 1980. *Handles* all types of books. No scripts. No unsolicited mss, nor any other material unless requested. No telephone calls. First approach by letter; send US postage or IRCs for reply, otherwise material not returned. No reading fee. *Commission* Home 15%; Foreign 20%. *UK Associate* **A. M. Heath & Co. Ltd**.

Ray Lincoln Literary Agency

Elkins Park House, Suite 107-B, 7900 Old York Road, Elkins Park PA 19027
☎001 215 635 0827   Fax 001 215 782 8882
Contact *Mrs Ray Lincoln*

FOUNDED 1974. *Handles* adult, young adult and children's fiction and non-fiction: biography, how-to, science, nature and history. Scripts as spin-offs from book mss only. No poetry or plays unless adaptations from published book. Keenly interested in adult biography, in all types of children's books (age five and upwards, not illustrated), in fine adult fiction, science and nature. No unsolicited mss; send query letter first, including IRCs for response. If interested, material will then be requested. No reading fee. Postage fee for projects handled by the agency. *Commission* Home & Dramatic 15%; Translation 20%.

Literary & Creative Artists Agency★

3543 Albemarle Street NW, Washington DC 20008
☎001 202 362 4688   Fax 001 202 362 8875
Contact *Muriel G. Nellis, Jane F. Roberts, Elizabeth Pokempner, Jennifer Steinbach, Leslie Toussaint*

FOUNDED 1981. *Specialises* in a broad range of general non-fiction. No poetry, pornography, academic or educational textbooks. No unsolicited mss; query letter in the first instance. Include IRCs for response. No reading fee. *Commission* Home 15%; Dramatic 20%; Translation 20–25%.

Sterling Lord Literistic, Inc.

65 Bleecker Street, New York NY 10012
☎001 212 780 6050
Contact *Peter Matson, Sterling Lord*

FOUNDED 1979. *Handles* all genres, fiction and non-fiction, plus scripts for TV and film. No unsolicited mss. Prefers letter outlining all non-fiction. No reading fee. *Commission* Home 15%; UK & Translation 20%. *Overseas associates* **Peters Fraser & Dunlop Group Ltd**, UK.

Richard P. McDonough, Literary Agent

34 Pinewood, Irvine CA 92604
☎001 949 654 5480   Fax 001 949 654 5481
Email: cestmoi@msn.com
Boston office: 37 Turner Road, Wellesley, MA 02482
☎ 001 781 235 8145 Fax 001 781 431 4661
Email: segrossman@aol.com
Contact *Richard P. McDonough (Irvine), Steve Grossman (Wellesley)*

FOUNDED 1986. General non-fiction and literary fiction. Film scripts should be addressed to *Steve Grossman*. No genre fiction. No unsolicited mss; query first and include IRCs. No reading fee. CLIENTS John Dufresne, Robert Gordon, Jane Holtz Kay, Mary Leonhardt, Thomas Lynch, M. R. Montgomery, William Sullivan. *Commission* 15%.

McIntosh & Otis, Inc.★

353 Lexington Avenue, New York NY 10016
☎001 212 687 7400   Fax 001 212 687 6894
President *Eugene H. Winick*
Adult Books *Sam Pinkus, Sean Ferrell, Whitney Calam, Barbara Kennedy*
Children's *Dorothy Markinko, Tracey Adams*
Motion Picture/Television *Evva Pryor*

FOUNDED 1928. Adult and juvenile literary fiction and non-fiction. No textbooks or scripts. No unsolicited mss. Query letter indicating nature of the work plus details of background. IRCs for response. No reading fee. *Commission* Home & Dramatic 15%; Foreign 20%. *UK Associates* **A. M. Heath & Co. Ltd**, London.

Denise Marcil Literary Agency, Inc.★

685 West End Avenue, Suite 9C, New York NY 10025
☎001 212 932 3110
President *Denise Marcil*

FOUNDED 1977. *Specialises* in non-fiction: health, alternative health and medicine, personal finance books, popular reference. Query letters only, with IRCs. CLIENTS include Richard McKenzie, Dwight Lee, Jinny Pitzber, Dr William Sears. *Commission* Home & Dramatic 15%; Foreign 20%.

Betty Marks

176 East 77th Street, Apt. 9F, New York NY 10021
☎001 212 535 8388
Contact *Betty Marks*

FOUNDED 1969. Works mostly with established/published authors. *Specialises* in journalists' non-fiction and novels. No unsolicited mss. Query letter and outline in the first instance. *Commission* Home 15%; Foreign 20%. *Overseas associates* **Abner Stein**, UK; Mohrbooks, Germany; International Editors, Spain & Portugal; Rosemary Buchman, Europe; Tuttle Mori, Japan.

The Evan Marshall Agency★
6 Tristam Place, Pine Brook NJ 07058–9445
☎001 973 882 1122   Fax 001 973 882 3099
Email: evanmarshall@TheNovelist.com
Website: www.TheNovelist.com
Contact *Evan Marshall*

FOUNDED 1987. *Handles* general adult fiction and non-fiction. No unsolicited mss; send query letter first. *Commission* Home 15%; UK & Translation 20%.

Mews Books Ltd
c/o Sidney B. Kramer, 20 Bluewater Hill, Westport CT 06880
☎001 203 227 1836   Fax 001 203 227 1144
Contact *Sidney B. Kramer, Fran Pollak*

FOUNDED 1970. *Handles* adult fiction and non-fiction, children's, pre-school and young adult. No scripts, short stories or novellas (unless by established authors). *Specialises* in cookery, medical, health and nutrition, scientific non-fiction, children's and young adult. Unsolicited material welcome. Presentation must be professional. Partial submissions should include summary of plot/characters, one or two sample chapters, personal credentials and brief on target market. No reading fee. If material is accepted, agency asks $350 circulation fee (4–5 publishers), which will be applied against commissions (waived for published authors). Charges for photocopying, postage expenses, telephone calls and other direct costs. Principal agent is an attorney and former publisher (a founder of Bantam Books). Offers consultation service through which writers can get advice on a contract or on publishing problems. *Commission* Home 15%; Film & Translation 20%. *Overseas associates* **Abner Stein**, UK.

Maureen Moran Agency
PO Box 20191, Parkwest Station, New York
NY 10025
☎001 212 222 3838   Fax 001 212 531 3464
Email: maureenm@erols.com
Contact *Maureen Moran*

Formerly Donald MacCampbell, Inc. *Handles* novels only. No scripts, non-fiction, science fiction, westerns or suspense. *Specialises* in romance. No unsolicited mss; approach by letter. No reading fee. *Commission* US Book Sales 10%; First Novels US 15%.

Howard Morhaim Literary Agency
841 Broadway, Suite 604, New York
NY 10003
☎001 212 529 4433   Fax 001 212 995 1112
Contact *Howard Morhaim*

FOUNDED 1979. *Handles* general adult fiction and non-fiction. No scripts. No children's or young adult material, poetry or religious. No unsolicited mss. Send query letter with synopsis and sample chapters for fiction; query letter with outline or proposal for non-fiction. No reading fee. *Commission* Home 15%; UK & Translation 20%. *Overseas associates* worldwide.

Henry Morrison, Inc.
PO Box 235, Bedford Hills NY 10507
☎001 914 666 3500   Fax 001 914 241 7846
Contact *Henry Morrison*

FOUNDED 1965. *Handles* general fiction, crime and science fiction, and non-fiction. No scripts unless by established writers. Unsolicited material welcome; but send query letter with outline of proposal (1–5 pp) in the first instance. No reading fee. *Commission* Home 15%; UK & Translation 20%.

Ruth Nathan Agency
53 East 34th Street, Suite 207, New York
NY 10016
☎001 212 481 1185   Fax 001 212 481 1185

FOUNDED 1984. *Specialises* in illustrated books, fine art & decorative arts, historical fiction with emphasis on Middle Ages, true crime, showbiz. Query first. No unsolicited mss. No reading fee. *Commission* 15%.

B. K. Nelson Literary Agency
139 S. Beverly Hills Drive, Site 323, Beverly Hills CA 90212
☎001 310 858 7006   Fax 001 310 858 7967
Website: www.cmonline.com/bknelson
President *Bonita K. Nelson*

FOUNDED 1979. *Specialises* in business, self-help, how-to, political, autobiography, celebrity biography. Major motion picture and TV documentary success. No unsolicited mss. Letter of inquiry. Reading fee charged. *Commission* 20%. Lecture Bureau for Authors founded 1994; Foreign Rights Catalogue established 1995; BK Nelson Infomercial Marketing Co. 1996, primarily for authors and endorsements, and Red Pepper Productions for motion picture production in 1998.

New Age World Services & Books
62091 Valley View Circle #2, Joshua Tree CA 92252
☎001 760 366 2833   Fax 001 760 366 2890
Contact *Victoria E. Vandertuin*

FOUNDED 1957. New Age fiction and non-fiction, young adult fiction and non-fiction, and poetry. No scripts, drama, missionary, biography, sports, erotica, humour, travel or cookbooks. *Specialises* in New Age, self-help, health and beauty, meditation, yoga, channelling, how-to, metaphysical, occult, psychology, theology, religion, lost continents, time travel. Unsolicited mss and queries welcome. Reading fee charged. *Commission* Home 15%; Foreign 20%.

New England Publishing Associates, Inc.★
Box 5, Chester CT 06412
☎001 860 345 7323   Fax 001 860 345 3660
Email: nepa@nepa.com
Contact *Elizabeth Frost-Knappman, Edward W. Knappman*

FOUNDED 1983. *Handles* non-fiction and (clients only) fiction. *Specialises* in current affairs, history, science, women's studies, reference, psychology, politics, biography, true crime. No textbooks or anthologies. No scripts. Unsolicited mss considered but query letter or phone call preferred first. No reading fee. CLIENTS include Lary Bloom, Kathryn Cullen-DuPont, Sharon Edwards, Elizabeth Lewin, Philip Ginsburg, Michael Golby, William Gross, Dandi Mackall, Mike Nevins, William Packard, John Philpin, Art Plotnik, Carol Rollyson, Robert Sherrill, Orion Magazine, Claude Summers, Ian Tattersall, Ann Waldron. *Commission* Home 15%. *Overseas associates* throughout Europe and Japan; Scott-Ferris, UK. Dramatic rights: **Renaissance**, Los Angeles.

The Betsy Nolan Literary Agency★
224 West 29th Street, 15th Floor, New York NY 10001
☎001 212 967 8200   Fax 001 212 967 7292
Contact *Betsy Nolan, Carla Glasser, Donald Lehr*

FOUNDED 1980. *Specialises* in non-fiction: popular culture, music, gardening, biography, childcare, cooking, how-to. Some literary fiction,

film & TV rights. No unsolicited mss. Send query letter with synopsis first. No reading fee. *Commission* Home 15%; Foreign 20%.

The Otte Co
9 Goden Street, Belmont MA 02178–3002
☎001 617 484 8505
Contact *Jane H. Otte, L. David Otte*

FOUNDED 1973. *Handles* adult fiction and nonfiction. No scripts. No unsolicited mss. Approach by letter. No reading fee. *Commission* Home 15%; Dramatic 7½%; Foreign 20%.

Richard Parks Agency★
138 East 16th Street, Suite 5B, New York NY 10003
☎001 212 254 9067
Contact *Richard Parks*

FOUNDED 1989. *Handles* general trade fiction and non-fiction: literary novels, mysteries and thrillers, commercial fiction, science fiction, biography, pop culture, psychology, self-help, parenting, medical, cooking, gardening, etc. No scripts. No technical or academic. No unsolicited mss. Fiction read by referral only. No reading fee. *Commission* Home 15%; UK & Translation 20%. *Overseas associates* **The Marsh Agency, Barbara Levy Literary Agency**.

James Peter Associates, Inc.★
PO Box 772, Tenafly NJ 07670
☎001 201 568 0760   Fax 001 201 568 2959
Contact *Bert Holtje*

FOUNDED 1971. Non-fiction only. 'Many of our authors are historians, psychologists, physicians – all are writing trade books for general readers.' No scripts. No fiction or children's books. *Specialises* in history, popular culture, business, health, biography and politics. No unsolicited mss. Send query letter first, with brief project outline, samples and biographical information. No reading fee. CLIENTS include Jim Wright, Alan Axelrod, Charles Phillips, Mike Chinoy, Carol Turkington. *Commission* 15%.

Stephen Pevner, Inc.
248 West 73rd Street, 2nd Floor, New York NY 10023
☎001 212 496 0474   Fax 001 212 496 0796
Contact *Stephen Pevner*

FOUNDED 1991. *Handles* pop culture, new fiction and film-related books. Also handles TV, film, theatre and radio scripts. Approach in writing with synopsis (include first chapters for a novel). No reading fee. *Commission* Home 15%.

Alison J. Picard Literary Agent

PO Box 2000, Cotuit MA 02635
☎001 508 477 7192   Fax 001 508 420 0762
Email: ajpicard@aol.com

Contact *Alison Picard*

FOUNDED 1985. *Handles* mainstream and literary fiction, contemporary and historical romance, children's and young adult, mysteries and thrillers; plus non-fiction. No short stories unless suitable for major national publications, and no poetry. Rarely any science fiction and fantasy. Particularly interested in expanding non-fiction titles. Approach with written query. No reading fee. *Commission* 15%. *Overseas associates* **A. M. Heath & Co. Ltd**, UK.

Pinder Lane & Garon-Brooke Associates Ltd★

159 West 53rd Street, New York NY 10019
☎001 212 489 0880   Fax 001 212 489 7104

Owner Agents *Dick Duane, Robert Thixton*
Vice President *Jean Free*
Agent *Nancy Coffey*

FOUNDED 1951. Fiction and non-fiction: history, historical romance, suspense/thrillers, political intrigue, horror/occult, self-help. No category romance, westerns or mysteries. No unsolicited mss. Approach by query letter. No reading fee. CLIENTS Virginia Coffman, Lolita Files, Eric Harry, Chris Heimerdinger, Michael Pinson, Rosemary Rogers, Richard Steinberg, Major Chris Stewart. *Commission* Home 15%; Dramatic 10–15%; Foreign 30%. *Overseas associates* **Abner Stein**, UK; Translation: Bernard Kurman.

Arthur Pine Associates, Inc.

250 West 57th Street, New York NY 10107
☎001 212 265 7330   Fax 001 212 265 4650

Contact *Richard S. Pine, Lori Andiman, Sarah Piel*

FOUNDED 1970. *Handles* fiction and non-fiction (adult books only). No scripts, children's, autobiographical (unless celebrity), textbooks or scientific. No unsolicited mss. Send query letter with synopsis, including IRCs in first instance. All material must be submitted to the agency on an exclusive basis with s.a.e. *Commission* 15%.

PMA Literary & Film Management, Inc.

Box 1817, Old Chelsea Sta., New York NY 10011
☎001 212 929 1222   Fax 001 212 206 0238
Email: pmalitfilm@aol.com
Website: www.pmalitfilm.com

President *Peter Miller*
Vice President *Delin Cormeny*
Associates *Steven Schattenberg, Allison Wolcott, Eric Wilinski*

FOUNDED 1976. Commercial fiction, non-fiction and screenplays. *Specialises* in books with motion picture and television potential, and in true crime. No poetry, pornography, non-commercial or academic. No unsolicited mss. Approach by letter with one-page synopsis. Editing service available for unpublished authors (non-obligatory). Fee recoupable out of first monies earned. CLIENTS Ann Benson, Vincent T. Bugliosi, Jay R. Bonansinga, Wensley Clarkson, Michael Eberhardt, Christopher Cook Gilmore, John Glatt, Chris Rogers, Ted Sennett, Nancy Taylor Rosenberg, Rob Thomas, Gene Walden, Steven Yount. *Commission* Home 15%; Dramatic 10–15%; Foreign 20–25%.

Susan Ann Protter Literary Agent★

110 West 40th Street, Suite 1408, New York NY 10018–3616
☎001 212 840 0480

Contact *Susan Protter*

FOUNDED 1971. *Handles* general fiction, mysteries, thrillers, science fiction and fantasy; non-fiction: history, general reference, biography, true crime, science, health and parenting. No romance, poetry, westerns, religious, children's or sport manuals. No scripts. First approach with letter, including IRCs. No reading fee. CLIENTS Lydia Adamson, Terry Bisson, John G. Cramer, David G. Hartwell, R. E. Klein, Kathleen McCoy PhD, Lynn Armistead McKee, Ian R. MacLeod, Rudy Rucker. *Commission* Home & Dramatic 15%; Foreign 25%. *Overseas associates* **Abner Stein**, UK; agents in all major markets.

Puddingstone Literary/ SBC Enterprises, Inc.

11 Mabro Drive, Denville NJ 07834–9607
☎001 973 366 3622

Contact *Alec Bernard, Eugenia Cohen*

FOUNDED 1972. *Handles* trade fiction, non-fiction, film and telemovies. No unsolicited mss. Send query letter with IRCs. No reading fee. *Commission* varies.

Quicksilver Books, Literary Agents

50 Wilson Street, Hartsdale NY 10530
☎001 914 946 8748

President *Bob Silverstein*

FOUNDED 1973. *Handles* literary fiction and mainstream commercial fiction: blockbuster, suspense, thriller, contemporary, mystery and historical; and general non-fiction, including self-help, psychology, holistic healing, ecology, environmental, biography, fact crime, New Age, health, nutrition, enlightened wisdom and spirituality. No scripts, science fiction and fantasy, pornographic, children's or romance. UK material must have universal appeal for the US market. Unsolicited material welcome but must be accompanied by IRCs for response, together with biographical details, covering letter, etc. No reading fee. CLIENTS Martin Goldsmith, Dick Gregory, Vasant Lad, Ted Libbey, Dorothy Nolte, Arthur Reber, Barrymore Scherer, Grace Speare, Melvin van Peebles. *Commission* Home & Dramatic 15%; Translation 20%.

Helen Rees Literary Agency*

123 N. Washington Street, 5th Floor, Boston MA 02114
☎001 617 723 5232 ext 233
Fax 001 617 723 5211

Contact *Joan Mazmanian*

FOUNDED 1982. *Specialises* in books on health and business; also handles biography, autobiography and history; quality fiction. No scholarly, academic or technical books; no scripts, science fiction, children's, poetry, photography, short stories, cooking; no unsolicited mss. Send query letter with IRCs. No reading fee. CLIENTS Adam Brandenburger, Donna Carpenter, James Champy, Alan Dershowitz, Alexander Dubcek, Harry Figgie Jr, Charles Fine, Senator Barry Goldwater, Senator John Kerry, Richard Lourie, Sandra Mackey, Barry Nalebuff, Sebastian Stuart, Elise Title, Price Waterhouse. *Commission* Home 15%; Foreign 20%.

Renaissance, A Literary/ Talent Agency

9220 Sunset Boulevard, Suite 302, Los Angeles CA 90069
☎001 310 858 5365   Fax 001 310 858 5389

President *Joel Gotler*
Literary Associates *Steven Fisher, Alan Nevins, Irv Schwartz, Brian Lipson*

FOUNDED 1934. Fiction and non-fiction; film and TV rights. No unsolicited mss. Send query letter with IRCs in the first instance. No reading fee. *Commission* Home 10–15%.

Rights Unlimited, Inc.*

101 West 55th Street, Suite 2D, New York NY 10019
☎001 212 246 0900   Fax 001 212 246 2114

Contact *Bernard Kurman*

FOUNDED 1985. *Handles* adult fiction, non-fiction. No scripts, poetry, short stories, educational or literary works. Unsolicited mss welcome; query letter with synopsis preferred in the first instance. No reading fee. *Commission* Home 15%; Translation 20%.

Rosenstone/Wender*

3 East 48th Street, 4th Floor, New York NY 10017
☎001 212 832 8330   Fax 001 212 759 4524

Contact *Phyllis Wender, Susan Perlman Cohen, Sonia E. Pabley*

FOUNDED 1981. *Handles* fiction, non-fiction, children's and scripts for film, TV and theatre. No material for radio. No unsolicited mss. Send letter outlining the project, credits, etc. No reading fee. *Commission* Home 15%; Dramatic 10%; Foreign 20%. *Overseas associates* La Nouvelle Agence, France; Andrew Nurnberg, Netherlands; The English Agency, Japan; Mohrbooks, Germany; Ole Licht, Scandinavia.

Shyama Ross 'The Write Therapist'

2000 North Ivar Avenue, Suite 3, Hollywood CA 90068
☎001 213 465 2630   Fax 001 213 465 8599

Contact *Shyama Ross*

FOUNDED 1979. *Handles* non-fiction trade books: New Age, health and fitness, philosophy, psychology, trends, humour, business, mysticism, religion; also fiction: thrillers, romance, suspense, mystery, contemporary. No scripts. Story analyst for screenplays. No Christian evangelical, travel, sleazy sex or children's. *Specialises* in all commercial non-fiction and fiction as well as literary. New writers welcome. Query by letter with brief outline of contents and background (plus IRCs). Fee charged ($125 for up to 50,000 words) for detailed analysis of mss. Professional editing also available (rates per page or hour). *Commission* Home & Film 15%; Translation 20%.

Jane Rotrosen Agency*

318 East 51st Street, New York NY 10022
☎001 212 593 4330   Fax 001 212 935 6985

Contact *Meg Ruley, Andrea Cirillo, Ruth Kagle, Stephanie Tade*

Handles commercial fiction: romance, horror, mysteries, thrillers and fantasy and popular non-fiction. No scripts, educational, professional or belles lettres. No unsolicited mss; send query letter in the first instance. No reading fee. *Commission* Home 15%; UK & Translation

20%. *Overseas associates* worldwide and film agents on the West Coast.

Victoria Sanders Literary Agency★

241 Avenue of the Americas, Suite 11H, New York NY 10014
☎001 212 633 8811   Fax 001 212 633 0525

Contact *Victoria Sanders, Diane Dickensheid*

FOUNDED 1993. *Handles* general trade fiction and non-fiction, plus ancillary film and television rights. CLIENTS Asha Bandele, Connie Briscoe, Michael Hetzer, Yolanda Joe, Alexander Smalls, J. M. Redmann and the estate of Zora Neale Hurston. *Commission* Home & Dramatic 15%; Translation 20%.

Sandum & Associates

144 East 84th Street, New York NY 10028
☎001 212 737 2011

Contact *Howard E. Sandum*

FOUNDED 1987. *Handles* all categories of general adult non-fiction, plus occasional fiction. No scripts. No children's, poetry or short stories. No unsolicited mss. Third-party referral preferred but direct approach by letter, with synopsis, brief biography and IRCs, is accepted. No reading fee. CLIENTS James Cowan, Bro. Victor d'Avila-Latourrette, Adele Getty, Barbara Lachman. *Commission* Home & Dramatic 15%; Translation & Foreign 20%. *Overseas associates* Scott Ferris Associates.

SBC Enterprises, Inc.

See **Puddingstone Literary**

Jack Scagnetti Talent & Literary Agency

5118 Vineland Avenue, Suite 102, North Hollywood CA 91601
☎001 818 762 3871

Contact *Jack Scagnetti*

FOUNDED 1974. Works mostly with established/published authors. *Handles* non-fiction, fiction, film and TV scripts. No reading fee for outlines. *Commission* Home & Dramatic 10% (scripts), 15% (books); Foreign 15%.

Schiavone Literary Agency, Inc.

236 Trails End, West Palm Beach FL 33413–2135
☎001 561 966 9294   Fax 001 561 966 9294
Email: profschia@aol.com

President *James Schiavone*

FOUNDED 1997. *Handles* fiction and non-fiction (all genres). *Specialises* in biography, autobiography, celebrity memoirs. No poetry or scripts. No

unsolicited mss; send query, brief biog-sketch, synopsis, outline and sample chapters with IRCs. No reading fee. CLIENTS Sandra E. Bowen, Lajla Kraichnan, Bernard Leopold, Michael Ugarte PhD. *Commission* Home 15%; Foreign & Translation 20%. *Overseas associates* in Europe.

Susan Schulman, A Literary Agency★

454 West 44th Street, New York NY 10036
☎001 212 713 1633/4/5
Fax 001 212 581 8830
Email: schulman@aol.com

FOUNDED 1979. *Specialises* in non-fiction of all types but particularly in psychology-based self-help for men, women and families. Other interests include business, the social sciences, biography, language and linguistics. Fiction interests include contemporary fiction, including women's, mysteries, historical and thrillers 'with a cutting edge'. Always looking for 'something original and fresh'. No unsolicited mss. Query first, including outline and three sample chapters with IRCs. No reading fee. Represents properties for film and television, and works with agents in appropriate territories for translation rights. *Commission* Home & Dramatic 15%; Translation 20%. *Overseas associates* Plays: **Rosica Colin Ltd** and **The Agency Ltd**, UK; Children's books: Marilyn Malin, UK, Commercial fiction: **MBA Literary Agents** UK.

Shapiro-Lichtman-Stein Talent Agency

8827 Beverly Boulevard, Los Angeles CA 90048
☎001 310 859 8877   Fax 001 310 859 7153

FOUNDED 1969. Works mostly with established/published authors. *Handles* film and TV scripts. Unsolicited mss will not be read. *Commission* Home & Dramatic 10%; Foreign 20%.

The Shepard Agency

Premier National Bank Building, Suite 3, 1525 Rt. 22, Brewster NY 10509
☎001 914 279 2900/3236
Fax 001 914 279 3239

Contact *Jean Shepard, Lance Shepard*

FOUNDED 1987. *Handles* non-fiction: business, food, self-help and travel; some fiction: adult, children's and young adult and the occasional script. No pornography. *Specialises* in business. Send query letter, table of contents, sample chapters and IRCs for resply. No reading fee. *Commission* Home & Dramatic 15%; Translation 20%.

Lee Shore Agency Ltd
The Sterling Building, 440 Friday Road,
Pittsburgh PA 15209
☎001 412 821 0440   Fax 001 412 821 6099
Email: LeeShore1@aol.com
Website:www.olworld.com/olworld/
   m_lshore/

Contact *Cynthia Sterling, Jennifer Blose,
   Kristine L. Habun*

FOUNDED 1988. *Handles* non-fiction, including
textbooks, and mass-market fiction: horror,
romance, mystery, westerns, science fiction.
Also some young adult and, more recently,
screenplays. *Specialises* in New Age, self-help,
how-to and quality fiction. No children's. No
unsolicited mss. Send IRCs for guidelines
before submitting work. Reading fee charged.
Commission Home 15%; Dramatic 20%.

Bobbe Siegel Literary Agency
41 West 83rd Street, New York NY 10024
☎001 212 877 4985   Fax 001 212 877 4985
Contact *Bobbe Siegel*

FOUNDED 1975. Works mostly with estab-
lished/published authors. *Specialises* in literary fiction, detective, suspense, historical, fantasy, biography, how-to, women's interest, fitness, health,
beauty, sports, pop psychology. No scripts. No
cookbooks, crafts, children's, short stories or
humour. First approach with letter including
IRCs for response. No reading fee. Critiques
given if the writer is taken on for representation.
CLIENTS include Michael Buller, Eileen Curtis,
Primo Levi, John Nordahl, Peter Siegel, Curt
Smith. *Commission* Home 15%; Dramatic &
Foreign 20%. (Foreign/Dramatic split 50/50
with sub-agent.) *Overseas associates* in various
countries, including **John Pawsey** in the UK.

The Evelyn Singer Agency, Inc.
PO Box 594, White Plains NY 10602
☎001 914 949 1147/914 631 5160
Contact *Evelyn Singer*

FOUNDED 1951. Works mostly with estab-
lished/published authors. *Handles* fiction and
non-fiction, both adult and children's. Adult:
health, biography, career, celebrity, political,
serious novels, suspense and mystery.
Children's: educational non-fiction for all ages
and fiction for the middle/teen levels. No picture books unless the author is or has an experienced book illustrator. No formula romance,
poetry, sex, occult, textbooks or specialised
material unsuitable for trade market. No
scripts. No unsolicited mss. First approach with

letter giving writing background, credits, pub-
lications, including date of publication and
publisher. IRCs essential. No phone calls. No
reading fee. 'Accepts writers who have earned
at least $25,000 from freelance writing.'
CLIENTS include John Armistead, Mary Elting,
Franklin Folsom, William F. Hallstead, Rose
Wyler. *Commission* Home 15%; Dramatic 20%;
Foreign 25%. *Overseas associates* **Laurence
Pollinger Limited**, UK.

Michael Snell Literary Agency
PO Box 1206, Truro MA 02666–1206
☎001 508 349 3718
President *Michael Snell*
Vice President *Patricia Smith*

FOUNDED 1980. Adult non-fiction, especially
science, business and women's issues. *Specialises*
in business and computer books (professional and
reference to popular trade how-to); general
how-to and self-help on all topics, from diet and
exercise to parenting, relationships, health, sex,
psychology and personal finance, plus literary
and suspense fiction. No unsolicited mss. Send
outline and sample chapter with return postage
for reply. No reading fee for outlines. Brochure
available on how to write a book proposal.
Author of *From Book Idea to Bestseller*, published
by Prima. Rewriting, developmental editing, col-
laborating and ghostwriting services available on
a fee basis. Send IRCs. *Commission* Home 15%.

Southern Writers
3004 Jackson Street, Suite A, Alexandria
LA 71301–4745
☎001 318 445 6550   Fax 001 318 445 6650
President *Emilie Griffin*

FOUNDED 1979. *Handles* fiction and non-fiction
of general interest. No scripts, short stories,
poetry, autobiography or articles. No unsolicited mss. Approach in writing with query.
Reading fee charged to authors unpublished in
the field. *Commission* Home 15%; Dramatic &
Translation 20%.

The Spieler Agency
154 West 57th Street, Room 135, New York
NY 10019
☎001 212 757 4439   Fax 001 212 333 2019
The Spieler Agency/West, 1328 Sixth Street,
#3, Berkeley, CA 94710
☎001 510 528 2616   Fax 001 510 528 8117

Contact *Joseph Spieler, Lisa M. Ross,
   John Thornton, Ada Muellner (New York);
   Victoria Shoemaker (Berkeley)*

FOUNDED 1980. *Handles* literary fiction and non-fiction. No how-to or genre romance. *Specialises* in history, science, ecology, social issues and business. No scripts. Approach in writing with IRCs. No reading fee. CLIENTS include James Chace, Evan Eisenberg, Paul Hawken, Joe Kane, Walter Laqueur, Akio Morita, Marc Reisner, Peter Senge, Jan Swafford. *Commission* Home 15%; Translation 20%. *Overseas associates* **Abner Stein**, **The Marsh Agency**, UK.

Philip G. Spitzer Literary Agency★
50 Talmage Farm Lane, East Hampton NY 11937
☎001 516 329 3650   Fax 001 516 329 3651
Contact *Philip Spitzer*

FOUNDED 1969. Works mostly with established/published authors. *Specialises* in general non-fiction and fiction – thrillers. No reading fee for outlines. *Commission* Home & Dramatic 15%; Foreign 20%.

Lyle Steele & Co. Ltd
Literary Agents
511 East 73rd Street, Suite 6, New York NY 10021
☎001 212 288 2981
President *Lyle Steele*

FOUNDED 1985. *Handles* general non-fiction and category fiction, including mysteries, thrillers, horror and occult. Also North American rights to titles published by major English publishers. No scripts unless derived from books already being handled. No romance. No unsolicited mss: query with IRCs in first instance. No reading fee. *Commission* 10%. *Overseas associates* worldwide.

Gloria Stern Agency★
2929 Buffalo Speedway, Suite 2111, Houston TX 77098
☎001 713 963 8360   Fax 001 713 963 8460
Contact *Gloria Stern*

FOUNDED 1976. *Specialises* in non-fiction, including biography, history, politics, women's issues, self-help, health, science and education; also adult fiction. No scripts, how-to, poetry, short stories or unsolicited mss. First approach by letter stating content of book, including one chapter, qualifications as author and IRCs. No reading fee. *Commission* Home 10–15%; Dramatic 10%; Foreign 20% shared; Translation 20% shared. *Overseas associates* **A. M. Heath & Co. Ltd**, UK, and worldwide.

Gloria Stern Agency (Hollywood)
12535 Chandler Boulevard, Suite 3, North Hollywood CA 91607
☎001 818 508 6296   Fax 001 818 508 6296
Contact *Gloria Stern*

FOUNDED 1984. *Handles* film scripts, genre (romance, detective, thriller and sci-fi) and mainstream fiction; electronic media. Accepts interactive material, games and electronic data. 'No books containing gratuitous violence.' Approach with letter, biography and synopsis. Reading fee charged by the hour. *Commission* Home 15%; Offshore 20%.

Gunther Stuhlmann Author's Representative
PO Box 276, Becket MA 01223
☎001 413 623 5170
Contact *Gunther Stuhlmann, Barbara Ward*

FOUNDED 1954. *Handles* literary fiction, biography and serious non-fiction. No film/TV scripts unless from established clients. No short stories, detective, romance, adventure, poetry, technical or computers. Query first with IRCs, including sample chapters and synopsis of project. '*We take on few new clients.*' No reading fee. CLIENTS Doris Alexander, Isabel Bolton, Julieta Campos, B. H. Friedman, Edward Margolies, Anaïs Nin, Richard Powers, Otto Rank. *Commission* Home 10%; Foreign 15%; Translation 20%.

The Tantleff Office★
375 Greenwich Street, Suite 603, New York NY 10013
☎001 212 941 3939   Fax 001 212 941 3948
Contact (scripts) *Jack Tantleff, Jill Bock, Charmaine Ferenczi, John B. Santoianni*

FOUNDED 1986. *Handles* primarily scripts for theatre, film and TV, and represents actors. Does not handle books. No unsolicited mss; queries only. No reading fee. CLIENTS include Brian Friel, Marsha Norman, Mark O'Donnell. *Commission* 10%.

2M Communications Ltd
121 West 27th Street, Suite 601, New York NY 10001
☎001 212 741 1509   Fax 001 212 691 4460
Contact *Madeleine Morel*

FOUNDED 1982. *Handles* non-fiction only: everything from pop psychology and health to cookery books, biographies and pop culture. No scripts. No fiction, children's, computers or science. No unsolicited mss; send letter with sample pages and IRCs. No reading fee. CLIENTS David

Steinman, Janet Wolfe, Donald Woods. *Commission* Home & Dramatic 15%; Translation 20%. *Overseas associates* Thomas Schluck Agency, Germany; Asano Agency, Japan; EAIS, France; Living Literary Agency, Italy; Nueva Agencia Literaria Internacional, Spain.

Van der Leun & Associates

22 Division Street, Easton CT 06612
☎001 203 259 4897

Contact *Patricia Van der Leun*

FOUNDED 1984. *Handles* fiction and non-fiction. No scripts. No science fiction, fantasy or romance. *Specialises* in art and architecture, science, biography and fiction. No unsolicited mss; query first, with proposal and short biography. No reading fee. CLIENTS include Robert Fulghum, Marion Winik, Arthur Zajonc. *Commission* 15%. *Overseas associates* **Abner Stein**, UK; Michelle Lapautre, France; English Agency, Japan; Carmen Balcells, Spain; Lijnkamp Associates, The Netherlands; Lucia Riff, South America; Susanna Zevi, Italy.

Wales Literary Agency, Inc.*

108 Hayes Street, Seattle WA 98109
☎001 206 284 7114   Fax 001 206 284 0190
Email: waleslit@aol.com

Contact *Elizabeth Wales, Adrienne Reed*

FOUNDED 1988. *Handles* quality fiction and non-fiction. No scripts except via sub-agents. No genre fiction, westerns, romance, science fiction or horror. Special interest in 'Pacific Rim', West, West Coast, and Pacific Northwest clients. No unsolicited mss; send query letter with publication list and writing sample. No reading fee. No Email queries longer than one page. *Commission* Home 15%; Dramatic & Translation 20%.

John A. Ware Literary Agency

392 Central Park West, New York NY 10025
☎001 212 866 4733   Fax 001 212 866 4734

Contact *John Ware*

FOUNDED 1978. *Specialises* in non-fiction: biography, history, current affairs, investigative journalism, science, inside looks at phenomena, medicine and psychology (academic credentials required). Also handles literary fiction, mysteries/thrillers, sport, oral history, Americana and folklore. Unsolicited mss not read. Send query letter first with IRCs to cover return postage. No reading fee. CLIENTS include Caroline Fraser, Jon Krakauer, Jack Womack. *Commission* Home & Dramatic 15%; Foreign 20%.

Waterside Productions, Inc.

2191 San Elijo Avenue, Cardiff by the Sea CA 92007–839
☎001 619 632 9190   Fax 001 619 632 9295
Email: bgladstone@compuserve.com

Contact *William Gladstone*

FOUNDED 1982. *Handles* general non-fiction: computers and technology, psychology, science, business, sports. All types of multimedia. No unsolicited mss; send query letter. No reading fee. *Commission* Home 15%; Dramatic 20%; Translation 25%. *Overseas associates* **Serafina Clarke**, UK; Asano Agency, Japan; Ulla Lohren, Sweden; Ruth Liepman, Germany; Vera Le Marie, EAIS, France; Bardon Chinese Media Agency, China; Grandi & Vitali, Italy; DRT, Korea; Mercedes Casanovas, Spain.

Watkins Loomis Agency, Inc.

133 East 35th Street, Suite 1, New York NY 10016
☎001 212 532 0080   Fax 001 212 889 0506

Contact *Katherine Fausset*

FOUNDED 1904. *Handles* fiction and non-fiction. No scripts for film, radio, TV or theatre. No science fiction, fantasy or horror. No reading fee. No unsolicited mss. Approach in writing with enquiry or proposal and s.a.e. *Commission* Home 15%; UK & Translation 20%. *Overseas associates* **Abner Stein**; **The Marsh Agency**, UK.

Wecksler-Incomco

170 West End Avenue, New York NY 10023
☎001 212 787 2239   Fax 001 212 496 7035

Contact *Sally Wecksler, Joann Amparan*

FOUNDED 1971. *Handles* literary fiction and non-fiction: business, reference, biographies, performing arts and heavily illustrated books. Send queries only. No unsolicited mss. No reading fee. Foreign rights. *Commission* Home 15%; Translation 20%; UK 20%.

Cherry Weiner Literary Agency

28 Kipling Way, Manalapan NJ 07726
☎001 732 446 2096   Fax 001 732 792 0506

Contact *Cherry Weiner*

FOUNDED 1977. *Handles* more or less all types of genre fiction: science fiction and fantasy, romance, mystery, westerns. No scripts. No non-fiction. No unsolicited mss. No submissions except through referral. No reading fee. *Commission* 15%. *Overseas associates* **Abner Stein**, UK; Thomas Schluck, Germany; International Editors Inc., Spain; Prava Prevodi Agency

(Eastern Europe), Serbia; Elaine Benisti Agency, France; English Agency (Japan) Ltd; Alex Korzhenevski Agency, Russia; Renaissance Media – movie agent.

Wieser & Wieser, Inc.
25 East 21st Street, New York NY 10010
☎001 212 260 0860   Fax 001 212 505 7186
Contact *Olga B. Wieser, George J. Wieser, Jake Elwell*

FOUNDED 1976. Works mostly with established/published authors. *Specialises* in literary and mainstream fiction, serious and popular historical fiction, and general non-fiction: business, finance, aviation, sports, photography, cookbooks, travel and popular medicine. No poetry, children's, science fiction or religious. No unsolicited mss. First approach by letter with IRCs. No reading fee for outlines. *Commission* Home & Dramatic 15%; Foreign 20%.

Ann Wright Representatives
165 West 46th Street, Suite 1105, New York NY 10036–2501
☎001 212 764 6770   Fax 001 212 764 5125
Contact *Dan Wright*

FOUNDED 1961. *Specialises* in screenplays for film and TV. Also handles novels, drama and fiction. No academic, scientific or scholarly. Approach by letter; no reply without IRCs. Include outline and credits only. New film and TV writers encouraged. No reading fee. CLIENTS Theodore Bonnet, Tom Dempsey, Lawrence Fallon, Jerry D. Hoffman, Paul L. Maier, Cordell Marks, Herbert Morote, Kevin O'Morrison, John Peer Nugent, David Reene, David Reynolds. Signatory to the Writers Guild of America Agreement. *Commission* Home – varies according to current trend (10–20%); Dramatic 10% of gross.

Writers House, Inc.★
21 West 26th Street, New York NY 10010
☎001 212 685 2400   Fax 001 212 685 1781
Contact *Albert Zuckerman, Amy Berkower, Merrilee Heifetz, Susan Cohen, Susan Ginsburg,*

Fran Lebowitz, Karen Solem, Robin Rue, John Hodgman, Simon Lipskar

FOUNDED 1974. *Handles* all types of fiction, including children's and young adult, plus narrative non-fiction: history, biography, popular science, pop and rock culture. *Specialises* in popular fiction, women's novels, thrillers and children's. Represents novelisation rights for film producers such as New Line Cinema. No scripts. No professional or scholarly. For consideration of unsolicited mss, send letter of enquiry, 'explaining why your book is wonderful, briefly what it's about and outlining your writing background'. No reading fee. CLIENTS include Virginia Andrews, Bryce Courtenay, Barbara Delinsky, Ken Follett, Neal Gaiman, Eileen Goudge, Stephen Hawking, Linda Howard, Michael Lewis, Robin McKinley, Ann Martin, Francine Pascal, Ridley Pearson, Nora Roberts, Cynthia Voigt, F. Paul Wilson. *Commission* Home & Dramatic 15%; Foreign 20%. Albert Zuckerman is author of *Writing the Blockbuster Novel*, published by **Little, Brown & Co.** and **Warner Paperbacks**.

Susan Zeckendorf Associates, Inc.★
171 West 57th Street, Suite 11B, New York NY 10019
☎001 212 245 2928   Fax 001 212 977 2643
President *Susan Zeckendorf*

FOUNDED 1979. Works with new/unpublished writers. *Specialises* in literary fiction, commercial women's fiction, international espionage, thrillers and mysteries. Non-fiction interests: science, parenting, music and self-help. No category romance, science fiction or scripts. No unsolicited mss. Send query letter describing mss. No reading fee. CLIENTS include Linda Dahl, James N. Frey, Marjorie Jaffe, Laurie Morrow, Una-Mary Parker, Jerry E. Patterson. *Commission* Home & Dramatic 15%; Foreign 20%. *Overseas associates* **Abner Stein**, UK; V. K. Rosemarie Buckman, Europe, South America; Tom Mori, Japan, Taiwan. Film & TV representative: Joel Gotler at **Renaissance**.

US Media Contacts in the UK

ABC News Intercontinental Inc.
8 Carburton Street, London W1P 7DT
☎0171 637 9222   Fax 0171 631 5084
Bureau Chief & Director of News Coverage, Europe, Middle East & Africa *Rex Granum*

Alaska Journal of Commerce
16 Cavaye Place, London SW10 9PT
☎0171 370 1737   Fax 0171 370 7751
Bureau Chief *Robert Gould*

The Associated Press
12 Norwich Street, London EC4A 1BP
☎0171 353 1515   Fax 0171 353 8118
Chief of Bureau/Managing Director *Myron L. Belkind*

The Baltimore Sun
11 Kensington Court Place, London W8 5BJ
☎0171 460 2200   Fax 0171 460 2211
Bureau Chief *Bill Glauber*

Bloomberg Business News
City Gate House, 39–45 Finsbury Square, London EC2A 1PX
☎0171 330 7500   Fax 0171 374 6138
London Bureau Chief *Guy Collins*

Boston Globe
61 Cholmeley Crescent, Highgate, London N6 5EX
☎0181 341 0126   Fax 0181 374 7631
Bureau Chief *Kevin Cullen*

Bridge News
78 Fleet Street, London EC4Y 1HY
☎0171 842 4000   Fax 0171 583 5032
Chief Correspondent (UK) *Timothy Penn*

Business Week
1 Albemarle Street, London W1
☎0171 491 8985   Fax 0171 409 7152
Bureau Chief *Stanley Reed*

Cable News Network Inc. (CNN)
CNN House, 19–22 Rathbone Place, London W1P 1DF
☎0171 637 6800   Fax 0171 637 6868
Bureau Chief *Thomas Mintier*

CBC Television and Radio
43/51 Great Titchfield Street, London W1P 8DD
☎0171 412 9200   Fax 0171 637 1892
London Bureau Manager *Sue Phillips*

CBS News
68 Knightsbridge, London SW1X 7LL
☎0171 581 4801   Fax 0171 581 4431
Vice President/Bureau Chief *John Paxson*

Chicago Tribune Press Service
169 Piccadilly, London W1V 9DD
☎0171 499 8769   Fax 0171 499 8781
Chief European Correspondent *Ray Moseley*

CNBC
8 Bedford Avenue, London WC1B 3AP
☎0171 927 6758   Fax 0171 636 2628
Bureau Chief *Karen Nye*

Cox Newspapers
PO Box 75, East Horsley, Surrey KT24 6WA
☎01483 281432   Fax 01483 285135
Correspondent *Bert Roughton Jr*

Dallas Morning News
35 Rusthall Avenue, London W4 1BW
☎0181 994 3248   Fax 0181 994 9438
European Bureau Chief *Gregory Katz*

Dow Jones Newswires
10 Fleet Place, Limeburner Lane, London EC4M 7QN
☎0171 832 9105   Fax 0171 832 9599
Senior Editor, Europe, Middle East & Africa *Arjen Bongard*

Fairchild Publications of New York (A division of ABC Media, Inc.)
20 Shorts Gardens, London WC2H 9AU
☎0171 240 0420   Fax 0171 240 0290
Bureau Chief *James Fallon*

Forbes Magazine
51 Charles Street, London W1X 7PA
☎0171 495 0120   Fax 0171 495 0170
Contributing Editor *Richard C. Morais*

Fox News Channel
6 Centaurs Business Park, Grant Way,
Isleworth, Middlesex TW7 5QD
☎0171 805 7143   Fax 0171 805 7140
Producer *Estelle Pratt*

Futures World News
2 Royal Mint Court, Dexter House, London
EC3N 4QN
☎0171 867 8867   Fax 0171 867 1368
London Bureau Chief *Barbara Kollmeyer*

The Globe and Mail
43–51 Great Titchfield Street, London
W1P 8DD
☎0171 323 0449   Fax 0171 323 0428
European Correspondent *Alan Freeman*

International Herald Tribune
40 Marsh Wall, London E14 9TP
☎0171 510 5718   Fax 0171 987 3470
London Correspondent *Tom Buerkle*
(See entry under **National Newspapers**)

Journal of Commerce
Totara Park House, 3rd Floor, 34/36 Gray's
Inn Road, London WC1X 8HR
☎0171 430 2495   Fax 0171 837 2168
Chief European Correspondent *Bruce Barnard*

Los Angeles Times
150 Brompton Road, London SW3 1HX
☎0171 823 7315   Fax 0171 823 7308
Bureau Chief *Marjorie Miller*

Market News International
167 Fleet Street, 8th Floor, London
EC4A 2EA
☎0171 353 4462   Fax 0171 353 9122
Bureau Chief *Jon Hurdle*

National Public Radio
Room G-10 East Wing, Bush House, Strand,
London WC2B 4PH
☎0171 557 1089   Fax 0171 379 6486

NBC News Worldwide Inc.
8 Bedford Avenue, London WC1B 2NQ
☎0171 637 8655   Fax 0171 636 2628
Bureau Chief *Chris Hampson*

The New York Times
66 Buckingham Gate, London SW1E 6AU
☎0171 799 5050   Fax 0171 799 2962
Chief Correspondent *William Hoge*

Newsweek
18 Park Street, London W1Y 4HH
☎0171 629 8361   Fax 0171 408 1403
Bureau Chief *Stryker McGuire*

People Magazine
Brettenham House, Lancaster Place, London
WC2E 7TL
☎0171 322 1134   Fax 0171 322 1125
Bureau Chief *Bryan Alexander*

Philadelphia Inquirer
17 Overstone Road, London W6 0AA
☎0181 846 8054   Fax 0181 741 8849
Correspondent *Fawn Vrazo*

Reader's Digest Association Ltd
11 Westferry Circus, Canary Wharf, London
E14 4HE
☎0171 715 8000   Fax 0171 715 8716
Editor-in-Chief, British Edition
    Russell Twisk
(See entries under **UK Publishers** and
Magazines)

Time Magazine
Brettenham House, Lancaster Place, London
WC2E 7TL
☎0171 499 4080   Fax 0171 322 1230
Bureau Chief *Barry Hillenbrand*
(See entry under **Magazines**)

USA Today
69 New Oxford Street, London
WC1A 1DG
☎0171 559 5859   Fax 0171 559 5895
Chief European Correspondent
    David Lynch

Voice of America
International Press Centre, 76 Shoe Lane,
London EC4A 3JB
☎0171 410 0960   Fax 0171 410 0966
Bureau Chief/Senior Editor *Paul Francuch*

Wall Street Journal
10 Fleet Place, London EC4M 7RB
☎0171 832 9200   Fax 0171 832 9201
London Bureau Chief *Gregory Steinmetz*

Washington Post
18 Park Street, London W1Y 4HH
☎0171 629 8958   Fax 0171 629 8950
Bureau Chief *T. R. Reid*

Who Weekly

Brettenham House, Lancaster Place, London
WC2E 7TL
☎0171 322 1118   Fax 0171 322 1199
Special Correspondent *Moira Bailey*

Worldwide Television News (WTN)

The Interchange, Oval Road, Camden Lock,
London NW1 7DZ
☎0171 410 5200   Fax 0171 410 8302
President *Robert E.Burke*

Commonwealth Publishers

Australia

ACER Press
19 Prospect Hill Road, Camberwell Victoria 3124
☎00 61 3 9277 555   Fax 00 61 3 9277 5678

FOUNDED 1930. *Publishes* Education, human relations, psychology, psychiatry.

Addison Wesley Longman Australia Pty Ltd
95 Coventry Street, South Melbourne Victoria 3205
☎00 61 3 9697 0666   Fax 00 61 3 9699 2041
Email: awlaus@awl.com.au
Website: www.awl.com.au

FOUNDED 1972. Australia's largest educational publisher.

Allen & Unwin Pty Ltd
9 Atchison Street, PO Box 8500, St Leonards, Sydney NSW 2065
☎00 61 2 9901 4088   Fax 00 61 2 9906 2218

FOUNDED 1976. *Publishes* general non-fiction, art, asian studies, business, cookery, earth sciences, economics, education, fiction, gay and lesbian, government, political science, health and nutrition, history, industrial relations, literature, literary criticism, essays, general science.

Edward Arnold (Australia) Pty Ltd
PO Box 885, Kew Victoria 3101
☎00 61 3 859 9011   Fax 00 61 3 859 9141

FOUNDED 1966. Part of **Hodder & Stoughton (Australia) Pty Ltd**. *Publishes* general nonfiction: accounting, Asian studies, career development, computer science, cookery, geography, geology, government, political science, health and nutrition, law, mathematics, psychology and psychiatry.

Blackwell Science Asia Pty Ltd
PO Box 378, South Carlton Victoria 3053
☎00 61 3 9347 0300   Fax 00 61 3 9347 5552

FOUNDED 1971. Part of Blackwell Science Ltd, UK. *Publishes* general science, medicine, nursing, dentistry, engineering, computer science, mathematics, physical sciences, physics, psychology, psychiatry.

Butterworths
PO Box 345, North Ryde NSW 2113
☎00 61 2 9335 3444   Fax 00 61 2 9335 4655

FOUNDED 1910. A division of Reed International Books Australia Pty Ltd. *Publishes* accounting, business and law.

Choice Books
57 Carrington Road, Marrickville NSW 2204
☎00 61 2 9577 3333   Fax 00 61 2 9577 3377

FOUNDED 1960. *Publishes* architecture and interior design, house and home, self-help, health and nutrition, travel.

Currency Press Pty Ltd
PO Box 2287, Strawberry Hills NSW 2012
☎00 61 2 9319 5877   Fax 00 61 2 9319 3649

FOUNDED 1971. Performing arts publisher – drama, theatre, music, dance, film and video.

Dangaroo Press
PO Box 1209, Sydney NSW 2001
☎00 61 4 954 5938   Fax 00 61 4 954 6531

FOUNDED 1978. *Publishes* general non-fiction, art, literature and literary criticism, essays, poetry, social sciences, women's studies.

E. J. Dwyer (Australia) Pty Ltd
Locked Bag 71, Alexandria NSW 2015
☎00 61 2 9550 2355   Fax 00 61 2 9519 3218

FOUNDED 1904. *Publishes* self-help, marketing, social sciences, sociology, religion, theology.

Harcourt Brace & Company Australia Pty Ltd
Locked Bag 16, Marrickville NSW 2204
☎00 2 9517 8999   Fax 00 2 9517 2249

Owner *Harcourt Brace & Company (USA)*

FOUNDED 1972. *Publishes* business, education, general science, medicine, nursing, dentistry, psychology, psychiatry, veterinary science, social sciences, mathematics.

HarperCollins Publishers Pty Ltd
PO Box 321, Pymble NSW 2073
☎00 61 2 9952 5000   Fax 00 61 2 9952 5555

Owner *HarperCollins Publishers Group*

FOUNDED 1872. *Publishes* fiction and general

non-fiction, biography, children's, gardening, humour, political science, regional interests, literature and literary criticism, essays, women's studies. DIVISIONS **General Illustrated Non-fiction** *Alison Presley*; **Children's** *Brian Cook*; **Mass Market Non-fiction** *Carolyn Walsh*.

Hodder & Stoughton (Australia) Pty Ltd

PO Box 885 Victoria 3101
☎00 61 3 859 9011   Fax 00 61 3 859 9141

Owner *Hodder & Stoughton Ltd (UK)*

FOUNDED 1958. *Publishes* general non-fiction and fiction.

Hyland House Publishing Pty Ltd

Hyland House, 387–389 Clarendon Street, South Melbourne Victoria 3205
☎00 61 3 9696 9064   Fax 00 61 3 9696 9065

FOUNDED 1976. *Publishes* general non-fiction, Asian studies, cookery, crafts, games and hobbies, essays, fiction, gardening, literature and literary criticism.

Jacaranda Wiley

33 Park Road, PO Box 1226, Milton Queensland 4064
☎00 61 7 3859 9755   Fax 00 61 7 3859 9715

Owner *John Wiley & Sons Inc. (USA)*

FOUNDED 1954. *Publishes* general non-fiction and education books.

Thomas C. Lothian Pty Ltd

11 Munro Street, Port Melbourne Victoria 3027
☎00 61 3 9645 1544   Fax 00 61 3 9646 4882

FOUNDED 1910. *Publishes* general non-fiction: business, health and nutrition, New Age, self-help.

Macmillan Education Australia Pty Ltd

Locked Bag 1400, South Yarra Victoria 3141
☎00 61 3 9825 1025   Fax 00 61 3 9825 1010

FOUNDED 1896. *Publishes* accounting, economics, education, geography, geology, political science, history, management, mathematics, physics, general science, social sciences, sociology.

Maxwell Macmillan Publishing (Australia) Pty Ltd

Locked Bag 44, Botany NSW 2019
☎00 61 2 316 9444   Fax 00 61 2 316 9484

FOUNDED 1968. *Publishes* general engineering, education, literature and literary criticism, essays, general science, psychology, psychiatry, social sciences and sociology.

McGraw-Hill Book Company Australia Pty Ltd

PO Box 239, Roseville NSW 2069
☎00 61 2 9417 4288   Fax 00 61 2 9417 8872

Owner *McGraw-Hill Inc. (USA)*

FOUNDED 1964. *Publishes* accountancy, education, health and nutrition, advertising, aviation, anthropology, architecture and interior design, art, chemistry, child care and development, computer science, criminology, economics, electronics, electrical engineering, general engineering, English as a second language, environmental studies, film and video, geography, geology, journalism, industrial relations, linguistics, management, maritime, mathematics, mechanical engineering, medicine, nursing, dentistry, philosophy, photography, physics, psychology, psychiatry, sport, social sciences and sociology.

Melbourne University Press

PO Box 278, Carlton South Victoria 3053
☎00 61 3 9347 3455   Fax 00 61 3 9349 2527

FOUNDED 1922. *Publishes* general non-fiction, biography, essays, history, literature and literary criticism, natural history, psychology, psychiatry, travel.

Openbook Publishers

PO Box 1368, Adelaide SA 5001
☎00 61 8 8223 5468   Fax 00 61 8 8223 4552

FOUNDED 1913. *Publishes* religious and education books.

Pan Macmillan Australia Pty Ltd

PO Box 124, Chippendale NSW 2008
☎00 61 2 9261 5611   Fax 00 61 2 9261 5047

Owner *Macmillan Publishers Ltd (UK)*

FOUNDED 1983. *Publishes* essays, fiction, literature and literary criticism.

Penguin Books Australia Ltd

PO Box 257, Ringwood Victoria 3134
☎00 61 3 9871 2400   Fax 00 61 3 9870 9618

FOUNDED 1946. *Publishes* general non-fiction and fiction; biography, cookery, humour, literature and literary criticism, essays, science fiction and fantasy, self-help, travel.

University of Queensland Press
PO Box 42, St Lucia Queensland 4067
☎00 61 7 3365 2127   Fax 00 61 7 3365 1988
FOUNDED 1948. *Publishes* general non-fiction and fiction, literature and literary criticism, essays, poetry.

Random House Australia Pty Ltd
29 Alfred Street, First Floor, Milsons Point
NSW 2061
☎00 61 2 9954 9966   Fax 00 61 2 9954 4562
Website: randomhouse.com.au

Associate company of **Random House UK Ltd**. *Publishes* fiction and non-fiction.

Reader's Digest (Australia) Pty Ltd
PO Box 4353, Sydney NSW 2001
☎00 61 2 9690 6111   Fax 00 61 2 699 8165
FOUNDED 1946. Associate company of **Reader's Digest Association Inc.** (USA). Educational publisher.

Reed Books Australia
20 Alfred Street, First Floor, Milsons Point
NSW 2061
☎00 61 2 9954 9966   Fax 00 61 2 9954 4562
Owner *Random House*
FOUNDED 1967. *Publishes* fiction and general non-fiction.

Rigby Heinemann
22 Salmon Street, Port Melbourne
Victoria 3207
☎00 61 3 9245 7111   Fax 00 61 3 9245 7333
Owner Reed Elsevier Plc
FOUNDED 1982. *Publishes* art, chemical engineering, environmental studies, geography, geology, health and nutrition, history, mathematics, physics.

Scholastic Australia Pty Limited
PO Box 579, Railway Crescent, Gosford
NSW 2250
☎00 61 24 328 3555   Fax 00 61 24 323 3827
Owner *Scholastic, Inc. (USA)*
FOUNDED 1968. *Publishes* education titles.

Science Press
Fitzroy & Chapel Streets, Marrickville
NSW 2204
☎00 61 2 516 1122   Fax 00 61 2 550 1915
FOUNDED 1945. Educational publisher.

Simon & Schuster Australia
PO Box 507, East Roseville NSW 2069
☎00 61 2 9417 3255   Fax 00 61 2 9417 2353
FOUNDED 1987. Part of **Simon & Schuster Consumer Group**, USA. *Publishes* general non-fiction.

Transworld Publishers Pty Ltd
Private Bag 12, Neutral Bay NSW 2089
☎00 61 2 9908 9900   Fax 00 61 2 9953 8563
Owner *Bertelsmann AG (Germany)*
FOUNDED 1980. *Publishes* non-fiction and fiction – romance, science fiction, humour.

University of Western Australia Press
The University of Western Australia,
Nedlands WA 6907
☎00 61 8 9380 3670   Fax 00 61 8 9380 1027
FOUNDED 1954. *Publishes* general non-fiction, essays, literature and literary criticism, history, social sciences and sociology, natural history, autobiography.

Canada

Addison Wesley Longman Canada
Box 580, 26 Prince Andrew Place, Don Mills
Ontario M3C 2T8
☎001 416 447 5101   Fax 001 416 443 0948
Website: www.awl.com/canada
FOUNDED 1967. Fourth-largest educational publisher in Canada. Acquired **HarperCollins'** educational list in 1997. Publishes in English and French.

Arnold Publishing Ltd
11016 127th Street, Edmonton Alberta
T5M 0T2
☎001 403 454 7477   Fax 001 403 454 7463
Website: www.arnold.ca/
FOUNDED 1967. Educational textbooks and CD-ROMS.

Butterworths Canada
75 Clegg Road, Markham Ontario L6G 1A1
☎001 905 479 2665   Fax 001 905 479 2826
Website: www.butterworths.ca
FOUNDED 1912. Division of Reed Elsevier plc. *Publishes* law and accountancy: books, CD-ROMs, journals, newsletters, law reports and newspapers.

Canadian Publishing Corp
164 Commander Boulevard, Scarborough
Ontario M1S 3C7
☎001 416 293 8141   Fax 001 416 293 9009
FOUNDED 1844. *Publishes* fiction, non-fiction
and school textbooks.

Canadian Scholars' Press, Inc
180 Bloor Street W, Suite 1202, Toronto
Ontario M5S 2V6
☎001 416 929 2774   Fax 001 416 929 1926
Email: info@cspi.org
Website: www.interlog.com/~cspi/cspi.html
FOUNDED 1987. *Publishes* scholarly books in
English and French.

Fenn Publishing Co Ltd
34 Nixon Road, Bolton Ontario L7E 1W2
☎001 905 951 6600   Fax 001 905 951 6601
Website: www.hbfenn.com
FOUNDED 1977. *Publishes* fiction and non-
fiction, children's.

Fitzhenry & Whiteside Limited
195 Allstate Parkway, Markham Ontario
L3R 4T8
☎001 905 477 9700   Fax 001 905 477 9179
Email: godwit@fitzhenry.ca
Website: www.fitzhenry.ca
FOUNDED 1966. *Publishes* reference and chil-
dren's books; educational material.

Golden Books Publishing (Canada) Inc
200 Sheldon Drive, Cambridge Ontario
N1R 5X2
☎001 519 623 3590   Fax 001 519 623 3598
FOUNDED 1942. *Publishes* (in English and
French) juvenile and adult books, Bibles, cookery, crafts, gardening.

Harcourt Brace & Co Canada Ltd
55 Horner Avenue, Toronto Ontario
M8Z 4X6
☎001 416 255 4491   Fax 001 416 255 4046
Website: www.harcourtbrace-canada.com
FOUNDED 1922. A subsidiary of **Harcourt
Brace & Co**. *Publishes* educational material.

HarperCollins Publishers Limited
55 Avenue Road, Suite 2900, Hazelton Lanes,
Toronto Ontario M5R 3L2
☎001 416 975 9334   Fax 001 416 975 9884
FOUNDED 1989. *Publishes* fiction and non-
fiction, children's and religious.

Irwin Publishing
325 Humber College Blvd., Toronto Ontario
M9W 7C3
☎001 416 798 0424   Fax 001 416 798 1384
Email: irwin@irwin-pub.com
Website: www.irwin-pub.com
FOUNDED 1945. *Publishes* (in English and
French) educational.

ITP Nelson
1120 Birchmount Road, Scarborough Ontario
M1K 5G4
☎001 416 752 9100   Fax 001 416 752 9646
Website: www.nelson.com/nelson.html
FOUNDED 1914. Division of Thomson Canada
Ltd. *Publishes* educational, professional and ref-
erence.

Little, Brown & Co (Canada) Ltd
148 Yorkville Avenue, Toronto Ontario
M5R 1C2
☎001 416 967 3888   Fax 001 416 967 4591
FOUNDED 1953. *Publishes* fiction and non-
fiction.

Macmillan Canada
29 Birch Avenue, Toronto Ontario M4V 1E2
☎001 416 963 8830   Fax 001 416 923 4821
FOUNDED 1905. Division of Canada Publishing
Corp. *Publishes* fiction and non-fiction.

McClelland & Stewart Inc
481 University Avenue, Suite 900, Toronto
Ontario M5G 2E9
☎001 416 598 1114   Fax 001 416 598 7764
FOUNDED 1906. *Publishes* fiction and non-
fiction, poetry.

McClelland–Bantam Inc
105 Bond Street, Toronto Ontario M5B 1Y3
☎001 416 340 0777   Fax 001 416 977 8488
FOUNDED 1977. Subsidiary of **Bantam
Doubleday Dell**. *Publishes* fiction and non-
fiction, mainly by Canadian authors.

McGill–Queen's University Press
3430 McTavish Street, Montreal Quebec
H3A 1X9
☎001 514 398 3750   Fax 001 514 398 4333
Email: mqup@printing.lan.mcgill.ca
Website: www.mcgill.ca/mqupress
FOUNDED 1969. *Publishes* (in English and
French) scholarly and non-fiction.

McGraw-Hill Ryerson Ltd

300 Water Street, Whitby Ontario L1N 9B6
☎001 905 430 5000   Fax 001 905 430 5020
Website: www.mcgrawhill.ca
FOUNDED 1944. Subsidiary of the McGraw-Hill Companies. *Publishes* education, professional and general trade.

New Star Books Ltd

2504 York Avenue, Vancouver BC V6K 1E3
☎001 604 738 9429   Fax 001 604 738 9332
Email: newstar@pinc.com
FOUNDED 1974. *Publishes* social issues and current affairs, fiction, literature, history, international politics, feminist, gay and lesbian studies.

Penguin Books Canada Ltd

10 Alcorn Avenue, Suite 300, Toronto
Ontario M4V 3B2
☎001 416 925 2249   Fax 001 416 925 0068
Email: oper@penguin.ca
Website: www.penguin.ca
FOUNDED 1974. *Publishes* fiction and non-fiction books and audio cassettes.

Prentice Hall Canada

1870 Birchmount Road, Scarborough Ontario
M1P 2J7
☎001 416 293 3621   Fax 001 416 299 2529
Website: www.phcanada.com
FOUNDED 1960. *Publishes* education, textbooks, reference and non-fiction.

Random House of Canada

2775 Matheson Blvd. East, Mississauga
Ontario L4W 4P7
☎001 905 624 0672   Fax 001 905 624 6217
FOUNDED 1944. *Publishes* fiction and non-fiction and children's.

Scholastic Canada Ltd

175 Hillmount Road, Markham Ontario
L6C 1Z7
☎001 905 883 5300   Fax 001 905 883 4113
Website: www.scholastic.ca
FOUNDED 1957. *Publishes* (in English and French) children's books and educational material.

Tundra Books Inc

481 University Avenue, Suite 802, Toronto
Ontario M5G 2E9
☎001 416 598 4786   Fax 001 416 598 0247
FOUNDED 1967. Division of **McClelland & Stewart Inc**. *Publishes* (in English and French) juvenile and art books.

John Wiley & Sons Canada Ltd

22 Worcester Road, Etobicoke Ontario
M9W 1L1
☎001 416 236 4433   Fax 001 416 236 4447
Website: www.wiley.com
FOUNDED 1968. *Publishes* professional, reference and textbooks.

Women's Press

517 College Street. Suite 302, Toronto
Ontario M6G 4A2
☎001 416 921 2425   Fax 001 416 921 4428
Email: wompress@web.apc.org
FOUNDED 1972. *Publishes* social issues, non-fiction, fiction and children's.

India

Addison Wesley Longman Pte Ltd

90 New Raidhani Enclave, Ground Floor,
Delhi 110 092
☎00 91 11 2059850   Fax 00 91 11 2059852
Owned by **Addison Wesley Longman** USA.
Educational publishers.

Affiliated East West Press Pvt Ltd

104 Nirmal Tower, 26 Barakhamba Road,
New Delhi 110 001
☎00 91 11 331 5398   Fax 00 91 11 326 0538
FOUNDED 1962. *Publishes* Aeronautics, aviation, agriculture, anthropology, biological sciences, chemistry, engineering (chemical, civil, electrical, mechanical), computer science, economics, electronics, mathematics, microcomputers, physical sciences, physics, general science, veterinary science, women's studies.

Arnold Heinman Publishers (India) Pvt Ltd

AB-9, 1st Floor, Safdarjung Enclave, New
Delhi 110 029
☎00 91 11 688 3422   Fax 00 91 11 687 7571
Associate company of **Edward Arnold (Publishers) Ltd**, UK. *Publishes* fiction, poetry, essays, literature, literary criticism, art, general engineering, government, political science, philosophy, religion, medicine, nursing and dentistry, social sciences and sociology.

S. Chand & Co Ltd

Ram Nagar, PO Box 5733, New Delhi
110 055
☎00 91 11 777 2080   Fax 00 91 11 777 7446
FOUNDED 1917. *Publishes* art, business, economics, government, political science,

medicine, nursing, dentistry, philosophy, general science, technology.

Current Books
Round West, Trichur 680 001
☎00 91 487 335642   Fax 00 91 487 335660
FOUNDED 1952. *Publishes* fiction and general non-fiction.

General Book Depot
PB 1220, 1691 Nai Sarak, Delhi 110 006
☎00 91 11 326 3695   Fax 00 91 11 371 2710
FOUNDED 1936. *Publishes* general nonfiction; business, career development, how-to, English as a second languages, language, linguistics, self-help, travel.

HarperCollins Publishers India Pty Ltd
7/61 Ansari Road, Daryaganj, New Delhi 110 002
☎00 91 11 327 8586   Fax 00 91 11 327 7294
Publishes fiction, poetry, biography and education.

Hind Pocket Books Private Ltd
18–19 Dilshad Garden Road, Delhi 110 095
☎00 91 11 202 046   Fax 00 91 11 202 332
Publishes fiction and general non-fiction; biography, how-to and self-help.

Jaico Publishing House
121–125 Mahatma Gandhi Road, Mumbai 400 023
☎00 91 22 267 4501   Fax 00 91 22 204 1673
FOUNDED 1945. *Publishes* biography, business, languages, linguistics, health and nutrition, cookery, law, criminology, astrology, occult, philosophy, religion, general engineering, economics, humour, history, government, political science, psychology, psychiatry.

Macmillan India
315/316 Raheja Chambers, 12 Museum Road, Bangalore 560 001
☎00 91 80 558 7878   Fax 00 91 80 558 8713
FOUNDED 1903. *Publishes* fiction, engineering (chemical and general), science (computer and general), history, philosophy, chemistry, medicine, nursing and dentistry, psychiatry, psychology, biological sciences, mathematics, social sciences, sociology, government, political science, management.

Munshiram Manoharlal Publishers Pvt Ltd
PO Box 5715, New Delhi 110 055
☎00 91 11 777 1668   Fax 00 91 11 777 3650
FOUNDED 1952. *Publishes* art, architecture and interior design, anthropology, archaeology, astrology, occult, religion (Buddhist, Hindu, Islamic), philosophy, history, language arts and linguistics, music, dance, drama, theatre, Asian studies.

National Book Trust India
India A–5, Green Park, New Delhi 110 016
☎00 91 11 664 020   Fax 00 91 11 685 1795
FOUNDED 1957. *Publishes* human relations and foreign countries.

National Publishing House
23 Daryaganj, New Delhi 110 002
☎00 91 11 327 4161
FOUNDED 1950. *Publishes* human relations, ethnicity, social sciences and sociology.

Orient Longman
3–6–272 Himayat Nagar, Hyderabad 500 029
☎00 91 842 240305   Fax 00 91 842 230100
FOUNDED 1948. *Publishes* fiction and general non-fiction; business, biography, biological sciences, chemistry, chemical and electrical engineering, child care and development, civil engineering, computer and general science, cookery, crafts, games, hobbies, economics, education, electronics, English as a second language, environmental studies, genealogy, geography, geology, government and political science, history, literature, literary criticism, essays, management, mathematics, medicine, nursing and dentistry, philosophy, physics, religion (Hindu), social sciences, sociology, travel, women's studies.

Oxford University Press
PO Box 43, New Delhi 110 001
☎00 91 11 202 1029   Fax 00 91 11 373 2312
FOUNDED 1912. *Publishes* business, biography, developing countries, economics, history, literature, literary criticism, essays, philosophy, religion (Hindu), sociology, natural history, politics, culture studies, gender studies, ecology, science and medicine.

Rajpal & Sons
1590 Madarsa Road, Kashmere Gate, Delhi 110 006
☎00 91 11 296 9812   Fax 00 91 11 296 7791
FOUNDED 1891. *Publishes* fiction, literature,

literary criticism, essays, human relations, general science.

Tata McGraw-Hill Publishing Co Ltd

4/12 Asaf Ali Road, 3rd Floor, New Delhi 110 002

☎00 91 11 278 251   Fax 00 91 11 327 8253

FOUNDED 1970. Parent company **The McGraw Hill Companies**, USA. *Publishes* general engineering and science, business, social sciences, sociology and management.

Vidyarthi Mithram Press

Baker Road, Kottayam 686 001

☎00 91 481 563281   Fax 00 91 481 562616

FOUNDED 1928. *Publishes* child care and development, cookery, drama and theatre, economics, biography, biological sciences, chemistry and chemical engineering, computer science.

A. H. Wheeler & Co Ltd

411 Surya Kiran Building, 19 K G Marg, New Delhi 110 001

☎00 91 11 331 2629 Fax 00 91 11 335 7798

FOUNDED 1879. *Publishes* computer science, behavioural sciences, accountancy, advertising, business, career development, civil engineering, communications.

New Zealand

Addison Wesley Longman New Zealand Ltd

Private Bag 102908, North Shore Mail Centre, Glenfield, Auckland 10

☎00 64 9 444 4968   Fax 00 64 9 444 4957

FOUNDED 1968. Educational publishers.

Butterworths of New Zealand Ltd

CPO Box 472, Wellington 1

☎00 64 4 385 1479   Fax 00 64 4 385 1598

FOUNDED 1914. *Publishes* accountancy, business, law and taxation.

Canterbury University Press

University of Canterbury, Private Bag 4800, Christchurch

☎00 64 3 364 2914   Fax 00 64 3 364 2044

FOUNDED 1960. *Publishes* general non-fiction; biography, biological sciences, history and natural history.

The Caxton Press

PO Box 25088, Christchurch

☎00 64 3 366 8516   Fax 00 64 3 365 7840

FOUNDED 1935. *Publishes* general non-fiction; biography, gardening and plants.

HarperCollins Publishers (New Zealand) Ltd

PO Box 1, Auckland

☎00 64 9 443 9400   Fax 00 64 9 443 9403

FOUNDED 1888. *Publishes* fiction, art, humour, natural history, religion, biography, gardening, sport, travel, self-help.

Hodder Moa Beckett Publishers Ltd

PO Box 3858, North Shore Mail Centre, Auckland

☎00 64 9 444 3640   Fax 00 64 9 444 3646

FOUNDED 1971. Owned by **Hodder Headline Ltd**, UK. *Publishes* fiction and general non-fiction.

University of Otago Press

PO Box 56, Dunedin

☎00 64 3 479 8807   Fax 00 64 3 479 8385

Email: university.press@otago.ac.nz

FOUNDED 1958. *Publishes* fiction, essays, literature, literary criticism, history, education, biography, anthropology, natural history, environmental studies, government and political science.

Random House New Zealand

Private Bag 102950, Auckland 10

☎00 64 9 444 7197   Fax 00 64 9 444 7524

Email: enquiries@randomhouse.co.uk

Website: www.randomhouse.co.uk

FOUNDED 1977. *Publishes* fiction and general non-fiction. Parent company **Random House Inc**, USA.

Reed Publishing (NZ) Ltd

Private Bag 34901, Birkenhead, Auckland 10

☎00 64 9 480 6039   Fax 00 64 9 419 1212

FOUNDED 1988. *Publishes* fiction and general non-fiction.

Scholastic New Zealand Ltd

Private Bag 94407, Greenmount, Auckland

☎00 64 9 274 8112   Fax 00 64 9 274 8114

FOUNDED 1962. Owned by **Scholastic, Inc.**, USA. Educational publishers.

Southern Press Ltd
R D 1, Porirua 6221
☎00 64 4 239 9063   Fax 00 64 4 349 9835
FOUNDED 1971. *Publishes* aviation, aeronautics, maritime, transport, technology, mechanical and civil engineering, archaeology.

Tandem Press
PO Box 34272, Birkenhead, Auckland 10
☎00 64 9 480 1452   Fax 00 64 9 480 1455
FOUNDED 1990. *Publishes* fiction and general non-fiction; cookery, business, alternative, ethnicity, health and nutrition, photography, psychology, psychiatry, self-help, women's studies.

Victoria University Press
PO Box 600, Wellington
☎00 64 4 496 6580   Fax 00 64 4 496 6581
Email: victoria-press@vuw.ac.nz
FOUNDED 1979. *Publishes* general science, government, political science, essays, poetry, literature, literary criticism, drama, theatre, history, social sciences and sociology, anthropology, language and linguistics, communications, law, architecture and interior design.

Viking Sevenseas NZ Ltd
PO Box 152, Paraparaumu, Wellington
☎00 64 4 297 1990
FOUNDED 1963. *Publishes* general non-fiction; astrology, occult, health and nutrition, medicine, nursing and dentistry, ethnicity.

South Africa

Books of Africa (Pty) Ltd
PO Box 1516, Capetown 8000
☎00 27 21 888316   Fax 00 27 21 888316
FOUNDED 1962. *Publishes* biography, history, ethnicity and art.

Butterworths South Africa
PO Box 792, Durban 4000
☎00 27 31 294147   Fax 00 27 31 286350
Publishes general science, medicine, nursing and dentistry, economics, education, law.

Flesch Financial Publications (Pty) Ltd
PO Box 3473, Cape Town 8000
☎00 27 21 461 7472   Fax 00 27 21 461 3758

FOUNDED 1966. *Publishes* aviation, aeronautics, maritime, animals, pets, business.

Heinemann Publishers (Pty) Ltd
66 Park Lane, Sandton, Johannesburg 2146
☎00 27 11 322 8600   Fax 00 27 11 322 8615
FOUNDED 1986. Parent company: **Reed Educational & Professional Publishing**, UK. *Publishes* economics, education, English as a second language, mathematics, mechanical engineering.

Maskew Miller Longman (Pty) Ltd
PO Box 396, Cape Town 8000
☎00 27 21 531 4049   Fax 00 27 21 531 4049
FOUNDED 1893. *Publishes* education, language and linguistics.

University of Natal Press
PB X01, Scottsville, Pietermaritzburg 3209
☎00 27 331 260 5225Fax 00 27 331 260 5599
FOUNDED 1947. *Publishes* essays, literature and literary criticism, natural history, history, women's studies.

Oxford University Press Southern Africa
PO Box 12119, N1 City 7463
☎00 27 21 595 4400   Fax 00 27 21 595 4439
FOUNDED 1915. Academic publishers. Parent company: **Oxford University Press**, UK.

Ravan Press (Pty) Ltd
PO Box 145, Randburg, Johannesburg 2125
☎00 27 11 789 7636   Fax 00 27 11 789 7653
FOUNDED 1972. Part of Hodder & Stoughton Educational South Africa. *Publishes* fiction and general non-fiction; anthropology, biography, business, economics, education, environmental studies, ethnicity, government, political science, history, labour and industrial relations, management, music, dance, social studies and sociology, women's studies.

Shuter & Shooter (Pty) Ltd
PO Box 109, Pietermaritzburg 3200
☎00 27 331 427419   Fax 00 27 331 943096
FOUNDED 1925. *Publishes* general non-fiction; biography, history, ethnicity, general science, technology, social sciences and sociology.

Struik Publishers (Pty) Ltd
PO Box 1144, Cape Town 8000
☎00 27 21 216740   Fax 00 27 21 4624379

FOUNDED 1962. *Publishes* child care and development, cookery, gardening, environmental studies, natural history.

Witwatersrand University Press
PO Wits, Johannesburg 2050
☎00 27 11 484 5907   Fax 00 27 11 484 5971

FOUNDED 1922. *Publishes* essays, literature and literary criticism, drama, theatre, history, business, anthropology, archaeology, natural history, religion (Jewish), medicine, nursing and dentistry.

Professional Associations and Societies

ABSA
See **Association for Business Sponsorship of the Arts**

ABSW
See **Association of British Science Writers**

Academi (Yr Academi Gymreig)
3rd Floor, Mount Stuart House, Mount Stuart Square, Cardiff CF10 6DQ
☎01222 472266   Fax 01222 492930
Email: academi@dial.pipex.com
Website: dspace.dial.pipex.com/academi
North Wales office: Tŷ Newydd,
Llanystumdwy, Cricieth, Gwynedd
LL52 0LW
☎01766 522817
Email: academi.gog@dial.pipex.com
Chief Executive *Peter Finch*

Academi is the trading name of Yr Academi Gymreig , the national society of Welsh writers. The Society exists to promote the literature of Wales. Yr Academi Gymreig was FOUNDED in 1959 as an association of Welsh language writers. An English language section was established in 1968. Membership, for those who have made a significant contribution to the literature of Wales, is by invitation. Membership currently stands at 300. The Academi runs courses, competitions (including the **Cardiff International Poetry Competition**), conferences, tours by authors, festivals and represents the interests of Welsh writers and Welsh writing both inside Wales and beyond. Its publications include *Taliesin*, a quarterly literary journal in the Welsh language, *The Oxford Companion to the Literature of Wales*, *The Welsh Academy English-Welsh Dictionary*, and a variety of translated works.

In 1998 the Academi won the franchise from the Arts Council of Wales to run the Welsh National Literature Promotion Agency. The new, much enlarged organisation now administers a variety of schemes including Writers on Tour, Writers Residencies and a number of literature development projects. It promotes an annual literary festival in North Wales, runs its own programme of literary activity and publishes *A470*, a bi-monthly literature information magazine. The Academi is also in receipt of a lottery grant to publish the first Welsh National Encyclopedia. This is expected to be ready towards the end of 2001.

Those with an interest in literature in Wales can become an associate of the Academi (which carries a range of benefits). Rates are £15 p.a. (waged); £7.50 (unwaged).

ALCS
See **Authors' Licensing & Collecting Society**

Alliance of Literary Societies
22 Belmont Crescent, Havant, Hampshire PO9 3PU
☎01705 475855   Fax 08700 560330
Website: www.sndc.demon.co.uk/als.htm
President *Gabriel Woolf*
Honorary Secretary *Mrs R. Culley*

FOUNDED 1974. Acts as a liaison body between member societies and, when necessary, as a pressure group. Deals with enquiries and assists in preserving buildings and places with literary connections and in the formation of new societies. Over 80 societies hold membership. A directory of literary societies and a list of speakers are maintained. Produces an annual fanzine, *Chapter One*, which is distributed to affiliated societies, carrying news of personalities, activities and events. Details of this and advertising rates from Kenneth Oultram, Editor, Chapter One, Clatterwick Hall, Little Leigh, Northwich, Cheshire CW8 4RJ (☎01606 891303).

Arvon Foundation
Totleigh Barton, Sheepwash, Beaworthy, Devon EX21 5NS
☎01409 231338   Fax 01409 231338
Email: t-barton@arvonfoundation.org
Website: www.arvonfoundation.org/index/
Lumb Bank, Heptonstall, Hebden Bridge, West Yorkshire HX7 6DF
☎01422 843714   Fax 01422 843714
Email: l-bank@arvonfoundation.org
Moniack Mhor, Teavarran, Kiltarlity, Beauly, Inverness-shire IV4 7HT
☎01463 741675
Email: m-mhor@arvonfoundation.org
President *Terry Hands*

Chairman *Sir Robin Chichester-Clark*
National Director *David Pease*
FOUNDED 1968. Offers people of any age (over 16) and any background the opportunity to live and work with professional writers. Five-day residential courses are held throughout the year at Arvon's three centres, covering poetry, fiction, drama, writing for children, songwriting and the performing arts. A number of bursaries towards the cost of course fees are available for those on low incomes, the unemployed, students and pensioners. Runs a biennial poetry competition (see under **Prizes**).

Association for Business Sponsorship of the Arts (ABSA)

Nutmeg House, 60 Gainsford Street, Butlers Wharf, London SE1 2NY
☎0171 378 8143   Fax 0171 407 7527
Email: absa@absa.org.uk
Website: www.absa.org.uk

ABSA exists to promote and encourage partnerships between the private sector and the arts, to their mutual benefit and to that of the community at large. It provides a wide range of services to over 300 business members as well as to 600 arts organisations and museums through the ABSA Development Forum. To enable individual business people to share their skills with the arts, ABSA manages the Placement Scheme and the NatWest Board Bank through its Business in the Arts programme. On behalf of the Department for Culture, Media and Sport and the Department of Education for Northern Ireland, Absa manages the Pairing Scheme, an incentive programme for new and established sponsors of the arts. Increasingly, ABSA is working with forward-looking businesses to determine the future of business/arts partnerships through its Creative Forum for Culture and the Economy. With the support of its Patron, HRH The Prince of Wales, it is exploring and developing new ways for business, the arts and society to interact. ABSA runs its programmes from London and through a network of offices nationwide.

Association of American Correspondents in London

12 Norwich Street, London EC4A 1BP
☎0171 353 1515   Fax 0171 936 2229
Contact *Sandra Marshall*
Subscription £90 (Organisations)
FOUNDED 1919 to serve the professional interests of its member organisations, promote social

cooperation among them, and maintain the ethical standards of the profession. (An extra £30 is charged for each department of an organisation which requires separate listing in the Association's handbook.)

Association of American Publishers, Inc

71 Fifth Avenue, 2nd Floor, New York, NY 10003 USA
☎001 212 255 0200   Fax 001 212 255 7007
Email: tmckee@aap.publishers.org
Website: www.publishers.org
Also at: 1718 Connecticut Avenue, NW, Washington, DC 20009
☎001 202 232 3335   Fax 001 202 745 0694
Contact *Tom McKee*
FOUNDED 1970. For information about subscription rates and membership, contact the Association's website.

Association of Authors' Agents

c/o Sheil Land Associates Ltd, 43 Doughty Street, London WC1N 2LF
☎0171 405 9351   Fax 0171 831 2127
President *Vivien Green*
Membership £50 p.a.
FOUNDED 1974. Membership voluntary. The AAA maintains a code of practice, provides a forum for discussion, and represents its members in issues affecting the profession.

Association of British Editors

Broadvision, 49 Frederick Road, Edgbaston, Birmingham B15 1HN
☎0121 455 7949   Fax 0121 454 6187
Email: info@broadv.u-net.com.uk
Executive Director/Honorary Secretary *Jock Gallagher*
Subscription £50 p.a.
FOUNDED 1985. Independent organisation for the study and enhancement of journalism worldwide. Established to protect and promote the freedom of the Press. Members are expected to 'maintain the dignity and rights of the profession; consider and sustain standards of professional conduct; exchange ideas for the advancement of professional ideals; work for the solution of common problems'. Membership is limited, but open to persons who have immediate charge of editorial or news policies in all media. *Publishes* quarterly (March, June, Sept., Dec.) *The British Editor*. Negotiates rates for articles re media freedom/standards.

Association of British Science Writers (ABSW)

23 Savile Row, London W1X 2NB
☎0171 439 1205   Fax 0171 973 3051
Administrator *Barbara Drillsma*
Membership £25 p.a.; £20 (Associate)

ABSW has played a central role in improving the standards of science journalism in the UK over the last 40 years. The Association seeks to improve standards by means of networking, lectures and organised visits to institutional laboratories and industrial research centres. Puts members in touch with major projects in the field and with experts worldwide. A member of the European Union of Science Journalists' Associations, ABSW is able to offer heavily subsidised places on visits to research centres in most other European countries, and hosts reciprocal visits to Britain by European journalists. Membership open to those who are considered to be *bona fide* science writers/editors, or their film/TV/radio equivalents, who earn a substantial part of their income by promoting public interest in and understanding of science. Runs the administration and judging of the **Glaxo Science Writers' Awards**, for outstanding science journalism in newspapers, journals and broadcasting.

Association of Christian Writers

73 Lodge Hill Road, Farnham, Surrey
GU10 3RB
☎01252 715746   Fax 01252 715746
Email: christian-writers@dial.pipex.com
Website: dspace.dial.pipex.com/christian-writers
Administrator *Mr W. G. Crawford*
Subscription £10 (Single); £12.50 (Family & Overseas)

FOUNDED in 1971 'to inspire and equip men and women to use their talents and skills with integrity to devise, write and market excellent material which comes from a Christian worldview. In this way we seek to be an influence for good and for God in this generation.' *Publishes* a quarterly magazine. Runs three training events each year, biennial conference, competitions, postal workshops, area groups, prayer support and manuscript criticism. Charity No. 1069839.

Association of Freelance Journalists

5 Beacon Flats, Kings Haye Road,
Wellington, Telford, Shropshire TF1 1RG
W'site:members.tripod.com/~media_2/afj.html
Founding President *Martin Scholes*
Subscription £30 p.a.

Offers membership to all who work in the field of journalism but especially local correspondents, stringers, freelance journalists, those at the beginning of their careers or long established. Also welcomes people who make a modest sum writing for the specialist press or those who write for a hobby and who want to make a career out of their writing. Members receive a laminated press card, regular newsletters, a free postal advice service, the opportunity to network with other members, a Website, discounts on products and services, etc. At present the AFJ is organising several new services including a free handbook to all members and a correspondence writing course with a 'substantial' discount to members.

Association of Freelance Writers

Sevendale House, 7 Dale Street, Manchester
M1 1JB
☎0161 228 2362   Fax 0161 228 3533
Contact *Angela Cox*
Subscription £29 p.a.

FOUNDED in 1995 to help and advise new and established freelance writers. Members receive a copy of *Freelance Market News* each month which gives news, views and the latest advice and guidelines about publications at home and abroad. Other benefits include one free appraisal of prose or poetry each year, reduced entry to **The Writers Bureau** writing competition, reduced fees for writing seminars and discounts on books for writers.

Association of Golf Writers

106 Byng Drive, Potters Bar, Hertfordshire
EN6 1UJ
☎01707 654112   Fax 01707 654112
Honorary Secretary *Mark Garrod*

FOUNDED 1938. Aims to cooperate with golfing bodies to ensure best possible working conditions.

Association of Illustrators

1–5 Beehive Place, London SW9 7QR
☎0171 733 9155   Fax 0171 733 1199
Contact *Samantha Taylor*

FOUNDED 1973 to promote illustration and illustrators' rights, and encourage professional standards. The AOI is a non-profit-making trade association dedicated to its members, to protecting their interests and promoting their work. Talks, seminars, a newsletter, regional groups, legal and portfolio advice as well as a number of related publications such as *Rights, The Illustrator's Guide to Professional Practice*, and *Survive, The Illustrator's Guide to a Professional Career*.

Association of Independent Libraries

Leeds Library, 18 Commercial Street, Leeds, West Yorkshire LS1 6AL
☎01132 453071
Chairman *Geoffrey Forster*

Established to 'further the advancement, conservation and restoration of a little-known but important living portion of our cultural heritage'. Members include the **London Library, Devon & Exeter Institution, Linen Hall Library** and **Plymouth Proprietary Library**.

Association of Learned and Professional Society Publishers

South House, The Street, Clapham, Worthing, West Sussex BN13 3UU
☎01903 871686   Fax 01903 871286
Secretary-General *Sally Morris*

FOUNDED 1972 to foster the publishing activities of learned societies and academic and professional bodies. Membership is limited to such organisations, those publishing on behalf of member organisations and those closely associated with the work of academic publishers.

Association of Scottish Motoring Writers

c/o Scottish and Universal Newspapers, 5/15 Bank Street, Airdrie ML6 6AF
☎01236 748048   Fax 01236 748098
Secretary *John Murdoch*
Subscription £45 (Full); £25 (Associate)

FOUNDED 1961. Aims to co-ordinate the activities of, and provide shared facilities for, motoring writers resident in Scotland. Membership is by invitation only.

Author-Publisher Network

SKS, St Aldhelm, 20 Paul Street, Frome, Somerset BA11 1DX
☎01373 451777
Chairman *Clive Brown*
Administrator *Vicky Knowles*
Subscription £25 (p.a.)

FOUNDED 1993. The association aims to provide an active forum for writers publishing their own work. An information network of ideas and opportunities for self-publishers. Explores the business and technology of writing and publishing. Regular newsletter, supplements, seminars and workshops, etc.

Authors North

c/o The Society of Authors, 84 Drayton Gardens, London SW10 9SB
☎0171 373 6642
Secretary *Peter Riley*

A group within **The Society of Authors** which organises meetings for members living in the North of England.

Authors' Club

40 Dover Street, London W1X 3RB
☎0171 499 8581   Fax 0171 409 0913
Secretary *Mrs Ann de la Grange*

FOUNDED in 1891 by Sir Walter Besant, the Authors' Club welcomes as members writers, agents, publishers, critics, journalists, academics and anyone involved with literature. Administers the **Authors' Club Best First Novel Award; Sir Banister Fletcher Award** and organises regular talks and dinners with well-known guest speakers. Membership fee: apply to secretary.

Authors' Licensing & Collecting Society (ALCS)

Marlborough Court, 14–18 Holborn, London EC1N 2LE
☎0171 395 0600   Fax 0171 395 0660
Email: alcs@alcs.co.uk
Website: www.alcs.co.uk
Acting Secretary General
   Dafydd Wyn Phillips
Subscription £5.88 incl. VAT (UK; free to members of **The Society of Authors, The Writers' Guild, NUJ, BAJ** and **CIOJ**); £5 (EU residents); £7 (Overseas)

FOUNDED 1977. The British collecting society for all writers and their heirs, ALCS is a non-profit organisation whose principle purpose is to ensure that hard-to-collect revenues due to authors are efficiently collected and speedily distributed. Established to give assistance to writers in their battle to make a better living through the protection and exploitation of collective rights, ALCS has distributed some £32m. to British writers since its creation. On joining, members license ALCS to administer on their behalf those rights which an author is unable to exercise as an individual or which are best handled on a collective basis. Chief among these are: photocopying, cable retransmission (including the fees for BBC Prime and BBC World Service programming), rental and lending rights (but not British Public Lending Right), off-air recording, electronic rights, the performing right and public reception of broadcasts. The society is a prime resource and a leading authority on copyright matters and writers' collective interests. It maintains a watching brief on all matters affecting copyright both in Britain and abroad, making representations to UK government authorities and the EU. Consult the ALCS Website or contact the office for application forms and further information.

BACB
See **British Association of Communicators in Business**

BAFTA (British Academy of Film and Television Arts)
195 Piccadilly, London W1V 0LN
☎0171 734 0022   Fax 0171 734 1792
Subscription £160 p.a. (Over 30); £78 p.a. (Under 30); £83 p.a. (Country); £72 p.a. (Overseas); £50 (Initial entry fee)

FOUNDED 1947. Membership limited to 'those who have contributed to the industry' over a minimum period of three years. Best known for its annual awards ceremonies, now held separately for film, television, children's programmes and interactive entertainment, the Academy runs a full programme of screenings, seminars, masterclasses, debates, lectures, etc. It also actively supports training and educational projects.

Also BAFTA Scotland, BAFTA Wales, BAFTA North, BAFTA LA, BAFTA East Coast (USA) run separate programmes and, in the case of Scotland and Wales, hold their own awards.

BAPLA (British Association of Picture Libraries and Agencies)
18 Vine Hill, London EC1R 5DX
☎0171 713 1780   Fax 0171 713 1211
Email: bapla@bapla.org.uk
Website: www.bapla.org.uk

Represents the interests of the British picture library industry. Works on UK and worldwide levels on such issues as copyright and technology. Offers researchers free telephone referrals from its database and through its Website. With access to 350 million images through its membership, BAPLA is a good place to start. *Publishes* a Directory, a definitive guide to UK picture libraries and a quarterly magazine, *Light Box*.

BASCA (British Academy of Songwriters, Composers and Authors)
The Penthouse, 4 Brook Street, London W1Y 1AA
☎0171 629 0992   Fax 0171 629 0993
Email: info@britishacademy.com
Chief Executive *Chris Green*

FOUNDED 1947. Europe's leading composers' organisation. The Academy represents the interests of composers and songwriters across all genres, providing advice on professional and artistic matters. Members receive the Academy's quarterly magazine and can attend fortnightly legal and financial seminars and creative workshops. The Academy administers Britain's annual awards for composers, the Ivor Novello Awards.

The Bibliographical Society
c/o The Wellcome Institute Library, 183 Euston Road, London NW1 2BE
☎0171 611 7244   Fax 0171 611 8703
President *D. J. McKitterick*
Honorary Secretary *D. Pearson*
Subscription £28 p.a.

Aims to promote and encourage the study and research of historical, analytical, descriptive and textual bibliography, and the history of printing, publishing, bookselling, bookbinding and collecting; to hold meetings at which papers are read and discussed; to print and publish works concerned with bibliography; to form a bibliographical library. Awards grants and bursaries for bibliographical research. *Publishes* a quarterly magazine called *The Library*.

Book Trust
Book House, 45 East Hill, London SW18 2QZ
☎0181 516 2977   Fax 0181 516 2978
Chief Executive *Brian Perman*
Subscription £25 p.a.; £28 (Overseas)

FOUNDED 1925. Book Trust, the independent educational charity promoting books and reading, includes Young Book Trust (formerly Children's Book Foundation). The Trust offers a book information service (free to the public); administers many literary prizes (including the **Booker**); carries out surveys, *publishes* useful reference books and resource materials; houses a children's book reference library, and promotes children's books through activities like Children's Book Week.

Booksellers Association of Great Britain & Ireland

Minster House, 272 Vauxhall Bridge Road, London SW1V 1BA

☎0171 834 5477   Fax 0171 834 8812

Email: 100437.2261@compuserve.com

Chief Executive *Tim Godfray*

FOUNDED 1895. The BA helps 3,300 independent, chain and multiple members to sell more books and reduce costs. It represents members' interests to publishers, Government, authors and others in the trade as well as offering marketing assistance, running training courses, conferences, seminars and exhibitions. Together with **The Publishers Association**, coordinates the World Book Day initiative. *Publishes* directories, catalogues, surveys and various other publications connected with the book trade and administers the **Whitbread Book of the Year and Literary Awards**.

British Academy of Film and Television Arts

See **BAFTA**

British Academy of Songwriters, Composers and Authors

See **BASCA**

British Association of Communicators in Business (BACB)

42 Borough High Street, London SE1 1XW

☎0171 378 7139   Fax 0171 387 7140

Email: bacb@globalnet.co.uk

Website: www.bacb.org

Membership Secretary *Sheila Ayinla*

FOUNDED 1949. The Association aims to be the 'market leader for those involved in corporate media management and practice by providing professional, authoritative, dynamic, supportive and innovative services'.

British Association of Journalists

88 Fleet Street, London EC4Y 1PJ

☎0171 353 3003   Fax 0171 353 2310

General Secretary *Steve Turner*

Subscription National newspaper staff, national broadcasting staff, national news agency staff: £12.50 a month. Other seniors, including magazine journalists, PRs and freelances who earn the majority of their income from journalism: £7.50 a month. Journalists under 24: £5 a month. Student journalists: Free.

FOUNDED 1992. Aims to protect and promote the industrial and professional interests of journalists.

British Association of Picture Libraries and Agencies

See **BAPLA**

British Centre for Literary Translation

University of East Anglia, Norwich, Norfolk NR4 7TJ

☎01603 592134/592785   Fax 01603 592737

Email: p.bush@uea.ac.uk

Contact *Dr Peter Bush*

FOUNDED 1989. Aims to promote literary translation and the status of the literary translator by working in the UK and overseas with translator associations and centres (e.g. European network of Translation Centres), cultural policy-makers, teachers and researchers of literary translation, Regional Arts Boards, publishers and the media, libraries and schools. Activities, mostly in collaboration with other organisations, include conferences (e.g. ITI biennial colloquia on literary translation) and seminars, workshops and readings. With European and other funding, BCLT runs a translator-in-residence programme for translators to spend one calendar month in Norwich. The first summer school for literary translation was held in July 1999. *Publishes* proceedings and reports of its activities where possible and a newsletter.

British Copyright Council

Copyright House, 29–33 Berners Street, London W1P 4AA

☎01986 788230   Fax 01986 788847

Email: copyright@bcc2.demon.co.uk

Contact *Janet Ibbotson*

Works for the national and international acceptance of copyright and acts as a lobby/watchdog organisation on behalf of creators, publishers and performers on copyright and associated matters. Publications include *Guide to the Law of Copyright and Rights in Performances in the UK*; *Photocopying from Books and Journals*. An umbrella organisation which does not deal with individual enquiries.

The British Council

10 Spring Gardens, London SW1A 2BN

☎0171 930 8466/Press Office: 0171 389 487

Fax 0171 839 6347

Website: www.britcoun.org

Head of Literature *Dr Alastair Niven*

The British Council promotes Britain abroad. It provides access to British ideas, talents, expertise and experience in education and training, books and periodicals, the English language, literature and the arts, sciences and technology. An independent, non-political organisation, the British Council works in 109 countries running a mix of offices, libraries, resource centres and English teaching operations.

British Equestrian Writers' Association

Priory House, Station Road, Swavesey, Cambridge CB4 5QJ
☎01954 232084   Fax 01954 231362
Contact *Gillian Newsum*
Subscription £15

FOUNDED 1973. Aims to further the interests of equestrian sport and improve, wherever possible, the working conditions of the equestrian press. Membership is by invitation of the committee. Candidates for membership must be nominated and seconded by full members and receive a majority vote of the committee.

British Film Commission

70 Baker Street, London W1M 1DJ
☎0171 224 5000   Fax 0171 224 1013
Email: info@britfilmcom.co.uk
Website: www.britfilmcom.co.uk
Press & Public Relations Manager
Tina McFarling

FOUNDED 1991 the BFC is funded through the Department for Culture, Media and Sport. Its remit is to promote the United Kingdom as an international production centre, to encourage the use of British artists and technicians, technical services, facilities and locations, and to provide wide-ranging support to those filming and contemplating filming in the UK.

British Film Institute

21 Stephen Street, London W1P 2LN
☎0171 255 1444   Fax 0171 436 7950
Website: www.bfi.org.uk
Membership from £11.95 p.a.

FOUNDED 1933. The BFI has undergone a major structural review, resulting in four new operational departments: Exhibition, Collections, Production and Education. Exists to promote greater understanding and appreciation of, and access to, film and moving image culture in the UK. Opened the BFI London IMAX Cinema on the South Bank in May 1999. *Publishes Sight*

and Sound and provides programming support to a network of regional film theatres. (See also entries for **BFI Production** and **BFI National Film Library**.)

British Guild of Beer Writers

The Maltings, Old School Lane, Stanford, Bedfordshire SG18 9JL
☎01462 851420   Fax 01462 813849
Email: bsb@tccnet.co.uk
Secretary *Barry Bremner*
Subscription £40 p.a.

FOUNDED 1988. Aims to improve standards in beer writing and at the same time extend public knowledge of beers and brewing. *Publishes* a directory of members with details of their publications and their particular areas of interest; this is then circulated to newspapers, magazines, trade press and broadcasting organisations. As part of the plan to improve writing standards and to achieve a higher profile for beer, the Guild offers annual awards, The Gold and Silver Tankard Awards, to writers and broadcasters judged to have made the most valuable contribution towards this end in their work. Meetings are held regularly.

British Guild of Travel Writers

Springfield, Hangersley Hill, Ringwood, Hampshire BH24 3JN
☎01425 470946
Chairman *Gary Buchanan*
Honorary Secretary *Adele Evans*
Subscription £75 p.a.

The professional association of travel writers, broadcasters, photographers and editors which aims to serve its members' professional interests by acting as a forum for debate, discussion and 'networking'. The Guild *publishes* an annual Year Book giving full details of all its members, holds monthly meetings and has a monthly newsletter. Members are required to earn the majority of their income from travel reporting.

British Science Fiction Association

1 Long Row Close, Everdon, Daventry, Northants NN11 3BE
☎01327 361661
Email: bsfa@enterprise.net
Membership Secretary *Paul Billinger*
Subscription £19 p.a. (Reduction for Unwaged)

FOUNDED originally in 1958 by a group of authors, readers, publishers and booksellers interested in science fiction. With a worldwide membership, the Association aims to promote the reading, writing and publishing of science fiction and to encourage SF fans to maintain contact with each other. Also offers postal writers workshop, a magazine chain and an information service. *Publishes Matrix* bi-monthly newsletter with comment and opinions, news of conventions, etc. Contributions from members welcomed; *Vector* bi-monthly critical journal – reviews of books and magazines; *Focus* bi-annual magazine with articles, original fiction and letters column. For further information, contact the Membership Secretary at the above address or on e-mail.

British Screen Finance
14–17 Wells Mews, London W1P 3FL
☎0171 323 9080   Fax 0171 323 0092
Contact *Simon Perry, Emma Berkofsky*

A private company aided by government grant; shareholders are Rank, Channel 4, Granada and Pathé. Exists to invest in British films specifically intended for cinema release in the UK and worldwide. Divided into two functions: project development (contact *Emma Berkofsky*), and production investment (contact *Simon Perry*). British Screen also manages the European Co-production Fund which exists to support feature films co-produced by the UK with other European countries. British Screen develops around 40 projects per year, and has invested in 125 British feature film productions in the last ten years.

British Society of Magazine Editors (BSME)
137 Hale Lane, Edgware, Middlesex HA8 9QP
☎0181 906 4664   Fax 0181 959 2137
Email: bsme@cix.compulink.co.uk
Contact *Gill Branston*

Holds regular industry forums and events as well as an annual awards dinner.

Broadcasting Press Guild
Tiverton, The Ridge, Woking, Surrey GU22 7EQ
☎01483 764895   Fax 01483 765882
Membership Secretary *Richard Last*
Subscription £15 p.a.

FOUNDED 1973 to promote the professional interests of journalists specialising in writing or broadcasting about the media. Organises monthly lunches addressed by leading industry figures, and annual TV and radio awards. Membership by invitation.

BSME
See **British Society of Magazine Editors**

Bureau of Freelance Photographers
Focus House, 497 Green Lanes, London N13 4BP
☎0181 882 3315   Fax 0181 886 5174
Membership Secretary *James Clancy*
Subscription £40 p.a. (UK);
    £50 p.a. (Overseas)

FOUNDED 1965. Assists members in selling their pictures through monthly *Market Newsletter* and offers advisory, legal assistance and other services.

Campaign for Press and Broadcasting Freedom
8 Cynthia Street, London N1 9JF
☎0171 278 4430   Fax 0171 837 8868
Email: freepress@cpbf.demon.co.uk
Website: www.cpbf.demon.co.uk
Subscription £15 p.a. (concessions available);
    £25 p.a. (Institutions/Organisations)

Broadly based pressure group working for more accountable and accessible media in Britain. Advises on right of reply and takes up the issue of the portrayal of minorities. Members receive *Free Press* (bi-monthly), discounts on publications and news of campaign progress.

The Caravan Writers' Guild
13 Groughlands Avenue, Hitchin, Hertfordshire SG4 0QT
☎01462 432877   Fax 01462 421795
Membership Secretary *D. King*
Subscription £5 Joining fee plus £10 p.a.

Guild for writers active in the specialist fields of caravan and camping journalism.

Careers Writers' Association
71 Wimborne Road, Colehill, Wimborne, Dorset BH21 2RP
☎01202 880320   Fax 01202 880320
Email: Barbara.Buffton@wsmail.co.uk
Membership Secretary *Barbara Buffton*

FOUNDED 1979. The association aims to promote high standards of careers writing, improve access to sources of information, provide a network for members to exchange information and experience, hold meetings on topics of relevance and interest to members. Also produces an occasional newsletter and maintains a membership list. Forges links with organisations sharing related interests, and maintains regular contact with national education and training bodies, government agencies and publishers.

Chartered Institute of Journalists

2 Dock Offices, Surrey Quays Road, London
SE16 2XU
☎0171 252 1187   Fax 0171 232 2302
General Secretary *Christopher Underwood*
Subscription £155

FOUNDED 1884. The Chartered Institute is concerned with professional journalistic standards and with safeguarding the freedom of the media. It is open to writers, broadcasters and journalists (including self-employed) in all media. Affiliate membership (£105) is available to part-time or occasional practitioners and to overseas journalists who can join the Institute's International Division. Members also belong to the IOJ (TU) – Institute of Journalists, an independent trade union which protects, advises and represents them in their employment or freelance work; negotiates on their behalf and provides legal assistance and support. The IOJ (TU) is a certificated trade union which represents members' interests in the workplace, and is also a constituent member of the National Council in the Training of Journalists and the Independent Unions Training Council.

Children's Book Circle

c/o Macmillan Publishers Ltd, 25 Eccleston Place, London SW1W 9NF
☎0171 881 8000   Fax 0171 881 8001
Membership Secretary *Gaby Morgan*

The Children's Book Circle provides a discussion forum for anybody involved with children's books. Monthly meetings are addressed by a panel of invited speakers and topics focus on current and controversial issues. Administers the **Eleanor Farjeon Award**.

Children's Book Foundation

See **Book Trust**

Circle of Wine Writers

30 Wimpole Street, London W1M 7AE
☎0171 486 6563
Membership £35 p.a.

FOUNDED 1962. Open to all *bona fide* authors, broadcasters, journalists and photographers currently being published, as well as lecturers and tutors, all of whom are professionally engaged in communicating about wines and spirits. Aims to improve the standard of writing, broadcasting and lecturing about wines, spirits and beers; to contribute to the growing knowledge and interest in wine; to promote wines and spirits of quality and to comment adversely on faulty products

or dubious practices; to establish and maintain good relations with the news media and the wine trade; to provide members with a strong voice with which to promote their views; to provide a programme of workshops, meetings, talks and tastings.

Cleveland Arts

Ground Floor, Gurney House, Gurney Street, Middlesbrough TS1 1JL
☎01642 262424   Fax 01642 262429
Contact *Buzzwords Development Worker*

Not one of the Regional Arts Boards, Cleveland Arts is an independent arts development agency working in the areas of Middlesbrough, Stockton on Tees, Hartlepool and Redcar & Cleveland. The company works in partnership with local authorities, public agencies, the business sector, schools, colleges, individuals and organisations to coordinate, promote and develop the arts – crafts, film, video, photography, music, drama, dance, literature, public arts, disability, Black arts, community arts. Buzzwords is the literature development unit which promotes writing classes, reading promotions, poetry readings and residencies, issues a free newsletter and assists local publishers and writers.

Clé, The Irish Book Publishers Association

43/44 Temple Bar, Dublin 2, Republic of Ireland
☎00 353 1 6706393   Fax 00 353 1 6706642
Email: cle@iol.ie
President *John Murphy*
Executive Director *Orla Martin*

FOUNDED 1970 to promote Irish publishing, protect members' interests and train the industry.

Comedy Writers' Association of Great Britain

61 Parry Road, Ashmore Park,
Wolverhampton, West Midlands WV11 2PS
☎01902 722729   Fax 01902 722729
Contact *Ken Rock*

FOUNDED 1981 to assist and promote the work of comedy writers. The Association is a self-help group designed to encourage and advise its members to sell their work. It is an international organisation with representatives in Britain, Germany, Cyprus, Sweden, Belgium, Luxembourg, Czechoslovakia, Denmark, Finland and Canada. International seminar with videos of foreign TV comedy programmes, bookshop and business club where members can discuss opportunities. Members often come together to work jointly on a variety of comedy projects for British and overseas productions. *Publishes* regular magazines and monthly market information.

Comhairle nan Leabhraichean/ The Gaelic Books Council

22 Mansfield Street, Glasgow G11 5QP
☎0141 337 6211   Fax 0141 353 0515
Chairman *Boyd Robertson*
Director *Ian MacDonald*

FOUNDED 1968 and now a charitable company with its own bookshop. Encourages and promotes Gaelic publishing by giving grants to publishers and writers; providing editorial and word-processing services; retailing Gaelic books; producing a catalogue of all Gaelic books in print, and answering enquiries about them.

Commercial Radio Companies Association

77 Shaftesbury Avenue, London W1V 7AD
☎0171 306 2603   Fax 0171 470 0062
Email: info@crca.co.uk
Chief Executive *Paul Brown*
Research and Communications Manager
  Rachell Fox
Political Analyst *Nick Irvine*

The CRCA is the trade body for the independent radio stations. It represents members' interests to Government, the **Radio Authority**, trade unions, copyright organisations and other bodies.

The Copyright Licensing Agency Ltd

90 Tottenham Court Road, London W1P 0LP
☎0171 631 5555   Fax 0171 631 5500
Email: cla@cla.co.uk
Website: www.cla.co.uk
Chief Executive *Peter Shepherd*

FOUNDED 1982 by the **Authors' Licensing and Collecting Society (ALCS)** and the **Publishers Licensing Society Ltd (PLS)**, the CLA administers collectively photocopying and other copying rights that it is uneconomic for writers and publishers to administer for themselves. The Agency issues collective and transactional licences, and the fees it collects, after the deduction of its operating costs, are distributed at regular intervals to authors and publishers via their respective societies (i.e. ALCS or PLS). Since 1986, CLA has distributed approximately £70 million.

Council for British Archaeology

Bowes Morrell House, 111 Walmgate, York YO1 2WA
☎01904 671417   Fax 01904 671384
Email: archaeology@csi.com
Website: www.britarch.ac.uk
Information Officer *Mike Heyworth*

FOUNDED 1944 to represent and promote archaeology at all levels. Its aims are to improve the public's awareness in and understanding of Britain's past; to carry out research; to survey, guide and promote the teaching of archaeology at all levels of education; to publish a wide range of academic, educational, general and bibliographical works (see **CBA Publishing**).

Council of Academic and Professional Publishers

See **The Publishers Association**

Crime Writers' Association (CWA)

PO Box 6939, Kings Heath, Birmingham B14 7LR
Secretary *Judith Cutler*
Membership £40 (Town); £35 (Country)

Full membership is limited to professional crime writers, but publishers, literary agents, booksellers, etc., who specialise in crime are eligible for Associate membership. The Association has regional chapters throughout the country, including Scotland. Meetings are held monthly in central London, with informative talks frequently given by police, scenes of crime officers, lawyers, etc., and a weekend conference is held annually in different parts of the country. Produces a monthly newsletter for members called *Red Herrings* and presents various annual awards.

The Critics' Circle

c/o The Stage (incorporating Television Today), 47 Bermondsey Street, London SE1 3XT
☎0171 403 1818 ext 106 (Catherine Cooper)
Fax 0171 357 9287
President *George Perry*
Honorary General Secretary *Charles Hedges*
Subscription £18 p.a.

Membership by invitation only. Aims to uphold and promote the art of criticism (and the commercial rates of pay thereof) and preserve the interests of its members: professionals involved in criticism of film, drama, music and dance.

Department for Culture, Media and Sport

2–4 Cockspur Street, London SW1Y 5DH
☎0171 211 6000   Fax 0171 211 6270

Senior Press Officer, Arts *Toby Sargent*

The Department for Culture, Media and Sport has responsibilities for Government policies relating to the arts, museums and galleries, public libraries, sport, broadcasting, Press standards, the built heritage, the film and music industries, tourism and the National Lottery. It funds **The Arts Council**, national museums and galleries, **The British Library** (including the new library building at St Pancras), the Public Lending Right and the Royal Commission on Historical Manuscripts. It is responsible within Government for the public library service in England, and for library and information matters generally, where they are not the responsibility of other departments.

Directory & Database Publishers Association

PO Box 23034, London W11 2WZ
☎0171 221 9089

Website: www.directory-publisher.co.uk
Contact *Rosemary Pettit*
Subscription £120 –£1200 p.a.

FOUNDED 1970 to promote the interests of *bona fide* directory and database publishers and protect the public from disreputable and fraudulent practices. The objectives of the Association are to maintain a code of professional practice to safeguard public interest; to raise the standard and status of directory publishing throughout the UK; to promote business directories as a medium for advertising; to protect the legal and statutory interests of directory publishers; to foster bonds of common interest among responsible directory publishers and to provide for the exchange of technical, commercial and management information between members. Meetings, seminars, conference, newsletter, awards, fairs.

Drama Association of Wales

The Library, Singleton Road, Splott, Cardiff CF2 2ET
☎01222 452200   Fax 01222 452277

Contact *Gary Thomas*

Runs a large playscript lending library; holds an annual playwriting competition (see under **Prizes**); offers a script-reading service (£10 per script) which usually takes three months from receipt of play to issue of reports. From plays submitted to the reading service, selected scripts are considered for publication of a short run (250–750 copies). Writers receive a percentage of the cover price on sales and a percentage of the performance fee.

Edinburgh Bibliographical Society

Rare Books Division, National Library of Scotland, George IV Bridge, Edinburgh EH1 1EW8 9LJ
☎0131 466 2806   Fax 0131 466 2807
Email: r.ovenden@nls.uk

Honorary Secretary *Richard Ovenden*
Subscription £10; £15 (Institution); £5 (Students)

FOUNDED 1890. Organises lectures on bibliographical topics and visits to libraries. *Publishes* a biennial journal called *Transactions*, which is free to members, and other occasional publications.

Educational Publishers Council
See **The Publishers Association**

Electronic Publishers' Forum
See **The Publishers Association**

The English Association

University of Leicester, University Road, Leicester LE1 7RH
☎0116 252 3982   Fax 0116 252 2301
Email: engassoc@le.ac.uk
Website: www.le.ac.uk/engassoc/

Chief Executive *Helen Lucas*

FOUNDED 1906 to promote understanding and appreciation of the English language and its literatures. Activities include sponsoring a number of publications and organising lectures and conferences for teachers, plus annual sixth-form conferences. Publications include *Year's Work in Critical and Cultural Theory, English, Use of English, English 4–11, Essays and Studies* and *Year's Work in English Studies*.

ETmA (Educational Television & Media Association)

37 Monkgate, York YO31 7PB
☎01904 639212   Fax 01904 639212
Email: josie.key@etma.u-net.com
Website: www.etma.org.uk

Administrator *Josie Key*

The ETmA is a 'dynamic association' comprising a wide variety of users of television and other electronic media in education. Annual awards scheme (video competition), and annual conferences. New members always welcome. CPD scheme.

Federation of Entertainment Unions

1 Highfield, Twyford, Nr Winchester, Hampshire SO21 1QR
☎01962 713134   Fax 01962 713288
Email: harris@interalpha.co.uk

Secretary *Steve Harris*

Plenary meetings six times annually and meetings of The Film and Electronic Media Committee six times annually on alternate months. Additionally, there are Training & European Committees. Represents the following unions: British Actors' Equity Association; Broadcasting Entertainment Cinematograph and Theatre Union; Musicians' Union; AEEU; **National Union of Journalists**; **The Writers' Guild of Great Britain**.

The Federation of Worker Writers and Community Publishers (FWWCP)

PO Box 540, Burslem, Stoke on Trent ST6 6DR
☎01782 822327   Fax 01782 822327
Email: fwwcp@cwcom.net
Website: www.fwwcp.mcmail.com

Administrator/Coordinator *Tim Diggles*

The FWWCP is a federation of writing groups who are committed to writing and publishing based on working-class experience and creativity. The FWWCP is the membership's collective national voice and has for some time been given funding by **The Arts Council**. Founded in 1976, it comprises around 50 member groups, each one with its own identity, reflecting its community and membership. They represent over 5000 people who regularly (often weekly) meet to offer constructive criticism, produce books and tapes, perform and share skills, offering creative and critical support. There are writers' workshops of long standing; adult literacy organisations; groups working mainly in oral and local history; groups and local networks of writers who come together to publish, train or perform; groups with a specific remit to further the aims of a section of the community such as the homeless or disabled. Although diverse in nature, member organisations share the aim to make writing and publishing accessible to people and encourage them to take an active, cooperative and democratic role in writing, performing and publishing. The main activities include training days and weekends to learn and share skills, a quarterly magazine, a quarterly broadsheet of members' writing, a major annual festival of writing and networking between member organisations. The FWWCP has published a number of anthologies and is willing to work with other organisations on publishing projects. Membership is only open to groups but individuals will be put in touch with groups which can help them, and become friends of the Federation. Contact the above address for an information leaflet.

Foreign Press Association in London

11 Carlton House Terrace, London SW1Y 5AJ
☎0171 930 0445   Fax 0171 925 0469

Contact *Davina Crole, Catherine Flury*
Membership (not incl. VAT) £103 p.a. (Full);
    £95.40 (Associate Journalists);
    £142.50 (Associate Non-Journalists)

FOUNDED 1888. Non-profit-making service association for foreign correspondents based in London, providing a variety of press-related services.

The Gaelic Books Council
See **Comhairle nan Leabhraichean**

The Garden Writers' Guild

c/o Institute of Horticulture, 14/15 Belgrave Square, London SW1X 8PS
☎0171 245 6943

Contact *Angela Clarke*
Subscription £20; (£15 to Institute of
    Horticulture members);
    £30 (Associate members)

FOUNDED 1990. Aims to revise the status and standing of gardening communicators. Administers an annual awards scheme. Operates a mailing service and organises press briefing days.

General Practitioner Writers' Association

West Carnliath, Strathtay, Perth PH9 0PG
☎01887 840380   Fax 01887 840380

Contact *Professor F. M. Hull*
Subscription £30 p.a.; £40 (Joint)

FOUNDED 1986 to promote and improve writing activities within and for general practices. Open to general practitioners, practice managers, nurses, etc. and professional journalists writing on anything pertaining to general practice. Very keen to develop input from interested parties who work mainly outside the profession. Regular workshops, discussions and a twice-yearly journal, *The GP Writer*.

Guild of Agricultural Journalists

Charmwood, 47 Court Meadow, Rotherfield,
East Sussex TN6 3LQ
☎01892 853187   Fax 01892 853551
Email: don.gomery@farmline.com

Honorary General Secretary *Don Gomery*
Subscription £30 p.a.

FOUNDED 1944 to promote a high professional standard among journalists who specialise in agriculture, horticulture and allied subjects. Represents members' interests with representative bodies in the industry; provides a forum through meetings and social activities for members to meet eminent people in the industry; maintains contact with associations of agricultural journalists overseas; promotes schemes for the education of members and for the provision of suitable entrants into agricultural journalism.

Guild of Editors

See **The Newspaper Society**

The Guild of Erotic Writers

CTCK PO Box 8431, Deptford, London
SE8 4BP
☎0973 767086

Contact *Elizabeth Coldwell, Zak Jane Keir*
Subscription £10 p.a. (cheques made
    payable to CTCK)

FOUNDED 1995. Aims to provide a network for all authors of erotic fiction, both published and unpublished and to promote erotica as a valid form of writing. Members receive quarterly newsletters and a tip sheet on getting work accepted, together with discounts on conferences and events, and a manuscript-reading service (also available to non-members at 'very competitive rates' – short stories £4.50 for members, £7 non-members).

The Guild of Food Writers

48 Crabtree Lane, London SW6 6LW
☎0171 610 1180   Fax 0171 610 0299
Email: gfw@gfw.co.uk

Administrator *Christina Thomas*
Subscription £45

FOUNDED 1975. The objects of the Guild include: 'to bring together professional food writers including journalists, broadcasters and authors, to print and issue an annual list of members, to extend the range of members' knowledge and experience by arranging discussions, tastings and visits, and to encourage the development of new writers by every means including competitions and awards. The Guild aims to contribute to the growth of public interest in, and knowledge of, the subject of food and to campaign for improvements in the quality of food.'

Guild of Motoring Writers

30 The Cravens, Smallfield, Surrey RH6 9QS
☎01342 843294   Fax 01342 844093

General Secretary *Sharon Scott-Fairweather*

FOUNDED 1944. Represents members' interests and provides a forum for members to exchange information.

Independent Publishers Guild

4 Middle Street, Great Gransden, Sandy,
Bedfordshire SG19 3AD
☎01767 677753   Fax 01767 677069
Email: sheila@ipg.uk.com

Secretary *Sheila Bounford*
Subscription approx. £75 p.a.

FOUNDED 1962. Membership open to independent publishers, packagers and suppliers, i.e. professionals in allied fields. Regular meetings, conferences, seminars, mailings and a quarterly bulletin.

Independent Television Association

See **ITV Network Ltd**

Independent Theatre Council

12 The Leathermarket, Weston Street,
London SE1 3ER
☎0171 403 1727/6698 (general/training)
Fax 0171 403 1745

Contact *Charlotte Jones*

The management association and representative body for small/middle-scale theatres (up to around 450 seats) and touring theatre companies. Negotiates contracts and has established standard agreements with Equity on behalf of all professionals working in the theatre. Negotiations with the **Theatre Writers' Union** and **The Writers' Guild** for a contractual agreement covering rights and fee structure for playwrights were concluded in 1991. Terms and conditions were renegotiated and updated in September 1998. Copies of the minimum terms agreement can be obtained from The Writers' Guild. *Publishes* a booklet, *A Practical Guide for Writers and Companies* (£3.50 plus p&p), giving guidance to writers on how to submit scripts to theatres and guidance to theatres on how to deal with them.

Institute of Copywriting

Honeycombe House, Bagley, Wedmore
BS28 4TD
☎01934 713563   Fax 01934 713492
Email: copy@inst.org
Website:dspace.dial.pipex.com/
    institute/copy.htm

Secretary *Alex Middleton*

FOUNDED 1991 to promote copywriters and
copywriting (writing publicity material). Maintains a code of practice. Membership is open to
students as well as experienced practitioners.
Runs training courses (see entry under **Writers'
Courses**). Has a list of approved copywriters.
Answers queries relating to copywriting. Contact
the Institute for a free booklet.

Institute of Translation and Interpreting (ITI)

377 City Road, London EC1V 1NA
☎0171 713 7600   Fax 0171 713 7650
Email: info@iti.org.uk
Website: www.iti.org.uk

FOUNDED 1986. The ITI is a professional association of translators and interpreters aiming to
promote the highest standards in translating and
interpreting. It has strong corporate membership and runs professional development courses
and conferences, sometimes in conjunction
with its language, regional and subject network.
Membership is open to those with a genuine
and proven involvement in translation and
interpreting (including students). ITI's Directory of Members, its bi-monthly Bulletin and
other publications are available from the
Secretariat. The Secretariat offers a free referral
service whereby enquirers can be given the
names of suitable members for any interpret-
ing/translating assignment. ITI is a full and
active member of FIT (International Federation
of Translators).

International Association of Puzzle Writers

42 Brigstocke Terrace, Ryde, Isle of Wight
PO33 2PD
☎01983 811688

Contact *Dr Jeremy Sims*
Annual membership fee £25

FOUNDED 1966 for writers of brainteasing puzzles, crosswords and word games, and for designers of games in general. Enquiries from publishers seeking material welcome. Aims to provide
support and information and to promote the art
of puzzle writing and games design to publishers,
games manufacturers and the general public.
Publishes bi-monthly newsletter – contributions
welcome. Members must have email. For further
information, send s.a.e. to the above address.

International Cultural Desk

6 Belmont Crescent, Glasgow G12 8ES
☎0141 339 0090   Fax 0141 337 2271
Email: icd@dial.pipex.com

Development Manager *Hilde Bollen*
Information Officer *Kerry Jardine*

FOUNDED 1994. Aims to assist the Scottish cultural community to operate more effectively in
an international context by providing timely
and targeted information and advice. The Desk
provides and disseminates information on
funding sources, international opportunities
and cultural policy development in Europe,
and also assists with establishing contacts internationally. The Desk is not a funding agency.
Publishes Communication, a bi-monthly information update about forthcoming international
opportunities across the whole range of cultural
and artistic activity, and *InFocus*, a series of
specialised guides with an international focus.

Irish Book Publishers Association

See **Clé**

Irish Copyright Licensing Agency Ltd

19 Parnell Square, Dublin 1,
Republic of Ireland
☎00 353 1 872 9202   Fax 00 353 1 872 2035

Administrator *Orla O'Sullivan*

FOUNDED 1992 by writers and publishers in
Ireland to provide a scheme through which
rights holders can give permission, and users of
copyright material can obtain permission, to
copy.

Irish Writers' Union

19 Parnell Square, Dublin 1 Republic of
Ireland
☎00 353 1 872 1302   Fax 00 353 1 872 6282

Secretary *Mara Rainwater*
Subscription £20 p.a.

FOUNDED 1986 to promote the interests and
protect the rights of writers in Ireland.

Isle of Man Authors

24 Laurys Avenue, Ramsey, Isle of Man
IM8 2HE
☎01624 815634

Secretary *Mrs Beryl Sandwell*

Subscription £5 p.a.

An association of writers living on the Isle of Man, which has links with **The Society of Authors**.

ITI
See **Institute of Translation and Interpreting**

ITV Network Ltd.
200 Gray's Inn Road, London WC1X 8HF
☎0171 843 8000   Fax 0171 843 8158
Website: www.itv.co.uk
Chief Executive *Richard Eyre*
Director of Programmes *David Liddiment*

The ITV Network Ltd., wholly owned by the ITV companies, independently commissions and schedules the television programmes which are shown across the ITV network. As a successor to the Independent Television Association, it also provides a range of services to the ITV companies where a common approach is required.

IVCA (International Visual Communication Association)
Bolsover House, 5–6 Clipstone Street, London W1P 8LD
☎0171 580 0962   Fax 0171 436 2606
Website: www.ivca.org
Chief Executive *Wayne Drew*

The IVCA is a professional association representing the interests of the users and suppliers of visual communications. In particular it pursues the interests of producers, commissioners and manufacturers involved in the non-broadcast and independent facilities industries and also business event companies. It represents all sizes of company and freelance individuals, offering information and advice services, publications, a professional network, special interest groups, a magazine and a variety of events including the UK's Film and Video Communications Festival.

The Library Association
7 Ridgmount Street, London WC1E 7AE
☎0171 636 7543   Fax 0171 436 7218
Email: info@la-hq.org.uk
Website: www.la-hq.org.uk
Chief Executive *Ross Shimmon*

The professional body for librarians and information managers, with 25,000 individual and institutional members. **Library Association Publishing** produces 30–35 new titles each year and has over 250 in print. The *LA Record* is the monthly magazine for members. Further information from Information Services, The Library Association.

The Media Society
56 Roseneath Road, London SW11 6AQ
Contact *Peter Dannheisser*
Subscription £25 p.a.; £10 Entry fee

FOUNDED 1973. A registered charity which aims to provide a forum for the exchange of knowledge and opinion between those in public and political life, the professions, industry and education. Meetings (about 10 a year) usually take the form of luncheons and dinners in London with invited speakers. The society also acts as a 'think tank' and submits evidence and observations to royal commissions, select committees and review bodies.

Medical Journalists' Association
2 St George's Road, Kingston-upon-Thames, Surrey KT2 6DN
☎0181 549 1019   Fax 0181 255 4964
Chairman *John Illman*
Honorary Secretary *Jenny Sims*
Subscription £30 p.a.

FOUNDED 1967. Aims to improve the quality and practice of medical and health journalism and to improve relationships and understanding between medical and health journalists and the health and medical professions. Regular meetings with senior figures in medicine and medico politics; teach-ins on particular subjects to help journalists with background information; weekend symposium for members with people who have newsworthy stories in the field; awards for medical journalists offered by various commercial sponsors, plus MJA's own award financed by members. *Publishes* a detailed directory of members and freelances and two-monthly newsletter.

Medical Writers' Group & Medical Prizes
The Society of Authors, 84 Drayton Gardens, London SW10 9SB
☎0171 373 6642   Fax 0171 373 5768
Email: authorsoc@writers.org.uk
Contact *Dorothy Wright*

FOUNDED 1980. A specialist group within **The Society of Authors** offering advice and help to authors of medical books. Administers Medical Prizes.

National Association of Writers Groups

The Arts Centre, Biddick Lane, Washington, Tyne & Wear NE38 2AB
☎0191 416 9751   Fax 0191 4311263
Contact *Brian Lister*

FOUNDED 1995 with the object of furthering the interests of writers' groups throughout the UK. A registered charity, No: 1059047, NAWG is strictly non-sectarian and non-political. *Publishes* a bi-monthly newsletter, distributed to member groups; gives free entry to competitions for group anthologies, poetry, short stories, articles, novels and sketches; holds an annual open festival of writing with 40 workshops, seminars, individual surgeries led by professional, high-profile writers. Membership is open to all writers' groups – there are no restrictions or qualifications required for joining; 120 groups are affiliated.

National Association of Writers in Education

PO Box 1, Sheriff Hutton, York YO60 7YU
☎01653 618429   Fax 01653 618429
Email: paul@nawe.co.uk
Website: www.nawe.co.uk
Contact *Paul Munden*
Subscription £12 p.a.

FOUNDED 1991. Aims to promote the contribution of living writers to education and to encourage both the practice and the critical appreciation of creative writing. Has over 400 members. Organises national conferences and training courses. A directory of over 1000 writers who work in schools, colleges and the community is available on-line. *Publishes* a magazine, *Writing in Education*, issued free to members thrice-yearly.

National Campaign for the Arts

Francis House, Francis Street, London SW1P 1DE
☎0171 828 4448   Fax 0171 931 9959
Email: newmail@artscampaign.org
Website: www.ecna.org/nca/
Director *Victoria Todd*

FOUNDED 1984 to represent the cultural sector in Britain and to make sure that the problems facing the arts are properly put to Government, at local and national level. The NCA is an independent body relying on finance from its members. Involved in all issues which affect the arts: public finance, education, broadcasting and media affairs, the fight against censorship, the rights of artists, the place of the arts on the public agenda and structures for supporting culture. Membership open to all arts organisations (except government agencies) and to individuals. Literature subscriptions available.

National Literacy Trust

Swire House, 59 Buckingham Gate, London SW1E 6AS
☎0171 828 2435   Fax 0171 931 9986
Email: contact@literacytrust.org.uk
Website: www.literacytrust.org.uk
Director *Neil McClelland*

FOUNDED 1993. A registered charity No: 1015539) which aims to work with others to enhance literacy standards in the UK, to encourage more reading and writing for pleasure and to seek to raise the profile of literacy in the context of social and technological change. Maintains a database of literacy initiatives in the UK, now available on its Website; provides training and consultancy on literacy, organises seminars and conferences, undertakes media campaigns and *publishes* a quarterly magazine, *Literacy Today* (subscription £14 p.a.). Runs Reading Is Fundamental, UK which provides books free to children and, in 1999, is organising the National Year of Reading for the government.

The National Small Press Centre

See **Organisations of Interest to Poets**

National Union of Journalists

Acorn House, 314 Gray's Inn Road, London WC1X 8DP
☎0171 278 7916   Fax 0171 837 8143
Email: acorn.house@uj.org.uk
Website: www.gn.apc.org/media/
General Secretary *John Foster*
Subscription £148.50 p.a. (Freelance) or
    1% of annual income if lower; minimum
    contribution £57.75

Represents journalists in all sectors of publishing, print and broadcast. Responsible for wages and conditions agreements which apply across the industry. Provides advice and representation for its members, as well as administering unemployment and other benefits. *Publishes* various guides and magazines: *Freelance Directory, Fees Guide, The Journalist* and *The Freelance* (see entry under **Magazines**).

NETWORKING for Women in Film, Video and Television

c/o Vera Media, 30–38 Dock Street, Leeds, West Yorkshire LS10 1JF
☎0113 242 8646   Fax 0113 242 8739
Email: networking@vera-media.co.uk

Website: www.networking-media.org
Contact *Jane Howarth, Al Garthwaite*
Subscription £15 p.a.

FOUNDED 1989. A membership organisation for women working, seeking work, studying or in any way involved in film, video or television. Media studies departments, libraries, careers services are also welcome to join. *Publishes* a quarterly 20–page newsletter with news of activities, upcoming events, reviews, information about production funds, courses, etc. and members-only Website for hot-off-the-keyboard items. Entries of up to 40 words may be sent for inclusion in the Members' Index circulated throughout the membership to assist geographical/interest-based networking and employment. Contributions to the newsletter are welcome from all members. Advice, help and a campaigning voice for women in media are also on offer.

New Playwrights Trust

Interchange Studios, 15 Dalby Street, London NW5 3NQ
☎0171 284 2818   Fax 0171 482 5292
Email: npt@easynet.co.uk

Executive Director *Jonathan Meth*
Subscription (information on rates available by post)

New Playwrights Trust is the national research and development organisation for writing for all forms of live and recorded performance. *Publishes* a range of information pertinent to writers on all aspects of development and production in the form of pamphlets, and a six-weekly journal which also includes articles and interviews on aesthetic and practical issues. NPT also runs a script-reading service and a link service between writers and producers, organises seminars and conducts research projects. The latter includes research into the use of bilingual techniques in playwriting (*Two Tongues*), documentation of training programmes for writers (*Going Black Under the Skin*) and an investigation of the relationship between live art and writing (*Writing Live*).

New Producers Alliance (NPA)

9 Bourlet Close, London W1P 7PJ
☎0171 580 2480   Fax 0171 580 2484
Email: admin@npa.org.uk
Website: www.npa.org.uk

FOUNDED 1992; current membership of over 1300. Aims to encourage the production of commercial feature films for an international audience and to educate and inform feature film producers, writers and directors. The NPA

is an independent networking organisation providing members with access to contacts, information, free legal advice and general help regarding film production. *Publishes* a monthly newsletter and organises meetings, workshops and seminars. The NPA does not produce films so please do not send scripts or treatments.

The New SF Alliance (NSFA)

c/o BBR Magazine, PO Box 625, Sheffield, South Yorkshire S1 3GY
Website: www.bbr-online.com/writers.

Contact *Chris Reed*

FOUNDED 1989. Committed to supporting the work of new writers and artists by promoting independent and small press publications worldwide. 'Help with finding the right market for your material by providing a mail-order service which allows you to sample magazines, and various publications including *Zene* magazine and *Scavenger's Newsletter* which feature the latest market news and tips.'

Newspaper Conference

See **The Newspaper Society**

The Newspaper Society

Bloomsbury House, 74–77 Great Russell Street, London WC1B 3DA
☎0171 636 7014   Fax 0171 631 5119
Email: ns@newspapersoc.org.uk
Website: www.newspapersoc.org.uk

Director *David Newell*

The association of publishers of the regional and local press, representing 1400 regional daily and weekly, paid for and free, newspaper titles in the UK. The Newspaper Conference is an organisation within the Society for London editors and representatives of regional newspapers. Bloomsbury House is also home to the Guild of Editors and to the Young Newspaper Executives' Association.

NPA

See **New Producers Alliance**

NSFA

See **The New SF Alliance**

Outdoor Writers' Guild

PO Box 520, Bamber Bridge, Preston, Lancashire PR5 8LF
☎01772 696732   Fax 01772 696732
Secretary *Terry Marsh*
Subscription £40p.a.; Joining fee £10
FOUNDED 1980 to promote, encourage and

assist the development and maintenance of professional standards among those involved in all aspects of outdoor journalism. Membership is not limited to writers but includes other outstanding professional media practitioners in the outdoor world such as broadcasters, photographers, filmmakers, editors, publishers and illustrators. *Publishes* a quarterly journal, *Bootprint*, and an annual *Handbook and Directory* (£25; free to members) as well as guidelines, codes of practice and advice notes. Presents five Awards for Excellence jointly with the Camping and Outdoor Leisure Association (COLA), and its own Award for Photographic Excellence.

PACT (Producers Alliance for Cinema and Television)

45 Mortimer Street, London W1N 7TD
☎0171 331 6000   Fax 0171 331 6700
Email: enquiries@pact.co.uk
Website: www.pact.co.uk

Chief Executive *Shaun Williams*
Membership Officer *David Alan Mills*

FOUNDED 1991. PACT is the trade association of the UK independent television and feature film production sector and is a key contact point for foreign producers seeking British co-production, co-finance partners and distributors. Works for producers in the industry at every level and operates a members' regional network throughout the UK with a divisional office in Scotland. Membership services include: a dedicated industrial relations unit; discounted legal advice; a varied calendar of events; business advice; representation at international film and television markets; a comprehensive research programme; various publications: a monthly magazine, an annual members' directory; affiliation with European and international producers' organisations; extensive information and production advice. Lobbies actively with broadcasters, financiers and governments to ensure that the producer's voice is heard and understood in Britain and Europe on all matters affecting the film and television industry.

PAPA

See **The Professional Authors' and Publishers' Association**

PEN

7 Dilke Street, London SW3 4JE
☎0171 352 6303   Fax 0171 351 0220
Email: enquiries@pen.org.uk
Website: www.pen.org.uk

General Secretary *Gillian Vincent*

Membership £40 (London/Overseas);
    £35 (members living over 50 miles from London)

English PEN is part of International PEN, a worldwide association of published writers which fights for freedom of expression and speaks out for writers who are imprisoned or harassed for having criticised their governments or for publishing other unpopular views. FOUNDED in London in 1921, International PEN now consists of 130 centres in almost 100 countries. PEN originally stood for poets, essayists and novelists, but membership is now open to published playwrights, editors, translators and journalists as well. A programme of talks and discussions is supplemented by a twice-yearly mailing and annual congress at one of the centres.

Performing Right Society

29–33 Berners Street, London W1P 4AA
☎0171 580 5544   Fax 0171 306 4455
Email: info@prs.co.uk
Website: www.prs.co.uk

Collects and distributes royalties arising from the performance and broadcast of copyright music on behalf of its composer, lyricist and music publisher members and members of affiliated societies worldwide.

Periodical Publishers Association (PPA)

Queens House, 28 Kingsway, London WC2B 6JR
☎0171 404 4166   Fax 0171 404 4167
Email: info1@ppa.co.uk
Website: www.ppa.co.uk

Contact *Daska Davis*

FOUNDED 1913 to promote and protect the interests of magazine publishers in the UK.

The Personal Managers' Association Ltd

1 Summer Road, East Molesey, Surrey KT8 9LX
☎0181 398 9796   Fax 0181 398 9796

Co-chairs *Marc Berlin, Tim Corrie*
Secretary *Angela Adler*
Subscription £250 p.a.

An association of artists' and dramatists' agents (membership not open to individuals). Monthly meetings for exchange of information and discussion. Maintains a code of conduct and acts as a lobby when necessary. Applicants screened. A high proportion of play agents are members of the PMA.

The Picture Research Association

Head Office: The Studio, 5A Alvanley Gardens, London NW6 1JD
☎0171 431 9886   Fax 0171 431 9887
Chairman *Emma Krikler*
Subscription Members: Introductory £40; Full £50; Associate £45.
 Magazine only: £25 per year quarterly

FOUNDED 1977 as the Society of Picture Researchers & Editors. The Picture Research Association is a professional body for picture researchers, managers, picture editors and all those involved in the research, management and supply of visual material to all forms of the media. The Association's main aims are to promote the interests and specific skills of its members internationally; to promote and maintain professional standards; to bring together those involved in the research and publication of visual material; to provide a forum for the exchange of information and to provide guidance to its members. Free advisory service for members, regular meetings, quarterly magazine, monthly newsletter and Freelance Register.

Player–Playwrights

9 Hillfield Park, London N10 3QT
☎0181 883 0371
Email: P-P@dial.pipex.com
President *Jack Rosenthal*
Contact *Peter Thompson* (at the above address)
Subscription £10 (Joining fee); £6 p.a.
 thereafter, plus £1 per attendance

FOUNDED 1948. A society giving opportunity for writers new to stage, radio and television, as well as others finding difficulty in achieving results, to work with writers established in those media. At weekly meetings (7.45–10.00 p.m., Mondays, St Augustine's Hall, Queen's Gate, London SW7), members' scripts are read or performed by actor members and afterwards assessed and dissected in general discussion. Newcomers and new acting members are always welcome.

Poetry Book Society

See **Organisations of Interest to Poets**

Poetry Ireland

See **Organisations of Interest to Poets**

The Poetry Society

See **Organisations of Interest to Poets**

Private Libraries Association

16 Brampton Grove, Kenton, Harrow, Middlesex HA3 8LG
☎0181 907 6802   Fax 0181 907 6802
Email: Frank@plantage.demon.co.uk
Honorary Secretary *Frank Broomhead*
Membership £25 p.a.

FOUNDED 1956. An international society of book collectors. The Association's objectives are to promote and encourage the awareness of the benefits of book ownership, and the study of books, their production, and ownership; to publish works concerned with this, particularly those which are not commercially profitable, to hold meetings at which papers on cognate subjects can be read and discussed. Lectures and exhibitions are open to non-members.

Producers Alliance for Cinema and Television

See **PACT**

The Professional Authors' and Publishers' Association (PAPA)

292 Kennington Road, London SE11 4LD
☎0171 582 1477   Fax 0171 582 4084
Contact *Tom Deegan, Andy Dempsey*

FOUNDED 1993 to provide self-publishing authors with an imprint, a book production, promotion and marketing service, thereby enabling them to avoid exploitation by so-called 'subsidy' or 'partnership' publishers. Authors using the Association's **New Millenium** imprint own the stock of books and receive the greater proportion of the profits on book sales.

The Publishers Association

1 Kingsway, London WC1B 6XF
☎0171 565 7474   Fax 0171 836 4543
Email: mail@publishers.org.uk
Website: www.publishers.org.uk
Chief Executive *Ronnie Williams, OBE*

The national UK trade association for books, learned journals, and electronic publications, with around 200 member companies in the industry. Very much a trade body representing the industry to Government and the European Commission, and providing services to publishers. *Publishes* the *Directory of Publishing* in association with **Cassell**. Also home of the General Books Council (trade books), the Educational Publishers Council (school books), PA's International Division (BDCI), the Council of

Academic and Professional Publishers, and the Electronic Publishers' Forum.

Publishers Licensing Society Ltd

5 Dryden Street, Covent Garden, London WC2E 9NW
☎0171 829 8486   Fax 0171 829 8488
Email: pls@dial.pipex.com
Website: www.pls.org.uk

Manager *Caroline Elmslie*

FOUNDED in 1981, the PLS obtains mandates from publishers which grant PLS the authority to license photocopying of pages from published works. Some licences for digitalisation of printed works are available. PLS aims to maximise revenue from licences for mandating publishers and to expand the range and repertoire of mandated publishers available to licence holders. It supports the **Copyright Licensing Agency (CLA)** in its efforts to increase the number of legitimate users through the issuing of licences and vigorously pursues any infringements of copyright works belonging to rights' holders.

Publishers Publicity Circle

48 Crabtree Lane, London SW6 6LW
☎0171 385 3708   Fax 0171 385 3708
Email: ppc-@lineone.net

Contact *Christina Thomas*

Enables book publicists from both publishing houses and freelance PR agencies to meet and share information regularly. Meetings, held monthly in central London, provide a forum for press journalists, television and radio researchers and producers to meet publicists collectively. A directory of the PPC membership is published each year and distributed to over 2500 media contacts.

The Queen's English Society

Fernwood, Nightingales, West Chiltington, Pulborough, West Sussex RH20 2QT
☎01798 813001   Fax 0181 870 2356

Honorary Membership Secretary
  David Ellis

Subscription: £10 p.a.; £12 p.a (Joint): £100 (Life)

ESTABLISHED in 1972 to promote and uphold the use of good English and to encourage the enjoyment of the language. Holds regular meetings to which speakers are invited, an annual luncheon and *publishes* a quarterly journal, *Quest*, for which original articles are welcome.

Radio Authority

Holbrook House, 14 Great Queen Street, London WC2B 5DG
☎0171 430 2724   Fax 0171 405 7062
Website: www.radioauthority.org.uk

The Radio Authority plans frequencies, awards licences, regulates programming and advertising, and plays an active role in the discussion and formulation of policies which affect the Independent Radio Industry and its listeners. The number of Independent Radio stations, now over 200, continues to increase with new licences being advertised on a regular basis.

The Romantic Novelists' Association

1 Beechwood Court, The Street, Syderstone, King's Lynn, Norfolk PE31 8TR
☎01485 578594   Fax 01485 578138
Email: john@hilaryjohnson.demon.co.uk

Contact *John Johnson*

Subscription Full & Associate: £25 p.a.; £30 (Overseas, non-EU); New Writers: £55; £60 (Overseas, non-EU)

Membership is open to published writers of romantic fiction (modern or historical), or those who have had two or more full-length serials published. Associate membership is open to publishers, editors, literary agents, booksellers, librarians and others having a close connection with novel writing and publishing. Membership, in the New Writers' Scheme, is available to writers who have not yet had a full-length novel published. New Writers must submit a manuscript each September. The mss receive a report from experienced published members and the reading fee is included in the subscription of £55. Meetings are held in London and the regions with interesting guest speakers. The *RNA News* is published quarterly and issued free to members. The Association makes two annual awards: **The Major Award** for the Romantic Novel of the Year, and **The New Writers Award** for the best published novel by a new writer.

Royal Festival Hall Literature Office

Performing Arts Department, Royal Festival Hall, London SE1 8XX
☎0171 921 0907   Fax 0171 928 2049

Head of Literature *Antonia Byatt*

The Royal Festival Hall presents a year-round literature programme covering all aspects of writing. Regular series range from New Voices to Fiction International and there is a biennial Poetry International Festival. Literature events are now programmed in the Voice Box, Purcell Room and Queen Elizabeth Hall. To join the free mailing list, phone 0171 921 0734.

Royal Society of Literature
1 Hyde Park Gardens, London W2 2LT
☎0171 723 5104   Fax 0171 402 0199
Email: RSLit@aol.com
President *Lord Jenkins of Hillhead*
Subscription £30 p.a.
FOUNDED 1820. Membership by application to the Secretary. Fellowships are conferred by the Society on the proposal of two Fellows. Membership benefits include lectures, discussion meetings and poetry readings in the Society's rooms. Lecturers have included Patrick Leigh Fermor, Germaine Greer, Seamus Heaney, John Mortimer and Tom Stoppard. Presents the **W. H. Heinemann Award** and the **Winifred Holtby Prize**.

Royal Television Society
Holborn Hall, 100 Gray's Inn Road, London WC1X 8AL
☎0171 430 1000   Fax 0171 430 0924
Email: royaltvsociety@btinternet.com
Website: www.rts.org.uk
Subscription £60 p.a.
FOUNDED 1927. Covers all disciplines involved in the television industry. Provides a forum for debate and conferences on technical, social and cultural aspects of the medium. Presents various awards including journalism, programmes, technology, design and commercials. *Publishes* Television Magazine nine times a year for members and subscribers.

Science Fiction Foundation
c/o Liverpool University Library, PO Box 123, Liverpool L69 3DA
☎0151 794 2696/2733   Fax 0151 794 2681
Email: asawyer@liverpool.ac.uk
Website:www.liv.ac.uk/
   ~asawyer/sffchome.html
Contact *Andy Sawyer*
The SFF is a national academic body for the furtherance of science fiction studies. *Publishes* a thrice-yearly magazine, *Foundation* (see entry under **Magazines**), which features academic articles and reviews of new fiction. It also has a reference library (see entry under **Library Services**), housed at Liverpool University.

Scottish Book Trust
The Scottish Book Centre, 137 Dundee Street, Edinburgh EH11 1BG
☎0131 229 3663   Fax 0131 228 4293
Email: scottish.book.trust@dial.pipex.com
Website: www.webpost.net/bts
Contact *Lindsey Fraser*
FOUNDED 1956. Scottish Book Trust works with schools, libraries, writers, artists, publishers, bookshops and individuals to promote the pleasures of reading to people of all ages. It provides a book information service which draws on the children's reference library (a copy of every children's book published in the previous twelve months), the Scottish children's book collection, a range of press cuttings on Scottish literary themes and a number of smaller collections of Scottish books. Scottish Book Trust administers **The Fidler Award** and the **Scottish Writer of the Year Award**; and *publishes* guides to Scottish books and writers, both adult and children's. Scottish Book Trust also produces a range of children's reading posters, literary guides, Scottish poetry posters and a set of six posters featuring contemporary Scottish writers.

Scottish Daily Newspaper Society
48 Palmerston Place, Edinburgh EH12 5DE
☎0131 220 4353   Fax 0131 220 4344
Email: info@sdns.org.uk
Director *Mr J. B. Raeburn*
FOUNDED 1915. Trade association representing publishers of Scottish daily and Sunday newspapers.

Scottish Library Association
Scottish Centre for Information & Library Services, 1 John Street, Hamilton, Strathclyde ML3 7EU
☎01698 458888   Fax 01698 458899
Email: sctlb@leapfrog.almac.co.uk
Website: www.slainte.napier.ac.uk
Director *Robert Craig*
FOUNDED 1908 to bring together everyone engaged in or interested in library work in Scotland. The Association has over 2300 members, covering all aspects of library and information work. Its main aims are the promotion of library services and the qualifications and status of librarians.

Scottish Newspaper Publishers Association
48 Palmerston Place, Edinburgh EH12 5DE
☎0131 220 4353   Fax 0131 220 4344
Email: info@snpa.org.uk

Website: www.snpa.org.uk
Director *Mr J. B. Raeburn*

FOUNDED around 1905. The representative body for the publishers of paid-for weekly and associated free newspapers in Scotland. Represents the interests of the industry to Government, public and other bodies and provides a range of services including marketing of *The Scottish Weekly Press*, industrial relations, and education and training. It is an active supporter of the Press Complaints Commission.

Scottish Print Employers Federation

48 Palmerston Place, Edinburgh EH12 5DE
☎0131 220 4353   Fax 0131 220 4344
Email: info@spef.org.uk
Director *Mr J. B. Raeburn*

FOUNDED 1910. Employers' organisation and trade association for the Scottish printing industry. Represents the interests of the industry to Government, public and other bodies and provides a range of services including industrial relations. Negotiates a national wages and conditions agreement with the Graphical, Paper and Media Union, as well as education, training and commercial activities. The Federation is a member of Intergraf, the international confederation for employers' associations in the printing industry. In this capacity its views are channelled on the increasing number of matters affecting print businesses emanating from the European Union.

Scottish Publishers Association

Scottish Book Centre, 137 Dundee Street, Edinburgh EH11 1BG
☎0131 228 6866   Fax 0131 228 3220
Email: enquiries@scottishbooks.org
Website: www.scottishbooks.org
Director *Lorraine Fannin*
Marketing Manager *Alison Rae*
SBMG/Training *Allan Shanks*
Administrator *Davinder Bedi*

The Association represents over 70 Scottish publishers, from multinationals to very small presses, in a number of capacities, but primarily in the cooperative promotion and marketing of their books. The SPA also acts as an information and advice centre for both the trade and general public. *Publishes* seasonal catalogues, membership lists, the annual *Directory of Publishing in Scotland* and regular newsletters. Represents members at international book fairs; runs an extensive training programme in publishing skills; carries out market research; and encourages export initia-

tives. Also provides administrative back-up for the Scottish Book Marketing Group, a cooperative venture with Scottish booksellers.

The Society of Authors in Scotland

Bonnyton House, Arbirlot, Angus DD11 2PY
☎01241 874131   Fax 01241 874131
Secretary *Eileen Ramsay*

The Scottish branch of **The Society of Authors**, which organises business meetings, social and bookshop events throughout Scotland.

The Society of Authors

84 Drayton Gardens, London SW10 9SB
☎0171 373 6642   Fax 0171 373 5768
Email: authorsoc@writers.org.uk
General Secretary *Mark Le Fanu*
Subscription £65/70 p.a.

FOUNDED 1884. The Society of Authors is an independent trade union with some 6500 members. It advises on negotiations with publishers, broadcasting organisations, theatre managers and film companies; assists with complaints and takes action for breach of contract, copyright infringement, etc. Together with **The Writers' Guild**, the Society has played a major role in advancing the Minimum Terms Agreement for authors. Among the Society's publications are *The Author* (a quarterly journal) and the *Quick Guides* series to various aspects of writing (all free of charge to members). Other services include vetting of contracts, emergency funds for writers, and various special discounts. There are groups within the Society for scriptwriters, children's writers and illustrators, educational writers, medical writers and translators. Authors under 35 or over 65, not earning a significant income from their writing, may apply for lower subscription rates. Contact the Society for a free booklet and a copy of *The Author*.

Society of Civil Service Authors

4 Top Street, Wing, Nr Oakham, Rutland LE15 8SE
Membership Secretary *Mrs Joan Hykin*
Subscription £15 p.a.

FOUNDED 1935. Aims to encourage authorship by present and past members of the Civil Service and to provide opportunities for social and cultural relationships between civil servants who are authors or who aspire to be authors. Annual competitions, open to members only, are held for short stories, poetry, sonnets, travel articles, humour, etc. Members receive *The Civil Service Author*, a bi-monthly magazine.

Occasional meetings in London, one or two weekends outside London.

Society of Freelance Editors and Proofreaders (SFEP)

Mermaid House, 1 Mermaid Court, London SE1 1HR
☎0171 403 5141   Fax 0171 407 1193
Email: admin@sfep.demon.co.uk
Website: www.sfep.org.uk

Chair *Kathleen Lyle*
Vice-chair *Simon de Pinna*
Secretary *Katie Lewis*
Subscription £50 p.a. (Individuals) plus £10 joining fee; Corporate membership available

FOUNDED 1988 in response to the growing number of freelance editors and their increasing importance to the publishing industry. Aims to promote high editorial standards by disseminating information through advice and training, and to achieve recognition of the professional status of its members. The Society also supports moves towards recognised standards of training and qualifications, and is currently putting in place accredited and registered membership of SFEP.

Society of Indexers

Globe Centre, Penistone Road, Sheffield, South Yorkshire S6 3AE
☎0114 2813060   Fax 0114 2813061
Email: admin@socind.demon.co.uk

Secretary *Liza Weinkove*
Administrator *Wendy Burrow*
Subscription £40 p.a.; £60 (Institutions)

FOUNDED 1957. *Publishes The Indexer* (bi-annual, April and October) and a quarterly newsletter. Issues an annual list of members and *Indexers Available (IA)*, which lists members and their subject expertise. In addition, the Society runs an open-learning course entitled *Training in Indexing* and recommends rates of pay (currently £13 per hour).

Society of Women Writers and Journalists

110 Whitehall Road, London E4 6DW
☎0181 529 0886
Email: swwriters@aol.com

Honorary Secretary *Jean Hawkes*
Subscription £25 (Town); £21 (Country); £15 (Overseas). £10 Joining fee

FOUNDED 1894. The first of its kind to be run as an association of women engaged in journalism. Aims to encourage literary achievement, uphold professional standards, and establish social contacts with other writers. Lectures given at monthly lunchtime meetings. Offers advice to members and has regular seminars, etc. *Publishes* a quarterly society journal, *The Woman Journalist*.

Society of Young Publishers

12 Dyott Street, London WC1A 1DF
Website: www.thesyp.demon.co.uk
Subscription £20 p.a.; £15 (Student/ unwaged)

Provides facilities whereby members can increase their knowledge and widen their experience of all aspects of publishing and holds regular social events. Open to those in related occupations, with associate membership available for over-35s. *Publishes* a monthly newsletter called *Inprint* and holds meetings on the last Wednesday of each month at **The Publishers Association**. Please enclose an s.a.e. when writing to the Society.

Sports Writers' Association of Great Britain

c/o Sport England External Affairs, 16 Upper Woburn Place, London WC1H 0QP
☎0171 273 1789   Fax 0171 383 0273
Subscription £23.50 p.a. incl. VAT (London); £11.75 (Regional)

FOUNDED 1948 to promote and maintain a high professional standard among journalists who specialise in sport in all its branches and to serve members' interests. *Publishes* a quarterly bulletin for members.

Theatre Writers' Union

See **The Writers' Guild of Great Britain**

The Translators Association

84 Drayton Gardens, London SW10 9SB
☎0171 373 6642   Fax 0171 373 5768
Email: authorsoc@writers.org.uk

Secretary *Gordon Fielden*

FOUNDED 1958 as a subsidiary group within **The Society of Authors** to deal exclusively with the special problems of literary translators into the English language. Members are entitled to all the benefits and services of the Association, in addition to those of the Society, without extra charge. These include free legal and general advice and assistance on all matters relating to translators' work, including the vetting of contracts and information about improvements in rates of remuneration. Membership is normally confined to translators who have had their work published in volume or serial form or produced in this country for stage, television or radio. Translators of work for industrial firms or government departments are in certain cases admitted to membership if their work, though not on general sale, is published by the organisation commissioning the work. The Association administers several prizes for translators of published work and maintains a database to enable members' details to be supplied to publishers who are seeking a translator for a particular work.

Voice of the Listener and Viewer
101 Kings Drive, Gravesend, Kent
DA12 5BQ
☎01474 352835   Fax 01474 351112
Email: vlv@btinternet.com

The citizen's voice in broadcasting is an independent, non-profit-making society working to ensure independence and high standards in broadcasting. It is also the only consumer body speaking for listeners and viewers on the whole range of broadcasting issues. VLV is funded by its members and is free from sectarian, commercial and political affiliations. Holds public lectures, seminars and conferences, and has frequent contact with MPs, civil servants, the BBC and independent broadcasters, regulators, academics and other consumer groups. VLV has responded to all parliamentary and public enquiries on broadcasting since 1984 and to all consultation documents issued by the ITC and Radio Authority since 1990. The VLV does not handle complaints.

W.A.T.C.H.
See **Writers and their Copyright Holders**

Welsh Academy
See **Academi**

Welsh Books Council (Cyngor Llyfrau Cymru)
Castell Brychan, Aberystwyth, Ceredigion
SY23 2JB
☎01970 624151   Fax 01970 625385
Email: castellbrychan@cllc.org.uk
Website: www.cllc.org.uk

Director *Gwerfyl Pierce Jones*
Head of Editorial Department
   Dewi Morris Jones

FOUNDED 1961 to stimulate interest in Welsh literature and to support authors. The Council distributes the government grant for Welsh language publications and promotes and fosters all aspects of both Welsh and Welsh-interest book production. Its Editorial, Design,

Marketing and Children's Books departments and wholesale distribution centre offer central services to publishers in Wales. Writers in Welsh and English are welcome to approach the Editorial Department for advice on how to get their manuscripts published.

Welsh Union of Writers
13 Tyn–y–Coed Road, Pentyrch, Cardiff
CF4 8NP
Email: wuw@btinternet.com
Secretary *Jean Henderson*
Subscription £10 p.a.; £5 Joining fee

FOUNDED 1982. Independent union. Full membership by application to persons born or working in Wales with at least one publication in a quality journal or other outlet. Associate membership now available for other interested supporters. Lobbies for writing in Wales, represents members in disputes; annual conference and occasional events, publications and twice-yearly newsletter.

Women in Publishing
c/o The Publishers Association, 1 Kingsway, 3rd Floor, Strand, London WC2B 6XF
Website: www.cyberiacafe.net/wip/

Contact *Information Officer*
Membership £20 p.a. (Individuals); £15
   (Unwaged); £25 (if paid for by company)

Aims to promote the status of women working within the publishing industry and related trades, to encourage networking, and to provide training for career and personal development. Meetings (with panels of speakers) held on the second Wednesday of the month at **The Publishers Association** at 6.30 pm. Monthly newsletter *WiPlash* and *Women in Publishing Directory*.

Women Writers Network (WWN)
23 Prospect Road, London NW2 2JU
☎0171 794 5861

Membership Secretary *Cathy Smith*
Subscription £30 p.a. (Full); £25 p.a.
   (Overseas); £20 p.a. ('Newsletter only' UK
   membership)

FOUNDED 1985. Provides a forum for the exchange of information, support, career and networking opportunities for working women writers. Meetings, seminars, excursions, newsletter and directory. Full membership includes free admission to monthly meetings, a directory of members and a monthly newsletter. Details from the Membership Secretary at the address above.

Writers and their Copyright Holders (W.A.T.C.H.)

The Library, The University of Reading,
PO Box 223, Whiteknights, Reading,
Berkshire RG6 6AE
☎0118 9318783   Fax 0118 9316636
Website:www.lib.utexas.edu/Libs/
HRC/WATCH

Contact *Dr David Sutton*

FOUNDED 1994. Provides an on-line database of information about the copyright holders of literary authors. The database is available free of charge on the Internet and the Web. W.A.T.C.H. is the successor project to the Location Register of English Literary Manuscripts and Letters, and continues to deal with location register enquiries.

The Writers' Guild of Great Britain (incorporating The Theatre Writers' Union)

430 Edgware Road, London W2 1EH
☎0171 723 8074   Fax 0171 706 2413
Email: postie@wggb.demon.co.uk
Website: www.writers.org.uk/guild

General Secretary *Alison V. Gray*
Annual subscription 1% of that part of the
    author's income earned in the areas in which
    the Guild operates, with a basic subscription
    of £80 and a maximum of £930

FOUNDED 1959. The Writers' Guild is the writers' trade union, affiliated to the TUC. It represents writers in film, radio, television, theatre and publishing. The Guild has negotiated agreements on which writers' contracts are based with the BBC, Independent Television companies, and **PACT** (the Producers' Alliance for Cinema and Television). Those agreements are regularly renegotiated, both in terms of finance and conditions. In 1997, the Guild membership joined with that of the Theatre Writers' Union to create a new, more powerful union.

In 1979, together with the Theatre Writers' Union, the Guild negotiated the first ever industrial agreement for theatre writers, the TNC Agreement, which covers the **Royal National Theatre**, the **Royal Shakespeare Company**, and the **English Stage Company**. Further agreements have been negotiated with the Theatrical Management Association which covers regional theatre and the **Independent Theatre Council**, the organisation which covers small theatres and the Fringe.

The Guild initiated a campaign over ten years ago which achieved the first ever publishing agreement for writers with the publisher W. H. Allen. Jointly with **The Society of Authors**, the campaign has continued and each year sees new agreements with more publishers. Perhaps the most important breakthrough came with **Penguin** in July 1990. The Guild now also has agreements covering **HarperCollins**, **Random House Group**, **Transworld** and others.

The Guild regularly provides individual help and advice to members on contracts, conditions of work, and matters which affect a member's life as a professional writer. Members are given the opportunity of meeting at craft meetings, which are held on a regular basis throughout the year. Writers can apply for Full Membership if they have one piece of written work for which payment has been received under a contract with terms not less than those negotiated by the Guild. Writers who do not qualify for Full Membership can apply for Candidate Membership. This is open to all those who wish to be involved in writing but have not yet had work published. The subscription fee for this is £35.

Yachting Journalists' Association

3 Friars Lane, Maldon, Essex CM9 6AG
☎01621 855943/0468 962936(mobile)
Fax 01621 852212
Email: petercookyja@compuserve.com

Honorary Secretary *Peter Cook*
Subscription £30 p.a.

To further the interest of yachting, sail and power, and to provide support and assistance to journalists in the field; current membership is just over 250 with 23 from overseas. A handbook, listing details of members and subscribing PR organisations, press facility recommendations, forthcoming events and other useful information, is published annually in April at a cost to non-members and non-advertisers of £5. Information for inclusion should be submitted by the end of February. The YJA organises the Yachtsman of the Year Awards which are in their 44th year. Presented annually at the beginning of January, they consist of the Yachtsman of the Year, Offshore Racing Yachtsman of the Year, Inshore Racing Yachtsman of the Year, Power Yachtsman of the Year, Endeavour and Young Sailor of the Year Awards.

Young Newspaper Executives' Association

See **The Newspaper Society**

Yr Academi Gymreig

See **Academi**

Choosing Your Words Carefully

The libel industry has gone quiet of late and a scandal–hungry press has been deprived of its most nourishing diet. The public loves the court battles in which the high and mighty gamble fortunes on lawyers' fees to defend their fake friend's reputation and honour. As John Mortimer has observed: 'Libel actions fulfil much the same function as the circus in the days of ancient Rome: the miseries of the masses are alleviated by the public suffering of the few, and there are a good many laughs to be got along the way.'

Where then is the next round of contestants? Their reluctance to chance their arm may have something to do with recent changes in the libel laws. Until recently, it was hard to escape from a libel by arguing that it was committed unintentionally. Your opponent had no need to prove that you intended to discredit him or even that he had been harmed by whatever you wrote. All that was necessary was to show that a hurt to reputation had been suffered. The 'offer to make amends' (by fulsome apology, for example) was available but was hedged by technicalities.

Now, under the 1996 Defamation Act, the rules have been tightened to allow for a speedy and relatively inexpensive resolution of disputes. If you did not intend to defame and can show that you were not reckless, you can avoid expensive litigation by offering a published apology, a sum in compensation and a settlement of costs. If the amount to be paid cannot be agreed mutually a judge can make an order.

There is a downside as Daniel Eilon, a solicitor with Campbell Hooper, points out: 'The offer of amends is not so much a defence as an orderly surrender. If you use it, you cannot plead any of the other recognised defences such as justification, fair comment, privilege and innocent dissemination.'

So what if you are in fighting mood? It is a complete defence to prove that a statement, however defamatory, is true in substance and in fact. The trouble with pleading justification, however, is that every significant detail of a statement must be proved to be true, a hard trick to pull.

Another line of defence is to prove that the words complained of are fair comment on a matter of public interest. The defence will fail if the defendant is shown to have been actuated by malice (merely disliking the plaintiff is insufficient) or the facts on which he based the comment were untrue. But fair comment allows for critics to do their worst. For over a century it has been the rule that 'Every latitude must be given to opinion and to prejudice … Mere exaggeration, or even gross exaggeration, would not make the comment unfair.'

Privilege covers 'fair and accurate' reports of public judicial proceedings while innocent dissemination applies only to distributors (not authors, editors or publishers). To rely on this defence, a defendant must show that he has taken reasonable care in relation to the publication of the statement; had no reason to believe that he was contributing to the publication of a defamatory statement; and no effective control over the maker of the statement. This defence came into force in 1996 and was aimed at protecting booksellers. But there is a catch. It now appears that by putting responsibility on 'agents' of author, editor and publisher, a bookseller might still be prosecuted because a court could argue that he has 'contributed to the publication of a defamatory statement'.

To choose any one of these defences is to cut off any line of retreat. There can be no resort to an offer to make amends.

Since 1996, the time limit for starting an action for defamation has been cut from three years to one, thus curbing the use of 'gagging writs' such as those used by the late Robert Maxwell. There is a new summary procedure under which every defamation claim can come before a judge at an early stage. The judge assesses whether the claim is suitable for summary disposal, or whether it should go for trial, with or without a jury. He has power to award damages up to £10,000. This makes it easier for an ordinary citizen to seek redress against a rich opponent who, otherwise, is liable to keep a trial going as long as possible in the hope that a plaintiff will run out of patience and money.

There is some hope that the lid has been put on outrageous libel awards now that the Court of Appeal can provide guidelines. Many reformers would go further. They want the responsibility of a jury to be limited to saying if damages should be substantial, moderate, nominal or contemptuous. The judge would then decide on the appropriate figure. A useful compromise would compel juries to explain their calculations. As Lord Donaldson has observed, 'having to give reasons puts a substantial premium on ensuring that the head rules the heart'.

Every writer is responsible for his own work. But this should not mean that when he makes mistakes he alone carries the can. Journalists are usually covered by their employers who take on the whole cost of a libel action. If it were otherwise many of our best known columnists would be out of business. When Alan Clark won his case against the London *Evening Standard* for 'passing off' a spoof diary as his own, the costs amounted to £250,000. How many journalists could afford that?

Book publishers are less protective of those who serve their commercial interests. A typical publishing contract includes a warranty clause which entitles the publisher to be indemnified by the author against damages and costs if any part of the work turns out to be libellous.

In fairness, it must be said that the indemnity is rarely invoked unless a publisher feels he has been deceived or misled. But, at the very least, the author should insist that his publisher has the manuscript read for libel and that his contract does not specify unlimited liability.

Libel insurance offers some sort of safeguard and a publisher who is insured is clearly preferable to one who is not. But most insurance policies carry severe limitations, not least a ceiling on the payout of damages. Also, reading for libel can be expensive for a book that is in any way controversial. As Richard West discovered when he wrote an investigative volume, 'The lawyer who read it for libel got £1000. The lawyer who wrote in to the publisher to complain on behalf of his client was probably paid about £5000.' Since West ended up with little more than £500 for his efforts he concluded he had chosen the wrong profession.

To make matters worse, the risks of encountering a libel action have increased substantially with the extension of 'no win, no fee' litigation to all claims for damages. It is already commonplace to hear solicitors advertising on commercial radio for prospective clients to come forward. Allowing actions to be funded by solicitors working for a success fee is bound to appeal to the easily offended. Even if a loony case fails to get to court, a cost-conscious publisher may choose to play safe by amending a text to a point where it loses its cutting edge and thus its sales appeal. It is not unknown for an entire book to be jettisoned to save on lawyers' bills.

Peter Marsh, a barrister specialising in defamation, offers these tips for writers about to embark on a controversial project.

'If the subject or subjects of critical comment are still alive, beware; if you are writing a book about real life incidents but have changed names to avoid identification, take extreme care in the choice of names for your characters; remember that damage to a person's reputation can be caused by innuendo. For example, to write of someone that most people thought he was taking advantage of the Inland Revenue may suggest some improper and unethical practice. If a living person is going to be the subject of comment which is expressly or implicitly derogatory, make absolutely sure your facts are correct and can be substantiated. Otherwise, your publisher is going to be propelled into the courtroom naked of a defence.'

Is there anything to be said for those who bring libel actions? No better summary of the risks and tribulations for all but the excessively rich appears in Adam Raphael's absorbing indictment, *Grotesque Libels*.

'The problems of a libel action can be stated quite simply. The law is highly technical and the pleadings so complex that even its skilled practitioners often differ on the most basic questions. The costs of the lawyers involved are so high that they make the fees charged by any other profession appear to be a mere bagatelle. The opportunities for obstruction and delay are such that it can take as long as five years to bring a libel action to court. When it eventually does reach the court, the damages left to the whim of a jury are so uncertain that the result is often no sounder than a dodgy fruit machine. A libel action has in fact more in common with a roulette wheel than justice. The net result for both plaintiffs and defendants is that such actions are a nightmare with only the lawyers able to sleep soundly.'

No wonder Bernard Levin asserts 'If I were libelled (I have frequently been) and were given the choice of suing or having all my toenails pulled out with red-hot pincers while listening to *Pelléas et Mélisande*, I think it would be a close run thing.'

As for those who are unable to keep out of the courts, the best advice comes from Tom Crone in his book on *Law and the Media*. The libel litigant, he says, must possess two prime qualities – 'a strong nerve and a deep pocket'.

Literary Societies

Most literary societies exist on a shoestring budget; it is a good idea to enclose an A5 s.a.e. with all correspondence needing a reply.

Margery Allingham Society

2B High Green, Winchelsea, East Sussex
TN36 4HB
☎01797 222363   Fax 01797 222363
Contact *Mrs Pamela Bruxner*
Subscription £8 p.a.

FOUNDED 1988 to promote interest in and study of the works of Margery Allingham. The Society *publishes* two issues of the newsletter, *The Bottle Street Gazette*, per year. Contributions welcome. Two social events a year. Open membership.

Jane Austen Society

Carton House, Redwood Lane, Medstead, Alton, Hampshire GU34 5PE
☎01705 475855   Fax 0870 056 0330
Email: rosemary@sndc.demon.co.uk
Website: www.sndc.demon.co.uk/jas.htm
Honorary Secretary *Susan McCartan*
Subscription UK: £10 (Annual); £15 (Joint); £30 (Corporate); £150 (Life); Overseas: £12 (Annual); £18 (Joint); £33 (Corporate); £180 (Life)

FOUNDED 1940 to promote interest in and enjoyment of Jane Austen's novels and letters. The society has branches in Bath & Bristol, Midlands, London, Oxford, Kent and Hampshire. There are independent Societies in North America and Australia.

William Barnes Society

75 Prince of Wales Road, Dorchester, Dorset DT1 1PS
☎01305 264405
Contact *Mrs Pamela Holden*
Subscription £6 p.a. (Single); £8 (Joint)

FOUNDED 1983 to provide a forum in which admirers of the Dorset poet could share fellowship and pleasure in his work. William Barnes (1801–86) is best known as the writer of Dorset dialect poetry. His interest in dialect prompted him to become a learned philologist and he published many papers in defence of native English against the incursions of French and Latin. Organises meetings and social events and *publishes* a newsletter in May and November.

The Baskerville Hounds

6 Bramham Moor, Hill Head, Fareham, Hampshire PO14 3RU
☎01329 667325
Chairman *Philip Weller*
Subscription £6 p.a.

FOUNDED 1989. An international Sherlock Holmes society specialising solely in studies of *The Hound of the Baskervilles* and its Dartmoor associations. *Publishes* a quarterly newsletter, an annual journal and specialist monographs. It also organises many social functions, usually on Dartmoor. Open membership.

The Beckford Society

15 Healey Street, London NW1 8SR
☎0171 267 7750   Fax 01985 213239
Secretary *Sidney Blackmore*
Subscription £10 (min.) p.a.

FOUNDED 1995 to promote an interest in the life and works of William Beckford (1760–1844) and his circle. Encourages Beckford studies and scholarship through exhibitions, lectures and publications, including an annual journal, *The Beckford Journal*, and occasional newsletters.

Arnold Bennett Society

106 Scotia Road, Burslem, Stoke on Trent, Staffordshire ST6 4ET
☎01782 816311
Secretary *Mrs Jean Potter*
Subscription £6 (Single); £7 (Family); £5 (Unwaged)

Aims to promote interest in the life and works of 'Five Towns' author Arnold Bennett and other North Staffordshire writers. Annual dinner. Regular functions in and around Buslem. Quarterly newsletter. Open membership.

E. F. Benson Society

The Old Coach House, High Street, Rye, East Sussex TN31 7JF
☎01797 223114   Fax 0171 580 0763
Secretary *Allan Downend*
Subscription £7.50 (UK/Europe); £12.50 (Overseas)

FOUNDED 1985 to promote the life and work of E. F. Benson and the Benson family. Organises social and literary events, exhibitions, talks and Benson interest walks in Rye. *Publishes* a quarterly newsletter and annual journal, *The Dodo*, postcards and reprints of E. F. Benson articles and short stories. Holds an archive which includes the Seckersen Collection (transcriptions of the Benson collection at the Bodleian Library in Oxford).

E. F. Benson/The Tilling Society
5 Friars Bank, Pett Road, Guestling, East Sussex TN35 4ET
Fax 01424 813237
Contact *Cynthia Reavell*
Subscription Full starting membership (members receive all back newsletters) £24 (UK); £28 (Overseas); or Annual Membership (members receive only current year's newsletters) £8 (UK); £10 (Overseas).

FOUNDED 1982 for the exchange of news, information and speculation about E. F. Benson, his works and, in particular, his *Mapp & Lucia* novels. Readings, discussions and twice-yearly newsletter. Acts as a clearing house for every sort of news and activity concerning E. F. Benson.

The Betjeman Society
35 Eaton Court, Boxgrove Avenue, Guildford, Surrey GU1 1XH
☎01483 560882
Honorary Secretary *John Heald*
Subscription £7 (Individual); £9 (Family); £3 (Student); £2 extra each category for Overseas members

Aims to promote the study and appreciation of the work and life of Sir John Betjeman. Annual programme includes poetry readings, lectures, discussions, visits to places associated with Betjeman, and various social events. Meetings are held in London and other centres. Regular newsletter and annual journal, *The Betjemanian*.

The Bewick Society
c/o The Dean's Office, Faculty of Arts and Design, University of Northumbria, Squires Building, Sandyford Road, Newcastle upon Tyne NE1 8ST
☎0191 227 3138   Fax 0191 227 4077
Chairman *Kenneth McConkey*
Subscription £7 p.a.

FOUNDED 1988 to promote an interest in the life and work of Thomas Bewick, wood-engraver and naturalist (1753–1828). Organises related events and meetings, and is associated with the Bewick birthplace museum.

Biggles & Co
See **The W. E. Johns Society**

Birmingham Central Literary Association
c/o Birmingham & Midland Institute, Margaret Street, Birmingham B3 3DS
☎0121 236 3591
Contact *The Honorary Secretary*

Holds fortnightly meetings at the Birmingham Midland Institute to discuss the lives and work of authors and poets. Holds an annual dinner to celebrate Shakespeare's birthday.

The George Borrow Society
The Gables, 112 Irchester Road, Rushden, Northants NN10 9XQ
☎01933 312965   Fax 01933 312965
President *Sir Angus Fraser, KCB TD*
Honorary Secretary *Dr James H. Reading*
Honorary Treasurer *Mrs Ena R. J. Reading*
Chairman/Editor *George Borrow Bulletin:*
   Dr Ann M. Ridler, St Mary's Cottage,
   61 Thame Road, Warborough,
   Wallingford, Oxford OX10 7EA
   ☎01865 858379 Fax 01865 858575
   Email: 113250.1724@compuserve.com
Subscription £10 p.a.

FOUNDED 1991 to promote knowledge of the life and works of George Borrow (1803–81), traveller, linguist and writer. The Society holds biennial conferences (with published proceedings) and informal intermediate gatherings, all at places associated with Borrow. *Publishes* the *George Borrow Bulletin* twice yearly, a newsletter containing scholarly articles, publications relating to Borrow, reports of past events and news of forthcoming events. Member of the **Alliance of Literary Societies** and corporate associate member of the Centre of East Anglian Studies (CEAS) at the University of East Anglia, Norwich (Borrow's home city for many years).

Elinor Brent-Dyer
See **Friends of the Chalet School**

British Fantasy Society
2 Harwood Street, Heaton Norris, Stockport, Cheshire SK4 1JJ
☎0161 476 5368 (after 6pm)
President *Ramsey Campbell*
Vice-President *Jan Edwards*
Secretary *Robert Parkinson*

Subscription from £20 p.a. (Apply to Secretary.)

FOUNDED 1971 for devotees of fantasy, horror and related fields in literature, art and the cinema. *Publishes* a regular newsletter with information and reviews of new books and films, plus related fiction and non-fiction magazines. Annual conference at which the **British Fantasy Awards** are presented. These awards are voted on by the membership and are not an open competition.

The Brontë Society

Brontë Parsonage Museum, Haworth, Keighley, West Yorkshire BD22 8DR
☎01535 642323   Fax 01535 647131
Contact *Membership Secretary*
Subscription £17 p.a. (UK/Europe); £7.50 (Student); £5 (Junior – up to age 14); £25 (Overseas); Joint subscriptions and life membership also available

FOUNDED 1893. Aims and activities include the preservation of manuscripts and other objects related to or connected with the Brontë family, and the maintenance and development of the museum and library at Haworth. The society holds regular meetings, lectures and exhibitions; and *publishes* information relating to the family, a bi-annual society journal *Transactions* and a bi-annual *Gazette*. Freelance contributions for either publication should be sent to the Publications Secretary at the address above.

The Browning Society

163 Wembley Hill Road, Wembley Park, Middlesex HA9 8EL
☎0181 904 8401
Honorary Secretary *Ralph Ensz*
Subscription £15 p.a.

FOUNDED 1969 to promote an interest in the lives and poetry of Robert and Elizabeth Barrett Browning. Meetings are arranged in the London area, one of which occurs in December at Westminster Abbey to commemorate Robert Browning's death.

The John Buchan Society

Limpsfield, 16 Ranfurly Road, Bridge of Weir PA11 3EL
☎01505 613116
Secretary *Russell Paterson*
Subscription £10 (Full/Overseas); £4 (Associate); £6 (Junior); £20 (Corporate); £90 (Life)

To perpetuate the memory of John Buchan and

to promote a wider understanding of his life and works. Holds regular meetings and social gatherings, *publishes* a journal, and liaises with the John Buchan Centre at Broughton in the Scottish borders.

The Burns Federation

The Dick Institute, Elmbank Avenue, Kilmarnock, Strathclyde KA1 3BU
☎01563 572469   Fax 01563 572469
Chief Executive *Shirley Bell*
Subscription £15 p.a.(Individual); £30 (Club subscription)

FOUNDED 1885 to encourage interest in the life and work of Robert Burns and keep alive the old Scottish Tongue. The Society's interests go beyond Burns himself in its commitment to the development of Scottish literature, music and arts in general. *Publishes* the quarterly *Burns Chronicle/Burnsian*.

The Byron Society

Byron House, 6 Gertrude Street, London SW10 0JN
☎0171 352 5112
Honorary Director, Byron Society *Mrs Elma Dangerfield OBE*
Subscription £20 p.a.

Also: Newstead Abbey Byron Society, Newstead Abbey, Newstead Abbey Park, Nottingham NG15 8GE
☎01623 797392
Contact *Mrs Maureen Crisp)*

FOUNDED 1876; revived in 1971. Aims to promote knowledge and discussion of Lord Byron's life and works, and those of his contemporaries, through lectures, readings, concerts, performances and international conferences. *Publishes* annually in April *The Byron Journal*, a scholarly journal – £5 plus £1 postage.

Randolph Caldecott Society

Clatterwick Hall, Little Leigh, Northwich, Cheshire CW8 4RJ
☎01606 891303 (day)/781731 (evening)
Honorary Secretary *Kenneth N. Oultram*
Subscription £7–£10 p.a.

FOUNDED 1983 to promote the life and work of artist/book illustrator Randolph Caldecott. Meetings held in the spring and autumn in Caldecott's birthplace, Chester. Guest speakers, outings, newsletter, exchanges with the society's American counterpart. (Caldecott died and was buried in St Augustine, Florida.) A medal in his memory is awarded annually in the US for children's book illustration.

The Carlyle Society, Edinburgh

Dept of English Literature, The University of Edinburgh, David Hume Tower, George Square, Edinburgh EH8 9JX
Fax 0131 650 6898
Email: ian.campbell@ed.ac.uk
Contact *The President*
Subscription £2 p.a.; £10 (Life); $20 (US)

FOUNDED 1929 to examine the lives of Thomas Carlyle and his wife Jane, his writings, contemporaries, and influences. Meetings are held about six times a year and occasional papers are published annually. Enquiries should be addressed to the President of the Society at the address above or to the Secretary at 15 Lennox Street, Edinburgh EH4 1QB.

Lewis Carroll Society

Acorns, Dargate, Near Faversham, Kent
ME13 9HG   Fax 01227 751339
Secretary *Sarah Stanfield*
Subscription Individual: £13 (UK);
£15 (Europe); £17 (Outside Europe);
£10 (Retired rate); £2 (Additional family members); Institutions: £26 (UK);
£28 (Europe); £30 (Outside Europe)

FOUNDED 1969 to bring together people with an interest in Charles Dodgson and promote research into his life and works. *Publishes* bi-annual journal *The Carrollian*, featuring scholarly articles and reviews; a newsletter (*Bandersnatch*) which reports on Carrollian events and the Society's activities; and *The Lewis Carroll Review*, a book reviewing journal. Regular meetings held in London with lectures, talks, outings, etc.

Lewis Carroll Society (Daresbury)

Clatterwick Hall, Little Leigh, Northwich, Cheshire CW8 4RJ
☎01606 891303 (day)/781731 (evening)
Honorary Secretary *Kenneth N. Oultram*
Subscription £5 p.a.

FOUNDED 1970. To promote the life and work of Charles Dodgson, author of the world-famous *Alice's Adventures*. Holds regular meetings in the spring and autumn in Carroll's birthplace, Daresbury, in Cheshire. Guest speakers, theatre visits and a newsletter. Appoints annually a 10-year-old 'Alice' who is available for public engagements.

Friends of the Chalet School

4 Rock Terrace, Coleford, Bath, Somerset BA3 5NF
☎01373 812705   Fax 01373 813517
Email: cridland@telecoll.co.uk
Contact *Ann Mackie-Hunter, Clarissa Cridland*
Subscription £7.50 p.a.; £6 (Under-18);
Outside UK: details on application

FOUNDED 1989 to promote the works of Elinor Brent-Dyer. The society has members worldwide; *publishes* four newsletters a year and runs a lending library.

The Raymond Chandler Society

6 Barkers Road, Nether Edge, Sheffield S7 1SE
☎0114 255 6302   Fax 0114 255 6302
Email: william.adamson@zsp.uni-ulm.de
UK Contact *Simon Beckett*
Subscription £15 p.a. (£7 concessions)

Although based in Germany, the Society has an international membership. Its foremost concerns are with Raymond Chandler's works and his influence and reception within a historical and contemporary context, but it is also concerned with the genre of the 'crime novel' in general. Presents the 'Marlowe' awards (see entry under **Prizes**). *Publishes* the *Chandler Yearbook*, a scholarly publication containing reviews and articles on crime writing in both English and German. The Society attends international conferences such as 'Dead on Deansgate' and 'Bouchercon', and organises the Chandler Symposium, usually held in Ulm, Germany in July.

The Chesterton Society UK

11 Lawrence Leys, Bloxham, Near Banbury, Oxfordshire OX15 4NU
☎01295 720869
Honorary Secretary *Robert Hughes, KHS*
Subscription £12.50 p.a.

FOUNDED 1964 to promote the ideas and writings of G. K. Chesterton.

The Children's Books History Society

25 Field Way, Hoddesdon, Hertfordshire EN11 0QN
☎01992 464885   Fax 01992 464885
Email: cbhs@abcgarrett.demon.co.uk
Membership Secretary *Mrs Pat Garrett*
Subscription £10 p.a.

ESTABLISHED 1969. Aims to promote an appreciation of children's books and to study their history, bibliography and literary content. The

Society holds approximately six meetings per year in London and a summer meeting to a collection, or to a location with a children's book connection. Three newsletters issued annually, also an occasional paper. The Society constitutes the British branch of the Friends of the Osborne and Lillian H. Smith Collections in Toronto, Canada, and also liaises with the **Library Association**. In 1990, the Society established its biennial Harvey Darton Award for a book, published in English, which extends our knowledge of some aspect of British children's literature of the past. 1998 joint-winners: John Goldthwaite *The Natural History of Make-Believe* and Peter Newbolt *G. A. Henty 1832–1902: a bibliographical study of his British editors with short accounts of his publishers, illustrators and designers etc.*

The John Clare Society

The Stables, 1A West Street, Helpston,
Peterborough PE6 7DU
☎01733 252678
Website: human.ntu.ac.uk/clare/clare.html
Honorary Secretary *Peter Moyse*
Subscription £9.50 (Individual);
£12.50 (Joint); £7.50 (Fully Retired);
£9.50 (Joint Retired); £10 (Group/
Library); £3 (Student, Full-time);
£12.50 sterling draft/$25 (Overseas)

FOUNDED 1981 to promote a wider appreciation of the life and works of the poet John Clare (1793–1864). Organises an annual festival in Helpston in July; arranges exhibitions, poetry readings and conferences; and *publishes* an annual society journal and quarterly newsletter.

Wilkie Collins Society

47 Hereford Road, Acton, London W3 9JW
Chairman *Andrew Gasson*
Membership Secretary *Paul Lewis*
Subscription £8.50 (UK); $12.50 (US/
outside Europe – remittance must be made
in UK sterling)

FOUNDED 1980 to provide information on and promote interest in the life and works of Wilkie Collins, one of the first English novelists to deal with the detection of crime. *The Woman in White* appeared in 1860 and *The Moonstone* in 1868. *Publishes* newsletters, reprints of Collins' work and an occasional journal.

The Arthur Conan Doyle Society

PO Box 1360, Ashcroft, British Columbia
Canada V0K 1A0
☎001 250 453 2045   Fax 001 250 453 2075
Email: ashtree@ash-tree.bc.ca

Website: www.ash-tree.bc.ca/acdsocy.html
Joint Organisers *Christopher Roden,
Barbara Roden*
Membership Contact *R. Dixon-Smith*,
59 Stonefield, Bar Hill, Cambridge CB3 8TE
Subscription £16 (UK); £16 (Overseas);
Family rates available

FOUNDED 1989 to promote the study and discussion of the life and works of Sir Arthur Conan Doyle. Occasional meetings, functions and visits. *Publishes* a bi-annual journal together with reprints of Conan Doyle's writings.

The Rhys Davies Trust

10 Heol Don, Whitchurch, Cardiff CF4 2AU
☎01222 623359   Fax 01222 529202
Contact *Meic Stephens*

FOUNDED 1990 to perpetuate the literary reputation of the Welsh prose writer, Rhys Davies (1901–78), and to foster Welsh writing in English. Organises competitions in association with other bodies such as **The Welsh Academy**, puts up plaques on buildings associated with Welsh writers, offers grant-aid for book production, etc.

The Dickens Fellowship

48 Doughty Street, London WC1N 2LF
☎0171 405 2127   Fax 0171 831 5175
Honorary General Secretary
Edward G. Preston
Subscription £5 (First year); £8.50 (Renewal)

FOUNDED 1902. The Society's particular aims and objectives are: to bring together lovers of Charles Dickens; to spread the message of Dickens, his love of humanity ('the keynote of all his work'); to remedy social injustice for the poor and oppressed; to assist in the preservation of material and buildings associated with Dickens. Annual conference. *Publishes* journal called *The Dickensian* (available at special rate to members) and organises a full programme of lectures, discussions, visits and conducted walks throughout the year. Branches worldwide.

Early English Text Society

Christ Church, Oxford OX1 1DP
Fax 01865 794199
Executive Secretary *R. F. S. Hamer* (at
address above)
Editorial Secretary *Dr H. L. Spencer* (at
Exeter College, Oxford OX1 3DP)
Membership Secretary *Dr W. E. J. Collier*
(at Buffers Cottage, Station Road, Hope,
Derbyshire S33 2RR)

Subscription £15 p.a. (UK); $30 (US); $35 (Canada)

FOUNDED 1864. Concerned with the publication of early English texts. Members receive annual publications (one or two a year) or may select titles from the backlist in lieu.

The Eighteen Nineties Society (incorporating The Francis Thompson Society)

97D Brixton Road, London SW9 6EE
☎0171 582 4690

Patron *HRH Princess Michael of Kent*
President *Countess of Longford CBE*
Chairman *Martyn Goff OBE*
Honorary Secretary G. *Krishnamurti*
Subscription £20 p.a. (UK); $35 (US)

FOUNDED 1963 to bring together admirers of the work of Francis Thompson, the Society widened its scope in 1972 to embrace the artistic and literary scene of the entire decade (Impressionism, Realism, Naturalism, Symbolism). Assists members' research into the literature and art of the period; mounts exhibitions; *publishes* an annual journal and quarterly newsletter, plus biographies of neglected writers and artists of the period under the general title of *Makers of the Nineties*.

The George Eliot Fellowship

71 Stepping Stones Road, Coventry, Warwickshire CV5 8JT
☎01203 592231

Contact *Mrs Kathleen Adams*
Subscription £10 p.a.; £100 (Life); Concessions for pensioners

FOUNDED 1930. Exists to honour George Eliot and promote interest in her life and works. Readings, memorial lecture, birthday luncheon and functions. Issues a quarterly newsletter and an annual journal. Awards an annual prize for a George Eliot essay.

Folly (Fans of Light Literature for the Young)

21 Warwick Road, Pokesdown, Bournemouth, Dorset BH7 6JW
☎01202 432562   Fax 01202 460059
Email: folly@sims.abel.co.uk

Contact *Mrs Sue Sims*
Subscription £6 p.a. (UK); £7 (Europe); £8.50 (Worldwide)

FOUNDED 1990 to promote interest in a wide variety of children's authors – with a bias towards writers of girls' books and school stories. *Publishes* three magazines a year.

The Franco-Midland Hardware Company

6 Bramham Moor, Hill Head, Fareham, Hampshire PO14 3RU
☎01329 667325

Chairman *Philip Weller*
Subscription £15 p.a.

FOUNDED 1989. 'The world's leading Sherlock Holmes correspondence study group and the most active Holmesian society in Britain.' *Publishes* bi-annual journal, a bi-annual news magazine and at least six specialist monographs a year. It provides certificated self-study courses and organises monthly functions at Holmes-associated locations. Open membership.

The Gaskell Society

Far Yew Tree House, Over Tabley, Knutsford, Cheshire WA16 0HN
☎01565 634668
Email: JoanLeach@aol.com
Website: www.lang.nagoya-ac.jp/~masuoka/ Gaskell.htm

Honorary Secretary *Joan Leach*
Subscription £8 p.a.; £12 (Overseas)

FOUNDED 1985 to promote and encourage the study and appreciation of the life and works of Elizabeth Cleghorn Gaskell. Meetings held in Knutsford, Manchester and London; residential study weekends and visits; annual journal and bi-annual newsletter. On alternate years holds either a residential weekend conference or overseas visit.

The Ghost Story Society

PO Box 1360, Ashcroft, British Columbia Canada V0K 1A0
☎001 250 453 2045   Fax 001 250 453 2075
Email: ashtree@ash-tree.bc.ca
Website: www.ash-tree.bc.ca/gss.html

Joint Organisers *Barbara Roden,*
Christopher Roden
Subscription UK: £13.50 (Surface mail)/ £15 (Airmail); $24 (US); $31 (Canadian)

FOUNDED 1988. Devoted mainly to supernatural fiction in the literary tradition of M. R. James, Walter de la Mare, Algernon Blackwood, E. F. Benson, A. N. L. Murphy, R. H. Malden, etc. *Publishes* a thrice-yearly journal, *All Hallows*, which includes new fiction in the genre and non-fiction of relevance to the genre.

Rider Haggard
Appreciation Society
27 Deneholm, Whitley Bay, Tyne & Wear
NE25 9AU
☎0191 252 4516   Fax 0191 252 4516
Email: 106251.3413@compuserve.com
Contact *Roger Allen*
Subscription £8 p.a. (UK); £10 (Overseas)
FOUNDED 1985 to promote appreciation of the
life and works of Sir Henry Rider Haggard,
English novelist, 1856–1925. News/books ex-
change, and meetings every two years.

James Hanley Network
Old School House, George Green Road,
George Green, Wexham, Buckinghamshire
SL3 6BJ
☎01753   578632
Email: gostick@altavista.net
Website:www.jameshanley.mcmail.com/
  INDEX.HTM
Network Coordinator *Chris Gostick*
An informal international association FOUNDED
in 1977 for all those interested in exploring and
publicising the works and contribution to lit-
erature of the novelist and dramatist James
Hanley (1901–1985). *Publishes* an annual
newsletter and more formal publications.
Occasional conferences are planned for the
future. All enquiries welcome.

The Thomas Hardy Society
PO Box 1438, Dorchester, Dorset DT1 1YH
☎01305 251501   Fax 01305 251501
Honorary Secretary *Miss Eileen Johnson*
Subscription £12 (Individual);
  £16 (Corporate); £15 (Individual Overseas);
  £20 (Corporate Overseas)
FOUNDED 1967 to promote the reading and
study of the works and life of Thomas Hardy.
Thrice-yearly journal, events and a biennial
conference.

The Henty Society
Fox Hall, Kelshall, Royston, Hertfordshire
SG8 9SE
☎01763 287208
Honorary Secretary *Mrs Ann J. King*
Subscription £13 p.a. (UK); £16 (Overseas)
FOUNDED 1977 to study the life and work of
George Alfred Henty, and to publish research,
bibliographical data and lesser-known works,
namely short stories. Organises conferences and
social gatherings in the UK and Canada, and
publishes quarterly bulletins to members.

Published in 1996: *G. A. Henty (1832–1902) a
Bibliographical Study* by Peter Newbolt.

Sherlock Holmes Society
(Northern Musgraves)
Fairbank, Beck Lane, Bingley, West Yorkshire
BD16 4DN
☎01274 563426
Contact *John Hall, Anne Jordan*
Subscription £17 p.a. (UK)
FOUNDED 1987 to promote enjoyment and
study of Sir Arthur Conan Doyle's Sherlock
Holmes through publications and meetings.
One of the largest Sherlock Holmes societies in
Great Britain. Honorary members include Bert
Coules, Richard Lancelyn Green, Edward
Hardwicke and Douglas Wilmer. Past hon-
orary members: Dame Jean Conan Doyle,
Peter Cushing and Jeremy Brett. Open mem-
bership. Lectures, presentations and consulta-
tion on matters relating to Holmes and Conan
Doyle available.

Sherlock Holmes
See **The Franco-Midland Hardware
Company**

Hopkins Society
35 Manor Park, Gloddaeth Avenue,
Llandudno LL30 2SE
☎01492 878334
Contact *Ambrose Boothby*
Subscription £7 p.a.
FOUNDED 1990 to celebrate the life and work
of Gerard Manley Hopkins; to inform members of any publications, courses or events
about the poet. Holds an annual lecture on
Hopkins in the spring; produces two newsletters a year; sponsors and organises educational
projects based on Hopkins' life and works.

W. W. Jacobs Appreciation Society
3 Roman Road, Southwick, West Sussex
BN42 4TP
☎01273 871017   Fax 01273 871017
Contact *A. R. James*
FOUNDED 1988 to encourage and promote the
enjoyment of the works of W. W. Jacobs, and
stimulate research into his life and works.
Publishes a quarterly newsletter free to those
who send s.a.e. (9x4ins). Contributions welcome but no payment made. Preferred lengths
600–1200 words. No subscription charge.
Biography, bibliography, directories of plays
and films are available for purchase.

Richard Jefferies Society

Eidsvoll, Bedwells Heath, Boars Hill, Oxford
OX1 5JE
☎01865 735678

Honorary Secretary *Lady Phyllis Treitel*
Membership Secretary *Mrs Margaret Evans*
Subscription £7 p.a. (Individual); £8 (Joint);
Life membership for those over 50

FOUNDED 1950 to promote understanding of
the work of Richard Jefferies, nature/country
writer, novelist and mystic (1848–87). Produces
newsletters, reports and an annual journal;
organises talks, discussions and readings. Library
and archives. Assists in maintaining the museum
in Jefferies' birthplace at Coate near Swindon.
Membership applications should be sent to
Margaret Evans, 23 Hardwell Close, Grove, Nr
Wantage, Oxon OX12 0BN.

Jerome K. Jerome Society

c/o Fraser Wood, Mayo and Pinson,
15/16 Lichfield Street, Walsall, West Midlands
WS1 1TS
☎01922 629000   Fax 01922 721065

Honorary Secretary *Tony Gray*
Subscription £7 p.a. (Ordinary);
    £25 (Corporate); £6 (Joint);
    £2.50 (Under 21/Over 65)

FOUNDED 1984 to stimulate interest in Jerome
K. Jerome's life and works (1859–1927). One
of the Society's principal activities is the support
of a small museum in the author's birthplace,
Walsall. Meetings, lectures, events and a twice-
yearly newsletter *Idle Thoughts*. Annual dinner
in Walsall near Jerome's birth date (2nd May).

The W. E. Johns Society

Canna, West Drive, Bracklesham Bay,
Chichester, West Sussex PO20 8PF
☎01243 671209

Contact *Jenny Schofield*
Subscription £8 p.a.

Publishes bi-annual magazine, *Biggles Flies Again*
and usually holds two meetings (in Hertford
and Nottingham) each year.

Johnson Society

Johnson Birthplace Museum, Breadmarket
Street, Lichfield, Staffordshire WS13 6LG
☎01543 264972

Hon. General Secretary *Mrs Norma Hooper*
Subscription £7.50 p.a.; £10 (Joint)

FOUNDED 1910 to encourage the study of the
life, works and times of Samuel Johnson
(1709–1784) and his contemporaries. The
Society is committed to the preservation of the
Johnson Birthplace Museum and Johnson
memorials.

Johnson Society of London

255 Baring Road, Grove Park, London
SE12 0BQ
☎0181 851 0173
Email: jsl@nbbl.demon.co.uk
Website: www.nbbl.demon.co.uk/index.html

Honorary Secretary *Mrs Z. E. O'Donnell*
Subscription £10 p.a.; £12.50 (Joint)

FOUNDED 1928 to promote the knowledge and
appreciation of Dr Samuel Johnson and his
works. Regular meetings from October to
April in the Vestry Hall of St Edmund the King,
Lombard Street in London on the second
Saturday of each month, and a commemoration
ceremony around the anniversary of Johnson's
death (December) held in Westminster Abbey.

The Just William Society

15 St James' Avenue, Bexhill-on-Sea,
East Sussex TN40 2DN
☎01424 216065

Secretary *Michael Vigar*
Treasurer *Phil Woolley*
Subscription £7 p.a. (UK); £10 (Overseas);
    £5 (Juvenile/Student); £15 (Family)

FOUNDED 1994 to further knowledge of
Richmal Crompton's *William* and *Jimmy* books.
An annual 'William' meeting is held in April,
although this is not currently organised by the
Society. The Honorary President of the Society
is Richmal Crompton's niece, Richmal Ashbee.

The Keats–Shelley Memorial Association (Inc)

(Registered office): 1 Lewis Road, Radford
Semele, Warwickshire CV31 1UB

Contact *Honorary Treasurer* (at 10 Lansdowne
    Road, Tunbridge Wells, Kent TN1 2NJ.
    ☎01892 533452 Fax 01892 519142)
Subscription £10 p.a.; £100 (Life)

FOUNDED 1909 to promote appreciation of the
works of Keats and Shelley, and their contemporaries. One of the Society's main tasks is the
preservation of 26 Piazza di Spagna in Rome as
a memorial to the British Romantic poets in
Italy, particularly Keats and Shelley. *Publishes* an
annual review of Romantic Studies called the
Keats-Shelley Review, arranges events and lectures for Friends and promotes bursaries and
competitive writing on Romantic Studies. The
review is edited by *Angus Graham-Campbell*, c/o
Eton College, Windsor, Berkshire SL4 6EA.

Kent & Sussex Poetry Society

23 Arundel Road, Tunbridge Wells, Kent
TN1 1TB
☎01892 530438

Honorary Secretary *Joyce Walter*
Subscription £10 p.a. (Full); £6
(Concessionary – country members living
farther afield, senior citizens, under-16s,
unemployed); £2 (per meeting)

FOUNDED 1946 to promote the enjoyment of
poetry. Monthly meetings, including readings
by major poets, and a monthly workshop.
Publishes an annual folio of members' work
based on Members' Competition, adjudicated
and commented upon by a major poet, and
runs an Open Poetry Competition (see entry
under **Prizes**) bi-annually.

The Kilvert Society

The Old Forge, Kinnersley, Hereford
HR3 6QB
☎01544 327426

Secretary *Mr M. Sharp*
Subscription £6 p.a.; £60 (Life)

FOUNDED 1948 to foster an interest in the
Diary, the diarist and the countryside he loved.
Publishes three newsletters each year; during
the summer holds three weekends of walks,
commemoration services and talks.

The Kipling Society

Tree Cottage, 2 Brownleaf Road, Brighton,
East Sussex BN2 6LB
☎01273 303719   Fax 01273 303719
Email: kipling@fastmedia.demon.co.uk
Website: www.kipling.org.uk

Honorary Secretary *Mr J. W. Michael Smith*
Subscription £20 p.a.

FOUNDED 1927. The Society's main activities
are: maintaining a specialised library in London;
answering enquiries from the public (schools,
publishers, writers and the media); arranging a
regular programme of lectures, especially in
London and in Sussex, and an annual luncheon
with guest speaker; maintaining a small museum
and reference at The Grange, in Rottingdean
near Brighton; issuing a quarterly journal. (For
the Kipling mailbox discussion list, email to:
mailbase@mailbase.ac.uk and send following
message: 'join rudyard-kipling' then sign your
name.) This is a literary society for all who enjoy
the prose and verse of Rudyard Kipling
(1865–1936) and are interested in his life and
times. Please contact the Secretary by letter, telephone or fax for further information.

The Kitley Trust

Toadstone Cottage, Edge View, Litton,
Derbyshire SK17 8QU
☎01298 871564

Contact *Rosie Ford*

FOUNDED 1990 by a teacher in Sheffield to
promote the art of creative writing, in memory
of her mother, Jessie Kitley. Activities include:
bi-annual poetry competitions; a 'Get Poetry'
Day (distribution of children's poems in shopping malls); annual sponsorship of a writer for a
school; campaigns; organising conferences for
writers and teachers of writing. Funds are provided by donations and profits (if any) from
competitions.

Charles Lamb Society

1A Royston Road, Richmond, Surrey
TW10 6LT
☎0181 940 3837

General Secretary *Mrs M. R. Huxstep*
Subscription £12 p.a. (Single); £18 (Joint &
Corporate); US$28 (Overseas Personal);
US$42 (Overseas Corporate)

FOUNDED 1935 to promote the study of the life,
works and times of English essayist Charles
Lamb (1775–1834). Holds regular monthly
meetings and lectures in London, organises
society events over the summer and an annual
luncheon in February. *Publishes* a quarterly
bulletin, *The Charles Lamb Bulletin*. Contributions of Elian interest are welcomed by the editor *Dr Duncan Wu* at Dept of English Literature,
University of Glasgow, Glasgow G12 8QQ.
(Email: dwu@englit.arts.gla.ac.uk/ ☎0141 332
3836). Membership applications should be sent
to the General Secretary at the Richmond
address above. The Society's library is housed in
the **Guildhall Library**, Aldermanbury, London
EC2P 2EJ (☎:0171 606 3030). Member of the
Alliance of Literary Societies. Registered
Charity No: 803222.

Lancashire Authors' Association

Heatherslade, 5 Quakerfields, Westhoughton,
Bolton, Lancashire BL5 2BJ
☎01942 791390

General Secretary *Eric Holt*
Subscription £9 p.a.; £12 (Joint); £1 (Junior)

FOUNDED 1909 for writers and lovers of
Lancashire literature and history. Aims to foster
and stimulate interest in Lancashire history and
literature as well as in the preservation of the
Lancashire dialect. Meets four times a year on
Saturday at various locations. *Publishes* a quarterly

journal called *The Record* which is issued free to members and holds eight annual competitions (open to members only) for both verse and prose. Comprehensive library with access for research to members.

The Philip Larkin Society

c/o Department of English, The University of Hull, Hull HU6 7RX
☎01482 847930   Fax 01482 465641
Email: j.booth@english.hull.ac.uk
Contact *Dr James Booth*
Subscription £18 (Full rate); £12 (Unwaged/ Senior Citizen); £8 (Student)

FOUNDED in 1995 to promote awareness of the life and work of Philip Larkin (1922–1985) and his literary contemporaries; to bring together all those who admire Larkin's work as a poet, writer and librarian; to bring about publications on all things Larkinesque. Organises a programme of events ranging from lectures to rambles exploring the countryside of Larkin's schooldays.

The D. H. Lawrence Society

Dept of French, University of Hull, Cottingham Road, Hull HU6 7RX
☎01482 465162   Fax 01482 465345
Email: c.greensmith@selc.hull.ac.uk
Contact *Dr Catherine Greensmith*
Subscription £10; £9 (Concession); £11 (Joint); £12 (European); £15 (Rest of World)

FOUNDED 1974 to increase knowledge and the appreciation of the life and works of D. H. Lawrence. Monthly meetings, addressed by guest speakers, are held in the library at Eastwood (birthplace of DHL). Organises visits to places of interest in the surrounding countryside, supports the activities of the D. H. Lawrence Centre at Nottingham University, and has close links with DHL Societies worldwide. *Publishes* two newsletters and one journal each year, free to members.

The T. E. Lawrence Society

PO Box 728, Oxford OX2 6YP
Contact *Gigi Horsfield*
Subscription £15 (UK); £20 (Overseas)

FOUNDED 1985 as a non-profit making, educational, registered charity to advance awareness of the life and work of Thomas Edward Lawrence and to promote research into his life and work. *Publishes* four newsletters and two journals per year. A biennial symposium is held, usually in Oxford, to bring members

together to share both academic and social interests. The Society encourages the formation of regional groups of which, currently, there are five: three in England (Northwest, London, Dorset), one in Europe (Netherlands) and one in the USA (Eastern States).

The Leamington Literary Society

15 Church Hill, Leamington Spa, Warwickshire CV32 5AZ
☎01926 425733
Honorary Secretary *Mrs Margaret Watkins*
Subscription £6 p.a.

FOUNDED 1912 to promote the study and appreciation of literature and the arts. Holds regular meetings every second Tuesday of the month (except August) at the Oddfellows Hall, Leamington Spa. The Society has published various books of local interest.

Lewes Monday Literary Club

c/o 12 Little East Street, Lewes, East Sussex BN7 2NU
☎01273 472658
Email: aliena@aubrey.mistral.co.uk
Contact *Mrs Christine Mason*
Subscriptions: £15 p.a.; £3 (Guest; per meeting)

FOUNDED in 1948 for the promotion and enjoyment of literature. Seven meetings are held during the winter on the last Monday of each month (from October to April) at the White Hart Hotel in Lewes. The Club attracts speakers of the highest quality and a balance between all forms of literature is aimed for. Guests are welcome to attend meetings.

Wyndham Lewis Society

18 Coltsfoot Road, Ware, Hertfordshire SG12 7NW
Email: swol@cableol.co.uk
Contact *Mrs Sam Brown*
Subscription £10 p.a. (UK/Europe); £12 p.a. (Institutions); US$25 (Rest of World); US$30 (Institutions, RoW) – all cheques payable to The Wyndham Lewis Society

FOUNDED 1974 to promote recognition of the value of Lewis's works and encourage scholarly research on the man, his painting and his writing. *Publishes* inaccessible Lewis writings; the annual society journal *The Wyndham Lewis Annual* plus two newsletters; and reproduces Lewis's paintings. The journal is edited by *Paul Edwards*, School of English, Bath Spa University College, Newton St. Loe, Bath BA2 9BN.

William Morris Society

Kelmscott House, 26 Upper Mall,
Hammersmith, London W6 9TA
☎0181 741 3735

Contact *David Rodgers*
Subscription £13.50 p.a.

FOUNDED 1953 to promote interest in the life, work and ideas of William Morris (1834–1923), English poet and craftsman.

Violet Needham Society

c/o 19 Ashburnham Place, London SE10 8TZ
☎0181 692 4562

Honorary Secretary *R. H. A. Cheffins*
Subscription £6 p.a. (UK & Europe);
£9 (outside Europe)

FOUNDED 1985 to celebrate the work of children's author Violet Needham and stimulate critical awareness of her work. *Publishes* thrice-yearly *Souvenir*, the Society journal with an accompanying newsletter; organises meetings and excursions to places associated with the author and her books. The journal includes articles about other children's writers of the 1940s and '50s and on ruritanian fiction. Contributions welcome.

The Edith Nesbit Society

73 Brookehowse Road, London SE6 3TH
Chairman *Nicholas Reed*
Secretary *Margaret McCarthy*
Subscription £5 p.a.; £7.50 (Joint);
£50 (Life)

FOUNDED in 1996 to celebrate the life and work of Edith Nesbit (1858–1924), best known as the author of *The Railway Children*. The Society's activities include a regular newsletter, booklets, talks and visits to relevant places.

The Wilfred Owen Association

17 Belmont, Shrewsbury, Shropshire
SY1 1TE
☎01743 235904

Chairman *Helen McPhail*
Subscription Adults £4 (£6 Overseas);
£2 (Senior Citizens/Students/
Unemployed); £10 (Groups/Institutions)

FOUNDED 1989 to commemorate the life and works of Wilfred Owen by promoting readings, visits, talks and performances relating to Owen and his work, and supporting appropriate academic and creative projects. Membership is international with 600 members. *Publishes* a newsletter twice a year. Speakers are available for schools or clubs, etc.

The Elsie Jeanette Oxenham Appreciation Society

32 Tadfield Road, Romsey, Hampshire
SO51 5AJ
☎01794 517149   Fax 01794 517149
Email: abbey@bufobooks.demon.co.uk
Websites: ds.dial.pipex.com/ct/ejo.html *and*
www.bufobooks.demon.co.uk/abbeylnk.htm
Contact *Ms Ruth Allen (Editor, The Abbey
Chronicle)*
Subscription £6 p.a.; enquire for Overseas rates

FOUNDED 1989 to promote the works of Elsie J. Oxenham. Publishes a newsletter, *The Abbey Chronicle*, three times a year.

Thomas Paine Society

43 Wellington Gardens, Selsey, West Sussex
PO20 0RF
☎01243 605730
Email: selseyrg@acunet.co.uk
Website: www.hkf.co.uk/tps

President *The Rt. Hon. Michael Foot*
Honorary Secretary/Treasurer *Eric Paine
(at address above)*
Subscription (Minimum) £10 p.a. (UK);
£20 (Overseas); £5 (Unwaged/Pensioners/
Students)

FOUNDED 1963 to promote the life and work of Thomas Paine, and continues to expound his ideals. Meetings, newsletters, lectures and research assistance. Membership badge. The Society has members worldwide and keeps in touch with American and French Thomas Paine associations. *Publishes* magazine, *Bulletin*, twice yearly (Editor: R. W. Morrell, 43 Eugene Gardens, Nottingham NG2 3LF) and holds occasional exhibitions and talks on Paine's life. Millennium Essay Writing Competition on the Life and Works of Thomas Paine (1737–1809).

Mervyn Peake Society

2 Mount Park Road, Ealing, London
W5 2RP
☎0181 566 9307   Fax 0181 991 0559
Email: 101367.1376@compuserve.com
Contact *Frank Surry*
Subscription £12 p.a. (UK & Europe);
£5 (Students/OAP/Unwaged);
£12 (Institutions); £14 (All other countries);
£16 (Institutions overseas)

FOUNDED 1975 to promote a wider understanding of Mervyn Peake's achievements as novelist, poet, painter and illustrator. Membership is open to all, irrespective of native language or country of residence. *Publishes The Mervyn Peake Review* annually and the *MPS Newsletter* quarterly. AGM held annually.

The John Polidori Literary Society

Ebenezer House, 31 Ebenezer Street, Langley Mill, Nottinghamshire NG16 4DA
Founder & President *Franklin Charles Bishop*
Subscription £20 p.a.

FOUNDED 1990 to promote and encourage appreciation of the life and works of John William Polidori MD (1795–1821) – novelist, poet, tragedian, philosopher, diarist, essayist, reviewer, traveller and one of the youngest students to obtain a medical degree (at the age of 19). He was one-time intimate of the leading figures in the Romantic movement and travelling companion and private physician to Lord Byron. He was a pivotal figure in the infamous Villa Diodati ghost story sessions in which he assisted Mary Shelley in the creation of her *Frankenstein* tale. Polidori introduced into literature the enduring icon of the vampire portrayed as an aristocratic, handsome seducer with his seminal work *The Vampyre – A Tale*, published in 1819. The birthplace of Polidori, in Great Pulteney Street, London, was honoured in 1998 by the erection of the City of Westminster Green Plaque. Members receive exclusive newsletters, invitations to social events and unique publications of the rare works of Polidori at subscriber rates. International membership in USA, Canada and France.

The Beatrix Potter Society

32 Etchingham Park Road, Finchley, London N3 2DT
☎0181 346 8031
Secretary *Mrs Marian Werner*
Subscription UK: £10 p.a. (Individual); £15 (Institution); Overseas: £15 (or US$25/Can./Aust.$30, Individual); £22 (US$35/Can./Aust.$47, Institution)

FOUNDED 1980 to promote the study and appreciation of the life and works of Beatrix Potter (1866–1943). Potter was not only the author of *The Tale of Peter Rabbit* and other classics of children's literature; she was also a landscape and natural history artist, diarist, farmer and conservationist, and was responsible for the preservation of large areas of the Lake District through her gifts to the National Trust. The Society upholds and protects the integrity of the inimitable and unique work of the lady, her aims and bequests. Holds regular talks and meetings in London with visits to places connected with Beatrix Potter.

Biennial International Study Conferences are held in the UK and occasionally in the USA. The Society has an active publishing programme.

The Powys Society

The Old School House, George Green Road, George Green, Wexham, Buckinghamshire SL3 6BJ
☎01753 578632
Email: gostick@altavista.net
Honorary Secretary *Chris Gostick*
Subscription £13.50 (UK); £16 (Overseas); £6 (Students)

The Society (with a membership of 350) aims to promote public education and recognition of the writings, thought and contribution to the arts of the Powys family; particularly of John Cowper, Theodore and Llewelyn, but also of the other members of the family and their close associates. The Society holds two major collections of Powys published works, letters, manuscripts and memorabilia. *Publishes* the *Powys Society Newsletter* in April, June and November and *The Powys Journal* in August. Organises an annual conference as well as lectures and meetings in Powys places.

The Arthur Ransome Society Ltd

Abbot Hall Art Gallery, Kirkland, Kendal, Cumbria LA9 5AL
☎01539 722464   Fax 01539 722494
Chairman *R. Wardale*
Secretary *Bill Janes*
Subscription £5 (Junior); £10 (Student); £15 (Adult); £20 (Family); £40 (Corporate); Overseas: £5 (Junior); £20 (Adult); £25 (Family); Concessions for retired persons

FOUNDED 1990 to celebrate the life and promote the works and ideas of Arthur Ransome, author of the world-famous *Swallows and Amazons* titles for children and biographer of Oscar Wilde. TARS seeks to encourage children and adults to engage in adventurous pursuits, to educate the public about Ransome and his works, and to sponsor research into his literary works and life.

The Followers of Rupert

31 Whiteley, Windsor, Berkshire SL4 5PJ
☎01753 865562
Membership Secretary *Mrs Shirley Reeves*
Subscription UK: £9.50; £11.50 (Joint); Europe, airmail: £10.50 (Individual); £12.50 (Joint); Worldwide, airmail: £12.50 (Individual); £14.50 (Joint)

FOUNDED in 1983. The Society caters for the growing interest in the Rupert Bear stories, past, present and future. *Publishes* the *Nutwood Newsletter* quarterly which gives up-to-date news of Rupert and information on Society activities. A national get-together of members – the Followers Annual – is held during the autumn in venues around the country.

The Ruskin Society (affiliated to The Ruskin Foundation)

49 Hallam Street, London W1N 5LN
☎0171 580 1894

Honorary Secretary *Dr Cynthia. J. Gamble*
Honorary Treasurer
  The Hon. Mrs Catherine Edwards
Subscriptions: £10 p.a. (payable on January 1st)

FOUNDED in 1997 to encourage a wider understanding of John Ruskin and his contemporaries. Organises lectures and events which seek not only to explain to the public at large the nature of Ruskin's theories but also to place these in a modern context. Promotes and organises publications and exhibitions in conjunction with the Ruskin Foundation.

The Ruskin Society of London

351 Woodstock Road, Oxford OX2 7NX
☎01865 310987/515962

Honorary Secretary *Miss O. E. Forbes-Madden*
Subscription £10 p.a.

FOUNDED 1986 to promote interest in John Ruskin (1819–1900) and his contemporaries. All aspects of Ruskinia are introduced. Functions are held in London. *Publishes* the annual *Ruskin Gazette*, a journal concerned with Ruskin's influence.

The Dorothy L. Sayers Society

Rose Cottage, Malthouse Lane,
Hurstpierpoint, West Sussex BN6 9JY
☎01273 833444   Fax 01273 835988
Website: www.sayers.org.uk/

Contact *Christopher Dean*
Subscription £14 p.a.; US$28 p.a.

FOUNDED 1976 to promote the study of the life, works and thoughts of Dorothy Sayers; to encourage the performance of her plays and publication of her books and books about her; to preserve original material and provide assistance to researchers. Acts as a forum and information centre, providing material for study purposes which would otherwise be unavailable. Annual seminars and other meetings. Co-

founder of the Dorothy L. Sayers Centre in Witham. *Publishes* bi-monthly bulletin, annual proceedings and other papers.

The Official Bernard Shaw Information Service

Yearnshaw House, 1 Vermont Road, Slough,
Berkshire SL2 2JP   Fax 01753 740923
Email: d_d.uttley@which.net
Contact *Diane S. Uttley*

ESTABLISHED in 1997 by writer and Shaw specialist Diane S. Uttley who was custodian of and lived in the writer's home, Shaw's Corner, from 1989 to 1997. The service is used by enthusiasts and academics; literary, theatrical and biographical.

The Shaw Society

51 Farmfield Road, Downham, Bromley,
Kent BR1 4NF
☎0181 697 3619   Fax 0181 697 3619

Honorary Secretary *Ms Barbara Smoker*
Subscription £10 p.a. (Individual); £15 (Joint)

FOUNDED 1941 to promote interest in the life and works of G. Bernard Shaw. Meetings are held on the last Friday of every month (except July, August and December) at Conway Hall, Red Lion Square, London WC1 (6.30pm for 7pm) at which speakers are invited to talk on some aspect of Shaw's life or works. Monthly playreadings are held on the first Friday of each month (except August). A 'Birthday Tribute' is held at Shaw's Corner, Ayot St Lawrence in Hertfordshire, on the weekend nearest to Shaw's birthday (26th July). *Publishes* a quarterly newsletter and a magazine, *The Shavian*, which appears approximately every nine months. (No payment for contributors.)

The Robert Southey Society

1 Lewis Terrace, Abergarwed, Resoluen,
Neath SA11 4DL
☎01639 711480

Contact *Robert King*
Subscription £10 p.a.

FOUNDED 1990 to promote the work of Robert Southey. *Publishes* an annual newsletter and arranges talks on his life and work. Open membership.

The Friends of Shandy Hall (The Laurence Sterne Trust)

Shandy Hall, Coxwold, York YO61 4AD
☎01347 868465   Fax 01347 868465
W'site:www.let.ruu.n1/2PeterdeVoogd/shandy

Honorary Secretary *Mrs J. Monkman*
Subscription £7 (Annual); £70 (Life)

Promotes interest in the works of Laurence Sterne and aims to preserve the house in which they were created (open to the public). *Publishes* annual journal, *The Shandean*. An Annual Memorial Lecture is delivered at Shandy Hall each summer.

Robert Louis Stevenson Club
5 Albyn Place, Edinburgh EH2 4NJ
☎0131 225 6665   Fax 0131 220 1015
Contact *Alistair J. R. Ferguson*
Subscription £10 p.a. (Individual); £80 (Life)

FOUNDED 1920 to promote the memory of Robert Louis Stevenson and interest in his works. *Publishes* yearbook and quarterly newsletter for members.

The R. S. Surtees Society
Manor Farm House, Nunney, Near Frome, Somerset BA11 4NJ
☎01373 836937   Fax 01373 836574
Contact *Orders and Membership Secretary*
Subscription £10

FOUNDED 1979 to republish the works of R. S. Surtees and others.

The Tennyson Society
Central Library, Free School Lane, Lincoln LN2 1EZ
☎01522 552862   Fax 01522 552858
Email: kathleenjefferson@lincolnshire.gov.uk
Honorary Secretary *Miss K. Jefferson*
Subscription £8 p.a. (Individual);
    £10 (Family); £15 (Corporate); £125 (Life)

FOUNDED 1960. An international society with membership worldwide. Exists to promote the study and understanding of the life and work of Alfred, Lord Tennyson. The Society is concerned with the work of the Tennyson Research Centre, 'probably the most significant collection of mss, family papers and books in the world'. *Publishes* annually the *Tennyson Research Bulletin*, which contains articles and critical reviews; and organises lectures, visits and seminars. Annual memorial service at Somersby in Lincolnshire.

The Edward Thomas Fellowship
Butlers Cottage, Halswell House, Goathurst, Bridgwater, Somerset TA5 2DH
☎01278 662856
Secretary *Richard Emeny*
Subscription £5 p.a. (Single); £7 p.a. (Joint)

FOUNDED 1980 to perpetuate and promote the memory of Edward Thomas and to encourage an appreciation of his life and work. The Fellowship holds a commemorative birthday walk on the Sunday nearest the poet's birthday, 3 March; issues newsletters and holds various events.

The Francis Thompson Society
See **The Eighteen Nineties Society**

The Trollope Society
9A North Street, Clapham, London SW4 0HN
☎0171 720 6789   Fax 0171 978 1815
Contacts *John Letts, Phyllis Eden*

FOUNDED 1987 to study and promote Anthony Trollope's works. Linked with the publication of the first complete edition of his novels.

Edgar Wallace Society
Kohlbergsgracht 40, 6462 CD Kerkrade, The Netherlands
☎00 31 455 67 0070   Fax 00 31 455 67 0060
Organiser *K. J. Hinz*
Subscriptions: £15 p.a.; £10 (Senior Citizens/Students); Overseas: £20; £15 (Senior Citizens/Students)

FOUNDED 1969 by Wallace's daughter, Penelope, to bring together all who have an interest in Edgar Wallace. Members receive a brief biography of Edgar by Penelope Wallace, with a complete list of all published book titles. A quarterly newsletter, *Crimson Circle*, is published in February, May, August and November.

The Walmsley Society
April Cottage, No 1 Brand Road, Hampden Park, Eastbourne, East Sussex BN22 9PX
☎01323 506447
Honorary Secretary *Fred Lane*
Subscription £8 p.a.; £10 (Family); £7 (Students/Senior Citizens)

FOUNDED 1985 to promote interest in the art and writings of Ulric and Leo Walmsley. Two annual meetings – one held at Robin Hood's Bay on the East Yorkshire coast, spiritual home of the author Leo Walmsley. The Society also seeks to foster appreciation of the work of his father Ulric Walmsley. *Publishes* a journal twice-yearly and newsletters, and is involved in other publications which benefit the aims of the Society.

Mary Webb Society
15 Melbourne Rise, Gains Park, Shrewsbury, Shropshire SY3 5DA
Website:www.wlv.ac.uk/~me1927/ mwebb.html/

Secretary *Mary Palmer*
Subscription £7.50 p.a.

FOUNDED 1972. Attracts members from the UK and overseas who are devotees of the literature of Mary Webb and of the beautiful Shropshire countryside of her novels. *Publishes* annual journal in September, organises summer schools in various locations related to the authoress's life and works. Archives; lectures; tours arranged for individuals and groups.

H. G. Wells Society
49 Beckingthorpe Drive, Bottesford, Nottingham NG13 0DN
Honorary Secretary *J. R. Hammond*
Subscription £14 (UK/EU);
   £17 (Overseas); £20 (Corporate);
   £8 (Concessions)

FOUNDED 1960 to promote an interest in and appreciation of the life, work and thought of Herbert George Wells. *Publishes The Wellsian* (annual) and *The H. G. Wells Newsletter* (bi-annual). Organises meetings and conferences.

The Charles Williams Society
3 The Rise, Islip, Kidlington, Oxfordshire OX5 2TG
Email: rsturch@compuserve.com
Contact *Honorary Secretary*

FOUNDED 1975 to promote interest in, and provide a means for, the exchange of views and information on the life and work of Charles Walter Stansby Williams (1886–1945).

The Henry Williamson Society
16 Doran Drive, Redhill, Surrey RH1 6AX
☎01737 763228
Membership Secretary *Mrs Margaret Murphy*
Subscription £12 p.a.; £15 (Family); £5 (Students)

FOUNDED 1980 to encourage, by all appropriate means, a wider readership and deeper understanding of the literary heritage left by the 20th-century English writer Henry Williamson (1895–1977). *Publishes* annual journal.

The P. G. Wodehouse Society
16 Herbert Street, Plaistow, London E13 8BE
Website:www.eclipse.co.uk/wodehouse
President *Richard Briars*
Membership Secretary *Helen Murphy*
Subscription £15 p.a.

Relaunched in May 1997 to advance the genius of P. G. Wodehouse. Publications include *Wooster Source* and the *By The Way* newsletter. Regular national and international group meetings. Members in most countries throughout the world. Society patrons include Rt. Hon. Tony Blair MP, Sir Edward Cazelet (Wodehouse's grandson) and Stephen Fry.

The Virginia Woolf Society of Great Britain
c/o 69 Rope Street, London SE16 1TF
☎0171 394 1050
Email: s.c.clarke@open.ac.uk
Contact *Stuart N. Clarke*
Subscriptions: £12 p.a.

FOUNDED 1999 to promote interest in the life and work of Virginia Woolf, author, essayist and diarist. The Society's activities include trips away, walks, reading groups and talks. *Publishes* a literary journal, *The Virginia Woolf Bulletin* 2/3 times yearly.

WW2 HMSO PPBKS Society
3 Roman Road, Southwick, West Sussex BN42 4TP
☎01273 871017   Fax 01273 871017
Contact *A. R. James*
Subscription £2 p.a.

FOUNDED 1994 to encourage collectors of, and promote research into HM Stationery Office's World War II series of paperbacks, most of which were written by well-known authors, although, in many cases, anonymously. *Publishes* bi-monthly newsletter for those who send s.a.e. (9x4ins). Contributors welcome; preferred length 600 – 1200 words but no payment made. Bibliography available for purchase (£3); Collectors' Guide (£5); Handbook, *Informing the People* (£10).

The Yeats Society
Yeats Memorial Building, Hyde Bridge, Sligo Republic of Ireland
☎00 353 71 42693   Fax 00 353 71 42780
Director *Marian Quinn*
Subscriptions: £15 (Single); £25 (Couple);
   £100 (Corporate); £10 (Overseas)

FOUNDED in 1958 to promote interest in the life and works of W. B. Yeats and to run the Yeats International Summer School and Yeats Winter Weekend School. Lectures are held monthly in partnership with the Institute of Technology, Sligo. Yeats' birthday celebration on 13th June. *Publishes* quarterly newsletter.

Poetry appreciation groups organised. Tours of Yeats country organised for visiting groups.

Yorkshire Dialect Society

51 Stepney Avenue, Scarborough, North Yorkshire YO12 5BW

Secretary *Michael Park*
Subscription £7 p.a.

FOUNDED 1897 to promote interest in and preserve a record of the Yorkshire dialect. *Publishes* dialect verse and prose writing. Two journals to members annually. Details of publications are available from the Librarian, YDS, School of English, University of Leeds, Leeds, West Yorkshire LS2 9JT.

Francis Brett Young Society

92 Gower Road, Halesowen, West Midlands B62 9BT
☎0121 422 8969

Honorary Secretary *Mrs Jean Hadley*
Subscription £7 p.a. (Individuals);
£10 (Couples sharing a journal);
£5 (Students); £7 (Organisations/
Overseas); £70 (Life); £100 (Joint, Life)

FOUNDED 1979. Aims to provide a forum for those interested in the life and works of English novelist Francis Brett Young and to collate research on him. Promotes lectures, exhibitions and readings; *publishes* a regular newsletter.

Arts Councils and Regional Arts Boards

The Arts Council of England
14 Great Peter Street, London SW1P 3NQ
☎0171 333 0100   Fax 0171 973 6590
Website: www.artscouncil.org.uk
Chairman *Gerry Robinson*
Chief Executive *Peter Hewitt*

The Arts Council of England is undergoing a substantial change of role and function which aims to serve the arts, artists and audiences more effectively. One of the guiding imperatives is the belief that arts activity should be funded as close to its source as possible. This will result in the devolution of Development Fund monies to Regional Arts Boards and, where appropriate, the delegation of Arts Council funded organisations to Regional Arts Boards.

For details of funding available in 2000/ 2001, please contact the Drama Department and the Literature Department.

The Arts Council/An Chomhairle Ealaion
70 Merrion Square, Dublin 2
☎00 353 1 6180200   Fax 00 353 1 6761302
Literature Officer *Sinead MacAodha*

The Irish Arts Council has programmes under six headings to assist in the area of literature and the book world: a) Writers; b) Literary Organisations; c) Publishers; d) Literary Magazines; e) Participation Programmes; f) Literary Events and Festivals. It also gives a number of annual bursaries (see **Arts Council Literature Bursaries, Ireland** under **Bursaries, Fellowships and Grants**).

The Arts Council of Northern Ireland
MacNeice House, 77 Malone Road, Belfast BT9 6AQ
☎01232 385200   Fax 01232 661715
Literature Arts Officer *John Brown*

Funds book production by established publishers, programmes of readings, literary festivals, writers-in-residence schemes and literary magazines and periodicals. Occasional schools programmes and anthologies of children's writing are produced. Annual awards and bursaries for writers are available. Holds information also on various groups associated with local arts, workshops and courses.

Scottish Arts Council
12 Manor Place, Edinburgh EH3 7DD
☎0131 226 6051   Fax 0131 476 7050
Website: www.sac.org.uk
Literature Director *Jenny Brown*
Literature Officer *Gavin Wallace*
Literature Secretary *Catherine Allan*

The Council's support for Scottish-based writers who have a track record of publication includes: bursaries (considered twice yearly); writing fellowships (posts advertised); international writing fellowships and translation fellowships. Also publishes lists of Scottish publishers, awards, literary magazines and literary agents.

The Arts Council of Wales
Museum Place, Cardiff CF1 3NX
☎01222 376500   Fax 01222 221447
Website: www.ccc-acw.org.uk
Senior Literature Officer *Tony Bianchi*
Senior Officer: Dance and Drama
   Anna Holmes

Funds literary magazines and book production; *Writers on Tour* and bursary schemes; **Welsh Academy, Welsh Books Council, Hay-on-Wye Literature Festival** and **Tŷ Newydd Writers' Centre** at Cricieth; also children's literature, annual awards and translation projects. The Council aims to develop theatrical experience among Wales-based writers through a variety of schemes – in particular, by funding writers on year-long attachments.

English Regional Arts Boards
5 City Road, Winchester, Hampshire SO23 8SD
☎01962 851063   Fax 01962 842033
Email: info@erab.org.uk
Website: www.arts.org.uk
Chief Executive *Christopher Gordon*
Assistant *Carolyn Nixson*

English Regional Arts Boards is the representative body for the 10 Regional Arts Boards (RABs) in England. Its Winchester secretariat provides project management, services and information for the members, and acts on their behalf in appropriate circumstances. Scotland, Northern Ireland and Wales have their own Arts Councils. The three former Welsh Regional Arts Associations are now absorbed into the Arts Council of Wales. RABs are support and development agencies for the arts in the regions. Policies are developed in response to regional demand, and to assist new initiatives in areas of perceived need; they may vary from region to region. The RABs are now responsible for the distribution of Arts Council Lottery funding for capital and revenue projects under £100,000.

SUPPORT FOR WRITERS

All the Regional Arts Boards offer support for professional creative writers through a range of grants, awards, advice, information and contacts. Interested writers should contact the Board in whose region they live or access the RAB pages on the website.

East Midlands Arts

Mountfields House, Epinal Way,
Loughborough, Leicestershire LE11 0QE
☎01509 218292   Fax 01509 262214
Email: info@ema@artsfb.org.uk
Literature Officer *Sue Stewart*
Drama Officer *Helen Flach*

Covers Leicestershire, Rutland, Nottinghamshire, Derbyshire (excluding the High Peak district) and Northamptonshire. A comprehensive information service for regional writers includes an extensive *Writers' Information Pack*, with details of local groups, workshops, residential writing retreats, publishers and publishing information, regional magazines which offer a market for work, advice on approaching the media, on unions, courses and grants. Also available is a directory of writers, primarily to aid people wishing to organise workshops, readings or writer's attachments. Writers' bursaries are granted for work on a specific project – all forms of writing are eligible except for local history and biography. Writing for the theatre can come under the aegis of both Literature and Drama. A list of writers' groups is available, plus *Foreword*, the literature newsletter.

Eastern Arts Board

Cherry Hinton Hall, Cambridge CB1 4DW
☎01223 215355   Fax 01223 248075
Literature Officer *Emma Drew*
Drama Officer *Alan Orme*

Cinema & Broadcast Media Officer
Martin Ayres

Covers Bedfordshire, Cambridgeshire, Essex, Hertfordshire, Norfolk and Suffolk. Policy emphasises quality and access. Support is given to publishers and literature promoters based in the EAB region, also to projects which develop audiences for literature performances and publishing, including electronic media. Bursaries are offered annually to individual published writers. Supplies lists of literary groups, workshops, local writing courses and writers working in the educational sector. Also provides advice on applying for National Lottery funds.

London Arts Board

Elme House, 3rd Floor, 133 Long Acre,
London WC2E 9AF
☎0171 240 1313/Help Line: 0171 670 2410
Fax 0171 670 2400
Principal Literature Officer *John Hampson*
Principal Drama Officer *Sue Timothy*

The London Arts Board is the Regional Arts Board for the Capital, covering the 32 boroughs and the City of London. Potential applicants for support for literature and other arts projects should contact the Board for information.

North West Arts Board

Manchester House, 22 Bridge Street,
Manchester M3 3AB
☎0161 834 6644   Fax 0161 834 6969
Email: nwarts-info@mcrl.poptel.org.uk
Media Officer – Literature *Bronwen*
Williams (Email: bwilliams@nwarts.co.uk)
Performing Arts Officer – Drama
Ian Tabbron (Email: itabbron@nwarts.co.uk)

NWAB covers Cheshire, Greater Manchester, Merseyside, Lancashire and the High Peak district of Derbyshire. Offers financial assistance to a great variety of organisations and individuals through a number of schemes, including Writers' Bursaries, Residencies and Placements and the Live Writing scheme. NWAB publishes a directory of local writers groups, a directory of writers and a range of information covering topics such as performance and publishing. For further details please contact the Literature or Drama Departments.

Northern Arts Board

9–10 Osborne Terrace, Jesmond, Newcastle
upon Tyne NE2 1NZ
☎0191 281 6334   Fax 0191 281 3276
Email: nab@norab.demon.co.uk
Website: www.poptel/org.uk/arts/

Head of Film, Media and Literature
Janice Campbell

Covers Cumbria, Durham, Northumberland, Teesside and Tyne and Wear, and was the first regional arts association in the country to be set up by local authorities. It supports both organisations and writers and aims to stimulate public interest in artistic events. Offers Writers Awards for published writers to release them from work or other commitments for short periods of time to enable them to concentrate on specific literary projects. It also has a film/TV script development fund operated through the Northern Production Fund. A separate scheme for playwrights is operated by the Northern Playwrights Society. Northern Arts makes drama awards to producers only. Also funds writers' residencies, and has a fund for publications. Contact list of regional groups available.

South East Arts
Union House, Eridge Road, Tunbridge Wells, Kent TN4 8HF
☎01892 507200   Fax 01892 549383
Email: info@seab.co.
Website: www.arts.org.uk
Literature Officer *Anne Downes*
Drama Officer *Judith Hibberd*

Covers Kent, Surrey, East Sussex, West Sussex, Brighton and Hove and Medway (excluding the London boroughs). Grant schemes accessible to all art forms in the areas of new work, presentation of work and venue development. Awards for individuals include training bursaries and writers' awards schemes. The literature programme aims to raise the profile of contemporary literature in the region and encourage creative writing and reading development projects. Priorities include live literature, writers and readers in residence and training bursaries for writers resident in the region. A regular feature on literature appears in the *Arts News* newsletter.

South West Arts
Bradninch Place, Gandy Street, Exeter, Devon EX4 3LS
☎01392 218188   Fax 01392 413554
Email: info@swa.co.uk
Website: www.swa.co.uk
Director of Media and Published Arts
David Drake
Media & Published Arts Administrator
Sara Williams

Covers Cornwall, Devon, Dorset (excluding Bournemouth, Christchurch and Poole), Gloucestershire, Somerset and the unitary authorities of Bristol, Bath and North East Somerset, South Gloucestershire, North Somerset, Torbay and Plymouth. The central theme running through the Board's aims are 'promoting quality and developing audiences for new work'. Specific policies aim to support the development and promotion of new writing and performance work in all areas of contemporary literature and published arts. There is direct investment in small presses and magazine publishers, literary festivals, writer residencies and training and marketing bursaries for individual writers. There is also a commitment to supporting the development of new writing in the performing arts.

Southern Arts
13 St Clement Street, Winchester, Hampshire SO23 9DQ
☎01962 855099   Fax 01962 861186
Email: info@southernarts.co.uk
Literature Officer *Keiren Phelan*
Film, Video & Broadcasting Officer
Jane Gerson
Theatre Officer *Nic Young*

Covers Berkshire, Buckinghamshire, Hampshire, the Isle of Wight, Oxfordshire, Wiltshire and South East Dorset. The Literature Department funds fiction and poetry readings, festivals, magazines, bursaries, a literature prize, publications, residencies and a scheme which subsidises writers working in education and the community.

West Midlands Arts
82 Granville Street, Birmingham B1 2LH
☎0121 631 3121   Fax 0121 643 7239
Literature Officer *Adrian Johnson*

There are special criteria across the art forms, so contact the Information Office for details of *New Work & Commissioning* and other schemes as well as for the *Reading (Correspondence Mss Advice) Service*. There are contact lists of writers, storytellers, writing groups, etc. WMA supports the regional publication, *Raw Edge Magazine*: contact PO Box 4867, Birmingham B3 3HD, and the Virtual Literature Centre for the West Midlands (and beyond) called 'Lit-net' (www.lit-net.org).

Yorkshire Arts
21 Bond Street, Dewsbury, West Yorkshire WF13 1AY
☎01924 455555   Fax 01924 466522
Email: <firstname.surname>.yha@artsfb.org.uk
Website: www.arts.org.uk

Literature Officer *Steve Dearden*
Drama Officer *Shea Connolly*
Administrator *Jill Leahy*

'Libraries, publishing houses, local authorities and the education service all make major contributions to the support of literature. Recognising the resources these agencies command, Yorkshire Arts actively seeks ways of acting in partnership with them, while at the same time retaining its particular responsibility for the living writer and the promotion of activities currently outside the scope of these agencies.' Funding goes to **Yorkshire Art Circus** (community publishing); poetry publishers **Arc Publications** and **Smith/Doorstop**; *Live Writing* and *Writing Development* are schemes which subsidise projects where a professional writer is employed as a performer or tutor. Support is also given to **Ilkley, Hull, Huddersfield** and Sheffield Literature Festivals. YA offers a bursary scheme for writers; holds lists of workshops and writers' groups throughout the region. *Publishes* an on-line directory of writers and *writeANGLES*, bimonthly newsletter. Contact the Administrator.

Verse and Worse

Barry Turner argues that bad writing has its uses

There should be prizes for the best bad writing. Everyday bad writing is just boring or frustrating. But truly awful writing can transcend its own inadequacies to rise to surreal heights. It becomes fascinating in spite of itself. It also stands as a dreadful warning to aspiring authors never to take themselves too seriously.

First of the immortals is William McGonagall who billed himself as 'poet and tragedian'. This Scottish bard entertained the citizens of Dundee selling broadsheets of his verses by day and giving pub recitations by night. Maybe 'entertain' is the wrong word for McGonagall's speciality was the composition of ballads of such thumping banality as to defy belief. Never at a loss for a subject he unfailingly chose the most mundane as with his tribute delivered, one imagines, with deadpan solemnity to the Beautiful Railway Bridge of the Silvery Tay:

> With your numerous arches and pillars in so grand array,
> And your central girders, which seem to the eye
> To be almost towering to the sky.
> The greatest wonder of the day,
> And a great beautification to the River Tay,
> Most beautiful to be seen,
> Near by Dundee and the Magdalen Green.

And so on for six more verses. Never one to leave bad alone, McGonagall followed up with an eulogy to the Newport railway.

> Across the Railway Bridge o' the Silvery Tay,
> Which was opened on the 12th of May,
> In the year of our Lord 1879,
> Which will clear all expenses in a very short time
> Because the thrifty housewives of Newport
> To Dundee will often resort,
> Which will be to them profit and sport,
> By bringing cheap tea, bread, and jam,
> And also some of Lipton's ham,
> Which will make their hearts feel light and gay,
> And cause them to bless the openingday
> Of the Newport Railway.

The sad climax to McGonagall's absorption with the Silvery Tay was the collapse of the railway bridge with a trainload of passengers.

Alas! I am very sorry to say
That ninety lives have been taken away
On the last Sabbath day of 1879,
Which will be remember'd for a very long time.

But he soon bounced back with his 'beautiful *new* railway bridge of the Silvery Tay, ... which will be a great protection on a windy day, so as the railway carriages won't be blown away.' He even managed to get in a plug for the engineers Messrs Barlow and Arrol with the wish that they would 'prosper for many a day'.

The spirit of McGonagall lives on in the vanity publishing of modern poetry. The only difference is that the poets of our own day are even less likely to produce lines that scan or rhyme. In awarding the McGonagall Prize for Bad Verse, the judges would be spoilt for choice.

It is unlikely that McGonagall was ever highly regarded by anyone but himself. However, other notoriously bad writers of his time boasted a devoted following who would willingly have manned the barricades to defend their idols against the cynics. The spread of elementary education in the late nineteenth century spawned a generation of tenth-rate popular novelists. In the lead were the purveyors of romantic fiction who told tales of unrequited passion behind the lace curtains. Their formula was to pile on the emotions stopping just short of raw sex. The effect could be compelling or ridiculous depending on taste.

A century ago names like Mrs Oliphant, Victoria Cross, 'The Duchess', Mrs Humphry Ward and Marie Corelli described, prematurely, as 'the world's worst novelist' were a guarantee of mass readership and fat royalty cheques. But if these were the Queens of the Circulating Library, as Alan Walbank has dubbed them, the Empress was unquestionably Amanda McKittrick Ros.

Having trained as a teacher in Dublin, Amanda Ros moved to Larne where she married the stationmaster. Inspired by Marie Corelli's barnstormer *The Sorrows of Satan*, she determined on her own novel. Published in 1897, *Irene Iddesleigh* is the story of a girl who marries an older man, elopes with a former lover and returns a broken woman.

Sympathise with me indeed! Ah, no! Cast your sympathy on the chill waves of troubled waters, fling it on the oases of futurity: dash it against the rock of gossip: or, better still, allow it to remain within the false and faithless bosom of buried scorn. Such were a few remarks of Irene as she paced the beach of limited freedom, alone and unprotected.

The Amanda Ros style was of old-fashioned melodrama. You could imagine her characters thumping their breasts or flinging a hand across the forehead to signify anguish or despair. But her trademark was verbosity. She was incapable of using one word when there was a choice of six, even in moments of greatest intimacy. In her second novel, *Delina Delaney*, a young lord of the manor falls in love with the daughter of a poor fisherman.

My darling virgin! my queen! my Delina! I am just in time to hear the toll of a parting bell strike its heavy weight of appalling softness against the weakest fibres of a heart of love, arousing and tickling its dormant action, thrusting the dart of evident separation deeper into its tubes of tenderness, and fanning the flame, already unextinguishable, into volumes of blaze.

The literary establishment saw Amanda as a joke. At Oxford the students founded an Amanda Ros Society to give weekly readings from her works. But the sheer awfulness of her books demanded an explanation. How was it possible for someone to write quite so badly and yet command a following. No less a critic than Aldous Huxley came up with a theory that the first conscious attempt to produce the artistic by an unsophisticated mind brings the desire to embellish.

'It is remarkable how late in the history of every literature simplicity is invented ... (Early writers became) ... intoxicated with their discovery of artifice. It was some time before the intoxication wore off and men saw that art was possible without artifice. Mrs Ros, an Elizabethan born out of her time, is still under the spell of that magical and delicious intoxication.'

Up to a point. The association of overblown prose with the unsophisticated mind gives too much credit to the intellectual. Today, some of the worst cases of verbosity are found in academia where arguments are judged to be the more impressive the longer it takes to express them.

But there are novelists too who overwrite. The computer is held partly to blame. All those lovely words flashing up on the screen, so neat and tidy. It takes willpower to wipe them out. Aspiring writers have a particular problem. Too often they imagine that extra words and convoluted sentences are all part of the literary performance. The biggest mistake of first-time authors is to try too hard to grab attention. An Amanda Ros prize for bad writing might help to convince them of this fundamental truth.

We need a special prize for dramatists. It is seldom appreciated that in having actors speak their words, playwrights are at an advantage over other writers. When the muse fails, the performers can still save the day. It is said of a great actor that he can command an audience by reciting the telephone directory. But all actors are used to wrestling with uninspired dialogue to shape it into something half presentable. Just read the stuff that gets to the West End. If it was judged on words alone half of it would not pass muster for a village hall.

Occasionally, actors take revenge by saying their lines exactly as the playwright intended. The result can be a classic – for all the wrong reasons. It happened, famously, in pre-war London when Walter Reynolds, an elderly author and impresario, got it into his head that the young people of Britain were letting the side down. A toughening of the sinews was called for and Reynolds believed he had the means to do it – a ramshackle play about the Boy Scouts and their bravery in the face of villainy climaxing in a rousing chorus of *Land of Hope and Glory*. It was called *Young England*. Patrick Ludlow, who starred as the scout leader, explains how a play with a serious message became the 'most glorious burlesque of all time'.

It was essential to say the corny lines sincerely. The greater the sincerity, the bigger the laugh. The casting helped to make it ludicrous. There's always something comic about grown up scouts; and I, with my frail figure, must have been a scream. Guy Middleton, hearty and robust, was equally ridiculous as a weedy rat-like conscientious objector. ... A very tall man with a falsetto voice played the supposedly fierce bailiff who turned a starving widow out of her cottage. ... The scouts were either little old men or effeminate young ones, who would have been better cast as girl guides. Their mincing added greatly to the fun of the marching number: 'Away we go to camp with all its pleasures.' And they went off slightly out of step, to ironic cheers. My yarn to the scouts never failed: 'I wish I could tell you how proud I am to have you youngsters all around me looking so spick and span – so clean, strong and healthy.' The desire to address this to the weediest types was irresistible. ... And how the audience adored my love scenes attired in a fantastic Ruritanian uniform: 'Are you happy?' 'My heart almost aches with happiness.' 'A miracle has come to me – I have never really lived till now.'

There have been other successful bad plays but never anything quite so unintentionally dreadful as this. At the first night the author roamed the aisles begging the audience not to laugh. But as the popularity of the show mounted and the full-house notices went up night after night, Walter Reynolds began to enjoy his notoriety. As if to prove that even in the hardest times the British could still laugh at themselves, *Young England* at the Victoria Palace became the hottest ticket in town. The play was serialised in the *Daily Express* and Margery Allingham was inspired by it to write the opening chapter of her detective novel, *Dancers in Mourning*. Walter Reynolds got rich and died, if not happy, at least knowing that he had made an exceptional contribution to the theatre.

In proposing a Reynolds prize for bad drama it might be wondered why the recognition of rotten scripts should be limited to the theatre. After all, much of what appears on screen is 'weary, stale, flat and unprofitable'. But screenplays are more team efforts (writer, director, producer, producer's girlfriend) in which the author cannot wholly be blamed for every inanity in the dialogue.

So there we have it: three prestigious awards for bad fiction, bad drama and bad poetry in want of a sponsor. Maybe one of those manufacturers whose product is accompanied by incomprehensible self-assembly instructions. As for nominations we might start with a politician author, a feminist playwright and one of several poets with Laureate aspirations. But the field is wide open and there are plenty of runners.

Readers are invited to nominate contemporary writers for Verse and Worse awards. The results will be published in the next edition of *The Writer's Handbook*. Write to Barry Turner at *The Writer's Handbook*, 34 Ufton Road, London N1 5BX.

Writers' Courses, Circles and Workshops

Courses

Courses are listed under country and county

ENGLAND

Berkshire

University of Reading
Centre for Continuing Education, London Road, Reading, Berkshire RG1 5AQ
☎0118 9318347

Creative writing courses usually include *Life into Fiction; Poetry Workshop; Getting Started; Writers Helping Writers* (with **Southern Arts**' help, the course includes visits from well-known writers); *Writing Fiction; Becoming Independent; Publishing Poetry* and *Scriptwriting*. There is also a support group for teachers of creative writing, a public lecture by a writer and a reading by students of their work, and various Saturday workshops. Tutors include the science fiction writer Brian Stableford, novelist Leslie Wilson and poets Jane Draycott, Elizabeth James and Susan Utting. Fees vary depending on the length of course. Concessions available.

Buckinghamshire

Missenden Abbey
Continuing Education
Chilterns Consortium, The Misbourne Centre, Great Missenden, Buckinghamshire HP16 0BN
☎01494 862904   Fax 01494 890087
Residential and non-residential weekend workshops and summer school. The 1999 programme included *Writing Magazine Articles and Getting Them Published; Writing for Television and Radio; A Creative Approach to Non-Fiction Writing; Writing Poetry.*

National Film & Television School
Beaconsfield Studios, Station Road, Beaconsfield, Buckinghamshire HP9 1LG
☎01494 671234   Fax 01494 674042
Email: cad@nftsfilm-tv.ac.uk
Website: www.nftsfilm-tv.ac.uk

Full-time screenwriting course designed for students who already have experience of writing in other fields, offering an intensive programme of writing combined with an understanding of the practical stages involved in the making of film and television drama. Range of work covers comedy, TV series and serials, short-film, adaptation for the screen and narrative. The ability to collaborate successfully is developed through exercises and projects shared with students in other specialisations. 'We encourage the formation of working partnerships which will continue after graduation.'

The Writers' Workshop
Barlows, Frieth, Nr High Wycombe, Buckinghamshire RG9 6PR
☎01442 871004
The Writers' Workshop runs regular daytime classes in creative writing, plus professional assessments and guidance, over three 10-week terms per year. Published writers and beginners are equally welcome.

Cambridgeshire

National Extension College
18 Brooklands Avenue, Cambridge CB2 2HN
☎01223 316644   Fax 01223 313586
Runs a number of home-study courses on writing. Courses include: *Essential Editing; Creative Writing; Writing for Money; Copywriting; Essential Desktop Publishing; Essential Design.* Contact the NEC for copy of the *Guide to Courses* which includes details of fees.

PMA Training
PMA House, Free Church Passage, St Ives, Cambridgeshire PE17 4AY
☎01480 300653   Fax 01480 496022
Email: admin@pma-group.com
Website: www.pma-group.co.uk
One-/two-/three-day editorial, PR, design and publishing courses held in central London.

High-powered, intensive courses run by Fleet Street journalists and magazine editors. Courses include: *News Writing; Journalistic Style; Feature Writing; Investigative Reporting; Basic Writing Skills*. Fees range from £150 to £600 plus VAT. Special rates for freelances.

Cheshire

The College of Technical Authorship – Distance Learning Course

The College of Technical Authorship, PO Box 7, Cheadle, Cheshire SK8 3BY
☎0161 437 4235   Fax 0161 437 4235

Distance learning courses for City & Guilds Tech 536, Part 1, Technical Communication Techniques, and Part 2, Technical Authorship. Individual tuition by correspondence and fax; includes some practical work done at home. Contact: John Crossley, DipDistEd, DipM, MCIM, FISTC, LCGI.

Cleveland

University of Leeds

Adult Education Centre, 37 Harrow Road, Middlesbrough, Cleveland TS5 5NT
☎01642 814987
Email: r.k.o'rourke@leeds.ac.uk

Creative writing courses held throughout Cleveland, North and West Yorkshire in the autumn, spring and summer terms. These are held weekly and as non-residential summer schools. Courses carrying undergraduate credit are part-time and offered in a range of subjects, at beginners, intermediate and advanced levels. Professional development courses for writers and Writing Development Workers which carry post-graduate credit are also offered. These include: *Black Writing Development; Creating Community Theatre; Writing and Cross Art Forms*. Contact *Rebecca O'Rourke* for details.

Cumbria

Higham Hall College

Bassenthwaite Lake, Cockermouth, Cumbria CA13 9SH
☎017687 76276   Fax 017687 76013

Winter and summer residential courses. Programme has included *Memoir Writing* and *Creative Writing*. Detailed brochure available.

Derbyshire

Real Writers

PO Box 170, Chesterfield, Derbyshire S40 1FE
Email: realwrtrs@aol.com
Website: www.turtledesign.com/RealWriters/

Correspondence service with personal tuition from working writers. In addition to the support and appraisal service, runs an annual short story competition. Send s.a.e. for details.

University of Derby

Student Information Centre, Kedleston Road, Derby DE22 1GB
☎01332 622236
Fax 01332 622754
Email: J.Bains@derby.ac.
    uk (prospectus requests only)
Website: www.derby.ac.uk
Contact *Graham Parker*

With upwards of 300 students, *Experience of Writing* runs sixteen modules as part of the undergraduate degree programme. These include: Storytelling, Poetry, Playwriting, Writing for TV and Radio, Screenwriting, the Short Story, Journalism, Writing for Children. The courses are all led by practising writers. The University has extended its creative writing provision with the MA in *Narrative Writing*, now in its third year.

Writers' Summer School, Swanwick

The Hayes, Swanwick, Derbyshire
Email: BCourtie@aol.com
Website: dspace.dial.pipex.com/roydev/

A week-long summer school of informal talks and discussion groups, forums, panels, quizzes and competitions, and 'a lot of fun'. Open to everyone, from absolute beginners to published authors. Held in August from late Saturday to Friday morning. Cost (1998) £192+, all inclusive. Contact the Secretary, *Brenda Courtie* at The Rectory, Blisworth NN7 3BZ (☎07050 630949).

Devon

Dartington College of Arts

Totnes, Devon TQ9 6EJ
☎01803 862224
Fax 01803 863569
Email: c.bergvall@dartington.ac.uk
    or registry@dartington.ac.uk
Website: www.dartington.ac.uk

BA(Hons) course in *Performance Writing*: exploratory approach to writing as it relates to performance. The course is part of a performance arts programme which encourages interdisciplinary work with Arts Management, Music, Theatre, Visual Performance. The programme includes a range of elective modules in digital media and emerging art forms which are available to all students. Contact Subject Director, Performance Writing: *Caroline Bergvall*.

Exeter Phoenix
Bradninch Place, Gandy Street, Exeter,
Devon EX4 3LS
☎01392 667055   Fax 01392 667599
Exeter Phoenix has regular literature events, focusing on readings by living poets and other writers and is often linked to aspects of a wider performance programme. Presents the annual Exeter International Poetry Prize and other projects such as the collection of the *New Exeter Book of Riddles*, published in 1999. Tutors in a wide range of writing skills run classes and workshops at the Phoenix, listed in the brochure of activities.

University of Exeter
Exeter, Devon EX4 4QW
☎01392 264580
BA(Hons) in *Drama* with a third-year and postgraduate option in *Playwriting*. Contact *Professor Peter Thomson*.

Dorset
Bournemouth University
School of Media Arts and Communication,
Poole House, Talbot Campus, Fern Barrow,
Poole, Dorset BH12 5BB
☎01202 595553   Fax 01202 595530
Three-year, full-time BA(Hons) course in *Scriptwriting for Film and Television*. Contact *Sue Sykes*, Programme Administrator.

Essex
National Council for the Training of Journalists
Latton Bush Centre, Southern Way, Harlow,
Essex CM18 7BL
☎01279 430009   Fax 01279 438008
Email: NCTJ@itecharlow.co.uk
Website: www.itecharlow.co.uk/nctj/
For details of journalism courses, both full-time

and via distance learning, please write to the NCTJ enclosing a large s.a.e.

Hampshire
Highbury College, Portsmouth
Dovercourt Road, Cosham, Portsmouth,
Hampshire PO6 2SA
☎01705 383131   Fax 01705 378382
Courses include: one-year *Pre-entry Magazine Journalism* (mainly post-graduate intake), run under the auspices of the Periodicals Training Council. 20-week *Pre-entry Newspaper Journalism* course, run under the auspices of the National Council for Training of Journalists. One-year Postgraduate Diploma in *Broadcasting Journalism*, run under the auspices of the Broadcast Journalism Training Council. Contact the Secretary, ☎01705 313287.

King Alfred's College
Winchester, Hampshire SO22 4NR
☎01962 841515   Fax 01962 842280
Website: www.wkac.ac.uk
Three-year degree course in *Drama, Theatre and Television Studies*, including *Writing for Devised Community Theatre* and *Writing for Television Documentary*. Contact the Admissions Office (☎01962 827262).
   MA course in *Theatre for Development* – one year, full-time course with major project overseas or in the UK. MA course in *Writing for Children* available on either a one- or two-year basis. Enquiries: Admissions Officer (☎01962 827235).

University of Southampton New College
Part-time/Adult Continuing Education, The Avenue, Southampton SO17 1BG
☎01703 592833   Fax 01703 597271
Email: vah@soton.ac.uk
Creative writing courses, writers' register and writers' workshops. Courses are held in local/regional centres. New for 1999/2000: Certificate of Higher Education in *Writing*.

Hertfordshire
West Herts College
Faculty of Visual Communication, Hempstead Road, Watford, Hertfordshire WD1 3EZ
☎01923 812654 (Admissions)
The 24-week postgraduate course in *Journalism, Radio and Advertising: Writing and Practice* covers

two options: *Writing for Prize Writing* and *Writing for Radio*. The college also offers a postgraduate diploma in *Publishing* with an option in *Multimedia Publishing*. Contact the Admissions Secretary on the number above.

Kent

University of Kent at Canterbury
Unit for Part-time Study, Keynes College, Canterbury, Kent CT2 7NP
☎01227 823662   Fax 01227 458745
Website: www.ukc.ac.uk/registry/UPS
Creative writing courses. Contact *Vicki Woolnough*.

Lancaster

Alston Hall
Alston Lane, Longridge, Preston, Lancashire PR3 3BP
☎01772 784661   Fax 01772 785835
Email: info@alstonhall.u-net.com
Website: www.alstonhall.u-net.com
Holds regular day-long creative writing workshops, also weekend residential courses. Brochure available.

Chrysalis – The Poet In You
Mashiters, Tatham, Lancaster LA2 8PH
☎015242 62996
Offers courses, workshops and one-to-one sessions. The course consists of Part 1, 'for those who feel drawn to reading more poetry as well as wanting to start to write their own', and Part 2, 'a more advanced course designed for those who are already writing and who want to go more deeply into its process and technique'. Brochure available from the address above.

Edge Hill College of Higher Education
St Helen's Road, Ormskirk, Lancashire L39 4QP
☎01695 575171
Offers a two-year, part-time MA in *Writing Studies*. Combines advanced-level writers' workshops with closely related courses in the poetics of writing and contemporary writing in English. There is also provision for MPhil- and PhD-level research in writing and poetics. A full range of creative writing courses is available at undergraduate level, in poetry and fiction writing which may be taken as part of a modular BA. Contact *Dr R. Sheppard*.

Lancaster University
Department of Creative Writing, Lonsdale College, Bailrigg, Lancaster LA1 4YN
☎01524 594169   Fax 01524 843934
Email: L.Anderson@lancaster.ac.uk
Offers practical graduate and undergraduate courses in writing fiction, poetry and scripts. All based on group workshops – students' work-in-progress is circulated and discussed. Visiting writers have included: Carol Ann Duffy, Kazuo Ishiguro, Bernard MacLaverty, David Pownall. Contact *Linda Anderson* for details.

Leicestershire

Leicester Adult Education College, Writing School
Wellington Street, Leicester LE1 6HL
☎0116 2334343   Fax 0116 2334344
Offers a wide range of creative writing and journalism courses throughout the year. The programme includes short modules of up to one-day and longer-taught courses. Choice of critical workshops. The Writing School specialises in supporting new and more experienced writers through to publication and has strong links with local media. Manuscript appraisal is available by post for short stories and articles. Occasional masterclasses and talks. Visiting writers have included Melvyn Bragg, Simon Brett, John Harvey, Roy Hattersley, Susan Hill, Rose Impey, Graham Joyce, Deric Longden and Andrew Motion. For course information and advice, contact *Valerie Moore*.

London

Black Coral Training
130 Lea Valley Techno Park, Ashley Road, London N17 9LN
☎0181 880 4860
Email: black.coral@virgin.net
Website: www.script-city.com
ScriptCity at Black Coral provides creative and professional training in screenwriting and story editing skills for writers, readers and script editors. Courses on offer: *Writing for Short Film Production*, Foundation & Intermediate; *Screenwriting*, Foundation, Intermediate & Advanced; *Working with Writers, Actors and Directors*, Foundation & Intermediate; *Script Reading*, Foundation; *Script Editing*, Foundation & Intermediate; *Writing for TV/Radio Drama*, Foundation & Intermediate; *New Perspectives* – a 10-month intensive script development and

marketing programme in association with professional editors and incorporating workshops and masterclasses. Prices from around £100 to £300, many concessions available. TV Intermediate courses carry 50% concessionary places.

The Central School of Speech and Drama

Embassy Theatre, Eton Avenue, London NW3 3HY
☎0171 722 8183   Fax 0171 722 4132

MA in *Advanced Theatre Practice*. One-year, full-time course aimed at providing a grounding in principal areas of professional theatre practice – *Writing, Dramaturgy, Directing, Performance, Puppetry* and *Design*, with an emphasis on collaboration between the various strands. Entrants to the *Writing* strand are required to submit two pieces of writing together with completed application form. Prospectus available. Writing and Dramaturgy Tutor: *Nick Wood*.

The City Literary Institute

Humanities Dept, Stukeley Street, London WC2B 5LJ
☎0171 430 0542   Fax 0171 405 3347

The Writing School offers a wide range of courses from *Radio Drama Writing* and *Writing for Children* to *Autobiographical Writing* and *Writing Short Stories*. The Department offers information and advice during term time.

City University

Northampton Square, London EC1V 0HB
☎0171 477 8268   Fax 0171 477 8256
Website: www.city.ac.uk/conted

Creative writing classes include: *Writer's Workshop; Wordshop* (poetry); *Writing Comedy; Playwright's Workshop; Writing Freelance Articles for Newspapers; Women Writer's Workshop; Creative Writing; Fiction Short and Long; Feature Journalism; Writing for Children*. Contact: Courses for Adults.

The Drill Hall

16 Chenies Street, London WC1B 7EX
☎0171 631 1353   Fax 0171 631 4468

Holds a number of writing classes and workshops. Regular tutors include Carol Barnes and Shaun Levin. Writers interested in *Writing for Performance* may also be interested in Claire Dowie and Colin Watkey's *Stand-Up Theatre Workshop*. Call for brochure on 0171 631 5107.

LNPF Writing School

See **London New Play Festival** under **Festivals**

The London Academy of Playwriting

75 Hillfield Park, London N10 3QU
☎0181 444 5228   Fax 0181 444 5228

Two-year, part-time, post-graduate course in playwriting. Directors: *Tony Dinner, Sonja Linden*.

London College of Printing

Elephant & Castle, London SE1 6SB
☎0171 514 6562/7667/6770
Email: b.daly@dali.linst.ac.uk
Website: www.linst.ac.uk/lcp/dali

Courses in journalism. Short courses run by DALI (Developments at the London Institute) at the Elephant & Castle address above: *Guide to Magazine Writing/News Writing/Feature Writing/ Freelance Journalism/Proof Reading/Subbing on the Screen*; also *Sub-editing and Law for Journalists*. Also offers 2-day specialist journalism courses in food writing, travel writing, writing for the music press, sports journalism and fashion writing. For individuals and companies there are 'tailor-made training' services. Prospectus and information leaflets available; ☎0171 514 6560.

London School of Journalism

22 Upbrook Mews, London W2 3HG
☎0171 706 3790   Fax 0171 706 3780
Email: info@lsjournalism.com
Website: www.home-study.com

Correspondence courses with an individual and personal approach. Students remain with the same tutor throughout their course. Options include: *Short Story Writing; Writing for Children; Poetry; Freelance Journalism; Improve Your English; English for Business; Journalism and Newswriting*. Fees vary but range from £215 for *Enjoying English Literature* to £395 for *Journalism and Newswriting*. Contact the Student Administration Office at the address above.

Middlesex University

School of Communication, Cultural & Media Studies, White Hart Lane, London N17 8HR
☎0181 362 5000   Fax 0181 362 6878

Undergraduate courses (full-time, part-time, associate) for those interested in writing, publishing and the media. Writing & Publishing Studies Set includes: *Editing* and *Marketing* (contact *Juliet Gardiner*); BA(Hons) Writing Programme includes: *Journalism, Scriptwriting and Narrative* and *Poetry Workshops* (contact *Susanna Gladwin*).

Roehampton Institute London

Department of Drama: Theatre, Film and Television, Roehampton Lane, London SW15 5PU

☎0181 392 3230   Fax 0181 392 3289

Email: j.ridgman@roehampton.ac.uk

Website: www.roehampton.ac.uk

Three-year BA(Hons) programmes in *Drama and Theatre Studies* and *Film and Television Studies* include courses on writing for stage and screen. Contact: *Jeremy Ridgman.*

Thames Valley University

St Mary's Road, London W5 5RF

☎0181 579 5000

Offers a course in *Scriptwriting for Television, Stage and Radio.* Aims to provide the fundamental principles of the craft of script writing.

University of Westminster

Harrow Campus, Watford Road, Harrow, Middlesex HA1 3TP

☎0171 911 5903

Part-time evening MAs available in *Journalism, Film and TV, Photography.* Summer courses in *Journalism and Broadcasting.*

Greater Manchester

Manchester Metropolitan University – The Writing School

Department of English, Geoffrey Manton Building, Rosamond Street West, off Oxford Road, Manchester M15 6LL

☎0161 247 1732/1   Fax 0161 247 6345

Closely associated with **Carcanet Press Ltd** and *PN Review,* The Writing School offers three principal 'routes' for students to follow: *Poetry, The Novel* and *Biography and Autobiography.* A key feature of the programme is regular readings, lectures, workshops and masterclasses by writers, publishers, producers, booksellers, librarians and agents. Tutors include Carol Ann Duffy, Jacqueline Roy and Jeffrey Wainwright.

University of Manchester

Department of English & American Studies, Arts Building, Oxford Road, Manchester M13 9PL

☎0161 275 3054   Fax 0161 275 3054

Email: alex.sherwood@man.ac.uk

Offers a one-year MA in *Novel Writing.* Contact: *Alex Sherwood.*

University of Salford

Postgraduate Admissions, Dept. of Media & Performance, Adelphi, Peru Street, Salford, Greater Manchester M3 6EQ

☎0161 295 6027

Email: s.horn@media-perf.salford.ac.uk

Website: www.salford.ac.uk

MA in *Television and Radio Scriptwriting.* Two-year, part-time course taught by professional writers and producers. Also offers a number of Masterclasses with leading figures in the radio and television industry.

Password Training Ltd

23 New Mount Street, Manchester M4 4DE

☎0161 953 4071   Fax 0161 953 4001

Password Training provides training for publishers, writers' groups and individual writers in Internet publishing, planning, production, design, marketing, costing and distribution. Clients have included the Federation of Worker Writers and Community Publishers, The Arts Council, Regional Arts Boards, Yorkshire Art Circus and Corridor Community Press. For further details, contact *Claire Turner.*

The Writers Bureau

Sevendale House, 7 Dale Street, Manchester M1 1JB

☎0161 228 2362   Fax 0161 236 9440

Comprehensive home-study writing course with personal tuition service from professional writers (fee: £249). Fiction, non-fiction, articles, short stories, novels, TV, radio and drama all covered in detail. Trial period, guarantee and no time limits. ODLQC accredited. Quote Ref. EH20. Free enquiry line: 0800 856 2008

The Writers Bureau College of Journalism

Address/☎l as The Writers Bureau above

Home-study course covering all aspects of journalism. Real-life assignments assessed by qualified tutors with the emphasis on getting into print and enjoying the financial rewards. Comprises 28 modules and three handbooks with special introductory offers. Ref: EHJ20. Free enquiry line: 0800 298 7008.

The Writers College

Address/☎ as The Writers Bureau above

The Art of Writing Poetry Course from The Writers Bureau sister college. A home-study course with a more 'recreational' emphasis. The 60,000 word course has 17 modules and lets you complete six written assignments for tutorial evaluation. Fees: £99. Quote Ref. EHP20. Free enquiry line: 0800 856 2008.

Merseyside

University of Liverpool

Centre for Continuing Education,
19 Abercromby Square, Liverpool L69 7ZG
☎0151 794 6900 (24 hours)
Fax 0151 794 2544

Courses include: *Introduction to Creative Writing; The Short Story and the Novel; Introduction to Writing Poetry; Introduction to Scripting for Radio and Television; Introduction to Writing Journalism; Science Fiction and Fantasy; Travel Writing; Biography and Autobiography; Writing for Children; Songwriting; Popular Music Journalism; Theatre Playwrights Workshop; Scripting Situation Comedy; Screenwriting: Film and Television; Scriptwriting for Women*. Most courses are run in the evening over 10 or 20 weeks but there are some linked Saturday and weekday courses on offer. Students have the option of accreditation towards a university award in Creative Writing. Some of the above courses are also part of the university's part-time Flexible Degree pathway (Comb. Hons., Arts). No pre-entry qualifications required. Fees vary with concessions for the unwaged and those in receipt of benefit. For further information and/or copy of current prospectus, phone or write to *Keith Birch*, Head of Creative Arts (address as above).

Norfolk

University of East Anglia

School of English & American Studies,
Norwich, Norfolk NR4 7TJ
☎01603 593262

UEA has a history of concern with contemporary literary culture. Among its MA programmes is one in *Creative Writing*, Stream 1: Prose Fiction; Stream 2: Poetry; Stream 3: Scriptwriting.

Nottinghamshire

The Nottingham Trent University

Humanities Faculty Office (Post Graduate Studies), Clifton Lane, Nottingham
NG11 8NS
☎0115 9418418   Fax 0115 9486632
Email: amanda.samuels@ntu.ac.uk
Website: human.ntu.ac.uk/foh/pg/
    mawriting.html

MA in *Writing*. Workshop-based, the course focuses on the development of your own feature-writing, fiction, life-writing and poetry. Current visiting professors: Michele Roberts and Miranda Seymour. Application forms available from the address above. For more information contact *Amanda Samuels* on 0115 8486335.

Somerset

Bath Spa University College

Newton Park, Bath BA2 9BN
☎01225 875875   Fax 01225 875444

Postgraduate Diploma/MA in *Creative Writing*. A course for creative writers wanting to develop their work. Teaching is by published writers in the novel, poetry, short stories and scriptwriting. In recent years, several students from this course have received contracts from publishers for novels, awards for poetry and short stories and have had work produced on BBC Radio. Contact Admissions Officer, *Clare Brandram Jones* for details.

Institute of Copywriting

Honeycombe House, Bagley, Wedmore, Somerset BS28 4TD
☎01934 713563   Fax 01934 713492
Email: copy@inst.org
Website:dspace.dial.pipex.com/
    institute/copy.htm

Comprehensive home-study course covering all aspects of copywriting, including advice on becoming a self-employed copywriter. Each student has a personal tutor who is an experienced copywriter and who provides detailed feedback on the student's assignments.

University of Bristol

Department of English, 3/5 Woodland Road, Bristol BS8 1TB
☎0117 954 6969   Fax 0117 928 8860
Email: rowena.fowler@bris.ac.uk
Website: www.bris.ac.uk/Depts/
    English-ce_creat.html

Courses: *Women and Writing*, for women who write or would like to begin to write (poetry, fiction, non-fiction, journals); *Certificate in Creative Writing*. Detailed brochure available.

Staffordshire

Keele University

The Centre for Continuing and Professional Education, Keele University, (Freepost ST1666), Newcastle under Lyme, Staffordshire ST5 5BG
☎01782 583436

Weekend courses on literature and creative writing. The 1998 programme included fiction writing and writing for children. Also runs study days where major novelists or poets read and discuss their work.

Surrey

Royal Holloway College
University of London, Egham Hill, Egham, Surrey TW20 0EX
☎01784 443922   Fax 01784 431018
Email: drama@rhbnc.ac.uk

Three-year BA course in *Theatre Studies* during which playwriting can be studied as an option in the second or third year. Contact *Dan Rebellato* or *David Wiles*.

University of Surrey
School of Educational Studies, University of Surrey, Guildford, Surrey GU2 5XH
☎01483 259750   Fax 01483 259522

The 'Learning for Life' programme includes several *Creative Writing* courses, held at the University, the Guildford Institute and throughout the county. The courses carry transferrable credits and can form part of an Honours Degree in Combined Studies. For details contact the Enrolment Secretary or *Dr Brian Crossley FRSA*, Lecturer and Subject Leader in Creative Writing.

Sussex

Chichester Institute of Higher Education
Bishop Otter Campus, College Lane, Chichester, West Sussex PO19 4PE
☎01243 816000   Fax 01243 816080

Postgraduate Certificate/Diploma/MA in *Creative Writing*. Contact *Ms Jan Ainsley*, Head of English Studies, for details.

The Earnley Concourse
Earnley, Chichester, West Sussex PO20 7JL
☎01243 670392   Fax 01243 670832
Email: info@earnley.co.uk
Website: www.earnley.co.uk

Offers a range of residential and non-residential courses throughout the year. Previous programme has included *Writing for Publication; You Can Sell What You Write*. Brochure available.

Scriptwriters Tutorials
Wish Hill, Sandy Lane, Mayfield, East Sussex TN20 6UE
☎01435 873914   Fax 0171 720 7047

Offers professional *one-to-one* scriptwriting tuition by working writers in film, television, radio or stage. Beginners, intermediate and advanced courses. Script evaluation service and correspondence courses. Tutors based in London, Oxford and the southern counties.

University of Sussex
Centre for Continuing Education, Education Development Building, Falmer, Brighton, East Sussex BN1 9RG
☎01273 678537   Fax 01273 678848

Postgraduate Diploma in *Dramatic Writing*: the student is treated as a commissioned writer working in theatre, TV, radio or film. One-year, part-time from April to March. Convenor: *Richard Crane*. Certificate in *Creative Writing*: short fiction, novel and poetry for imaginative writers. One-year, part-time. Convenor: *Richard Crane*. Postgraduate Diploma in *Creative Writing and Personal Development*: for writers working in care services and self exploration. Convenor: *Celia Hunt*. Contact for all courses: *Yvonne Barnes*.

Other accredited courses on campus and at locations in East and West Sussex. Contact: *Lisa Templeton*.

Tyne & Wear

University of Newcastle upon Tyne
Centre for Lifelong Learning, Newcastle upon Tyne NE1 7RU
☎0191 222 5680

Writing-related courses include: *Writing From the Inside Out; Dramatic Writing for Film, TV and Radio; Writing Workshops*. Contact the Secretary, Adult Education Programme.

Warwickshire

University of Warwick
Open Studies, Continuing Education Department, Coventry, Warwickshire CV4 7AL
☎01203 523831

Creative writing courses held at the university or in regional centres. Subjects include: *Starting to Write; Prose and Poetry Writing; Writing for Radio; Screenwriting for Beginners*. A one-year certificate in *Creative Writing* is available.

Focus on Fiction
71 Bucknill Crescent, Hillmorton, Rugby CV21 4HE
☎01788 560972

Correspondence course with one-to-one tuition from professional published writers and literary agents. Offers support, encouragement, contacts and advice. £25 (£35 outside UK) registration fee includes personal organiser with over 400 pages of advice, tips and course notes. A small fee is then paid with each item sent in for appraisal. Covers all genres of fiction writing: writing for women's magazines, science fiction, horror, crime, erotica, writing for children and teenagers, fantasy and caters for all levels of ability. Also runs an annual short story competition, **The Phillip Good Memorial Prize** (see **Prizes**).

West Midlands

Sandwell College
Smethwick Campus, Crocketts Lane, Smethwick B66 3BU
☎0121 556 6000

Creative writing courses held afternoons/evenings, from September to July. General courses covering short stories, poetry, autobiography, etc. Also women's writing courses. Contact *Roz Goddard*.

University of Birmingham
School of Continuing Studies, Edgbaston, Birmingham B15 2TT
☎0121 414 5607/7259   Fax 0121 414 5619

Certificate of Higher Education in *Creative Writing* – two years, part-time. Day and weekend classes, including creative writing, literature, theatre. Courses are held at locations throughout Birmingham, the West Midlands, Hereford, Worcester and Shropshire. Detailed course brochures are available from the above address. Please specify which course you are interested in.

The University also offers an MA course in *Playwriting Studies* established by David Edgar in 1970. Contact *David Edgar* at the Department of Drama and Theatre Arts (☎0121 414 5790).

Wiltshire

Marlborough College
Marlborough, Wiltshire SN8 1PA
☎01672 892388/9   Fax 01672 892476
Email: summer.school@marlboroughcollege.
    wilts.sch.uk

Summer school with literature and creative writing included in its programme. Caters for residential and day students. Brochure available giving full details and prices.

Yorkshire

Hull College
Queen's Gardens, Hull, East Yorkshire HU1 3DG
☎01482 329943   Fax 01482 219079

Offers part-time day/evening writing courses in *Novel Writing* and *Short Story Writing*, at Hull College, Park Street Centre. Courses begin each academic term. Writers are encouraged to contribute stories for a collection. Contact: *Gwynneth Yates.*

The Northern School of Film and Television
Leeds Metropolitan University, 2 Queen Square, Leeds, West Yorkshire LS2 8AF
☎0113 2831900   Fax 0113 2831901
Email: nsftv@lmu.ac.uk
Website: www.lmu.ac.uk

The NSFTV offers a Postgraduate Diploma/MA course in *Fiction Screenwriting*. One to two years, full-time. Currently, graduates working on *The Bill, Emmerdale, Coronation Street,* three features and other professional projects. Contact: *Ian Macdonald.*

Open College of the Arts
Houndhill, Worsbrough, Barnsley, South Yorkshire S70 6TU
☎01226 730495   Fax 01226 730838
Email: open.arts@ukonline.co.uk
Website:www.ukonline.co.uk/
    open.arts/index.htm

The OCA correspondence course, *Starting to Write,* offers help and stimulus, without an emphasis on commercial success, from experienced writers/tutors. Subsequent levels available include specialist poetry, fiction and biographical writing courses. Audio–cassette versions of these courses are available. New *Creative Writing* course helps student writers understand how readers interact with their writing.

Sheffield Hallam University
School of Cultural Studies, Sheffield Hallam University, Collegiate Crescent, Sheffield S10 2BP
☎0114 2254408   Fax 0114 2254363
Offers MA in *Creative Writing* (one-year, full-time; also part-time).

University College Bretton Hall
School of English, Faculty of Arts, University College Bretton Hall, West Bretton, Wakefield, West Yorkshire WF4 4LG
☎01924 830261   Fax 01924 832006
Offers one-year full-time/two-year part-time MA course in *Creative Writing* designed for competent though not necessarily published writers. Contact *Rob Watson* for details.

University College, Scarborough

North Riding College, Filey Road,
Scarborough, North Yorkshire YO11 3AZ
☎01723 362392   Fax 01723 362392
Website: www.ucscarb.ac.uk

BA Single Honours and Combined Honours
Degree in which *Theatre Studies* contains *Writing
for Theatre*. Contact: *Dr Eric Prince*. University
College Scarborough also works closely with the
Stephen Joseph Theatre and its artistic director
Alan Ayckbourn. The theatre sustains a policy
for staging new writers. (See entry under
Theatre Producers.) The College hosts the
annual National Student Drama Festival which
includes the International Student Playscript
Competition (details from The National Information Centre for Student Drama at UCS;
email: nsdf@ucscarb.ac.uk or from *Clive Wolfe*
on 0181 883 4586).

University of Sheffield

Division of Adult Continuing Education,
196–198 West Street, Sheffield S1 4ET
☎0114 2227000   Fax 0114 2227001
Creative writing courses and workshops.

IRELAND

Dingle Writing Courses Ltd

Ballintlea, Ventry, Co. Kerry, Republic of
Ireland
☎00 353 66 9159052 Fax 00 353 66 9159052

A summer and autumn programme of weekend
and five-day residential courses for beginners
and experienced writers alike. Tutored by professional writers the courses take place in 'an
inspirational setting overlooking Inch strand'.
The 1999 programme offers poetry, fiction,
starting to write, travel and writing for theatre.

Tutors include Jennifer Johnston, Thomas
Lynch and Graham Mort. Writing courses for
schools are also available. Brochures and further
information available from directors, *Abigail Joffe*
or *Nicholas McLachlan* at the address above.

University of Dublin
(Trinity College)

Graduates Studies Office, Arts Building,
Trinity College, Dublin 2, Republic of Ireland
☎00 353 1 608 1561   Fax 00 353 1 671 2821
Email: evansd@tcd.ie

Offers an M.Phil. *Creative Writing* course. A one-
year, full-time course intended for students who

are seriously committed to writing, are practising, or prospective authors. Contact Admissions
at the address above.

Queen's University of Belfast

Institute of Continuing Education, Belfast
BT7 1NN
☎01232 273323
Email: ice@qub.ac.uk
Website: www.qub.ac.uk/ice

Courses have included *Creative Writing* and
Journal Writing.

University of Ulster

Short Course Unit, Room 17C21, University
of Ulster, Belfast BT37 0QB
☎01232 365131

Creative writing course/workshop, usually held
in the autumn and spring terms. Concessions
available. Contact the Administrative Officer.

SCOTLAND

University of Aberdeen

Centre for Continuing Education, Regent
Building, Regent Walk, Aberdeen
AB24 3FX
☎01224 272449   Fax 01224 272478

Creative writing evening class held weekly,
taught by published author. Participants may join
at any time.

University of Dundee

Institute for Education and Lifelong Learning,
Nethergate, Dundee DD1 4HN
☎01382 344128

Various creative writing courses held at the
University and elsewhere in Dundee, Perthshire
and Angus. Detailed course brochure available.

Edinburgh University

Centre for Continuing Education,
11 Buccleuch Place, Edinburgh EH8 9LW
☎0131 650 4400   Fax 0131 667 6097
Email: cce@ed.ac.uk
Website: www.cce.ed.ac.uk

Several writing-orientated courses and summer
schools. Beginners welcome. Intensive two-
week course *Playwriting*, held in July, culminates
in a rehearsed reading by professional actors and
recorded on video for participants to take away.
Free tuition in word-processing and use of computer room. Course brochure available.

University of Glasgow

Department of Adult and Continuing Education, 59 Oakfield Avenue, Glasgow G12 8LW

☎0141 330 4032/4394 (Brochure/Enquiries)

Runs writers' workshops and courses at all levels; all friendly and informal. Daytime and evening meetings. Tutors are all experienced published writers in various fields.

University of St Andrews

School of English, The University, St Andrews, Fife KY16 9AL

☎01334 462666   Fax 01334 462655

Offers postgraduate study in *Creative Writing*. Candidates choose two topics from: *Fiction: The Novel; Craft and Technique in Poetry; The Short Story*, and also write their own poetry and/or prose for assessment.

7:84 Summer School

See **7:84 Theatre Company Scotland** under **Theatre Producers**

University of Stirling

Division of Academic Innovation and Continuing Education, Airthrey Castle, Stirling FK9 4LA

☎01786 467953   Fax 01786 463398

Offers 10-week courses from the beginning of February, held in Airthrey Castle.

113 Writers Workshop: aspiring writers are invited to join a lively and friendly group which offers help and stimulus with many different kinds of writing. The workshop format means students produce a fair body of writing and receive feedback and encouragement. A 10-week course, held on Thursday evenings.

112 Creative Writing: Absolute Beginners: a course designed for those who would like to write but lack the confidence or experience for a writers' workshop. Held on Monday evenings. For further information or an application form, contact *Paula Douglas*, Open Studies Secretary at the address above.

WALES

Tŷ Newydd Writers' Centre

Llanystumdwy, Cricieth, Gwynedd LL52 0LW

☎01766 522811   Fax 01766 523095

Email: tynewydd@dial.pipex.com

Residential writers' centre set up by the Taliesin Trust with the support of the **Arts Council of Wales** to encourage and promote writing in both English and Welsh. Most courses run from Monday evening to Saturday morning. Each course has two tutors and takes a maximum of 16 participants. The centre offers a wide range of specific courses for writers at all levels of experience. Early booking essential. Fee £320 (single)/£295 (twin-bedded) inclusive. People on low incomes may be eligible for a grant or bursary. Course leaflet available. (See also **Organisations of Interest to Poets**.)

University of Glamorgan

Treforest, Pontypridd CF37 1DL

☎01443 482551

MPhil in *Writing* – a two-year part-time Masters degree for writers of fiction and poets. ESTABLISHED 1993. Contact *Professor Tony Curtis* at the School of Humanities and Social Sciences.

Also, BA in Theatre and Media Drama. Modules include *Scriptwriting: Theatre, Radio, TV and Video*. Contact *Steven Blandford*.

University of Wales, Bangor

Department of English, College Road, Bangor LL57 2DG

☎01248 382102   Fax 01248 382102

Offers undergraduate and postgraduate degrees in creative writing, including *Writing Fiction, Writing Poetry, Writing for the Theatre, Writing for Film and the Media*. Modules also available in contemporary literature, adaptation, film studies, modern American and British fiction, poetry and drama, children's literature and women's writing, and the opportunity to combine study with other creative and performing arts, languages or film studies. PhD course in *Creative and Critical Writing*. Visiting writers have included Margaret Atwood, Ted Hughes, and Nobel prize winners Derek Walcott and William Golding.

Circles and Workshops

Directory of Writers' Circles

Oldacre, Horderns Park Road,
Chapel-en-le-Frith, High Peak SK23 9SY
☎01298 812305
Email: jillie@cix.co.uk
Website: www.cix.co.uk/~oldacre/

Comprehensive directory of writers' circles, containing contacts and addresses of more than 600 groups and circles meeting throughout the country. Some overseas entries too. Available from *Jill Dick* at the address above; £5 post free.

Annual Writers' Conference

'Chinook', Southdown Road, Winchester,
Hampshire SO21 2BY
☎01962 712307 Email: WriterConf@aol.com
Website: www.gmp.co.uk/writers/conference

Conference Director *Barbara Large*

Having grown over the past 18 years from a creative writing workshop, this event is now the foremost writers' conference in the country, attracting international authors, playwrights, poets, agents and editors who give workshops, mini courses, editor appointments, lectures and seminars to help writers harness their creativity and develop technical skills. 15 writing competitions are attached to the conference. All first-place winners are published in *The Best of* series annually. The 2000 Conference will be held over the weekend of 30 June – 2 July at King Alfred's University College, Winchester, with workshops from 3 – 7 July. The Bookfair offers delegates a wide choice of exhibits including Internet author services, publishers, booksellers, printers and associations.

Carmarthern Writers' Circle

Lower Carfan, Tavern Spite, Whitland,
Pembrokeshire SA34 0NP
☎01994 240441

FOUNDED 1989. The Circle meets on the second Monday of every month upstairs at the Queen's Hotel in Carmarthen. Both beginners and experienced writers are welcome. Activities include competitions, workshops and 'poets and pints' evenings. For more information, contact *Jenny White* at the address above.

Children's Novel Writers' Folio

See **Short Story Writers' Folio**

Chiltern Writers' Group

Marsh Green House, Bassetsbury Lane,
High Wycombe HP11 1QY
☎01494 451654

Invites writers, publishers, editors and agents to speak at its monthly meetings at Wendover Public Library. Regular newsletter and competitions. Annual subscription: £15; concessions: £10. Non-members meeting: £3. Contact *Diana Atkinson* at the address above.

Concordant Poets Folios

87 Brookhouse Road, Farnborough,
Hampshire GU14 0BU

Founded through popular demand over ten years ago to encourage and assist poets, while studying techniques and possible marketing outlets. Each poem included is discussed and advised upon from several different viewpoints, with poets gaining valuable knowledge while building (via postal method) a circle of friends with mutual interests. Whether beginner, intermediate or advanced, there is a suitable place in one of the folios. For details and enrolment form please send s.a.e. to *Barbara Horsfall*.

The Cotswold Writers' Circle

Dar-es-Salaam, Beeches Park, Hampton Fields, Minchinhampton, Gloucestershire
GL6 9BA
☎01453 882912

Contact *Charles Hooker*

The Circle meets fortnightly in Cirencester. Circle activities include organising and running two competitions, publishing an anthology of Circle work, organising a writing workshop, etc. Contact *Charles Hooker*, Honorary Treasurer, for details of the Circle's activities.

'Sean Dorman' Manuscript Society

Cherry Trees, Crosemere Road, Cockshutt,
Ellesmere, Shropshire SY12 0JP
☎01939 270293

FOUNDED 1957. The Society provides mutual help among writers and aspiring writers in England, Wales and Scotland. By means of circulating manuscript parcels, members receive constructive criticism of their own work and read and comment on the work of others. Each 'Circulator' has up to nine participants and members' contributions may be in any medium: short stories, chapters of a novel, poetry, magazine articles, etc. Members may join two such circulators if they wish. Each circulator has a technical section and a letters section in which friendly communication between members is encouraged, and all are of a general nature apart from one, specialising in mss for the Christian market. Full details and application forms available on receipt of s.a.e. Director: *Mary Driver*. Subscription: £6.50 p.a.

East Anglian Writers
52 Riverside Road, Norwich, Norfolk
NR1 1SR
☎01603 629088   Fax 01603 629088
Contact *Anthony Vivis*

A group of over 80 professional writers living in Norfolk and Suffolk. Informal pub meetings, occasional speakers' evenings and contact point for professional writers new to the area.

Equinoxe Screenwriting Workshops
Association Equinoxe, 4 Square du Roule,
75008 Paris France
☎00 33 1 5353 4488   Fax 00 33 1 5353 4489

FOUNDED 1993, with Jeanne Moreau as president, to promote screenwriting and to establish a link between European and American film production. In association with Canal+, Sony Pictures Entertainment and Media Programme of the European Union, Equinoxe supports young writers of all nationalities by creating a screenwriting community capable of appealing to an international audience. Open to selected professional screenwriters able to speak either English or French fluently. To-date, Equinoxe has helped 120 European and American authors to perfect and promote scripts. 26 of these have been brought to the screen and a further six are in production. Contact *Claire Dubert* for further information.

Euroscript
114 Whitfield Street, London W1P 5RW
☎0171 387 5880   Fax 0171 387 5880
Email: euroscript@netmatters.co.uk
Website: www.euroscript.co.uk

Euroscript, a MEDIA programme of the EU to advance European scriptwriting, is a distance training project working in EU languages. It develops screenplays, reads, selects and promotes scripts and writers. Also runs workshops and supports writers' groups. Two story competitions per year: deadlines 30 April and 31 October. Write or access the Website for further information.

Gay Authors Workshop
BM Box 5700, London WC1N 3XX
☎0181 520 5223

Established 1978 to encourage and support lesbian/gay writers. Regular meetings and a newsletter. Contact: *Kathryn Byrd*. Membership: £7; £3 unwaged.

Historical Novel Folio
17 Purbeck Heights, Mount Road, Parkstone, Poole, Dorset BH14 0QP
☎01202 741897

An independent postal workshop – single folio dealing with any period before World War II. Send s.a.e. for details. Contact: *Doris Myall-Harris*.

The International Inkwell
See entry under **Miscellany**

Kops and Ryan Advanced Playwriting Workshops
41B Canfield Gardens, London NW6 3JL
☎0171 624 2940/263 8740
Tutors *Bernard Kops, Tom Ryan*

Three ten-week terms per year beginning in September. Students may join course any term. Workshops on Tuesday, 7–10 pm or Thursday, 7–10 pm, or Saturday, 2–5 pm. Small groups. Focus on structure, character, language, meaning and style through written and improvised exercises; reading scenes from students' current work; and readings of full-length plays. Two actors attend each session. Call for details.

London Screenwriters' Workshop
114 Whitfield Street, London W1P 5RW
☎0171 387 5511
Website: www.lsw.org.uk

Established by writers in 1983 as a forum for contact, information and tuition. LSW helps new and developing writers in the film, TV and video industries. Organises a continuous programme of workshops, events with industry figures, seminars and courses. Free monthly events and magazine newsletter every two months. Contact: *Ben Davies*. Membership: £30 p.a..

London Writer Circle
Flat D, 49 Christchurch Street,
London SW3 4AS
☎0171 351 6377

FOUNDED 1924. Aims to help and encourage writers of all grades. Monthly evening meetings with well-known speakers on aspects of literature and journalism, and workshops for short story writing, poetry and feature writing. Occasional social events and quarterly magazine. Subscription: £16 (London); £9 (Country); £6 (Overseas). Contact: *Pamela Birley* at the address above.

Nottingham Writers Contact

U.A.E.C. Centre, 16 Shakespeare Street, Nottingham NG1 4GF
☎01159 288913

A group of professional and amateur writers which meets every third Saturday in the month at the U.A.E.C. Centre, 10.00 am – 12.30 pm. 'If you are visiting the city, contact Keith Taylor at the telephone number above.'

NWP (North West Playwrights)

18 St Margaret's Chambers, 5 Newton Street, Manchester M1 1HL
☎0161 237 1978   Fax 0161 237 1978
FOUNDED 1982. Award-winning organisation whose aim is to develop and promote new theatre writing. Operates a script-reading service, classes and script development scheme and *The Lowdown* newsletter. Services available only to North West writers.

QueenSpark Books

See entry under **Small Presses**

Scribo

1/31 Hamilton Road, Boscombe, Bournemouth, Dorset BH1 4EQ
☎01202 302533

Scribo (established for more than 20 years) is a postal workshop for novelists. Mss criticism foilos cover fantasy/sci-fi, crime/thrillers, mainstream, women's fiction, literary. Forums offer information, discussion on all topics relating to writing and literature. No annual subscription. £5 joining fee only. Contact: *Kay Sylvester* at the address above. S.a.e., please.

Short Story Writers' Folio/ Children's Novel Writers' Folio

5 Park Road, Brading, Sandown, Isle of Wight PO36 0HU
☎01983 407697

Postal workshops – members receive constructive criticism of their work and read and offer advice on fellow members' contributions. Send an s.a.e. for further details. Contact: *Mrs Dawn Wortley-Nott*.

Society of Sussex Authors

Bookends, Lewes Road, Horsted Keynes, Haywards Heath, West Sussex RH17 7DP
☎01825 790755   Fax 01825 790755
Contact *Michael Legat*

FOUNDED 1968 to promote the interests of its members and of literature, particularly within the Sussex area. Regular meetings and exchange of information; plus social events. Membership restricted to writers who live in Sussex and who have had at least one book commercially published, or other writings used professionally. Meetings are held six times a year in Lewes. Annual subscription: £10.

The South and Mid-Wales Association of Writers (S.A.M.W.A.W.)

c/o I.M.C. Consulting Group, Denham House, Lambourne Crescent, Cardiff CF4 5ZW
☎01222 761170   Fax 01222 761304
Contact *Julian Rosser*

FOUNDED 1971 to foster the art and craft of writing in all its forms. Provides a common meeting ground for writers, critics, editors, adjudicators from all over the UK and abroad. Organises an annual residential weekend conference and a day seminar in May and October respectively. Holds competitions, two for members only and two which are open to the public, in addition to **The Mathew Pritchard Award for Short Story Writing**. Subscription: £7 (Single); £12 (Joint).

South Eastern Writers' Association

47 Sunningdale Avenue, Leigh-on-Sea, Essex SS9 1JY
☎01702 477083   Fax 01702 477083
President *Marion Hough*

FOUNDED 1989 to bring together experienced and novice writers, in an informal atmosphere. Non-profit-making, the Association holds an annual residential weekend each spring at Bulphan, Essex. Free workshops and discussion groups included in the overall cost. Previous guest speakers: Simon Brett, George Layton, Maureen Lipman, Terry Pratchett, Jack Rosenthal, Bernard Cornwell.

Southport Writers' Circle

32 Dover Road, Southport, Merseyside PR8 4TB
Runs a poetry competition (see entry under **Prizes**). Contact: *Hilary Tinsley*.

Southwest Scriptwriters

149 St Andrew's Road, Montpelier, Bristol
BS6 5EL
☎0117 9445424   Fax 0117 9445413

FOUNDED 1994 to offer encouragement and advice to those writing for stage, screen, radio and TV in the region. The group attracts professional writers, enthusiasts and students and meets regularly at the Theatre Royal, Bristol to read aloud and provide critical feedback on members' work, discuss writing technique and exchange market information. Catherine Johnson, writer-in-residence at the Bristol Old Vic, acts as Honorary President. Subscription: £5 p.a. Contact the Secretary, *John Colbom* for details.

Speakeasy – Milton Keynes Writers' Group

46 Wealdstone Place, Springfield, Milton Keynes MK6 3JG
☎01908 663860

Invites lovers of the written and spoken word to their monthly meetings on the first Friday of each month, 7.45pm. Full and varied programme including Local Writers Nights where work can be read and performed. Contact: *Martin Brocklebank*. Also runs an Annual Open Creative Writing Competition. Send s.a.e. for entry form to address above.

Sussex Playwrights' Club

2 Brunswick Mews, Hove, East Sussex
BN3 1HD
☎01273 730106

FOUNDED 1935. Aims to encourage the writing of plays for stage, radio and TV by giving monthly dramatic readings of members' work by experienced actors, mainly from local drama groups. Gives constructive, critical suggestions as to how work might be improved, and suggests possible marketing. Membership is not confined to writers but to all who are interested in theatre in all its forms, and all members are invited to take part in such discussions. Guests are always welcome at a nominal £1. Meetings held at New Venture Theatre, Bedford Place, Brighton, East Sussex. Subscription: £5 p.a. Contact the Chairman, *Dennis Evans* for details.

Ver Poets

Haycroft, 61–63 Chiswell Green Lane,
St Albans, Hertfordshire AL2 3AL
☎01727 867005

Chairman *Ray Badman*
Editor/Organiser *May Badman*

FOUNDED 1966 to promote poetry and to help poets. With postal and local members, holds meetings in St Albans; runs a poetry bookstall for members' and other groups' publications; publishes members' work in anthologies and organises competitions, including the annual **Ver Poets Open** competition. Gives help and advice and makes information available to members about other poetry groups, events and opportunities for publication. Membership: £10 p.a.; £12.50 or US$25 (Overseas).

West Country Writers' Association

81 Crock Lane, Bothenhampton, Bridport,
Dorset DT6 4DQ
☎01308 421833   Fax 01305 767111

President *Christopher Fry*
Honorary Secretary *Mrs Caroline Strickland*

FOUNDED 1951 in the interest of published authors with an interest in the West Country. Meets to discuss news and views and to listen to talks. Conference and newsletters. Annual subscription: £10 p.a.

Workers' Educational Association

National Office: Temple House, 17 Victoria Park Square, London E2 9PB
☎0181 983 1515   Fax 0181 983 4840

FOUNDED in 1903, the WEA is a voluntary body with members drawn from all walks of life. It runs writing courses and workshops throughout the country and all courses are open to everyone. Branches in most towns and many villages, with 13 district offices in England and one in Scotland. Contact your district WEA office for courses in your region. All correspondence should be addressed to the District Secretary.

Cheshire, Merseyside & West Lancashire: 7/8 Bluecoat Chambers, School Lane, Liverpool L1 3BX (☎0151 709 8023)

Eastern: Botolph House, 17 Botolph Lane, Cambridge CB2 3RE (☎01223 350978)

East Midlands: 16 Shakespeare Street, Nottingham NG1 4GF (☎01159 475162)

London: 4 Luke Street, London EC2A 4NT (☎0171 388 7261/387 8966)

Northern: 51 Grainger Street, Newcastle upon Tyne NE1 5JE (☎0191 232 3957)

North Western: 4th Floor, Crawford House, University Precinct Centre, Oxford Road, Manchester M13 9GH (☎0161 273 7652)

South Eastern: 4 Castle Hill, Rochester, Kent ME1 1QQ (☎01634 842140)

South Western: Martin's Gate Annexe, Bretonside, Plymouth, Devon PL4 0AT (☎01752 664989)

Thames & Solent: 6 Brewer Street, Oxford OX1 1QN (☎01865 246270)

Western: 40 Morse Road, Redfield, Bristol BS5 9LB (☎01179 351764)

West Mercia: 78–80 Sherlock Street, Birmingham B5 6LT (☎0121 666 6101)

Yorkshire North: 6 Woodhouse Square, Leeds, W. Yorkshire LS3 1AD (☎01132 453304)

Yorkshire South: Chantry Buildings, 6–20 Corporation Street, Rotherham S60 1NG (☎01709 837001)

Scottish Association: Riddle's Court, 322 Lawnmarket, Edinburgh EH1 2PG (☎0131 226 3456)

Writers in Oxford

41 Kingston Road, Oxford OX2 6RH
☎01865 513844   Fax 01865 510017

FOUNDED 1992. Open to published authors, playwrights, poets and journalists. Linked to **The Society of Authors** but organised locally.

Arranges a programme of meetings, seminars and social functions. Publishes newsletter, *The Oxford Writer*. Subscription: £15 p.a. Contact the Secretary, *Maggie Black* for details.

Yorkshire Playwrights

3 Trinity Road, Scarborough, North Yorkshire YO11 2TD
☎01723 367449   Fax 01723 367449
Email: ScarTam@aol.com

FOUNDED 1989 out of an initiative by Jude Kelly and William Weston of the **West Yorkshire Playhouse**. A group of professional writers of plays for stage, TV and radio whose aims are to encourage the writing and performance of new plays in Yorkshire. Open to any writers living in Yorkshire who are members, preferably, of the **The Writers' Guild/Theatre Writers Union**, or **The Society of Authors**. Contact the Administrator, *Ian Watson* for an information sheet.

Miscellany

Arjay Research

20 Rookery View, Little Thurrock, Grays,
Essex RM17 6AS
☎01375 372199   Fax 01375 372199

Contact *Roger W. Jordan*

All aspects of international merchant shipping
and naval research undertaken by former shipping archivist and editor. Extensive maritime
library and comprehensive databases on *inter
alia* ships wrecked/lost and passenger and cruise
ships. Terms by arrangement.

Authors' Research Services

32 Oak Village, London NW5 4QN
☎0171 284 4316

Contact *Richard Wright*

Research and document supply service, particularly to authors, academics and others without
easy access to London libraries and sources of
information. Also indexing of books and journals. Rates negotiable.

Brooks Krikler Research

455 Finchley Road, London NW3 6HN
☎0171 431 9886   Fax 0171 431 9887
Email: bkr@pictures.demon.co.uk

Contact *Emma Krikler*

Provides a full picture-research service to all
those involved in publishing and the media.
Educational and non-educational books, magazines, advertising, CD-ROM and multimedia,
brochures, video and computer games manufacturers and designers. The service includes finding, editing and providing images, negotiating all
reproduction charges inclusive of full copyright
clearance. Has special arrangements with photographic libraries worldwide and a variety of photographers can undertake commissioned work.
An on-line service is available with all requests.

The International Inkwell,
a writers' retreat

Cafe du Livre, Rue de la Mairie, 11170
Montolieu, Aude France
☎00 33 468 248117   Fax 00 33 468 248321
Email: 11320.616@compuserve.com

London address: 96 Edith Grove, Chelsea,
London SW10
☎01304 369799   Fax 0171 352 3951

Contact *Lucia Stuart*

Set in the French medieval village of
Montolieu, which boasts 14 bookshops to a
population of 800, The International Inkwell
rents rooms for writers. Open from June to
September, groups are welcome for writing
courses, reading weeks or forums. For further
details contact Lucia Stuart at the address in
France from May to September or the London
address from November to April.

J. P. Lethbridge

245 St Margaret's Road, Ward End,
Birmingham B8 2DY
☎0121 783 0548

Contact *J. P. Lethbridge*

Experienced historical researcher. Searching
through old newspapers and checking birth,
marriage and death certificates a speciality.
Special interest in crime. Rates negotiable.

The Literary Consultancy

PO Box 12939, London N8 9WA
☎0181 372 3922   Fax 0181 372 3922
Email: swifttlc@dircon.co.uk

Contact *Rebecca Swift*

Founded by former publishers to offer an editorial service and advice for aspiring writers.
Will provide an appraisal of fiction and most
categories of non-fiction. Charges range from
£40 for a short story to £300 for a full mss of
300 pages.

Murder Files

Marienau, Brimley Road, Bovey Tracey,
Devon TQ13 9DH
☎01626 833487   Fax 01626 835797
Email: UKMurders@aol.com
Website: www.UKMurders@aol.com

Contact *Paul Williams*

Crime writer and researcher specialising in UK
murders. Can provide information on thousands of well-known and less well-known cases
dating from 1400. Copies of press cuttings
relating to murder available for cases from 1920
onwards. Research also undertaken for general

enquirers, writers, TV, radio, video, etc. Rates on application.

New Authors Showcase

Rivendell, Kingsgate Close, Torquay, Devon TQ2 8QA
☎01803 326617   Fax 01803 326617
Email: newauthors@compuserve.com
Website: ourworld.compuserve.com/
   homepages/newauthor

Contact *Barrie E. James*

Formed in August 1997. A modern Internet site for new unpublished authors to display their work to publishers. Web pages available for published authors to advertise their work. All literary work considered, including poetry. No reading fee. First approach should be by regular mail including s.a.e.

Roger Palmer Limited, Media Contracts and Copyright

23c Tavistock Place, London WC1H 9SE
☎0171 383 5454   Fax 0171 383 3234
Email: contracts@rogerpalmer.co.uk

Contact *Roger Palmer, Stephen Aucutt, Angela Elkins*

ESTABLISHED 1993. Drafts, advises on and negotiates all media contracts (on a regular or *ad hoc* basis) for publishers, literary and merchandising agents, authors, packagers, charities and others. Manages and operates clients' complete contracts functions, undertakes contractual audits, devises contracts and permissions systems, advises on copyright and related issues and provides training and seminars on an individual or group basis. Growing private client list, with special rates for members of **The Society of Authors** and **The Writers' Guild**. Roger Palmer (Managing Director) was for many years Contracts and Intellectual Property Director of the Hodder & Stoughton Group; Stephen Aucutt (Director) was previously Contracts Manager for Reed Children's Books, and Angela Elkins has considerable experience in publishing, music and broadcasting.

Patent Research

Dachsteinstr. 12a, D–81825 Munich, Germany
☎00 49 89 430 7833

Contact *Gerhard Everwyn*

All world, historical patents for researchers, authors, archives, museums and publishers. Rates on application.

Teral Research Services

45 Forest View Road, Moordown, Bournemouth, Dorset BH9 3BH
☎01202 516834   Fax 01202 516834

Contact *Terry C. Treadwell*

All aspects of research undertaken but specialises in all military, aviation, naval and defence subjects, both past and present. Extensive book and photographic library, including one of the best collections of World War One aviation photographs. Terms by arrangement.

Melanie Wilson

Ten Steps, Church Street, Seagrave LE12 7LT
☎01509 812806   Fax 01509 812334
Email: MelanieWilson@compuserve.com

Contact *Melanie Wilson*

Comprehensive research service for books, magazines, newspapers, documentaries, films, radio, education, TV drama. Includes free worldwide booksearch service and groundwork for factual basis for all media presentations, particularly in historical research, costume and textiles, crafts, food and cooking, weapons and uniforms, traditional storytelling, past technology, living history displays and exhibitions.

Press Cuttings Agencies

The Broadcast Monitoring Company

89½ Worship Street, London EC2A 2BE
☎0171 377 1742   Fax 0171 377 6103
Website: www.bmc.co.uk

Television, radio, national and European press monitoring agency. Cuttings from national and all major European press available seven days a week, with early morning delivery. Also monitoring of all news and current affairs programmes – national, international and satellite. Retrospective research service and free telephone notification. Sponsorship evaluation from all media sources.

Durrants Press Cuttings Ltd

Discovery House, 28–42 Banner Street, London EC1Y 8QE
☎0171 674 0200   Fax 0171 674 0222

Wide coverage of all print media sectors; foreign press in association with agencies abroad; current affairs and news programmes from UK broadcast media. High speed, early morning press cuttings from the national press. Overnight delivery via courier to most areas or first-class mail. Well presented, laser printed, A4 cuttings. Monthly reading fee of £70 plus 85p per cutting.

International Press-Cutting Bureau

224–236 Walworth Road, London SE17 1JE
☎0171 708 2113   Fax 0171 701 4489
Contact *Robert Podro*

Covers national, provincial, trade, technical and magazine press. Cuttings are normally sent twice weekly by first-class post and there are no additional service charges or reading fees. Subscriptions for 100 and 250 cuttings are valid for six months. Larger subscriptions expire after one year even if the total number of cuttings subscribed for has not been reached. 100 cuttings £246.75 (including VAT); 250 £528.75.

Press Express

3rd Floor, 53–56 Great Sutton Street, London EC1V 0DE
☎0171 689 0123   Fax 0171 251 1412
Contact *Charles Stuart-Hunt*

High-speed overnight press cuttings.

The Prominent Information Company

Bear Wharf, 27 Bankside, London SE1 9DP
☎0171 203 3500   Fax 0171 203 0101
Contact *Gary Forrest*

Offers an overnight national press monitoring service with same day, early morning delivery. Also coverage of regional papers and weekly/monthly business/trade magazines. Rates on application.

Romeike & Curtice

Hale House, 290–296 Green Lanes, London N13 5TP
☎0800 289543   Fax 0181 882 6716
Email: info@romeike.com
Website: www.romeike.com
Contact *Mary Michael*

Monitors national and international dailies and Sundays, provincial papers, consumer magazines, trade and technical journals, teletext services as well as national radio/TV networks. Back research, advertising checking services and Internet monitoring are also available.

We Find It (Press Clippings)

103 South Parade, Belfast BT7 2GN
☎01232 646008   Fax 01232 646008
Contact *Avril Forsythe*

Specialises in Northern Ireland press and magazines, both national and provincial. Rates on application.

Bursaries, Fellowships and Grants

Aosdána
An Chomhairle Ealaíon (The Arts Council),
70 Merrion Square, Dublin 2,
Republic of Ireland
☎00 353 1 6180200   Fax 00 353 1 6761302
Website: www.artscouncil.ie
Registrar of Aosdána *Patricia Quinn*
Assistant Registrar *Dermot McLaughlin*

Aosdána is an affiliation of creative artists engaged in literature, music and the visual arts, and consists of not more than 200 artists who have gained a reputation for achievement and distinction. Membership is by competitive sponsored selection and is open to Irish citizens or residents only. Members are eligible to receive an annuity for a five-year term to assist them in pursuing their art full-time.
Award IR£8720 (annuity).

Arts Council Literature Bursaries, Ireland
An Chomhairle Ealaíon (The Arts Council),
70 Merrion Square, Dublin 2,
Republic of Ireland
☎00 353 1 6180200   Fax 00 353 1 6761302
Website: www.artscouncil.ie
Literature Officer *Sinead MacAodha*

Bursaries in literature awarded to creative writers of fiction, poetry and drama in Irish and English to enable concentration on, or completion of, specific projects. A limited number of bursaries may be given to non-fiction projects. Open to Irish citizens or residents only. Final entry date 3rd April.
Award IR£3000–8000 (£6,000–16,000 over two years).

Arts Council Theatre Writing Bursaries
Arts Council of England, 14 Great Peter Street, London SW1P 3NQ
☎0171 973 6431   Fax 0171 973 6983
Contact *John Johnston*

Intended to provide experienced playwrights with an opportunity to research and develop a play for the theatre independently of financial pressures and free from the need to write for a particular market. Bursaries are also available for theatre translation projects. Writers must be resi-dent in England. Writers resident in Wales, Scotland or Northern Ireland should approach their own Arts Council. Final entry date 6 January 2000.
Award £3500.

The Authors' Contingency Fund
The Society of Authors, 84 Drayton Gardens,
London SW10 9SB
☎0171 373 6642   Fax 0171 373 5768

This fund makes modest grants to published authors who find themselves in sudden financial difficulties. Contact the **Society of Authors** for an information sheet and application form.

The Authors' Foundation
The Society of Authors, 84 Drayton Gardens,
London SW10 9SB
☎0171 373 6642   Fax 0171 373 5768

Annual grants to writers whose publisher's advance is insufficient to cover the costs of research involved. Application by letter to The Authors' Foundation giving details, in confidence, of the advance and royalties, together with the reasons for needing additional funding. Grants are sometimes given even if there is no commitment by a publisher, so long as the applicant has had a book published and the new work will almost certainly be published. About £50,000 is distributed each year. Contact the **Society of Authors** for an information sheet. Final entry date 31 May.

The K. Blundell Trust
The Society of Authors, 84 Drayton Gardens,
London SW10 9SB
☎0171 373 6642   Fax 0171 373 5768

Annual grants to writers whose publisher's advance is insufficient to cover the costs of research. Author must be under 40, has to submit a copy of his/her previous book and the work must 'contribute to the greater understanding of existing social and economic organisation'. Application by letter. Contact the **Society of Authors** for an information sheet. Final entry date 31 May 1999

Alfred Bradley Bursary Award
c/o Network Radio Drama, BBC North,
New Broadcasting House, Oxford Road,
Manchester M60 1SJ
☎0161 244 4254   Fax 0161 244 4248

Email: melanie.harris@bbc.co.uk

Contact *Melanie Harris*

ESTABLISHED 1992. Biennial award in commemoration of the life and work of the distinguished radio producer Alfred Bradley. Aims to encourage and develop new writing talent in the BBC North region. There is a change of focus for each award; the theme for the 1998 award was Drama. Entrants must live or work in the North region. The award is given to help authors to pursue a career in writing for radio. Support and guidance is given from regional BBC radio producers. Previous winners: Lee Hall, Mandy Precious.

Award Up to £6000 over 2 years.

British Academy Small Personal Research Grants

10 Carlton House Terrace, London SW1Y 5AH
☎0171 969 5200   Fax 0171 969 5300

Contact *Assistant Secretary, Research Grants*

Quarterly award to further original creative research at postdoctoral level in the humanities and social sciences. Entrants must no longer be registered for postgraduate study, and must be resident in the UK. Final entry dates end of September, November, February and April.

Award maximum £5000.

Cholmondeley Awards

The Society of Authors, 84 Drayton Gardens, London SW10 9SB
☎0171 373 6642   Fax 0171 373 5768

FOUNDED 1965 by the late Dowager Marchioness of Cholmondeley. Annual noncompetitive awards for the benefit and encouragement of poets of any age, sex or nationality, for which submissions are not required. 1998 winners: Roger McGough, Robert Minhinnick, Anne Ridler, Ken Smith.

Award (total) £8000.

The Economist/ Richard Casement Internship

The Economist, 25 St James's Street, London SW1A 1HG
☎0171 839 7000

Contact *Science Editor (re. Casement Internship)*

For a journalist under 24 to spend three months in the summer writing for *The Economist* about science and technology. Applicants should write a letter of introduction along with an article of approximately 600 words suitable for inclusion in the Science and Technology Section. Competition details normally announced in the magazine late January and 4–5 weeks allowed for application.

European Jewish Publication Society

37–43 Sackville Street, London W1X 2DL
☎0171 333 8111   Fax 0171 333 0660

Contact *Dr Colin Shindler, Dr Sidney Brichto*

ESTABLISHED in 1995 to help fund the publication of books of European Jewish interest which would otherwise remain unpublished. Helps with the marketing, distribution and promotion of such books. Publishers who may be interested in publishing works of Jewish interest should approach the Society with a proposal and manuscript in the first instance. Books which have been supported include: *Double or Nothing* Thelma Ruby and Peter Frye; *The Slow Mirror and Other Stories* Sonja Lyndon and Sylvia Paskin; *Jewish Carpets* Anton Felton; *Selected Poems of Lotte Kramer* Lotte Kramer.

Grant £3000 (maximum)

Fulbright Awards

The Fulbright Commission, Fulbright House, 62 Doughty Street, London WC1N 2LS
☎0171 404 6880   Fax 0171 404 6834
Website: www.fulbright.co.uk

Contact *Programme Director*

The Fulbright Commission has a number of scholarships given at postgraduate level and above, open to any field (science and the arts) of study/research to be undertaken in the USA. Length of award is typically an academic year. Application deadline for postgraduate awards is usually late October/early November of preceding year of study; and late March/early April for distinguished scholar awards. Further details and application forms are available on the Commission's Website. Alternatively, send A4 envelope with sufficient postage for 100g with a covering letter explaining which level of award is of interest.

Fulton Fellowship

David Fulton (Publishers) Ltd, Ormond House, 26/27 Boswell Street, London WC1N 3JD
☎0171 405 5606   Fax 0171 831 4840
Email: david.fulton@fultonbooks.co.uk
Website: www.fultonbooks.co.uk

Contact *David Fulton*

The Fulton Fellowship in Special Education was ESTABLISHED in 1995 with The Centre for the Study of Special Education, Westminster

College, Oxford. The Fellowship, worth £2000, has been extended to offer schools as well as individual teachers the chance to share work their staff have done or are doing collaboratively through written publication to a wider audience. 1997 Fellow: St John's School, Kempston, Bedford.

The Tony Godwin Award

The Tony Godwin Memorial Trust,
c/o Laurence Pollinger Limited,
18 Maddox Street, London W1R 0EU
☎0171 629 9761   Fax 0171 629 9765
Email: TGMT@bigfoot.com
Contact *Lesley Hadcroft*
Chairman *Iain Brown* (0171 627 4244)

Biennial award established to commemorate the life of Tony Godwin, a prominent publisher in the 1960s/70s. Open to all young people (under 35 years old) who are UK nationals and working, or intending to work, in publishing. The award provides the recipient with the means to spend at least one month as the guest of an overseas publishing house in order to learn about international publishing. The recipient is expected to submit a report upon return to the UK. Final entry date for next award: 31 December, 1999. Previous winners: George Lucas (Hodder), Richard Scrivener (Penguin), Fiona Stewart (HarperCollins).
Award Bursary of approx. US$5000.

Eric Gregory Trust Fund

The Society of Authors, 84 Drayton Gardens, London SW10 9SB
☎0171 373 6642   Fax 0171 373 5768

Annual competitive awards of varying amounts are made each year for the encouragement of young poets under the age of 30 who can show that they are likely to benefit from an opportunity to give more time to writing. Open only to British-born subjects resident in the UK. Final entry date, 31 October. Contact the **Society of Authors** for further information. 1998 winners: Mark Godwin, Joanne Limburg, Patrick McGuinness, Kona Macphee, Esther Morgan, Christiana Whitehead, Frances Williams.
Award (total) £24,500.

The Guardian Research Fellowship

Nuffield College, Oxford OX1 1NF
☎01865 278520   Fax 01865 278676
Contact *Warden's Secretary*

One-year fellowship endowed by the Scott Trust, owner of *The Guardian*, to give someone working in the media the chance to put their experience into a new perspective, publish the outcome and give a *Guardian* lecture. Applications welcomed from journalists and management members, in newspapers, periodicals or broadcasting. Research or study proposals should be directly related to experience of working in the media. Accommodation and meals in college will be provided, and a 'modest' supplementary stipend might be arranged to ensure the Fellow does not lose out from the stay. Advertised annually in November.

Hawthornden Castle Fellowship

Hawthornden Castle, The International Retreat for Writers, Lasswade, Midlothian EH18 1EG
☎0131 440 2180
Administrator *Adam Czerniawski*

ESTABLISHED 1982 to provide a peaceful setting where published writers can work without disturbance. The Retreat houses five writers at a time, who are known as Hawthornden Fellows. Writers from any part of the world may apply for the fellowships. No monetary assistance is given, nor any contribution to travelling expenses, but once arrived at Hawthornden, the writer is the guest of the Retreat. Applications on forms provided must be made by the end of September for the following calendar year. Previous winners include: Les Murray, Alasdair Gray, Helen Vendler, Olive Senior, Hilary Spurling.

Francis Head Bequest

The Society of Authors, 84 Drayton Gardens, London SW10 9SB
☎0171 373 6642   Fax 0171 373 5768

Provides grants to published British authors over the age of 35 who need financial help during a period of illness, disablement or temporary financial crisis. Contact the **Society of Authors** for an information sheet and application form.

Ralph Lewis Award

University of Sussex Library, Brighton,
East Sussex BN1 9QL
☎01273 678158   Fax 01273 678441

ESTABLISHED 1985. Triennial award set up by Ralph Lewis, a Brighton author and art collector who left money to fund awards for promising manuscripts which would not otherwise be published. The award is given in the form of a grant to a UK-based publisher in respect of an agreed three-year programme of publication of literary works by new authors or by established authors using new styles or forms. No direct applications from writers. Previous winners: **Peterloo Poets** (1989–91); **Serpent's Tail** (1992–94); **Stride Publications** (1997–99).

London Arts Board: Publishing New Writing Fund

London Arts Board, Elme House, 133 Long Acre, London WC2E 9AF
☎0171 240 1313   Fax 0171 670 2400
Email: john.hampson@lonab.co.uk

Aims to support and develop small presses and literary magazines in the publishing of new or under-represented fiction and poetry. This fund is only open to groups for whom publishing is a central activity. Deadline for applications is in August. Contact the Principal Literature Officer for further details and an application form.

Macaulay Fellowship

An Chomhairle Ealaíon (The Arts Council), 70 Merrion Square, Dublin 2, Republic of Ireland
☎00 353 1 6180200   Fax 00 353 1 6761302
Literature Officer *Sinead MacAodha*

To further the liberal education of a young creative artist. Candidates for this triennial award must be under 30 on 30 June, or 35 in exceptional circumstances, and must be Irish citizens or residents. The Fellowship is offered on rotation between Music, Visual Arts and Literature (Visual Arts in 2000).
   Award IR£3500.

The John Masefield Memorial Trust

The Society of Authors, 84 Drayton Gardens, London SW10 9SB
☎0171 373 6642   Fax 0171 373 5768

This trust makes occasional grants to professional poets (or their immediate dependants) who are faced with sudden financial problems. Contact the **Society of Authors** for an information sheet and application form.

Somerset Maugham Trust Fund

The Society of Authors, 84 Drayton Gardens, London SW10 9SB
☎0171 373 6642   Fax 0171 373 5768

The annual awards arising from this Fund are designed to encourage young writers to travel and to acquaint themselves with other countries. Candidates must be under 35 and their publishers must submit a published literary work in volume form in English. They must be British subjects by birth. Final entry date 31 December. Presentation in June. 1998 winners: Rachel

Cusk *The Country Life*; Jonathan Rendall *This Bloody Mary Is the Last Thing I Own*; Kate Summerscale *The Queen of Whale Cay*; Robert Twigger *Angry White Pyjamas*.
   Awards £5000 each.

The Airey Neave Trust

40 Charles Street, London W1X 7PB
☎0171 495 0554   Fax 0171 491 1118
Contact *Hannah Scott*

INITIATED 1989. Annual research fellowships for up to three years – towards a book or paper – for serious research connected with national and international law, and human freedom. Must be attached to a particular university in Britain. Interested applicants should come forward with ideas, preferably before March in any year.

New London Writers Awards

London Arts Board, Elme House, 133 Long Acre, London WC2E 9AF
☎0171 240 1313   Fax 0171 670 2400
Email: john.hampson@lonab.co.uk
Contact *John Hampson*

ESTABLISHED 1993/94. Five bursaries, of £3,500 each, are awarded annually to London writers. Application form available from the address above. Final entry date: 15 October 1999. The five winners in 1997/98 were Jill Dawson, Mario Petrucci, Maurice Riordan, Ardashir Vakil and Sarah Waters.

Newspaper Press Fund

Dickens House, 35 Wathen Road, Dorking, Surrey RH4 1JY
☎01306 887511   Fax 01306 876104
Director/Secretary *Peter Evans*

Aims to relieve distress among journalists and their dependants. Limited help available to non-member journalists. Continuous and/or occasional financial grants; also retirement homes for eligible beneficiaries. Further information and subscription details available from The Secretary or via the Reuter Foundation Website on: www.foundation.reuters.com.npf

Northern Arts Literary Fellowship

Northern Arts, 10 Osborne Terrace, Jesmond, Newcastle upon Tyne NE2 1NZ
☎0191 281 6334   Fax 0191 281 3276
Contact *Film, Media & Literature Department*

A competitive fellowship. Contact Northern Arts for details.

Northern Arts Writers Awards

New Writing North, 7/8 Trinity Chare, Quayside, Newcastle upon Tyne NE1 3DF
☎0191 232 9991   Fax 0191 230 1883
Contact *Published & Broadcast Arts Department*

Bi-annual awards, offered to established authors resident in the Northern Arts area on the basis of literary merit. Application spring/summer. Also available, one-month residencies at the Tyrone Guthrie Centre, Ireland.
Award Variable.

The PAWS (Public Awareness of Science) Drama Script Fund

The PAWS Office, OMNI Communications, Osborne House, 111 Bartholomew Road, London NW5 2BJ
☎0171 267 2555/voice mail: 0171 428 0961
Fax 0171 482 2394
Contacts *Barrie Whatley, Andrew Millington*

ESTABLISHED 1994. Annual award aimed at encouraging television scriptwriters to include science and engineering scenarios in their work. Grants (currently £2000) are given to selected writers to develop their script ideas into full treatments; prizes are awarded for the best of these treatments (Grand Prix currently £5000). The PAWS Fund holds meetings enabling writers to meet scientists and engineers and also offers a contacts service to put writers in 'one-to-one' contact with specialists who can help them develop their ideas. See also **The PAWS Midas Prize** under **Prizes**.

Pearson Playwrights' Scheme

3 Burlington Gardens, London W1X 1LE
☎01730 810688
Contact *Jack Andrews*

Awards four bursaries to playwrights. Applicants must be sponsored by a theatre which then submits the play for consideration by a panel. Each award allows the playwright a twelve-month attachment. Applications invited via theatres in September 1999. For up-to-date information, contact *Jack Andrews*.

The Margaret Rhondda Award

The Society of Authors, 84 Drayton Gardens, London SW10 9SB
☎0171 373 6642   Fax 0171 373 5768

Competitive award given to a woman writer as a grant-in-aid towards the expenses of a research project in journalism. Contact the **Society of Authors** for an information sheet. Triennial (next awarded: 2002). Final entry date 31 December 2001.
Award approx. £1000.

The Royal Literary Fund

3 Johnson's Court, off Fleet Street, London EC4A 3EA
☎0171 353 7150   Fax 0171 353 1350
Secretary *Mrs Fiona Clark*

Grants and pensions are awarded to published authors in financial need, or to their dependants. Examples of author's works are needed for assessment by Committee. Write for further details and application form.

Southern Arts Writer's Award

13 St Clement Street, Winchester, Hampshire SO23 9DQ
☎01962 855099   Fax 01962 861186
Contact *Literature Officer*

Offers an annual award of £3500 to a published writer living in the region to assist a specific project. Awards can be used to cover a period of unpaid leave while writing from home, to finance necessary research and travel, or to purchase equipment. Final entry date: October – please contact for date nearer the time.

Laurence Stern Fellowship

Department of Journalism, City University, Northampton Square, London EC1V 0HB
☎0171 477 8224   Fax 0171 477 8594
Website: www.city.ac.uk/journalism
Contact *Bob Jones*

FOUNDED 1980. Awarded to a young journalist experienced enough to work on national stories. It gives them the chance to work on the national desk of the *Washington Post*. Benjamin Bradlee, the *Post*'s Vice-President-at-Large, selects from a shortlist drawn up in March/April. 1998 winner: Caroline Daniel. Full details available on the Website.

David Thomas Prize

The Financial Times (W), 1 Southwark Bridge, London SE1 9HL
☎0171 873 3000   Fax 0171 873 3924
Managing Editor *Robin Pauley*

FOUNDED 1991. Annual award in memory of

David Thomas, *FT* journalist killed on assignment in Kuwait in April 1991, whose 'life was characterised by original and radical thinking, coupled with a search for new subjects and orthodoxies to challenge'. The award will provide an annual study/travel grant to enable the recipient to take a career break to explore a theme in the fields of industrial policy, Third World development or the environment. Entrants may be of any nationality; age limits vary.

A given theme, which changes from year to year, is announced in the early autumn. The 1997 theme was: 'What is the future of work?'. Entrants should submit up to 800 words on the theme, together with a brief c.v. and proposal outlining how the award could be used to explore the theme further. Award winners will be required to write an essay of 1500–2000 words at the end of the study period which will be considered for publication in the newspaper. Final entry date end December/early January.

Prize £3000 travel grant.

Tom-Gallon Trust

The Society of Authors, 84 Drayton Gardens, London SW10 9SB
☎0171 373 6642   Fax 0171 373 5768

A biennial award is made from the Trust Fund to fiction writers of limited means who have had at least one short story accepted for publication. Authors wishing to enter should send a list of their already published fiction, giving the name of the publisher or periodical in each case and the approximate date of publication; one short story; a brief statement of their financial position; an undertaking that they intend to devote a substantial amount of time to the writing of fiction as soon as they are financially able to do so; their date of birth; and s.a.e.s for acknowledgement and for the return of work submitted. Final entry date 20 September 2000.

Award £1000.

The Betty Trask Awards

The Society of Authors, 84 Drayton Gardens, London SW10 9SB
☎0171 373 6642   Fax 0171 373 5768

These annual awards are for authors who are under 35 and Commonwealth citizens, awarded on the strength of a first novel (published or unpublished) of a traditional or romantic nature. The awards must be used for a period or periods of foreign travel. Final entry date 31 January. Contact the **Society of Authors** for an infor-

mation sheet. Previous winners: Kiran Desai *Hullabaloo in the Guava Orchard*; Gail Anderson-Dargatz *The Cure for Death by Lightning*; Nick Earls *Zigzag Street*; Tobias Hill *Underground*; Phil Whitaker *Eclipse of the Sun*.

Award (total) £25,000.

The Travelling Scholarships

The Society of Authors, 84 Drayton Gardens, London SW10 9SB
☎0171 373 6642   Fax 0171 373 5768

Annual, non-competitive awards for the benefit of British authors, to enable them to travel abroad. 1998 winners: Dorothy Nimmo, Dilys Rose, Paul Sayer.

Award (total) £6000.

UEA Writing Fellowship

University of East Anglia, University Plain, Norwich, Norfolk NR4 7TJ
☎01603 592734   Fax 01603 593522
Director of Personnel & Registry Services
J. R. L. Beck

ESTABLISHED 1971. Awarded to a writer of established reputation in any field for a period of six months, January to end June. The duties of the Fellowship are discussed at an interview. It is assumed that one activity will be the pursuit of the Fellow's own writing. In addition the Fellow will be expected to (a) offer an undergraduate creative writing workshop in the School of English and American Studies during the Spring semester; (b) make contact with groups around the county. An office and some limited secretarial assistance will be provided, and some additional funds will be available to help the Fellow with the activities described above. Applications for the fellowship should be lodged with the Director of Personnel & Registry Services in the autumn; candidates should submit at least two examples of recent work. Previous winner: Ali Smith.

Award £7000 plus free flat on campus.

The David T. K. Wong Fellowship

School of English and American Studies, University of East Anglia, Norwich, Norfolk NR4 7TJ
☎01603 592810   Fax 01603 507728

An annual fellowship founded by retired Hong Kong senior civil servant, journalist and businessman, David Wong, to give writers the chance to produce a work of fiction in English set in the

Far East. The aim of the Fellowship is 'to promote better understanding of the Far East and excellence in the writing of literature'. Applications will be considered from published and unpublished writers of any age and nationality.

An original piece of fiction must be submitted with an application form, available from the above address, by 31 October. 1998 winner: Po Wah Lam.

Award £25,000.

Prizes

ABSW/Glaxo Science Writers' Awards

Association of British Science Writers, 23 Savile Row, London W1X 2NB
☎0171 439 1205   Fax 0171 973 3051
ABSW Administrator *Barbara Drillsma*

A series of annual awards for outstanding science journalism in newspapers, journals and broadcasting.

J. R. Ackerley Prize

English Centre of International PEN, 7 Dilke Street, London SW3 4JE
☎0171 352 6303   Fax 0171 351 0220
Commemorating the novelist/autobiographer J. R. Ackerley, this prize is awarded for a literary autobiography, written in English and published in the year preceding the award. Entry restricted to nominations from the Ackerley Trustees only ('please do not submit books'). 1998 winner: Kathryn Fitzherbert *True to Both Myselves*.

Acorn-Rukeyser Chapbook Contest

Mekler & Deahl, Publishers, 237 Prospect Street South, Hamilton, Ontario, Canada L8M 2Z6
☎001 905 312 1779   Fax 001 905 312 8285
Email: meklerdeahl@globalserve.net
Contact *James Deahl, Gilda Mekler*

ESTABLISHED in 1996, this annual award is named after the poets Milton Acorn and Muriel Rukeyser in order to honour their achievements as populist poets. Poets may enter as many as 30 poems for a fee of £5. Final entry date: 31 October. Contact the above address for a copy of the rules. 1998 winner: Walt Peterson *In the Waiting Room of the Speedy Muffler King*.
  Prize (US) $100 and publication of the manuscript.

Age Concern Book of the Year

See **The Seebohm Trophy**

Aldeburgh Poetry Festival Prize

Reading Room Yard, The Street, Brockdish, Diss, Norfolk IP21 4JZ
☎01379 668345   Fax 01379 668844
Festival Coordinator *Michael Laskey*

ESTABLISHED 1989 by the Aldeburgh Poetry Trust. Sponsored by the Aldeburgh Bookshop for the best first collection published in Britain or the Republic of Ireland in the preceding twelve months. Open to any first collection of poetry of at least 40 pp. Final entry date: 1 October. Previous winners include: Donald Atkinson, Susan Wicks, Gwyneth Lewis, Glyn Wright, Robin Robertson, Tamar Yoseloff.
  Prize £500, plus an invitation to read at the following year's festival.

Alexander Prize

Royal Historical Society, University College London, Gower Street, London WC1E 6BT
☎0171 387 7532   Fax 0171 387 7532
Contact *Literary Director*

Awarded for a historical essay of not more than 8000 words. Competitors may choose their own subject for the essay, but must submit their choice for approval in the first instance to the Literary Director of the Royal Historical Society.
  Prize £250.

Allied Domecq Playwright Award

c/o Ketchum Sponsorship, Tower House, 8–14 Southampton Street, London WC2E 7HA
☎0171 379 3234   Fax 0171 465 8241
Contact *Lucy McCrickard, Nathalie Curry*

ESTABLISHED 1995. Biennial award, founded by Allied Domecq and the **Bush Theatre** in London, to encourage new writing talent. Open to writers (over the age of 18) who have not yet had a play produced professionally. Entrants must submit a 1000-word outline plus examples of previously completed work. First winner: Jacinta Stringer.
  Prize £5000 to help with development of the outline; if appropriate, the play will be staged at the Bush Theatre.

An Duais don bhFilíocht i nGaeilge

An Chomhairle Ealaíon (The Arts Council), 70 Merrion Square, Dublin 2, Republic of Ireland
☎00 353 1 6180200   Fax 00 353 1 6761302
Literature Officer *Sinead MacAodha*

Triennial award for the best book of Irish poetry.

Works must have been published in the Irish language in the preceding three years. Next award in 2001.
Prize £3000.

Hans Christian Andersen Awards

IBBY, Nonnenweg 12, Postfach CH-4003, Basel, Switzerland
☎00 41 61 272 2917   Fax 00 41 61 272 2757
Email: ibby@eye.ch
Website: www.ibby.org
Executive Director *Leena Maissen*

The highest international prizes for children's literature: The Hans Christian Andersen Award for Writing ESTABLISHED 1956; The Hans Christian Andersen Award for Illustration ESTABLISHED 1966. Candidates are nominated by National Sections of IBBY (The International Board on Books for Young People). Biennial prizes are awarded, in even-numbered years, to an author and an illustrator whose body of work has made a lasting contribution to children's literature. Next award 2000. 1998 winners: Award for Writing: Katherine Paterson (USA); Award for Illustration: Tomi Ungerer (France).
Award Gold medals.

Eileen Anderson Central Television Drama Award

Central Broadcasting, Central Court, Gas Street, Birmingham B1 2JT
☎0121 634 4240   Fax 0121 634 4414
Head of Regional Affairs *Kevin Johnson*

ESTABLISHED 1987 with money left by the late Dr Eileen Anderson and contributed to by **Central Television**, this is an annual award to encourage new theatre writing in the Midlands. Open to all new plays or an adaptation commissioned or premièred by a building-based theatre company in the Central region. Previous winners include: David Edgar *Pentecost* (premièred at the **Royal Shakespeare Company**'s The Other Place in Stratford); Sean Street *Honest John* (premièred on Community Tour by the **Royal Theatre Northampton**); Vilma Hollingbery & Michael Napier Brown *Is This the Day?* (premièred at the Royal Theatre Northampton); Lucy Gannon *Wicked Old Nellie* (**Derby Playhouse**); Timberlake Wertenbaker *The Love of the Nightingale* (commissioned by the Royal Shakespeare Company's The Other Place); Pam Gem's *The Blue Angel* (premièred at the Royal Shakespeare Company's The Other Place) and Rod Dungate for *Playing By The Rules* (premièred at the **Birmingham Repertory Theatre**).

Prize £2000 for the winner; a plaque and £2000 to the commissioning theatre (to be used to develop new work).

Angus Book Award

Angus Council Cultural Services, County Buildings, Forfar DD8 3WF
☎01307 473256   Fax 01307 462590
Contact *Gavin Drummond (Director of Cultural Services)*

ESTABLISHED 1995. Designed to try to help teenagers develop an interest in and enthusiasm for reading. Eligible books are read and voted on by third-year schoolchildren in all eight Angus secondary schools. 1999 winner: Tim Bowler *River Boy*.
Prize £250 cheque, plus trophy in the form of a replica Pictish stone.

Annual Theatre Book Prize

See **The Society for Theatre Research Annual Theatre Book Prize**

Arvon Foundation International Poetry Competition

Kilnhurst, Kilnhurst Road, Todmorden, Lancashire OL14 6AX
☎01706 816582   Fax 01706 816359
Website: www.arvonfoundation.org/index
Contact *David Pease*

ESTABLISHED 1980. Biennial competition (next in 2000) for poems written in English and not previously broadcast or published. There are no restrictions on the number of lines, themes, age of entrants or nationality. No limit to the number of entries. Entry fee: £5 per poem. Previous winners: Paul Farley *Laws of Gravity*; Don Paterson *A Private Bottling*.
Prize (1st) £5000 and £5000 worth of other prizes sponsored by Duncan Lawrie Limited.

Authors' Club First Novel Award

Authors' Club, 40 Dover Street, London W1X 3RB
☎0171 499 8581   Fax 0171 409 0913
Contact *Mrs Ann de la Grange*

ESTABLISHED 1954. This award is made for the most promising work published in Britain by a British author, and is presented at a dinner held at the Authors' Club in April. Entries for the award are accepted from publishers by the end of November of the year in question and must be full-length – short stories are not eligible. 1998 winner: Jackie Kay *Trumpet*.
Award £750.

BAAL Book Prize

BAAL Publications Secretary, Centre for Language & Communication, University of Wales, Cardiff, PO Box 94, Cardiff CF1 3XB
☎01222 874243   Fax 01222 874242
Email: sarangi@cardiff.ac.uk

Contact *Dr Srikant Sarangi*

Annual award made by the British Association for Applied Linguistics to an outstanding book in the field of applied linguistics. Final entry at the end of Oct/Nov. Nominations from publishers only. Previous winners: Ruth Lesser and Lesley Milroy *Linguistics and Aphasia*; *Dictionary of British Sign Language*; Susan Berk-Seligson *The Bilingual Courtroom*; Joshua A. Fishman *Reversing Language Shift*; Deborah Cameron *Verbal Hygiene*; Marco Jacquemet *Credibility in Court*; Ana Celia Zentella *Growing Up Bilingual*.

The Barclays Bank Prize

See **Lakeland Book of the Year Awards**

Verity Bargate Award

The Soho Theatre Company, 21 Dean Street, London W1V 6NE
☎0171 287 5060   Fax 0171 287 5061

Contact *Paul Syrett, Literary Manager*

To commemorate the late Verity Bargate, founder and director of the **Soho Theatre Company**. This award is presented bi-annually for a new and unperformed full-length play. Send s.a.e. for details; if submitting scripts, enclose one s.a.e. script-size and one standard-size. The Soho Theatre Company also runs many courses for new writers. Previous winners: Toby Whithouse, Adrian Pagan, Frazer Grace, Lyndon Morgans, Diane Samuels, Judy Upton, Angela Meredith.

Award £1500, plus production by the Soho Theatre Company.

The Herb Barrett Award

Mekler & Deahl, Publishers, 237 Prospect Street South, Hamilton, Ontario, Canada L8M 2Z6
☎001 905 312 1779   Fax 001 905 312 8285
Email: meklerdeahl@globalserve.net

Contact *James Deahl*

ESTABLISHED in 1996, this annual award is named in honour of Herb Barrett, founder of the Hamilton Chapter of the Canadian Poetry Association. Poets may enter one or two haiku for a fee of £5, or three or more haiku for a fee of £7.50. Final entry date: 30 November. Contact the address above for a copy of the rules.

1998 winners: Timothy Russell, A. C. Missias, Ferris Gilli.

Prize (US) $150, $100 and $50; anthology publication for the winners and all other worthy entries.

The Shaunt Basmajian Chapbook Award

Canadian Poetry Association, PO Box 22571, St George Postal Outlet, Toronto, Ontario, Canada M5S 1V0
Email: cpa@zap.wwdc.com

Contact *CPA National Coordinator*

ESTABLISHED 1996. Annual award named in honour of poet Shaunt Basmajian, a founder of the Canadian Poetry Association. Up to 24 pages of poetry may be submitted for an entry fee of Canadian $15. Open to any type of poetry. A copy of the rules is available from the above address.

Prize (Canadian) $100 and publication of the winning manuscript.

H. E. Bates Short Story Competition

See **Words & Pictures Literary & Photographic Competition**

BBC Wildlife Magazine Awards for Nature Writing

BBC Wildlife Magazine, Broadcasting House, Whiteladies Road, Bristol BS8 2LR
☎0117 9738402   Fax 0117 9467075

Annual competition for professional and amateur writers. The competition was suspended in 1997 and at the time of going to press plans for its future resumption were unknown.

BBC Wildlife Magazine Poetry Awards

PO Box 229, Bristol BS99 7JN
☎0117 9738402   Fax 0117 9467075

Contact *Rosamund Kidman Cox*

Annual award for a poem, the subject of which must be the natural world and/or our relationship with it. Entrants may submit one poem only of no more than 50 lines with the entry form which appears in the magazine. Closing date for entries varies from year to year.

Prizes Poet of the Year: £500, publication in the magazine, plus reading of the poem on Radio 4's *Poetry Please*; eight runners-up prizes: £75 plus publication in the magazine; four young poets awards.

David Berry Prize

Royal Historical Society, University College London, Gower Street, London WC1E 6BT
☎0171 387 7532   Fax 0171 387 7532

Annual award for an essay of not more than 10,000 words on Scottish history. Candidates may select any subject from the relevant period, providing it has been submitted to, and approved by, the Council of the Royal Historical Society.
Prize £250.

Besterman Medal

See **The Library Association Besterman Medal**

The BFC Mother Goose Award

Books for Children, Brettenham House, Lancaster Place, London WC2E 7TL
☎0171 322 1422   Fax 0171 322 1488
Contact *Marisa Ryder, Editorial Coordinator*

ESTABLISHED 1979. Annual award for the most exciting newcomer to British children's book illustration. 1999 winner: Niamh Sharkey *The Gigantic Turnip* and *Tales of Wisdom and Wonder*.
Prize £1000, plus Golden Egg trophy.

Birdwatch Bird Book of the Year

c/o Birdwatch Magazine, 3D/F Leroy House, 436 Essex Road, Islington, London N1 3QP
☎0171 704 9495
Contact *Dominic Mitchell*

ESTABLISHED in 1992 to acknowledge excellence in ornithological publishing – an increasingly large market with a high turnover. Annual award. Entries, from publishers, must offer an original and comprehensive treatment of their particular ornithological subject matter and must have a broad appeal to British-based readers. 1999 winner: *The Handbook of Bird Identification for Europe and the Western Palearctic* Mark Beaman and Steve Madge.

James Tait Black Memorial Prizes

University of Edinburgh, David Hume Tower, George Square, Edinburgh EH8 9JX
☎0131 650 3619   Fax 0131 650 6898
Contact *Department of English Literature*

ESTABLISHED 1918 in memory of a partner of the publishing firm of **A. & C. Black Ltd**. Two prizes, one for biography and one for fiction.

Closing date for submissions: 30 September. Each prize is awarded for a book published in Britain in the previous twelve months. Prize winners are announced in December each year. 1998 winners: Peter Ackroyd *The Life of Thomas More*; Beryl Bainbridge *Master Georgie*.
Prizes £3000 each.

The Robert Bloomfield Awards for Rustic Poetry

Hilton House (Publishers), Hilton House, 39 Long John Hill, Norwich, Norfolk NR1 2JP
☎01603 449845
Contact *Michael K. Moore*

Annual competition to publicise the works of the Suffolk poet and to promote descriptive poetry with a rural theme, drawing attention to the wonders of nature in the British and Irish countryside and emphasising the necessity for protecting the environment and wildlife. Entry forms available from 2 January on receipt of s.a.e. or IRC. Closing date: 30 September. 1998 winners: Frances Winfield, Lynne Wycherley.
Prizes to the value of £550 for individual poems. Special prizes for best collections of 6 to 10 poems. Prize winners will be published in Awards Yearbook.

Boardman Tasker Award

14 Pine Lodge, Dairyground Road, Bramhall, Stockport, Cheshire SK7 2HS
☎0161 439 4624   Fax 0161 439 4624
Contact *Dorothy Boardman*

ESTABLISHED 1983, this award is given for a work of fiction, non-fiction or poetry, whose central theme is concerned with the mountain environment and which can be said to have made an outstanding contribution to mountain literature. Authors of any nationality are eligible, but the book must have been published or distributed in the UK for the first time between 1 November 1998 and 31 October 1999. Entries from publishers only. 1998 winner: Peter Steele *Eric Shipton, Everest and Beyond*.
Prize £2000 (at Trustees' discretion).

Booker Prize for Fiction

Book Trust, Book House, 45 East Hill, London SW18 2QZ
☎0181 516 2973   Fax 0181 516 2978
Contact *Sandra Vince*

The leading British literary prize, set up in 1968

by Booker McConnell Ltd, with the intention of rewarding merit, raising the stature of the author in the eyes of the public and increasing the sale of the books. The announcement of the winner has been televised live since 1981, and all books on the shortlist experience a substantial increase in sales. Eligible novels must be written in English by a citizen of Britain, the Commonwealth, the Republic of Ireland or South Africa, and must be published in the UK for the first time between 1 October and 30 September of the year of the prize. Self-published books are no longer accepted. Entries are accepted from UK publishers who may each submit not more than two novels within the appropriate scheduled publication dates. The judges may also ask for certain other eligible novels to be submitted to them. Annual award. 1998 winner: Ian McEwan *Amsterdam*. Previous winners include: James Kelman *How Late It Was, How Late*; Ben Okri *The Famished Road*; Michael Ondaatje *The English Patient*; Barry Unsworth *Sacred Hunger*; Roddy Doyle *Paddy Clarke Ha, Ha, Ha*; Pat Barker *The Ghost Road*; Graham Swift *Last Orders*; Arundhati Roy *God of Small Things*.
 Prize £20,000 winner; £1000, shortlist.

Author of the Year Award
Booksellers Association of
Great Britain and Ireland
272 Vauxhall Bridge Road, London
SW1V 1BA
☎0171 834 5477   Fax 0171 834 8812
Contact *Administrator*
Founded as part of the BA Annual Conference to involve authors more closely in the event. Authors must be British or Irish. Not an award open to entry but voted on by the BA's membership. 1998 winner: Louis de Bernières *Captain Corelli's Mandolin*.
 Award £1000 plus trophy.

Border Television Prize
See **Lakeland Book of the Year Awards**

The BP Natural World Book Prize
Book Trust, Book House, 45 East Hill,
London SW18 2QZ
☎0181 516 2973   Fax 0181 516 2978
Contact *Sandra Vince*
ESTABLISHED in 1996 as an amalgamation of the Natural World Book Prize (the magazine of the Wildlife Trusts) and the BP Conservation Book Prize. Award for a book on creative conservation of the environment. Entries from UK publishers

only. 1998 winner: David Attenborough *The Life of Birds*.
 Prizes (1st) £5000; Runner-up: £1000.

Bridport Arts Centre
The Bridport Prize
Arts Centre, South Street, Bridport, Dorset
DT6 3NR
☎01308 427183   Fax 01308 427183
Contact *Bridport Prize Administrator*
Annual competition for poetry and short story writing. Unpublished work only, written in English. Winning stories are read by leading London literary agent and an anthology of prize-winning entries is published. Also runs a Young Writers' Competition with variable prizes. Final entry date: 30 June (1 May for Young Writers' award). Send s.a.e. for entry forms.
 Prizes £2,500, £1000 and £500 in each category, plus supplementary runners-up prizes.

Katharine Briggs Folklore Award
The Folklore Society, University College
London, Gower Street, London WC1E 6BT
☎0171 387 5894
Contact *The Convenor*
ESTABLISHED 1982. An annual award in November for the book, published in Britain and Ireland between 1 June and 30 May in the previous calendar year, which has made the most distinguished non-fiction contribution to folklore studies. Intended to encourage serious research in the field which Katharine Briggs did so much to establish. The term folklore studies is interpreted broadly to include all aspects of traditional and popular culture, narrative, belief, custom and folk arts.
 Prize £50, plus engraved goblet.

British Book Awards
Publishing News, 39 Store Street, London
WC1E 7DB
☎0171 692 2900   Fax 0171 419 2111
Email: mailbox@publishingnews.co.uk
Website: www.publishingnews.co.uk
ESTABLISHED 1988. Viewed by the book trade as the one to win, 'The Nibbies' are presented annually in February. The 1999 Awards were in the following categories: Children's Book; Supply Chain; Editor; Publisher Marketing; Bookshop Marketing; Illustrated Book; Sales Representative; Newcomer; Design and Production; Lifetime Achievement; Author; Book; Independent Bookseller; Chain

Bookseller; Services to Bookselling; Publisher. Each winner receives the prestigious Nibbie and the awards are presented to those who have made the most impact in the book trade during the previous year. Previous winners have included: Louis de Bernières, Alan Bennett, Salman Rushdie, Dava Sobel, Sebastian Faulks, Jung Chang, Anne Fine, Books etc., Waterstone's, Ottakar's, and the publishers **Transworld**, **Fourth Estate**, **Little**, **Brown** and **Random House**. For further information contact: Merric Davidson, 12 Priors Heath, Goudhurst, Cranbrook, Kent TN17 2RE (☎/Fax 01580 212041).

British Comparative Literature Association/British Centre for Literary Translation Competition

School of Modern Languages, University of East Anglia, Norwich, Norfolk NR4 7AZ
Email: JBoase-Beier@uea.ac.uk
Website: www.bcla.org/trancomp.htm
Competition Secretary Dr Leon Burnett

ESTABLISHED 1983. Annual competition open to unpublished literary translations from all languages. Maximum submission 25 pages.
  Prizes (1st) £350; (2nd) £200; (3rd) £100; plus publication for all winning entries in the Association's annual journal *Comparative Criticism* (**Cambridge University Press**). Other entries may receive commendations.

British Fantasy Awards

2 Harwood Street, Heaton Norris, Stockport, Cheshire SK4 1JJ
☎0161 476 5368 (after 6 p.m.)
Secretary Robert Parkinson

Awarded by the **British Fantasy Society** by members at its annual conference for Best Novel and Best Short Story categories, among others. Not an open competition. Previous winners include: Ramsey Campbell, Dan Simmonds, Michael Marshall Smith, Thomas Ligotti.

British Literature Prize
See **David Cohen British Literature Prize**

British Press Awards

Press Gazette, Quantum House, 19 Scarbrook Road, Croydon, Surrey CR9 1LX
☎0181 565 4200   Fax 0181 565 4395
'The Oscars of British journalism'. Open to all British morning and Sunday newspapers sold nationally and news agencies. March event. Run by *Press Gazette*.

British Science Fiction (Association) Award

The Bungalow, 27 Lower Evingar Road, Whitchurch, Hampshire RG28 7EY
☎01256 893253
Email: cphill@enterprise.net
Award Administrator Chris Hill

ESTABLISHED 1966. The BSFA awards a trophy each year in three categories – novel, short fiction and artwork – published in the preceding year. Previous winners: Mary Doria Russell *The Sparrow* (novel); Stephen Baxter *War Birds* (short fiction); SMS *The Black Blood of the Dead.*.

James Cameron Award

City University, Department of Journalism, Northampton Square, London EC1V 0HB
☎0171 477 8221   Fax 0171 477 8594
Contact The Administrator

Annual award for journalism to a reporter of any nationality, working for the British media, whose work is judged to have contributed most during the year to the continuance of the Cameron tradition. Administered by City University Department of Journalism. 1998 winner: Jonathan Steele, *The Guardian*.

Cardiff International Poetry Competition

PO Box 438, Cardiff CF1 6YA
☎01222 492025   Fax 01222 492930
Contact Margaret Harlin

ESTABLISHED 1986. An annual competition for unpublished poems in English of up to 50 lines. Closing date in December.
  Prize (total) £5000.

Carey Award

Society of Indexers, Globe Centre, Penistone Road, Sheffield, South Yorkshire S6 3AE
☎0114 2813060   Fax 0114 2813061
Email: admin@socind.demon.co.uk
Secretary Liza Weinkove

A private award made by the Society to a member who has given outstanding services to indexing. The recipient is selected by Council with no recommendations considered from elsewhere.

Carnegie Medal
See **The Library Association Carnegie Medal**

The Raymond Chandler Society's 'Marlowe' Award for Best International Crime Novel

Heidenheimerstr. 106, 89075 Ulm Germany
☎0114 255 6302 (UK contact)
Fax 0114 255 6302
Email: william.adamson@zsp.uni-ulm.de
Contact *Simon Beckett (UK), Dr William R. Adamson (Germany)*

ESTABLISHED 1991. Annual award to the best English language crime novel. Awards also for best German language crime novel and best German language crime short story. Entry details from UK contact number. Submissions direct to the Society. Previous international 'Marlowe' winners include: Sara Paretsky, Minette Walters, Michael Connelly.

Sid Chaplin Short Story Competition

Shildon Town Council, Civic Centre Square, Shildon, Co Durham DL4 1AH
☎01388 772563   Fax 01388 775227
Contact *Mrs J. M. Stafford*

FOUNDED 1986. Annual themed short story competition (1998 subject was 'The Changing World'). Maximum 3000 words; £2 entrance fee (Juniors free). All stories must be unpublished and not broadcast and/or performed. Application forms available from September 1999. *Prizes* (1st) £300; (2nd) £150; (3rd) £75; (Junior) £50.

Children's Book Award

The Federation of Children's Book Groups, The Old Malt House, Aldbourne, Wiltshire SN8 2DW
☎01672 540629   Fax 01672 541280
Coordinator *Marianne Adey*

ESTABLISHED 1980. Awarded annually for best book of fiction suitable for children. Unique in that it is judged by the children themselves. Previous winners include: Dick King-Smith *Harriet's Hare*; Ian Strachan *The Boy in the Bubble*; Mick Inkpen *Threadbear*; Robert Swindells *Room 13*; Elizabeth Laird *Kiss the Dust*; Jaqueline Wilson *The Suitcase Kid* and *Double Act*; J.K. Rowling *Harriett Potter and the Philosopher's Stone*.

Award A silver and oak sculpture made by Graham Stewart and Tim Stead, plus portfolio of letters, drawings and comments from the children who took part in the judging; category winners receive silver bowls designed by the same artists and portfolios.

Children's Book Circle Eleanor Farjeon Award

See **Eleanor Farjeon Award**

Arthur C. Clarke Award for Science Fiction

60 Bournemouth Road, Folkestone, Kent CT19 5AZ
☎01303 252939   Fax 01303 252939
Email: mks_pk@cix.co.uk
Administrator *Paul Kincaid*

ESTABLISHED 1986. The Arthur C. Clarke Award is given yearly to the best science fiction novel with first UK publication in the previous calendar year. Both hardcover and paperback books qualify. Made possible by a generous donation from Arthur C. Clarke, this award is selected by a rotating panel of judges nominated by the **British Science Fiction Association**, the **Science Fiction Foundation** and the Science Museum. 1998 winner: Mary Doria Russell *The Sparrow*.

Award £1000 plus trophy.

The Cló Iar-Chonnachta Literary Award

Cló Iar-Chonnachta Teo, Indreabhán, Conamara, Co. Galway Republic of Ireland
☎00 353 91 593307   Fax 00 353 91 593362
Website: www.wombat.ie/clc
Editor *Nóirín Ní Ghrádaigh*

An annual prize for a newly written and unpublished work in the Irish language. Awarded in 1999 for the best collection of poems or long play and in 2000 for the best novel. Last date of entry for 2000 Award: 18 December 1999. 1998 winner: Joe Steve Ó Neachtain for his collection of short stories, *Clochmhóin*.

Prize IR£5000.

David Cohen British Literature Prize

Arts Council of Great Britain, 14 Great Peter Street, London SW1P 3NQ
☎0171 333 0100   Fax 0171 973 6520
Literature Director *Gary McKeone*
Literature Assistant *Valerie Olteanu*

ESTABLISHED 1993. By far the most valuable literature prize in Britain, the British Literature Prize, launched by the **Arts Council**, is awarded biennially. Anyone is eligible to suggest candidates and the award recognises writers who use the English language and who are British citizens, encompassing dramatists as well as novelists, poets and essayists. The prize is for a lifetime's achievement rather than a single play or book and is donated by the David Cohen Family Charitable Trust in association with Coutts Bank. The David Cohen Trust was set up in 1980 by David Cohen, general practitioner and son of a property developer. The Trust has helped composers, choreographers, dancers, poets, playwrights and actors. The Council is providing a further £10,000 to enable the winner to commission new work, with the dual aim of encouraging young writers and readers. 1999 winner: William Trevor. Previous winners: Dame Muriel Spark., Harold Pinter, V. S. Naipaul.

Award £30,000, plus £10,000 towards new work.

The Commonwealth Writers Prize
Book Trust, Book House, 45 East Hill,
London SW18 2QZ
☎0181 516 2973   Fax 0181 516 2978
Contact *Sandra Vince*

ESTABLISHED 1987. An annual award to reward and encourage the upsurge of new Commonwealth fiction. Any work of prose or fiction is eligible, i.e. a novel or collection of short stories. No drama or poetry. The work must be written in English by a citizen of the Commonwealth and be first published in the year before its entry for the prize. Entries must be submitted by the publisher to the region of the writer's Commonwealth citizenship. The four regions are: Africa, Eurasia, S. E. Asia and South Pacific, Caribbean and Canada. 1999 winners: Murray Bail *Eucalyptus* (Best Book); Kerri Sakamoto *The Electrical Field* (Best First Book).

Prizes £10,000 for Best Book; £3000 for Best First Book; 8 prizes of £1000 for each best and first best book in four regions.

The Thomas Cook/*Daily Telegraph* Travel Book Award
Thomas Cook Publishing, PO Box 227,
Peterborough PE3 6PU
☎01733 503566   Fax 01733 503596
Email: joan.lee@thomascook.com
Contact *Jennifer Rigby, Publishing*

FOUNDED in 1980 by The Thomas Cook Group. Annual award given to the author of the book, published (in the English language) in the previous year, which most inspires the reader to want to travel. Submissions by publishers only. 1998 winner: Tim Mackintosh-Smith *Yemen: Travels in Dictionary Land*.

Award £7500.

The Duff Cooper Prize
54 St Maur Road, London SW6 4DP
☎0171 736 3729   Fax 0171 731 7638
Contact *Artemis Cooper*

An annual award for a literary work of biography, history, politics or poetry, published by a recognised publisher (member of **The Publishers Association**) during the previous 12 months. The book must be submitted by the publisher, not the author. Financed by the interest from a trust fund commemorating Duff Cooper, first Viscount Norwich (1890–1954). 1998 winner: Richard Holmes *Coleridge*.

Prize £3000.

Rose Mary Crawshay Prize
The British Academy, 10 Carlton House Terrace, London SW1Y 5AX
☎0171 969 5200   Fax 0171 969 5300
Website: www.britac.ac.uk
Contact *British Academy Secretary*

ESTABLISHED 1888 by Rose Mary Crawshay, this prize is given for a historical or critical work by a woman of any nationality on English literature, with particular preference for a work on Keats, Byron or Shelley. The work must have been published in the preceding three years.

Prizes Normally two of approximately £500 each.

Crime Writers' Association (Cartier Diamond Dagger)
PO Box 6939, Kings Heath, Birmingham B14 7LT
Contact *The Secretary*

An annual award for a lifetime's oustanding contribution to the genre. 1999 winner: Margaret Yorke.

Crime Writers' Association (John Creasey Memorial Dagger for Best First Crime Novel)
PO Box 6939, Kings Heath, Birmingham B14 7LT
Contact *The Secretary*

ESTABLISHED 1973 following the death of crime writer John Creasey, founder of the **Crime Writers' Association**. This award, sponsored by **Chivers Press**, is given annually for the best crime novel by an author who has not previously published a full-length work of fiction. Nominations from publishers only. 1998 winner: Denise Mina *Garnet Hill*.

Award Dagger, plus cheque.

Crime Writers' Association (The CWA/The Macallan Gold Dagger for Non-Fiction)

PO Box 6939, Kings Heath, Birmingham B14 7LT

Contact *The Secretary*

Annual award for the best non-fiction crime book published during the year. Nominations from publishers only. 1998 winner: Gitta Sereny *Cries Unheard*.

Award Dagger, plus cheque (sum varies).

Crime Writers' Association (The CWA/The Macallan Gold and Silver Daggers for Fiction)

PO Box 6939, Kings Heath, Birmingham B14 7LT

Contact *The Secretary*

Two annual awards for the best crime fiction published during the year. Nominations for Gold Dagger from publishers only. 1998 winners: James Lee Burke *Sunset Limited* (Gold); Nicholas Blincoe *Manchester Slingback* (Silver).

Award Dagger, plus cheque (sum varies).

Crime Writers' Association (The CWA/The Macallan Short Story Dagger)

PO Box 6939, Kings Heath, Birmingham B14 7LT

Contact *The Secretary*

ESTABLISHED 1993. An award for a published crime story. Publishers should submit three copies of the story by 30 September. 1998 winner: Jerry Sykes *Roots*.

Prize Dagger, plus cheque.

Curtis Brown Prize

Curtis Brown Group Ltd, Haymarket House, 28/29 Haymarket, London SW1Y 4SP

☎0171 396 6600   Fax 0171 396 0110

Email: cb@curtisbrown.co.uk

Contact *Giles Gordon (cbscot@globalnet.co.uk)*

ESTABLISHED 1998. Annual prize for the best novel, in the opinion of Curtis Brown, written by a student on the MA in Novel Writing programme run by the University of Manchester. Open to all those not currently represented by a literary agent or under contract to a publisher.

Prize £1000. (Curtis Brown reserves the right to offer to act as literary agent to the winner.)

Harvey Darton Award

See **The Children's Books History Society** under **Literary Societies**

The Hunter Davies Prize

See **Lakeland Book of the Year Awards**

Isaac & Tamara Deutscher Memorial Prize

School of African and Asian Studies, University of Sussex, Brighton, East Sussex BN1 9RH

☎01273 606755

Email: J.P.Rosenberg@Sussex.ac.uk

Secretary *Dr Justin Rosenberg*

An annual award in recognition of, and as an encouragement to, outstanding research in or about the Marxist tradition. Made to the author of an essay or full-scale work published or in manuscript. Final entry date 1 May.

Award £250.

George Devine Award

17A South Villas, London NW1 9BS

☎0171 267 9793 (evenings)

Contact *Christine Smith*

Annual award for a promising new playwright writing for the stage in memory of George Devine, artistic director of the **Royal Court Theatre**, who died in 1965. The play, which can be of any length, does not need to have been produced. Send two copies of the script, plus outline of work, to Christine Smith by the end of March. Information leaflet available.

Prize £7500.

Denis Devlin Memorial Award for Poetry

An Chomhairle Ealaíon (The Arts Council), 70 Merrion Square, Dublin 2, Republic of Ireland

☎00 353 1 6180200   Fax 00 353 1 6761302

Literature Officer *Sinead MacAodha*

Triennial award for the best book of poetry in English by an Irish poet, published in the preceding three years. Next award 2001.

Award £1500.

Dog Watch Open Poetry Competition

267 Hillbury Road, Warlingham, Surrey CR6 9TL

☎01883 622121

Contact *Michaela Edridge*

ESTABLISHED 1993. Dog Watch is a charity that rescues and finds new homes for badly abused dogs. The annual prize is awarded only to authors of unpublished works. Final entry date is 1st September each year and entrants should send s.a.e. for details.

Prize (1st) £50; (2nd) £30; (3rd) £20.

Drama Association of Wales Playwriting Competition

The Library, Singleton Road, Splott, Cardiff CF2 2ET

☎01222 452200   Fax 01222 452277

Contact *Gary Thomas*

Annual competition held to promote the writing of one-act plays in English and Welsh of between 20 and 45 minutes' playing time. The theme of the competition is changed each year (the 1999 title was *Awakening*). Application forms from the above address.

Prizes awarded for Best Play for an All Female Cast; Best Play in the Welsh Language; Best Play for a Children's/Youth Cast; Best Author Under 25; Best Adult Play; Best Overall Play.

Eccles Prize

Columbia Business School, 834 Uris Hall, 3022 Broadway, New York NY 10027, USA

☎001 212 854 2747   Fax 001 212 854 3050

Contact *Office of Public Affairs*

ESTABLISHED 1986 by Spencer F. Eccles in commemoration of his uncle, George S. Eccles, a 1922 graduate of the Business School. Annual award for excellence in economic writing. One of the US's most prestigious book prizes. Books must have a business theme and be written for a general audience. Previous winners: *The Warburgs* Ron Chernow; *A Stream of Windows: Unsettling Reflections on Trade, Immigration and Democracy* Jagdish Bhagwati.

The T.S. Eliot Prize

The Poetry Book Society, Book House, 45 East Hill, London SW18 2QZ

☎0181 870 8403/
877 1615 (24 hr answerphone)

Contact *Clare Brown, Director*

ESTABLISHED 1993. Annual award named after T. S. Eliot, one of the founders of the **Poetry Book Society**. Open to books of new poetry published in the UK and Republic of Ireland during the year and over 32 pages in length. At least 75 per cent of the collection must be previously unpublished in book form. Final entry date is in August. Previous winners: Ciaran Carson *First Language*; Paul Muldoon *The Annals of Chile* ; Mark Doty *My Alexandria*; Les Murray *Subhuman Redneck Poems*; Don Paterson *God's Gift to Women*; Ted Hughes *Birthday Letters*.

The Encore Award

The Society of Authors, 84 Drayton Gardens, London SW10 9SB

☎0171 373 6642   Fax 0171 373 5768

ESTABLISHED 1990. Awarded for the best second published novel of the year. Final entry date 30 November. Details from the **Society of Authors**. 1998 joint winners: Alan Warner *These Demented Lands* and Timothy O'Grady *I Could Read the Sky*.

Prize (total) £7500.

Envoi Poetry Competition

Envoi, 44 Rudyard Road, Biddulph Moor, Stoke on Trent, Staffordshire ST8 7JN

☎01782 517892

Contact *Roger Elkin*

Run by *Envoi* poetry magazine. Competitions are featured regularly, with prizes of £200, plus three annual subscriptions to *Envoi*. Winning poems along with full adjudication report are published. Send s.a.e. to Competition Secretary, 17 Millcroft, Bishops Stortford, Hertfordshire CM23 2BP.

European Literary Prize/ European Translation Prize

See **The Aristeion Prize**

Euroscript

See entry under **Writers' Courses, Circles and Workshops**

Exeter International Poetry Prize

See **Exeter Phoenix** under **Writers' Courses, Circles and Workshops**

Geoffrey Faber Memorial Prize

Faber & Faber Ltd, 3 Queen Square, London WC1N 3AU

☎0171 465 0045   Fax 0171 465 0034

ESTABLISHED 1963 as a memorial to the founder and first chairman of **Faber & Faber**, this prize is awarded in alternate years for the volume of verse and the volume of prose fiction published in the UK in the preceding two

years, which is judged to be of greatest literary merit. Authors must be under 40 at the time of publication and citizens of the UK, Commonwealth, Republic of Ireland or South Africa. 1999 winner: Gavin Kramer *Shopping*.
Prize £1000.

Eleanor Farjeon Award

c/o Children's Book Circle, The Watts Publishing Group, 96 Leonard Street, London EC2A 4RH
☎0171 739 2929   Fax 0171 739 2318
Contact *Susan Barry*

This award, named in memory of the much-loved children's writer, is for distinguished services to children's books either in this country or overseas, and may be given to a librarian, teacher, publisher, bookseller, author, artist, reviewer, television producer, etc. Nominations from members of the **Children's Book Circle**. 1998 winner: *Gina Pollinger*.
Award £750.

The Fidler Award

c/o Scottish Book Trust, The Scottish Book Centre, 137 Dundee Street, Edinburgh EH11 1BG
☎0131 229 3663   Fax 0131 228 4293
Email: scottish.book.trust@dial.pipex.com
Website: www.webpost.net/bts

Sponsored by Hodder Children's Books for an unpublished novel for children aged 8–12, to encourage authors new to writing for this age group. The award is administered by **Scottish Book Trust**. Authors should not previously have had a novel published for this age group. Final entry date: end October. Previous winners: Theresa Breslin *Simon's Challenge*; Catherine McPhail *Run Zan Run*; John Smirthwaite *The Falcon's Crest*; Mark Leyland *Slate Mountain*.
Award £1000, plus publication.

Fish (Publishing) Short Story Prize

Fish Publishing, Durrus, Bantry, Co Cork Republic of Ireland
☎00 353 27 61246
Email: fishpublishing@tinet.ie
Website: www.sleeping-giant.ie/fishpublishing
Contact *Clem Cairns, Jula Walton*

ESTABLISHED 1994. Annual international award which aims to discover, encourage and publish exciting new literary talent. Stories of 5000 words maximum which have not been published previously may be entered. An entry fee of £8 is charged for the first entry and £5 per entry if more than one is entered. (£5 for pensioners, unemployed and full-time students.) Closing date: 30 November. Previous winners: Molly McCloskey *The Stranger*; Karl Iagnemma *Dog Days*; Richard O'Reilly *Scrap Magic*. Honorary Patrons: Roddy Doyle and Dermot Healy.
Prize £1000; the best 15 stories are published in an anthology.

Sir Banister Fletcher Award

Authors' Club, 40 Dover Street, London W1X 3RB
☎0171 499 8581   Fax 0171 409 0913
Contact *Mrs Ann de la Grange*

This award was created by Sir Bannister Fletcher, who was president of the **Authors' Club** for many years. The prize is presented annually for the best book on architecture or the fine arts published in the preceding year. Submissions: Fletcher Award Committee, RIBA, 66 Portland Place, London W1N 4AD. Previous winners: Richard Weston *Alvar Aalto*; Dr Megan Aldrich *Gothic Revival*; Professor Thomas Markus *Building and Power*; John Onians *Bearers of Meaning: Classical Orders in Antiquity*; Sir Michael Levey *Giambattista Tiepolo: His Life and Art*; John Allan *Berthold Lubetkin – Architecture and The Tradition of Progress*; Professor David Watkin *Sir John Soane, Enlightenment Thought and the Royal Academy*.
Award £750.

The John Florio Prize

See **The Translators Association Awards**

The Forward Prizes for Poetry

Colman Getty PR, Carrington House, 126–130 Regent Street, London W1R 5FE
☎0171 439 1783   Fax 0171 439 1784
Contact *Liz Sich, Margot Weale*

ESTABLISHED 1992. Three awards, sponsored by Forward Publishing, Waterstone's and Tolman Cunard, for the best collection of poetry, the best first collection of poetry, and the best single poem which is not already part of an anthology or collection. All entries must be published in the UK or Eire and submitted by poetry publishers (collections) or newspaper and magazine editors (single poems). Individual entries of poets' own work are not accepted. 1998 winners: Ted Hughes, Paul Farley, Sheenagh Pugh.
Prizes £10,000 for best collection; £5000

for best first collection; £1000 for best single poem

Anne Frankel Prize

Sight and Sound, British Film Institute, 21 Stephen Street, London W1P 2LN
☎0171 255 1444   Fax 0171 436 2327
Website: www.bfi.org.uk
Contact *The Administrator*

ESTABLISHED 1991. Annual prize for young film critics in memory of the late Anne Frankel, who wrote on film. Age limit for entrants is 25. Entrants must submit three examples of their film writing which must have been published in local or national newspapers and periodicals (these can include student newspapers). Final entry date usually end October.
Prize £500.

The Frogmore Poetry Prize

The Frogmore Press, 18 Nevill Road, Lewes, East Sussex BN7 1PF
Contact *Jeremy Page*

ESTABLISHED 1987. Awarded annually and sponsored by the Frogmore Foundation. The winning poem, runners-up and short-listed entries are all published in the magazine. Previous winners have been: David Satherley, Caroline Price, Bill Headdon, John Latham, Diane Brown, Tobias Hill, Mario Petrucci, Gina Wilson, Ross Cogan.
Prize The winner receives 100 guineas and a life subscription to the biannual literary magazine *The Frogmore Papers*.

David Gemmell Cup

Hastings' Writers Group, 39 Emmanuel Road, Hastings, East Sussex TN34 3LB
☎01424 442471
Contact *Mrs R. Bartholomew*

ESTABLISHED 1988. Annual award to encourage writers of short fiction (1500 words) resident in East and West Sussex, Kent, Surrey, London and London boroughs. Final entry date: end of August; entry forms, which are essential, are available from May (enclose s.a.e). The competition is organised by Hastings Writers' Group and is presented by its sponsor David Gemmell. 1998 winner: Jocelyn Kemp.
Prizes (1st) £250 plus David Gemmell Cup; (2nd) £150; (3rd) £100; (4th) £50; (5th) £30; (6th) £20. Additionally, certificates of commendation issued at the discretion of the judge, David Gemmell.

The Gladstone History Book Prize

Royal Historical Society, University College London, Gower Street, London WC1E 6BT
☎0171 387 7532   Fax 0171 387 7532
Contact *Executive Secretary*

A new annual award for the best new work on any historical subject which is not primarily related to British history, published in the UK in the preceding calendar year. The book must be the author's first (solely written) history book and be an original and scholarly work of historical research.
Prize £1000.

Glaxo Science Writers' Awards

See **ABSW/Glaxo Science Writers' Awards**

Glenfiddich Awards

4 Bedford Square, London WC1B 3RA
☎0171 255 1100   Fax 0171 631 0602

A series of awards to writers and broadcasters who have contributed most to the civilised appreciation of food and drink through articles, books, illustration and photography published in the UK. Also covers TV and radio programmes, as well as a Special Award for outstanding work or event. 1998 winners: Food Book of the Year: *The Book of Jewish Food* Claudia Roden; Drink Book of the Year: *The Wild Bunch* Patrick Matthews; Food Writer of the Year: Philippa Davenport for work in the *Financial Times*; Drink Writer of the Year: Richard Ehrlich for work in the *Independent on Sunday*; Magazine Cookery Writer of the Year: Philippa Davenport for work in *Country Living*; Newspaper Cookery Writer of the Year: Simon Hopkinson for work in *The Independent*; Restaurant Writer of the Year: Fay Maschler for work in the *Evening Standard*; Wine Writer of the Year: Richard Neill for work in *Decanter* and *The Daily Telegraph*; Regional Writer of the Year: Gillian Glover for work in *The Scotsman*; Television Programme of the Year: *A Cook on the Wild Side*, presented and produced by Hugh Fearnley-Whittingstall, directed by Andrew Palmer, executive producer Eleanor Stephens (Keo Films for Ch4 in association with Stephens Kerr); Radio Programme of the Year: no award made; Visual Award: Jason Lowe for photography in *Malt Whisky* by Charles MacLean; 1998 Special Awards: Ann Bagnall, Southover Press and *The Food Programme*, BBC Radio 4; 1998 Glenfiddich Trophy Winner: Fay Maschler.
Award Overall winner (chosen from the

category winners) £3000, plus the Glenfiddich Trophy (which is held for one year); category winners £800 each, plus a case of Glenfiddich Single Malt Scotch Whisky and an engraved commemorative quaich.

The Phillip Good Memorial Prize

QWF Magazine, 71 Bucknill Crescent, Hillmorton, Rugby CV21 4HE
Contact *Competition Secretary*

ESTABLISHED in 1997, the competition is run by *QWF Magazine* and a percentage of the entry fee goes to the Brain Research Trust. The prize commemorates the memory of Phillip Good (late husband of QWF editor, Jo Good) and is for short stories of less than 5000 words in any style or genre (except children's). Open entry. Entrants may request in–depth critique of their stories for an extra fee. For entry forms send s.a.e. to the address above.
Prizes (total) £525 plus free subscription to *QWF Magazine*.

Edgar Graham Book Prize

c/o Department of Geography, School of Oriental and African Studies, Thornhaugh Street, Russell Square, London WC1H 0XG
☎0171 691 3418   Fax 0171 691 3432
Contact *The Secretary*

ESTABLISHED 1984. Biennial award in memory of Edgar Graham. Aims to encourage research work in Third World agricultural and industrial development. Open to published works of original scholarship on agricultural and/or industrial development in Asia and/or Africa. No edited volumes. Next award 2000; final entry date 31 March 2000.
Prize £1500.

Kate Greenaway Medal

See **The Library Association Kate Greenaway Medal**

The Guardian Children's Fiction Award

The Guardian, 119 Farringdon Road, London EC1R 3ER
☎0171 239 9694   Fax 0171 713 4366
Children's Book Editor *Julia Eccleshare*

ESTABLISHED 1967. Annual award for an outstanding work of fiction for children aged seven and over by a British or Commonwealth author, first published in the UK in the preceding year, excluding picture books. Final entry date: late January. No application form necessary. Previous winners: Henrietta Branford *Fire, Bed and Bone*;

Melvin Burgess *Junk*; Lesley Howarth *MapHead*; Rachel Anderson *Paper Faces*; Hilary McKay *The Exiles*; William Mayne *Low Tide*; Sylvia Waugh *The Mennyms*; Philip Pullman *Dark Materials I: Northern Lights*; Alison Prince *The Sherwood Hero*.
Award £1500.

The Guardian Fiction Prize

The Guardian, 119 Farringdon Road, London EC1R 3ER
☎0171 239 9694   Fax 0171 713 4366
Contact *Literary Editor*

ESTABLISHED 1965. An annual award for a novel published by a British, Irish or Commonwealth writer, which is chosen by the literary editor in conjunction with the paper's regular reviewers of fiction. 1998 winner: Jackie Kay *Trumpet*.
Prize £5000.

Hastings National Poetry Competition

See **The Hastings International Poetry Festival** under **Festivals**

W. H. Heinemann Award

Royal Society of Literature, 1 Hyde Park Gardens, London W2 2LT
☎0171 723 5104   Fax 0171 402 0199
Email: RSlit@aol.com

ESTABLISHED 1945. Works of any kind of literature may be submitted by publishers under this award, which aims to encourage genuine contributions to literature. Books must be written in the English language and have been published in the previous year; translations are not eligible for consideration, nor are single poems, nor collections of poems by more than one author, nor may individuals put forward their own work. Preference tends to be given to publications which are unlikely to command large sales: poetry, biography, criticism, philosophy, history. Final entry date: 15 December. Up to three awards may be given. Previous winner: Graham Robb *Victor Hugo*.
Prize £5000.

Felicia Hemans Prize for Lyrical Poetry

University of Liverpool, PO Box 147, Liverpool, Merseyside L69 3BX
☎0151 794 2458   Fax 0151 794 2454
Contact *The Registrar*

ESTABLISHED 1899. Annual award for published or unpublished verse. Open to past or present members and students of the University of

Liverpool. One poem per entrant only. Closing date 1 May.

Prize £30.

Heywood Hill Literary Prize

10 Curzon Street, London W1Y 7FJ
☎0171 629 0647

Contact *John Saumarez Smith*

ESTABLISHED 1995 by the Duke of Devonshire to reward a lifetime's contribution to the enjoyment of books. Three judges chosen annually. No applications are necessary for this award. 1998 joint winners: Norman Lewis and Richard Ollard.

Prize £10,000.

William Hill Sports Book of the Year

Greenside House, Station Road, Wood Green, London N22 4TP
☎0181 918 3731　　　　Fax 0181 918 3728

Contact *Graham Sharpe*

ESTABLISHED 1989. Annual award introduced by Graham Sharpe of bookmakers William Hill. Sponsored by William Hill and thus dubbed the 'bookie' prize, it is the first, and only, Sports Book of the Year award. Final entry date: September. 1998 winner: Robert Twigger *Angry White Pyjamas*.

Prize (reviewed annually) £10,000 package including £7500 cash, hand-bound copy, £1000 free bet and a day at the races. Runners-up prizes.

Hilton House Poet of the Year/ Open Competitions

Hilton House (Publishers), Hilton House, 39 Long John Hill, Norwich, Norfolk NR1 2JP
☎01603 449845

Contact *Michael K. Moore*

ESTABLISHED 1995. Annual awards to promote interest in poetry and to encourage high standards. Unpublished poems only, of up to 30 lines; no limit to number of entries. Best poems selected will be published in Hilton House anthology series for that year. Entrants for all competitions must apply for rules and entry forms. Final entry dates: 31st March (Poet of the Year); 31st August (Open Competition). 1998 winners: David Rogers, Andrew Farmer, Allister Fraser MBE, Beryl Fleming. *Prizes* (for both competitions) 1st £200; 2nd £100; 3rd £150.

Also Hilton House Poet of the Year Best Collection/Open Competition Best Collection – for collections of 6–10 poems. Entry dates as above. *Prizes* (for Individual Poems) £300 1st; £150 2nd; £50 3rd; (for Best Collection) 1st 30 books containing prizewinner's collection; 2nd 20 books; 3rd 10 books.

Calvin & Rose G. Hoffman Prize

King's School, Canterbury, Kent CT1 2ES
☎01227 595501

Contact *The Headmaster*

Annual award for distinguished publication on Christopher Marlowe, established by the late Calvin Hoffman, author of *The Man Who was Shakespeare* (1955) as a memorial to himself and his wife. For unpublished works of at least 5000 words written in English for their scholarly contribution to the study of Christopher Marlowe and his relationship to William Shakespeare. Final entry date: 1 September. 1998 winner: Prof. David Riggs.

Winifred Holtby Prize

Royal Society of Literature, 1 Hyde Park Gardens, London W2 2LT
☎0171 723 5104　　　　Fax 0171 402 0199
Email: RSlit@aol.com

ESTABLISHED 1966 by Vera Brittain who gave a sum of money to the RSL to provide an annual prize in honour of Winifred Holtby who died at the age of 37. Administered by the **Royal Society of Literature**. The prize is for the best regional novel of the year written in the English language. The writer must be of British or Irish nationality, or a citizen of the Commonwealth. Translations, unless made by the author himself of his own work, are not eligible for consideration. If in any year it is considered that no regional novel is of sufficient merit the prize money may be awarded to an author, qualified as aforesaid, of a literary work of non-fiction or poetry, concerning a regional subject. Publishers are invited to submit works (three copies of each) published during the current year to the Secretary, labelled 'Winifred Holtby Prize'. Final entry date: 15 December. Previous winners: Eden Robinson *Traplines*; Rohinton Mistry *A Fine Balance*; Jim Crace *Signals of Distress*.

Prize £800.

L. Ron Hubbard's Writers of the Future Contest

PO Box 218, East Grinstead, West Sussex RH19 4GH

Contest Administrator *Andrea Grant-Webb*

ESTABLISHED 1984 by L. Ron Hubbard to encourage new and amateur writers of science fiction, fantasy and horror. Quarterly awards with an annual grand prize. Entrants must submit a short story of up to 10,000 words, or a novelette less than 17,000 words, which must not have not been published previously. The contest is open only to those who have not been published professionally. Previous winners: Roge Gregory, Malcolm Twigg, Janet Martin, Alan Smale, Ken Rand. Send s.a.e. for entry form.

Prizes (1st) £640, (2nd) £480 and (3rd) £320 each quarter; Annual Grand Prize: £2500. All winners are awarded a trip to the annual L. Ron Hubbard Achievement Awards which include a series of professional writers' workshops, and are published in the *L. Ron Hubbard Presents Writers of the Future* anthology.

Ilkley Literature Festival Poetry Competition

Manor House Museum, Ilkley, West Yorkshire LS29 9DT
☎01943 601210

Contact *David Porter*

Annual open poetry competition run by the **Ilkley Literature Festival**. Final entry date: August each year. Entry fee: £2.50 per poem.
Prize (total) £600.

The Richard Imison Memorial Award

The Society of Authors, 84 Drayton Gardens, London SW10 9SB
☎0171 373 6642   Fax 0171 373 5768

Contact *The Secretary, The Broadcasting Committee*

Annual award established 'to perpetuate the memory of Richard Imison, to acknowledge the encouragement he gave to writers working in the medium of radio, and in memory of the support and friendship he invariably offered writers in general, and radio writers in particular'. Administered by the **Society of Authors** and generally sponsored by the Peggy Ramsay Foundation, the purpose is 'to encourage new talent and high standards in writing for radio by selecting the radio drama by a writer new to radio which, in the opinion of the judges, is the best of those submitted.' An adaptation for radio of a piece originally written for the stage, television or film will not be eligible. Any radio drama first transmitted in the UK between 1 January and 31 December by a writer or writers new to radio, is eligible, provided the work is an original piece for radio and it is the first dramatic work by the writer(s) that has been broadcast. Submission may be made by any party to the production in the form of two copies of an audio cassette (not-returnable) accompanied by a nomination form. 1998 winner: Katie Hims *The Earthquake Girl*.
Prize £1500.

The Independent/ Scholastic Story of the Year

Postal box address changes each year (see below)

ESTABLISHED 1993. Open competition for the best short story for children aged 6–9. One story per entrant (between 1500–2500 words). Details of the competition, including the postal box address, are published in *The Independent* in March/April of each year.

Prize £2000; two runners-up of £500 each. The winning story will be published in the newspaper and in an anthology published by **Scholastic Children's Books**, along with a selection of the best entries.

The International IMPAC Dublin Literary Award

Dublin City Public Libraries, Administrative Headquarters, Cumberland House, Fenian Street, Dublin 2, Republic of Ireland
☎00 353 1 6619000   Fax 00 353 1 6761628
Email: dubaward@iol.ie
Website: www.iol.ie/~dubcilib

ESTABLISHED 1995. Sponsored by Dublin Corporation and a US-based productivity improvement firm, IMPAC, this prize is awarded for a work of fiction written and published in the English language or written in a language other than English and published in English translation. Initial nominations are made by municipal public libraries in major and capital cities worldwide, each library putting forward up to three books to the international panel of judges in Dublin. 1999 winner: Andrew Miller *Ingenious Pain*.

Prize IR£100,000 (if the winning book is in English translation, the prize is shared IR£75,000 to the author and IR£25,000 to the translator).

International Reading Association Literacy Award

International Reading Association, 800 Barksdale Road, PO Box 8139, Newark, Delaware 19714–8139, USA
☎001 302 731 1600   Fax 001 302 731 1057

Director of Research *Alan E. Frostrup, Executive Director*

The International Reading Association is a non-profit education organisation devoted to improving reading instruction and promoting literacy worldwide. In addition to the US $10,000 award presented each year on International Literacy Day (September 8), the organisation gives more than 25 awards in recognition of achievement in reading research, writing for children, media coverage of literacy, and literacy instruction.

International Student Playscript Competition
See **University College, Scarborough** under **Writers' Courses, Circles and Workshops**

Irish Times International Fiction Prize
The Irish Times Ltd, 10–16 D'Olier Street, Dublin 2, Republic of Ireland
☎00 353 1 679 2022   Fax 00 353 1 670 9383
Email: ewalsh@Irish-times.ie
Administrator, Book Prizes
Gerard Cavanagh

FOUNDED 1989. Biennial award to the author of a work of fiction written in the English language and published in Ireland, the UK or the US in the two years of the award. Next award to be announced in October 1999, the short list having been announced in September. Books are nominated by literary critics and editors only. Previous winners: J. M. Coetzee *The Master of Petersburg*; E. Annie Proulx *The Shipping News*; Norman Rush *Mating*; Louis Begley *Wartime Lies*; Seamus Deane *Reading in the Dark*.
Prize IR£7500.

Irish Times Irish Literature Prizes
The Irish Times Ltd, 10–16 D'Olier Street, Dublin 2, Republic of Ireland
☎00 353 1 679 2022   Fax 00 353 1 670 9383
Email: ewalsh@Irish-times.ie
Administrator, Book Prizes
Gerard Cavanagh

FOUNDED 1989. Biennial prizes awarded in four different categories: fiction (a novel, novella or collection of short stories), non-fiction prose (history, biography, autobiography, criticism, politics, sociological interest, travel, current affairs and belles-lettres), poetry (collection or a long poem or a sequence of poems, or a revised/updated edition of a previously published selection/collection) and (since 1999) for a work in the Irish language (fiction, poetry or non-fiction). The author must have been born in

Ireland or be an Irish citizen, but may live in any part of the world. Books are nominated by literary editors and critics, and are then called in from publishers. Previous winners: Paddy Devlin *Straight Left* (non-fiction); Kathleen Ferguson *A Maid's Tale* (fiction); Robert Greacen *Collected Poems*; Brian Keenan *An Evil Cradling*; John MacKenna *The Fallen and Other Stories*.
Prizes IR£5000 each category.

The Jennings Brothers Prize
See **Lakeland Book of the Year Awards**

Jewish Quarterly Literary Prizes
PO Box 2078, London W1A 1JR
☎0171 629 5004   Fax 0171 629 5110
Contact *Gerald Don*

Formerly the H. H. Wingate Prize. Annual awards (one for fiction and one for non-fiction) for works which best stimulate an interest in and awareness of themes of Jewish interest. Books must have been published in the UK in the year of the award and be written in English by an author resident in Britain, the Commonwealth, Israel, Republic of Ireland or South Africa. Previous winners: Anne Michaels *Fugitive Pieces*; Claudia Roden *The Book of Jewish Food*; Amos Oz *Black Box*; Anton Gill *The Journey Back from Hell*; Bernice Rubens *Kingdom Come*; Leo Abse *Wotan My Enemy*; Ronald Harwood *Home*; Alan Isler *The Prince of West End Avenue*; Theo Richmond *Konin: A Quest*; Clive Sinclair *The Lady With the Laptop*; W. G. Sebald *The Emigrants*.
Prizes Fiction: £4000; Non-fiction: £3000.

The Samuel Johnson Prize for Non-fiction
The Booksellers Association, Minster House, 272 Vauxhall Bridge Road, London SW1V 1BA
☎0171 834 5477   Fax 0171 834 8812
Email: 100437.2261@compuserve.com
Contact *Gill Cronin*

ESTABLISHED 1998. Annual prize sponsored by an anonymous retired British businessman to reward the best of non-fiction. Eligible categories include the arts, autobiography, biography, business, commerce, current affairs, history, natural history, popular science, religion, sport and travel. Entries submitted by publishers only.
Prize £30,000; £2500 to each shortlisted author.

Mary Vaughan Jones Award

Cyngor Llyfrau Cymru (Welsh Books Council), Castell Brychan, Aberystwyth, Dyfed SY23 2JB
☎01970 624151   Fax 01970 625385
Email: castellbrychan@cllc.org.uk
Website: www.wbc.org.uk
Contact *The Administrator*

Triennial award for distinguished services in the field of children's literature in Wales over a considerable period of time.
Award Silver trophy.

Keats–Shelley Prize

Keats–Shelley Memorial Association, 117 Cheyne Walk, London SW10 0ES
☎0171 352 2180   Fax 0171 352 6705
Website: www.demon.co.uk.heritage/
  Keats.House.Rome
Contact *Harriet Cullen*

ESTABLISHED 1998. Annual award to promote the study and appreciation of Keats and Shelley, especially in the universities, and of creative writing inspired by the younger romantic poets. Sponsored by the Folio Society. Two categories: essay and poem; open to all ages and nationalities. Previous winners: Sarah Wootton, Rukmini Maria Callimachi.
Prize £2000 distributed between the winners of the two categories.

Kent & Sussex Poetry Society Open Competition

13 Ruscombe Close, Southborough, Tunbridge Wells, Kent TN4 0SG
☎01892 543862
Chairman *Clive R. Eastwood*

Annual competition. Entry fee £3 per poem, maximum 40 lines.
Prizes (total) £1000.

Kent Short Story Competition

Kent Literature Festival, The Metropole Arts Centre, The Leas, Folkestone, Kent CT20 2LS
☎01303 255070
Contact *Ann Fearey*

ESTABLISHED 1992. For a short story of up to 3000 words by anyone over the age of 16. Sponsored by Midland Bank and supported by Saga and Shepway District Council. Send s.a.e. for entry forms, available from March.
Prizes (1st) £275; (2nd) £150; (3rd) £100.

Kraszna-Krausz Book Awards

122 Fawnbrake Avenue, London SE24 0BZ
☎0171 738 6701   Fax 0171 738 6701
Email: k-k@dial.pipex.com
Administrator *Andrea Livingstone*

ESTABLISHED 1985. Annual award to encourage and recognise oustanding achievements in the publishing and writing of books on the art, practice, history and technology of photography and the moving image (film, television, video and related screen media). Books in any language, published worldwide, are eligible. Entries must be submitted by publishers only. Prizes for books on still photography alternate annually with those for books on the moving image (1999: moving image). Previous winners: Herbert Molderings *Umbo: Otto Umbehr 1902–1980*; Ann Thomas (ed.) *Beauty of Another Order: Photography in Science*; Ruth Vasey *The World According to Hollywood, 1918–1939*; Richard Taylor *The Encyclopedia of Animation Techniques*.
Prizes £5000 in each of the main categories; £1000 special commendations.

Lakeland Book of the Year Awards

Cumbria Tourist Board, Ashleigh, Holly Road, Windermere, Cumbria LA23 2AQ
☎015394 44444   Fax 015394 44041
Contact *Sheila Lindsay*

Five annual awards set up by Cumbrian author Hunter Davies and the Cumbria Tourist Board. The **Hunter Davies Prize** was established in 1984 and is awarded for the book which best helps visitors or residents enjoy a greater love or understanding of any aspect of life in Cumbria and the Lake District. Three further awards were set up in 1993 with funding from the private sector: **The Tullie House Prize** is for the book which best helps develop a greater appreciation of the built and/or natural environment of Cumbria; **The Barclays Bank Prize** is for the best small book on any aspect of Cumbrian life, its people or culture, and **The Border Television Prize** is for the book which best illustrates the beauty and character of Cumbria. A new award was established in 1997: **The Jennings Brothers Prize for the Best Guide Book**. Final entry date mid-March. 1998 winners: Hunter Davies Prize and Border Television Prize: Mary E. Burkett and Valerie M. Rickerby *Percy Kelly: A Cumbrian Artist*; Barclays Bank Prize: Kathleen Jones *A Passionate Sisterhood*; Tullie House Prize: Jane Renouf *Alfred Heaton Cooper –*

Painter of Landscapes; Jennings Brothers Prize: William Rollinson *The Cumbrian Dictionary*.
Prize £100 and certificate.

Lancashire County Library/NWB Children's Book of the Year Award

Lancashire County Library Headquarters, County Hall, PO Box 61, Preston, Lancashire PR1 8RJ
☎01772 264040   Fax 01772 264043
Manager, Young People's Service
Jean Wolstenholme

ESTABLISHED 1986. Annual award sponsored by the National Westminster Bank for a work of original fiction suitable for 11–14-year-olds. The winner is chosen by 13–14-year-old secondary school pupils in Lancashire. Books must have been published between 1 September and 31 August in the year of the award and authors must be UK residents. Final entry date: 1 September each year. Recent winners: Elizabeth Hawkins *The Sea of Peril*; Elizabeth Laird *Joy*. 1999 winner: Nigel Hinton *Out of the Darkness*. To celebrate the tenth anniversary of the award, all previous winners were judged for the 'Books Across Europe Award'. Ian Strachan's *The Boy in the Bubble* was voted the overall winner.
Prize £500 plus engraved glass decanter.

The Library Association
Besterman Medal
7 Ridgmount Street, London WC1E 7AE
☎0171 636 7543   Fax 0171 436 7218

ESTABLISHED 1970. Sponsored by Whitaker. Awarded annually for an outstanding bibliography or guide to literature first published in the UK during the preceding year. Recommendations for the award are invited from members of **The Library Association**, publishers and others. Among criteria taken into consideration in making the award are: authority of the work and quality of articles or entries; accessibility and arrangement of the information; scope and coverage; quality of indexing; adequacy of references; accuracy of information; physical presentation; and the originality of the work. Previous winners include: Heather Creaton *Bibliography of Printed Works on London History to 1939*; John McIlwaine *Africa: A Guide to Reference Material*; Katherine Pantzer *A Short-title Catalogue of Books Printed in England, Scotland, Ireland and English Books Printed Abroad 1475–1640 Vol 3*.
Award Medal.

The Library Association
Carnegie Medal
7 Ridgmount Street, London WC1E 7AE
☎0171 636 7543   Fax 0171 436 7218

ESTABLISHED 1936. Presented for an outstanding book for children written in English and first published in the UK during the preceding year. This award is not necessarily restricted to books of an imaginative nature. 1998 winner: Tim Bowler *River Boy*. Previous winners include: Melvyn Burgess *Junk*; Anne Fine *Flour Babies*; Theresa Breslin *Whispers in the Graveyard*.
Award Medal.

The Library Association
Kate Greenaway Medal
7 Ridgmount Street, London WC1E 7AE
☎0171 636 7543   Fax 0171 436 7218

ESTABLISHED 1955. Presented annually for the most distinguished work in the illustration of children's books first published in the UK during the preceding year. 1998 winner: P. J. Lynch *When Jessie Came Home from the Sea*. Previous winners include: Helen Cooper *The Baby Who Wouldn't Go To Bed*; Alan Lee *Black Ships Before Troy*; Gregory Rogers *Way Home*.
Award Medal.

The Library Association
McColvin Medal
7 Ridgmount Street, London WC1E 7AE
☎0171 636 7543   Fax 0171 436 7218

ESTABLISHED 1970. Sponsored by Whitaker. Annual award for an outstanding reference book first published in the UK during the preceding year. Books eligible for consideration include: encyclopedias, general and special; dictionaries, general and special; biographical dictionaries; annuals, yearbooks and directories; handbooks and compendia of data; atlases. Recommendations invited from members of **The Library Association**, publishers and others. Previous winners include: Colin Matthew *The Gladstone Diaries*; Ray Desmond *Dictionary of British and Irish Botanists*; Edward Peget-Tomlinson *The Illustrated History of Canal and River Navigation*.
Award Medal.

The Library Association
Walford Award
7 Ridgmount Street, London WC1E 7AE
☎0171 636 7543   Fax 0171 436 7218

Awarded to an individual who has made a

sustained and continual contribution to British bibliography over a period of years. The nominee need not be resident in the UK. The award is named after Dr A. J. Walford, a bibliograper of international repute. Previous winners include: Prof. Stanley Wells, Prof. J. D. Pearson and Prof. R. C. Alston

Award Cash prize and certificate.

The Library Association Wheatley Medal

7 Ridgmount Street, London WC1E 7AE
☎0171 636 7543   Fax 0171 436 7218

ESTABLISHED 1962. Sponsored by Whitaker. Annual award for an outstanding index first published in the UK during the preceding three years. Whole work must have originated in the UK and recommendations for the award are invited from members of **The Library Association**, the **Society of Indexers**, publishers and others. Previous winners include: Elizabeth Moys *British Tax Encyclopedia*; Paul Nash *The World of Environment 1972–1992*; Richard Raper *The Works of Charles Darwin*.

Award Medal.

Lichfield Prize

c/o Tourist Information Centre, Donegal House, Bore Street, Lichfield, Staffordshire WS13 6NE
☎01543 252109   Fax 01543 417308
Email: tic@lichfield-tourist.co.uk
Website: www.lichfieldtourist.co.uk

Contact *Mrs Alison Bessey* (at Lichfield District Council on 01543 414000 ext. 2047)

ESTABLISHED 1988. Biennial award initiated by Lichfield District Council to coincide with the Lichfield Festival. Run in conjunction with James Redshaw Booksellers of Lichfield and 1997 Prize co-sponsors, **Hodder & Stoughton** publishers. Awarded for a previously unpublished novel based upon the geographical area of Lichfield district, contemporary or historical, but not futuristic. Previous winners include: Valerie Kershaw *Rockabye*; Gary Coyne *The Short Caution*. Next award 1999. Final entry date in April of award year.

Prize £5000, plus possible publication.

Literary Review Grand Poetry Competition

See *Literary Review* under **Magazines**

The London Writers Competition

Room 224a, The Town Hall, Wandsworth High Street, London SW18 2PU
☎0181 871 8711   Fax 0181 871 8712

Contact *Wandsworth Arts Office*

Arranged by Wandsworth Borough Council in association with Waterstone's. An annual competition, open to all writers of 16 or over who live, work or study in the Greater London area. Work must not have been published previously. There are three sections: poetry, short story and play.

Prizes £1000 for each section, with a first prize of £600. Poetry and story winners are published and the winning play is produced in a London venue.

Longman–History Today Book of the Year Award

c/o History Today, 20 Old Compton Street, London W1V 5PE
☎0171 534 8000

Contact *Peter Furtado, Marion Soldan*

ESTABLISHED 1993. Annual award set up as joint initiative between the magazine *History Today* and publisher Longman (**Pearson Education**) to mark the past links between the two organisations, to encourage new writers, and to promote a wider public understanding of, and enthusiasm for, the study and publication of history. Submissions are made by publishers only. Previous winners: Michael Richards *A Time of Silence*; Amanda Vickery *A Gentleman's Daughter*; Andrew Gordon *The Rules of the Game: Jutland and British Naval Command*; Orlando Figes *A People's Tragedy: The Russian Revolution 1891–1924*; Paul Binski *Westminster Abbey and the Plantagenets*; Nicholas Timmins *Five Giants: A Biography of the Welfare State*.

Prize £1000 (see *History Today* from July 1999).

Sir William Lyons Award

The Guild of Motoring Writers, 30 The Cravens, Smallfield, Surrey RH6 9QS
☎01342 843294   Fax 01342 844093

Contact *Sharon Scott-Fairweather*

An annual competitive award to encourage young people in automotive journalism and to foster interests in motoring and the motor industry. Entrance by two essays and interview with Awards Committee. Applicants must be British, aged 17–23 and resident in UK. Final entry date 31 August. Presentation date in December.

Award £1000 plus trophy.

The Macallan/Scotland on Sunday Short Story Competition

Scotland on Sunday, 20 North Bridge, Edinburgh EH1 1YT

☎0131 243 3602   Fax 0131 220 2443

Contact *Rosemary Goring*

ESTABLISHED 1990. Annual competition to recognise the best in new Scottish writing. Stories are accepted from those who were born or are living in Scotland, or from Scots living abroad. Up to three stories per applicant permitted. Maximum 3000 words per story. Final entry date in March. The top 20 entries are published in a book in conjunction with the **Scottish Arts Council**. Previous winners: Alan Spence, Ali Smith, Chris Dolan, Michael Faber, Anne Donovan.

Prizes 1st £6000; 2nd £600; four runners-up receive £100 each. Winning story is published in *Scotland on Sunday* and four of six shortlisted will be broadcast on BBC Radio Scotland.

McColvin Medal

See **The Library Association McColvin Medal**

W. J. M. Mackenzie Book Prize

Political Studies Association, School of Politics, University of Nottingham, Nottingham NG7 2RD

☎0115 9514797   Fax 0115 9514797

PSA Executive Director *Victoria Leach*

ESTABLISHED 1987. Annual award to best work of political science published in the UK during the previous year. Submissions from publishers only. Final entry date in June. Previous winners: James Mayall *Nationalism and International Society*; Brian Barry *Theories of Justice;* Avi Shlaim *Collusion Across the Jordan*; Colin Crouch *Industrial Relations and European State Tradition*; Iain Hampsher-Monk *A History of Modern Political Thought*; Patrick Dunleavy *Democracy, Bureaucracy and Public Choice*; Ivor Crewe and Anthony King *The S.D.P.*; Archie Brown *The Gorbachev Factor*.

Prize £100, plus travel/attendance at three-day annual conference.

McKitterick Prize

Society of Authors, 84 Drayton Gardens, London SW10 9SB

☎0171 373 6642   Fax 0171 373 5768

Contact *Awards Secretary*

Annual award for a full-length adult work in the English language, first published in the UK or

unpublished. Open to writers over 40 who have not had any adult novel published other than the one submitted. Closing date 16 December. 1998 winner: Eli Gottlieb *The Boy Who Went Away*.

Prize £4000.

Enid McLeod Prize

Franco-British Society, Room 623, Linen Hall, 162–168 Regent Street, London W1R 5TB

☎0171 734 0815   Fax 0171 734 0815

Executive Secretary *Mrs Kate Brayn*

ESTABLISHED 1982. Annual award to the author of the work of literature published in the UK which, in the opinion of the judges, has contributed most to Franco-British understanding. Any full-length work written in English by a citizen of the UK, Commonwealth, Republic of Ireland, Pakistan, Bangladesh and South Africa. No English translation of a book written originally in any other language will be considered. Nominations from publishers for books published between 1 January and 31 December of the year of the prize. Previous winners: Jan Ousby *Occupation – The Ordeal of France 1940–44*; Gillian Tindall *Célestiné, Voices from a French Village*; Jonathan Keates *Stendhal*; Sebastian Faulks *Birdsong*; Margaret Crosland *Simone de Beauvoir – The Woman and Her Work*; Frank Giles *The Locust Years*.

Prize Cheque.

Macmillan Prize for a Children's Picture Book

Macmillan Children's Books, 25 Eccleston Place, London SW1W 9NF

☎0171 881 8000   Fax 0171 881 8001

Contact *Marketing Dept., Macmillan Children's Books*

Set up in order to stimulate new work from young illustrators in art schools, and to help them start their professional lives. Fiction or non-fiction. **Macmillan** have the option to publish any of the prize winners.

Prizes (1st) £1000; (2nd) £500; (3rd) £250.

Macmillan Silver PEN Award

The English Centre of International PEN, 7 Dilke Street, London SW3 4JE

☎0171 352 6303   Fax 0171 351 0220

Sponsored by **Macmillan Publishers**. An annual award for a volume of short stories written in English by a British author and published in the UK in the year preceding the prize. Nominations by the PEN Executive Committee only. Please do not submit books. 1998 winner:

Tobias Hill *Skin*. Previous winners: Jane Gardham *Going into a Dark House*; Nicola Barker *Love Your Enemies*; Clive Sinclair *The Lady With the Laptop*.

Prize £500, plus silver pen.

The Mail on Sunday Novel Competition

Postal box address changes each year (see below)

Annual award ESTABLISHED 1983. Judges look for a story/character that springs to life in the 'tantalising opening 50–150 words of a novel'. Details of the competition, including the postal box address, are published in *The Mail on Sunday* in July/August. Previous winners: Jude Rodger, Nicola Richardson, Michael Ryan, Kate Spencer, Karen Martin, Pat Simpson.

Awards (1st) £400 book tokens and a weekend writing course at the **Arvon Foundation**; (2nd) £300 tokens; (3rd) £200 tokens; three further prizes of £150 tokens each.

The Mail on Sunday/John Llewellyn Rhys Prize

Book Trust, Book House, 45 East Hill, London SW18 2QZ

☎0181 516 2973   Fax 0181 516 2978

Contact *Sandra Vince*

ESTABLISHED 1942. An annual young writer's award for a memorable work of any kind. Entrants must be under the age of 35 at the time of publication; books must have been published in the UK in the year of the award. The author must be a citizen of Britain or the Commonwealth, writing in English. Previous winners: Matthew Kneale *Sweet Thames*; Jason Goodwin *On Foot to the Golden Horn*, Melanie McGrath *Motel Nirvana*. 1998 winner: Phil Whitaker *Eclipse of the Sun*.

Prize (1st) £5000; £500 for shortlisted entries.

Marsh Award for Children's Literature in Translation

Roehampton Institute London, Froebel College, Roehampton Lane, London SW15 5PJ

☎0181 392 3000   Fax 0181 392 3664

Contact *Dr Gillian Lathey*

ESTABLISHED 1995 and sponsored by the Marsh Christian Trust, the award aims to encourage translation of foreign children's books into English. It is a biennial award (next award: 1998), open to British translators of books for 4–16-year-olds, published in the UK by a British publisher. Any category will be considered with the exception of encyclopedias and reference books. No electronic books. First winner: Anthea Bell *A Dog's Life* by Christine Nostlinger. 1999 winner: Patricia Crampton for her translation of *The Final Journey* by Gudrun Pausewang.

Prize £750.

Marsh Biography Award

The English-Speaking Union, Dartmouth House, 37 Charles Street, London W1X 8AB

☎0171 493 3328   Fax 0171 495 6108

Email: lucy_passmore@esu.org

Website: www.esu.org

Contact *Lucy Passmore*

A biennial award for the most significant biography published over a two-year period by a British publisher. Next award October 1999. Previous winners: Hugh & Mirabel Cecil *Clever Hearts*; Patrick Marnham *The Man Who Wasn't Maigret*; Selina Hastings *Evelyn Waugh*. 1997 winner: Jim Ring *Erskine Childers*.

Award £3500, plus silver trophy presented at a dinner.

Kurt Maschler Award

Book Trust, Book House, 45 East Hill, London SW18 2QZ

☎0181 516 2973   Fax 0181 516 2978

Contact *Sandra Vince*

ESTABLISHED 1982. Annual award for 'a work of imagination in the children's field in which text and illustration are of excellence and so presented that each enhances, yet balances the other'. Books published in the current year in the UK by a British author and/or artist, or by someone resident for ten years, are eligible. Previous winners: William Mayne and Jonathan Heale (illus.) *Lady Muck*. 1998 winner: Anthony Browne *Voices in the Park*.

Award £1000 plus bronze Emil trophy.

MCA Book Prize

Kinross & Render, 192–198 Vauxhall Bridge Road, London SW1V 1DX

☎0171 592 3100   Fax 0171 931 9641/0

Contact *Janet Awe, Jonathan Sinnatt*

ESTABLISHED 1993. Annual award sponsored by the Management Consultancies Association to recognise and reward books that contribute stimulating, original and progressive ideas on management. Entries should have been published first in the UK during the calendar year of the Award and written by British subjects living in the UK. Submissions by publishers only. 1998 winner: Shiv S. Mathur and Alfred Kenyon *Creating Value: Shaping Tomorrow's Business*.

Prizes £5000 for best management book published. In addition, a special commendation for younger writers, carrying an award of £2000 for best management book by a writer under 40 may be given.

Medical Prizes
The Society of Authors, 84 Drayton Gardens, London SW10 9SB
☎0171 373 6642   Fax 0171 373 5768
Contact *Dorothy Wright*

Annual award in five categories: basic book, advanced author book, advanced edited book, medical history, first textbook, dental book, published in the UK in the year preceding the awards. Previous winners: Anne Stephenson *A Textbook of General Practice*; Michael Donaghy *Neurology*; David Weedon *Skin Pathology*; Leslie Collier, Albert Balows, Max Sussman *Topley & Wilson's Microbiology and Microbial Infections, 9th ed.*; David Ellison, Seth Love, Leila Chimelli, Brian Harding, Jim Lowe, Gareth W. Roberts, Harry V. Vinters *Neuropathology*; Peter Richards, Simon Stockhill *The New Learning Medicine, 14th ed.*; Rogan J. Corbridge *Essential ENT Practice*.

Prizes £1000 (each category).

Mere Literary Festival Open Competition
The Mere & District Linkscheme, Limpers Hill, Mere, Wiltshire BA12 6BD
☎01747 860475
Contact *Mrs Adrienne Howell (Events Organiser)*

Annual open competition which alternates between short stories and poetry. The winners are announced at the Mere Literary Festival during the second week of October. The 2000 competition is for short stories with a closing date for entries in July. For further details, including entry fees and form, contact the address above from 1 March with s.a.e.

Cash prizes

Meyer-Whitworth Award
Arts Council of England, 14 Great Peter Street, London SW1P 3NQ
☎0171 973 6431   Fax 0171 973 6983
Contact *John Johnston*

In 1908 the movement for a National Theatre joined forces with that to create a memorial to William Shakespeare. The result was the Shakespeare Memorial National Theatre Committee, the embodiment of the campaign for a National Theatre. This award, bearing the name of but two protagonists in the movement, has been established to commemorate all those who worked for the SMNT. Endowed by residual funds of the SMNT, the award is intended to help further the careers of UK playwrights who are not yet established, and to draw contemporary theatre writers to the public's attention. The award is given to the writer whose play most nearly satisfies the following criteria: a play which embodies Geoffrey Whitworth's dictum that 'drama is important in so far as it reveals the truth about the relationships of human beings with each other and the world at large'; a play which shows promise of a developing new talent; a play in which the writing is of individual quality. Nominations from professional theatre companies. Plays must have been written in the English language and produced professionally in the UK in the 12 months preceding the award. Candidates will have had no more than two of their plays professionally produced.

Award £8000.

MIND Book of the Year/ Allen Lane Award
Granta House, 15–19 Broadway, London E15 4BQ
☎0181 519 2122 ext. 225 Fax 0181 522 1725

ESTABLISHED 1981. Annual award, in memory of Sir Allen Lane, for the author of a book published in the current year (fiction or non-fiction), which furthers public understanding of mental health problems. 1998 winner: Jenny Diski *Skating to Antarctica. Award* £1000.

The Mitchell Prize for Art History/The Eric Mitchell Prize
c/o The Burlington Magazine, 14–16 Duke's Road, London WC1H 9AD
☎0171 388 8157   Fax 0171 388 1230
Executive Director *Caroline Elam*

ESTABLISHED 1977 by art collector, philanthropist and businessman, Jan Mitchell, to draw attention to exceptional achievements in the history of art. Consists of two prizes: The Mitchell Prize, given for an outstanding and original contribution to the study and understanding of visual arts, and The Eric Mitchell Prize, given for the most outstanding first book in this field. The prizes are awarded to authors of books in English that have been published in the previous 12 months. The prizes were not awarded in 1999 but will be resumed in 2000. Books are submitted by publishers before the end of February. Previous winners: The Mitchell Prize: *Nicolas Poussin* Elizabeth Cropper and Charles Dempsey; The Eric Mitchell Prize: *The Triumph of Vulcan* Suzanne Brown Butters.

Prizes $15,000 (Mitchell Prize); $5000 (Eric Mitchell Prize)

Scott Moncrieff Prize
See **The Translators Association Awards**

The Montagu of Beaulieu Trophy
Guild of Motoring Writers, 30 The Cravens, Smallfield, Surrey RH6 9QS
☎01342 843294   Fax 01342 844093
Contact *Sharon Scott-Fairweather*

First presented by Lord Montagu on the occasion of the opening of the National Motor Museum at Beaulieu in 1972. Awarded annually to a member of the **Guild of Motoring Writers** who, in the opinion of the nominated jury, has made the greatest contribution to recording in the English language the history of motoring or motor cycling in a published book or article, film, television or radio script, or research manuscript available to the public.
Prize Trophy.

Brian Moore Short Story Award
Creative Writers' Network, 15 Church Street, Belfast BT1 1ER
☎01232 312361   Fax 01232 434669
Contact *Anne Harris, Noel McBride*

ESTABLISHED 1996. Annual award to encourage creative writing in Northern Ireland. Awarded in association with the *Belfast Telegraph*, winning entries are usually published by them around Christmas. Two categories: published and unpublished writers; final entry date in September. Previous winners: Hugh McGrattan, Sally Wheeler. *Prizes* (total) £1800 and trophies.

The Mother Goose Award
See **The BFC Mother Goose Award**

Shiva Naipaul Memorial Prize
The Spectator, 56 Doughty Street, London WC1N 2LL
☎0171 405 1706   Fax 0171 242 0603
Contact *Emma Bagnall*

ESTABLISHED 1985. Annual prize given to an English language writer of any nationality under the age of 35 for an essay of not more than 4000 words describing a culture alien to the writer. Final entry date is 30 April. Previous winner: Sadakat Kadri.
Prize £3000.

NASEN Special Educational Needs Book Awards
The Educational Publishers Council, The Publishers Association, 1 Kingsway, London WC2B 6XF
☎0171 565 7474   Fax 0171 836 4543

ESTABLISHED 1992. Organised by the National Association for Special Education Needs (NASEN) and the **Educational Publishers Council**. Two awards: *The Children's Book Award*, for the book that most successfully provides a positive image of children with special needs; *The Academic Book Award* celebrates the work of authors and editors who have made an outstanding contribution to the theory and practice of special education. Books must have been published in the UK within the year preceding the award. 1998 winners: Dick King-Smith *The Crowstarver* (Children's); Gary Thomas, David Walker, Julie Webb *The Making of the Inclusive School* (Academic).
Prize £500.

National Poetry Competition (in association with BT)
The Poetry Society, 22 Betterton Street, London WC2H 9BU
☎0171 420 9880   Fax 0171 240 4818
Contact *Competition Organiser (WH)*

One of Britian's major open poetry competitions. Closing date: 31 October. Poems on any theme, up to 40 lines. For rules and entry form send s.a.e. to the Competition Organiser at the above address.
Prizes (1st) £5000; (2nd) £1000; (3rd) £500; plus 10 commendations of £50. From 1999–2001 there will be six additional prizes courtesy of British Telecommunications plc.

Nestlé Smarties Book Prize
Book Trust, Book House, 45 East Hill, London SW18 2QZ
☎0181 516 2973   Fax 0181 516 2978
Contact *Sandra Vince*

ESTABLISHED 1985 to encourage high standards and stimulate interest in books for children, this prize is given for a children's book (fiction), written in English by a citizen of the UK or an author resident in the UK, and published in the UK in the year ending 31 October. There are three age-group categories: 5 and under, 6–8 and 9–11. 1998 winners: *Cowboy Baby* Sue Heap (5 and under, gold); *The Last Gold Diggers* Harry Horse (6–8, gold); *Harry Potter and the Chamber of Secrets* J. K. Rowling (9–11, gold).

Prizes in each category: £2,500 (gold); £1000 (silver); £500 (bronze).

The New Writer Poetry Prizes

The New Writer, PO Box 60, Cranbrook, Kent TN17 2ZR
☎01580 212626   Fax 01580 212041
Contact *Merric Davidson*

ESTABLISHED 1997. Annual award founded by *The New Writer* poetry editor and poet, Abi Hughes-Edwards. Open to all poets writing in the English language for an original, previously unpublished poem or collection of six to ten poems. Final entry date: 20 November. Previous winners: Mark Granier, Ros Barber, Celia de Fréine, John Hilton.

Prizes Up to 20 prizes from £20 to £600 plus publication in collection.

Nobel Prize

The Nobel Foundation, PO Box 5232, 102 45 Stockholm Sweden
☎00 46 8 663 0920   Fax 00 46 8 660 3847
Website: www.nobel.se
Contact *Information Section*

Awarded yearly for outstanding achievement in physics, chemistry, physiology or medicine, literature and peace. FOUNDED by Alfred Nobel, a chemist who proved his creative ability by inventing dynamite. In general, individuals cannot nominate someone for a Nobel Prize. The rules vary from prize to prize but the following are eligible to do so for Literature: members of the Swedish Academy and of other academies, institutions and societies similar to it in constitution and purpose; professors of literature and of linguistics at universities or colleges; Nobel Laureates in Literature; presidents of authors' organisations which are representative of the literary production in their respective countries. British winners of the literature prize, first granted in 1901, include Rudyard Kipling, John Galsworthy and Winston Churchill. Recent winners: Seamus Heaney; Camilio Jose Cela (Spain); Octavio Paz (Mexico); Nadine Gordimer (South Africa); Derek Walcott (St Lucia); Toni Morrison (USA); Kenzaburo Oe (Japan); Wislawa Szymborska (Poland); Dario Fo (Italy). Nobel Laureate in Literature 1998: José Saramago (Portugal).

Prize 1997: SEK7,600,000 (about £700,000), increasing each year to cover inflation.

The Noma Award for Publishing Africa

PO Box 128, Witney, Oxfordshire OX8 5XU
☎01993 775235   Fax 01991 709265
Email: maryljay@aol.com
Contact *Mary Jay, Secretary to the Managing Committee*

ESTABLISHED 1979. Annual award, founded by the late Shoichi Noma, President of Kodansha Ltd, Tokyo, to encourage the publication of works by African writers and scholars within Africa. The award is for an outstanding book, published in Africa by an African writer, in three categories: scholarly and academic; literature and creative writing; children's books. Entries, by publishers only, by 28 February for a title published in the previous year. Maximum number of three entries. Previous winners: Paul Tiyambe Zeleza *A Modern Economic History of Africa – Vol 1: The Nineteenth Century*; Marlene van Niekerk *Triomf*; Kitia Touré *Destins Parallèles*; A. Adu Boahen *Mfantsipim and the Making of Ghana: A Centenary History 1876–1976*; Peter Adwok Nyaba *The Politics of Liberation in South Sudan; An Insider's View*.

Prize US$10,000 and presentation plaque.

C. B. Oldman Prize

Aberdeen University Library, Queen Mother Library, Meston Walk, Aberdeen AB24 3UE
☎01224 272592   Fax 01224 487048
Email: rturbet@abdn.ac.uk
Contact *Richard Turbet*

ESTABLISHED 1989 by the International Association of Music Libraries, UK Branch. Annual award for best book of music bibliography, librarianship or reference published the year before last (i.e. books published in 1998 considered for the 2000 prize). Previous winners: Michael Twyman, Andrew Ashbee, Michael Talbot, Donald Clarke, John Parkinson, John Wagstaff, Stanley Sadie, William Waterhouse, Richard Turbet.

Prize £150.

Orange Prize for Fiction

Book Trust, 45 East Hill, London SW18 2QZ
☎0181 516 2973   Fax 0181 516 2978
Contact *Sandra Vince*

ESTABLISHED 1996. Annual award founded by a group of senior women in publishing to 'create the opportunity for more women to be rewarded for their work and to be better known by the reading public'. Awarded for a full-length novel written in English by a woman of any nationality, and published in the UK between 1 April and 31 March of the following year. 1998 winner: Carol Shields *Larry's Party*.

Prize £30,000 and a work of art (a limited edition bronze figurine to be known as 'The Bessie' in acknowledgement of anonymous prize endowment).

Orange Prize for Screenwriting/ Pathé Production Prize

Pathé Pictures, 14–17 Kent House, London W1N 8AR
☎0171 323 5157   Fax 0171 631 3568
Contact *Vicki Patterson*

ESTABLISHED 1999. Together with partners, Orange, Pathé Pictures has launched a two-tier screenwriting and promotion award aimed specifically at new writing talent. The Orange Prize for Screenwriting and the Pathé Production Prize undertakes to find three feature-length scripts by new writers each year. Winners will receive a cash prize and go into development at Pathé, after which one script will be chosen for production and distribution throughout the UK. First winners: Bernard Wright *Frankie's Come Back*; Clive Bradley *Priceless*; Sara Sugarman *Pavarotti in Dad's Room*.

The Orwell Prize

The Political Quarterly, (Literary Editor), 8a Bellevue Terrace, Edinburgh EH7 4DT
☎0131 557 2517   Fax 0131 557 2517
Contact *Bernard Crick*

Jointly ESTABLISHED in 1993 by the George Orwell Memorial Fund and the *Political Quarterly* to encourage and reward writing in the spirit of Orwell's 'What I have most wanted to do ... is to make political writing into an art'. Two categories: book or pamphlet; newspaper and/or articles, features, columns, or sustained reportage on a theme. Submissions by editors, publishers or authors. 1998 winners: Polly Toynbee (journalism); Lady Hollis (book).

Prizes £1000 for each category.

Outposts Poetry Competition

Outposts, 22 Whitewell Road, Frome, Somerset BA11 4EL
☎01373 466653
Contact *Roland John*

Annual competition for an unpublished poem of not more than 60 lines run by **Hippopotamus Press**.

Prizes (1st) £500, (2nd) £200, (3rd) £100.

OWG/COLA Awards for Excellence

Outdoor Writers' Guild, PO Box 520, Bamber Bridge, Preston, Lancashire PR5 8LF
☎01772 696732   Fax 01772 696732
Contact *Terry Marsh*

ESTABLISHED 1980. Annual award by the **Outdoor Writers' Guild** and the Camping & Outdoor Leisure Association to raise the standard of outdoor writing, journalism and broadcasting. Winning categories include best guidebook, best outdoor book, best feature, best photojournalism, best technical report. Open to OWG members only. Final entry date March.

Prize (total) £1250.

Catherine Pakenham Award

The Sunday Telegraph, 1 Canada Square, Canary Wharf, London E14 5DT
☎0171 538 6259   Fax 0171 513 2512
Contact *Lucy Goodwin*

ESTABLISHED in 1970, the award is designed to ecourage women journalists as they embark on their careers. Open to women aged 18–25 who have had at least one piece of work published. Previous winners: Elizabeth Brooks, Esther Oxford, Polly Toynbee.

Award £1000 and a writing commission with one of the Telegraph publications; three runner-up prizes of £200 each.

The Parker Romantic Novel of the Year

The Old Bakehouse, 36 Eastgate, Hallaton, Market Harborough, Leicester LE16 8UB
☎01858 555602
Contact *Award Organiser*

ESTABLISHED 1960. Formerly known as the Romantic Novelists' Association Major Award. Sponsorship for the 2000 award is by Parker Pen. Annual award for the best romantic novel of the year, open to non-members as well as members of the **Romantic Novelists' Association**. Novels must be published between specified dates which vary year to year. Authors must be based in the UK. 1999 winner: Clare Chambers *Learning to Swim*. Contact the Organiser for entry form.

Award £5000.

The PAWS (Public Awareness of Science) Midas Prize

The PAWS Office, OMNI Communications, Osborne House, 111 Bartholomew Road, London NW5 2BJ
☎0171 267 2555/voice mail: 0171 428 0961
Fax 0171 482 2394

Contact *Barrie Whatley, Andrew Millington*

ESTABLISHED 1998. Annual prize awarded to the writer and producer of the best television drama, first transmitted in the year up to the end of October, that bears in a significant way on science or engineering. The drama may be a single play or an episode of a series, serial or soap. It need not necessarily be centred on a science or engineering theme, although clearly it can be. The context and quality of the drama and the audience size all weigh alongside the science in making the Award. To enter a programme or suggest that a programme should be entered, contact the PAWS office above. 1998 winner: episode of *McCallum*.

Prize £5000.

Peer Poetry Competition

26(wh) Arlington House, Bath Street, Bath, Somerset BA1 1QN
☎01225 445298

Contact *Paul Amphlett*

Winners are chosen by poets and subscribers to *Peer Poetry* magazine. £10 paid for all qualifying groups of several poems; *Peer Poetry* prints all qualifying entries. 'No size limits, eclectic range, for 35+ poets.' No entry form required. No entry fee for existing subscribers. New submissions: £4.50 for a complete group of poems comprising approximately 200 lines, 1000 words, presented double-column, single sides, name and address on top line of reverse. Closing dates: end April/October. Two s.a.e.s, A5 size, required. Articles and letters welcome. Magazine subscription £12 for 2 issues, incl. p&p (UK), single issue £7. Please enclose list of poems.

PEN Awards

See **Macmillan Silver PEN Award**; **The Stern Silver PEN Non-Fiction Award**

Peterloo Poets Open Poetry Competition

The Old Chapel, Sand Lane, Calstock, Cornwall PL18 9QU
☎01822 833473

Contact *Lynn Chambers*

ESTABLISHED 1986. Annual competition for unpublished English language poems of not more than 40 lines. Final entry date 2 March. Previous winners: John Watts, David Craig, Rodney Pybus, Debjani Chatterjee, Donald Atkinson, Romesh Gunesekera, Shafi Ahmed, Anna Crowe, Carol Ann Duffy, Mimi Khalvati, John Lyons, M. R. Peacocke, Carol Shergold, David Simon, Maureen Wilkinson, Chris Woods.

Prize £3000 (1st); plus 10 prizes of £50.

Poetry Business Competition

The Studio, Byram Arcade, Westgate, Huddersfield, West Yorkshire HD1 1ND
☎01484 434840   Fax 01484 426566

Contact *The Competition Administrator*

ESTABLISHED 1986. Annual award which aims to discover and publish new writers. Entrants should submit a manuscript of poems. Entry fee: £15. Winners will have their work published by the **Poetry Business** under the Smith/Doorstop imprint. Final entry date: end of October. Previous winners include: Pauline Stainer, Michael Laskey, Mimi Khalvati, David Morley, Julia Casterton, Liz Cashdan, Moniza Alvi, Selima Hill. Send s.a.e. for full details.

Prize Publication of full collection; runners-up have pamphlets; 20 complimentary copies. Also cash prize (£1000) to be shared equally between all winners.

Poetry Life Poetry Competition

1 Blue Ball Corner, Water Lane, Winchester, Hampshire   SO23   0ER
Email: abishop@virgin.net
Website: freespace.virgin.net/poetry.life/

Contact *Adrian Bishop*

ESTABLISHED 1993. Open competition for original poems in any style which have not been published in a book. Maximum length of 80 lines. Entry fee of £3 per poem. Send s.a.e. for details.

Prize £500 (1st); £100 (2nd); £50 each (3rd & 4th).

The Poetry Society's National Poetry Competition

See **National Poetry Competition**

Peter Pook Humorous Novel Competition

See **Emissary Publishing** under **UK Publishers**

The Portico Prize

The Portico Library, 57 Mosley Street, Manchester M2 3HY
☎0161 236 6785   Fax -161 236 6803
Contact *Miss Emma Marigliano*

ESTABLISHED 1985. Administered by the Portico Library in Manchester. Biennial award (odd-numbered years) for a work of fiction or non-fiction published between the two closing dates. Set wholly or mainly in the North-West of England, including Cumbria and the High Peak District of Derbyshire. Previous winners include: John Stalker *Stalker*; Alan Hankinson *Coleridge Walks the Fells*; Jenny Uglow *Elizabeth Gaskell: A Habit of Stories*.
Prize £2500.

The Dennis Potter Television Play of the Year Award

Room 6022, BBC TV Centre, Wood Lane, London W12 7RJ
☎0181 225 9513

ESTABLISHED 1994 in memory of the late television playwright to 'bring out courageous and imaginative voices'. Annual award for writers who have not had single plays produced on television. Nominees are put forward by independent and BBC producers. 1998 winner: Nick Stafford *Pity*.
Prize A production commission for a 30-minute drama.

Premio Langhe Ceretto – Per La Cultura Del Cibo

Biblioteca Civica 'G. Ferrero', Via Paruzza 1, 12051 Alba Italy
☎00 39 173 290092   Fax 00 39 173 362075
Contact *Gianfranco Maggi*

ESTABLISHED 1991. Annual award, founded by the wine company F. Lli Ceretto, for published works dealing with historical, scientific, dietological, gastronomical or sociological aspects of food and wine. Previous winners: E. Gowers, A. Kanafani-Zahar, J. Bottero, S. L. Kaplan.

The Premio Valle Inclán

See **The Translators Association Awards**

The Mathew Prichard Award for Short Story Writing

95 Celyn Avenue, Lakeside, Cardiff CF2 6EL
Competition Secretary *Mrs Betty Persen*
Organiser *Philip Beynon*

ESTABLISHED 1996 to provide sponsorship and promote Wales and its writers. Competition open to all writers in English; the final entry date is 1 March each year.
Prizes (1st) £1000; (2 runners-up) £250 each.

Pro Dogs Open Creative Writing & Photographic Competition

Pro Dogs National Charity, 4 New Road, Ditton, Kent ME20 6AD

Open competition for unpublished poems, stories or photographs on any theme. Results are published in *Argos*, the journal of Pro Dogs National Charity. Closing date: 1 October 1999. Entry forms available from the address above.
Prizes (in each section) £200 (1st); £150 (2nd); £75 (3rd).

Pulitzer Prizes

The Pulitzer Prize Board, 709 Journalism, Columbia University, New York NY 10027, USA
☎001 212 854 3841/2
Website: www.pulitzer.org

Awards for journalism in US newspapers, and for published literature, drama and music by American nationals. Deadlines: 1 February (journalism); 1 March (music); 1 March (drama); 1 July for books published between 1 Jan–30 June, and 1 Nov for books published between 1 July–31 Dec (literature). Previous winners include: Steven Millhauser *Martin Dressler: The Tale of an American Dreamer*; Frank McCourt *Angela's Ashes*; Lisel Mueller *Alive Together: New and Selected Poems*; Richard Kluger *Ashes to Ashes: America's Hundred-Year Cigarette War, the Public Health and the Unabashed Triumph of Philip Morris*.

Puppy Lifeline Short Story and Poetry Competition

Farplace, Sidehead, Westgate, Co Durham DL13 1LE
☎01388 517397   Fax 01388 517044
Email: farplace@msn.com
Contact *Jan Edwards, National Fundraising Officer*

ESTABLISHED 1997 to help raise funds for Puppy Lifeline's rescue and rehoming work. Annual competition for writers and poets. Closing date for entries is 31 July each year. Submissions can be any length up to 5000 words; entry fee of £3 per short story and £2 per poem, payable to Puppy Lifeline. Send s.a.e. for details.
Prizes £100 (story); £60 (poem) plus runners-up prizes.

Real Writers
PO Box 170, Chesterfield, Derbyshire S40 1FE
Email: realwrtrs@aol.com
Website: www.turtledesign.com/RealWriters/
ESTABLISHED 1994. Annual short story competition. Entry fee: £5. Optional critiques. Entry forms, rules and further details available from the address above; send s.a.e. for details.
Prize (1st) £1000.

Trevor Reese Memorial Prize
Institute of Commonwealth Studies,
University of London, 28 Russell Square,
London WC1B 5DS
☎0171 862 8844   Fax 0171 255 2160
Contact *Seminar and Conference Secretary*
ESTABLISHED 1979 with the proceeds of contributions to a memorial fund to Dr Trevor Reese, Reader in Commonwealth Studies at the Institute and a distinguished scholar of imperial history (d.1976). Biennial award (next award 2000) for a scholarly work, usually by a single author, in the field of Imperial and Commonwealth History published in the preceding two academic years. Final entry date: March 2000. All correspondence relating to the prize should be marked 'Trevor Reese Memorial Prize'.
Prize £1000.

Regional Press Awards
Press Gazette, Quantum House, 19 Scarbrook Road, Croydon, Surrey CR9 1LX
☎0181 565 4200   Fax 0181 565 4395

Comprehensive range of journalist and newspaper awards for the regional press. Five newspapers of the year, by circulation and frequency, and a full list of journalism categories. Open to all regional journalists, whether freelance or staff. July event. Run by the *Press Gazette*.

Renault UK Journalist of the Year Award
Guild of Motoring Writers, 30 The Cravens, Smallfield, Surrey RH6 9QS
☎01342 843294   Fax 01342 844093
Contact *Sharon Scott-Fairweather*
Originally the Pierre Dreyfus Award and ESTABLISHED 1977. Awarded annually by Renault UK Ltd in honour of Pierre Dreyfus, president director general of Renault 1955–75, to the member of the **Guild of Motoring Writers** who is judged to have made the most outstanding journalistic effort during the year.
Prize (1st) £1500, plus trophy.

The Rhône-Poulenc Prizes for Science Books
COPUS, c/o The Royal Society, 6 Carlton House Terrace, London SW1Y 5AG
☎0171 451 2579/2580   Fax 0171 451 2693
Contact *Imelda Topping*
ESTABLISHED 1988 by COPUS (Committee on the Public Understanding of Science) with the Science Museum. Sponsored by Rhône-Poulenc. Annual awards for popular non-fiction science and technology books judged to contribute most to people's understanding of science. Books must have first been written in the English language and must have been published in the UK in the calendar year 1 January - 31 December 1999. The prizes, totalling £32,000, are divided between two categories: the Rhône-Poulenc Prize awarded for a book for general readership, and the Junior Prize for books written primarily for young people. Final entry date: January. 1998 winners: Jared Diamond *Guns, Germs and Steel*; David Lambert *The Kingfisher Book of Oceans* (Junior Prize).
Prizes Rhône-Poulenc Prize £10,000; Junior Prize £10,000; £1000 for every shortlisted author.

Rhyme International Prize
c/o Orbis Magazine, 27 Valley View, Primrose, Jarrow, Tyne & Wear NE32 5QT
☎0191 4897055   Fax 0191 4301297
Contact *Mike Shields*
Email: Mshields12@aol.com *or*
    MikeShields@compuserve.com
ESTABLISHED 1982. Annual competition aimed at promoting rhyming poetry. Minimum entry fee £5 (£2.50 per poem). Entries may fall into two categories: rhymed poems of less than 50 lines; or formal: sonnet, villanelle, etc. Final entry date: end September.
Prize (total) £1500.

John Llewellyn Rhys Prize
See **The Mail on Sunday/John Llewellyn Rhys Prize**

Rio Tinto David Watt Memorial Prize
Rio Tinto plc, 6 St James's Square, London SW1Y 4LD
☎0171 930 2399   Fax 0171 930 3249
Contact *The Administrator*
INITIATED in 1987 to commemorate the life and work of David Watt. Annual award, open to writers currently engaged in writing for English

language newspapers and journals, on international and political affairs. The winners are judged as having made 'outstanding contributions towards the greater understanding and promotion of national and international political issues'. Entries must have been published during the year preceding the award. Final entry date 31 March. The 1998 winner was Simon Jenkins for his article 'Missionary Diplomacy', published in *The Times*.

Prize £5000.

Romantic Novelists' Association Major Award
See **The Parker Romantic Novel of the Year**

Rooney Prize for Irish Literature
Rooney Prize, Strathin, Templecarrig, Delgany, Co. Wicklow, Republic of Ireland
☎00 353 1 287 4769   Fax 00 353 1 287 2595
Contact *Jim Sherwin, Grainne Davis*

ESTABLISHED 1976. Annual award to encourage young Irish writing to develop and continue. Authors must be Irish, under 40 and published. A non-competitive award with no application procedure.

Prize IR£5000.

Royal Economic Society Prize
c/o University of York, York YO10 5DD
☎01904 433575   Fax 01904 433575
Contact *Prof. Mike Wickens*

Annual award for the best article published in *The Economic Journal*. Open to members of the Royal Economic Society only. Next award 2000. Final entry date: December 1999. Previous winners: Drs O. P. Attanasio & Guglielmo Weber; Prof. M. H. Pesaran; Prof. J. Pemberton.

Prize £3000.

Royal Society of Literature Awards
See **Winifred Holtby Memorial Prize** and **W. H. Heinemann Prize**

Runciman Award
Anglo-Hellenic League, c/o The Hellenic Centre, 16–18 Paddington Street, London W1M 4AS
☎0171 486 9410
Contact *The Administrator*

ESTABLISHED 1985. Annual award, founded by the Anglo-Hellenic League to promote Anglo-Greek understanding and friendship, for a work

wholly or mainly about some aspect of Greece or the Hellenic scene, which has been published in its first English edition in the UK during the previous year and listed in Whitaker's Books in Print. Named after Sir Steven Runciman, former chairman of the Anglo-Hellenic League. The Award may be given for a work of fiction, drama or non-fiction; concerned academically or non-academically with the history of any period; biography or autobiography, the arts, archaeology; a guide book or a translation from the Greek of any period. Final entry date in February; award presented in May. Previous winners include: *The Empire of Manuel I Kommenos 1143–1180* Paul Magdalino; *Crete: the Battle and the Resistance* Antony Beevor; *A Concise History of Greece* Richard Clogg; *An Introduction to Modern Greek Literature* Roderick Beaton; *The Diffusion of Classical Art in Antiquity* Sir John Boardman; *Siren Feasts* Andrew Dalby; *Painting the Soul: Icons, Death Masks and Shrouds* Robin Cormack.

Awards of at least £2000.

Sagittarius Prize
Society of Authors, 84 Drayton Gardens, London SW10 9SB
☎0171 373 6642   Fax 0171 373 5768

ESTABLISHED 1990. For first published novel by an author over the age of 60. Final entry date: mid-December. Full details available from the **Society of Authors**. 1998 winner: A. Sivanandan *When Memory Dies*.

Prize £2000.

The Saltire Literary Awards
Saltire Society, 9 Fountain Close, 22 High Street, Edinburgh EH1 1TF
☎0131 556 1836   Fax 0131 557 1675
Administrator *Kathleen Munro*

ESTABLISHED 1982. Annual awards, one for Book of the Year, the other for Best First Book by an author publishing for the first time. Open to any author of Scottish descent or living in Scotland, or to anyone who has written a book which deals with either the work and life of a Scot or with a Scottish problem, event or situation. Nominations are invited from editors of leading newspapers, magazines and periodicals. Previous winners: The Scotsman/Saltire Scottish Book of the Year: *The Sopranos* Alan Warner; The Post Office/Saltire Best First Book: *The Pied Piper's Poison* Christopher Wallace and *Two Clocks Ticking* Dennis O'Donnell.

Prizes £5000 (Scottish Book); £1500 (First Book).

Sandburg-Livesay Anthology Contest

Mekler & Deahl, Publishers, 237 Prospect Street South, Hamilton, Ontario, Canada L8M 2Z6
☎001 905 312 1779   Fax 001 905 312 8285
Email: meklerdeahl@globalserve.net
Contact *James Deahl, Gilda Mekler*

FOUNDED 1996. Annual award named after the poets Carl Sandburg and Dorothy Livesay to honour their achievement as populist poets. Up to ten poems may be entered for a fee of £5. A copy of the rules is available from the above address. Final entry date: 31 October. 1998 winners: Peggy Poole (UK), Gillian Harding-Russell (Canada).

Prizes (1st) US$200; (2nd) US$100; (3rd) US$50; anthology publication for the winners and all other worthy entries.

Aileen and Albert Sanders Memorial Trophy

13 Milton Crescent, Leicester LE4 0PA
Contact *Ivan Sanders*

Annual poetry competition. Entry fees: £5 for up to two poems, £10 for up to five (maximum per competitor). Rules and entry forms available from the address above; enclose s.a.e. 1999 winner: K. V. Skene.

Prizes 1st £500 plus trophy and certificate; nine runners-up prizes and certificates.

Schlegel–Tieck Prize
See **The Translators Association Awards**

Scottish Arts Council Book Awards

Scottish Arts Council, 12 Manor Place, Edinburgh EH3 7DD
☎0131 226 6051   Fax 0131 476 7050
Email: gavin.wallace.sac@artsfb.org.uk
Literature Officer *Gavin Wallace*

A number of awards are given biannually (spring and autumn) to authors of published books in recognition of high standards in fiction or non-fiction from new or established writers. Authors should be Scottish or resident in Scotland, or books must be of Scottish interest. Applications from publishers only.

Award £1000 each.

Scottish Arts Council Children's Book Awards

Scottish Arts Council, 12 Manor Place, Edinburgh EH3 7DD
☎0131 226 6051   Fax 0131 476 7050
Email: gavin.wallace.sac@artsfb.org.uk
Literature Officer *Gavin Wallace*

A number of awards are given annually (spring) to authors of published books in recognition of high standards in children's fiction or non-fiction from new or established writers. Awards are made in three categories: picture books for children, books aimed at 6–9 years, and books aimed at 10+ years. Authors should be Scottish or resident in Scotland, or books must be of Scottish interest. Applications from publishers only.

Award £1000 each.

Scottish Book of the Year
See **The Saltire Literary Awards**

Scottish Historical Book of the Year in Memory of Agnes Mure Mackenzie

The Saltire Society, 9 Fountain Close, 22 High Street, Edinburgh EH1 1TF
☎0131 556 1836   Fax 0131 557 1675
Administrator *Kathleen Munro*

ESTABLISHED 1965. Annual award in memory of the late Dr Agnes Mure Mackenzie for a published work of distinguished Scottish historical research of scholarly importance (including intellectual history and the history of science). Editions of texts are not eligible. The 1998 award is open to books published between 1st January 1999 and 31st December 1999. Nominations are invited and should be sent to the Administrator. Previous winner: Stephen Boardman *The Early Stewart Kings, Robert II and Robert III.*

Prize Bound and inscribed copy of the winning publication.

Scottish International Open Poetry Competition

42 Tollerton Drive, Irvine, Ayrshire KA12 0ER
Contact *The Administrator*

ESTABLISHED in 1972 in association with Ayrshire Writers and Artists Society by Henry Mair and patronised by Hugh MacDiarmid. Open to poets worldwide for poems written in English or Scots and which have not been published or broadcast. All entries to be accompanied by an s.a.e. or IRCs (for international entries). Contact the administrator for further details.

Prizes 1st £100 and The MacDiarmid Trophy; Scottish section, The Clement Wilson Trophy; International Trophy.

The Scottish Writer of the Year Award

c/o Scottish Book Trust, The Scottish Book Centre, 137 Dundee Street, Edinburgh EH11 1BG
☎0131 229 3663   Fax 0131 228 4293
Email: scottish.book.trust@dial.pipex.com
Website: www.webpost.net/bts
Contact *Kathryn Ross*
ESTABLISHED 1987. Awarded for the best substantial work of an imaginative nature, including TV and radio scripts and writing for children (for 8–16 years), first published, performed, filmed or transmitted between 1st August and 31st July. Writers born in Scotland, or who have Scottish parents, or who have been resident in Scotland for a considerable period, or who take Scotland as their inspiration are all eligible. Submissions accepted in English, Scots or Gaelic. Recent winners: Janice Galloway, Edwin Morgan and James Kelman.
Prize £10,000, plus £1,000 to each of the other four shortlisted writers.

SCSE Book Prizes

School of Education Studies, University of Reading, Bulmershe Court, Reading, Berkshire RG6 1HY
☎01189 318861   Fax 01189 318863
Contact *Professor P. Croll*
Annual awards given by the Standing Conference on Studies in Education for the best book on education published during the preceding year and for the best book by a new author. Nomination by members of the Standing Conference and publishers.
Prizes £1000 and £500.

The Seebohm Trophy – Age Concern Book of the Year

1268 London Road, London SW16 4ER
☎0181 765 7200/0181 765 7456
Contact *Vinnette Marshall, Jane Marsh*
ESTABLISHED 1995. Annual award in memory of the late Lord Seebohm, former President of Age Concern England. Awarded to the author and publisher of a non-fiction title published in the previous calendar year which, in the opinion of the judges, is most successful in promoting the well-being and understanding of older people. Final entry by the end of March for presentation in October. 1998 winner: *Dementia Reconsidered* Tom Kitwood.
Prize £1000 (author); Trophy (publisher), for one year.

SEEDS International Poetry Contest

412–701 King Street West, Toronto, Ontario Canada M5V 2W7
Email: writers@pathcom.com
Website: www.pathcom.com/~writers
International competition for poems which are optimistic expressions of life, society and nature (the theme of *SEEDS* magazine). No electronic submissions. Entry fee: US$15. Deadlines at the end of April and October.
Prizes 1st $100 and publication in *SEEDS* magazine and Website.

Bernard Shaw Translation Prize

See **The Translators Association Awards**

Signal Poetry for Children Award

Thimble Press, Lockwood, Station Road, South Woodchester, Stroud, Gloucestershire GL5 5EQ
☎01453 873716/872208   Fax 01453 878599
Contact *Nancy Chambers*
This award is given annually for particular excellence in one of the following areas: single-poet collections published for children; poetry anthologies published for children; the body of work of a contemporary poet; critical or educational activity promoting poetry for children. All books for children published in Britain are eligible regardless of the original country of publication. Unpublished work is not eligible. Previous winners include: Philip Gross *The All-Nite Café*; Helen Dunmore *Secrets*.
Award Substantial article-citation in each May issue of the journal *Signal*; £100 plus certificate designed by Michael Harvey.

André Simon Memorial Fund Book Awards

5 Sion Hill Place, Bath BA1 5SJ
☎01225 336305   Fax 01225 421862
Contact *Tessa Hayward*
ESTABLISHED 1978. Three awards given annually for the best book on drink, best on food and special commendation in either. Previous winners: Claudia Roden *The Book of Jewish Food*; Clive Coats *Côte d'Or*; Maria Kaneva-Johnson *The Melting Pot – Balkan Food and Cookery*; Janet Mendel *Traditional Spanish Cooking*; Sophie D. Coe and Michael D. Coe *The True History of Chocolate* (special commendation).
Awards £2000 (best books); £1000 (special commendation); £200 to shortlisted books.

WH Smith Annual Literary Award

WH Smith Group PLC, Nations House, 103
Wigmore Street, London W1H 0WH
☎0171 409 3222 Fax 0171 629 3600
Contact *Corporate Affairs*

FOUNDED 1959. Annual prize awarded to a
UK, Republic of Ireland or Commonwealth
citizen for the most oustanding contribution to
English literature, published in English in the
UK in the preceding year. Writers cannot sub-
mit work themselves. 1999 winner: Beryl
Bainbridge *Master Georgie*. Four previous win-
ners have gone on to win the Nobel Prize for
Literature – Derek Walcott, Nadine Gordimer,
Patrick White and Seamus Heaney.
Prize £10,000.

WH Smith's Thumping Good Read Award

WH Smith PLC, Greenbridge Road,
Swindon, Wiltshire SN3 3LD
☎01793 616161 Fax 01793 562590
Contact *Catherine Hickson*

ESTABLISHED 1992 to promote new writers of
popular fiction. Books must have been published
in the 12 months preceding the award. Submissions, made by publishers, are judged by a
panel of customers to be the most un-put-down-
able from a shortlist of six. Final entry date:
February each year. 1998 winner: Douglas
Kennedy *The Big Picture*.
Award £5000.

The Society for Theatre Research Annual Theatre Book Prize

c/o The Theatre Museum, 1e Tavistock
Street, London WC2E 7PA
☎01304 379179
Email: e.cottis@btinternet.com
Website: www.unl.ac.uk/str

ESTABLISHED 1997. Annual award for books, in
English, of original research into any aspect of
the history and technique of the British Theatre.
Not restricted to authors of British nationality
nor books solely from British publishers. No
submissions; independent judges rely on their
personal observations during the year. 1998
winner: Peter Brook *The Threads of Time: An
Autobiography*.
Award £400.

Sony Radio Awards

Alan Zafer & Associates, 47–48 Chagford
Street, London NW1 6EB
☎0171 723 0106 Fax 0171 724 6163
Email: zafer@compuserve.com
Contact *Alan Zafer*

ESTABLISHED 1981 by the **Society of Authors**.
Sponsored by Sony and presented in association
with the Radio Academy. Annual awards to
recognise excellence in radio broadcasting.
Entries must have been broadcast in the UK
between 1 January and 31 December in the year
preceding the award. The categories for the
awards are reviewed each year.

Southern Arts Literature Prize

Southern Arts, 13 St Clement Street,
Winchester, Hampshire SO23 9DQ
☎01962 855099 Fax 01962 861186
Contact *Literature Officer*

ESTABLISHED 1991, this prize is awarded annually
to an author living in the **Southern Arts** region
for the most promising work of prose or poetry
published during the year. The 1999 prize will
be awarded for fiction. Previous winner: James
Knowlson *Damned to Fame* (biography).
Prize £1000, plus a craft commission to the
value of £600.

Southport Writers' Circle Poetry Competition

32 Dover Road, Southport, Merseyside
PR8 4TB
Contact *Mrs Hilary Tinsley*

For previously unpublished work. Entry fee: £2
first poem, plus £1 for each subsequent entry.
Open category (any subject any form) and
humorous category; maximum 40 lines. Closing
date: end April. Poems must be entered under a
pseudonym, accompanied by a sealed envelope
marked with the pseudonym and title of poem,
containing s.a.e. Entries must be typed on A4
paper and be accompanied by the appropriate fee
payable to Southport Writers' Circle. No application form is required. Envelopes should be
marked 'Poetry Competition'. Postal enquiries
only. No calls.
Prizes (1st) £150; (2nd) £75; five runners-
up of £10 in each category.

Springbeach Press Annual Anthology Competition

Springbeach Press, 11 Vernon Close,
Eastbourne, East Sussex BN23 6AN
Email: sian@springbeachpress.freeserve.co.uk
Contact *S. Ross*

ESTABLISHED 1998. Annual competition for a
collection of eight unpublished poems, each
under 60 lines, any style or subject. Entry fee:

£5. Final entry date: last day of March. Entry forms essential; send s.a.e. for full details.

Prize £200, plus 50 copies of the prizewinner's published collection.

Ian St James Awards

c/o The New Writers' Club, PO Box 60, Cranbrook, Kent TN17 2ZR
☎01580 212626   Fax 01580 212041
ESTABLISHED 1989. Administered by the New Writers' Club. Presented annually to approximately 10 writers of short stories. These awards are 'an opportunity for talented and as yet unpublished writers to achieve recognition'. Ian St James is a successful novelist who hopes to attract both literary and commercial fiction from aspiring writers. Winning entries are published in a paperback anthology, the most recent, *Pulse Fiction*. The Ian St James Awards are open to international writers who have not had a novel or novella previously published. Final entry date: 30 April each year. Previous award winners who have gone on to novel publication include: Kate Atkinson, Louise Doughty, Alan Dunn, Sylvia Baker, Carrie Worrall, Francesca Clementis, Julia Darling, Mike McCormack, Hwee Hwee Tan, Tobias Hill, Lorna Fergusson, Elizabeth Harris, Anna McGrail. Entry forms available from around October from above address.

Award Top prize: £2000 plus runners-up cash prizes. Shortlisted stories are published throughout the year in *The New Writer* magazine.

Stand Magazine Poetry Competition

Stand Magazine, 179 Wingrove Road, Newcastle upon Tyne NE4 9DA
☎0191 273 3280
Contact *The Administrator*
Biennial award for poems written in English and not yet published, broadcast or under consideration elsewhere. Next award 2000. Final entry date: 30 June 2000. Send s.a.e. for entry form.

Prize (total) £2500.

Stand Magazine Short Story Competition

Stand Magazine, 179 Wingrove Road, Newcastle upon Tyne NE4 9DA
☎0191 273 3280
Contact *The Administrator*
Biennial award for short stories written in English and not yet published, broadcast or under consideration elsewhere. Next award

2001. Closing date: 30 June 2001. Send s.a.e. for entry form.

Prize (total) £2500.

Staple Open Poetry Competition

Tor Cottage, 81 Cavendish Road, Matlock, Derbyshire DE4 3HD
☎01629 582764
Contact *Donald Measham*
Annual open competition run by *Staple* magazine. Final entry date: 31 December.

Prizes (1st) £500 and £50 of Carcanet books of poet's choice; (2nd) £150 and £25 of Carcanet books; (3rd) £50 and 50 prizes of £10 plus publication of all winning poems in *Staple* magazine.

The Stern Silver PEN Non-Fiction Award

English Centre of International PEN, 7 Dilke Street, London SW3 4JE
☎0171 352 6303   Fax 0171 351 0220
ESTABLISHED 1986 and sponsored, from 1997, by the family of James Stern in memory of their father. An annual award for an outstanding work of non-fiction written in English and published in England in the year preceding the prize. Nominations by the PEN Executive Committee only. Please do not submit books. 1998 winner: Ian Ousby *The Occupation of France*.

Prize £1000, plus silver pen.

Sunday Times Award for Excellence in Writing

The Sunday Times, 1 Pennington Street, London E1 9XW
☎0171 782 5770   Fax 0171 782 5798
ESTABLISHED 1987. Annual award to fiction and non-fiction writers. The panel consists of *Sunday Times* journalists, publishers and other figures from the book world. Previous winners: Anthony Burgess, Seamus Heaney, Stephen Hawking, Ruth Rendell, Muriel Spark, William Trevor, Martin Amis, Ted Hughes, Harold Pinter. No applications; prize at the discretion of the Literary Editor.

Sunday Times Award for Small Publishers

Independent Publishers Guild, 4 Middle Street, Great Gransden, Sandy, Bedfordshire SG19 3AD
☎01767 677753   Fax 01767 677069
Email: sheila@ipg.uk.com
Contact *Sheila Bounford*

ESTABLISHED 1988, the first winner was **Fourth Estate**. Open to any publisher producing between five and forty titles a year, which must primarily be original titles, not reprints. Entrants are invited to submit their catalogues for the last twelve months, together with two representative titles. Previous winners: **Nick Hern Books**; **Tarquin Publications**; **Ellipsis**; **Bradt Publications**.

Sunday Times Young Writer of the Year Award

The Society of Authors, 84 Drayton Gardens, London SW10 9SB
☎0171 373 6642   Fax 0171 373 5768
Contact *Awards Secretary*

ESTABLISHED 1991. Annual award given on the strength of the promise shown by a full-length published work of fiction, non-fiction, poetry or drama. Entrants must be British citizens, resident in Britain and under the age of 35 at the closing date of 31 December. The work must be by one author, in the English language, and published in Britain during the 12 months prior to the closing date. Full details available from the **Society of Authors**. Previous winners: Patrick French *Liberty or Death*; Francis Spufford *I May Be Some Time*; Katherine Pierpoint *Truffle Beds*; Andrew Cowan *Pig*.
Prize £5000.

Tabla Poetry Competition

Department of English, University of Britsol, 3–5 Woodland Road, Bristol BS8 1TB
Fax 0117 9288860
Email: stephen.james@bristol.ac.uk
Contact *Stephen James*

ESTABLISHED 1991. Annual award for poems of any length which have not been published or broadcast. Minimum age of entrants must be 16. Final entry date: end of August. No poems by email, please. Winning and other selected entries are published, alongside leading names, in the annual *Tabla Book of New Verse*. Previous winners: Chris Beckett, Paul F. Cowlan.
Prizes 1st £200; 3 runners–up, £100 each.

The Talkies

15 Prescott Place, London SW4 6BS
☎0171 819 1116   Fax 0171 819 1122/33
Email: info@squareonepublishing.co.uk
Contact *Peter Dean, Sean King, Samantha Warren*

Annual award ESTABLISHED in 1995 by *Talking Business* magazine to recognise the best in spoken word publishing, production, design and retailing. There are 20 awards with the 'Talkie of the Year' being picked from the winners of all the categories. Contact *Talking Business* for entry form. Final entry date: late July. Previous Talkie of the Year winners: *Alan Bennett Diaries*; *This Sceptred Isle*; *Spoonface Steinberg*; *Ambush at Fort Bragg*.
Prizes Framed certificate for all winners, plus trophy for Best Reader and Talkie of the Year.

Reginald Taylor and Lord Fletcher Essay Prize

Journal of the British Archaeological Association, Institute of Archaelogy, 36 Beaumont Street, Oxford OX1 2PG
Contact *Dr Martin Henig*

A biennial prize, in memory of the late E. Reginald Taylor and of Lord Fletcher, for the best unpublished essay, not exceeding 7500 words, on a subject of archaeological, art history or antiquarian interest within the period from the Roman era to AD 1830. The essay should show *original* research on its chosen subject, and the author will be invited to read the essay before the Association. The prize is now included in the British Archaeological Awards scheme and the presentation will be made along with the other awards in November 2000. The essay may be published in the journal of the Association if approved by the Editorial Committee. Closing date for entries is 1 June 2000. All enquiries by post please. No phone calls. Send s.a.e. for details.
Prize £300 and a medal.

The Teixeira Gomes Prize

See **The Translators Association Awards**

David Thomas Prize

See entry under **Bursaries, Fellowships and Grants**

Anne Tibble Poetry Competition

See **Words & Pictures Literary & Photographic Competition**

The Times Educational Supplement Book Awards

Times Educational Supplement, Admiral House, 66–68 East Smithfield, London E1 9XY
☎0171 782 3000   Fax 0171 782 3200
Email: friday@tes.co.uk
Website: www.tes.co.uk
Contact *Awards Administrator*

ESTABLISHED 1973. Annual awards made for the best non-fiction books used in schools. The books must have been published in Britain. Previous winners: Junior Information Book Award: *What's the Big Idea? Time and the Universe* Mary and John Gribbin; Senior Information Book Award: *Big Bang* Heather Cooper and Nigel Henbest. The subject for the schoolbook award changes each year. The subject for 1999 is Music. 1998 Mathematics Award winners: Primary Mathematics Schoolbook Award: *Learning Mathematics in the Nursery: Desirable Approaches* The Early Childhood Mathematics Group; Secondary Mathematics Schoolbook Award: *Nelson Secondary Maths Extension Book* Jim Noonan, Paula Barker, Terry Bevis, Gay Cain, Brian Martin, Christine Mitchell, Robert Powell, Gwen Wood.

The Tir Na N-Og Award

Cyngor Llyfrau Cymru (Welsh Books Council), Castell Brychan, Aberystwyth, Dyfed SY23 2JB
☎01970 624151   Fax 01970 625385
Email: castellbrychan@cllc.org.uk
Website: www.wbc.org.uk

An annual award given to the best original book published for children in the year prior to the announcement. There are three categories: Best Welsh Fiction; Best Welsh Non-fiction; Best English Book with an authentic Welsh background.

Awards £1000 (each category).

TLS/Blackwells Poetry Competition

Times Literary Supplement, Admiral House, 66–68 East Smithfield, London E1 9XY
☎0171 782 3000

Contact *Mick Imlah (Poetry Editor, TLS)*

ESTABLISHED 1997. Annual open competition. Final entry date: 1 November. 1998 winner: James Lasden.

Prizes £2000; three runners-up £500 each.

Marten Toonder Award

An Chomhairle Ealaíon (The Arts Council), 70 Merrion Square, Dublin 2, Republic of Ireland
☎00 353 1 6180200   Fax 00 353 1 6761302

Music Officer *Maura Eaton*

A triennial award for creative writing. Next award will be offered in Music in 2000. Given to an established writer in recognition of achievement. Open to Irish citizens or residents only.

Award IR£4000.

The Translators Association Awards

The Translators Association, 84 Drayton Gardens, London SW10 9SB
☎0171 373 6642   Fax 0171 373 5768

Contact *Dorothy Wright*

Various awards for translations into English from, for example, Dutch and Flemish (The Vondel Translation Prize), French (Scott Moncrieff Prize), German (Schlegel-Tieck Prize), Italian (The John Florio Prize), Portuguese (The Teixeira Gomes Prize), Spanish (The Premio Velle Inclán), and Swedish (Bernard Shaw Translation Prize). Contact the **Translators Association** for full details.

The Betty Trask Prize

See entry under **Bursaries, Fellowships and Grants**

The Trewithen Poetry Prize

Chy-an-Dour, Trewithen Moor, Stithians, Truro, Cornwall TR3 7DU
Contact *Competition Secretary*

ESTABLISHED 1995 in order to promote poetry with a rural theme. Entry forms available from the address above (enclose s.a.e.). Closing date: 31 October. Entry fee of £3 for first poem, £1.75 for subsequent entries. Previous winners include: Elizabeth Rapp, David Smart, Ann Drysdale, Roger Elkin.

Prizes (total) £800 plus publication in *The Trewithen Chapbook.*

The Tullie House Prize

See **Lakeland Book of the Year Awards**

T. E. Utley Memorial Award

111 Sugden Road, London SW11 5ED
☎0171 228 3900

Contact *The Secretary*

Annual award ESTABLISHED 1988 in memory of the political journalist T. E. Utley. In 1996, two awards were given for unpublished essays by aspiring journalists who were still at school or university.

Prizes £2500 (under 25); £1500 (under 18).

The V. B. Poetry Prize

20 Clifton House, Club Row, London E2 7HB
Fax 0171 729 8358
Email: LOOKLEARN@aol.com

Contact *Nicholas Morgan*

Annual open competition for original single unpublished poems, any style, maximum length 40 lines. Entry fee: £3 for first two poems,

£1.50 for each additional poem. Closing date: 31 March 2000. Send s.a.e. for full details and entry form.

Prize £400 (1st), £100 (2nd), £50 (3rd). Winning poems will be published on the Look and Learn Productions' Website.

Ver Poets Open Competition

Haycroft, 61–63 Chiswell Green Lane, St Albans, Hertfordshire AL2 3AL
☎01727 867005

Contact *May Badman*

Various competitions are organised by **Ver Poets**, the main one being the annual Open for unpublished poems of no more than 30 lines written in English. Entry fee: £2.50 per poem. Entries must be made under a pseudonym, with name and address on form or separate sheet. *Vision On*, the anthology of winning and selected poems, and the adjudicators' report are normally available from mid-June. Final entry date: 30 April. Back numbers of the anthology are available for £2, post-free.

Prizes (1st) £500; (2nd) £300; two runners-up £100.

Vogue Talent Contest

Vogue, Vogue House, Hanover Square, London W1R 0AD
☎0171 499 9080   Fax 0171 408 0559

Contact *Frances Bentley*

ESTABLISHED 1951. Annual award for young writers and journalists (under 25 on 1 January in the year of the contest). Final entry date is in April. Entrants must write three pieces of journalism on given subjects.

Prizes £1000, plus a month's paid work experience with *Vogue*; (2nd) £500.

The Vondel Translation Prize

See **The Translators Association Awards**

Wadsworth Prize for Business History

Business Archives Council, 101 Whitechapel High Street, London E1 7RE
☎0171 247 0024

Chairman *Mrs Lenore Symons*

ESTABLISHED 1978. Annual award for the best book published on British business history. Previous winners: Dr Richard Saville *Bank of Scotland, A History 1695–1995*; Dr T. R. Gourvish and Dr R. Wilson *The British Brewing Industry: A History*.

Prize £500.

Arts Council of Wales Book of the Year Awards

Arts Council of Wales, Museum Place, Cardiff CF1 3NX
☎01222 376500   Fax 01222 221447

Contact *Tony Bianchi*

Annual non-competitive prizes awarded for works of exceptional literary merit written by Welsh authors (by birth or residence), published in Welsh or English during the previous calendar year. There is one major prize in English, the Book of the Year Award, and one major prize in Welsh, Gwobr Llyfr y Flwyddyn. Shortlists of three titles in each language are announced in April; winners announced in May.

Prizes £3000 (each); £1000 to each of four runners-up.

Walford Award

See **The Library Association Walford Award**

The Harri Webb Prize

10 Heol Don, Whitchurch, Cardiff CF4 2AU
☎01222 623359   Fax 01222 529202

Contact *Meic Stephens*

ESTABLISHED 1995. Annual competition to commemorate the Welsh poet, Harri Webb (1920–94), for a single poem in any of the categories in which he wrote: ballad, satire, song, polemic or a first collection of poems. The poems are chosen by three adjudicators; no submissions. 1998 winner: David Hughes.

Prize £100/£200.

The Weidenfeld Translation Prize

European Humanities Research Centre, The Queen's College, Oxford OX1 4AW
☎01865 279183/244701   Fax 01865 790819
Email: david.constantine@queens.ox.ac.uk

Contact *The Fellows' Secretary or David Constantine*

ESTABLISHED in 1996 by publisher Lord Weidenfeld to encourage good translation into English. Annual award to the translator(s) of a work of fiction, poetry or drama written in any living European language. Submissions from publishers only. For further information, contact Dr David Constantine at the Queen's College address above. 1998 winner: Guido Waldman *Silk* by Alessandro Baricco.

Prize £1000.

The Wellcome Trust Prize

Consultation and Education Dept., The Wellcome Trust, 210 Euston Road, London NW1 2BE
☎0171 611 7221   Fax 0171 611 8269
Email: r.birse@wellcome.ac.uk
Website: www.wellcome.ac.uk
Contact *Ruth Birse, Suzanne King*

ESTABLISHED 1997. Biennial award for a book that 'will educate, captivate and inspire the non-specialist lay reader', to be written by a professional life scientist who is unpublished and resident in the UK or Ireland. Contact the Wellcome Trust for rules and guidelines or visit the Website. The winning book will be published by **Weidenfeld & Nicolson**. Previous winner: Dr Guy Brown.
Prize £25,000 (in four instalments, depending on progress of the book)

Wellington Town Council Award

Civic Offices, Tan Bank, Wellington, Telford, Shropshire TF1 1LX
☎01952 222935   Fax 01952 222936
Contacts *Martin Scholes, Derrick Drew*

ESTABLISHED 1995. Annual short story competition to promote the ancient town of Wellington, now part of the Wellington annual literary festival. Open to all for a minimum fee of £2.50; prizes are sponsored so all entry fee monies go to charity. 1998 winners: Jane McNulty (Overall winner); Phil Thane (Best Shropshire Entry); Jill Thomas (Best Story for Children).
Prizes Trophies and money.

Wheatley Medal

See **The Library Association Wheatley Medal**

Whitbread Book Awards

Minster House, 272 Vauxhall Bridge Road, London SW1V 1BA
☎0171 834 5477   Fax 0171 834 8812
Contact *Gillian Cronin*

ESTABLISHED 1971. Publishers are invited to submit books for this annual competition designed for writers who have been resident in Great Britain or the Republic of Ireland for three years or more. The awards are made in two stages. First, nominations are selected in four categories: novel, first novel, biography and poetry. One of these is then voted by a panel of judges as Whitbread Book of the Year. 1998 winners: Justin Cartwright *Leading the Cheers* (novel); Giles Foden *The Last King of Scotland* (first novel); Amanda Foreman *Georgiana, Duchess of Devonshire* (biography); Ted Hughes *Birthday Letters* (poetry and Book of the Year). For the first time in 1996, the Children's Award was separated out to become the Whitbread Children's Book of the Year Award, the 1998 winner being David Almond for *Skellig*.
Awards £21,000 (Book of the Year); £10,000 (Children's Book of the Year); £2000 (adult category winners).

Whitfield Prize

Royal Historical Society, University College London, Gower Street, London WC1E 6BT
☎0171 387 7532   Fax 0171 387 7532
Contact *Executive Secretary*

ESTABLISHED 1977. An annual award for the best new work within a field of British history, published in the UK in the preceding calendar year. The book must be the author's first (solely written) history book and be an original and scholarly work of historical research. Final entry date: end December.
Prize £1000.

John Whiting Award

Arts Council of England, 14 Great Peter Street, London SW1P 3NQ
☎0171 973 6431   Fax 0171 973 6983
Contact *John Johnston*

FOUNDED 1965. Annual award to commemorate the life and work of the playwright John Whiting (*The Devils, A Penny for a Song*). Any writer who has received during the previous two calendar years an award through the **Arts Council's Theatre Writing Schemes** or who has had a première production by a theatre company in receipt of annual subsidy is eligible to apply. Awarded to the writer whose play most nearly satisfies the following criteria: a play in which the writing is of special quality; a play of relevance and importance to contemporary life; a play of potential value to the British theatre. Closing date for entries: 6 January 2000.
Prize £6000.

Alfred and Mary Wilkins International £2000 Prize Memorial Poetry Competition

Birmingham & Midland Institute, 9 Margaret Street, Birmingham B3 3BS
☎0121 236 3591   Fax 0121 212 4577
Administrator *Mr P. A. Fisher*

An annual competition for an unpublished

poem, not exceeding 40 lines, written in English by an author over the age of 15. The poem should not have been entered for any other poetry competition. Nineteen prizes awarded in all.

Prizes (total) £2000.

H. H. Wingate Prize
See **Jewish Quarterly Literary Prizes**

Wolf Web
PO Box 136, Norwich, Norfolk NR3 3LJ
☎01603 440944   Fax 01603 440940
Contact *Tricia Frances*

Sayana Wolf Trust publishes *Wolf Web Quarterly* and runs one poetry competiton annually. Unpublished poems only on the theme of 'wolf'. All profits go to the work of The Sayana Wolf Trust who fund personal development, educational and community projects for British and North American children and adults. For more details, send s.a.e. to the above address.

Prizes reflect the amount of entries received.

Wolfson History Prizes
Wolfson Foundation, 8 Queen Anne Street, London W1M 9LD
☎0171 323 5730   Fax 0171 323 3241
Contact *Executive Secretary*

ESTABLISHED 1972. An award made annually to authors of published historical works, with the object of encouraging historians to communicate with general readers as well as with their professional colleagues. Previous winners include: Fiona MacCarthy *William Morris*; John G. C. Rohl *The Kaiser and His Court: Wilhelm II and the Government of Germany*; Lord Skidelsky *John Maynard Keynes: The Economist as Saviour 1920–1937*.

Prizes vary each year.

Words & Pictures Literary & Photographic Competition
Events Team, Directorate of Environment Services, Northampton Borough Council, Cliftonville House, Bedford Road, Northampton NN4 7NR
☎01604 238791   Fax 01604 238796
Email: events@northampton.gov.uk

A combination of four competitions: National Literary Competition; Short Story Competition for the H. E. Bates Prize; Poetry Competition for the Anne Tibble Prize; and National Photographic Competition. Short stories must not be of more than 2000 words and poems not exceed 20 lines. Entries should be typed on one side of the paper only; entry fee of £4 per competition. Send s.a.e. for full details and entry form.

World Wide Writers Award
Suite 22, Ashley Business Centre, Briggs House, Commercial Road, Poole, Dorset BH14 0JR
☎01202 716043   Fax 01202 740995
Email: writintl@globalnet.co.uk
Website: www.users.globalnet.co.uk/~wrtintl
Contact *John Jenkins, Mary Hogarth*

ESTABLISHED 1997. Quarterly and annual competitions for original, unpublished short stories of between 2500 and 5000 words. Entries are published in *World Wide Writers* magazine. Entry fee of £6. Closing dates: end of January, March, June and September. Previous winners: Sally Zigmond, Shirley Nunes, Judi Moore, Gerald Phillipson, Brian Dixon, L. Morgana Braveraven. *Prize* £3000 and Waterford glass trophy.

The Writers Bureau Poetry and Short Story Competition
The Writers Bureau, Sevendale House, 7 Dale Street, Manchester M1 1JB
☎0161 228 2362
Competition Secretary *Angela Cox*

ESTABLISHED 1994. Annual award. Poems should be no longer than 40 lines and short stories no more than 2000 words. £4 entry fee. Closing date: 31 July 2000.

Prizes in each category: (1st) £500; (2nd) £250; (3rd) £150; (4th) 2 prizes of £50.

Yorkshire Open Poetry Competition
See **Ilkley Literature Festival Poetry Competition**

Yorkshire Post Book of the Year Award
Yorkshire Post, PO Box 168, Wellington Street, Leeds, West Yorkshire LS1 1RF
☎0113 2432701 ext 1704   Fax 0113 2388909
Contact *Margaret Brown*

An annual award for the book (either fiction or non-fiction) which, in the opinion of the judges, is the best work published in the preceding year. Closing date: 31 December. Previous winner: John Ehrman *The Younger Pitt, Vol. III: The Consuming Struggle.*

Prize £1200.

Young Science Writer Award
The Daily Telegraph, 1 Canada Square,
Canary Wharf, London E14 5DT
☎0171 538 6259

Contact *Vicky Hurley*

ESTABLISHED 1987, this award is designed to bridge the gap between science and writing, challenging the writer to come up with a piece in no more than 700 words that is friendly, informative and, above all, understandable. Open to two age groups: 16–19 and 20–28.

Award Winners and runners-up receive cash prizes and have the opportunity to have their pieces published on the science pages of *The Daily Telegraph*. The winner also gets an all expenses paid trip.

Supplementary Income
What writers make from lending and copying

There can be few authors who have yet to hear of Public Lending Right, the state-funded scheme for recompensing authors for books borrowed from public libraries. The number of writers on the PLR register increased again this year to a total of 28,586. With just £5 million available for distribution at a rate of 2.07p. per loan, over a third of recipients got less than £100 and another third, nothing at all. With little hope of a substantially increased grant, the PLR administrators are going slow on various ideas for extending their brief. Little is now heard of rewarding authors of reference books which are consulted but rarely taken out on loan or of applying PLR to talking books or loans from school and university libraries.

By contrast, the **Authors' Licensing & Collecting Society**, which collects and redistributes payments for photocopying, cable retransmission and electronic exploitation, is only too keen to spread its wings. The reason is that the ALCS is not tied down by government. The money it has for distribution – some £19 million last year – increases along with its scope as a collecting agency.

In the early days the ALCS acted as the link with VG Wort, the German collecting agency which paid over fees collected for British authors whose books were borrowed from German libraries. Soon it was the turn of scriptwriters to benefit, this time from cable retransmission throughout Benelux. By the early 1990s, ALCS was receiving money from BBC World Service programmes shown in Europe and from radio transmissions to the Benelux countries and to Ireland.

But the biggest boost to revenue came from licensing deals on photocopying. While income from broadcast sources continues to grow (educational 'off air' recording where schools are licensed to record programmes for later use is now on the list) photocopying money accounts for 65 per cent of ALCS income.

Recent initiatives include a scheme allowing authors 'equitable remuneration' for the rental of videos and other recordings of their work.

Membership of the ALCS is via one of the writers' organisations. If, say, you are a member of the **Society of Authors** you automatically belong to the ALCS and will profit accordingly. On the other hand, it is as well to register items of work as they become available to the public. Not all media promoters hand over fees willingly. Every bit of additional information gathered by the ALCS helps it to become more effective as a policing as well as a collecting agency.

PLR application forms and details can be obtained from: The Registrar, PLR Office, Bayheath House, Prince Regent Street, Stockton on Tees, Cleveland TS18 1DF. ☎*01642 604699*

The Authors' Licensing & Collecting Society (ALCS), is at Marlborough Court, 14–18 Holborn, London EC1N 2LE. ☎*0171 395 0600; email: alcs@alcs.co.uk*

Library Services

Aberdeen Central Library

Rosemount Viaduct, Aberdeen AB25 1GW
☎01224 652500   Fax 01224 641985

Open 9.00 am to 7.00 pm Monday to
Thursday; 9.00 am to 5.00 pm Friday
(Reference & Local Studies: 9.00 am to
8.00 pm); 9.00 am to 5.00 pm Saturday.
Branch library opening times vary.

Open access
General reference and loans. Books, pamphlets, periodicals and newspapers; videos, CDs and cassettes; arts equipment lending service; recording studio; DTP, Internet and WP for public access; photographs of the Aberdeen area; census records, maps; on-line database, patents and standards. The library offers special services to housebound readers. Non-resident administrative fee for audiovisual and lending services.

Armitt Library

Ambleside, Cumbria LA22 9BL
☎015394 31212   Fax 015394 31313

Open 10.00 am to 12.30 pm and 1.30 pm to
4.00 pm Monday to Friday.

Free access (To view original material please give prior notice)
A small but unique reference library of rare books, manuscripts, pictures, antiquarian prints and museum items, mainly about the Lake District. It includes early guidebooks and topographical works, books and papers relating to Ruskin, H. Martineau, Charlotte Mason and others; fine art including work by W. Green, J. B. Pyne, John Harden, K. Schwitters, and Victorian photographs by Herbert Bell; also a major collection of Beatrix Potter's scientific watercolour drawings and microscope studies. Museum and Exhibition open seven days per week from 10.00 am to 5.00 pm. Entry fee.

The Athenaeum, Liverpool

Church Alley, Liverpool L1 3DD
☎0151 709 7770   Fax 0151 709 0418
Email: library @athena.force9.net
Website: www.athena.force9.co.uk

Open 9.00 am to 4.00 pm Monday to Friday

Access To club members; researchers by application only
General collection, with books dating from

the 15th century, now concentrated mainly on local history with a long run of Liverpool directories and guides. *Special collections* Liverpool playbills; William Roscoe; Blanco White; Robert Gladstone; 18th-century plays; 19th-century economic pamphlets; the Norris books; Bibles; Yorkshire and other genealogy. Some original drawings, portraits, topographical material and local maps.

Bank of England Information Centre

Threadneedle Street, London EC2R 8AH
☎0171 601 4715/4846   Fax 0171 601 4356

Open 9.30 am to 5.30 pm Monday to Friday

Access For research workers by prior arrangement only, when material is not readily available elsewhere
50,000 volumes of books and periodicals. 3000 periodicals taken. UK and overseas coverage of banking, finance and economics. *Special collections* Central bank reports; UK 17th–19th-century economic tracts; Government reports in the field of banking.

Barbican Library

Barbican Centre, London EC2Y 8DS
☎0171 638 0569

Open 9.30 am to 5.30 pm Monday,
Wednesday, Thursday, Friday; 9.30 am to
7.30 pm Tuesday; 9.30 am to 12.30 pm
Saturday

Open access
Situated on Level 2 of the Barbican Centre, this is the Corporation of London's largest lending library. Limited study facilities are available. In addition to a large general lending department, the library seeks to reflect the Centre's emphasis on the arts and includes strong collections, including videos, on painting, sculpture, theatre, cinema and ballet, as well as a large music library with books, scores, cassettes and CDs (sound recording loans available at a small charge). Also houses the City's main children's library and has special collections on finance, natural resources, conservation, socialism and the history of London. Service available for housebound readers. A literature events programme is organised by the Library which supplements and provides cross-

arts planning opportunities with the Barbican Centre artistic programme.

Barnsley Public Library

Central Library, Shambles Street, Barnsley, South Yorkshire S70 2JF
☎01226 773930   Fax 01226 773955
Email: Librarian@Barnsley.ac.uk
Website: www.barnsley.ac.uk/sites/library/index.htm
Open Lending & Reference: 9.30 am to 7.00 pm Monday and Wednesday; 9.30 am to 5.30 pm Tuesday and Friday; 9.30 am to 1.00 pm Thursday; 9.30 am to 4.00 pm Saturday. Please telephone to check hours of other departments.

Open access
General library, lending and reference. Archive collection of family history and local firms; local studies: coalmining, local authors, Yorkshire and Barnsley; European Business Information Unit; music library (books, CDs, records, tapes); Open Learning collection with study support; ICT/Internet connections; large junior library. (Specialist departments are closed on certain weekday evenings and Saturday afternoons.)

BBC Written Archives Centre

Peppard Road, Caversham Park, Reading, Berkshire RG4 8TZ
☎0118 946 9280/1/2   Fax 0118 946 1145
Contact *Jacqueline Kavanagh*
Open 9.30 am to 5.30 pm Monday to Friday

Access For reference, by appointment only on Wednesday to Friday.

Holds the written records of the BBC, including internal papers from 1922 to 1974 and published material to date. Charges for certain services.

Bedford Central Library

Harpur Street, Bedford MK40 1PG
☎01234 350931/270102 (Reference Library)
Fax 01234 342163
Open 9.30 am to 7.00 pm Monday and Wednesday; 9.30 am to 5.30 pm Tuesday, Thursday, Friday; 9.30 am to 5.00 pm Saturday

Open access
Lending library with a wide range of stock, including books, music (CDs and cassettes), audio books and videos; reference information library, children's library, local history library, Internet facilities, gallery and coffee bar.

Belfast Public Libraries: Central Library

Royal Avenue, Belfast BT1 1EA
☎01232 243233   Fax 01232 332819
Open 9.30 am to 8.00 pm Monday and Thursday; 9.30 am to 5.30 pm Tuesday, Wednesday, Friday; 9.30 am to 1.00 pm Saturday

Open access To lending libraries; reference libraries by application only

Over 2 million volumes for lending and reference. *Special collections* United Nations/UNESCO depository; complete British Patent Collection; Northern Ireland Newspaper Library; British and Irish government publications. The Central Library offers the following reference departments: General Reference; Irish and Local Studies; Business and Law; Electronic Information Services; Fine Arts, Language and Literature; Music and Recorded Sound. The lending library, supported by twenty branch libraries and two mobile libraries, offers special services to hospitals, prisons and housebound readers.

BFI National Library

21 Stephen Street, London W1P 2LN
☎0171 255 1444   Fax 0171 436 2338
Website: www.bfi.org.uk
Open 10.30 am to 5.30 pm Monday and Friday; 10.30 am to 8.00 pm Tuesday and Thursday; 1.00 pm to 8.00 pm Wednesday; Telephone Enquiry Service operates from 10.00 am to 5.00 pm

Access For reference only; annual and limited day membership available

The world's largest collection of information on film and television including periodicals, cuttings, scripts, related documentation, personal papers. Information available through SIFT (Summary of Information on Film and Television).

Birmingham and Midland Institute

9 Margaret Street, Birmingham B3 3BS
☎0121 236 3591   Fax 0121 212 4577
Administrator & General Secretary
Philip Fisher
Access For research, to students (loans restricted to members)
ESTABLISHED 1855. Later merged with the Birmingham Library (now renamed the Priestley Library), which was founded in 1779. The Priestley Library specialises in the humanities, with approximately 100,000 volumes in stock. Founder member of the **Association of**

Independent Libraries. Meeting-place of many affiliated societies including many devoted to poetry and literature.

Birmingham Library Services
Central Library, Chamberlain Square,
Birmingham B3 3HQ
☎0121 303 4511
Website: www.birmingham.gov.uk

Open 9.00 am to 8.00 pm Monday to Friday;
9.00 am to 5.00 pm Saturday

Over a million volumes. *Research collections* include the Shakespeare Library; War Poetry Collection; Parker Collection of Children's Books and Games; Johnson Collection; Milton Collection; Cervantes Collections; Early and Fine Printing Collection (including the William Ridler Collection of Fine Printing); Joseph Priestley Collection; Loudon Collection; Railway Collection; Wingate Bett Transport Ticket Collection; Labour, Trade Union and Co-operative Collections. Photographic Archives: Sir John Benjamin Stone; Francis Bedford; Francis Frith; Warwickshire Photographic Survey; Boulton and Watt Archive; Charles Parker Archive; Birmingham Repertory Theatre Archive and Sir Barry Jackson Library; Local Studies (Birmingham); Patents Collection; Song Sheets Collection; Oberammergau Festival Collection.

Bradford Central Library
Princes Way, Bradford, West Yorkshire
BD1 1NN
☎01274 753600   Fax 01274 395108
Open 9.00 am to 7.30 pm Monday to Friday;
9.00 am to 5.00 pm Saturday

Open access
Wide range of books and media loan services. Comprehensive reference and information services, including major local history collections and specialised business information service. Bradford Libraries runs *Reader2Reader*, a ground-breaking, reader-centred literature development project.

Brighton Central Library
Church Street, Brighton, East Sussex BN1 1UE
☎01273 290800   Fax 01273 296951
Open 10.00 am to 7.00 pm Monday to Friday
(closed Wednesday); 10.00 am to 4.00 pm
Saturday
Reference Library ☎01273 296969
Fax 01273 296965

Access Limited stock on open access; all material for reference use only

FOUNDED 1869, the library has a large stock covering most subjects. Specialisations include art and antiques, history of Brighton and Sussex, family history, local illustrations, TSO, business and large bequests of antiquarian books and ecclesiastical history.

Bristol Central Library
College Green, Bristol BS1 5TL
☎0117 9276121   Fax 0117 9221081
Open 9.30 am to 7.30 pm Monday, Tuesday
and Thursday; 9.30 am to 5.00 pm
Wednesday, Friday and Saturday

Open access
Lending, reference, art, music, commerce and local studies are particularly strong.

British Architectural Library
Royal Institute of British Architects,
66 Portland Place, London W1N 4AD
☎0171 580 5533   Fax 0171 631 1802
Email: bal@inst.riba.org
Website: www.riba.org/library/index.htm

Members' Information Line (Premium rate):
0891 234 444; Public Information Line
(Premium rate): 0891 234 400

Open 1.30 pm to 5.00 pm Monday; 10.00 am
to 8.00 pm Tuesday; 10.00 am to 5.00 pm
Wednesday, Thursday, Friday; 10.00 am to
1.30 pm Saturday

Access Free to RIBA members; non-members must buy a day ticket (£10/£5 concessions, but on Tuesdays between 5–8.00 pm and Saturdays £5/£2.50); subscriber membership available (write for details); loans available to RIBA and library members only

Collection of books, drawings, manuscripts, photographs and periodicals, 400 of which are indexed. All aspects of architecture, current and historical. Material both technical and aesthetic, covering related fields including: interior design, landscape architecture, topography, the construction industry and applied arts. Brochure available; queries by telephone, letter or in person. Charge for research (min. charge £30).

The British Library
Admission to St Pancras Reading Rooms

The British Library does not provide access to all those who request admission to use its research facilities but operates an admissions policy which grants access to those who need to use the collection because they cannot find the material they require in other libraries.

Admission is by interview and applicants are required to demonstrate that they need access to the reading rooms because: (a) material they need to consult is not available elsewhere; (b) their work or studies require the facilities of a large research library; (c) they need access to the Library's public records.

For further information, contact the Reader Admissions Office, The British Library, 96 Euston Road, London NW1 2DB. Email: reader-admission@bl.uk ☎0171 412 7677 Fax 0171 412 7794

British Library Business Information Service (BIS)

96 Euston Road, London NW1 2DB
Email: business-information@bl.uk
Website: www.bl.uk

Free enquiry service: ☎0171 412 7977
Fax 0171 412 945
Priced enquiry service: ☎0171 412 7457
Fax 0171 412 7453
Open 9.30 am to 5.00 pm Monday to Saturday. At the time of going to press, opening times had not been confirmed; telephone for details

Open access
BIS holds the most comprehensive collection of business information literature in the UK. This includes market research reports and journals, directories, company annual reports, trade and business journals, house journals, trade literature and CD-ROM services.

British Library Early Printed Collections

96 Euston Road, London NW1 2DB
☎0171 412 7673   Fax 0171 412 7577
Email: rare-books@bl.uk
Website: www.bl.uk

Open 9.30 am to 6.00 pm Monday and Thursday; 9.30 am to 8.00 pm Tuesday and Wednesday; 9.30 am to 5.00 pm Friday and Saturday.

Access By British Library reader's pass
Reader services and advance reservations
☎0171 412 7676   Fax 0171 412 7609
Email: reader-services-enquiries@bl.uk

The Early Printed Collections Department, which is an integral part of British Library Reader Services and Collection Development, selects, acquires, researches and provides access to material in the humanities collections printed in the British Isles to 1914 and in Western European languages before 1851. The collec-

tions are available in the Rare Books and Music Reading Room at St Pancras which also functions as the focus for the British Library's extensive collection of humanities microforms.

Further information about Early Printed Collections can be found at the British Library Website

British Library Humanities Reading Room

96 Euston Road, London NW1 2DB
☎0171 412 7676   Fax 0171 412 7609
Email: reader-services-enquiries@bl.uk
Website: www.bl.uk

Open 9.30 am to 6.00 pm Monday and Thursday; 9.30 am to 8.00 pm Tuesday and Wednesday; 9.30 am to 5.00 pm Friday and Saturday

Access By British Library reader's pass
This reading room is the focus for the Library's modern collections service in the humanities. It is on two levels, Humanities 1 and Humanities 2 and provides access to the Library's comprehensive collections of books and periodicals in all subjects in the humanities and social sciences and in all languages apart from Oriental languages. These collections are not available for browsing at the shelf. Material is held in closed access storage and needs to be identified and ordered from store using an on-line catalogue. A selective open access collection on most humanities subjects can be found in Humanities 1 whilst in Humanities 2 there are open access reference works relating to periodicals and theses, to recorded sound and to librarianship and information science.

To access British Library catalogues, go to the Website at: opac97.bl.uk

British Library Manuscript Collections

96 Euston Road, London NW1 2DB
☎0171 412 7513   Fax 0171 412 7745
Email: mss@bl.uk
Website: www.bl.uk

Open 9.30 am to 5.00 pm Monday to Saturday

Access Reading facilities only, by British Library reader's pass; a written letter of recommendation is required for certain categories of material

Two useful publications, *Index of Manuscripts in the British Library*, Cambridge 1984–6, 10 vols, and *The British Library: Guide to the Catalogues and Indexes of the Department of Manuscripts* by M. A. E. Nickson help to guide the researcher through this vast collection of manuscripts dating from Ancient Greece to the present day. Approximately 300,000 mss, charters, papyri and seals are housed here.

For information on British Library collections and services, visit the Website. To access main British Library catalogues, go to the Website at: opac97.bl.uk (NB Manuscript catalogues not yet available on-line).

British Library Map Library
96 Euston Road, London NW1 2DB
☎0171 412 7702   Fax 0171 412 7780
Email: maps@bl.uk
Website: www.bl.uk

Open 9.30 am to 5.00 pm Monday to Saturday

Access By British Library reader's pass

A collection of two million maps, charts and globes with particular reference to the history of British cartography. Maps for all parts of the world in a wide range of scales and dates, including the most comprehensive collection of Ordnance Survey maps and plans. *Special collections* King George III Topographical Collection and Maritime Collection, and the Crace Collection of maps and plans of London.

For information on British Library collections and services, visit the Website.

To access main British Library catalogues, go to the Website at: opac97.bl.uk (NB Map Library catalogue on CD-ROM; not yet available on-line.)

British Library Music Collections
96 Euston Road, London NW1 2DP
☎0171 412 7772   Fax 0171 412 7751
Email: music-collections@bl.uk
Website: www.bl.uk

Open 9.30 am to 6.00 pm Monday and Thursday; 9.30 am to 8.00 pm Tuesday and Wednesday; 9.30 am to 5.00 pm Friday and Saturday

Access By British Library reader's pass

Special collections The Royal Music Library (containing almost all Handel's surviving autograph scores) and the Paul Hirsch Music Library. Also a large collection (about one and a quarter million items) of printed music and about 100,000 items of manuscript music, both British and foreign.

For information on British Library collections and services, visit the Website.

To access British Library catalogues, go to the Website at: opac97.bl.uk (NB Only the current music catalogue – printed music acquired after 1980 – is available through the Internet. The retrospective music catalogues and the catalogues of manuscripts are not yet available on-line.)

British Library National Sound Archive
96 Euston Road, London NW1 2DB
☎0171 412 7440   Fax 0171 412 7441
Website: www.bl.uk/collections/sound-archive

Open 9.30 am to 6.00 pm Monday and Thursday; 9.30 am to 8.00 pm Tuesday and Wednesday; 9.30 am to 5.00 pm Friday and Saturday

Listening service (by appointment)

Northern Listening Service
British Library Document Supply Centre, Boston Spa, West Yorkshire: 9.15 am to 4.30 pm Monday to Friday

Open access
An archive of over 1,000,000 discs and more than 170,000 tape recordings, including all types of music, oral history, drama, wildlife, selected BBC broadcasts and BBC Sound Archive material. Produces a thrice-yearly newsletter, *Playback*.

For information on British Library National Sound Archive collections and services, visit the Website.

To access British Library catalogues, go to the Website at: opac97.bl.uk

British Library Newspaper Library
Colindale Avenue, London NW9 5HE
☎0171 412 7353   Fax 0171 412 7379
Email: newspaper@bl.uk
Website: www.bl.uk/collections/newspaper

Open 10.00 am to 4.45 pm Monday to Saturday (last newspaper issue 4.15 pm)

Access By British Library reader's pass or Newspaper Library pass (available from and valid only for Colindale)

English provincial, Scottish, Welsh, Irish, Commonwealth and selected overseas foreign newspapers from *c*.1700 are housed here. London newspapers from 1801 and many weekly periodicals are also in stock. (London newspapers pre-dating 1801 are housed at the new library building in St Pancras – 96 Euston Road, NW1 2DB – though many are available at Colindale Avenue on microfilm.) Readers are advised to check availability of material in advance.

For information on British Library Newspaper Library collections and services, visit the Website.

To access British Library catalogues, go to the Website at: opac97.bl.uk

British Library Oriental and India Office Collections

96 Euston Road, London NW1 2DB
☎0171 412 7873   Fax 0171 412 7641
Email: oioc-enquiries@bl.uk
Website: www.bl.uk

Open 9.30 am to 5.00 pm Monday to Saturday

Open access By British Library reader's pass (identification required)

A comprehensive collection of printed volumes and manuscripts in the languages of North Africa, the Near and Middle East and all of Asia, plus official records of the East India Company and British government in India until 1947. Also prints, drawings and paintings by British artists of India.

For information on British Library collections and services, visit the Website.

To access British Library catalogues, go to the Website at: opac97.bl.uk

British Library Science Reference and Information Service Reading Room

96 Euston Road, London NW1 2DB
☎0171 412 7494/7496 (General Enquiries)
Fax 0171 412 7495
Email: scitech@bl.uk
Website: www.bl.uk

British/EPO patent equiries: 0171 412 7919
Business enquiries: 0171 412 7454/7977
   (Business quick enquiry line available 9.00 am to 5.00 pm Monday to Friday)
Open 9.30 am to 5.00 pm Monday to Friday (check before visiting); 10.00 am to 1.00 pm Saturday

Engineering, business information on companies, markets and products, physical science and technologies. British, European and Patent Co-operation Treaty patents and trade marks.

For information on British Library collections and services, visit the Website.

To access British Library catalogues go to the Website at: opac97.bl.uk

British Library Social Policy Information Service

96 Euston Road, London NW1 2DB
☎0171 412 7536   Fax 0171 412 7761
Website: www.bl.uk/services/sirs/spis.html

Open 9.30 am to 5.00 pm Monday to Saturday. At the time of going to press, opening times had not been confirmed; telephone for details

Access By British Library reader's pass

Provides an information service on social policy, public administration, and current and international affairs, and access to current and historical official publications from all countries and intergovernmental bodies, including House of Commons sessional papers, UK legislation, UK electoral registers, up-to-date reference books on official publications and on the social sciences, a major collection of statistics and a browsing collection of recent social science books and periodicals. Also offers a priced research service providing literature surveys, current awareness and topic briefings for clients on demand.

To access British Library catalogues, go to the Website at: opac97.bl.uk

British Museum Department of Ethnography Library

6 Burlington Gardens, London W1X 2EX
☎0171 323 8031   Fax 0171 323 8013

Open 10.00 am to 4.45 pm Monday to Friday

Access By ticket-holders only. Tickets are given to scholars and postgraduate students, with special privileges accorded to Fellows of the Royal Anthropological Institute. Reference tickets are issued to *bona fide* researchers provided that the material is not available elsewhere. Undergraduates are admitted only if engaged in a research project

In 1976 the important library of the Royal Anthropological Institute (RAI) was donated to the Department of Ethnography Library and the RAI continues to support the library with donations of books and periodicals.

The collection consists of books (120,000), periodicals (1000 current titles), congress reports, newsletters, maps, microforms, manuscripts. It covers every aspect of anthropology: cultural anthropology (notably material culture and the arts), archaeology, biological anthropology and linguistics, together with such related fields as history, sociology, description and travel. Geographically the collection's scope is worldwide. Particular strengths are in British Commonwealth, Eastern Europe and the Americas. Mesoamerica is well represented as the library holds the Sir John Eric Thompson (1898–1970) collection.

British Psychological Society Library

c/o Psychology Library, University of London, Senate House, Malet Street, London WC1E 7HU
☎0171 862 8451   Fax 0171 862 8480
Email: ull@ull.ac.uk

Open Term-time: 9.00 am to 9.00 pm
Monday to Thursday; 9.00 am to 6.30 pm
Friday; 9.30 am to 5.30 pm Saturday
(Holidays: 9.00 am to 6.00 pm Monday to
Friday; 9.30 am to 5.30 pm Saturday)

Access Members only; Non-members £7 day
ticket

Reference library, containing the British
Psychological Society collection of periodicals
– over 140 current titles housed alongside the
University of London's collection of books and
journals. Largely for academic research. General queries referred to Swiss Cottage Library in
London which has a very good psychology
collection.

Bromley Central Library

London Borough of Bromley - Leisure &
Community Services, High Street, Bromley,
Kent BR1 1EX
☎0181 460 9955   Fax 0181 313 9975

Open 9.30 am to 6.00 pm Monday,
Wednesday, Friday; 9.30 am to 8.00 pm
Tuesday and Thursday; 9.30 am to 5.00 pm
Saturday

Open access

A large selection of fiction and non-fiction
books for loan, both adult and children's. Also
videos, CDs, cassettes, language courses, open
learning packs for hire. Other facilities include
a business information service, CD-ROM,
computer hire, internet, local studies library,
'Upfront' teenage section, large reference
library with photocopying, fax, microfiche and
film facilities and specialist 'Healthpoint' and
'Careerpoint' sections.

Specialist collections include: H. G. Wells,
Walter de la Mare, Crystal Palace, The Harlow
Bequest, and the history and geography of
Asia, America, Australasia and the Polar
regions.

CAA Library and Information Centre

Aviation House, Gatwick Airport, West
Sussex RH6 0YR
☎01293 573725   Fax 01293 573181

Open 9.30 am to 4.30 pm Monday to Friday;
10.00 am to 4.30 pm first Wednesday of the
month

Open access

Books, periodicals and reports on air transport, air traffic control, electronics, radar and
computing.

Cambridge Central Library (Reference Library & Information Service)

7 Lion Yard, Cambridge CB2 3QD
☎01223 712014   Fax 01223 712018
Email: cambridge.central.library@camcnty.
gov.uk

Open 9.30 am to 7.00 pm Monday,
Wednesday, Thursday; 9.30 am to 5.00 pm
Tuesday and Friday; 12 noon to 7.00 pm
Wednesday; 9.30 am to 5.00 pm Saturday

Open access

Large stock of books, periodicals, newspapers, maps, plus comprehensive collection of
directories and annuals covering UK, Europe
and the world. Microfilm and fiche reading and
printing services. On-line access to news and
business databases. News databases on CD-
ROM; Internet access. Monochrome and
colour photocopiers.

Camomile Street Library

12–20 Camomile Street, London EC3A 7EX
☎0171 247 8895   Fax 0171 377 2972

Open 9.30 am to 5.30 pm Monday to Friday

Open access

Corporation of London lending library.
Wide range of fiction and non-fiction books
and language courses on cassette, foreign fiction, paperbacks, maps and guides for travel at
home and abroad, children's books, a selection
of large print, and collections of music CDs
and of videos.

Cardiff Central Library

Frederick Street, St David's Link, Cardiff
CF1 4DT
☎01222 382116   Fax 01222 871599
Email: library@cardlib.demon.co.uk

Open 9.00 am to 6.00 pm Monday, Tuesday,
Wednesday, Friday; 9.00 am to 7.00 pm
Thursday; 9.00 am to 5.30 pm Saturday

General lending library with the following
departments: leisure, music, children's, local
studies, information, science and humanities.

Carmarthen Public Library

St Peter's Street, Carmarthen SA31 1LN
☎01267 224830   Fax 01267 221839

Open 9.30 am to 7.00 pm Monday, Tuesday,
Wednesday Friday; 9.30 am to 5.00 pm
Thursday and Saturday

Open access

Comprehensive range of fiction, non-fiction,
children's books and reference works in English

and in Welsh. Large local history library – newspapers/census returns on microfilm. Internet and CD-ROM facilities. Large Print books, books on tape, CDs, cassettes, and videos available for loan.

Catholic Central Library
Lancing Street, London NW1 1ND
☎0171 383 4333   Fax 0171 388 6675
Open 10.30 am to 5.00 pm Monday,
   Tuesday, Thursday, Friday; 10.30 am to
   8.00 pm Wednesday
Open access For reference (non-members must sign in; loans restricted to members)
   Contains books, many not readily available elsewhere, on theology, religions worldwide, scripture and the history of churches of all denominations.

The Centre for the Study of Cartoons and Caricature
See entry under **Picture Libraries**

City Business Library
1 Brewers Hall Garden, London EC2V 5BX
☎0171 638 8215   Fax 0171 332 1847
☎0171 480 7638 (recorded information)
Open 9.30 am to 5.00 pm Monday to Friday
Open access
   Local authority public reference library run by the Corporation of London. Books, pamphlets, periodicals and newspapers of current business interest, mostly financial. Aims to satisfy the day-to-day information needs of the City's business community, and in so doing has become one of the leading public resource centres in Britain in its field. Strong collection of directories for both the UK and overseas, plus companies information, market research sources, management, law, banking, insurance, statistics and investment. No academic journals or textbooks.

Commonwealth Institute
Commonwealth Resource Centre,
Kensington High Street, London W8 6NQ
☎0171 603 4535   Fax 0171 602 7374
Email: info@commonwealth.org
Website: www.commonwealth.org.uk
Open 10.00 am to 4.00 pm Monday to
   Saturday
Access For reference (Loan service available to 'Friends' of the CI)
   The Commonwealth Literature Library includes fiction, poems, drama and critical writings. *Special collection* Books and periodicals on

the 54 Commonwealth countries. Also a collection of directories and reference books on the Commonwealth and information on arts, geography, history and literature, cultural organisations and bibliography.

Commonwealth Secretariat Library
Marlborough House, Pall Mall, London
SW1Y 5HX
☎0171 747 6164   Fax 0171 747 6168
Email: library@commonwealth.int
Website: www.thecommonwealth.org
Open 9.15 am to 5.00 pm Monday to Friday
Access For reference only, by appointment
   Extensive reference source concerned with economy, development, trade, production and industry of Commonwealth countries; also human resources including women, youth, health, management and education.

Corporation of London Libraries
See **Barbican Library; Camomile Street Library; City Business Library; Guildhall**

Coventry Central Library
Smithford Way, Coventry, Warwickshire
CV1 1FY
☎01203 832314   Fax 01203 832440
Email: covinfo@discover.co.uk
Open 9.00 am to 8.00 pm Monday, Tuesday,
   Thursday; 9.30 am to 8.00 pm Wednesday;
   9.00 am to 5.00 pm Friday; 9.00 am to
   4.30 pm Saturday
Open access
   Located in the middle of the city's main shopping centre. Approximately 120,000 items (books, cassettes and CDs) for loan; plus reference collection of business information and local history. *Special collections* Cycling and motor industries; George Eliot; Angela Brazil; Tom Mann Collection (trade union and labour studies); local newspapers on microfilm from 1740 onwards. Over 500 periodicals taken. 'Peoplelink' community information database available.

Derby Central Library
Wardwick, Derby DE1 1HS
☎01332 255398   Fax 01332 369570
Open 10.00 am to 7.00 pm Monday,
   Tuesday, Thursday, Friday; 10.00 am to
   1.00 pm Wednesday and Saturday

LOCAL STUDIES LIBRARY
25B Irongate, Derby DE1 3GL
☎01332 255393

Open 10.00 am to 7.00 pm Monday and Tuesday; 10.00 am to 5.00 pm Wednesday, Thursday, Friday; 10.00 am to 1.00 pm Saturday

Open access
General library for lending, information and Children's Services. The Central Library also houses specialist private libraries: Derbyshire Archaeological Society; Derby Philatelic Society. The Local Studies Library houses the largest multimedia collection of resources in existence relating to Derby and Derbyshire. The collection includes mss deeds, family papers, business records including the Derby Canal Company, Derby Board of Guardians and the Derby China Factory.

Devon & Exeter Institution Library
7 Cathedral Close, Exeter, Devon EX1 1EZ
☎01392 251017
Website: www.ex.ac.uk/~ijtilsed/lib/
devonex.html

Open 9.00 am to 5.00 pm Monday to Friday

Access Members only (Temporary membership available)
FOUNDED 1813. Contains over 36,000 volumes, including long runs of 19th-century journals, theology, history, topography, early science, biography and literature. A large and growing collection of books, journals, newspapers, prints and maps relating to the South West.

Doncaster Libraries and Information Services
Central Library, Waterdale, Doncaster, South Yorkshire DN1 3JE
☎01302 734305   Fax 01302 369749

Open 9.30 am to 6.00 pm Monday to Friday; 9.30 am to 4.00 pm Saturday

Open access
Books, cassettes, CDs, videos, picture loans. Reading aids unit for people with visual handicap; activities for children during school holidays, including visits by authors, etc. Occasional funding available to support literature activities.

Dorchester Library (part of Dorset County Library)
Colliton Park, Dorchester, Dorset DT1 1XJ
☎01305 224440/224448   Fax 01305 266120

Open 10.00 am to 7.00 pm Monday; 9.30 am to 7.00 pm Tuesday, Wednesday, Friday; 9.30 am to 5.00 pm Thursday; 9.00 am to 4.00 pm Saturday

Open access
General lending and reference library, including Local Studies Collection, special collections on Thomas Hardy, The Powys Family and William Barnes. Periodicals, children's library, CD-ROMs and video lending service.

Dundee District Libraries
Central Library, The Wellgate, Dundee DD1 1DB
☎01382 434000 (434866 after 5.00pm)
Fax 01382 434642

Open Lending Departments: 9.30 am to 7.00 pm Monday, Tuesday, Thursday, Friday; 10.00 am to 7.00 pm Wednesday; 9.30 am to 5.00 pm Saturday. General Reference Department: 9.30 am to 9.00 pm Monday, Tuesday, Thursday, Friday; 10.00 am to 7.00 pm Wednesday; 9.30 am to 5.00 pm Saturday. Local History Department: 9.30 am to 5.00 pm Monday, Tuesday, Friday, Saturday; 10.00 am to 7.00 pm Wednesday; 9.30 am to 7.00 pm Thursday.

Access Reference services available to all; lending services to those who live, work, study or were educated within Dundee City
Adult lending, reference and children's services. Art, music, audio and video lending services. Internet access. Schools service (Agency). Housebound and mobile services. *Special collections*: The Wighton Collection of National Music; The Wilson Photographic Collection; The Lamb Collection.

English Nature
Northminster House, Peterborough, Cambridgeshire PE1 1UA
☎01733 455000   Fax 01733 568834
Email: enquiries@english-nature.org.uk
Website: www.english-nature.org.uk

Open 8.30 am to 5.00 pm Monday to Thursday; 8.30 am to 4.30 pm Friday;

Access To *bona fide* students only. Telephone library for appointment on 01733 455094
Information on nature conservation, nature reserves, SSSIs, planning, legislation, etc.

Equal Opportunities Commission Library
Overseas House, Quay Street, Manchester M3 3HN
☎0161 833 9244   Fax 0161 835 1657

Open 10.00 am to 12.00 pm & 2.00 pm to 4.00 pm Monday to Friday

Access For reference
Books and journals on equal opportunities

and gender issues. Equal Opportunities Commission publications.

Essex County Council Libraries
County Library Headquarters, Goldlay Gardens, Chelmsford, Essex CM2 0EW
☎01245 284981   Fax 01245 492780
Email: essexlib@essexcc.gov.uk

Essex County Council Libraries has 74 static libraries throughout Essex as well as 13 mobile libraries and three special-needs mobiles. Services to the public include books, newspapers, periodicals, CDs, cassettes, videos, pictures, CD-ROM and Internet access as well as postal cassettes for the blind and subtitled videos. Specialist subjects and collections are listed below at the relevant library.

Chelmsford Library
PO Box 882, Market Road, Chelmsford, Essex CM1 1LH
☎01245 492758   Fax 01245 492536
Open: 9.00 am to 7.00 pm Monday to Friday; 9.00 am to 5.00 pm Saturday

Science and technology, business information and social sciences.

Colchester Library
Trinity Square, Colchester, Essex CO1 1JB
☎01206 245900   Fax 01206 245901
Open: 9.00 am to 7.30 pm Monday, Tuesday, Wednesday, Friday; 9.00 am to 5.00 pm Thursday and Saturday

Local studies, music scores and education. Harsnett collection (early theological works 16th/17th-century); Castle collection (18th-century subscription library); Cunnington collection; Margaret Lazell collection; Taylor collection.

Harlow Library
The High, Harlow, Essex CM20 1HA
☎01279 413772   Fax 01279 424612
Open: 9.00 am to 7.00 pm Monday to Friday; 9.00 am to 5.00 pm Saturday
Fiction, language and literature. Sir John Newson Memorial collection; Maurice Hughes Memorial collection.

Loughton Library
Traps Hill, Loughton, Essex IG10 1HD
☎0181 502 0181   Fax 0181 508 5041
Open: 9.30 am to 7.00 pm Monday, Tuesday, Wednesday, Friday; 9.30 am to 1.30 pm Thursday; 9.00 am to 5.00 pm Saturday (closed Thursday)

National Jazz Foundation Archive.

Saffron Walden Library
2 King Street, Saffron Walden, Essex CB10 1ES
☎01799 523178   Fax 01799 513642
Open: 9.00 am to 7.00 pm Monday, Tuesday, Thursday, Friday; 9.00 am to 5.00 pm Saturday (closed Wednesday)
Victorian studies collection.

Witham Library
18 Newland Street, Witham, Essex CM8 2AQ
☎01376 519625   Fax 01376 501913
Open: 9.00 am to 7.00 pm Monday, Tuesday, Thursday, Friday; 9.00 am to 5.00 pm Saturday (closed Wednesday)
Drama. Dorothy L. Sayers and Maskell collections.

The Fawcett Library
London Guildhall University, Calcutta House, Old Castle Street, London E1 7NT
☎0171 320 1189   Fax 0171 320 1188
Email: fawcett@lgu.ac.uk
Website: www.lgu.ac.uk/fawcett/main.htm

Open University term-time: 10.15 am to 8.30 pm Monday; 9.00 am to 8.30 pm Wednesday; 9.00 am to 5.00 pm Thursday and Friday. During University vacation: 9.00 am to 5.00 pm Monday, Wednesday to Friday

Open access Members of staff and students at London Guildhall University and to *bona fide* researchers employed in higher education institutions funded by the (UK) Funding Councils and DENI. Otherwise, full membership including limited borrowing rights £30, or £7 for full-time students and the unwaged. Day fee (reference only) £3, or £1.50 for students and the unwaged. Bring a student ID card or similar to claim concessionary rate and two passport-type photographs if intending to join as an annual member

The Fawcett Library, national research library for women's history, is the UK's oldest and most comprehensive research library on all aspects of women in society, with both historical and contemporary coverage. The Library includes materials on feminism, work, education, health, the family, law, arts, sciences, technology, language, sexuality, fashion and the home. The main emphasis is on Britain but many other countries are represented, especially the Commonwealth and the Third World. Established in 1926 as the library of the London Society of Women's Service (formerly

Suffrage), a non-militant organisation led by Millicent Fawcett. In 1953 the Society was renamed after her and the library became the Fawcett Library.

Collections include: women's suffrage, work, education; women and the church, the law, sport, art, music; abortion, prostitution. Mostly British materials but some American, Commonwealth and European works. Books, journals, pamphlets, archives, photographs, posters, postcards, audiovisual materials, artefacts, scrapbooks, albums and press cuttings dating mainly from the 19th century although some materials date from the 17th century.

NB In autumn 2000 The Fawcett Library will become the core of the new National Library of Women. This requires moving to new premises (very close to the present site) and consequently The Fawcett Library will be closed to personal readers for part of the year. Intending readers are advised to contact the Library directly or consult the Website.

Foreign and Commonwealth Office Library

King Charles Street, London SW1A 2AH
☎0171 270 3925   Fax 0171 270 3270
Website: www.fco.gov.uk

Access By appointment only

An extensive stock of books, pamphlets and other reference material on all aspects of historical, socio-economic and political subjects relating to countries covered by the Foreign and Commonwealth Office. Particularly strong on colonial history, early works on travel, and photograph collections, mainly of Commonwealth countries and former colonies, c. 1850s–1960s.

Forestry Commission Library

Forest Research Station, Alice Holt Lodge, Wrecclesham, Farnham, Surrey GU10 4LH
☎01420 22255   Fax 01420 23653
Email: library@forestry.gov.uk
Website: www.forestry.gov.uk

Open 9.00 am to 5.00 pm Monday to Thursday; 9.00 am to 4.30 pm Friday

Access By appointment for personal visits

Approximately 20,000 books on forestry and arboriculture, plus 500 current journals. CD-ROMS include TREECD (1939 onwards). Offers a Research Advisory Service for advice and enquiries on forestry (☎01402 23000) with a charge for consultations and diagnosis of tree problems exceeding 10 minutes.

French Institute Library

17 Queensberry Place, London SW7 2DT
☎0171 838 2144   Fax 0171 838 2145
Email: library@ambrinsie.ambafrance.org.uk
Head Librarian *Odile Grandet*
Deputy Head Librarian *Sandrine Malotaux*

Open 12.00 pm to 7.00 pm Tuesday to Friday; 12 noon to 6.00 pm Saturday

Open access For reference and consultation (loans restricted to members)

A collection of over 40,000 volumes mainly centred on French cultural interests with special emphasis on language, literature and history. Books in French and English. Collection of 2000 videos; 250 periodicals; 2000 CDs (French music); 200 CD-ROMs; Children's library (8000 books); also a special collection about 'France Libre'. Inter-library loans; quick information service; Internet access. Group visits on request.

John Frost Newspapers

8 Monks Avenue, Barnet, Hertfordshire EN5 1DB
☎0181 440 3159   Fax 0181 440 3159
Contact *John Frost, Andrew Frost*

A collection of 60,000 original newspapers (1630 to the present day) and 100,000 press cuttings available, on loan, for research and rostrum work (TV and audiovisual documentaries/presentations). Historic events, politics, sports, royalty, crime, wars, personalities, etc., plus many in-depth files.

Gloucestershire County Library Arts & Museums Service

Quayside House, Shire Hall, Gloucester GL1 2HY
☎01452 425020   Fax 01452 425042
Email: gclams@gloscc.gov.uk
Website: www.gloscc.gov.uk

Open access

The service includes 39 local libraries – call the number above for opening hours; and six mobile libraries – telephone 01452 425039 for timetable/route enquiries.

Goethe-Institut Library

50 Princes Gate, Exhibition Road, London SW7 2PH
☎0171 596 4040   Fax 0171 594 0230
Email: Library@London.goethe.org
Librarian *Marilen Daum*
Open 11.00 am to 8.00 pm Monday to Thursday; 10.00 am to 1.00 pm Saturday

Library specialising in German literature and books/audiovisual material on German culture and history: 25,000 books (4,800 of them in English), 140 periodicals, 14 newspapers, 2600 audiovisual media (including 1000 videos), selected press clippings on German affairs from the German and UK press, information service, photocopier, video facility. Also German language teaching material for teachers and students of German.

Greater London Record Office
See **London Metropolitan Archives**

Guildford Institute of University of Surrey Library
Ward Street, Guildford, Surrey GU1 4LH
☎01483 562142

Librarian *Clare Miles*

Open 10.00 am to 3.00 pm Tuesday, Thursday, Friday; 10.00 am to 4.30 pm Wednesday (15-minute closure each day at 12.00 am)

Open access To members only but open to enquirers for research purposes

FOUNDED 1834. Some 10,000 volumes of which 7500 were printed before the First World War. The remaining stock consists of recently published works of fiction, biography and travel. Newspapers and periodicals also available. *Special collections* include an almost complete run of the *Illustrated London News* from 1843-1906, a collection of Victorian scrapbooks, and about 400 photos and other pictures relating to the Institute's history and the town of Guildford.

Guildhall Library
Aldermanbury, London EC2P 2EJ
☎See below   Fax 0171 600 3384
Website: www.corpoflondon.gov.uk

Access For reference (but much material is kept in storage areas and is supplied to readers on request; proof of identity is required for consultation of certain categories of stock)

Part of the Corporation of London libraries. Seeks to provide a basic general reference service but its major strength, acknowledged worldwide, is in its historical collections. The library is divided into three sections, each with its own catalogues and enquiry desks. These are: Printed Books; Manuscripts; the Print Room.

PRINTED BOOKS
Open 9.30 am to 5 pm Monday to Saturday
NB closes occasionally on Saturdays

following Bank Holidays; check for details
☎0171 332 1868/1870

Strong on all aspects of London history, with wide holdings of English history, topography and genealogy, including local directories, poll books and parish register transcripts. Also good collections of English statutes, law reports, parliamentary debates and journals, and House of Commons papers. Home of several important collections deposited by London institutions: the Marine collection of the Corporation of Lloyd's, the Stock Exchange's historical files of reports and prospectuses, the Clockmakers' Company library and museum, the Gardeners' Company, Fletchers' Company, the Institute of Masters of Wine, International Wine and Food Society and Gresham College.

MANUSCRIPTS
Open 9.30 am to 4.45 pm Monday to Saturday (no requests for records after 4.30 pm) NB closes occasionally on Saturdays following Bank Holidays; check for details
☎0171 332 1863
Email: manuscripts.guildhall@ms.corpoflondon. gov.uk

Website: ihr.sas.ac.uk/gh/

The official repository for historical records relating to the City of London (except those of the Corporation of London itself, which are housed at the Corporation Records Office). Records date from the 11th century to the present day. They include archives of most of the City's parishes, wards and livery companies, and of many individuals, families, estates, schools, societies and other institutions, notably the Diocese of London and St Paul's Cathedral, as well as the largest collection of business archives in any public repository in the UK. Although mainly of City interest, holdings include material for the London area as a whole and beyond.

PRINT ROOM
Open 9.30 am to 5.00 pm Monday to Friday
☎0171 332 1839
Email: john.fisher@ms.corpoflondon.gov.uk
Website: collage.nhil.com

An unrivalled collection of prints and drawings relating to London and the adjacent counties. The emphasis is on topography, but there are strong collections of portraits and satirical prints. The map collection includes maps of the capital from the mid-16th century to the present day and various classes of Ordnance Survey maps. Other material includes photographs, theatre bills and programmes, trade cards, book plates and playing cards as well as a sizeable collection of Old Master prints. Over 30,000 items have been digitally imaged on Collage, including topographical prints, some maps, a small number of photographs and all the Guildhall art collection.

Guille–Alles Library
Market Street, St Peter Port, Guernsey, Channel Islands GY1 1HB
☎01481 720392   Fax 01481 712425
Open 9.00 am to 5.00 pm Monday, Tuesday, Thursday, Friday, Saturday; 9.00 am to 8.00 pm Wednesday

Open access For residents; payment of returnable deposit by visitors. CD-ROM collection: £10 for 2-year subscription
Lending, reference and information services.

Health Information Library (Westminster)
Marylebone Library, Marylebone Road, London NW1 5PS
☎0171 641 1039   Fax 0171 641 1028
Open 9.30 am to 8.00 pm Monday, Tuesday, Thursday, Friday; 10.00 am to 8.00 pm Wednesday; 9.30 am to 5.00 pm Saturday; 1.30 pm to 5.00 pm Sunday

Open access
Located in Westminster's Marylebone public library. Books, pamphlets and periodicals covering all aspects of medicine and the health services. 90 journals on current medicine.

Herefordshire Libraries and Information Service
Shirehall, Hereford HR1 2HY
☎01432 359830/278254   Fax 01432 359668
Website: www.hereford-worcester.gov.uk
Open Opening hours vary in the libraries across the county

Access Information and reference services open to anyone; loans to members only (membership criteria: resident, being educated, working, or an elector in the county or neighbouring authorities; temporary membership to visitors. Proof of identity and address required)
Information service, reference and lending libraries. Non-fiction and fiction for all age groups, including normal and large print, spoken word cassettes, sound recordings (CD and cassette), videos, maps, local history, CD-ROMs at Hereford and Leominster Libraries, on-line information service including Internet access to certain specified (public information) Websites.

Special collections Cidermaking; Beekeeping; Alfred Watkins; John Masefield; Pilley.

University of Hertfordshire Library
College Lane, Hatfield, Hertfordshire AL10 9AD
☎01707 284677   Fax 01707 284670
Websites: www.herts.ac.uk/lrc/campus/ hatfield (*or* hertford, stalbans *or* watford)
Open Term-time: 24 hours a day; closes 11.00 pm Saturday; 11.00 am to 11.00 pm Sunday; Holidays: 8.30 am to 8.00 pm Monday to Friday; 11.00 am to 6.00 pm Saturday; closed Sunday

Access For reference; loans available to members of HERTIS.
280,000 volumes and 2000 journals in science technology and social science, including law, across all five of the university's campuses. There are four other site libraries: at the Business School at Hertford, at the Watford campus near Radlett (education and humanities), at the Art & Design building in Hatfield and at the Law School in St Albans. Desk research, postal interlibrary loans and consultancy undertaken by HERTIS Information and Research Unit which is based at Hatfield and has capacity for up to 300 subscribing companies and organisations.

HERTIS
See **University of Hertfordshire Library**

Highgate Literary and Scientific Institution Library
11 South Grove, London N6 6BS
☎0181 340 3343   Fax 0181 340 5632
Open 10.00 am to 5.00 pm Tuesday to Friday; 10.00 am to 4.00 pm Saturday (closed Sunday and Monday)
Annual membership £35 (single); £55 (household)
25,000 volumes of general fiction and non-fiction, with a children's section and extensive local archives. *Special collections* on local history, London, and local poets Samuel Taylor Coleridge and John Betjeman.

Highland Libraries, The Highland Council, Cultural and Leisure Services
Library Support Unit, 31A Harbour Road, Inverness IV1 1UA
☎01463 235713   Fax 01463 236986
Open Library opening hours vary to suit local

needs. Contact Administration and support services for details (8.00 am to 6.00 pm Monday to Friday)

Open access
Comprehensive range of lending and reference stock: books, pamphlets, periodicals, newspapers, compact discs, audio and video cassettes, maps, census records, genealogical records, photographs, educational materials, etc. Highland Libraries provides the public library service throughout the Highlands with a network of 40 static and 12 mobile libraries.

Holborn Library
32–38 Theobalds Road, London WC1X 8PA
☎0171 413 6345/6

Open 10.00 am to 7.00 pm Monday and Thursday; 10.00 am to 6.00 pm Tuesday and Friday; 10.00 am to 5.00 pm Saturday (closed all day Wednesday)

Open access
London Borough of Camden public library. Includes a law collection and the London Borough of Camden Local Studies and Archive Centre.

Sherlock Holmes Collection (Westminster)
Marylebone Library, Marylebone Road, London NW1 5PS
☎0171 641 1039   Fax 0171 641 1044
Email: c.cooke@dial.pipex.com

Open 9.30 am to 5.00 pm Monday, Tuesday, Thursday, Friday; 10.00 am to 5.00 pm Wednesday (closed Saturday)

Telephone for access By appointment only
Located in Westminster's Marylebone Library. An extensive collection of material from all over the world, covering Sherlock Holmes and Sir Arthur Conan Doyle. Books, pamphlets, journals, newspaper cuttings and photos, much of which is otherwise unavailable in this country. Some background material.

Imperial College Central Library
See **Science Museum Library**

Imperial War Museum
Department of Printed Books, Lambeth Road, London SE1 6HZ
☎0171 416 5000   Fax 0171 416 5374

Open 10.00 am to 5.00 pm Monday to Saturday (restricted service Saturday; closed on Bank Holiday Saturdays and last two full weeks of November for annual stock check)

Access For reference (but at least 24 hours' notice must be given for intended visits)
A large collection of material on 20th-century life with detailed coverage of the two world wars and other conflicts. Books, pamphlets and periodicals, including many produced for short periods in unlikely wartime settings; also maps, biographies and privately printed memoirs, and foreign language material. Additional research material available in the following departments: Art, Documents, Exhibits and Firearms, Film, Sound Records, Photographs. Active publishing programme based on reprints of rare books held in library. Catalogue available.

Instituto Cervantes
102 Eaton Square, London SW1W 9AN
☎0171 235 0324   Fax 0171 235 0329
Email: biblon@cervantes.es

Open 12.30 pm to 6.30 pm Monday; 9.30 am to 6.30 pm Tuesday to Thursday; 9.30 am to 5.00 pm Friday; 9.30 am to 1.30 pm Saturday

Open access For reference and lending
Spanish literature, history, art, philosophy. The library houses a collection of books, periodicals, videos, slides, tapes, CDs, cassettes, films and CD-ROMs specialising entirely in Spain and Latin America.

Italian Institute Library
39 Belgrave Square, London SW1X 8NX
☎0171 235 1461   Fax 0171 235 4618

Open 10.00 am to 1.00 pm and 2.00 pm to 5.00 pm Monday to Friday

Open access For reference
A collection of over 21,000 volumes relating to all aspects of Italian culture. Texts are mostly in Italian, with some in English.

Jersey Library
Halkett Place, St Helier, Jersey JE2 4WH
☎01534 59991 (Lending)/59992 (Reference)
Fax 01534 69444   Email: piano@itl.net
Website: www.itl.net/vc/europe/jersey/education/library/index.html

Open 9.30 am to 5.30 pm Monday, Wednesday, Thursday, Friday; 9.30 am to 7.30 pm Tuesday; 9.30 am to 4.00 pm Saturday

Open access
Books, periodicals, newspapers, CDs, cassettes, CD-ROMs, videos, microfilm, specialised local studies collection, public Internet access.

Kent County Central Library
Kent County Council Arts & Libraries,
Springfield, Maidstone, Kent ME14 2LH
☎01622 696511   Fax 01622 753338

Open 9.30 am to 5.30 pm Monday,
Wednesday, Friday; 9.30 am to 6.00 pm
Tuesday; 9.30 am to 7.00 pm Thursday;
10.00 am to 5.00 pm Saturday

Open access
50,000 volumes available on the floor of the
library plus 250,000 volumes of non-fiction,
mostly academic, available on request to staff.
English literature, poetry, classical literature,
drama (including playsets), music (including
music sets). Strong, too, in sociology, art history,
business information and government publications. Loans to all who live or work in Kent;
those who do not may consult stock for reference or arrange loans via their own local library
service.

Lansdowne Library
Meyrick Road, Bournemouth, Dorset
BH1 3DJ
☎01202 556603   Fax 01202 291781

Open 10.00 am to 7.00 pm Monday; 9.30 am
to 7.00 pm Tuesday, Thursday, Friday; 9.30
am to 5.00 pm Wednesday; 9.00 am to 1.00
pm Saturday

Open access
Main library for Bournemouth with separate
lending, reference and music departments.
Collection of government publications; children's section, periodicals.

The Law Society
113 Chancery Lane, London WC2A 1PL
☎0171 316 5764/320 5810/5811/5884
Fax 0171 242 1309
Website: www.lawsociety.org.uk
Head of Press Office *David McNeill*
Press Relations Manager *Catherine Slaytor*
Open 9.00 am to 5.00 pm with out-of-hours
answerphone and mobile phone back-up

Access Library restricted to solicitors/mem-
bers but press office available to all journalists
for advice, information and assistance.
　Provides all information about solicitors, the
legal profession in general, law reform issues, etc.

Leeds Central Library
Calverley Street, Leeds, West Yorkshire
LS1 3AB
☎0113 2478274   Fax 0113 2478426

Open 9.00 am to 8.00 pm Monday and

Wednesday; 9.00 am to 5.30 pm Tuesday
and Friday; 9.30 am to 5.30 pm Thursday;
10.00 am to 5.00 pm Saturday

Open access to lending libraries; Reference
material on request

Lending Library covering all subjects.

Music Library contains scores, books, video
and audio.

Information for Business Library holds
company information, market research, statistics, directories, journals and computer-based
information.

Art Library (in Art Gallery) has a major collection of material on fine and applied arts.

Local Studies Library contains an extensive
collection on Leeds and Yorkshire, including
maps, books, pamphlets, local newspapers, illustrations and playbills. Census returns for the
whole of Yorkshire also available. International
Genealogical Index and parish registers.

Research & Study Library with over
270,000 volumes, including extensive files of
newspapers and periodicals plus all government
publications since 1960. *Special collections*
include military history, Judaic, early gardening
books, and mountaineering.
　Leeds City Libraries has an extensive network of 65 branch and mobile libraries.

Leeds Library
18 Commercial Street, Leeds, West Yorkshire
LS1 6AL
☎0113 2453071   Fax 0113 243 8218

Open 9.00 am to 5.00 pm Monday to Friday

Access To members; research use upon application to the librarian
　FOUNDED 1768. Contains over 120,000
books and periodicals from the 15th century to
the present day. *Special collections* include
Reformation pamphlets, Civil War tracts,
Victorian and Edwardian children's books and
fiction, European language material, spiritualism and psychical research, plus local material.

Lincoln Central Library
Free School Lane, Lincoln LN2 1EZ
☎01522 510800   Fax 01522 535882

Open 9.30 am to 7.00 pm Monday to Friday;
9.30 am to 4.00 pm Saturday

Open access to the library; appointment
required for the Tennyson Research Centre
　Lending and reference library. Special collections include Lincolnshire local history
(printed and published material, photographs,

maps, directories and census data) and the Tennyson Research Centre (contact *Susan Gates*).

Linen Hall Library

17 Donegall Square North, Belfast BT1 5GD
☎01232 321707   Fax 01232 438586

Librarian *John Gray*

Open 9.30 am to 5.30 pm Monday to Friday;
9.30 am to 4.00 pm Saturday

Open access For reference (loans restricted to members)

FOUNDED 1788. Contains about 200,000 books. Major Irish and local studies collections, including the Northern Ireland Political Collection relating to the current troubles (c. 90,000 items).

Literary & Philosophical Society of Newcastle upon Tyne

23 Westgate Road, Newcastle upon Tyne NE1 1SE
☎0191 232 0192   Fax 0191 261 2885

Librarian *Pat Southern*

Open 9.30 am to 7.00 pm Monday, Wednesday, Thursday, Friday; 9.30 am to 8.00 pm Tuesday; 9.30 am to 1.00 pm Saturday

Access Members; research facilities for *bona fide* scholars on application to the Librarian

200-year-old library of 140,000 volumes, periodicals (including 130 current titles), classical music on vinyl recordings and CD, plus a collection of scores. A programme of lectures and recitals provided. Recent publications include: *The Reverend William Turner: Dissent and Reform in Georgian Newcastle upon Tyne* Stephen Harbottle; *History of the Literary and Philosophical Society of Newcastle upon Tyne, Vol. 2 (1896–1989)* Charles Parish; *Bicentenary Lectures 1993* ed. John Philipson.

Liverpool City Libraries

William Brown Street, Liverpool LE3 8EW
☎0151 225 5429   Fax 0151 207 1342
Email: central@lvpublib.demon.co.uk

Open 9.00 am to 7.30 pm Monday to Thursday; 9.00 am to 5.00 pm Friday; 10.00 am to 4.00 pm Saturday

Open access

Humanities Reference Library A total stock in excess of 120,000 volumes and 24,000 maps, plus book plates, prints and autographed letters. *Special collections* Walter Crane and Edward Lear illustrations, Kolmscott Press, Audubon.

Business and Technology Reference Library Extensive stock dealing with all aspects of science, commerce and technology, including British and European standards and patents and trade directories.

Audio Visual Library Extensive stock relating to all aspects of music. Includes 128,000 volumes and music scores, 18,500 records, and over 3000 cassettes and CDs. *Special collections* Carl Rosa Opera Company Collection and Earl of Sefton's early printed piano music.

Record Office and Local History Department Printed and audiovisual material relating to Liverpool, Merseyside, Lancashire and Cheshire, together with archive material mainly on Liverpool. Some restrictions on access, with 30-year rule applying to archives.

London College of Printing: Department of Learning Resources

Elephant and Castle, London SE1 6SB
☎0171 514 6527   Fax 0171 514 6597

Access By arrangement

The Department of Learning Resources operates from the two sites of the college at: Elephant & Castle and Back Hill (Clerkenwell). Books, periodicals, slides, CD-ROMs, videos and computer software on all aspects of the art of the book, printing, management, film/photography, graphic arts, plus retailing. *Special collections* Private Press books and the history and development of printing and books.

The London Library

14 St James's Square, London SW1Y 4LG
☎0171 930 7705   Fax 0171 766 4766
Email: membership@londonlibrary.co.uk
Website: webpac.londonlibrary.co.uk

Librarian *Mr A. S. Bell*

Open 9.30 am to 5.30 pm Monday to Saturday (Thursday till 7.30 pm)

Access For members only (£130 p.a., 1998)

With over a million books and 8400 members, The London Library 'is the most distinguished private library in the world; probably the largest, certainly the best loved'. Founded in 1841, it is a registered charity and wholly independent of public funding. Its permanent collection embraces most European languages as well as English. Its subject range is predominantly within the humanities, with emphasis on literature, history, fine and applied art, architecture, bibliography, philosophy, religion, and topography and travel. Some 6000–7000 titles are added yearly. Most of the stock is on open shelves to which members have free access. Members may take out up to 10 volumes; 15 if they live more than 20 miles from the Library. The comfortable Reading Room has an annexe for users of personal computers. There are photocopiers and CD-ROM workstations, and the Library also offers a postal loans service.

Prospective members are required to submit a refereed application form in advance of admission, but there is at present no waiting list for membership. The London Library Trust may make grants to those who are unable to afford the full annual fee; details on application.

London Metropolitan Archives

40 Northampton Road, London EC1R 0HB
☎0171 332 3820   Fax 0171 833 9136
Email: lma@ms.corpoflondon.gov.uk
Minicom 0171 278 8703

Open 9.30 am to 4.45 pm Monday,
  Wednesday, Friday; 9.30 pm to 7.30 pm
  Tuesday and Thursday

Access For reference only
  Formerly, the Greater London Record Office Library. Covers all aspects of the life and development of London, specialising in the history and organisation of local government in general, and London in particular. Books on London history and topography, covering many subjects. Also London directories dating back to 1677, plus other source material including Acts of Parliament, Hansard reports, statistical returns, atlases, yearbooks and many complete sets of newspapers and magazines.

Lord Louis Library

Orchard Street, Newport, Isle of Wight
PO30 1LL
☎01983 527655/823800 (Reference Library)
Fax 01983 825972

Open 9.30 am to 5.30 pm Monday to Friday
  (Saturday till 5.00 pm)

Open access
  General adult and junior fiction and non-fiction collections; local history collection and periodicals. Also the county's main reference library.

Manchester Central Library

St Peters Square, Manchester M2 5PD
☎0161 234 1900   Fax 0161 234 1963
Email: mclib@libraries.manchester.gov.uk
Website: www.manchester.gov.uk/
  mccdlt/index.htm

Open 10.00 am to 8.00 pm Monday to
  Thursday; 10.00 am to 5.00 pm Friday and
  Saturday; Commercial and European Units:

10.00 am to 6.00 pm Monday to Thursday;
10.00 am to 5.00 pm Friday and Saturday

Open access
  One of the country's leading reference libraries with extensive collections covering all subjects. Departments include: Commercial, European, Technical, Social Sciences, Arts, Music, Local Studies, Chinese, General Readers, Language & Literature. Large lending stock and VIP (visually impaired) service available.

Marylebone Library (Westminster)

See **Health Information Library; Sherlock Holmes Collection**

Ministry of Agriculture, Fisheries and Food

Nobel House, 17 Smith Square, London SW1P 3JR
☎0171 238 3000   Fax 0171 238 6591

MAFF Helpline 0645 335577 (local call rate)
  – general contact point which can provide information on the work of MAFF, either directly or by referring callers to appropriate contacts. Available 9.00 am to 5.00 pm Monday to Friday (excluding Bank Holidays)

Open 9.30 am to 5.00 pm Monday to Friday

Access For reference (but at least 24 hours notice must be given for intended visits)
  Large stock of volumes on temperate agriculture.

The Mitchell Library

North Street, Glasgow G3 7DN
☎0141 287 2999   Fax 0141 287 2815
Website: www.glasgow.gov.uk/gcl/ref.htm

Open 9.00 am to 8.00 pm Monday to
  Thursday; 9.00 am to 5.00 pm Friday and
  Saturday

Open access
  Europe's largest public reference library with stock of over 1,200,000 volumes. It subscribes to 46 newspapers and more than 2000 periodicals. There are collections in microform, records, tapes and videos, as well as CD-ROMs, illustrations, photographs, postcards, etc.

  The library is divided into a number of subject departments including the Arts department which contains a number of special collections, e.g. the Robert Burns Collection (5000 vols), the Scottish Poetry Collection (12,000 items) and the Scottish Drama Collection (1650 items).

Morrab Library

Morrab House, Morrab Gardens, Penzance,
Cornwall TR18 4DA
☎01736 364474

Librarian *L. Lowdon, BA, ALA*

Open 10.00 am to 4.00 pm Tuesday to
Friday; 10.00 am to 1.00 pm Saturday

Access Non-members may use the library for
a small daily fee, but may not borrow books

Formerly known as the Penzance Library. An
independent subscription lending library of over
60,000 volumes covering virtually all subjects
except modern science and technology, with
large collections on history, literature and religion. There is a comprehensive Cornish collection of books, newspapers and manuscripts
including the Borlase letters; a West Cornwall
photographic archive; many runs of 18th- and
19th-century periodicals; a collection of over
2000 books published before 1800.

National Library of Scotland

George IV Bridge, Edinburgh EH1 1EW
☎0131 226 4531/459 4531
Fax 0131 622 4803
Email: enquiries@nls.uk
Website: www.nls.uk

Open Main Reading Room: 9.30 am to
8.30 pm Monday, Tuesday, Thursday,
Friday; 10.00 am to 8.30 pm Wednesday;
9.30 am to 1.00 pm Saturday. Map Library:
9.30 am to 5.00 pm Monday, Tuesday,
Thursday, Friday; 10.00 am to 5.00 pm
Wednesday; 9.30 am to 1.00 pm Saturday.
Scottish Science Library: 9.30 am to
5.00 pm Monday, Tuesday, Thursday,
Friday; 10.00 am to 8.30 pm Wednesday.

Access To reading rooms and Map Library, for
research not easily done elsewhere, by reader's
ticket

Collection of over 7 million volumes. The
library receives all British and Irish publications.
Large stock of newspapers and periodicals. Many
special collections, including early Scottish
books, theology, polar studies, baking, phrenol-
ogy and liturgies. Also large collections of maps,
music and manuscripts including personal
archives of notable Scottish persons.

National Library of Wales

Aberystwyth, Ceredigion SY23 3BU
☎01970 632800   Fax 01970 615709
Website: www.llgc.org.uk

Open 9.30 am to 6.00 pm Monday to Friday;
9.30 am to 5.00 pm Saturday (closed Bank
Holidays and first week of October)

Access To reading rooms and map room by
reader's ticket, available on application

Collection of over 4 million books and including large collections of periodicals, maps,
manuscripts and audiovisual material. Particular
emphasis on humanities in printed foreign material, and on Wales and other Celtic areas in all
collections.

National Library of Women

See **The Fawcett Library**

National Meteorological Library and Archive

London Road, Bracknell, Berkshire RG12 2SZ
☎01344 854841   Fax 01344 854840
Email: metlib@meto.gov.uk

Open Library & Archive: 8.30 am to 4.30 pm
Monday to Friday; Archive closed between
1.00 pm and 2.00 pm

Access By Visitor's Pass available from the
reception desk; advance notice of a planned
visit is appreciated

The major repository of most of the important
literature on the subjects of meteorology, clima-
tology and related sciences. The Library houses a
collection of books, journals, articles and scientific papers, plus published climatological data
from many parts of the world. The Technical
Archive (The Scott Building, Sterling Centre,
Eastern Road, Bracknell, Berks RG12 2PW,
☎01344 855960; Fax 01344 855961) holds the
document collection of meteorological data and
charts from England, Wales and British overseas
bases, including ships' weather logs. Records
from Scotland are stored in Edinburgh and those
from Northern Ireland in Belfast.

The Natural History Museum Library

Cromwell Road, London SW7 5BD
☎0171 938 9191   Fax 0171 938 9290
Email: library@nhm.ac.uk
Website: www.nhm.ac.uk/info/library/
index.html

Open 10.00 am to 4.30 pm Monday to Friday

Access To *bona fide* researchers, by reader's
ticket on presentation of identification (telephone first to make an appointment)

The library is in five sections: general; botany;
zoology; entomology; earth sciences. The sub-
department of ornithology is housed at the
Zoological Museum, Akeman Street, Tring,
Herts HP23 6AP (☎01442 834181). Resources
available include books, journals, maps, manuscripts, drawings and photographs covering all

aspects of natural history, including palaeontology and mineralogy, from the 14th century to the present day. Also archives and historical collection on the museum itself.

Newcastle upon Tyne City Library

Princess Square, Newcastle upon Tyne
NE99 1DX
☎0191 261 0691   Fax 0191 261 1435

Open 9.30 am to 8.00 pm Monday and Thursday; 9.30 am to 5.00 pm Tuesday, Wednesday, Friday; 9.00 am to 5.00 pm Saturday

Open access
Extensive local studies collection, including newspapers, illustrations and genealogy. Also business, science, humanities and arts, educational guidance unit, open learning resource centre, marketing advice centre. Patents advice centre.

Norfolk Library & Information Service

Norfolk and Norwich Central Library, Central Lending Service, 71 Ber Street, Norwich, Norfolk NR1 3AD
☎01603 215215
Website: www.norfolk.gov.uk/council/departments/lis/libhome.htm

Central Reference & Information Service and Norfolk Studies

Gildengate House, Upper Green Lane, Norwich, Norfolk NR3 1AX
☎01603 215222   Fax 01603 215258

Open Lending Library, Reference and Information Service and Norfolk Studies: 10.00 am to 8.00 pm Monday to Friday; 9.00 am to 5.00 pm Saturday

Open access
Reference and lending library with wide range of stock for loan, including books, recorded music, music scores, plays and videos. Houses the 2nd Air Division Memorial Library and has a strong Local Studies Library. Extensive range of reference stock including business information. On-line database and CD-ROM services. Public fax and colour photocopying, access to the Internet. Information brokerage provides in-depth research services.

Northamptonshire Libraries & Information Service

Library HQ, PO Box 259, 27 Guildhall Road, Northampton NN1 1BA
☎01604 620262   Fax 01604 626789

Since 1991, the Libraries and Information

Service have run two to three programmes of literary events for adults each year. Programmes so far have included visiting authors, poetry readings, workshops and other events and activities. The programmes are supported by regular touring fiction displays, writers' advice sessions and dedicated notice boards in libraries across the county.

Northumberland Central Library

The Willows, Morpeth, Northumberland
NE61 1TA
☎01670 534518/534514   Fax 01670 534513

Open 10.00 am to 8.00 pm Monday, Tuesday, Wednesday, Friday; 9.30 am to 12.30 pm Saturday (closed Thursday)

Open access
Books, periodicals, newspapers, cassettes, CDs, video, microcomputers, CD-ROM, Internet access, prints, microforms, vocal scores, playsets, community resource equipment. *Special collections* **Northern Poetry Library**: 13,000 volumes of modern poetry (see entry under **Organisations of Interest to Poets**); Cinema: comprehensive collection of about 5000 volumes covering all aspects of the cinema; Family History.

Nottingham Central Library

Angel Row, Nottingham NG1 6HP
☎0115 9152828   Fax 0115 9152840

Open 9.30 am to 7.00 pm Monday to Friday; 9.00 am to 1.00 pm Saturday

Open access
General public lending library: business information, on-line information, the arts, local studies, religion, community languages, literature. Videos, periodicals, spoken word, recorded music, CD-ROM service – textual information on CD-ROM on public access machines. Internet on public access. *Special collection* on D. H. Lawrence. Extensive back-up reserve stocks. Drama and music sets for loan to groups.

Nottingham Subscription Library Ltd

Bromley House, Angel Row, Nottingham
NG1 6HL
☎0115 9473134

Librarian *Julia Wilson*

Open 9.30 am to 5.00 pm Monday to Friday; also first Saturday of each month from 10.00 am to 12.30 pm

Access For members only

FOUNDED 1816. Collection of 30,000 books including local history, topography, biography, travel and fiction.

Office for National Statistics

1 Drummond Gate, London SW1V 2QQ
☎0171 533 6262   Fax 0171 533 6261
Email: info@ons.gov.uk
Website: www.ons.gov.uk

Open 9.30 am to 4.30 pm Monday to Friday
All published Census data from 1801 onwards for the UK. Population and health statistics from 1837 onwards. Some foreign censuses and statistics (incomplete; most are out-housed and require one week's notice for retrieval). International statistics (WHO, UN, etc). Government Social Survey reports, 1941 onwards. Wide range of other Government statistical publications, business and economic statistics, EUROSTAT publications. Small stock of books on demography, vital registration, epidemology, survey methodology, census taking.

Orkney Library

Laing Street, Kirkwall, Orkney KW15 1NW
☎01856 873166   Fax 01856 875260

Open 9.00 am to 8.00 pm Monday to Friday; 9.00 am to 5.00 pm Saturday. Archives: 9.00 am to 1.00 pm and 2.00 pm to 4.45 pm Monday to Friday

Open access
Local studies collection. Archive includes sound and photographic departments.

Oxford Central Library

Westgate, Oxford OX1 1DJ
☎01865 815549   Fax 01865 721694

Open Call 01865 815509 for details
General lending and reference library including the Centre for Oxfordshire Studies. Also periodicals, audio visual materials, music library, children's library and Business Information Point.

PA News Library

292 Vauxhall Bridge Road, London SW1V 1AE
☎0171 963 7012   Fax 0171 963 7065

Open 8.00 am to 8.00 pm Monday to Friday; 8.00 am to 6.00 pm Saturday; 9.00 am to 5.00 pm Sunday

Open access
PA News, the 24-hour national news and information group, offers public access to its press cutting archive. Covering a wide range of subjects, the library includes over 14 million cuttings dating back to 1928. Personal callers welcome or research undertaken by in-house staff.

Penzance Library

See **Morrab Library**

City of Plymouth Library and Information Services

Central Library, Drake Circus, Plymouth, Devon PL4 8AL   Fax 01752 385905
Website: www.plymouth.gov.uk/star/ library.htm

Open access

CENTRAL LIBRARY LENDING DEPARTMENTS:
Lending ☎01752 385912

Children's Department ☎01752 385916

Music & Drama Department ☎01752 385914 Email: music@plymouth.gov.uk

Open 9.30 am to 7.00 pm Monday and Friday; 9.30 am to 5.30 pm Tuesday, Wednesday, Thursday; 9.30 am to 4.00 pm Saturday

The Lending departments offer books on all subjects; language courses on cassette and foreign language books; the Holcenberg Jewish Collection; books on music and musicians, drama and theatre; music parts and sets of music parts; play sets; videos; song index; cassettes and CDs.

CENTRAL LIBRARY REFERENCE DEPARTMENTS:
Reference ☎01752 385907/8
Email: ref@plymouth.gov.uk

Business Information ☎01752 385906
Email: keyinfo@plymouth.gov.uk

Local Studies & Naval History Department ☎01752 385909
Email: localstudies@plymouth.gov.uk

Open 9.00 am to 7.00 pm Monday to Friday; 9.00 am to 4.00 pm Saturday

The Reference departments include an extensive collection of Ordnance Survey maps and town guides; community and census information; marketing and statistical information; Patents and British Standards; books on every aspect of Plymouth; naval history; Mormon Index on microfilm; Baring Gould manuscript of 'Folk Songs of the West'.

Plymouth Proprietary Library

Alton Terrace, 111 North Hill, Plymouth, Devon PL4 8JY
☎01752 660515

Librarian *Camilla M. Blackman*

Open Monday to Saturday from 9.30 am (closing time varies)

Access To members; visitors by appointment only

FOUNDED 1810. The library contains approximately 17,000 volumes of mainly 20th-century work. Member of the **Association of Independent Libraries**.

The Poetry Library
See entry under **Organisations of Interest to Poets**

Polish Library
238–246 King Street, London W6 0RF
☎0181 741 0474   Fax 0181 746 3798

Open 10.00 am to 8.00 pm Monday and Wednesday; 10.00 am to 5.00 pm Friday; 10.00 am to 1.00 pm Saturday (library closed Tuesday and Thursday)

Access For reference to all interested in Polish affairs; limited loans to members and *bona fide* scholars only through inter-library loans

Books, pamphlets, periodicals, maps, music, photographs on all aspects of Polish history and culture. *Special collections* Emigré publications; Joseph Conrad and related works; Polish underground publications; bookplates.

Poole Central Library
Dolphin Centre, Poole, Dorset BH15 1QE
☎01202 673910   Fax 01202 670253

Open 10.00 am to 7.00 pm Monday; 9.30 am to 7.00 pm Tuesday to Friday; 9.00 am to 1.00 pm Saturday

Open access

General lending and reference library, including Healthpoint health information centre, business information, children's library, periodicals and newspapers.

Press Association Library
See **PA News Library**

Harry Price Library of Magical Literature
University of London Library, Senate House, Malet Street, London WC1E 7HU
☎0171 862 8470   Fax 0171 862 8480
Website: www.ull.ac.uk

Open 9.30 am to 6.00 pm Monday to Friday; 9.30 am to 1.00 pm, 2.00 pm to 5.15 pm Saturday (by prior appointment only); Monday evenings in term time (by prior appointment only)

Restricted access For reference only, restricted to members of the University and *bona fide* researchers (apply in writing); items must be requested from, and consulted in, the Special Collections Reading Room

Over 14,000 volumes and pamphlets on psychic phenomena and pseudo-phenomena; books relating to spiritualism and its history, to hypnotism, telepathy, astrology, conjuring and quackery.

Public Record Office
Ruskin Avenue, Kew, Richmond, Surrey TW9 4DU
☎0181 876 3444   Fax 0181 878 8905
Email: enquiry@pro.gov.uk
Website: www.pro.gov.uk

Also at: The Family Record Centre, 1 Myddleton Street, London EC1R 1UW

Open 9.00 am to 5.00 pm Monday, Wednesday, Friday; 10.00 am to 7.00 pm Tuesday; 9.00 am to 7.00 pm Thursday; 9.30 am to 5.00 pm Saturday

Access For reference, by reader's ticket, available free of charge on production of proof of identity (UK citizens: banker's card or driving licence; non-UK: passport or national identity card. Telephone for further information)

Over 168 kilometres of shelving house the national repository of records of central Government in the UK and law courts of England and Wales, which extend in time from the 11th–20th century. Medieval records and the records of the State Paper Office from the early 16th–late 18th century, plus the records of the Privy Council Office and the Lord Chamberlain's and Lord Steward's departments. Modern government department records, together with those of the Copyright Office dating mostly from the late 18th century. Under the Public Records Act, records are normally only open to inspection when they are 30 years old.

Reading Central Library
Abbey Square, Reading, Berkshire RG1 3BQ
☎0118 901 5955   Fax 0118 901 5954

Open 9.30 am to 5.00 pm Monday and Wednesday; 9.30 am to 7.00 pm Tuesday, Thursday, Friday; 9.30 am to 4.00 pm Saturday

Open access

Lending library; reference library; local studies library, bringing together every aspect of the local environment and human activity in Berkshire; business library; music and drama library. Special collections: Mary Russell Mitford; local illustrations.

Public meeting room available.

Religious Society of Friends Library

Friends House, 173 Euston Road, London NW1 2BJ

☎0171 663 1135   Fax 0171 663 1001

Email: library@quaker.org.uk

Website: www.quaker.org.uk

Open 1.00 pm to 5.00 pm Monday, Tuesday, Thursday, Friday; 10.00 am to 5.00 pm Wednesday

Open access A letter of introduction from someone in good standing is required for researchers who are not members of the Society

Quaker history, thought and activities from the 17th century onwards. Supporting collections on peace, anti-slavery and other subjects in which Quakers have maintained long-standing interest. Also archives and manuscripts relating to the Society of Friends.

Richmond Central Reference Library

Old Town Hall, Whittaker Avenue, Richmond, Surrey TW9 1TP

☎0181 940 5529   Fax 0181 940 6899

Email: ref@richmond.gov.uk

Open 10.00 am to 6.00 pm Monday, Thursday, Friday (Tuesday till 1.00 pm; Wednesday till 8.00 pm and Saturday till 5.00 pm)

Open access

General reference library serving the needs of local residents and organisations.

Royal Geographical Society Library (with the Institute of British Geographers)

1 Kensington Gore, London SW7 2AR

☎0171 591 3040   Fax 0171 591 3001

Email: library@rgs.org

Website: www.rgs.org

Open 11.00 am to 5.00 pm Monday to Friday

Access to the library and reading rooms restricted to use by Fellows and members

Books and periodicals on geography, topography, cartography, voyages and travels. The Map Room, open since 1854 to the general public for reference purposes only, houses map and chart sheets, atlases and RGS-sponsored expedition reports. Photographs on travel and exploration

are housed in the picture library, for which an appointment is necessary. (See entry under **Picture Libraries**.)

Royal Society Library

6 Carlton House Terrace, London SW1Y 5AG

☎0171 451 2606   Fax 0171 930 2170

Open 10.00 am to 5.00 pm Monday to Friday

Access For research only, to *bona fide* researchers; contact the Library in advance of first visit

History of science, scientists' biographies, science policy reports, and publications of international scientific unions and national academies from all over the world.

RSA (Royal Society for the Encouragement of Arts, Manufactures & Commerce)

8 John Adam Street, London WC2N 6EZ

☎0171 930 5115   Fax 0171 839 5805

Email: library@rsa-uk.demon.co.uk

Website: www.rsa.org.uk

Curator *Susan Bennett*

Open 9.30 am to 1.00 pm Monday to Friday and 2.00pm to 5.00 pm Wednesdays only

Access to Fellows of RSA; by application and appointment to non-Fellows

Archives of the Society since 1754. A collection of approximately 5000 volumes; international exhibition material.

Royal Society of Medicine Library

1 Wimpole Street, London W1M 8AE

☎0171 290 2940   Fax 0171 290 2939

Email: library@roysocmed.ac.uk

Website: www.roysocmed.ac.uk

Open 9.00 am to 8.30 pm Monday to Friday; 10.00 am to 5.00 pm Saturday

Access For reference only, on introduction by Fellow of the Society (temporary membership may also be granted)

Books and periodicals on general medicine, biochemistry and biomedical science. Extensive historical material.

Royal Statistical Society Library

University College London, Gower Street, London WC1E 6BT

☎0171 387 7050 ext. 2628

Fax 0171 380 7727/7373

Email: d.chatarji@ucl.ac.uk

Contact *D Chatarji*

Access RSS Fellows registered with University

College London Library

Statistics (theor and methodology), mathematical statistics, applied statistics, econometrics.

Science Fiction Foundation Research Library

Liverpool University Library, PO Box 123, Liverpool L69 3DA
☎0151 794 2696/2733   Fax 0151 794 2681
Email: asawyer@liverpool.ac.uk
Website: www.liv.ac.uk/~sawyer/
    sffchome.html

Contact *Andy Sawyer*
Website: www.liv.ac.uk/~asawyer/
    sffchome.html

Access For research, by appointment only (telephone first)

This is the largest collection outside the US of science fiction and related material – including autobiographies and critical works. *Special collection* Runs of 'pulp' magazines dating back to the 1920s. Foreign-language material (including a large Russian collection), and the papers of the Flat Earth Society. The collection also features a growing range of archive and manuscript material, including the Eric Frank Russell archive. The University of Liverpool also holds the Olaf Stapledon and John Wyndham archives.

Science Museum Library

Imperial College Road, London SW7 5NH
☎0171 938 8234   Fax 0171 938 9714
Email: smlinfo@nmsi.ac.uk
Website: www.nmsi.ac.uk/library

Open 9.30 am to 9.00 pm Monday to Friday (closes 5.30 pm outside academic terms); 9.30 am to 5.30 pm Saturday

Open access Reference only; no loans

National reference library for the history and public understanding of science and technology, with a large collection of source material. Operates jointly with Imperial College Central Library.

Scottish Poetry Library

See entry under **Organisations of Interest to Poets**

Sheffield Libraries and Information Services

Central Library, Surrey Street, Sheffield S1 1XZ
☎0114 273 4711   Fax 0114 2735009
Website (Central Library): www.earl.org.uk/
    partners/ sheffield/index.html

Sheffield Archives

52 Shoreham Street, Sheffield S1 4SP
☎ 0114 2039395   Fax 0114 2039398
Email: sheffield.archives@dial.pipex.com

Open 9.30 am to 5.30 pm Monday to Thursday; 9.00 am to 1.00 pm and 2.00 pm to 4.30 pm Saturday (documents should be ordered by 5.00 pm Thursday for Saturday)

Access By reader's pass

Holds documents relating to Sheffield and South Yorkshire, dating from the 12th century to the present day, including records of the City Council, churches, businesses, landed estates, families and individuals, institutions and societies.

Arts and Social Sciences Reference Service

☎0114 2734747/8

Open 10.00 am to 8.00 pm Monday; 9.30 am to 5.30 pm Tuesday and Friday; 9.30 am to 8.00 pm Wednesday; 9.30 am to 4.30 pm Saturday (closed Thursday)

Access For reference only

A comprehensive collection of books, periodicals and newspapers covering all aspects of arts (excluding music) and social sciences.

Music and Video Service

☎0114 2734733

Open as for Arts and Social Sciences above

Access For reference (loans to ticket holders only)

An extensive range of books, CDs, cassettes, scores, etc. related to music. Also a video cassette loan service.

Local Studies Service ☎0114 2734753

Open as for Arts & Social Sciences above (except Wednesday 9.30 am to 5.30 pm)

Access For reference (but advance notice advisable)

Extensive material covering all aspects of Sheffield and its population, including maps, photos and videos.

Business, Science and Technology Reference Services

☎0114 2734736/7 or 2734742

Open as for Arts & Social Sciences above

Access For reference only

Extensive coverage of science and technology as well as commerce and commercial law. British patents and British and European standards with emphasis on metals. Hosts the

World Metal Index. The business section holds a large stock of business and trade directories, plus overseas telephone directories and reference works with business emphasis.

Sheffield Information Service
☎0114 2734760/1 or 2734712
Fax 0114 2757111
Email: nd54@dial.pipex.com
Website\; dis.shef.ac.uk/help_yourself

Open 10.00 am to 5.30 pm Monday; 9.30 am to 5.30 pm Tuesday, Wednesday, Friday; 9.30 am to 4.30 pm Saturday (closed. Thursday)·

Full local information service covering all aspects of the Sheffield community and a generalist advice service on a sessional basis.

Children's and Young People's Library Service
☎0114 2734734

Open 10.30 am to 5.00 pm Monday and Friday; 1.00 pm to 5.00 pm Tuesday and Wednesday; 9.30 am to 4.30 pm Saturday (closed Thursday)

Books, spoken word sets, videos; under-five play area; teenage reference section; readings and promotions; storytime sessions.

Shetland Library
Lower Hillhead, Lerwick, Shetland ZE1 0EL
☎01595 693868   Fax 01595 694430
Email: info@shetland-library.gov.uk
Website: www.shetland-library.gov.uk

Open 10.00 am to 7.00 pm Monday, Wednesday, Friday; 10.00 am to 5.00 pm Tuesday, Thursday, Saturday

General lending and reference library; extensive local interest collection including complete set of *The Shetland Times, The Shetland News* and other local newspapers on microfilm and many old and rare books; audio collection including talking books/newspapers. Junior room for children. Disabled access and Housebound Readers Service (delivery to reader's home). Mobile library services to rural areas. Open Learning Service. Same day photocopying service. Publishing programme of books in dialect, history, literature.

Shoe Lane Library
Hill House, Little New Street, London EC4A 3JR
☎0171 583 7178

Open 9.30 am to 5.30 pm Monday,

Wednesday, Thursday, Friday; 9.30 am to 6.30 pm Tuesday

Open access
Corporation of London general lending library, with a comprehensive stock of 50,000 volumes, most of which are on display.

Shrewsbury Library
Castlegates, Shrewsbury, Shropshire SY1 2AS
☎01743 255300   Fax 01743 255309
Website: www.shropshire-cc.gov.uk

Open 9.30 am to 5.00 pm Monday and Wednesday; 9.30 am to 1.00 pm Thursday; 9.30 am to 7.30 pm Tuesday and Friday; 9.30 am to 4.00 pm Saturday

Open access
The largest public lending library in Shropshire. Books, cassettes, CDs, talking books, videos, language courses. Open Learning, homework and study centre with public use computers for word processing, CD-ROMs and Internet access. Strong music, literature and art book collection. Reference and local studies provision in adjacent buildings.

Southend-on-Sea Borough Libraries
Central Library, Victoria Avenue, Southend-on-Sea, Essex SS2 6EX
☎01702 612621   Fax 01702 469241
Email: sos@dial.pipex.com

Open 9.00 am to 7.00 pm Monday to Friday; 9.00 am to 5.00 pm Saturday

Open access
Southend-on-Sea Libraries have seven libraries and two mobile libraries. The Central Library has a major arts collection and also specialist collections on history and travel.

Spanish Institute Library
See **Instituto Cervantes**

St Bride Printing Library
Bride Lane, London EC4Y 8EE
☎0171 353 4660   Fax 0171 583 7073
Open 9.30 am to 5.30 pm Monday to Friday

Open access
Corporation of London public reference library. Appointments advisable for consultation of special collections. Every aspect of printing and related matters: publishing and bookselling, newspapers and magazines, graphic design, calligraphy and type, papermaking and bookbinding. One of the world's largest specialist

collections in its field, with over 40,000 volumes, over 3000 periodicals (200 current titles), and extensive collection of drawings, manuscripts, prospectuses, patents and materials for printing and typefounding. Noted for its comprehensive holdings of historical and early technical literature.

Suffolk County Council Libraries & Heritage

St Andrew House, County Hall, St Helens Street, Ipswich, Suffolk IP4 1LJ
☎01473 583000   Fax 01473 584549
Email (general enquiries):
  infolink@libher.suffolkcc.gov.uk
Website: www.suffolkcc.gov.uk/
  libraries_and_heritage/

Open Details on application to St Andrew House above. Major libraries open six days a week

Access A single user registration card gives access to the lending service of 41 libraries across the county

Full range of lending and reference services. Free public access to the Internet and multimedia CD-ROMs in all libraries. Catalogue with self-service facilities for registered borrowers available on the Website. *Special collections* include Suffolk Archives and Local History Collection; Benjamin Britten Collection; Edward Fitzgerald Collection; Seckford Collection and Racing Collection (Newmarket). The Suffolk Infolink service gives details of local groups and societies and is available in libraries throughout the county.

Sunderland City Library and Arts Centre

28–30 Fawcett Street, Sunderland, Tyne & Wear SR1 1RE
☎0191 514 1235   Fax 0191 514 8444

Open 9.30 am to 7.30 pm Monday and Wednesday; 9.30 am to 5.00 pm Tuesday, Thursday, Friday; 9.30 am to 4.00 pm Saturday

The city's main lending and reference library. Local studies and children's sections, plus sound and vision department (CDs, cassettes, videos, CD-ROMs, talking books). The City of Sunderland also maintains community libraries of varying size, offering a range of services, plus mobile libraries. A Books on Wheels service is available to housebound readers; the Schools Library Service serves teachers and schools.

Swansea Central Reference Library

Alexandra Road, Swansea SA1 5DX
☎01792 615753/615757   Fax 01792 615759
Email: swanlib@demon.co.uk

Open 9.00 am to 7.00 pm Monday, Tuesday, Wednesday, Friday; 9.00 am to 5.00 pm Thursday and Saturday. The library has a lending service but hours tend to be shorter – check in advance (☎01792 654065).

Access For reference only (Local Studies closed access: items must be requested on forms provided)

General reference material (approx. 100,000 volumes); also British standards, statutes, company information, maps, European Community information. Local studies: comprehensive collections on Wales; Swansea & Gower; Dylan Thomas. Local maps, periodicals, illustrations, local newspapers from 1804. B&w and colour photocopying facilities, access to the Internet and microfilm/microfiche copying facility.

Swiss Cottage Central Library

88 Avenue Road, London NW3 3HA
☎0171 413 6533/4

Open 10.00 am to 7.00 pm Monday and Thursday; 10.00 am to 6.00 pm Tuesday and Friday; 10.00 am to 5.00 pm Saturday (closed all day Wednesday)

Open access

Over 300,000 volumes in the lending and reference libraries and 300 periodicals (200 current titles). Home of the London Borough of Camden's Information and Reference Services.

Theatre Museum Library & Archive

1e Tavistock Street, London WC2E 7PA
☎0171 836 7891   Fax 0171 836 5148
Website: www.vam.ac.uk

Open 10.30 am to 4.30 pm Tuesday to Friday

Access By appointment only

The Theatre Museum was founded as a separate department of the Victoria & Albert Museum in 1974 and moved to its own building in Covent Garden in 1987. The museum (open Tuesday to Sunday 11.00 am to 7.00 pm) houses permanent displays, temporary exhibitions, a studio theatre, and organises a programme of special events, performances, lectures, guided visits and workshops. The library houses the UK's largest performing arts research collections, including books, photographs, designs, engravings, programmes, press cuttings, etc. All the performing arts are covered but strengths are in the areas of theatre, dance, musical theatre and stage design. The Theatre Museum has acquired much of the British Theatre Association's library and is providing reference access to its collections of play texts and critical works.

Thurrock Council Leisure, Libraries & Cultural Services Department

Grays Library, Orsett Road, Grays, Essex RM17 5DX
☎01375 383611   Fax 01375 370806

Open 9.00 am to 7.00 pm Monday, Tuesday, Thursday; 9.00 am to 5.00 pm Wednesday, Friday, Saturday; branch library opening times vary

Open access
General library lending and reference through nine libraries and a mobile library. Services include books, magazines, newspapers, audiocassettes, CDs, videos, pictures and language courses. Large collection of Thurrock materials. Periodicals collection (not on public access).

Truro Library

Union Place, Pydar Street, Truro, Cornwall TR1 1EP
☎01872 279205 (Lending)/272702 (Reference

Open 9.30 am to 5.00 pm Monday to Thursday; 9.30 am to 7.00 pm Friday; 9.30 am to 1.00 pm Saturday

Books, cassettes, CDs and videos for loan through branch or mobile networks. Reference, music and drama. *Special collections* on local studies.

United Nations Information Centre

Millbank Tower (21st Floor), 21–24 Millbank, London SW1P 4QH
☎0171 630 1981   Fax 0171 976 6478
Email: info@uniclondon.org
Website: www.unitednations.org.uk

Open Library: 9.00 am to 1.00 pm and 2.00 pm to 5.30 pm Monday to Thursday

Open access By appointment only
A full stock of official publications and documentation from the United Nations.

Western Isles Libraries

Public Library, 19 Cromwell Street, Stornoway, Isle of Lewis
☎01851 703064   Fax 01851 705657

Open 10.00 am to 5.00 pm Monday to

Thursday; 10.00 am to 7.00 pm Friday; 10.00 am to 1.00 pm Saturday

Open access
General public library stock, plus local history and Gaelic collections including maps, printed music and cassettes; census records and Council minutes; music collection (cassettes). Branch libraries on the isles of Barra, Benbecula, Harris and Lewis.

City of Westminster Archives Centre

10 St Ann's Street, London SW1P 2XR
☎0171 641 5180   Fax 0171 641 5179

Open 9.30 am to 7.00 pm Monday, Tuesday, Thursday, Friday; 9.30 am to 9.00 pm Wesdnesday; 9.30 am to 5.00 pm Saturday

Access For reference
Comprehensive coverage of the history of Westminster and selective coverage of general London history. 22,000 books, together with a large stock of maps, prints, photographs, and theatre programmes.

Westminster Music Library

Victoria Library, 160 Buckingham Palace Road, London SW1W 9UD
☎0171 641 2192   Fax 0171 641 2181
Email: westmuslib@dial.pipex.com
Website: www.earl.org.uk/music/ westminster/composers

Open 11.00 pm to 7.00 pm Monday to Friday; 10 am to 5.00 pm Saturday

Open access
Located at Victoria Library, this is the largest public music library in the South of England, with extensive coverage of all aspects of music, including books, periodicals and printed scores. No recorded material, notated only. Lending library includes a small collection of CDs, cassettes and videos.

Westminster Reference Library

35 St Martin's Street, London WC2H 7HP
Fax 0171 641 4640
Website: www.earl.org.uk/partners/ westminster/gateway.html
General Reference & Performing Arts:
☎0171 641 4636
Business and Official Publications:
☎0171 641 4634

Open 10.00 am to 8.00 pm Monday to Friday; 10.00 am to 5.00 pm Saturday

Access For reference only

A general reference library with emphasis on the following: Art & Design (see separate entry); Performing Arts – theatre, cinema, radio, television and dance; Official Publications – major collection of HMSO publications from 1947, plus parliamentary papers dating back to 1906, and a ten-year file of key statistical publications from OECD, UN, UNESCO, etc.; Business – UK directories, trade directories, company and market data; Official EU Depository Library – carries official EU material; Periodicals – long files of many titles. One working day's notice is required for government documents, some monographs and most older periodicals.

Westminster Reference Library – Art & Design Library

35 St Martin's Street, London
WC2H 7HP
☎0171 641 4638   Fax 0171 641 4640

Open 10.00 am to 8.00 pm Monday to
Friday; 10.00 am to 5.00 pm Saturday

Access For reference only (stacks are closed to the public)

Located on the second floor of the City of Westminster's main reference library. An excellent reference source for fine and applied arts, including antiques, architecture, ceramics, coins, costume, crafts, design, furniture, garden history, interior decoration, painting, sculpture, textiles. Complete runs of major English Language periodicals such as *Studio*; exhibition catalogues; guidebooks to historic houses, castles, gardens and churches. Some older books and most periodicals earlier than 1980 are in storage and at least one day's notice is required before they can be obtained.

The Wiener Library

4 Devonshire Street, London W1N 2BH
☎0171 636 7247   Fax 0171 436 6428
Email: lib@wl.u-net.com

Open 10.00 am to 5.30 pm Monday to Friday

Access By letter of introduction (readers needing to use the Library for any length of time should become members)

Private library – one of the leading research centres on European history since the First World War, with special reference to the era of totalitarianism and to Jewish affairs. Founded by Dr Alfred Wiener in Amsterdam in 1933, it holds material that is not available elsewhere. Books, periodicals, press archives, documents, pamphlets, leaflets and brochures. Much of the material can be consulted on microfilm.

Vaughan Williams Memorial Library

English Folk Dance and Song Society, Cecil Sharp House, 2 Regent's Park Road, London NW1 7AY
☎0171 284 0523   Fax 0171 284 0523

Open 9.30 am to 5.30 pm Monday to Friday

Access For reference to the general public, on payment of a daily fee; members may borrow books and use the library free of charge

A multi-media collection: books, periodicals, manuscripts, tapes, records, CDs, films, videos. Mostly British folk culture and how this has developed around the world. Some foreign language material, and some books in English about foreign cultures. Also, the history of the English Folk Dance and Song Society.

Dr Williams's Library

14 Gordon Square, London WC1H 0AG
☎0171 387 3727   Fax 0171 388 1142

Open 10.00 am to 5.00 pm Monday,
Wednesday, Friday; 10.00 am to 6.30 pm
Tuesday and Thursday

Open access To reading room (loans restricted to subscribers)

Annual subscription £10; ministers of
religion and certain students £5

Primarily a library of theology, religion and ecclesiastical history. Also philosophy, history (English and Byzantine). Particularly important for the study of English Nonconformity.

Wolverhampton Central Library

Snow Hill, Wolverhampton WV1 3AX
☎01902 552025   Fax 01902 552024

Open 9.00 am to 7.00 pm Monday to
Thursday; 9.00 am to 5.00 pm Friday and
Saturday

Archives & Local Studies Collection

42–50 Snow Hill, Wolverhampton WV2 4AB
☎01902 552480

Open 10.00 am to 5.00 pm Monday,
Tuesday, Friday, 1st and 3rd Saturday of
each month; 10.00 am to 7.00 pm
Wednesday; closed Thursday (Limited
archive production between 12.00 pm and
2.00 pm; archives must be booked in
advance on Saturdays)

General lending and reference libraries, plus children's library. Also audiovisual library holding cassettes, CDs, videos and music scores. Internet access.

Worcestershire Libraries and Information Service

Cultural Services, County Hall, Spetchley Road, Worcester WR5 2NP
☎01905 766231   Fax 01905 766240
Website: www.worcestershire.gov.uk

Open Opening hours vary in the 22 libraries and mobile libraries covering the county; all full-time libraries open at least one evening a week until 7.00 pm or 8.00 pm, and on Saturday until 1 pm; part-time libraries vary

Access Information and reference services open to anyone; loans to members only (membership criteria: resident, being educated, working, or an elector in the county or neighbouring authorities; temporary membership to visitors. Proof of identity and address required)

Information service, and reference and lending libraries. Non-fiction and fiction for all age groups, including normal and large print, spoken word cassettes, sound recordings (CD, cassette, some vinyl), videos, maps, local history, CD-ROMs for reference at main libraries, on-line information service including Internet access to certain specified (public information) Websites. *Special collections* Carpets and Textiles; Needles & Needlemaking; Stuart Period; A. E. Housman.

York Central Library

Museum Street, York YO1 7DS
☎01904 655631   Fax 01904 611025

Lending Library

Open 9.30 am to 8.00 pm Monday, Tuesday, Friday; 9.30 am to 5.30 pm Wednesday and Thursday; 9.30 am to 4.00 pm Saturday

General lending library including videos, CDs, music cassettes, audio books and children's storytapes.

Reference Library

Open 9.00 am to 8.00 pm Monday, Tuesday, Wednesday, Friday; 9.00 am to 5.30 pm Thursday; 9.00 am to 4.00 pm Saturday

General reference library; organisations database; local studies library for York and surrounding area; business information service; microfilm/fiche readers for national and local newspapers; census returns and family history resource; general reference collection. Maintains strong links with other local history resource centres, namely the Borthwick Institute, York City Archive and York Minster Library. CD-ROM and Internet facilities.

Young Book Trust Children's Reference Library

Book House, 45 East Hill, London SW18 2QZ
☎0181 516 2977   Fax 0181 516 2978

Open 9.00 am to 5.00 pm Monday to Friday (by appointment only)

Access For reference only

A comprehensive collection of children's literature, related books and periodicals. Aims to hold most of all children's titles published within the last two years. An information service covers all aspects of children's literature, including profiles of authors and illustrators. Reading room facilities.

Zoological Society Library

Regent's Park, London NW1 4RY
☎0171 449 6293   Fax 0171 586 5743

Open 9.30 am to 5.30 pm Monday to Friday

Access To members and staff; non-members by application and on payment of fee

160,000 volumes on zoology including 5000 journals (1300 current) and a wide range of books on animals and particular habitats. Slide collection available and many historic zoological prints.

Picture Libraries

A–Z Botanical Collection Ltd
192 Goswell Road, London EC1V 7DT
☎0171 253 0991   Fax 0171 253 0992
Website: www.a-z.picture-library.com

Contact *James Wakefield*

300,000 transparencies, specialising in plants and related subjects.

Acme
See **Popperfoto**

Action Plus
54–58 Tanner Street, London SE1 3PH
☎0171 403 1558   Fax 0171 403 1526

Specialist sports and action library with a vast comprehensive collection of small-format colour and b&w images covering all aspects of over 140 professional and amateur sports from around the world. As well as personalities, events, venues, etc, also covers themes such as success, celebration, dejection, teamwork, effort and exhaustion. Offers same-day despatch of pictures or alternatively, clients with modem or ISDN links can receive digital images direct.

Lesley & Roy Adkins Picture Library
Longstone Lodge, Aller, Langport, Somerset TA10 0QT
☎01458 250075   Fax 01458 250858
Email: Adkins_Archaeology@
compuserve.com

Colour coverage of archaeology, heritage and related subjects in the UK, Europe, Egypt and Turkey. Subjects include towns, villages, housing, landscape and countryside, churches, temples, castles, monasteries, art and architecture, gravestones and tombs, and antiquarian views. Prompt service. No service charge if pictures are used.

The Advertising Archive Limited
45 Lyndale Avenue, London NW2 2QB
☎0171 435 6540   Fax 0171 794 6584

Contact *Suzanne or Larry Viner*

With over one million images, the largest collection of British and American press ads and magazine cover illustrations in Europe. Material from 1870 to the present day. Visitors by appointment. Research undertaken; rapid service, competitive rates. Exclusive UK agents for *Saturday Evening Post* cover illustrations including artwork of Norman Rockwell and Josef Leyendecker.

AKG London Ltd, The Arts and History Picture Library
10 Plato Place, 72–74 St Dionis Road, London SW6 4TU
☎0171 610 6103   Fax 0171 610 6125
Email: enquiries@akg-london.co.uk
Website: www.akg-london.co.uk

Contact *Julia Engelhardt*

Collection of 150,000 images with computerised access to 10 million more kept in the Berlin AKG Library. *Specialises* in art, archaeology, history, topography, music, personalities and film.

Bryan & Cherry Alexander Photography
Higher Cottage, Manston, Sturminster Newton, Dorset DT10 1EZ
☎01258 473006   Fax 01258 473333
Email: arcticfoto@aol.com
Website: members.aol.com/arcticfoto/

Contact *Cherry Alexander*

Arctic and Antarctic specialists; indigenous peoples, wildlife and science in polar regions; Norway, Iceland, Siberia and Alaska.

Allsport (UK) Ltd
3 Greenlea Park, Prince George's Road, London SW19 2JD
☎0181 685 1010   Fax 0181 648 5240
Email: lmartin@allsport.co.uk
Website: www.allsport.com

Contact *Lee Martin*

A large specialist library with 6 million colour transparencies, covering 140 different sports and top sports personalities. Represented in 27 countries worldwide. Digital wiring facilities through Macintosh picture desk. Online digital archive access available via ISDN and Internet.

AlphaStock Picture Library
Greenheys Business Centre, 10 Pencroft Way, Manchester M15 6JJ
☎0161 226 8000   Fax 0161 226 2022
Email: pictures@alphastock.co.uk
Website: www.alphastock.co.uk

Wide selection of subjects from the UK and abroad. Mostly colour, some b&w. Industry, business, sport, farming, scenic, personalities, jazz musicians (and some classical), space, and many more. Special collection on the North West of England. Commissions undertaken.

Alvey & Towers
9 Rosebank Road, Countesthorpe, Leicestershire LE8 5YA
☎0116 2779184   Fax 0116 2779184
Email: alveytower@aol.com

Contact *Emma Rowen*

Houses two separate collections; one covering the modern railway industry and all related supporting industries, the other features a more general 'lifestyle' collection with the emphasis on people and day-to-day living plus a substantial selection of transport images.

Andes Press Agency
26 Padbury Court, London E2 7EH
☎0171 613 5417   Fax 0171 739 3159
Email: photos@andespress.demon.co.uk

Contact *Val Baker, Carlos Reyes*

80,000 colour transparencies and 300,000 b&w, specialising in social documentary, world religions, Latin America and Britain.

Heather Angel/Biofotos
Highways, 6 Vicarage Hill, Farnham, Surrey GU9 8HJ
☎01252 716700   Fax 01252 727464
Email: Natvision@btinternet.com

Contacts *Lindsay Bamford, Valerie West*

Constantly expanding worldwide natural history, wildlife and landscapes: polar regions, tropical rainforest flora and fauna, all species of plants and animals in natural habitats from Africa, Asia (notably China and Malaysia), Australasia, South America and USA, urban wildlife, pollution, biodiversity, global warming. Also worldwide gardens and cultivated flowers. Transparencies only loaned to publishers after contract exchanged with author.

Animal Photography
4 Marylebone Mews, New Cavendish Street, London W1M 7LF
☎0171 935 0503   Fax 0171 487 3038
Email: thompson@animal-photography.co.uk

Colour and b&w coverage of horses, dogs, cats, zoos, the Galapagos Islands, East Africa. Pictures from other photographers are not accepted.

Ansel Adams
See **Corbis Images**

Aquarius Picture Library
PO Box 5, Hastings, East Sussex TN34 1HR
☎01424 721196   Fax 01424 717704

Contact *David Corkill*

Over one million images specialising in cinema past and present, television, pop music, ballet, opera, theatre, etc. The library includes various American showbiz collections. Film stills date back to the beginning of the century. Interested in film stills, the older the better. Current material is supplied by own suppliers.

Aquila Wildlife Images
PO Box 1, Studley, Warwickshire B80 7JG
☎0152785 2357   Fax 0152785 7507

Natural history library specialising in birds, British and European wildlife, North America, Africa and Australia, environmental subjects, farming, habitats and related subjects, domestic animals and pets.

Arcaid
The Factory, 2 Acre Road, Kingston upon Thames, Surrey KT2 6EF
☎0181 546 4352   Fax 0181 541 5230
Email: arcaid@arcaid.co.uk
Website: www.arcaid.co.uk

The built environment, historic and contemporary architecture and interior design by leading architectural photographers. Covers international and British subjects, single images and series, with background information. Visitors welcome by appointment. Commissions undertaken.

Architectural Association Photo Library
34–36 Bedford Square, London WC1B 3ES
☎0171 887 4078/4086   Fax 0171 414 0782

Contact *Valerie Bennett, Vera Wong, Anna Drury*

200,000 35mm transparencies on architecture, historical and contemporary. Archive of large-format b&w negatives from the 1920s and 1930s.

Ardea London Ltd
35 Brodrick Road, London SW17 7DX
☎0181 672 2067   Fax 0181 672 8787
Email: ardea@ardea.co.uk

Specialist natural history photographic library supplying original transparencies of animals, birds, plants, fish, reptiles and amphibians in their natural habitat worldwide and domestic pets. Coverage includes landscapes, conservation and environmental images.

Art Directors & Trip Photo Library
57 Burdon Lane, Cheam, Surrey SM2 7BY
☎0181 642 3593/661 7104
Fax 0181 395 7230
Email: images@tripphoto.demon.co.uk
Website: www.tripphoto.demon.co.uk
Contact *Helene Rogers, Bob Turner*

Englarged newly-merged library with over 750,000 images. Extensive coverage of all countries, lifestyles, religion, peoples, etc. Backgrounds a speciality. Catalogues available free to professionals.

Artbank Illustration Library
8 Woodcroft Avenue, London NW7 2AG
☎0181 906 2288   Fax 0181 906 2289
Email: info@artbank.ltd.uk
Website: www.artbank.ltd.uk

Illustration and art library holding thousands of images by many renowned contemporary illustrators. Large-format transparencies. Catalogue available on faxed request. Represents a diverse group of UK and American illustrators for commissioned work. Portfolios available for viewing.

Aspect Picture Library Ltd
40 Rostrevor Road, London SW6 5AD
☎0171 736 1998/731 7362
Fax 0171 731 7362
Email: Aspect.Ldn@btinternet.com
Website: www.aspect-picture-library.co.uk

Colour and b&w worldwide coverage of countries, events, industry and travel, with large files on art, namely paintings, space, China and the Middle East.

Audio Visual Services
Imperial College School of Medicine at St Mary's, London W2 1PG
☎0171 886 1739   Fax 0171 724 7349
Contact *B. Tallon*

Colour and b&w, mostly 35mm colour. Clinical medicine, contemporary and historical, including HIV-AIDS material and history of penicillin. Commissions undertaken.

Australia Pictures
28 Sheen Common Drive, Richmond TW10 5BN
☎0181 898 0150/876 3637
Fax 0181 898 0150/876 3637

Contact *John Miles*

Collection of 4000 transparencies covering all aspects of Australia: Aboriginal people, paintings, Ayers Rock, Kakadu, Tasmania, underwater, reefs, Arnhem Land, Sydney. Also Africa, Middle East and Asia.

Aviation Images – Mark Wagner
42B Queens Road, London SW19 8LR
☎0181 944 5225   Fax 0181 944 5335
Contact *Mark Wagner*

250,000+ aviation images, civil and military, technical and generic. Mark Wagner is the photographer for *Flight International* magazine. Member of **BAPLA** and RAeS.

Aviation Photographs International
15 Downs View Road, Swindon, Wiltshire SN3 1NS
☎01793 497179   Fax 01793 434030

The 250,000 colour photos comprise a comprehensive coverage of army, naval and airforce hardware ranging from early pistols to the latest ships. Extensive coverage of military and civil aviation includes modern together with many air-to-air views of vintage/warbird types. Commissions undertaken for additional photography and research.

Aviation Picture Library
116 The Avenue, St Stephens, West Ealing, London W13 8JX
☎0181 566 7712   Fax 0181 566 7714
Email: avpix@avnet.co.uk
Contact *Austin John Brown, Chris Savill*

Specialists in the aviation field but also a general library which includes travel, architecture, transport, landscapes and skyscapes. *Special collections*: aircraft and all aspects of the aviation industry; aerial obliques of Europe, USA, Caribbean and West Africa; architectural and town planning. Commissions undertaken on the ground and in the air.

Axel Poignant Archive
115 Bedford Court Mansions, Bedford Avenue, London WC1B 3AG
☎0171 636 2555   Fax 0171 636 2555
Contact *Roslyn Poignant*

Anthropological and ethnographic subjects, especially Australia and the South Pacific. Also Scandinavia (early history and mythology), Sicily and England.

Barnaby's Picture Library

Barnaby House, 19 Rathbone Street, London
W1P 1AF
☎0171 636 6128   Fax 0171 637 4317
Email: barnabyspicturelibrary@ukbusiness.com
Website: www.ukbusiness.com/
   barnabyspicturelibrary
Contact *Mary Buckland*

Colour and b&w coverage of a wide range of
subjects: nature, transport, industry and historical, including a collection on Hitler. Etchings
throughout history.

Barnardos Photographic and Film Archive

Tanners Lane, Barkingside, Ilford, Essex
IG6 1QG
☎0181 550 8822   Fax 0181 550 0429
Contact *John Kirkham*

Specialises in social history (1874 to present day),
child care, education, war years, emigration/
migration. Half a million prints, slides, negatives.
Images are mainly b&w, colour since late
1940s/early 50s. Archive of 200 films dating back
to 1905. Visitors by appointment Mon–Fri 9.30
am to 4.30 pm.

Colin Baxter Photography Limited

Woodlands Industrial Estate, Grantown-on-
Spey PH26 3NA
☎01479 873999   Fax 01479 873888
Email: colin.baxter@zetnet.co.uk
Contact *Colin B. Kirkwood (Marketing), Mike
   Rensner (Editorial)*

Over 50,000 images specialising in Scotland.
Also the Lake District, Yorkshire, the
Cotswolds, France, Iceland and a special collection on Charles Rennie Mackintosh's work.
Publishes books, calendars, postcards and greetings cards on landscape, cityscape and natural
history containing images which are primarily,
but not exclusively, Colin Baxter's. Also publishers of the *Worldlife Library* of natural history
books.

BBC Natural History Unit Picture Library

Broadcasting House, Whiteladies Road,
Bristol BS8 2LR
☎0117 9746720   Fax 0117 9238166
Email: nhu.picture.library@bbc.co.uk
Contacts *Helen Gilks, Sue Fogden*

A collection of 80,000 transparencies of wildlife
of the world. Other subjects covered include
plants, landscapes, environmental issues and photos relating to the making of the Natural History
Unit's films. Wildlife sound recordings and film
footage also available.

The Photographic Library Beamish, The North of England Open Air Museum

Beamish, The North of England Open Air
Museum, Beamish, County Durham
DH9 0RG
☎01207 231811   Fax 01207 290933
Email: Beamish@neoam.demon.co.uk
Website: www.merlins.demon.co.uk/beamish
Keeper of Resource Collections *Jim Lawson*

Comprehensive collection; images relate to the
North East of England and cover agricultural,
industrial, topography, advertising and shop
scenes, people at work and play. Also on laser
disk for rapid searching. Visitors by appointment weekdays.

Francis Bedford

See **Birmingham Library Services** under
Library Services

Ivan J. Belcher Colour Picture Library

57 Gibson Close, Abingdon, Oxfordshire
OX14 1XS
☎01235 521524   Fax 01235 521524

Extensive colour picture library specialising in
top-quality medium-format transparencies
depicting the British scene. Particular emphasis
on tourist, holiday and heritage locations,
including famous cities, towns, picturesque harbours, rivers, canals, castles, cottages, rural scenes
and traditions photographed throughout the
seasons. Mainly of recent origin, and constantly
updated.

Andrew Besley PhotoLibrary

2 Reawla Lane, Reawla, Near Hayle,
Cornwall TR27 5HQ
☎01736 850086   Fax 01736 850086
Email: bes.pix@btinternet.com
Contact *Andrew Besley*

Specialist library of 20,000 images of West
Country faces, places and moods.

Bettmann Archive

See **Corbis Images**

BFI Stills, Posters and Designs

British Film Institute, 21 Stephen Street,
London W1P 2LN

☎0171 255 1444   Fax 0171 323 9260

Holds images from more than 60,000 films and
TV programmes on 6 million b&w prints and
over 500,000 colour transparencies. A further
20,000 files hold portraits of film and TV personalities and cover related general subjects such as
studios, equipment, awards. Also holds original
posters and set and costume designs. Visitors welcome by appointment only (from 11.00 am to
5.00 pm).

Blackwoods Picture Library

See **Geoslides Photography**

Anthony Blake Photo Library

54 Hill Rise, Richmond, Surrey TW10 6UB

☎0181 940 7583   Fax 0181 948 1224

Email: anthonyblake.photo@virgin.net

'Europe's premier source' of food and wine related images. From the farm and the vineyard to
the plate and the bottle. Cooking and kitchens,
top chefs and restaurants, country trades and
markets, worldwide travel with an extensive
Italian section. Many recipes available to accompany transparencies. Free brochure available.

Peter Boardman Collection

See **Chris Bonnington Picture Library**

Boats & Boating Features
(Keith Pritchard)

9 High Street, Southwell, Portland, Dorset
DT5 2EH

☎01305 861006/0378 307301

Fax 01305 861006

Email: keith@boating-features.demon.co.uk

Website: www.boating-features.demon.co.uk

Contact *Keith Pritchard*

Around 20,000 colour transparencies of small
craft, historic and modern boats up to 100ft,
boating events, people and places in Britain and
overseas.

Chris Bonington Picture Library

Badger Hill, Nether Row, Hesket
Newmarket, Wigton, Cumbria CA7 8LA

☎016974 78286   Fax 016974 78238

Email: frances@bonington.com

Website: www.bonington.com

Contact *Frances Daltrey*

Based on the personal collection of climber and
author Chris Bonington and his extensive travels

and mountaineering achievements; also work by
Doug Scott and other climbers, including the
Peter Boardman and Joe Tasker Collections.
Full coverage of the world's mountains, from
British hills to Everest, depicting expedition
planning and management stages, the approach
march showing inhabitants of the area, flora and
fauna, local architecture and climbing action
shots on some of the world's highest mountains.

Boulton and Watt Archive

See **Birmingham Library Services** under
Library Services

The Bridgeman Art Library

17–19 Garway Road, London W2 4PH

☎0171 727 4065   Fax 0171 792 8509

Email: info@bridgeman.co.uk

Website: www.bridgeman.co.uk

Rights & Marketing Executive
Beatrice Thomas

Fine art photo archive acting as an agent to
more than 750 museums, galleries and picture
owners around the world. Large-format colour
transparencies of paintings, sculptures, prints,
manuscripts, antiquities and the decorative arts.
The Library is currently expanding at the rate
of 500 new images each week and has offices in
Paris and New York. Collections represented
by the library include the British Library, the
National Galleries of Scotland, the National
Library of Australia, and the National Gallery
of South Africa. Catalogues of stock are available in printed form and on CD-ROM. 'Please
call for a free brochure or visit our Website on
the Internet.'

British Library Reproductions

British Library, 96 Euston Road, London
NW1 2DB

☎0171 412 7614   Fax 0171 412 7771

Email: bl-repro@bl.uk

Website: www.bl.uk

Twelve million books and approximately five
million other items available for photography,
microfilming or photocopying by Library staff.
Specialist subjects include illuminated manuscripts, stamps, music, maps, botanical and zoological illustration, portraits of historical figures,
history of India and South East Asia. The library
has a small but unique collection of colour and
b&w images mainly covering royalty, religion,
medieval life and world maps plus a selection of
natural history. All copies should be ordered as
far in advance as possible. However, for photographs for commercial reproduction a picture

library service is available which enables orders to be processed more quickly. Customers are welcome to browse.

Brooklands Museum Picture Library
Brooklands Museum, Brooklands Road, Weybridge, Surrey KT13 0QN
☎01932 857381   Fax 01932 855465
Contact *John Pulford (Curator of Collections), Julian Temple (Curator of Aviation)*

About 40,000 b&w and colour prints and slides. Subjects include: Brooklands Motor Racing 1907–1939; British aviation and aerospace 1908–present day – particularly BAC, Hawker, Sopwith and Vickers aircraft built at Brooklands.

Hamish Brown Scottish Photographic
26 Kirkcaldy Road, Burntisland, Fife KY3 9HQ
☎01592 873546
Contact *Hamish M. Brown*

Colour and b&w coverage of most topics and areas of Scotland (sites, historic, buildings, landscape, mountains), also travel and mountains abroad, Ireland and Morocco. Commissions undertaken.

Simon Brown, Nature and Landscape Photographer
36 Sandymount Road, Wath–upon–Dearne, Rotherham, South Yorkshire S63 7AE
☎01709 874322/0966 538821 (mobile)
Fax 01709 874322
Website: www.redstart.net
Contact *Simon Brown*

20,000 images of the nature and landscape of the British Isles with particular emphasis on the Peak District, Northumberland and North Wales. Predominantly colour transparencies with some monochrome material. Works to commission or from stock. Self publishers welcome; full research service in life sciences, history, photography and moutaineering. More information available on the Website; 'click on photography and search by my name'.

Bubbles Photolibrary
23A Benwell Road, London N7 7BL
☎0171 609 4547/ISDN – 0171 697 9807
Fax 0171 607 1410
Email: BUBBLESPHOTOS@
    compuserve.com

Pregnancy, babies, children, teenagers, general lifestyle, health, old age, medical, still lives of food.

Camera Press
21 Queen Elizabeth Street, London SE1 2PD
☎0171 378 1300   Fax 0171 278 5126

Quality studio images of celebrities, photo-features, news, personality portraits, humour, royals, fashion and beauty.

Camera Ways Ltd Picture Library
Court View, Stonebridge Green Road, Egerton, Ashford, Kent TN27 9AN
☎01233 756454   Fax 01233 756242
Email: CAMERAWAYS@compuserve.com
Contacts *Derek, Caryl, Jonathan, Steve*

Founded by award-winning film-maker and photographer, Derek Budd, the digital scanned library specialises in rural activities and natural history. It contains 35mm and 6x4.5mm, colour and b&w images as well as 16mm film and video footage on Beta SP and digital Betacam formats. Coverage includes: wildlife habitats, flora and fauna of Britain and Europe, traditional country crafts and people, village scenes, landscapes, gardens, coastal and aquatic life, dinosaurs, aerial surveys, storm damage and M.O.D. reserves. A creative service is available from their Technical Artist & Wildlife Illustrator; commissions undertaken in all aspects of commercial multi-media photography, 16mm film, broadcast and corporate video production.

Capital Pictures
49–51 Central Street, London EC1V 8AB
☎0171 253 1122   Fax 0171 253 1414
Contact *Phil Loftus*

500,000 images. *Specialises* in photographs of famous people from the worlds of showbusiness, rock and pop, television, politics, royalty and film stills.

The Casement Collection
Erin Lodge, Jigs Lane South, Warfield, Berkshire RG42 3DR
☎01344 302067   Fax 01344 303158

Colour and b&w travel library, particularly strong on North America and the Gulf. Not just beaches and palm trees. Based on Jack Casement's collection, with additions by other photographers. Digitised images available.

J. Allan Cash Ltd
204 Northfield Avenue, London W14 9SJ
☎0181 840 4141   Fax 0181 566 2568

Colour and b&w coverage of travel, natural history, people, space, sport, industry, agriculture and many other subjects. New material regularly contributed by 300-plus photographers.

The Centre for the Study of Cartoons and Caricature
The Templeman Library, University of Kent at Canterbury, Canterbury, Kent CT2 7NU
☎01227 823127   Fax 01227 823127
Email: J.M.Newton@ukc.ac.uk
Website: libservb.ukc.ac.uk/cartoons/

Contacts *Jane Newton*

A national research archive of over 85,000 20th century cartoons and caricatures, supported by a library of books, papers, journals, catalogues and assorted ephemera. A computer database provides for quick and easy catalogued access. A source for exhibitions and displays as well as a picture library service. *Specialises* in historical, political and social cartoons from British newspapers.

CEPHAS Picture Library
Hurst House, 157 Walton Road, East Molesey, Surrey KT8 0DX
☎0181 979 8647   Fax 0181 224 8095
Email: mickrock@cephas.co.uk
Website: www.cephas.co.uk

The wine industry and vineyards of the world is the subject on which Cephas has made its reputation. 100,000 images, mainly original 6x7s, make this the most comprehensive and up-to-date archive in Britain. Almost all wine-producing countries and all aspects of the industry are covered in depth. Spirits, beer and cider also included. A major food and drink collection now also exists, through preparation and cooking, to eating and drinking. Call for free 114-page catalogue.

Christel Clear Marine Photography
Roselea, Church Lane, Awbridge, Near Romsey, Hampshire SO51 0HN
☎01794 341081   Fax 01794 340890
Email: christel.clear@btinternet.com

Contact *Nigel Dowden, Christel Dowden*

Over 70,000 images on 35mm and 645 transparency: yachting and boating from Grand Prix sailing to small dinghies, cruising locations and harbours. Recent additions include angling, fly fishing and travel. Visitors by appointment.

Christian Aid Photo Section
PO Box 100, London SE1 7RT
☎0171 523 2235   Fax 0171 620 0719

Pictures are mainly from Africa, Asia and Latin America, relating to small-scale, community-based programmes. Mostly development themes: agriculture, health, education, urban and rural life.

Christie's Images
1 Langley Lane, London SW8 1TH
☎0171 582 1282   Fax 0171 582 5632
Email: cimages@compuserve.com
Website: www.christies.com/christiesimages/

Contact *Camilla Young*

The UK's largest fine art photo library. 150,000 images of fine and decorative art. An extensive list of subjects is covered through paintings, drawings and prints of all periods as well as silver, ceramics, jewellery, sculpture, textiles and many other decorative and collectable items. Staff will search files and database to locate specific requests or supply a selection for consideration. Visits by appointment.

The Cinema Museum
The Master's House, Old Lambeth Workhouse, off Renfrew Road, London SE11 4TH
☎0171 840 2200   Fax 0171 840 2299
Email: martin@cinemamuseum.org.uk

Colour and b&w coverage (including stills) of the motion picture industry throughout its history, including the Ronald Grant Archive. Smaller collections on theatre, variety, television and popular music.

John Cleare/Mountain Camera
Hill Cottage, Fonthill Gifford, Salisbury, Wiltshire SP3 6QW
☎01747 820320   Fax 01747 820320
Email: cleare@btinternet.com

Colour and b&w coverage of mountains and wild places, climbing, ski-touring, trekking, expeditions, wilderness travel, landscapes, people and geographical features from all continents. *Specialises* in the Himalaya, Andes, Antarctic, Alps and the British countryside, and a range of topics from reindeer in Lapland to camels in Australia, from whitewater rafting in Utah to ski-mountaineering in China. Commissions and consultancy work undertaken. Researchers welcome by appointment. Member of **BAPLA** and the OWG.

The Clifton Archive
71 Broadmead Road, Folkestone, Kent
CT19 5AW
☎01303 850524   Fax 01303 850524
Contact *Alan Clifton*

Established in 1956 by photographer Alan Clifton. A collection of 300,000 b&w 35mm negatives and 200,000 colour 35mm transparencies which includes a large travel section and over 500 personalities.

Close-Up Picture Library
14 Burnham Wood, Fareham, Hampshire
PO16 7UD
☎01329 239053
Director *David Stent*

Specialises in the close-up angle of all aspects of life: people, places, animal and bird-life and the environment in general. Also a wide range of pictures covering travel in Europe and the Orient, multicultural, ethnic and educational issues. Photographers with quality material always welcome: no minimum initial submission; 50% commission on 35mm.

Stephanie Colasanti
38 Hillside Court, 409 Finchley Road,
London NW3 6HQ
☎0171 435 3695   Fax 0171 435 9995
Email: stephani@photosource.co.uk
Website: www.photosource.co.uk/
    photosource/stephanie

Colour coverage of Europe, Africa, Asia, United Arab Emirates, the Caribbean, USA, Australia, New Zealand, the Pacific Islands and South America: people, animals, towns, agriculture, landscapes, carnivals, markets, archaeology, religion and ancient civilisations. Travel assignments undertaken. Medium-format transparencies (2″ square).

Michael Cole Camerawork
The Coach House, 27 The Avenue,
Beckenham, Kent BR3 2DP
☎0181 658 6120   Fax 0181 658 6120
Website: www.tennisphotos.com
Contact *Michael Cole, Derrick Bentley*

Probably the largest and most comprehensive collection of tennis pictures in the world; incorporating the library of Le Roye Productions, a company which covered Wimbledon from 1945–70, and MCC coverage of all major tennis events, worldwide, since 1970. Also small travel picture library: English countryside, Venice,

Moscow, USA, etc. 200,000 35mm colour slides, 3,600 2¼ inch and 6x7cm colour transparencies, 270,000 b&w negatives and a vast quantity of b&w movie film.

Collections
13 Woodberry Crescent, London N10 1PJ
☎0181 883 0083   Fax 0181 883 9215
Email: collections@btinternet.com
Contact *Laura Boswell, Brian Shuel*

Extensive coverage of the British Isles from Shetland to the Channel Islands, from Connemara to East Anglia, including people, customs, workers, religions, pastimes, as well as places and things. Incorporates the landscapes of Fay Godwin and, recently, the Irish agency Image Ireland. Also a major 'Family Life' collection from pregnancy through to old age, with particular emphasis on child development and education. Visitors are welcome but by appointment.

Comstock Photolibrary
21 Chelsea Wharf, 15 Lots Road, London
SW10 0QJ
☎0171 351 4448   Fax 0171 352 8414
Contact *Julie Steinberg*

Extensive coverage of business, people, industry, science, futuristic, world travel, landscapes, medical and natural history. Also desktop photography and CD-ROM. Free catalogues on request. Provides access to over four million images.

Concannon Golf History Library
11 Cheyne Gardens, Westcliff, Bournemouth,
Dorset BH4 8AS
☎01202 766145
Contact *Dale Concannon*

Private collection of historic golfing images 1750–1950. Players, courses, Ryder Cup, Open championship, golf architecture, memorabilia, US golf. Specialist advice. Commissions undertaken.

Corbis Images
12 Regents Wharf, All Saints Street, London
N1 7RL
☎0800 7319995/7315558 Fax 0171 278 1408
Email: info@uk.corbis.com
Website: www.corbisimages.com
Contacts *Anna Calvert*

A unique and comprehensive resource containing more than 25 million images, with other 1.4

million of them available on-line. The images come from professional photographers, museums, cultural institutions and public and private collections worldwide, including images from the Bettmann Archive, Ansel Adams, Lynn Goldsmith, the Turnley Collection and Hulton Deutsch. Subjects include history, travel, celebrities, events, science, world art and cultures. Free catalogues are available or register for a free password to search, save and order on-line.

Sylvia Cordaiy Photo Library

45 Rotherstone, Devizes, Wiltshire SN10 2DD
☎01380 728327   Fax 01380 728328
Email: 113023.2732@compuserve.com

Over 130 countries on file from the obscure to main stock images – Africa, North, Central and South America, Asia, Atlantic, Indian and Pacific Ocean islands, Australasia, Europe, polar regions. Covers travel, architecture, ancient civilisations, people worldwide, environment, wildlife, natural history, Antarctica, domestic pets, livestock, marine biology, veterinary treatment, equestrian, ornithology, flowers. UK files cover cities, towns villages, coastal and rural scenes, London. Transport, railways, shipping and aircraft (military and civilian). Aerial photography. Backgrounds and abstracts. Also the Paul Kaye B/W archive.

Country Collections

Unit 9, Ditton Priors Trading Estate, Bridgnorth, Shropshire WV16 6SS
☎01746 712533/861330

Contact *Robert Foster*

Small select collection of colour transparencies specialising in sundials, Celtic culture, villages, churches and ancient monuments. Assignments undertaken.

Country Images Picture Library

27 Camwood, Clayton Green, Bamber Bridge, Preston, Lancashire PR5 8LA
☎01772 321243   Fax 01772 321243
Email: terrymarsh@countrymatters.
  demon.co.uk

Contact *Terry Marsh*

35mm colour coverage of landscapes and countryside features generally throughout the UK and France, in particular Cumbria, North Yorkshire, Lancashire, southern Scotland, Isle of Skye, Wales, Cornwall, French Alps, French Pyrenees, Provence and Australia. Commissions undertaken.

Country Life Picture Library

King's Reach Tower, Stamford Street, London SE1 9LS
☎0171 261 6337   Fax 0171 261 6216

Contact *Camilla Costello*

Over 150,000 b&w negatives dating back to 1897, and 15,000 colour transparencies. Country houses, stately homes, churches and town houses in Britain and abroad, interiors of architectural interest (ceilings, fireplaces, furniture, paintings, sculpture), and exteriors showing many landscaped gardens, sporting and social events, crafts, people and animals. Visitors by appointment. Open Tuesday to Friday.

Philip Craven Worldwide Photo-Library

Surrey Studios, 21 Nork Way, Nork, Banstead, Surrey SM7 1PB
☎01737 373737   Fax 01737 373737

Contact *Philip Craven*

Extensive coverage of British scenes, cities, villages, English countryside, gardens, historic buildings and wildlife. Worldwide travel and wildlife subjects on medium- and large-format transparencies.

CTC Picture Library

CTC Publicity, Longfield, Midhurst Road, Fernhurst, Haslemere, Surrey GU27 3HA
☎01428 655007   Fax 01428 641071
Email: ctcpub@globalnet.co.uk

Contact *Neil Crighton*

One of the biggest specialist libraries in the UK with 250,000 slides covering world and UK agriculture, horticulture, and environmental subjects. Also a small section on travel.

Cumbria Picture Library

See **Eric Whitehead Photography**

Sue Cunningham Photographic

56 Chatham Road, Kingston upon Thames, Surrey KT1 3AA
☎0181 541 3024   Fax 0181 541 5388
Email: pictures@scphotographic.com

Extensive coverage of many geographical areas: South America (especially Brazil), Eastern Europe from the Baltic to the Balkans, various African countries, Western Europe including the UK. Colour and b&w. Member of **BAPLA**.

Dalton–Watson Collection

See **The Ludvigsen Library Limited**

James Davis Travel Photography

65 Brighton Road, Shoreham, West Sussex
BN43 6RE
☎01273 452252   Fax 01273 440116
Email: eyeubiquitous@msn.com

Travel collection: people, places, emotive scenes
and tourism. Constantly updated by James Davis
and a team of photographers, both at home and
abroad. Same-day service available.

The Defence Picture Library

Sherwell House, 54 Staddiscombe Road,
Plymouth, Devon PL9 9NB
☎01752 401800   Fax 01752 402800
Email: DPL@defencepictures.demon.co.uk

Contact *David Reynolds, Jessica Kelly, James
Rowlands, Andrew Chittock*

Leading source of military photography covering all areas of the UK Armed Forces, supported
by a research agency of facts and figures. More
than 350,000 images with a significant number
on CD-ROM. Campaigns in Aden, the
Falklands, Ulster, the Gulf and Yugoslavia covered. Specialist collections include the Royal
Marine Commandos and Parachute Regiment
training. Visitors welcome by appointment.

Douglas Dickins Photo Library

2 Wessex Gardens, Golders Green, London
NW11 9RT
☎0181 455 6221

Worldwide colour and b&w coverage, specialising in Asia, particularly India, Indonesia and
Japan. Meeting educational requirements on
landscape, archaeology, history, religions, customs, people and folklore.

C M Dixon

The Orchard, Marley Lane, Kingston,
Canterbury, Kent CT4 6HJ
☎01227 830075   Fax 01227 831135

Colour coverage of ancient civilisations, archaeology and art, ethnology, mythology, world religion, museum objects, geography, geology,
meteorology, landscapes, people and places from
many countries including most of Europe, former USSR, Ethiopia, Iceland, Jordan, Morocco,
Sri Lanka, Tunisia, Turkey, Egypt, Uzbekistan.

Dominic Photography

4B Moore Park Road, London SW6 2JT
☎0171 381 0007   Fax 0171 381 0008

Contact *Zoë Dominic, Catherine Ashmore*

Colour and b&w coverage of the entertainment world from 1957 onwards: dance, opera,
theatre, ballet, musicals and personalities.

Philip Dunn Picture Library

18 Tyning Terrace, Bath, Somerset BA1 6ET
☎01225   461741/0860   523599
Email: philip.dunn@btinternet.com
Website: www.btinternet/~philip.dunn

Contact *Philip Dunn*

Constantly expanding collection of some
50,000 b&w/colour images of travel, people,
activities and places in Britain and overseas.
Commissions undertaken.

E. T. Archive

4th Floor, 184 Drummond Street, London
NW1 3HP
☎0171 388 8848   Fax 0171 388 8849
Email: et.archive@dial.pipex.com

26,000 colour transparencies covering fine art
and history.

Patrick Eagar Photography

5 Ennerdale Road, Kew Gardens, Surrey
TW9 3PG
☎0181 940 9269   Fax 0181 332 1229

Colour and b&w coverage of cricket from 1965.
Test matches, overseas tours and all aspects of the
sport. Also a constantly expanding wine library
(colour) of vineyards, grapes, cellars and wine-
makers of France, Italy, Germany, Lebanon,
Australia, New Zealand, South Africa (and
England). Digital photograph transmission by
modem.

Ecoscene

The Oasts, Headley Lane, Passfield, Liphook,
Hampshire GU30 7RX
☎01428 751056   Fax 01428 751057
Email: sally@ecoscene.com
Website: www.ecoscene.com

Contact *Sally Morgan*

Expanding colour library of over 80,000 transparencies specialising in all aspects of the environment: pollution, conservation, recycling,
restoration, natural history, habitats, education,
landscapes, industry and agriculture. All parts of
the globe are covered with specialist collections
covering Antarctica, Australia, North America.
Sally Morgan, who runs the library, is a professional ecologist and expert source of information on all environmental topics. Photographic
and writing commissions undertaken.

Edifice

14 Doughty Street, London WC1N 2PL
☎0171 242 0740   Fax 0171 267 3632
Email: info@edificephoto.com
Website: www.edificephoto.com

Contact *Philippa Lewis, Gillian Darley*

Colour coverage of architecture, buildings of all possible descriptions, gardens, urban and rural landscape. *Specialises* in details of ornament, period style and material. British Isles, USA, Africa, Europe and Japan all covered. Detailed list available, visits by appointment.

English Heritage Photographic Library

23 Savile Row, London W1X 1AB
☎0171 973 3338   Fax 0171 973 3027
Email: celia.sterne@english-heritage.org.uk

Contact *Celia Sterne*

Images of English castles, abbeys, houses, gardens, Roman remains, ancient monuments, battlefields, industrial and post-war buildings, interiors, paintings, artifacts, architectural details, conservation, archaeology.

Mary Evans Picture Library

59 Tranquil Vale, Blackheath, London SE3 0BS
☎0181 318 0034   Fax 0181 852 7211
Email: lib@mepl.co.uk

Collection of historical illustrations documenting social, political, cultural, technical, geographical and biographical themes from ancient times to the recent past (up to mid-20th century). Photographs, prints and ephemera backed by large book and magazine collection. Many special collections including Sigmund Freud, the **Fawcett Library** (women's rights), the paranormal, the Meledin Collection (20th-century Russian history) and individual photographers such as Roger Mayne and Grace Robertson. Brochure sent on request. Compilers of the *Picture Researcher's Handbook* every three years by PIRA.

Express Newspapers Syndication

Ludgate House, 245 Blackfriars Road, London SE1 9UX
☎0171 922 7903/5/6   Fax 0171 922 7871

Manager *Jamie Maskey*

Two million images updated daily, with strong collections on personalities, royalty, showbiz, sport, fashion, nostalgia and events. Electronic transmission available. Daily news and feature service.

Eye Ubiquitous

65 Brighton Road, Shoreham, East Sussex BN43 6RE
☎01273 440113   Fax 01273 440116
Email: eyeubiquitous@msn.com

Contact *Paul Seheult*

General stock specialising in social documentary worldwide, including the work of Tim Page, and now incorporating the **James Davis Travel Library** (see entry).

Chris Fairclough Colour Library
See **Image Select International**

Falklands Pictorial

Vision House, 16 Broadfield Road, Heeley, Sheffield, South Yorkshire S8 0XJ
☎0114 2589299   Fax 0114 2550113

Colour and b&w photographs showing all aspects of Falklands life from 1880 to the present day.

Famous Pictures and Features

Studio 4, Limehouse Cut, 46 Morris Road, London E14 6NQ
☎0171 510 2500   Fax 0171 510 2510
Email: famous@compuserve.com
Website: www.famous.uk.com

Pictures and features agency with a growing library of interviews and colour transparencies dating back to 1985. Portrait, party and concert shots of rock and pop stars plus international entertainers, film and TV celebrities. The library is supplied by a team of photographers and journalists from the UK and around the world, keeping it up-to-date on a daily basis.

Farmers Weekly Picture Library

Quadrant House, The Quadrant, Sutton, Surrey SM2 5AS
☎0181 652 4914   Fax 0181 652 4005
Email: farmers.library@rbi.co.uk
Website: www.fwi.co.uk

Library Manager *Barry Dixon*

Britain's largest agricultural picture library holds more than 200,000 transparencies covering all aspects of farming, country life and the environment. The collection is continually updated.

ffotograff

10 Kyveilog Street, Pontcanna, Cardiff CF1 9JA
☎01222 236879   Fax 01222 229326

Contact *Patricia Aithie*

Library and agency specialising in travel, exploration, the arts, architecture, traditional culture, archaeology and landscape. Based in Wales but specialising in the Middle and Far East; Yemen and Wales are unusually strong aspects of the library. Churches and cathedrals of Britain and Crusader castles. Abstract paintings and detailed photographic textures suitable for book covers. Digital transfer by ISDN and modem available.

Financial Times Pictures

1 Southwark Bridge, London SE1 9HL
☎0171 873 3671   Fax 0171 873 4606
Email: richard.pigden@ft.com

Photographs from around the world ranging from personalities in business, politics and the arts, people at work and other human interests and activities. 'FT Graphics are outstanding in their ability to make complex issues comprehensible.' Delivery via Modem, ISDN, email or Newscom.

Fine Art Photographic Library Ltd

2A Milner Street, London SW3 2PU
☎0171 589 3127   Fax 0171 584 1944
Contact Linda Hammerbeck

Over 20,000 large-format transparencies, with a specialist collection of 19th-century paintings.

Fire-Pix International

68 Arkles Lane, Anfield, Liverpool,
Merseyside L4 2SP
☎0151 260 0111/Mobile: 0777 5930419
Fax 0151 250 0111
Email: tonymyers@firepixint.demon.co.uk
Website: www.firepixint.demon.co.uk
Contact Tony Myers

The UK's only fire photo library. 17,000 images of fire-related subjects, firefighters, fire equipment manufacturers. Website contains 16 different categories from historical fire to abstract flame. Member of **BAPLA**.

Fogden Wildlife Photos

Basement, 10 Bellevue, Bristol BS8 1DA
☎0117 923 8849   Fax 0117 923 8543
Email: susan.fogden@virgin.net
Contact Susan Fogden

Natural history collection, with special reference to rain forests and deserts. Emphasis on quality rather than quantity; growing collection of around 10,000 images.

Food Features

Hardwicke Court, Waverley Lane, Farnham,
Surrey GU9 8ES
☎01252 781433   Fax 01252 784091
Email: frontdesk@foodpix.co.uk
Website: www.foodpix.co.uk
Contacts Steve Moss, Alex Barker

Specialised high-quality food and drink photography, features and tested recipes. Clients' specific requirements can be incorporated into regular shooting schedules.

Ron & Christine Foord Colour Picture Library

155B City Way, Rochester, Kent ME1 2BE
☎01634 847348   Fax 01634 847348

Specialist library with over 1000 species of British and European wild flowers, plus garden flowers, trees, indoor plants, pests and diseases, mosses, lichen, cacti and the majority of larger British insects.

Forest Life Picture Library

231 Corstorphine Road, Edinburgh
EH12 7AT
☎0131 314 6411   Fax 0131 314 6285
Email: n.campbell@forestry.gov.uk
Contact Douglas Green, Neill Campbell

The official image bank of the Forestry Commission, the library provides a single source for all aspects of forest and woodland management. The comprehensive subject list includes tree species, scenic landscapes, employment, wildlife, flora and fauna, conservation, sport and leisure.

Werner Forman Archive Ltd

36 Camden Square, London NW1 9XA
☎0171 267 1034   Fax 0171 267 6026
Email: wfa@btinternet.com
Website: www.btinternet.com/~wfa

Colour and b&w coverage of ancient civilisations, oriental and primitive societies around the world. A number of rare collections. Subject lists available.

Format Photographers

19 Arlington Way, London EC1R 1UY
☎0171 833 0292   Fax 0171 833 0381
Email: format@formatphotogs.demon.co.uk
Contact Maggie Murray

Over 100,000 documentary images in colour and b&w covering education, health, disability and women's issues in the UK and abroad.

Formula One Pictures

Suite 8, King Harold Court, Sun Street,
Waltham Abbey, Essex EN9 1ER
☎01992 787800   Fax 01992 714366
Email: jt@f1pictures.demon.co.uk
Website: www.f1pictures.com

Contacts *John Townsend, Erika Townsend*

500,000 35mm colour slides, b&w and colour
negatives of all aspects of Formula One grand
prix racing including driver profiles and portraits.

Robert Forsythe Picture Library

16 Lime Grove, Prudhoe, Northumberland
NE42 6PR
☎01661 834511   Fax 01661 834511
Email: robert@forsythe.demon.co.uk
Website: www.forsythe.demon.co.uk/

Contact *Robert Forsythe, Fiona Forsythe*

25,000 transparencies of industrial and transport
heritage; plus a unique collection of 50,000 items
of related publicity ephemera from 1945. Image
finding service available. Robert Forsythe is a
transport/industrial heritage historian and consultant. Nationwide coverage, particularly strong
on Northern Britain. A bibliography of published material is available.

Fortean Picture Library

Henblas, Mwrog Street, Ruthin LL15 1LG
☎01824 707278   Fax 01824 705324
Email: janet.bord@forteanpix.demon.co.uk
Website: www.forteanpix.demon.co.uk/

Contact *Janet Bord*

30,000 colour and 45,000 b&w images: mysteries and strange phenomena worldwide, including
ghosts, UFOs, witchcraft and monsters; also
antiquities, folklore and mythology. Subject list
available.

The Fotomas Index

12 Pickhurst Rise, West Wickham, Kent
BR4 0AL
☎0181 776 2772   Fax 0181 776 2772

Contact *John Freeman*

General historical collection, mostly pre-1900.
Subjects include London, topography, art, satirical, social and political history. Large portrait section.

The Francis Frith Collection

Frith's Barn, Teffont, Salisbury, Wiltshire
SP3 5QP
☎01722 716376   Fax 01722 716881
Email: john_buck@francisfrith.com
Website: www.francisfrith.com

Contact *John Buck*

330,000 b&w and sepia photographs of British
topography from 1860 to 1969 depicting 7000
British towns and villages.

John Frost Newspapers

See under **Library Services**

Andrew N. Gagg's Photo Flora

Town House Two, Fordbank Court,
Henwick Road, Worcester WR2 5PF
☎01905 748515
Email: gagg@cwcom.net
Website:www.gagg.mcmail.com/
  photoflora.htm

Specialist in British and European wild plants,
flowers, ferns, grasses, trees, shrubs, etc. with
colour coverage of most British and many
European species (rare and common) and habitats; also travel in India, Nepal, Egypt, China,
Thailand and Tibet.

Galaxy Picture Library

1 Milverton Drive, Ickenham, Uxbridge,
Middlesex UB10 8PP
☎01895 637463   Fax 01895 623277
Email: galaxypix@compuserve.com
Website: ourworld.compuserve.com/
  homepages/galaxypix

Contact *Robin Scagell*

Specialises in astronomy, space, telescopes,
observatories, the sky, clouds and sunsets.
Composites of foregrounds, stars, moon and
planets prepared to commission. Editorial service
available.

Garden and Wildlife Matters Photo Library

'Marlham', Henley's Down, Battle, East
Sussex TN33 9BN
☎01424 830566   Fax 01424 830224
Email: gardens@ftech.co.uk
Website: web.ftech.net/~gardens

Contact *Dr John Feltwell*

Collection of 100,000 6x4 and 35mm images.
General gardening techniques and design; cottage gardens and USA designer gardens. 7000
species of garden plants. Flowers, wild and house
plants, trees and crops. Environmental, ecological and conservation pictures, including sea, air,
noise and freshwater pollution, SE Asian and
Central and South American rainforests; Eastern
Europe, Mediterranean. Recycling, agriculture,
forestry, horticulture and oblique aerial habitat
shots from Europe, USA. High-quality images

required. Digital images supplied worldwide by ISDN.

The Garden Picture Library
Unit 12, Ransome's Dock, 35 Parkgate Road, London SW11 4NP
☎0171 228 4332   Fax 0171 924 3267

Contact *Sally Wood*

'Our inspirational images of gardens, plants and gardening offer plenty of scope for writers looking for original ideas to write about.' Special collections include al fresco food, floral graphics and the still life photography of Linda Burgess. From individual stock photos to complete features, photographers submit material from the UK, Europe, USA and Australia on 35mm and medium formats. In-house picture research can be undertaken on request. Visitors to the library are welcome by appointment and copies of promotional literature are available on request.

Leslie Garland Picture Library
69 Fern Avenue, Jesmond, Newcastle upon Tyne, Tyne & Wear NE2 2QU
☎0191 281 3442   Fax 0191 209 1094
Email: garland@cableinet.co.uk

Contact *Leslie Garland, ABIPP, ARPS*

Subjects areas: Northumberland, Durham, Tyne & Wear, Cumbria, North Yorkshire, with growing collections of Lancashire, Merseyside, Greater Manchester and Derbyshire. Also Scotland, Norway and Sweden. Major cities, towns, sights and scenes, heritage, etc. Applied science and engineering – bridges, cranes, ship building, chemical plants, field studies, geography and geology, physics and chemistry experiments, etc., and a range of still-life studies of miscellaneous subjects – household objects, cats eyes, hydraulic rams, galvanised steel, crash barriers, etc. Most on medium format. Brochure available. Commissions undertaken.

Ed Geldard Picture Collection
7 Ellergreen House, Nr Burnside, Kendal, Cumbria LA9 5SD
☎01539 728609

Contact *Ed Geldard*

Approximately 15,000 colour transparencies and b&w negs, all by Ed Geldard, specialising in mountain landscapes: particularly the mountain regions of the Lake District; and the Yorkshire limestone areas, from valley to summit. Commissions   undertaken.   Books   published: *Wainwright's Tour of the Lake District* and *Wainwright in the Limestone Dales* and *The Lake District*.

Genesis Space Photo Library
Greenbanks, Robins Hill, Raleigh, Bideford, Devon EX39 3PA
☎01237 471960   Fax 01237 472060
Email: tim@spaceport.co.uk
Website: www.spaceport.co.uk

Contact *Tim Furniss*

Contemporary and historical colour and b&w spaceflight collection including rockets, spacecraft, spacemen, Earth, moon and planets. Stock list available on request.

Geo Aerial Photography
4 Christian Fields, London SW16 3JZ
☎0181 764 6292/0115 9819418
Fax 0181 764 6292/0115 9815474/9819418
Email: geo.aerial@geo-group.demon.co.uk

Contact *Kelly White*

Established 1990 and now a growing collection of aerial oblique photographs from the UK, Scandinavia, Asia and Africa – landscapes, buildings, industrial sites, etc. Commissions undertaken.

GeoScience Features
6 Orchard Drive, Wye, Kent TN25 5AU
☎01233 812707   Fax 01233 812707
Email: gsf@geoscience.demon.co.uk

Fully computerised and comprehensive library containing the world's principal source of volcanic phenomena. Extensive collections, providing scientific detail with technical quality, of rocks, minerals, fossils, microsections of botanical and animal tissues, animals, biology, birds, botany, chemistry, earth science, ecology, environment, geology, geography, habitats, landscapes,   macro/microbiology,   peoples,   sky, weather, wildlife and zoology. Over 300,000 original colour transparencies in medium- and 35mm-format. Subject lists and CD-ROM catalogue available on application. Incorporates the RIDA photolibrary.

Geoslides Photography
4 Christian Fields, London SW16 3JZ
☎0181 764 6292
Fax 0181 764 6292/0115 9819418
Email: geoslides@geo-group.demon.co.uk

Contact *John Douglas*

Established in 1968. Landscape and human interest subjects from the Arctic, Antarctica, Scandinavia, UK, Africa (south of Sahara), Middle East, Asia (south and southeast); also Australia, via Blackwoods Picture Library. Also specialist collections of images from British India (the Raj) and Boer War.

Getty Images (incorporating Tony Stone Images & The Hulton Getty Collection)

101 Bayham Street, London NW1 0AY
☎0171 544 3333　　　　Fax 0171 544 3334
Email: info@getty-images.com

Contact *Sales Dept.*

With over 15 million images, the collection is the largest picture resource in Europe with images from ancient history through the early years of photography up to the present day. As well as many old newspaper archives, the extensive contemporary collections cover lifestyles, travel, science, business.

Lynn Goldsmith

See **Corbis Images**

Martin and Dorothy Grace

40 Clipstone Avenue, Mapperley, Nottingham NG3 5JZ
☎0115 9208248　　　　Fax 0115 9626802
Email: graces@lineone.net

Colour coverage of Britain's natural history, specialising in trees, shrubs and wild flowers. Also ferns, birds and butterflies, habitats, landscapes, ecology. Member of **BAPLA**.

Ronald Grant Archive

See **The Cinema Museum**

Greater London Photograph Library

See **London Metropolitan Archives**

Sally and Richard Greenhill

357A Liverpool Road, London N1 1NL
☎0171 607 8549　　　　Fax 0171 607 7151
Email: library.greenhill@shadow.org.uk
Website: www.shadow.org.uk/photolibrary

Photo Librarian *Vanessa Jones*

Colour and b&w photos of a social documentary nature: child development, pregnancy and birth, education and urban scenes in London and Northern England. Also Modern China 1971–95, Hong Kong, USA, longhouse life in Sarawak, and other material from around the world.

V. K. Guy Ltd

Silver Birches, Troutbeck, Windermere, Cumbria LA23 1PN
☎015394 33519　　　　Fax 015394 32971

Contact *Vic Guy, Pauline Guy, Mike Guy, Paul Guy, Nicola Guy*

British landscapes and architectural heritage. 20,000 5″x4″ transparencies, suitable for tourism brochures, calendars, etc. Colour catalogue available.

Angela Hampton 'Family Life Picture Library'

Holly Tree House, The Street, Walberton, Arundel, West Sussex BN18 0PH
☎01243 555952　　　　Fax 01243 555952

Contact *Angela Hampton*

Over 50,000 transparencies on all aspects of contemporary lifestyle, including pregnancy, childbirth, babies, children, parenting, behaviour, education, medical, holidays, pets, family life, relationships, teenagers, women and men's health, over-50's and retirement. Also comprehensive stock on domestic and farm animal life. Isle of Wight travel pictures in 35mm. Commissions undertaken. Offers fully illustrated text packages on most subjects and welcomes ideas for collaboration from writers with proven, successful background.

Tom Hanley

61 Stephendale Road, London SW6 2LT
☎0171 731 3525　　　　Fax 0171 731 3525

Colour and b&w coverage of London, England, Europe, Canada, India, the Philippines, Brazil, China, Japan, Korea, Taiwan, the Seychelles, Cayman Islands, USA. Also pop artists of the '60s, First World War trenches, removal of London Bridge to America, and much more. Current preoccupation with Greece, Turkey, Spain and Egypt, ancient and modern.

Robert Harding Picture Library

58–59 Great Marlborough Street, London W1V 1DD
☎0171 287 5414　　　　Fax 0171 631 1070

Over two million colour images covering a wide range of subjects – travel, people, architecture, scenics, sport, lifestyle, food, industry and agriculture. Syndication of many titles from IPC Magazines, BBC Magazines and Burda Group.

Harpur Garden Library

44 Roxwell Road, Chelmsford, Essex CM1 2NB
☎01245 257527　　　　Fax 01245 344101
Email: harpur.garden.library@dial.pipex.com

Contact *Jerry Harpur, Marcus Harpur, Rae Spencer-Jones*

Jerry Harpur's personal collection of gardens in Britain, France, Australia, South Africa, the US,

Morocco, Argentina, Chile and Japan (35mm and 6x7, colour). Inspired partly by contemporary designers and horticulturalists but also includes historic gardens: formal gardens, front and back gardens, plant associations, gardens in all four seasons, garden containers, fences, hedges, herbs, hillsides, seaside, lawns, paths, paving, rock, arbours, scented, fruit and vegetables, ornaments, water and integrated gardens.

Jim Henderson Photographer & Publisher

Crooktree, Kincardine O'Neil, Aboyne, Aberdeenshire AB34 4JD
☎01339 882149   Fax 01339 882149
Email: JHende7868@aol.com
Website: www.sldirect.co.uk/jhenderson/
Contact *Jim Henderson, AMPA, ARPS*

Scenic and general activity coverage of the North-East Scotland/Grampian region and Highlands for tourist, holiday and activity illustration. Specialist collection of over 100 Aurora Borealis displays from 1989–1999 in Grampian and co-author of *The Aurora* (pub. 1997). Large collection of recent images of Egypt: Cairo through to Abu-Simbel. Commissions undertaken.

Heritage and Natural History Photographic Library

37 Plainwood Close, Summersdale, Chichester, West Sussex PO19 4YB
☎01243 533822   Fax 01243 533822
Contact *Dr John B. Free*

Specialises in insects (particularly bees and beekeeping), tropical and temperate agriculture and crops, archaeology and history worldwide.

John Heseltine Picture Library

Mill Studio, Frogmarsh Mill, South Woodchester, Gloucestershire GL5 5ET
☎01453 873792   Fax 01453 873793
Email: Johnhes@aol.com
Contact *John Heseltine*

Over 100,000 colour transparencies of landscapes, architecture, food and travel with particular emphasis on Italy and the UK.

Christopher Hill Photographic Library

17 Clarence Street, Belfast BT2 8DY
☎01232 245038   Fax 01232 231942
Email: ChrisHillPhotographic@btinternet.com
Website: www.scenic-ireland.com

Contact *Janet Smyth*

A comprehensive collection of landscapes of Northern Ireland, from Belfast to the Giant's Causeway, updated daily. Images of farming, food and industry. 'We will endeavour to supply images overnight.'

Hobbs Golf Collection

5 Winston Way, New Ridley, Stocksfield, Northumberland NE43 7RF
☎01661 842933   Fax 01661 842933
Email: hobbs.golf@btinternet.com
Contact *Michael Hobbs*

Specialist golf collection: players, courses, art, memorabilia and historical topics (1300 to present day). 40,000+ images – mainly 35mm colour transparencies and b&w prints. Commissions undertaken. Author of 30 golf books.

David Hoffman Photo Library

21 Norman Grove, London E3 5EG
☎0181 981 5041/0468 402932
Fax 0181 980 2041
Email: info:hoffmanphotos.demon.co.uk
Website: www.hoffmanphotos.demon.co.uk
Contact *David Hoffman*

Commissioned photography and stock library with a strong emphasis on social issues built up from 35mm journalistic and documentary work dating from the late 1970s. Files on drugs and drug use, policing, disorder, riots, major strikes, youth protest, homelessness, housing, environmental demonstrations and events, waste disposal, alternative energy, industry and pollution. Wide range of images especially from UK and Europe but also USA, Canada, Venezuela and Thailand. General files on topical issues and current affairs plus specialist files from leisure cycling to local authority services.

Holt Studios International Ltd

The Courtyard, 24 High Street, Hungerford, Berkshire RG17 0NF
☎01488 683523   Fax 01488 683511
Commercial Director *Andy Morant*

Specialist photo library covering world agriculture and horticulture both from a pictorial and a technical point of view. Commissions undertaken worldwide.

The Bill Hopkins Collection

See **The Special Photographers Library**

Houghton's Horses/ Kit Houghton Photography

Radlet Cottage, Spaxton, Bridgwater, Somerset TA5 1DE

☎01278 671362   Fax 01278 671739

Email: kit@enterprise.net

Contact *Kit Houghton, Debbie Cook*

Specialist equestrian library of over 200,000 transparencies on all aspects of the horse world, with images ranging from the romantic to the practical, step-by-step instructional and competition pictures in all equestrian disciplines worldwide. On-line picture delivery with ISDN facility.

Houses and Interiors

192 Goswell Road, London EC1V 7DT

☎0171 253 0991   Fax 0171 253 0992

Manager *Victoria Norman*

40,000 images of houses and gardens. Large format and 35mm. Specialises in reselling of illustrated articles and features for magazines. Member of **BAPLA**.

Chris Howes/ Wild Places Photography

51 Timbers Square, Roath, Cardiff CF2 3SH

☎01222 486557   Fax 01222 486557

Email: wildpp@globalnet.co.uk

Contact *Chris Howes, Judith Calford*

Expanding collection of over 50,000 colour transparencies and b&w prints covering travel, topography and natural history worldwide, plus action sports such as climbing. *Specialist areas* include caves, caving and mines (with historical coverage using engravings and early photographs), wildlife, landscapes and the environment, including pollution and conservation. Europe (including Britain), USA, Africa and Australia are all well represented within the collection. Commissions undertaken.

Hulton Deutsch

See **Corbis Images**

The Hulton Getty Picture Collection

See **Getty Images**

Huntley Film Archive

78 Mildmay Park, Islington, London N1 4PR

☎0171 923 0990   Fax 0171 241 4929

Contact *Amanda Huntley*

Originally a private collection, the library is now a comprehensive archive of rare and vintage documentary film dating from 1895. 30,000–35,000 films on all subjects of a documentary nature, plus 50,000 feature film stills. Hollywood and the British film studios plus a television archive of rare stills and films.

Jacqui Hurst

66 Richford Street, Hammersmith, London W6 7HP

☎0181 743 2315/07970 781336

Fax 0181 735 0382

Contact *Jacqui Hurst*

A specialist library of traditional and contemporary designers and crafts, regional food producers and markets. The photos form illustrated essays of how something is made and finish with a still life of the completed object. The collection is always being extended and a list is available on request. Commissions undertaken.

Hutchison Picture Library

118B Holland Park Avenue, London W11 4UA

☎0171 229 2743   Fax 0171 792 0259

Email: library@hutchisonplc.demon.co.uk

Worldwide contemporary images from the straight-forward to the esoteric and quirky. With over half a million documentary colour photographs on file and more than 200 photographers continually adding new work, this is an ever-growing resource covering people, places, customs and faiths, agriculture, industry and transport. *Special collections* include the environment and climate, family life (including pregnancy and birth), ethnic minorities worldwide (including Disappearing World archive), conventional and alternative medicine, and music around the world. Search service available.

Illustrated London News Picture Library

20 Upper Ground, London SE1 9PF

☎0171 805 5585   Fax 0171 805 5905

Engravings, photographs and illustrations from 1842 to the present day, taken from magazines published by Illustrated Newspapers: *Illustrated London News; Graphic; Sphere; Tatler; Sketch; Illustrated Sporting and Dramatic News; Illustrated War News 1914–18; Bystander; Britannia & Eve.* Social history, London, Industrial Revolution, wars, travel. Brochure available. Visitors by appointment.

The Image Bank
17 Conway Street, London W1P 6EE
☎0171 312 0300   Fax 0171 391 9111
4 Jordan Street, Manchester M15 4PY
☎0161 236 9226   Fax 0161 236 8723 57
Melville Street, Edinburgh EH3 7HL
☎0131 225 1770   Fax 0131 225 1660 11
Upper Mount Street, Dublin 2
☎00 353 1 676 0872   Fax 00 353 1 676 0873
Contact, London *Ivan Purdie*
Contact, Manchester *Rowan Young*
Contact, Edinburgh *Roddy McRae*
Contact, Dublin *Brid Harrington*

Stock photography, illustration and film footage. Over 20 million constantly updated images from 450 photographers and 337 illustrators. Free catalogue available. Creative advertising, editorial and corporate commissions undertaken. For magazines, partworks and books, contact the publishing department. Visitors welcome.

Image Ireland
See **Collections**

Image Select International
2nd Floor, Heron House, 109 Wembley Hill Road, Wembley, Middlesex HA9 8DY
☎0181 900 2898   Fax 0181 900 9969
Contact *Darren Wisden*

History archive plus the Chris Fairclough Colour Library (general colour library with special collections on religion, education, travel, children, people and places) and the Ann Ronan Collection (history, science and technology).

Images Colour Library
Ramillies House, 1–2 Ramillies Street, London W1V 1DF
☎0171 734 7344   Fax 0171 287 3933
15/17 High Court Lane, The Calls, Leeds, West Yorkshire LS2 7EU
☎0113 2433389   Fax 0113 2425605

A general contemporary library specialising in top-quality advertising, editorial and travel photography. Catalogues available. Visitors welcome. Also holds the **Landscape Only** collection (see entry).

Images of Africa Photobank
11 The Windings, Lichfield, Staffordshire WS13 7EX
☎01543 262898   Fax 01543 417154
Email: info@imagesofafrica.co.uk
Contact *Jacquie Shipton*

Owner *David Keith Jones, ABIPP, FRPS*

Over 135,000 images covering 14 African countries: Botswana, Egypt, Ethiopia, Kenya, Malawi, Namibia, Rwanda, South Africa, Swaziland, Tanzania, Uganda, Zaire, Zambia and Zimbabwe. 'Probably the best collection of photographs of Kenya in Europe.' Wide range of topics covered. Particularly strong on African wildlife with over 80 species of mammals including many sequences showing action and behaviour. Popular animals like lions and elephants are covered in encyclopedic detail. More than 100 species of birds and many reptiles are included. Other strengths include National Parks & Reserves, natural beauty, tourism facilities, traditional and modern people. Most work is by David Keith Jones, ABIPP, FRPS; several other photographers are represented. Colour brochure available.

Images of India
See **Link Picture Library**

Imperial War Museum Photograph Archive
All Saints Annexe, Austral Street, London SE1 4SL
☎0171 416 5333/5338   Fax 0171 416 5355
Email: photos@iwm.org.uk

A national archive of over five million photographs illustrating all aspects of 20th century conflict. Emphasis on the two world wars but includes material from other conflicts involving Britain and the Commonwealth. Majority of material is b&w, although holdings of colour material increases with more recent conflicts. Visitors welcome by appointment, Mon–Fri, 10.00 am. to 5.00 pm.

The Interior Archive Ltd
15 Grand Union Centre, West Row, London W10 5AS
☎0171 370 0595   Fax 0181 960 2695
Contact *Karen Howes*

Several thousand images of interiors, architecture, design and gardens.

International Photobank
Loscombe Barn Farmhouse, West Knighton, Dorchester, Dorset DT2 8LS
☎01305 854145   Fax 01305 853065

Over 300,000 transparencies, mostly medium-format. Colour coverage of travel subjects: places, people, folklore, events. Assignments undertaken for guide books and brochure photography.

The Isle of Wight Photo Library

The Old Rectory, Calbourne, Isle of Wight
PO30 4JE
☎01983 531247   Fax 01983 531253
Contact *The Librarian*

Stock material represents all that is best on the
Isle of Wight – landscapes, seascapes, architecture, gardens, boats.

Robbie Jack Photography

45 Church Road, Hanwell, London W7 3BD
☎0181 567 9616   Fax 0181 567 9616
Email: rjackphoto@aol.com
Contact *Robbie Jack*

Built up over the last 14 years, the library contains over 250,000 colour transparencies of the
performing arts – theatre, dance, opera and
music. Includes West End shows, the RSC and
Royal National Theatre productions, English
National Opera and Royal Opera. The dance
section contains images of the Royal Ballet,
English National Ballet, the Rambert Dance
Company, plus many foreign companies. Also
holds the largest selection of colour material
from the Edinburgh International Festival.
Researchers are welcome to visit by appointment.

Jayawardene Travel Photo Library

7A Napier Road, Wembley, Middlesex
HA0 4UA
☎0181 902 3588   Fax 0181 902 7114
Contact *Rohith Jayawardene*

120,000 colour transparencies, specialising in
worldwide travel and travel-related subjects.
Most topics featured have been covered in
depth, with more than 500 different images per
destination. Regularly updated, all are originals
and shot in 35mm- and medium-format.
Commissions undertaken. New photographers
welcome (please telephone first) – minimum
initial submission: 200 transparencies.

Trevor Jones Thoroughbred Photography

The Hornbeams, 2 The Street, Worlington,
Suffolk IP28 8RU
☎01638 713944   Fax 01638 713945
Contact *Trevor Jones, Gill Jones*

Extensive library of high-quality colour transparencies depicting all aspects of thoroughbred
horse racing dating from 1987. Major group
races, English classics, studs, stallions, mares and
foals, early morning scenes, personalities,
jockeys, trainers and prominent owners. Also
international work: USA Breeders Cup, Arc de
Triomphe, French Classics, Irish Derby, Dubai
racing scene, Japan Cup and Hokkaido stud
farms; and more unusual scenes such as racing on
the sands at low tide, Ireland, and on the frozen
lake at St Moritz. Visitors by appointment.

Katz Pictures

Zetland House, 5–25 Scrutton Street, London
EC2A 4LP
☎0171 377 5888   Fax 0171 377 5558
Contact *Alyson Whalley*

Contains an extensive collection of colour and
b&w material covering a multitude of subjects
from around the world – business, environment,
industry, lifestyles, politics plus celebrity portraits
from the entertainment world. Also Hollywood
portraits and film stills dating back to the twenties. Represents *Life* and *Time* magazines for syndication in the UK and can offer a complete
selection of material spanning over 50 years; also
the Mansell Collection.

David King Collection

90 St Pauls Road, London N1 2QP
☎0171 226 0149   Fax 0171 354 8264
Contact *David King*

250,000 b&w original and copy photographs and
colour transparencies of historical and present-
day images. Russian history and the Soviet
Union from 1900 to the fall of Khrushchev; the
lives of Lenin, Trotsky and Stalin; the Tzars,
Russo-Japanese War, 1917 Revolution, World
War I, Red Army, the Great Purges, Great
Patriotic War, etc. Special collections on China,
Eastern Europe, the Weimar Republic, John
Heartfield, American labour struggles, Spanish
Civil War. Open to qualified researchers by
appointment, Monday to Friday, 10 am – 6 pm.
Staff will undertake research; negotiable fee for
long projects. David King's latest photographic
book, *The Commissar Vanishes*, documents the
falsification of photographs and art in Stalin's
Russia.

The Kobal Collection

4th Floor, 184 Drummond Street, London
NW1 3HP
☎0171 383 0011   Fax 0171 383 0044

Colour and b&w coverage of Hollywood
films: portraits, stills, publicity shots, posters,
ephemera. Visitors by appointment.

Kos Picture Source Ltd
7 Spice Court, Ivory Square, Plantation
Wharf, London SW11 3UE
☎0171 801 0044   Fax 0171 801 0055
Email: images@kospictures.com

Specialists in water-related images, from yachting and super-yachts to windsurfing, canoeing
and ice skeeting. Seascapes, underwater images
and a worldwide travel section.

Landscape Only
Ramillies House, 1–2 Ramillies Street,
London W1V 1DF
☎0171 734 7344   Fax 0171 287 3933

Part of the **Images Colour Library**. A premier
landscape collection, featuring the work of top
photographers Charlie Waite, Nick Meers, Joe
Cornish and many others. Colour brochure
available.

Frank Lane Picture Agency Ltd
Pages Green House, Wetheringsett,
Stowmarket, Suffolk IP14 5QA
☎01728 860789   Fax 01728 860222
Email: pictures@flpa-images.co.uk
Website: www.flpa-images.co.uk

Colour and b&w coverage of natural history,
environment, pets and weather. Represents
Sunset from France, Foto Natura from Holland
and works closely with Eric and David Hosking,
plus 270 freelance photographers.

Last Resort Picture Library
Manvers Studios, 12 Ollerton Road, Tuxford,
Newark, Nottinghamshie NG22 0LF
☎01777 870166   Fax 01777 871739
Email: LRPL@dmimaging.co.uk
Website: www.dmimaging.co.uk

Contact *Jo Makin*

Images of agriculture, architecture, education,
landscape, industry, food, people at work,
computing and new technology. Images cover
a wide variety of areas rather than specialising,
ranging from the everyday to the obscure.

LAT Photographic
Somerset House, Somerset Road, Teddington
TW11 8RU
☎0181 251 3000   Fax 0181 251 3001

Motor sport collection of over 70 million
images dating from 1920 to the present day.

André Laubier Picture Library
4 St James Park, Bath BA1 2SS
☎01225 420688   Fax 01225 420688

An extensive library of photographs from 1935
to the present day in 35mm- and medium-
format. Main subjects are: archaeology and architecture, art and artists (wood carving, sculptures,
contemporary glass), botany, historical buildings,
sites and events, landscapes, nature, leisure sports,
events, experimental artwork and photography,
people and travel. Substantial stock of many
other subjects including: birds, buildings and
cities, folklore, food and drink, gardens, transport. Special collection: Images d'Europe
(Austria, Britain, France, Greece, S. W. Ireland,
Italy, Spain, Turkey and former Yugoslavia) and
Norway. Private collection: World War II to D-
Day. List available on request. Photo assignments, artwork, design, and line drawings undertaken. Correspondence welcome in English,
French or German.

Lebrecht Music Collection
58b Carlton Hill, London NW8 0ES
☎0171 625 5341/372 8233
Fax 0171 625 5341
Email: lebrechtcoll@claranet
Website: www.lebrecht.coll.clara.net./

Contact *Elbie Lebrecht*

30,000 prints and transparencies covering classical music, from antiquity to 21st century mini-
malists. Instruments, opera singers, concert halls
and opera houses, composers and musicians.

The Erich Lessing Archive of Fine Art & Culture
c/o AKG London Ltd, The Arts and History
Picture Library, 10 Plato Place, 72–74 St
Dionis Road, London SW6 4TU
☎0171 610 6103   Fax 0171 610 6125
Email: enquiries@akg-london.co.uk
Website: www.akg-london.co.uk

Computerised archive of large-format transparencies depicting the contents of many of the
world's finest art galleries as well as ancient
archaeological and biblical sites. CD-ROM
available. Represented by AKG London Ltd.

Life File Ltd
76 Streathbourne Road, London SW17 8QY
☎0181 767 8832   Fax 0181 672 8879
Email: S.TAYLOR@IBM.net

Contact *Simon Taylor*

300,000 images of people and places, lifestyles,
industry, environmental issues, natural history
and customs, from Afghanistan to Zimbabwe.
Stocks most of the major tourist destinations
throughout the world, including the UK.

Lindley Library, Royal Horticultural Society

80 Vincent Square, London SW1P 2PE
☎0171 821 3053   Fax 0171 828 3022

Contact *Jennifer Vine*

18,000 original drawings and approx. 8000 books with hand-coloured plates of botanical illustrations. Appointment is absolutely essential; all photography is done by own photographer.

Link Picture Library

33 Greyhound Road, London W6 8NH
☎0171 381 2261/2433   Fax 0171 385 6244
Email: lib@linkpics.demon.co.uk
Website: www.linkphotographers.co.uk

Contacts *Orde Eliason*

100,000 images of South Africa, India, China, Vietnam and Israel. A more general collection of colour transparencies from 100 countries worldwide. Link Picture Library and its partner, Images of India, has an international network and can source material not in its file from Japan, USA, Holland, Scandinavia, Germany and South Africa. Original photographic commissions undertaken.

London Aerial Photo Library

PO Box 25, Ashwellthorpe, Norwich, Norfolk NR16 1HL
☎01508 488320   Fax 01508 488282
Email: aerialphotos@btinternet.com

Contact *Sandy Stockwell*

80,000 colour negatives of aerial photographs covering most of Britain, with particular emphasis on London and surrounding counties. No search fee. Photocopies of library prints are supplied free of charge to enquirers. Welcomes enquiries in respect of either general subjects or specific sites and buildings.

The London Film Archive

78 Mildmay Park, Islington, London N1 4PR
☎0171 923 4074   Fax 0171 241 4929
Email: films@huntleyarchives.com
Website: www.huntleyarchives.com

Contact *Robert Dewar*

A newly-established archive which concentrates on all aspects of commercial, political and social life in the City and suburbs of London. The collection is primarily a film collection but also has stills, glass plate negatives, posters, advertising and documents of London interest.

London Metropolitan Archives

40 Northampton Road, London EC1R 0HB
☎0171 332 3820/Minicom: 0171 278 8703
Fax 0171 833 9136
Email: lma@ms.corpoflondon.gov.uk

Contact *The Senior Librarian*

Approximately 500,000 images of London, mostly topographical and architectural. Subjects include education, local authority housing, transport, the Thames, parks, churches, hospitals, war damage, pubs, theatres and cinemas. Also major redevelopments like the South Bank, The City, Covent Garden and Docklands.

London Transport Museum Photographic Library

39 Wellington Street, London WC2E 7BB
☎0171 379 6344   Fax 0171 497 3527

Contacts *Hugh Robertson, Simon Murphy, Martin Harrison-Putnam*

Around 100,000 b&w images from the 1860s and 10,000 colour images from c.1975. *Specialist collections* poster archive, underground construction, corporate design and architecture, street scenes, London Transport during the war. Collection available for viewing by appointment on Monday, Wednesday and Friday. No loans system but prints and transparences can be purchased.

The Ludvigsen Library Limited

73 Collier Street, London N1 9BE
☎0171 837 1700   Fax 0171 837 1776
Email: ludvigsen@mail.bogo.co.uk
Website: www.ludvigsen.com

Contact *Paul Parker*

Approximately 400,000 images (both b&w and many colour transparencies) of automobiles and motorsport, from 1920s through 1980s. Glass plate negatives from the early 1900s; Formula One, Le Mans, motor car shows, vintage, antique and classic cars from all countries. Includes the Dalton-Watson Collection and noted photographers such as John Dugdale, Edward Eves, Peter Keen, Max le Grand, Karl Ludvigsen, Rodolfo Mailander, Ove Nielsen, Stanley Rosenthall and others. Extensive information research facilities for writers and publishers.

Lupe Cunha Photos

19 Ashfields Parade, London N14 5EH
☎0181 882 6441   Fax 0181 882 6303
Email: lupe.cunha@btinternet.com
Website: www.lupecunha.com

Children, health, pregnancy and general women's interest. Also special collection on Brazil. Commissions undertaken.

MacQuitty International Photographic Collection

7 Elm Lodge, River Gardens, Stevenage Road, London SW6 6NZ
☎0171 385 6031/384 1781
Fax 0171 384 1781

Contact *Dr Miranda MacQuitty*

Colour and b&w collection on aspects of life in over 70 countries: dancing, music, religion, death, archaeology, buildings, transport, food, drink, nature. Visitors by appointment.

Magnum Photos Ltd

Moreland Buildings, 2nd Floor, 5 Old Street, London EC1V 9HL
☎0171 490 1771   Fax 0171 608 0020
Email: magnum@magnumphotos.co.uk

Head of Library *Heather Vickers*

FOUNDED 1947 by Cartier Bresson, George Rodger, Robert Capa and David 'Chim' Seymour. Represents over 50 of the world's leading photo-journalists. Coverage of all major world events from the Spanish Civil War to present day. Also a large collection of personalities.

The Raymond Mander & Joe Mitchenson Theatre Collection

The Mansion, Beckenham Place Park, Beckenham, Kent BR3 2BP
☎0181 658 7725   Fax 0181 663 0313

Contact *Richard Mangan*

Enormous collection covering all aspects of the theatre: plays, actors, dramatists, music hall, theatres, singers, composers, etc. Visitors welcome by appointment.

Mansell Collection

See **Katz Pictures**

S & O Mathews Photography

The Old Rectory, Calbourne, Isle of Wight PO30 4JE
☎01983 531247   Fax 01983 531253

Library of colour transparencies of landscapes, gardens and flowers.

Institution of Mechanical Engineers

1 Birdcage Walk, London SW1H 9JJ
☎0171 973 1265   Fax 0171 222 4557
Website: www.imeche.org.uk

Senior Librarian & Archivisst *Keith Moore*

Historical and contemporary images on mechanical engineering. Open 9.15 am to 5.30 pm, Mon. to Fri. Telephone for appointment.

Medimage

32 Brooklyn Road, Coventry CV1 4JT
☎01203 668652   Fax 01203 668562

Contact *Anthony King, Catherine King*

Medium format colour transparencies of Mediterranean countries covering a wide range of subjects – agriculture, archaeology, architecture, arts, crafts, education, festivals, flora, geography, history, industry, landscapes, markets, recreation, seascapes, sports and transport. The collection is added to on a regular basis and photographic commissions are undertaken. No search fees. Pictures by other photographers are not accepted.

Meledin Collection

See **Mary Evans Picture Library**

Lee Miller Archives

Farley Farm House, Chiddingly, Near Lewes, East Sussex BN8 6HW
☎01825 872691   Fax 01825 872733
Email: archives@leemiller.co.uk
Website: www.leemiller.co.uk

The work of Lee Miller (1907–77). As a photojournalist she covered the war in Europe from early in 1944 to VE Day with further reporting from the Balkans. Collection includes photographic portraits of prominent Surrealist artists: Ernst, Eluard, Miró, Picasso, Penrose, Carrington, Tanning, and others. Surrealist and contemporary art, poets and writers, fashion, the Middle East, Egypt, the Balkans in the 1930s, London during the Blitz, war in Europe and the liberation of Dachau and Buchenwald.

Mirror Syndication International

22nd Floor, 1 Canada Square, Canary Wharf, London E14 5AP
☎0171 293 3700   Fax 0171 293 2712
Email: desk@mirpix.com
Website: www.mirrorpix.com

Managing Director *Frank Walker*

Major photo library specialising in current affairs, personalities, royalty, sport, pop and glamour, plus extensive British and world travel pictures. Major motion picture archive up to 1965. Agents for Mirror Group Newspapers. Syndicator of photos and text for news/features.

Monitor Syndication

17 Old Street, London EC1V 9HL
☎0171 253 7071   Fax 0171 250 0966

Colour and b&w coverage of leading international personalities. Politics, entertainment, royals, judicial, commerce, religion, trade unions, well-known buildings. Also an archive library dating back to 1870, and a specialist file on Lotus cars. Syndication to international, national and local media.

Moroccan Scapes

Seend Park, Seend, Wiltshire SN12 6NZ
☎01380 828533   Fax 01380 828630
Email: chris@morocco-travel.com

Contact *Chris Lawrence*

Specialist collection of Moroccan material: scenery, towns, people, markets and places, plus the Atlas Mountains. Over 16,000 images.

Motoring Picture Library

National Motor Museum, Beaulieu,
Hampshire SO42 7ZN
☎01590 612345   Fax 01590 612655
Email: nmmt@compuserve.com

Contact *Jonathan Day*

Three-quarters of a million b&w images, plus 80,000 colour transparencies covering all forms of motoring history from 1880s to present day. Commissions undertaken. Own studio.

Mountain Camera

See **John Cleare**

Moving Image Communications Ltd

The Basement, 2–4 Dean Street, London
W1V 5RN
☎0171 437 5688   Fax 0171 437 5649
Email: moving_image@compuserve.com
Website: www.moving-image@co.uk

Contact *Michael Maloney*

11,000 hours of quality archive and contemporary images; computer catalogued for immediate access. Collections include: Britain 1925–98, The Cuban Archive, Medical Technology, 1950's Classic Travelogues, Subaqua Films, Space Exploration, Vintage Slapstick, British Airways 1984–98, Seascapes and Landscapes, TVAM Interviews/Funnies 1983–92, Lonely Planet. In addition, Moving Image provides an external research and copyright clearance service. In-house researchers can locate images using long-established contacts with footage sources worldwide.

Museum of Antiquities Picture Library

University and Society of Antiquaries of Newcastle upon Tyne, Newcastle upon Tyne NE1 7RU
☎0191 222 7846   Fax 0191 222 8561
Email: m.o.antiquities@ncl.ac.uk
Website: www.ncl.ac.uk/~nantiq

Contact *Lindsay Allason-Jones*

25,000 images, mostly b&w, of special collections including: Hadrian's Wall Archive (b&ws taken over the last 100 years); Gertrude Bell Archive (during her travels in the Near East, 1900–26); and aerial photographs of archaeological sites in the North of England. Visitors welcome by appointment.

Museum of London Picture Library

150 London Wall, London EC2Y 5HN
☎0171 814 5604/5   Fax 0171 600 1058
Email: picturelib@museumoflondon.org.uk

The Museum of London Picture Library tells the story of London from its earliest settlers to the present day. Suffragettes: photographs and memorabilia; Museum Objects: gallery and reserve collections – Prehistoric, Roman, Saxon, Medieval, Stuart, Georgian, Victorian, London Now; Photographs: social history of the capital – working life, East End, inter-war years, the Blitz, post-war; Prints and Caricatures: political and social satire, architecture; Paintings: dating from the 17th century, portraits, landscapes, cityscapes.

National Galleries of Scotland Picture Library

National Galleries of Scotland, Belford Road, Edinburgh EH4 3DR
☎0131 624 6319   Fax 0131 315 2963

Contacts *Deborah Hunter, Helen Nicoll*

Over 30,000 b&w and several thousand images in colour of works of art from the Renaissance to present day. Specialist subjects cover fine art (painting, sculpture, drawing), portraits, Scottish, historical, still life, photography and landscape. Colour leaflet, scale of charges and application forms available on request.

National Maritime Museum Picture Library

Greenwich, London SE10 9NF
☎0181 312 6631/6704   Fax 0181 312 6533

Contact *David Taylor, Lindsey Macfarlane*

Over three million maritime-related images and artefacts, including oil paintings from the 16th century to present day, prints and drawings, historic photographs, plans of ships built in the UK since the beginning of the 18th century, models, rare maps and charts, instruments, etc. Over 50,000 items within the collection are now photographed and with the Historic Photographs Collection form the basis of the picture library's stock.

National Medical Slide Bank
See **Wellcome Trust Medical Photographic Library**

National Meteorological Library and Archive
See under **Library Services**

National Monuments Record
National Monuments Record Centre, Kemble Drive, Swindon, Wiltshire SN2 2GZ
☎01793 414600   Fax 01793 414606
Email: infor@rchme.gov.uk
Website: www.rchme.gov.uk
The National Monuments Record is the first stop for photographs and information on England's heritage. Over 12 million photographs, documents and drawings are held. English architecture from the first days of photography to the present, air photographs covering every inch of England from the first days of flying to the present, and archaeological sites. The record is now the public archive of English Heritage and includes the material gathered by the Royal Commission on the Historical Monuments of England in its 90-year history. The London office specialises in the architecture of the capital city – for more information phone 0171 208 8200.

National Portrait Gallery Picture Library
St Martin's Place, London WC2H 0HE
☎0171 312 2473/4/5/6 or 306 0055
Fax 0171 312 2464/306 0092/0056
Email: tmorgan@npg.org.uk
Website: www.npg.org.uk
Contact *Tom Morgan*
Access to over 700,000 portraits of famous British men and women dating from the middle ages to the present. Various formats/media.

National Railway Museum Picture Library
Leeman Road, York YO26 4XJ
☎01904 621261   Fax 01904 611112
1.5 million images, mainly b&w, covering every aspect of railways from 1866 to the present day. Visitors by appointment.

The National Trust Photographic Library
36 Queen Anne's Gate, London SW1H 9AS
☎0171 447 6788   Fax 0171 447 6767
Email: photolibrary@ntrust.org.uk
Website: www.nationaltrust.org.uk/ photolibrary
Contact *Ed Gibbons*
Collection of mixed-format transparencies covering landscape and coastline throughout England, Wales and Northern Ireland; also architecture, interiors, gardens, paintings and conservation, plus a new collection of wildlife photographs. Award-winning brochure available on request. Profits from the picture library are reinvested in continuing the work of the Trust.

Natural History Museum Picture Library
Cromwell Road, London SW7 5BD
☎0171 938 9122/9035   Fax 0171 938 9169
Email: nhmpl@nhm.ac.uk
Website: www.nhm.ac.uk/images
Contact *Martin Pulsford, Lodvina Mascarenhas*
12,000 large-format transparencies on natural history and related subjects: extinct animals, dinosaurs, fossils, anthropology, minerals, gemstones, fauna and flora. No wildlife pictures but many images of historic natural history art. Commissions of museum specimens undertaken.

Natural History Photographic Agency
See **NHPA**

Natural Science Photos
33 Woodland Drive, Watford, Hertfordshire WD1 3BY
☎01923 245265   Fax 01923 246067
Colour coverage of natural history subjects worldwide. The work of some 150 photographers, it includes angling, animals, birds, reptiles, amphibia, fish, insects and other invertebrates, habitats, plants, fungi, geography, weather, scenics, horticulture, agriculture, farm animals and registered dog breeds. Researched by experienced scientists Peter and Sondra Ward. Visits by appointment. Commissions undertaken.

Nature Photographers Ltd

West Wit, New Road, Little London, Tadley, Hampshire RG26 5EU
☎01256 850661   Fax 01256 851157
Email: nature.photos@clara.net

Contact *Dr Paul Sterry*

Over 150,000 images on worldwide natural history and environmental subjects. The library is run by a trained biologist and experienced author on his subject.

Peter Newark's Pictures

3 Barton Buildings, Queen Square, Bath BA1 2JR
☎01225 334213   Fax 01225 480554

Over one million images covering world history from ancient times to the present day. Incorporates two special collections: American history in general with strong Wild West collection; and the military collection: military/naval personalities and events. Subject list available. Visitors welcome by appointment.

NHPA (Natural History Photographic Agency)

Little Tye, 57 High Street, Ardingly, West Sussex RH17 6TB
☎01444 892514   Fax 01444 892168
Email: nhpa@nhpa.co.uk
Website: www.nhpa.co.uk

Library Manager *Tim Harris*

Extensive coverage on all aspects of natural history – animals, plants, landscapes, environmental issues, gardens and pets. 120 photographers worldwide provide a steady input of high-quality transparencies. Specialist files include the unique high-speed photography of Stephen Dalton, extensive coverage of African and American wildlife, also rainforests, marine life and the polar regions. UK agents for the ANT collection of Australasian material. Loans are generally made direct to publishers; individual writers must request material via their publisher.

NRSC – Air Photo Group

Arthur Street, Barwell, Leicestershire LE9 8GZ
☎01455 849227   Fax 01455 841785

Contact *Joanne Burchnall*

Leading supplier of earth observation data, including satellite imagery, aerial photography and airborne remote sensing.

Odhams Periodicals Library

See **Popperfoto**

Only Horses Picture Agency

27 Greenway Gardens, Greenford, Middlesex UB6 9TU
☎0181 578 9047   Fax 0181 575 7244

Colour and b&w coverage of all aspects of the horse. Foaling, retirement, racing, show jumping, eventing, veterinary, polo, breeds, personalities.

Open University Photo Library

Room 163 A Block, Walton Hall, Milton Keynes MK7 6AA
☎01908 658408   Fax 01908 653313

Contact *Debbie Nicholls-Brien*

Education, industry and social welfare collection. 65,000 mainly b&w images dating from the early 1970s.

Oxford Picture Library

1 North Hinksey Village, Oxford OX2 0NA
☎01865 723404   Fax 01865 725294

Contact *Annabel Webb, Chris Andrews, Angus Palmer*

Specialist collection on Oxford: the city, university and colleges, events, people, spires and shires; also the Cotswolds, architecture and landscape from Stratford-upon-Avon to Bath; the Chilterns and Henley on Thames, with aerial views of all of the above; plus Channel Islands, especially Guernsey and Sark. General collection includes wildlife, trees, plants, clouds, sun, sky, water and teddy bears. Commissions undertaken.

Oxford Scientific Films Photo Library

Lower Road, Long Hanborough, Oxfordshire OX8 8LL
☎01993 881881   Fax 01993 882808
Email: photo.library@osf.uk.com
Website: www.osf.uk.com

Senior Account Manager *Suzanne Aitzetmuller*

Account Managers *Jo Glass, Sarah Fox*

Collection of 300,000 colour transparencies of wildlife and natural science images supplied by over 300 photographers worldwide, covering all aspects of wildlife plus landscapes, weather, seasons, plants, environment, anthropology, habitats, industry, space, creative textures and backgrounds, and geology. Macro and micro photography. UK agents for Animals Animals, USA, Okapia, Germany and Dinodia, India.

Research by experienced researchers for specialist and creative briefs. Visits welcome, by appointment.

PA News Photo Library

PA News Centre, 292 Vauxhall Bridge Road, London SW1V 1AE
☎0171 963 7038/7039   Fax 0171 963 7066
Website: www.pa.press.net/info/paphotos/main.html

PA News, the 24-hour national news and information group, offers public access to its photographic archives. Photographs, dating from 1890 to the present day, cover everything from news and sport to entertainment and royalty, with around 50 new pictures added daily. Personal callers welcome (10.00 am to 4.00 pm weekdays) or research undertaken by in-house staff.

Hugh Palmer

Knapp House, Shenington, Near Banbury, Oxfordshire OX15 6NE
☎01295 670433   Fax 01295 670709
Email: hupalmer@msn.com

Extensive coverage of gardens from Britain and Europe, as well as rural landscapes and architecture. Medium-format transparencies from numerous specialist commissions for books and magazines.

Panos Pictures

1 Chapel Court, Borough High Street, London SE1 1HH
☎0171 234 0010   Fax 0171 357 0094
Email: pics@panos.co.uk
Website: www.panos.co.uk

Documentary colour and b&w library specialising in Third World and Eastern Europe, with emphasis on environment and development issues. Leaflet available. Fifty per cent of all profits from this library go to the Panos Institute to further its work in international sustainable development.

Papilio Natural History & Travel Library

44 Palestine Grove, Merton, London SW19 2QN
☎0181 687 2202   Fax 0181 640 2011
Email: justine@papilio.demon.co.uk
Website: www.papilio.demon.co.uk

Contact *Robert Pickett, Justine Bowler*

Over 100,000 colour transparencies of natural history, including birds, animals, insects, flowers, plants, fungi and landscapes; plus travel worldwide including people, places and cultures. Commissions undertaken. Colour catalogue and digital slide show on disk available; call for further information. Visits by appointment only. Member of **BAPLA**.

Charles Parker Archive

See **Birmingham Library Services** under **Library Services**

David Paterson Photo-Library

88 Cavendish Road, London SW12 0DF
☎0181 673 2414   Fax 0181 675 9197
Email: paterson@wildcountry.uk.com
Website: www.wildcountry.uk.com

Travel, landscapes, nature from the UK, Europe, North Africa, the Himalayas, Japan, Scotland and the USA.

Ann & Bury Peerless Picture Library

St David's, 22 King's Avenue, Minnis Bay, Birchington-on-Sea, Kent CT7 9QL
☎01843 841428   Fax 01843 848321

Contact *Ann or Bury Peerless*

Specialist collection on world religions: Hinduism, Buddhism, Jainism, Christianity, Islam, Sikhism. Geographical areas covered: India, Afghanistan (Bamiyan Valley of the Buddhas), Pakistan, Bangladesh, Sri Lanka, Cambodia (Angkor Wat), Java (Borobudur), Bali, Thailand, Russia, Republic of China, Spain, Poland. 10,000 35mm colour transparencies.

Performing Arts Library

52 Agate Road, London W6 0AH
☎0181 748 2002   Fax 0181 563 0538
Email: performingartspics@pobox.com
Website: www.performingartslibrary.co.uk

Colour and b&w pictures of all aspects of the performing arts, including classical music, opera, theatre, ballet and contemporary dance, musicals, concert halls, opera houses and festivals.

Photo Resources

The Orchard, Marley Lane, Kingston, Canterbury, Kent CT4 6JH
☎01227 830075   Fax 01227 831135

Colour and b&w coverage of archaeology, art, ancient art, ethnology, mythology, world religion, museum objects.

Photofusion

17A Electric Lane, London SW9 8LA
☎0171 738 5774   Fax 0171 738 5509
Email: library@photofusion.org
Website: www.photofusion.org

Contact *Liz Somerville*

Colour and b&w coverage of contemporary social issues including babies and children, disability, education, the elderly, environment, family, health, housing, homelessness, people and work. Brochure available.

The Photographers' Library

81A Endell Street, London WC2H 9AJ
☎0171 836 5591   Fax 0171 379 4650
Email: photographerslibrary@
  compuserve.com

Covers people, lifestyles, commerce, holiday people, travel destinations, industry, landscapes, health. Brochure available.

Photomax

118–122 Magdalen Road, Oxford OX4 1RQ
☎01865 241825   Fax 01865 794511
Email: photomax@compuserve.com

Contact *Max Gibbs, Barry Allday*

All aspects of the aquarium hobby are covered: aquarium fish, tropical freshwater, tropical marine, coldwater, marine invertebrates (tropical), freshwater invertebrates, aquarium plants, fish diseases/parasites, water lilies. Commissions undertaken.

Photos Horticultural

169 Valley Road, Ipswich, Suffolk IP1 4PJ
☎01473 257329   Fax 01473 233974
Email: library@photos.keme.co.uk
Website: www.photos-horticultural.co.uk

Colour coverage of all aspects of gardening in Britain and abroad, including extensive files on plants in cultivation and growing wild.

PictureBank Photo Library Ltd

Parman House, 30–36 Fife Road, Kingston upon Thames, Surrey KT1 1SY
☎0181 547 2344   Fax 0181 974 5652

Over 400,000 colour transparencies covering people (girls, couples, families, children), travel and scenic (UK and world), moods (sunsets, seascapes, deserts, etc.), industry and technology, environments and general. Commissions undertaken. Visitors welcome. Member of **BAPLA**. New material on medium/large format welcome.

Pictures Colour Library

4th Floor, The Italian Building, 41 Dockhead, London SE1 2BS
☎0171 252 3300   Fax 0171 252 3345
Email: pictures@dial.pipex.com

Location, lifestyle, food, still life, sport, animals, industry and business. Visitors welcome.

Pitkin Unichrome Ltd

Healey House, Dene Road, Andover, Hampshire SP10 2AA
☎01264 409200   Fax 01264 334110
Email: guides@pitkin.u-net.com
Website: www.britguides.com

Contact *Jan Kean*

Colour transparencies of London, Bath, major ciies, cathedrals. No visitors. Mail order. Also publishers of guide books, calendars and postcards.

H. G. Ponting

See **Popperfoto**

Popperfoto

The Old Mill, Overstone Farm, Overstone, Northampton NN6 0AB
☎01604 670670   Fax 01604 670635
Email: popperfoto@msn.com
Website: www.popperfoto.com

Home to over 14 million images, covering 150 years of photographic history. Renowned for its archival material, a world-famous sports library and stock photography. Popperfoto's credit line includes Reuters, Bob Thomas Sports Photography, UPI, Acme, INP, Planet, Paul Popper, Exclusive News Agency, Victory Archive, Odhams Periodicals Library, Illustrated, Harris Picture Agency, and H. G. Ponting which holds the Scott 1910–1912 Antarctic expedition. Colour from 1940, b&w from 1870 to the present. Major subjects covered worldwide include events, personalities, wars, royalty, sport, politics, transport, crime, history and social conditions. Material available on the same day to clients throughout the world. Mac-desk available. Researchers welcome by appointment. Free catalogue available.

PPL Photo Agency Ltd

68 East Ham Road, Littlehampton, West Sussex BN17 7BE
☎01903 730614   Fax 01903 730618
Email: ppl@mistral.co.uk
Website: www.pplmedia.com

Contacts *Barry Pickthall, Eunice Bergin*

2 million pictures of sailing and boating, water-sports, travel, water and coastal scenes. British Steel Multimedia Library – all aspects of steel and steel making. Construction, science and technology, transport, mining and industry.

Premaphotos Wildlife

Amberstone, 1 Kirland Road, Bodmin, Cornwall PL30 5JQ
☎01208 78258   Fax 01208 72302
Email: premaphotos@compuserve.com
Website: www.premaphotos.co.uk

Contact *Jean Preston-Mafham, Library Manager*

Natural history worldwide. Subjects include flowering and non-flowering plants, fungi, slime moulds, fruits and seeds, galls, leaf mines, seashore life, mammals, birds, reptiles, amphibians, insects, spiders, habitats, scenery and cultivated cacti. Commissions undertaken. Visitors welcome. 'Make sure your name is on our mailing list to receive regular, colourful mailers.'

Professional Sport International Ltd

8 Apollo Studios, Charlton Kings Road, London NW5 2SA
☎0171 482 2311   Fax 0171 482 2441
Email: pictures@prosport.co.uk
Website: www.prosport.co.uk

Colour and b&w coverage of tennis, soccer, athletics, golf, cricket, boxing, winter sports and many minor sports. Major international events including the Olympic Games, World Cup soccer and all Grand Slam tennis events. Also news and feature material supplied worldwide. Computerised library with in-house processing and studio facilities; Macintosh photo transmission services available for editorial and advertising.

Public Record Office
Image Library

Ruskin Avenue, Kew, Richmond, Surrey TW9 4DU
☎0181 392 5225   Fax 0181 392 5266
Email: image-library@pro.gov.uk

Contact *Jo Matthews, Paul Johnson*

British and colonial history from the Domesday Book to the 1960s, shown in photography, maps, illuminations, posters, advertisements, textiles and original manuscripts. Approximately 20,000 5"x4" and 35mm colour transparencies and b&w negatives. Open: 9.00 am to 5.30 pm, Monday to Friday.

Punch Cartoon Library

Trevor House, 100 Brompton Road, London SW3 1ER
☎0171 225 6710/6711   Fax 0171 225 6712
Email: library@punch.co.uk

Owner *Liberty Publishing*
Library Manager *Miranda Taylor*

Gives access to the 500,000 cartoons published in *Punch* magazine between 1841–1992. The library has a 500+ subject listing and can search on any subject. Social history, politics, fashion, fads, famous people and more by the world's most famous cartoonists, including Tenniel, du Maurier, Pont, Fougasse, E. H. Shepard and Emett.

PWA International Ltd

City Gate House, 399–425 Eastern Avenue, Gants Hill, Ilford, Essex IG2 6LR
☎0181 518 2057   Fax 0181 518 2241
Email: pwaint@dircon.co.uk

Contact *Terry Allen*

Leading comprehensive library of story illustrations comprising work by some of the UK's best-known illustrators, including book covers and magazines. Also over half a million images of beauty, cookery and craft.

Railfotos

Millbrook House Ltd., Unit 1, Oldbury Business Centre, Pound Road, Oldbury, West Midlands B68 8NA
☎0121 544 2790
Fax 0121 253 6836 (quote Millbrook House)

One of the largest specialist libraries dealing comprehensively with railway subjects worldwide. Colour and b&w dating from the turn of the century to present day. Up-to-date material on UK, South America and Far East (except Japan), especially China. Visitors by appointment.

Redferns Music Picture Library

7 Bramley Road, London W10 6SZ
☎0171 792 9914   Fax 0171 792 0921
Email: info@redferns.com
Website: www.redferns.com

Music picture library covering every aspect of popular music from 1920's jazz to present day. Over 12,000 artists on file plus other subjects including musical instruments, recording studios, crowd scenes, festivals, etc. Brochure available.

Remote Source
See **Royal Geographical Society Picture Library**

Retna Pictures Ltd
Ground Floor, 53–56 Great Sutton Street, London EC1V 0DG
☎0171 490 0578   Fax 0171 490 0577
Email: chris@retna.demon.co.uk

Colour and b&w coverage of international rock and pop performers, actors, actresses, entertainers and celebrities. Also a general stock library covering a wide range of subjects, including travel, people, sport and leisure, flora and fauna, and the environment.

Retrograph Nostalgia Archive Ltd
164 Kensington Park Road, London W11 2ER
☎0171 727 9378/9426   Fax 0171 229 3395
Email: MBreese999@aol.com
Website: www.Retrograph.com

Contact *Jilliana Ranicar-Breese*

'Number One for nostalgia!' A vast archive of commercial and decorative art (1860–1960). Worldwide labels and packaging for food, wine, chocolate, soap, perfume, cigars and cigarettes; fine art and commercial art journals, fashion and lifestyle magazines, posters, Victorian greetings cards, scraps, Christmas cards, Edwardian postcards, wallpaper and gift-wrap sample books, music sheets, folios of decorative design and ornament – Art Nouveau and Deco; hotel, airline and shipping labels; memorabilia, tourism, leisure, food and drink, transport and entertainment. Lasers for book dummies, packaging, mock-ups, film/TV action props. Colour brochure on request. Picture research service. Design consultancy service. Victorian-style montages conceived, designed and styled (RetroMontages).

Rex Features Ltd
18 Vine Hill, London EC1R 5DX
☎0171 278 7294/3362   Fax 0171 696 0974

Established in the 1950s. Colour and b&w coverage of news, politics, personalities, show business, glamour, humour, art, medicine, science, landscapes, royalty, etc.

Ann Ronan Collection
See **Image Select International**

Royal Air Force Museum
Grahame Park Way, Hendon, London NW9 5LL
☎0181 205 2266   Fax 0181 200 1751

Contact *Christine Gregory*

About a quarter of a million images, mostly b&w, with around 1500 colour in all formats, on the history of aviation. Particularly strong on the activities of the Royal Air Force from the 1870s to 1970s. Researchers are requested to enquire in writing only.

The Royal Collection
Windsor Castle, Windsor, Berks SL4 1NJ
☎01753 868286   Fax 01753 620046

Contact *Shruti Patel, Nicole Mitchell*

Photographic material of items in the Royal Collection, particularly oil paintings, drawings and watercolours, works of art, and interiors and exteriors of royal residences. 35,000 colour transparencies plus 25,000 b&w negatives.

Royal Geographical Society Picture Library
1 Kensington Gore, London SW7 2AR
☎0171 591 3060   Fax 0171 591 3061
Website: www.rgs.org/picturelibrary

Contact *Joanna Scadden, Sharon Martins*

A strong source of geographical and historical images, both archival and modern, showing the world through the eyes of photographers and explorers dating from the 1830s to the present day. The Remote Source Collection provides up-to-date transparencies from around the world, highlighting aspects of cultural activity, environmental phenomena, anthropology, architectural design, travel, mountaineering and exploration. Offers a professional and comprehensive service for both commercial and academic use.

The Royal Photographic Society
The Octagon, Milsom Street, Bath BA1 1DN
☎01225 462841   Fax 01225 448688

Contact *Debbie Ireland*

History of photography, with an emphasis on pictorial photography as an art rather than a documentary record. Photographic processes and cameras, landscape, portraiture, architecture, India, Victorian and Edwardian life.

RSPB Images
21-22 Great Sutton Street, London EC1V 0DN
☎0171 608 7325   Fax 0171 608 0770

Contact *Zoe Beech*

Colour and b&w images of birds, butterflies,

moths, mammals, reptiles and their habitats. Also colour images of all RSPB reserves. Growing selection of various habitats. Over 52,000 slides available digitally or in any desired format.

RSPCA Photolibrary

RSPCA Trading Limited, Causeway, Horsham, West Sussex RH12 1HG
☎01403 223150   Fax 01403 241048
Email: photolibrary@rspca.org.uk
Photolibrary Manager *Andrew Forsyth*

Over 40,000 colour transparencies and over 5000 b&w/colour prints. A comprehensive collection of natural history images whose subjects include mammals, birds, domestic and farm animals, amphibians, insects and the environment, as well as a unique photographic record of the RSPCA's work. Also includes the Wild Images collections. Catalogue available. No search fees.

Russia and and Eastern Images

'Sonning', Cheapside Lane, Denham, Uxbridge, Middlesex UB9 5AE
☎01895 833508   Fax 01895 831957
Email: easteuropix@btinternet.com

Architecture, cities, landscapes, people and travel images of Russia and the former Soviet Union. Considerable background knowledge available and Russian language spoken.

Salamander Picture Library

8 Blenheim Court, Brewery Road, London N7 9NT
☎0171 700 7799   Fax 0171 700 3918/3572
Contact *Terry Forshaw*

Approximately 250,000 images, colour and b&w, of American history, collectables, cookery, crafts, military, natural history, space and transport.

Peter Sanders Photography

24 Meades Lane, Chesham, Buckinghamshire HP5 1ND
☎01494 773674   Fax 01494 773674/771372
Email: petersanders.photography@
   btinternet.com
Contact *Peter Sanders, Hafsa Garwatuk*

The world of Islam in all its aspects from religion and industry to culture and arts. Areas included are Saudi Arabia, Africa, Asia, Europe and USA. Now expanding to all religions.

Science & Society Picture Library

Science Museum, Exhibition Road, London SW7 2DD
☎0171 938 9750   Fax 0171 938 9751
Email: piclib@nmsi.ac.uk
Website: www.nmsi.ac.uk/piclib/
Contact *Angela Murphy, Venita Paul*

25,000 reference prints and 100,000 colour transparencies, incorporating many from collections at the Science Museum, the National Railway Museum and the National Museum of Photography Film and Television. Collections illustrate the history of science, industry, technology, medicine, transport and the media. Plus three archives documenting British society in the twentieth century.

Science Footage Limited

29 Bridge Street, Hitchin, Hertfordshire SG5 2DF
☎01462 421110   Fax 01462 421092
Email: admin@science-pictures.ltd.uk
Website: www.science-pictures.led.uk
Contact *Judy Spears, Mary Hansford*

Part of Science Pictures Limited, a TV production company. Over 5000 images: medical, botanical, microscopy, scanning electron microscopy; also small collection of animal pictures. Film and video footage available.

Science Photo Library

327–329 Harrow Road, London W9 3RB
☎0171 432 1100   Fax 0171 286 8668
Email: info@sciencephoto.co.uk
Website: www.sciencephoto.com

FOUNDED 1979. Over 120,000 images of science, medicine and technology.

The Scottish Highland Photo Library

Croft Roy, Crammond Brae, Tain, Ross-shire IV19 1JG
☎01862 892298   Fax 01862 892298
Email: shpl@cali.co.uk
Contact *Hugh Webster*

150,000 colour transparencies of the Scottish Highlands and Islands. Not just a travel library; images cover industry, agriculture, fisheries and many other subjects of the Highlands and Islands. Submissions from photographers welcome. Commissions undertaken. Call for free catalogue.

Scottish Media Newspapers

195 Albion Street, Glasgow G1 1QP
☎0141 552 6255   Fax 0141 553 2642

Over six million images: b&w and colour photographs from *c.*1900 from the *Herald* (Glasgow) and *Evening Times*. Current affairs, Scotland, Glasgow, Clydeside shipbuilding and engineering, personalities, World Wars I and II, sport.

Seaco Picture Library

Sea Containers House, 20 Upper Ground, London SE1 9PF
☎0171 805 5831   Fax 0171 805 5807

Contact *Maureen Elliott*

Approx. 250,000 images of containerisation, shipping, fast ferries, manufacturing, fruit farming, ports, hotels and leisure.

Mick Sharp Photography

Eithinog, Waun, Penisarwaun, Caernarfon, Gwynedd LL55 3PW
☎01286 872425   Fax 01286 872425

Contacts *Mick Sharp, Jean Williamson*

Colour transparencies (6x4.5cm and 35mm) and black & white prints (5"x4" and 6x4.5cm negatives) of subjects connected with archaeology, ancient monuments, buildings, churches, countryside, environment, history, landscape, past cultures and topography from Britain and abroad. Photographs by Mick Sharp and Jean Williamson, plus access to other specialist collections on related subjects. Commissions undertaken.

Phil Sheldon Golf Picture Library

40 Manor Road, Barnet, Hertfordshire EN5 2JQ
☎0181 440 1986   Fax 0181 440 9348
Email: GolfSnap@aol.com

An expanding collection of over 400,000 quality images of the 'world of golf'. In-depth worldwide tournament coverage including every Major championship & Ryder Cup since 1976. Instruction, portraits, trophies and over 300 golf courses from around the world. Also the Dale Concannon collection covering the period 1870 to 1940 and the classic 1960s collection by photographer Sidney Harris.

Skishoot–Offshoot

Hall Place, Upper Woodcott, Whitchurch, Hampshire RG28 7PY
☎01635 255527   Fax 01635 255528
Email: skishoot@surfersparadise.net

Contact *Jane Blount, Fiona Foote*

Skishoot ski and snowboarding picture library has 200,000 images. Offshoot travel library specialises in France.

The Skyscan Photolibrary

Oak House, Toddington, Cheltenham, Gloucestershire GL54 5BY
☎01242 621357   Fax 01242 621343
Email: info@skyscan.co.uk
Website: www.skyscan.co.uk

As well as the Skyscan Photolibrary collection of unique balloon's-eye views of Britain, the library now includes the work of photographers from across the aviation spectrum; air to ground, aviation, aerial sports – 'in fact, anything aerial!'. Links have been built with photographers across the world; photographs can be handled on an agency basis and held in house, or as a brokerage where the collection stays with the photographer; terms 50/50 for both. Commissioned photography undertaken. Enquiries welcome.

Snookerimages (Eric Whitehead Photography)

PO Box 33, Kendal, Cumbria LA9 4SU
☎015394 48894   Fax 015394 48294
Email: eric@snookerimages.co.uk
Website: www.snookerimages.co.uk

Over 20,000 images of snooker. Also holds the Cumbria Picture Library; the agency covers local news events, PR and commercial material.

SOA Photo Library

87 York Street, London W1H 1DU
☎0171 258 0202   Fax 0171 258 01881
Email: soaphotos@btinternet.com
Website: www.soa-photoagency.co.uk

Contact *Brigitte Bott, Lorna Allen, Emma Davies*

85,000 colour slides, 15,000 b&w photos covering *Stern* productions, sports, travel & geographic, advertising, social subjects. Representatives of Voller Ernst, Interfoto, Picture Press and many freelance photographers. Free catalogues available.

Solo Syndication Ltd

49-53 Kensington High Street, London W8 5ED
☎0171 376 2166   Fax 0171 938 3165

Syndication Manager *Trevor York*
Sales *Danny Howell, Nick York*
Online transmissions *Geoff Malyon*
(☎0171 937 3866)

Three million images from the archives of the *Daily Mail, Mail on Sunday, Evening Standard* and

Evening News. Hard prints or Mac-to-mac delivery. 24–hour service.

Sotheby's Picture Library

34–35 New Bond Street, London W1A 2AA
☎0171 293 5383   Fax 0171 293 5062

Contact *Joanna Ling, Sue Daly*

The library mainly consists of over 30,000 selected transparencies of pictures sold at Sotheby's. Images from the 15th to the 20th century. Oils, drawings, watercolours and prints. 'Happy to do searches or, alternatively, visitors are welcome by appointment.'

South American Pictures

48 Station Road, Woodbridge, Suffolk
IP12 4AT
☎01394 383963/383279   Fax 01394 380176
Email: morrison@south-american-pic.com
Website: www.south-american-pic.com

Contact *Marion Morrison*

Colour and b&w images of South/Central America, Cuba, Mexico and New Mexico (USA), including archaeology and the Amazon. Frequently updated. There is an archival section, with pictures and documents from most countries.

The Special Photographers Library

21 Kensington Park Road, London W11 2EU
☎0171 221 3489   Fax 0171 792 9112
Email: info@specialphoto.co.uk
Website: www.specialphoto.co.uk

Contacts *Chris Kewbank*

Represents over 100 contemporary fine art photographers who are unusual in style, technique or subject matter. Also has exclusive access to the Bill Hopkins Collection – an archive of thousands of vintage pictures dating back to the early 20th century.

Spectrum Colour Library

41–42 Berners Street, London W1P 3AA
☎0171 637 1587   Fax 0171 637 3681
Email: keith@sridge.demon.co.uk
Website: www.sclpix.co.uk

A large collection including travel, sport, people, pets, scenery, industry, British and European cities, etc. All pictures are also available in digital format. Visitors welcome by appointment.

Frank Spooner Pictures Ltd

Unit B7, Hatton Square, 16–16A Baldwin's Gardens, London EC1N 7US
☎0171 632 5800   Fax 0171 632 5828
Email: fsp/pix@compuserve.com

Subjects include current affairs, show business, fashion, politics, travel, adventure, sport, personalities, films, animals and the Middle East. Represented in more than 30 countries and handles UK distribution of Harry Benson, and Gamma Presse Images and Roger-Viollet of Paris. Commissions undertaken.

The Still Moving Picture Co.

67A Logie Green Road, Edinburgh EH7 4HF
☎0131 557 9697   Fax 0131 557 9699
Email: stillmovingpictures@compuserve.com

Contact *John Hutchinson, Sue Hall*

250,000 colour, b&w and 16mm film coverage of Scotland and sport. The largest photo and film library in Scotland, holding the Scottish Tourist Board library among its files. Scottish agents for **Allsport (UK) Ltd**.

Still Pictures' Whole Earth Photolibrary

199 Shooters Hill Road, Blackheath, London SE3 8UL
☎0181 858 8307   Fax 0181 858 2049
Email: info@stillpictures.com
Website: www.stillpictures.com

Contacts *Theresa de Salis, Mark Edwards*

FOUNDED 1970, the library is a leading source of pictures illustrating the human impact on the environment, Third World development issues, industrial ecology, nature and wildlife, endangered species and habitats. 250,000 colour medium-format transparencies, 100,000 b&w prints. Over 300 leading photographers from around the world supply the library with stock pictures. Write, phone or fax for Still Pictures' Environment and Third World catalogue and Still Pictures' Nature and Wildlife catalogue.

Stockfile

5 High Street, Sunningdale, Berkshire
SL5 0LX
☎01344 872249   Fax 01344 872263
Email: info@stockfile.co.uk

Contact *Jill Behr, Steven Behr*

Specialist cycling- and skiing-based collection covering most aspects of these activities, with emphasis on mountain biking. Expanding adventure sports section.

Sir John Benjamin Stone
See **Birmingham Library Services** under
Library Services

Joe Tasker Collection
See **Chris Bonnington Picture Library**

Tate Gallery Picture Library
Tate Gallery Publishing Ltd, Millbank,
London SW1P 4RG
☎0171 887 8867/90   Fax 0171 887 8900
Email: carlotta.gelmetti@tate.org.uk   and
christopher.webs
Website: www.tate.org.uk

Contact *Carlotta Gelmetti, Chris Webster*

Approximately 8000 images of British art from
the 16th century; international 20th century
painting and sculpture. Artists include William
Blake, William Hogarth, J. M. W. Turner,
Dante Gabriel Rossetti, Barbara Hepworth,
Henry Moore, Stanley Spencer, Pablo Picasso,
Mark Rothko, Salvador Dali, Lucien Freud and
David Hockney. Colour transparencies of more
than half the works in the main collection are
available for hire. For a fee, new photography is
available depending on the location and condition of the art work. B&w prints of nearly all
the works in the collection can be purchased.
Colour slides and prints can be made on request
providing a colour transparency exists. Picture
researchers must make an appointment to visit
the library. All applications must be made by fax
or letter.

Telegraph Colour Library
The Innovation Centre, 225 Marsh Wall,
London E14 9FX
☎0171 293 2939   Fax 0171 293 2930

Contact *Craig Mullaly*

Leading stock photography agency covering a
wide subject range: business, sport, people,
industry, animals, medical, nature, space, travel
and graphics. Free catalogue available. Same-day
service to UK clients.

3rd Millennium Music Ltd
22 Avon, Hockley, Tamworth, Staffordshire
B77 5QA
☎01827 286086   Fax 01827 286086
Email: Neil3MMLtd@aol.com
Website: members.aol.com/Neil3MMLtd/
 NWCC.htm

Managing Director *Neil Williams*

Archive specialising in classical music ephemera,
particularly portraits of composers, musicians,
conductors and opera singers comprising of old
and sometimes very rare photographs, postcards,
antique prints, cigarette cards, stamps, First Day
Covers, concert programmes, Victorian newspapers, etc. Also modern photos of composer
references such as museums, statues, busts, paintings, monuments, memorials and graves. Other
subjects covered include ballet, musical instruments, concert halls, opera houses, 'music in art',
manuscripts, opera scenes, music-caricatures,
bands, orchestras and other music groups.

Bob Thomas Sports Photography
See **Popperfoto**

Patrick Thurston Photolibrary
10 Willis Road, Cambridge CB1 2AQ
☎01223 352547   Fax 01223 366274

Colour photography of Britain: scenery, people, museums, churches, coastline. Also various
countries abroad. Commissions undertaken.

Rick Tomlinson Marine Photo Library
18 Hamble Yacht Services, Port Hamble,
Hamble, Southampton, Hampshire
SO31 4NN
☎01703 458450   Fax 01703 458350

Contacts *Rick Tomlinson, Julie Birchall*

ESTABLISHED 1985. *Specialises* in marine subjects.
60,000 35mm transparencies of yachting, racing,
cruising, Whitbread Round the World Race,
Tall Ships, RNLI Lifeboats, Antarctica, wildlife
and locations.

Topham Picturepoint
PO Box 33, Edenbridge, Kent TN8 5PB
☎01342 850313   Fax 01342 850244

Contact *Alan Smith*

Eight million contemporary and historical
images, ideal for advertisers, publishers and the
travel trade. Delivery on-line.

B. M. Totterdell Photography
Constable Cottage, Burlings Lane, Knockholt,
Kent TN14 7PE
☎01959 532001   Fax 01959 532001

Contact *Barbara Totterdell*

Specialist volleyball library covering all aspects
of the sport.

Tessa Traeger Library

7 Rossetti Studios, 72 Flood Street, London
SW3 5TF
☎0171 352 3641   Fax 0171 352 4846
Food, gardens, travel and artists.

Travel Ink Photo & Feature Library

The Old Coach House, 14 High Street,
Goring on Thames, Nr Reading, Berkshire
RG8 9AR
☎01491 873011   Fax 01491 875558
Email: info@travel-ink.co.uk
Website: www.travel-ink.co.uk
Contact *Abbie Enock*

Around 100,000 colour images covering about
130 countries (including the UK). Close links
with other specialist libraries mean most topics
can be accessed. Subjects include travel, tourism,
lifestyles, business, industry, transport, children,
religion, history, activities. Specialist collections
on Hong Kong (including construction of the
Tsing Ma bridge), Greece, North Wales,
Germany, the Cotswolds, France, and many others.

Peter Trenchard's Image Store Ltd

The Studio, West Hill, St Helier, Jersey,
Channel Islands JE2 3HB
☎01534 769933   Fax 01534 89191
Contact *Peter Trenchard, FBIPP, AMPA, PPA*

Slide library of the Channel Islands - mainly
tourist and financial-related. Commissions
undertaken.

Tropical Birds Photo Library

PO Box 100, Mansfield, Nottinghamshire
NG20 9NZ
☎01623 846430   Fax 01623 846430
Contact *Rosemary Low*

Transparencies (35mm) of parrots and other
tropical birds, and tropical butterflies. Also
colour and b&w prints and large format transparencies of parrots. Specialises in parrots: more
than 250 species.

Tropix Photographic Library

156 Meols Parade, Meols, Wirral, Merseyside
L47 6AN
☎0151 632 1698   Fax 0151 632 1698
Email: tropixphoto@postmaster.co.uk
Website: www.merseyworld.com/tropix/
Contact *Veronica Birley*

Specialists on the developing world in all its
aspects. Environmental topics worldwide.
Assignment photography UK and overseas.

'New collections welcome. Must be 35mm or
larger colour transparencies, top professional
quality only, taken 1996 or later. When submitting images, send postage stamps (only) to the full
value of return cost. Do not write or stick anything on the mounts. The images we want to
accept will be flagged up for you to prepare
according to our guidelines.'

True North Picture Source

5 Brunswick Street, Hebden Bridge, West
Yorkshire HX7 6AJ
☎01422 845532   Fax 01422 845532
Email: john@trunorth.demon.co.uk
Website: www.trunorth.demon.co.uk
Contact *John Morrison*

30,000 transparencies on 35mm and 6x4.5cm
format on the life and landscape of the north of
England, photographed by John Morrison.

Turnley Collection
See **Corbis Images**

Ulster Museum (National Museums and Galleries of Northern Ireland)

Botanic Gardens, Belfast BT9 5AB
☎01232 383000 ext 3113   Fax 01232 383103
Email: patricia.mclean.um@nics.gov.uk
Contact *Mrs Pat McLean*

Specialist subjects: art – fine and decorative, late
17th–20th century, particularly Irish art, archaeology, ethnography, treasures from the Armada
shipwrecks, geology, botany, zoology, local history and industrial archaeology. Commissions
welcome for objects not already photographed.

Universal Pictorial Press & Agency Ltd

29–31 Saffron Hill, London EC1N 8FW
☎0171 421 6000   Fax 0171 421 6006
News Editor *Peter Dare*

Photo archive dates back to 1944 and contains
approximately four million pictures. Colour
and b&w coverage of news, royalty, politics,
sport, arts, and many other subjects. Commissions undertaken for press and public relations. Fully interactive digital photo archive in
addition to bulletin board accessible via ISDN
or modem. Full digital scanning, retouching
and transmission facilities.

UPI
See **Popperfoto**

V & A Picture Library

Victoria and Albert Museum, South Kensington, London SW7 2RL
☎0171 938 8352/8354/8452/9645
Fax 0171 938 8353
Email: picture.library@vam.ac.uk

60,000 colour and half a million b&w photos of decorative and applied arts, including ceramics, ivories, furniture, costumes, textiles, stage, musical instruments, toys, Indian, Far Eastern, Islamic objects, sculpture, painting and prints, from medieval to present day.

Valley Green

Barn Ley, Valley Lane, Buxhall, Stowmarket, Suffolk IP14 3EB
☎01449 736090   Fax 01449 736090
Contact *Joseph Barrere*

Masses of perennials – 'all correctly labelled'. Over 10,000 hardy plant transparencies in stock, plus watercolours and line drawings available. Commissions undertaken as well as commercial copywriting.

Venice Picture Library

2a Milner Street, London SW3 2PU
☎0171 589 3127   Fax 0171 584 1944

25,000 35mm images of Venice, its buildings, people, animals and atmosphere. Member of **BAPLA**.

Victory Archive

See **Popperfoto**

The Vintage Magazine Company Ltd

203–213 Mare Street, London E8 3QE
☎0181 533 7588   Fax 0181 533 7283
Email: piclib.vintage@ndirect.co.uk
Website: www.vinmag.com

A large collection of movie stills and posters, photographs, illustrations and advertisements covering music, glamour, social history, theatre posters, ephemera, postcards.

The Charles Walker Collection

Ramillies House, 1–2 Ramillies Street, London W1V 1DF
☎0171 734 7344   Fax 0171 287 3933

One of the foremost collections in the world on subjects popularly listed as 'Mystery, myth and magic'. The collection includes astrology, occultism, witchcraft and many other related areas. Catalogue available.

John Walmsley Photo Library

April Cottage, Warners Lane, Albury Heath, Guildford, Surrey GU5 9DE
☎01483 203846
Fax 01483 203846
Email: johnwalmsleyphotos@compuserve.com

Specialist library of learning/training/working subjects. Comprehensive coverage of learning environments such as playgroups, schools, colleges and universities. Images reflect a multiracial Britain. Plus a section on complementary medicine with over 30 therapies from acupuncture and yoga to more unusual ones like moxibustion and metamorphic technique. Commissions undertaken. Subject list available on request.

Christopher Ware Pictures

65 Trinity Street, Barry, Glamorgan CF62 7EX
☎01446 732816/0802 865999 (Mobile)
Fax 01446 732816
Contact *Christopher Ware*

Large collection of images (b&w and colour) of S. E. Wales, including Barry docks and the Steam Graveyard, railways, Vale of Glamorgan landscapes, civil and military aircraft over the last 40 years. Images available on CD-ROM or via email. Digital post-production. Commissions. Other photographers' work not accepted.

Warwickshire Photographic Survey

See **Birmingham Library Services** under **Library Services**

Waterways Photo Library

39 Manor Court Road, Hanwell, London W7 3EJ
☎0181 840 1659   Fax 0181 567 0605

A specialist photo library on all aspects of Britain's inland waterways. Top-quality 35mm- and medium-format colour transparencies, plus a large collection of b&w. Rivers and canals, bridges, locks, aqueducts, tunnels and waterside buildings. Town and countryside scenes, canal art, waterway holidays, boating, fishing, windmills, watermills, watersports and wildlife.

Philip Way Photography

2 Green Moor Link, Winchmore Hill, London N21 2ND
☎0181 360 3034
Contact *Philip Way*

Over 5000 images of St Paul's Cathedral –

historical exteriors, interiors and events (1982–1997).

Wellcome Trust Medical Photographic Library

210 Euston Road, London NW1 2BE
☎0171 611 8348   Fax 0171 611 8577
Email: photolib@wellcome.ac.uk
Website: www.wellcome.ac.uk

Contact *Michele Minto, Julie Dorrington*

Approximately 160,000 images on the history of medicine and human culture worldwide, including modern clinical medicine. Incorporates the National Medical Slide Bank.

Eric Whitehead Photography

PO Box 33, Kendal, Cumbria LA9 4SU
☎015394 48894   Fax 015394 48284

Incorporates the Cumbria Picture Library. The agency covers local news events, PR and commercial material, also leading library of snooker images (see **Snookerimages**).

Wild Images

See **RSPCA Photolibrary**

Wilderness Photographic Library

Mill Barn, Broad Raine, Sedbergh, Cumbria LA10 5ED
☎015396 20196   Fax 015396 21293

Contact *John Noble*

Striking colour images from around the world, from polar wastes to the Himalayas and Amazon jungle. Subjects: mountains, Arctic, deserts, icebergs, wildlife, rainforests, glaciers, geysers, exploration, caves, rivers, eco-tourism, people and cultures, canyons, seascapes, marine life, weather, volcanoes, mountaineering, skiing, geology, conservation, adventure sports, national parks.

David Williams Picture Library

50 Burlington Avenue, Glasgow G12 0LH
☎0141 339 7823   Fax 0141 337 3031

Colour coverage of Scotland and Iceland. Smaller collections of the Faroes, France, Spain, Portugal, Czech Republic, Hungary and various other European countries; also Western USA. Landscapes, historical sites, buildings, geology and physical geography. Medium format and 35mm. Catalogue available. Commissions undertaken.

Vaughan Williams Memorial Library

English Folk Dance and Song Society, Cecil Sharp House, 2 Regent's Park Road, London NW1 7AY
☎0171 284 0523   Fax 0171 284 0523

Mainly b&w coverage of traditional/folk music, dance and customs worldwide, focusing on Britain and other English-speaking nations. Photographs date from the late 19th century to the 1990s.

The Wilson Photographic Collection

See **Dundee District Libraries** under **Library Services**

Windrush Photos, Wildlife and Countryside Picture Agency

99 Noah's Ark, Kemsing, Sevenoaks, Kent TN15 6PD
☎01732 763486   Fax 01732 763285

Contact *David Tipling*

Specialists in birds (worldwide) and British wildlife. A large collection of black and white images covering British wildlife and angling, and shooting scenes dating back to the 1930s. High quality photographic and features commissions are regularly undertaken for publications in the UK and overseas. The agency acts as ornithological consultants for all aspects of the media.

Woodfall Wild Images

17 Bull Lane, Denbigh, Denbighshire LL16 3SN
☎01745 815903   Fax 01745 814581
Email: WWImages@btinternet.com

Contacts *David Hill*

Specialist environmental, conservation, landscape and wildlife photographic library. A constantly expanding collection of images reflecting the natural world and man's effect upon it, both positively and negatively. Please call for a brochure, stock cards or prospective photographer notes. New specialist panoramic coverage available.

World Pictures

85a Great Portland Street, London W1N 5RA
☎0171 437 2121/436 0440
Fax 0171 439 1307
Email: Worldpictures@btinternet.com

Contacts *David Brenes, Carlo Irek*

600,000 colour transparencies of travel and emotive material.

WWF UK Photolibrary

Panda House, Weyside Park, Catteshall Lane, Godalming, Surrey GU7 1XR
☎01483 426444   Fax 01483 426409

Contact *Rosie Lynch*

Specialist library covering natural history, endangered species, conservation, environment, forests, habitats, habitat destruction, and pollution in the UK and abroad. 10,000 colour slides (35mm).

Yemen Pictures

28 Sheen Common Drive, Richmond
TW10 5BN
☎0181 898 0150/876 3637
Fax 0181 898 0150

Large collection (4000 transparencies) covering all aspects of Yemen – culture, people, architecture, dance, qat, music. Also Africa, Australia, Middle East, and Asia.

York Archaeological Trust Picture Library

Cromwell House, 13 Ogleforth, York YO1 7FG
☎01904 663000   Fax 01904 640029
Email: postmaster@yorkarch.demon.co.uk
Website: www.yorkarch.demon.co.uk

Specialist library of rediscovered artifacts, historic buildings and excavations, presented by the creators of the highly acclaimed Jorvik Viking Centre. The main emphasis is on the Roman, Anglo-Saxon and Viking periods.

The John Robert Young Collection

61 De Montfort Road, Lewes, East Sussex BN7 1SS
☎01273 475216   Fax 01273 475216

Contact *Jennifer Barrett*

50,000 transparencies and monochrome prints on travel, religion and military subjects.

Balancing the Books –
Tax and the Writer

'No man in the country is under the smallest obligation, moral or other, to arrange his affairs as to enable the Inland Revenue to put the largest possible shovel in his stores.

The Inland Revenue is not slow, and quite rightly, to take every advantage which is open to it ... for the purpose of depleting the taxpayer's pockets. And the taxpayer is, in like manner, entitled to be astute to prevent as far as he honestly can the depletion of his means by the Inland Revenue.'
Lord Clyde, *Ayrshire Pullman v Inland Revenue Commissioners, 1929*

Income Tax

What is a professional writer for tax purposes?
Writers are professionals while they are writing regularly with the intention of making a profit; or while they are gathering material, researching or otherwise preparing a publication.

A professional freelance writer is taxed under Case II of Schedule D of the *Income and Corporation Taxes Act 1988*. The taxable income is the amount receivable, either directly or by an agent, on his behalf, less expenses wholly and exclusively laid out for the purpose of the profession. If expenses exceed income, the loss can either be carried forward and set against future income from writing or set against other income which is subject to tax in the same year. If tax has been paid on that other income, a repayment can be obtained, or the sum can be offset against other tax liabilities. Special loss relief can apply in the opening years of the profession. Losses made in the first four years can be set against income of up to three earlier years.

Where a writer receives very occasional payments for isolated articles, it may not be possible to establish that these are profits arising from carrying on a continuing profession. In such circumstances these 'isolated transactions' may be assessed under Case VI of Schedule D of the *Income and Corporation Taxes Act 1988*. Again, expenses may be deducted in arriving at the taxable income but, if expenses exceed income, the loss can only be set against the profits from future isolated transactions, or other income assessable under Case VI.

In the tax year 1996/97 a new tax system came into effect called Self Assessment. Under Self Assessment the onus is on the individual to declare income and expenses correctly. Each writer therefore has to decide whether profits arise from a professional or occasional activity. The consequences of getting it wrong can be expensive by way of interest, penalties and surcharges on additional tax subsequently found to be due. If in any doubt the writer should seek professional advice.

Income

A writer's income includes fees, advances, royalties, commissions, sale of copyrights, reimbursed expenses, etc., from any source anywhere in the world whether or not brought to the UK (non UK resident or domiciled writers should seek professional advice).

Agents

It should be borne in mind that the agent stands in the shoes of the principal. It is not always realised that when the agent receives royalties, fees, advances, etc. on behalf of the author those receipts became the property of the author on the date of their receipt by the agent. This applies for Income Tax and Value Added Tax purposes.

Expenses

A writer can normally claim the following expenses:

(a) Secretarial, typing, proofreading, research. Where payment for these is made to the author's wife or husband they should be recorded and entered in the spouse's tax return as earned income which is subject to the usual personal allowances. If payments reach relevant levels, PAYE should be operated.

(b) Telephone, faxes, Internet costs, computer software, postage, stationery, printing, equipment maintenance, insurance, dictation tapes, batteries, any equipment or office requisites used for the profession.

(c) Periodicals, books (including presentation copies and reference books) and other publications necessary for the profession, but amounts received from the sale of books should be deducted.

(d) Hotels, fares, car running expenses (including repairs, petrol, oil, garaging, parking, cleaning, insurance, road fund tax, depreciation), hire of cars or taxis in connection with:

   (i)   business discussions with agents, publishers, co-authors, collaborators, researchers, illustrators, etc.

   (ii) travel at home and abroad to collect background material.

   As an alternative to keeping details of full car running costs, a mileage rate can be claimed for business use. This rate depends on the engine size and varies from year to year. This is known as the Fixed Profit Car Scheme and is available to writers whose turnover does not exceed the VAT registration limit, currently £51,000.

(e) Publishing and advertising expenses, including costs of proof corrections, indexing, photographs, etc.

(f) Subscriptions to societies and associations, press cutting agencies, libraries, etc., incurred wholly for the purpose of the profession.

(g)   Rent, council tax and water rates, etc., the proportion being determined by the ratio of the number of rooms used exclusively for the profession, to the total number of rooms in the residence. But see note on *Capital Gains Tax* below.

(h)   Lighting, heating and cleaning. A carefully calculated figure of the business use of these costs can be claimed as a proportion of the total.

(i)   Agent's commission, accountancy charges and legal charges incurred wholly in the course of the profession including cost of defending libel actions, damages in so far as they are not covered by insurance, and libel insurance premiums. However, where in a libel case damages are awarded to punish the author for having acted maliciously the action becomes quasi-criminal and costs and damages may not be allowed.

(j)   TV and video rental (which may be apportioned for private use), and cinema or theatre tickets, if wholly for the purpose of the profession.

(k)   Capital allowances for business equipment, e.g. car, TV, radio, hi-fi sets, tape and video recorders, dictaphones, computers, printers, scanners, typewriters, office furniture, photographic equipment. Allowances vary in the Finance Acts. At present there is a First Year Allowance (for the year to 30 June 1998, 50%, and 1999, 40%) of the cost of equipment purchased in those years. Subsequently there is an annual Writing Down Allowance of 25% of the reducing balance. On motor cars the allowance is 25% in the first year and 25% of the reducing balance in each successive year limited to £3000 each year. (In the case of motor cars bought before 11 March 1992 the limit is £2000 each year.) The total allowances claimed over the lifetime of any asset must not exceed the difference between the cost and eventual sale price. Allowances will be reduced to exclude personal (non-professional) use where necessary.

(l)   Lease rent. The cost of lease rent of equipment is allowable; also on cars, subject to restrictions for private use, and for expensive cars.

(m)   Other expenses incurred wholly and exclusively for professional purposes. (Entertaining expenses are not allowable in any circumstances.)

NB It is always advisable to keep detailed records. Diary entries of appointments, notes of fares and receipted bills are much more convincing to the Inland Revenue than round figure estimates.

The Self Assessment regime makes it a legal requirement for proper accounting records to be kept. These records must be sufficient to support the figures declared in the tax return.

In addition to the above, tax relief is available on:

(a)   Premiums to pension schemes such as the *Society of Authors Retirement Benefits Scheme*. Depending on age, up to 40% of net earned income can be paid into a personal pension plan.

(b)   Covenants to charities.

(c) Gift Aid payments to charities. Currently single payment of £250 or more.
(d) *Millennium Relief* Gifts for relief in poor countries ends on 31 December 2000

Capital Gains Tax

The exemption from Capital Gains Tax which applies to an individual's main residence does not apply to any part of that residence which is used exclusively for business purposes. The effect of this is that the appropriate proportion of any increase in value of the residence since 31 March 1982 can be taxed when the residence is sold, subject to adjustment for inflation to March 1998 and subsequent length of ownership, at the individual's highest rate of tax.

Writers who own their houses should bear this in mind before claiming expenses for the use of a room for writing purposes. Arguments in favour of making such claims are that they afford some relief now, while Capital Gains Tax in its present form may not stay for ever. Also, where a new house is bought in place of an old one, the gain made on the sale of the first study may be set off against the cost of the study in the new house, thus postponing the tax payment until the final sale. For this relief to apply, each house must have a study and the author must continue his profession throughout. On death there is an exemption of the total Capital Gains of the estate.

Alternatively, writers can claim that their use is non-exclusive and restrict their claim to the cost of extra lighting, heating and cleaning to avoid any Capital Gains Tax liability.

Can a writer average out his income over a number of years for tax purposes?

Under Section 534 of the *Income and Corporation Taxes Act 1988*, a writer may in certain circumstances spread over two or three fiscal years lump sum payments whenever received and royalties received during two years from the date of first publication or performance of work. Points to note are:

(a) If the period of preparing and writing the work exceeds twelve months but does not exceed twenty-four months, one-half of the advances and/or royalties will be regarded as income from the year preceding that of receipt. If the period of preparing and writing exceeds twenty-four months, one-third of the amount received would be regarded as income from each of the two years preceding that of receipt.

(b) For a writer on a very large income, who otherwise fulfils the conditions required, a claim under these sections could result in a tax saving. If his income is not large he should consider the implication, in the various fiscal years concerned, of possible loss of benefit from personal and other allowances and changes in the rates of income tax.

It is also possible to average out income within the terms of publishers' contracts, but professional advice should be taken before signature. Where a husband and wife collaborate as writers, advice should be taken as to whether a formal partnership agreement should be made or whether the publishing agreement should be in joint names.

Is a lump sum paid for an outright sale of the copyright or is part of the copyright exempt from tax?

No. All the money received from the marketing of literary work, by whatever means, is taxable. Some writers, in spite of clear judicial decisions to the contrary, still seem to think that an outright sale of, for instance, the film rights in a book is not subject to tax.

Remaindering

To avoid remaindering authors can usually purchase copies of their own books from the publishers. Monies received from sales are subject to income tax but the cost of books sold should be deducted because tax is only payable on the profit made.

Is there any relief where old copyrights are sold?

Section 535 of the *Income and Corporation Taxes Act 1988* gives relief where not less than ten years after the first publication of the work the author of a literary, dramatic, musical or artistic work assigns the copyright therein wholly or partially, or grants any interest in the copyright by licence, and:

(a)   the consideration for the assignment or grant consists wholly or partially of a lump sum payment, the whole amount of which would, but for this section, be included in computing the amount of his/her profits or gains for a single year of assessment, and

(b)   the copyright interest is not assigned or granted for a period of less than two years.

In such cases, the amount received may be spread forward in equal yearly instalments for a maximum of six years, or, where the copyright or interest is assigned or granted for a period of less than six years, for the number of whole years in that period. A 'lump sum payment' is defined to include a non-returnable advance on account of royalties.

It should be noted that a claim may not be made under this section in respect of a payment if a prior claim has been made under Section 534 of the *Income and Corporation Taxes Act 1988* (see section on spreading lump sum payments over two or three years) or vice versa. Relief under Sections 534 and 535 has now been withdrawn from partnerships.

Are royalties payable on publication of a book abroad subject to both foreign tax as well as UK tax?

Where there is a Double Taxation Agreement between the country concerned and the UK, then on the completion of certain formalities no tax is deductible at source by the foreign payer, but such income is taxable in the UK in the ordinary way.

When there is no Double Taxation Agreement, credit will be given against UK tax for overseas tax paid. A complete list of countries with which the UK has conventions for the avoidance of double taxation may be obtained from FICO, Inland Revenue, St John's House, Merton Road, Bootle, Merseyside L69 9BB, or the local tax office.

Residence abroad

Writers residing abroad will, of course, be subject to the tax laws ruling in their country of residence, and as a general rule royalty income paid from the United Kingdom can be exempted from deduction of UK tax at source, providing the author is carrying on his profession abroad. A writer who is intending to go and live abroad should make early application for future royalties to be paid without deduction of tax to FICO, address as above. In certain circumstances writers resident in the Irish Republic are exempt from Irish Income Tax on their authorship earnings.

Are grants or prizes taxable?

The law is uncertain. Some Arts Council grants are now deemed to be taxable, whereas most prizes and awards are not, though it depends on the conditions in each case. When submitting the Self Assessment annual returns, such items should be excluded, but reference made to them in the 'Additional Information' box on the self-employment (or partnership) pages.

What is the item 'Class 4 N.I.C.' which appears on my Self Assessment return?

All taxpayers who are self-employed pay an additional national insurance contribution if their earned income exceeds a figure which varies each year. This contribution is described as Class 4 and is calculated when preparing the return. It is additional to the self-employed Class 2 (stamp) contribution but confers no additional benefits and is a form of levy. It applies to men aged under 65 and women under 60.

Value Added Tax

Value Added Tax (VAT) is a tax currently levied at 17.5% on:
- (a) the total value of taxable goods and services supplied to consumers,
- (b) the importation of goods into the UK,
- (c) certain services or goods from abroad if a taxable person receives them in the UK for the purpose of their business.

Who is taxable?

A writer resident in the UK whose turnover from writing and any other business, craft or art on a self-employed basis is greater than £51,000 annually, before deducting agent's commission, must register with HM Customs & Excise as a taxable person. Turnover includes fees, royalties, advances, commissions, sale of copyright, reimbursed expenses, etc. A business is required to register:

■ at the end of any month if the value of taxable supplies in the past twelve months has exceeded the annual threshold; or

■ if there are reasonable grounds for believing that the value of taxable supplies in the next twelve months will exceed the annual threshold.

Penalties will be claimed in the case of late registration. A writer whose turnover is below these limits is exempt from the requirements to register for VAT, but may apply for voluntary registration, and this will be allowed at the discretion of HM Customs & Excise.

A taxable person collects VAT on outputs (turnover) and deducts VAT paid on inputs (taxable expenses) and where VAT collected exceeds VAT paid, must remit the difference to HM Customs & Excise. In the event that input exceeds output, the difference will be refunded by HM Customs & Excise.

Inputs (Expenses)

Taxable at the standard rate if supplier is registered	Taxable at the zero or special rate	Not liable to VAT
Rent of certain commercial premises	Books (zero)	Rent of non–commercial premises
Advertisements in newspapers, magazines, journals and periodicals	Coach, rail and air travel (zero)	Postage
Agent's commission (unless it relates to monies from overseas)	Agent's commission (on monies from overseas)	Services supplied by unregistered persons
Accountant's and solicitors fees for business matters	Domestic gas and electricity (5%)	Subscriptions to the Society of Authors, PEN, NUJ, etc.
Agency services (typing, copying, etc.)		Insurance
Word processors, typewriters and stationery		
Artists' materials		
Photographic equipment		
Tape recorders and tapes		
Hotel accommodation		*Outside the scope of VAT*
Taxi fares		
Motorcar expenses		PLR (Public Lending Right)
Telephone		Profit shares
Theatres and concerts		Investment income
NB This list is not exhaustive		

Outputs (Turnover)

A writer's outputs are taxable services supplied to publishers, broadcasting organisations, theatre managements, film companies, educational institutions, etc. A taxable writer must invoice, i.e. collect from, all the persons (either individuals or organisations) in the UK for whom supplies have been made, for fees, royalties or other considerations plus VAT. An unregistered writer cannot and must not invoice for VAT. A taxable writer is not obliged to collect VAT on royalties or other fees paid by publishers or others overseas. In practice, agents usually collect VAT for the registered author.

Remit to Customs

The taxable writer adds up the VAT which has been paid on taxable inputs, deducts it from the VAT received and remits the balance to Customs. Business with HM Customs is conducted through the local VAT offices of HM Customs which are listed in local telephone directories, except for VAT returns which are sent direct to the Customs & Excise VAT Central Unit, Alexander House, 21 Victoria Avenue, Southend on Sea, Essex SS99 1AA.

Accounting

A taxable writer is obliged to account to HM Customs & Excise at quarterly intervals. Returns must be completed and sent to VAT Central Unit by the dates shown on the return. Penalties can be charged if the returns are late.

It is possible to account for the VAT liability under the Cash Accounting Scheme (leaflet 731), whereby the author accounts for the output tax when the invoice is paid or royalties, etc., are received. The same applies to the input tax, but as most purchases are probably on a 'cash basis', this will not make a considerable difference to the author's input tax. This scheme is only applicable to those with a taxable turnover of less than £350,000 and, therefore, is available to the majority of authors. The advantage of this scheme is that the author does not have to account for VAT before receiving payments, thereby relieving the author of a cash flow problem.

It is also possible to pay VAT by nine estimated direct debits, with a final balance at the end of the year (see leaflet 732). This annual accounting method also means that only one VAT return is submitted.

Registration

A writer will be given a VAT registration number which must be quoted on all VAT correspondence. It is the responsibility of those registered to inform those to whom they make supplies of their registration number. The taxable turnover limit which determines whether a person who is registered for VAT may apply for cancellation of registration is £49,000.

Voluntary registration

A writer whose turnover is below the limits may apply to register. If the writer is paying a relatively large amount of VAT on taxable inputs – agent's commission, accountant's fees, equipment, materials, or agency services, etc. – it may make a significant improvement in the net income to be able to offset the VAT on these inputs. A writer who pays relatively little VAT may find it easier, and no more expensive, to remain unregistered.

Fees and royalties
A taxable writer must notify those to whom he makes supplies of the Tax Registration Number at the first opportunity. One method of accounting for and paying VAT on fees and royalties is the use of multiple stationery for 'self-billing', one copy of the royalty statement being used by the author as the VAT invoice. A second method is for the recipient of taxable outputs to pay fees, including authors' royalties, without VAT. The taxable writer then renders a tax invoice for the VAT element and a second payment, of the VAT element, will be made. This scheme is cumbersome but will involve only taxable authors. Fees and royalties from abroad will count as payments of the exported services and will accordingly be zero-rated.

Agents and accountants
A writer is responsible to HM Customs for making VAT returns and payments. Neither an agent nor an accountant nor a solicitor can remove the responsibility, although they can be helpful in preparing and keeping VAT returns and accounts. Their professional fees or commission will, except in rare cases where the adviser or agent is himself unregistered, be taxable at the standard rate and will represent some of a writer's taxable inputs.

Income Tax – Schedule D
An unregistered writer can claim some of the VAT paid on taxable inputs as a business expense allowable against income tax. However, certain taxable inputs fall into categories which cannot be claimed under the income tax regulations. A taxable writer, who has already claimed VAT on inputs, cannot charge it as a business expense for the purposes of income tax.

Certain services from abroad
A taxable author who resides in the United Kingdom and who receives certain services from abroad must account for VAT on those services at the appropriate tax rate on the sum paid for them. Examples of the type of services concerned include: services of lawyers, accountants, consultants, provision of information and copyright permissions.

Inheritance Tax

Inheritance Tax was introduced in 1984 to replace Capital Transfer Tax, which had in turn replaced Estate Duty, the first of the death taxes of recent times. Paradoxically, Inheritance Tax has reintroduced a number of principles present under the old Estate Duty.

The general principle now is that all assets owned at death are chargeable to tax (currently 40%) except the first £231,000 of the estate and any assets passed to a surviving spouse or a charity. Gifts made more than seven years before death are exempt, but those made within this period are taxed on a sliding scale. No tax is payable at the time of making the gift.

In addition, each individual may currently make gifts of up to £3000 in any year and these will be considered to be exempt. A further exemption covers any number of annual gifts not exceeding £250 to any one person.

If the £3000 is not fully utilised in one year, any unused balance can be carried forward to the following year (but no later). Gifts out of income, which do not reduce one's living standards, are also exempt if they are part of normal expenditure.

At death all assets are valued; they will include any property, investments, life policies, furniture and personal possessions, bank balances and, in the case of authors, the value of copyrights. All, with the sole exception of copyrights, are capable (as assets) of accurate valuation and, if necessary, can be turned into cash. The valuation of copyright is, of course, complicated and frequently gives rise to difficulty. Except where they are bequeathed to the owner's husband or wife, very real problems can be left behind by the author.

Experience has shown that a figure based on two to three years' past royalties may be proposed by the Inland Revenue in their valuation of copyright. However, this may not be reasonable and may require negotiation. If a book is running out of print or if, as in the case of educational books, it may need re-vision at the next reprint, these factors must be taken into account. In many cases the fact that the author is no longer alive and able to make personal appear-ances, or provide publicity, or write further works, will result in lower or slower sales. Obviously, this is an area in which help can be given by the publishers, and in particular one needs to know what their future intentions are, what stocks of the books remain, and what likelihood there will be of reprinting.

There is a further relief available to authors who have established that they have been carrying on a business, normally assessable under Case II of Schedule D, for at least two years prior to death. It has been possible to establish that copyrights are treated as business property and in these circumstances, Inheritance Tax 'business property relief' is available. This relief at present is 100% so that the tax saving can be quite substantial. The Inland Revenue may wish to be assured that the business is continuing and consideration should therefore be given to the appointment, in the author's will, of a literary execu-tor who should be a qualified business person or, in certain circumstances, the formation of partnership between the author and spouse, or other relative, to ensure that it is established the business is continuing after the author's death.

If the author has sufficient income, consideration should be given to building up a fund to cover future Inheritance Tax liabilities. One of a number of ways would be to take out a whole life assurance policy which is assigned to the children, or other beneficiaries, the premiums on which are within the annual exemption of

£3000. The capital sum payable on the death of the assured is exempt from inheritance tax.

Anyone wondering how best to order his affairs for tax purposes should consult an accountant with specialised knowledge in this field. Experience shows that a good accountant is well worth his fee which, incidentally, so far as it relates to professional matters, is an allowable expense.

The information contained in this section has been prepared by Pat Kernon and Ian Spring of Moore Stephens, Chartered Accountants, who will be pleased to answer questions on tax problems. Please write to Pat Kernon, c/o The Writer's Handbook, *34 Ufton Road, London N1 5BX.*

Company Index

The following codes have been used to classify the index entries:

Subject Index